Los Angeles

AND ITS ENVIRONS IN THE TWENTIETH CENTURY

Los Angeles

AND

ITS ENVIRONS IN THE TWENTIETH CENTURY

A BIBLIOGRAPHY OF A METROPOLIS

compiled under the auspices

of the

Los Angeles Metropolitan History Project

Foreword by MRS. FLETCHER BOWRON

Edited with an Introduction by

DOYCE B. NUNIS, JR.

The Ward Ritchie Press
Los Angeles 1973

MAYOR

Thomas Bradley

LOS ANGELES CITY COUNCIL

John S. Gibson, Jr., *President*	Billy G. Mills
Ernani Bernardi	Louis R. Nowell
Marvin Braude	Pat Russell
Edmund D. Edelman	Arthur K. Snyder
John Ferraro	Robert J. Stevenson
Gilbert W. Lindsay	Joel Wachs
Donald D. Lorenzen	Robert M. Wilkinson

COPYRIGHT © 1973 BY THE CITY OF LOS ANGELES
LIBRARY OF CONGRESS CATALOG CARD NUMBER 70-161669
ISBN 0378-02581-3
PRINTED IN THE UNITED STATES OF AMERICA
BY THE PRINTING DIVISION, SUPPLIES DEPARTMENT
CITY OF LOS ANGELES

Dedicated to the Memory of

FLETCHER BOWRON

1887-1968

"His was a life of service"

Fletcher Bowron was Mayor of the City of Los Angeles from 1938 to 1953. Becoming mayor as the result of a recall election inspired by an aroused citizenry, he instituted reforms and changed the whole course of city government. His leadership laid the foundations for good government and a professional municipal service.

So strong was the moral force of his administration that he has been referred to as "the conscience" of the city.

Prior to becoming Mayor, he had served as Judge of the Superior Court of the County of Los Angeles from 1926 to 1938. Again elected to the bench in 1956, he retired in 1962. He was known for his judicial temperament, compassion, integrity, fearlessness and thorough knowledge of the law. During the time he served, he played an important role in bringing about significant improvements in the judicial system.

Honored, respected, beloved, he would have wished no higher tribute than to be called "a good citizen."

ACKNOWLEDGMENTS

In her Foreword, Mrs. Bowron has acknowledged the assistance rendered by a number of individuals in bringing this bibliography to publication. In addition to those who have been singled out for special recognition, the following individuals and institutions have also added their measure.

For special searches and for responding to a variety of requests, we wish to thank the following librarians: Wilma J. Dewey and Virginia Frinell, Municipal Reference Library, Los Angeles City Hall; Gay Boughourian, Los Angeles Police Department Library; Phyllis Absalom, Los Angeles Department of Water and Power Library; Helen Bennett, Head Reference Librarian, California State University, Northridge; Marion L. Buckner, Senior Librarian, California Room, San Diego Public Library; Herbert S. Fox, Senior Reference Librarian, California State University, Fresno; Mary Gormly, Reference Librarian, California State University, Los Angeles; Margaret Hinshaw, Miles Merwin, and Murray A. Beman, all librarians in the Reference Department, Honnold Library, Claremont Colleges, Claremont; Beryl Hoskin, Reference Librarian, University of Santa Clara; Irene Moran, Reference Librarian, Bancroft Library, University of California, Berkeley; Frances Purser, Reference Librarian, California State University, Humboldt; Donald L. Read, Head Librarian, Social Science Department, California State University, Long Beach; Virginia Reilly, Librarian, Los Angeles Board of Education; Margaret D. Uridge, Head, General Reference Service, General Library, and John Macpherson of her staff, University of California, Berkeley; Imogene Woods, Reference Librarian, University of California, Davis.

Other librarians who have been of assistance to us are: Christine I. Andrew, Senior Reference Librarian, and Rutherford D. Rogers, University Librarian, Yale University, New Haven, Conn.; Joseph A. Belloli, Senior Reference Librarian, Stanford University; Barbara Dalkey, Reference and Bibliography Division, California State University, San Jose; Marion Henderson, Reference Librarian, Clark University, Worcester, Mass.; Norma Hovden, Chief Reference Librarian, University of Minnesota, Minneapolis; J. Frank Jones, Reference Department, University of the Pacific, Stockton; Donald McKie, Head, Reference Department, University of California, San Diego; Dorothy O'Malley, Librarian, Marymount College, Los Angeles; Allan R. Ottley, formerly Head, California Section, California State Library, Sacramento; Mary S. Pierce, Reference Librarian, University of Redlands; Florence M. Power, Head, Reference Services, Pasadena Public Library; Laurie Robinson, Acquisition Librarian, California State University, San Diego; Martha Townsend, Chief Reference Librarian, Santa Monica Public Library; Judith Wainright, Head, Reference Department, University of San Francisco; Helen Whitson, Librarian, California State University, San Francisco; Stanley M. Williamson, Associate Dean, Graduate Division, University of California, Santa Cruz; Jay Willisar and Peter A. Evans, California Historical Society Library, San Francisco.

Others who have responded to specific requests include: Dr. Thomas F. Andrews, Assistant Professor of History, Pasadena College; Mary Ann Carter and Claire Phipps, librarians in California State University, Chico; Kimball C. Elkins, Curator, Harvard University Archives, Harvard University, Cambridge, Mass.; James P. Else, United Methodist Conference Archivist, Theology Library, Claremont; Lois A. Forwalter and Beverly Sperring, librarians in the University of Chicago; Frances Henselman, City Librarian, Long Beach Public Library; E. Kay Kirkman, Librarian, Los Angeles Temple, Church of Jesus Christ of Latter Day Saints; Edward Livengood, Reference Librarian, California State University, Fullerton; Thomas V. Schmidt, Reference Department, Catholic University of America, Washington, D.C.; Ernest Siegel, Central Library, Los Angeles Public Library; Anna Mary Urban, Librarian, University of Maryland, College Park; Benjamin Whitten, Librarian, Whittier College.

It is a pleasure to thank Rev. Francis J. Weber, Archivist, Archdiocese of Los Angeles, for a number of courtesies. A bibliographer himself, he generously provided access to his work on the history of the Catholic Church in California. John Bruckman of the Central Library, Los Angeles Public Library, provided expert guidance in the selection and standardization of the categories which were adopted for use in the bibliography.

This bibliography represents the culmination of an important phase of the Metropolitan Los Angeles History Project which was initiated by the late Fletcher Bowron, Mayor of the City of Los Angeles, 1938-1953, after his retirement as Judge of the Superior Court of the County of Los Angeles.

Shortly before his retirement, Judge Bowron was approached by the Office of Oral History at the University of California, Los Angeles, and asked to undertake an "oral history" of his eventful life, with particular emphasis on his long tenure as Mayor of the City of Los Angeles. After several ensuing interviews, the Judge became concerned as to whether or not an "oral history" was the best approach to the project. This concern grew. His sense of integrity and inborn demand for truth and honesty which had been hallmarks of his mayoralty administration and his years on the bench would not permit him to accept the possibility that errors in facts, either as to dates, names, places, or sequence of events, might appear in his oral memoirs.

Stimulated by this concern, he began to consider an alternative to an oral history of his life. During the course of his fifteen years as Mayor of Los Angeles, he had become aware of the great need for an authentic history of the Los Angeles area since the turn of the century. As he weighed the matter, a plan gradually began to take shape. He came to the conclusion that what was needed was a history that would tell of the rise of this modern metropolis, not just a summary of his role in some of the events which had helped shape that development. He fully realized that many individuals had played important roles in a variety of fields of endeavor. Motivated by that belief, he formulated a plan which he hoped would result in a true picture of the growth and development of Los Angeles and its environs in the twentieth century. Thus, in 1962, the Metropolitan Los Angeles History Project was inaugurated.

In an outline of his plan, Judge Bowron stated the project's objective:

". . . The purpose of this project is the compilation of an authentic history of Los Angeles City and County during the twentieth century, with particular reference to the factors contributing to the making of a great metropolitan area . . . . The growth of Los Angeles from a small inland town to become the center of one of the great metropolitan areas of the world is a remarkable story that has not been adequately told. Unless the facts are collected and recorded during the lifetime of persons now in being, they will never be preserved . . ."

From the outset of the project, the research was "confined to the period since 1900," with special attention devoted to the "examination of official records of the City and County and contacts with the various organizations, firms, and corporations, as well as individuals who have had an important part in events that have contributed in the making" of this metropolis as we know it today.

The Metropolitan History Project envisioned two resultant accomplishments: first, a factual history of the greater Los Angeles area since 1900; second, the collection and preservation of significant historical materials. These were divided into two categories: interviews with individuals who had played significant roles in their respective fields; documents and manuscripts which recorded important developments pertaining to the region.

With the encouragement of former Chancellor Franklin D. Murphy of the University of California, Los Angeles, Judge Bowron set to work. Gradually, as the work progressed, he came to realize the enormity of the task he had undertaken. What was needed was a lifetime of assiduous historical endeavor. Aware of the time factor, he sought assistance from local professors of history and graduate students, urging them to undertake specific investigations on a variety of subjects. Some tangible and helpful results were realized, but there remains a largely untapped and very promising field for future effort.

To assist in the activities of the project, The Haynes Foundation initially provided a small grant. Dr. Gordon Watkins, now deceased, but then director of the foundation, was enthusiastic in his endorsement. Assistance and cooperation were given by the State of California under two governors in making available office facilities in the State Building in Los Angeles. Later, in 1968,

Dr. C. Erwin Piper, City Administrative Officer, requested and received authorization from the Mayor and the Los Angeles City Council to provide the project with office space and staff assistance. With the continuing assistance and support of Dr. Piper and Carl F. Pahl, Assistant City Administrative Officer, the first phase of the project has now been successfully completed.

After Judge Bowron's death in September, 1968, I felt deeply committed to continuing his work, to bring to fruition insofar as possible his dedicated efforts and hopes, and research was continued. In February, 1970, in order to provide advice and assistance on policy matters relating to the project, the Metropolitan Los Angeles History Project Advisory Committee was formed under the chairmanship of The Honorable Kenneth N. Chantry, formerly Presiding Judge of the Superior Court of the County of Los Angeles.

Upon reviewing the work already done, the committee concluded, as had Judge Bowron, that a tremendous amount of research would still be required to carry out the original objective of completing a definitive history of the Los Angeles metropolitan area.

Counsel was sought of Dr. Doyce B. Nunis, Jr., who had first interviewed the Judge for the Office of Oral History of the University of California, Los Angeles, and who had assisted him in the initial phases of launching the Metropolitan Los Angeles History Project. Dr. Nunis had resigned the directorship of the oral history program in 1965 to accept appointment to the faculty of the Department of History of the University of Southern California, and had just returned from a term in England as Visiting Professor of American History at the University of Birmingham. After lengthy discussions and a careful examination and assessment of the materials and files collected through the Judge's six years of research, it was Dr. Nunis' opinion that within the material lay the foundation core of a much needed comprehensive bibliography. The Advisory Committee was consulted and it was agreed that the immediate project goal should be the completion and publication of a bibliography of the history of the metropolitan area, 1900-1970. It was the consensus that such a bibliography would lay the groundwork for future historical studies of Los Angeles and its environs and would thus serve as a basis for the comprehensive studies which Judge Bowron originally envisioned. The Committee concluded that the publication of the bibliography would make available a tool which would aid immeasurably laymen and scholars alike who might be interested in the many-sided aspects of the development of metropolitan Los Angeles.

This phase of the project is now finished. It represents many hours of research and careful attention to detail not only by a small staff, but by others who gave generously as a public service their valuable time, their knowledge and professional skill because they shared Judge Bowron's realization of the importance of assembling at this time the available material that should go into an authentic history. It has been not only an endeavor for historical purposes, but an expression of appreciation for the ideals and accomplishments of a man who had devoted his entire adult life to public service, who left an indelible imprint on the growth, development and character of this metropolis, who changed the course of the City at a time when corruption was rampant by establishing honest, efficient government, and who, even after a well-earned retirement, undertook this prodigious task because he considered it to be in the public interest.

Deep and sincere thanks and appreciation go to the many who have made this publication possible: to The Haynes Foundation for the initial assistance given through a grant; to the project staff who did the day-to-day research and detail work with enthusiasm and devotion — Elsie Tistaert, Assistant Director and Secretary, for her loyal support, skills and expert knowledge of the many requirements of such an exacting task, who worked often at great personal sacrifice and always with heartfelt interest; and Robert C. Post, graduate history student, for his diligent, intelligent work as chief researcher. On the staff at various times, others who made significant contributions were Anna Marie Hager, who was President of the Southern California Historical Society, Anne H. Stites, and Edward L. Parker. To Elizabeth Stewart, Chief Clerk City Administrative Officer, appreciation is due for her help in solving many problems.

Policy advice and assistance have been provided through the Advisory Committee: The Honorable Kenneth N. Chantry, Judge of the Superior Court (ret.), Chairman; Dr. John C. Bollens, Professor of Political Science, University of California, Los Angeles; Wallace N. Jamie, civic leader, lecturer and business executive; Dr. Doyce B. Nunis, Jr.,

Professor of History, University of Southern California; Rudolph Ostengaard, Vice President, United California Bank (ret.); Dr. C. Erwin Piper, City Administrative Officer, City of Los Angeles; George Rigby, Chief Administrative Analyst (ret.), City of Los Angeles; and Gordon Whitnall, Planning Consultant.

We wish to express sincere thanks to Dr. C. Erwin Piper and Carl F. Pahl whose interest and support made the continuation of the project possible and whose guidance has been most important.

To George Rigby go very special thanks. His interest, understanding, guidance, never-failing and ever-available wise counsel and kindliness not only were a constant source of encouragement and assistance, but bridged over what was a very difficult period. His continued assistance in the final difficult stages of printing and publishing was invaluable.

We are grateful to Lyman H. Jones, City Librarian, for helpful suggestions and professional advice; to Ruth Palmer, Librarian, Municipal Reference Library, now retired, who gave much valuable assistance and whose interest and belief in the importance of the work were of great encouragement to Judge Bowron from the inception of the project.

Ward Ritchie of The Ward Ritchie Press has been most generous in helping with the technical details of publication. We appreciate his personal interest and assistance in this phase of the work.

I wish to express deep personal gratitude to Dr. Franklin D. Murphy for the initial encouragement he gave Judge Bowron, and to Edward W. Carter, civic leader, prominent business executive and long-time friend with whom he counseled in the early stages of the development of the idea and at whose suggestion The Haynes Foundation grant was sought. I should also like to express personal thanks to former Supervisor Warren M. Dorn of the County of Los Angeles for assistance given at times when it was most helpful.

There are many others who should be named — many who spent time and effort in providing information and whose interest and belief in the value of the project gave support and encouragement. To them go the thanks of all who worked on the project and those who in the future will make use of this bibliography.

Lastly, it would indeed be most difficult to express fully the appreciation due the man who was willing, purely as a public service, to undertake the demanding task of serving as Editor-in-Chief, Dr. Doyce B. Nunis, Jr. It was he who first excited Judge Bowron's interest in the project, who assisted him in getting the work started, whose professional advice aided in the decision to make the publication of the bibliography the immediate project goal, and then, not only provided the necessary expertise for such an undertaking, but himself participated tirelessly in the relentless, detailed work required. He only, of those concerned with the bibliography, had any conception of the amount of tedious, time-consuming, careful, sometimes grueling work that would be necessary. Yet, despite the heavy demands on his time as professor of history, editor of the "Southern California Quarterly," writer and lecturer, he undertook the work of Editor-in-Chief and gave tirelessly, generously, always graciously and cheerfully, of his time, talent and experience. As an historian he knew the importance of this work and was willing to devote himself to it. Without him it could not have been done. With him, we feel a distinguished work of great value and importance has been produced. To him it has truly been a labor of love: love for the city of his adoption; love for history for its own sake; and appreciation, admiration, respect and understanding of the man who initiated the project and to whose memory this work is dedicated, Fletcher Bowron.

Mrs. Fletcher Bowron, Director
Metropolitan Los Angeles History Project

August 1973

TABLE OF CONTENTS

INTRODUCTION

> No bibliography is, in an absolute sense, complete. It calls
> for discrimination and discretion, and I hope that no one is
> under any illusion that long lists are always better than
> short lists. *More* may mean *worse* if the bibliographer does
> not discipline himself within the terms of the task he has
> been set.
>
> George Watson, *CBEL. The Making of the Cambridge
> Bibliography* (Los Angeles, 1965), p. 11.

This bibliography is unique in the annals of the history of Los Angeles. It is the first attempt to collect, annotate, and catalogue materials which relate to the many-sided aspects of this twentieth-century California metropolitan area. As such, it is hoped that it will serve as a fount of information which will prove helpful to the general public, both interested citizens and scholars. Another hope is that it will stimulate more research and investigation into neglected aspects of the growth and development of the city and its environs in this century. Much remains to be done; the opportunities for additional study are numerous, if one examines the entries which follow.

What emerges in the bibliography is essentially a profile of what has been written on Los Angeles, 1900-1970. Significantly, four categories emphasize the basic problems which have confronted the area: education, public transportation, traffic, and water supply. These four subjects have by far the greatest number of entries. At the same time, biographies of local citizens have received considerable attention. Perhaps that may be explained by human vanity. But, on the other hand, such pressing issues as ecology, fire protection, housing, law enforcement, medicine, public health, planning, population, social problems, urban renewal, and welfare have hardly received the attention afforded to such subject categories as labor and religion.

If the bibliography could be graphed on the basis of the number of entries in each category, what one would find in essence would be the needs and opportunities for research into greater Los Angeles in this century. The gaps are there; the need to fill them with sound research is great. Only when these gaps are filled can the history of Los Angeles and its environs in the twentieth century be finally written.

In way of suggestion as to what might be undertaken, one can begin with agriculture. The assessment of the impact of agriculture on the evolution of greater Los Angeles' economic development has not been systematically examined, no more than the influence of the aircraft industry and trade. Although we have limited histories of the development of the Los Angeles harbor, we have no economic treatment of the same subject. And certainly, the whole picture of business history, be it in finance, banking, commerce, industry, petroleum, or real estate, cries out for in-depth attention.

From the aesthetic side, there does not exist a comprehensive treatment of architecture and architects in greater Los Angeles. As for culture, we only have snippets of the history of music and art, but relatively little on dance, opera, and theatre. Even those items touching on music and art are fragments of a rich mosaic that has given rise to the myth that Los Angeles is a cultural desert rather than a long-time cultural oasis.

Nor has anyone dealt with what might be called mass entertainment, specifically radio and television. The evolution and role of communication via the air waves is a neglected chapter in the metropolitan area's history. The same could be said for the printed media, newspapers and periodicals. One illustration: there is no history of *La Opinion*, the area's distinguished Spanish language newspaper, nor of *The Eagle*, an equally distinguished Negro newspaper. And if you were to ask someone about *Fortnight Magazine* or *Los Angeles Saturday Night*, *Arts & Architecture* or *Frontier Magazine*, the paucity of information would be found in the *Guide to Serial Publications*.

A great deal has been written about the moving picture industry and sports, but little has been done about the relationship of these two activities in respect to greater Los Angeles. Although long hailed as the world capital for these two activities, one has to search hard for an integrated treatment of the two subjects and the role they have played in building the area's communities.

One could continue this litany of the needs and opportunities for research, but three more examples will suffice. A history of the many-sided aspects of municipal government cry out for close investigation and study, as does the history of local politics. The relationship of local levels of government to the state and national government begs for due attention as well.

It was in consideration of these many neglected topics which need to be studied and written about that this bibliography was actually spawned. Hopefully, this bibliography will help to stimulate and to serve those who seek to address themselves to the quest of researching and writing about Los Angeles and its environs.

From the outset of compiling this bibliography of Los Angeles and its environs in the twentieth century, two primary guidelines have been kept in view. First, that every facet of the making of this metropolitan area should be scrutinized. Second, that certain limits had to be imposed. It was hoped that the end result would be a tool which would serve a wide audience—high school and college students, business and professional men and women, civil and public servants, scholars and ordinary citizens—in essence, any one who had a question about, or who sought background reading on, any aspect of life in greater Los Angeles. Such was the goal.

Keeping that broad objective in mind, the two guidelines that were imposed on material included in the bibliography were a constant reference. There were "the terms of the task" which served as rules to be applied on the inclusion or rejection of entries. As to the first guideline, careful examination of entries has been adhered to with only slight deviation. The bulk of the bibliography's entries have been screened, with one major exception—not all the graduate theses included have been personally examined. Where there was any question as to their appropriateness to the bibliography, then a search was made. Otherwise, it is safe to state that 95% of all entries which have been included have been scrutinized. In compiling the bibliography, entries which are not self-evident as to content as deduced from the title have been annotated for reference clarity.

In applying the second guideline, limitations on materials included, certain standards have been maintained. Four specific categories of material have been excluded: governmental documents, be they municipal, county, state or federal; scientific works; newspapers; manuscript collections.

It would have been a herculean task to have searched governmental documents since they are so widely scattered, especially municipal and county documents. On several occasions, however, a few very significant agency documents have been listed as well as extraordinary published governmental documents, but the very nature of such material made them exceptional. They simply could not be overlooked. Fortunately, there are collections of federal documents existing, for example, the University of California, Los Angeles, is a depository; it also collects state documents as well. It is to be hoped that the city and county of Los Angeles will give thought to establishing a depository for municipal and county documents, and maintain the collection with a systematic program of record management.

Scientific works were omitted because they are so specialized. Here again there are aids to finding these materials, such as the *Index Medicus* which is maintained for medical studies, reports, findings, etc.

The omission of newspapers should be obvious: the bulk alone would require a search team of great size and years of researching to compile references. It is a sad commentary that the major newspapers for the city of Los Angeles are not indexed. Yet, one can go to the State Library, Sacramento, and have ready access to excellent indices to San Francisco and Sacramento papers. These indices are kept current. One can go to the California Room in the San Diego Public Library and find the San Diego newspapers indexed. That index, too, is kept current. But all we have available for Los Angeles is the incompleted index to the Los Angeles *Star* which was undertaken by the Department of Special Collections at UCLA some years ago, but which remains unfinished because of lack of funds. Thus the largest metropolitan area in California does not have an index to its newspapers easily available for the use of students, scholars, and interested citizens.

Since manuscripts, like documents, are so widely scattered, including numerous collections which remain in private hands, no effort was made to incorporate them into this bibliography. Happily, a massive effort is underway, sponsored by the Library of Congress, to publish a descriptive catalogue of all known manuscript collections in public repositories in the United States. This impressive undertaking has already produced over a half-dozen massive volumes of catalogued collections, made accessible through excellent subject indices. When this great task is completed, manuscript collections which relate to Los Angeles and its environs can be readily located. Regrettably, many manuscript collections will not be listed in this important publication program—they will have been destroyed by some unknowing public employee or some unthinking family member or personal friend. Preservation of manuscripts, letters, scrapbooks, photographs, and the like should be a primary concern of both governmental agencies and private individuals. Only by preserving the records of our past can we write its history in the future.

In addition to the four categories discussed above which have been excluded from incorporation in this bibliography, articles found in "fan" magazines have been omitted whether they relate to entertainment, business or sports. It was felt that such periodicals contribute relatively little of significance. Certain popular magazines have also been excluded; for example, *Sports Illustrated* and *Ladies Home Journal*. Although widely read, popular magazines are already indexed and anyone interested in locating material in them can turn to a variety of published indices. Lastly, news magazines have not been thoroughly canvassed. Like newspapers, news magazines would demand a large search staff. Besides, most of them have their contents indexed in one or more of the available indices. However, a few select entries have been included from such publications if the coverage was of sufficient merit to warrant attention. No effort has been made, then, to duplicate listings which are conveniently found in the *Readers' Guide to Periodical Litera-*

ture, or the many indices published by the H. W. Wilson Company.

Specifically, in compiling entries for inclusion in the bibliography, efforts were made to undertake definitive searches of those periodicals which related directly to Los Angeles and its environs, with emphasis being given to those publications which are not indexed in any of the available guides to periodical literature. Thus, journals which dealt with utilities, petroleum, water, traffic, municipal affairs, and cultural activities were given close scrutiny and complete coverage. At the same time, an exhaustive search was made in the field of unpublished master's theses and doctoral dissertations. All institutions of higher learning in California were carefully canvassed in respect to master's theses, but no effort was made to include a national search because of the difficulties such an endeavor would encounter. However, since finding aids are available for doctoral dissertations on the national level, here the search was made feasible.

In the final structuring of the bibliography, the entries were distributed into categories. This has meant in a number of instances the inclusion of an item in more than one category. Such duplicate entry has been rigorously held to the absolute minimum.

No bibliography which breaks new ground, which for the first time undertakes a specific task, can be labelled definitive. That may be especially true of this first effort in trying to provide a major bibliographical guide to published materials relating to Los Angeles and its environs. But what is presented here is a foundation on which can be built a more comprehensive and definitive bibliography in the decades to come. If our objectives are fully realized, namely to provide a reliable source of information on the topics selected and to stimulate further study, research, and writing on Los Angeles and its environs, this bibliography will have served well its purpose.

Doyce B. Nunis, Jr.
Editor-in-Chief

University of Southern California
Los Angeles

A Bibliography of a Metropolis

AGRICULTURE

1. Adamson, M. H. "Los Angeles County's Big Agricultural Year." *Southern California Business* 8 (May 1929): 16-7+.

2. Ainsworth, Ed[ward M.]. *Journey with the Sun, the Story of Citrus in Its Western Pilgrimage.* Los Angeles, 1968. 54 pp.

3. "Beating the Crop Record." *Southern California Business* 6 (May 1927): 16-7.
   Agricultural production, mainly Los Angeles County.

4. Boyd, Jessie. "Historical Import of the Orange Industry in Southern California [1769-1915]." Master's thesis, University of California, Berkeley, 1922. 126 pp.

5. Burnight, Ralph F. "The Japanese Problem in Agricultural Districts of Los Angeles County." Master's thesis, University of Southern California, 1920. 70 pp.

6. Burtnett, Gerald B. "Mushrooms No Upstart Business." *Southern California Business* 11 (April 1932): 24.
   Whittier mushroom "houses" of C. W. Savery.

7. Chambers, Clarke A. *California Farm Organizations: A Historical Study of the Grange, the Farm Bureau, and the Associated Farmers, 1929-1941.* Berkeley and Los Angeles, 1952. 277 pp.

8. Clark, Robert. "Down to Earth." *Westways* 35 (August 1943): 10-1.
   Pasadena, the city with the most wartime "Victory Gardens" in the U.S.

9. Clarke, David A., Jr. "Costs, Pricing, and Conservation in Wholesale Milk Delivery in Los Angeles." Doctoral dissertation, University of California, Berkeley, 1951. 163 pp.

10. Cleland, Robert Glass, and Hardy, Osgood. *The March of Industry.* Los Angeles, 1929. 322 pp.
    History of California industry and agriculture from earliest period to 1920s.

11. Clements, George P. "After All, Los Angeles Is a County." *Southern California Business* 11 (June 1932): 8-9.
    Los Angeles County agriculture.

12. ———— "The Agricultural Future of Los Angeles County." *Los Angeles Realtor* 4 (March 1925): 17+.

13. ———— "L.A. County Leads in Farm Products." *Southern California Business* 1 (September 1922): 40-1.

14. Davidson, Jack R. "Economic Efficiency and Firm Adjustment for Market Milk Production in the Southern Metropolitan Milkshed of California." Doctoral dissertation, University of California, Berkeley, 1960. 246 pp.

15. Donovan, Richard A. "Smudge Over Sunkist." *Reporter* 3 (July 4, 1950): 22-4.
    Brief history of the California Fruit Growers Exchange.

16. Downing, Carl B. "County Agricultural Extension Administration." Master's thesis, Claremont Graduate School, 1965. 79 pp.

17. Eder, Herbert M. "Some Aspects of the Persistence of Agriculture in the San Fernando Valley, California." Master's thesis, University of California, Los Angeles, 1960. 139 pp.

18. Ewing, Paul A. *The Agricultural Situation in the San Fernando Valley, California.* Washington, D.C., 1939. 128 pp.

19. Fielding, Gordon J. "Dairying in the Los Angeles Milkshed: Factors Affecting Character and Location." Doctoral dissertation, University of California, Los Angeles, 1961. 199 pp.

20. ———— "The Los Angeles Milkshed: A Study of the Political Factor in Agriculture." *Geographical Review* 54 (1964): 1-12.
    Effect of production and price regulation, and land-use zoning, 1928-1959.

21. Fletcher, Lehman B. "Growth and Adjustment of the Los Angeles Milkshed: A Study in the Economies of Location." Doctoral dissertation, University of California, Berkeley, 1960. 247 pp.

22. Fogelberg, Neptune, and McKay, A. W. *The Citrus Industry and the California Fruit Growers Exchange System.* Washington, D.C., 1940. 109 pp.

23. Froehde, F. C. "How Pomona Makes Money Selling Sewage Effluent for Irrigation Use." *Western City* 6 (January 1930): 39-40+.

24. Gardner, Kelsey B., and McKay, A. W. *The California Fruit Growers Exchange System.* Washington, D.C., 1950. 124 pp.

Revision of U.S. Farm Credit Association, Circular C-121: *The Citrus Industry and the California Fruit Growers Exchange System* by Nepthune Fogelberg and A. W. McKay. Washington, D.C., 1940.

25. Gast, Ross H. "An Acre and Liberty—With a Pay Check: A New Way of Life, the Small Farm Home for Factory and City Workers, Proves Practical in Los Angeles County." *Southern California Business* 9 (June 1930): 18-9+.

26. ———— "Handling the Cold Storage Problem." *Southern California Business* 4 (September 1925): 20+.

Los Angeles area.

27. ———— "Why People Seek Small Farm Homes." *Southern California Business* 12 (April 1933): 18-9.

28. Geissinger, W. B. " 'Sunkist' Measures Its Market." *Southern California Business* 12 (March 1933): 10-1.

29. ———— "Thirty Years of Orange Advertising." *California Magazine of the Pacific* 28 (April 1938): 10-1+.

30. Gleason, George. *The Fifth Migration . . . California Migratory Agricultural Worker Situation.* Prepared for the Los Angeles Committee for Church and Community Cooperation. [Los Angeles, 1940]. 29 pp.

31. Glendora Citrus Association. *Glendora Citrus Association, 1895-1945.* Glendora, [1945?]. [24] pp.

32. Gregor, Howard F. "Urban Pressures on California Land." *Land Economics* 33 (1957): 311-25.

Explains reasons for shrinkage in amount of land devoted to agriculture.

33. ———— "Urbanization of Southern California Agriculture." *Tijdschrift voor Economische en Social Georgrafie* 12 (December 1963): 273-8.

34. "Hitting a New Crop Level." *Southern California Business* 6 (February 1927): 14-5+.

Agricultural production, Los Angeles County.

35. Holloway, B. R. "Southwest Agriculture Centers in Los Angeles." *Southern California Business* 8 (March 1929): 12-3+.

36. Jacobs, Josephine K. "Sunkist Advertising." Doctoral dissertation, University of California, Los Angeles, 1966. 383 pp.

37. Jessup, Roger W. "Los Angeles County's Dairy Industry." *California Magazine of the Pacific* 42 (June 1952): 17+.

38. Joralmon, L. B. "Southern California Dairying as a Business and as a Stabilizer of Land Values." *Los Angeles Realtor* 4 (March 1925): 14-5.

39. Kugelmass, Joe. "Bossy Punches a Time Clock." *Westways* 41 (January 1949): 10-1.

Dairy industry in Los Angeles.

40. Law, George. "Where Arid Lands Yield Abundantly: That Part of the Great Mojave Desert Known as Antelope Valley Has Been Made One of the Most Productive Sections in Southwest." *Southern California Business* 2 (May 1923): 10-1.

41. "Los Angeles County Leads in Crops." *Southern California Business* 2 (December 1923): 30.

Leads U.S. in value of crops.

42. "Los Angeles County Leads in Dairy Products." *Southern California Business* 7 (July 1928): 24+.

43. "Los Angeles County's Income from Agricultural Production." *California Journal of Development* 20 (July 1930): 20.

44. "Los Angeles Garbage Feeds 40,000 Hogs on Fontana Farm." *Engineering News-Record* 95 (August 6, 1925): 208-12.

45. MacCurdy, Rahno M. *The History of the California Fruit Growers Exchange.* Los Angeles, 1925. 106 pp.

Appended are a number of California Fruit Growers Exchange (CFX) documents.

46. McNaughton, J. A. "The Livestock Industry in Southern California; Its Importance and Its Problems." *Los Angeles Realtor* 4 (May 1925): 19+.

47. Mehren, George L. "An Economic Analysis of the Voluntary Control Programs in the California Orange Industry." Doctoral dissertation, University of California, Berkeley, 1942. 463 pp.

48. Nadeau, Remi. "Wheat Ruled the Valley." *Westways* 55 (April 1963): 18-21.

Wheat ranching in San Fernando Valley, 1869-1910.

49. Naftzger, A. H. "Marketing California Oranges and Lemons." *Land of Sunshine* 14 (March 1901): 247-58.

50. Nevins, John A. "The Puente Area; A Study of Changing Agricultural Land Use." Master's thesis, University of California, Los Angeles, 1951. 107 pp.

51. Norman, Emmett B. *Early Industry: Picking, Packing and Marketing.* [N.p., n.d.]. 45 pp.

A personal history of the citrus industry in Duarte.

52. Northcutt, John Orlando. "Farmers Go to Market by Wire." *Southern California Business* 3 (October 1924): 18+.

Mutual F.O.B. Auction Company, Los Angeles, for marketing produce by telegraph.

53. "Palm Ranch, Where the Turkeys Come From." *Los Angeles Saturday Night* 10 (November 23, 1929): 7.

Turkey breeding farm near Palmdale.

54. Platt, George E. "Dairies and Dollars." *Los Angeles Realtor* 5 (June 1926): 14+.

Los Angeles County leads state in volume of dairy production.

55. Poronto, H. E. "Why Chicago Came to Los Angeles." *Southern California Business* 2 (August 1923): 21+.

Development of Los Angeles stockyards.

56. Prizer, J. A. "Selling California's Gigantic Citrus Crop." *Southern California Business* 8 (December 1929): 12-3+.

Sunkist.

57. Pulling, Hazel A. "A History of California's Range-Cattle Industry, 1770-1912." Doctoral dissertation, University of Southern California, 1944. 393 pp.

58. Raup, H[allock] F. "Land-Use and Water-Supply Problems in Southern California: Market Gardens of the Palos Verdes Hills." *Geographical Review* 26 (April 1936): 264-9.

Discusses role of critical climatic factors.

59. ———. "Transformation of Southern California to a Cultivated Land." *Annals of the Association of American Geographers* 49 supplement (September 1959): 58-78.

From mission agriculture to modern irrigation.

60. Ryerson, Knowles. "Truck Crop Development and Possibilities in Los Angeles County and Environs." *Los Angeles Realtor* 4 (March 1925): 13+.

61. "Selling Sunkist Abroad." *California Journal of Development* 25 (May 1935): 13.

62. Seltzer, Raymond E. "The Competitive Position of the Los Angeles Cattle Market." Doctoral dissertation, University of California, Berkeley, 1957. 224 pp.

63. Stone, George C. "Financing the Orange Industry in California." *Pomona Valley Historian* 2 (1966): 159-74; 3 (1967): 31-46.

64. Stump, Frank V. "The Great Southwest Trade Field: Farm Land Values of Los Angeles County and Neighboring States Far Outstrip Figures of Large Eastern Territory." *Southern California Business* 1 (June 1922): 12-3.

65. ———. "Valley Awakes to Fulfill a Promise." *Southern California Business* 3 (December 1924): 37-8+.

Beginning of agricultural development in Antelope Valley.

66. Thorpe, C. "Leading the Country in Agriculture." *Southern California Business* 5 (July 1926): 12-3.

Los Angeles County.

67. Updegraff, Winston R. "Here's How and Why Municipal Garbage Feeds 10,000 Hogs on a Southern California Ranch." *Western City* 28 (April 1952): 44-5.

Los Angeles metropolitan garbage feeds hogs in Saugus-Newhall area. Hogs were returned to Los Angeles and sold to slaughter houses.

68. Van Nostrand, Randolph. "Our Factories Improve Our Meats: Livestock Show to Demonstrate Use of Vegetable Oil By-Products in Fattening Cattle." *Southern California Business* 10 (November 1931): 16.

Los Angeles.

69. Von Blon, John L. "The Olive's Royal Swartness Speaks an Ancient Spanish Line." *Westways* 26 (March 1934): 16-8+.

History of olive growing in California.

70. Williamson, Harold F. "Some Phases of the Citrus-By-Product Industry of Southern California." Master's thesis, University of Southern California, 1927. 43 pp.

71. Zierer, Clifford M. "The Citrus Fruit Industry of the Los Angeles Basin." *Economic Geography* 10 (1934): 53-73.

AIRCRAFT INDUSTRY AND TRADE

72. "[Allan] Loughead Completes Sales Tour: Changes Made in Lockheed Vega." *Western Flying* 4 (December 1928): 84.

73. Allen, Arthur P., and Schneider, Betty V. H. *Industrial Relations in the California Aircraft Industry.* Berkeley, 1956. 59 pp.

74. Arnett, Eugene V. "An Analysis of the Southern California Airframe Industry's Longe Range Manpower Planning for Engineering Requirements." Master's thesis, University of Southern California, 1957. 113 pp.

Airplane industry workers.

75. "At Lockheed—Novel Miller for Aircraft Parts." *Western Machinery and Steel World* 32 (December 1941): 604-6.

76. "Aviation History Made by Douglas Aircraft." *Western Machinery and Steel World* 29 (July 1938): 245-6+.

Mostly about DC-4, newest and largest commercial airship.

77. Barber, Farrell. *History of Aircraft Accessories Corporation.* [Kansas City, Mo., 1943]. 51 pp.

78. "Boeing Douglas Vega in Joint Flying Fortress Program." *Western Machinery and Steel World* 32 (July 1941): 320-1.

79. Buckel, Carl W. "An Investigation of the Functioning of Methods and Facilities Departments in Local Aircraft Industries." Master's thesis, University of Southern California, 1958. 127 pp.

80. Burtnett, Gerald B. "He Crashed into Business." *Southern California Business* 9 (March 1930): 18+.

Arrigo Balboni's second-hand aircraft parts business, Los Angeles.

81. Chapin, Seymour L. "Garrett and Pressurized Flight: A Business Built on Thin Air." *Pacific Historical Review* 35 (1966): 329-43.

John Clifford Garrett and the AiResearch Manufacturing Company, a Los Angeles firm that pioneered in pressurized flight.

82. Chapman, Merle J. "An Aircraft Specialty Manufacturer Tools Up." *Western Machinery and Steel World* 31 (August 1940): 302-3.

Aircraft Accessories Corp., Glendale.

83. "City of the Angels: Aviation's Boom Town." *Fortune* 23 (March 1941): 90-5+.

84. Clapp, Edwin J. *Los Angeles Should Be the Home of Aircraft Industries.* Los Angeles, 1926. 11 pp.

85. Collins, James H. "But Douglas Already Had a Trophy: 'Collier's' Fine Award Just Turns Our Home Town Attention to the Big Plant in Santa Monica." *Southern California Business* 15 (August 1936): 10-1.

86. ———— "First the Dare-Devil—Then the Dollar: Record-Breaking Airplanes Built in Burbank Also the Ships that Make Money with Passengers." *Southern California Business* 10 (December 1931): 10-1.

Lockheed Aircraft.

87. ———— "Outpost—National Air Defense: Douglas Staff and Plant Second to None in Military Aircraft—And May We Keep It So!" *Southern California Business* 10 (December 1931): 8-9.

88. ———— "This New Air Product — 'Pay Load': Douglas Carries It Up Higher in the Big Sleeper

Transports for American Airlines." *Southern California Business* 15 (January 1936): 8-9.

Douglas DST (DC-4), built at Santa Monica plant.

89. ——"Through Those Skeleton Years." *Southern California Business* 14 (August 1935): 10-1.

Kinner Airplane & Motor Corp., Glendale.

90. Crane, H. T. "Latest Lighting Developments Used in Santa Monica Aircraft Plant." *Western City* 12 (September 1936): 41-2.

Douglas plant.

91. Cunningham, William G. *The Aircraft Industry, A Study in Industrial Location.* Los Angeles, 1951. 247 pp.

92. Douglas, Donald W. "Planes Twelve Months in the Year." *California Magazine of the Pacific* 28 (March 1938): 5-6+.

93. "Douglas Aircraft Installs Largest Self-Contained Hydraulic Press." *Western Machinery and Steel World* 28 (October 1937): 380-1.

Santa Monica.

94. "Douglas B-19 Army Super-Bomber: World's Largest Airplane Nears Test Stage." *Western Machinery and Steel World* 32 (January 1941): 18-20.

Santa Monica.

95. Duncan, Ray. "The Aerospace Economy: Go or No Go?" *Los Angeles* 7 (February 1964): 26+.

96. Eaton Manufacturing Company. *A Chronicle of the Aviation Industry in America, 1903-1947. A Salute to the Aviation Industry.* Cleveland, Ohio, 1948. 98 pp.

1947-1948 Supplement also issued.

97. Elliott, Arlene. "The Rise of Aeronautics in California, 1849-1940." *Southern California Quarterly* 52 (1970): 1-32.

98. "Expansion Program and Methods of an Aircraft Parts Manufacturer." *Western Machinery and Steel World* 31 (November 1940): 410-2.

Wells Aircraft Parts Co., Los Angeles.

99. "50,000 Lockheed-Vega Employees." *Western Machinery and Steel World* 32 (December 1941): 619.

100. "First Fast Cargo Planes Built Here." *Southern California Business* 12 (February 1933): 13.

Northrup Aircraft, Los Angeles.

101. "Flying Automobile Appears." *Los Angeles Saturday Night* 15 (October 20, 1934): 2.

The "Fre-Wing," invented by G. Wilbur Cornelius, to be manufactured at Van Nuys.

102. Forker, Don. "The First Western Aircraft Exposition." *Southern California Business* 8 (November 1929): 20-1.

Los Angeles.

103. Gardner, Harold F. "A Study of the Utilization of Engineers and Scientists in a Selected Segment of the Los Angeles Aerospace Industry." Master's thesis, San Fernando Valley State College, 1969. 92 pp.

104. "Giants and Near Giants: Air Navigation Week Sees Ever-Larger Planes Projected." *Literary Digest* 120 (October 19, 1935): 28-9.

Mainly about Glenn L. Martin.

105. Glines, Carroll V. *Grand Old Lady; Story of the DC-3.* Cleveland, 1959. 250 pp.

Contains material about Douglas Aircraft Company of Santa Monica.

106. "A Great New Plant for Northrop Aircraft." *Western Machinery and Steel World* 31 (April 1940): 128-32.

Hawthorne.

107. Griffin, James V. "Manufacturing and Testing of Air Liners." *Western Machinery and Steel World* 28 (December 1937): 438-9+.

Lockheed Aircraft, Burbank.

108. Hamilton, Andrew. "Aerojet: From the Depths of the Sea to Outer Space." *Westways* 55 (January 1963): 8-10.

109. —— "Aerospace: Umpire for the Air Force." *Westways* 54 (July 1962): 10-2.

Aerospace Corporation, whose "mission is to 'accelerate the advancement of space and technology.'"

110. ——— "Douglas: The Lengthened Shadow." *Westways* 56 (February 1964): 11-3.

Douglas Aircraft Co.

111. ——— "Lockheed—Seaplane to Space." *Westways* 55 (December 1963): 12-4.

112. ——— "Northrop: Where Technologies Are Mastered." *Westways* 55 (March 1963): 8-10.

113. ——— "Rocketdyne: Roar of the Future." *Westways* 53 (October 1961): 4-6.

114. ——— "Shangri-La for Deep Thinkers." *Westways* 54 (February 1962): 4-6.

Hughes Aircraft "think tank" in Malibu.

115. Himmel, Nieson S. "Aerospace Firms Design Cars for Los Angeles Transit Link." *Aviation Week and Space Technology* 92 (June 15, 1970): 18.

116. Holt, Raymond M. "Wings for War." *Westways* 48 (May 1956): 22-3.

Early Los Angeles aircraft industry.

117. "Huge Plane Moved to Base in Pieces." *Western Construction News* 21 (August 1946): 104.

Howard Hughes' 700-passenger wooden airplane.

118. Kiele, William C. "A Survey of the Industry-Wide Training Program of the Northrop Aeronautical Institute." Master's thesis, University of Southern California, 1949. 139 pp.

Located in Hawthorne.

119. Kumar, Rosetta A. C. "Development of United States Aircraft Industry from 1914 to 1956." Master's thesis, University of California, Berkeley, 1963. 60 pp.

References to the Southern California scene.

120. "Lockheed Aircraft's Role in California's Airplane Production." *Western Machinery and Steel World* 31 (June 1940): 200-7.

121. "Lockheed Builds Nation's Largest Cafeteria." *The Architect and Engineer* 156 (February 1944): 16+.

122. "Lockheed Joins New Holding Company." *Western Flying* 6 (July 1929): 100.

123. "Los Angeles Plant Manufactures Aircraft Hydraulic Equipment." *Western Machinery and Steel World* 30 (May 1939): 150-2.

Aircraft Precision Parts, Inc.

124. Mappelbeck, John. "Now the Used Plane Broker." *Southern California Business* 10 (December 1931): 16.

Aero Brokerage Service Co.

125. Marx, Wesley. "Our Aerospace Industry: Will It Runaway, Too?" *Los Angeles* 5 (February 1963): 25+.

Los Angeles.

126. ——— "The Quick Change from Rocketry to Diversity." *Los Angeles* 3 (October 1961): 25-7.

Los Angeles aircraft industry.

127. "Millions Pour into Western Industry: Fokker Refinanced." *Western Flying* 4 (November 1928): 38-9+.

Formation of Fokker Aircraft Corp. of America by James A. Talbott of Los Angeles (head of Richfield Oil Co.).

128. Mitchell, Charles K. "An Analysis of Technical Recruiting in the Missile Industry of Southern California." Master's thesis, University of Southern California, 1959. 128 pp.

129. "Moreland Building Aircraft Factory." *Western Flying* 5 (April 1929): 172.

Moreland Aircraft, adjacent to Mines Field, Los Angeles.

130. Morgan, F. P. *The Origin and History of Convair Pomona.* [n.p., n.d.]. 31 pp.

131. "New Headquarters Building for Aerojet-General." *Western Flying* 44 (March 1964): 14.

El Monte.

132. "New Lockheed Proposal Envisions Air Vehicle of Unique Design and Performance." *Western Flying* 44 (May-June 1964): 15.

133. "No Errors! Lockheed Watchword." *Western Machinery and Steel World* 32 (July 1941): 356-7.

134. "North American Presents the Navion: The First Personal Airplane to Be Announced by a Major West Coast Manufacturer." *Western Flying* 26 (May 1946): 32-3+.

135. "Operations in Aircraft Specialty Shop." *Western Machinery and Steel World* 31 (July 1940): 277.

Aircraft Specialties & Supply Co., Santa Monica.

136. "The Pacific Coast's Only Builder of Radial Aircraft Engines." *Western Machinery and Steel World* 31 (July 1940): 274-5.

Kinner Motors, Inc., Glendale.

137. Pederson, Carlton A. "A Case Study of Lockheed Aircraft Corporation's Program for the Selection of Management Personnel." Doctoral dissertation, Stanford University, 1946. 139 pp.

138. Poole, A. W. "Where the Aviation Industry Centers." *Southern California Business* 8 (May 1929): 9-10+.

Los Angeles County.

139. Rae, John B. *Climb to Greatness: The American Aircraft Industry, 1920-1960*. Cambridge, Mass., 1968. 280 pp.

140. "Round-the-Clock Schedule for Vega and Lockheed." *Western Machinery and Steel World* 32 (July 1941): 344-5.

141. Rudeen, John E. "Analysis of Differentials in the Structure of Engineer Salaries in the Southern California Aircraft Industry." Master's thesis, University of Southern California, 1958. 70 pp.

142. Seidenbaum, Art. "From Here to the Moon." *Los Angeles* 3 (January 1962): 14-9.

Role of Los Angeles firms in Apollo space program.

143. Smalley, Calvin. "Selling the Air to Your Boss: Southern California Aircraft Engineers Helped Most by Adding Comfort to Speed." *Southern California Business* 13 (July 1954): 10-1.

144. "A Southern California Aircraft Tool Shop." *Western Machinery and Steel World* 31 (September 1940): 342-3.

Airco Tool Co., Santa Monica.

145. Squier, Carl B. "Speed — A Los Angeles Idea: We Build It into Planes That Are Fastest and Flying with Pay Load, at Least Cost." *Southern California Business* 13 (May 1934): 9-10.

Lockheed Aircraft Corp.

146. Stark, James W. "Forecasting Maintenance Requirements for Complex Electronic Equipment in the Aircraft Industry: Los Angeles." Master's thesis, University of Southern California, 1958. 109 pp.

147. Strosnider, R. H. " 'Forward' — Burbank." *Los Angeles Realtor* 8 (November 1928): 32.

Ascribes Burbank's progress to growth of movie industry and airplane manufacture.

148. Taylor, Frank J., and Wright, Lawton. *Democracy's Air Arsenal*. New York, 1947. 208 pp.

Accounts of the rise of the aircraft manufacturing industry; Aircraft Production Council World War II; Boeing, Consolidated, Vultee, Douglas, Lockheed, North American, Northrop, and Ryan.

149. Thomas, Milton G. "An Analytical Study of the Industrial Relations Program at Northrop Aircraft, Inc." Master's thesis, University of Southern California, 1948. 163 pp.

150. "The Trends of Today in Airplanes and Motors: An Analysis of the Exposition." *Western Flying* 4 (October 1928): 44-5.

Held in Los Angeles.

151. Turner, Q. G. "Vega Streamlines Production with Ultramodern Plant." *Western Machinery and Steel World* 32 (February 1941): 58-60.

Vega Airplane Co., Burbank.

152. Tyran, Michael R. "Mechanized Financial Forecasting at Lockheed Aircraft Corporation." Master's thesis, University of Southern California, 1962. 191 pp.

Use of electronic data processing in business forecasting.

153. U. S. Department of Labor. Bureau of Labor Statistics. *Southern California Aircraft Workers in Wartime*. Washington, D.C. 1946. 17 pp.

154. "Vultee: Where Aircraftsmen Are Setting New Production Records with Modern Equipment." *Western Machinery and Steel World* 31 (June 1940): 208-12.

155. "Wings for the World: Aircraft Manufacturing at the Plant Producing the DC-4, World's Largest Land Plane." *Western Machinery and Steel World* 30 (July 1939): 190-3.

Douglas Aircraft, Santa Monica.

156. " 'Wings for the World' by California's Great Douglas Plants." *Western Machinery and Steel World* 31 (June 1940): 192-9.

157. "World's Largest and Most Powerful Airplane: United States Army Giant Bomber the Douglas B-19." *Western Machinery and Steel World* 31 (October 1940): 370-1.

158. "Young Santa Monica Firm Produces Vital Components and Systems for World Wide Aerospace Sales." *Western Flying* 44 (May-June 1964): 23.

Radar Relay, Inc.

AIRPORTS

159. Amrine, William J., and Amrine, Susan. "Brackett Field: Dirt Strip to Modern Airport." *Pomona Valley Historian* 6 (1970): 72-86; 126-38.

160. Ball, Stanley A. "Los Angeles Airport Extended: Biggest Hand-Leveling Job in the West Paves the Way for One of the Greatest Airports in the Country." *Western Construction News* 24 (June 1949): 94-6.

161. Beadle, W. N. "Los Angeles Gets FIDO: First Commercial Airport Uses Fog-Dispersal System to Achieve Weather-Free Landings." *American City* 64 (May 1949): 126-7.

162. "Beginning of an Era." *Outlook* 151 (March 13, 1929): 421-2.

Grand Central Air Terminal, said to be first airport devoted strictly to commercial aviation.

163. Belinn, C. M. "Municipal Planning for Helicopters." *American City* 67 (January 1952): 92-3.

By President of Los Angeles Airways, Inc.

164. Black, Don. "Big Business Growing Wings: 'Men at Work' Make Up a Large Part of the Air Travel In and Out of Los Angeles." *Southern California Business* 15 (July 1936): 12-3.

165. Brashear, H. R. "Shall Los Angeles Have a Municipal Airport for Commerce?" *Southern California Business* 6 (September 1927): 14-5+.

166. "Building a Jet-Age Terminal." *Western Construction* 36 (May 1961): 46-7.

Los Angeles International Airport.

167. "Burbank's Model Airport." *Pacific Municipalities* 44 (March 1930): 94.

United Airport.

168. Carpenter, Ford A. "Why Los Angeles Needs a First Class Airport." *Southern California Business* 5 (January 1927): 16-7.

169. Charleville, J. W. "Glendale Dedicates New Air Terminal." *Pacific Municipalities* 43 (March 1929): 99-100.

Grand Central Air Terminal.

170. "Constructing a Dustless Landing Strip for Air Terminal at Los Angeles." *Engineering News-Record* 102 (April 25, 1929): 660-2.

Grand Central Air Terminal, Glendale.

171. Cook, R. H. "Pilots, Carriers Debate FAA Plan to Alleviate Los Angeles Noise." *Aviation Week and Space Technology* 72 (January 4, 1960): 26-7.

172. "Curtiss Buys Two Western Airports." *Western Flying* 5 (June 1950): 114.

Alameda Airport and Grand Central Air Terminal, Glendale.

173. "The Dedication of L.A. Metropolitan." *Western Flying* 5 (January 1929): 88-9.

Los Angeles Metropolitan Airport, Van Nuys.

174. Ditzel, Paul. "A Field for Plane Watching." *Westways* 56 (October 1964): 40.

Van Nuys Airport.

175. "Downtown Heliport for Los Angeles." *California Magazine of the Pacific* 40 (September 1950): 30.

176. "Downtown Los Angeles Heliport to Aid Air Industry." *The Architect and Engineer* 182 (August 1950): 9.

177. "Federal Aid to Western Airports Will Exceed $8.8 Million in 1957." *Western City* 32 (July 1956): 34-5.

Includes several Los Angeles County airports.

178. "First FIDO at Commercial Airport: Dense

Fog at Los Angeles Municipal Airport Can Now Be Dispersed in 1½ Min. to Provide Round-the-Clock Safe Landing Conditions after Installation of the Country's First Commercial FIDO." *Western Construction News* 24 (April 1949): 77-8+.
Method of intensive fog dispersal (FIDO).

179. "Four L. A. Airlines Move to New Airport." *Western Flying* 26 (November 1946): 74.

180. Goodnow, Marc N. "Architectural Aspects of Pacific Airports." *The Architect and Engineer* 103 (November 1930): 29-42.
Southern California airports: Western Air Express, Alhambra; LeHigh Airport, Los Angeles; Grand Central Airport Terminal, Glendale; United Airport, Burbank.

181. Graham, Ben S. "Career Mastery: A Study of Growth and Decline of Occupational Identity Among Air Traffic Controllers at Los Angeles International Airport." Doctoral dissertation, University of California, Los Angeles 1969. 325 pp.

182. Hawkes, Russell. "Work Advances on Los Jet Airport." *Aviation Week and Space Technology* 75 (July 3, 1961): 40-1.

183. Himmel, N. S. "Airlines Expand Los Angeles Facilities." *Aviation Week and Space Technology* 92 (May 4, 1970): 44-6.

184. Keally, Francis. "Architectural Treatment of the Airport." *The Architect and Engineer* 103 (November 1930): 43-51.
Grand Central Air Terminal, Glendale, and Curtiss Flying Service, Los Angeles.

185. Kendall, Thomas R. "Asphalt Stabilized Runways Built as Part of Extensive Development Program at Los Angeles Municipal Airport 13 Miles from City." *American City* 54 (July 1939): 55-6.

186. Kessler, Richard. "Can Service Ten Planes at a Time." *American City* 83 (May 1968): 137.
Hawthorne Municipal Airport.

187. Kochevar, Ronald J. "Congestion Problems and Some Possible Solutions at Major U.S. Airports with Emphasis on Los Angeles International Airport." Master's thesis, University of California, Los Angeles, 1970. 150 pp.

188. "The Landscape Development of the Los Angeles Airport." *The Architect and Engineer* 174 (August 1948): 10-6.

189. "League Urges Purchase of Mines Field." *Municipal League of Los Angeles Bulletin* 6 (August 1, 1929): [11].

190. Littrell, Gaither. "L. A. Faces Its Airport Problem." *Flying* 42 (April 1948): 36-7+.
Airport congestion.

191. Long Beach Chamber of Commerce. *Information about Long Beach, California: A Statistical Exhibit Prepared for Presentation to the Civil Aeronautics Board, Washington, D.C.* Long Beach, 1944. 29 pp.
Argument for airport facilities.

192. Los Angeles County. Regional Planning Commission. *A Comprehensive Report on the Master Plan of Airports for the Los Angeles County Regional Planning District.* Los Angeles, 1940. 165 pp.

193. "Los Angeles Expands Its Airport." *Aviation Week and Space Technology* 71 (September 21, 1959): 50.

194. "Los Angeles Revises Jet Approach Plan." *Aviation Week and Space Technology* 71 (October 26, 1959): 116-7.

195. "Los Angeles Starts Jet Age Terminal." *Aviation Week* 67 (December 2, 1957): 41-2.

196. "Los Angeles Votes Bond Issues for Airport, Sewage Treatment." *Western City* 21 (May 1945): 29.

197. Marx, Wesley, "Proud New Home for the Jet Liners." *Los Angeles* 2 (April 1961): 14-7.
Los Angeles International Airport.

198. McKinstry, F. D. "An Illuminating Article." *Western City* 6 (April 1930): 18.
Lighting the Los Angeles Municipal Airport and the Rose Bowl.

199. Miller, A. A. "Municipal Airport Grows from 80 to 365 Acres." *American City* 38 (April 1928): 144.
Long Beach.

200. "Mines Field — Airport or Political Grave-yard?" *Municipal League of Los Angeles Bulletin* 6 (February 1, 1929): [5].

201. "Municipal Airport Operation in the West." *Western City* 37 (June 1961): 17-22+; (July 1961): 36-40.

Includes Long Beach, Los Angeles, Santa Monica and Torrance.

202. "Portable Lounge for Air Travelers." *American City* 81 (November 1966): 23.

"A load-carrying helicopter or flying crane [a 'Skylounge'] may help solve the perplexing problem of getting passengers from downtown to airport and back again. The experiment will take place in the Los Angeles area using a craft like that used in Viet Nam for transporting ground forces."

203. "Renewing Long Beach Runways." *Western Construction* 44 (July 1969): 74+.

Long Beach Municipal Airport.

204. Ronnie, Art. "Wilshire and Fairfax: Aviation Center." *Westways* 52 (January 1960): 20-1.

Describes activities between 1919 and 1921 at two of the city's first three airports, De Mille Field No. 2 and Chaplin Airdrome.

205. "Runway Dedication: An Approach to the Problem of the Vanishing Urban Airport." *Western Flying* 27 (August 1947): 20-2.

Discusses Los Angeles.

206. Stahl, Sheldon W. "The Los Angeles International Airport—An Economic Analysis." Doctoral dissertation, University of California, Los Angeles, 1964. 268 pp.

207. Stromme, George. "$200,000 Airpark." *Western Flying* 26 (January 1946): 32-3.

Whiteman Airpark, Pacoima.

208. "TWA Builds New L.A. Nose Hangar." *Western Construction News* 22 (February 1947): 85.

209. "Two Major West Coast Cities Expand Airport Facilities." *Western City* 15 (June 1939): 44-5.

Los Angeles and Portland.

210. Wheeler, Henry O. "United Aircraft Spend-ing $2,500,000 for Development." *Southern California Business* 8 (November 1929): 9-11.

United Airport, Burbank.

211. Young, Clarence M. "FIDO Clears the Fog for Los Angeles." *American City* 63 (October 1948): 177.

Airport fog-dispersal system.

ARCHITECTURE AND ARCHITECTS

212. Adams, Charles G. "Whittier Union High School." *The Architect and Engineer* 103 (December 1930): 91-5.

213. "Adding to the Mission Play House." *Southern California Business* 7 (January 1929): 46.

San Gabriel.

214. Alexandria Hotel. *The Alexandria*. [Los Angeles, 1915?]. [4] pp.

215. "All-Marble Building for I. Magnin & Co., Los Angeles." *The Architect and Engineer* 137 (June 1939): 19-22.

216. Allan, Fitz John. "Hacienda La Brea Reflects Old Spanish Days." *California Graphic* 5 (March 3, 1928): 5.

217. Allen, Harris C. "Architecture in Los Angeles." *Overland Monthly* 85 (May 1927): 138.

218. —— "It Can Happen Here." *The Architect and Engineer* 129 (May 1937): 13-7.

Gordon B. Kaufmann's San Pedro High School and Los Angeles Times Building.

219. —— "Recent Theaters Designed by G. Albert Lansburgh, Architect." *The Architect and Engineer* 71 (November 1922): 47-69.

Includes Hill Street Theater and Shrine Auditorium, Los Angeles.

220. Alley, A. W. "A Southern California House in Japanese Style." *The Architect and Engineer of California* 21 (July 1910): 62-3.

Greene & Greene house in Pasadena.

221. "The Allied Architects [of Los Angeles]." *Municipal League of Los Angeles Bulletin* 2 (January 20, 1925): 13-6.

222. Allison, David C. "Seven Years of Architectural Control in Palos Verdes." *The Architect and Engineer* 100 (January 1930): 53-74.

223. —— "The Work of Mr. Myron Hunt, F.A.I.A." *The Architect and Engineer of California* 53 (April 1918): 38-68.

224. Alpaugh, Norman W. "The Asbury Apartments, Los Angeles." *The Architect and Engineer* 85 (May 1926): 43-9.

225. "Anti-Earthquake Roller Bearings Installed in L.A. Building Addition." *Western Construction News* 21 (November 1946): 111.
   Sears, Roebuck & Company.

226. "Apartments Designed for Single People." *Architectural Record* 109 (June 1951): 178-83.
   Brentwood Garden Apartments, Los Angeles.

227. Arfwedson, Carl G., and Morgridge, Howard H. "From Barracks to Beauty: El Camino College, Southern California." *The Architect and Engineer* 187 (November 1951): 14-22+.

228. Austin, John C. "The Al Malaikah Temple, Los Angeles." *The Architect and Engineer* 85 (June 1926): 79-90.

229. —— *Architecture in Southern California.* Los Angeles, 1905. Unp.

230. —— "The Los Angeles City Hall: Construction Well under Way on Structure 440 Ft. High to Cost $5,000,000." *Western Construction News* 2 (June 25, 1927): 48-9.

231. —— "Says Collapse Started from the Top." *The Architect and Engineer of California* 7 (November 1906): 46-7.
   Bixby Hotel, Long Beach.

232. Bach, Richard F. "The Southwest Museum Los Angeles Cal.—Summer Hunt & S. R Burns, Architects." *Architectural Record* 42 (July 1917): 19-26.
   Also history and activities of the museum.

233. Bailey, Stuart W. "The Gamble House, 1908: An Analytical Description of a Residence in Pasadena, California, in View of Some of the Influences Affecting Its Design." Master's thesis, Claremont Graduate School, 1954. 222 pp.

234. Bakewell, John, Jr. "The Pasadena City Hall." *The Architect and Engineer* 93 (June 1928): 35-9.

235. Bangs, Jean Murray. "Greene and Greene." *Architectural Forum* 89 (October 1948): 80-9.

236. Banham, Reyner. *Los Angeles; the Architecture of Four Ecologies.* New York, 1971.

237. "The Bank That Stayed." *Architectural Forum* 114 (February 1961): 82-5.
   Rebuilding of the Security First National Bank, Sixth and Spring streets, Los Angeles.

238. Barber, Lloyd D. "Building a Great University: Some Construction Problems." *The Architect and Engineer* 103 (October 1930): 91-2.
   UCLA.

239. Beanfield, R. McC. "Unusual Engineering Features of an Immense Theatre Building." *Proceedings of the American Society of Civil Engineers* 53 (December 1927): 2645-74.
   The Al Malaikah Temple, Los Angeles. A condensation of this article appears thusly: Beanfield, R. McC. "Unusal Engineering Features of the Al Malaikah Temple, Los Angeles." *American Architect* 133 (May 5, 1928): 625-34.

240. "Beautiful Beaux Arts Building: Los Angeles' New Music Center." *Saturday Night* 7 (March 26, 1927): 1-2.
   Beaux Arts Building, Eighth and Beacon streets, with some 175 studios, as well as auditorium, recital halls, offices, and stores.

241. "Beauty Plus Utility: A New Municipal Water and Power Office Complex Provides Landmark Attractiveness for Downtown Los Angeles." *American City* 81 (March 1966): 114+.

242. Berkeley, Ellen P. "Workshop in Watts." *Architectural Forum* 130 (January-February 1969): 58-63.
   The Urban Workshop, a group of black architects and planners.

243. Bingham, E. "Grauman Theater a Work of Art." *The Architect and Engineer* 73 (May 1923): 76-7.

244. "Bold Departure from Traditional Bank Design: Citizens National Trust and Savings Bank, Los Angeles." *Architectural Record* 104 (October 1948): 116-21.

245. Bole, James R. "All Prestressed and Precast Warehouse: $5.68 Per Sq. Ft." *Western Construction* 28 (September 1953): 65-7.
   Warehouse at Long Beach Harbor.

246. Boyd, John T., Jr. "A Jury of Artists Appraises the Architecture of Los Angeles." *Architectural Record* 48 (November 1920): 461-2.

247. Bradley Bungalow Co. *The Bungalow De Luxe*. [Los Angeles, c1912]. [30] pp.

248. Brady, Frances. "The Spanish Revival in California Architecture." Master's thesis, California State College at Long Beach, 1962. 211 pp.

249. "A British Criticism of the New Los Angeles City Hall." *The Architect and Engineer* 91 (November 1927): 63.

250. Brockway, Leon C. "A New Working Plant for the First Congregational Church of Pasadena, California." *The Architect and Engineer of California* 50 (August 1917): 59-65.

251. Brown, D. Scott. "Development Proposal for Dodge House Park." *Arts & Architecture* 83 (April 1966): 16.

252. ———— "Will Salvation Spoil the Dodge House?" *Architectural Forum* 125 (October 1966): 68-71.
   "Apparent rescue" of Irving Gill's Dodge House.

253. Brown, Robert G. "The California Bungalow in Los Angeles; A Study in Origins and Classification." Master's thesis, University of California, Los Angeles, 1964. 90 pp.

254. Brunnier, Henry J. "Structural Aspects of University Buildings." *The Architect and Engineer* 103 (October 1930): 49-83.
   UCLA.

255. Brush, George C. "New Office Building Construction Problems in Los Angeles Area." *Western Housing* 36 (October 1952): 10+.

256. Bulen, Mary. "Mary Andrews Clark Residence." *Los Angeles Saturday Night* 15 (February 2, 1935): 4.
   Residence originally built as a memorial for mother of William Andrews Clark.

257. "Bullock's Wilshire Boulevard Store — Los Angeles." *The Architect and Engineer* 99 (December 1929): 45-51.

258. "Bullock's Wilshire Department Store, Los Angeles." *Architectural Record* 67 (January 1930): 51-64.

259. Bungalowcraft Company. . . . *California Bungalow Homes*. 3rd ed. Los Angeles, c1911. 128 pp.

260. "Burbank City Hall." *The Architect and Engineer* 154 (August 1943): 18-23.

261. Burkhart, Max E. "The Architectural Requirements of a Television Center." Master's thesis, University of Southern California, 1951. 76 pp.
   CBS Television City.

262. "CBS—Television City—Los Angeles." *Arts & Architecture* 70 (January 1953): 20-3.
   Architects, William L. Pereira and Charles Luckman.

263. "California Club's Picturesque New Home on Flower Street." *Los Angeles Saturday Night* 9 (March 23, 1929): 1+.

264. "California Fruit Growers Exchange, Los Angeles, California." *American Architect* 148 (April 1936): 69-74.

265. "A California Theater of Reinforced Concrete." *The Architect and Engineer of California* 17 (May 1909): 67-73.
   Majestic Theater, Los Angeles.

266. "Camp Buildings Designed for Easy Erection and Reuse." *Western Construction* 35 (March 1960): 74+.
   Los Angeles County Road Department prison camp.

267. Campbell, H. M. "Lynwood Dedicates Modern City Hall." *American City* 69 (April 1954): 153.

268. "Century City, Los Angeles' New Ultra-Uptown Alcoa Building on 20th Century-Fox's Old Movie Lot." *Business Week* (July 23, 1966): 98-101.

269. "The Century Plaza: A Resort in Mid-City." *Architectural Record* 140 (August 1966): 124-7.

270. "Century Plaza Hotel/Minoru Yamasaki & Associates, Architects." *Arts & Architecture* 81 (December 1964): 24-5.

271. Charleville, J. W. "Civic Auditorium Dedicated by Pasadena." *Pacific Municipalities* 46 (March 1932): 93.

272. "City Hall by Victor Gruen Associates, Architects." *Arts & Architecture* 79 (October 1962): 12-3.
Redondo Beach.

273. Cline, William H. "The New Orpheum Theater Building, Los Angeles." *The Architect and Engineer of California* 26 (September 1911): 34-50.

274. "College Library by Kistner and Wright, Architects." *Arts & Architecture* 80 (June 1963): 18-9.
Cerritos College.

275. "Colorful High-Rise Is Tallest in L.A." *Architectural Record* 130 (October 1961): 139-41.
Tishman Realty and Construction Company Office Building.

276. "A Community Hotel by Richard J. Neutra and Robert E. Alexander, Architects." *Arts & Architecture* 70 (September 1953): 18-9+.
San Pedro. Planned, but never built.

277. "Competition for St. John's Church, Los Angeles." *The Architect and Engineer* 68 (February 1922): 75-7.

278. "Complex Elements Integrated Through Master Planning." *Architectural Record* 131 (March 1962): 167-70.
Los Angeles Orthopaedic Hospital.

279. "Concrete Cottages in California." *The Architect and Engineer of California* 31 (January 1913): 67-72.
Cottages in Sierra Madre by Irving Gill.

280. Connolly, John. "A Survey of Nineteenth Century Building in Los Angeles." Master's thesis, University of Southern California, 1962. 367 pp.
Filled with high-gloss, enlarged illustrations.

Provides background for twentieth-century building still existing.

281. Cook, Wilbur D. "The Howard E. Huntington Estate." *The Architect and Engineer of California* 11 (December 1907): 48-51.
Pasadena.

282. "County's New Fire Houses Set a High Standard of Neighborhood Architecture." *American City* 42 (May 1930): 112-3.

283. Coyle, Ray F. "A New Shop in Los Angeles." *The Architect and Engineer* 64 (February 1921): 70-5.
I. Magnin.

284. "Craig Ellwood Associates, Architect." *Arts & Architecture* 83 (November 1966): 28-31.
Plant for Scientific Data Systems, El Segundo.

285. Crawford, Roland H. "The Mirror Building, Los Angeles." *The Architect and Engineer* 176 (February 1949): 14-29.

286. Croly, Herbert D. "The California Country House." *Sunset Magazine* 18 (November 1906): 50-65. Reprinted in *The Architect and Engineer of California* 7 (December 1906): 24-39.
Architecture of Myron Hunt, Elmer Grey, A. Benton, and Greene & Greene in Los Angeles.

287. Daugherty [sic], Emmett E. "New Courthouse Progress Report." *Los Angeles Bar Bulletin* 31 (January 1956): 66-7.
[Author's correct name Doherty.]

288. "The Demonstration Health-House, Los Angeles." *Architectural Record* 67 (April 1930): 433-9.
Richard Neutra's "Lovell House."

289. "Design for Los Angeles Hall of Justice." *The Architect and Engineer* 69 (June 1922): 85-6.

290. "Design of Sierra Madre Library Includes Community Center Plan." *Western City* 32 (April 1956): 69.

291. "Designer of Ritz Carlton Reveals Plans." *Los Angeles Saturday Night* 10 (March 29, 1930): 7.
Proposed Hollywood Ritz-Carlton Hotel, designed by Gordon B. Kaufmann.

292. Doherty, Emmett E. "Superior Courts House a Reality." *Los Angeles Bar Bulletin* 24 (May 1949): 259+.

County Board of Supervisors awards contract for new Superior Courts Building.

293. Easton, Bob. "Architecture at UCLA and Berkeley." *California Engineer* 42 (May 1964): 6-8.

294. "Edison Company's Projected New Building." *Los Angeles Saturday Night* 8 (July 28, 1928): 2.

Fifth and Grand, Los Angeles.

295. Edminson, Ross W. "Some Houses in Southern California Designed by B. Cooper Corbett, A.I.A." *The Architect and Engineer of California* 40 (February 1915): 39-49.

Los Angeles architect and his work.

296. "The Elks Building, Los Angeles, Calif." *Architectural Record* 59 (April 1925): 357.

297. Ellis, Marion L. "Need for Earthquake Proof Construction in School Buildings as Revealed by the History of Earthquakes in California." Master's thesis, University of Southern California, 1934. 175 pp.

298. Evans, E. A. "Recent Work of Messrs. Walker and Eisen." *The Architect and Engineer* 82 (August 1925): 51-89.

299. ———— "United Artists Theater, Los Angeles." *The Architect and Engineer* 94 (August 1928): 35-8.

300. Evans, L. T. "Foundations for the Prudential Building, Los Angeles." *The Architect and Engineer* 180 (February 1950): 13+.

Adjacent to Hancock Park and La Brea Tar Pits.

301. "Exhibition House Group, Los Angeles, California. Arranged by Miss Marie Louise Schmidt." *Architectural Forum* 65 (July 1936): 37-46.

Los Angeles houses costing less than $5,000, designed by Neutra, Byers, Keeley & Estop, and Williams.

302. Flood, Frances. "A Study of Architecture of the Period 1869-1900 Existing in Los Angeles in 1940." Master's thesis, University of Southern California, 1941. 153 pp.

303. "Forty Tons of Mosaic." *Amercian Artist* 33 (August 1969): 18-21+.

Mathematical Sciences Building, UCLA.

304. "$14,000,000 Hotel for Los Angeles." *The Architect and Engineer* 166 (August 1946): 25+.

Statler Center.

305. "Fourth Exhibition of the Architectural League of the Pacific Coast." *The Architect and Engineer of California* 32 (March 1913): 46-71.

Exhibition presented under the auspices of the Los Angeles Architectural Club.

306. "Fraternity House by Carleton Monroe Winslow, Architect." *Arts & Architecture* 81 (August 1964): 17.

USC.

307. Gallion, Arthur B. "Architecture of the Los Angeles Region." *Architectural Record* 119 (May 1956): 159-66.

308. "Garden Apartment-Houses of the West." *The Architect and Engineer of California* 57 (June 1919): 72-8.

Sierra Madre apartments by Irving Gill.

309. Garren, William I. "Architecture and the Motion Picture." *The Architect and Engineer* 63 (October 1920): 66-70.

Goldwyn Studios, Culver City.

310. Gebhard, David. "L.A.—The Stuccoed Box." *Art in America* 58 (May-June 1970): 130-3.

Critique of Los Angeles architecture.

311. ———— "The Spanish Colonial Revival in Southern California (1895-1930)." *Journal of the Society of Architectural Historians* 26 (May 1967): 131-47.

312. ————, and Winter, Robert. *A Guide to Architecture in Southern California.* Los Angeles, 1965. 164 pp.

Primarily pictorial; an excellent work.

313. Gibbs, Dwight. "The Carthay Circle Theatre, Los Angeles." *The Architect and Engineer* 95 (November 1928): 63-6.

314. "Glendale Custom Designs Its New Municipal Office Building." *Western Ctiy* 42 (October 1966): 66-7.

315. Goldman, Ronald E. "Hillside Housing Project." *Arts & Architecture* 80 (September 1963): 14-5+.

Project designed for site in hills of South Pasadena.

316. Goodnow, Marc N. "Architectural Aspects of Pacific Airports." *The Architect and Engineer* 103 (November 1930): 29-42.

Southern California airports: Western Air Express, Alhambra; LeHigh Airport, Los Angeles; Grand Central Air Terminal, Glendale; United Airport, Burbank.

317. ———— "Distinction and Dollars in New Southern California Architecture." *Southern California Business* 6 (November 1927): 20+.

Mainly Los Angeles.

318. Gordon, Dudley C. "El Alisal: The House That Lummis Built." *Historical Society of Southern California Quarterly* 35 (1953): 19-28.

319. ———— *El Alisal: The Lummis Home; Its History and Architecture, California State Monument No. 531.* [Los Angeles, 1964]. 11 pp.

Charles Fletcher Lummis (1859-1928) and his home.

320. Gregg, Gardner W. "Civic Center Plan." *Municipal League of Los Angeles Bulletin* 2 (March 1925): 13-4.

By "one of the publicity agents of the Allied Architects."

321. ———— "Los Angeles' Bold Plans for a Civic Center." *National Municipal Review* 14 (July 1925): 406-9.

322. Grey, Elmer. "Fifth Annual Architectural Exhibit at Los Angeles." *The Architect and Engineer of California* 44 (March 1916): 39-68.

323. ———— "On the Design of Certain Modern Church Edifices." *Architectural Record* 34 (December 1913): 544-56.

First Church of Christ, Scientist, Los Angeles, on Alvarado Street.

324. ———— "What a Home in California Should Mean." *The Architect and Engineer of California* 47 (December 1916): 38-61.

Los Angeles architecture.

325. Gustafson, Paul E. "New School Unit Fills Today's Education Needs." *The Architect and Engineer* 141 (June 1940): 43+.

Richard Neutra's Emerson Junior High School, Los Angeles.

326. Hadley, Homer M. "New Home of the California Fruit Growers Exchange, Los Angeles." *The Architect and Engineer* 124 (February 1936): 9-14.

327. Hales, George P. *Los Angeles City Hall.* Los Angeles, c1928. 63 pp.

328. Hall, George D. "An Eastern Architect's Impressions of Los Angeles." *The Architect and Engineer* 61 (May 1920): 90-1.

329. ———— "The Estate of Mr. W. L. Dodge, Hollywood, California." *The Architect and Engineer* 61 (April 1920): 87-90.

Irving Gill's "Dodge House."

330. Hamilton, Frederick. "Recent Work of Albert C. Martin, Architect." *The Architect and Engineer* 85 (June 1926): 43-73.

Los Angeles architect and his works, including Los Angeles City Hall.

331. Hamilton, William. "Administration Center for Los Angeles." *The Architect and Engineer* 124 (January 1936): 11-5.

332. Hanley, Anne. "A Sampling of Modern Religious Architecture in Southern California." *Westways* 62 (August 1970): 36-44.

Pictorial; brief text.

333. Hansen, Frank A. "Beverly Hills City Hall." *Western City* 8 (December 1932): 17-8.

334. Harris, Frank, and Bonenberger, Weston, eds. *A Guide to Contemporary Architecture in California.* Los Angeles, 1951. 91 pp.

335. "Harris Hall of Architecture Dedicated." *The Architect and Engineer* 140 (January 1940): 8+.

USC.

336. *Hellman Building, 4th and Main Sts., Los Angeles, California.* [Los Angeles, 1909]. [15] pp.

337. Holden, H. H. "Natural Beauty of Palos Verdes Hills Enhanced by Proper Adaptation of

Architectural Designs." *Hydraulic Engineering* 4 (June 1928): 321-3.

338. "Hollywood's Outstanding Bank Structure." *Los Angeles Saturday Night* 9 (November 24, 1928): 7.

First National Trust and Savings Bank, Hollywood Boulevard at Highland, Los Angeles.

339. Honnold, Douglas. *Southern California Architecture, 1956-1969*. New York, 1956. 96 pp.

340. "Honor Awards: American Institute of Architects, Southern California and Pasadena Chapters." *Arts and Architecture* 69 (January 1952): 24-32.

Most in Los Angeles County.

341. "Hospital Designed for Quakes." *Western Construction News* 20 (April 1945): 87-90.

Birmingham General Hospital, Van Nuys.

342. *Hotel Alexandria, Los Angeles, California.* [Los Angeles, 1910?]. 22 pp.

343. *Hotel Green* [San Francisco, c1905]. 16 pp. Another edition: [Los Angeles, 19(10?)]. [48] pp.

Pasadena.

344. Howe-Prell, Bette. "Richard Neutra's Home." *Southern California Prompter* 2 (February 1961): 32-4.

Neutra and his works in Los Angeles, including his own home on Silverlake Boulevard.

345. Hunt, Myron. *Palos Verdes—Where Bad Architecture Is Eliminated.* [Los Angeles?, 1927?]. 15 pp.

Reprinted from *Pacific Coast Architect,* April 1927.

346. ———— "The Pasadena, California, Stadium." *American Architect* 128 (October 20, 1925): 341-6.

Rose Bowl.

347. ———— "The Work of Messrs. Allison & Allison." *The Architect and Engineer of California* 42 (September 1915): 39-75.

Los Angeles architects and their works.

348. Hunter, Paul R., and Reichardt, Walter L. *Residential Architecture in Southern California.* [Los Angeles?], 1939. [111] pp.

349. Hunter, Thomas B. "Features of Mechanical Layout of University of California Buildings." *The Architect and Engineer* 103 (October 1930): 85-90.

UCLA.

350. Huntington Hotel. *The Huntington, Pasadena, California.* [Pasadena?, 19——]. [24] pp.

351. "Huntington Park Builds City Hall." *Western City* 24 (February 1948): 30-1.

352. Hyers, Faith H. "The New Los Angeles Library." *Libraries* 31 (February 1926): 74-7.

Description of new Los Angeles Library completed in May 1926.

353. ———— "The New Public Library, Los Angeles." *The Architect and Engineer* 87 (November 1926): 77-82.

354. ———— "Significance of Los Angeles' New Library." *Library Journal* 51 (August 1926): 633-6.

355. ———— "Utility and Beauty in the New Los Angeles Public Library." *Libraries* 31 (October 1926): 408-10.

Description of library, opened to public July 6, 1926.

356. ———— "Where Simplicity Means Beauty." *Sunset* 57 (December 1926): 17+.

Los Angeles Public Library.

357. "IBM Aerospace Headquarters by Eliot Noyes and Associates, Architects." *Arts & Architecture* 81 (October 1964): 14-7.

Westchester.

358. Irvin, Leslie A. "Los Angeles Processing Plant Utilizes Steel Framing on Top of Concrete Flat Slab." *Civil Engineering* 20 (July 1950): 30-2.

Lever Bros. Company.

359. "Islamic Mosque by Pierre Koenig, Architect." *Arts & Architecture* 81 (September 1964): 33.

Moslem Association of America, Los Angeles.

360. "J. W. Robinson Company: New Department Store, Beverly Hills, California." *The Architect and Engineer* 188 (March 1952): 10-5.

361. James, George W. "The Christian Science Ar-

chitecture of Los Angeles." *Out West,* new series, 4 (August 1912): [71]-9.

362. ——— "'Fashioned by Nature.'" *Out West,* new series, 5 (March-April 1913): [141]-53.
Rustic construction and landscaping Los Angeles.

363. Jennings, Frederick W. "The Architecture and Landscape Architecture of Los Angeles and Vicinity." *The Architect and Engineer* 62 (August 1920): 47-94.

364. ——— "The Los Angeles City Hall." *The Architect and Engineer* 93 (May 1928): 35-9.

365. ——— "Los Angeles the Home of Many High Class Apartment Houses." *The Architect and Engineer of California* 34 (September 1913): 65-75.

366. ——— "Recent Hotel Architecture in California." *The Architect and Engineer* 80 (January 1925): 49-69.
Half of this article concerns the Los Angeles Biltmore, "largest hotel west of Chicago."

367. ——— "A Theater Designed in the Egyptian Style." *The Architect and Engineer* 72 (March 1923): 77-84.
Grauman's Egyptian Theater, Hollywood.

368. Jones, Fred'k. W. "Some Notable Architecture in Southern California." *The Architect and Engineer* 72 (March 1923): 47-74.
Los Angeles and vicinity.

369. Keally, Francis. "Architectural Treatment of the Airport." *The Architect and Engineer* 103 (November 1930): 43-51.
Grand Central Air Terminal, Glendale, and Curtiss Flying Service, Los Angeles.

370. Keough, T. E. "Failure of the Bixby Hotel: Official Reports of the Special Committee from the San Francisco Cement Workers Union." *The Architect and Engineer of California* 7 (December 1906): 67-70.
Long Beach hotel.

371. Kinsey, Kersey. "From Desert to Glamor: San Fernando Valley Federal Savings and Loan Association, San Fernando, California." *The Architect and Engineer* 202 (July 1955:) 14-7+.

372. Knight, Arthur, and Elisofon, Eliot. *The Hollywood Style.* New York, 1969. 216 pp.

373. Lansburgh, G. Albert. "The El Capitan Theatre and Department Store Building, Hollywood." *The Architect and Engineer* 88 (February 1927): 35-43.

374. "'Lay' Votes Spotlight Los Angeles Buildings." *Architectural Record* 87 (March 1940): 16-8.
Survey of Angelenos on architectural preferences among local buildings: most popular, Union Station, NBC, and I. Magnin.

375. Leonard, John B. "The Failure of the Bixby Hotel." *The Architect and Engineer* 7 (November 1906): [85-92].
Long Beach hotel.

376. "Lightweight Aggregate Volume Tops Records on Statler Building Project." *Western Construction* 26 (August 1951): 72-4.
Statler Center, Los Angeles.

377. "Limit of Height of Buildings May Be Eliminated in Los Angeles." *Western Housing* 39 (March 1956): 10+.

378. Lindeberg, Harrie T. "Some Observations on Domestic Architecture." *The Architect and Engineer of California* 33 (June 1913): 46-72.
Los Angeles.

379. "Lofty Office Building Has—Gunited Lightweight Spandrel Walls." *Western Construction News* 24 (May 1949): 79-80.
General Petroleum Corp., Los Angeles.

380. "Los Angeles Automobile Service Station Embodies Newest Features." *The Architect and Engineer* 164 (January 1946): 8-9.

381. "Los Angeles Biltmore Hotel, Los Angeles, Cal." *Architectural Record* 54 (November 1923): 523.

382. "Los Angeles County Civic Center." *The Architect and Engineer* 136 (March 1939): 29.

383. Los Angeles County Museum. *Irving Gill, 1870-1936 . . . in Collaboration with the Art Center in La Jolla.* Los Angeles, 1958. 58 pp.

384. "Los Angeles Harbor Terminal, A Joint Venture by Kistner, Wright & Wright, Architects & Engineers; Edward H. Fickett, Architect; and S. B. Barnes & Associates." *Arts & Architecture* 80 (August 1963): 26-7+.

385. "Los Angeles Has First Steel Lamella Roof on Pacific Coast." *The Architect and Engineer* 107 (October 1931): 67-9.

Coca Cola warehouse.

386. "Los Angeles in a New Image." *Life* 48 (June 20, 1960): 74-87+.

387. Los Angeles. Municipal Art Commission. *Roots of California Contemporary Architecture, by Esther McCoy.* [An Exhibition of the work of Irving Gill, Greene & Greene, Bernard Maybeck, Richard Neutra, R. M. Schindler, Frank Lloyd Wright.] [Los Angeles, 1956]. [20 pp.]

388. "Los Angeles' New Depot." *The Architect and Engineer* 35 (December 1913): 84.

Southern Pacific Railroad Terminal.

389. "Los Angeles Stock Exchange Artistic Bronze Doors." *Los Angeles Saturday Night* 11 (January 10, 1931): 7.

390. "Low Camp: A Kook's Tour of Southern California's Fast-Disappearing Un-Real Estate." *Los Angeles* 10 (November 1965): 34-5.

Los Angeles "Pop-Architecture" — commercial buildings shaped like animals, hot dogs, hats and other such objects.

391. "A Low-Cost Church in Los Angeles." *Architectural Record* 76 (November 1934): 346-7.

Photographs and plan of Our Lady of Lebanon Church on Brooklyn Avenue.

392. Luitjens, Helen. *The Elegant Era; A Sketchbook of the Ornate Architecture and Delicate Detail of Yesterday's Southland.* [Palm Desert, Calif., 1968]. Unp.

393. "Magnificent New Home of Southern California Edison Company." *Los Angeles Saturday Night* 11 (February 21, 1931): 7.

Architectural and structural features of building at Fifth and Grand, Los Angeles.

394. "A Mail Order Store Building in Los Angeles, California." *Architectural Record* 64 (July 1928): 65-9.

Sears, Roebuck & Co., Ninth and Soto streets.

395. "The Majestic Theatre Building at Los Angeles." *Engineering Record* 59 (January 30, 1909): 128.

396. "A Mammoth Vitrified Clay Pipe Plant." *The Architect and Engineer* 30 (September 1912): 84.

Pacific Sewer Pipe Company, Los Angeles.

397. Mann, William F. "Investigation of Sawtooth Construction for Secondary School Building in Los Angeles." Master's thesis, University of Southern California, 1937. 227 pp.

398. "A Manufacturing Building in Los Angeles, Cal." *American Architect* 126 (December 17, 1924): 589-90.

Theme Hosiery Co.

399. "Many Plan and Structural Innovations in Dorsey High School." *Architectural Record* 84 (September 1938): 39-48.

400. Mark, David. "New Chapel for San Gabriel Mission." *Westways* 50 (March 1958): 28-9.

401. Martins, Victor L. "A Study of Public Schools in Southern California Damaged by the Earthquake of March 10, 1933." Master's thesis, University of Southern California, 1933. 146 pp.

402. Maybeck, Bernard R. "Reflections on the Grauman Metropolitan Theater, Los Angeles." *The Architect and Engineer* 73 (June 1923): 99-102.

403. McCoy, Esther. "A. Quincy Jones and Frederick E. Emmons." *Arts & Architecture* 83 (May 1966): 8-13.

Los Angeles architects.

404. ——— "Lloyd Wright." *Arts & Architecture* 83 (October 1966): 22-6.

His buildings in Los Angeles.

405. ——— *Modern California Houses: Case Study Houses 1945-1962.* New York, 1962. 215 pp.

406. ——— "Roots of California Contemporary Architecture." *Arts & Architecture* 73 (October 1956): 14-7+.

407. ——— "Social Sciences Building by Maynard Lyndon, Architect." *Arts & Architecture* 83 (December 1966): 8-12.

UCLA.

408. ——— "A Vast Hall Full of Light, the Bradbury Building." *Arts & Architecture* 70 (April 1953): 20-1+.

Los Angeles building famous for its design.

409. ——— "Wilshire Boulevard." *Western Architect and Engineer* 222 (September 1961): 25-51.

410. McC[oy], E[sther], and T[ravers], D[avid]. "Editorial—Irving Gill's Dodge House: 1916-1965." *Arts & Architecture* 82 (September 1965): 11.

Los Angeles architectural landmark demolished.

411. "Medical Building Expertly Designed." *Western Construction News* 24 (May 1949): 96.

Thatcher Medical Center, Pasadena.

412. "Merchandising Center: A New Robinson's Store." *Arts & Architecture* 69 (April 1952): 37-9+.

Beverly Hills, by Periera & Luckman, and Charles O. Matcham.

413. "Merchandising Center: A New Store for Bullock's." *Arts & Architecture* 68 (December 1951): 29-31.

Westwood, by Welton Becket and Associates.

414. "The Merritt Building, Los Angeles." *The Architect and Engineer* 41 (April 1915): 53-7.

415. "Mid-Wilshire Medical Building." *Arts & Architecture* 68 (September 1951): 28-31.

By Victor Gruen.

416. "Mid-Wilshire Medical Building, Beverly Hills, Los Angeles." *The Architect and Engineer* 187 (December 1951): 16-21.

417. Miller, Arthur. " 'Always Plan Largely': Architect Lloyd Wright Recalls Ideas His Famous Father Had for Los Angeles, and Blasts Current Civic Planning." *Los Angeles* 3 (February 1962): 21-2.

418. "Milliron Department Store, Westchester District, Los Angeles." *The Architect and Engineer* 179 (November 1949): 20-8.

419. *Miradero, the Country Home of L. C. Brand, Los Angeles County, California.* [Los Angeles, n.d.]. 28 pp.

420. "The Mission Type School House." *The Architect and Engineer of California* 14 (September 1908): 34-42.

Madison School, Pasadena.

421. Mitchell, Roy C. "Huge Concrete Girders and Trusses in New Theater." *Engineering News-Record* 91 (July 5, 1923): 4-9.

Grauman's Metropolitan Theater, Sixth and Hill, Los Angeles.

422. "Modern Art in New Richfield Building." *Los Angeles Saturday Night* 9 (December 15, 1928): 7.

Some architectural features of this building designed by Morgan, Walls & Clements.

423. "Modern Hospital: Mount Sinai in Los Angeles." *Arts & Architecture* 73 (June 1956): 18-20.

By Welton Becket and Associates, and Palmer, Krisel and Lindsay.

424. "More Is Less." *Arts & Architecture* 80 (October 1963): 10+.

Dodge House.

425. "Morningside High School, Inglewood, California." *The Architect and Engineer* 202 (September 1955): 30.

426. Morris, Mary E. "Pomona: The American Story of Change as Revealed in the Architecture of an Ordinary Community." Master's thesis, Claremont Graduate School, 1953. 292 pp.

427. Morrow, Irving F. "Ancient California Architecture." *The Architect and Engineer* 68 (January 1922): 47-69.

Myron Hunt's Flintridge Country Club, near Pasadena.

428. ——— "A Notable Architectural Achievement—The University Club of Los Angeles." *The Architect and Engineer* 72 (January 1923): 47-85.

429. ——— "The Pasadena Public Library." *The Architect and Engineer* 91 (October 1927): 35-41.

430. ——— "A Restored Spanish Adobe." *The Architect and Engineer* 65 (April 1921): 47-55.

C. E. Noyes residence, Pasadena.

431. ——— "A Revival of Adobe Buildings." *The Architect and Engineer* 69 (April 1922): 47-57.

Adobe homes in Los Angeles area.

432. ——— "The Women's Athletic Club of Los Angeles." *The Architect and Engineer* 82 (September 1925): 55-75.

433. "Municipal Electric Utility Architecture." *Los Angeles Saturday Night* 8 (January 21, 1928): 2.

Architecture of stations belonging to the Los Angeles Bureau of Power and Light.

434. Neely, Jo. "A Dream Come True." *The Architect and Engineer of California* 53 (May 1918): 80-6.

New Grauman Theatre, Third and Broadway, Los Angeles.

435. Neff, Wallace. *Architecture of Southern California; A Selection of Photographs, Plans, and Scale Details from the Work of Wallace Neff.* Chicago, [c1964]. 144 pp.

436. "Neutra and Alexander Design Fine Arts Building with Handsome Sun Controls." *Architectural Record* 131 (April 1962): 144-5.

San Fernando Valley State College.

437. "Neutra Obliges a Colorful Tenant with Adaptable Interiors." *Interiors* 111 (February 1952): 84-91.

American Crayon Company, Los Angeles.

438. "The New Administration Center Plan for Los Angeles." *Architectural Record* 57 (May 1925): 474-5.

Plan submitted by Allied Architects' Association.

439. "New Beverly-Wilshire Apartment Hotel." *Los Angeles Saturday Night* 8 (December 24, 1927): 2+.

$4 million apartment hotel designed by Walker & Eisen.

440. "New City Hall Is Designed to Dominate Los Angeles Landscape." *American City* 37 (November 1927): 666.

441. *The New Hotel Clark.* [Los Angeles?, 1917?]. [7] pp.

442. "New Limit-Height Title Insurance and Trust Company Building." *Los Angeles Saturday Night* 8 (June 9, 1928): 2.

443. "New Los Angeles Builders Exchange." *The Architect and Engineer* 187 (November 1951): 11+.

444. "New Research Laboratories: McCulloch Motors Corporation, Los Angeles, California." *The Architect and Engineer* 182 (September 1950): 26-7.

445. "New State Building in Los Angeles Dedicated with Impressive Ceremony." *California Highways and Public Works* 10 (July 1932): 24-5.

446. "Newest Building in Photographic Center, Hollywood, California." *The Architect and Engineer* 186 (August 1951): 16-8+.

Western Division of Graflex, Inc.

447. "Newly-Opened Trading Floor of the California Stock Exchange." *Los Angeles Saturday Night* 10 (January 18, 1930): 1+.

California Stock Exchange, Seventh and Main streets.

448. "Newspaper Plant by George Vernon Russell and Eduardo Jose Samaniego, Associated Architects." *Arts & Architecture* 72 (August 1955): 19.

La Opinion (Spanish language newspaper), Fifteenth and Main streets.

449. "Notable Features of New Stock Exchange Building." *Los Angeles Saturday Night* 9 (June 29, 1929): 11.

Los Angeles.

450. Nystrom, Richard K. "UCLA, an Interpretation Considering Architecture and Site." Doctoral dissertation, University of California, Los Angeles, 1968. 294 pp.

451. "Oceanarium By Pereira and Luckman, Architects." *Arts & Architecture* 71 (November 1954): 22-3.

Marineland.

452. O'Connor, Ben H. "School House Trends in Southern California." *The Architect and Engineer* 144 (February 1941): 35-42.

El Segundo High School.

453. O'Dodd, George V. " 'The Castle on the Hill' (Yama Shiro)." *The Architect and Engineer* 73 (June 1923): 87-94.

Hollywood Hills "Castle" of Messrs. Adolph and Eugene Bernheimer.

454. Oehl, Gordon L. "Esthetics of Public Buildings Emphasized at La Puente City Hall Dedication." *Western City* 42 (July 1966): 46-7.

455. "Office Building and Auditorium by Richard J. Neutra . . . & Robert E. Alexander." *Arts & Architecture* 74 (July 1957): 14-5.

Amalgamated Clothing Worers of America, Los Angeles.

456. "Office Building by Victor Gruen and Associates." *Arts & Architecture* 74 (June 1957): 12-3.

Tishman Realty and Construction Company, Los Angeles.

457. "The Office Building of Tomorrow: $8,000,000 General Petroleum Building—Los Angeles." *The Architect and Engineer* 177 (June 1949): 16+.

458. "Olympic Stadium in Los Angeles." *Architectural Record* 70 (December 1931): 419-24.

Los Angeles Coliseum.

459. "One Convertible Plan, the Basic Design for a 100-Unit Subdivision, Allows One Customer to Change a Standard House to Fit His Own Family Requirements of Size and Use." *Architectural Forum* 90 (April 1949): 126-8.

Mar Vista District of Los Angeles.

460. Orbison, R[obert] V. "A Worthy Center for the 'Crown City.' " *American City* 35 (November 1926): 678-9.

New Pasadena City Hall.

461. "Pacific Borax Plant a Notable Industrial Achievement." *The Architect and Engineer* 80 (March 1925): 81-2.

Plant located on Mormon Island in Los Angeles Harbor.

462. "Pacific Electric Subway Terminal, Los Angeles." *The Architect and Engineer* 82 (July 1925): 68-70.

463. "Parklabrea Apartments." *The Architect and Engineer* 156 (February 1944): 19+.

464. "Parklabrea Housing Project." *Arts & Architecture* 67 (January 1950): 39-43.

465. "Parklabrea, Los Angeles." *Architectural Record* 99 (May 1946): 88-90.

466. "Partial Collapse of the Bixby Hotel at Long Beach." *The Architect and Engineer of California* 7 (November 1906): 44-5.

467. "Pasadena's New Public Library." *Saturday Night* 7 (February 19, 1927): 17.

Designed by Myron Hunt and H. C. Chambers, the first building to be completed in new Pasadena Civic Center.

468. Perliter, S. "Building Poured by Pumpcrete." *Western Construction News* 22 (June 1947): 90-100.

This and the following article concern the May Co., Crenshaw, Los Angeles.

469. ———— "Construction of West Coast Building Proves Economical Use of Pumped Concrete." *Civil Engineering* 17 (June 1947): 20-3.

470. "The Pilgrim Church at Pomona, California." *The Architect and Engineer of California* 30 (August 1912): 63-5.

471. "Police Facilities Building, Los Angeles, California." *The Architect and Engineer* 193 (May 1953): 7-9.

472. "Police Facilities Building, Los Angeles, California." *The Architect and Engineer* 205 (May 1955): 8-13.

473. "Police Facility Building by Welton Becket & Associates, Architects, and J. E. Stanton, Associated Architect." *Arts & Architecture* 73 (July 1956): 12-3.

Los Angeles Police Building (Parker Center).

474. Politi, Leo C. *Bunker Hill, Los Angeles: Reminiscences of Bygone Days.* Palm Desert, 1964. [65] pp.

475. "Precast Concrete Auditorium by Flewelling & Moody, Architects." *Arts & Architecture* 81 (May 1964): 16-7.

Culver City.

476. Price, Matlack. "Great Modern Hotels of America, Their Leadership in Architecture and

Interior Design: The Los Angeles-Biltmore." *Arts and Decoration* 21 (June 1924): 25-8.

477. "Proposed Fashion Building for Los Angeles." *The Architect and Engineer* 162 (September 1945): 14+.

478. "Recently Completed Pacific Finance Building Marks Growth." *Los Angeles Saturday Night* 8 (April 14, 1928): 2.

Office building on South Hope Street.

479. "Redevelopment Project Submitted to the Santa Monica, California, Redevelopment Agency by Maynard Lyndon, A. Quincy Jones, Frederick E. Emmons, Associated Architects." *Arts & Architecture* 78 (May 1961): 16-8.

Ocean Park project.

480. Reed, Frank. "Unique Helical Stairway Is within Center Well: Tower in Southwest Museum, Los Angeles, Contains Probably the Only Reinforced-Concrete Stairway of Its Kind in the World." *Engineering Record* 73 (January 15, 1916): 82.

481. Regan, Michael. *Mansions of Los Angeles.* Los Angeles, 1965. 79 pp.

Pictorial with text.

482. —— *Stars, Moguls, Magnates—The Mansions of Beverly Hills.* Los Angeles, 1966. 79 pp.

Domestic architecture, Beverly Hills.

483. "A Reinforced Concrete Church in Los Angeles, Cal." *Engineering Record* 59 (March 20, 1909): 312-3.

Second Church of Christ, Scientist, on West Adams.

484. "A Research Park by Victor Gruen Associates for Great Lakes Properties, Inc." *Arts & Architecture* 75 (October 1958): 14-5.

Palos Verdes.

485. "Result of Competition for Pasadena Civic Center Buildings." *The Architect and Engineer* 76 (March 1924): 77-80.

486. Reynolds, Del M. "Casa Verdugo, the Renovation of a Famous Hacienda." *Out West,* new series, 1 (February 1911): 182-90.

487. "The Richfield Building, Los Angeles." *Architectural Record* 67 (June 1930): 505-10.

488. "Richfield Building, Los Angeles, California." *American Architect* 139 (May 1931): 44-5.

489. Robinson, Alcyon. "Industry and Artistry in Club Home: New Lines of Architecture and Decoration Mark the New Building Recently Completed by the University Club." *Southern California Business* 1 (October 1922): 25+.

Los Angeles.

490. Roehrig, Frederick L. "Los Angeles Power and Light Plants." *The Architect and Engineer* 99 (November 1929): 75-9.

491. Roller, Albert F. "World Headquarters Office Building, Rexall Drug Company, Los Angeles, California." *The Architect and Engineer* 171 (October 1947): 19-27+.

492. Rosenheim, Alfred F. "Los Angeles Woefully Lacking in Beautiful Municipal Buildings." *The Architect and Engineer of California* 36 (July 1914): 78-9.

493. —— "A Mammoth Department Store." *The Architect and Engineer of California* 6 (August 1906): 36-9.

Hamburger Building, Eighth and Broadway, Los Angeles.

494. Sachse, Richard. "Proposed Railroad Grade Crossing Elimination and New Passenger and Freight Terminals for Los Angeles." *The Architect and Engineer* 62 (September 1920): 47-58.

495. Sanders, Harry, Jr. "Two Streamlined Ticket Offices." *The Architect and Engineer* 150 (August 1942): 42-3.

Union Pacific Railroad and United Airlines offices, Los Angeles.

496. Schippers, Donald J. "Walker & Eisen: Twenty Years of Los Angeles Architecture, 1920-1940." *Southern California Quarterly* 46 (1964): 371-91.

An explanation for the architecture of this era of boom and bust. This firm is credited with the planning of $40,000,000-worth of buildings—apartments, hotels, offices, theatres, banks, and department stores.

497. Schulze, Henry A. "Says Bixby Hotel Construction Was Not True Reinforced Concrete." *The Architect and Engineer of California* 7 (December 1906): 71-3.

Investigation into causes of Long Beach hotel collapse.

498. Schuyler, Montgomery. "Round about Los Angeles." *Architectural Record* 24 (December 1908): 430-40.

Descriptive article.

499. Simmons, Matty. *On the House. Decorations by Fabres.* New York, 1955. 259 pp.

Los Angeles and San Francisco restaurant interior designs (decor).

500. Simmons, Joseph. "The Bixby Hotel Disaster as Viewed by a Brick Man." *The Architect and Engineer of California* 7 (December 1906): 51-2.

Long Beach Hotel.

501. "Sixteen Southern California Architects Exhibit Contemporary Trends in Group Showing at Scripps College." *Arts & Architecture* 67 (April 1950): 22-33.

Most of the house design exhibited are in Los Angeles County.

502. "A Skyscraper Fight." *Architectural Record* 29 (February 1911): 186-7.

Fight over proposal to erect a building taller than the Los Angeles 180-foot limit.

503. "Solving Los Angeles' Greatest Waterproofing Problem." *The Architect and Engineer of California* 31 (January 1913): 79-80.

Los Angeles Times Building.

504. "Some California Architecture as Seen in the Work of C. W. Buchanan, Architect." *The Architect and Engineer of California* 12 (February 1908): 38-47.

Pasadena.

505. "Some of the Work of Sumner P. Hunt and A. Wesley Eager, Architects." *The Architect and Engineer of California* 11 (November 1907): 34-48.

Los Angeles architects and their works.

506. "Southern California Architecture Given Recognition." *The Architect and Engineer* 78 (September 1924): 53-91.

Los Angeles area.

507. "Southland's Finest Theater Completed." *Los Angeles Saturday Night* 8 (December 10, 1927): 2.

$3.5 million United Artists Theatre on Broadway, designed by Walker & Eisen.

508. "Space Frame Costs Less Than $4 a Square Foot." *Architectural Record* 139 (March 1966): 181-4.

Pauley Pavilion, UCLA.

509. "State Edifices in South Dedicated; Governor James Rolph Is Chief Speaker." *California Highways and Public Works* 9 (March 1931): 5-6+.

State Building, Los Angeles; Long Beach Armory.

510. "Statler Center, Los Angeles." *Architectural Record* 109 (March 1951): 89-104.

511. Stephenson, Allen B. and Perkins, John W. "Inglewood's New Branch Library Shows Distinctive Design." *Western City* 42 (March 1966): 38-9.

512. "Student Housing by Richard Dorman & Associate Architects." *Arts & Architecture* 79 (December 1962): 18.

USC.

513. "Student Residence Hall by Welton Becket and Associates, Architects." *Arts & Architecture* 79 (December 1962): 29.

UCLA.

514. "Sunset Tower: Tallest Building in Los Angeles County." *Los Angeles Saturday Night* 13 (December 31, 1932): 6.

515. "Tallest Skyscraper in Southern California." *California Magazine of the Pacific* 56 (February 1966): 8+.

Union Bank Building, Los Angeles.

516. Tanner, Laura. "Newest Straw-in-the-Wind: The Bel-Air Hotel." *House Beautiful* 89 (August 1947): 60-3.

517. "Theatrical." *Out West,* new series, 1 (February 1911): 196-200.

New Orpheum Theater, Los Angeles.

518. Thomas, B. X. "The Long Beach, Calif., Water Department Shows How to Construct an Administration Building That Is . . . Functional and Beautiful." *American City* 78 (January 1963): 141-2.

519. Thomas, Frank J. "The Bradbury Building." *Westways* 47 (May 1955): 28-9.

520. Thomas, Gil. "The Face Changers." *Los Angeles* 8 (September 1964): 44-7.
Los Angeles architects and architecture.

521. Thompson, Elisabeth K. "Los Angeles." *Architectural Record* 143 (April 1968): 181-8.

522. "Three Privately Developed Apartment Houses." *Pencil Points* 25 (January 1944): 51-6.
Kelton Apartments, near Wilshire Blvd.; Strathmore Apartments, Westwood, and Landfair Apartments, Westwood, all designed by Richard Neutra.

523. *Thru My Window at Southgate; Southgate Gardens formerly the Famous Cudahy Ranch.* Los Angeles, [1918]. 31 pp.
Views of Southgate homes.

524. Tichenor, Paul. "A Review of the Construction Problems on the $12,000,000—Eastland Shopping Center Project." *Western Construction* 32 (May 1957): 63+.
West Covina.

525. "Transition 1935-1955 Architectural Design: Work of Architect Raphael S. Soriano." *The Architect and Engineer* 205 (May 1955): 14-21+.
Los Angeles architect and his work, including Jewish Community Chest Center, Los Angeles.

526. Travers, David. "Notes in Passing." *Arts & Architecture* 83 (April 1966): 9.
Dodge House.

527. Trood, S. P. "[Allied] Architects Association Prepares Civic Center Plan." *American City* 32 (May 1925): 573+.
Los Angeles.

528. ———— "Los Angeles Architects Combine for Public Service: Have Association Which Plans and Constructs Public Buildings at Regular Fees for Common Profit of Profession." *Engineering News-Record* 95 (August 20, 1925): 312-3.

529. "Two Southern California Churches." *The Architect and Engineer* 61 (May 1920): 77-83.
Wilshire District Presbyterian and Hollywood Christian Church.

530. Uhl, George M. "Los Angeles City Health Building Shows Functional Planning Design." *Western City* 31 (January 1955): 46-7.

531. "Unified Health and Welfare Centers of Los Angeles County, California." *Architectural Record* 77 (June 1935): 445-9.

532. "Unique Oviatt Building and Store." *Los Angeles Saturday Night* 8 (May 19, 1928): 17.
Men's store on Olive Street designed by Walker & Eisen.

533. "Unique Subway Terminal Building." *Los Angeles Saturday Night* 8 (March 17, 1928): 2.
Pacific Electric.

534. "The United Artists' Theater, Los Angeles: Contains Heaviest Structural Steel Girder Fabricated in the Far West." *Western Construction News* 2 (November 10, 1927): 39.

535. "University of Southern California Founders Hall, Los Angeles." *The Architect and Engineer* 183 (October 1950): 10-3+.

536. "University Religious Center by Killingsworth-Brady & Associates." *Art & Architecture* 84 (January 1967): 22-3.
USC.

537. "Utility and Art Blend in Sunkist Building." *Los Angeles Saturday Night* 16 (December 21, 1935): 8.

538. Vandervoort, Paul, II. "Burbank's New City Hall." *American City* 58 (September 1943): 55.

539. "A View of the Pacific." *Time* 62 (December 21, 1953): 41.
Morman Temple, Los Angeles.

540. Whittlesey, Charles F. "California's Largest Reinforced Concrete Building." *The Architect and Engineer of California* 4 (March 1906): 17-27.
Auditorium at Fifth and Olive streets, Los Angeles.

541. Whittlesey, H. C. "Construction Notes on Villa Riviera, Long Beach, California." *Western Construction News* 3 (December 10, 1928): 756-7.

14-story apartment building.

542. Whitworth, D. M. "Wanted: A Wealthy House-keeper." *Westways* 57 (November 1965): 4-7+.

History of "Greystone" estate and its future.

543. "William L. Pereira and Associates, Architects." *Arts & Architecture* 82 (May 1965): 16-7.

Los Angeles County Museum of Art.

544. Wilson, Lewis Eugen. "Eggshell Shape Gives Strength to—Tunnel-Like Wood Arch Theater." *Western Construction News* 24 (May 1949): 86-7.

Baldwin Hills Theater, Leimert Park.

545. Winslow, Carleton M. "Chapman Park Hotel, Los Angeles Offers Unique Housing Plan for Its Guests." *The Architect and Engineer* 129 (June 1937): 23-32.

546. Withey, H. T. "Some Phases of School-House Construction." *American Architect* 106 (November 4, 1914): 273-7.

Includes Santa Monica High School and Whittier High School.

547. Woollett, William L. "Architects' Services a Necessity." *Los Angeles Saturday Night* 8 (November 5, 1927): 17.

Argues need for an architect's analysis of problem of designing new Civic Center and Plaza.

548. —— "Architecture of the Pacific Southwest Exposition, Long Beach, California." *The Architect and Engineer* 94 (August 1928): 57-9.

549. —— "Concrete and Creative Architecture." *The Architect and Engineer* 73 (May 1923): 51-75.

Grauman's Metropolitan Theater, Los Angeles.

550. —— "Los Angeles Civic Center." *The Architect and Engineer* 74 (August 1923): 73-4.

551. —— "More Anent the Los Angeles Civic Center." *The Architect and Engineer* 74 (September 1923): 89-91.

552. "The Work of Alfred F. Rosenheim, Architect." *The Architect and Engineer of California* 8 (March 1907): 34-49.

Los Angeles architect whose works included Hellman Building, 1903, and Christian Science churches.

553. "The Work of John Parkinson and Edwin Bergstrom." *The Architect and Engineer of California* 22 (September 1910): 34-69.

Los Angeles architects and their work; large commercial buildings.

554. "The Work of Norman F. Marsh." *The Architect and Engineer of California* 31 (December 1912): 46-66.

Los Angeles architect and his works which included many churches and schools, and the one-time Columbia Hospital.

555. Wray, Albert. "Statler Hotel and Office Building to Be Completed by June, 1952." *Western Housing* 34 (April 1951): 9+.

556. Yates, Peter. "Music." *Arts & Architecture* 71 (May 1954): 33-5.

New music building at Long Beach City College.

AVIATION

557. Anderson, Arnold T. "Commercial Aviation in Southern California." *Los Angeles Realtor* 8 (June 1929): 7-8+.

558. "Annual Aviation Speed Classic: Municipal Airport, July 1, 2, 3 and 4." *Los Angeles Saturday Night* 13 (June 24, 1933): 10.

1933 National Air Races.

559. "Aviation in Southern California." *Los Angeles Realtor* 7 (September 1928): 7-8+.

560. Barber, Horatio. *The Aeroplane Speaks.* 9th ed. New York, 1928. 148 pp.

561. Battle, Don. "Balloon Lost." *Westways* 53 (July 1961): 8-9.

Describes plight of five balloon riders who took off from a Tournament Park carnival in March, 1909 with Captain A. E. Mueller, who got off course and had to set down on top of Strawberry Peak and await rescue.

562. Black, Archibald. *The Story of Flying.* Rev. ed. New York, 1943. 272 pp.

563. Clare, Kenneth G. *Southern California Regional Airport Study*. Prepared by the Stanford Research Institute, Southern California Laboratories, South Pasadena. South Pasadena, 1964. 231 pp.

564. Clements, Mary Jo. "The First United States Air Meet." *Westways* 47 (June 1955): 22-3.

Dominguez Air Meet, January 1910.

565. Cuthbert, A. E. "Preparations at Los Angeles Municipal Airport." *Aero Digest* 23 (July 1933): 19.

566. Dektar, Cliff. "Whirlybirds Are Watching Over Us." *Westways* 49 (July 1957): 12-3.

Use of helicopters in Los Angeles County.

567. Ditzel, Paul. "The Day Los Angeles Had *Zeppelin* Fever." *Westways* 61 (March 1969): 2-5; (April 1969): 24-6+.

568. Douglas, Donald W. "Southern California's Highways of the Skies." *Touring Topics* 12 (May 1920): 16-7+.

Los Angeles aviation.

569. Edholm, Charlton L. "The Noble Sport of Aviation." *Out West* 32 (January 1910): 2-28.

Dominguez Air Meet, 1910.

570. "Everywhere by Air from Los Angeles." *Southern California Business* 10 (December 1931): 12-3.

571. "Eyes Up! Two Million of Them." *Western Flying* 4 (October 1928): 39+.

1928 National Air Races and Aeronautical Exposition, Mines Field, Los Angeles.

572. Ferris, Dick. "The People's Aviation Meet." *Out West*, new series, 3 (January 1912): 70-3.

Aviation in Los Angeles.

573. Field, Charles K. "On the Wings of To-day: An Account of the First International Aviation Meet in America, at Los Angeles, California." *Sunset* 34 (March 1910): 245-52.

Dominguez Air Meet, 1910.

574. Hanshue, Harris M. "Selling It on the Wing: No Time Was Lost in Putting to Work Our Two Lines of Air Service." *Southern California Business* 10 (March 1931): 10-1.

Transcontinental and Western Air, and American Airways.

575. "Helicopter Mail Service Tested in Los Angeles Area." *Western Flying* 26 (July 1946): 38.

576. "Helicopter Taxis Are Part of Air Terminal Design." *Interiors* 105 (January 1946): 74-5.

577. Henderson, Cliff. "Attracting the World Flyers." *Southern California Business* 7 (August 1928): 12-3+.

National Air Races at Los Angeles.

578. Holder, Chas. F. "Mining with an Airship." *Out West* 32 (March 1910): 275-7.

Plans for using airships designed by T. S. C. Lowe of Pasadena in freighting to and from inaccessible mines.

579. Hull, Theodore T. "Planning Nation's Greatest Air Races." *Southern California Business* 7 (May 1928): 12-3+.

1928 National Air Races, Los Angeles.

580. ———— "Southland Leads Aerial March." *Southern California Business* 6 (January 1928): 9-10+.

Commercial aviation.

581. Irwin, Randall. "A 10-Day Show in 4 Fast Days." *Southern California Business* 12 (May 1933): 18.

1933 National Air Races, Los Angeles.

582. Karst, Harry E. "Covered Wagons in the Air: Looking Back to Western Air Express Beginnings —First Flight April 17, 1926." *Southern California Business* 15 (April 1936): 10-1.

583. Kesselring, C. B. (Kess). "Blind Copter Flying Techniques Disclosed." *Aviation Week* 55 (November 5, 1951): 74-7.

Los Angeles Airways, first helicopter service to win an instrument air-worthiness certificate.

584. Ketcham, C. T. "Aviation to Hasten Development of San Fernando Valley." *Los Angeles Realtor* 8 (November 1928): 33+.

585. Knight, William H. "The Lowe Passenger Airship." *Out West* 32 (January 1910): 29-34.

T. S. C. Lowe of Pasadena.

586. Leadabrand, Russ. "Glendale's Amazing Rooftop Dirigible." *Westways* 49 (November 1957): 26-7.

587. Longyear, W. D. "Take Airplanes for Instance." *Southern California Business* 8 (August 1929): 9-11+.

Aviation developments in Los Angeles area.

588. Los Angeles. Chamber of Commerce. *Los Angeles County Spreads Her Wings. History of National Air Races.* [Los Angeles, c1929]. 30 pp.

589. "Los Angeles Airways Costly Strike Ends." *Aviation Week and Space Technology* 92 (May 11, 1970): 26.

590. "Los Angeles Gets First Helicopter Mail." *Western Flying* 27 (July 1947): 30.

591. MacKay, M. G. "When Curtiss Flew 40 M.P.H.: The Story of the First Air Meet." *Western Flying* 4 (September 1928): 54-7+.

Dominguez Air Meet, 1910.

592. Maynard, Harry Y. "Howdy, Neighbor! We're in the Same Block with Every Town in the Land— 48 Hours by Air." *Southern California Business* 10 (December 1931): 6-7.

Los Angeles as air transport focal-point.

593. Mayor, George W. "The Growth of Air Freight and Its Effect on the Marketing Strategy of Shippers with Special Reference to Manufacturers of Industrial Goods in the Long Beach, California, Area." Master's thesis, University of Southern California, 1961. 128 pp.

594. McClure, Paul T. "Some Projected Effects of Jet Noise on Residential Property Near Los Angeles International Airport by 1970." Master's thesis, University of Southern California, 1969. 155 pp.

595. Messinger, Robert E. "Evaluation of the Uses of Corporate Aircraft by Certain Southern California Manufacturers." Master's thesis, University of Southern California, 1961. 288 pp.

596. Moseley, C. C. "Southland Leads in Air Mail." *Southern California Business* 7 (August 1928): 14-5+.

597. ——— "30 Hours Nearer New York." *Southern California Business* 5 (March 1926): 9-11.

A Los Angeles firm, Western Air Express, awarded Los Angeles — Salt Lake City airmail contract.

598. Nadeau, Remi. "Gathering of the Early Birds." *Westways* 52 (February 1960): 4-6.

Dominguez Air Meet, 1910.

599. Neal, J. Wesley. "America's First International Air Meet." *Historical Society of Southern California Quarterly* 43 (1861): 369-414.

Full documentation of Dominguez Air Meet, 1910.

600. Newmark, Marco R. "The Aviation Meet of 1910." *Historical Society of Southern California Quarterly* 28 (1946): 103-8.

A shorter revision appears in the author's *Jottings in Southern California History.* (Los Angeles, 1955): 57-61.

601. Niblo, Fred. "Contact! Camera!" *Western Flying* 4 (December 1928): 40-1+.

Role of flying in film industry.

602. ———, and Kellogg, Virginia. "When Hollywood Flies." *Western Flying* 6 (November 1929): 44-5+.

603. Phillips, Jerry. "Rendezvous in the Sky." *Westways* 59 (July 1967): 26-9.

Describes an attempt to make an emergency airplane repair while circling above Clover Field, Santa Monica, sometime in the early 1920s.

604. Powell, William J. *Black Wings.* Los Angeles, 1934. 218 pp.

Written by a Los Angeles aviator, contains reference to some local Negro aviators.

605. "Results of the National Air Races, Los Angeles, California." *Aero Digest* 23 (August 1933): 20-1+.

606. Ronnie, Art. "Catalina and the Air Age." *Westways* 54 (August 1962): 8-9.

Flight to and from Catalina from 1912 (year of

Glenn Martin's "greatest over water flight in history") to the 1950s (a routine commuter run).

607. Sibley, Hi. "California Goes up in the Air!" *Westways* 36 (August 1944): 6-7.

Dominguez Air Meet, 1910.

608. "TWA Adopts Airborne Radar." *Western Flying* 27 (June 1947): 22.

Developed by Hughes Aircraft.

609. "There Was Another Air Meet." *Southern California Business* 7 (September 1928): 16-7+.

Dominguez Air Meet, 1910.

610. Western Air Lines. *Wings Over the West: The Story of America's Oldest Airline.* [Los Angeles, 1951?]. 48 pp.

BANKS AND BANKING; FINANCE

611. Akin, William H. "Exchange Business in a Class by Itself." *Out West,* new series, 6 (July-August 1913): 72.

Optimistic projection of Los Angeles' future.

612. Armstrong, Leroy, and Denny, J. O. *Financial California: An Historical Review of the Beginnings and Progress of Banking in the State.* San Francisco, 1916. 191 pp.

Largely San Francisco, but some material on Los Angeles.

613. Arnold, Robert K. *The California Economy, 1947-1980.* Menlo Park, 1961. 456 pp.

Statewide overview.

614. Bank of America. Municipal Bond Department. *Metropolitan Los Angeles.* [San Francisco, 1961]. 38 pp.

615. Bauer, Dorothy A. "The Economic Significance of Savings and Loan Associations with Emphasis on Los Angeles County." Master's thesis, University of Southern California, 1953. 207 pp.

616. Brown, Eugene M. "An Investigation of the Opinions and Attitudes of Selected Business Groups in the Los Angeles Area Toward Regulation W." Master's thesis, University of Southern California, 1954. 83 pp.

Regulation W is a control by the Federal Reserve Board over private credit.

617. "Business Barometer Hits High Mark: Bank Clearings, One of the Best Gauges of Business Conditions, Show Los Angeles to Be Rapidly Gaining." *Southern California Business* 2 (August 1923): 26.

618. Case, Frederick E. *Los Angeles Real Estate; A Study of Investment Experience.* Los Angeles, c1960. 103 pp.

619. Cleland, Robert Glass, and Putnam, Frank B. *Isaias W. Hellman and the Farmers and Merchants Bank.* San Marino, 1965. 136 pp.

Chapters V-VIII on twentieth century.

620. Collins, James H. "How the Money Flies: Our Banks Have the Speediest Clearing Service in the World, Based on Air Mail." *Southern California Business* 11 (July 1932): 12-3.

Los Angeles banks.

621. ———— "Our Stock Market — A Duplex: No Other City Has Such a Big Wall Street Public, Apart from Spring Street's Clientele." *Southern California Business* 15 (February 1936): 8-9.

Los Angeles Stock Exchange.

622. Comstock, Theo. B. "Staying Qualities of Los Angeles Investments." *Out West,* new series, 6 (July-August 1913): 60-8.

623. Coons, Arthur G. "The Economic Implications of Metropolitan Planning," in *Los Angeles: Preface to a Master Plan.* Ed. by George W. Robbins and L. Deming Tilton. Los Angeles, 1941. Pp. 267-82.

624. Cox, John R. "Institutional Mortgage Lending in the Los Angeles Metropolitan Area, 1953-54 and 1957-58." Doctoral dissertation, University of Southern California, 1963. 344 pp.

625. Cross, Ira B. *Financing an Empire: History of Banking in California.* Chicago, San Francisco, and Los Angeles, 1927. 4 volumes.

Author emphasizes San Francisco and northern California, but there is considerable material on the Los Angeles region.

626. Dee, Gilbert. "Consumer Lending Control by Los Angeles Commercial Banks." Master's thesis, University of Southern California, 1959. 90 pp.

627. Dockson, R. R. *Growth Patterns, the Dynamic Los Angeles Area.* Los Angeles, 1958. 32 pp.

628. Douglas, J. R. *The Bank and Community; A History of the Security Trust and Savings Bank of Los Angeles, 1889-1929.* Los Angeles, 1929. 62 pp.

629. Dustin, C. Mial. *Milestones in History. The Citizens National Bank of Los Angeles, California, Spring and Fifth Street.* Los Angeles, 1915. 20 pp.

630. Elliott, Edward. "Los Angeles Banks and Their Relation to the Economic Development of the Southwest." *Los Angeles Saturday Night 150th Birthday of Los Angeles: Fiesta and Pre-Olympiad,* Special Issue (1931): [8].

631. "Employee's Credit Union in California Plant." *Western Machinery and Steel World* 31 (December 1940): 461.
   Axelson Manufacturing Co., Los Angeles.

632. "Expanding the Unusual." *Business Week* (August 28, 1965): 68-70+.
   Union Bank of Los Angeles.

633. Farmers and Merchants National Bank of Los Angeles. *The Farmers and Merchants National Bank of Los Angeles, April 10, 1871-April 10, 1921.* Los Angeles, 1921. 34 pp.

634. "Financing in Los Angeles." *Electric Railway Journal* 42 (December 13, 1913): 1258.
   Los Angeles Railway.

635. German American Trust and Savings Bank. *Twenty-Five Years of Growth; A Quarter Century of Achievement.* Los Angeles, [1915]. [20] pp.

636. Gillies, James, and Berger, Jay S. *Profile of the Los Angeles Metropolis — Its People and Its Homes.* Part 4: *Financing Homeownership: The Borrowers, the Lenders, and the Homes.* Los Angeles, 1965. 77 pp.

637. Grebler, Leo, and Gillies, James. *Junior Mortgage Financing in Los Angeles County, 1958-1959.* Los Angeles, 1960. 71 pp.

638. Haglund, Roger W. "The Door to Banking Opportunity: It's the 'Institute,' Where Bank People Train — Los Angeles Has the Second Largest Chapter." *Southern California Business* 11 (October 1932): 16.

639. Hellman, Irving H. "Bank Records Tell Amazing Story." *Southern California Business* 2 (January 1924): 35+.
   Describes Los Angeles banking activities.

640. "Impressive New Home of Los Angeles Stock Exchange." *Los Angeles Saturday Night* 11 (January 3, 1931): 6.

641. James, Marquis. *Biography of a Bank: The Story of the Bank of America.* New York, 1954. 566 pp.
   History of a great banking house with much on the financial history of California from 1900 until recent times.

642. Jones, Frederick W. "The Los Angeles Stock Exchange." *The Architect and Engineer* 104 (March 1931): 25-45.

643. "Kaspare Cohn Builded Well." *Los Angeles Saturday Night* 8 (October 15, 1927): 2.
   Founder of the Union Bank & Trust Co., and the growth of that institution.

644. Lehman, Anthony L. "From Finance to Pharmacy." *Pomona Valley Historian* 3 (1967): 108-11.
   Claremont.

645. "Los Angeles Leads Again." *Southern California Business* 3 (August 1924): 31.
   Los Angeles Stock Exchange establishes stock ticker service.

646. "Los Angeles Stock Exchange to Have New Home." *Los Angeles Realtor* 8 (June 1929): 13+.

647. Maxwell, Morgan. "A Description of the Periodic Investment Plan Which Originated in the Los Angeles Stock Exchange in February, 1954." Master's thesis, University of Southern California, 1955. 106 pp.

648. Miller, Carl P. "The Year on the Los Angeles Stock Exchange." *Southern California Business* 8 (February 1929): 38+.

649. Monte, Joseph L. "Part-Time Female Employees — A Partial Solution to the Staffing Problem in the Banking Industry of the Los Angeles Metropolitan Area." Master's thesis, University of Southern California, 1958. 98 pp.

650. "Near Top in Wealth and Purchasing Power." *Southern California Business* 8 (February 1929): 30+.

Comparison of Los Angeles County, other California counties, and wealthy counties in rest of United States.

651. Nicholson, H. C. "Banking for the World's Sunrise: We Should Be Ready to Finance a Greater Harbor Trade Than Ever." *Southern California Business* 11 (October 1932): 10-1.

652. "Pan American Bank's Unique Record: Notable Three-Months' History." *Los Angeles Saturday Night* 7 (April 2, 1927): 2.

Rapidity with which new accounts opened is said to illustrate "the city's financial elasticity and the stability of its institutions and citizenship."

653. Pettingell, Frank H. "Where the Stock Mart Carries On." *Southern California Business* 3 (November 1924): 20+.

History of Los Angeles Stock Exchange.

654. Reynolds, D. M. "Banks Offer Cosmopolitan Service: Financial Institutions of Los Angeles Provide Unity of Operation That Means Much to Business Interest of Large Field." *Southern California Business* 1 (September 1922): 68+

655. Roberts, Myron. "The Liberation of Wall Street West." *Los Angeles* 14 (July 1969): 28-31+.

Los Angeles branch of the Pacific Coast Stock Exchange, 618 South Spring.

656. Rosemead, Calif. Economic Inventory Committee. *The Economic Resources of the City of Rosemead, California.* Rosemead, 1961. 115 pp.

657. Sartori, J. F. "Here Is a $1,000,000,000 Banking City." *Southern California Business* 5 (December 1926): 28+.

Los Angeles.

658. Schnitman, L. Seth. "Looking Down from Business Heights." *Southern California Business* 3 (January 1925): 7-8+.

Los Angeles boom as indicated by bank clearings.

659. Schroeder, W[illia]m H. "No Terrifying Red Tape: How a Bank Simplifies Your World Trade Financing, Credits and Collections." *Southern California Business* 11 (February 1932): 10-1.

Citizens National Trust & Savings Bank, Los Angeles.

660. Security First National Bank of Los Angeles. Reasearch Department. *The Growth and Economic Stature of the South Coast Area of Los Angeles County.* [Los Angeles, 1963]. 64 pp.

661. ────── *Southern California Report; A Study of Growth and Economic Stature.* Los Angeles, 1965. 160 pp.

662. Slonaker, Charles W. "An Investigation of Mortgage Lending in Los Angeles County." Master's thesis, University of Southern California, 1948. 134 pp.

663. Stevens, George T. "Public Employee Credit Unions in the Los Angeles Area." Master's thesis, University of Southern California, 1940. 136 pp.

664. "Survey of the Banking Industry of Los Angeles." *Saturday Night* 6 (October 2, 1926): 1-2.

665. Tidyman, Clayton R. "An Investigation of Recent Trends in Junior Mortgage Financing in Los Angeles County." Doctoral dissertation, University of Southern Calfiornia, 1957. 316 pp.

666. Tillis, Harry A., and Watt, George R. *City of Industry: Its Economic Characteristics and Significance, 1957-1970.* Prepared by the Stanford Research Institute, Southern California Laboratories, South Pasadena, 1964. [Various pagings.]

667. Tritt, Robert E. "The Economic Environment in Which Los Angeles Firms Make Decisions with Respect to Investment in the European Economic Community." Doctoral dissertation, University of Southern California, 1965. 234 pp.

668. Williams, Douglas. "Financing a Big Industries." *Southern California Business* 3 (July 1924): 13+.

Describes growth of Los Angeles industrial banking.

669. Workman, W. H. "Usury Is Rampant in Los Angeles." *Southern California Business* 13 (June 1934): 18.

Author was president of the First Industrial Loan Co. of California.

BIBLIOGRAPHY

670. Bleich, Pamela A. "A Study of Graduate Research in California History in California Colleges and Universities." *California Historical Society Quarterly* 43 (1964): 231-45, 331-44; 44 (1965): 35-50, 139-63, 237-50, 333-48; 45 (1966): 149-61.

Based on the author's master's thesis, "A Study of Research Topics for Advanced Degrees in California History." University of Southern California, 1960. 299 pp.

671. Blumann, Ethel, and Thomas, Mabel W., eds. *California Local History: A Centennial Bibliography*. Stanford, 1950. 576 pp.

Superceded by Margaret M. Rocq revised edition, 1970.

672. Brinnell, Joseph. *A Bibliography of California Ornithology*. Santa Clara, 1909. 166 pp.

673. Brown, Charlotte Maud. *Catalina Island, Limited Bibliography*. [Los Angeles: By the author, 1927]. 4 pp.

674. Chapin, Edward L. Jr. *A Selected Bibliography of Southern California Maps*. Berkeley and Los Angeles, 1953. 124 pp.

Lists 624 maps from Imperial, Kern, Los Angeles, and other Southern California counties. Based on author's "A Selected Cartobibliography of Southern California," Master's thesis, University of California, Los Angeles, 1950. 451 pp.

675. Cowan, Robert Ernest, and Cowan, Robert Granniss. *A Bibliography of the History of California, 1510-1930*. San Francisco, 1933. 3 vols. Reissued 1964, 1 vol.

676. Durrenberger, Robert; Pitt, Leonard, and Preston, Richard. *The San Fernando Valley: A Bibliography*. San Fernando, 1966. 32 pp.

677. Goodman, John Bartlett, III. "An Annotated Bibliography of California County Histories: The First One Hundred-Eleven Years, 1855-1966." Los Angeles, 1966. 2 vols.

Unpublished manuscript, but xerox copies available at UCLA and the Huntington Library.

678. Hager, Anna Marie. "Los Angeles 1884-1914 in Books." *The Branding Iron* (of the Los Angeles Corral of Westerners) 71 (1964): 5-8.

679. ——, and Hager, Everett Gordon, comps. *Cumulative Index — Westways, Touring Topics, 1909-1959*. Los Angeles, 1961. 505 pp.

Numerous Los Angeles area references indexed.

680. —— and ——, comps. *The Historical Society of Southern California Bibliography of All Published Works 1884-1957*. Los Angeles, 1958. 184 pp.

Seventy-three years of the *Annual Publication* and *Quarterly* are annotated.

681. Historical Records Survey, California. Southern California Historical Records Survey Project. Works Progress Administration. *Inventory of the County Archives of California, No. 20*. Los Angeles, [194?]. 172 pp.

682. Jamison, Judith N. *Public Planning in the Los Angeles Region; A Bibliography*. Los Angeles, 1948. 54 pp.

683. Layne, J[oseph] Gregg. *Books of the Los Angeles District*. Los Angeles, 1950. 61 pp.

684. Leuthold, David A. *California Politics and Problems, 1900-1963: A Selective Bibliography*. Berkeley, 1965. 64 pp.

Mimeographed.

685. Los Angeles Public Library. *The Government of Metropolitan Areas, a Bibliography*. Los Angeles, 1947. [Various pagination.]

686. Magistretti, William. "A Bibliography of Historical Materials in the Japanese Language on the West Coast Japanese." *Pacific Historical Review* 12 (1943): 67-73.

687. Occidental Life Insurance Company of California. *A Directory of Newspapers in Los Angeles and Orange Counties*. Prepared by the News Bureau, Occidental Life Insurance Company of California. Los Angeles, 1962. 62 pp.

688. Powell, Lawrence Clark. *Los Angeles Bibliography*. Menlo Park, 1968. 4 pp.

Reprint from Paul C. Johnson, ed. *Los Angeles. Portrait of an Extraordinary City*. Menlo Park, 1964.

689. Rocq, Margaret M., ed. *California Local History. A Bibliography and Union List of Library Holdings*. 2nd ed., rev. and enlarged. Stanford, 1970. 611 pp.

690. Slobodek, Mitchell. *A Selective Bibliography of California Labor History.* Los Angeles, 1964. 265 pp.

691. Stern, Norton B., ed. *California Jewish History: A Descriptive Bibliography.* Glendale, 1967. 175 pp.

Annotated with call numbers. Includes general, city, county historical studies as well as entries on wholly Jewish theme.

692. University of California. Los Angeles. School of Education. *Subject Index of Theses and Dissertations in Education for 1934-1962.* Los Angeles, 1963. 124 pp.

Lists all items relating to the Los Angeles area.

693. Weber, Francis J. "A Bibliography of California Bibliographies." *Southern California Quarterly* 50 (1968): 5-32.

Reprinted as a separate under same title.

694. ———— *A Select Guide to California Catholic History.* Los Angeles, 1966. 227 pp.

695. ———— *A Select Los Angeles Bibliography, 1872-1970.* Los Angeles, [1970]. 44 pp.

BIOGRAPHY

696. Ainsworth, Ed[ward M.]. *Maverick Mayor, a Biography of Sam Yorty of Los Angeles.* Garden City, N.Y., 1966. 256 pp.

697. ———— *Memories in the City of Dreams . . . A Tribute to Harry Chandler . . .* Los Angeles, 1959. 40 pp.

698. ———— *Pot Luck; Episodes in the Life of E. Parker Lyon.* Hollywood, 1940. 201 pp.

Founder of Arcadia's "Pony Express Museum," now defunct.

699. Alexander, J. A. *The Life of George Chaffey: The Story of Irrigation Beginnings in California and Australia.* Melbourne, Australia, 1928. 382 pp.

700. Alexander, Jack. "Private Life of a Catholic Cardinal." *Saturday Evening Post* 226 (September 12, 1953): 28-9+.

James Francis Cardinal McIntyre.

701. Alger, H. O. "The American Dream: A New Nixon (Don, This Time) Success Story." *Frontier* 7 (May 1956): 12-3.

Don Nixon, Richard Nixon's brother.

702. Arlt, Gustave O. "Edward A. Dickson: A Eulogy Delivered at the Funeral Service." *Historical Society of Southern California Quarterly* 38 (1956): 3-8.

703. Armitage, Merle. *Accent on Life.* Ames, Iowa, [c1965]. 386 pp.

One-time resident in the Los Angeles area.

704. ———— *Success Is No Accident: The Biography of William Paul Whitsett.* Yucca Valley, 1959. 326 pp.

Pioneer San Fernando Valley real estate developer.

705. Armour, Richard. *Drug Store Days; My Youth Among the Pills and Potions.* New York, 1959. 184 pp.

Autobiographical memoirs of Santa Monica.

706. "Artist's Career Ended." *Los Angeles Saturday Night* 15 (November 10, 1934): 12.

Obituary of Fannie E. Duvall.

707. Ashton, George. "Upton Sinclair." Master's thesis, University of California, Berkeley, 1951. 176 pp.

708. "Au Revoir: Spencer V. Cortelyou Concludes 38 Years of Loyal State Service." *California Highways and Public Works* 28 (September-October 1949): 19-23+.

Was Assistant State Highway Engineer in charge of District VII, which includes metropolitan Los Angeles.

709. "Banker-Author: Jackson A. Graves." *Los Angeles Saturday Night* 11 (November 15, 1930): 7+.

710. Barger, Bob Dale. "Raymond Haight, California's 'Angry' Young Man: The Biography of a Political Activist." Doctoral dissertation, University of Southern California, 1967. 233 pp.

711. "Barker Bros.' New President." *Los Angeles Saturday Night* 15 (January 26, 1935): 9.

Paul Quattlander.

712. Barry, Iris. *D. W. Griffith: American Film Master.* New York, 1940. 39 pp.

713. —— *D. W. Griffith, American Film Master.* With an Annotated List of Films by Eileen Bowser. New York, 1965. 88 pp.

714. Barry, Richard. "Profile: Our City's Country Judge—The Dual Life of Walter Evans." *The Los Angeles Bar Bulletin* 37 (April 1962): 189-91.

715. Bass, Charlotta A. *Forty Years; Memoirs from the Pages of a Newspaper.* Los Angeles, 1960. 198 pp.
Autobiography by the long-time editor of *The California Eagle.*

716. Batman, Richard. "D. W. Griffith: The Lean Years." *California Historical Society Quarterly* 44 (1965): 195-204.

717. Beck, Frederick K. *Second Carrot from the End.* New York, 1946. 160 pp.
Roger C. Dahlhjelm and the Farmers Market.

718. Bell, Lawrence. "Glenn L. Martin," in *America's Fifty Foremost Business Leaders.* Ed. by Bertie C. Forbes. New York, 1948. Pp. 298-306.

719. Bingham, Edwin R. "Charles F. Lummis and His Magazine." Doctoral dissertation, University of California, Los Angeles, 1950. 430 pp.

720. —— *Charles F. Lummis, Editor of the Southwest.* San Marino, 1955. 218 pp.
Based in part on the author's doctoral dissertation.

721. Bixby, Fred Hathaway. *Bixbyana, This House and the Hathaway-Bixby Story.* Long Beach, 1962. 22 pp.
Pioneer Long Beach families.

722. Blomgren, William. "Aimee Semple McPherson and the Foursquare Gospel, 1921-1944." Master's thesis, Stanford University, 1952. 103 pp.

723. Bloom, Hannah. "God Is a Millionaire." *Frontier* 2 (December 1950): 5-9.
Dr. James W. Fifield, pastor of the First Congregational Church of Los Angeles, and head of "Spiritual Mobilization."

724. —— "Norris Poulson." *Frontier* 4 (July 1953): 6.
Newly-elected Los Angeles mayor described as a "dependable, obedient party servant," lacking "the imagination, originality, adroitness, and conceit that political eminance demands."

725. —— "The Passing of 'Red' Hynes." *Nation* 175 (August 1952): 91-2.
Captain William F. Hynes, one-time head of the Los Angeles Police Department's "Red Squad."

726. Bogardus, Emory S. "In Memoriam: Rockwell D. Hunt, 1868-1966." *California Historical Society Quarterly* 47 (1968): 89-91.

727. Bourdon, Roger J. "George Wharton James, Interpretor of the Southwest." Doctoral dissertation, University of California, Los Angeles, 1966. 375 pp.

728. Branson, Helen K. *Let There Be Life; The Contemporary Account of Edna L. Griffin, M.D.* Pasadena, [c1947]. 135 pp.

729. Bravermann, Barnet. "David Wark Griffith: Creator of Film Form." *Theatre Arts* 29 (April 1945): 240-50.

730. Brickley, Donald P. *Man of the Morning: The Life and Work of Phineas F. Bresee.* Kansas City, Mo., 1960. 297 pp.
Biography of the man who founded the Nazarene Church in Los Angeles in 1895. Based on the author's doctoral dissertation at the University of Pittsburgh. Survey of church in Southern California, pp. 132-68.

731. Bridge, Norman. *The Marching Years.* New York, 1920. 292 pp.
Autobiography.

732. Buhrman, Robert. "O'Malley the Younger." *Los Angeles* 14 (May 1969): 46-8+.
Peter O'Malley, Walter O'Malley's son.

733. —— "Pancho Gonzales' Next to Last Hurrah." *Los Angeles* 14 (July 1969): 32-3+.
Professional tennis star who grew up in East Los Angeles.

734. —— "Where Have You Gone, Golden Boys?" *Los Angeles* 13 (September 1968): 30+.

Ronnie Knox, football player and Art Aragon, boxer.

735. Bulen, Mary H. "Municipal Judge May D. Lahey." *Los Angeles Saturday Night* 15 (March 16, 1935): 13.

Los Angeles jurist.

736. Burdette, Robert J. *Robert J. Burdette; His Message.* Ed. by Clara B. Burdette. Pasadena, [c1922]. 460 pp.

737. Burlingame, Roger. "From Barnstorming to Bombers: Glenn Martin, Pioneer Plane Builder." *Popular Science* 139 (September 1941): 51-8.

738. [Buschlen, John Preston]. *Senor Plummer; The Life and Laughter of an Old California.* By Don Juan [*pseud.*]. Los Angeles, 1943 [c1942]. 242 pp.

739. Bynum, Lindley, and Jones, Idwal. *Biscailuz, Sheriff of the New West.* New York, 1950. 208 pp.

Eugene Biscailuz.

740. "[C. C.] Julian's Spectacular Exit." *Los Angeles Saturday Night* 14 (March 31, 1934): 3.

Suicide of this "confidence crook extraordinary."

741. Cannom, Robert C. *Van Dyke and the Mythical City, Hollywood.* Culver City, [c1948]. 424 pp.

Motion picture director Woodbridge Strong Van Dyke, 1889-1943, and the movie industry.

742. Carew, Harold D. "Adventures of a Literary Detective." *Westways* 30 (July 1938): 20-1.

Dr. Lodewyk Bendikson of the Huntington Library.

743. ———— "Arbiter Elegantarium in the Realm of California Books." *Touring Topics* 22 (January 1930): 32-4.

Robert E. Cowan.

744. ———— "The Boss of Boulder Dam." *Touring Topics* 21 (August 1929): 32-4+.

Dr. Elwood Mead.

745. ———— "Chronicler of Gringo California." *Westways* 30 (January 1938): 28-9.

Prof. Robert Glass Cleland.

746. ———— "Don of the Archives." *Touring Topics* 21 (December 1929): 28-30.

Prof. Max Farrand of the Huntington Library.

747. ———— " 'El Obispo' of Pomona." *Touring Topics* 22 (March 1930): 32-4+.

Prof. Joseph Pijoan of Pomona College.

748. ———— "He Proved that Einstein Was Right." *Touring Topics* 21 (March 1929): 32-4+.

Charles E. St. John of the Mount Wilson Solar Observatory.

749. ———— "A Man of Many Worlds." *Touring Topics* 20 (October 1928): 28-30+.

George Ellery Hale.

750. ———— "The Man Who Split the Atom." *Touring Topics* 20 (September 1928): 32-4+.

Dr. Robert Andrews Millikan of the California Institute of Technology.

751. ———— "A Modern Model in Educators." *Touring Topics* 21 (September 1929): 32-4+.

Susan Miller Dorsey.

752. ———— "One Among the Wise Men." *Touring Topics* 23 (October 1931): 26-7+.

Henry Raup Wagner.

753. ———— "Toiler in the Vineyard of Books." *Touring Topics* 21 (February 1929): 32-4+.

George Watson Cole of the Huntington Library.

754. Carlisle, Rodney P. "The Political Ideas and Influence of William Randolph Hearst, 1928-1936." Doctoral dissertation, University of California, Berkeley, 1965. 200 pp.

755. Carr, O. O. *Tribute to the Memory of Josiah Hopkins.* Hollywood, [c1937]. 30 pp.

756. Carrillo, Leo. *The California I Love.* Englewood Cliffs, N.J., 1961. 280 pp.

Autobiography.

757. [Carroll, John Alexander]. "Charles Fletcher Lummis, 1859-1928." *Arizona and the West* 1 (1959): 302-4.

A brief summary of the life and contributions of this Los Angeles cultural leader, including a selected list of publications both by and about Lummis.

758. Carson, Robert. "Homage to the Movies' Last Eagle." *Los Angeles* 11 (April 1966): 40-3+.

Paul Mantz, Hollywood stunt flier.

759. Cerwin, Herbert. *In Search of Something; The Memoirs of a Public Relations Man.* Los Angeles, [1966]. 318 pp.

760. Chaffee, Burns. *My First Eighty Years. The Life Story of a California Surgeon.* Los Angeles, 1960. 264 pp.

761. Chamberlain, Arthur H. "Mark Keppel: A Personal Tribute to a Good Man." *Overland Monthly* 86 (August 1928): 289+.

Obituary.

762. Chamberlain, Henry. "Back of the Background." *Westways* 45 (May 1953): 16-7.

Lee Chamberlain, first president of the Automobile Club of Southern California.

763. Champlin, C. D. " 'Aimee': For 25 Years, the Name of Evangelist Aimee Semple McPherson Was Synonymous with Southern California. Her Brass Bands, Pageants, Hell-Fearing Sermons — and Her Disappearance — Made Her Famous Around the World." *Southern California Prompter* 2 (February 1961): 16-9.

764. Chapman, Alice M. "Madame Severance, the Founder of Women's Clubs." Master's thesis, University of Southern California, 1930. 91 pp.

Caroline Severance.

765. "Chicano Columnist." *Newsweek* 75 (June 22, 1970): 61.

Reuben Salazar of the Los Angeles *Times.*

766. Christy, George. "Reminiscing with Dave Chasen." *Los Angeles* 14 (August 1969): 44-7.

Beverly Hills restaurateur.

767. "Civic and Literary Work of Orra E. Monnette." *Los Angeles Saturday Night* 11 (November 15, 1930): 7.

Banker, writer, and long-time member of the Los Angeles Public Library Board.

768. Claypool, Vincent B. "John Amherst Sexson, Educator." Doctoral dissertation, University of California, Los Angeles, 1948. 529 pp.

769. Clover Sam[uel] T. "California Men of Notable Constructive Ability: XXXV. Charles Collins Teague." *Saturday Night* 5 (August 15, 1925): 1-2.

770. ———— "California Men of Notable Constructive Ability: XLV. Dr. John Randolph Haynes." *Saturday Night* 6 (February 6, 1926): 1-2.

Physician and reform leader.

771. ———— "California Men of Notable Constructive Ability: XXXII. Dr. Milbank Johnson." *Saturday Night* 5 (July 11, 1925): 1.

Physician, a founder of Automobile Club of Southern California, and one-time president of the Southwest Museum.

772. ———— "California Men of Notable Constructive Ability: XXXIX. Elmanson Avery McCarthy." *Saturday Night* 5 (October 31, 1925): 1.

Los Angeles area land subdivider.

773. ———— "California Men of Notable Constructive Ability: XXXVI. Frank Hervey Pettingell." *Saturday Night* 5 (September 19, 1925): 1.

President of the Los Angeles Stock Exchange.

774. ———— "California Men of Notable Constructive Ability: XXI. Fred Lawrence Baker." *The Argonaut* 96 (March 28, 1925): 1.

President of the Los Angeles Steamship Company.

775. ———— "California Men of Notable Constructive Ability: XL. Frederick William Braun." *Saturday Night* 5 (November 14, 1925): 1-2.

Los Angeles merchant.

776. ———— "California Men of Notable Constructive Ability: XIV. George Chaffey." *The Argonaut* 96 (February 7, 1925) 1.

777. ———— "California Men of Notable Constructive Ability: VIII. George Ellery Hale." *The Argonaut* 96 (December 27, 1924): 1+.

778. ———— "California Men of Notable Constructive Ability: XIX. George Ira Cochran." *The Argonaut* 96 (March 14, 1925): 1-2.

President, Pacific Mutual Life Insurance Company.

779. ———— "California Men of Notable Construc-

tive Ability: X. Harry Chandler." *The Argonaut* 96 (January 10, 1925): 1+.

Publisher, Los Angeles *Times*.

780. ——— "California Men of Notable Constructive Ability: XLVI. Harry H. Culver." *Saturday Night* 6 (February 27, 1926): 1-2.

Real estate developer.

781. ——— "California Men of Notable Constructive Ability: VI. Henry Edwards Huntington." *The Argonaut* 96 (December 13, 1924): 1+.

782. ——— "California Men of Notable Constructive Ability: XXXIII. J. Dabney Day." *Saturday Night* 5 (August 1, 1925): 1-2.

Los Angeles banker.

783. ——— "California Men of Notable Constructive Ability: IV. John Barnes Miller." *The Argonaut* 96 (November 29, 1924): 1-2.

784. ——— "California Men of Notable Constructive Ability: XXII. John Willis Baer." *Saturday Night* 5 (April 4, 1925): 1.

Banker, church leader and president of Occidental College, 1906-1916.

785. ——— "California Men of Notable Constructive Ability: II. Joseph Francis Sartori." *The Argonaut* 96 (November 15, 1924): 1-2.

Banker.

786. ——— "California Men of Notable Constructive Ability: XXVI. Joseph Scott." *Saturday Night* 5 (May 9, 1925): 1.

Lawyer.

787. ——— "California Men of Notable Constructive Ability: V. Paul Shoup." *The Argonaut* 96 (December 6, 1924): 1.

788. ——— "California Men of Notable Constructive Ability: XXXVIII. Percy H. Clark." *Saturday Night* 5 (October 24, 1925): 1.

A major developer of Beverly Hills.

789. ——— "California Men of Notable Constructive Ability: XXXVII. Robert M. Clarke." *Saturday Night* 5 (October 17, 1925): 1.

One-time jurist.

790. ——— "California Men of Notable Construc-

tive Ability: XLI. Walter Robey Simons." *Saturday Night* 6 (December 19, 1925): 1-2.

Los Angeles brick merchant.

791. ——— "California Men of Notable Constructive Ability: XVII. William Andrews Clark, Jr." *The Argonaut* 96 (February 28, 1925): 1.

Los Angeles philanthropist.

792. ——— "California Men of Notable Constructive Ability: XX. William May Garland." *The Argonaut* 96 (March 21, 1925): 1.

793. ——— "California Men of Notable Constructive Ability: XXIII. William Mulholland." *Saturday Night* 5 (April 18, 1925): 1.

794. ——— "California Men of Notable Constructive Ability: XLIII. William Preston Harrison." *Saturday Night* 6 (January 16, 1926): 1-2.

Noted art collector.

795. ——— "California Men of Notable Constructive Ability: XXX. William Taylor McArthur." *Saturday Night* 5 (June 6, 1925): 1.

One-time president of the Los Angeles County Medical Association.

796. ——— "California Men of Notable Constructive Ability: XXIX. William Wales Mines." *Saturday Night* 5 (May 23, 1925): 1.

797. ——— "Masterly Retail Merchants of Los Angeles: II. Andrew Mullen, II." *Saturday Night* 6 (May 8, 1926): 1-2.

798. ——— "Masterly Retail Merchants of Los Angeles: III. Harry Philp." *Saturday Night* 6 (May 15, 1926): 1+.

Manager of the Broadway Department Store.

799. ——— "Masterly Retail Merchants of Los Angeles: I. John Gillespie Bullock." *Saturday Night* 6 (May 1, 1926): 1-2.

800. ——— "Pioneer Electric Railway Builder of Southern California: Eli P. Clark." *Saturday Night* 6 (May 22, 1926): 1-2.

801. ——— *A Pioneer Heritage.* Los Angeles, 1932. 291 pp.

G. Allan Hancock, a descendant of two distinguished California pioneers, Count Agostin Haraszthy and Major Henry Hancock.

802. Coblentz, Edmond D., ed. *William Randolph Hearst. A Portrait In His Own Words.* New York, 1952. 309 pp.

803. Cohn, Alfred A., and Chisholm, Joseph. *"Take the Witness!"* New York, 1934. 315 pp.
Los Angeles attorney Earl Rogers (1970-1922).

804. Cole, Cornelius. *The Memoirs of Cornelius Cole, Ex-Senator of the United States from California.* New York, 1908. 354 pp.

805. Cole, George L. *Medical Associates of My Early Days in Los Angeles.* Los Angeles, 1930. [134] pp.
Reprint from 1930 *Los Angeles County Medical Association Bulletins.*

806. Cooper, Belle. "A Tribute to Mrs. John R. Haynes." *Los Angeles Saturday Night* 15 (December 8, 1934): 7.
Obituary.

807. Cooper, Charles W. *The A. Wardman Story.* Whittier, 1961. 96 pp.
Whittier pioneer.

808. Costello, William. *The Facts About Nixon: An Unauthorized Biography.* New York, 1960. 306 pp.
Richard Nixon.

809. Counselman, Bill. "Saga of Wilson Mizner." *Westways* 27 (February 1935): 16-7+.

810. Covington, Floyd C. "Greene of Los Angeles." *Crisis* 40 (March 1933): 57-8.
An account of Y.M.C.A. secretary, Thomas A. Greene.

811. Craft, Robert. "Huxley at Home." *Frontier* 3 (September 1952): 18-9.
Aldous Huxley.

812. Crandall, Shannon. "Memories of Men and Business in California, 1887-1931: The Reminiscences of Shannon Crandall." Pt. II. *Claremont Quarterly* 15 (1958): 41-58.

813. Crowther, Bosley. *Hollywood Rajah: The Life and Times of Louis B. Mayer.* New York, [1960]. 339 pp.

814. Croy, Homer. *Star Maker; The Story of D. W. Griffith.* New York, 1959. 210 pp.

815. Cunningham, Frank. *Sky Master, the Story of Donald Douglas.* Philadelphia, 1943. 321 pp.

816. Curti, Carlo. *Skouras, King of Fox Studios.* Los Angeles, [1967]. 311 pp.

817. Dace, Catherine. "Early San Fernando: Memoirs of Mrs. Catherine Dace." Ed. with introduction by Elizabeth I. Dixon. *Southern California Quarterly* 44 (1962): 219-67.
Recollections of the grand-daughter of Senator Charles Maclay, founder of the City of San Fernando, and daughter of Henry C. Hubbard, a promoter of annexation of the valley to the city of Los Angeles.

818. Dalmas, Herbert. "Woman Guardian of L. A. Charities." *Coronet* 37 (April 1955): 73-6.
Evelyn Spaulding, general manager of the Los Angeles Social Service Department, and her fight against charity rackets.

819. Darrow, Clarence S. *The Story of My Life.* New York, 1932. 465 pp.

820. Davis, Donald G. "The Ionaco of Gaylord Wilshire." *Southern California Quarterly* 49 (1967): 425-53.
Examines Wilshire's motives and beliefs, and his hopes for promoting an electrical device designed to rid people of a variety of ills.

821. Dean, Arthur. "Los Angeles and a Man." *Industrial Education Magazine* 26 (May 1925): 351-2.
Vierling Kersey.

822. ——— "Los Angeles and a School." *Industrial Education Magazine* 27 (July 1925): 5-6.
William S. Kienholz, director of Vocational Education in Los Angeles.

823. ——— "Los Angeles and a Woman." *Industrial Education Magazine* 26 (April 1925): 319-20.
Susan M. Dorsey.

824. De Mille, Agnes G. *Dance to the Piper*. Boston, 1952. 342 pp.
Autobiography.

825. De Mille, Cecil B. *The Autobiography of Cecil B. De Mille*. Ed. by Donald Hayne. New York, 1959. 465 pp.

826. De Mille, William C. *Hollywood Saga*. New York, 1939. 319 pp.
Autobiography.

827. de Packman, Ana Begue. "In Memoriam." *Historical Society of Southern California Quarterly* 41 (December 1959): 291-8.
Recounts the accomplishments of Marco Ross Newmark and Roger John Sterrett.

828. Dickert, Lois. "How to Succeed in Business by Being Charming." *Los Angeles* 4 (September 1962): 37-9.
"The schoolmarm of charm, Caroline Leonetti," and her modeling school.

829. Dixon, Mary Patricia. *Ernest Dawson*. Los Angeles, 1967. 79 pp.
[Xeroxed, but bound volume.]

830. "Doheny's Career Saga of the Oil Business." *Petroleum World* 32 (October 1935): 16-7.
Obituary, Edward L. Doheny.

831. Donovan, Joseph J., S.J., ed. *Joseph Scott, Moralist, Lawyer, Orator*. Los Angeles, 1940. Unp.

832. Drinkwater, John *The Life and Adventures of Carl Laemmle*. New York, 1931. 288 pp.
Motion picture luminary, 1867-1939.

833. Dumke, Glenn S. "The Career of James F. Crank: A Chapter in the History of Western Transportation." *Huntington Library Quarterly* 6 (1943): 313-32.

834. Duncan, Ray. " 'Fighting Bob' Shuler: The Holy Terror." *Los Angeles* 7 (March 1964): 38-41+.
One-time minister of Trinity Methodist Church, Los Angeles.

835. ———— "Gene Autry, the Cowboy as Tycoon." *Los Angeles* 6 (July 1963): 42-7.
Autry's enterprises, including the Los Angeles Angels baseball team, and the Continental Hotel.

836. ———— "The Lucrative Limbo of Johnny Green." *Los Angeles* 5 (May 1963): 56-9.
Hollywood composer.

837. ———— "Mehta's Magic Fire." *Los Angeles* 10 (December 1965): 28-32+.
Zubin Mehta, musical director of the Los Angeles Philharmonic Orchestra.

838. Dwiggins, Don. *Hollywood Pilot; The Biography of Paul Mantz*. Garden City, N.Y., 1967. 249 pp.

839. Earle, Henry E. "An Old-Time Collector: Reminiscences of Charles F. Lummis." *California Folklore Quarterly* 1 (April 1942): 179-83.

840. Edelstein, J. M., ed. *A Garland for Jake Zeitlin*. Los Angeles, 1967. 131 pp.
Several biographical essays on this famed Los Angeles bookseller.

841. Edmonds, P. G. *Hollywood R. I. P.* Evanston, Ill., 1963. 158 pp.
Biographical and legal.

842. "Eli P. Clark: An Appreciation." *Los Angeles Saturday Night* 11 (January 24, 193[1]): 3.
Obituary.

843. Farrand, Max. "Frederick Jackson Turner at the Huntington Library." *Huntington Library Bulletin* 3 (February 1933): 156-64.

844. Fayne, John J. "Lowe—the Ingenious American." *Westways* 38 (July 1946): 7.
T.S.C. Lowe.

845. Fernandez, F. "Cardinal McIntyre, Great Figure in the Church." *Claridad* 3 (1953): 171-202.
James Francis Cardinal McIntyre.

846. Field, Ben. "Charles Fletcher Lummis." *Overland Monthly* 87 (July 1929): 197-203+.

847. Finney, Guy W. *Mericos H. Whittier, His Career; The Story of a California Oil Pioneer, Civic Leader, and Humanitarian* [*1857-1925*]. [Los Angeles, c1940]. 115 pp.

848. "First Gentleman of California." *Saturday Night* 44 (July 10, 1937): 7.
William May Garland.

849. FitzGerald, Richard E. "John Huston: Hollywood Writer-Director; A Study of the Early Career, the Period 1941-1948." Master's thesis, University of California, Los Angeles, 1968. [?] pp.

850. Flake, Rhita. "William Ralph LaPorte: Physical Educator, Administrator, Innovator." Doctoral dissertation, University of Southern California, 1968. 164 pp.

851. "Fletcher Bowron." *Western City* 14 (October 1938): 15.

852. Fornas, Virgil W. "Charles L. Lowman: His Role in Physical Education." Doctoral dissertation, University of Southern California, 1968. 205 pp.

Famed Los Angeles physician.

853. Foster, A. M. "Samuel Goldwyn," in *America's Fifty Foremost Business Leaders*. Ed. by Bertie C. Forbes. New York, 1948. Pp. 176-83.

854. "Founder of the Nazarene Church Called." *California Christian Advocate* 64 (November 25, 1915): 13.

Death of Phineas F. Bresee in Los Angeles.

855. Francis, Devon. "Glenn L. Martin's First 40 Years." *Flying* 46 (January 1950): 21-6+.

856. Frank, Herman W. *Scrapbook of a Western Pioneer*. Los Angeles, [c1934]. 256 pp.

Autobiography.

857. "Frank G. Bonelli." *Western Housing* 43 (March 1960): 8+.

858. "Frank Wiggins: Born November 8, 1849, Died October 18, 1924." *Southern California Business* 3 (November 1924): 2 unnumbered pages inserted between pp. 26-27.

Obituary.

859. Fretz, Lewis A. "Upton Sinclair: The Don Quixote of American Reform." Doctoral dissertation, Stanford University, 1970. 345 pp.

860. Friedman, Ralph. "The Cautiously Daring Young Man." *Frontier* 9 (December 1957): 11-4.

Assemblyman William Munnell.

861. ———— "The Eager Samaritan." *Frontier* 9 (January 1958): 7-12.

Kenneth Hahn.

862. "From Mt. Lebanon to Los Angeles: Sketch of Pharis A. Be-Hannesey." *Los Angeles Saturday Night* 8 (November 12, 1927): 13.

Noted furniture dealer.

863. "Garland Building and Its Creative Owner." *Los Angeles Saturday Night* 8 (May 26, 1928): 2.

William May Garland.

864. Gauguin, Lorraine. "Les Biches." *Los Angeles* 14 (May 1969): 34-6+.

Joyce Haber and Rona Barrett, Hollywood gossip columnists. [Author's name is misspelled Gaugin.]

865. ———— "Up From Boyle Heights: Tony the Quinn." *Los Angeles* 14 (March 1969): 34-5+.

Anthony Quinn.

866. Gaydowski, John D. "Dr. Townsend and His Plan, 1867-1934." Master's thesis, University of California, Los Angeles, 1969. 230 pp.

Dr. Francis Townsend of Long Beach.

867. "George Chaffey: Constructionist." *Los Angeles Saturday Night* 12 (March 5, 1932): 3.

Obituary.

868. Gerry, Vance. *Some Fond Remembrances of a Boy Printer at the Castle Press*. South Laguna, 1968. 11 pp.

869. Gessner, Robert. "The Moving Image." *American Heritage* 11 (April 1960): 30-5+.

The three Americans who "created the art of the motion picture": Thomas A. Edison, "motion captured"; Edwin S. Porter, "motion organized"; and D. W. Griffith, "motion interpreted."

870. Getty, Paul J. *My Life and Fortunes*. New York, 1963. 300 pp.

871. Gibson, Mary S. *Caroline M. Severance: Pioneer, 1820-1914*. Los Angeles, 1925. 15 pp.

872. Girvin, E. A. *Phineas F. Bresee: A Prince in Israel*. Kansas City, Mo., 1916. 463 pp.

Founder of the Nazarene Church in Los Angeles, which sponsors Pasadena College (see pp. 178-81 for early history). Survey of the church in Southern California, pp. 101-36.

873. Glasscock, C[arl] B. "Lucky Baldwin Days at Santa Anita." *Westways* 27 (December 1935): 26-7.

874. —— *Lucky Baldwin; The Story of an Unconventional Success.* New York, 1935. 308 pp.

875. "Glenn L. Martin: A Biography." *Aviation Week* 51 (July 25, 1944): 12.

876. Goben, John D. *"Aimee," the Gospel Gold Digger.* New York, 1932. 73 pp.
Aimee Semple McPherson.

877. Goldwyn, Samuel. *Behind the Screen.* New York, 1923. 263 pp.
Autobiography.

878. Gordon, Dudley C. "Charles F. Lummis, Litt. D., Librarian Extraordinary and Founder of the Bibliosmiles." *California Librarian* 22 (January 1961): 17-22.

879. —— "Charles F. Lummis: Pioneer American Folklorist." *Western Folklore* 28 (1969): 175-81.

880. —— "Charles Fletcher Lummis, Cultural Pioneer of the Southwest." *Arizona and the West* 1 (Winter 1959): 305-16.

881. Graham, Sheilah. *Confessions of a Hollywood Columnist.* New York, 1969. 309 pp.

882. Graves, Jackson A. *California Memories, 1857-1930.* Los Angeles, 1930. 330 pp.
Autobiography.

883. —— *My Seventy Years in California, 1857-1927.* Los Angeles, 1927. 478 pp.

884. Gray, Blanche. *Ruffled Petticoat Days.* Culver City, 1953. 147 pp.
Autobiography.

885. Green, Harriet L. *Gilmore Brown, Portrait of a Man—And an Idea.* Pasadena, 1933. [21] pp.
Founder of Pasadena Playhouse.

886. "Greetings to 'Dr. John.'" *Los Angeles Saturday Night* 13 (June 17, 1933): 6.
Tribute to John R. Haynes on his 80th birthday.

887. Haase, John. "The Broad from the Waterfront." *Los Angeles* 15 (June 1970): 44-6+.
Sylvia Zanich, said to be "the most powerful woman in San Pedro politics."

888. Hall, Wilbur. "How Doheny Did It: He Became One of America's Richest Men. You Could Achieve Some Measure of His Success by Using His Methods." *Sunset* 41 (July 1918): 21-3.
Edward L. Doheny.

889. [Halsey, Mina D.]. *A Tenderfoot in Southern California.* By M. D. Yeslah [*pseud.*]. New York, 1908. 149 pp.

890. Hammer, Eleanor R. "Louis Woodson Curtis, Music Educator." Master's thesis, University of California, Los Angeles, 1961. 98 pp.
One-time director of music for the Los Angeles City Schools.

891. Hanna, Phil T. "Nestor on the Amerinds." *Touring Topics* 24 (February 1932): 20-1+.
Frederick Webb Hodge.

892. Harmer, Ruth M. "Man without a Category." *Frontier* 9 (January 1958): 13-5.
Stanley Mosk.

893. Harrington, Johns. "Bone-Digger for Science." *Westways* 33 (January 1941): 26-7.
Mark Raymond Harrington of the Southwest Museum.

894. Harris, Nicholas B. *Famous Crimes by Nick Harris, Famous Pacific Coast Criminologist.* Los Angeles, 1933. 95 pp.
Autobiographical in part.

895. Harris, Robert. "Showman Saint of Temple Street." *Frontier* 7 (January 1956): 12-5.
Eugene Biscailuz.

896. Harrison, Charles Y. *Clarence Darrow.* New York, 1931. 380 pp.

897. Hart, William S. *My Life East and West.* Boston and New York, 1929. 362 pp.

898. Haverland, Della. "Charles Fletcher Lummis." *Pacific Bindery Talk* 7 (September 1934): 115-9.

899. Hazelton, Elizabeth C. *Poppy of the San Fernando Valley.* Los Angeles, 1928. 43 pp.

A family history.

900. Heinly, Burt A. "The Aladdin of the Aqueduct." *Sunset* 28 (April 1912): 465-7.

William Mulholland.

901. "Henry W. O'Melveny." *Bar Bulletin* 16 (June 1941): 218.

Obituary.

902. Hertrich, William. *The Huntington Botanical Gardens, 1905-1949; Personal Recollections of William Hertrich, Curator Emeritus.* San Marino, 1949. 167 pp.

903. Hewett, Edgar L. *Lummis, the Inimitable.* Santa Fe, N. Mex., 1944. 14 pp.

Charles Fletcher Lummis.

904. "Highway Engineer E. E. East Retires from Automobile Club." *California Highways and Public Works* 36 (July-August 1957): 22.

An early proponent of a freeway system for Los Angeles.

905. Hill, Evelyn. "The King of Calabasas." *Westways* 47 (September 1955): 4-5.

Miguel Leonis.

906. Hincker, Richard G. "The Speakership of the California Assembly: Jesse Unruh, Fifty-Four Speaker." Master's thesis, San Jose State College, 1966. 102 pp.

Inglewood assemblyman.

907. Hindman, Flint. "Daniel Freeman, Scholar and Rancher." *Historical Society of Southern California Quarterly* 33 (1951): 179-212.

908. Hindman, Jo. "Grace Freeman Howland." *Historical Society of Southern California Quarterly* 38 (1956): 255-62.

909. Holland, Maurice, and Smith, Thomas M. *Architects of Aviation.* New York, 1951. 214 pp.

The final chapter is on Glenn Martin.

910. Hopper, Hedda. *From Under My Hat.* Garden City, N. Y., 1952. 311 pp.

Autobiography.

911. Hughes, Carol. "Mrs. A. S. C. Forbes." *Saturday Night* 46 (January 28, 1939): 24-5.

912. Hunt, Rockwell D. *"Mr. California"; Autobiography.* San Francisco, 1956. 380 pp.

One-time professor of history and first dean of the Graduate School at University of Southern California. Born in 1868; died in 1966.

913. Hutchinson, W. H. *Oil, Land and Politics: The California Career of Thomas Robert Bard.* Norman, Okla., 1965. 2 vols.

914. Hyland, Dick, and Monroe, Keith. "He Made the Coast See Red." *Saturday Evening Post* 225 (October 25, 1952): 26-7+.

One-time USC football coach Jess Hill.

915. *In Memoriam.* [Los Angeles, 1949?]. 20 pp.

Charles Keyser Edmunds.

916. *In Memoriam.* Claremont, 1935. 31 pp.

Nathaniel W. Stephenson.

917. "In the Public Eye. Introducing: Charles R. Baird." *Western Housing* 28 (December 1945): 16.

Glendale city manager.

918. "In The Public Eye. Introducing: County Supervisor Leonard J. Roach." *Western Housing* 28 (May 1946): 28.

919. "In The Public Eye. Introducing: Harold A. Henry." *Western Housing* 28 (March 1946): 18.

Los Angeles city councilman, 15th District.

920. "In The Public Eye. Introducing: Harold W. Kennedy." *Western Housing* 28 (February 1946): 24.

Los Angeles County counsel.

921. "In The Public Eye. Introducing: T. Fenton Knight." *Western Housing* 28 (April 1946): 16.

Member of California Legislature, 48th District.

922. Irwin, William H. *The House That Shadows Built.* Garden City, N. Y. 1928. 293 pp.

Adolph Zukor.

923. J. G. "California Men of Notable Constructive Ability: XXXIV. Ezra F. Scattergood." *Saturday Night* 5 (August 8, 1925): 1.

924. J. J. L. "California Men of Notable Constructive Ability: XLII. Chester Wallace Brown." *Saturday Night* 6 (January 9, 1926): 1-2.

Petroleum geologist.

925.—— "California Men of Notable Constructive Ability: XLIV. Isadore Eisner." *Saturday Night* 6 (January 30, 1926): 1.

Los Angeles realtor.

926. Jackson, Donald. "The Young Richard Nixon." *Life* 69 (November 6, 1970): 54+.

927. "Jackson A. Graves: An Appreciation." *Los Angeles Saturday Night* 13 (February 18, 1933): 3.

Obituary.

928. James, George W. "Charles F. Lummis: A Unique Literary Personage of Modern America." *National Magazine* 27 (October 1912): 129-43.

929. —— "J. Bond Francisco, Musician and Painter." *Out West*, new series, 6 (September 1913): 78-94.

930. —— "William Lees Judson, Painter." *Out West*, new series, 5 (May 1913): 242-54.

One-time head of the USC College of Fine Arts.

931. Jensen, Joan M. "After Slavery: Caroline Severance in Los Angeles." *Southern California Quarterly* 58 (1966): 175-86.

932. "John G. Bullock: Practical Idealist." *Los Angeles Saturday Night* 13 (September 23, 1933): 3.

Obituary.

933. "John Willis Baer's Personality." *Los Angeles Saturday Night* 11 (February 14, 1931): 3.

Obituary of one-time president of Occidental College.

934. Johnson, John L. "Harry Russell Sanders: Coach and Teacher." Doctoral dissertation, University of California, Los Angeles, 1965. 302 pp.

One-time UCLA football coach.

935. Johnson, Wynonah B. "Aimee S. McPherson and Her Work." *Saturday Night* 4 (November 3, 1923): 5+.

936. Johnston, Alva. *The Great Goldwyn.* New York, [1937]. 99 pp.

Samuel Goldwyn.

937. —— "Hero For Business Reasons." *New Yorker* 18 (November 28, 1942): 24-8+; (December 5, 1942): 26-34+.

Glenn L. Martin.

938. Keatley, Vivien B. "Siren of the Sawdust Trail." *Coronet* 42 (August 1957): 52-8.

Aimee Semple McPherson.

939. Keats, John. *Howard Hughes.* New York, [1966]. 304 pp.

Howard Robard Hughes, born 1905.

940. Kellon, Francis. "Llewellyn and Jotham Bixby: Pioneer California Businessmen." Master's thesis, University of Southern California, 1951. 93 pp.

941. [Kerr, Willis Holmes]. *Willis Holmes Kerr, Librarian Emeritus, Claremont College* . . . Claremont, 1952. 19 pp.

942. Kershner, Frederick D., Jr. "George Chaffey and the Irrigation Frontier." *Agricultural History* 27 (October, 1953): 115-22.

943. Kilner, William H. B. *Arthur Letts, 1862-1923, Man and Merchant, Steadfast Friend, Loyal Employer.* Los Angeles, 1927. 273 pp.

Founder of Los Angeles' Broadway Department Store.

944. King, Carrington. "Ed Pauley Is Washington 'Mystery Man.'" *Petroleum World* 39 (May 1942): 21.

945. Knowles, Ruth S. *The Greatest Gamblers; The Epic of American Oil Exploration.* New York, 1959. 346 pp.

Includes material on Edward L. Doheny (1856-1940) and Lyman Stewart (1840-1923).

946. Knudsen Creamery Co. of California. [*Tribute to Thorkild R. Knudsen*]. Los Angeles, 1965. [24] pp.

947. Knutsen, George E. "Upton Sinclair; The Urge to Reform." Master's thesis, University of Southern California, 1965. 120 pp.

948. Koury, Phil A. *Yes, Mr. De Mille.* New York, 1959. 319 pp.

Cecil B. De Mille.

949. Kruckeberg, Henry W. *George Christian Roeding 1868-1928: The Story of California's Leading Nurseryman and Fruit Grower.* Los Angeles, 1930. 109 pp.

950. Krueger, Robert B. "Profile: Grant B. Cooper, President of Los Angeles Bar Association for 1960." *Los Angeles Bar Bulletin* 35 (February 1960): 107-9.

951. Kruszynski, Eugene S. "Ernest Carroll Moore: Educational Historian." Doctoral dissertation, University of California, Los Angeles, 1963. 259 pp.

Much of his career spent at UCLA.

952. La Bounty, Hugh O. "Edwin Augustus Lee: Portrait of an Educator." Doctoral dissertation, University of California, Los Angeles, 1961. 347 pp.

One-time dean of the UCLA School of Education.

953. Lahart, Edward. "Upton Sinclair: Still an Unabashed Reformer and Optimist." *Frontier* 17 (August 1966): 13-4.

954. Langlie, Warren M. "Arnold Schoenberg as a Teacher." Doctoral dissertation, University of California, Los Angeles, 1960. 200 pp.

955. Larkin, Edgar L. "Thaddeus S. C. Lowe and Lewis Swift. A Tribute and Appreciation." *Out West*, new series, 5 (February 1913): 92-100.

956. Lasky, Jesse Louis. *I Blow My Own Horn.* With Don Weldon. New York, 1957. 284 pp.

Autobiography.

957. Lavell, Ruth G. "Sheriff Eugene W. Biscailuz: An Administrative Biography [1883-1958]." Master's thesis, University of Southern California, 1962. 69 pp.

958. Lee, Charles L. "A Case Study in Educational Leadership: Willard E. Goslin." Doctoral dissertation, Stanford University, 1949. 176 pp.

One-time superintendent of Pasadena City Schools.

959. Lee, James. "Mr. Donald Douglas." *Saturday Night* 45 (February 12, 1938): 11+.

960. LeRoy, Mervyn. *It Takes More Than Talent.* New York, 1953. 300 pp.

Autobiography.

961. Libby, Bill. "Here Comes Jack Kent Cooke." *Los Angeles* 11 (February 1966): 30-2+.

Sports promoter.

962. —— "The Long Week of Roman Gabriel." *Los Angeles* 11 (November 1966): 36-40.

Quarterback of the Los Angeles Rams.

963. —— "O'Malley: Looking Back on the First 10." *Los Angeles* 12 (September 1967): 46-50.

Walter O'Malley, owner of the Los Angeles Dodgers.

964. Lippincott, J[oseph] B. "William Mulholland —Engineer, Pioneer, Raconteur." *Civil Engineering* 11, Part I. "His Start in Life and His Service in the Los Angeles City Water Company." (February 1941): 105-7; Part II. "The Owens Valley Aqueduct and Later Work." (March 1941): 161-4.

965. Lissner, Meyer. "Bill Mulholland." *American Magazine* 73 (April 1912): 674-6.

966. Los Angeles Jewish Community Council. *Judge Harry A. Hollzer, 1880-1946.* [Los Angeles, n.d.]. 17 pp.

967. Luttrell, Raymond S. "Mark Keppel—His Life and Educational Career." Doctoral dissertation, University of California, Los Angeles, 1951. 334 pp.

968. Lyman, Edward D. *Homer P. Earle.* Los Angeles, 1946. 20 pp.

969. Mahood, Ruth I., ed. *Photographer of the Southwest, Adam Clark Vroman, 1856-1916.* Los Angeles, 1961. 127 pp.

Brief biographical sketch; rest chiefly pictorial.

970. "Makers of Los Angeles: A. H. Koebig." *Out West* 32 (April 1910): 327.

971. "Makers of Los Angeles: Alfred F. Webster." *Out West* 32 (April 1910): 332.

972. "Makers of Los Angeles: Alfred G. R. Schloesser." *Out West* 32 (April 1910): 331.

973. "Makers of Los Angeles: Dick Ferris." *Out West* 32 (April 1910): 321.

974. "Makers of Los Angeles: Edward Double." *Out West* 32 (April 1910): 320.

975. "Makers of Los Angeles: Fielding J. Stilson." *Out West* 32 (April 1910): 329.

976. "Makers of Los Angeles: George C. Peckham." *Out West* 32 (April 1910): 329.

977. "Makers of Los Angeles: George G. Gillette." *Out West* 32 (April 1910): 323.

978. "Makers of Los Angeles: George H. Hupp." *Out West* 32 (April 1910): 324.

979. "Makers of Los Angeles: Henry Hauser." *Out West* 32 (April 1910): 324.

980. "Makers of Los Angeles: Horace M. Russell." *Out West* 32 (April 1910): 330.

981. "Makers of Los Angeles: Ion L. Clark." *Out West* 32 (April 1910): 318.

982. "Makers of Los Angeles: James A. Gibson." *Out West* 32 (April 1910): 322.

983. "Makers of Los Angeles: John Denair." *Out West* 32 (April 1910): 319.

984. "Makers of Los Angeles: Joseph R. Loftus." *Out West* 32 (April 1910): 328.

985. "Makers of Los Angeles: Julius Hauser." *Out West* 32 (April 1910): 325.

986. "Makers of Los Angeles: Lynden E. Behymer." *Out West* 32 (April 1910): 317.

987. "Makers of Los Angeles: W. F. Holt." *Out West* 32 (April 1910): 326.

988. "Makers of Los Angeles: Wilkes Wheatley." *Out West* 32 (April 1910): 332.

989. Marcosson, Isaac F. *A Little Known Master of Millions, the Story of Henry E. Huntington, Constructive Capitalist.* Boston, 1914. [30 pp.]

990. Marquis, Neeta. "William B. Bowen, Philanthropist." *Out West,* new series, 3 (January 1912): 57-61.

[Bowen's correct middle initial was M.]

991. Marshall, James. *Elbridge A. Stuart, Founder of Carnation Company.* Los Angeles, 1949. 238 pp.

992. Marston, George W. *Over the Years, Recollections of George White Marston, Trustee Since 1887, Pomona College, October 14, 1937.* [Claremont, 1937]. [26] pp.

993. Martin, George R. *The Clarke Story. Chauncey Dwight Clarke, Marie Rankin Clarke, and the Claremont Colleges.* Claremont, 1964. 37 pp.

994. Martin, I. G. *Dr. P. F. Bresee and the Church He Founded.* [Kansas City, Mo.], 1937. 53 pp.

995. Marx, Wesley. "Dan Reeves: The Impresario of Risk." *Los Angeles* 6 (July 1963): 30+.
Owner of the Los Angeles Rams.

996. ———. "Parker: The Cop as Crusader." *Los Angeles* 4 (August 1962): 18+.
One-time Los Angeles Police Chief William Henry Parker, III.

997. ———. "Watkins of Watts: What One Man Can Do." *Reporter* 38 (January 25, 1968): 36-8.
Ted Watkins.

998. "Master of Merchandising: Harry Philp." *Los Angeles Saturday Night* 13 (July 15, 1933): 10.
Manager of the Broadway Department Store.

999. Mathews, Linda M. "Chief Reddin: New Style at the Top." *Atlantic Monthly* 223 (March 1969): 84-6+.
Thomas Reddin, former Chief, Los Angeles Police Department.

1000. Maulsby, Orlando W. *Rolling Stone, the Autobiography of O. W. Maulsby.* Los Angeles, 1931. 130 pp.
Author came to rest at Whittier around 1906 and became an orange grower and active in the California Fruit Growers Exchange.

1001. Mavity, Nancy Barr. *Sister Aimee.* Garden City, N. Y., 1931. 360 pp.
Aimee Semple McPherson.

1002. Mazo, Earl. *Richard Nixon: A Political and Personal Portrait.* New York, [1959]. 309 pp.

1003. [McCarthy, John Russell]. *Joseph Francis Sartori, 1858-1946.* Los Angeles, 1948. 120 pp.

1004. ———— "Los Angeles' Bad, Bad Boy." *Westways* 26 (February 1934): 26-7+.
Journalist Harry Carr.

1005. ———— "Those Who Write: Dr. Robert Cleland Has Two Hobbies—He Rides One, the Other Rides Him." *Saturday Night* 46 (January 28, 1939): 35.

1006. ———— "Water: The Story of Bill Mulholland." *Pacific Saturday Night* 45. Published in 15 installments as follows:
Prologue (October 30, 1937): 4-5.
Chapter 1 (November 6, 1937): 4-5.
Chapter 2 (November 13, 1937): 4-5.
Chapter 3 (November 20, 1937): 4-5.
Chapter 4 (November 27, 1937): 4-5.
Chapter 5 (December 4, 1937): 28-9.*
Chapter 6 (December 11, 1937): 28-9.
Chapter 7 (December 18, 1937): 28-9.
Chapter 8 (December 25, 1937): 24-5.
Chapter 9 (January 1, 1938: 32-3.
Chapter 10 (January 15, 1938): 32-3.
Chapter 11 (January 29, 1938): 32-3.
Chapter 12 (February 12, 1938): 30-1.
Chapter 13 (February 26, 1938): 38-9.
Chapter 14 (March 12, 1938): 36-8.
Chapter 15 (March 26, 1938): 31.
[*Beginning with this installment, word *Pacific* dropped from title of periodical.]

1007. McCoy, Esther. *Five California Architects.* New York, 1960. 200 pp.
Bernard Maybeck, the two Greene brothers, Irving Gill, and R. M. Schindler.

1008. ———— *Richard Neutra.* New York, 1960. 128 pp.

1009. McDowell, Evelyn. "New Pastor for Church." *Los Angeles Saturday Night* 15 (January 26, 1935): 4.
Dr. James W. Fifield, Jr., pastor of First Congregational Church of Los Angeles.

1010. McGregor, Georgette F. "The Educational Career of Susan Miller Dorsey." Doctoral dissertation, University of California, Los Angeles, 1949. 310 pp.

1011. McIntire, Charles. "The King of Home Builders." *Out West,* new series, 6 (September 1913): 124-7.
Charles A. Elder of the Los Angeles Investment Co.

1012. McPherson, Aimee Semple. *In the Service of the King: The Story of My Life.* New York, 1927. 316 pp.
Autobiography.

1013. ———— *The Story of My Life.* [Ed. by Raymond W. Becker]. Hollywood, 1951. 246 pp.

1014. ———— *This Is That; Personal Experiences, Sermons and Writings of Aimee Semple McPherson.* Los Angeles, 1921. 672 pp. 2nd ed., [1923]. 791 pp.

1015. McWilliams, Carey. "Southern California Begins to Write. IV. Challis Silvay: 'A Bright, Authentic Stain.'" *Los Angeles Saturday Night* 8 (November 26, 1927): 4-5.
Poet who lived at Ocean Park.

1016. ———— "Southern California Begins to Write. XVII. Clarkson Crane." *Los Angeles Saturday Night* 9 (November 17, 1928): 5.

1017. ———— "Southern California Begins to Write. XII. Edith Summers Kelley: Realist." *Los Angeles Saturday Night* 8 (April 28, 1928): 4-5.

1018. ———— "Southern California Begins to Write. XVI. George Wycherley Kirkman: Historian." *Los Angeles Saturday Night* 8 (September 8, 1928): 4-5.

1019. ———— "Southern California Begins to Write. XX. Henry Chester Tracy: Scientific Humanist." *Los Angeles Saturday Night* 9 (March 2, 1929): 5.

1020. ———— Southern California Begins to Write. V. Herman George Scheffauer: An Appreciation." *Los Angeles Saturday Night* 8 (December 3, 1927): 4-5.

1021. ———— "Southern California Begins to Write. XVIII. Hildegarde Flanner." *Los Angeles Saturday Night* 9 (January 19, 1929): 5.

1022. —— "Southern California Begins to Write. III. Jake Zeitlin: American Poet." *Los Angeles Saturday Night* 8 (November 19, 1927): 4-5.

1023. —— "Southern California Begins to Write. VIII. Jane O'Sullivan: In Love With Hills." *Los Angeles Saturday Night* 8 (January 28, 1928): 4-5.

1024. —— "Southern California Begins to Write. XIII. Jim Tully: Literary Hobo." *Los Angeles Saturday Night* 8 (May 12, 1928): 4-5.

1025. —— "Southern California Begins to Write. XXI. Ken Nakazawa." *Los Angeles Saturday Night* 9 (March 30, 1929): 5.

1026. —— "Southern California Begins to Write. I. Louis Adamic: Ex-Crusader." *Los Angeles Saturday Night* 8 (October 22, 1927): 4-5.
Adamic then resided in San Pedro.

1027. —— "Southern California Begins to Write. X. Paul Jordan-Smith: Bibliophile." *Los Angeles Saturday Night* 8 (March 3, 1928): 5.

1028. —— "Southern California Begins to Write. XIV. Sydney King Russell: A Changing Flame." *Los Angeles Saturday Night* 8 (July 21, 1928): 4-5.

1029. —— "Southern California Begins to Write. VI. Upton Sinclair: Two Impressions." *Los Angeles Saturday Night* 8 (December 24, 1937): 4-5.

1030. —— "Southern California Begins to Write. IX. Wallace Smith: Throws Bricks at the Moon." *Los Angeles Saturday Night* 8 (February 18, 1928): 4-5.

1031. —— "Southern California Begins to Write. XV. Welford Beaton: Film Critic." *Los Angeles Saturday Night* 8 (August 4, 1928): 4-5.

1032. Mears, Joe. "It Takes Brains to Run a Forest." *Westways* 47 (November 1955): 6-7.
William V. Mendenhall, supervisor of Angeles National Forest.

1033. "Measure of a Mayor." *Time* 61 (April 20, 1953): 27.
Fletcher Bowron.

1034. Medeiros, Francine M. "Edward A. Dickson: A Study in Progressivism." Master's thesis, University of California, Los Angeles, 1968. 97 pp.

1035. "Memorial Resolutions Adopted by the Board of Trustees of the Los Angeles Bar Association: In Memoriam, Isidore B. Dockweiler." *Los Angeles Bar Bulletin* 22 (March 1947): 194-6.

1036. "Memorial to Edward S. Shattuck." *Los Angeles Bar Bulletin* 41 (January 1966): 132-3.
Obituary.

1037. Meredith, De Witt. *G. Allan Hancock: A Pictorial Account of One Man's Score in Fourscore Years.* [San Jose, 1964]. 281 pp.
Primarily pictorial.

1038. Meredith, Francis. "Cool Cooper." *Los Angeles* 14 (March 1969): 26-8+
Attorney Grant B. Cooper.

1039. Michelson, Arthur U. *From Judaism and Law to Christ and Grace.* Los Angeles, 1943. 144 pp.
Autobiography.

1040. Miller, Diane Disney. *The Story of Walt Disney.* New York, 1957. 247 pp.

1041. Miller, Eleanor. *When Memory Calls.* Gardena, 1936. 225 pp.
Autobiography.

1042. Miller, Richard C. "The Lion of Los Angeles: Harrison Gray Otis and the Los Angeles Times, Emphasizing 1903-1912." Master's thesis, Claremont Graduate School, 1956. 227 pp.

1043. —— "Otis and His Times: The Career of Harrison Gray Otis of Los Angeles." Doctoral dissertation, University of California, Berkeley, 1961. 545 pp.

1044. Miller, Virgil E. *Splinters from Hollywood Tripods; Memoirs of a Cameraman.* New York, [1964]. 130 pp.

1045. Millier, Arthur. "Citizen Disney." *Los Angeles* 8 (November 1964): 32+.
Walt Disney.

1046. Millikan, Robert A. *The Autobiography of Robert A. Millikan.* New York, 1950. 311 pp.

1047. "Millikan Pays Tribute to Judge Gavin W. Craig." *Los Angeles Bar Bulletin* 23 (March 1948): 217-8+.

Remarks of Charles E. Millikan, senior vice president of Los Angeles Bar Association, on Judge Craig, deceased.

1048. Monroe, Keith. "California's Dedicated Detective." *Harper's Magazine* 214 (June 1957): 57-9.

Ed Bliss, chief investigator for Los Angeles County Public Defender's Office.

1049. Moon, Henry L. "Loren Miller, Legal Scholar." *Crisis* 74 (August-September 1967): 346-7.

Los Angeles Negro judge.

1050. Morgan, John T. "Our American Mayors: VIII. Mayor George E. Cryer of Los Angeles." *National Municipal Review* 18 (January 1928): 27-32.

1051. Morosco, Helen M., and Dugger, Leonard P. *Life of Oliver Morosco, the Oracle of Broadway.* Caldwell, Idaho, 1944. 391 pp.

Included are chapters on his theatre activities in Los Angeles.

1052. Morrison, Lorrin L. "Noah Levering: A Biographical Sketch." *Historical Society of Southern California Quarterly* 40 (1958): 211-22.

Commemorative sketch of a founder of the Historical Society of Southern California; also included are lists of the Society's officers and notes on Major E. W. Jones, James Miller Guinn, George Butler Griffin, Dr. J. D. Moody, Walter R. Bacon, George Finley Bovard, Rockwell D. Hunt, Arthur Ellis, J. Gregg Layne, Henry Raup Wagner, and Robert Glass Cleland.

1053. "Mulholland . . . Man of Broad Vision." *Southern California Business* 8 (September 1929): 15.

William Mulholland.

1054. Munk, Joseph A. *Activities of a Life-Time.* Los Angeles, 1924. 221 pp.

Autobiography.

1055. Nadeau, Remi. "The Men Who Opened the Valley." *Westways* 55 (May 1963): 24-7.

Hobart J. Whitley and other San Fernando Valley land developers.

1056. Neal, T[homas] [A.]. "In Retrospect—Ernest Dawson," [Horn's] *Magazine for Booklovers* 1 (January 1948): 10-1+.

1057. Neff, Merlin L. *For God and C.M.E.; A Biography of Percy Tilson Magan upon the Historical Background of the Educational and Medical Work of Seventh-Day Adventists.* Mountain View, [1964]. 341 pp.

1058. Newmark, Leo. *California Family Newmark: An Intimate History.* Santa Monica, 1970. 110 pp.

1059. Newmark, Marco R. "Charles Fletcher Lummis." *Historical Society of Southern California Quarterly* 32 (1950): 45-60.

Reprinted as "Bohemian and Genius—Charles F. Lummis" in the author's *Jottings in Southern California History* (Los Angeles, 1955): 103-29.

1060. ———— "The Community Builders of Los Angeles—Dr. Joseph P. Widney," in *Jottings in Southern California History* (Los Angeles, 1955): 89-93.

1061. ———— "The Community Builders of Los Angeles—Judge Robert Maclay Widney," in *Jottings in Southern California History* (Los Angeles, 1955): 81-9.

1062. ————"Dr. Philip Semen." *Historical Society of Southern California Quarterly* 41 (March 1959): 79.

Scholar and civic leader.

1063. ———— "A Friend of Abraham Lincoln—Cornelius Cole," in *Jottings in Southern California History* (Los Angeles, 1955): 101-2.

1064. ———— "The Gift of Leadership — Colonel William M. Garland," in *Jottings in Southern California History* (Los Angeles, 1955): 127-8.

1065. ———— "Great Journalist—Harrison Gray Otis," in *Jottings in Southern California History* (Los Angeles, 1955): 103-6.

1066. ———— "Historical Profiles: Alexander Campbell." *Historical Society of Southern California Quarterly* 37 (1955): 69.

1067. ———— "Historical Profiles: Andrew M. Chaffey." *Historical Society of Southern California Quarterly* 37 (1955): 70-1.

1068. ———— "Historical Profiles: Dr. Joseph Kurtz." *Historical Society of Southern California Quarterly* 37 (1955): 372-3.

1069. —— "Historical Profiles: Dr. Walter Lindley." *Historical Society of Southern California Quarterly* 38 (1956): 292-4.

1070. —— "Historical Profiles: Edward L. Doheny." *Historical Society of Southern California Quarterly* 37 (1955): 76-8.

1071. —— "Historical Profiles: Eli P. Clark." *Historical Society of Southern California Quarterly* 37 (1955): 71-2.

1072. —— "Historical Profiles: Ferdinand K. Rule." *Historical Society of Southern California Quarterly* 37 (1955) 284-5.

1073. —— "Historical Profiles: Frank Wiggins." *Historical Society of Southern California Quarterly* 37 (1955): 359-61.

1074. —— "Historical Profiles: Fred W. Blanchard." *Historical Society of Southern California Quarterly* 37 (1955): 370-1.

1075. —— "Historical Profiles: Harris Newmark." *Historical Society of Southern California Quarterly* 37 (1955): 186-7.

1076. —— "Historical Profiles: Henry M. Robinson." *Historical Society of Southern California Quarterly* 38 (1956): 289-90.

1077. —— "Historical Profiles: Homer Lea." *Historical Society of Southern California Quarterly* 37 (1955) 177-84.

Reprinted as "Dreamer and Prophet — Homer Lea" in the author's *Jottings in Southern California History* (Los Angeles, 1955): 134-44.

1078. —— "Historical Profiles: Isaac N. Van Nuys." *Historical Society of Southern California Quarterly* 38 (1956): 91-3.

1079. —— Historical Profiles: Isidore B. Dockweiler." *Historical Society of Southern California Quarterly* 37 (1955): 75-6.

1080. —— "Historical Profiles: J. M. Guinn." *Historical Society of Southern California Quarterly* 37 (1955): 82-4.

1081. —— "Historical Profiles: John C. Austin." *Historical Society of Southern California Quarterly* 36 (1954): 342-3.

Reprinted as "Profile of a Great Architect—John C. Austin" in the author's *Jottings in Southern California History* (Los Angeles, 1955): 132-3.

1082. —— "Historical Profiles: John R. Haynes." *Historical Society of Southern California Quarterly* 37 (1955): 84-6.

1083. —— "Historical Profiles: Joseph Mesmer." *Historical Society of Southern California Quarterly* 37 (1955): 185.

1084. —— "Historical Profiles: Joseph Scott." *Historical Society of Southern California Quarterly* 36 (1954): 255-7.

Reprinted as "An Horatio Alger Story—Joseph Scott" in the author's *Jottings in Southern California History* (Los Angeles, 1955): 128-31.

1085. —— "Historical Profiles: Judge Ygnacio Sepulveda." *Historical Society of Southern California Quarterly* 37 (1955): 285.

1086. —— "Historical Profiles: Kaspare Cohn." *Historical Society of Southern California Quarterly* 37 (1955): 368-70.

1087. —— "Historical Profiles: Louis M. Cole." *Historical Society of Southern California Quarterly* 37 (1955): 73-4.

1088. —— "Historical Profiles: Madame Caroline Severance." *Historical Society of Southern California Quarterly* 38 (1956): 294-6.

Reprinted as " 'The Mother of Woman's Clubs' —Madame Caroline Severance" in the author's *Jottings in Southern California* (Los Angeles, 1955): 98-101.

1089. —— "Historical Profiles: Marshall Stimson." *Historical Society of Southern California Quarterly* 37 (1955): 287-8.

1090. —— "Historical Profiles: Max Meyberg." *Historical Society of Southern California Quarterly* 38 (1956): 290-2.

1091. —— "Historical Profiles: Miss Mary Foy." *Historical Society of Southern California* 37 (1955): 366-8.

1092. —— "Historical Profiles: Reginaldo F. del

Valle." *Historical Society of Southern California Quarterly* 37 (1955): 74-5.

Reprinted as "A Serviceable Career—Reginaldo F. Del Valle" in the author's *Jottings in Southern California History* (Los Angeles, 1955): 75-6.

1093. —— "Historical Profiles: William G. Kerckhoff." *Historical Society of Southern California Quarterly* 37 (1955): 364-6.

1094. —— "Historical Profiles: William Orcutt." *Historical Society of Southern California Quarterly* 37 (1955): 187-8.

1095. —— "Inventor and Publisher—Edwin T. Earl," in *Jottings in Southern California History* (Los Angeles, 1955): 145.

1096. —— *Jottings in Southern California History.* Los Angeles, 1955. 162 pp.

The last half of the book consists of brief biographies of notable Los Angeles citizens. See individual entries in *Biography*.

1097. —— "Master of Finance — Isaias W. Hellman," in *Jottings in Southern California History* (Los Angeles, 1955): 77-81.

1098. —— "Railroad Builder—Henry E. Huntington," in *Jottings in Southern California History* (Los Angeles, 1955): 146-8.

1099. Nolan, William F. *John Huston, King Rebel.* Los Angeles, [1965]. 247 pp.

1100. Norton, Richard H. *Reminiscences of an Agitator: With a Diagonisis and a Remedy for Present Economic Conditions.* Los Angeles, 1912. 91 pp.

1101. O'Connor, J. H. "Judge William B. McKesson." *Los Angeles Bar Bulletin* 19 (March 1944): 223.

1102. O'Melveny, Henry W. *William G. Kerckhoff; A Memorial.* Los Angeles, 1935. 75 pp.

1103. Orcutt, William W. *Memorabilia of William Warren Orcutt, 1869-1942.* Los Angeles, 1945. 93 pp.

1104. Orme, Reginald G. "William H. Snyder: Biography of an Educational Adventurer." Doctoral dissertation, University of California, Los Angeles, 1950. 394 pp.

1105. Otis, Harrison Gray. *A Letter from Harrison Gray Otis* [1914]. Los Angeles, 1917. 15 pp.

Contains a brief biographical sketch.

1106. "Our Public Officials: John Anson Ford, Los Angeles County Supervisor." *Western Housing* 28 (February 1946): 13.

1107. Page, James R. *I. N. Van Nuys, 1835-1912.* Los Angeles, 1944. 34 pp.

1108. [Parkinson, John]. *Incidents by the Way.* [Los Angeles, c1935]. 342 pp.

Autobiography of the designer of many Los Angeles buildings, including the City Hall

1109. Parsons, Louella (Oettinger). *The Gay Illiterate.* Garden City, N.Y., 1944. 194 pp.

Autobiography.

1110. Pasadena Symphony Association. *In Celebration of the Eightieth Birthday of Richard Lert.* Los Angeles, 1965. 27 pp.

Biographical sketch.

1111. "Passing of a Pioneer." *Los Angeles Saturday Night* 13 (May 27, 1933): 10.

Obituary of Louis Denni, dairyman and Signal Hill oil operator.

1112. Penchef, Esther H. "The Sociological Thought of Clarence Marsh Case: Its Origins, Development, Significance, and Its Relation to the Contributions of Other Sociologists." Doctoral dissertation, University of Southern California, 1947. 223 pp.

1113. Peyton, Thomas R. *Quest for Dignity, an Autobiography of a Negro Doctor.* Los Angeles, [c1950]. 156 pp.

1114. Pindell, M. L. *From a Country Doctor to a Radiologist in Beverly Hills, California.* New York, [1967]. 211 pp.

1115. Pohlmann, John O. "Alphonzo E. Bell: A Biography." *Southern California Quarterly* 46 (1964): 197-222, 315-50.

Based on the author's same titled Master's thesis, Occidental College, 1963. 135 pp.

1116. Pottenger, Francis M. *The Fight Against Tuberculosis; An Autobiography.* New York, [c1952]. 276 pp.

1117. Powell, Lawrence Clark. "California Classics Reread: *The Cattle on a Thousand Hills*." *Westways* 61 (April 1969): 14-7+.

Prof. Robert Glass Cleland.

1118. ———— "California Classics Reread: Charles Fletcher Lummis and *The Land of Sunshine*." *Westways* 62 (January 1970): 20-3+.

1119. ———— "California Classics Reread: *Farewell, My Lovely*." *Westways* 61 (March 1969): 6-9.

Los Angeles novelist Raymond Chandler.

1120. ———— "California Classics Reread: George Wharton James, *The Wonders of the Colorado Desert*." *Westways* 62 (February 1970): 4-7+.

1121. ———— "California Classics Reread: Idwal Jones and *The Vineyard*." *Westways* 62 (March 1970): 18-21+.

1122. ———— "California Classics Reread: Upton Sinclair's *Oil!*" *Westways* 62 (September 1970): 14-7+.

1123. ———— "Climbing the Ladder: Excerpt from Fortune and Friendship." *Library Journal* 93 (January 1, 1968): 49-53.

Autobiographical.

1124. ———— *Recollections of an Ex-Bookseller*. Los Angeles, 1950. 17 pp.

1125. Putnam, Frank B. "Teresa Urrea, 'The Saint of Cabora.'" *Southern California Quarterly* 55 (1963): 245-64.

Life of a young woman thought to have miraculous curative powers, who lived in Los Angeles for a time during the early twentieth century.

1126. R. O. F. "California Men of Notable Constructive Ability: XII. Daniel Moore Linnard." *The Argonaut* 96 (January 24, 1925): 1+.

Hotelman whose enterprises included the Maryland, Huntington, and Vista Del Arroyo hotels in Pasadena.

1127. "Raconteur and Writer: John T. Gaffey." *Los Angeles Saturday Night* 11 (November 15, 1930): 6-7.

1128. Rand, Carl W. *Joseph Pomeroy Widney,*

Physician and Mystic. Ed. by Doris Sanders. Los Angeles, 1970. 133 pp.

1129. Raulston, Marion C. *Memoirs of Owen Humphrey Churchill [1841-1916] and His Family*. Los Angeles, 1950. [97] pp.

1130. Reagan, Ronald. *Where's the Rest of Me?* With Richard G. Hubler. New York, [1965]. 316 pp.

1131. "Retires After Forty Active Years." *Los Angeles Saturday Night* 43 (July 4, 1936): 13.

Harry Philp, manager of the Broadway Department Store.

1132. Rice, Cy. *Defender of the Damned: Gladys Towles Root*. New York, [1964]. 258 pp.

1133. Richardson, James H. *For the Life of Me; Memoirs of a City Editor*. New York, 1954. 312 pp.

James Hugh Richardson (1894-1963), one-time editor of the Los Angeles *Herald,* and city editor of the Los Angeles *Examiner.*

1134. Riley, Frank. "Ahmanson: A 1967 Interview." *Los Angeles* 12 (January 1967): 32-3+.

Howard Ahmanson, Los Angeles financier.

1135. Ring, Frances. "My Boss, Scott Fitzgerald." *Los Angeles* 7 (January 1964): 34-6.

F. Scott Fitzgerald in Encino and Hollywood.

1136. Riznik, Joseph Q. "California Racket Buster." *American Magazine* 125 (June 1938): 14-5+.

Clifford E. Clinton.

1137. "Robert Ernest Cowan, 1862-1942." *California Library Association Bulletin* 4 (September 1942): 12.

Obituary.

1138. Roberts, Belle M. *A Word in Appreciation of Charles Heston Peirson*. Los Angeles, [1926]. 27 pp.

1139. Rolle, Andrew F. "Robert Glass Cleland, 1885-1957: An Historian's Appreciation." *Historical Society of Southern California Quarterly* 40 (1958): 81-3.

1140. Romer, Margaret. "Pioneer Builders of Los Angeles: A Series of Personality Sketches of Some of the Men and Women Who Helped Transform the Pueblo of Los Angeles into a Modern American City." *Historical Society of Southern California Quarterly* 43 (1961): 97-103, 342-9.

Included are Lynden E. Behymer and Susan M. Dorsey.

1141. ———— "The Story of Martin Aguirre, Famed Los Angeles County Sheriff." *Historical Society of Southern California Quarterly* 43 (1961): 125-36.

1142. Roger, William L. "The Man Who Might Be President: Richard Nixon's Success Story from the Inside." *Frontier* 6 (September 1955): 7-9+.

1143. Ruddy, Ella G., ed. *The Mother of Clubs.* Los Angeles, 1906. 191 pp.

On Caroline M. Severance (Seymore) who resided in Los Angeles, 1875-1906. Founder of first woman's club in the United States and of the Los Angeles Friday Morning Club.

1144. Russell, J[oe] H. *Heads and Tails . . . and Odds and Ends.* Los Angeles, 1963. 97 pp.

Autobiographical sequel to author's *Cattle on the Conejo* with many references to Los Angeles County communities and personalities.

1145. Ryder, David W. "Donald W. Douglas," in *America's Fifty Foremost Business Leaders.* Ed. by Bertie C. Forbes. New York, 1948. Pp. 92-9.

1146. St. Johns, Adela Rogers. *Final Verdict.* New York, 1962. 512 pp.

Earl Rogers.

1147. ———— *First Step up Toward Heaven: Hubert Eaton and Forest Lawn.* Englewood Cliffs, N. J., [1959]. 293 pp.

1148. Salzman, Maurice. "Charles Fletcher Lummis: The Very Last of the Mohicans." *Progressive Arizona and the Great Southwest* 8 (January 1929): 14-8.

1149. "Sam of Watts." *Arts & Architecture* 68 (July 1951): 23-5.

Simon Rodia, builder of the Watts Towers.

1150. Schad, Robert O. "Henry E. Huntington: The Founder and the Library." *Huntington Library Bulletin* 1 (May 1931): 3-32.

1151. Schickel, Richard. *The Disney Version.* New York, 1968. 384 pp.

Published in London, 1968, under the title of *Walt Disney.* A lengthy summation was published as "Bringing Forth the Mouse." *American Heritage* 19 (April 1968): 24-9+.

1152. Scott, Audrey. *I Was a Hollywood Stunt Girl.* Philadelphia, [1969]. 119 pp.

Actually a stunt man.

1153. Scruggs, Baxter S. *Man in Our Community; The Biography of L. G. Robinson of Los Angeles, California.* Gardena, 1937. 134 pp.

Louis George Robinson, a black man who migrated to Los Angeles from Georgia in 1904; Los Angeles County civil servant; active in Y.M.C.A.

1154. Sennett, Mack. *King of Comedy. As Told to Cameron Shipp.* Garden City, N. Y., 1954. 284 pp.

1155. Shank, Theodore J. "Garnet Holme: California Pageant Maker." Master's thesis, University of California, Los Angeles, 1953. 158 pp.

1156. Sherer, Caroline S. *How Much He Remembered; The Life of John Calvin Sherer, 1852-1949.* [N.p.], 1952. 64 pp.

1157. Shippey, Lee. *The Luckiest Man Alive.* Los Angeles, 1959.

Autobiography of Los Angeles' colorful long-time journalist.

1158. Shuler, Robert P. *"McPhersonism"; A Study of Healing Cults and Modern Day "Tongues" Movements, Containing Summary of Facts as to Disappearances and Reappearances of Aimee Semple McPherson.* [Los Angeles, 1924?]. 128 pp.

1159. ———— *"Miss X."* Los Angeles, [1926?]. 96 pp.
Aimee Semple McPherson.

1160. "Sidelights on Business Success Through Half a Century." *Los Angeles Saturday Night* 14 (June 16, 1934): 11.
Herman W. Frank of Harris & Frank.

1161. Simonson, Harold P. *Francis Grierson.* New York, 1966. 158 pp.

Based on the author's doctoral dissertation, Northwestern University, 1958.

1162. —— "Zona Gale's Acquaintance with Francis Grierson." *Historical Society of Southern California Quarterly* 41 (March 1959): 11-6.

Describes Grierson's unusual death and Zona Gale's efforts to help him financially.

1163. Simpson, W[illia]m A. "They Wrote Their Names in Deeds: Los Angeles Will Long Remember John Bullock for Water, as It Will George Ward for Power." *Southern California Business* 12 (October 1933): 14.

1164. Sinclair, Helen. "He Ran His Business by a Book: That Book Was the Bible—And Lyman Stewart Left the Bible Institute and the Union Oil Company." *Southern Calfiornia Business* 9 (October 1930): 26-7.

1165. Smith, Bertha H. "The Policewoman." *Good Housekeeping Magazine* 52 (March 1911): 296-8.

Alice Sterbins Wells, first female police officer in Los Angeles.

1166. Smith, Jack. "A Day in the City: Echoes of Aimee." *Westways* 62 (April 1970): 11-3+.

Aimee Semple McPherson's exploits during the 1920s.

1167. Smith, Sarah Hathaway (Bixby). *Adobe Days; Being the Truthful Narrative of the Events in the Life of a California Girl on a Sheep Ranch and in El Pueblo de Nuestra Senora de Los Angeles* . . . Cedar Rapids, Iowa, 1925. 208 pp. Rev. ed., 1926. 217 pp. 3rd rev. ed., Los Angeles, 1931. 148 pp.

1168. Smythe, William E. "Charles Amadon Moody. The Man and the Citizen." *Out West,* new series, 1 (December 1910): 68.

Pioneer in the Good Government Movement in Los Angeles.

1169. Somerville, J. Alexander. *Man of Color, an Autobiography by Dr. J. Alexander Somerville; Factual Report on the Status of the American Negro Today.* Los Angeles, [c1949]. 170 pp.

1170. Spalding, William A. *William Andrew Spalding, Los Angeles Newspaperman; An Autobiographical Account* [1852-1941]. Ed. with an introduction by Robert V. Hine. San Marino, 1961. 156 pp.

1171. "Spencer Cortelyou." *California Highways and Public Works* 41 (September-October 1962): 46.

Obituary of the engineer called the "Father of Freeways."

1172. Steckhan, H. O. "Pasadenans Write for Boys and Girls." *California Graphic* 5 (January 7, 1928): 5.

Carl and Grace Moon.

1173. [Steele, Rober V. P.]. *Storming Heaven. The Lives and Turmoils of Minnie Kennedy and Aimee Semple* McPherson. By Lately Thomas [*pseud.*]. New York, 1970. 364 pp.

1174. —— The Vanishing Evangelist. By Lately Thomas [*pseud.*]. New York, 1959. 334 pp.

The Aimee Semple McPherson kidnapping affair.

1175. Steffens, Lincoln. *Autobiography.* New York, 1931. 2 vols.

1176. Stern, Norton B. "Abraham Mooser—First Jewish Businessman of Santa Monica, California [1884-1931]." *Western States Jewish Historical Quarterly* 1 (1969): 109-27.

1177. —— *Mannie's Crowd. Emanuel Lowenstein* [*1857-1939*], *Colorful Character of Old Los Angeles.* Los Angeles, 1970. 136 pp.

1178. Stimson, Marshall. *Fun, Fights, and Fiestas in Old Los Angeles. An Autobiography.* Los Angeles, 1966. 322 pp.

1179. —— "A Los Angeles Jeremiah, Homer Lea: Military Genius and Prophet." *Historical Society of Southern California Quarterly* 24 (1949): 5-13.

1180. Stocker, Joseph. "Matt Weinstock: Mr. L.A." *Frontier* 2 (June 1951): 11-3.

Los Angeles newspaper columnist.

1181. Stone, Irving. *Clarence Darrow for the Defenes.* New York, [1941]. 570 pp. London, [1949]. 504 pp.

1182. "Successful Woman Educator Publicly Recognized: XXXI. Mrs. Susan M. Dorsey." *Saturday Night* 5 (June 13, 1925): 1.

1183. Sutton, Ernest V. *A Life Worth Living.* Pasadena, 1948. 350 pp.

Author worked as a compositor for various Los Angeles newspapers.

1184. Talbert, T[homas] B. *My Sixty Years in California: Memoirs of Pioneer Days of Long Beach.* Huntington Beach, 1952. 125 pp.

1185. Talmachoff, Peter J. "The Wizard of the West." *Museum Alliance Quarterly* 8 (Fall 1969): 12-7.

Edward H. Amet, early motion picture figure, who later resided in Newhall.

1186. Taylor, Frank J. "Booster No. 1." *Saturday Evening Post* 214 (April 4, 1942): 20-1+.

Donald K. Thomas, managing director of the All Year Club of Southern California.

1187. ———— "Heretic in The Promised Land: Los Angeles' Own Jiminy Cricket." *Saturday Evening Post* 213 (December 21, 1940): 27+.

Dr. George P. Clements, head of the Agricultural Department of the Los Angeles Chamber of Commerce.

1188. ———— "It Costs $1000 to Have Lunch with Harry Chandler." *Saturday Evening Post* 212 (December 16, 1939): 8-9+.

Partly biography and partly history of twentieth-century Los Angeles.

1189. ———— "Man with a Borrowed Shoestring." *Saturday Evening Post* 217 (December 2, 1944): 24-5+.

Manchester Boddy and the revival of the Los Angeles *Daily News.*

1190. Taylor, Ken. "Howard Hughes: A Sketch in Two Parts." *Pacific Saturday Night* 45 (November 27, 1937): 15+; (December 4, 1937): 35+.

[The word *Pacific* dropped from title of issue containing second installment (December 4).]

1191. Thomas, Bob. *Selznick.* Garden City, N. Y., 1970 381 pp.

David O. Selznick.

1192. ———— *Thalberg; Life and Legend.* Garden City, N. Y., 1969. 415 pp.

1193. "Thomas Bradley, Rising Political Star in the West." *Ebony* 24 (June 1969): 126-8+.

1194. "Those Tireless Chandlers." *Newsweek* 47 (April 30, 1956): 60+.

The Chandler family of Los Angeles, the *Times,* and its other enterprises.

1195. Thrapp, Dan. "Theodore Payne—Plantsman." *Westways* 53 (August 1961): 14-5.

Los Angeles horticulturist and nurseryman who campaigned to preserve California's native plants.

1196. *To Remember Gregg Anderson; Tributes by Members of the Columbiad Club, the Rounce and Coffin Club, the Roxburghe Club, the Zamorano Club.* [Los Angeles], 1949. [98] pp.

1197. Townsend, Francis E. *New Horizons.* Chicago, 1943. 246 pp.

Autobiography of the proponent of the "Townsend Plan"; born 1867; died 1936.

1198. Treanor, Thomas C. *John Treanor, a Sketch of His Life, with Excerpts from His Letters [1883-1935].* Los Angeles, 1937. 85 pp.

1199. Turner, Justin G., and Stern, Norton B. "Marco Ross Newmark, 1878-1959: First Jewish Historian of the Southland," *Western States Jewish Historical Quarterly* 1 (1968): 3-8.

1200. "Two Prominent Western Engineers Die." *Western Construction News* 10 (August 1935): 239-40.

Obituaries of William Mulholland and D. C. Henny.

1201. Underwood, Agness. *Newspaperwoman.* New York, 1949. 297 pp.

Reporter and city editor of the Los Angeles *Evening Herald and Express,* 1926-1968

1202. Vaughan, Ruben V. "*Doc.*" *The Print of My Remembrance; An Autobiography.* Hollywood, [c1955]. [?] pp.

Doc Vaughn, Avalon's official greeter.

1203. ———— *Doc's Catalina Diary.* Ed. by Betta R. Tigge. [N.p., 1956]. 74 pp.

1204. Vidor, King W. *A Tree Is a Tree*. New York, 1953. 315 pp.

Autobiography of a Hollywood director.

1205. Voorhis, Jerry [Horace J.]. *Confessions of a Congressman*. Garden City, N. Y., 1947. 365 pp.

1206. W. B. J. "California's Best Loved Composer Tells of Early Struggles: Carrie Jacobs Bond." *Saturday Night* 5 (September 12, 1925): 1-2.

1207. Wagner, Henry R. *Bullion to Books; Fifty Years of Business and Pleasure*. Los Angeles, 1942. 370 pp.

1208. —— *Sixty Years of Book Collecting*. [San Francisco], 1952. 51 pp.

1209. Wagner, Rob, and Hughes, Robert. *Two Decades; The Story of a Man of God, Hollywood's Own Padre*. Los Angeles, 1936. Unp.

Rev. Neal Dodd, pastor of Hollywood's "Little Church Around the Corner."

1210. Wagner, Walter. *The Golden Fleecers*. Garden City, N. Y., 1966. 278 pp.

Autobiography.

1211. Ward, Natalie J. "James Arnold Blaisdell: A Study of His Professional Career." Doctoral dissertation, 1960. 329 pp.

Founder of the Associated Colleges at Claremont.

1212. Warde, Frederick B. *Fifty Years of Make-Believe*. Los Angeles, 1923. 314 pp.

Life span, 1851-1935.

1213. Warner, Jack L. *My First Hundred Years in Hollywood*. With Dean Jennings. New York, [1965]. 331 pp.

1214. Warren, Althea H. "Don Carlos: Southern Californiac Among Librarians." *California Librarian* 14 (June 1953): 213-5.

Charles Fletcher Lummis.

1215. Warren, Lawrence. "Lester Horton: California Dance Pioneer." Master's thesis, University of California, Los Angeles, 1968. 126 pp.

1216. Watkins, Louise W. *Henry Edwards Hunt-*

ington; A Character Sketch of a Great Man. [Gardena, 1928]. 27 pp.

1217. Watson, Jane W. *The Seaver Story*. Claremont, 1960. 30 pp.

Biography of Frank Roger Seaver.

1218. Watts, Richard, Jr. "D. W. Griffith." *New Theatre* 3 (November 1936): 6-8.

1219. "We Boys" Class of the First Methodist Episcopal Church Sunday School. *The Beautiful Life of Eva Todd Burch*. Los Angeles, 1912. [?] pp.

1220. Weber, Francis J. *George Thomas Montgomery, California Churchman*. Los Angeles, 1966. 57 pp.

1221. —— "Irish-Born Champion of the Mexican-Americans." *California Historical Society Quarterly* 49 (1970): 233-49.

Los Angeles Archbishop John J. Cantwell.

1222. —— *Thomas James Conaty. Pastor—Educator—Bishop*. Los Angeles, 1969. 81 pp.

1223. Weinland, Henry A. *Now the Harvest; Memories of a County Agricultural Agent*. New York, 1957. 96 pp.

1224. West, Jessamyn. *To See the Dream*. New York, 1957. 314 pp.

An outgrowth of the author's journal kept when she was spending part of her time at home in Napa and part of it in Hollywood as a script writer.

1225. Weyer, Sister M. Anita, I.H.M. "Joseph Scott: A Life of Service." *Southern California Quarterly* 58 (1966): 241-64.

1226. White, Leslie T. *Me, Detective*. New York, c1936. 302 pp.

Autobiography, including a brief chapter on Doheny case.

1227. Whiting, Perry. *Autobiography of Perry Whiting: Pioneer Building Material Merchant of Los Angeles*. Ed. by John A. Davies. Los Angeles, 1930. 334 pp.

1228. Whitney, Caspar. *Charles Adelbert Canfield*. New York, 1930. 217 pp.

Canfield (1848-1913) was an oil entrepreneur in Los Angeles and the southern San Joaquin Valley.

1229. Widney, Joseph P. *Joseph Pomeroy Widney* [*1841-1938*] . . . *Founder of the Los Angeles County Medical Association and the College of Medicine of the University of Southern California* . . . San Francisco, 1936. 10 pp.

Reprint of his four-part article, "The Lure of Medical History," *California and Western Medicine* 44, Pt. 1 (April 1936): 292-5; Pt. 2 (May 1936): 396-401; Pt. 3 [subtitle] "Rational or Liberal Medicine" (June 1936): 513-7; 45 (July 1937): 58-61.

1230. Wiener, Rosalind. "How a Woman Member of the City Council Sees Her Job." *American City* 69 (April 1954): 119.

Miss Wiener was elected to the Los Angeles City Council in 1953 at the age of 22. Autobiographical in part.

1231. "William A. Bowen." *Los Angeles Bar Association Bulletin* 12 (October 21, 1937): 53.

Obituary.

1232. "William Mulholland—Maker of Los Angeles—Pioneer in Southern California's Ceaseless Quest for Water—His Energy and Vision Have Made Possible the Colorado River Aqueduct." *Western Construction News and Highways Builder* 8 (August 1933): 330.

1233. Williams, Charles. *Story of Aimee McPherson, Was She Kidnapped?* 2nd ed. Los Angeles, c1926. 36 pp.

1234. Wilson, Carol G. "A Business Pioneer in Southern California [William R. Staats]." *Historical Society of Southern California Quarterly* 26 (1944): 139-61; 27 (1945): 23-31, 93-103.

1235. ———— *California Yankee: William R. Staats, Pioneer Builder.* Claremont, 1946. 184 pp.

1236. Wilson, Joyce R. "Yvonne Brathwaite." *Urban West* 2 (December 1968): 11+.

An account of a Negro member of the California State Assembly from Baldwin Hills.

1237. Wolsey, Serge G. *Call House Madame: The Story of the Career of Beverly Davis.* San Francisco, 1942. 442 pp.

Memoir laid in Los Angeles during the early twentieth century.

1238. Wood, Robin. *Howard Hawks.* Garden City, N. Y., 1968. 200 pp.

1239. "The Work of One Woman." *Southern California Business* 5 (November 1926): 26+.

Mrs. Harriet W. R. Strong, first regular female member of the Los Angeles Chamber of Commerce.

1240. Wright, Helen. *Explorer of the Universe: A Biography of George Ellery Hale.* New York, 1966. 480 pp.

1241. Yorty, Samuel W. *The Yorty Years; The Story of Sam Yorty's Leadership as Mayor of Los Angeles Since 1961.* [Los Angeles, 1969]. 48 pp.

A political biography prepared for the 1961 mayoralty election.

1242. Youle, W. E. *Sixty-Three Years in the Oil Fields.* Los Angeles, 1926. 59 pp.

Autobiography of Los Angeles oil man (died 1926).

1243. Young, Nellie May. *William Stewart Young, Builder of California Institutions: An Intimate Biography.* Glendale, 1967. 196 pp.

1244. "Young in Heart." *Time* 92 (September 20, 1968): 62+.

UCLA chancellor Charles Young.

1245. Zamorano Club. *In Memoriam; Tributes Paid at the Bier of Henry Raup Wagner.* [Los Angeles, 1957]. 41 pp.

1246. Zukor, Adolph. *The Public Is Never Wrong; The Autobiography of Adolph Zukor.* In collaboration with Dale Kramer. New York, 1953. 309 pp.

BIOGRAPHY—COLLECTIVE

1247. Armstrong, Alice Catt, ed. *Who's in Los Angeles County 1952-53; Two Thousand Illustrated Biographies of Leading Men and Women of Achievement in Los Angeles County.* Los Angeles, 1952. 439 pp.

Includes hundreds of motion picture and entertainment industry biographies.

1248. Beasley, Delilah L. *The Negro Trail Blazers of California.* Los Angeles, 1919. Reprint, San Francisco, 1968. 317 pp.

1249. Benedict, Pierce E., ed. *History of Beverly Hills . . . In Two Parts, Narrative and Biographical.* Beverly Hills, 1934. 235 pp.

1250. Blair, William L., ed. *Pasadena Community Book; In Two Parts, Narrative and Biographical.* Pasadena, [c1943]. 789 pp. 1947 ed., 476 pp.

Subsequent editions are cited under the name of Clarence F. Shoop.

1251. Bowen, Edith B., comp. *Annals of Early Sierra Madre.* Sierra Madre, 1950. 206 pp.

1252. Burdette, Robert J., ed. *Greater Los Angeles and Southern California, Portraits and Personal Memoranda.* Chicago, 1910. 295 pp.

1253. —— *Greater Los Angeles and Southern California, Their Portraits and Chronological Record of Their Careers.* Chicago and Los Angeles, 1906. 240 pp.

1254. Burton, George W. *Men of Achievement in the Great Southwest. A Story of Pioneer Struggles During Early Days in Los Angeles and Southern California.* [Los Angeles], 1904. 149 pp.

1255. Case, Walter H., ed. *History of Long Beach . . . In Two Parts, Narrative and Biographical.* Long Beach, 1935. 336 pp. 3rd ed., 1948. 431 pp.

1942 ed. entitled *Long Beach Blue Book;* 1948 ed., *Long Beach Community Book.*

1256. —— *History of Long Beach and Vicinity . . . In Which Is Incorporated the Early History Written by the Late Jane Elizabeth Harnett.* Chicago, 1927. 2 vols.

1257. Cline, William H. *Twelve Pioneers of Los Angeles, 1928.* Los Angeles, [1928?]. [37] pp.

Harry Chandler, Eli P. Clark, Jackson A. Graves, Henry William O'Melveny, Gen. M. H. Sherman, George I. Cochran, Michael J. Connell, Lucien J. Brunswig, Joseph F. Sartori, Frank Putnam Flint, William P. Jeffries, and Frank A. Garbutt.

1258. Cole, George L. *Medical Associates of My Early Days in Los Angeles.* Los Angeles, 1930. [134] pp.

Reprint from 1930 *Los Angeles Country Medical Association Bulletins.*

1259. Colver, Seth I., ed. *The Historical Volume and Reference Works, Covering Arcadia, Azusa, Baldwin Park, Bradbury, Charter Oak, Claremont, Covina, Duarte, El Monte, Glendora, Irwindale, La Verne, Monrovia, Pomona, San Dimas, South El Monte, West Covina.* Arlington, 1964. 962 pp.

1260. Condon, James E. *Condon's Blue Book of Wealth; A List of 8,500 People Who Possess Wealth Aggregating More Than $1,000,000,000, Compiled from the Tax Records of Los Angeles City and County and Ventury County, California, Separately Classified and Alphabetically Arranged.* Los Angeles, 1917. 197 pp. 2nd ed., 1920. 189 pp.

1261. —— *Southern California Blue Book of Money. Taxpayers Assessed on $5,000 and Upwards in Los Angeles, Pasadena, South Pasadena, Long Beach, Pomona, Monrovia, Arcadia, Santa Monica, Venice, etc., also San Diego.* Los Angeles, 1913. 137 pp.

1262. *Constructive Californias: Men of Outstanding Ability Who Have Added Greatly to the Golden State's Prestige.* Los Angeles, 1926. 214 pp.

1263. Davis, Charles F., ed. *History of Monrovia and Duarte.* Monrovia, 1938. 229 pp.

1264. —— *The Monrovia Blue Book, A Historical and Biographical Record of Monrovia and Duarte.* Monrovia, 1943. 147 pp.

Based in part upon the author's *History of Monrovia and Duarte,* published in 1938.

1265. —— *Monrovia-Duarte Community Book.* Monrovia, 1957. 384 pp.

1266. Driscoll, Roy L., ed. *Pomona Valley Community Book.* Pomona, 1950. 445 pp.

1267. Forbes, Bertie C. *Men Who Are Making the West.* New York, 1923. 343 pp.

Includes a number of Los Angeles figures.

1268. Fowler, John. [*Spreading Joy*]. [Los Angeles, 1937]. 51 pp.

Personal reminiscences of pioneer families in

California, especially in Los Angeles. Originally published as a column, "Spreading Joy," in the Los Angeles *California Eagle,* the Los Angeles *Tribune,* and other Negro newspapers.

1269. Fox, Charles D. *Mirrors of Hollywood, with Brief Biographies of Favorite Film Folk.* New York, 1925. 143 pp.

1270. Graves, Jackson. *Celts Who Have Helped Build Up Los Angeles; An Address Delivered before the Celtic Club of Los Angeles . . . April 11th, 1916, at the Sierra Madre Club, Los Angeles, California.* [Los Angeles?, 1916?]. 26 pp.

1271. Guinn, James M. *Historical and Biographical Record of Los Angeles and Vicinity, Containing a History of the City from Its Earliest Settlement as a Spanish Pueblo to the Closing Year of the 19th Century. Also Containing Biographies of Well-Known Citizens of the Past and Present.* Chicago, 1901. 940 pp.

Important for biographies at the turn of the century.

1272. ——— *Historical and Biographical Record of Southern California . . .* Chicago, 1902. 1019 pp.

1273. ——— *A History of California and an Extended History of Its Southern Coast Counties . . .* Los Angeles, 1907. 2 vols.

1274. ——— *A History of California and an Extended History of Los Angeles and Environs.* Los Angeles, 1915. 3 vols.

1275. ——— *Southern California, Its History and Its People.* Los Angeles, [c1907]. 2 vols.

Differs from 1902 edition entiled *Historical and Biographical Record of Southern California . . .*

1276. Hamilton, Lloyd P., ed. *Inglewood Community Book.* Inglewood, 1949. 443 pp.

1277. *History of Pomona Valley, California, with Biographical Sketches.* Los Angeles, 1920. 818 pp.

1278. Hopkins-Smith, pub. *Pasadena and Pasadenans in Honor of Pasadena's Fiftieth Birthday.* [Pasadena, 1924]. 56 pp.

1279. Hubbard, Carson B., ed. *History of Huntington Park . . . In Two Parts, Narrative and Biographical.* Huntington Park, 1935. 257 pp.

1280. Hunt, Rockwell D. "Some California Educators I Have Known." *Historical Society of Southern California Quarterly* 39 (September 1957): 217-26.

Author speaks from a long career in educational circles, furnishing valuable asides on a number of local leaders.

1281. Ives, Sarah N. *Altadena.* Compiled for the Altadena Historical and Beautification Society. Pasadena, c1938. 351 pp.

1282. Jones, Helen L. "Some California Hermits." *Out West* 21 (December 1904): 517-33.

Some from Los Angeles.

1283. Keffer, Frank M. *History of San Fernando Valley. In Two Parts, Narrative and Biographical.* Glendale, 1934. 329 pp.

1284. Kress, George H. *A History of the Medical Profession of Southern California.* Los Angeles, 1910. 209 pp. 2nd ed., 1910. 209 pp.

Only a few copies of the initial edition survive. The rest was destroyed in the bombing of the Los Angeles *Times.*

1285. Krythe, Maymie R., ed. *The Historical Volume and Reference Works, Covering Long Beach.* Arlington, 1965. Bound with James L. Stamps, ed., *The Historical Volume and Reference Works, Covering Artesia, Bellflower, Bell Gardens, Compton, Dairy Valley, Downey, Lynwood, Montebello, Norwalk, Paramount, South Gate.* 898 pp.

1286. Los Angeles Examiner. *Notables of the Southwest.* Los Angeles, 1912. 438 pp.

1287. Los Angeles. Municipal Art Department. *Mayors of Los Angeles.* [Los Angeles], 1965. 76 pp.

1288. Los Angeles Times. *Men of Achievement in the Great Southwest . . . A Story of Pioneer Struggles During Early Days in Los Angeles and Southern California . . . 1904.* [Los Angeles], 1904. 149 pp.

1289. Loyer, Fernand, and Beaudreau, Charles, assisted by Beaudreau, Catherine, eds. *Le Guide Francais de Los Angeles et du Sud de la Californie.* Los Angeles, [c1932]. 221 pp.

1290. McGroarty, John S. *California of the South: A History.* Chicago, 1933. 4 vols.

Vol. I is a history of Los Angeles and vicinity; vols. II-IV consist of biographical sketches.

1291. —— *History of Los Angeles County; With Selected Biography of Actors and Witnesses in the Period of the County's Greatest Growth and Achievement.* Chicago, 1923. 3 vols.

Vol. I, historical; vols. II-III, are biographical.

1292. —— *Los Angeles from the Mountains to the Sea.* Chicago and New York, 1921. 3 vols.

Vol. I is historical; vols. II and III are biographical.

1293. Monroe, George L., ed. *Burbank Community Book. In Two Parts, Narrative and Biographical.* Burbank, 1944. 216 pp.

1294. Moody, Charles A., ed. "Makers of Los Angeles." *Out West* 30 (April 1909): [311]-420.

1295. Northrup, William M., ed. *Alhambra (San Gabriel-Monterey Park) Community Book . . . In Two Parts, Narrative and Biographical.* Alhambra, 1944. 249 pp. 2nd ed., 1949. 179 pp.

1296. ——, and Thompson, Newton W., eds. *History and Alhambra . . . In Two Parts, Narrative and Biographical.* Alhambra, 1936. 219 pp.

1297. Overholt, Alma (Staheli). *The Catalina Story.* Comp. and ed. under the auspices of the Catalina Island Museum Society. Avalon, 1962. 96 pp.

1298. Palmer, Edwin O. *History of Hollywood.* Hollywood, 1937. 2 vols. Rev. and extended edition, 1938. 294 pp.

1299. Parcher, Carroll W., ed. *Glendale Community Book.* Glendale, 1957. 1039 pp.

1300. Perlman, William J., and Ussher, Bruno D. *Who's Who in Music and Dance in Southern California.* Los Angeles, 1933. 299 pp.

1301. Pioneers of Los Angeles County, Los Angeles. *Historical Record and Souvenir.* Los Angeles, 1923. 283 pp.

1302. Porter, Florence C., and Trask, Helen B., eds. *Maine Men and Women in Southern California.* Los Angeles, 1913. 144 pp.

1303. Press Reference Library (Southwest ed.) . . . *Being the Portraits and Biographies of Progressive Men of the Southwest . . .* Los Angeles, 1912. 500 pp.

1304. Robinson, William W., ed. *Zamorano Choice, Selections from the Zamorano Club's Hoja Volante 1934-1966.* Los Angeles, 1966. 128 pp.

Contains a number of biographical and historical sketches pertinent for the Los Angeles area.

1305. Rodman, Willoughby. *History of the Bench and Bar of Southern California.* Los Angeles, 1909. 267 pp.

1306. Rosenberg, Roy. *History of Inglewood . . . Narrative and Biographical.* Inglewood, 1938. 215 pp.

1307. Saunders, Richard D., ed. *Music and Dance in California and the West.* Hollywood, 1948. 311 pp.

Biographical sketches included.

1308. Sherer, John C. *History of Glendale and Vicinity.* Glendale, 1922. 476 pp.

1309. Shippey, Lee. *Folks Ushud Know, Interspersed with Songs of Courage.* Sierra Madre, 1930. 96 pp.

1310. —— *Personal Glimpses of Famous Folks and Other Selections from the Lee Side of L.A.* Sierra Madre, 1929. 96 pp.

1311. Shoop, C[larence] F., ed. *Pasadena Community Book.* Pasadena, 1951. 584 pp.

1312. ——; Blair, William L.; and Arnold, Ralph, eds. *Pasadena Community Book: Ralph Arnold Edition.* Pasadena, 1955. 472 pp.

1313. Spalding, William A., comp. *History and Reminiscences. Los Angeles City and County, California.* Los Angeles, [1931]. 3 vols. Vols. 2-3 have title: *History of Los Angeles City and County . . . Biographical.*

1314. Stamps, James L., ed. *The Historical Volume and Reference Works, Covering Artesia, Bellflower, Bell Gardens, Compton, Dairy Valley, Downey, Lynwood, Montebello, Norwalk, Paramount, South Gate.* Arlington, 1965. 898 pp. Bound with Krythe, Maymie R., ed., *The Historical Volume and Reference Works, Covering Long Beach.*

1315. Studer, Robert P., ed. *The Historical Volume and Reference Works, Including Alhambra, Monterey Park, Rosemead, San Gabriel, South San Gabriel, Temple City.* Los Angeles, 1962. 836 pp.

1316. Swain, John G. (Jack), ed. *The Historical Volume and Reference Works, Covering Bassett, City of Industry, La Habra, La Mirada, La Puente, Pico Rivera, Santa Fe Springs, Walnut, Whittier.* Whittier, 1963. 1052 pp.

1317. Warren, Charles S., ed. *History of Santa Monica Bay Region. In Two Parts, Narrative and Biographical.* Santa Monica, 1934. [308] pp.

1318. ———— *Santa Monica Blue Book.* Santa Monica, 1941. 365 pp.

1319. ———— *Santa Monica Community Book.* Santa Monica, 1944. 210 pp. 2nd ed., 1948. 231 pp.

1320. Weber, Francis J. *Catholic Footprints in California.* Newhall, 1970. 235 pp.

Contains, among some 125 sketches, thirteen biographical accounts of important twentieth-century Los Angeles area Catholic laity and religious personages.

1321. ———— *Readings in California Catholic History.* Los Angeles, 1967. 265 pp.

Contains a number of twentieth-century historical sketches on Los Angeles area Catholic institutions and personalities.

1322. ———— *Sacerdotal Necrology for the Archdiocese of Los Angeles* [*1846-1966*]. Los Angeles, 1966. [52] pp.

1323. White, Carl F. *Santa Monica Community Book.* Los Angeles, 1953. [?] pp.

1324. Wiley, John L. *History of Monrovia.* Pasadena, 1927. 291 pp.

1325. Wood, John W. *Pasadena, California: Historical and Personal . . .* [Pasadena], 1917. 565 pp.

1326. Zierold, Norman J. *The Child Stars.* New York, [1965]. 250 pp.

BUSINESS, COMMERCE, AND INDUSTRY

1327. Allen, George H. "A Study of Planning Factors Affecting Manufacturing Development in the Mature Satellite City; Glendale, California." Master's thesis, University of Southern California, 1963. 202 pp.

1328. Allen, Hubert. "Compton Prepares to Show Its Wares." *Southern California Business* 6 (February 1927): 26+.

1329. Allen, Hugh. "Rubber—A Very Good Customer: What This Industry Buys Here in Materials and Goods for Its 'City' of 26,000 Customers." *Southern California Business* 13 (June 1934): 12-3.

1330. Allen, Paul F. "Tourists in Southern California — 1875-1903." Master's thesis, Claremont Graduate School, 1940. 149 pp.

1331. The Ambassador. *The Guest at the Ambassador.* [N.p., n.d.]. [13] pp.

1332. Anderson, A. O. "Screw Machine Parts and How They Are Produced in a Los Angeles Plant." *Western Machinery and Steel World* 29 (July 1938): 224-6.

1333. Arnoll, A. G. "Our City's Sub-Normal Industries." *Southern California Business* 1 (February 1922): 17.

Los Angeles.

1334. "The Assembly Line in a California Industrial Trailer Plant." *Western Machinery and Steel World* 31 (October 1940): 374-5.

Fruehauf Trailer Co., Los Angeles.

1335. Austin, John C. "1933 Construction—Afoot and Earmarked." *Southern California Business* 12 (April 1933): 10-1.

Mostly Los Angeles projects.

1336. ———— "Pioneering the World's Second Tire Center." *Southern California Business* 8 (February 1929): 9-10+.

Los Angeles second to Akron in tire manufacture.

1337. "Automobile Club Moves in New Home." *Southern California Business* 2 (April 1923): 29+.

Adams and Figueroa, Los Angeles.

1338. "Automobile Club of Southern California Celebrates." *Los Angeles Realtor* 5 (December 1925): 35.

25th Anniversary.

1339. "Automobile Club's Fine Record." *Los Angeles Saturday Night* 11 (July 4, 1931): 3.

Efforts of Automobile Club of Southern California to equalize expenditures on state highways north and south.

1340. "Azusa Displays Industrial Trend." *Southern California Business* 4 (October 1925): 11-2.

1341. "Back to Elegance." *Newsweek* 75 (June 29, 1970): 74.

Renovation of Alexandria Hotel, Los Angeles, built in 1906.

1342. Baker, Arthur. "When a Market Becomes a Magnet: During the Lean Years, Los Angeles Has Been Made a Buying Center That Commands." *Southern California Business* 15 (October 1936): 10-1.

1343. Baker, Fred L. "Forming New Iron and Steel Center." *Southern California Business* 1 (September 1922): 30+.

Fabrication of iron and steel products in Los Angeles area.

1344. "Ball Bearing Reclamation in California Factory." *Western Machinery and Steel World* 32 (May 1941): 246-7.

Precision Bearing Inc., Los Angeles.

1345. Barber, John E. "Twelve Months of Prosperity." *Southern California Business* 4 (December 1925): 9+.

State of business in Los Angeles and Southern California.

1346. Barker Bros., Los Angeles. *Barker Brothers, 1880-1955.* Los Angeles, [c1955]. 9 pp.

75th Anniversary.

1347. Bayles, T. W. "A Study of the Principles and Practices of Los Angeles County Retail Cooperatives." Master's thesis, University of Southern California, 1938. 101 pp.

1348. "Beautiful, Artistic Hollywood Cemetery." *Los Angeles Saturday Night* 10 (May 31, 1930): 7.

1349. Bell, Charline. "In Business 160 Years: The Bottle Water Man Took over the Old Spanish 'Aguador's' Trade and Made This the Biggest Bottle Water Town in the Land." *Southern California Business* 9 (June 1930): 24+.

1350. ———. "Rancho Furniture Goes National: Tables and Chairs and Things, on Old Los Angeles Pueblo Lines, Find Buyers Everywhere." *Southern California Business* 12 (November 1933): 16-7.

1351. Benjamin, McDonald P. "California's Fruit and Vegetable Canning Industry: An Economic Study." Doctoral dissertation, University of California, Los Angeles, 1961. 363 pp.

1352. Bennison, Faye G. "Making Glass in Southern California." *Southern California Business* 7 (April 1928): 12-3+.

Los Angeles.

1353. Bidwell, M. Wolford. "Southern California Leads in Sardine Fishing & Packing." *Southern California Business* 5 (May 1926): 9-10.

Los Angeles harbor area.

1354. Binder, R. W. "Largest Steel Frame Plant Finished Soon." *Western Construction News* 22 (June 1947): 84-6.

General Motors, Van Nuys.

1355. Blum, Jack E. "An Analysis of Educational Aid Plans in Southern California Industry." Master's thesis, University of Southern California, 1960. 138 pp.

1356. Boesmiller, Al. C. "Furnishing Office Buildings Throughout the World." *Southern California Business* 7 (March 1928): 14-5+.

Los Angeles manufacture of office furniture.

1357. Bomar, Thomas F. "Building a Western Textile Center." *Southern California Business* 4 (February 1925): 9+.

Los Angeles.

1358. Bond, James D. "An Analysis of Sales Forecasting Techniques of Manufacturers with Special Reference to Los Angeles Area Firms." Master's thesis, University of Southern California, 1957. 157 pp.

1359. Bone, James F. "Who? What? Where? in

Furniture: Putting the Yardstick on the Western Market to Guide the Los Angeles Manufacturer." *Southern California Business* 14 (July 1935): 24.

1360. "Born on an Old Battlefield: From the Deadly Rate War of the 1890's Grew the Insurance Exchange, Now 40 Years Old." *Southern California Business* 14 (May 1935): 18.

Los Angeles Insurance Exchange.

1361. Boyd, C. T. "Building Charts Tell Graphic Story." *Southern California Business* 3 (February 1924): 19+.

More than $200 million worth of Los Angeles construction in 1923.

1362. Breeden, Marshall. "Los Angeles Factories Make Radio Cabinets." *Southern California Business* 8 (May 1929): 20+.

1363. ——— "Making Stringed Instruments in Los Angeles." *Southern California Business* 8 (July 1929): 39+.

1364. Brent, W. L. "What Have We Industrially?" *Los Angeles Realtor* 5 (February 1926): 13+.

Los Angeles industrial statistics.

1365. "Bringing the Railway and Its Freight Customer Together: Los Angeles Union Terminal Company Is Now Building Fireproof Warehouses in Which the City's Chief Wholesale Business Will Be Centered." *Electric Railway Journal* 50 (July 7, 1917): 6-7.

1366. Brininstool, F. M. "Making Paint in Los Angeles." *Southern California Business* 4 (January 1926): 12-3.

1367. Brisbin, Bryce J. "An Analysis of the Problems Involved in the Selection and Training of Salesmen in the Electronics Industry in Southern California." Master's thesis, University of Southern California, 1960. 130 pp.

1368. "Broadway-Hollywood's Expanding Innovations." *Los Angeles Saturday Night* 11 (April 25, 1931): 7.

Department store said to occupy "the most strategic location in Hollywood."

1369. "Broadway's Thirty-Seventh Anniversary, 1896-1933." *Los Angeles Saturday Night* 13 (March 18, 1933): 10.

History and activities of department store founded by Arthur Letts.

1370. Broomfield, Joan F. "The Fishery Industry of Southern California." Master's thesis, University of California, Los Angeles, 1949. 86 pp.

1371. Brothen, Gerald C. "The Development of the Lumbering Industry in Southern California." Master's thesis, San Fernando Valley State College, 1967. 95 pp.

1372. Brown, Markley C. "An Analysis of the Economic Factors That Establish Optimum Locations for Major Hollywood Office Buildings." Master's thesis, University of California, Los Angeles, 1961. 101 pp.

1373. Brown, Robert A. "The Use of Standard Time Data with Emphasis on the Los Angeles County Area." Master's thesis, University of Southern California, 1952. 160 pp.

Time study in industry.

1374. Brubaker, Sterling L. "The Impact of Federal Government Activities on California's Economic Growth, 1930-1954." Doctoral dissertation, University of California, Berkeley, 1959. 356 pp.

1375. Buckley, Geo[rge] B. "70 Millions for 1937 Buildings: And That's a Conservative Forecast—Our 1936 Prediction Was Exceeded by 12 Millions." *Southern California Business* 16 (January 1937): 8-9.

1376. "Building a New Furniture Center." *Southern California Business* 6 (October 1927): 9-10+.

Los Angeles.

1377. Bulen, Mary H. " 'The Carolina Pines.' " *Los Angeles Saturday Night* 15 (March 30, 1935): 4.

Hollywood restaurant.

1378. "Bullock's-Wilshire Ultra Modern Store." *Los Angeles Saturday Night* 9 (September 21, 1929): 7.

1379. Burden, Jean. "Nostalgia Is His Business." *Westways* 53 (March 1961): 12-3.

Colombo's Lilac Farm at Acton, said to be possibly the world's largest.

1380. Burford, S. W. "Uniform Conditions to Follow Rock Products Merger." *Southern California Business* 8 (April 1929): 9-11+.

Formation of Consolidated Rock Products Co.

1381. Burtnett, Gerald R. "Sold with a Wiggle in the Tail." *Southern California Business* 12 (September 1933): 20.

Leigh G. Garnsky, Los Angeles County live trout retailer.

1382. Byron Jackson Co. . . . *Annual Statement: 1951.* [N.p., 1952?]. 15 pp.

Contains a brief history of the firm.

1383. Cable, Donovan C. "An Investigation of C P F F Government Contracts in Smaller Firms of the Los Angeles Area." Master's thesis, University of Southern California, 1957. 115 pp.

C P F F—Cost-Plus-Fixed Fee.

1384. California Shipbuilding Corp. *Calship, an Industrial Achievement.* [Los Angeles, 1946]. 197 pp.

1385. "California Acquires Its First Steel Tube Mill." *Petroleum World* 41 (February 1944): 30-3.

Pacific Tube Co., Los Angeles.

1386. "California Research Corporation Opens New Laboratory at La Habra." *Petroleum World* 46 (February 1949): 22-3.

1387. "Captain [Paul] Chandler New Head of Los Angeles Marine Exchange." *Southern California Business* 6 (July 1927): 18+.

1388. "Carburizing Equipment in Southern California Plant." *Western Machinery and Steel World* 30 (April 1939): 112-3.

Emsco Derrick & Equipment Co., Los Angeles.

1389. Chandler, Norman. "There Is Always a Convention in Town." *Southern California Business* 9 (January 1930): 18-9.

1390. Chaney, Finis J. "Analysis of Antitrust Submarket Policy and Its Ability to Maintain Competition as Evidenced by Investigation of the Los Angeles and Kansas City Retail Food Markets." Doctoral dissertation, University of Southern California, 1970. 266 pp.

1391. "Charms of New Hotel Flintridge." *Los Angeles Saturday Night* 8 (December 3, 1927): 13.

Opening of luxury hotel in "residential park" backed by ex-Senator Frank P. Flint.

1392. "Chevrolet Assembly Plant, Van Nuys, California." *The Architect and Engineer* 182 (September 1950): 22-3.

1393. Cho, Tai Jun. "Development of Fisheries and the Distribution of Fishery Products for the Los Angeles Region." Master's thesis, University of California, Los Angeles, 1969. 113 pp.

1394. "City Develops Downtown Travel Center: West Sixth Street Becomes Starting Point for Everywhere." *Los Angeles Saturday Night* 16 (January 11, 1936): 7+.

Concentration of travel agencies on West Sixth Street.

1395. "A City's Business Told in Billions: Industrial Leaders Themselves Do Not Stop to Consider the Tremendous Volume of Transactions in Los Angeles." *Southern California Business* 2 (June 1923): 9.

"The total business transacted in Los Angeles during the first five months of 1923 amounted to $3,400,625,000."

1396. Claus, Cynthia. "Hollywood Knickerbocker." *Apartment Journal* 17 (January 1935): 8-9.

Hotel business.

1397. ———— "The Rampart." *Apartment Journal* 18 (November 1935): 8-9+.

Los Angeles apartment house, built 1910.

1398. ———— "Sunset Tower." *Apartment Journal* 19 (November 1936): 10-1.

1399. ———— "The Town House." *Apartment Journal* 18 (May 1936): 10-1+.

1400. Clayton, James L. "Defense Spending: Key to California's Growth." *Western Political Quarterly* 15 (1962): 280-93.

1401. Cleland, Robert G. and Hardy, Osgood. *The March of Industry.* Los Angeles, 1929. 322 pp.

History of California industry and agriculture from earliest period to 1920s.

Business, Commerce, and Industry 1402-1422

1402. Clover, Madge. "Majestic, Modern Vista del Arroyo." *Los Angeles Saturday Night* 11 (December 20, 1930): 7.
Pasadena Hotel overlooking Arroyo Seco.

1403. "A Coast Plant Supplying World-Wide Market for Hard-Facing Metals." *Western Machinery and Steel World* 32 (December 1941): 600-3.
Stoody Company, Whittier.

1404. "Coffee and . . . Its Place in Los Angeles Import Market." *Southern California Business* 5 (June 1926): 18-9.

1405. Collier, Robert W. "An Analysis of the Large-Scale Single-Family Residential Builder in Los Angeles, Orange and Ventura Counties." Doctoral dissertation, University of Southern California, 1967. 213 pp.

1406. Collins, James H. "Back to Quality—The Los Angeles Idea: Downtown Merchants Adopt Certain Prices Below Which They Will Not Advertise." *Southern California Business* 11 (December 1932): 8-9.

1407. ——— "But People Still Wanted Radios: With the Right Set, at the Right Price, Los Angeles Manfacturers Did Well in 1930." *Southern California Business* 10 (April 1931): 12-3.

1408. ——— "Let's Take Stock of Motors: Progressive Policies Have Made This the World's Second Largest Automotive Center." *Southern California Business* 15 (June 1936): 8-9.
Los Angeles.

1409. ——— "Los Angeles Grows by a Formula: In 12 Years, It Has Advanced Our County from 27th Place to 6th Place in Manufacturing." *Southern California Business* 12 (September 1933): 18-9.

1410. ——— "On the Map as a Garment Town." *Southern California Business* 10 (March 1931): 12-3.
Los Angeles.

1411. ——— "Rubber Is a Good Citizen." *Southern California Business* 16 (September 1937): 8-13.
Los Angeles rubber manufacture.

1412. ——— "This Company Welcomes Change: As Car Makers Come to the Coast, U.S. Spring & Bumper Add Facilities for Supplying Them."

Southern California Business 15 (June 1936): 10-1.
Los Angeles manufacturer.

1413. ——— "Working with the Noble Gases: A Los Angeles Laboratory Adds Something That Neon Lacked—Candlepower for Lighting." *Southern California Business* 12 (March 1933): 8-9.
Krypton gas.

1414. ——— "The World Looks Here for Good Ideas: For Los Angeles Does Things in New Ways—How the Chamber [of Commerce] Can Help Develop Your Idea." *Southern California Business* 12 (October 1933): 10-1.

1415. "Columbia Becomes Part of U. S. Steel Corporation." *Southern California Business* 8 (December 1929): 16-7+.
Columbia Steel, Torrance.

1416. "Composting Gets a Tryout . . . In An Experimental Plant Operating in San Fernando, Calif." *American City* 80 (April 1965): 99-102.
Salvage and Conversion Systems Inc., San Fernando.

1417. "Conventions Bring Millions to Dealers." *Southern California Business* 6 (July 1927): 16+.
Los Angeles.

1418. "Converting Brewery into Cotton Mill." *Southern California Business* 1 (May 1922): 11.
Imperial Cotton Mills, Los Angeles.

1419. Coons, Arthur Gardner. *Defense Industry and Southern California's Economy.* Pacific Southwest Academy of Political and Social Science, *Publication No. 20.* Los Angeles, 1941. 12 pp.

1420. Covington, Floyd G. "How to Enter the Negro Market: It Numbers 40,000 Customers in Los Angeles, Who Have Their Likes and Dislikes." *Southern California Business* 12 (February 1933): 14.

1421. Cramer, Tom M. "Wilmington Refinery." *Pioneer* 4 (October 1962): 14-5.
U. S. Borax & Chemical Co. plant.

1422. Crandall, Shannon. "Great Goodrich Plant in Operation." *Southern California Business* 7 (May 1928): 9-11+.
Rubber plant, Los Angeles.

1423. —— "Industrial Los Angeles County." *Southern California Business* 8 (June 1929): 9-11+.

1424. —— "Putting the Willys-Overland Plant in Operation." *Southern California Business* 8 (March 1929): 9-11+.

Auto assembly plant, Los Angeles.

1425. —— "$200,000,000 Output of Metal Working Industries." *Southern California Business* 7 (July 1928): 14+.

Los Angeles and vicinity.

1426. Croker, Richard S. *Historical Account of the Los Angeles Mackerel Fishery.* Division of Fish & Game, *Fish Bulletin No. 52.* Terminal Island, 1938. 62 pp.

1427. Cummings, Ridgely. "Why Los Angeles Is a 'Lousy Cab Town.'" *Los Angeles* 14 (November 1969): 49.

Taxicab service in Los Angeles area.

1428. Cunningham, Glenn. "Automobile and Aircraft Industries," in *California and the Southwest.* Ed. by Clifford M. Zierer. New York, 1956. Pp. 287-97.

1429. Cutler, Allan. "World Eats Los Angeles Canned Goods." *Southern California Business* 1 (September 1922): 48+.

1430. Dable, Daniel K. "An Analysis of the Linseed Oil Industry with Special Emphasis on the Los Angeles County Area." Master's thesis, University of Southern California, 1946. 104 pp.

1431. Daniel, Mann, Johnson & Mendenhall. *A Presentation of the Work of Daniel, Mann, Johnson & Mendenhall.* [Los Angeles, 196?]. Unp.

1432. Daum, W. H. "Los Angeles Industrially and the Industrial Real Estate Situation in Los Angeles Today." *Los Angeles Realtor* 4 (February 1925): 10-1.

1433. Davis, J. Allen. *The Friend to All Motorists: The Story of the Automobile Club of Southern California Through 65 Years, 1900-1963.* [Los Angeles, 1967]. 272 pp.

1434. Davis, J. M. "We Sell Die Castings in 26 States." *Southern California Business* 12 (November 1938): 8-9.

Union Die Casting Co., Los Angeles.

1435. Day, J. Dabney. "Bring Cotton Mills Close to Crop: Textile Establishments of New England Are Moving Close to Raw Material—Los Angeles Offers Advantages to Manufacturers." *Southern California Business* 2 (October 1923): 11+.

1436. —— "Los Angeles as a Great Consuming Market." *Southern California Business* 6 (April 1927): 28+.

1437. De Dapper, Jay W. "The Marketing Characteristics of the Southern California Chemical Industry." Master's thesis, University of Southern California, 1955. 130 pp.

1438. "De Forest Moving 'Lab' Here." *Southern California Business* 9 (September 1930): 29.

Lee De Forest, inventor of vacuum tube, moves business to Los Angeles.

1439. DeMond, C[hester] W. *Price, Waterhouse & Co. in America. A History of a Public Accounting Firm.* New York, 1951. 356 pp.

Much on activities of this famous firm in California and the West.

1440. "Die Casting—Business Barometer." *Southern California Business* 15 (February 1936): 18.

Los Angeles.

1441. Dienes, Kalman I. *Problems of Transition in Pomona Valley.* Claremont, c1949. 88 pp.

Economic conditions in Pomona.

1442. "Dizzy Figures in Mail Trading: Careful Survey Shows That the Orders Coming to Los Angeles Houses from Distance Reach Astounding Number." *Southern California Business* 2 (May 1923): 9+.

1443. Dockson, R. R. *Growth Patterns, the Dynamic Los Angeles Area.* Los Angeles, 1958. 32 pp.

1444. "'Doing the Whole Job!' from Engineering to Assembly." *Western Machinery and Steel World* 32 (July 1941): 342-3.

National Machine Products Co., Los Angeles.

1445. Dollar, Robert. "In Reach of Half the World's

People." *Southern California Business* 5 (December 1926): 9-11.

Dollar Steamship Co. to make Los Angeles its West Coast terminus.

1446. Donovan, Richard. "Pushing a Tray to the Promised Land." *Reporter* 5 (January 9, 1951): 34-6.

Clifton's Cafeteria, Los Angeles.

1447. Douglas, A. W. "A Cool Million on Our Doorstep." *Southern California Business* 16 (October 1937): 21.

Los Angeles tire retreading industry.

1448. Doyle, Katherine. "A Factory Here Since 1860." *Southern California Business* 10 (July 1931): 14-5.

Los Angeles Soap Co.

1449. —— "Here's Another 'Do You Know?'" *Southern California Business* 10 (December 1931): 18.

Los Angeles leads country in venetian blind manufacture.

1450. —— "Safety Lights for Wide Open Spaces: Living in Automobile Country, We Have Been Clever at Inventing Special Auto Lamps." *Southern California Business* 11 (March 1932): 18.

Los Angeles manufacturers.

1451. —— "Still Here—the Stage Coach Era: But Today We Design, Build and Ride in Our California-Type Motor Coaches." *Southern California Business* 11 (January 1932): 8-9.

Pickwick Motor Coach Works, Inglewood.

1452. Dunkle, John R. "The Tourist Industry of Southern California: A Study in Economic and Cultural Georgraphy." Master's thesis, University of California, Los Angeles, 1950. 148 pp.

1453. Eastman, George L. "Industrial Development in Southern California." *Southern California Business* 7 (July 1928): 9-11+.

1454. Eberle, George J. "The Business District," in *Los Angeles: Preface to a Master Plan.* Ed. by George W. Robbins and L. Deming Tilton. Los Angeles, 1941. Pp. 127-44.

1455. Ebersole, Morris R. "Fair Winds in the Yacht Industry." *Southern California Business* 8 (June 1929): 14+.

1456. "Echoes from the Story on the Los Angeles Statler." *Hotel Monthly* 61 (March 1953): 58+.

1457. Ehrenreich, Joseph W. "Some Implications of the Projected Transit Plan upon the Movement of Retail Trade in the Los Angeles Metropolitan Area." Master's thesis, University of Southern California, 1948. 100 pp.

1458. "Electric Roads to Serve Large Market: Newly Formed Company Announces Immediate Start on Construction of Union Market Terminal in Heart of Los Angeles." *Electric Railway Journal* 47 (April 22, 1916): 782-3.

1459. Elliott, Clifford A. "Los Angeles Wholesale Terminal: Rival of Bush Terminal Erected in Los Angeles at Cost of $10,000,000—Served Exclusively by Pacific Electric Railway Company." *Electric Railway Journal* 59 (January 14, 1922): 78-9.

1460. Erickson, Kathryn. "Furniture Fashions: Los Angeles, a Leader in Furniture Field, Offers New Ideas at Forthcoming Style Show." *Apartment Journal* 21 (June 1939): 14-5+.

1461. "Fabrication of Steel Structures." *Southern California Business* 2 (November 1923): 24.

Los Angeles structural steel industry.

1462. "Fabrication Plant of Consolidated Steel Corporation." *Western Machinery and Steel World* 32 (January 1941): 6-7.

Maywood.

1463. Fairhead, George E. "Eucalyptus, the Hardwood of the Present." *Out West* 31 (December 1909): 952-65.

Los Angeles manufacture of furniture and buildings made of eucalyptus.

1464. "Fashion Warfare: Los Angeles Boosts Fund to Sell City as Style Capital of the World." *Business Week* (March 25, 1944): 48.

Associated Apparel Manufacturers of Los Angeles.

1465. Ferguson, Homer L. "Speaking of Los Angeles' Opportunity." *Southern California Business* 6 (March 1927): 12-3+.

Enumerates industrial advantages of Los Angeles.

1466. Ferguson, James R. "Gas Fired Heat Treating Equipment in a Los Angeles Plant." *Western Machinery and Steel World* 29 (March 1938): 73.
Abegg & Reinhold Co., Ltd., Los Angeles.

1467. Fessier, Mike, Jr. "Westside's Ingenious Innkeepers." *Los Angeles* 11 (January 1966): 59+.
The "Great Beverly Hills Hotel War."

1468. Findley, James C. "The Economic Boom of the 'Twenties in Los Angeles." Doctoral dissertation, Claremont Graduate School, 1958. 456 pp.

1469. Finney, Guy W. "A 'Growing Pain' in Bullock's Progress." *California Graphic* 5 (April 14, 1928): 7+.
Los Angeles *Times* and advertising for Bullock's.

1470. "Firestone Comes West." *Southern California Business* 6 (September 1927): 9-11.
Firestone Tire & Rubber plant, Los Angeles.

1471. Fitzgerald, Gerald. "Concrete Carries Heavy Traffic at [Los Angeles] Wholesale Terminal." *Pacific Municipalities* 37 (February 1923): 55-6.
General description of terminal and its facilities.

1472. "$5,000 to Be Clean." *Out West,* new series, 1 (May 1911): 369-76.
California Macaroni Company, Los Angeles.

1473. "Flintridge Biltmore All-Year Resort." *Los Angeles Saturady Night* 9 (December 22, 1928): 7.

1474. Forbes, B. C. "Building the New Southwest Empire." *Southern California Business* 4 (August 1925): 7-8.
Los Angeles manufacturing.

1475. Ford, Corey. "The Stars Are Dave's Dish." *Collier's* 124 (July 16, 1949): 27+.
Dave Chasen, Hollywood restaurant operator.

1476. "Ford Company to Expand L.A. Plant." *Southern California Business* 1 (January 1923): 23+.

1477. "Ford Plant One of Many New Los Angeles Industries." *Business Week* (April 16, 1930): 13.

1478. "Four New Skyscrapers Projected for Los Angeles in Fortnight: Construction of Downtown Office Buildings Is Given Impetus." *Los Angeles Realtor* 4 (March 1925): 21.
Los Angeles Investment Co., Tenth and Broadway; Medico-Dental Building, Eighth and Francisco; Builders Exchange Building, Seventh and Los Angeles; Lutheran Hospital, Fifteenth and Hope.

1479. "4th New Plant in 3 Years Doubles Output of Aircraft Tools." *Western Machinery and Steel World* 32 (July 1941): 338-9.
Aircraft Tools Inc., Los Angeles.

1480. Frazee, J. K. "Pressed Steel Is 'Big Stuff.'" *Southern California Business* 10 (October 1931): 18-9.
New department of Ford Motor Co., Long Beach.

1481. ——— "These Horns Lead the Parade: Why and How Los Angeles Makes the Highest-Price Band Instruments in the World." *Southern California Business* 11 (August 1932): 18.

1482. "Fred Harvey Hollywood Restaurant Enlarges to Meet Increasing Local Demand." *Hotel Monthly* 59 (February 1951): 41-2.

1483. Fredericks, John D. "The Orient Our Natural Trade Field: When Los Angeles Becomes Widely Known in the Far East as an Important Industrial Center Commercial Relations Will Increase." *Southern California Business* 1 (December 1922): 11-2.

1484. ——— "Welcome to Our Exposition Visitors." *Southern California Business* 1 (September 1922): 21.

1485. ——— "Welding Together the New Empire: The Residents of Los Angeles, the San Joaquin Valley, the Imperial, Arizona, Utah and Nevada Are One People in Aims." *Southern California Business* 1 (June 1922): 17+.

1486. "Freight Handling System for a Warehouse." *Engineering Record* 66 (December 28, 1912): 714-5.
Unique telpherage system at M. A. Newmark & Co.

1487. French, William F. "A Study of Location Factors for Industrial Plants in and about Los

Angeles, California." Master's thesis, University of Southern California, 1926. 160 pp.

1488. Friedly, Philip H. "An Economic Base and Income Multiplier Study of Redondo Beach, California." Master's thesis, University of Southern California, 1964. 119 pp.

Describes economic conditions.

1489. Friedman, Donald A. "The Distributed Lag as Reflected by Construction in the City of Los Angeles, 1955-1967." Doctoral dissertation, University of California, Los Angeles, 1969. 157 pp.

1490. Fritzler, Geoffrey G. "Directorships and Communications Between Directors and Officers in Selected Small and Medium-Sized Corporations in Southern California." Master's thesis, University of Southern California, 1964. 121 pp.

1491. "From a One-Man Shop to a Precision Organization." *Western Machinery and Steel World* 32 (July 1941): 340-1.

Airco Tool Co., Santa Monica.

1492. "The Furniture Mart's Own Book." *Southern California Business* 14 (March 1935): 24.

Catalog for furniture dealers, Los Angeles.

1493. Fuston, Virginia E. "A Study of Sources of Fashion Information Utilized by Buyers of Better Dresses in Los Angeles." Master's thesis, University of Southern California, 1951. 117 pp.

1494. Garland, William M. "Mixing Games and Business Profitability." *Southern California Business* 3 (December 1924): 15+.

Suggestions on ways Los Angeles businessmen can capitalize on Olympic Games.

1495. "Gas Equipment in Southern California Auto Plant." *Western Machinery and Steel World* 28 (March 1937): 88-9.

Southern California Division of General Motors, Los Angeles.

1496. Gassaway, Gordon. "Making an Automobile Club Count." *Sunset* 35 (November 1915): 990-8.

Auto Club of Southern California, Los Angeles.

1497. German American Trust and Savings Bank, Los Angeles. *Twenty Five Years of Growth; A Quarter Century of Achievement.* Los Angeles, 1915. [20] pp.

1498. Gill, Corringon. "Five Congested Production Areas Designated on West Coast." *Western City* 20 (February 1944): 25-6.

Includes Los Angeles.

1499. Glasscock, G. A. " 'Thar She Blows' as Southern California Launches Whaling Industry." *Southern California Business* 6 (April 1927): 14-5+.

1500. Glenn, Fletcher M. "A Study of Factors Entering into the Demand for Neon Signs in the Los Angeles Area." Master's thesis, University of Southern California, 1954. 108 pp.

1501. "Golden Anniversary of J. W. Robinson Company." *Los Angeles Saturday Night* 13 (March 4, 1933): 7.

1502. Golding, Cedric J. "A Comparative Analysis of Executive Salaries in Manufacturing Industries in the Los Angeles Metropolitan Area." Master's thesis, University of Southern California, 1960. 200 pp.

1503. Goodman, Charles S. *The Location of Fashion Industries: With Special Reference to the California Apparel Market. Michigan Business Studies* X, No. 2 (Ann Arbor, 1948). 105 pp.

1504. Goodnow, Marc N. "The House That Jack Now Builds." *Southern California Business* 6 (February 1927): 12-3+.

Growth of Los Angeles building materials and household equipment manufacture.

1505. "Goodyear-Zeppelin Plant May Locate in Los Angeles." *Southern California Business* 7 (February 1928): 12-3+.

1506. "Great Los Angeles Building Boom." *Western Construction* 37 (April 1962): 30-3.

1507. "Greater Los Angeles Biltmore's Features." *Los Angeles Saturday Night* 9 (October 20, 1928): 7.

Grand Avenue addition to hotel.

1508. Halpert, Saul. "The Mammoth Chain Store Monopoly in Los Angeles." *Frontier* 11 (November 1959): 5-9.

Describes the "trend towards growing concentration of ownership and control of retail food outlets" in Los Angeles.

1509. Hamilton, Andrew. "Golden Electronics Complex." *Westways* 54 (October 1962): 12-4.

Industiral history of Thompson Ramo Wooldridge, Inc.

1510. ———. "Henry Would Be Amazed!" *Westways* 54 (August 1962): 4-6.

Industrial history of Aeronutronic [Ford Motor Co.].

1511. ———. "Insurance for Survival." *Westways* 53 (December 1961): 10-1.

RAND Corp.

1512. Hamilton, Lloyd P. "Coming to the Front in Furniture." *Southern California Business* 3 (January 1925): 15+.

Los Angeles furniture manufacture.

1513. Hamilton, Robert R. "An Analysis of Executive Development Programs in the Los Angeles Area." Master's thesis, University of Southern California, 1957. 217 pp.

1514. Hampton, Edgar L. "How the 'Back Country' Comes In." *Southern California Business* 3 (December 1924): 7-8.

Extent and significance of Los Angeles' "Back Country" in business.

1515. ———. "The Whole World for a Market." *Southern California Business* 3 (November 1924): 7-8+.

Los Angeles manufacturing and marketing.

1516. Hampton, Wade W. "Metal Congress Comes to Los Angeles." *Southern California Business* 7 (January 1929): 12-3+.

1517. Hancock, Ralph. *The Forest Lawn Story.* Los Angeles, [1955]. 160 pp.

1518. Hanna, Phil T. *The Wheel and the Bell; The Story of the First Fifty Years of the Automobile Club of Southern California.* Los Angeles, 1950. 18 pp.

1519. Hardesty, Wayne L. "Management Consulting for Small Businesses: Selected Cases in the Southern California Area." Master's thesis, University of Southern California, 1963. 270 pp.

1520. Harman, F. L. S. "The Central Manufacturing District." *Southern California Business* 1 (September 1922): 76+.

Los Angeles.

1521. ———. "The Filling of New Los Angeles Office Buildings." *Southern California Business* 4 (October 1925): 10+.

1522. ———. "A Topping Business—General Insurance." *Southern California Business* 12 (November 1933): 10-1.

Los Angeles.

1523. "Heavy Gain in Building Marks First Five Months of 1925 in Los Angeles." *Los Angeles Realtor* 4 (June 1925): 11+.

1524. Heerema, Martin P. "A Study of the Retailing of Used Automobiles in the City of Los Angeles." Master's thesis, University of Southern California, 1952. 114 pp.

1525. Heilman, Howard H. "Synthetic Rubber Program in Southern California." *Petroleum World* 44 (March 1947): 51-5.

1526. Hill, James H. "Enough Clay for the World's Dishes: Few Persons Realize the Importance of Los Angeles as a Western Pottery Center—List of Products Is Growing at Amazing Rate." *Southern California Business* 1 (September 1922): 142+.

1527. ———. "Exchanging Products with Hawaii: Result of Chamber of Commerce Excursion to Mid-Pacific Isles Has Been an Increase in Trade Relations with Los Angeles Firms." *Southern California Business* 1 (December 1922): 7-8.

1528. Hilliard, Merle. "An Emperical Study of Delegation as Practiced by Presidents of Small and Medium-Sized Firms in Southern California." Doctoral dissertation, University of Southern California, 1970. 225 pp.

1529. Hillinger, Charles. "The Gold That Was Plucked." *Westways* 41 (August 1949): 16-7.

Ostrich farming in Los Angeles.

1530. Hine, C. C. "Again, We Can Bid for National Markets." *Southern California Business* 12 (November 1933): 8-9.

Los Angeles County manufacturers.

1531. ———— "Bargains That Lead to Beggary: Public Opinion Must Deal with the Below-Cost Selling That Steadily Undermines the Community." *Southern California Business* 11 (July 1932): 8-9.

1532. ———— "Now It's Batteries." *Southern California Business* 8 (October 1929): 9-11.

Willard Battery Co.

1533. ———— "Yes, Chicken-Feed—But Worth $10,-000,000." *Southern California Business* 12 (May 1933): 12-3.

Los Angeles County manufacture of livestock feeds.

1534. Hirsh, Milton A. "Garment Manufacturing in Southern California Is High in Quality as Well as in Volume." *Southern California Business* 5 (August 1926): 26+.

Los Angeles.

1535. ———— "The Los Angeles Industrial and Trade Exposition." *Southern California Business* 5 (June 1926): 16-7+.

1536. Hoadley, Carlyle. "'Murder' Was His Market Problem." *Southern California Business* 12 (September 1933): 16.

Murray Director Company, Los Angeles exterminator firm (pest control).

1537. Hoagland, Leslie S. "Making a Cemetery a Civic Asset Instead of a Civic Liability." *American City* 35 (July 1926): 66-8.

Forest Lawn Memorial Park, Glendale.

1538. "Hollywood Institution." *Time* 44 (July 3, 1944): 74+.

Restaurant La Rue.

1539. "Hollywood Knickerbocker Apartment Hotel." *Los Angeles Saturday Night* 9 (July 13, 1929): 7.

1540. "Home Port's Fine Steamship Service." *Saturday Night* 4 (September 1, 1923): 25.

Los Angeles Steamship Company.

1541. Horning, David C. "Management Engineering in the Los Angeles Area." Master's thesis, University of Southern California, 1950. 158 pp.

1542. Hornstein, Samuel. "Supplying Fish for Every Nation." *Southern California Business* 8 (May 1929): 14+.

Los Angeles sardine industry.

1543. "Hotel Figueroa, Financed and Operated Wholly by Women." *Saturday Night* 6 (August 21, 1926): 1.

1544. "Hotel Mayfair's Bid for Popularity." *Saturday Night* 7 (January 29, 1927): 18.

Formal opening of thirteen-story hotel at West Seventh and Hartford.

1545. *Hotel Virginia, Long Beach.* Los Angeles, 1910. 16 pp.

1546. "How the Municipal Market of Long Beach Was Established." *Pacific Municipalities* 33 (February 1919): 63-6.

1547. "'How to Attract Industrial Development' Is No Problem for This Unique Community." *Western City* 42 (August 1966): 44-5.

City of Industry.

1548. Hubbell, K. T. "A New Million Dollar Industry." *Southern California Business* 7 (April 1928): 18-9+.

Los Angeles fur apparel industry.

1549. Hunter, Sherley. "Touching Los Angeles Industrialism." *Southern California Business* 2 (November 1923): 12+.

"A city may have a large number of large plants in a particular classification of industry—and still not be a great industrial city."

1550. Hutchings, Edward, Jr. "Little—But Far Out." *Westways* 54 (November 1962): 7-9.

Industrial history of Electro-Optical Systems, Inc.

1551. Hyatt, Bob. "Midget Monsters of Outer Space." *Westways* 55 (January 1955): 14-6.

Industrial history of International Rectifier Corp.

1552. "Hydraulic Presses for Southern California Plants." *Western Machinery and Steel World* 31 (March 1940): 110.

North American Aviation, Inc., Inglewood, and U.S. Spring & Bumper Co., Los Angeles.

1553. "In Alhambra . . . Diversified Heavy Metal Fabricating." *Western Machinery and Steel World* 32 (August 1941): 422-5.

C.F. Braun & Co.

1554. "In Stride with Heat-Treating Developments." *Western Machinery and Steel World* 32 (July 1941): 351-5.

Abegg & Reinhold Co., Ltd., Los Angeles.

1555. " 'Industrial Hollywood' to Vie with Movie Colony." *Saturday Night* 7 (July 16, 1927): 1.

Hollywood business and industry.

1556. "Industrialist's Dream Realized in West's First Steel Tube Mill." *Apartment Journal* 26 (May 1944): 10-1+.

Pacific Tube Co., Los Angeles.

1557. "Industries Close to Billion Point: Survey Shows That Los Angeles Plants Earned More Last Year Than Did All the Railroads in the United States." *Southern California Business* 2 (July 1923): 11.

1558. "International Mart and Its Scope." *Saturday Night* 7 (June 11, 1927): 11.

Central retailing facility, Washington and Hill streets.

1559. " 'It Can Be Done in California': Coast Plant Makes Records in Automatic Screw Machine Products with Modern Equipment." *Western Machinery and Steel World* 28 (December 1937): 448-9.

Pacific Screw Products Corp., Los Angeles.

1560. "It's the Los Angeles Idea! We Lead in Making the 'Tin Ear.' " *Southern California Business* 13 (February 1934): 14.

Universal Microphone Co.

1561. Ivey, Herbert D. "Have We the Soil for Big Business?" *Southern California Business* 9 (December 1930): 12-3.

Outlook for business expansion.

1562. Izzard, Alex E., Jr. "The Factors Influencing the Agglomeration of the Electronics Industry in San Fernando Valley." Master's thesis, University of California, Los Angeles, 1961. 130 pp.

1563. "J. F. Sartori Explains How Los Angeles Is Country's Bright Spot Industrially." *Los Angeles Saturday Night* 2 (August 13, 1921): section 2, page 5.

1564. Jacobs, Paul. "The Most Cheerful Graveyard in the World." *Reporter* 19 (September 18, 1958): 26-30.

Forest Lawn, Glendale.

1565. Johnston, Lyle F. "Analysis of Training Techniques for Industrial Relations Personnel in Southern California Industry." Master's thesis, University of Southern California, 1958. 157 pp.

1566. Jones, James L. "An Investigation of the Agent Selection and Sales Training Activities of the Golden State Mutual Life Insurance Company." Master's thesis, University of Southern California, 1956. 136 pp.

1567. Jones, William C. "Corporate Evolution of the Southern California Edison Company and Its Financial History from 1909 to 1928." Master's thesis, University of Southern California, 1929. 134 pp.

1568. Kamei, Toshio. "An Inquiry into the Industrial Relations Program of the Restaurant Industry in Los Angeles." Master's thesis, University of Southern California, 1952. 142 pp.

1569. Kaschenbach, Edwin J. "A Study of Retailing in Los Angeles in Order to Determine the Advisability of Establishing a Research Bureau." Master's thesis, University of Southern California, 1924. 87 pp.

1570. Kasun, Jacqueline R. *Some Social Aspects of Business Cycles in the Los Angeles Area, 1920-1950.* Los Angeles, 1954. 155 pp.

1571. Kauffmann, E. H. "Parcel Post in Foreign Trade: Los Angeles Should Be Made an Exchange Station for the Distribution of Packages to the Orient." *Southern California Business* 1 (March 1922): 14+.

1572. Keller, Paul F. "Corporate Financial Support of Community Activities; Programs of Selected Southern California Companies." Master's thesis, University of Southern California, 1963. 77 pp.

Charitable contributions.

1573. Kelso, A. P. "Large Stress Relieving Oven in a Southern California Plant." *Western Machinery and Steel World* 29 (May 1938): 143+.
C. F. Braun & Co., Alhambra.

1574. Kern, Frank L. "Hawaii, Los Angeles and Company." *Southern California Business* 3 (September 1924): 15+.
Trade between Los Angeles and Hawaiian Islands.

1575. ———— "Los Angeles as Hawaii's Shopping Center." *Southern California Business* 5 (June 1926): 20-2+.

1576. Kidner, Frank Le Roy, and Neff, Philip. *Los Angeles, the Economic Outlook.* Los Angeles, 1945. 151 pp.
Under the same title, a condensation was prepared by Molly Levin. Los Angeles, 1946. 24 pp.

1577. Kinney, Arthur W. "Home Industry and Home Prosperity." *Out West* 43 (April 1916): 173-4.
Los Angeles.

1578. Kling, S. J. "58 Varieties of California-Made Wood Products from Imported Raw Lumber." *Southern California Business* 5 (July 1926): 24-5.
Furniture business.

1579. ———— "In the Midst of Furniture Making." *Southern California Business* 4 (September 1925): 17+.

1580. Klotz, Esther H. "Pomona's Palomares Hotel." *Pomona Valley Historian* 6 (1970): 32-9.

1581. Kratzer, Henry W. "An Appraisal of the Better Business Bureau Operations in the Los Angeles Area, 1930-1939." Master's thesis, University of Southern California, 1940. 82 pp.

1582. Krec, Ted. "Sweet Old Days in Los Alamitos." *Westways* 48 (June 1956): 20-1.
Los Alamitos Sugar Co., one-time sugar-beet processing plant.

1583. Kreider, S. L. "Japan and Southern California as Trade Allies." *Southern California Business* 5 (October 1926): 16-7+.

1584. Lacy, William. "Iron and Steel." *Southern California Business* 5 (July 1926): 16-7+.
Los Angeles steel industry.

1585. ———— "Southern California Makes Steel: An Industrial Re-discovery." *Southern California Business* 5 (February 1926): 12-3+.
Los Angeles steel industry.

1586. Land, Ruth E. "Use of Advertising Media by Certain Men's Clothing Retailers in San Francisco and Los Angeles." Master's thesis, University of California, Berkeley, 1940. 134 pp.

1587. Larson, J. David. "Australia Has Turned the Corner and Los Angeles Is Her Nearest Large American Market—But We Must Sell Australians on That!" *Southern California Business* 13 (March 1934): 8-9.

1588. ———— "Hawaii Also Has Business Romance: The Crossroads of the Pacific, American in Its Tastes, Gives Los Angeles an Ever Growing Market." *Southern California Business* 12 (March 1933): 19.

1589. Lassiter, Edward B. "An Analysis of Garment Manufacturing in the Los Angeles Area [1786-1953]." Master's thesis, University of Southern California, 1953. 128 pp.

1590. "Leading in Auto Registration and Sales." *Southern California Business* 6 (March 1927): 16-7.
Los Angeles.

1591. Leeming, Arthur T. "Los Angeles as a Wholesale Center." Master's thesis, University of California, Berkeley, 1938. 124 pp.

1592. LeFevre, Dorothy J. "Geographic Aspects of the Private Swimming Pool Industry in Los Angeles." Master's thesis, University of California, Los Angeles, 1961. 105 pp.

1593. Lehman, Anthony L. "From Finance to Pharmacy." *Pomona Valley Historian* 3 (1967): 108-11.
Claremont.

1594. Leichter, Jack. "Where Art and Enthusiasm Create a Great Hotel." *Los Angeles Saturday Night* 43 (April 18, 1936): 15.
The Town House, Los Angeles.

1595. "Lever Brothers Plant in Los Angeles." *Western Construction* 25 (September 1950): 82-4.

1596. Levoy, Sydonia M. "The Federal Textile Fiber Products Identification Act as a Factor in the Selection of Blouses and Shirts by Santa Monica City College Students." Master's thesis, University of California, Los Angeles, 1961. 73 pp.

1597. "Life Visits Clifton's Cafeteria." *Life* 17 (November 27, 1944): 102-5.

1598. Lindberg, E. R. "Handling a $13,000,000 Fish Catch." *Southern California Business* 7 (October 1928): 16-7+.
Los Angeles fishing industry.

1599. Lindvall, F. C. "Pacific Railway Equipment Company's High-Speed Rail Coaches Now Building at Consolidated Steel's Los Angeles Plant." *Western Machinery and Steel World* 31 (July 1940): 278-9.

1600. Lingle, D. M. "Industrial Hollywood." *Los Angeles Realtor* 8 (November 1928): 27+.

1601. Linton, Robert. "An Automotive Center in the Making: We Will Come into Production as Our Industrial Facilities Are Linked to Assembly Plants." *Southern California Business* 11 (March 1932): 6-7.

1602. —— "How the Clay Industry Has Grown." *Southern California Business* 7 (May 1928): 14-5+.
Los Angeles.

1603. —— " 'Ivory' Was Named Out of the Bible." *Southern California Business* 9 (February 1930): 28-9+.
Procter & Gamble Factory, Long Beach.

1604. Lippincott, J. B. "Engineering Contributions to the Development of California Described by Distinguished Speaker at Los Angeles Meeting." *The Architect and Engineer* 122 (July 1935): 47-51; (August 1935): 41-8.

1605. Los Angeles. Chamber of Commerce. *Facts About Industrial Los Angeles.* Los Angeles, 1921. Unp.

1606. —— *Los Angeles Today.* Los Angeles, 1920. 32 pp.
Industrial attributes described.

1607. —— *Report on the Electronics Industry, Los Angeles Metropolitan Area.* Los Angeles, [c1955]. 47 pp.

1608. Los Angeles Examiner. *A Working Sales Control of the Southern California Market Area.* [Los Angeles], 1947. 151 pp.

1609. Los Angeles Times. *The Country of Los Angeles, America's 3rd Market.* Los Angeles, 1948. 4 vols. in 2. Unp.

1610. "Los Angeles Acclaims Nation's Greatest Machinery Building." *Western Machinery and Steel World* 32 (April 1941): 170-1.
Moore Machinery Co.

1611. "Los Angeles Becomes Style Center Built Around Sportswear." *Business Week* (September 14, 1940): 42.

1612. "Los Angeles Company Starts Production of Radio Sets." *Southern California Business* 1 (July 1922): 14.
Blue Bird Talking Machines.

1613. "Los Angeles County Has Third of State's Wealth." *Southern California Business* 3 (July 1924): 12.

1614. "Los Angeles Dedicates Its Most Modern, Advanced Plant for Die-Casting Service." *Western Machinery and Steel World* 31 (November 1940): 404-9.
Harvill Aircraft Die Casting Corp., Los Angeles.

1615. "L.A. Factories Beat Whole States." *Southern California Business* 2 (January 1924): 26.
Claims that Los Angeles industrial plants turned out more goods in 1923 than did the entire state of Connecticut, or Maine, New Hampshire, and Vermont combined.

1616. "Los Angeles Farmer's Market." *Sunset* 122 (February 1959): 46.

1617. "Los Angeles Fireproofing Industry." *Southern California Business* 6 (June 1927): 32.

1618. "Los Angeles Furniture Goes to Hawaii." *Southern California Business* 8 (March 1929): 36.

1619. "Los Angeles Has Even Break in Trade

Op[p]ortunities." *Southern California Business* 1 (July 1922): 8+.

1620. "Los Angeles Leads in Motor Vehicle Sales." *Southern California Business* 1 (August 1922): 26.

1621. "Los Angeles' Little Cutters." *Fortune* 31 (May 1945): 134-9+.

Los Angeles Garment Industry.

1622. "Los Angeles-Made Pumps Draw Water for Our Thirsty Troops over World." *Apartment Journal* 26 (June 1944): 9+.

Peerless Pump Co.

1623. "Los Angeles' New Industrial Record." *Southern California Business* 6 (November 1927): 22+.

Value of output.

1624. "L.A. Proves Profitable Site for Tire Plant." *Southern California Business* 1 (June 1922): 42.

Goodyear Tire & Rubber Corp.

1625. "L.A. Spends More Than Most States." *Southern California Business* 2 (October 1923): 33.

Declares that the more than $8,600,000,000 to be spent in Los Angeles in 1923 would buy all the minerals produced in U.S. mines in 1922.

1626. "The Los Angeles Spirit." *Time* 45 (January 1, 1945): 58-9.

Barker Brothers Corp.

1627. "Los Angeles the New Tire Center." *Southern California Business* 6 (May 1927): 9-10+.

1628. "Los Angeles to Become Wool Center." *Southern California Business* 1 (December 1922): 19.

1629. "Los Angeles to Have New Truck Plant." *Southern California Business* 2 (June 1923): 28.

Kleiber Motor Truck Co. of San Francisco building Los Angeles plant.

1630. Los Angeles Warehouse for Allegheny Ludlum." *Western Machinery and Steel World* 32 (August 1941): 426-7.

1631. Louis, Henry W. "How New Industry Helps Old." *Southern California Business* 6 (August 1927): 10-1.

New Los Angeles industries.

1632. ——— "Los Angeles Garments Set Styles." *Southern California Business* 1 (September 1922): 78+.

1633. "A Lowly Worm." "A Book Found the World Around." *Southern California Business* 12 (June 1953): 16.

Los Angeles Manufacturers' Directory.

1634. Lynch, Samuel D. "Racing Car Capital of the World." *Westways* 41 (June 1949): 16-7.

Los Angeles area, home of such leading race-car engine and chassis builders as Meyer & Drake Engineering, Kurtis-Kraft, Inc., Lou Moore, Bud Winfield, and Art Sparks, as well as many owners and drivers of Indianapolis cars.

1635. Mack, Don. "Sturdy Life Rafts Made Here Protect Our Seamen." *Apartment Journal* 26 (July 1944): 8-9+.

Weber Showcase & Fixture Co., Los Angeles.

1636. "Making Better Venetian Blinds." *Southern California Business* 15 (April 1936): 18.

National Venetian Blind Co., Los Angeles.

1637. Manker, F. H., and Alexander, Dan. "At the Foot of Mt. San Antonio." *Trails Magazine* 4 (Spring 1937): 6-15.

History of San Antonio Canyon, mining and resorts. Latter half on the twentieth century.

1638. "The Manufacture of Air Conditioning Equipment in Southern California." *Western Machinery and Steel World* 30 (March 1939): 76-9.

Utility Fan Corp., Los Angeles.

1639. "Manufacturing of Mailing Machines: Equipment and Methods in a Pacific Coast Factory." *Western Machinery and Steel World* 31 (February 1940): 62-7.

National Postal Meter Co., Los Angeles.

1640. Maples, Robert L. "The Southern California Kelp Industry; A Study in the Utilization of a Natural Resource." Master's thesis, San Fernando Valley State College, 1966. 89 pp.

1641. Mappelback, John. "And What Do You Think Sells Paint?" *Southern California Business* 14 (July 1935): 12-3.

Los Angeles paint manufacture.

1642. ——— "A Big Industry That Few of Us Know." *Southern California Business* 14 (November 1935): 16.

Oil equipment manufacturers.

1643. ——— "A Big New Market at the Door: Auto Assembly Plants Buy Many Things Outside—It's a Tempting Market, But Not Any Too Easy." *Southern California Business* 15 (February 1936): 12-3.

Los Angeles manufactures.

1644. ——— "The Days of Old, the Days of—Zinc!" *Southern California Business* 12 (October 1933): 16-7.

Argues need for an electrolytic refinery for zinc extraction in Los Angeles.

1645. ——— "If It's Rubber—What Do You Lack? Our Miscellaneous Rubber Goods Factories Make Everything from Battery Boxes to Baby's Pants." *Southern California Business* 13 (September 1934): 12-3.

1646. ——— "In Pumps, We Are Old, Big, Clever." *Southern California Business* 14 (October 1935): 12-3.

Los Angeles pump manufacture.

1647. ——— "Leading the Parade in Tires: Better Than 1 in 10 Now Made in Los Angeles County— And We're Growing Faster." *Southern California Business* 15 (June 1936): 12-3.

1648. ——— "Let the Customers Get at the Goods." *Southern California Business* 13 (December 1934): 12-3.

Los Angeles store fixture industry.

1649. ——— "Our Factories Have Diversity: Hundreds of Smaller Plants, Making Many Products, Are the Sign of Industrial Health." *Southern California Business* 16 (May 1937): 14-5.

Los Angeles County.

1650. ——— "Porcelain—Hard and True." *Southern California Business* 10 (April 1931): 16.

Los Angeles manufacture.

1651. ——— "Press the Starter and Get—Payrolls." *Southern California Business* 12 (December 1933): 18-9.

Battery manufacture.

1652. ——— "S-P-E-E-D Is His Main Product: Right Here in Los Angeles, Harry Miller Has Built Cars That Made Racing History." *Southern California Business* 11 (October 1932): 18-9.

1653. ——— "Too Delicate for Foreign Trade: Neon Signs Won't Stand Ocean Shipment—But Parts Have Grown into Good Export Business." *Southern California Business* 10 (August 1931): 18-9.

Los Angeles manufacture.

1654. ——— "We Lead in Warehousing: Splendid Facilities, at Low Rates, Make Los Angeles County the West's Pivotal Center." *Southern California Business* 11 (July 1932): 24.

1655. ——— "A White Spot in Fire Insurance: Once a Dark Spot, Los Angeles Started a Big Clean-up, and Got Better Rates." *Southern California Business* 11 (April 1932): 14.

1656. "The March of the Cities: Another Successful Municipal Market" *World's Work* 27 (November 1913): 114.

Municipally operated food markets in Los Angeles.

1657. Marion, Guy E. "How Shall We Cut Your Pie? Many Are the Ways of Dividing Los Angeles City and County for Business Purposes." *Southern California Business* 13 (February 1934): 18-9.

1658. Marriner, John E. *History of Shipbuilding in the Harbors of San Pedro Bay.* Long Beach, 1959. 41 pp.

1659. Marshall, Frank F., and MacBride, Dexter. "Outer Highways: A Study in Successful Planning for Major Retail Business Development." *California Highways and Public Works* 27 (May-June 1948): 1-7.

Crenshaw Shopping Center.

1660. Mathison, Richard R. "The Club Story. A Motorist's History of the Automobile and the Automobile Club in Southern California." *Westways* 59-60 (June 1967-December 1968): various pagination (18 parts with different titles for each segment).

1661. ——— *Three Cars in Every Garage; A Motorist's History of the Automobile and the Auto-*

mobile Club in Southern California. Garden City, N. Y., 1968. 257 pp.

1662. "May Company's Ultra-Modern Food Market." *Los Angeles Saturday Night* 11 (September 5, 1931): 12.

Eighth and Broadway.

1663. Mayor, George W. "The Growth of Air Freight and Its Effect on the Marketing Strategy of Shippers with Special Reference to Manufacturers of Industrial Goods in the Long Beach, California, Area." Master's thesis, University of Southern California, 1961. 128 pp.

1664. McGaffey, Ernest. "Automobile Club Celebrates Silver Anniversary." *Southern California Business* 4 (January 1926): 10.

1665. ———— "Good Samaritans of the Highway." *Southern California Business* 3 (August 1924): 17.

Emergency roadside service of Automobile Club of Southern California.

1666. McGarry, D. F. "B. F. Goodrich Rubber Company Comes to Los Angeles." *Southern California Business* 6 (June 1927): 9-11.

1667. McGuire, Joseph W. *Comparative Prices of Selected Consumer Items: Honolulu, San Francisco, Los Angeles*. Honolulu, 1963. 41 pp.

1668. McNaughton, J. A. "Los Angeles Stockyards Show Aids Development of the West." *California Journal of Development* 20 (October 1930): 19+.

1669. ———— "Union Stock Yards Will Prove Boon." *Southern California Business* 1 (September 1922): 108+.

1670. Merrill, F. H. "The Growth of the Chemical Industry in Southern California." *Southern California Business* 5 (July 1926): 30+.

Mostly Los Angeles.

1671. Merrill, James M. "A History of the Los Angeles Steamship Company [1920-1937]." Master's thesis, Clarement Graduate School, 1948. 104 pp.

1672. Messinger, Robert E. "Evaluation of the Uses of Corporate Aircraft by Certain Southern California Manufacturers." Master's thesis, University of Southern California, 1961. 228 pp.

1673. "Metal Cutting Tools and Industrial Supplies for Southern California Shops." *Western Machinery and Steel World* 32 (December 1941): 643-6.

Almquist Bros. & Viets, Los Angeles.

1674. Michael, A. F. "Steel and Cast Iron, the Base for Porcelain Ware: A Big Furnace in Southern California for Processing a Wide Variety of Articles." *Western Machinery and Steel World* 30 (December 1939): 378-9.

U. S. Porcelain Enameling Corp., Los Angeles.

1675. "Mike's Place." *Time* 56 (November 6, 1950): 96+.

Romanoff's Restaurant, Hollywood.

1676. "Milestone! A New Plant for Die Casting Firm in Los Angeles." *Western Machinery and Steel World* 31 (July 1940): 266-7.

Harvill Aircraft Die Casting Corp.

1677. Miller, H. A. "The Milk a Metropolis Consumes." *Southern California Business* 4 (August 1925): 22+.

Covers production, bottling, and marketing in Los Angeles.

1678. ———— "Stock Men Now Have a Real Market." *Southern California Business* 1 (November 1922): 21+.

Los Angeles Union Stockyards.

1679. ———— "Where Meat Packing Is a Big Item." *Southern California Business* 4 (November 1925): 9+.

Los Angeles.

1680. Miller, W. Everett. "When Automobiles Were F.O.B. Los Angeles." *Westways* 42 (December 1950): 20-1.

Various makes of cars manufactured in Los Angeles.

1681. Minea, William K. "A Comparative Study of Industrial Engineering Practices in Some Los Angeles Industries." Master's thesis, University of Southern California, 1956. 120 pp.

1682. "Mr. Schine Goes West." *Time* 48 (December 23, 1946): 83-4.

Fight for control of Los Angeles Ambassador Hotel.

1683. Mitchell, Lee. "A Survey of the Wholesale Drapery and Upholstering Fabric Trade in the Los Angeles Area." Master's thesis, University of Southern California, 1948. 69 pp.

1684. Mittelbach, Frank G., and Gillies, James. *Management in the Light Construction Industry— A Study of Contractors in Southern California.* Los Angeles, 1962. 109 pp.

1685. "A Modern Plant for Manufacturing Pumps in Southern California." *Western Machinery and Steel World* 30 (February 1939): 48-51.
   Kimball-Krogh Pump Division of Victor Equipment Co., Los Angeles.

1686. Monnette, Orra C. "Industrial Southern California." *Southern California Business* 5 (July 1926): 9-11+.
   Los Angeles area.

1687. Moore, Charles I. D. *The Pacific Mutual Life Insurance Company of California; A History of the Company and the Development of Its Organization, the Sixtieth Anniversary 1868-1928.* [Los Angeles, 1928]. 304 pp.

1688. Moreland, G. Elmer. "Oil Industry Speeds Equipment Production." *Southern California Business* 8 (December 1929): 9-11+.
   Los Angeles area manufacturers.

1689. Moreland, Watt L. "The Auto Manufacturing and Assembling Industry in Los Angeles." *Southern California Business* 5 (November 1926): 9-11+.

1690. Morgen, Lewis. "A Study of the Independent Ladies Ready-to-Wear Retailer in Southern California." Master's thesis, University of Southern California. 1962. 103 pp.

1691. Mortimer, Frank C. "Why Southern California Should Be a Greater Wool Center." *Southern California Business* 5 (July 1926): 28.
   Describes Los Angeles' advantageous position for development of extensive wool manufacture.

1692. "Motorists Served by Fine Organization." *Los Angeles Saturday Night* 11 (November 15, 1930): 11.
   Thirtieth anniversary of Auto Club of Southern California.

1693. "Mullen & Bluett Clothing Company." *Out West* 32 (April 1910): [382-3].

1694. Neff, Philip; Baum, Lisette C. and Heilman, Grace E. *Favored Industries in Los Angeles.* Los Angeles, 1948. 25 pp.

1695. ———, and Weifenbach, Annette. *Business Cycles in Los Angeles.* The Haynes Foundation, Pamphlet Series No. 15. Los Angeles, 1949. 25 pp.

1696. ——— and ———. *Business Cycles in Selected Industrial Areas.* Los Angeles, 1949. 274 pp.

1697. Nelson, Howard J., and Foster, Gerald. *Ventura Boulevard: A String Type Shopping Street* Los Angeles, 1958. 63 pp.

1698. "New Ambassador Hotel, One of Finest in World, to Open on Wilshire Blvd., January 1." *Los Angeles Saturday Night* 1 (December 25, 1920): 2.

1699. "The New Hollywood Hotel and Apartments." *Western Housing* 42 (July 1958): 12.

1700. "New Industries Produce Millions." *Southern California Business* 3 (February 1924): 32.
   Value of Los Angeles silk, wood, cotton, and steel output in 1924 predicted at $130,000,000.

1701. "New Industries Show Their Wares." *Southern California Business* 8 (May 1929): 22.
   Los Angeles area.

1702. "The New Maltby Home." *Western Machinery and Steel World* 31 (December 1940): 474-6.
   Edward D. Maltby [Bearing] Co., Los Angeles.

1703. "New Produce Terminal Formally Opened." *Los Angeles Realtor* 7 (December 1927): 37.
   Los Angeles.

1704. Newmark, Marco R. "It Has Everything But Customers: A Complete Retail Grocery Store Built as a Model by a Los Angeles Wholesaler." *Southern California Business* 11 (December 1932): 16-7.

1705. "Ninth and Broadway Wholesale Center Building." *Los Angeles Saturday Night* 10 (October 5, 1929): 7.

New nine-story wholesale building on property once owned by Harrison Gray Otis.

1706. Nunis, Doyce B., Jr. *Past Is Prologue. A Centennial Profile of Pacific Mutual Life Insurance Company.* Los Angeles, 1968. 78 pp.

1707. O'Brien, P. P. "Handling Mail a Business Enterprise." *Southern California Business* 3 (October 1924): 11+.
Los Angeles postal service.

1708. ———— "Uncle Sam's Los Angeles Industry." *Southern California Business* 6 (October 1927): 16+.
Los Angeles postal service.

1709. "Of Major Interest in Retail World: Bullock's, Incorporated, Acquires [Arthur] Letts' Estate Interest, Insuring Retention of Present Management." *Los Angeles Saturday Night* 7 (October 1, 1927): 9.

1710. "An Old Company Moves into a New Home." *Los Angeles Realtor* 7 (June 1928): 25.
New $4 million Spring Street headquarters of Title Insurance and Trust Company.

1711. "Oldest Pottery — Newest Kiln." *Southern California Business* 14 (January 1935): 18.
Pacific Clay Products, Los Angeles.

1712. "Only Large City to Show Building Gain." *Southern California Business* 7 (March 1928): 22.
Los Angeles.

1713. Oppenheim, Ramsey. *Los Angeles, Land of Destiny, a Narrative of a Market.* [Los Angeles], 1941. 32 pp.

1714. Orr, G. V. "Motor Cars—We Really Build Them." *Southern California Business* 10 (June 1931): 20-1.
Los Angeles.

1715. Osborn, William E. "An Analysis of the Organization for Distribution of Frozen Foods in Southern California." Master's thesis, University of Southern California, 1956. 69 pp.

1716. Otis, Harrison Gray. "Los Angeles — A Sketch." *Sunset* 24 (January 1910): 12-6.
Economic conditions.

1717. "The Outlook Ahead Was Never Brighter." *Southern California Business* 2 (December 1923): 28.
Asserts that business in Los Angeles for 1923 will top that for 1922 by approximately $2 billion.

1718. "Pack It Cleverly and with Beauty — In Glass." *Southern California Business* 12 (November 1933): 18-9.
Los Angeles area glass industry.

1719. Packard, John. "The Role of the Tourist Hotel in California Development to 1900." Master's thesis, University of Southern California, 1953. 152 pp.

1720. Palmer, W. Morgan. "Our Four Hundred Million Friends: Orientals Refer to 'Old Gold Mountains' of California; Opening New Channels of Trade to Los Angeles." *Southern California Business* 1 (February 1922): 14+.

1721. Panunzio, Constantine. *Self-Help Coorperatives in Los Angeles.* University of California, Los Angeles, *Publications in Social Science,* Vol. 8. Los Angeles, 1939. 148 pp.

1722. Peerman, Dean. "The Marble Orchard." *Frontier* 15 (November 1963): 11-3.
Forest Lawn, Glendale.

1723. Pegrum, Dudley F. *Urban Transport and the Location of Industry in Metropolitan Los Angeles.* Los Angeles, 1963. 46 pp.

1724. "Perino's of Los Angeles." *Esquire* 73 (May 1970): 36.
Restaurant.

1725. Perkins, Arthur B. "Mining Camps of the Soledad." *Historical Society of Southern California Quarterly* 40 (1958): 149-73; 285-303; 373-92.
Copper, gold, borax, oil—all of these brought people into the area near the northwesterly boundary of Los Angeles County. The third part contains information about the twentieth-century business ventures.

1726. Pesante, Jesslyn. "The Relationship of the Interior Decorator to the Home Furnishings Industry in Southern California." Master's thesis, University of Southern California, 1962. 150 pp.

1727. Phillips, Lee A. "Leading the West as a Steel Center." *Southern California Business* 8 (March 1929): 14-5+.

Los Angeles.

1728. Phillips, Sidney. "A Birthday for Glamour Manor: The Golden Anniversary of the Beverly Hills Hotel Recalls an Era of Glitter, Wit—and the 'Original Rat-Pack.'" *Los Angeles* 4 (November 1962): 34-7.

1729. "Picturesque Charms of the Mandarin Market." *Los Angeles Saturday Night* 10 (March 8, 1930): 17.

Open-air market in Hollywood.

1730. Pierce, George O. "A Study of the General Contracting Industry in Southern California." Master's thesis, University of Southern California, 1947. 78 pp.

1731. "Pioneer Industrial Marches On." *Apartment Journal* 26 (December 1944): 11+.

Los Angeles Soap Co., established 1860.

1732. "Placing Los Angeles on the Style Center Map." *Southern California Business* 4 (December 1925): 14.

1733. "Plant Departments and Equipment — Los Angeles Shipbuilding and Dry Dock Co." *Western Machinery and Steel World* 32 (January 1941): 2-5.

1734. Pollack, Evelyn H. "Development of Chemical and Nuclear Radiation Protection Programs in Selected Firms in the Los Angeles Area." Master's thesis, University of Southern California, 1962. 91 pp.

1735. Pollard, Genia. "Recent Development in Commerce and Industry in Southern California Using Vernon as a Type." Master's thesis, University of Southern California, 1928. 81 pp.

1736. Pollard, W. L. "Retail Stores Among World Leaders." *Southern California Business* 1 (September 1922): 146+.

Los Angeles.

1737. Pollock, Allen K. "Los Angeles." *California Magazine of the Pacific* 49 (June 1959): 12.

Convention activity in Los Angeles County.

1738. "Precision Plant in South." *Western Machinery and Steel World* 32 (February 1941): 66-7.

Vard Mechanical Laboratory, Pasadena.

1739. "The Prestige Acropolis." *Time* 87 (June 10, 1966): 62.

Century Plaza Hotel.

1740. Probert, William J. "An Approach to the Identification of Factors in Organization Effectiveness: Use of the Critical Incident Technique at Long Beach Naval Shipyard." Master's thesis, University of Southern California, 1956. 116 pp.

1741. "Producing Soap for Half the Nation." *Southern California Business* 1 (October 1922): 28.

Los Angeles Soap Co.

1742. "Products of Merit: Steelbilt, Inc." *Arts & Architecture* 68 (September 1951): [43-58].

Los Angeles manufacturer of sliding glass door and window frames.

1743. "A Progressive Steel Foundry Operates Efficiently with Modernized Equipment." *Western Machinery and Steel World* 31 (November 1940): 414-6.

Kay-Brunner Steel Products, Alhambra.

1744. "Purex Moves in New Plant." *Southern California Business* 16 (October 1937): 18.

Purex Corp., South Gate.

1745. Putnam, Frank B. "Pico's Building: Its Genealogy and Biography." *Historical Society of Southern California Quarterly* 39 (1957): 74-89.

Los Angeles.

1746. Radell, David R. "'Mom 'n' Pop' Grocery Stores in the Boyle Heights Section of Los Angeles, California: A Study of Site and Situation." Master's thesis, California State College at Los Angeles, 1961. 61 pp.

1747. Rand Corporation. *The Rand Corporation. The First Fifteen Years.* Santa Monica, 1963. 46 pp.

1748. Raphael, Marc L. "Babin's Kosher Restaurants—A Los Angeles Odyssey," *Western States Jewish Historical Quarterly* 1 (1969): 174-81.

1749. Rathbun, Morris M. "The Los Angeles

Wholesale Market." *American City* 19 (July 1918): 59.

1750. *The Raymond . . . Pasadena, California.* [San Francisco, c1904]. [16] pp.

Famous hotel.

1751. "Reaching Out over the Seven Seas: Los Angeles Products, in Rapidly Increasing Volume, Are Carried by World's Largest Vessels to All Foreign Markets." *Southern California Business* 2 (March 1923): 9-10+.

1752. Reis, Clem. "The Salesmanager Tackles His Costs: 500 Sales Executives in the Los Angeles Area Join Efforts to Meet This Serious Problem." *Southern California Business* 11 (May 1932): 10-1.

1753. Remenih, Maurine M. "The New Technology of Toyland: Using Space-age Production Methods, Airtight Security Checks, and Former Missile Engineers, Hawthorne's Mattel, Inc. Has Built the Talking Doll into a National Obsession." *Los Angeles* 6 (December 1963): 42-5.

1754. "Revolution in L. A. Retailing." *Business Week* (December 4, 1948): 86-7.

"Orbach's policy of strictly cash, no alterations, no deliveries, price-cutting, startles Los Angeles' old-line merchants. . . . "

1755. Rezvani, Mohammad. "The Problem of Management in Relocation of Industrial Plants in the City of Industry." Doctoral dissertation, University of Southern California, 1961. 208 pp.

1756. Rice, M. B. "The Trail to Rainbow's End: A Man Who Has Made a Study of the State Says San Joaquin Trade Awaits Los Angeles." *Southern California Business* 1 (February 1922): 11+.

1757. Richardson, William H. "Making $3,000,000 Worth of Musical Instruments." *Southern California Business* 7 (May 1928): 22-3+.

Yearly production, Los Angeles and vicinity.

1758. Riddiford, Henry. "Could Build a Walk Around the World: Coastwise Lumber Imports, Valued at Over $15,000,000 Give Indication of Continued Activity in All Lines of Construction." *Southern California Business* 1 (April 1922): 19+.

Los Angeles.

1759. Riley, Frank. "Los Angeles Needs a Foreign Policy." *Los Angeles* 13 (April 1968): 32-3.

Particularly a Far-Eastern policy, because trade is a significant factor in its economy. Article seems to be at least partly facetious.

1760. Robbins, George W. "Transport: The Movement of Commodities," in *Los Angeles: Preface to a Master Plan.* Ed. by George W. Robbins and L. Deming Tilton. Los Angeles, 1941. Pp. 115-25.

1761. Roberts, Myron. "Son of 'the Octopus.'" *Los Angeles* 5 (March 1963): 25-7+.

Music Corporation of America (MCA), at Universal City.

1762. Robinson, John W. "Baldy Summit Inn." *Pomona Valley Historian* 6 (1970): 64-71.

1763. Roedel, Phil M. "A Review of the Pacific Mackeral (Pneumatophorus Diego) Fishery of the Los Angeles Region with Special Reference to the Years 1939-1951." *California Fish and Game* 38 (April 1952): 252-73.

1764. Roesti, Robert M. "Economic Analysis of Factors Underlying Pricing in the Southern California Tuna Canning Industry." Doctoral dissertation, University of Southern California, 1960. 336 pp.

1765. Rolfe, Frank. "The Economic Factors in the Development of Los Angeles." Master's thesis, University of Southern California, 1924. 233 pp.

1766. "The Rose Marie Reid Story." *Western Housing* 41 (October 1957): 13.

Los Angeles manufacturer of sportswear and bathing suits.

1767. Rouleau, Art, and Rouleau, Barbara. "Flower Merchants of Wall Street." *Westways* 57 (September 1965): 28-9.

The cut-flower business in Los Angeles.

1768. Russell, Josiah. "Economic Development of the Glass Industry in Southern California." Master's thesis, University of Southern California, 1938. 74 pp.

1769. Sanford, F[loyd] E. "The Stock Exchange as a Machine." *Southern California Business* 10 (January 1931): 22.

Los Angeles Stock Exchange.

1770. Sanford J. E. "History of Los Angeles Stock Exchange." *Los Angeles Saturday Night 150th Birthday of Los Angeles: Fiesta and Pre-Olympiad.* Special Issue (1931): [10].

[Author's correct name is Floyd E. Sanford.]

1771. Sangster, R. D. "Glass Industry in the Los Angeles District." *Southern California Business* 6 (December 1927): 10+.

1772. —— "An Industrial $25,000,000 Gain." *Southern California Business* 6 (January 1928): 12-3+.

Los Angeles, 1926 to 1927.

1773. —— "Los Angeles' Industry Leads Coast." *Los Angeles Realtor* 7 (January 1927): 17+.

1774. —— "Our Own Story of Rubber: The Commanding Position of Los Angeles Shown in Rapid Growth of Tire Industry." *Southern California Business* 11 (November 1932): 12-3.

1775. —— "Pig Iron from California." *Southern California Business* 5 (October 1926): 12-3+.

Mostly Los Angeles area.

1776. —— "Reading Our Future in Copper: A Fact Story About Los Angeles' Advantages and Opportunities with the Red Metal." *Southern California Business* 12 (June 1953): 18-9.

1777. —— "Yes, We Have No Smokestacks: And Likewise No Tenements—Latest Figures About the Factories in Our Big Garden Community." *Southern California Business* 11 (August 1932): 12-3.

1778. Saunders, Leslie R. "The Industrial Development of Greater Los Angeles." *Los Angeles Realtor* 4 (September 1925): 14-5.

1779. Schleicher, A. "Diversified Industrial Progress of Los Angeles District." *Southern California Business* 7 (November 1928): 9-11+ .

1780. Schnitman, L. Seth. "The Postoffice Tells a Vivid Story." *Southern California Business* 4 (March 1925): 15+.

Los Angeles postal receipts.

1781. Schwartz, Frederick L. "The Economics of Specialty Restaurants with Particular Reference to Los Angeles." Master's thesis, University of Southern California, 1951. 240 pp.

1782. Scott, Mellier G. *Cities Are for People; The Los Angeles Region Plans for Living* . . . Pacific Southwest Academy, *Publication 21.* Los Angeles, 1942. 109 pp.

Industrial history of Los Angeles with suggestions for the future.

1783. Scott, Roderick. "Meat Packing Among the Leaders." *Southern Cailfornia Business* 6 (November 1927): 14-5+.

Fourth among Los Angeles industries.

1784. Seidenbaum, Art. "The Kingdom of the Keys." *Los Angeles* 4 (July 1962): 44-6.

Los Angeles "Key Clubs" (restaurants) including Caves Des Roys, Millionaire Club, Playboy Club.

1785. Seiter, Howard H. "His Line Is—Bad News for Bandits." *Southern California Business* 10 (September 1931): 16-7.

Los Angeles safe manufacturer.

1786. "A Self-Help Program Stirs a Negro Slum." *Business Week* (March 25, 1967): 67-8+.

"Operation Bootstrap," Watts.

1787. "Seventy Million Dollars in Silk." *Southern California Business* 2 (June 1923): 21.

Golden State Silk Mills, to be built at Hermosa Beach.

1788. Shanley, Francis P. "Over $250,000,000 Invested in Guest Rooms." *Southern California Business* 5 (February 1926): 9-11.

Facilities for Los Angeles visitors.

1789. Shaw, George. "In Avalon, Catalina Island, All the Industry and All the Problems Come from People" *Western City* 24 (July 1948): 26-8.

1790. Sherman, Edwin A. "Getting Funds on Warehouse Receipts." *Southern California Business* 2 (September 1923): 22+.

By the manager of the Southern California Field Warehouse Department of Lawrence Warehouse Company.

1791. Sherman, Mary N. "The Bazaar That Failure Built: Colorful, Crowded, Country-in-the-Cityish

Los Angeles' Own Farmers Market . . . A World-Renowned Success Story and How It All Began." *Southern California Prompter* 1 (October 1960): 23-5.

1792. Shinn, Richard D. "The Location of the Apparel Industry in Los Angeles." Master's thesis, University of Southern California, 1962. 172 pp.

1793. Shipp, Cameron. "Farmers Market." *Holiday* 6 (August 1949): 64-70.

1794. "The Shopping District of Northwest Los Angeles." *Los Angeles Realtor* 6 (November 1926): 28+.

Hollywood.

1795. "Signal and Dispatching System for Interurban Railways.'" *Electric Railway Journal* 32 (July 4, 1908): 242-3.

Simmen Automatic Railway Signal Co., Los Angeles.

1796. "Silverwood's New Wilshire Boulevard Store." *Los Angeles Saturday Night* 9 (September 14, 1929): 7.

1797. Simons, Seward C. "Dressing Up Los Angeles." *Southern California Business* 7 (February 1928): 18-20+.

Apparel industry.

1798. ———— "Milling Flour for the Southwest." *Southern California Business* 4 (April 1925): 10-1+.

Los Angeles millers.

1799. ———— "The West's Greatest Garment Center." *Southern California Business* 4 (October 1925): 17+.

Los Angeles.

1800. Simpson, Vivian. "Also Built Here—Business Motor Bodies." *Southern California Business* 13 (July 1934): 18.

1801. "Sixty Conventions Scheduled for Los Angeles." *Southern California Business* 6 (December 1927): 16-7+.

1802. Smith, Hadley E. "A Review of Plant Location Theory and a Questionnaire Study of Plant Location in Los Angeles County." Master's thesis, University of Southern California, 1954. 73 pp.

1803. Smith, Jack. "A Day in the City: Of Ships and Shops." *Westways* 60 (August 1968): 7-9+.

Ports of Call, San Pedro.

1804. ———— "A Day in the City: Samarkand on Fairfax." *Westways* 61 (March 1969): 22-4.

Farmers' Market.

1805. Southern California Research Council. *The Los Angeles Economy: Its Strengths and Weaknesses.* Los Angeles and Pomona, 1953. 39 pp.

1806. ———— *The Next Fifteen Years — The Los Angeles Metropolitan Area 1955-1970.* Los Angeles and Pomona, 1955. 60 pp.

1807. "Southern California Exporting Activities Championed by New Bureau." *Southern California Business* 6 (July 1927): 9+.

Los Angeles District Office of Bureau of Foreign and Domestic Commerce.

1808. "A Southern California Tool Company Expands into a New Plant." *Western Machinery and Steel World* 31 (July 1940): 258-9.

Modern Die & Stamping Co., Los Angeles.

1809. "Southern Pacific Cabooses Roll off Assembly Line." *Western Machinery and Steel World* 32 (March 1941): 106-7.

Los Angeles.

1810. "Southland's Home Port Steamship Line." *Saturday Night* 3 (February 17, 1923): 24.

Los Angeles Steamship Company.

1811. Sparks, Frank H. "The Location of Industry: An Analysis of Some of the Factors Which Have Affected the Location of Industry in the Ten Southern Counties of California." Doctoral dissertation, University of Southern California, 1941. 261 pp.

1812. "Spectacular Expansion of Los Angeles Industries." *Apartment Journal* 24 (July 1941): 23.

1813. "Stacking Up New Factory Records." *Southern California Business* 4 (November 1925): 26.

Los Angeles manufacturing.

1814. "Stacking Up Some New Records." *Southern California Business* 3 (September 1924): 24.

Statistics showing how "Los Angeles is rounding out biggest year in her history and 1925 promises to be even better."

1815. Staniford, Edward F. *Business Decentralization in Metropolitan Los Angeles.* [Los Angeles, 1960]. 57 pp.

1816. Stanley, Norman S. "Modern Los Angeles." *Western Housing* 41 (November 1957): 8.

Statistics on industry, commerce, and construction.

1817. —— *No Little Plans, the Story of the Los Angeles Chamber of Commerce.* [Los Angeles?, 1956?]. 32 pp.

Reprinted from *Southern California Business,* September 1956.

1818. Steinman, Alfred A. "Small Industrial Firms That Failed in the Los Angeles Area During the Postwar Period." Master's thesis, University of Southern California, 1950. 88 pp.

1819. Stevens, I. M. "New Products to Be 'Made in Los Angeles': Our Factory Growth Has Come by Making What We Purchase—and the End Has Not Been Reached." *Southern California Business* 12 (April 1933): 16-7.

1820. Stewart, Marion. "Fresh as Morning Dew Is Produce in Farmers' Market Where Shopping Becomes an Exciting Experience." *Los Angeles Saturday Night* 43 (April 25, 1936): 9.

1821. Stump, Frank V. "City's Industries Near Billion Mark." *Southern California Business* 1 (July 1922): 12-3.

Los Angeles.

1822. —— "Los Angeles Fisheries Take Lead." *Southern California Business* 4 (March 1925): 9-10.

1823. "Styles from City of Los Angeles." *Southern California Business* 5 (February 1926): 28+.

1824. Sutherland, Delos. "Following the Trail of King Steel." *Southern California Business* 2 (August 1923): 13+.

Five hundred percent growth in Los Angeles steel industry, 1918-1923.

1825. Sutherland, H. M. "Aluminum Foundry in Southern California." *Western Machinery and Steel World* 30 (January 1939): 13+.

Aluminum Alloy Casting Co., Los Angeles.

1826. Swift, John C. "The Tuna Fishery Industry of Southern California." Master's thesis, University of California, 1956. 210 pp.

1827. "A Tale of Retailing That Gives a True Picture of Los Angeles as a Shopping Center." *Southern California Business* 5 (March 1926): 12-3.

Statistics on per-capita income and retail trade.

1828. Tamaru, Takuji. "An Analysis of the Factors Which Have Influenced the Location of the Apparel Industry in Los Angeles." Master's thesis, University of Southern California, 1951. 107 pp.

1829. "Tenth Anniversary of the May Company Store." *Los Angeles Saturday Night* 13 (March 25, 1933): 10.

1830. "A 30-Foot Modern Planer Installed in Los Angeles Plant." *Western Machinery and Steel World* 31 (June 1940): 236-7.

Axelson Manufacturing Co., Los Angeles.

1831. "Thousands Moving Bag and Baggage." *Southern California Business* 2 (December 1923): 24.

Moving the possessions of the 132,000 new residents of Los Angeles in 1923.

1832. "Three Sources Yield Many Millions." *Southern California Business* 3 (October 1924): 31.

Los Angeles income from manufacturing, agriculture, and tourism estimated to be $1.744 billion in 1924.

1833. "Transition to Defense Production." *Western Machinery and Steel World* 32 (September 1941): 458-61.

Utility Fan Corp., Los Angeles.

1834. "Trend of Industrial Expansion in City and County." *Los Angeles Saturday Night 150th Birthday of Los Angeles: Fiesta and Pre-Olympiad.* Special Issue (1931): [19].

1835. "Truck Subway Serves Stores." *Western Construction News* 21 (April 1946): 98-100.

Crenshaw Shopping Center.

1836. Truesdail, Roger W. "Finding Dollars in Fish Cannery Wastes." *Southern California Business* 12 (March 1933): 18.

Truesdail Bio-Chemical Laboratories, Los Angeles.

1837. "The Undiscovered City." *Fortune* 39 (June 1949): 76-83.

Industry in Los Angeles.

1838. Union Bank, Los Angeles. *Growth Pattern: The Dynamic Los Angeles Metropolitan Area.* [Los Angeles, 1958]. 30 pp.

1839. Valleau, Delmar S. "Management Succession and Preselection—A Survey of Staffing Practices in the United States and Los Angeles Areas." Doctoral dissertation, University of California, Los Angeles, 1967. 296 pp.

Because results are based on the demand that responses to a detailed questionnaire be kept secret, this work must be used with caution.

1840. van Buskirk, Robert. "The Development of a Marketing Program for a Downtown Los Angeles Club and Its Attendant Problems." Master's thesis, University Southern California, 1958. 156 pp.

1841. Van Rensler, George. "A Metropolitan Institution, the Alexandria Hotel of Los Angeles." *Out West,* new series, 9 (March 1915): 101-4.

1842. "Vertical Miller with Jig Boring Features in Southern California Shop." *Western Machinery and Steel World* 32 (February 1941): 86-7.

Toolcraft Manufacturing Co., Los Angeles.

1843. Vogelsang, H. C. "What Cotton Really Means to Southern California." *Southern California Business* 5 (February 1926): 16-7+.

"Los Angeles the Cotton Center of the West."

1844. Wade, Frederick W. "Proposed Plan to Determine the Causes of Business Failures in the City of Los Angeles." Master's thesis, University of Southern California, 1952. 173 pp.

1845. Wales, R. Ellis. "Monumental Total of Small Things: Many of the Large Los Angeles Industries of Today Started in a Small Way—Hundreds of Others Promise to Become Great." *Southern California Business* 1 (September 1922): 132+.

1846. "War Finds Los Angeles Rubber Industry Ready." *Apartment Journal* 28 (September 1945): 10-1.

1847. Warren, Van C. "Each Mining Unit Also a Consumer Unit: This Year, $5,000,000 Will Be Spent for Equipment Alone, in Mine Projects Tributary to Los Angeles—And Millons More for Consumer Goods." *Southern California Business* 12 (April 1933): 20-1.

1848. "Water and Power Attract Industries." *Southern California Business* 4 (March 1925): 12-3+.

Los Angeles.

1849. Waterbury, L. A. "Market and Warehouses Form Large Building Group." *Engineering News-Record* 80 (January 24, 1918): 167-8.

Los Angeles Union [Produce] Terminal Co.

1850. Watson, Elizabeth V. "The Consumers' Cooperative Movement in Los Angeles County." Master's thesis, University of Southern California, 1935. 52 pp.

1851. Weinberg, Hershel. "A Consolidated Wholesale Produce Terminal for Los Angeles—A Location, Operation and Facilities Study." Master's thesis, University of Southern California, 1959. 127 pp.

1852. Weiner, Harvey. "Folklore in the Los Angeles Garment Industry." *Western Folklore* 23 (1964): 17-21.

1853. "Welding the Bonds of Business: Visits Between Industrial and Commercial Interests of Los Angeles and San Joaquin Valley Have Brought Valuable Results." *Southern California Business* 2 (April 1923): 11-2.

1854. "The West Coast Presents a Modern Grinding Plant." *Western Machinery and Steel World* 29 (July 1938): 227-9.

Coast Centerless Grinding Co., Los Angeles.

1855. "The West's Great Furniture Center." *Southern California Business* 1 (January 1923): 16+.

Los Angeles.

1856. Wharton, Mel. "Henry Ford's 36th Child." *Southern California Business* 9 (June 1930): 28-9.

Assembly plant, Long Beach.

1857. Wharton, Mel. "Machinery — Largest West of Chicago: Metal-Working Here Is a $150,000,000 Business, Well-Balanced, Resourceful, and with a Future." *Southern California Business* 11 (May 1932): 12-3.

1858. "What Rubber Buys." *Southern California Business* 16 (September 1937): 20-1.

Los Angeles.

1859. "What Rubber Makes Here Besides Tires." *Southern California Business* 16 (September 1937): 14-9.

Los Angeles.

1860. "Where Advertising Money Is Well Spent." *Southern California Business* 6 (April 1927): 9+.

Los Angeles industrial advertising.

1861. "Where Purchasing Power Runs High: Southland Cities Show Surprising Figures, One Month Going Ahead of the Aggregate of Whole States in Other Sections." *Southern California Business* 2 (April 1923): 13.

1862. "Where We Now Stand in Factories." *Southern California Business* 10 (June 1931): 14.

Los Angeles.

1863. "Where Western Buy-Ways Meet." *Southern California Business* 6 (July 1927): 24+.

Los Angeles Trade and Manufacturers' Exhibitions.

1864. Whitworth, D. M. "Commerce Casual." *Westways* 57 (April 1965): 22-4.

The "Swap Meet," Los Angeles' version of the "Flea Market."

1865. "Why Not from Los Angeles." *Southern California Business* 5 (March 1926): 16-7.

States reasons why Los Angeles should take lead in auto accessory exports.

1866. Wiles, Herman L. "Factors Affecting the Concentration of the Electronics Industry in Southern California." Master's thesis, University of Southern California, 1961. 135 pp.

1867. Williams, Willard W. "Ordered Confusion." *Westways* 40 (February 1948): 6-7.

City Market of Los Angeles.

1868. Williams, William J. "Attacking Poverty in the Watts Area: Small Business Development under the Economic Opportunity Act of 1964." Master's thesis, University of Southern California, 1966. 273 pp.

1869. Williamson, Mrs. M. Burton. "Abalone Industry of the California Coast." *Out West* 28 (June 1908): 487-94.

Includes Catalina, Pt. Fermin, Palos Verdes, White's Point.

1870. Willy, J. Knight, *et al. The Story of the Los Angeles Statler.* Evanston, Ill., 1953. 64 pp.

A reprint of the text from *The Hotel Monthly* 61 (January 1953): 27-88.

1871. "Willys-Overland Comes to Los Angeles." *Southern California Business* 7 (May 1928): 16-7+.

Automobile manufacturer.

1872. Wilson, Bertha J. "A Study of the Educational Significance of the Women's Garment Industry in Los Angeles, California." Master's thesis, University of Southern California, 1935. 125 pp.

1873. Witter, Jere. "The Wild Reign of Captain Tony and His Floating Casinos." *Los Angeles* 9 (March 1965): 40-3.

Tony Cornero's offshore gambling ships, the *Rex* and the *Lux*—1930s and early '40s.

1874. Woehlke, Walter V. "The Land of Sunny Homes: A Survey of Economic Conditions and Causes in Southern California, the Suburban Garden of the Far West." *Sunset* 34 (March 1915): 463-72.

Los Angeles area.

1875. ———— "Smoke-Stacks on the Pacific." *Sunset* 31 (December 1913): 1161-71.

Includes Los Angeles industry.

1876. Wood, Stanley. "The Industries of Los Angeles." *Out West,* new series, 7 (January 1914): 65-8.

1877. ———— "Los Angeles in Its March of Progress." *Out West,* new series, 6 (December 1913): 245-54.

1878. "A World Cross Roads of Shops." *Southern California Business* 16 (June 1937): 18.

Hollywood.

1879. Young, David H. "Making Silk in California." *Southern California Business* 5 (June 1926): 14-5.

Golden State Silk Mills, Inc., Hermosa Beach.

1880. Young, John P. "Industrial Background," in *Los Angeles: Preface to a Master Plan.* Ed. by George W. Robbins and L. Deming Tilton. Los Angeles, 1941. Pp. 61-73.

1881. ———, ed. *Los Angeles: Its Economic and Financial Position.* Los Angeles, 1936. 31 pp.

1882. Zierer, Clifford M., ed. *California and the Southwest.* New York, 1956. 376 pp.

Focused in large part on Los Angeles region. Includes chapters on airplane and entertainment industries, and auto assembly.

1883. "Zoning Case Voiding 'Home Industry' Prohibition to Be Appealed." *Western City* 14 (February 1938): 13.

Los Angeles County.

1884. Zukin, Joseph. "Over $50,000,000 in Wearing Apparel." *Southern California Business* 7 (January 1929): 28-9+.

Los Angeles apparel industry.

CHAMBER OF COMMERCE

1885. Arnoll, A. G. "The Los Angeles Chamber of Commerce: An Appraisal of Three Years of Activities 1930 to 1932, Inclusive." *Southern California Business* 13 (January 1934): 12-34.

1886. ——— "Those Responsible for New Building." *Southern California Business* 4 (April 1925): 22+.

Building Committee, Los Angeles Chamber of Commerce.

1887. Baur, John E. "The Chamber of Commerce Cornerstones: Milestones in Los Angeles Progress." *Historical Society of Southern California Quarterly* 38 (1956): 61-70.

1888. Baus, Herbert M. "A Chamber Sells Nationally: Trade Ambassadors of Los Angeles Keep Local Business Men Informed as to Better Outlets, New Markets, Trade Possibilities in Their Domestic Trade Territory." *Nation's Business* 27 (February 1939): 27-8+.

"Trade ambassador" system of the Los Angeles Chamber of Commerce.

1889. Bayer, Charles P. "Taking Los Angeles County East." *Southern California Business* 7 (January 1929): 14-5+.

Field Service and Exposition Department, Los Angeles Chamber of Commerce.

1890. Boone, Andrew R. "Los Angeles Chamber of Commerce: And the Part It Played in Building an Industrial Empire." *California Magazine of Pacific Business* 27 (April 1937): 26-9+.

1891. "Break Ground for New Chamber Home." *Southern California Business* 2 (May 1923): 24.

Los Angeles Chamber of Commerce Building, Twelfth and Hill.

1892. "Bringing New Industries to Town." *Southern California Business* 4 (February 1925): 16+.

Industrial Department, Los Angeles Chamber of Commerce.

1893. Burke, Carleton F. "New Building Is Filling Rapidly." *Southern California Business* 4 (June 1925): 24+.

Los Angeles Chamber of Commerce Building.

1894. "Chamber of Commerce in New Home." *Los Angeles Realtor* 4 (February 1925): 9.

Los Angeles.

1895. Cole, William B. "From Board of Trade to Chamber of Commerce." *The Downey Historical Society Annual* 2 (1967-68): 42-57.

1896. Cooke, Charles A. "Los Angeles as a Convention Center." *Southern California Business* 3 December 1924): 20+.

1897. Fredericks, John D. "A New Home for the Chamber." *Southern California Business* 1 (February 1922): 10+.

Los Angeles.

1898. Graff, Frederic. "The Development of the Industrial Program of the Pasadena Chamber of Commerce [1872-1953]." Master's thesis, University of Southern California, 1953. 189 pp.

1899. Heywood, Ferd. H. "Chamber Moves into New Home." *Southern California Business* 4 (February 1925): 15+.

Los Angeles.

1900. "An Important New Department." *Southern California Business* 6 (March 1927): 26.

Real Estate, City and County Planning Department, Los Angeles Chamber of Commerce.

1901. "Inglewood Chamber Builds New Home." *Southern California Business* 4 (September 1925): 34.

1902. Kirker, G. B. "Putting a Trade Exposition Together." *Southern California Business* 5 (August 1926): 20+.

Los Angeles Industrial and Trade Exposition.

1903. Kling, S. J. "One Good Show Deserves Another." *Southern California Business* 5 (September 1926): 11+.

Los Angeles Chamber of Commerce Industrial and Trade Exposition.

1904. Layne, J. Gregg. "Chamber of Commerce Milestones—Six Decades of Public Service." *Historical Society of Southern California* 30 (1948): 205-7.

1905. Leimert, Walter H. "Business Is Where the People Are." *Los Angeles Realtor* 7 (February 1927): 17.

Promotional efforts of the Los Angeles Chamber of Commerce and the All-Year Club of Southern California.

1906. "Looking Forward to New Home." *Southern California Business* 1 (September 1922): 99+.

Los Angeles Chamber of Commerce.

1907. MacDonough, E. F. "How to Trade in the 4th Market Area: Good Data for Seller and Buyer Can Be Had in Publications of the Los Angeles Chamber." *Southern California Business* 10 (November 1931): 18-9.

1908. Mappelbeck, John. "What Would You Like to Know? Many Kinds of Information Are Available in the Periodicals Published by the Chamber." *Southern California Business* 16 (August 1937): 12-3.

Los Angeles.

1909. Newmark, Marco R. "A Short History of the Los Angeles Chamber of Commerce." *Historical Society of Southern California Quarterly* 27 (1945): 57-80.

1910. "Paying Attention to the Visitor." *Southern California Business* 4 (May 1925): 19+.

Convention Department, Los Angeles Chamber of Commerce.

1911. Purcell, F. J. "Harbor to Welcome 50,000 Guests: Ships and Sailors from World Ports Join Junior Chamber of Commerce for May 16 Celebration." *Los Angeles Saturday Night* 43 (May 9, 1936): 16.

"Harbor Day."

1912. Shoup, Paul. "Los Angeles at the Western Meeting of U. S. Chamber of Commerce." *Southern California Business* 4 (December 1925): 10+.

1913. "Torrance Chamber's New Home." *Southern California Business* 16 (December 1937): 20.

1914. "Unraveling Some Knotty Tangles." *Southern California Business* 4 (July 1925): 24+.

Research Department, Los Angeles Chamber of Commerce.

1915. Walsh, Marie T. "To Mark Early Los Angeles: Stories of the City's Pueblo Days Are Being Gathered by This Women's Organization." *Southern California Business* 13 (October 1934): 12-3.

History and Landmarks Division, Women's Auxiliary, Los Angeles Chamber of Commerce.

1916. Whitcomb, Lou La Blonge. "The Business Women's Committee." *Southern California Business* 6 (August 1927): 32.

Los Angeles Chamber of Commerce.

CULTURE

CULTURE—GENERAL

1917. Bogardus, Emory S. *Southern California, a Center of Culture.* Los Angeles, 1940. 90 pp.

1918. Champlin, Charles. "A Warm Climate for Cultural Life." *Life* 48 (June 20, 1960): 89-90.

"Growing accent on the arts" in Los Angeles.

1919. Gordon, Dudley C. *An Entertaining Guidebook to the Cultural Assets of Metropolitan Los Angeles.* Los Angeles, 1940. 64 pp.
Museums, galleries and libraries.

1920. "Inglewood Concentrates on Culture in the Community." *Western City* 46 (March 1970): 27.

1921. Kentle, Jean B. "Los Angeles as an Aesthetic Center." *Saturday Night* 4 (May 26, 1923): 17.

1922. Los Angeles. Chamber of Commerce. Women's Community Service Auxiliary. *Southern California Competitive Festival of the Allied Arts.* Los Angeles, 1934. 32 pp.

1923. ———— Civic Bureau of Music and Art. *Los Angeles County Culture and the Community . . .* Los Angeles, 1927. 68 pp. 2nd ed., [1929?]. 80 pp.

1924. Stevens, Jean. "Pasadena's Bid for 7½ Acres of Culture." *Southern California Prompter* 2 (February 1961): 22-3.
Proposed Carmelita Cultural Center.

1925. Wray, Albert. "D'Oporto Studio House Is Los Angeles' First 'Hotel Des Artistes.'" *Western Housing* 32 (October 1948): 12+.

CULTURE—ART

1926. Alliot, Hector. "Alexander Stirling Calder." *Out West* 31 (September 1909): 765-84.
Sculpture by Calder at Throop Institute (Cal Tech), the YMCA, and other Los Angeles-area locations.

1927. "Art Loving Public of Los Angeles Receives Rare Gift in the Opening of the Henry Huntington Library." *Los Angeles Realtor* 7 (March 1928): 25+.

1928. "Art Museum for Posterity." *Los Angeles Saturday Night* 13 (September 16, 1933): 4.
Advocates new Los Angeles Art Museum.

1929. "Art Rides High at a Great University." *Life* 42 (May 20, 1957): 92-101+.
UCLA.

1930. Bryan, Robert S. "Sam Rodia and the Children of Watts." *Westways* 59 (August 1967): 3-6.
Watts Towers.

1931. Carthay Circle Theatre. *California, 1826-1926.* [Catalog of Paintings Hung in the Tower Room of the Carthay Circle Theatre; Issued by the Historical Committee of the Carthay Center.] [Los Angeles, 1926]. 32 pp.

1932. [Chapin, Lou V.]. *Art Work on Southern California.* San Francisco, 1900. 12 parts in 2 vols.

1933. Committee for Simon Rodia's Towers in Watts. *The Watts Towers.* [Los Angeles, 1961]. 11 pp.

1934. Cummings, Ridgely. "Freedom to Hammer." *New Republic* 132 (May 23, 1955): 14-5.
Controversy over Bernard Rosenthal sculpture at Los Angeles Police Building.

1935. Diamond, Susan J. "Should We Set Fire to Our Art Museum?" *Los Angeles* 13 (February 1968): 30-1+.
Los Angeles.

1936. Federal Art Project. Southern California. *Southern California Creates.* [N.p., 1939]. 51 pp.

1937. Fiske, Turbese L. "Growing Colony of Mexican Artists." *Saturday Night* 3 (February 17, 1923): 5.
Los Angeles.

1938. Grey, Elmer. "The Fine Arts in America." *The Architect and Engineer* 147 (October 1941): 35-45.
Partly about Huntington Art Gallery, San Marino.

1939. Hampton, Edgar L. "Los Angeles as an American Art Centre." *Current History* 24 (September 1926): 858-65.

1940. Harrison, Preston. "Art Museum for Posterity." *Los Angeles Saturday Night* 13 (September 9, 1933): 5.
Discusses possibility of new Los Angeles Art Museum.

1941. ———— "Permanent Museum within Reach." *Los Angeles Saturday Night* 14 (October 14, 1933): 5.
Los Angeles Art Museum.

1942. Higgins, Winifred H. "Art Collecting in the Los Angeles Area, 1910-1960." Doctoral dissertation, University of California, Los Angeles, 1963. 504 pp.

1943. "History of Printed Word in Murals." *Los Angeles Saturday Night* 12 (September 10, 1932): 4.

Treasure Room of Doheny Memorial Library, U.S.C., dedicated September 12, 1932.

1944. Hyers, Faith H. "New Sculptures at the Library." *Los Angeles Saturday Night* 11 (November 15, 1930): 5.

Lee Lawrie sculptures at Los Angeles Public Library.

1945. James, George W. "A Vision for Los Angeles." *Out West,* new series, 5 (May 1913): 221-41.

Sculpture.

1946. Judson, Horace T. "William Lees Judson Memorial Window." *Los Angeles Saturday Night* 44 (October 24, 1936): 15.

Tribute to "the dean of early Southern California painters" at the California State Exposition Building in Exposition Park.

1947. Kendig, Francis. "Fine Arts Center in Hancock Park." *Los Angeles Saturday Night* 44 (December 26, 1936): 10.

Project said to be "moving along."

1948. Langsner, Jules. "Fantasy in Steel, Concrete and Broken Bottles." *Arts & Architecture* 76 (September 1959): 27-8.

Watts Towers.

1949. ———— "Rico Lebrun." *Arts & Architecture* 74 (June 1957): 20-1+.

The work of a Los Angeles artist.

1950. ————, and Selz, Peter. "Kinetics in L.A.: Charles Mattox's Restless Sculptures and John Whitney's Computer-Generated Films Forecast a Happy Alliance Between Art and Modern Technology." *Art in America* 55 (May-June 1967): 107-8.

1951. Los Angeles County Museum. *California Centennials Exhibition of Art. Section I: "Historic California." Section II: "Artists of California,*

1949." September 30, through November 13, 1949. Los Angeles, 1949. 148 pp.

1952. ———— *Simon Rodia's Towers in Watts, a Photographic Exhibition by Seymour Rosen.* Sponsored by the Contemporary Art Council and the Committee for Simon Rodia's Towers in Watts. [Text by Paul LaPorte.] Los Angeles, 1962. [24 pp.]

1953. Los Angeles. Municipal Art Commission. *1961 Progress Report. 50th Anniversary.* [Los Angeles, 1961]. [14] pp.

1954. Lynch, Samuel D. "Science Protects Art." *Westways* 57 (August 1965): 8-10+.

Various devices and procedures for protection of treasures in the Los Angeles County Art Museum.

1955. Madian, Jon. *Beautiful Junk: A Story of the Watts Towers.* Boston and Toronto, 1968. 44 pp.

1956. Martin, M. M., Sister, "The Establishment of a Commission of Sacred Art in the Archdiocese of Los Angeles." Master's thesis, University of Southern California, 1944. 160 pp.

1957. Millier, Arthur. "Frank Perls: Knight-Errant of the Art World." *Los Angeles* 12 (April 1967): 40-3.

Owner of gallery in Beverly Hills.

1958. ———— "The Years with Ross (Kenneth): The City Owes Much of Its Cultural Course to the Man at Barnsdall Park." *Los Angeles* 4 (October 1962): 54-5.

1959. "Municipal Art Center Is New Long Beach Facility." *Western City* 27 (August 1951): 36.

1960. Nelson, Elmer S. *Treasures of the Past.* Los Angeles, 1929. [33] pp.

Reprint of an article, descriptive of the Huntington Library and Art Gallery, which appeared in three parts in the *Pacific Mutual News.*

1961. Norman-Wilcox, Gregor. "A Collection Which Gives Los Angeles Distinction." *Los Angeles Saturday Night* 44 (November 14, 1936): 15.

Chinese art display, Los Angeles County Art Museum.

1962. ———— "Los Angeles Museum Receives Many Gifts." *Los Angeles Saturday Night* 43 (August 1, 1936): 9.

1963. Pomfret, John E. *The Henry E. Huntington Library and Art Gallery, from Its Beginning to 1969.* San Marino, 1969. 241 pp.

1964. Quélin, René de. "This Te Deum Is Sung in Glass." *International Studio* 76 (January 1923): 360-1.

Louis C. Tiffany's Favrile Glass in the First Methodist Church, Los Angeles.

1965. Security-First National Bank, Los Angeles. *The Ranch of the Gathering of the Waters.* Los Angeles, 1934. 18 pp.

"The Story of the Murals in the Beverly Hills Branch of the Security-First National Bank of Los Angeles."

1966. Smith, Jack. "A Day in the City: Gallery Night on La Cienega." *Westways* 60 (May 1968): 9-11.

Los Angeles.

1967. ———— "A Day in the City: Miracle on 107th Street." *Westways* 62 (August 1970): 6-8+.

Simon Rodia's Watts Towers.

1968. Splitter, Henry W. "Art in Los Angeles Before 1900." *Historical Society of Southern California Quarterly* 41 (1959) 38-57; 117-38; 247-56.

A necessary background for understanding the community's attitude toward art in the twentieth century. Among turn-of-the-century artists, included are William Lees Judson, who became Dean of the Art Department of the University of Southern California, and Paul de Longpré, who achieved worldwide fame as a painter of flowers.

1969. "A Stained Glass Craftsman, Horace T. Judson, Looks at the 20th Century." *The Architect and Engineer* 191 (November 1952): 8-15.

Judson Studios of Los Angeles.

1970. "Three Views of La Cienega." I. "The Galleries," by Arthur Miller. II. "The Collector," by William Fadiman. III. "The Opening," by Barbara Wilkins. *Los Angeles* 11 (July 1966): 31-6.

Los Angeles' La Cienega Boulevard art galleries.

1971. Travers, David. "American Sculpture of the Sixties." *Arts & Architecture* 84 (June 1967): 6-9.

Los Angeles County Museum of Art.

1972. "UCLA's Outstanding Displays of Modern Sculpture." *Sunset* 138 (February 1967): 96-7.

1973. Wark, Robert R. "Arabella Huntington and the Beginnings of the Art Collection." *Huntington Library Quarterly* 32 (1968-9): 309-31.

1974. "What Does a Municipal Art Commission Do?" *American City* 40 (March 1929): 141.

Activities of Los Angeles Municipal Art Commission.

1975. Winslow, Carleton M. "Los Angeles Mural Painter Stimulates Public Interest in Art." *The Architect and Engineer* 106 (July 1931): 55-8.

Lucile Lloyd.

1976. Yates, Peter. "Ethnic Art at UCLA." *Arts & Architecture* 83 (May 1966): 18-22.

1977. ———— "The Wellcome Collection Exhibition of Ethnic Art at the University of California, Los Angeles." *Arts & Architecture* 83 (May 1966): 30-2.

CULTURE—MUSIC

1978. Arlen, Walter. "A Music Center." *Library Journal* 78 (June 15, 1953): 1067-9.

Music in greater Los Angeles.

1979. Armitage, Merle. "Los Angeles—The Home of Grand Opera." *Southern California Business* 7 (October 1928): 18-9+.

1980. Asseyev, Tamara C. "The Development of the Los Angeles Music Center Project." Master's thesis, University of California, Los Angeles, 1968. 86 pp.

1981. Balch, Allan C. "Hollywood Bowl: Its Place in the Community." *Los Angeles Realtor* 7 (November 1927): 31+.

1982. ———— "Symphonies Under the Stars." *Southern California Business* 6 (May 1927): 34.

Hollywood Bowl.

1983. "Beaux Arts Building, Music Center of Los Angeles." *Saturday Night* 7 (May 28, 1927): 1.
   Activities and programs at the center since its opening.

1984. Bell, Charline. "The Bowl Is Kind to Artists." *Southern California Business* 9 (July 1930): 22.
   Hollywood Bowl.

1985. Boddy, Manchester. "Discord Amid Harmony: Los Angeles Culture Front Squabbles over Subsidized Opera." *Saturday Night* 45 (October 22, 1938): 12-5.

1986. Borcherdt, Donn. "Armenian Folk Songs and Dances in the Fresno and Los Angeles Areas." *Western Folklore* 18 (1959): 1-12.

1987. Brackenbury, Don. "The Long Beach Civic Light Opera." *Frontier* 12 (December 1960): 21-2.

1988. Brite, Raymond. " 'Concertized Opera' to Feature Bowl Season." *Southern California Business* 8 (July 1929): 20+.

1989. Brookwell, George. *Saturdays in the Hollywood Bowl*. Hollywood, [c1940]. 93 pp.

1990. Buhrman, Robert. "The Philharmonic Takes to the Streets." *Los Angeles* 15 (May 1970): 38-41+.
   "Contempo '70"—an effort to increase attendance at concerts of the Los Angeles Philharmonic and to give exposure to the works of significant modern composers.

1991. Cadman, Charles W. "How the Pacific Coast Is Growing Musically—I. Los Angeles." *The Musician* 16 (November 1911): 734-5.
   Enumeration of musical activtities in Los Angeles.

1992. Davenport, Charles. "The Music Center and Mrs. C." *Los Angeles* 3 (May 1962): 40-3.
   Music Center and Mrs. Dorothy Buffum Chandler.

1993. Duncan, Ray. "A Connoisseur's Key to the Music Center." *Los Angeles* 8 (December 1964): 30-2+.
   Los Angeles Music Center.

1994. Fasoli, Guy A. "An Occupational Study of the Vocations in Music in the Los Angeles Area." Master's thesis, University of Southern California, 1942. 82 pp.

1995. " 'Festival Year' for the Bowl Symphony Orchestra." *Saturday Night* 5 (June 20, 1925): 1.
   Hollywood Bowl's fourth season.

1996. "Free Grand Opera at Greek Theater, Griffith Park." *Los Angeles Saturday Night* 11 (June 20, 1931): 13.
   Opening of Greek Theater, June 26, 1931.

1997. Garland, William M. "The Philharmonic Orchestra of Los Angeles." *Los Angeles Realtor* 7 (November 1927): 41+.

1998. Heim, Frank. "The Grand Opera Season." *Southern California Business* 8 (October 1929): 24+.

1999. Hillyer, Anthony [*pseud.*]. *The Hollywood Bowl*. Ed. by Thomas P. Stricker. Los Angeles, [c1939]. 16 pp.

2000. "The Hollywood Bowl as a Civic Asset." *Los Angeles Realtor* 4 (May 1925): 14.

2001. "Hollywood Bowl Breakfast Talks." *Los Angeles Saturday Night* 13 (August 5, 1933): 7.
   Tuesday morning lectures during Bowl season.

2002. "Hollywood Bowl—World Famous." *Los Angeles Realtor* 7 (July 1927): 17.

2003. "Hollywood—Salzburg of America." *California Magazine of the Pacific* 28 (May 1938): 7+.

2004. [Huyck, Charles L.]. *"Die Walkure," a Classic Feat of Broadcasting, October 18, 1926.* [Los Angeles?, 1926]. 13 pp.
   Transmission from Los Angeles to San Francisco of the first opera broadcast by telephone.

2005. Hyers, Faith H. "Music at the Library." *Library Journal* 64 (April 1, 1939): 252.
   Daily noon-hour concerts, offered through the Art and Music Department of the Los Angeles Public Library.

2006. Jones, Isabel M. *Hollywood Bowl*. New York and Los Angeles, 1936. 203 pp.

2007. Kendig, Francis. "All Roads Lead to Hollywood." *Saturday Night* 44 (August 14, 1937): 10.
   Hollywood Bowl performances.

2008. ———— "The Battle of the Hollywood Bowl." *Saturday Night* 44 (July 31, 1937): 12.
Opinions of performers and personnel of Hollywood Bowl versus those of the public as to the quality of performances there.

2009. Krec, Ted. "Blowing Their Horns for Long Beach." *Westways* 50 (November 1958): 22-3.
Anecdotal history of municipal band.

2010. Lacey, Franklin. *Highlights on Twenty Years of Civic Light Opera.* Los Angeles, [1957]. [20] pp.
Los Angeles.

2011. Larson, Esther. "The History of Music in Los Angeles." Master's thesis, University of Southern California, 1930. 64 pp.

2012. Los Angeles Times. *Music Center: A Living Memorial to Peace.* [Los Angeles], 1964. 119 pp.
Issued as a supplement to the Los Angeles *Times* edition of December 6, 1964.

2013. "Los Angeles as a Music Center." *Saturday Night* 5 (May 10, 1924): 25+.

2014. "Los Angeles Selects Sites for New Buildings." *American City* 62 (March 1947): 93.
War Memorial auditorium and opera house.

2015. Lynch, Samuel D. "Behind the Scenes at the Hollywood Bowl." *Westways* 55 (July 1963): 2-4.

2016. Marty, Belle M. "The Activities and Personnel of Non-Professional Musical Organizations in Long Beach, California." Master's thesis, University of Southern California, 1941. 94 pp.

2017. McCarthy, E. Avery. "Symphonic Music as a Civic Force Affecting Realty Values." *Los Angeles Realtor* 6 (December 1926): 19+.
Los Angeles Philharmonic.

2018. McClintock, Madeline. "Penny-a-Day Banks Helped to Obtain the Hollywood Bowl." *American City* 40 (March 1929): 112-3.

2019. "The Music Program in Los Angeles." *Playground and Recreation* 24 (June 1930): 177+.
Los Angeles Department of Playground and Recreation.

2020. Northcutt, John O. *The Hollywood Bowl Story.* Hollywood, 1962. 30 pp.

2021. ———— *Magic Valley, the Story of Hollywood Bowl.* Los Angeles, 1967. 159 pp.

2022. ———— *Symphony, the Story of the Los Angeles Philharmonic Orchestra.* [Los Angeles, 1963]. 80 pp.

2023. "A Pageant of Symphonic Drama." *Los Angeles Saturday Night* 14 (September 15, 1934): 1-2.
Hollywood Bowl.

2024. "Philharmonic Orchestra Enters Eleventh Season." *Los Angeles Saturday Night* 10 (October 19, 1929): 7.
Includes history of philharmonic and role of William Andrews Clark, Jr.

2025. Sayers, Charles. "The Development of the Community Orchestra in Selected Cities of Los Angeles County." Master's thesis, Occidental College, 1948. 197 pp.

2026. Smith, Caroline E. *The Philharmonic Orchestra of Los Angeles, the First Decade, 1919-1929.* Los Angeles, 1930. 283 pp.

2027. Stricker, Thomas P. *Hollywood Bowl.* Los Angeles, [c1939]. 16 pp.

2028. Sutherland, Henry A. "Requiem for the Los Angeles Philharmonic Auditorium." *Southern California Quarterly* 47 (1965): 303-31.
Sketches the uses made of the auditorium before The Music Center was built, as well as other locations for the theatre arts and music.

2029. Swan, Howard. *Music in the Southwest 1825-1950.* San Marino, 1952. 316 pp.
Chapter X-XV on twentieth-century Los Angeles.

2030. "The Symphony under the Stars: Hollywood Bowl." *Los Angeles Realtor* 6 (November 1926): 27.

2031. Tritt, Edward C. "The Community Symphony Orchestra; A Study of the Historical Development, Present Activities, Personnel and Inner Organization of Eight Community Orchestras in Southern California." Doctoral dissertation, Indiana University, 1961. 309 pp.

2032. Weissman, David. "Battin' the Baton Around." *Saturday Night* 44 (August 14, 1937): 5.
Interview with Dr. Otto Klemperer.

2033. "What Opera Means to Los Angeles." *Southern California Business* 5 (October 1926): 33.

2034. Will, Arthur J. "Proposed County of Los Angeles Civic Auditorium and Music Center." *California Magazine of the Pacific* 46 (September 1956): 20-2.

CULTURE—POPULAR AND PUBLIC ENTERTAINMENT

2035. "Another Fair Tries Monorail." *American City* 78 (February 1963): 111.
Los Angeles County Fair.

2036. "Augmenting the County Fair." *Southern California Business* 6 (September 1927): 22.
Expansion of Los Angeles County Fairgrounds.

2037. Bennett, J. B. "Our County Fair Has Showmanship." *Southern California Business* 10 (September 1931): 14.

2038. Boone, Andrew R. "Fifty Years of Roses." *California Magazine of the Pacific* 28 (December 1938): 17+.
The Tournament of Roses, Pasadena.

2039. Brown, Gilbert. "What the Tenderfoot Is Told About Los Angeles." *Westways* 28 (March 1936): 30-1.
Sightseeing tours.

2040. Buhrman, Robert. "The New Nightlife." *Los Angeles* 15 (May 1970): 48-53.
Current Los Angeles night-club scene.

2041. —— "Tourism in Los Angeles . . . Is It all Done with Mirrors? That Isn't Los Angeles the Tourist Sees, But an Unreal Melange of Movie Tours, Amusement Parks and Hokum . . ." *Los Angeles* 14 (August 1969): 29-32.

2042. Bush, Carl. "Hollywood Dresses Up." *Los Angeles Realtor* 8 (November 1928): 19+.
Second annual fashion festival.

2043. Celvin, Paul. "Pasadena Does the Impossible." *Westways* 60 (January 1968): 2-5
The Tournament of Roses.

2044. Chapin, Alonzo F. *A Book of the Crown City and Its Tournament of Roses, Pasadena, California.* [Pasadena, 1907?]. Unp.

2045. Connor, J. Torrey. "La Fiesta de Los Angeles." *Sunset* 8 (April 1902): 267.

2046. Curran, C. P. "County Fair Attracts over 150,000." *Southern California Business* 8 (September 1929): 56+.

2047. Dalen, Edith. "Whose Zoo?" *Westways* 35 (July 1943): 10-1.
The Grace Wiley Zoo, in North Long Beach, specializing in reptiles.

2048. Diehl, Digby. "The Surprising Harbor." *Los Angeles* 11 (August 1966): 24-9.
San Pedro's Ports O'Call Village.

2049 Economic Research Associates. *Economic Planning for the Long Beach World's Fair, 1966-1967, Phase II Report.* Los Angeles, 1962. Various pagings.

2050. —— *Progress Memorandum [on] Facilities for the Performing Arts at the California World's Fair, 1967-1968.* [Los Angeles], c1962. 37 pp.

2051. —— *Synopsis [of] Economic Impact of the California World's Fair, Long Beach, California, 1967-1968, Prepared for International Exposition for Southern California, Inc.* [Los Angeles?, 1962]. 25 pp.

2052. "Electric Float Parade in Los Angeles." *Street Railway Journal* 28 (August 25, 1906): 301-2.

2053. Fessier, Mike, Jr. "Sunset Boulevard's New Bohemia." *Los Angeles* 10 (December 1965): 34-7+.
Change on Sunset Strip: "Entertainment on the Strip is now provided by the hair, the clothes, the talk of the invading army."

2054. Geissinger, James A. "Los Angeles in Festive Spirit: Missions, Priests,. Dons and Señoritas of 150 Years Ago Reappear with a Hollywood Accent." *Christian Century* 48 (October 7, 1931): 1258-9.
"Los Angeles Celebrates 150 Years of History."

2055. "Grand-Daddy of Fiestas." *Westways* 33 (June 1941): 6-7.
Photo story on San Fernando Fiesta.

2056. "The Great Fair." *Southern California Business* 7 (September 1928): 30+.
Los Angeles County Fair.

2057. Grinnell, Elizabeth. "New Year's Rose Tourney." *Sunset* 10 (February 1903): 286-9.
Pasadena.

2058. ———— "Pasadena's Rose Tournament." *Sunset* 12 (February 1904): 331-4.

2059. Hassler, Dorothy K. "That Day in Pasadena." *Westways* 55 (December 1963): 4-7.
The Tournament of Roses.

2060. Holder, Stirrup. "Los Angeles Horse Show in Retrospect." *California Graphic* 5 (February 18, 1928): 8+

2061. *In Its Fifty-fifth Year, the Tournament of Roses, Present — Memories of the Past — a Challenge for the Future.* [N.p., 1944]. [36] pp.

2062. "Interest Centers in Great Pageant." *Southern California California Business* 1 (August 1922): 20-1.
Pageant of Progress and Industrial Exposition, Exposition Park, Los Angeles.

2063. International Exposition for Southern California. *California World's Fair, 1967-68, Dedicated to the Dignity of Man.* [Long Beach?, 1964]. [37] pp.

2064. James, George W. "Tournament of Roses in Pasadena. New Year's 1912." *Out West,* new series, 2 (November 1911): [259]-61.

2065. Jessup, Roger W. "World's Fair for Los Angeles." *California Magazine of the Pacific* 34 (December 1944): 15+.

2066. Los Angeles County Fair. *Historical Pageant, La Fiesta del Rancho San Jose, Pomona, Commemorating the One Hundredth Anniversary of the Settlement of Pomona Valley, Los Angeles County Fair, Sunday, September 20, 1936.* Pomona, 1936. 30 pp.

2067. "Los Angeles County Fair 'Silver Jubilee.'"
California Magazine of the Pacific 42 (September 1952): 22.

2068. "Los Angeles County Fair 'The American Way.'" *California Magazine of the Pacific* 44 (September 1954): 25.

2069. "Los Angeles' Great Opportunity." *Los Angeles Saturday Night* 15 (August 10, 1935): 3.
Plans for 1938 Pacific Exposition.

2070. "Los Angeles La Fiesta, 1932." *Overland Monthly* 90 (September 1932): 222.
Labor Day festivities celebrating founding of Los Angeles.

2071. "Los Angeles Makes Debut as Industrial and Manufacturing Center with Big Trade Exposition and Buyers' Display." *Los Angeles Saturday Night* 2 (August 20, 1921): section 2, pp. 4-5.

2072. Lunden, Samuel E. *Community Development Through an Exposition for Los Angeles.* Los Angeles, 1944. 42 pp.

2073. Marquis, Neeta. "Our Annual Bookplate Show." *Los Angeles Saturday Night* 8 (May 19, 1928): 4-5.
Show at Los Angeles Museum put on by Los Angeles Bookplate Association.

2074. Marshall, Jim. "Everybody's Night Club." *Collier's* 113 (May 13, 1944): 24.
Hollywood Palladium.

2075. McNaughton, J. A. "The Christmas Live Stock Show." *Southern California Business* 8 (November 1929): 12-3+.
Los Angeles Union Stockyards.

2076. "Our Builders Plan First Big Exhibit." *Southern California Business* 6 (November 1927): 24.
Builders Exposition of Southern California.

2077. Parks, Marion. "La Fiesta de Los Angeles." *Los Angeles Saturday Night 150th Birthday of Los Angeles: Fiesta and Pre-Olympiad.* Special Issue (1931): [4].

2078. ———— "La Fiesta de Los Angeles—Retrospect." *Overland Monthly* 89 (October 1931): 11+.

2079. "Pasadena Rose Tournament Internationally Famous." *Touring Topics* 8 (December 1916): 7-10.

2080. "Planning the West's Greatest Fair." *Southern California Business* 5 (September 1926): 22+.
Los Angeles County Fair.

2081. "Planning World's Fair Around Permanent Civic Improvements: Los Angeles Considers an International Exposition with Large-Scale Survival Value." *American City* 59 (July 1944): 87.

2082. Plusfours, Cholly. "Why the County Fair?" *Southern California Business* 9 (September 1930): 20.

2083. Power, B. M. "The West Los Angeles Flower Show and Trade Exposition." *Southern California Business* 8 (April 1929): 18+

2084. Pridham, R. W. "A Permanent Industrial Exhibit." *Southern California Business* 4 (March 1925): 33+.
Exhibit at Los Angeles Chamber of Commerce.

2085. Randolph, Teasdale. "Occidental Exposition in a Mediterranean Setting." *Los Angeles Saturday Night* 8 (July 21, 1928): 2+.
Pacific Southwest Exposition at Long Beach.

2086. Rodriguez, Raul. "Flight Through the Heavens." *Westways* 31 (April 1939): 18-9.
Griffith Planetarium, Los Angeles.

2087. "Rounding Out Plans for Pageant of Progress." *Southern California Business* 1 (July 1922): 19+.
Los Angeles Trade Exposition, Exposition Park.

2088. Ryckman, John W., ed. *Story of an Epochal Event in the History of California: The Pacific Southwest Exposition . . . 1928.* [Long Beach, 1929]. 292 pp.

2089. Schiff, Ludwig. "Planning a Regal Downtown Yuletide." *Southern California Business* 8 (November 1929): 14-5+.
Los Angeles Christmas decorations.

2090. Scott, Charles F. "Los Angeles on Parade." *Overland Monthly* 89 (August-September 1931): 7+.
"Where to go and what to see in the Fiesta City."

2091. Seidenbaum, Art. "The Strip Comes to the Strip." *Los Angeles* 2 (May 1961): 30-1.
Sunset Strip adopts "striptease."

2092. "Showing the Goods Los Angeles Can Produce." *Southern California Business* 4 (September 1925): 14.
Permanent exihibit at Chamber of Commerce.

2093. Smith, Jack. "A Day in the City: Afloat in a Beer Garden." *Westways* 61 (January 1969): 6-8+.
Busch Gardens.

2094. ———— "A Day in the City: Listening to the Dolphins." *Westways* 62 (March 1970): 8-10+.
Marineland.

2095. ———— "A Day in the City: Star Trek." *Westways* 61 (June 1969): 10-2.
Universal Studios.

2096. ———— "Some of My Favorite Places Are Tourist Traps." *Los Angeles* 15 (July 1970): 46-8.

2097. Staley, Genevieve M. "Our Second Annual 'Cruise Show'." *Southern California Business* 16 (October 1937): 10-1.
Los Angeles manufacturers of sports apparel.

2098. Stewart, Rex. "Days and Nights When the Music Wouldn't Stop." *Los Angeles* 11 (September 1966): 44-6+.
"A veteran trumpeter recalls an era when jazz boomed from every club and dance hall in Los Angeles, and Central Avenue hosted the greats till dawn."

2099. Stone, Irving. *Rose Bowl Town.* [N.p., n.d.]. 47 pp.
An amusing history of Pasadena with interesting bits about the Rose Tournament, people who have been connected with it, and how people feel about it.

2100. Talbot, Katherine. "Here Comes the Parade." *Westways* 47 (December 1955): 4-5.
Rose Parade, Pasadena.

2101. "The Trade Exposition Develops New Business." *Southern California Business* 5 (October 1926): 22+.
Los Angeles.

2102. "The Trends of Today in Airplanes and Motors. An Analysis of the [Los Angeles] Exposition." *Western Flying* 4 (October 1928): 44-5.

2103. Vedder, Clyde B. "An Analysis of the Taxi-Dance Hall as a Social Institution, with Special Reference to Los Angeles and Detroit." Doctoral dissertation, University of Southern California, 1947. 311 pp.

2104. Wales, R. Ellis. "Success Attends Great Exposition." *Southern California Business* 1 (October 1922): 11-2+.
Los Angeles Trade Exposition.

2105. Woollett, William L. "Pacific Southwest Exposition." *Los Angeles Saturday Night* 8 (August 25, 1928): 5.
Long Beach.

2106. Wyler, Lorraine. "Glimpses of the Los Angeles County Fair." *Los Angeles Saturday Night* 10 (September 20, 1930): 17.

CULTURE—THEATRE

2107. Allen, John A. "A Study of the Theatre in Relation to the Welfare of Los Angeles [1859-1912]." Master's thesis, University of Southern California, 1912. 44 pp.

2108. Ballantine, Bill. "Turnabout Theatre." *Holiday* 8 (September 1950): 11+
Combination marionette and live variety show, Hollywood.

2109. Barnett, Martha. "A Historical Sketch of the Professional Theater in the City of Los Angeles to 1911." Master's thesis, University of Southern California, 1930. 67 pp.

2110. Bartlett, Randolph. "Combining the Stock Companies." *Out West,* new series, 2 (July 1911): 73-9.
Theatrical enterprises, Los Angeles.

2111. Braden, George W. "Municipal and School Outdoor Theatres in California." *American City*
Includes Little Lattice Playhouse, Hollywood; Occidental College Hillside Theatre; Pomona College Greek Theatre.

2112. Claus, Cynthia. "The Pasadena Play House." *Apartment Journal* 18 (June 1936): 10-1+.

2113. Day, Harriett. " 'Back Stage' of the Pilgrim-age Play." *Saturday Night* 4 (August 25, 1923): 5+.
Hollywood.

2114. Dowling, Paul H. "The Masque of the Nativity: A Triumph in Municipal Pageantry." *American City* 15 (December 1916): 655-7.
"Story of the Nativity" presented at Exposition Park "by volunteer actors and singers before 15,000 people of Los Angeles."

2115. Doyle, Katherine. "A Real Home for the Pilgrimage Play." *Southern California Business* 10 (June 1931): 16.
Hollywood.

2116. Duncan, Ray "The Four Seasons: There's a New Theatre at the End of Every Freeway This Summer, But the Boom in the Suburbs Has Created a Raging Theatrical Controversy Downtown." *Los Angeles* 7 (June 1964): 30-4+

2117. Eckley, Dan M. "The World's Longest Run; A Descriptive and Analytical Study of the Los Angeles Theatre Mart's Twenty-Six Years of Continuous Production of the 'The Drunkard,' and Its Musical Companion, 'The Wayward Way.' " Master's thesis, University of California, Los Angeles, 1962. 193 pp.

2118. Feigelman, Miriam. "Pasadena Playhouse." *Apartment Journal* 21 (July 1938): 18+.

2119. Fitzgerald, Thomas E. "An Historical Study of the Formation, Growth, and Development of the Downey Children's Theatre." Master's thesis, University of California, Los Angeles, 1969. 131 pp.

2120. Foote, Robert O. "Epoch-Marking Pasadena Community Playhouse." *Saturday Night* 5 (May 16, 1925): 1-2.

2121. Gartler, Ruth M. "A Historical Study of the Mason Operahouse in Los Angeles." Master's thesis, University of California, Los Angeles, 1966. 88 pp.

2122. Greene, Patterson. "Professional Theatre on Campus." *Theatre Arts* 47 (February 1963): 62-3+.
Theatre Group makes use of UCLA facilities.

2123. Grey, Elmer. "The Romance of the Pasadena Community Playhouse." *The Architect and Engineer* 97 (June 1929): 61-5.

2124. Griffith, Van M. "A Greek Theatre with Modern Improvements." *American City* 41 (November 1929): 145-6.
Los Angeles.

2125. ——— "Los Angeles Park Commission Plans New Greek Theatre." *Pacific Municipalities* 43 (September 1929): 368+.

2126. "Griffith Park's Greek Theatre." *Los Angeles Saturday Night* 9 (June 1, 1929): 20.
Theatre plans announced.

2127. Hilberman, David. "The Production Design and Lighting of the UCLA Opera Workshop Production of the Mother of Us All." Master's thesis, University of California, Los Angeles, 1965. 87 pp.

2128. Holcomb, Robert. "The Federal Theatre in Los Angeles." *California Historical Society Quarterly* 41 (1962): 131-47.

2129. ——— "The Federal Theatre in the Los Angeles Area [1935-1939]." Master's thesis, University of Southern California, 1956. 108 pp.

2130. Holden, O. W. "Marvelous Acoustics Found in Greek Theater." *Pacific Municipalities* 46 (May 1932): 169-70.
Los Angeles.

2131. Holland, Jack. "An Historical Study of Ken Murray's 'Blackouts'." Master's thesis, University of California, Los Angeles, 1961. 149 pp.
Hollywood.

2132. *Hollywood Play House*. [Los Angeles, n.d.]. 32 pp.

2133. "Hollywood's New Theatre." *Saturday Night* 6 (April 17, 1926): 1-2.
El Capitan.

2134. Hook, Ted. "Los Angeles' Civic Theatre Invites the Ballet." *Dance Magazine* 27 (April 1953): 30.

2135. Jones, Earl H. "The History of the Pilgrimage Play: 1920-1929." Master's thesis, University of California, Los Angeles, 1965. 144 pp.
Los Angeles.

2136. Kelly, Richard J. "A History of the Los Angeles Greek Theatre under the Management of James A. Doolittle and the Los Angeles Greek Theatre Association 1952-1969: The Professional Theatre Producer as a Lessee of City Government." Doctoral dissertation, University of Southern California, 1970. 420 pp.

2137. Kenefick, Ruth M. "The Power and Position of the Spanish and Mexican Folk Dance in Southern California." Master's thesis, Claremont Graduate School, 1936. 69 pp.

2138. Knight, Emerson. "Outdoor Theatres and Stadiums in the West." *The Architect and Engineer* 78 (August 1924): 53-92.
Includes many in Los Angeles area, such as Hollywood Bowl, Rose Bowl, and Exposition Park.

2139. Korf, Jean P. "The Use of Standard Theatrical Skills in the Presentation of Three Short Scenes Acted by Patients of the Brentwood Neuropsychiatric Hospital." Master's thesis, University of California, Los Angeles, 1956. 221 pp.

2140. Lawrence, Jodi. "The Method Goes West." *Los Angeles* 13 (May 1968): 46-53.
Actors Studio West in Hollywood.

2141. Lewis, Madalynne (Solomon). "Some Mexican Folk Dances as Found in Los Angeles, California." Master's thesis, University of California, Los Angeles, 1941. 209 pp.

2142. Litle, Selma E. "The Padua Hills Project Introduces Mexican Folk Lore into California Culture." Master's thesis, University of California, Los Angeles, 1943. 40 pp.

2143. Litle, Velma. "A Study of the Significance of Folk Dances of Three National Dance Groups in Los Angeles." Master's thesis, University of California, Los Angeles, 1943. 47 pp.
Swedish, Czechoslovakian, and Hungarian.

2144. "Los Angeles to Have Greek Theatre." *Playground and Recreation* 23 (January 1930): 630+.
Description of financing and facilities.

2145. Lowman, J. J. "Little Theatres Now in Vogue." *Saturday Night* 4 (June 16, 1923): 17.
Los Angeles.

2146. Luitjens, Helen. "The Contribution of Puppetry to the Art Life of Los Angeles [1859-1943]."

Master's thesis, University of Southern California, 1943. 121 pp.

2147. Lynch, Samuel D. "Theaters under the Stars." *Westways* 53 (July 1961): 4-7.
Outdoor theatres in Southern California.

2148. Maxwell, Everett C. "A Modern Miracle— The Pasadena Community Playhouse." *Overland Monthly* 90 (August 1932): 175.

2149. McKim, Paul N. "A Survey of the Federal Theatre Project of Los Angeles — 1936-1938 — As Observed in the Los Angeles *Examiner* and Los Angeles *Times*." Master's thesis, University of California, Los Angeles, 1953. 392 pp.

2150. Merenbach, Eula S. "The Value and Use of Religious Drama in Certain Selected Churches in Los Angeles." Master's thesis, University of Southern California, 1935. 124 pp.

2151. Merken, Helen J. "A History of the Turnabout Theater." Master's thesis, University of California, Los Angeles, 1967. 167 pp.
Hollywood.

2152. Miller, John. "Vertical Signs in a Horizontal City." *Marquee* 2 (December 1970): 3-5.
Motion picture theater signs in Los Angeles.

2153. Mouring, Muriel A. "Henry 'Terry' Duffy: The West-Coast's Leading Actor Producer." Master's thesis, University of California, Los Angeles, 1969. 112 pp.

2154. "Outdoor Matinees for Children." *Recreation* 34 (May 1940): 99-100.
Summer matinees at municipal playgrounds presented by the Los Angeles Department of Playground and Recreation.

2155. Owen, J. Thomas. "The Theatre in Los Angeles." *Museum Alliance Quarterly* 1 (1963): 32-7.

2156. "Pasadena Community Players." *Saturday Night* 7 (May 7, 1927): 2.
The new Pasadena Playhouse after two years of operation.

2157. "Pasadena the Scene of Unique Dramatic Festival." *Los Angeles Saturday Night* 15 (May 18, 1935): 4.
Inauguration of annual Midsummer Drama Festival at Pasadena Playhouse.

2158. Pederson, La Delle. "The Long Beach Community Players, 1929-1968." Master's thesis, California State College at Long Beach, 1968. 201 pp.

2159. Peters, Charles F. "A Historical Survey of the Biltmore Theater." Master's thesis, California State College at Long Beach, 1969. 313 pp.
Los Angeles.

2160. "Pilgrimage Play Attracts Tourists to Los Angeles." *Southern California Business* 1 (July 1922): 42.

2161. Pontius, D. W. "New Home of the Mission Play." *Southern California Business* 6 (April 1927): 30.
Mission Playhouse, San Gabriel.

2162. "Preparing for 'The Miracle'." *Southern California Business* 5 (December 1926): 26+.
"Super-Pageant-Drama" staged at Los Angeles Shrine Auditorium.

2163. Rickner, Don L. "Turnabout Theatre, Hollywood, 1941-1956." Master's thesis, California State College, Fullerton, 1966. 200 pp.

2164. Salvi, Delia N. "The History of the Actor's Laboratory, Inc." Doctoral dissertation, University of California, Los Angeles, 1969. 340 pp.
Hollywood theatrical group, 1941-1950.

2165. "Santa Monica—The City of the Christmas Story." *American City* 73 (December 1958): 71-2+.
Dramatization of Christmas story.

2166. Schallert, Edwin. "Famous American Theatres." *Theatre Arts* 41 (April 1957): 64.
Biltmore Theatre, Los Angeles.

2167. ———— "Los Angeles: A Retarded Destiny." *Theatre Arts* 40 (June 1956): 72-3+.

2168. Scheff, Aimee. "Leontovich Builds a California Theatre." *Theatre Arts* 36 (May 1952): 100.
Eugenie Leontovich and her studio-workshop on La Cienega.

2169. Seiler, Conrad. "Los Angeles Must Be Kept Pure." *Nation* 122 (May 19, 1926): 548-9.
Sarcastic account of arrest and prosecution of actors in Los Angeles production of O'Neill's "Desire Under the Elms."

2170. Simpson, Margaret H. "Padua Hills Mexican Theater: An Experiment in Inter-Cultural Relations." Master's thesis, Claremont Graduate School, 1944. 83 pp.

2171. "Sixth Season of America's 'Passion Play'." *Saturday Night* 5 (June 27, 1925): 1.

History and description of Hollywood Pilgrimage Play.

2172. Sorrels, Roy W. "The Los Angeles Theatre Activities of Oliver Morosco." Master's thesis, California State College at Long Beach, 1966. 138 pp.

2173. Steckhan, H. O. "Genuine Producing Theatre for Los Angeles." *California Graphic* 5 (October 15, 1927): 10+.

Henry Kolker's work on a Los Angeles theatre.

2174. Swisher, V. H. "UCLA's Committee on Fine Arts Productions Brings Performances to School and Community." *Dance Magazine* 41 (June 1967): 33-5.

2175. "Theatrical." *Out West,* new series, 1 (December 1910): 37-40.

Los Angeles described as "best show town" west of Chicago.

2176. Thomas, Dwight, and Griepenkerl, Mary G. "Pelican Productions." *Theatre Arts* 31 (December 1947): 68-70.

Organization founded by John Houseman to present plays at Coronet Theatre, Los Angeles.

2177. Thünen, Frances H. "A Historical Study of the Circle, the Players' Ring and the Players' Ring Gallery Theatres in Hollywood from 1945-1966." Master's thesis, University of Southern California, 1968. 445 pp.

2178. Williamson, C. J. S. "Los Angeles Dedicates New $200,000 Greek Theatre." *Western City* 6 (November 1930): 12-4.

2179. Wright, Willard H. "The Mission Play: A Pageant of the History of the Franciscan Missions in California." *Sunset* 29 (July 1912): 93-100.

San Gabriel.

2180. Zolotow, Maurice. "Land of Nod." *Theatre Arts* 40 (April 1956): 73-4+.

A critical analysis of theatre in Los Angeles.

DESCRIPTION AND TRAVEL

2181. Abbe, Patience; Abbe, Richard and Abbe, Johnny. *Of All Places!* New York, 1937. 233 pp.

Los Angeles.

2182. [Abbott, James W.]. *Among Cities Los Angeles Is the World's Greatest Wonder—Why?* [Los Angeles, 1914]. 32 pp.

2183. Adair, Charles H. *The Long Beach Story; Some Delineating Words and Drawings about a Western Pueblo and How It Became an Eventful City by the Sea.* Long Beach, 1963. Unp.

2184. ———— *Los Angeles, the Miracle City.* Los Angeles, 1931. 33 pp.

2185. Adamic, Louis. "Los Angeles! There She Blows!" *Outlook and Independent* 155 (August 13, 1930): 563-5+.

2186. ———— *The Truth about Los Angeles.* Girard, Kan., c1927. 64 pp.

2187. Adler, Pat[ricia]. "Watts: A Legacy of Lines." *Westways* 58 (August 1966): 22-4.

2188. Adler, Renata. "A Reporter at Large: Fly Trans-Love Airways." *New Yorker* 43 (February 25, 1967): 116+.

Sunset Strip.

2189. Alderman, Frances L., and Wilson, Amber M. *About Los Angeles.* Boston, 1948. 313 pp.

2190. Alhambra. Board of Trade. *Alhambra, the Gateway to the San Gabriel Valley.* [Alhambra?, 1909]. [16] pp.

2191. ————. Chamber of Commerce. *Descriptive Booklet of the City of Alhambra.* Los Angeles, 1915. 31 pp.

2192. *Alhambra, California.* Beverly Hills, 1964. 36 pp.

2193. "Anatomy of a Super City." *Los Angeles* 12 (October 1967): 24-30.

Los Angeles.

2194. Anderson, J. Lee. "Hollywood: The Myth Becomes a City." *Los Angeles* 7 (February 1964): 28-31+.

2195. "Army Guns Open Up at Unknown 'Foe.'" *Life* 12 (March 9, 1942): 22-3.

Enemy aircraft scare over Los Angeles, February 25, 1942.

2196. Atwood, Albert W. "Money from Everywhere." *Saturday Evening Post* 195 (May 12, 1923): 10-1+.

Los Angeles boom of 1920s "very closely connected with the golden inflow from the outside." The people who make up this inflow described as being, to a large extent, "a huge, aimless, idle mob, milling about in search of amusement."

2197. Augsburg, Paul D. *Advertising Did It! The Story of Los Angeles*. 4th ed., Los Angeles, [c1922]. 11 pp.

2198. Ayres, Harold M. *Redondo Beach on the Rim of the Western Sea*. Redondo Beach, [1914]. 32 pp.

2199. Baker, Faye. "Victor Gruen: 'Maybe It Is All Improvisation.'" *Los Angeles* 4 (November 1962): 30+.

Gruen's observations on Los Angeles.

2200. Banham, Reyner. "L. A. Is - - - Exactly Like London." *Los Angeles* 13 (November 1968): 34-5+.

2201. Barrington, Pauline. "Characters of Vermont Avenue." *Saturday Night* 4 (November 3, 1923): 21+.

2202. ———— "Spring Street, Calla [*sic*] Primavera." *Saturday Night* 4 (May 12, 1923): 16.

2203. ———— "Street of Los Angeles: Broadway." *Saturday Night* 4 (June 23, 1923): 5+.

2204. Bartlett, Dana W. "An Industrial Garden City: Torrance." *American City* 9 (October 1913): 310-4.

2205. Bascomb, Robert. "The Great White Elephant." *Los Angeles* 13 (July 1968): 28-31+.

Catalina Island.

2206. Basso, Hamilton. "Los Angeles." *Holiday* 7 (January 1950): 26-47.

2207. Baugh, Ruth E. "Los Angeles, the Sunshine City." *Home Geographic Monthly* 1 (June 1932): 25-30.

2208. *Beautiful Santa Monica, By-the-sea* . . . [Los Angeles, 1905-06]. [30] pp.

2209. Bell, Charlotte. "Monrovia." *Out West* 24 (May 1906): 471-4.

2210. Benton, Frank W. *Hollywood, California, All the Year*. [Los Angeles, 1922]. [48] pp.

Chiefly pictorial.

2211. ———— *Long Beach, California; Mighty and Magnificent*. Los Angeles, 1924. Unp.

2212. ———— *Semi-Tropic California: The Garden of the World, Including a Concise History of Panama and the Panama Canal, with Map, and the Missions of California*. Los Angeles, 1914. 87 pp.

Includes information on Los Angeles agriculture, commerce, industry, and water development.

2213. Bernard, J. P. *Non-Tourist Los Angeles*. [San Francisco, 1959]. 60 pp.

2214. Berry, Alice E. (Bush). *The Bushes and the Berrys*. Los Angeles, 1941. 183 pp.

Two families that migrated to Los Angeles around the turn of the century; descriptive of many places in the area.

2215. Beverly Hills. Chamber of Commerce. *Beverly Hills, California, Midway Between Los Angeles and the Sea*. [Beverly Hills, 192-?]. [24] pp.

2216. Bicknell, Edmund, comp. *Ralph's Scrapbook: Illustrated by His Own Camera and Collection of Photographs* . . . Lawrence, Mass., 1905. 453 pp.

Pictorial.

2217. Bisby, R. L. "Long Beach; Here's Showing How the Fastest Growing Town Going Grows." *Out West, new series,* 3 (June 1912): 407-17.

This is a booster article hawking not only tourism but the harbor, the Pike, shipbuilding and commerce.

2218. Black, Glenn L. "The Case of the 'Tied' Island." *Westways* 46 (June 1954): 8-9.

Palos Verdes Peninsula.

2219. Bliven, Bruce. "Los Angeles: The City That Is Bacchanalian—In a Nice Way." *New Republic* 51 (July 13, 1927): 197-200.

2220. Bobrow, Robert. "Calabasas: Growing Out of Its Gourd." *Westways* 61 (February 1969): 16-9.

2221. ———— "El Segundo—Second to None?" *Westways* 59 (July 1967): 13-5.

2222. ———— "Long Beach: Has Iowa Lost Its Port?" *Westways* 60 (January 1968): 16-9.

2223. ———— "Redondo Beach: Renaissance on the South Bay." *Westways* 59 (December 1967): 28-31.

2224. ———— "San Gabriel—The Ancestral Egg." *Westways* 58 (September 1966): 2-4.

2225. ———— "San Pedro: New Season for an Old Salt." *Westways* 60 (November 1968): 28-30.

2226. ———— "Will Cybernetics Spoil Los Angeles?" *Westways* 57 (June 1965): 6-8+.

A number of quotations that embody diverse opinions on Los Angeles.

2227. ———— "Wilshire Boulevard: A Profile." *Westways* 54 (April 1964): 5-8; (May 1964): 3-6.

2228. Breeden, Marshall. *The Romantic Southland of California*. Los Angeles, 1928. 207 pp.

Includes the region south of Santa Barbara and Bakersfield, with more than 1,000 California place names defined.

2229. Brilliant, Ashleigh E. "Some Aspects of Mass Motorization in Southern California, 1919-1929." *Southern California Quarterly* 47 (1965): 191-206.

A study of variant attitudes of motorist, pedestrian, and police as the car culture of Los Angeles took shape.

2230. Brison, J. Oliver. "Long Beach—'The California Riviera.' " *Pacific Municipalities* 39 (January 1925): 5-7.

2231. Bristol, William M. "Encompassing Mount San Antonio." *Touring Topics* 8 (January 1917): 10-4.

2232. Broke, W. S. "Preserving Historical Data." *Out West, new series,* 2 (July 1911): 65-72.

A plea for efforts to discover and preserve early photographs of Los Angeles, along with some comparative photos of certain sites showing how they have changed since the 1880s.

2233. Brook, Harry E. *Los Angeles, California. The City and County.* Los Angeles, 1924. 78 pp.

2234. [————]. *Los Angeles, the Chicago of the Southwest.* Los Angeles, 1904. 16 pp.

2235. Buhrman, Robert. "Calling the Queen Mary . . . Can You Hear Us? Please Acknowledge." *Los Angeles* 15 (July 1970): 38-41+.

Long Beach and the *Queen Mary,* a prospective museum and tourist attraction.

2236. *Burbank, California.* Encino, 1970. 72 pp.

2237. Burdick, Eugene "The Sun and Its Worshipers: The World of Los Angeles Revolves Around the Sun, Which All Year Long Tans, Tranquilizes, Titillates Its Gilded Young and Old." *Holiday* 22 (October 1957): 64-7+.

2238. Busch, Noel F. "The San Fernando Valley." *Holiday* 10 (December 1951): 108-15+.

Mainly about movie stars and restaurants, but includes a brief historical account.

2239. Bush, Elizabeth. "Venice of America." *Semi-Tropical California* 8 (July 1918): 9-15.

2240. Butterfield, Roger. "Los Angeles Is the Damdest Place . . . The City That Started with Nothing But Sunshine Now Expects to Become the Biggest in the World." *Life* 15 (November 22, 1943): 102-4+.

Historical sketch of Los Angeles from 1781, statistics on business and industry, and an enumeration of salient contemporary characteristics.

2241. "By the Crescent's Shimmering Sands." *Touring Topics* 14 (April 1922): 28-9+.

Santa Monica.

2242. "California: The Pink Oasis." *Time* 54 (July 4, 1949): 5-15.

Also contains biographical data on Mayor Fletcher Bowron.

2243. *Canoga Park, California.* [Beverly Hills, 1964?]. 44 pp.

2244. Carr, Harry. "Is Los Angeles Worth Defending? Congress, the Navy and the General Staff Say 'No'—What Does the Pacific Coast Say?" *Sunset* 38 (February 1917): 9-12.

2245. —— *Los Angeles: City of Dreams.* New York, 1935. 403 pp.
Romantic, sketchy, journalistic style.

2246. Carson, Robert. " 'Upper' Los Angeles." *Los Angeles* 11 (January 1966): 56-8+.
Los Angeles' westside.

2247. Cassatt, Jay D. "Santa Monica. To Become America's Finest Resort and All-the-Year-Round Home Place." *Out West,* new series, 6 (July-August 1913): 47-9.

2248. "Catalina a Popular Vacation Land." *Los Angeles Realtor* 4 (May 1925): 31-2.

2249. "Catalina, the Play-Isle of the Pacific." *Los Angeles Saturday Night* 10 (June 7, 1930): 7.
Another similar description appears in volume 11 (December 27, 1930): 7.

2250. Channing, Grace E. "The Meeting of Extremes." *Out West* 19 (September 1903): 239-49.
Compares Los Angeles to Rome.

2251. Chanslor, Roy. "San Fernando Valley." *Holiday* 22 (October 1957): 82-3.

2252. Chapman, John L. *Incredible Los Angeles.* New York, 1967. 271 pp.

2253. "Circling San Fernando Valley." *Touring Topics* 24 (May 1932): 27.

2254. "The City of Los Angeles." *Journal of National Educational Association* 19 (December 1930): 293-6.
General description.

2255. *City of Rosemead.* [Beverly Hills, 1964?]. Unp.

2256. "City of the Angeles: It's Still an Age of Miracles." *Newsweek* 42 (August 3, 1953): 64-6.
Various facets of Los Angeles' growth.

2257. Clarke, Maurice. "The Phenomenon by the Pacific—Los Angeles County." *Westways* 42 (May 1950): 8-10.

2258. Claus, Cynthia. "Japanese Ghost Town." Subtitle: " 'Little Tokyo' in Los Angeles, as foreign as the city for which it was named . . ." *Apartment Journal* 24 (May 1942): 8+.

2259. Climie, Margaret S. "Southern California in American Fiction." Master's thesis, University of Southern California, 1925. 138 pp.

2260. Clover, Sam T. "Seventh Street: Our Fifth Avenue." *Saturday Night* 5 (September 26, 1925): 2.
Los Angeles.

2261. Clyde, Norman. "Over the Crests of Southland Urban Mountains: The Chronicle of a Mountaineer's Jaunt Along the Summits of the Peaks That Encircle Metropolitan Southern California." *Touring Topics* 24 (April 1932): 10-21+.

2262. Collins, James H. "Los Angeles: Ex-Crossroads Town." *World's Work* 59 (August 1930): 53-6+.

2263. *Compton, California.* Encino, 1969. [41] pp.

2264. Comstock, Sarah. "The Great American Mirror: Reflections from Los Angeles." *Harper's Monthly* 156 (May 1928): 715-23.
Author spent "several weeks in observing with evergrowing wonder this astonishing American city." Discusses Los Angeles as "The Paradise of the Corn Belt," bizarre architecture, wierd religion, "Blood-Red Eucalyptus in Bloom," educational institutions, and other topics.

2265. Consigny, Jean Marie. "San Rafael." *Saturday Night* 45 (September 10, 1938): 26.
Raymond Gould's Pasadena estate.

2266. Coonradt, Frederic. "Can Bombs Wreck L.A.?" *Saturday Night* 44 (October 21, 1937): 5-6.
Possible effects of an air attack on Los Angeles.

2267. Copeland, George D. "Beautiful Hotels and Apartment Houses Legion in Film Capital." *Los Angeles Realtor* 6 (November 1926): 30-1.
Hollywood.

2268. Cotton, Zola V. "Montebello, the City of Flowers." *Pacific Municipalities* 43 (October 1929): 439-41.

2269. Crossman, Carl D. *Alhambra Booster Book; A Guide for Newcomers.* [Alhambra, c1932]. 20 pp.

2270. Croswell, Mary E. *Story of Hollywood.* Hollywood, 1905. 34 pp.

2271. *Culver City, California.* Beverly Hills, [1964?]. 24 pp.

2272. Daggett, C. D. "Pasadena, the City of Homes." *Land of Sunshine* 14 (April 1901): 345-60.

2273. Daingerfield, Rex. "The Tourist in Glamourland." *Los Angeles* 2 (August 1961): 29-31.
Hollywood tourism.

2274. Dame, John B. "California's Venice." *Sunset* 16 (November 1905): 32-6.

2275. ——— "Under Pasadena's Palms." *Sunset* 16 (February 1906): 360-5.

2276. Damon, George A. *Picturesque Pasadena.* [Pasadena, 19-?]. 55 pp.

2277. Davenport, Charles. "The Look of the City, Is Beauty within Reach?" *Los Angeles* 3 (April 1962): 18-27.

2278. Davis, Charles F., pub. *Picturesque Monrovia.* [Monrovia, 1929]. 64 pp.

2279. Davis, Harold H., ed. *This Is Claremont.* Claremont, 1941. 147 pp.

2280. Decker, Charles E., comp. *Altadena "the Beautiful." "The Paradise of the Foothills."* [Altadena, 1926]. 48 pp.

2281. Deegan, Robert E. "The Unclosed Frontier." *American* 98 (February 8, 1958): 534-6.
Enumerates certain concepts necessary to an understanding of the Los Angeles metropolitan area, such as "Growth & Change," and "Motion on Wheels."

2282. DeRoos, Robert. "Los Angeles." *National Geographic Magazine* 122 (October 1962): 451-501.

2283. "A Designer's Sight-Seeing in Los Angeles." *Interiors* 119 (April 1960): 124-7.

2284. DeWolfe, Terry E. "A Fearless Walk from Venice to Glendale." *Los Angeles* 14 (August 1969): 40-3.

2285. Dezendorf, Alfred. "In Sunshine and Surf." *Sunset* 10 (December 1902): 150-3.
Long Beach.

2286. Diamond, Susan J. "The Umbrellas of Los Angeles." *Los Angeles* 13 (August 1968): 28-31+.
Jacques Demy's film about Los Angeles.

2287. Dickert, Lois. "The Los Angeles Career Girl." *Los Angeles* 8 (November 1964): 26-31+.

2288. Division News Company, Los Angeles. *Picturesque Santa Catalina Island; Photogravures.* Los Angeles, 1900. 137 pp.

2289. Dole, Arthur M. "How Los Angeles Grows." *Sunset* 16 (December 1905): 176-88.

2290. *Downey, California.* Beverly Hills, 1966. 48 pp.

2291. Duncan, Gerald. "The San Fernando: Valley of Surprises." *Coronet* 29 (March 1951): 92-5.

2292. Duncan, Ray. "Pasadena: The Old Order Changeth." *Los Angeles* 6 (December 1963): 34+.

2293. Edholm, Charlton L. "The Seaward Suburbs of Los Angeles." *Out West* 30 (May 1909): 423-65.

2294. *El Monte—South El Monte.* Beverly Hills, 1968. 64 pp.

2295. "The Environment." *Los Angeles* 12 (January 1967): 27-31.
Comments on such topics as smog, population, transportation, and industry.

2296. "The Face of L.A.—1970: Ten Years from Today, Los Angeles Will Have a Dramatic New Shape, Form and Face and a Whole New Set of Problems." *Southern California Prompter* 1 (September 1960): 16-9.

2297. Fadiman, Clifton. "Mining-Camp Megalopolis: Sprawling, Brawling, Galling Los Angeles Makes Pleasure a Business and Plays at Working Hard." *Holiday* 38 (October 1965): 8+.

2298. Fairfield, S. M. "San Fernando." *Out West* 26 (January 1907): 95-100.

2299. "The Far Country." *Time* 86 (September 24, 1965): 23-4.
Watts.

2300. Fessier, Mike, Jr. "Walden Pond: Malibou [*sic*] Annex." *Los Angeles* 11 (August 1966): 38-9.
Two hidden lake communities, Lake Malibou [*sic*] and Lake Sherwood.

2301. Findlay, Bruce A. "What'll Folks Read

About Los Angeles?" *Southern California Business* 11 (November 1932): 10-1.
Most popular topics for Los Angeles publicity.

2302. Forbes, B. C. "Cities in the Making." *Overland Monthly* 88 (October 1930): 305+.
Includes prophecies on future of Los Angeles.

2303. "Four Seashore Capitals." *Touring Topics* 14 (August 1922): 25+.
Includes Naples and Alamitos Bay.

2304. "14 Resolutions for Los Angeles: What Does the City Need Most in 1961?" *Southern California Prompter* 2 (Holiday Issue [December 1960 and January 1961]): 16-8.

2305. Fox, Christy. "Los Angeles Beckons." *Independent Woman* 19 (December 1940): 392-3.
Points of interest in Los Angeles and vicinity, for delegates to 1940 Convention of National Federation of Business and Professional Woman's Clubs, Inc.

2306. Friend, Herve. *Redondo Hotel and Vicinity; 16 Miles from Los Angeles, Redondo Beach, California*. Los Angeles, [19-?]. [24] pp.

2307. "From All Quarters They Come to Us: Tourists Pour into Los Angeles and the Southland at the Rate of More Than 100,000 a Month, Many of Them to Remain Here." *Southern California Business* 2 (February 1923): 21.

2308. "From Los Angeles of 1952 to Los Angeles of 2052." *American City* 67 (May 1952): 7.
Mayor Bowron presides at burying of time capsule at Pershing Square.

2309. Gage, Harriet H. "Long Beach." *Out West* 23 (December 1905): 613-24.

2310. Garrett, Garet. "Los Angeles in Fact and Dream." *Saturday Evening Post* 203 (October 18, 1930): 6-7+.

2311. Gates, Charles F. "Automobile Pioneering in Los Angeles." *Touring Topics* 12 (January 1920): 16-7+.
Mainly about attempts to set intercity speed records.

2312. Gates, Eleanor. "Pasadena—Paradise Regained: Terrestrial Elysium of Gold and Gardens in the Land of Winter Roses—Heavenly Abode Between Snowpeaks and Orange Groves—'Mid Pleasures and Palaces There's No Place Like Home Except a Pasadena Bungalow." *Sunset* 27 (December 1911): 603-16.

2313. Gibbon, Thomas E. "The Future Progress of Los Angeles." *Out West*, new series, 6 (September 1913): 115-23.

2314. Gilbert, Leland R. "Azusa-California: Prosperous City of Southland." *Pacific Municipalities* 45 (March 1931): 121-3.

2315. Gilbert, Richard. *City of the Angels*. London, 1964. 221 pp.
A young Englishman's account of Los Angeles as it appeared to him while he was in residence at UCLA.

2316. *Glendale, California, the Jewel City*. Glendale, [1912?]. 44 pp.

2317. Glendale Merchants Association. *Glendale, Your Home*. Glendale, 1928. 52 pp.

2318. Gray, Arthur L., Jr. "Los Angeles: Urban Prototype." *Land Economics* 35 (1959): 232-42.
"The Los Angeles region demonstrates great significance as the progenitor of urban change throughout the United States."

2319. *Greater Los Angeles Illustrated*. [Los Angeles, 1907?]. 192 pp.

2320. Griffith, Alfred P. "Azusa the Canyon City." *Out West*, new series, 3 (March 1912): [202]-7.

2321. "Growth 'Normal' in L. A. Area." *Business Week* (February 22, 1941): 22+.

2322. Hamilton, Andrew. "Our Number One Name-Caller." *Westways* 57 (June 1965): 20-1.
Edmund Passler of the Los Angeles Bureau of Engineering, whose job it is to select 150-200 new street names annually.

2323. Hampton, Edgar L. "Los Angeles, a Miracle City." *Current History* 24 (April 1926): 35-42.
Laudatory description.

2324. Hanna, Hugh S. "The Llano del Rio Cooperative Colony." *Monthly Review of the U. S. Bureau of Labor Statistics* 2 (January 1916): 19-23.

2325. Hannau, Hans W. *Los Angeles.* Garden City, 1967. 59 pp.
Pictorial.

2326. Harmon, Ginger. "The Downtowners' Guide to Downtown." *Los Angeles* 15 (December 1970): 46-8.
Los Angeles.

2327. Harris, H[erbert] E. "Whittier." *Out West* 18 (January 1903): 121-36.

2328. ——— *Whittier, California.* Whittier, 1909. 16 pp.

2329. Hart, Lincoln. *"Our Town."* [Los Angeles], 1942. 55 pp.

2330. Hashem, Edfan A. "Development of the University Neighborhood; The University of Southern California." Master's thesis, University of Southern California, 1954. 177 pp.
Los Angeles.

2331. Hawthorne, Hildegarde. *Romantic Cities of California.* New York, 1939. 456 pp.
Included are Long Beach, Los Angeles, Hollywood, and Pasadena.

2332. Heald, Weldon F. "The Happy Land." *Westways* 44 (August 1952): 8-9.
Los Angeles at the turn of the century.

2333. Heisley, George D. "Seeing America." *Out West* 30 (February-March 1909): [193-225].
Los Angeles.

2334. Henselman, Frances. "Your 1954 Convention City: Long Beach: 'Bay of the Smokes.'" *California Librarian* 14 (June 1954): 216-7.

2335. Herrick, Elisabeth W. *Curious California Customs.* Los Angeles, [c1934]. 110 pp. 2nd ed., [c1935]. 225 pp.

2336. Hillinger, Charles. *The California Islands.* Los Angeles, 1958. 165 pp.
Santa Catalina Island, pp. 29-69. Part of the material in this book originally appeared in the Los Angeles *Times.*

2337. Hine, Al. "Millionaires' Manor." *Holiday* 10 (August 1951): 98-103.
Hotel Bel-Air, Los Angeles.

2338. Hollywood. Board of Trade. "Hollywood, the City of Homes." *Out West* 21 (July 1904): 97-112.

2339. "Hollywood—Los Angeles Other Half." *Los Angeles Realtor* 7 (November 1927): 35-9+.

2340. Holmes, Roger. "Venice—Abbott Kinney's Dream City." *Westways* 49 (November 1957): 6-7.

2341. Hopkins, Una N. "The Señorita at the Gateway: Los Angeles." *Craftsman* 28 (May 1915): 172-8.

2342. Hosmer, Helen. "Arrivederci, Venice." *American West* 5 (March 1968): 43-8.
Brief childhood recollection.

2343. Hoy, Eugene. *So This is Glendale.* Glendale, c1939. Unp.

2344. Hunter, Sherley. *Why Los Angeles Will Become the World's Greatest City.* Los Angeles, 1923. 42 pp.

2345. Industrial Association of the San Fernando Valley. *San Fernando Valley, Los Angeles, California.* North Hollywood, 1965. 1 vol. Unp.
Cities and towns in San Fernando Valley.

2346. Inglewood. Board of Trade. *Inglewood: The City That Grows.* Inglewood, 1910. 32 pp.

2347. Isenberg, Irwin, ed. *The City in Crisis.* New York, 1968. 246 pp.
Contains two essays on Los Angeles: "Watts—'Remarkably the Same,'" by John C. Waugh, pp. 50-4, and "On-the-Spot in Watts," by Anne Henehan, pp. 54-63.

2348. James, George W. "From Alpine Snow to Semi-Tropical Sea. A New Year's Day Journey in Southern California." *Out West,* new series, 4 (December 1912): 370-6.
Pasadena to Long Beach.

2349. ——— "Los Angeles, a Moral City." *Out West,* new series, 5 (March-April 1913): 199-210.

2350. ——— "Pasadena the City of Beautiful Homes." *Out West,* new series, 4 (December 1912): 397-411.

2351. James, Warren B. "Saturday Night: Diary

of a Los Angeles Cabbie." *Los Angeles* 14 (November 1969): 46-8+.

2352. Jarmuth, John. "Glendora the Magic City." *Southern California Business* 3 (August 1924): 10+.

2353. Jillson, E. R. "Ocean Park. What, Where and Why." *Out West* 24 (April 1906): 355-62.

2354. Jones, E. S. "The Work of Dressing Up a City." *Southern California Business* 7 (November 1928): 24-5+.
Decorating Los Angeles for various conventions.

2355. Jones, J. A. "Glendora." *Out West*, new series, 3 (March 1912): [208]-10.

2356. Jones, Jack. *The View from Watts.* [N.p., 1965?]. [28] pp.
Reprint of a series of articles from the Los Angeles *Times*, October 1965.

2357. ———— *The View from Watts Today.* [N.p., 1967?]. [28] pp.
Reprint of a series of articles from the Los Angeles *Times*, July 1967.

2358. Keeler, Charles A. *Southern California.* Los Angeles, [1902]. 139 pp.

2359. Kellogg (W. K.) Arabian Horse Ranch, Pomona. *The Romance of Pomona Ranch.* [Np., n.d.]. 32 pp.

2360. Kendall, Sidney C. *Long Beach, California.* Long Beach, [c1905]. 59 pp.

2361. ———— "Long Beach. The City by the Sea." *Out West* 18 (June 1903): 783-98.

2362. Kinney, Abbott. "Sanitary Santa Monica." *Sunset* 4 (January 1900): 98-102.
Kinney says that Santa Monica is a very healthful place to live indeed.

2363. Kopp, Glenn, and Miller, Geoff. "Our Backyard Riviera." *Los Angeles* 2 (April 1961): 18-21.
Canals in Southern California: Naples (Long Beach) and Venice.

2364. *Lakewood, California.* [Beverly Hills, 1964]. 28 pp.

2365. Langley, Nancy. "G.I. Santa Anita." *Westways* 35 (December 1943): 12-3.
Santa Anita Racetrack during World War II, first as a Japanese internment center, then as army ordnance training center.

2366. ———— "Venice in Beavers and Bustles." *Westways* 27 (February 1935): 24-5+.
Description of Venice, mostly in the days of Abbott Kinney.

2367. "Lankershim, the Gateway of the San Fernando Valley." *Out West*, new series, 7 (June 1914): 295-6.

2368. Leadabrand, Russ. "From Wrightwood to La Canada." *Westways* 58 (November 1966): 20-2+.

2369. ———— "The Garden on Indian Hill." *Westways* 51 (April 1959): 4-6.
Claremont.

2370. ———— "Let's Explore a Byway—Through the San Fernando and Simi Valleys." *Westways* 54 (December 1962): 13.

2371. ———— "Now the Big T Has a Future." *Westways* 50 (October 1958): 10-1.
Big Tujunga Canyon.

2372. Leonard, J. S. "Monrovia: The Gem of the Foothills." *Out West*, new series, 3 (March 1912): [195]-201.

2373. Lewis, Edward G. *Palos Verdes, Los Angeles.* [Atascadero, 1922?]. 31 pp.

2374. Lewis, Sinclair. "Gold, Inc." *Newsweek* 11 (February 21, 1938): 21.
Author declares that the novelist who can answer "a few million" questions about "the million or two of plain people" in Los Angeles can "make a saga greater than Turgenieff's."

2375. Lilly, Joseph. "Metropolis of the West." *North American Review* 232 (September 1931): 239-45.
Concluding sentence: "I wonder what disconcerts Los Angeles most: the number of crimes or the ruralness of their [sic] character?"

2376. Lindsay, Cynthia (Hobart). *The Natives Are Restless.* Philadelphia and New York, 1960. 223 pp.
Discusses and emphasizes the bizarre in the Los

Angeles area. Published abroad under the title, *The Climate of Lunacy; An Unnatural History of Southern California.* London, [c1960]. 174 pp.

2377. "Living Atop a Civic Mushroom." *Newsweek* 49 (April 1, 1957): 36-42.
Los Angeles and its relentless horizontal diffusion, the epitome of "the newly emerged suburban way of life."

2378. Llewellyn, F. "Pomona." *Out West* 18 (March 1903): 397-412.

2379. "Long Beach." *Out West* 17 (July 1902): 137.

2380. "Long Beach Auditorium Disaster." *Engineering Record* 67 (June 7, 1913): 628-9.
Thirty-four killed in floor collapse of auditorium on municipal pier.

2381. Long Beach. Board of Trade. *Souvenir of Long Beach.* Long Beach and Los Angeles, 1900. Unp.

2382. ———. Chamber of Commerce. *Long Beach; A Descriptive and Statistical Manual.* Long Beach, 1932. 82 pp.

2383. ———. Municipal Convention and Publicity Bureau. *Long Beach, California . . . 50th Anniversary, Xth Olympiad Souvenir.* Long Beach, 193[3]. 23 pp.

2384. "Long Beach—the Surprising." *Touring Topics* 14 (July 1922): 27-8.

2385. Los Angeles. Chamber of Commerce. *Los Angeles and Vicinity.* Los Angeles, 1904. Unp.

2386. ——— *Los Angeles County, California.* Los Angeles, 1925. 59 pp.

2387. ———. Research Committee. *From Ciudad to Metropolis; Research Reveals the 60-Year Progress of Los Angeles in Twenty-One Aspects.* Los Angeles, 1948. [43] pp.

2388. Los Angeles County. Chamber of Commerce. *Know Los Angeles County: Communities, Wealth, History, Features, Economic Trends.* Los Angeles, 1938. 81 pp. 2nd ed., [c1939]. Prepared by William J. Dunkerley under the direction of Leonard E. Read. 76 pp.

2389. ——— *Los Angeles County, California: Claremont Edition.* Los Angeles, 1923. 24 pp.

2390. ——— *Los Angeles County, California: Eagle Rock Edition.* Los Angeles, c1933. 64 pp.

2391. ——— *Los Angeles: "The Magic City and County."* Los Angeles, 1951. 48 pp.

2392. ——— *A Summer Tourist in Southern California: Huntington Park Edition.* Los Angeles, 1931. [48] pp.

2393. Los Angeles Examiner. *What About Los Angeles?* Los Angeles, 1920. 25 pp.

2394. Los Angeles Morning Herald. *Land of Heart's Desire, Southern California, Its People, Homes and Pleasures, Art and Architecture.* Los Angeles, 1911. 117 pp.

2395. "Los Angeles at 160." *Newsweek* 18 (September 15, 1941): 16-7.

2396. "Los Angeles: Center of Vulgarity." *Esquire* 66 (December 1966): 178-9.
"Clippings for a doomsday book"—excerpts from various periodicals.

2397. *Los Angeles, the Metropolis of the West.* [N.p., c1929]. 32 pp.

2398. *Los Angeles, the Old and the New.* [Los Angeles, 1911]. 96 pp.
Supplement to *Western Insurance News* 8, No. 12 (1911). Los Angeles in 1910-11.

2399. *Los Angeles, the Wonder City; A Pictorial Representation . . .* [Los Angeles, c1931]. [96] pp.

2400. Lowry, Buck. "Malibu: How You've Changed." *Los Angeles* 5 (January 1963): 34-8.

2401. Lummis, Charles F. "The Right Hand of the Continent." *Out West* 16 (June 1902): 569-95; 17 (July 1902): 2-32; (August 1902): 138-71; (September 1902): 269-99; (October 1902): 398-428; (November 1902): 526-56; (December 1902): 654-83; 18 (January 1903): 2-31; (February 1903): 138-68; (March 1903): 286-316; (April 1903): 414-31; (May 1903): 550-68; (June 1903): 698-713.
Compares California cities, particularly Los Angeles, to others in the United States.

2402. ———— "Southern California." *The Mentor* 4 (December 15, 1916): 1-12.

Mainly on Los Angeles.

2403. Luria, Rafe. "Venice in Limbo." *Westways* 56 (September 1964): 18-21.

2404. *Lynwood, California.* Beverly Hills, 1966. [37] pp.

2405. *Lynwood on Long Beach Boulevard.* Los Angeles, [c1919?]. 22 pp.

2406. Mackenzie, Armine D. "The Los Angeles Paradox." *Wilson Library Bulletin* 27 (April 1953): 617-9.

The paradox: "Most of the concepts in the popular mind about the [Los Angeles] region date back to periods which no longer exist."

2407. "Manhattan, Hermosa and Redondo." *Touring Topics* 14 (June 1922): 30-1.

2408. Marien, Francis J. "Los Angeles and the Idea of a City." *America* 98 (November 30, 1957): 261.

Author contends that only "those who confuse size with greatness" think Los Angeles is a great city." . . . it has no personality and no poet." Los Angeles is not a great city because "the inhabitants of this area are faceless, abstract, national stereotypes . . ."

2409. Martin, Lannie H. "Whittier, the City of Opportunities." *Out West,* new series, 3 (April 1912): 257-60.

2410. Marvin, George. "Nuestra Señora de Los Angeles. The Magic Mecca of Southern California." *Outlook* 140 (August 5, 1925): 491-4.

2411. Marx, Wesley. "The 'City' of Wilshire." *Los Angeles* 6 (August 1963): 26-30+.

The "Miracle Mile" expands.

2412. ————, and Thomas, Gil[bert]. "The Westside Story." *Los Angeles* 3 (February 1962): 16-20.

West Los Angeles development.

2413. Matson, Clarence H. "The Los Angeles of Tomorrow." *Southern California Business* 3 (September 1924): 18+; (October 1924): 27+; (November 1924): 22+.

2414. Matthews, J. L. "Covina 'A City Among the Orange Groves.'" *Out West* 26 (May 1907): 477-81.

2415. Maulsby, F. R. *Antelope Valley, California.* [San Francisco, 1913]. 14 pp.

2416. McBroom, Patricia. "The Ducal Life in Northridge." *Los Angeles* 6 (September 1963): 42-7.

2417. McCulloch, Frank. "Los Angeles: What It Is, What It Might Be." *Los Angeles* 7 (January 1964): 42-5+.

2418. McGaffey, Ernest. "Los Angeles . . . City of Destiny." *Southern California Business* 5 (January 1927): 14-5+.

2419. McGroarty, John S. *A Year and a Day; Westwood Village, Westwood Hills.* [Los Angeles, 193-?]. 16 pp.

2420. McMichael, Stanley L. "The Future of Los Angeles as Seen by an Easterner." *Los Angeles Realtor* 4 (January 1925): 9.

2421. Mears, Joe. "Roses and Feather Dusters: Notes on Pasadena When the Tournament of Roses Was in Its Infancy and the Mount Lowe Railway Was a Sensation." *Westways* 27 (March 1935): 18-9+.

2422. Meinell, H. M. "The Novel Streets of Venice, Cal." *Pacific Municipalities* 21 (November 1909): 99-100.

Canals.

2423. [Meline, F. L., Inc.]. *Los Angeles, the Metropolis of the West . . .* Los Angeles, 1929. 32 pp.

" . . . The Frank Meline company recently completed an exhaustive survey covering every phase of the growth and development of Los Angeles . . . This book contains a brief synopsis of the most important facts of the survey. . . . "

2424. Mezerik, A. G. "Journey in America." *New Republic* 111 (December 18, 1944): 830-1.

Part of a series on "what is being done—and left undone—in various regions of the United States to prepare for the peace."

2425. Miller, A. A. *Your Long Beach Home.* Long Beach, 1927. 63 pp.

2426. Miller, Max C. *It Must Be the Climate.* New York, 1941. 262 pp.
Los Angeles area.

2427. Mitchell, John W. "Los Angeles: In the Making." *American City* 2 (April 1910): 148-57.

2428. "Monrovia Hits the Industrial Trail." *Southern California Business* 3 (June 1924): 20.

2429. *Montebello, California.* Encino, 1969. 28 pp.

2430. Moody, Charles A. "Azusa." *Land of Sunshine* 14 (February 1901): 163-78.

2431. Motley, Willard F. "Small Town Los Angeles." *Commonweal* 30 (June 30, 1939): 251-2.
Author declares that "weather, street cars, orange juice and naivete go to make up a loveable city."

2432. "Motor-Borne Los Angeles Gives Industry That Open-Air Touch." *Business Week* (May 18, 1957): 172-8+.
The auto as a "way of life" in Los Angeles.

2433. "Mount Wilson and the Angeles Crest." *Westways* 27 (November 1935): 39-42.

2434. Murray, Jim. "Los Angeles: Once Upon a Time It *Was* Dreamsville." *Los Angeles* 15 (July 1970): 36-7.

2435. Nadeau, Remi. "The New California: A Society of Strangers?" *Los Angeles* 6 (October 1963): 44-5.
Los Angeles County.

2436. *Naples; An Artistic Dream and Its Realization.* Los Angeles, 1905. Unp.

2437. "A New Look at San Fernando Valley: Everything about the Valley Is Geared Toward Tomorrow: The Homes, the Industry and the Standard of Living . . . It Has Become a Test Laboratory for the Nation." *Southern California Prompter* 1 (September 1960): 20-3.

2438. "A New Mayor, A New Councilwoman . . . and 400 New Angels Every Day." *Life* 35 (June 13, 1953): 23-9.

2439. "New Peak-Load of Tourists Coming." *Southern California Business* 2 (November 1923): 26+.

Estimate that 1,600,000 tourists will have visited Los Angeles by the end of 1923.

2440. Newton, A. Edward. "The Course of Empire." *Atlantic Monthly* 150 (September 1932): 298-304.
Author discusses a variety of topics, including the Huntington Library, filling stations, the automobile, Hollywood, bookshops, libraries, and religion.

2441. *North Hollywood, California; Gateway to the San Fernando Valley.* Beverly Hills, 1966. 32 pp.

2442. "Now Through 1970: This Is Where It's Happening." *Los Angeles* 11 (January 1966): 24-6.
Los Angeles.

2443. O'Day, Edward F. *Bel-Air Bay; A Country Place by the Sea.* [Los Angeles], 1927. 30 pp.

2444. "Oranges, Mountains & Surf." *California Highways and Public Works* 45 (May-June 1966): 13-7.
Los Angeles and vicinity.

2445. Osborne, Sherrill B. *Whittier, California.* [Whittier, 1904?]. [16] pp.

2446. Otis, Harrison Gray. "Los Angeles—A Sketch." *Sunset* 24 (January 1910): 12-6.
Following article, pp. 17-48, sixty-four photographs are presented.

2447. "Out in the San Fernando Valley." *Southern California Business* 7 (August 1928): 16+.

2448. "Over 600,000 Motorists Will Come." *Southern California Business* 3 (April 1924): 14.
Southern California tourism in 1924.

2449. Overholt, Alma. "At the Catalina Isthmus." *Los Angeles Saturday Night* 10 (July 5, 1930): 6.

2450. ——— "At the New Catalina." *Los Angeles Saturday Night* 9 (May 11, 1929): 7.
William Wrigley's plan to develop island as a resort, 1919-1929.

2451. ——— "Catalina Island's Greatly Enhanced Charms." *Los Angeles Saturday Night* 8 (June 23, 1928): 2.
Describes the "many added attractions for vacationists."

2452. ——— "Magic of Change Adds New Charms to Catalina Island." *Los Angeles Saturday Night* 14 (June 9, 1934): 10.

2453. Owens, Charles H., and Seewerker, Joseph. *Nuestro Pueblo. Los Angeles, City of Romance.* Boston, 1940. 185 pp.

2454. Padua Hills, Inc. *Padua Hills; A Residential Community of Distinction.* [N.p., 1935?]. [5] pp.

2455. *Palmdale. Romance and Drama in the Valley of Sunshine, Being a Story of Old Palmdale.* Los Angeles, 1914. [?] pp.

2456. *Paramount, California.* Encino, 1968. 24 pp.

2457. Parker, William. "Pueblo to Metropolis: Los Angeles." *Travel* 74 (November 1939): 18-21+.

2458. Pasadena. Chamber of Commerce. *Picturesque Pasadena.* Pasadena, n.d. 55 pp.

2459. ———. Chamber of Commerce and Civic Association. *Pasadena, Summer and Winter.* [Pasadena], 1922. [32] pp. 2nd ed., 1923. [24] pp.

2460. Perkins, Mary M. "Impressions of the Los Angeles Biltmore." *Saturday Night* 4 (September 29, 1923): 14-5.

2461. Perry, George S. "The Cities of America: Los Angeles." *Saturday Evening Post* 218 (December 15, 1945): 14-5+.

2462. Phillips, Freeman. "Life in L.A." *American Mercury* 72 (May 1951): 552-5.

2463. Pictorial American, Publishers. *Greater Los Angeles Illustrated, the Most Progressive Metropolis of the Twentieth Century.* Los Angeles, [1907?]. 224 pp.

2464. *A Pictorial Tour of Southern California.* San Francisco, 1936. Unp.

2465. Pierce, Paul "Panther". *Take an Alternate Route.* Los Angeles, 1968. 159 pp.
   A look of freeways and expressway travel.

2466. "The Play Isle of the Pacific . . . Catalina." *Southern California Business* 6 (March 1927): 18-9+.

2467. Politi, Leo C. *Bunker Hill, Los Angeles: Reminiscences of Bygone Days.* Palm Desert, 1964. [65] pp.

2468. *Pomona and Vicinity.* Pomona, c19[06?]. [22 pp.]

2469. Potter, Bernard. *Los Angeles, Yesterday and Today.* Los Angeles, 1950. 201 pp.

2470. Powell, Lawrence Clark. "Reading on the Malibu." *California Librarian* 16 (October 1955): 287-8+.

2471. [Pratt, L. M., & Co.]. *Altadena.* Los Angeles, 1905. 40 pp.

2472. Rand, Christopher. *Los Angeles: The Ultimate City.* New York, 1967. 205 pp.
   "The Ultimate City 1—Upward and Outward." *New Yorker* 42 (October 1, 1966): 56-60+;
   "The Ultimate City—The Management of Innovation." (October 8, 1966): 64-6+;
   "The Ultimate City—Technology and Frontiersmanship." (October 15, 1966): 64-6+.
   Rand's articles appeared in the feature headed "Profiles."

2473. Rankin, Gil. "Santa Monica, the Pearl of the Pacific." *Pacific Municipalities* 35 (August 1921): 286-9.

2474. Rattray, Will. "Enchanting Canals Yield to Flashy Motorways." *Southern California Business* 8 (June 1929): 12-3+.
   Venice.

2475. Rayfield, Joan R. "The Languages of a Bilingual Community." Doctoral dissertation, University of California, Los Angeles, 1960. 237 pp.
   A descriptive study of a group of Jewish people residing along the Venice and Santa Monica ocean front.

2476. "Redondo Beach, California." *Out West* 29 (August 1908): 159-68.

2477. "Redondo Beach in Summer and Winter." *Out West*, new series, 2 (November 1911): 264-5.

2478. Reese, Herbert H. *The Kellogg Arabians; Their Background and Influence.* In collaboration with Gladys Brown Edwards. Los Angeles, 1958. 222 pp.
   Kellogg Ranch, Pomona.

2479. Reid, D. "Whittier." *Out West* 25 (September 1906): 295-302.

2480. Reynolds, Ann C. *Wild Goat Trails of Catalina . . .* Avalon, 1941. 40 pp.

2481. Rickard, T. A. "Los Angeles—The Wonder City of America." *Engineering News-Record* 91 (October 4, 1923): 554-8.
  Various facets of the Los Angeles scene during the boom of the 1920s.

2482. Rieder, Michael, pub. *Pasadena, the Crown of the Valley.* Los Angeles, c1905. [64] pp.

2483. —— *Santa Catalina Island.* Los Angeles, c1905. 32 pp.

2484. Riley, Frank. "An All-Purpose Marathon Walk from Boyle Heights to the Beach." *Los Angeles* 13 (August 1968): 24-7+.

2485. —— "The New Los Angeles Woman. Under 25: A Rejection of Stereotype." *Los Angeles* 12 (April 1967): 30-2+.

2486. —— "Why Los Angeles Isn't a 'Swinging City.'" *Los Angeles* 11 (September 1966): 24-7.
  Author asserts that Los Angeles is kept from "swinging up to its potential" by such ailments as "lack of political leadership," "lack of a sense of city," "fragmentation of the power structure, "fiscal yo-yo," and "creeping conformity."

2487. Roberts, Glenys. "The Return of Witchcraft." *Los Angeles* 12 (June 1967): 28-31+.
  "Witches, clairvoyants, wizards" and haunted houses in the Los Angeles area.

2488. Roberts, Myron. "Good Bye 60's and Amen." *Los Angeles* 14 (December 1969): 32-5+.
  Los Angeles during the 1960s.

2489. —— "The Human City." *Los Angeles* 15 (July 1970): 32-3+.
  Survey of city in the decade, 1960-70.

2490. —— "Is Los Angeles about to Become a City?" *Los Angeles* 12 (June 1967): 24-5+.

2491. —— "A Whitey's Tour of Watts." *Los Angeles* 13 (June 1968): 27+.

2492. ——, and Thompson, Louis. "Why Christmas Is Different in Los Angeles." *Los Angeles* 15 (December 1970): 33-7.

2493. Robinson, William W. "Los Angeles, Everybody's Town." *The Kiwanis Magazine* 33 (January 1948): 28-9+.

2494. —— *What They Say about Los Angeles.* Pasadena, 1942. 88 pp.
  Comments by visitors, 1769-1941.

2495. [Rodd, Marcel]. *Souvenir-Album. Los Angeles, Hollywood, and the Southland at a Glance.* Hollywood, [c1942]. 96 pp.

2496. Rogers, Florence G. "Los Angeles' Street Types." *Saturday Night* 4 (June 16, 1923): 19+.
  Los Angeles' "distinctly individual public characters."

2497. Ross, Robert E. *Wings over the Marshes. Shooting Scenes from an Old Log Book.* London, 1948. 151 pp.
  Turn-of-the-century account of Los Angeles.

2498. Rutter, Alice M. "Lynwood, the City of Homes." *Pacific Municipalities* 43 (October 1929): 436-7.

2499. San Fernando. Chamber of Commerce. *San Fernando, California.* San Fernando, 1964. 33 pp.

2500. *San Fernando, California.* Beverly Hills, 1967. 24 pp.

2501. San Gabriel. Women's Chamber of Commerce. *San Gabriel.* San Gabriel, 1915. 26 pp.

2502. Sanders, Francis C. S. *California as a Health Resort.* San Francisco, 1916. 300 pp.
  Alhambra included.

2503. *Santa Fe Springs.* Beverly Hills, 1968. [21] pp.

2504. "Santa Monica." *Pacific Municipalities* 35 (February 1921): 70-2.

2505. *Santa Monica, California.* Beverly Hills, 1969. 88 pp.

2506. *Santa Monica. The Famous Pacific Ocean Resort of Southern California.* Santa Monica, [c1915]. 14 pp.

2507. "Santa Monica's Progress." *Pacific Municipalities* 9 (August 1903): 18-9.

2508. Saunders, Charles F. "Winter on the Isle of Summer." *Sunset* 26 (February 1911): 205-9.
Santa Catalina Island.

2509. Scanland, J. M. " 'Chinatown's' Fading Local Color." *Saturday Night* 4 (July 14, 1923): 20+.
Los Angeles.

2510. Scherer, James A. B. "What Kind of a Pittsburgh Is Los Angeles." *World's Work* 41 (February, 1921): 382-92.
General description of Los Angeles.

2511. Scott, Johnie. "How It Is—My Home Is Watts." *Harper's Magazine* 233 (October 1966): 47-8.

2512. See, Carolyn. "Los Angeles: The Hippie Invasion." *Los Angeles* 12 (May 1967): 30-2+.

2513. Seidenbaum, Art. "A New Look at San Fernando Valley." *Southern California Prompter* 1 (September 1960): 20-3.

2514. Sengel, Jerome (Jerry). "Hollywood." *Los Angeles Realtor* 5 (October 1925): 13-4.
Indices of growth and prosperity.

2515. Shay, Dorothy. "Romantic Santa Catalina—Famed in Song and Story." *Apartment Journal* 23 (January 1941): 14-5+.

2516. Shelton, Wilson E. "San Pedro by Night." *Los Angeles Saturday Night* 10 (September 20, 1930): 5.
Impressionistic description.

2517. Shippey, Lee. *The Los Angeles Book.* Boston, 1950. 117 pp.
Pictorial.

2518. Shirk, Adam H. "Los Angeles Important Center of Magic." *California Graphic* 5 (December 10, 1927): 5.

2519. Smith, Bertha H. "Beside the All-the-Year-Sea." *Sunset* 27 (July 1911): 63-5.
Life at the Hotel Virginia, Long Beach.

2520. ——— "Homes of Pasadena: Something about the California City Where on New Year's Day They Battle with Roses Instead of Snowballs." *Sunset* 14 (November 1904): 33-6.

2521. ——— "The Making of Los Angeles: A Study of the Astonishing Growth of California's Southland City—Oranges, Palms and Fast Rising Skyscrapers—Present Population Close to 300,000." *Sunset* 19 (July 1907): 237-54.

2522. Smith, Jack. "A Day in the City: Away to Avalon." *Westways* 62 (September 1970): 25-7+.

2523. ——— "A Day in the City: Christmas on Olvera Street." *Westways* 60 (December 1968): 8-10.

2524. ——— "A Day in the City: Down by the Depot." *Westways* 62 (February 1970): 12-4+.
Los Angeles.

2525. ——— "A Day in the City: Downtown." *Westways* 61 (November 1969): 21-3+.
Los Angeles.

2526. ——— "A Day in the City: The Pacific Pleasures of Santa Monica." *Westways* 60 (June 1968): 6-8.

2527. ——— "A Day in the City: Sights and Scents Celetial." *Westways* 62 (June 1970): 23-5+.
Chinatown.

2528. ——— "A Day in the City: Temples and Tempura." *Westways* 61 (February 1969): 7-9.
Little Tokyo.

2529. ——— "A Day in the City: A Walk Through Old Hollywood." *Westways* 60 (November 1968): 8-10+.

2530. ——— " 'It Can Be Walked.' " *Los Angeles* 12 (August 1967): 28-9.
Downtown Los Angeles.

2531. ——— "Sightseeing Along Wilshire Blvd." *Southern California Prompter* 1 (July 1960): 14-6.
"From Grand Ave. to the Sea: 16 miles, 400 blocks . . . $50,000 a foot."

2532. Smith, Richard A. "Los Angeles, Prototype of Supercity." *Fortune* 71 (March 1965): 98-101+.

2533. Smith, Robert L. "Is Hollywood on Its Great White Way?" *Los Angeles Realtor* 7 (November 1927): 16-8.

Author poses this question: "Is the 'Great White Way' of New York's Times Square to have its western counterpart in Hollywood?"

2534. Smythe, William E. "Significance of Southern California." *Out West* 32 (April 1910): 286-303.

2535. *South Gate, California.* Beverly Hills, 1968. [25] pp.

2536. "South Gate Grows and Prospers." *Southern California Business* 5 (March 1926): 34.

2537. South Pasadena. Board of Trustees. *South Pasadena.* South Pasadena, 1906. Unp.

2538. Southern California Pasadena Expositions Commission. *Southern California, Comprising the Counties of Imperial, Los Angeles, Orange, Riverside, San Bernardino, San Diego, Ventura.* [San Diego? 1914]. 263 pp.

2539. *Southern California at a Glance.* Los Angeles, 1930. 192 pp.

2540. "Southern California's 'Isle of Dreams.'" *Touring Topics* 14 (May 1922): 20-2.
Santa Catalina.

2541. "Sprawling Los Angeles Gets a New Skyline." *Business Week* (December 13, 1969): 68-9+.

2542. "Squaresville U.S.A. vs. Beatsville." *Life* 47 (September 21, 1959): 31-7.
Picture story contrasting "life" in Venice, California, and Hutchinson, Kansas.

2543. "The State of Our Future." *Los Angeles* 12 (January 1967): 24-5+.

2544. Stevens, Jean H. "Society Among the Angels." *Los Angeles* 2 (July 1961): 25-7.
Survey of Los Angeles "Society."

2545. Stewart, David A. *Voyageur . . . to the San Fernando Valley.* Sherman Oaks, 1964. 80 pp.
Travel.

2546. "Still the Tourist Stream Flows." *Southern California Business* 3 (September 1924): 20+.
Los Angeles tourists and new permanent residents.

2547. "Story of the Queen of the Angels." *Overland Monthly* 41 (April 1903): 310-5.

2548. Stump, Frank V. "Alhambra Is on Her Way." *Southern California Business* 3 (July 1924): 14-5+.
Beginning of industrialization.

2549. ———— "An Artistic Industrial Youngster." *Southern California Business* 3 (May 1924): 12-3+.
Torrance.

2550. ———— "Burbank Has a Word to Offer." *Southern California Business* 3 (April 1924): 10-2.
Burbank's industrial boom and other aspects of progress.

2551. ———— "Some Towns Can't Help Flourishing." *Southern California Business* 3 (September 1924): 12-3+.
Inglewood.

2552. *Sunny California from the Mountains to the Sea: Los Angeles and Vicinity.* [Los Angeles, n.d.]. [42] pp.

2553. Sunset Books and Sunset Magazine. *Los Angeles; Portrait of an Extraordinary City.* Ed. by Paul C. Johnson. Menlo Park, 1968. 304 pp.

2554. Sutton, Horace. "Ever-Ever Land." *Saturday Review* 41 (April 5, 1958): 23-5.
Description of Forest Lawn, Glendale.

2555. Switzer, G. W. "San Fernando, King of the Fernando Valley." *Out West,* new series, 7 (June 1914): 291-5.

2556. Talbot, Katherine. "The San Fernando Valley." *Pacific Pathways* 2 (January 1948): 37+.

2557. Thomas, Gilbert. "Los Angeles 67/77: A Fantasy (?) View." *Los Angeles* 12 (January 1967): 18-22.

2558. ———— "The Young Side of Town: South Bay." *Los Angeles* 9 (May 1965): 34-9.
Changes in the South Bay, Playa Del Rey to Redondo.

2559. Thrall, Will H. "Millard's Canyon." *Trails Magazine* 6 (Spring 1939): 15-6+.

2560. ———— "Old Days on the Big Tujunga." *Trails Magazine* 5 (Winter 1938): 6-10.

2561. ——— "Scenic Mt. Lowe." *Trails Magazine* 6 (Spring 1939): 5-14.

2562. Tibon, Gutierre. *Los Angeles.* Mexico, 1955. 65 pp.

2563. *Torrance, California.* Beverly Hills, 1967. 40 pp.

2564. *Torrance, the Modern Industrial City.* Los Angeles, [1913]. 32 pp.

2565. "Troubled Los Angeles—Race Is Only One of Its Problems." *U. S. News and World Report* 59 (August 30, 1965): 58-62.

2566. Truitt, W. H. "Pomona." *Out West,* new series, 4 (August 1912): [130]-6.

2567. Truman, Ben[jamin] C. [text]. *Los Angeles. The Queen City of the Angels.* Los Angeles, 1904. 63 pp.
   Pictorial.

2568. ——— *Southern California.* Los Angeles, 1903. Unp.
   Pictorial.

2569. "The Upper West Fork." *Trials Magazine* 4 (Summer 1937): 14-6+.
   Describes upper west fork of San Gabriel River, its resorts, lodges, and ranger stations. Mainly early twentieth century.

2570. "Van Nuys." *Out West,* new series, 7 (June 1914): 296.

2571. "Venice." *Out West* 32 (April 1910): [384-5].

2572. "Venice, the Convention City." *Pacific Municipalities* 27 (October 1913): 531-8.

2573. "A Visit to Movieland: The Film Capital of the World—Los Angeles." *Forum* 63 (January 1920): 16-29.

2574. von Engeln, O.D. "Geography of Los Angeles, California." *Annals of Association of American Geographers* 20 (March 1930): 29-30.

2575. von Vieregg, G. "Santa Monica: The City of Many Sides." *Sunset* 28 (June 1912): 773-4.

2576. Wagg, Peter A. [*pseud.?*]. *Southern Califor-*

nia Exposed. Ed. by Homer Fort. [Los Angeles, 1915]. 24 pp.

2577. Wagner, Anton. *Los Angeles: Werden, Leben und Gestalt der Zweiimillionenstadt in Sudkalifornien.* Leipzig, [Germany], 1935. 295 pp.

2578. Waring, G. P., ed. "Alhambra. A City of Homes in Orange Groves. Interviews with Prominent Residents." *Out West,* new series, 3 (April 1912): 266-73.

2579. "The Way Long Beach Bounded Ahead." *Southern California Business* 3 (December 1924): 17-8+.
   Various indices of growth and prosperity.

2580. Weaver, John D. "The Good Tolerant Life of the Hollywood Hills." *Holiday* 47 (April 1970): 60-3+.

2581. Webster, David K. "Los Angeles." *Frontier* 3 (June 1952): 12-4.
   Los Angeles described as "the most stimulating ci[t]y in America and one of the most beautiful."

2582. Weinstein, Robert A. "From San Pedro Due South to Catalina Island." *Museum Alliance Quarterly* 6 (Winter 1968): 4-9.

2583. Weinstock, Matt. *My L. A.* New York, 1947. 239 pp.
   Random characterizations of Los Angeles people and places.

2584. Westwood Hills Press. *Westwood Hills Pictorial.* Los Angeles, [1946]. 54 pp.

2585. ——— *Westwood Hills, Westwood Village, Los Angeles, California, America's Most Unique Shopping Center. "A Village within a City."* [Westwood? 193-?]. 37 pp.

2586. Wharton, Mel. "Alhambra the Twice-Chosen: First, the Padres Picked the Valley for Fertility, and Now Industry Builds a Stronghold at Its Portal." *Southern California Business* 11 (September 1932): 10-1.

2587. ——— "The Ego That Is Long Beach: Ten Years Ago, A Sunny Seaside 'Town,' Today a Belligerent Industrial City — How Did It Get That Way?" *Southen California Business* 9 (1930): 12-3.

2588. ———— "Nothing Stands Still in Glendale." *Southern California Business* 9 (October 1930): 12-3.

2589. ———— "Pomona—A Large Little City." *Southen California Business* 12 (January 1933): 10-1.

2590. ———— "The Port That Never Found Its Sea-Legs: Planned as a Great Harbor, Santa Monica Became, Instead, a Notable Place to Live." *Southern California Business* 11 (January 1932): 10-1.

2591. ———— "Torrance — Our Own Gary." *Southern California Business* 10 (June 1931): 12-3.

2592. " 'What Kind of City Do You Chaps Want?' " *Los Angeles* 8 (July 1964): 35-40.
   Question is posed, "What should be Los Angeles' goals and roles?"

2593. "What's the Matter with Los Angeles?" *Out West,* new series, 10 (May 1916): 187-93.
   A symposium.

2594. White, Mowbray. "Santa Catalina Island." *Out West, new series,* 8 (November 1914): 282-7.

2595. Whittier. Chamber of Commerce. *Whittier, Los Angeles County, California* . . . [Whittier], 1917. [16] pp. 2nd ed., [1923]. 35 pp.

2596. Whitworth, D. M. "Sunset Strip — A Protean Fable." *Westways* 56 (November 1964): 4-7; (December 1964): 8-11.

2597. Wiggins, Frank. "Why Should They Spin Such Yarns?" *Southern California Business* 3 (October 1924): 9+.
   Alleged "persistent, and well organized effort . . . being made throughout the east and middle west to injure the southwest, Los Angeles, and Southern California."

2598. Wight, Frank C. "Observations on a Pacific Coast Trip: Los Angeles the Crowded." *Engineering News-Record* 86 (January 13, 1921): 56-7.

2599. Wilkins, Barbara. "A Moveable Feast: Los Angeles' Celebrity Circuit." *Los Angeles* 13 (October 1968): 34-7.

2600. Willard, Howard W. "American Cities: A Series of Metropolitan Travelcharts." *Woman's Home Companion* 54 (July 1927): 15+.
   Article headed, "Los Angeles," with an historical sketch, points of interest, and suggested itinerary.

2601. Williams, Iza. *Santa Catalina Island.* Los Angeles, 1904. [48] pp. 2nd ed., 1905.

2602. Williford, Stanley O. "Watts — Five Years Later." *Black Politician* 2 (October 1970): 20-3.

2603. "Wilshire to the Sea." *Fortune* 57 (May 1958): 129-36.
   Photographs taken along Wilshire Blvd.

2604. Wilson, Edmund. "The City of Our Lady the Queen of the Angels." *New Republic* 69 (December 2, 1931): 67-8; (December 9, 1931): 89-93.

2605. Wilson, James Q. "The Young People of North Long Beach." *Harper's Magazine* 239 (December 1969): 83-90.
   Impressionistic study of folkways and attitudes of high-school youth in North Long Beach, where the author, head of the Department of Government at Harvard, grew up.

2606. Woehlke, Walter V. "Angels in Overalls." *Sunset* 28 (March 1912): 261-72.
   "Being a True and Veracious Account of Workday Life in the Angelic Region . . ."

2607. ———— "The Rejuvenation of San Fernando." *Sunset* 33 (February 1914): 357-66.

2608. Wolfe, Bernard. "Manners and Morals on the Sunset Strip." *Esquire* 56 (August 1961): 48-54.

2609. Wooster, Ernest S. *Communities of the Past and Present.* Newllano, La., 1924. 156 pp.
   Lengthy sections on the Llano Colony. The same author has published like accounts in *Sunset* 53 (July 1924): 21-23, 80-82; (August 1924): 21-23, 59-60; (September 1924): 30-33, 75-80; and in the *Nation* 117 (October 10, 1923): 378-80.

2610. "World's Greatest City in Prospect." *World's Work* 47 (December 1923): 140-2.
   Los Angeles.

2611. Wright, Willard. "Los Angeles—The Chemically Pure," in *The Smart Set Anthology.* Ed. by

Burton Rascoe and Groff Conklin. New York, 1934. Pp. 90-102.

Essay details how Los Angeles epitomizes "Municipal Prudery," but ends on optimistic note that in the future may lie "a metropolis wealthy and diverse, commercially powerful and artistically wise."

2612. Wybro, Jesse M. "Van Nuys, the City of Aladdin's Lamps." *Out West,* new series, 2 (December 1911): 51-3.

2613. Yavno, Max, and Shippey, Lee. *The Los Angeles Book.* Boston, 1950. 117 pp.

Photographs by Yavno with description by Shippey.

2614. "The Young Giant of the Southwest." *Southern California Business* 1 (January 1923): 19+.

Los Angeles.

2615. Zierer, Clifford M., ed. *California and the Southwest.* New York, 1956. 376 pp.

Largely focused on the Los Angeles area in such topics as the aircraft, automobile, and motion picture industries.

2616. ——— "San Fernando, a Type of Southern California Town." *Annals of the Association of American Geographers* 24 (1934): 1-28.

DESCRIPTION AND TRAVEL—GUIDEBOOKS

2617. Ault, Phillip H. *How to Live in California: A Guide to Work, Leisure, and Retirement There and in the Southwest.* New York, 1961. 298 pp.

2618. Bartlett, Lanier, and Bartlett, Virginia S. *Los Angeles in Seven Days, Including Southern California.* New York, 1932. 298 pp.

2619. Blumer, J. G., ed. *A Dictionary of Sierra Madre and a Guide, Philosopher and Friend for Tourists, Travellers and Investors.* Los Angeles, 1906. 66 pp.

2620. Brunner, Francis. *Southern California's Prettiest Drive; A Tour Along the Crescent Shore of Santa Monica Bay and Up into the Picturesque Canyons of the Santa Monica Mountains.* Santa Monica, [1925?]. 32 pp.

2621. Cass, W. W. "A Catalina Safari." *Westways* 60 (February 1969): 2-5.

2622. Christy, George. *The Los Angeles Underground Gourment. A Complete Guide to Dining in the Los Angeles Area . . .* New York, 1970. 159 pp.

2623. *Complete Visitors Guide of Los Angeles, Hollywood, Pasadena, Beverly Hills, Long Beach, Santa Monica, the Beaches and Southern California.* [Los Angeles, 1948]. 96 pp.

2624. Connor, J. Torrey. *Saunterings in Summerland.* Los Angeles, 1902. 80 pp.

2625. Cooper, Frederic T. *Rider's California, a Guide-Book for Travelers.* New York, 1925. 667 pp.

2626. Crow, John A. *California as a Place to Live.* New York, 1953. 246 pp.

Climate, geography, jobs, education, towns and cities, farming, housing, business opportunities, resorts.

2627. Cunningham, Glenn, ed. *Day Tours—Geographical Journeys in the Los Angeles Area.* Palo Alto, 1964. 288 pp.

Includes the San Gabriel, Santa Monica and San Bernardino mountains, Antelope Valley and the Ridge Route.

2628. Drury, Aubrey. *California, an Intimate Guide; From the Days of the Mission Fathers to the Celebration Surrounding One Hundred Years of Statehood.* New York, 1947. 592 pp.

2629. "Exploring the Motor Roads Around Los Angeles." *Touring Topics* 7 (February 1915): 10-7.

2630. "First International Recreation Congress, Los Angeles, July 23 to 29, 1932." *Western City* 8 (July 1932): 9-13.

Includes tours of Los Angeles and Pasadena.

2631. Gebhard, David, and Winter, Robert. *A Guide to Architecture in Southern California.* Los Angeles, 1965. 164 pp.

2632. Gordon, Dudley. *An Entertaining Guidebook to the Cultural Assets of Metropolitan Los Angeles.* Los Angeles, 1940. 64 pp.

Museums, galleries and libraries.

2633. Haggart, Stanley Mills. *TWA's Budget Guide to Los Angeles.* New York, 1969. 144 pp.

2634. Halliday, Ruth S. *Stars on the Crosswalks; An Intimate Guide to Hollywood.* Sherman Oaks, 1958. 100 pp.

2635. Halsey, Mina D. *A Tenderfoot in Southern California.* New York, 1918. 162 pp.

Everyday experiences of a tourist in Southern California and Los Angeles. Originally published under the name M.D. Yeslah [*pseud.*].

2636. Harris, Frank, and Bonenberger, Weston, eds. *A Guide to Contemporary Architecture in California.* Los Angeles, 1951. 91 pp.

2637. Hepburn, Andrew, ed. *Rand McNally Guide to Southern California.* Chicago and New York, 1968. 174 pp.

2638. ——— *Southern California.* Boston, 1959. Rev. ed., 1962. 160 pp.

2639. Houston, Robert d'Auria. *This Is Los Angeles: A Complete Guide Book.* Los Angeles, [1950]. 176 pp.

2640. Hunt, John, ed. *El Pueblo de Nuestra Senora de Los Angeles. Los Angeles Official Handbook for Visitors.* Los Angeles, 1969. 126 pp.

2641. James, George W. *Travelers' Handbook to Southern California.* Pasadena, 1904. 507 pp.

2642. Johnson, Humphrey C. *Scenic Guide to Southern California.* Susanville, 1946. 103 pp.

2643. Leadabrand, Russ. *Exploring California Byways, from King's Canyon to the Mexican Border.* Los Angeles, 1967. 164 pp.

Chapter VII, "Along the San Andreas Earthquake Fault Line," pp. 62-9, and Chapter VIII, "The Historic Saugas-Newhall 'Country,'" pp. 70-8, describe areas in Los Angeles County.

2644. ——— *Exploring California Byways—II. In and Around Los Angeles.* Los Angeles, 1968. 184 pp.

2645. ——— *Exploring California Byways, IV. Mountain Country. Trips for a Day or a Weekend.* Los Angeles, 1970. 142 pp.

Chapter IV, "Into the San Gabriel" (pp. 46-57) covers the mountains of Los Angeles County.

2646. ——— *A Guidebook to the Mojave Desert of California. Including Death Valley, Joshua Tree National Monument and the Antelope Valley.* Los Angeles, 1966. 180 pp.

Chapter II through V (pp. 16-43) deal with southwestern Antelope Valley, including Palmdale and Lancaster.

2647. ——— *A Guidebook to the San Bernardino Mountains of California.* Rev. ed. Los Angeles, 1964. 117 pp.

Includes Lake Arrowhead and Big Bear.

2648. ——— *A Guidebook to the San Gabriel Mountains of California.* Rev. ed., Los Angeles, 1964. 117 pp.

2649. ——— "Into the San Gabriels," in *Exploring California Byways IV: Mountain Country.* Los Angeles, 1970. Pp. 47-57.

2650. Los Angeles. Chamber of Commerce. *Los Angeles To-day City and County.* Los Angeles, c1927. 48 pp.

Attractive living conditions described.

2651. Los Angeles Times. *Southern California's Standard Guide Book, 1910 . . .* Los Angeles, [1910]. 231 pp.

2652. *Los Angeles and Southern California Guide Book and Room, Board, and Hotel Directory . . . . Also Describing All Points of Interest In and Around Los Angeles.* [Los Angeles, 1907?]. 240 pp.

2653. Mackey, Margaret G. *Cities in the Sun.* Los Angeles, 1938. 181 pp.

2654. ——— *Going Places In and Near Los Angeles.* Los Angeles, 1940. 235 pp.

2655. ——— *Los Angeles. Proper and Improper.* Los Angeles, 1938. 131 pp.

2656. McClees, E. D. *Suburban Trips: Eight Delightful Trips Out of Los Angeles via Pacific Electric and L.A. Inter-Urban Railways.* Los Angeles, 1904. 64 pp.

2657. Miner, Frederick R. *Outdoor Southland of California.* Los Angeles, 1923. 229 pp.

A collection of forty essays on a variety of topics.

2658. Muench, Joyce R. *West Coast Portrait.* New York, 1946. 168 pp.

Pacific Coast travel.

2659. Murphy, Bill. *The Dolphine Guide to Los Angeles and Southern California.* Garden City, N. Y., 1962. 399 pp.

2660. —— *Los Angeles, Wonder City of the West: A Pictorial Guide and Souvenir.* San Francisco, c1959. Unp.

2661. Murphy, Thomas D. *On Sunset Highways; A Book of Motor Rambles in California.* Boston, 1921. 379 pp.

2662. National Recreation Association. *Leisure Time Resources in Greater Los Angeles and Adjacent Areas; Directory of Community Activities, Organizations . . .* Comp. by Harold W. Lathrop. New York, 1955. 224 pp.

2663. Nichols, Howard S. *Los Angeles County California.* Los Angeles, 1925. 52 pp.

2664. North American Press Association, San Francisco. *Standard Guide: Los Angeles, San Diego and the Panama-California Exposition.* San Francisco, 1914. 143 pp.

2665. Noyes, Brenda. *Los Angeles Epicurean Directory. The First Source Book of the Finest Markets, Food Suppliers, and Culinary Services in Metropolitan Los Angeles.* Los Angeles, 1969. 139. pp.

2666. O'Dell, Scott. *County of the Sun. Southern California, an Informal History and Guide.* Cornwall, N. Y., 1957. 310 pp.

2667. Parks, Marion. *Doors to Yesterday. A Guide to Old Los Angeles.* Los Angeles, 1932. 16 pp.

2668. Phillips, Alice M., comp. *Los Angeles, a Guide Book Compiled Under the Direction of Dr. E. C. Moore, Martin C. Neuner, Robert O. Hoedel, by Alice Mary Phillips for the National Educational Association.* Los Angeles, 1907. 151 pp.

2669. *Rand McNally Guide to Los Angeles and Environs . . .* New York, c1925. 237 pp.

2670. Reid, Hiram A. *Pasadena Handbook; Giving Name and Location of Over Two Hundred Natural Objects, Historic Sights and Structures, Places of Interest, Mountain Features, etc., in and around Pasadena.* Pasadena, 1905. 19 pp.

2671. Roth, Beulah (Spigelgass). *Los Angeles: An Unusual Guide to Unusual Shopping.* Los Angeles, [1967]. 159 pp.

2672. —— *Where to Find It in Los Angeles; An Unusual Guide to Unusual Shopping, 1970-71.* Los Angeles, [1970]. 159 pp.

2673. Rotholtz, Benjamin. *Wilson's Illustrated and Descriptive Souvenir and Guide to Los Angeles and Near-by Towns.* Los Angeles, [1901]. 157 pp.

2674. Sherer, John C. "Glendale, California." *Out West* 26 (June 1907): 572-7.

2675. —— "Glendale. The City of Beautiful Homes." *Out West,* new series, 3 (April 1912): 274-81.

2676. Spink, T. P., ed. *Los Angeles Red Book.* Los Angeles, 1927. 136 pp.

2677. Sunset Books and Sunset Magazine, eds. *Southern California: A Discovery Book.* Menlo Park, 1959. 127 pp. 2nd ed., 1964. 128 pp.

2678. —— *Sunset Beachcombers' Guide to the Pacific Coast.* Ed. by Bob Thompson. Menlo Park, 1968. 112 pp.

2679. Taylor, Katherine A. *The Los Angeles Tripbook.* New York, 1928. 94 pp.

2680. *The Ten Southern California Counties.* Beverly Hills, 1959. 78 pp.

Includes Los Angeles County.

2681. The Traveler (formerly Newmans' Guide). *Directory Guide and Handbook of Los Angeles and Southern California.* [Los Angeles], 1909. 64 pp.

2682. Van Tuyle, Bert, comp. *Know Your Los Angeles; An Unusual Guide Book.* Los Angeles, c1938. 44 pp. 2nd ed., [1940?]. 68 pp. 3rd ed., 1941. 44 pp.

2683. Wilson, Harry W. *Wilson's Guide to Avalon the Beautiful, and the Island of Santa Catalina.* 2nd. Los Angeles, 1914. [26] pp.

2684. Wood, Ruth K. *The Tourists' California.* New York, 1915. 408 pp.

2685. Woon, Basil D. *Incredible Land; A Jaunty Baedeker to Hollywood and the Great Southwest.* New York, 1933. 374 pp.

2686. Works Progress Administration. Federal Writers' Program *Los Angeles, a Guide to the City and Its Environs.* New York, 1941. 433 pp. Rev. 2nd ed., 1951. 441 pp. New rev. [3rd] ed. by Harry Hansen, 1967. 733 pp.

ECOLOGY

ECOLOGY—AIR

2687. Afflerbaugh, C. B. "It's O.K. in Los Angeles: New Type Incinerator Passes Strict Tests in Smog-Conscious Los Angeles County and Receives Official Permit." *American City* 70 (December 1955): 72-4.

2688. "Air Pollution 'Dragnet': Los Angeles Uses Special Force of Air-Pollution Detectives." *American City* 72 (March 1957): 139.

2689. "Airplanes Spot the Heavy Smokers on a Smoggy Day in L. A. Town." *Business Week* (September 14, 1957): 25.

2690. Albers, J. C. "First Unit of New Glendale Incinerator in Operation Passes Performance and Air Pollution Tests." *Western City* 28 (July 1952): 31-3.

2691. "Auto Exhaust Accused for L. A. Smog." *American City* 71 (July 1956): 20.
Accusation made by Air Pollution Foundation.

2692. Blewett, Stephen E. "Air Pollution Is a Growing Problem for Many Western Cities." *Western City* 25 (April 1949): 29-31.
Includes Los Angeles.

2693. "Blight on the Land of Sunshine." *Life* 37 (November 1, 1954): 17-9.
Smog.

2694. Boffey, P. M. "Smog: Los Angeles Running Hard, Standing Still." *Science* 161 (September 6, 1968): 990-5.

2695. Carroll, James L. "A Survey of the Biologi-

cal Implications of Air Pollution to the California School Health Program." Master's thesis, Claremont Graduate School, 1958. 241 pp.

2696. "Clear Los Angeles Smog: The Techniques for Dealing with the Los Angeles Smog Are Now Available, and Scientists Close to the Problem Urge Less Talk and More Action." *Science News Letter* 66 (December 11, 1954): 371.

2697. Ditzel, Paul. "Smog." *Westways* 61. Four parts:
"The Familiar Recipe." (June 1969): 22-5.
"Focus on the Automobile." (July 1969): 12-5.
"Prospects for Control." (September 1969): 14-7.
"The Search for Other Sources of Power." (October 1969): 14-7.

2698. Duncan, Ray. "Pollution in Paradise, the Blot on the Sunny Face of Los Angeles: Smog." *Holiday* 22 (October 1957): 74-5+.

2699. Eckels, Richard P. "Los Angeles Pioneers in the Fight Against Smog." *Reporter* 11 (December 30, 1954): 30-4.

2700. Fisher, George H. "Poison in the Air: Los Angeles Is Losing the Fight Against Smog." *Frontier* 10 (October 1959): 5-9+.

2701. ——— "Twenty Years of Smog in Los Angeles." *Frontier* 16 (June 1965): 10-4.

2702. Griswold, S. Smith. "The Official Word. . . . What Multiple Dwelling Owners Must Do to Assist in the Abatement of SMOG." *Western Housing* 40 (September 1956): 11+.

2703. Haagen-Smit, A. J. "Air Conservation." *Science* 128 (October 17, 1958): 869-78.

2704. ——— "The Air Pollution Problem in Los Angeles." *Engineering and Science* 14 (December 1950): 7-13.

2705. ——— "The Control of Air Pollution: It Is Now Clear That Smog Is Not Only Annoying But also Injurious to Health. Los Angeles Is a Leading Example of a City That Has Analyzed the Sources of Its Smog and Taken Steps to Bring Them under Control." *Scientific American* 210 (January 1964): 24-31.

2706. Harmer, Ruth. "Danger in the Air." *Frontier* 7 (November 1955): 5-7.

2707. Hedrich, O. H. "Odor-Control Experiments at Pasadena." *Civil Engineering* 5 (September 1935): 564-7.

2708. Heyer, N. Robert. "Smog Sleuths." *Popular Mechanics* 91 (April 1949): 178-81+.
Scientists of the Stanford Research Institute.

2709. Jones, Jack. "Smog Crisis in Los Angeles. Strong Words, Weak Action While Polluted Air Chokes the City." *Frontier* 5 (November 1953): 5-6.

2710. Kennedy, Harold W. *The History, Legal and Administrative Aspects of Air Pollution Control in the County of Los Angeles.* Report submitted to the Board of Supervisors of the County of Los Angeles. [Los Angeles], 1953. 83 pp.
The author completed a similarly entitled study as a Master's thesis, University of Southern California, 1954. 195 pp.

2711. ———— "Legal Aspects of Air Pollution Control with Particular Reference to the County of Los Angeles." *Southern California Law Review* 27 (July, 1954): 373-98.

2712. ———— "Levels of Responsibility for the Administration of Air Pollution Control Programs." *Proceedings* of the National Conference on Air Pollution 1958, *Public Health Service Publication No. 654.* Washington, D. C., 1959. Pp. 389-400.

2713. ———— "The Mechanics of Legislative and Regulatory Action." *Proceedings* of the National Conference on Air Pollution, 1962, *Public Health Service Publication No. 1022.* Washington, D. C., 1963. Pp. 306-14.

2714. ————, and Porter, A.O. "Air Pollution: Its Control and Abatement." *Vanderbilt Law Review* 8 (June, 1955): 854.

2715. Larson, G. P. "Medical Research and Control in Air Pollution." *American Journal of Public Health and Nation's Health* 42 (May 1952): 549-56.

2716. "League Committee Recommends No Smog Law Change at This Time." *Western City* 24 (December 1948): 40.
Includes Los Angeles County cities.

2717. Los Angeles County. Air Pollution Control District. *Crossing the Smog Barrier: A Factual Account of Southern California's Fight Against Air Pollution.* Los Angeles, [1957]. 22 pp.
Based on material from local newspapers.

2718. ———— *Smog. Los Angeles Fights Back!* [Los Angeles, 1956]. 12 pp.

2719. Los Angeles Times. *Where We Stand on the Smog Problem, What's Been Done, What's Ahead.* Los Angeles, 1961. 28 pp.

2720. "Los Angeles Channels Public Support with Fact-Laced Information Program." *American City* 73 (June 1958): 164+.
Public Information Division of Los Angeles Air Pollution Control District.

2721. "Los Angeles Counts Benefits of Ban on Trash Burnings." *American City* 74 (February 1959): 88.
Reduction of air pollution, decrease in number of fires.

2722. "Los Angeles: Forgotten Sun." *Newsweek* 28 (December 23, 1946): 27.

2723. Los Angeles in Torment: The Valley of Smog." *Fortune* 51 (April 1955): 144-5.
Causes of air pollution.

2724. "Los Angeles Pinpoints Auto Exhaust as Uncontrolled Air Pollution Source." *American City* 73 (May 1958): 126.
Conclusion reached as the result of studies by the Air Pollution Foundation, San Marino.

2725. Meyer, Larry L. "Air Pollution: The Motor Vehicle's Role." *Westways* 55 (August 1963): 13-6.

2726. ———— "Air Pollution: The Persistent Foe." *Westways* 55 (July 1963): 18-20.

2727. Middleton, J. T.; Kendrick, J. B. Jr., and Schwalm, H. W. "Smog in the South Coastal Area." *California Agriculture* 4 (November 1950): 7.

2728. Neiburger, Morris. "Smog Today & Smog Tomorrow." *Nation* 201 (December 6, 1965): 432-5.
Article follows an introduction titled, "Is the Automobile Incurable?"

2729. ———— "Weather Modification and Smog." *Science* 126 (October 4, 1957): 637-45.

Causes of smog in Los Angeles and possibilities of eliminating it.

2730. Nicholson, Arnold. "Los Angeles Battles the Murk." *Saturday Evening Post* 232 (December 19, 1959): 17-9+.

"Each day its autos and industry pour more than 2000 tons of smog-forming pollutants into the air. A report from the city which leads the fight against a growing urban menace."

2731. Niese, R. B. "Blowing the Lid Off Los Angeles' Smog Pot." *American Mercury* 90 (January 1960): 85-8.

Poses question, "Will Los Angeleans ever draw another clean breath?"

2732. "19 Cities in Los Angeles County Cited as Smog Violators." *Western City* 24 (May 1948): 48.

2733. Packard, Francis H. "The Politics of Smog." *Frontier* 7 (April 1956): 11-2.

County Supervisors accused of refusing to "enact and enforce necessary regulations."

2734. "Progress on Smog But Not Enough." *Frontier* 14 (October 1963): 14.

2735. Reith, John W. "Los Angeles Smog." *Yearbook of the Association of Pacific Coast Geographers* 13 (1951): 24-31.

2736. Rheingold, Paul D. "Air Pollution: Lawsuit as Social Action?" *Arts & Architecture* 84 (January 1967): 12-3+.

Excerpted from *Trial* magazine.

2737. Riley, Frank. "How to Escape the Smog (Almost): Postponing Doomsday: A Do-It-Yourself Smog Rating of Southern California Communities." *Los Angeles* 15 (August 1970): 30-3+.

2738. Robinson, H. E. "Huntington Park Incinerator Smoke Reduced by Catalysts." *Western City* 29 (August 1953): 58-9.

2739. Rumford, William B. "Smog Abatement Administration with Special Reference to California." Master's thesis, University of California, Berkeley, 1959. 127 pp.

2740. Schiller, Ronald. "The Los Angeles Smog." *National Municipal Review* 44 (December 1955): 558-64.

2741. Scott, Herbert J. "Beverly Hills Incinerator Meets All City and Smog Control Requirements." *Western City* 24 (December 1948): 21-3.

2742. Senn, Charles L. "General Atmospheric Pollution: Los Angeles 'Smog.'" *American Journal of Public Health and Nation's Health* 38 (July 1948): 962-5.

2743. "Smog Experts Condemn Los Angeles Refuse Burning." *American City* 70 (February 1955): 141+.

2744. "Smog—Why We Have It and What Is Being Done to Eliminate It." *Western Housing* 40 (August 1956): 8-9+.

2745. Stead, Frank M. "Air Pollution: How to Get Rid of Smog." *Arts & Architecture* 84 (January 1967): 10-1+.

2746. Stewart, Frank. "Smog Circus in L.A." *Frontier* 6 (December 1954): 12-3.

2747. Union Oil Co. of California. *Smog: Questions and Answers on This Community Problem* Los Angeles, n.d. 22 pp.

2748. Wendt, W[ilhelmine]. "Death on the Installment Plan." *Frontier* 10 (March 1959): 5-7+.

Argues necessity of eliminating smog.

2749. ——— *Smog Over Los Angeles.* [Los Angeles, c1959]. 53 pp.

2750. White, Magner. "The Air Apparent." *Los Angeles* 3 (May 1962): 27-9.

Los Angeles smog.

2751. "Why Los Angeles Area Has Smog." *Western City* 28 (August 1952): 53-4.

2752. Will, Arthur J. "We're Fighting Smog in Los Angeles." *California Magazine of the Pacific* 45 (March 1955): 25+.

2753. "Will Stop Air Pollution from Chemically Reactive Solvents." *American City* 82 (May 1967): 148+.

Los Angeles County Board of Supervisors adopts Rule 66, a regulation controlling the use of chemically reactive solvents in paint thinners, dry-cleaning fluids and ink.

2754. Zaren, A. M., and Rand, W. E. "Smog." *Scientific American* 186 (May 1952): 15-9.
Includes report on air-pollution studies done in Los Angeles.

ECOLOGY—CONSERVATION

2755. Alexander, Louis J. "One Chemical, Three Treatments at El Segundo Water Works." *American City* 54 (September 1939): 51-3+.

2756. Battle, Don. "Ancients of the Angeles Forest." *Westways* 54 (October 1962): 33.
Limber pines of the Angeles National Forest, very old trees which resemble the bristlecone pines of the White Mountains.

2757. Baumann, Paul. "Reclaimed Waste Water Possible Source for Fresh Water Barrier to Stem Sea Intrusion." *Western City* 33 (September 1957): 42-3.

2758. Boesen, Victor. "And the Hills Came Tumbling Down." *Frontier* 17 (April 1966): 10-5.
Land slippage.

2759. Bonderson, Paul R. "Cooperative Water Pollution Control Proved of Value in California." *Western City* 34 (October 1958): 26-8.

2760. Cecil, George H. *Conservation in Los Angeles County.* Los Angeles City School District School, *Publication No. 275.* [Los Angeles], 1935. 82 pp. 2nd ed., 1937. 95 pp.

2761. ———— "Increased County Funds for Watershed Protection." *Southern California Business* 8 (July 1929): 22-3.

2762. Chapman, George B. "Tree Planting and Maintenance in City of Beverly Hills." *Western City* 13 (March 1937): 33-4.

2763. Clark, I. L. K. "Park Commission of Burbank Enlists United Efforts of Citizens in 2,200-acre Reforestation Enterprise." *American City* 39 (August 1928): 109-10.

2764. "A Concerned Citizen Views the Beauty Gap." *Los Angeles* 13 (April 1968): 30-1.
Los Angeles.

2765. Cram, C. M. "Beach Erosion in Southern California." *Civil Engineering* 6 (December 1936): 808-9.

2766. Crowder, R[obert] E. "Beautification Trends in Urban Drillsites of the Los Angeles Basin." *Summary of Operations California Oil Fields* 51 (1965): 53-65.

2767. Dasmann, Raymond F. *The Destruction of California.* New York, 1966. 223 pp.

2768. Derby, Ray L. "Chlorinating Method Improved at Los Angeles." *Civil Engineering* 5 (September 1935): 558-61.

2769. Eldridge, Arthur. "Salvage from Rubbish in Los Angeles." *American City* 42 (May 1930): 19.

2770. Emery, Richard W. "Putting a Madcap River to Work." *Popular Mechanics* 86 (July 1946): 154-7+.
Describes how sand swept down Los Angeles River during high water is trapped at Long Beach and utilized for dikes and fill.

2771. Goudey, R[aymond] F. "Solving Boron Problems in Los Angeles Water Supply." *Western Construction News* 11 (September 1936): 295-7.

2772. Hall, L. Glenn. "Street Tree Beautification in Cities of the West." *Western City* 8 (July 1932): 25-7.
Includes Los Angeles and Beverly Hills.

2773. Hamilton, Andrew. "The Fight for Beauty: Los Angeles Citizens Prove Elimination of Eyesores Good Business, Contagious Example." *National Civic Review* 51 (February 1962): 66-9.
A condensation appears thusly: "The Lesson Los Angeles Learned: Civic Beauty Is Good Business." *Reader's Digest* 80 (March 1962): 212-4+.

2774. ———— "Undersea Housing Projects." *Westways* 57 (May 1965): 18-9.
Old auto wrecks submerged off Redondo Beach for fish to use as spawning grounds.

2775. Hedger, Harold E. "Los Angeles Considers Reclaiming Sewage Water to Recharge Underground Basins." *Civil Engineering* 20 (May 1950): 39-40.

2776. Holden, H. H. "Natural Beauty of Palos Verdes Hills Enhanced by Proper Adaptation of Architectural Designs." *Hydraulic Engineering* 4 (June 1928): 321-3.

2777. Hurlbut, William W. "Water and the West —The Relationship of Reclamation to Municipal Supply." *Western City* 23 (July 1947): 26-46.
   Deals with many western cities including Los Angeles.

2778. Johnson, A. G. "Beach Protection—Erosion, Pollution Mar Shores." *Western Construction News* 18 (June 1943): 259-62.
   Partly on Los Angeles County.

2779. Keller, Lewis. "No Sound Statutory Objections to Fluoridation of City Water Supplies in California Holds." *Western City* 28 (July 1952): 34-6.

2780. Laverty, Finley B. "Report Describes How Sea-Water Intrusion Is Stemmed in Recent Experimental Project by Flood Control Districts." *Western City* 31 (October 1955): 59-61+.

2781. Lillard, Richard G. *Eden in Jeopardy. Man's Prodigal Meddling with His Environment: The Southern California Experience.* New York, 1966. 329 pp.

2782. "Los Angeles to Test Purified Sewage as Water Source." *American City* 75 (October 1960): 21.

2783. Luippold, G. T. "The Use of Liquid Chlorine in Southern California for Purification and Sanition." *Hydraulic Engineering* 5 (November 1929): 30-5.

2784. Marlette, John W. "The Breakwater at Redondo Beach, California, and Its Effect on Erosion and Sedimentation." Master's thesis, University of Southern California, 1954. 80 pp.

2785. McKee, W. F. "The CCC in Southern California." *Southern California Business* 14 (February 1955): 9.
   Fort MacArthur Civilian Conservation Corps.

2786. Miller, James E. "Vegetation and Its Relationship to Land Use in the Santa Monica Mountains, California." Master's thesis, University of California, Los Angeles, 1969. 159 pp.

2787. Mount, William. "Burbank Builds Mountain Road, Parking Area with Rubbish Reclamation Fill." *Western City* 26 (February 1950): 30-5.

2788. Nadeau, Remi. "A Tree Grows in Los Angeles." *Westways* 51 (March 1959): 18-9.
   Planting of "street trees" in Los Angeles. A project launched by Valley M. Knudson and Charles M. Jones.

2789. "New Large Scale Experiment on How to Stem Sea Water Intrusion Authorized. Twelve Areas Now Affected." *Western City* 27 (September 1951): 32-5.
   Los Angeles basin included.

2790. Olewiler, Grant M., Jr. "Beach and Harbor Destruction Fought by Erosion Control Projects." *Western City* 34 (April 1958): 42-4.

2791. Ostrom, Elinor. "Public Entrepreneurship: A Case Study in Ground Water Basin Management." Master's thesis, University of California, Los Angeles, 1965. 2 vols.

2792. Palmer, Frank L. "Water Conservation in Pomona Valley." *Pomona Valley Historian* 3 (1967): 74-87.

2793. Parkhurst, John D. "The Market for 'Used' Water . . . Proves Brisk Enough to Require a Second Water-Reclamation Plant." *American City* 83 (March 1968): 78+.
   County Sanitation Districts Plant No. 1 in Pomona and new Plant No. 2.

2794. Parsons, Robert. "A Study of 1961-1962 Winter Rain Damage on Certain Firegrounds in the Major Watersheds of Los Angeles County." Master's thesis, University of Southern California, 1963. 79 pp.

2795. Pickett, Arthur. "Stop Ground-Water Pollution." *American City* 69 (August 1954): 95-6.
   "Los Angeles County is perhaps unique . . . because of its comprehensive protection program for underground water supplies."

2796. Poland, J. F. "Saline Contamination of Coastal Ground Water in Southern California." *Western City* 19 (October 1943): 46-50.
   Includes Los Angeles County.

2797. "Reclamation of Water From Sewage: Board

of Engineers Recommends Program for Los Angeles County to Provide a Supplemental Supply for Replenishment of Groundwater Resources and for Industry." *Western Construction News* 24 (November 15, 1949): 77-8.

2798. "Reclamation of Water from Sewage Safe and Feasible, Report Holds." *Western City* 25 (September 1949): 20.
  Report of Los Angeles County Sanitation District and Flood Control District.

2799. Reeves, Richard W. "Modifications of Drainage in the El Segundo Sand Hills of Coastal Southern California." Master's thesis, University of Southern California, Los Angeles, 1964. 139 pp.

2800. Reinhardt, R. T. "Storm Water Crossing over Outfall Sewer: Los Angeles Installation Involves Forty Foot Drop in Approximately One Hundred and Sixty-two Feet; Guard Against Erosion." *Western City* 7 (October 1931): 18.

2801. Robinson, John. "Can We Save Our Beaches?" *Westways* 59 (June 1967): 18-9.
  Explains why the quantity of sand being deposited along the coastline is diminishing.

2802. Romig, B. Eugene. "City Works with Private Companies to Develop New Wilderness Area." *Western City* 45 (March 1969): 28.
  Whittier.

2803. Rosecrans, W. S. "Woodman, Spare That Tree!" *Los Angeles Realtor* 5 (September 1926): 15+.
  Advises subdividers against cutting an excessive number of trees.

2804. "Salvaging Water Waste in the Los Angeles Coastal Basin." *California Highways and Public Works* 8 (July-August 1930): 15-6+.

2805. Shafer, Elsa. "The Civilian Conservation in the Angeles National Forest." Master's thesis, California State College at Los Angeles, 1966. 298 pp.

2806. Shanteau, Willard E. "Monrovia's Chemical-Controlled Weeds Reduce Cutting and Burning Expense." *Western City* 30 (December 1954): 29.

2807. Sharp, Frederick W., and Van Wagner, James H. "Pomona's On-Going Water Conservation and Re-Use Program." *Western City* 43 (April 1967): 23-6.

2808. Smith, Chester A. "Water Purification in Southern California." *Western Construction News* 6 (August 25, 1931): 443-8.
  Includes Los Angeles area.

2809. Stevenson, Ralph A. "Beverly Hills Tries Ferric Chloride." *Western Construction News* 7 (March 25, 1932): 167-8.
  Beverly Hills Filtration Plant No. 2.

2810. Updegraff, Winston R. "California Future Requires Replenishment of Ground Water Supply." *Western City* 30 (November 1954): 46-8.
  Long Beach.

2811. ——— "Minimum Standards, Pollution Control Approved by California Section AWWA [American Water Works Association]." *Western City* 24 (November 1948): 34-44.

2812. Van Norman, H. A. "How Los Angeles Keeps Its Water Pure." *American City* 40 (June 1929): 117-9.

2813. Vogel, Alice M. "Human Alteration of the Ecology of a Portion of the Los Angeles Basin: UCLA as an Example." Master's thesis, University of California, Los Angeles, 1968. 286 pp.

2814. Warren, Viola L. "The Eucalyptus Crusade." *Southern California Quarterly* 44 (1962): 31-42.

2815. "Water Conservation Program for Los Angeles County: Bond Issue of $35,300,000 to Provide Flood Storage and Replenish Underground Sources — High Dams Among Projects." *Engineering News-Record* 92 (June 26, 1924): 1088-90.

2816. "Water Quality Criteria Considered by Pollution Control Board." *Western City* 26 (May 1950): 24-7.
  Partly on Los Angeles.

2817. Wilson, Carl. "Chlorine Control of Certain Algae Growth in Los Angeles Reservoir." *Western City* 7 (October 1931): 25-8.

2818. Wilson, Carl. "Los Angeles Successfully Reclaims Sewage for Replenishment of Underground Water Supplies. *Western Construction News* 5 (September 25, 1930): 473-4.

2819. Woehl, Daniel C. "Forestry Camps in Los

Angeles County: Their Origin and Early Development." Master's thesis, University of Southern California, 1965. 71 pp.

2820. Wood, Richard J. "Cudahy Spearheads Conversion of Dump Site to New Civic Center—School Complex." *Western City* 42 (December 1966) : 45.

2821. Yates, June C. "Utilization of Completed Landfills in Metropolitan Los Angeles." Master's thesis, California State College at Los Angeles, 1966. 84 pp

ECOLOGY—REFUSE DISPOSAL

2822. Arlen, Don. "The Busy Beachcombers of Long Beach." *Western City* 43 (September 1967) : 60.
Maintaining cleanbeaches.

2823. Arnold, C. E. "Why Los Angeles County Adopted Cut-and-Cover Refuse Disposal." *American City* 66 (May 1951) : 92-3.

2824. Bargman, Robert D. " 'SAMMIS' Is the Latest Improvement in Los Angeles Refuse Collection Program." *Western City* 45 (February 1969) : 19-20.
SANMIS—Sanitation Management Information System. SANMIS is misspelled SAMMIS in title.

2825. Bowerman, F. R. "Los Angeles' Answer to the Long Haul Problem: Ban on Home Incinerators Creates Need for Special Trailers and Transfer Stations as Refuse Load Increases." *American City* 73 (October 1958) : 132-4.

2826. "Cleaning Vacant Lots and Streets in Pasadena, Calif." *American City* 54 (June 1939) : 98-9.

2827. Conti, L. F. "Special Equipment and Careful Supervision in Los Angeles County Remove Objections to Garbage Disposal by Hog Feeding." *American City* 43 (December 1930) : 86-9.

2828. Dorton, Randall M. "Santa Monica to Have New 200 Ton Incinerator under Lease Plan." *Western City* 27 (March 1951) : 33.

2829. Farnam, William F. "The Considerable Advantages of One-Man Refuse Collection . . . Include Twice as Much Production Per Man-Hour and a Phenomenal Drop in the Accident Rate." *American City* 84 (April 1969) : 87-8.
Inglewood.

2830. "Garbage Disposal by Feeding It Raw to Hogs on Way Out in California." *Western City* 30 (July 1954) : 51+.
Includes Los Angeles County.

2831. "Garbage Specifications of Santa Monica." *Pacific Municipalities* 17 (October 1907) : 66.
Garbage pickup program.

2832. "Gold in City Dump." *Business Week* (January 31, 1942) : 57-9.
"Mining" tin and other strategic metals from the Los Angeles city dump.

2833. Gruendyke, B. P. "Los Angeles County Machine-Cleans Its Beaches." *American City* 66 (June 1951) : 122-3.
Parks and Recreation Department's beach "Sanitizer."

2834. Haug, Lester A., and Davidson, Stanley. "Refuse Collection and Disposal Survey Indicates Changing Trends in 118 Western Cities." *Western City* 40 (April 1964) : 26-34; (May 1964) : 25-31.
Includes many Los Angeles County cities.

2835. "How 61 Cities Exercise Some Degree of Industrial Wastes Control." *Western City* 31 (May 1955) : 54-5.
Includes many Los Angeles County cities.

2836. "Incineration of Rubbish Recommended for Los Angeles Metropolitan Area." *Western City* 21 (August 1945) : 26-8.

2837. "Incinerator Recommended for Refuse Disposal in L. A. County." *Western City* 23 (May 1947) : 19.

2838. Ingham, Edwin A., and Jarrett, William M. "Alhambra to Build New Incinerator." *Western City* 25 (January 1949) : 27-9.

2839. Jarrett, W[illiam] M. "Operational Experience — Alhambra Incinerator and City Dump." *Western City* 29 (March 1953) : 59+.

2840. ———, and Larson, Linnie C. "Alhambra

Incinerator Undergoes Stiff Tests; Operation Costs Estimated." *Western City* 26 (May 1950): 32-5.

2841. Jessup, J[ohn] J. "Five Per Cent of City Budget Paid for Refuse Disposal." *American City* 49 (March 1934): 15.
Los Angeles.

2842. Johnson, Worth. "41 Years of Refuse Collection in Long Beach." *Western City* 38 (May 1962): 34-5.

2843. —— "Long Beach Uses 'Mock Up Area' to Test Safety Operations in Refuse Collection." *Western City* 36 (December 1960): 37-8.

2844. King, Maurice M. "New Incinerator for Santa Monica." *Western City* 28 (August 1952): 45-7.

2845. —— "Stationary Compactor at Refuse Transfer Station Saves Santa Monica $60,000 Per Year." *Western City* 37 (February 1961): 42-3.

2846. Larson, Linne C. "Beverly Hills Constructing 300 Ton Per Day Incinerator." *Western City* 23 (April 1947): 29-31.

2847. "Long Beach Refuse Collection and Disposal $4.28 Per Capita." *Western City* 34 (February 1958): 56-7.

2848. "Los Angeles Area Cities Struggle with Complicated Refuse Program." *Western City* 27 (August 1951): 35.

2849. "Los Angeles Constructs 800-Ton Refuse Incinerator." *Engineering News-Record* 99 (July 14, 1927): 54-5.

2850. Lynch, George E., and Metz, William. "Destruction of Combustible Refuse in Cities — How Beverly Hills Does It." *Western City* 12 (August 1936): 20-1+.

2851. Metz, William R. "Problems of Garbage Collection in Beverly Hills." *American City* 44 (June 1931): 17.

2852. "More on Grinders in Los Angeles." *American City* 67 (January 1952): 19.
Food-waste grinders (garbage disposals).

2853. "New 800-Ton Incinerator for Los Angeles." *Western Construction News* 2 (April 10, 1927): 51-3.

2854. "No Garbage . . . Because the 7,200 Homes in the Lakewood Park [*sic*], Calif., Housing Development Are Equipped with Food-Waste Disposal Units." *American City* 66 (September 1951): 104-5.

2855. Parkhurst, John D. "Sanitation Districts Implement Long-Range Refuse Plan for Los Angeles County." *Western City* 46 (April 1970): 15+.

2856. Pearson, Erman A., and Gotaas, Harold B. "Refuse Collection and Disposal Practice in California." *Western City* 28 (December 1952): 43-7.
Includes some Los Angeles County cities.

2857. Pickett, Arthur. "Refuse-Disposal Problems . . . And How Metropolitan Los Angeles Is Handling Them." *American City* 67 (August 1952): 96-7+.

2858. Rawn, A. M. "Los Angeles Experience Favors Central Garbage-Grinder Stations." *American City* 66 (April 1951): 122-3.

2859. —— "Planned Refuse Disposal for Los Angeles County." *Civil Engineering* 26 (April 1956): 41-5.

2860. ——, and Bowerman, F. R. "A Refuse Collection and Disposal Plan for 27 Cities and County Urban Areas: Elimination of Back Yard Burners and Central Grinding of Garbage to Sewers Proposed to Serve 1,800,000 Population; Financing Would Be by Ad Valorem Tax." *Western City* 26 (December 1950): 28-34.
Los Angeles County.

2861. "Santa Monica Considers Incinerator." *Western City* 23 (November 1947): 25.

2862. "Santa Monica's Weed Ordinance." *Pacific Municipalities* 16 (April 1907): 84-5.
Law requiring destruction of weeds in vacant lots.

2863. Scott, H. J. "Incinerator Handles Garbage-less Refuse." *American City* 64 (February 1949): 123+.
Beverly Hills.

2864. Sharp, Fred. "Pomona Awards Contract for

225 Ton Capacity Incinerator." *Western City* 25 (November 1949): 41.

2865. Shelley, Chet. "Montebello Solves Salvage Problem." *Western City* 19 (December 1943): 17.

2866. Simons, Seward C. "Garbage and Rubbish Disposal in Los Angeles, Calif." *Engineering News* 76 (October 12, 1916): 677-80.

2867. "South Pasadena Institutes Rear Yard Refuse Service with New Equipment." *Western City* 26 (December 1950): 35.

2868. "Special Equipment and Careful Supervision in Los Angeles County Remove Objections to Garbage Disposal by Hog Feeding." *American City* 43 (December 1930): 86-9.

2869. Stewart, R. W. "Garbage Collection and Disposal." *Pacific Municipalities* 42 (February 1928): 45-8.

2870. ———— "Garbage Collection and Disposal in Los Angeles." *American City* 38 (April 1928): 155+.

2871. Stone, Ralph, and Bowerman, Francis R. "Municipal Incinerators in California." *Western City* 28 (January 1952): 36-8.

Includes several Los Angeles County cities. Los Angeles was first California city to have a municipal incinerator.

2872. Taylor, John R. "A Survey of Refuse Disposal in Los Angeles." *American City* 48 (May 1933): 55-7.

2873. "35 Los Angeles Area Cities Included in New District Refuse Study." *Western City* 25 (November 1949): 42.

2874. "Three-Phase Long-Range Refuse Disposal Plan Is Proposed for 39 Cities in Los Angeles Area by Sanitation Districts Staff." *Western City* 31 (September 1955): 42-7.

2875. Tibbett, William M., and Carroll, William J. "Are Grease Traps Necessary for Restaurant Sewer Operation? Two Studies in the Los Angeles Area Disclose That They Are Not—the Cost Is Greater Than Possible Benefits." *American City* 66 (July 1951): 98-100.

2876. "To Help Combat Smog Los Angeles Embarks on City-Wide Collection of Combustible Refuse with Fleet of 178 New Vehicles." *Western City* 33 (April 1957): 36-9.

2877. Updegraff, Winston R. "Collection and Disposal of Garbage and Refuse in California Cities." *Western City* 19 (October 1943): 16-23; (November 1943): 19-25.

Includes many Los Angeles County cities.

2878. ————, and Bartle, Richard. "Refuse Collection and Disposal in 156 California Cities." *Western City* 25 (July 1949): 37-40; (August 1949): 23-34; (September 1949): 34-5.

Includes many Los Angeles County cities.

2879. ————, and Bowerman, Francis R. "Refuse Collection and Disposal in 194 Western Cities." *Western City* 34 (May 1958): 32-40; (June 1958): 32-3+; (July 1958): 28-34.

2880. Watson, K. S. "Solving Community Garbage Problems by the Use of Disposers." *Western City* 40 (April 1964): 36-9.

Mostly Los Angeles County cities.

2881. Wilhelms, Meno. "Hawthorne's Refuse Collection Provides New Sanitary Containers." *Western City* 32 (August 1956): 47.

2882. Williams, Alan J. "Mayor Poulson Proposes Collection of Combustible Rubbish by City." *Western Housing* 38 (May 1955): 8+.

2883. Zapf, Fritz, and Giles, Henry. "Mammoth Trucks and Mini Scooters . . . Cooperate to Cut the Cost of Refuse Collection." *The American City* 82 (January 1967): 77-9.

Pasadena.

ECOLOGY—SEWAGE CONTROL

2884. Aldrich, L[loyd M.]. "Sewer Maintenance Operations in Los Angeles." *American City* 50 (July 1935): 11.

2885. ————, and Smith, H. G. "Los Angeles' $41,000,000 Hyperion Project Ends Beach Contamination." *Civil Engineering* 18 (July 1948): 18-23+.

2886. Allin, J. H. "Pasadena Sewer Is Extended: Recently Completed Extension to the West Side Outfall Sewer of the City of Pasadena, Calif., Will Relieve the Overtaxed Sewer System and Correct the Resulting Unsanitary Conditions." *Western Construction News* 18 (December 1943): 551-3.

2887. Allin, T. D. "Pasadena Sewer Farm." *Pacific Municipalities* 12 (February 1905): 3-8.

2888. "Arcadia Builds Sewerage System." *Western City* 24 (August 1948): 22.

2889. Arnold, C. E. "Altadena, Calif., Builds Sewers to Protect Water Supply." *American City* 66 (November 1951): 127.

2890. "Beach Again Closed by Quarantine." *Western City* 23 (September 1947): 24.
Santa Monica Bay polluted by sewage.

2891. "Beach Pollution Control Speeded by Huge Chlorination Plant: Installation Includes Seven of Largest Size Chlorinators Made; Operation During Summer Bathing Season Will Cost City of Los Angeles Approximately $1000 Daily." *Western City* 23 (January 1947): 16-8.

2892. Belt, Elmer. "Sanitary Survey of Sewage Pollution of Santa Monica Bay." *Western City* 19 (June 1943): 17-22.

2893. "Big Wye for Hyperion Outfall." *Public Works* 91 (March 1960): 121.

2894. Bowlus, Fred D. "60 percent of Population Served by 40 California Ocean Outfall Sewers from San Francisco Bay to Mexican Border." *Western City* 31 (April 1955): 42-4.

2895. Brown, Reuben F. "Down to the Sea by Sewer—How It Was Done and What Was Found." *Western City* 12 (December 1936): 13-5+.
Fifty-mile Los Angeles County Outfall Sewer.

2896. Carpenter, S. E. "Ocean Outfall Sewers for Avalon, California." *Western Construction News* 5 (September 25, 1930): 475-6.
Catalina Island.

2897. "Chlorination to Clear Portion of Sewage Contaminated Beach." *Western City* 22 (February 1946): 16-7.
Santa Monica Bay.

2898. "Comprehensive Sewer Plan Proposed for Los Angeles County." *National Municipal Review* 14 (September 1925): 579.

2899. "Contracts Totaling $2,500,000 Awarded for Sewer Tunnel at Los Angeles." *Western Construction News* 10 (July 1935): 205.

2900. Davis, H. E. "Development of the Los Angeles Sewer System." *California Engineer* 4 (December 1925): 107-8.

2901. "Dual Fuel Engines Gain Favor in Sewage Treatment Plants: Columbus, Ohio, and Los Angeles, Calif., Sewage-Plant Improvements Include Use of Gas-Oil Engines to Meet Their Power Needs." *American City* 65 (April 1950): 88-9.

2902. Earle, W. C. "Pasadena Activated Sludge Sewage Treatment Plant." *Western Construction News* 4 (March 10, 1929): 131-9.

2903. "Enlisting Citizen Cooperation for Sewage Treatment and Other Coastline Improvements." *American City* 60 (February 1945): 78.
Summary of *Coastline Plans and Action,* a pamphlet by Donald F. Griffin and Charles W. Eliot advocating development of the Los Angeles metropolitan coastline.

2904. Farrand, William. "Centrifugally Cast Concrete Pipe Used for New Venice Outfall Sewer Line." *Hydraulic Engineering* 4 (December 1928): 753-5.

2905. "Findings of Los Angeles Sewage Disposal Commission." *Engineering News-Record* 86 (June 30, 1921): 1117-8.

2906. Froehde, F. C. "How Pomona Makes Money Selling Sewage Effluent for Irrigation Use." *Western City* 6 (January 1930): 39-40+.

2907. Garrison, Walt. "Growth of a Sewerage System—A Matter of Evolution." *Western City* 45 (April 1969): 13-4.
Los Angeles County Sanitation Districts.

2908. Goudey, R. F. "Disposal of Sewage Sludge at Pasadena." *American City* 39 (December 1928): 101-2.

2909. ——— "Plans for Sewage Reclamation in the Los Angeles Metropolitan Area." *Engineering News-Record* 106 (March 12, 1931): 443-6.

2910. —— "Report on New Outfall Sewer." *Municipal League of Los Angeles Bulletin* 3 (August 1925): 12-3.
Hyperion.

2911. —— "Sewage Reclamation Plant for Los Angeles." *Western Construction News* 5 (October 25, 1930): 519-25.

2912. Graham, E. H., Jr. "New Ocean and Land Outfall Sewers in Los Angeles' $60 Million Program." *Western City* 32 (April 1956): 34-6+.

2913. Hincks, Harvey W. "Sludge Disposal at the Pasadena Plant." *Civil Engineering* 5 (September 1935): 561-4.

2914. "Hyperion Screening Plant to Be Modified." *Western Construction News and Highways Builder* 9 (February 1934): 69.
Hyperion sewage treatment plant.

2915. Jarmuth, John. "Handling a Big Sewer Proposition." *Southern California Business* 4 (August 1925): 17+.
Los Angeles Metropolitan sewer system.

2916. Jones, Helen L. "Description of Pasadena Sewer Farm." *Pacific Municipalities* 10 (March 1904): 39-47.

2917. Kennedy, Robert E. "Long Beach, Calif.— Sewer Ball Cleans Lines: Tests with a Beach Ball Develop a Method That Keeps Sewers Clear and Free-Flowing." *American City* 63 (July 1948): 94-5.

2918. Knowlton, W. T. "Disposal of Los Angeles City Sewage." *Municipal League of Los Angeles Bulletin* 4 (January 31, 1927): 7-8.

2919. —— "Los Angeles Sewage Disposal Plans Assuming Final Form." *Engineering News-Record* 90 (June 7, 1923): 1000-1.

2920. —— "New Ocean Outfall and Screens for Los Angeles Sewage." *Engineering News-Record* 86 (February 24, 1921): 331-2.
Hyperion.

2921. —— "Progress on North Outfall Sewer for City of Los Angeles." *Engineering News-Record* 92 (April 24, 1924): 730-1.

2922. "Large Screening Plant Handles Los Angeles Sewage." *Engineering News-Record* 96 (June 3, 1926): 898-900.
Hyperion.

2923. "Largest Sewage-Treatment Plant in Country Will Correct Beach Pollution: Hyperion Plant at Los Angeles Will Serve 150-Square-Mile Area with Three Million Inhabitants." *American City* 64 (February 1949): 84-5+.

2924. Larson, Linne C. "Cast-Iron Intercepting Sewer at San Pedro." *Western Construction News and Highways Builder* 7 (September 25, 1932): 540.

2925. "Los Angeles Allots Two Million for New Sewer." *Western Construction News* 20 (December 1945): 92.
Mayor Fletcher Bowron signs appropriation for new Hyperion outfall.

2926. "Los Angeles Builds Novel Temporary Outfall Sewer under Order of Court." *Pacific Municipalities* 38 (September 1924): 322.

2927. "Los Angeles Builds Sewer System in a Town 250 Mi. Away." *Western Construction News and Highways Builder* 9 (February 1934): 69.
Lone Pine.

2928. "Los Angeles County Sanitation Districts." *Western Construction News* 3 (July 25, 1928): 485-7.

2929. "Los Angeles County Sanitation Districts Find—Derrick Key to Deep Water Pipe Laying." *Western Construction* 31 (November 1956): 42-3+.
White Point.

2930. "Los Angeles Plans 'Water Reclamation'." *American City* 65 (February 1950): 11.
Sewage reclamation.

2931. "L.A. Sewer Pipe and Trench Specifications: City, County, and County Sanitation District Engineers Adopt Uniform Set of Specifications for Use by Public Agencies Constructing Sewers in Los Angeles County." *Western Construction News and Highways Builder* 8 (March 10, 1933): 143-6.

2932. "Los Angeles Tackles Sewage Problem." *Western Construction News* 20 (May 1945): 93.
Rehabilitation of Hyperion sewage treatment plant.

2933. "Los Angeles Votes Bond Issues for Airport, Sewage Treatment." *Western City* 21 (May 1945): 29.

2934. Machado, Frederick. "50 Miles of Sewer Maintenance Per Year No Strain in Culver City's New Program." *Western City* 38 (April 1962): 31.

2935. "Making Sewer Maintenance Safe: The Los Angeles Bureau of Maintenance and Sanitation Establishes Some Standards Based on Experience Where the Problem Is Critical." *American City* 59 (January 1944): 48-9.

2936. Miller, David R. "Outfall Pipeline Pulled 7 Mi. to Sea." *Western Construction* 32 (July 1957): 23-6.
Hyperion.

2937. "New Construction Will Double Los Angeles Co. Sewerage." *Western Construction News* 23 (September 1948): 81-4.

2938. "New Hyperion Outfall in Service." *Western City* 25 (December 1949): 33.

2939. Nikolitch, Milan. "Sewerage System of Los Angeles and Sewage Irrigation in Southern California." Master's thesis, University of California, Berkeley, 1906. 48 pp.

2940. "Nine Dual Fuel Diesel Engines a Feature of Hyperion Plant." *Western City* 25 (September 1949): 41.

2941. Noel P. D. "Bathing Beaches and the Sewage." *Municipal League of Los Angeles Bulletin* 6 (October 1, 1928): [6-7].

2942. Orbison, R[obert] [V.]. "How the Activated Sludge Process of Sewage Disposal Is Working in Pasadena." *Pacific Municipalities* 31 (November 1917): 594-606.
[Typographical error uses middle initial "B."]

2943. "Outfall Sewer Extension Proposed for Los Angeles Studies." *Western City* 22 (August 1946): 54.

2944. Pardee, Lyall A. "Double-Barreled Clay-Pipe Sewer . . . Solves a Difficult Corrosion Problem." *American City* 81 (December 1966): 82-3.

Part of the La Cienega and San Fernando Valley Relief Sewer.

2945. Parkes, Geoffrey A. "Los Angeles Aims at Perfection: New Hyperion Activated-Sludge Plant Incorporates Thorough Treatment, Power Development, and Fertilizer Production." *American City* 6 (June 1951): 79-81+.

2946. ———. "Los Angeles New 245 M.G.D. Hyperion Treatment Plant Nears Completion: Primary Portion to Be Placed in Operation This Summer; Activated Sludge Plant Combines Sludge Digestion, Power Generation and Fertilizer Production; Cost Is $41 Million." *Western City* 26 (April 1950): 28-37.

2947. ———. "Sewage Plant Features Sludge and Gas Handling." *Western Construction News* 11 (November 1936): 355-7.
Terminal Island.

2948. "Pre-Stressed Concrete Tanks at Hyperion: Los Angeles Constructing Nation's Largest High-rate Activated Sludge Plant for Treatment of Sewage—Outstanding Feature of the $41,000,000 Construction Is Prestressing of 18 Circular Concrete Digestion Tanks." *Western Construction News* 24 (October 15, 1949): 86-9.

2949. "Preventive Maintenance Provides Savings for Long Beach Sewer Care." *Western City* 35 (April 1959): 29+.

2950. "Quarantine of Beach from Pollution Reduces Use to Minimum." *Western City* 20 (February 1944): 19.
Santa Monica Bay polluted by sewage.

2951. Rawn, A. M. "Downey-Bellflower Sanitary Trunk Sewer." *Western Construction News* 6 (May 10, 1931): 222.

2052. ———. "Novel Sludge Digestion Tanks Completed." *Civil Engineering* 1 (August 1931): 997-1000.
Joint disposal plant of Los Angeles Sanitation Districts.

2953. ———. "Western Water and Sewage Programs: Sanitation in L.A. County." *Western Construction News* 22 (July 1947): 97.

2954. Reeves, Carl H. "Maintaining 400 Miles of

Lateral Sewers." *Western City* 7 (February 1931): 38-9.
Los Angeles County.

2955. "Report Points Out Los Angeles Sanitation Needs." *Western City* 15 (December 1939): 31.

2956. Reynolds, Leon R. "Sewage Treatment in the Far West." *Western City* 23 (July 1947): 49-57.
Discusses various western cities, including Los Angeles.

2957. "Sanitary Engineers Report on Ocean Pollution by L.A. Sewer." *Western Construction News* 18 (September 1943): 399.

2958. "Saturday Night's Library of Civic Projects: Sewage, a City's Indigestion." *Pacific Saturday Night* 44 (October 9, 1937): 2-8A.
Describes Los Angeles sewage disposal and needed improvements.

2959. Sawyer, W. C. "Mar Vista Avenue Sewer District and Pumping Plant, Los Angeles." *Western Construction News* 2 (November 10, 1927): 38-9.

2960. Schneider, W. A. "1 Lubricant Replaces 20 at Los Angeles Hyperion Sewage-Treatment Plant." *American City* 68 (December 1953): 102-3.

2961. "Sending Sewage to Sea Saves the Los Angeles Sands." *Business Week* (September 21, 1957): 84-5+.
"To Make Sure Its Famous Beaches Will Never Again Be Contaminated By A Leaking Sewer Outlet, Los Angeles Is Building Two Spectacular Underwater Pipelines."

2962. "Sewage Sterilization Experiments Made by Los Angeles." *Western City* 22 (May 1946): 54+.

2963. "Sewage Treatment Plant for Los Angeles." *American City* 59 (December 1944): 11.
Metcalf and Eddy plan for Hyperion.

2964. "Sewer Tunnel and Outfall to Complete Program for Los Angeles Districts." *Western Construction News* 10 (December 1935): 340-2.
White Point.

2965. "Sharp Tunneling Practice for White Point Outfall." *Western Construction* 30 (September 1955): 47-8.
Los Angeles County Sanitation Districts.

2966. Shaw, John C. "Los Angeles Sanitary Sewer Program." *Pacific Municipalities* 43 (April 1929): 154-5.

2967. "Shoreline Development Study for Los Angeles." *American City* 59 (August 1944): 11.
Study compiled under sponsorship of the Greater Los Angeles Citizens Committee, Inc., calls attention to pollution of Santa Monica Bay because of inadequacy of Hyperion treatment plant.

2968. "Should Long Beach Vote $3,400,000 to Help Pour County Sewage into the Sea?" *Municipal League of Los Angeles Bulletin* 7 (March 1, 1930): [1-8].
Includes:
"Sewage Laws and Their Administration," by W. E. Hinshaw, pp. [1-2];
"Sewage Needs of the Harbor District," by E. D. Seward, pp. [2-4];
"Modern Sanitation for Los Angeles," by W. T. Knowlton, pp. [5-7]; and
"How Pasadena Solves Her Sewage Problem," by City Engineer Hooper [*sic*], pp. [7-8].

2969. Smith, H. G. "Los Angeles Incinerates Sewage Screenings." *Civil Engineering* 4 (June 1934): 293-5.
Hyperion.

2970. ———. "Los Angeles Sewage Plant Redesigned and Enlarged." *Western Construction News* 11 (April 1936): 112-3.
Hyperion.

2971. ———. "New Sewage Treatment Plant for the City of Los Angeles." *Western City* 12 (January 1936): 22.
Hyperion.

2972. Strother, Vane. "New Los Angeles Sewer Outfall." *Western Construction News* 22 (November 1947): 80-3.
Hyperion.

2973. "Swimming Forbidden as Sewage Pollutes Beach." *Western Construction News* 18 (July 1943): 301.
Santa Monica Bay.

2974. Taylor, A. A. "Signal Hill Sewers and Sewage Treatment Plant." *Western Construction News and Highways Builder* 8 (September 1933): 369-72.

2975. "Trailer-Mounted Sewer Cleaner Removes Roots and Deposits: Crew of Three and Machine Make Five Set-Ups Daily in Cleaning Los Angeles Sewers." *American City* 54 (October 1939): 50-1.

2976. "A $24,000,000 Program to Improve Los Angeles Sewers." *Western Construction News* 13 (May 1938): 190-1.

2977. $21,000,000 Sewage Treatment Plant and Ocean Outfall Recommended." *Western City* 20 (May 1944): 20-1.
Metcalf and Eddy plan for Hyperion.

2978. $2,000,000 Sanitary Sewer System Being Placed in Altadena Area." *Western City* 28 (June 1952): 62-3.

2979. "Use of Sewage Sludge Gas for Pump Operation Shows Economics." *Western City* 12 (March 1936): 38-9.
Los Angeles County Sanitation Districts.

2980. Van Norman, H. A. "Open Sea Construction of a Concrete Pipe Sewer Outfall." *Engineering News-Record* 95 (August 20, 1925): 292-4.
Hyperion.

2981. Veatch, F. M. "Activated-Sludge Plant for Three Small California Cities." *Engineering News-Record* 97 (July 1, 1926): 10-3.
Pomona, Claremont and LaVerne.

2982. Warren, A. K. "Los Angeles County Metropolitan Sewer: Permit Granted by State Board of Health for Construction of 5000-ft. Submarine-Tunnel Outfall Sewer at White Point—$10,000,000 Construction Program to Proceed." *Western Construction News* 2 (May 10, 1927): 45.

2983. —— "Metropolitan Sewer Plan for Los Angeles County." *Engineering News-Record* 94 (June 18, 1925): 1026.

2984. Williamson, C. J. S. "Industry's Wastes Go to Sea: The East Side's New Outfall Sewer, WPA Job, Solves the Problem for All Time." *Southern California Business* 16 (August 1937): 10-1.
Los Angeles.

2985. Wilson, Arthur L. "Sewage Treatment Design Is Serious Business . . . in Los Angeles Where the City Is Embarking on a Record-Breaking Study of a Persistent Pollution Problem." *American City* 71 (October 1956): 101-4.

2986. Woodworth, Robert M. "Long Beach Adds Two Automatic Relift Pumping Plants to Sewage System." *Hydraulic Engineering* 5 (October 1929): 13-4+.

2987. Wyman, A. H. "Two Comminutors Increase Fertilizer Recovery at Pasadena Sewage Treatment Plant." *Western City* 13 (April 1937): 44-5.

EDUCATION

EDUCATION—GENERAL

2988. Adams, Glen W. "The Unesco Controversy in Los Angeles, 1951-1953. A Case Study of the Influences of Right-Wing Groups on Urban Affairs." Doctoral dissertation, University of Southern California, 1970. 166 pp.

2989. Allen, Harlie B. "The Administration of an Educational Program in a Changing Neighborhood." Master's thesis, University of California, Los Angeles, 1955. 180 pp.

2990. Allen, Mary L. *Education or Indoctrination.* Caldwell, Idaho, 1956. 216 pp.
The Pasadena public school controversy, 1950-51.

2991. Alves, Euro F. "Evaluating Supervisory Training in Los Angeles County." Master's thesis, University of Southern California, 1963. 114 pp.

2992. American Civil Liberties Union. Southern California Branch. *A Call for Integrated Schools.* [Los Angeles, 1963?]. 23 pp.
Relates mainly to Los Angeles.

2993. Anderson, Chloe C. "A Study of the Health Work of the Schools of Long Beach, California." Master's thesis, University of Southern California, 1922. 263 pp.

2994. Ashcraft, Julian H. "A Classified Compilation of Administrative Policies in Physical Education for Long Beach Schools." Master's thesis, University of Southern California, 1940. 210 pp.

2995. Ashe, Bertram L. "A Study of Lay Advisory Committees in Los Angeles County." Master's thesis, University of Southern California, 1960. 83 pp.

2996. Austin, James A. "A Survey of the Los Angeles County Special Schools." Master's thesis, University of Southern California, 1956. 97 pp.

2997. Baird, Victor W. "A Survey of What the Teachers of the El Monte School District Believe Their Role Should Be in Public Relations." Master's thesis, University of Southern California, 1955. 73 pp.

2998. Bamber, Edwin E. "Faculty Meetings in Pomona Schools." Master's thesis, Claremont Graduate School, 1960. 88 pp.

2999. Banks, Reginald G. "Development of Salary Schedules for Burbank School Teachers." Master's thesis, University of Southern California, 1938. 152 pp.

3000. Barden, Harold E. "A Survey of the Department of Research and Guidance of the Los Angeles City Schools." Master's thesis, University of Southern California, 1933. 107 pp.

3001. Barlow, Melvin L. "A History of Trade and Industrial Education in Los Angeles." Doctoral dissertation, University of California, Los Angeles, 1949. 373 pp.

3002. Barnes, Myron C. "An Evaluation of a Proposed Local Teacher Retirement System for the City of Los Angeles." Master's thesis, University of Southern California, 1934. 120 pp.

3003. Barrett, Robert E. "Evaluation of In-Service Education Needs in the Lawndale School District." Master's thesis, University of Southern California, 1961. 104 pp.

3004. Bloom, Clarence H. "Teacher Orientation Practices of Los Angeles County School Districts." Master's thesis, University of Southern California, 1953. 71 pp.

3005. Boesen, Victor. "Why I Quit Teaching." *Reporter* 11 (July 6, 1954): 18-21.
    Describes effect on Los Angeles teachers of the Dilworth Act, requiring a loyalty oath.

3006. Boone, A[ndrew] R. "From Play Jobs to Real Jobs: Vocational Training from Kindergarten to High School Fits Students to Follow Careers in Industry." *Popular Science* 137 (October 1940): 102-4.
    Los Angeles.

3007. Boothe, Barbara, and Pollard, Shirley. "The Role of the Child Welfare and Attendance Worker in the Los Angeles City Schools." Master's thesis, University of Southern California, 1960. 61 pp.

3008. Bowling, William C. "A Curriculum Analysis of the School District of San Gabriel, California." Master's thesis, Chico State College, 1955. 392 pp.

3009. Boyington, Chester J. "The Cost of Government and the Support of Education for Los Angeles County, California." Master's thesis, University of Southern California, 1935. 228 pp.

3010. Brophy, Helen E. "A Study of the Problems of Interrelationships as Reported by the School Nurses of the Pasadena City Schools." Master's thesis, University of California, Los Angeles, 1956. 123 pp.

3011. Brown, W[illia]m B. "New Approaches to Curriculum Building in the Los Angeles City Schools." *School and Society* 42 (September 1935): 332-4.

3012. Buhrman, Robert. "The Wayward Bus: Has Integration Made a Wrong Turn?" *Los Angeles* 15 (March 1970): 28-31+.
    Judge Alfred Gitelson's integration decision.

3013. California Taxpayers Association. *Survey of the Pasadena City Schools.* Los Angeles, 1931. 331 pp.

3014. Callahan, Robert B. "In-Service Training in the Los Angeles City School Districts." Master's thesis, University of Southern California, 1950. 128 pp.

3014. Carl, Ernest W. "School Building Survey of Pomona." Master's thesis, Claremont Graduate School, 1933. 122 pp.

3016. Carlson, Carl H. "The Historical Development of the Advisement Service of the Los Angeles City Schools [1945 to 1953]." Master's thesis, University of Southern California, 1953. 156 pp.

3017. Carr, Dorothy B. "Teaching Homebound Pupils by Telephone in Los Angeles." Doctoral dissertation, University of California, Los Angeles, 1965. 219 pp.

3018. Caughey, John W. *Segregation Blights Our Schools: An Analysis Based on the 1966 Official Report on Racial and Ethnic Distribution School by School Throughout the Los Angeles System.* Los Angeles, 1967. 20 pp.

3019. ———— "Segregation Increases in Los Angeles: District Survey Shows Racial Concentrations Still Characterize Most of City's Schools. *California Teachers Association Journal* 64 (October 1968): 39-41.

3020. ————, and Caughey, LaRee. *School Segregation on Our Doorstep: The Los Angeles Story.* Los Angeles, 1966. 103 pp.

3021. Chapin, Alice C. "Organization of Speech Correction Classes in Los Angeles City Schools." *Quarterly Journal of Speech Education* 13 (1927): 24-9.

3022. Chiljan, Diane G. "An Investigation of the Utilization of the Education Radio Series, 'People, Places, and Things,' in Schools of Los Angeles County." Master's thesis, University of California, Los Angeles, 1958. 116 pp.

3023. Clark, Jessica B. "The Operation of the Emergency Education Program in Los Angeles, California." Master's thesis, University of Southern California, 1935. 140 pp.

3024. Cleland, Donald M. "Historical Study of the Santa Monica City Schools." Doctoral dissertation, University of California, Los Angeles, 1952. 281 pp.

3025. Clifton, A. R. "The Schools of Los Angeles County." *Overland Monthly* 89 (July 1931): 17+.

3026. Cloud, Roy W. *Education in California; Leaders, Organizations and Accomplishments of the First Hundred Years.* Stanford, [1952]. 296 pp.
General history.

3027. Collins, Mary E. "A Study of the 1936-37 Programs of the Parent-Teachers Associations of Los Angeles." Master's thesis, University of Southern California, 1938. 107 pp.

3028. Conrad, Warren C. "The Los Angeles City Public Schools." *Overland Monthly* 89 (July 1931): 13.

3029. Cooper, Jeannette. "A Survey of the Student Aid Program of the National Youth Administration in the Santa Monica School System." Master's thesis, University of Southern California, 1941. 93 pp.

3030. Cornelison, Bernice M. "Critical Study of Certain Experiments Carried on in an Expanded Educational Program in the Church Schools of Los Angeles and Vicinity." Master's thesis, University of Southern California, 1930. 114 pp.

3031. Coss, Joe G. "The Schools of Downey: One Hundred Years from 1867 to 1967." *The Downey Historical Society Annual* 1 (1966-67): 11-23.

3032. Couch, Gretchen P. "Adjustment Problems in Child Welfare and Attendance Service in the Glendale City Schools, 1932-38." Master's thesis, University of Southern California, 1940. 320 pp.

3033. Crebs, Clara (Wells). *History of the Los Angeles Federation, Tenth District California Congress of Mothers and Parent-Teacher Associations from May 1, 1911 to May 1, 1922.* [N.p., n.d.]. 178 pp.

3034. Cunliffe, William. "Public Opinion Techniques in the Public School Relations Program, with Special Reference to the Long Beach City Schools During the Years 1912-32." Master's thesis, Claremont Graduate School, 1939. 215 pp.

3035. Cunningham, Ray M. "A Pupil Population Study in the City of Long Beach, California." Master's thesis, University of Southern California, 1931. 36 pp.

3036. Daniels, Preston W. "The Effect of Unauthorized Activity on the Incidence of Injury in the Los Angeles City Schools, 1961 and 1962; A Comparative Study." Master's thesis, University of California, Los Angeles, 1963. 78 pp.

3037. Diether, Ray O. "The Professional Preparation and Improvement While in Service of the Teachers of Berkeley, Oakland and Los Angeles." Master's thesis, University of California, Berkeley, 1921. 63 pp.

3038. "The Dismissal of Dr. Sutherland." *Municipal League of Los Angeles Bulletin* 2 (August 15, 1924): [13-15].

Refusal of the Board of Education to renew the appointment of Dr. Arthur H. Sutherland, Director of Psychological Research for the city school system.

3039. Doak, Helen P. "The Induction of New Teachers into the Educational Program of Los Angeles County." Master's thesis, University of Southern California, 1946. 166 pp.

3040. Docter, Robert L. "Survey of Los Angeles Public Opinion Concerning Education." Master's thesis, University of Southern California, 1957. 117 pp.

3041. Donner, Ruth. "A History of the Governmental Provisions for Public Education in Los Angeles [1781-1934]." Master's thesis, University of Southern California, 1934. 152 pp.

3042. Dorsey, Susan M. "Contributions of Part-Time Education in Los Angeles," in National Education Association *Proceedings and Addresses.* Washington, D.C. 1922. Pp. 558-60.

3043. ———— "Investing $61,000,000 in Child Education." *Southern California Business* 5 (March 1926): 15+.

Los Angeles schools.

3044. ———— $17,400,000 for Los Angeles Schools." *American City* 27 (November 1922): 420-1.

School bond measure passed by 15 to 1 majority.

3045. Douglass, Inez D. "Study of the Clauses of Truancy Among Girls in Los Angeles." Master's thesis, University of Southern California, 1921. 48 pp.

3046. Downey, John H. "Population and Enrollment Forecast of the Arcadia Unified School District." Master's thesis, University of Southern California, 1955. 91 pp.

3047. Dumke, Herbert W. "A Study of the Organization and Function of the Los Angeles City School Cafeterias." Master's thesis, University of Southern California, 1934. 201 pp.

3048. Eales, John R. "A Brief, General History of the Los Angeles City School System." Doctoral dissertation, University of California, Los Angeles, 1956. 331 pp.

3049. Eason, Charles L. "An Analysis of the Social Attitudes and Causal Factors of Negro Problem Boys of the Los Angeles City Schools." Master's thesis, University of Southern California, 1936. 96 pp.

3050. Eckert, Earl W. "A Survey of Summer School Programs in Los Angeles County, 1959." Doctoral dissertation, University of Southern California, 1962. 529 pp.

3051. Edkar, Maxwell E. "A Survey of the Community Resources That May Be Utilized by the Schools of Montebello, California." Master's thesis, University of Southern California, 1941. 96 pp.

3052. "Educational Advantages of City and County." *Los Angeles Saturday Night 150th Birthday of Los Angeles: Fiesta and Pre-Olympiad.* Special Issue (1931): [15].

3053. Ehmann, Gerhard E. "Teacher Evaluation of Selected Aspects of the Long Beach Schools Curriculum Development Plan." Master's thesis, University of California, Los Angeles, 1948. 123 pp.

3054. Elder, George R. "A Critical Evaluation of Weekday Religious Education in Selected Los Angeles School Areas." Master's thesis, University of Southern California, 1950. 142 pp.

3055. Elmak, Ali Mohamed Ali. "The Los Angeles Joint Salary Survey." Master's thesis, University of Southern California, 1966. 146 pp.

3056. Falk, Charles J. *"The Development and Organization of Education in California.* New York, [1968]. 264 pp.

While the main focus is on the state as a whole, there are occasional references to Los Angeles.

3057. Farquar, Gloria. "Retreat from Reason: The Attack on UNESCO." *Frontier* 4 (November 1952): 5-7.

Controversy in Los Angeles over a teacher's manual called "The E in UNESCO."

3058. Feitshans, F. R. "The Realtor and the Public Schools." *Los Angeles Realtor* 5 (September 1926): 17+.

Public school enrollment and building as index of Los Angeles growth.

3059. Ferrier, W[illiam] W. *Ninety Years of Education in California (1846-1936).* Berkeley, 1937. 413 pp.

References to education in Los Angeles area.

3060. Fife, Lorin M., Jr. "The Factors Causing Teacher Terminations in the Los Angeles City School Districts." Master's thesis, University of Southern California, 1959. 104 pp.

3061. Finch, Arnold E. "The Relationship of In-Service Education to Competence of Selected Teachers of the Los Angeles City School Districts." Doctoral dissertation, University of California, Los Angeles, 1964. 213 pp.

3062. Finney, Guy W. "Mrs. Dorsey Points to Better Ways." *California Graphic* 5 (March 17, 1928): 7+.

Mrs. Susan M. Dorsey heads Los Angeles public school system.

3063. Fodor, John T. "An Analysis of the School Health Program in Seventy-One Schools within the Los Angeles City School Districts." Master's thesis, University of California, Los Angeles, 1958. 151 pp.

3064. Francis, J. H. "High Points in the Los Angeles Plan," in National Education Association *Proceedings and Addresses.* (Washington, D.C., 1916). Pp. 988-93.

3065. Freeman, Sherman H. "Board of Education-Superintendent Relationships in the Los Angeles City School System, 1853-1920." Doctoral dissertation, University of California, Los Angeles, 1951. 684 pp.

3066. Fryer, Roy. "Early Schools of Pomona Valley." *Pomona Valley Historian* 3 (1967): 56-69.

3067. Gaffey, William T., Jr. "The Recruitment, Selection and Induction of Classified Personnel in Unified School Districts of Los Angeles County." Doctoral dissertation, University of Southern California, 1963. 217 pp.

3068. Gearhart, May. "The Art Course in the Los Angeles City Schools." *School Arts Magazine* 25 (March 1926): 404-7.

3069. Goff, Walter E. "A Study of Certain Incentives in Attracting and Retaining Teachers (Limited to Three Major Universities in Southern California)." Doctoral dissertation, University of California, Los Angeles, 1959. 165 pp.

3070. Gordon, Edmond D. "Problem Boys in the Special Schools of Los Angeles." Master's thesis, University of Southern California, 1936. 123 pp.

3071. Gordon, Leslie O. "A Study of the Comparable Factors of Attendance Service in the Los Angeles and San Diego City Schools." Master's thesis, University of Southern California, 1935. 148 pp.

3072. Goudy, Eliz. "Radio Broadcasting Information to Teachers." *Education* 60 (May 1940): 612-7.

3073. Gould, Linwood P. "The Los Angeles Citizens' Commission for the Public Schools: 1952-1955." Master's thesis, University of Southern California, 1955. 157 pp.

3074. Goulet, Frank X. "The Development, Status, and Trend of Special Supervision in the Los Angeles City Schools." Master's thesis, University of Southern California, 1928. 116 pp.

3075. Gray, C. Delmar. "A Study of the Educational Value of Extra-School Agencies in the City of Pomona." Master's thesis, Clarement Graduate School, 1934. 128 pp.

3076. Grover, Martha T. "Problems of Adapting the Social Studies Program of the Los Angeles County Course of Study to a School District of Low Socio-Economic Level." Master's thesis, University of Southern California, 1952. 96 pp.

3077. Hafner, Gene E. "The History of the East Whittier City School District . . ." Master's thesis, Whittier College, 1957. 94 pp.

3078. Hammer, Gerald K. "Charles Alpheus Bennett, Dean of Manual Arts." Doctoral dissertation, University of California, Los Angeles, 1962. 364 pp.

Leader in vocational education.

3079. Hanna, Byron C. "His Depression Job Was

Schools: Maybe Our Biggest Business—And from 1929 Frank Bouelle Had It, Brickbats and All." *Southern California Business* 16 (April 1937) : 8-9.

Los Angeles Superintendent of Schools, 1929-1937.

3080. Harper, Evelyn S. "A Survey of the Eugene Street Development Center in Los Angeles." Master's thesis, University of Southern California, 1934. 171 pp.

Center for mentally handicapped children.

3081. Harper, Howard K. "A Survey of Public Transportation in the Los Angeles City School Districts." Master's thesis, University of Southern California, 1934. 130 pp.

3082. Harrington, Audrey L. "The Effects of Correction of Physical Defects on the Progress of Pupils in Selected Los Angeles City Schools." Master's thesis, University of California, Los Angeles, 1956. 67 pp.

3083. Harris, James C. "Teacher Transfers from Schools in Low Socio-Economic Areas of the Los Angeles City Schools." Doctoral dissertation, University of Southern California, 1970. 166 pp.

3084. Harrison, Dwight T. "An Evaluation of Salary Rates Paid Employees in Selected Non-Certificated Service Positions of the Los Angeles City District." Master's thesis, University of Southern California, 1938. 118 pp.

3085. Hawks, William J. "Effects of Equalization Plans in Los Angeles County." Master's thesis, University of Southern California, 1935. 168 pp.

School finances.

3086. Haynes, Clarence E. "Interagency Cooperation in Los Angeles County. Relationships Between School Districts and City Recreation Departments." Master's thesis, Claremont Graduate School, 1970. 49 pp.

3087. Hebel, Vernon E. "Educational Provision for the Physically Handicapped Child in the Los Angeles City Schools." Master's thesis, University of Southern California, 1933. 138 pp.

3088. Hendrick, Irving G. "Academic Revolution in California. A History of Events Leading to the Passage and Implementation of the 1961 Fisher Bill on Teacher Certification." *Southern Califor-*

nia Quarterly 49 (1967) : 127-66, 253-95, 359-406.

Based on authors doctoral dissertation, University of California, Los Angeles, 1964.

3089. Hennessey, Mark A. "Saving Los Angeles from the U.N." *Reporter* 7 (November 11, 1952) : 28-31.

Describes background of ban placed by the Los Angeles School Board on a pamphlet entitled "The E in UNESCO."

3090. Hilton, Leon E. "Educational Facilities for the Deaf Child in the Public Schools of Los Angeles County." Master's thesis, University of Southern California, 1952. 73 pp.

3091. Howell, Harry M. "Salary Survey and Job Analysis of Non-Certificated Personnel in Los Angeles City Schools." Master's thesis, University of Southern California, 1936. 81 pp.

3092. Hoyt, Edwin L. "Correlations of Civil Service Tests with Three Successive Service Ratings Based on Cases Obtained from the Non-Certified Personnel Division of the Los Angeles City School District." Master's thesis, University of Southern California, 1940. 73 pp.

3093. Hulburd, David. *This Happened in Pasadena.* New York, 1951. 166 pp.

Recounts a bitter disagreement between the Board of Education and the superintendent of the Pasadena Public Schools in 1950.

3094. Hull, Osman R. *Survey of the Alhambra Public Schools.* University of Southern California, *Studies No. 5.* Los Angeles, 1929. 107 pp.

3095. ———, and Ford, Willard S. *Survey of the Los Angeles City Schools.* Los Angeles, 1934. 395 pp.

3096. Hume, Jessie H. "The Organization and Administration of the Los Angeles School Libraries." Master's thesis, University of Southern California, 1935. 241 pp.

3097. Hunter, Madeline C. "Stirrings in the Big Cities: Los Angeles." *NEA Journal* 51 (April 1962) : 18-20.

3098. Hutchens, Jens H. "The Annual Report of the Office of the County Superintendent of

Schools." Doctoral dissertation, University of California, Los Angeles, 1950. 135 pp.

3099. Isbitz, Sarah F. "An Analysis of the Stanford Reading Tests in Relation to the Los Angeles City Schools District Curriculum." Master's thesis, University of Southern California, 1967. 95 pp.

3100. Jacobs, Paul. "Assault on UNESCO." *Commonweal* 62 (May 27, 1955): 210-1.

UNESCO as key issue in Los Angeles school board election.

3101. Jarmuth, John. "Foothill Cities Make Education an Industry by Centering Private Schools." *Southern California Business* 5 (February 1926): 24+.

San Gabriel Valley.

3102. ——— "Private Schools — Another Industry." *Southern California Business* 3 (January 1925): 17+.

Los Angeles area.

3103. Johns, Mary E. "An Evaluation of the Health Instruction Program of the Whittier City School District." Master's thesis, University of California, Los Angeles, 1957. 124 pp.

3104. Johnsen, Henry M. "An Evaluation of the Remedial Reading Program in Certain Los Angeles City Schools." Master's thesis, University of California, Los Angeles, 1956. 73 pp.

3105. Johnson, Charles E. "A Survey of the Public Schools' Parent Education Program in Santa Monica, California." Master's thesis, University of California, Los Angeles, 1948. 115 pp.

3106. Johnson, DeWayne B. "A Historical Analysis of the Criticisms Concerning Teaching about the United Nations Educational, Scientific, and Cultural Organization in the Los Angeles City Schools." Doctoral dissertation, University of California, Los Angeles, 1955. 378 pp.

3107. Johnson, Donald W. "A Study of the Factors in the Exodus of Permanent Teachers from the Los Angeles City Schools During the Period 1935 to 1947." Master's thesis, University of California, Los Angeles, 1948. 162 pp.

3108. Johnson, Fern P. "Science News in the Los

Angeles Press: A Curriculum Study." Master's thesis, University of Southern California, 1936. 113 pp.

3109. Jones, Frank H. "A Survey of the Montebello School-Housing and Building Program." Master's thesis, University of Southern California, 1936. 90 pp.

3110. Jones, Helen L. *Schools.* Los Angeles, 1952. *Metropolitan Los Angeles. A Study in Integration,* Vol. XII, The Haynes Foundation, *Monograph Series No. 29.* 107 pp.

3111. Karayan, Robert H. "The Determination of a Plan for Parent Teacher Conferences in the Compton City Schools." Master's thesis, University of Southern California, 1953. 63 pp.

3112. Katz, Saul. "Migration: A Study of Migration in the Los Angeles City Schools and the Los Angeles County Schools [1934 to 1954]." Master's thesis, University of Southern California, 1954. 98 pp.

3113. Kendall, Robert. *White Teacher in a Black School.* New York, [1964]. 241 pp.

Negroes and education in Los Angeles; teachers.

3114. Kerby, Phil. "Minorities Oppose Los Angeles School System: Persistent Segregation." *Christian Century* 85 (September 4, 1968): 1119-22. Discussion in 85 (October 16, 1968): 1310; (November 20, 1968): 1482.

3115. Kidd, David C. "An Evaluation of the Publicity Methods Used by the Los Angeles City Schools in the 1959 Tax Election." Master's thesis, University of Southern California, 1960. 84 pp.

3116. Knight, Kenneth N. "Predictors of Teaching Success in the Los Angeles City Schools." Doctoral dissertation, University of Southern California, 1963. 206 pp.

3117. Kunou, C. A. "Features in Manual Education for Children and Adults." *Industrial Education Magazine* 27 (December 1925): 180-2.

Activities of the Manual Education Department of the Los Angeles City Schools.

3118. Kusché, Karl. "The Development of UNESCO in Los Angeles 1948-1952." Master's thesis, University of Southern California, 1953. 129 pp.

3119. Lacq, Jasper N., Jr. "The Financial Administration of City School Systems with Particular Reference to the Los Angeles City School System." Master's thesis, University of Southern California, 1923. 133 pp.

3120. Landers, J. P. "An Evaluation of the Physical Education Program for Physically Handicapped Children in the Los Angeles City Schools." Master's thesis, University of Southern California, 1945. [?] pp.

3121. Landrum, John W. "The Effects of the Los Angeles County Neighborhood Youth Corps Program on the Performance of Enrollees in School." Doctoral dissertation, University of Southern California, 1967. 218 pp.

3122. Laughlin, Tom. "Stop Educating Our Normal Children in Retarded Schools!" *Los Angeles* 2 (September 1961): 26-8.

Author, co-founder of Sophia School in Santa Monica, discusses Montessori System.

3123. Lee, Frances. "Vocational Training in Institutions for Dependent Children in Los Angeles Area." Master's thesis, University of Southern California, 1935. 145 pp.

3124. "Letter to the Board of Education of Los Angeles." *School and Society* 12 (July 24, 1920): 83-4.

Los Angeles high school teachers protest their low salaries.

3125. Lewerenz, Alfred S. "New Developments in Evaluating Achievement in the Public Schools of Los Angeles." *Education* 71 (December 1950): 237-44.

Evaluation program of the Los Angeles City Schools.

3126. Lewis, David C. "A Study of the Southern California City Superintendents Group, 1923-1963." Doctoral dissertation, University of California, Los Angeles, 1966. 434 pp.

3127. Lewis, Helene C. "A Program of Organization for the Opening and Closing Days of the School Year in the Los Angeles City School District." Master's thesis, University of California, Los Angeles, 1958. 97 pp.

3128. Lewis, John C. "The Standard of Living of the Teachers of the Compton City School District." Master's thesis, University of Southern California, 1952. 124 pp.

3129. Lickley, Ernest J. "Los Angeles Schools." *School Review* 15 (June 1907): 459-62.

Random aspects of city school system.

3130. ———— "A Social and Educational Study of 1,554 Cases of Truancy in the Special Schools of Los Angeles." Master's thesis, University of Southern California, 1917. 101 pp.

3131. Lloyd, James W. "The Administration of the Orientation and In-Service Education Program for New Teachers in the Los Angeles City School System." Doctoral dissertation, University of California, Los Angeles, 1960. 299 pp.

3132. "The Local Public School Situation." *Municipal League of Los Angeles Bulletin* 6 (September 1, 1929): [1-2].

3133. Los Angeles. Board of Education. *Los Angeles City Schools and the War.* Los Angeles, 1918. 84 pp.

3134. ———— *The Reconstruction Program of the Los Angeles City Schools, 1933-35 Inclusive.* [Los Angeles, n.d.]. 19 pp.

3135. Los Angeles City School District. *Education of the Physically Handicapped in Los Angeles City Schools.* Los Angeles, 1931. 38 pp.

3136. "Los Angeles Builds a School for the Crippled." *Architectural Record* 82 (November 1937): 30-1.

Washington Boulevard Orthopaedic School.

3137. Lynch, Chester. "A History of the Glendale Public Schools from 1879 to 1957 with Emphasis on School Organization and Administration." Master's thesis, Occidental College, 1957. 196 pp.

3138. Magee, Lawrence T. "Historical Developments Affecting the Administration of the Office of the Los Angeles County Superintendent of Schools [1849 to 1955]." Doctoral dissertation, University of Southern California, 1955. 251 pp.

3139. Mahakian, K. John. "A Plan for a System of Cooperative Purchasing Among School Districts of Los Angeles County." Master's thesis, University of Southern California, 1939. 125 pp.

3140. Martin, August H. "A Study fo Special Promotion of Pupils in the Long Beach Schools with Reference to Their Subsequent School Progress." Master's thesis, University of Southern California, 1923. 158 pp.

3141. Marx, Wesley. "A New Look in Education." *Los Angeles* 4 (September 1962): 24-7.
Public and private schools in Los Angeles.

3142. Mauller, Robert L. "A Comparison of In-Service Workshops with the Los Angeles City School In-Service Point Projects." Master's thesis, University of Southern California, 1957. 98 pp.

3143. Maxfield, Richard W. "A Study of Factors Alleged to Cause Custodial Separation in the Los Angeles City School Districts." Doctoral dissertation, University of California, Los Angeles, 1965. 158 pp.

3144. Maxwell, William C. "An Investigation of Boy Delinquency in Long Beach, California, and Its Implications for the Public Schools." Master's thesis, University of Southern California, 1935. 356 pp.

3145. McCartney, A. Kenneth. "An Inquiry into the Territorial Extension of the Los Angeles Public Schools." Master's thesis, Occidental College, 1940. 167 pp.

3146. McConnell, Tille F. "A Comparison of Reading Grades Before and After the Earthquake in Long Beach." Master's thesis, University of Southern California, 1934. 39 pp.

3147. McCoy, John H. "Educational News in the Los Angeles Press." Master's thesis, University of Southern California, 1933. 109 pp.

3148. McCunn, Drummond J. "A Study of Pasadena and Its Public Schools: Analysis of the Factors Contributing to Educational Leadership in a Community." Doctoral dissertation, University of California, Los Angeles, 1950. 314 pp.

3149. McDonald, George J. "The Wider Use of the School Plant in Los Angeles." Master's thesis, University of Southern California, 1917. 98 pp.

3150. McKinnon, Mary Concepta, Sister. "The Educational Work of the California Institute of the Sisters of the Immaculate Heart of Mary." Master's thesis, University of California, Los Angeles, 1937. 151 pp.
Also includes note of collegiate work.

3151. Mercereau, George W. "A Study of the Relative Value of Electrical Equipment in Terms of Usage and Cost Based on Los Angeles, Long Beach and Pasadena School Systems." Master's thesis, University of Southern California, 1933. 104 pp.

3152. Metts, Albert C. "An Evaluation of the County School Organization in California as It Functions in Los Angeles County." Doctoral dissertation, University of Southern California, 1932. 291 pp.

3153. Miller, Raymond B. "A Survey of the School System of Long Beach, California." Master's thesis, Stanford University, 1921. Unp.

3154. Morehouse, William H. "A Survey of Health and Corrective Physical Education in the Los Angeles City Schools." Master's thesis, University of Southern California, 1936. 158 pp.

3155. Morris, Perry S. "A Survey of Pupil Personnel in the Azusa City Schools." Master's thesis, University of Southern California, 1935. 201 pp.

3156. National Commission for the Defense of Democracy Through Education. *The Pasadena Story; An Analysis of Some Forces and Factors That Injured a Superior School System.* [Washington, D.C.], 1951. 39 pp.

3157. Neher, Gerwin C. "A Survey of the Health Services of the Los Angeles City Schools." Master's thesis, University of Southern California, 1934. 200 pp.

3158. "A New School Building Every Week." *Southern California Business* 3 (May 1924): 24+.
"When [Los Angeles] can score an increase daily school attendance that is greater than the combined increase of the cities of Chicago, Philadelphia, Pittsburgh, San Francisco and St. Louis, it may be said to be about the fastest growing metropolis the world has ever known."

3159. Newsom, Alfred D. "The Relative Efficiency of Large and Small Schools in Glendale." Master's thesis, University of Southern California, 1935. 120 pp.

3160. North, William E. *Catholic Education in Southern California.* Washington, D. C., 1936. 227 pp.

3161. Ogle, Robert. "An Integrated Approach to the Social Studies in the Los Angeles City School District, Using History as the Unifying Principle." Master's thesis, Occidental College, 1958. 155 pp.

3162. Ostrom, Vincent A. "School Board Politics —An Analysis of Non-Partisanship in the Los Angeles City Board of Education." Master's thesis, University of California, Los Angeles, 1945. 206 pp.

3163. Owen, Alfred. "Development of Overhead Rates in Maintenance Work in the Los Angeles City School Districts." Master's thesis, University of Southern California, 1956. 156 pp.

3164. Parker, John D. "Executive Development in the Public Service: An Analysis of Executive and High Level Administrative Personnel Background and Behavior in the Classified Divisions of the Los Angeles City School District." Master's thesis, University of Southern California, 1965. 83 pp.

3165. Perden, Philip W. "The Administration of Education for Physically Handicapped Children in the Los Angeles City Schools." Master's thesis, University of Southern California, 1943. 103 pp.

3166. Perret, Anne L., Sister. "Development of Diocesan Supervision in the Archdiocese of Los Angeles." Doctoral dissertation, University of California, Los Angeles, 1967. 348 pp.

3167. ———— "The Roles of the Diocesan and of the Community Supervisors in the Roman Catholic School System in the Western States." Master's thesis, University of California, Los Angeles, 1962. 107 pp.

Includes Los Angeles Archdiocese.

3168. Persons, A. Madelyn. "News and Editorials Concerning the Los Angeles Public Schools." Master's thesis, University of Southern California, 1952. 133 pp.

3169. Pierson, Celia D. "The Program of Educational Counseling in the Los Angeles City Schools." Master's thesis, University of California, Berkeley, 1928. 224 pp.

3170. Poe, Elizabeth. "Segregation in Los Angeles Schools." *Frontier* 13 (October 1962): 12-3.

3171. "Policies and Procedures of the Special Departments in the Los Angeles Public Schools." *Industrial Arts Magazine* 15 (September 1926): 339.

3172. Polkinghorn, Rena I. "Physical Education Work in the Los Angeles City Schools." Master's thesis, University of Southern California, 1923. 198 pp.

3173. Powell, Earle B. "Educational Programs of County-Operated Camps and Ranch Homes for Juvenile Delinquents in Southern California." Master's thesis, Claremont Graduate School, 1951. 73 pp.

3174. "Pressures in Los Angeles." *New Republic* 127 (September 22, 1952): 7.

Controversy over whether or not to integrate "Unesco subject matter" into Los Angeles City School curriculum.

3175. Probst, Ruth A. "Development of Business Education in the Public Schools of Los Angeles [1884 to 1933]." Master's thesis, University of Southern California, 1933. 113 pp.

3176. Purdy, Robert J. "The Impact of State Requirements upon the Budget and Program of the Los Angeles City Schools, 1940-41 to 1963-64." Doctoral dissertation, University of California, Los Angeles, 1965. 230 pp.

3177. Randall, Harriett B. "Health Is for Teachers Too." *NEA Journal* 40 (October 1951): 467-8.

Report on study of teacher absences in the Los Angeles school system.

3178. Randall, Lucretia T. "A Survey of Art Appreciation in the Los Angeles City Schools." Master's thesis, University of California, Los Angeles, 1965. 109 pp.

3179. Ransom, Robert E. "Parent Reactions to the Los Angeles City Schools Camping Program." Master's thesis, University of Southern California, 1955. 58 pp.

3180. Rathwell, Grace K. "Public School News in the Los Angeles Press." Master's thesis, University of Southern California, 1935. 105 pp.

3181. Reece, Thomas E. "The Area Superintendent in the Los Angeles City School System Today and Tomorrow." Doctoral dissertation, University of California, Los Angeles, 1966. 187 pp.

3182. Riedel, Gerhardt. "General Fund Disbursement Differentials Occurring Since Unification of the Culver City Unified School District." Master's thesis, University of California, Los Angeles, 1964. 85 pp.

3183. Robinson, Alcyon. "Los Angeles School System." *School and Society* 17 (June 2, 1923): 609-12.

3184. Robinson, Hugh A. "An Analysis of the Opinions of Parents, Pupils, and Educators Toward Physical Education in Selected Schools in the Los Angeles Area." Master's thesis, University of California, Los Angeles, 1956. 162 pp.

3185. Roorbach, Eloise J. "A Practical School System Aimed to Develop Children's Character and Personality: A Western Idea." *Craftsman* 22 (September 1912): 640-9.

Los Angeles school system under Superintendent I. H. Francis.

3186. Root, Florence E. "The Growth and Development of Special Education in the City Schools of Pasadena, California." Master's thesis, University of Southern California, 1936. 158 pp.

3187. Rountree, Lynn. "Where Pomona People Get Their Information about Schools." Master's thesis, Claremont Graduate School, 1957. 88 pp.

3188. Seaman, C. E. "Problems of Los Angeles' School Board." *Saturday Night* 3 (December 16, 1922): 19-20.

3189. "A Selective Directory of Private Schools." *Los Angeles* 4 (September 1962): 28-9.

Nearly all in Los Angeles area.

3190. Shifren, Seymour. "Narcotic Education in Two Selected Communities of Los Angeles County." Master's thesis, University of California, Los Angeles, 1955. 99 pp.

3191. Shuck, Leslie E. "A Survey of Guidance Practices in Covina." Master's thesis, University of Southern California, 1958. 148 pp.

3192. Singer, Stanley L. "Organization and Administration of a Guidance Center: A Study of Three Years of Operation of the Advisement Service of the Los Angeles City Schools." Master's thesis, University of Southern California, 1949. 129 pp.

3193. Singleton, Robert, and Bullock, Paul. "Some Problems in Minority-Group Education in the Los Angeles Public Schools." *Journal of Negro Education* 32 (1963): 137-45.

3194. Smallenburg, Harry W. "Selection, Segregation and Training of Behavior Problem Boys in Los Angeles." Master's thesis, University of Southern California, 1935. 211 pp.

3195. Smith, F. D. "Work of City Supervision," in National Education Association *Proceedings and Addresses*. Washington, D.C., 1923. Pp. 694-95.

3196. Snider, William W. "A Historical Study of School District Organization in Los Angeles County [1838 to 1959]." Doctoral dissertation, University of Southern California, 1959. 280 pp.

3197. Snoddy, Jennings L. "A Survey of the Methods Used in Adjusting the Truant Boy in the Los Angeles Schools." Master's thesis, University of Southern California, 1932. 105 pp.

3198. Soref, Irwin. "A History of Jewish Education in Los Angeles, 1850-1937." Master's thesis, College of Jewish Studies, Chicago, 1949. 115 pp.

A translation of the original Hebrew text is available.

3199. Spring, Carl C. "The Effect of Annexation upon Los Angeles County School Systems." Master's thesis, University of Southern California, 1935. 200 pp.

3200. Stephens, Ruth M. B. "Practices in the Los Angeles City Schools in Dealing with Socially Maladjusted Girls." Master's thesis, University of Southern California, 1940. 131 pp.

3201. Stevens, Edwin A. "Opportunities for Re-education of the Juvenile Delinquent in Los Angeles County." Master's thesis, University of Southern California, 1951. 93 pp.

3202. Stirdivant, Clarence E. "Recruitment, Examination, and Assignment of Certificated Personnel in the Los Angeles City School Districts." Master's thesis, University of California, Los Angeles, 1949. 99 pp.

3203. Sussman, Allen R. "A History of Discipline in the Los Angeles City School System." Master's thesis, University of California, Los Angeles, 1964. 118 pp.

3204. Sutherland, Lawrence E. "A Survey of the Pasadena Merit System." Master's thesis, University of Southern California, 1936. 90 pp.

3205. Thomas, John. "Saved Again!" *Frontier* 4 (September 1953) : 9-10.

Los Angeles Board of Education refuses to allow the reinstatement of "UNESCO teaching" in the Los Angeles schools.

3206. Voelker, Joseph O. "An Analysis of the 1960 County-Wide School Support Plan in Los Angeles County." Master's thesis, University of California, Los Angeles, 1963. 67 pp.

3207. Walters, Flora B. "A History of Education in Long Beach." Master's thesis, University of Southern California, 1939. 130 pp.

3208. Watrous, Valerie. "Los Angeles Schools." *Pacific Municipalities* 44 (September 1930) : 345-8.

3209. ——— "Los Angeles Schools." *Pacific Municipalities* 45 (January 1931) : 13-6.

3210. Webb, Grvan W. "The History of the Department of Health and Corrective Physical Education of the Los Angeles City Schools [1889-1938]." Master's thesis, University of Southern California, 1938. 260 pp.

3211. Weinberg, Carl. "Education Level and Perceptions of Los Angeles Negroes of Educational Conditions in a Riot Area." *Journal of Negro Education* 36 (1967) : 377-84.

3212. Welch, Frank G. "Freedom of Teaching in California, 1920-1930." Doctoral dissertation, University of California, Los Angeles, 1965. 383 pp. Some references to Los Angeles area.

3213. "A Western City—Pattern for North?" *U. S. News & World Report* 68 (March 16, 1970) : 32-3.

Judge Alfred Gitelson's school integration decision.

3214. Whitaker, Hazel G. "A Study of Gifted Negro Children in the Los Angeles City Schools." Master's thesis, University of Southern California, 1931. 86 pp.

3215. White, Larry C. "A Study of Termination Questionnaires Completed by Former Nonteaching Employees of the Los Angeles City School Districts." Master's thesis, University of Southern California, 1959. 97 pp.

3216. Wright, Frank M. "A Survey of the El Monte School District, El Monte, California." Master's thesis, University of Southern California, 1930. 338 pp.

Includes elementary and secondary schools.

3217. Yukie, Thomas S. "An Analysis of the Administrative Factors Affecting the Use of School Facilities for Recreation During After-School Hours in Selected Communities in Los Angeles County." Master's thesis, University of California, Los Angeles, 1952. 203 pp.

EDUCATION—ELEMENTARY

3218. Abrahamson, Harry W. "Survey of the Educational Program of Whittier Christian Elementary Schools." Master's thesis, University of Southern California, 1961. 196 pp.

3219. "An Advance Step in Los Angeles School Garden Instruction." *Pacific Garden* 10 (September 1914) : 13.

3220. Airy, Carolyn. "Present Practices of Reporting to Parents in Los Angeles County Elementary School Districts." Master's thesis, University of Southern California, 1950. 106 pp.

3221. Anderson, Herbert C. "The Status of Men in Elementary Teaching in the Los Angeles City Schools." Master's thesis, University of Southern California, 1955. 197 pp.

3222. Arbor, Bernice B. "A Historical Study of the Kindergarten Program in Los Angeles, California [1876 to 1964]." Master's thesis, University of Southern California, 1965. 78 pp.

3223. Barnum, Bernice W. "A Critical Evaluation of Current Practices in Democratic Administration in the Los Angeles Elementary Schools." Master's thesis, University of Southern California, 1949. 70 pp.

3224. Bates, Elizabeth. *A Study of the Development of Elementary Education in Los Angeles.* [Los Angeles, 1955]. 115 pp.

An outgrowth of the author's master's thesis, University of Southern California, 1928.

3225. ——— "A Study of the Development of Elementary Education in Los Angeles City." Master's thesis, University of Southern California, 1928. [?] pp.

3226. Beckman, Esther A. "Nursery Education: Its Development and Current Practices in Los Angeles County." Master's thesis, University of California, Los Angeles, 1949. 135 pp.

3227. Boettcher, Nina T. "A Survey and Critical Analysis of the Educational and Health Status of the Pupils in a Large Los Angeles Elementary School." Master's thesis, University of Southern California, 1938. 185 pp.

Home Gardens School.

3228. Cahan, Ruth. "The Implementation of the John Dewey Philosophy in the University Elementary School, University of California at Los Angeles." Master's thesis, University of California, Los Angeles, 1958. 248 pp.

3229. Capri, Roger. "A Population and Enrollment Survey of the Grant Elementary School Attendance Area, Santa Monica City." Master's thesis, University of Southern California, 1949. 79 pp.

3230. Cole, Dale H. "Comparative Factors of the Palos Verdes School District and the Lenox Elementary School District Affecting the Prospective Use of Merit Rating for Teachers." Master's thesis, University of Southern California, 1960. 110 pp.

3231. Colwell, Helen P. "A Model Plan for the Instrumental Music Program in the Redondo Beach Elementary Schools." Master's thesis, University of California, Los Angeles, 1964. 148 pp.

3232. Cowles, Kathryn E. "Duties of Elementary Vice Principals in Los Angeles City Schools." Master's thesis, University of California, Los Angeles, 1958. 157 pp.

3233. Dible, Isabel W. "A Study of the A-to-Z Spelling-Through-Writing Program as Used in the Elementary Schools of Santa Monica, California." Master's thesis, University of California, Los Angeles, 1953. 168 pp.

3234. Dorough, Joe D. "An Analysis of the Dismissal of Unsatisfactory Teachers in the Los Angeles County Public Elementary Schools." Master's thesis, University of Southern California, 1958. 99 pp.

3235. Ducker, Sydney A. "Practices in the Articulation and Orientation of Elementary School Pupils to Los Angeles City Junior High Schools." Doctoral dissertation, University of California, Los Angeles, 1968. 148 pp.

3236. Eckardt, Augusta K. "The Functioning of the Spanish Language Program in the Elementary Schools of Los Angeles." Master's thesis, University of Southern California, 1948. 96 pp.

3237. Emanuel, Rose, Sister. "The Parish Schools of Our Lady Queen of the Angels." *Historical Society of Southern California Quarterly* 43 (1961) : 446-59.

3238. Flagg, Etta P. "Los Angeles School Board Maintains Sixteen Day Nurseries." *School Life* 10 (May 1925) : 178-9.

3239. Forrest, William B. "Extent and Cause of Teacher Turnover in Los Angeles County Elementary Schools." Master's thesis, University of Southern California, 1953. 93 pp.

3240. Furnivall, Fred. "A Proposed Study for the Teaching of Mexican-American Children Based upon a Survey of a Mexican Rural Community and a Mexican Urban Community." Master's thesis, Claremont Graduate School, 1948. 74 pp.

3241. Gibbs, Jeanie W. *Memoirs of the Pasadena Children's Training Society.* Pasadena, 1930. 44 pp.

3242. Giles, James F. "An Evaluation of the Experimental Parent-Teacher Conferences in the Elementary Schools of El Segundo, California." Master's thesis, University of Southern California, 1953. 110 pp.

3243. Glendora Foot-hills School. *The Glendora Foot-hills School upon the George D. Whitcomb Foundation.* [Glendora? 1921]. 56 pp.

3244. Gray, Avery J. "Teaching School Children to Save Millions." *Southern California Business* 7 (February 1928): 30-1+.
   Los Angeles banks' School Savings Association.

3245. Gray, Mary R. "The Education of Children in the School Gardens of Los Angeles." *Craftsman* 24 (August 1913): 472-9.
   Gardening as part of the curriculum in the Los Angeles City Schools.

3246. Hollzer, Rose M. "Some Parent-Education Practices in Selected Nursery Schools in Los Angeles County." Master's thesis, University of California, Los Angeles, 1951. 229 pp.

3247. Horowitz, Norman H. "Differences Between Successful and Unsuccessful Candidates for the Elementary School Principalship in the Los Angeles City Schools." Doctoral dissertation, University of California, Los Angeles, 1968. 241 pp.

3248. Hoyme, Theresa M. "The History of the Redondo Beach City School District." Master's thesis, University of Southern California, 1967. 70 pp.

3249. Hunter, Allan A. "Auspicious Start for Weekday Plan: Los Angeles Registers 5,000 Children in Religious Classes." *Christian Century* 61 (November 1, 1944): 1264.

3250. Hunter, Mildred W. "A Study of the Remedial Reading Program in One of the Elementary Districts of the Los Angeles City School System, September, 1954-June, 1955." Master's thesis, University of California, Los Angeles, 1955. 79 pp.

3251. Johnson, Donald W. "A Critical Study of Elementary Teacher Turnover in Southern California." Doctoral dissertation, University of California, Los Angeles, 1950. 323 pp.

3252. Johnson, Lucille W. "A Survey of the Orientation and Induction Practices for Beginning Teachers in the Elementary Schools of Santa Monica." Master's thesis, University of California, Los Angeles, 1951. 146 pp.

3253. Kanigher, Herbert. "Elementary In-Service Education in the City of Los Angeles." Master's thesis, University of Southern California, 1963. 135 pp.

3254. Knox, Charles, and Parker, James W. "A Study of Elementary School Follow-Up Cases Serviced by Area VI Los Angeles City Schools Child Welfare and Attendance Branch." Master's thesis, University of Southern California, 1959. 58 pp.

3255. Kravetz, Nathan. "A Study of the Education of Gifted Children in the Los Angeles City Elementary Schools." Doctoral dissertation, University of California, Los Angeles, 1954. 154 pp.

3256. Lee, Gilbert E. "An Overview of the Elementary Agriculture Program of the Los Angeles City Schools [1912 to 1959]." Master's thesis, University of Southern California, 1960. 81 pp.

3257. Lehman, Inez W. "Evaluation of the Individual Child Study Groups in Long Beach, California." Master's thesis, Stanford University, 1952. 112 pp.

3258. Lewerenz, Alfred S. "The Use of Scholastic Aptitude Test Data in Elementary School Educational Administration." *Education* 56 (November 1935): 154-61.
   Educational Research and Guidance Section of the Los Angeles City Schools.

3259. Litsinger, Dolores A. "The Theory and Method of Social Studies Instruction at the University Elementary School, U.C.L.A." Doctoral dissertation, University of California, Los Angeles, 1962. 555 pp.

3260. Lucas, William L. "The Nonteaching Clerical Tasks of Elementary Teachers in the Los Angeles Unified School District." Doctoral dissertation, University of California, Los Angeles, 1966. 133 pp.

3261. Luhman, Robert P. "Recent Trends on Men Teachers in Primary Education in Los Angeles

County." Master's thesis, University of Southern California, 1952. 95 pp.

3262. MacCono, Mary D. "A Survey of the Health and Physical Education Programs of the Harbor District Elementary Schools of Los Angeles City." Master's thesis, University of Southern California, 1945. 125 pp.

3263. MacKay, Hugh G. "The Agency Play Room in the Placement of Pre-School Children." Master's thesis, University of Southern California, 1949. 91 pp.

3264. Mair, Marion S. "An Analysis and Comparison of Preschool Education in Child Development Centers in Los Angeles, California, City Schools with Play Centres for the Development of Maori Children in Auckland, New Zealand." Master's thesis, University of Southern California, 1966. 120 pp.

3265. McNeil, Albert J. "A Study of the Special Music Education Program in the Elementary Schools of Los Angeles." Master's thesis, University of Southern California, 1952. 50 pp.

3266. Merchant, Alma G. "Health Instruction in Pomona Elementary Schools." Master's thesis, University of Southern California, 1940. 70 pp.

3267. Mobley, Josephine. "Records and Reports in the Nursery Schools of the Los Angeles Metropolitan Area." Master's thesis, University of Southern California, 1945. 299 pp.

3268. Moore, Luella Z. "History of Curricularized Health Education in Los Angeles City Elementary Schools [1827 to 1931]." Master's thesis, University of Southern California, 1931. 97 pp.

3269. Morrison, Isabelle W. "A Survey of Pupil Personnel of the Ramona School (Los Angeles City)." Master's thesis, University of Southern California, 1943. 108 pp.

3270. Moyes, Rhea B. "A Pupil Personnel Survey of the Highland Elementary School, in Inglewood, California." Master's thesis, University of Southern California, 1944. 187 pp.

3271. Nicholson, Samuel R. "A Playground Surfacing Study for the Elementary Schools of Los Angeles." Master's thesis, University of Southern California, 1952. 104 pp.

3272. Noskoff, Faye H. "A Study of the Effect of the Divided Opening Program on Reading Achievement of First Grade Children in the City of Burbank." Master's thesis, University of California, Los Angeles, 1955. 43 pp.

3273. "Pacific Military Academy: School for Boys." *Los Angeles Saturday Night* 13 (August 5, 1933): 10.
Private school founded by Harry H. Culver.

3274. Peters, Mary M. "The Segregation of Mexican American Children in the Elementary Schools of California—Its Legal and Administrative Aspects." Master's thesis, University of California, Los Angeles, 1948. 192 pp.

3275. Phelan, Arthur E. "The Administration of the University Elementary School of the University of California, Los Angeles, 1882-1957." Doctoral dissertation, University of California, Los Angeles, 1961. 438 pp.

3276. Pollich, R. E. "Experiment in Moral Education." *Elementary School Journal* 26 (May 1926): 674-82.
Grant School, Los Angeles. Purpose of experiment was "to develop habits, ideals, and attitudes of citizenship in the Grant District through school, home, and community activities, and to secure material that might prove of value to others interested in the subject."

3277. Potts, Ida S. "The Nature and Organization of the Primary School in Los Angeles." Master's thesis, University of Southern California, 1940. 75 pp.

3278. Raikes, Naomi M. "The Role of the Elementary Principal in Guidance in the Los Angeles City Schools." Master's thesis, University of Southern California, 1955. 112 pp.

3279. Reece, Thomas E. "A Survey of the City Terrace School." Master's thesis, University of Southern California, 1950. 165 pp.

3280. Reed, Beth. "A Survey of Retardation in a Los Angeles Elementary School." Master's thesis, University of Southern California, 1929. 100 pp.

3281. Richard, Olga M. "Art Education in Los Angeles Elementary Schools: An Investigation." Master's thesis, University of California, Los Angeles, 1957. 128 pp.

3282. Richardson, Allen T. "A Follow-Up of Four Hundred Forty Behavior-Problem Boys Enrolled in the Fort-Hill School (1927-1928)." Master's thesis, University of Southern California, 1932. 33 pp.

3283. Riddlebarger, Glenn A. "The Inequalities of Educational Opportunities in the Los Angeles County Elementary Schools." Master's thesis, University of Southern California, 1937. 256 pp.

3284. Riley, Edward F. "A History of the Organization and Administration of the Elementary Schools in the La Puente High School District." Master's thesis, Claremont Graduate School, 1962. 89 pp.

3285. Rose, Helene L. "A Guide for Student Teachers, James A. Garfield School, Long Beach, California." Master's thesis, University of Southern California, 1952. 99 pp.

3286. Sams, Harry R. A. "The Influence of the Association of Elementary School Administrators of Los Angeles on Education." Master's thesis, University of Southern California, 1957. 92 pp.

3287. Samuels, Charles T. "A Comparative Study of the Nature and Amount of Civic Information Possessed by Children of the Sixth Grade Level of Los Angeles County Schools." Master's thesis, University of Southern California, 1934. 108 pp.

3288. Scannell, Patrick. "A Survey of Playground Activities and Recreational Interests of School Children in Los Angeles City." Master's thesis, University of Southern California, 1935. 123 pp.

3289. "The School Survey of Los Angeles." *Elementary School Journal* 17 (September 1916): 8-10.

3290. Scoles, Robert. "A Proposed Plan of Outdoor Education Integrated with the Sixth Grade Curriculum of the Los Angeles County Schools." Master's thesis, Occidental College, 1949. 125 pp.

3291. Shafer, Paul F. "The Administrative Organization of Certain Los Angeles City Elementary Schools." Master's thesis, University of Southern California, 1937. 90 pp.

3292. Shiels, Albert. "Report on a Self-Directed System of Kindergarten Supervision." *Elementary School Journal* 18 (November 1917): 206-9.

3293. Smith, Paul R. "A Diagnostic Educational Survey of the Lawndale Elementary Schools." Master's thesis, University of Southern California, 1935. 140 pp.

3294. Snyder, Martha D. "Procedures Employed by Teachers in Teaching Development Rooms in Los Angeles Elementary Schools." Master's thesis, University of Southern California, 1929. 87 pp.

3295. *Souvenir of the Silver Jubilee of Saint Mary's School, 1907-1932.* Los Angeles, 1932. Unp.

3296. Spain, William D. "A Study of the Attitudes of Catholic Parochial School Children Towards Mexicans in Southern California." Master's thesis, The Catholic University of America, 1962. 64 pp.

3297. Spencer, George J. "An Evaluation of the Criteria Used in the Selection of Elementary Teacher Personnel in the Los Angeles Area." Master's thesis, University of Southern California, 1955. 121 pp.

3298. Spengler, Marie H. "In-Service Training of Teachers in Compton Elementary Schools." Master's thesis, University of Southern California, 1952. 96 pp.

3299. Stearns, Oletha. "A Pupil Personnel Analysis of Van Nuys Elementary School." Master's thesis, University of Southern California, 1940. 108 pp.

3300. Stichter, Charles R. "Criteria for the Administration and Supervision of Organized Play in Elementary Schools of the Los Angeles City School District." Master's thesis, University of California, Los Angeles, 1950. 89 pp.

3301. Stone, Wilson M. "The Recreation Needs of Grammar School Boys in the West Los Angeles Area." Master's thesis, University of California, Los Angeles, 1947. 46 pp.

3302. Stoval, Zettie B. "A Study of Supply Management in Selected New Elementary Schools in

Los Angeles City Unified School District." Master's thesis, University of Southern California, 1963. 79 pp.

3303. Tipton, Elis. "History of San Dimas Grammar School." *Pomona Valley Historian* 4 (1968): 131-7.

3304. Trotter, Velma M. "The Status of Music, Dancing, Art, and Dramatic Instruction in a Selected Group of Mexican Elementary Schools in Los Angeles County." Master's thesis, University of Southern California, 1940. 133 pp.

3305. Turner, Grace M. "A Study of the Neighborhood Schools of Los Angeles [1903 to 1923]." Master's thesis, University of Southern California, 1923. 63 pp.

3306. Verhusen, Alex. "A Survey of the Intelligence and Achievement Status of the Pupils of a Los Angeles City School." Master's thesis, University of Southern California, 1940. 125 pp.

South Park Elementary School.

3307. Warner, Helen S. "The Education of Frail Children." *Elementary School Journal* 30 (October 1929): 136-41.

Solano Avenue School, Los Angeles.

3308. Whitcomb, Emeline. "Children of Many Nationalities Receive Practical Instruction." *School Life* 11 (March 1926): 138-9.

Amelia Street School, in the midst of a multi-national part of Los Angeles.

3309. Wilberg, Esther. "An Evaluation of Supervision in the Elementary Schools of Santa Monica, California." Master's thesis, Stanford University, 1945. 114 pp.

3310. Willson, Ralph E. "The Administrative Organization of Specialized Reading Programs in the Elementary Schools of Los Angeles County." Doctoral dissertation, University of Southern California, 1966. 278 pp.

3311. Wood, Gertrude. "An Evaluation Study of the Child Study Program in Los Angeles County." Doctoral dissertation, University of Southern California, 1955. 372 pp.

3312. "The Work of the Intermediate Schools of Los Angeles." *Elementary School Journal* 15 (March 1915): 361-77.

3313. Ynigo, Alexander. "Mexican-American Children in an Integrated Elementary School: An Investigation of Their Academic Performance and Social Adjustment." Master's thesis, University of Southern California, 1957. 86 pp.

EDUCATION—SECONDARY

3314. Abbott, John L. "An Enrollment and Drop-Out Study of Six Representative Secondary Schools in Los Angeles." Doctoral dissertation, University of Southern California, 1939. 297 pp.

3315. Adams, Richard L. "Current Practices and Recommendations in Relation to Interscholastic Athletics in Selected Junior High Schools in the Los Angeles Area." Master's thesis, University of California, Los Angeles, 1958. 68 pp.

3316. Agnew, Allen M. "Evaluation Criteria for Business Law in California High Schools." Doctoral dissertation, University of California, Los Angeles, 1966. 344 pp.

References to Los Angeles area.

3317. Alexander, Violet L. "A Study of the School and Social Life of Some Unadjusted Pupils at Whittier Union High School." Master's thesis, University of Southern California, 1945. 137 pp.

3318. Aliberti, Orlando J. "A Survey of the Follow-Up Programs within the Senior High Schools of Los Angeles County." Master's thesis, University of California, Los Angeles, 1947. 97 pp.

3319. Allen, Grace T. "Adults Tomorrow." *Woman's Home Companion* 71 (October 1944): 38+.

Cadet nursery school teachers, Lincoln High School, Los Angeles.

3320. Anderson, Reg L. "The Administration of Off-Campus Disciplinary Problems in Seven Selected Secondary Schools of the Los Angeles City High School District." Master's thesis, University of California, Los Angeles, 1955. 122 pp.

3321. Anderton, Ray L. "An Investigation of the Aims, Services, and Needs of the In-Service Education Program Offered by the Southern California School Band and Orchestra Association." Master's thesis, University of California, Los Angeles, 1956. 48 pp.

3322. Andrus, Ethel P. "Education Thru Socialization," in National Educational Association *Addresses and Proceedings* 55 (1917): 275-81.

Author's experiences at Lincoln High School.

3323. Armantrout, Guy E. "An Evaluation of the Extra-Curricular Activities of the Eliot Junior High School of Pasadena, California." Master's thesis, University of Southern California, 1934. 170 pp.

3324. Bainbridge, Augusta C. "Practical Hygiene in One California High School." *Out West*, new series, 2 (October 1911): 250-2.

Los Angeles Polytechnic.

3325. Barnelle, Virginia M. P. "A Survey of the Entertainment Experiences and Interests of Two Graduating Classes of Santa Monica High School." Master's thesis, University of California, Los Angeles, 1951. 80 pp.

3326. Bates, Dorothy. "A Study of Delinquent Girls in a Pasadena High School." Master's thesis, University of Southern California, 1940. 137 pp.

McKinley Junior High School.

3327. Bauer, Sheila M. "A Study of the Science Courses in the Los Angeles City Secondary Schools, 1950 Through 1962." Doctoral dissertation, University of California, Los Angeles, 1962. 192 pp.

3328. Beard, E. Alice. "A Study of the Mexican Pupils in the Fremont Junior High School, Pomona, California, 1940-1941." Master's thesis, Claremont Graduate School, 1941. 68 pp.

3329. Behrman, Marguerite B. "An Evaluation of the Work of the Nurse-Instructor in the Secondary Schools of Los Angeles." Master's thesis, University of Southern California, 1937. 156 pp.

3330. Bowen, Charles G. "Variability in Class Size in Large Southern California High Schools as Related to Pupil-Teacher Ratios and Other Factors." Master's thesis, Claremont Graduate School, 1958. 51 pp.

3331. Bowman, Howard A. "Pupil Marking Practices in Los Angeles City Senior High Schools." Doctoral dissertation, University of Southern California, 1956. 324 pp.

3332. Brown, Floyd J. "The Nature of the Interview; A Study of Office Procedures in Los Angeles Junior High Schools." Master's thesis, University of Southern California, 1934. 81 pp.

3333. Cavanaugh, Doretha M. "Five-Year Follow-Up of Whittier Union High School Graduates." Master's thesis, University of Southern California, 1934. 205 pp.

3334. Clark, Willis W. "A Study of Factors Relating to Mastery of Skills in Reading, Arithmetic, and Written Expression in Los Angeles County Senior High Schools." Doctoral dissertation, University of Southern California, 1941. 192 pp.

3335. Claus, Cynthia. "Frank Wiggins Trade School." *Apartment Journal* 17 (February 1935): 10+.

Los Angeles.

3336. Clay, Betty L. P. "A Survey of Units and Courses in Family Life Education in the Curricula of Selected Public Secondary Schools in Los Angeles County." Master's thesis, University of California, Los Angeles, 1956. 98 pp.

3337. Compton, Edwin R. "Instructional Problems in Unified Types of Teaching in the Los Angeles Junior High Schools." Master's thesis, University of Southern California, 1935. 151 pp.

3338. Connell, Eleanor H. "A Pupil Personnel Study of a Large Junior High School in Los Angeles." Master's thesis, University of Southern California, 1933. 74 pp.

3339. Connor, Mary, Sister. "A Vocational Guidance Program for Sacred Heart of Mary High School." Master's thesis, University of California, Los Angeles, 1949. 120 pp.

3340. Cordill, Tunis S. "Church Life Activities and Attitudes of San Dimas High School Students; A Socio-Religious Survey Made in San Dimas, California, 1932-1933." Master's thesis, Claremont Graduate School, 1933. 134 pp.

3341. Corey, Stephen M. "A Class for Chronic Failures." *School Review* 56 (March 1948): 132-4.

Thomas Jefferson High School, Los Angeles.

3342. "Courses in Training for Social Leadership." *School Review* 44 (May 1936): 327-9.

Abraham Lincoln High School, Los Angeles.

3343. Cox, Arthur W. "A Study of Selected Problems of the Junior High Schools of Long Beach, California." Master's thesis, Stanford University, 1928. Unp.

3344. Crane, Frank. "Real Teaching." *NEA Journal* 17 (October 1928) : 203-4.

Metropolitan High School, Los Angeles, for part-time schooling of 16- to 18-year-olds who are working full-time.

3345. Crawshaw, Marshall R. "The Development of the Driver Education and Training Program in the Los Angeles City Schools, 1945 to 1949." Doctoral dissertation, University of California, Los Angeles, 1950. 162 pp.

Published under same title. Los Angeles, 1950. 162 pp.

3346. Davis, N. Evelyn. "A Study of Junior Business Training Needs in George Washington Junior High School, Pasadena." Master's thesis, Stanford University, 1928. Unp.

3347. De Saix, Rena A. "Organization and Administration of Selected Aspects of Family Life Education at Woodrow Wilson High School, Los Angeles." Master's thesis, University of California, Los Angeles, 1956. 131 pp.

3348. Dinkel, Robert E. "Algebra Prognosis: Predicting Algebra Achievement in Culver City Junior High." Master's thesis, University of California, Los Angeles, 1954. 91 pp.

3349. Drury, John M. "A Study of Drama in the Los Angeles City High Schools (1952-1953) Academic Preparation of Drama Teachers; Drama Curriculums; and Direction Methods." Master's thesis, University of California, Los Angeles, 1954. 135 pp.

3350. Duncan, Vernon P. "Student Participation in School Government in the Senior High Schools of Los Angeles, California." Master's thesis, University of Southern California, 1948. 113 pp.

3351. Dyck, Henry O., Jr. "The Organization of the Los Angeles Continuation High Schools under the Fifteen-Hour Law." Master's thesis, University of Southern California, 1931. 81 pp.

3352. Dyer, Lydia E. "Some Aspects of the Progressive Education Movement and Applications in Certain Los Angeles Secondary Schools." Master's thesis, University of Southern California, 1935. 109 pp.

3353. Elliott, Essie L. "Types of Home Economics Courses for Boys in Los Angeles." *Journal of Home Economics* 23 (December 1931) : 118-9.

3354. Elmgren G. Theodore. "A Survey of Practices of Teaching English in Industrial Arts Classes in the High Schools of L.A." Master's thesis, University of California, Los Angeles, 1955. 111 pp.

3355. Engberg, C. Evan. "Trends in Enrollments and Offerings in Long Beach Senior High Schools." Master's thesis, University of Southern California, 1934. 117 pp.

3356. Ennis, George W. "The Juvenile Traffic School of Los Angeles County." Master's thesis, University of Southern California, 1935. 140 pp.

3357. Ericson, E. E. "Trade School Education on a Large Scale." *Industrial Education Magazine* 27 (April 1926) : 332-4.

Frank Wiggins Trade School, Los Angeles.

3358. "Failure in Los Angeles." *Times* 58 (December 10, 1951) : 93.

Tests given 8th and 11th grade students; Superintendent Maurice Blair characterizes their showing as "wretched."

3359. Fargo, George A. "Criteria for Evaluating the Content of Selected Reading Materials for Mexican-American Pupils in Los Angeles Junior High School Classes for the Mentally Retarded." Master's thesis, University of California, Los Angeles, 1959. 98 pp.

3360. Fenwick, Arthur M. "A Modern City's High-School System — Los Angeles." *School Review* 24 (February 1916) : 116-29.

3361. "The Modern High School." *Educational Review* 54 (June 1917) : 38-48.

Manual Arts High School, Los Angeles.

3362. Fields, Earl B. "Factors Associated with Non-Attendance in a Los Angeles Junior High School." Master's thesis, University of Southern California, 1948. 127 pp.

Horace Mann Junior High School.

3363. Foreman, Ruth E. "A Personnel Survey of the Student Body of the Monrovia-Arcadia-Duarte High School, Monrovia, California." Master's thesis, University of Southern California, 1941. 147 pp.

3364. Freeman, George H. "A Comparative Investigation of the School Achievement and Socio-Economic Background of the Japanese-American Students and the White-American Students of Gardena High School." Master's thesis, University of Southern California, 1938. 92 pp.

3365. Frick, Mary E. "Histories of the Metropolitan High School, and the Huntington Park Opportunity School." Master's thesis, University of Southern California, 1931. 116 pp.

3366. Frishman, Harry. "End to a Dead End." *NEA Journal* 36 (March 1947): 231.
   Occupational classes, Business and Technology Division of Long Beach public schools.

3367. Garrison, Irving M. "An Investigation in Integrative Programs in Los Angeles Senior High Schools." Master's thesis, University of Southern California, 1936. 209 pp.

3368. Genevro, George W. "A History of Industrial Arts in the Long Beach City Schools." Doctoral dissertation, University of California, Los Angeles, 1966. 318 pp.

3369. George, Bettie H. "An Evaluation of First Semester Typewriting in Selected Junior High Schools in the City of Los Angeles." Master's thesis, University of California, Los Angeles, 1945. 147 pp.

3370. Giddings, Harriet G. "An Evaluation of the Educational Program of Metropolitan High School, Los Angeles, California." Master's thesis, University of Southern California, 1935. 170 pp.

3371. "Girls' Collegiate School Begins Its Forty-First Year." *Los Angeles Saturday Night* 12 (September 3, 1932): 7.
   History and activities of Girls' Collegiate School, Glendora.

3372. Glassey, Margaret F. "Helping the Social Living Program." *Wilson Library Bulletin* 15 (March 1941): 570-3.
   Emerson Junior High School, Los Angeles.

3373. Goldsmith, J. Lyman. "Committee of 300 Plans School Shops." *Industrial Arts and Vocational Education* 45 (March 1956): 63-7.
   Los Angeles City Schools.

3374. Gooden, Robert B. "Harvard School — A Southland School for Boys." *Los Angeles Saturday Night* 8 (August 18, 1928): 2.
   A private boys' school under the Episcopal Dioceses of Los Angeles.

3375. Goodwin, Lorraine L. "A Follow-Up Study of the Graduates of Leadership Training in One Los Angeles City High School." Master's thesis, University of California, Los Angeles, 1962. 106 pp.
   University High School.

3376. Graham, Jessie. "Business Education in Los Angeles Schools." *NEA Journal* 40 (May 1951): 336-8.

3377. Graham, Luelva B. "A Survey of Counseling Needs as Reported by Negro Female Students in the Twelfth Grade of the Los Angeles Area." Master's thesis, University of California, Los Angeles, 1967. 76 pp.

3478. Grainage, Floyd M. "Trade and Technical Education in the Long Beach City Schools." Doctoral dissertation, University of California, Los Angeles, 1967. 230 pp.

3379. Graves, Clayborn L. "Analysis of the Current Expenses in Los Angeles County High Schools, 1927-28 to 1936-37." Master's thesis, University of Southern California, 1940. 111 pp.

3380. Grill, Nannette L. "A Case Study of the In-School Television Viewing Habits of 38 Students Participating in the Culver City High School's Basic Skills Program." Master's thesis, University of California, Los Angeles, 1969. 92 pp.

3381. Hall, Burton P. "Interscholastic Athletics in the Junior High Schools of Los Angeles County." Master's thesis, University of Southern California, 1940. 121 pp.

3382. Hall, Lee R. "Comparative Homogeneity of Various Groupings of Grades Seven to Fourteen in the Glendale City Schools." Master's thesis, University of Southern California, 1933. 208 pp.

3383. Hamilton, Andrew. "Tournament for Troubleshooters." *Westways* 61 (April 1969) : 27-8.

Contest among auto mechanics students to find mechanical malfunctions.

3384. Harmer, Ruth M. "The World in a High School." *Americas* 10 (September 1958) : 3-7.

Belmont High School, Los Angeles: "The most 'integrated' educational institution in the United States."

3385. "Harvard School Enters Its Thirty-Second Year." *Los Angeles Saturday Night* 11 (August 1, 1931) : 6.

A private boys' school under the Episcopal Diocese of Los Angeles.

3386. "Harvard School Enters Its Thirty-Third Year." *Los Angeles Saturday Night* 12 (August 6, 1932) : 7.

3387. "Harvard School Enters Thirtieth Year." *Los Angeles Saturday Night* 9 (August 3, 1929) : 7.

3388. "Harvard School Long Famous for Thorough Training." *Los Angeles Saturday Night* 14 (July 28, 1934) : 9.

3389. "Harvard School's Projected New Home." *Los Angeles Saturday Night* 12 (February 20, 1932) : 6.

Relocation from Western Ave. and Venice Blvd. to Beverly (now Sunset) Blvd. and Sepulveda.

3390. Haskell, Eugene R. "A Proposed Program of Music-Drama for High Schools in Los Angeles County, California." Master's thesis, University of California, Los Angeles, 1944. 115 pp.

3391. Hatfield, Salley J. "The Dietary Practices of Students in Grades Seven Through Twelve in the Inglewood Unified School District." Master's thesis, University of California, Los Angeles, 1962. 157 pp.

3392. Hayman, Darcy S. "A Survey of Repositories in the Los Angeles Area and Their Potential Contribution to the Teacher of Art in the Secondary Schools of the Los Angeles City School System." Master's thesis, University of California, Los Angeles, 1953. 81 pp.

3393. Herman, Joseph S. "Financing Student Body Activities in Los Angeles Schools." Doctoral dissertation, University of California, Los Angeles, 1966. 175 pp.

3394. Herschberger, Mary E. "A Follow-Up Study of Junior High School Adjustment of Pupils Graduated from the University Elementary School of the University of California at Los Angeles." Master's thesis, University of Southern California, 1939. 80 pp.

3395. "Hollywood School for Girls' New Era of Progress." *Los Angeles Saturday Night* 11 (August 22, 1931) : 12.

Reorganization of school on non-profit basis.

3396. Horton, Helen M. "Occupations for Graduates of Los Angeles High Schools." Master's thesis, University of Southern California, 1928. 133 pp.

3397. "Ideal Setting for the Marborough School for Girls." *Los Angeles Saturday Night* 12 (August 27, 1932) : 6+.

History and activities of private girls' school, Wilshire District.

3398. Jack, Clyde A. "A Study of the Commercial Curriculum in Pomona High School and Its Relation to the Commercial Opportunities Available in Pomona." Master's thesis, Claremont Graduate School, 1949. 119 pp.

3399. Jensen, Mary G. "The Rise and Expansion of Public Secondary Education in the Los Angeles City High School District." Master's thesis, University of California, Berkeley, 1941. 461 pp.

3400. Johnson, Milo P. "The Trade and Industrial Education of Negroes in the Los Angeles Area." Master's thesis, University of California, Los Angeles, 1945. 86 pp.

3401. *Junipero Serra High School.* Gardena, 1951. Unp.

3402. Kennedy, M. C. *A Half Century's History of the Academy of the Holy Names.* Pomona, 1948. Unp.

3403. Kersey, Vierling. "An Analysis of Part-Time Organization and Administration Based on the Provisions of the California Compulsory Education Act, Passed May 27, 1919, Dealing More Particularly with the Problems of Organization and Administration of Part-Time Education in the City of Los Angeles." Master's thesis, University of Southern California, 1922. 74 pp.

3404. Kienholz, William S. "The Frank Wiggins Trade School." *Southern California Business* 5 (April 1926): 32+.

Los Angeles.

3405. Kurth, Myrtle. "A Study of Four Racial Groups in a Pasadena Junior High School." Master's thesis, University of Southern California, 1941. 143 pp.

McKinley Junior High School.

3406. Laidlaw, Virginia T. "Historical Development of Business Education in the Public Evening High Schools of Southern California." Master's thesis, University of Southern California, 1934. 148 pp.

Emphasis on Los Angeles, 1917-1934.

3407. Lambert, Edward L. "Comparison of Industrial Employment Standards with High School Graduation Requirements for Terminal Point Students in the Los Angeles Area." Master's thesis, University of Southern California, 1960. 190 pp.

3408. Larsen, Cecil E. "Control Patterns in an Interracial School; The Thomas Jefferson High School in East Los Angeles." *Sociology and Social Research* 30 (1946): 383-90.

3409. Lawrence, John D. "The Application of Criteria to Textbooks in the Secondary Schools of Los Angeles County." Doctoral dissertation, University of Southern California, 1961. 141 pp.

3410. *Leaves from a Marlborough Diary, 1888-1939, Dedicated to the Memory of Mary E. Caswell.* [Hollywood, 1939]. 95 pp.

Marlborough School Golden Jubilee, Los Angeles.

3411. Leitner, Roni J. "Teacher Observation of Pupil Health at Dana Junior High School, Los Angeles." Master's thesis, University of California, Los Angeles, 1956. 112 pp.

3412. Lloyd, James W. "An Investigation of Certain Needs of Students and Former Students of the Beverly Hills High School." Master's thesis, University of California, Los Angeles, 1939. 78 pp.

3413. *Los Angeles Catholic Girls High School.* N.p., n.d. 8 pp.

Historical background of Conaty High School.

3414. "Los Angeles to Have Largest Vocational Institution: Frank Wiggins Trade School Will Accommodate 7,500 Students." *Industrial Arts Magazine* 16 (January 1927): 15-7.

3415. Lovell, Ronald P. "Book Censorship in Southern California High Schools as Symbolized by the Case of *The Catcher in the Rye*." Master's thesis, University of California, Los Angeles, 1961. 103 pp.

3416. Lynch, Rose de Lima, Sister. "Appraisal of the Curriculum of St. Mary's Academy, Los Angeles." Doctoral dissertation, University of California, Berkeley, 1959. 235 pp.

3417. Lyon, Laura L. "Investigation of the Program for the Adjustment of Mexican Girls to the High Schools of the San Fernando Valley." Master's thesis, University of Southern California, 1933. 74 pp.

3418. Makepeace, F. G. "The Instructional Costs of Vocational Subjects in the Senior High Schools of Los Angeles." Master's thesis, University of Southern California, 1930. 92 pp.

3419. Malloy, John J., S.D.B. *Saint John Bosco High School.* Bellflower, 1955. Unp.

3420. Mandel, Bernard. "The Economic Understandings of Culver City High School Seniors." Master's thesis, University of California, Los Angeles, 1968. 94 pp.

3421. Marshall, Marvin L. "The Tenth Grade Guidance Course in the Los Angeles City High Schools." Doctoral dissertation, University of Southern California, 1968. 280 pp.

3422. Martin, Janet P. "Implications for Business Education and Counseling from a Follow-Up Study of Graduates of Baldwin Park High School." Master's thesis, University of California, Los Angeles, 1963. 93 pp.

3423. Martin, Marie Y. "An Evaluation of the Work Experience Program in the Los Angeles City High Schools." Doctoral dissertation, University of Southern California, 1954. 406 pp.

3424. Mason, Anna M. "A Study of the Pupil Personnel of Alexander Hamilton High School of Los Angeles." Master's thesis, University of Southern California, 1940. 95 pp.

3425. McCoy, Enid E. "Study Techniques of Los Angeles Junior High School Pupils." Master's thesis, University of Southern California, 1941. 120 pp.

3426. McCray, Nathan S. "A Study of School Products: The Graduating Class of June 1946 Monrovia-Arcadia-Duarte High School." Master's thesis, Claremont Graduate School, 1953. 192 pp.

3427. McGuigan, Joseph E. "The Bases for Transference of Senior High School Students from Regular to Special Schools in Los Angeles in 1940." Master's thesis, University of Southern California, 1941. 83 pp.

3428. McMurry, Vera L. "An Investigation of a Group of Children of Superior Mental Ability in a Six Year High School in Los Angeles." Master's thesis, University of Southern California, 1931. 92 pp.

3429. McNicholas, Thomas F. "A Critical Study of Guidance Programs in Catholic Secondary Schools in Los Angeles." Master's thesis, University of California, Los Angeles, 1943. 101 pp.

3430. Miglionica, Mary B. "A Study of Differences and Relationships Between Educational Achievement and Class Size in Twenty-Six Selected High Schools in the Archdiocese of Los Angeles." Doctoral dissertation, University of Southern California, 1958. 260 pp.

3431. Miller, E. Arnold. "The Coordination of Athletics in the Los Angeles City High Schools." Master's thesis, University of Southern California, 1955. 123 pp.

3432. Miller, Lillian S. "An Analysis of the Types and Interests of Students Found in the Polytechnic Evening High School of Los Angeles." Master's thesis, University of Southern California, 1927. 71 pp.

3433. Miller, Ross V. "The History, Organization, and Administration of Safety Education in the Junior High Schools of Los Angeles." Master's thesis, University of Southern California, 1935. 150 pp.

3434. Mitchell, Carl G. "A Comparison of the Values of High and Low Creative Seventh Grade Students in Selected Junior High Schools in the Los Angeles District." Doctoral dissertation, University of Southern California, 1967. 429 pp.

3435. "Model Plant for Harvard School Approved for New Home on West Los Angeles Campus." *Los Angeles Saturday Night* 12 (March 12, 1932): 10.

3436. Monroe, Wallace C. "Revision and Reorganization of Bell Gardens Junior High School Faculty Handbook." Master's thesis, University of Southern California, 1949. 101 pp.

3437. Montgomery, G. Millage. "Special Arrangements for One School's Bright Pupils." *School Review* 47 (May 1939): 328-30.
Dorsey High School, Los Angeles.

3438. Murphy, Reginald T. "Internal Administrative Oraginzation in Secondary Schools of the Los Angeles City Unified School District." Doctoral dissertation, University of Southern California, 1970. 161 pp.

3439. Murray, Marion M. "A Study of Pupil Elimination at Whittier Union High School." Master's thesis, University of Southern California, 1938. 90 pp.

3440. Murray, Verl. "A Comparative Study of the Boys of Whittier State School and Monrovia-Arcadia-Duarte High School as to Play Information and Athletic Achievement." Master's thesis, University of Southern California, 1930. 141 pp.

3441. Nicholson, Aloys E. "The Problems Involved in Establishing a Course of Instruction in Driver Training in the Los Angeles City Senior High Schools." Master's thesis, University of Southern California, 1947. 148 pp.

3442. Nicoll, John. "A Study of the Self- and Social Adjustment Patterns of Equated Mexican-American Groups Entering Excelsior High School, Norwalk, California, from Both Mixed and Segregated Elementary Schools." Master's thesis, Claremont Graduate School, 1949. 85 pp.

3443. Nihart, Claude E. "Industrial Arts and Vocational Education in the Convention City." *Industrial Arts and Vocational Education* 36 (December 1947): 397-401.

Los Angeles.

3444. ———— "Radio Training in the Los Angeles Schools." *Industrial Arts and Vocational Education* 33 (June 1944): 227.

3445. ———— "Vocational Guidance in the Industrial-Arts Curriculum." *Industrial Arts and Vocational Education* 37 (November 1948): 343-6.

Los Angeles City Schools.

3446. Nold, Virginia R. "A Follow-Up Study of an Unselected Group of Graduates of Benjamin Franklin High School, Los Angeles." Master's thesis, University of Southern California, 1938. 152 pp.

3447. Nussbaum, Dinette (Zimmerman). "Journalism in the Senior High Schools of Los Angeles County." Master's thesis, University of Southern California, 1933. 100 pp.

3448. O'Connor, Rose C. "A Handbook for Counselors in Los Angeles City Junior High Schools." Master's thesis, University of Southern California, 1950. 64 pp.

3449. Ohme, Herman. "Evaluation of a Modified Daily Schedule at Culver City High School." Doctoral dissertation, University of Southern California, 1968. 277 pp.

3450. Olson, Eugene F. "An Analytic Study of Ninth Grade Guidance in the Los Angeles City Junior High Schools." Doctoral dissertation, University of California, Los Angeles, 1948. 169 pp.

3451. Olson, Velma J. "A Critical Evaluation of the Business Guidance Program in Los Angeles." Master's thesis, University of Southern California, 1942. 102 pp.

3452. Ondrasik, Barbara A. "A Case Study of the Student Government Program of Horace Mann Junior High School." Master's thesis, University of Southern California, 1960. 110 pp.

3453. Osburn, Gertrude M. "Analyzing Student Difficulties in Spanish in a Los Angeles Junior High School with Remedial Suggestions." Master's thesis, University of Southern California, 1928. 65 pp.

3454. Overman, Wallace L. "An Evaluation Survey of the Health and Physical Education Programs of the Junior High Schools of Los Angeles." Master's thesis, University of Southern California, 1941. 109 pp.

3455. Pack, Lloyd C. "The Professional Preparation of Vice-Principals in the Los Angeles City High School District." Doctoral dissertation, University of California, Los Angeles, 1956. 361 pp.

3456. Parker, Alida W. "Some Effects of the UCLA - Beverly Hills High School Cooperative Program." Master's thesis, University of California, Los Angeles, 1962. 127 pp.

3457. Parry, Jack E. "An Analysis and Appraisal of Library Instruction in the Secondary Schools of Los Angeles County." Master's thesis, University of California, Los Angeles, 1953. 143 pp.

3458. Penn, Nolan. "Racial Influence on Vocational Choice." *Journal of Negro Education* 35 (1966): 88-9.

A study of 75 students in a junior high school in Compton.

3459. Perry, Glenn E. "Juvenile Delinquency in the Junior and Senior High Schools of Los Angeles: Its Prevalence, Manifestations, and Causes." Master's thesis, University of Southern California, 1937. 75 pp.

3460. Perry, Richard H. "Policies Pertaining to Hiring and Teaching Assignments of Coaches of Interscholastic Teams in Southern California Secondary Schools." Doctoral dissertation, University of Southern California, 1968. 181 pp.

3461. Petersen, Lena M. "Free Reading in the Junior High Schools of Los Angeles." Master's thesis, University of Southern California, 1932. 158 pp.

3462. Phillips, Rodney E. "The Use of Community Resources by Teachers of Eleventh and Twelfth Grade Mathematics and Physical Science in the Public High Schools of Los Angeles." Doctoral dissertation, University of California, Los Angeles, 1960. 292 pp.

3463. Pilmer, Richard. "An Appraisal of the Effectiveness of Health Instruction at Venice High School." Master's thesis, University of California, Los Angeles, 1957. 111 pp.

3464. Pitts, James C. "The Organization and Administration of School Clubs in the Jefferson High School of Los Angeles, California." Master's thesis, University of Southern California, 1941. 74 pp.

3465. Popenoe, Herbert. "The Distribution of Costs of Instruction in the Junior and Senior High Schools of the City of Los Angeles, California." Master's thesis, University of Southern California, 1926. 77 pp.

3466. Porter, Persis B. "A Study of the Fluctuation of Public Evening High School Attendance in Los Angeles." Master's thesis, University of Southern California, 1928. 130 pp.

3467. Possemato, Paul M. "The Student Voluntary Exchange Phase of the APEX Program, Los Angeles Unified School District: 1967-1968." Doctoral dissertation, University of Southern California, 1969. 252 pp.

3468. *Ramona Convent Jubilee.* Los Angeles, 1965. 88 pp.

Los Angeles Catholic secondary school.

3469. Rawlins, Marcus D. "A Career Pattern Study of Secondary Principals in the Los Angeles City Schools." Doctoral dissertation, University of California, Los Angeles, 1964. 397 pp.

3470. Read, William J., Jr. "Problems of Secondary Substitute Teachers in the Los Angeles City School District." Master's thesis, University of Southern California, 1958. 99 pp.

3471. Reed, Harold J. "Disseminating Occupational Information in Los Angeles County." *Personnel and Guidance Journal* 33 (March 1955): 389-92.

3472. Reinhard, James C. "A Personnel Survey of the Student Body of Central Junior High School, Los Angeles." Master's thesis, University of Southern California, 1935. 161 pp.

3473. Reiter, John L. "A Follow-Up Study of 431 High School Seniors Counseled by the Advise-ment Service of the Los Angeles City Schools." Doctoral dissertation, University of California, Los Angeles, 1953. 191 pp.

3474. Rich, Ruth. "Identification of Health Education Needs of High School Students in the Los Angeles City School Districts." Doctoral dissertation, University of California, Los Angeles, 1959. 264 pp.

3475. Richardson, Adeline (Claff). "A Follow-Up Study of Negro Girl Graduates of a Los Angeles High School." Master's thesis, University of Southern California, 1941. 105 pp.

3476. Riley, Frank. "The Student Drug Kick." *Los Angeles* 10 (October 1965): 58-61.

Drug use by Los Angeles high school students.

3477. Robinson, Alcyon. "City to Lead Vocational Training." *Southern California Business* 1 (April 1922): 40+.

Los Angeles.

3478. ———— "Los Angeles Trains for Production." *Journal of the National Education Association* 12 (June 1923): 227-8.

"Experimental work in cooperative classes for vocational training."

3479. Robok, Horace M. "An Open Air Theater on the [Santa Monica] High School Grounds." *American City* 26 (April 1922): 340-1.

3480. Rosenberg, Lewis B. "History and Development of Industrial Arts Education in Los Angeles [1881 to 1939]." Master's thesis, University of Southern California, 1939. 147 pp.

3481. Rossi, Dale R. "A Study of the Occupational Opportunities in the Food Service Industry in the Santa Monica Area for Secondary School Students with Home Economics Skills." Master's thesis, University of California, Los Angeles, 1966. 51 pp.

3482. Rozolis, James T. "A Critical Study of the Relationship Between the Biological Science Courses in the Selected High Schools and Those at the University of California, Los Angeles, 1960-1965." Doctoral dissertation, University of California, Los Angeles, 1966. 618 pp.

3483. Ruess, William R., Jr. "The Vice Principal

and the Supervision of the Interscholastic Athletic Program in the Los Angeles High Schools." Master's thesis, University of California, Los Angeles, 1956. 76 pp.

3484. Ruffcorn, Georgia. "A Survey of the Courses in Child Development in the Secondary Schools of Los Angeles County." Master's thesis, University of Southern California, 1934. 140 pp.

3485. Ryel, Chrystle C. "A Survey of the Guidance Programs in the Five Juinor High Schools of the Compton Union Secondary District." Master's thesis, University of Southern California, 1949. 144 pp.

3486. Sands, Elizabeth. "A Survey of the Guidance Practices in the Junior High Schools of Los Angeles." Master's thesis, University of Southern California, 1941. 190 pp.

3487. Sandy, Maurice O. "The History of the California Interscholastic Federation, Southern Section, 1914-1954." Master's thesis, University of California, Los Angeles, 1954. 152 pp.

3488. "Santa Monica High School." *Pacific Municipalities* 35 (March 1921): 25-6.

3489. Sargent, Elise H. "A Study of the Girls' Welfare Centers of the Los Angeles School System." Master's thesis, University of Southern California, 1932. 157 pp.

3490. Sargent, Harry. "The History of Secondary Education in the City of Los Angeles." Master's thesis, University of Southern California, 1940. [?] pp.

3491. Scharer, Norman B. "The Development of Public Secondary Education in Alhambra, California." Doctoral dissertation, University of Califoration, Los Angeles, 1947. 317 pp.

3492. "School Orchestras in Los Angeles." *The Musician* 20 (June 1915): 373.

Orchestra Department of Los Angeles City Schools.

3493. Sellwood, John J. "The Corrective Physical Education Programs in Sixteen Los Angeles County High Schools." Master's thesis, University of Southern California, 1946. 86 pp.

3494. Sharon, John B. "Trends in Vocational Agricultural Education in Los Angeles County, 1950-1960." Master's thesis, Claremont Graduate School, 1964. 38 pp.

3495. Sheets, Kenneth L. "The Physical Fitness of High School Boys Graduating from Los Angeles and Santa Monica Public Schools." Master's thesis, University of California, Los Angeles, 1959. 57 pp.

3496. Shepard, John B. "The Preparation and Duties of the Boys' Physical Education Department Heads in the Los Angeles Senior High Schools." Master's thesis, University of Southern California, 1932. 241 pp.

3497. Sherman, Sadie E. "A Critical Survey of General Music Classes in the Junior High Schools of Los Angeles." Master's thesis, University of Southern California, 1937. 131 pp.

3498. Shroff, Piroja D. "Seventh Grade Art Curriculum and Instruction in the Public Schools of Los Angeles County." Doctoral dissertation, University of Southern California, 1961. 203 pp.

3499. Smill, Rose A. "The Role of the Health Coordinator in Los Angeles High Schools." Master's thesis, University of Southern California, 1943. 143 pp.

3500. Smith, Bertha H. "Mothering a Thousand Girls." *Good Housekeeping Magazine* 51 (December 1910): 688-91.

Los Angeles Polytechnic High School.

3501. Snowbarger, Vernon A. "Factors Associated with Truancy Among Boys in Selected Junior High Schools of Los Angeles County." Doctoral dissertation, University of Southern California, 1954. 155 pp.

3502. Sobey, Christel L. A. "Teacher Tenure and Turnover in the High Schools of Los Angeles County from September 1923 to September 1928 Inclusive." Master's thesis, University of Southern California, 1929. 136 pp.

3503. "Sports and Studies Balance at Carl Curtis School." *Los Angeles Saturday Night* 14 (August 4, 1934): 7.

Private co-educational school near Beverly and Fairfax, Los Angeles.

3504. Starter, Marvin S. "A Comparative Study of the Social Adjustment Programs in Two Los Angeles City Secondary Schools." Master's thesis, University of California, Los Angeles, 1965. 72 pp.

Marshall Junior High School and Warren High School.

3505. Stevens, W. Bertrand. "Aims of Harvard School for Boys." *Los Angeles Saturday Night* 13 (July 29, 1933): 11.

A private boys' school under the Episcopal Diocese of Los Angeles.

3506. Stimson, Marshall. "History of Los Angeles High School." *Historical Society of Southern California Quarterly* 24 (1942): 99-109.

3507. Stonebraker, Miles J. "A Survey of the Teaching of Shakespeare in Selected Secondary Schools of Los Angeles County." Master's thesis, University of California, Los Angeles, 1958. 127 pp.

3508. Strange, Glessie. "A Survey of Extra-Curricular Activities at the Santa Monica High School." Master's thesis, University of Southern California, 1949. 82 pp.

3509. Sullivan, Ethel (MacKenzie). "Case Studies of Employed Ninth Grade Graduates of a Los Angeles Junior High School; A Record of Seventy-Eight Employed Graduates and the Use They Make of Shop Information and Acquired Skill in Connection with Their Jobs." Master's thesis, University of Southern California, 1932. 60 pp.

3510. Switzer, W. J. "La Puente Surveys Its Curricular Progress in Geography." *The Journal of Geography* 61 (1962): 259-61.

La Puente Union High School District.

3511. Tappe, Virgil A. "A Survey of the Activities Carried on in the Home Shops of Los Angeles Junior High School Boys." Master's thesis, University of Southern California, 1936. 169 pp.

3512. Thomas, Charlotte B. "The Status of Crafts in the Los Angeles High Schools." Master's thesis, University of Southern California, 1935. 191 pp.

3513. Thomas, Kenneth R. "The History of Industrial Arts in the City of Pasadena." Doctoral dissertation, University of California, Los Angeles, 1967. 419 pp.

3514. Thomas, Mary E. "The Housing of Junior High School Programs in the City of Los Angeles." Master's thesis, University of Southern California, 1928. 52 pp.

3515. Thurman, Wesley B. "Unit Costs of Supplies in the Four-Year High Schools of Los Angeles County." Master's thesis, University of Southern California, 1931. 102 pp.

3516. Trieb, Jeanette B. "Supervisory Responsibilities of Physical Education Department Heads (Girls) in the Los Angeles City High Schools." Master's thesis, University of Southern California, 1934. 162 pp.

3517. Trillingham, Clinton C. "Administrative Devices for Stimulating Scholarship in the Junior High Schools of Los Angeles County." Master's thesis, University of Southern California, 1931. 185 pp.

3518. Turner, Winnifred T. "An Analysis of the Population of the Public Evening High School in Los Angeles." Master's thesis, University of Southern California, 1931. 95 pp.

3519. "An Unusual Program to Provide for Individual Differences." *School Review* 45 (November 1937): 643-5.

David Starr Jordan High School, Los Angeles.

3520. Van Barneveld, Mary. "Administration of Registration, Records, and Allied Student Problems in the Larger Senior High Schools of Los Angeles." Master's thesis, University of Southern California, 1931. 152 pp.

3521. Voorhis, Horace J. "The Education of the Institution Boy: A General Outline of Policies for the Voorhis School for Boys." Master's thesis, Claremont Graduate School, 1928. 341 pp.

3522. ———— *The Story of the Voorhis School for Boys.* San Dimas, 1932. 20 pp.

3523. Walther, Henry W. "A Survey of the Employment and Subsequent History Records of Behavior Problem Boys Who Have Passed Through the Welfare Centers of the Los Angeles City Schools." Master's thesis, University of Southern California, 1937. 111 pp.

3524. Webb, Carolyn K., and Dooley, Milton D. "A Comparative Study of the Effect of Transiency on Academic, Personal and Social Adjustment of Eleventh Grade Pupils." Master's thesis, University of Southern California, 1964. 108 pp.

3525. Weingarten, Kurt P. "Some Implications for Business Education from a Follow-Up of Graduates of Nine Los Angeles High Schools." Master's thesis, University of California, Los Angeles, 1950. 99 pp.

3526. Weiss, Benjamin. "An Analysis of Continuation Students in Los Angeles." Master's thesis, University of Southern California, 1931. 84 pp.

3527. "Westlake School and Holmby College." *Los Angeles Saturday Night* 12 (August 20, 1932): 7.
   Sketch of Los Angeles private school.

3528. "Westlake School for Girls and Holmby College." *Los Angeles Saturday Night* 10 (August 23, 1930): 7.

2529. Weyer, Joseph E. "A Survey of the Non-Academic Curricula of the Catholic Secondary Schools in the Archdiocese of Los Angeles." Master's thesis, University of California, Los Angeles, 1950. 172 pp.

3530. White, Muriel M. "The Visiting Teacher Program at Mark Keppel High School of Alhambra, California." Master's thesis, University of Southern California, 1948. 153 pp.

3531. Wittington, Harriett E. "The Administration of Senior High School Libraries in Los Angeles." Master's thesis, University of Southern California, 1929. 136 pp.

3532. Wickes, Una S. "Analysis and Assessment of the Pasadena High School Guidance Program." Doctoral dissertation, University of California, Los Angeles, 1957. 288 pp.

3533. Williams, Maurice C. "Instructional Assistance Needed by English and Social Studies Teachers in the Secondary Schools of Los Angeles County." Doctoral dissertation, University of California, Los Angeles, 1958. 206 pp.

3534. Williams, Rebecca M. "Administration of Guidance and Counseling in the Los Angeles Senior High Schools During the Last Three Decades: 1935-1965." Doctoral dissertation, University of California, Los Angeles, 1966. 481 pp.

3535. Winkler, Elizabeth A. "Opportunities for Science Specialization in Los Angeles City Junior High Schools." Master's thesis, University of California, Los Angeles, 1959. 94 pp.

3536. Yates, Harold W. "A History of the Brea-Olinda Union High School District: A Thesis." "Master's thesis, Whittier College, Whittier. Unp.

EDUCATION—ADULT

3537. Amidon, Beulah. "Home Teachers in the City." *Survey* 56 (June 1, 1926): 304-7+.
   Home teaching in Los Angeles, particularly for recent immigrants.

3538. Atherton, Sadie C. "The Trade Extension School of Los Angeles, California." *Industrial-Arts Magazine* 14 (June 1925): 218-21.

3539. Blanchard, Gladys M. "The Administration and Supervision of the Americanization Department of the Evening Schools of Los Angeles." Master's thesis, University of Southern California, 1935. 140 pp.

3540. Callender, Ruth F. "A Study of Special Day Americanization and Citizenship Classes in the Los Angeles City Schools." Master's thesis, University of Southern California, 1949. 136 pp.

3541. Cooperider, Louise. "History of the Americanization Department in the Los Angeles City Schools." Master's thesis, University of Southern California, 1934. 149 pp.

3542. Darling, Lu Ann W. "From Mop to Typewriter . . . Clerical Training for Disadvantaged Adults." *NEA Journal* 56 (October 1967): 28-9.
   Clerical training program, UCLA.

3543. Davidson, Adele K. "A History of the California Association for Adult Education." Doctoral dissertation, University of California, Los Angeles, 1960. 303 pp.
   Study is not focused on Los Angeles, but does contain some material on the Los Angeles County Council of Adult Education.

3544. Davis, Pete. "Recreational Training Opportunities in Los Angeles." Master's thesis, University of Southern California, 1940. 131 pp.

3545. Davis, Thomas J. "Schools That Reach the Homes of Immigrants." *American City* 17 (December 1917): 511-6.

Neighborhood schools of Los Angeles.

3546. "Defense Training in South Pasadena Part of Adult Education Program." *Western City* 18 (July 1942): 21-2.

3547. De Prez, Richard H. "A Study of Continuation Education in the South Bay Union High School District." Master's thesis, University of Southern California, 1965. 65 pp.

3548. Dickert, Lois. "How to Succeed in Business by Being Charming." *Los Angeles* 4 (September 1962): 37-9.

Brief biography of "the schoolmarm of charm, Caroline Leonetti," and how her school got started.

3549. Doyle, Katherine. "Yes, We Have Invisible Exports: For Here Is a Los Angeles School with 20,000 Students in Latin America." *Southern California Business* 9 (October 1930): 18-9.

"Escuela Nacional de Automotores."

3550. Felburg, William F. "Organization and Administration of Continuation Education in Los Angeles County." Master's thesis, University of Southern California, 1953. 90 pp.

3551. Ferris, Chester. "The Los Angeles Example." *Review of Reviews* 53 (January 1916): 18-2.

Dana Bartlett and others secure a series of measures "by which to educate the immigrant in the meaning and spirit of our American institutions."

3552. "First Negro History Class in Los Angeles City Schools at Dorsey Adult School." *Negro History Bulletin* 25 (1961): 18-9+.

3553. Freeland, John L. "A Critical Incident Study of Public Health Inspection and Restaurant Employee Training Programs in the City of Los Angeles." Master's thesis, University of Southern California, 1953. 152 pp.

3554. Funk, Ruth L. "A Historical Study of Metropolitan School of Business, 1935-1942." Master's thesis, University of Southern California, 1946. 123 pp.

3555. Gerber, Charlotte B. "A Study of the Los Angeles Training School for Household Employees." Master's thesis, University of Southern California, 1940. 128 pp.

3556. Harth, Dorothy G. "The Los Angeles Bureau of Music from 1950 to 1960: Its Implications for Adult Music Education." Master's thesis, University of Southern California, 1961. 77 pp.

3557. Jackson, George A. "A History of the Adult Education Program in the Los Angeles Public Schools." Doctoral dissertation, University of California, Los Angeles, 1957. 295 pp.

3558. Johnston, William J. "Minors in Classes for Adults in Twenty-Seven Los Angeles City Adult Schools." Doctoral dissertation, University of California, Los Angeles, 1965. 252 pp.

3559. Kahan, Melanie J. "Parent Education Through Child Development Classes; A Study of the Origins, Development and Present Program of the Los Angeles City School Adult Education Branch." Master's thesis, University of California, Los Angeles, 1959. 260 pp.

3560. Kelso, C. C. "A New Plan of Naturalization." *Journal of the National Education Association* 17 (November 1928): 237-8.

Naturalization granted upon presentation of a diploma from a course in "Citizenship," a plan assertedly initiated in Los Angeles.

3561. Kirschman, Richard. "Actors 'On Cue' for Watts Workshop." *Urban West* 2 (February 1969): 13+.

Interviews with Sidney Poitier, Greg Morris and Talmadge Sprott concerning the Douglass House Foundation, an adult educational enterprise, Los Angeles.

3562. Lamson, Pauline. "Vocational Rehabilitation Through the Food Trades at the Frank Wiggins Trade School." Master's thesis, University of Southern California, 1935. 132 pp.

3563. Langley, Nancy. "Maritime Catalina." *Westways* 36 (July 1944): 6-7.

U.S. Maritime Service Training Station, one of four in the country, at Catalina Island.

3564. "Large Airport Planned in L. A. to Conduct School and Factory." *Western Flying* 4 (November 1928): 92.

Site on West Jefferson picked by Joseph Kreutter, Inc., as location of factory, shops and aviation academy.

3565. Lawrence, Beverly G. "Planning, Conducting, and Evaluating an Adult Education Class in Parent Education for Mothers of Elementary School Age Children in Monrovia and Duarte." Master's thesis, University of California, Los Angeles, 1956. 145 pp.

3566. Lea, Howard P. "A Survey of the Attitudes of Los Angeles City Teachers Who Teach Both Regular Session and Adult Classes Towards Their Adult Teaching Assignment." Master's thesis, University of California, Los Angeles, 1958. 116 pp.

3567. Lynch, Pauline F. "The Status of Domestic Service in Los Angeles." Master's thesis, University of Southern California, 1929. 65 pp.

Domestic servants.

3568. Mezirow, Jack D. "The Coordinating Council Movement in Los Angeles County and Its Implications for Adult Education." Doctoral dissertation, University of California, Los Angeles, 1955. 604 pp.

3569. Osborn, Charles H. "A Guide for Adult School Counselors in the Whittier Union High School District." Master's thesis, University of Southern California, 1958. 52 pp.

3570. Parrott, Wanda Sue. "Studio Watts Workshop." *Arts in Society* 5 (1968): 510-9.

The story of an arts workshop established in 1965 mainly for the integration into society of school dropouts.

3571. "Polytechnic's Unique Law Classes." *Saturday Night* 7 (July 23, 1927): 3.

Evening law classes at Los Angeles Polytechnic High School.

3572. Reed, Clarence M. "The Physical Education Needs and Desires of Adult School Men in Los Angeles." Master's thesis, University of Southern California, 1934. 87 pp.

3573. Ride, Dale B. "Public Education for the Aging—A Determination of the Educational Desires of the Aging and Recommendations for More Adequately Involving Them in the Santa Monica Adult Education Program." Doctoral dissertation, University of California, Los Angeles, 1954. 142 pp.

3574. Riley, Frank. "The Hidden Campus." *Los Angeles* 9 (April 1965): 34-40.

Los Angeles adult education.

3575. Stewart, Robert M. "An Evaluation of the Guidance Program in the Los Angeles City Adult Schools." Doctoral dissertation, University of California, Los Angeles, 1967. 165 pp.

3576. Sylvester, Kathryn D. "History of the Organization of the Adult Education Department of the Long Beach City Schools." Master's thesis, University of Southern California, 1940. 138 pp.

3577. Trautwein, Mary C. "A History of the Development of Schools for the Foreign-Born Adults in Los Angeles." Master's thesis, University of Southern California, 1928. 137 pp.

Period covered is 1817 to 1928, with emphasis on 1890 to 1928.

3578. Willey, Frank G. "A Study of Worker's Education in the Greater Los Angeles Area." Master's thesis, Claremont Graduate School, 1951. 272 pp.

EDUCATION—HIGHER

3579. Adams, Flora A. "Chinese Student Life at the University of Southern California." Master's thesis, University of Souther California, 1935. 117 pp.

3580. Allison, William L. "The Variability of Denominational Affiliation Among Students of the University of Southern California." Master's thesis, University of Southern California, 1955. 111 pp.

3581. Anderson, Herbert C. *A Brief History of the Printing Department of Los Angeles Trade-Technical Junior College . . . Including Biographical Sketches of the Printing Instructors and the Bruce McCallister Memorial Award, 1924-1952.* Los Angeles, 1952. 69 pp.

3582. "Art Rides High at a Great University." *Life* 42 (May 20, 1957): 92-101+.

UCLA.

3583. Atkinson, Byron H. "Attitudinal Differences of Fraternity and Non-Fraternity Men at the University of California, Los Angeles." Doctoral dissertation, University of California, Los Angeles, 1960. 120 pp.

3584. ———— "Social and Financial Adjustment of Veterans at UCLA." *School and Society* 72 (July 8, 1950): 24-7.

3585. ———— "Veteran Performance at the University of California at Los Angeles." Master's thesis, University of California, Los Angeles, 1949. 65 pp.

3586. Aumack, Gordon D. "A Twenty-Year Study of the Success after Transfer of Compton Junior College Students." Doctoral dissertation, University of California, Los Angeles, 1953. 249 pp.

3587. Baer, John W. "The 'Small' College in Southern California." *Out West* 30 (February-March 1909): 172-5.

Occidental College, of which Baer was president.

3588. Baker, David. "A Study of the Interrelationships and Effectiveness of Modes of Admission for the 1958 Freshman Class in the College of Letters, Arts, and Sciences at the University of Southern California." Master's thesis, University of Southern California, 1962. 22 pp.

3589. Ball, Joseph A. "Community Support Is Needed to Build the U.S.C. Law Center." *Long Beach Bar Bulletin* 12 (June 1966): 5-7.

3590. Beach, Alice. " 'Dere Professor'—What Folks Want to Know About Astronomy." *Westways* 33 (February 1941): 16-7.

Mt. Wilson Observatory.

3591. Beck, Julian. "The History of Legal Education in Los Angeles County." Master's thesis, University of Southern California, 1935. 108 pp.

3592. Becker, Tamer S. "Perceptions and Attituinal Changes Among Foreign Students on the UCLA Campus." Doctoral dissertation, University of California, Los Angeles, 1966. 323 pp.

3593. Benson, Ellis M. "A Time and Sequence Analysis of Critical Steps in the Establishment of California Public Junior Colleges." Doctoral dissertation, University of California, Los Angeles, 1962. 369 pp.

3594. Berry, Aubrey L. "An Eight-Year Study of Teacher Guidance and Placement by the Office of Teacher Placement, University of California, Los Angeles." Doctoral dissertation, University of California, Los Angeles, 1948. 471 pp.

3595. Beyer, L. Remmy. "The Anniversary of the University of Southern California Graduate School." *School and Society* 61 (March 1945): 134.

3596. Blumenberg, Eleanor B. "The University of Southern California Teacher Corps Rural-Migrant Program: A Descriptive Analysis of the First Cycle." Doctoral dissertation, University of Southern California, 1970. 286 pp.

3597. Boehm, George A. W. "Bringing Engineers Up to Date." *Fortune* 67 (May 1963): 120-1+.

Six-week training program sponsored by General Electric and UCLA.

3598. Bogardus, Emory S., ed. *Graduate Studies in a World Reborn; The Proceedings of the Thirty-fifth Anniversary of the Founding of the Graduate School of the University of Southern California, January 25-28, 1945.* Los Angeles, 1945. 216 pp.

3599. Borum, May. "A History of the Pasadena Community Playhouse [1916-1928]." Master's thesis, University of Southern California, 1928. 173 pp.

3600. Brackett, Charles H. "The History of Azusa College and the Friends, 1900-1965." Master's thesis, University of Southern California, 1967. 152 pp.

3601. Brackett, Frank P. *Granite and Sagebrush; Reminiscences of the First Fifty Years of Pomona College.* Los Angeles, 1944. 251 pp.

3602. Bradway, John S. "The Beginning of the Legal Clinic of the University of Southern California." *Southern California Law Review* 2 (1929): 252-76.

3603. ———— "Work of the Legal Clinic of the University of Southern California." *The Bar Association Bulletin* 4 (October 18, 1928): 54-8.

3604. Brazzale, Ray; Rito, Rosa, and Wakelee, Earl. "Mobility of Social Work Graduates of the University of Southern California, School of Social Work, 1950-1954." Master's thesis, University of Southern California, 1963. 96 pp.

3605. Brown, Jane W. "An Analysis of Selected Data Pertaining to Master's Degrees in Education at the University of Southern California." Master's thesis, University of Southern California, 1961. 152 pp.

3606. Bundy, Stuart M. "Prediction of Success in the Doctoral Program of the School of Education of the University of Southern California." Doctoral dissertation, University of Southern California, 1968. 109 pp.

3607. Burg, Jules S. "A Survey of Past Participants of the NDEA Institute in Counseling and Guidance at the University of Southern California." Master's thesis, University of Southern California, 1967. 27 pp.

3608. Burroughs, Franklin T. "Foreign Students at U.C.L.A.; A Case-Study in Cross-Cultural Education." Doctoral dissertation, University of California, Los Angeles, 1964. 239 pp.

3609. Gaffray, Donald B. "The U.S.C. Law Center." *Long Beach Bar Bulletin* 12 (June 1966): 9-11.

3610. California Institute of Technology. Industrial Relations Center. *Caltech's Industrial Relations Section Twenty-Year Report, 1939-1959.* Pasadena, [1960?]. 29 pp.

3611. —— *Our First Twenty-Five Years, 1939-1964.* [Pasadena, 1964?]. 37 pp.

3612. "The California State Normal School at Los Angeles." *The Architect and Engineer of California* 37 (May 1914): 93-111.

3613. Carew, Harold D. "Beauty Wed to Use." *Wesways* 30 (February 1938): 26-7.
   "The world's newest art," industrial design, as taught at the Southern California Graduate School of Design in Pasadena, headed by Dr. Walter Baermann.

3614. —— "Handmaidens of the Sciences." *Westways* 31 (November 1939): 20-1.
   California Institute of Technology.

3615. Caughey, John W. "A University in Jeopardy." *Harpers Magazine* 201 (November 1950): 68-75.
   The California loyalty oath controversy as seen by one UCLA professor profoundly involved.

3616. Cha, Marn Jai. "An Empirical Evaluation of the Effects of an Educational Program in Public Administration: One University Experience." Master's thesis, University of Southern California, 1967. 132 pp.

3617. Chang, Stella L. "A Descriptive Study of the Curriculum, Personnel and Facilities of Commercial and Professional Institutions in the Greater Los Angeles Area Offering Training to Students in Television Performance." Master's thesis, University of California, Los Angeles, 1958. 127 pp.

3618. Chisholm, James C. "A Comparison of Academic Success of Veterans Counseled at the University of Southern California Veterans Guidance Center Who Followed Through on Their Decision on Course of Study with Those Who Changed Their Decision." Master's thesis, University of Southern California, 1950. 69 pp.

3619. Clark, Donald S. "Placing College Men and Women: 3. California Institute of Technology." *Southern California Business* 17 (June 1938): 20.

3620. Clark, Edwin C. "The Upward or Outward Extension of Education in Burbank, California." Doctoral dissertation, Stanford University, 1955. 198 pp.
   Junior college program.

3621. Clark, Sandra J. "An Exploratory Analysis of Educational Opportunity Program (EOP) Women Students in a UCLA Residence Hall." Doctoral dissertation, University of California, Los Angeles, 1969. 211 pp.

3622. Clarke, Edith M. "A Course in Study in Health Education for the Women of the Los Angeles Junior College." Master's thesis, University of Southern California, 1935. 232 pp.

3623. Claus, Cynthia. "As the Twig Is Bent: The George Pepperdine Foundation; Its Aim and Purpose." *Apartment Journal* 19 (June 1937): 12+.

3624. Cleland, Robert G. *The History of Occidental College, 1887-1937.* Los Angeles, 1937. 115 pp.

3625. Cole, Eleanor H. "An Investigation of the Frequency, Variety, and Intensity Problems Reported by Selected Women Physical Education Majors at the University of California at Los Angeles." Doctoral dissertation, University of California, Los Angeles, 1956. 174 pp.

3626. Collins, James H. "Meet Our Cosmopolitan Student Body: Young People from 50 Lands, at Our Colleges, Mean Much in Contacts for the Future." *Southern California Business* 13 (April 1934): 12-3.

3627. Comm, Walter. "A Historical Analysis of Vocational Education: Land-Grant Colleges to California Junior Colleges, 1862-1940." Master's thesis, University of Southern California, 1967. 190 pp.

3628. Cook, Herbert R. "An Evaluative Study of a General Education Course in Life Science at Long Beach City College." Master's thesis, University of California, Los Angeles, 1961. 82 pp.

3629. Cooper, Charles W. *Whittier: Independent College in California, Founded by Quakers, 1887.* Los Angeles, 1967. 405 pp.

3630. Covert, Spencer E. "A Follow-Up Study of the Doctoral Graduates in Education at the University of Southern California." Master's thesis, University of Southern California, 1947. 55 pp.

3631. Cranston, M. W. "U.S.C. School of Religion Moves." *Christian Century* 73 (July 18, 1956): 855-6.

3632. Dager, Eleanor T. "A Descriptive Study of the Development of Educational Television Production and Policy at the University of California at Los Angeles, 1950-1954." Master's thesis, University of California, Los Angeles, 1956. 126 pp.

3633. Dakin, Wirt B., and Howson, Carl R. "History of the Medical School [Part III]." *Southern California Alumni Review* 16 (February 1935): 6-7+.

Second and final twentieth-century intallment.

3634. Daniels, Clinton C. "Economic Education in the Junior Colleges of California." Master's thesis, University of Southern California, 1963. 136 pp.

3635. De Nevers, Margaret Y. "A Study of Possible Significant Personality Differences Between Undergraduate and Graduate Students in Education at the University of California at Los Angeles." Master's thesis, University of California, Los Angeles, 1955. 94 pp.

3636. Diaconoff, Phil, and Washburn, C.G. "Engineering on the Los Angeles Campus." *California Engineer* 26 (December 1947): 17+.

UCLA College of Engineering.

3637. Dickson, Edward A. *University of California at Los Angeles, Its Origin and Formative Years.* Los Angeles, 1955. 61 pp.

3638. Diem, Grace A. "A Study of Students' Opinions in Regard to Home Economics at the University of California at Los Angeles." Master's thesis, University of California, Los Angeles, 1951. 88 pp.

3639. Dillahunt, Barbara S. "Comparison of Social Attitudes of UCLA Undergraduate Women Living in a Coeducational Residence and Those Living in an All Women's Dormitory." Master's thesis, University of California, Los Angeles, 1962. 47 pp.

3640. Dodson, Leigh M. "Analysis of Student Personnel Problems and Counseling Practises in Los Angeles City College." Doctoral dissertation, University of California, Los Angeles, 1951. 341 pp.

3641. Dole, Arthur M. "An Era in Pomona College History." *Out West,* new series, 1 (February 1911): 191-4.

3642. Dunn, Dora G. "An Evaluation of the Understanding Possessed by Prospective Teachers at Pepperdine College of Basic, Necessary Mathematical Concepts." Master's thesis, University of California, Los Angeles, 1965. 77 pp.

3643. Dunn, Velma C. "A Survey of the Leisure-Time Activities of Undergraduate Students at the University of Southern California." Master's thesis, University of Southern California, 1942. 109 pp.

3644. "18,500 Extension Students." *Los Angeles Saturday Night* 44 (September 26, 1936): 5.

UCLA Extension Division.

3645. Eitzen, David D. "The Possibility of Developing Studies in Pastoral Counseling in the School of Religion of the University of Southern California." Master's thesis, University of Southern California, 1937. 88 pp.

3646. Emery, Warren G. "A Survey and Evaluation of the Physical Education Program at the California Institute of Technology." Master's thesis, University of California, Los Angeles, 1959. 150 pp.

3647. Farrar, Ronald D. "The Non-Visa Foreign Student at Los Angeles City College: A Study of the Relation of Various Administraive and Academic Factors to the Immigrant Student." Doctoral dissertation, University of California, Los Angeles, 1968. 229 pp.

3648. Feeler, William. "History of Whittier College." Master's thesis, University of Southern California, 1919. 78 pp.

3649. Fernald, Grace M. "Certain Points Concerning Remedial Reading as It Is Taught at the University of California." *Education* 67 (March 1947) : 442-58.

UCLA.

3650. Fetty, Homer D. "The Feasibility of an Alternate Work-Study Program on College Level for Los Angeles Area." Doctoral dissertation, University of Southern California, 1951. 225 pp.

3651. *The First Decade of Long Beach State College, 1949-1959.* [Long Beach, 1960]. 191 pp.

3652. "First Degrees Granted in Audio Engineering." *Radio & Television News* 44 (July 1950): 102+.

B.S. degress conferred by College of Audio Engineering of the "University of Hollywood."

3653. Flakoll, Adrian. "A Study of the Classification Plan for Certificated Positions in the Los Angeles City Junior College District." Master's thesis, Occidental College, 1950. 83 pp.

3654. Florell, David M. "The Origin and History of the School of Education, University of California, Los Angeles." Doctoral dissertation, University of California, Los Angeles, 1946. 485 pp.

3655. Foreman, Mildred L. "Placing College Men and Women: 1. University of California at Los Angeles." *Southern California Business* 17 (April 1938) : 20.

3656. Fox, Frederick. "A History of the Extended Day Programs of the Los Angeles Junior Colleges." Doctoral dissertation, University of California, Los Angeles, 1960. 265 pp.

3657. Fuller, Charlotte J. "An Evaluation of the Effectiveness of a Business Communications Course in Helping UCLA School of Business Administration Students Improve in the Mechanics of English." Master's thesis, University of California, Los Angeles, 1966. 48 pp.

3658. Furukawa, Fred M. "An Analysis and Appraisal of Transfer Credit Courses via a Commercial Television Channel from Selected Community Colleges in Los Angeles County." Doctoral dissertation, University of Southern California, 1969. 143 pp.

3659. Futrell, Louis W. "An Analysis of the Course in Personal Health Problems at the University of Southern California." Master's thesis, University of Southern California, 1949. 67 pp.

3660. Gardner, David P. *The California Oath Controversy.* Berkeley and Los Angeles, 1967. 329 pp.

Based on author's doctoral dissertation.

3661. ——— "The University of California Loyalty Oath Controversy, 1949-1952." Doctoral dissertation, University of California, Berkeley, 1966. 395 pp.

References to UCLA.

3662. Gates, Charles. "The History and the Development of the California Institute of Technology." Master's thesis, University of Southern California, 1935. 67 pp.

3663. Gates, Samuel E. "A History of the University of Southern California, 1900-1928." Master's thesis, University of Southern California, 1929. 303 pp.

3664. Gaw, Allison. *A Sketch of the Development of Graduate Work in the University of Southern California, 1910-1935.* Los Angeles, 1935. 64 pp.

3665. Gay, Leslie F., Jr. "History of the University

of Southern California." Master's thesis, University of Southern California, 1910. 301 pp.

3666. "Gift of Kerckhoff Hall." *Los Angeles Saturday Night* 11 (January 31, 1931): 7.
Gift of Mrs. William G. Kerckhoff to UCLA.

3667. Giguette, Eulalia M. "A Follow-Up Study of the Remedial Reading Clinic of the University of Southern California." Doctoral dissertation, University of Southern California, 1935. 212 pp.

3668. Giles, Mary. "A Critical Appraisal of the Program of Supervising Teaching Provided for a Group of Prospective Teachers Given Emergency Training at the University of California at Los Angeles." Master's thesis, University of California, Los Angeles, 1946. 88 pp.

3669. Given, John N. "The Attitudes and Opinions of Selected Community Groups Toward Junior College Education in Los Angeles." Doctoral dissertation, University of California, Los Angeles, 1957. 431 pp.

3670. Goodhew, Edna F. *Echoes from Half a Century.* Los Angeles, [1960]. 322 pp.
History of Los Angeles Pacific College.

3671. Greene, Patterson. "Professional Theatre on Campus." *Theatre Arts* 47 (February 1963): 62-3+.
Theatre Group makes use of UCLA facilities.

3672. Greif, Pamela J. "An Evaluation of a Minority Fellowship Program at the Graduate School of Education, U.C.L.A. 1968-1969." Master's thesis, University of California, Los Angeles, 1970. 45 pp.

3673. "Grinding the 200-Inch Mirror for the Mt. Palomar Telescope." *Western Machinery and Steel World* 28 (August 1937): 266-7.
Work done at California Institute of Technology, Pasadena.

3674. Gustafsson, Carl W. "A Survey of the Development of Counseling and Guidance Services in Colleges, Universities and Communities of Southern California Resulting from the Advisement and Guidance Program of the Veterans Administration." Master's thesis, University of Southern California, 1948. 58 pp.

3675. Hale, George E. *Ten Years of a Mountain Observatory. A Brief Account of the Mount Wilson Solar Observatory of the Carnegie Institute of Washington.* Washington, D.C., 1915. 91 pp.

3676. Halpert, Ruth L. "A Study of the Sources, Manifestations, and Magnitude of Stress Among Student Teachers at UCLA." Doctoral dissertation, University of California, Los Angeles, 1966. 114 pp.

3677. Hamilton, Andrew. "California: The World's Largest University." *Coronet* 26 (May 1949): 36-40.

3678. ———, and Jackson, John B. *UCLA on the Move During Fifty Golden Years, 1919-1969.* Los Angeles, 1969. 230 pp.
Heavily illustrated.

3679. Hand, Wayland D. "Folklore and Mythology at UCLA: Folklore, Mythology, Folk Music, and Ethnomusicology." *Western Folklore* 23 (January 1964): 35-7.

3680. Hanley, Anne. "D.C.I.—The Self-Fulfilling Phophecy." *Westways* 61 (November 1969): 17-20.
Delinquency Control Institute of USC's School of Public Administration.

3681. "Harper Hall: Further Step in Group Plan." *Los Angeles Saturday Night* 12 (March 5, 1932): 7.
New central library and administration building of Claremont Colleges.

3682. Harris, Herbert E. *The Quaker and the West; The First Sixty Years of Whittier College.* [N.p., 1948]. 175 pp.

3683. Hashem, Erfan A. "Develpoment of the University Neighborhood; The University of Southern California." Master's thesis, University of Southern California, 1954. 177 pp.

3684. Hazard, Pauline. "History of the Mount Wilson Observatory." Master's thesis, University of Southern California, 1931. 73 pp.

3685. Heron, Lilian E. "An Analysis of the Graduates of the School of Merchandising at the University of Southern California from 1930 to 1936 Inclusive." Master's thesis, University of Southern California, 1938. 130 pp.

3686. Herrscher, Barton R. "Patterns of Attainment and the Environmental Press at UCLA

Student Groups." Doctoral dissertation, University of California, Los Angeles, 1967. 248 pp.

3687. Hill, Herbert W., ed. *Proceedings, Twenty-Fifth Anniversary Celebration of the Inauguration of Graduate Studies, the University of Southern California, 1910-1935.* Los Angeles, 1936. 255 pp.

3688. Hill, Laurance L. *Six Collegiate Decades—The Growth of Higher Education in Southern California.* Los Angeles, 1929. 111 pp.

3689. Hoedinghaus, George E. "Report of the 1934 Housing Investigation, University of Southern California." Master's thesis, University of Southern California, 1934. 102 pp.

Student housing.

3690. "Holmby College, a Junior College for Young Women." *Los Angeles Saurday Night* 14 (August 18, 1934): 7.

3691. Hood, Mantle. "Folklore and Mythology at UCLA: The Ethnomusicology Program." *Western Folklore* 23 (January 1964): 37-8.

3692. "How Doctors Are Made." *Time* 68 (July 2, 1956): 44.

UCLA Medical School.

3693. Hungerford, Curtiss, R. "A Study in University Administrative Leadership: Rufus B. von KleinSmid and the University of Southern California, 1921 to 1935." Doctoral dissertation, University of Southern California, 1967. 307 pp.

3694. Hunt, Rockwell D. *The First Half-Century.* Los Angeles, 1930. 109 pp.

History of USC.

3695. ——— "The Semi-Centennial of the University of Southern California." *Overland Monthly* 88 (April 1930): 103-4+.

3696. Hunter, Paul R. "Occidental College a Well Planned Institution." *The Architect and Engineer* 139 (October 1939): 17-25.

3697. Ifeagwu, Chukuemeka O. "The University and the Community; A Case Study in Responsibility." Doctoral dissertation, University of Southern California, 1956. 235 pp.

USC.

3698. *An Illustrated History of Saint Vincent's College.* Los Angeles, 1908. 96 pp.

3699. "Imposing New School of Law Building U.S.C." *Saturday Night* 6 (February 20, 1926): 9.

3700. Jervey, Edward D. "The Methodist Church and the University of Southern California." *Historical Society of Southern California Quarterly* 40 (1958): 58-69.

3701. Jessup, Roger W. "Los Angeles County Medical Education Center." *California Magazine of the Pacific* 46 (June 1956): 20+.

3702. Johnson, Clyde S. "Student Self-Government: A Preliminary Survey of the Background and Development of Extra-Class Activities at the University of California at Los Angeles." Doctoral dissertation, University of California, Los Angeles, 1948. 411 pp.

3703. Joy, Alfred H. "Astronomy on Mount Wilson." *Trails Magazine* 4 (Summer 1937): 11-3.

3704. "Jubilee at Occidental College." *Los Angeles Saturday Night* 44 (November 7, 1936): 8.

Golden Jubilee accompanied by pledge to donate a new auditorium by Charles H. Thorne.

3705. "Junior College: Los Angeles Two-Year School Is Biggest in the U.S." *Life* 20 (May 13, 1946): 99-103.

Los Angeles City College.

3706. Keithley, Erwin M. "A Study of Business Education Graduates of the University of California, Los Angeles, with Implications for Modifying Curricula in Business Teacher Education." Doctoral dissertation, University of California, Los Angeles, 1952. 412 pp.

3707. Kibbe, Helen. "Factors Involved in the Elimination of Undergraduate Students from the University of California at Los Angeles." Master's thesis, University of California, Los Angeles, 1937. 72 pp.

3708. Kiele, William C. "A Survey of the Industry-Wide Training Program of the Northrop Aeronautical Institute." Master's thesis, University of Southern California, 1949. 139 pp.

Located in Hawthorne.

3709. King, Kermit C. "The Historical Development of University Extension at the University of California, with Particular Reference to Its Organization in the Southern Area." Doctoral dissertation, University of California, Los Angeles, 1947. 308 pp.

3710. Knott, James P. *History of Pasadena College.* Pasadena, 1960. 124 pp.

3711. Lalane, Melba de la Motte Brown. [*sic*] "Conditions Associated with Women Student Withdrawals at the University of Southern California." Doctoral dissertation, University of Southern California, 1953. 408 pp.

3712. Lang, Bernie. "Pilots Go to College for Safety: USAF Sponsors Six-Week Course for Flying Officers at USC as Part of Accident Prevention Program." *Aviation Week* 60 (March 29, 1954): 50+.

3713. Lauria, Joseph L. "A Study of the Male Elementary Teachers in Training at the University of California, Los Angeles, During the Post-War Period 1945-1950." Master's thesis, University of California, Los Angeles, 1955. 62 pp.

3714. "Law Schools of Los Angeles County." *The Los Angeles Bar Bulletin* 39 (October 1964): 486-7.

3715. Lay, Clemewell. "Placing College Men and Women: 6. Claremont, Pomona and Scripps Colleges, Claremont, California." *Southern California Business* 17 (September 1938): 18.

3716. Layne, J[oseph] Gregg. "A Quarter Century at the University of California at Los Angeles." *Historical Society of Southern California Quarterly* 26 (1944): 123-7.

3717. LeBoutillier, Cornelia. "Placing College Men and Women: 7. Occidental College." *Southern California Business* 17 (October 1938): 18.

3718. Lemmon, Lucille. "Continuing Education for Social Workers: A University of Southern California Questionnaire." Master's thesis, University of Southern California, 1950. 89 pp.

3719. Levitt, Leon. "A History to 1953 of the School of Education of the University of Southern California." Doctoral dissertation, University of Southern California, 1970. 514 pp.

3720. Lewis, Margaret H. "Counseling Service a New Aid for Women: Modern Methods Employed by Dr. Bessie A. McClenahan of U.S.C. Prove Practical." *Los Angeles Saturday Night* 43 (March 28, 1936): 7.

3721. Lindsay, Jeffrey. "Space Frames and Structural Physics." *Arts & Architecture* 74 (July 1957): 17-9.
Report of a seminar given to a group of UCLA industrial design students, the purpose of which was to acquaint them with the nature of structural physics as applied to space frame construction.

3722. "Lipid Research Lab to Be Set Up at UCLA." *Science News Letter* 75 (March 7, 1959): 153.

3723. "Long Beach Acquires and Gives to State 330-Acre Site for College." *Western City* 27 (February 1951): 41.

3724. Los Angeles City College. *Twenty-Five Years of Community Service; A History of Los Angeles City College.* Los Angeles, 1954. 26 pp.

3725. "Los Angeles Library School." *Library Journal* 62 (January 15, 1937): 82.
Transferal from Public Library to USC.

3726. "Los Angeles Plans for an Agricultural College." *Western Construction News* 19 (June 1944): 76.

3727. "Los Angeles Premiere." *Time* 54 (October 3, 1949): 36.
Opening of UCLA Law School.

3728. Macgowan, Kenneth. "Film in the University." *Saturday Review of Literature* 32 (May 14, 1949): 61-2.
UCLA.

3729. "New Arts Go to College." *Theatre Arts* 31 (July 1947): 51-5.
New Department of Theatre Arts at UCLA.

3730. Malcolm, Richard W. "An Analysis of Selected Conditional Admissions at the University of Southern California." Doctoral dissertation, University of Southern California, 1966. 203 pp.

3731. Malnekoff, Jon L. "The First Fifty Years;

A History of the Department of Physical Education of the University of California, Los Angeles, 1915-1965." Master's thesis, University of California, Los Angeles, 1970. 144 pp.

3732. "The Man from U.C.L.A." *Time* 88 (October 21, 1966): 98.

Franklin D. Murphy and the upgrading of UCLA to the status of a top-rank university.

3733. Marsh, W. C. "Make U.C.L.A. Campus Public Cultural Center." *Los Angeles Saturday Night* 44 (January 23, 1937): 15.

Describes efforts "to bring to the attention of every resident the existing Cultural Center at the university."

3734. Martin, James R. *The University of California (in Los Angeles); A Resume of the Selection and Acquisition of the Westwood Site.* Los Angeles, 1925. 317 pp.

3735. "Master Plan for Long Beach State College." *Arts & Architecture* 80 (April 1963): 14-5.

3736. Maxwell, Richard C. "The School of Law." *University of California Los Angeles Law Review* 10 (1962): 11-4.

Reviews accomplishments of UCLA Law School.

3737. Mayer, Martin. "University in the Sun." *Esquire* 56 (November 1961): 112-7.

UCLA.

3738. McAdie, Alexander; Hale, George E. and Du Bois, Stanley. "In Galileo's Footsteps: On This Summit of California's Sierra Madre Today Is Being Solved the Ultimate Problem of the Evolution of the Universe—The World of Science Watching Results." *Sunset* 22 (February 1909): [133-43].

Mt. Wilson Observatory.

3739. McAlmon, Victoria M. "The Development of Occupational Courses in the Los Angeles Junior College." Master's thesis, University of Southern California, 1931. 88 pp.

3740. McFadden, Jean K. "Survey of Medical Secretarial and Medical Office-Assistant Majors at Los Angeles City College with Implications for Changes in Curriculum." Doctoral dissertation, University of California, Los Angeles, 1969. 81 pp.

3741. McGraw, Edward J. "A Study of the Compulsory and Voluntary Training of Reserve Officers for the Army at University of California, Los Angeles, from 1955-1965." Master's thesis, University of California, Los Angeles, 1966. 141 pp.

3742. McGinnis, John F. "A Forecast of Junior College Needs to 1975 in Los Angeles County and City." Doctoral dissertation, University of Southern California, 1958. 409 pp.

3743. McGinnis, Lowell M. "An Appraisal of Former Student Teachers' Reactions to Their Student Teaching Experiences in Social Studies at the University of California, Los Angeles." Doctoral dissertation, University of California, Los Angeles, 1954. 293 pp.

3744. McHargue, Robert M. "The Early History of Los Angeles Pierce College: Its Genesis, Foundation, and Transition, 1943-1956." Doctoral dissertation, University of California, Los Angeles, 1965. 303 pp.

3745. McLaughlin, Laurence K. "Student Population in University of California Extension Classes." Doctoral dissertation, University of California, Los Angeles, 1951. 227 pp.

3746. Merlino, Maxine O. "A History of the California State Normal Schools; Their Origin, Growth, and Transformation into Teachers Colleges." Doctoral dissertation, University of Southern California, 1962. 374 pp.

3747. Meyer, Larry L. "D.C.I. and the Problem of Juvenile Crime." *Westways* 56 (July 1964): 12-5; (August 1964): 12-4.

Delinquency Control Institute at USC.

3748. "Microradiographic Lab Established at UCLA." *Science News Letter* 74 (July 19, 1958): 40.

3749. Mink, James V. "The UCLA Story." *UCLA Alumni Magazine* 36-37 (September 1961 to May-June 1962): published in 8 parts.

3750. Molony, William R. "History of the Medical School [Part II]." *Southern California Alumni Review* 16 (January 1935): 6-7+.

(First installment dealing with the pre-twentieth century history of the USC Medical School appeared in the December 1934 issue.)

3751. Moore, Ernest Carroll. *I Helped Make a University*. Los Angeles, 1952. 175 pp.

The story of UCLA by its first provost.

3752. ——— "The Purpose of a University: It Is a Laboratory for Truth-Seeking, Not a Public Market for the Propagandist." *Southern California Business* 14 (September 1935): 20.

3753. Mount Saint Mary's College. *The New Mount Saint Mary's College Now Being Erected on Mount Saint Mary in the Santa Monica Hills in Los Angeles, with a Foreword by the Right Reverend J. J. Cantwell* . . . [Los Angeles, 1930]. [6] pp.

3754. Moyse, George U. "A Study of Basic Elements in a Program of Vocational Guidance for the Glendale Junior College." Master's thesis, University of Southern California, 1932. 126 pp.

3755. Muelder, Wallace R. "Factors Involved in the Elimination of Veteran and Non-Veteran Undergraduate Students from the University of Southern California." Master's thesis, University of Southern California, 1947. 63 pp.

3756. Muir, Gladys E. "The Founding of La Verne College." *Pomona Valley Historian* 6 (1970): 93-109.

3757. ——— *La Verne College, Seventy-Five Years of Service.* [La Verne, 1967]. 115 pp.

3758. Neches, Vivian F. "A Follow-Up Study of Legal Secretarial Majors at Los Angeles City College with Implications for Changes in Curriculum." Master's thesis, University of California, Los Angeles, 1964. 199 pp.

3759. "New College of Architecture and Fine Arts Combined with a New Art Gallery in Los Angeles." *Architectural Record* 87 (April 1940): 39-43.

USC.

3760. "New Colleges." *Time* 29 (June 14, 1937): 48+.

George Pepperdine College.

3761. Nicklin, John R. "Characteristics of Students in a Credit Course by Television Offered by the University of California Extension, Southern Area." Doctoral dissertation, University of California, Los Angeles, 1955. 186 pp.

3762. Norton, Edwin C. *The Dean Speaks Again; Giving Hitherto Unpublished Excerpts from Personal Papers, Diaries, and Letters.* Claremont, 1955. 125 pp.

Pomona College, Claremont.

3763. Nystrom, Richard K. "UCLA, An Interpretation Considering Architecture and Site." Doctoral dissertation, University of California, 1968. 294 pp.

3764. Obst, Frances M. "A Study of Selected Psychometric Charcteristics of Home Economics and Non-Home Economics Women at the University of California, Los Angeles." Doctoral dissertation, University of California, Los Angeles, 1955. 70 pp.

3765. ——— "UCLA's New Home Management House." *Practical Home Economics* 31 (October 1952): 28-30+.

3766. Patrick, James G. "The Role of Intimate Groups in the Personality Development of Selected College Men." Doctoral dissertation, University of Southern California, 1933. 219 pp.

3767. Paxman, Marlys E. "The Development of Medical Education at the University of Southern California." Master's thesis, University of Southern California, 1966. 127 pp.

3768. Pendray, G. Edward. *Men, Mirrors, and Stars.* New York, 1935. 339 pp. Rev. ed., 1969. 341 pp.

Mount Wilson Observatory.

3769. Peterson, Dorothy O. "A Survey of Graduates with a Bachelor of Science Degree in Home Economics from the University of California, Los Angeles, from 1939 to 1949." Master's thesis, University of California, Los Angeles, 1951. 85 pp.

3770. Peterson, John R. "Guidance, Counciling, Attitude and Aptitude Testing in the Department of Theater Arts at the University of California at Los Angeles from March, 1948 to June, 1949." Master's thesis, University of California, Los Angeles, 1949. 111 pp.

3771. Pettit, Clare. "The Effect of the Public Junior College on the Small Senior Colleges in

Southern California." Master's thesis, Occidental College, 1929. 135 pp.

3772. Pfeiffer, Clyde E. "An Attitudinal Study of the Educational Program at John Muir College, Pasadena, Calif." Doctoral dissertation, University of California, Los Angeles, 1951. 529 pp.

3773. —— "A History of Pasadena Junior College." Master's thesis, Occidental College, 1941. 218 pp.

3774. Powell, Carolyn D. "The Perceptions and Opinions of a Selected Group of University of Southern California Students with Regard to Their Experiences as Volunteer Tutors." Master's thesis, University of Southern California, 1965. 74 pp.

3775. Powell, Lawrence Clark. "Beanfields, Builders, and Books: The First Quarter Century of the Los Angeles Campus of the University of California." *Historical Society of Southern California Quarterly* 36 (1954): 312-21.

3776. —— "The Library School at U.C.L.A." *California Librarian* 21 (October 1960): 251-2.

3777. —— "A University Librarian Takes Pen in Hand." *Library Journal* 71 (April 1, 1946): 461-3.

Consists mainly of excerpts from Powell's second "Occasional Letter to the Faculty" (December 1945).

3778. —— "U.C.L.A. Arranges Preprofessional Program for Library Students." *Library Journal* 73 (November 1948): 1655.

3779. Priddy, Earl. "A Historical Study of Speech Education at the University of Southern California [1880-1950]." Doctoral dissertation, University of Southern California, 1961. 513 pp.

3780. Reichert, Stephen B., Jr. "The Four-Year Junior College Movement in California." Doctoral dissertation, University of California, Los Angeles, 1957. 306 pp.

Deals largely with Pasadena, Compton and Pomona.

3781. —— "Some Aspects of the Student Activities Program at John Muir College." Master thesis, University of California, Los Angeles, 1951. 99 pp.

Pasadena.

3782. Reid, Howard T. "Types, Frequencies, and Urgency of Problems Encountered Among Students in Public Junior Colleges of Los Angeles County." Master's thesis, University of Southern California, 1949. 260 pp.

3783. Reid, Maryanne. "The Role of the Dormitory Social Program in Teaching Social Competence to Undergraduate Women with a Description of the UCLA Women's Dormitory Social Program." Master's thesis, University of California, Los Angeles, 1955. 68 pp.

3784. Reinhard, Robert H. "A Survey Study of a Proposed Junior College District to Include the El Segundo, Inglewood and Redondo High School Districts." Master's thesis, University of California, Los Angeles, 1936. 123 pp.

3785. Richards, John A. "Utilization of Engineers Graduated from the University of Southern California." Master's thesis, University of Southern California, 1961. 96 pp.

Higher Ed.

3786. Roaney, John. "The Caltech Man." *Los Angeles* 3 (January 1962): 21-3.

3787. Roberts, Eugene L. "An Investigation of the Leisure Time Activities of Faculty Members of the University of Southern California." Master's thesis, University of Southern California, 1935. 171 pp.

3788. Roberts, Myron. "The Brain Gain." *Los Angeles* 15 (September 1970): 34-7.

New Cal Arts campus.

3789. —— "A Brief Survey of Small Private Colleges." *Los Angeles* 11 (September 1966): 48-9.

Los Angeles area.

3790. —— "Life at an Off-Ramp U: Or, God and Man at Cal State L.A." *Los Angeles* 13 (September 1968): 29.

3791. —— "Who's Really Teaching at UCLA?" *Los Angeles* 14 (March 1969): 20-2+.

The teaching assistant system.

3792. Robinson, Giles. "An Historical Study of Dramatic Activities at the University of Southern California [1880 to 1957]." Master's thesis, University of Southern California, 1957. 135 pp.

3793. Rodda, George H., Jr. "A Three-Year Follow-Up Study of the Pasadena City College Fourteenth Year Graduates." Master's thesis, University of Southern California, 1956. 52 pp.

3794. Rogers, Florence. "Triumvirate Celebration at Pomona." *California Graphic* 5 (October 1, 1927): 19+.

Beginnings of Claremont Colleges.

3795. Rogers, Nola S. "A Study of Certain Personality Characteristics of Sorority and Non-Sorority Women at the University of California, Los Angeles." Doctoral dissertation, University of California, Los Angeles, 1952. 118 pp.

3796. Rolle, Andrew F. *Occidental College: The First Seventy-Five Years, 1887-1962.* Los Angeles, 1962. 191 pp.

3797. Rosenoff, Wayne E. "The Evaluation of Participation in the Intramural Program at the University of California, Los Angeles." Master's thesis, University of California, Los Angeles, 1950. 128 pp.

3798. Ross, Penelope. "Pasadena Community Playhouse Objectives." *Los Angeles Saturday Night* 9 (January 5, 1929): 15.

3799. "Rufus Rex, Ex." *Time* 47 (April 29, 1946): 75.

Retirement of Rufus Bernhard von KleinSmid after twenty-four years as president of USC.

3800. Rulison, Kathleen D. "The Analysis and Appraisal of the Listening Course at Los Angeles City College." Master's thesis, University of California, Los Angeles, 1952. 112 pp.

3801. Ryan, James E. "The History of Manual Training Teacher Education in the California State Normal Schools." Doctoral dissertation, University of California, Los Angeles, 1964. 481 pp.

3802. Salisbury, William. "Los Angeles' New Art Institute." *Magazine of Art* 30 (November 1937): 660-3.

3803. "School of Library Service at U.S.C." *Pacific Bindery Talk* 9 (October 1936): 26-7.

3804. "School with a Style." *Arts & Architecture* 70 (December 1953): 12-7.

Immaculate Heart College.

3805. Scothorn, Carol. "UCLA Project: Modern Dance Classics Become Part of the Repertory at a Leading University." *Dance Magazine* 35 (November 1961): 54-5.

3806. Servín, Manuel P., and Wilson, Iris H. *Southern California and Its University: A History of USC, 1880-1964.* Los Angeles, 1969. 319 pp.

3807. "Short Course for Public Officials Enrolled 717 Last Year: University of Southern California Prepares for Fifth Annual School." *Western City* 8 (March 1932): 24+.

3808. Shoup, Gail L. "The Pasadena Community Playhouse: Its Origins and History from 1917 to 1942." Doctoral dissertation, University of California, Los Angeles, 1968. 390 pp.

3809. Showman, Frank, Jr. "A Comparative Study of the Academic Records of a Group of Los Angeles City College Transfers Before and After Transfer to the University of California at Los Angeles." Master's thesis, University of Southern California, 1958. 184 pp.

3810. Smith, Jack. "A Day in the City: Open Home in Westwood." *Westways* 60 (October 1968): 19-21+.

Open House at UCLA.

3811. Smith, Timothy L. *Called Unto Holiness; The Story of the Nazarenes: The Formative Years.* Kansas City, Mo., 1962. 413 pp.

The launching of Pasadena College discussed on pp. 137-40.

3812. Snyder, William H. "Curriculum Development." *Journal of National Education Association* 22 (March 1933): 87-8.

Los Angeles Junior College.

3813. Sorensen, Royal W. "California Institute of Technology's Million-Volt Laboratory." *Journal of Electricity* 53 (October 1, 1924): 242-4.

3814. Stadtman, Verne A. *The University of California, 1868-1968.* New York, [1970]. 594 pp.

3815. Stewart, Cecil C. "A Follow-Up Study of Pasadena Junior College Graduates." Doctoral dissertation, Stanford University, 1942. Unp.

3816. "Student Project at the University of Southern California." *Arts & Architecture* 64 (June 1947): 34-5.

Project devised by Gregory Ain for students of School of Architecture.

3817. "The Study of Chinese at the University of Southern California." *School and Society* 60 (November 1944): 311.

As an aid to study of Chinese language, students in Department of Asiatic Studies put on series of plays entirely in Chinese.

3818. Sumner, Charles B. *The Story of Pomona College.* Boston and New York, c1914. 417 pp.

3819. Thompson, Joseph V. "The Social Work Generalist; A Study of Recent Graduates of the University of Southern California School of Social Work." Doctoral dissertation, University of Southern California, 1969. 256 pp.

3820. Thrall, Will H. "Mount Wilson—the Observatory and the Toll Road Company." *Trail Magazine* 4 (1937): 6-10.

3821. Topping, Norman H. *The University of Southern California: An Institution and a Community.* New York, 1966. 28 pp.

3822. "The Ultimate University?" *Los Angeles* 14 (March 1969): 22-3.

"Experimental College" at UCLA, in which courses are supervised largely by the students themselves.

3823. "A University Is Born." *Radio & Television* 42 (November 1949): 52-3.

"University of Hollywood," which offers an eighteen-month course leading to a B. S. in audio engineering.

3824. University of California, Los Angeles. *The University: An Introduction to the Los Angeles Campus.* Berkeley, 1936. 52 pp.

3825. ———. Alumni Association. *California of the Southland, a History of the University of California at Los Angeles.* Los Angeles, 1937. 95 pp.

3826. "U.C.L.A.'s 20-Year Plan for Health Sciences." *Architectural Record* 142 (September 1967): 198-201.

Description and plans of the Center for the Health Sciences.

3827. "University of California Plans $27,000,000 Post-War Building Program." *The Architect and Engineer* 158 (August 1944): 8+.

Includes UCLA.

3828. University of Southern California. *Now They Belong to the Ages.* Los Angeles, 1927. 23 pp.

3829. ——— *The Second Fifty Years.* Los Angeles, 1927. 28 pp.

3930. ——— *The Semicentennial Celebration of the Founding of the University of Southern California . . . 1880-1930.* Ed. by Herbert W. Hill. Los Angeles, 1930. 211 pp.

3831. ——— *Twenty-Five Years of Building Better Government.* Los Angeles, 1955. 72 pp.
USC School of Public Administration.

3832. ———. General Alumni Association. *Cardinal and Gold; A Pictorial and Factual Record of the Highlights of Sixty Years of Progress on the Southern California Campus with Views and News of Some of the 17,000 Students Who Played Their Part in the Growth of a Great University, 1880-1940.* W. Ballentine Henley and Arthur E. Neelley, eds. Los Angeles, 1939. 151 pp.

3833. ———. School of Library Science. Alumni Association. *Directory of Graduates, 1892-1950* [of the] *Library School, Los Angeles Public Library, and School of Library Science, University of Southern California.* Los Angeles, 1951. 39 pp.

3834. "University's Fiftieth Anniversary." *Los Angeles Saturday Night* 10 (November 2, 1929): 3.
USC.

3835. Van Note, Samuel E. "A Follow-Up Study of the Former Students of Los Angeles Pacific College." Master's thesis, University of Southern California, 1941. 157 pp.

3836. Vickers, Samuel E. "Long Beach Gets New State College Through Community Action." *American City* 66 (April 1951): 111.

3837. VonBoenigk, Winifred P. "An Analysis of the Activities of the Elementary Student Teaching Coordinator Associated with the University of California at Los Angeles and the Public Elementary School." Master's thesis, University of California, Los Angeles, 1958. 98 pp.

3838. Von Hofe, Harold. "Intensive Language Study at the University of Southern California." *School and Society* 58 (November 1943): 430-1.

3839. Walker, Margarette W. "An Analysis of the Doctoral Program in Education at the University of Southern California." Doctoral dissertation, University of Southern California, 1953. 330 pp.

3840. Ware, Louise. "Placing College Men and Women: 5. Woodbury College." *Southern California Business* 17 (August 1938): 18.

3841. Warren, Viola Lockhart. "The Old College of Medicine." *Historical Society of Southern California Quarterly* 41 (1959): 299-317; 42 (1960): 41-56.

3842. Webber, Vivienne L. "The Performance of Home Economics and Non-Home Economics Teacher Education Majors at the University of California, Los Angeles on the American Council on Education Psychological Examination for College Freshmen." Master's thesis, University of California, Los Angeles, 1957. 93 pp.

3843. Weber, Francis J. "What Ever Happened to Saint Vincent's College?" *The Pacific Historian* 14 (1970): 76-90.

3844. Wells, John K. "A Study of the Net Expense of Selected Curricular Programs at East Los Angeles College." Doctoral dissertation, University of California, Los Angeles, 1966. 120 pp.

3845. Wharton, Mel. "Pasadena — Campus of Universe Makers." *Southern California Business* 10 (January 1931): 12-3.
   Cal Tech.

3846. "What Loyola Means to Los Angeles." *Los Angeles Saturday Night* 9 (October 6, 1928): 4.
   Proposed new site for Loyola University in Del Rey Hills.

3847. White, Alson P. "Special Problems in Management of Facilities at a Government-Owned University-Operated Laboratory." Master's thesis, University of Southern California, 1968. 172 pp.
   Caltech.

3848. White, Mulvey. "Placing College Men and Women: 2. University of Southern California." *Southern California Business* 17 (May 1938): 18.

3849. "Why the Chouinard School of Art Has Succeeded." *Los Angeles Saturday Night* 10 (March 15, 1930): 7.

3850. Williams, James A. "Collegiate In-Service Training Policies of the Public Jurisdictions Located within the Los Angeles Metropolitan Area." Master's thesis, University of Southern California, 1940. 80 pp.

3851. Woellner, Frederic P. "A Stubborn Professor's Idea: The Idea Has Now Become U.C.L.A.— Let Us Pay Tribute to Dr. Ernest Carroll Moore." *Southern California Business* 15 (September 1936): 8-9.

3852. Worden, William L. "U.C.L.A.'s Red Cell: Case History of College Communism." *Saturday Evening Post* 223 (October 21, 1950): 42-3+.

3853. "World's Largest Telescope on Mt. Wilson." *Touring Topics* 10 (February 1918): 7-10.

3854. Wulk, Jerry E. "A Comparative Follow-Up Study of Academic Scholarship Freshman and Regular Status Freshman Students at the University of Southern California." Doctoral dissertation, University of Southern California, 1956. 133 pp.

3855. Yates, Peter. "Musical Leadership at Two Southern California Universities." *Arts & Architecture* 70 (September 1953): 9-10+.
   USC and UCLA.

3856. Yeremian, Thais S. "A Comparative Study of Divergent Thinking Ability and Academic Achievement of Students in the Honors Program at the University of Southern California." Doctoral dissertation, University of Southern California, 1967. 160 pp.

3857. Zucker, Alfred. "An Investigation of Factors Contributing to and Interfering with the Successful Achievement of Remedial English

Course Objectives in Los Angeles City Junior Colleges." Doctoral dissertation, University of California, Los Angeles, 1966. 208 pp.

FIRE PROTECTION

3858. Aiassa, George, and Weatherbee, Calvin. "West Covina's Fire Apparatus Is Designed for Efficiency and Safety." *Western City* 42 (February 1966) : 27.

3859. Alford, A. B. "New Telephone Fire Alarm System Installed at Whittier." *Western City* 32 (August 1956) : 32-3.

3860. Benner, J. J. "Fire Department 'Stars' in Movie Planned for School Use." *Western City* 29 (September 1953) : 37.

Torrance.

3861. Brunstrom, Raymond E., Jr. "An Analysis of the Utilization of Local Fire Companies for Fire Prevention Activity in Twelve Selected Southern California Cities." Master's thesis, University of Southern California, 1969. 149 pp.

3862. Byers, Charles Alma. "A New Type of Fire Boat for Los Angeles: Motorizing the Floating Fire Department Proves Highly Successful." *American City* 21 (November 1919) : 413-4.

3863. Canfield, Lloyd B. "Beverly Hills Cuts Insurance Rates with New Fire Alarm System." *Western City* 15 (July 1939) : 19-21.

3864. Clark, Paul R. "The History and Development of the Department of Fire of the City of Los Angeles [1870 to 1934]." Master's thesis, University of Southern California, 1934. 223 pp.

3865. Crockett and Conklin. *Souvenir [of the] Los Angeles Fire Department.* [Los Angeles], 1900. 116 pp.

3866. "Culver City Finances Fire Station Under Lease-Purchase Plan." *Western City* 26 (August 1950) : 26.

3867. Davis, Joseph J. "Tank Trucks for Sure-Fire Water." *American City* 54 (June 1939) : 87-8.

Trucks used by County Fire Department.

3868. Dektar, Cliff. "Whirlybirds Are Watching Over Us." *Westways* 49 (July 1957) : 12-3.

Helicopters in Los Angeles County, particularly as used in fire-fighting and rescue work.

3869. Ditzel, Paul. "Dial 'O' for Rescue." *Westways* 56 (November 1964) : 29.

Fire rescue service in San Fernando Valley.

3870. Donoghue, James R. *Intergovernmental Cooperation in Fire Protection in the Los Angeles Area.* Bureau of Governmental Research, University of California, Los Angeles, *Studies in Local Government No. 7.* Los Angeles, 1943. 126 pp.

3871. Ernest, Richard E. "Candidate Dysfunction from Oral Interview Portions of Civil Service Examinations for Promotion in the Los Angeles Fire Department." Master's thesis, University of Southern California, 1965. 153 pp.

3872. Farrell, Milton R. "An Analysis of the Feasibility of Consolidating the Forty-Six Fire Departments in Los Angeles County." Master's thesis, University of Southern California, 1956. 148 pp.

3873. "The Fire Department and Its Relations with Local Public." *Western City* 11 (April 1935) : 11-5.

Includes views of: R. J. Scott, Chief, Los Angeles Fire Department; L. B. Canfield, Chief, Beverly Hills Fire Department; A. H. Lankford, Chief, Glendale Fire Department.

3874. "Fire Headquarters at Torrance Result of State-Wide Survey Ideas." *Western City* 33 (December 1957) : 44.

3875. "Fortifying Against Ravages of Fire." *Southern California Business* 4 (October 1925) : 26+.

Egyptian Ballroom at Ocean Park.

3876. "Glendale Fire Department Possesses Modern Equipment." *Pacific Municipalities* 45 (May 1931) : 232-3.

3877. Goedhard, Neil. "Covina Puts Fire Prevention Visits Program to Many Uses." *Western City* 34 (March 1958) : 32-4.

3878. Grady, Anthony J. "A Study of the Mutual Aid Problems in the Fire Service in Los Angeles County." Master's thesis, University of Southern California, 1959. 97 pp.

3879. Griswold, S. Smith. "A Survey of the Los Angeles County Fire Protection Districts and Proposed Plan of Reorganization." Master's thesis, Stanford University, 1934. 231 pp.

3880. "Helicopters Fight Glendale Fires." *American City* 72 (October 1957): 185.

3881. Homrighausen, George A. "Police, Fire and Health Departments of Los Angeles [1850-1939]." Master's thesis, University of Southern California, 1939. 290 pp.

3882. Johnson, Virgina. "Boys Who Play with Fire—For Keeps." *Westways* 37 (June 1945): 8-9.
"Problem boys" fight fires instead of going to reform school.

3883. "Los Angeles Fire Automobile." *Journal of Electricity, Power and Gas* 20 (June 27, 1908): 403.
Emergency fire vehicle operated by Los Angeles Gas & Electric Co.

3884. Mathison, Richard R. "Have Fire—Can't Handle!" *Westways* 51 (September 1959): 26-7.
City of Los Angeles Mountain Patrol.

3885. Mendenhall, W[illia]m V. "Fire Lookouts of the Angeles." *Trails Magazine* 1 (Autumn 1934): 10.
Angeles National Forest.

3886. ———— "Fire Protection of the Angeles Forest." *Trails Magazine* 1 (Summer 1934): 9.

3887. Miller, William L. "Los Angeles Fire Department Races with City Growth." *American City* 73 (September 1958): 112-4.

3888. Moniot, A.M., and Wasmansdorff, C.W. "How Glendale's 'All Out' Fire and Police System Functions." *Western City* 17 (June 1941): 30-1.

3889. Mount, William J. "The Effects of the Provisions for Police, Fire, Health, and Special District Services by Los Angeles County in the Unincorporated Fringe Areas." Master's thesis, University of Southern California, 1951. 110 pp.

3890. O'Donovan, Patrick J. "Pasadena City Council Considers Retroactive Fire Control Legislation." *Western Housing* 31 (April 1948): 10+.

3891. "Old Pasadena Reservoir a Fire-Truck Repair Shop." *American City* 54 (August 1939): 60.

3892. Pemberton, J. E. "Early Fire Control in Los Angeles County." *Trails Magazine* 3 (Spring 1936): 15.

3893. "Pomona's Fire Alarm System." *Pacific Municipalities* 12 (May 1905): 113.

3894. Scott, R. J. "Real Estate and the Fire Department." *Los Angeles Realtor* 5 (January 1926): 19+.
Los Angeles.

3895. Sherwood, Frank P., and Markey, Beatrice. *The Mayor and the Fire Chief: The Fight Over Integrating the Los Angeles Fire Department.* The Inter-University Case Program, *Case Series No. 43.* University, Ala., 1959. 24 pp.

3896. Smith, J. A. "Palos Verdes Fire Department Builds Its Own Equipment." *Western City* 34 (March 1958): 39.

3897. "South Pasadena Takes Step Toward Fire and Police Integration." *Western City* 28 (February 1952): 56.

3898. Stanbro, Russ. "New Long Beach Squad Wagon Wins Praise from Its Crew." *Western City* 26 (June 1950): 51.
New fire truck said to be "a complete Fire Department in itself by the crews assigned to it."

3899. Sullivan, H. W. "L.A.'s Police Helicopter Detects Fires and Traffic Jams." *American City* 75 (August 1960): 169.

3900. Taylor, W. J. "Five Year Fire Improvement Program Succeeds in Obtaining Class 3 Rating for Burbank." *Western City* 36 (May 1960): 24+.

3901. Trump, James K. *The Administration of Fire Districts in the Los Angeles Metropolitan Area.* Los Angeles, 1950. 176 pp.
Based on the author's master's thesis, University of Southern California, 1950. 176 pp.

3902. ————; Donoghue, James R., and Kroll, Morton. *Fire Protection.* Los Angeles, 1952. *Metropolitan Los Angeles. A Study in Integration,* Vol. VI, The Haynes Foundation, *Monograph Series No. 23.* 173 pp.

3903. ——, and Kroll, Morton. *County Administered Fire Protection: A Case Study in a Metropolitan Area.* Los Angeles, 1951. 86 pp.

Los Angeles.

3904. Wetherbee, Calvin, and Cowen, Paul. "West Covina's 'Topsy' Fire Department Just Grew Up with City Development." *Western City* 36 (May 1960): 22.

3905. "Why and How of Fire Losses in 38 Western Cities." *Western City* 6 (March 1930): 9-12.

Includes Los Angeles County cities.

3906. Will, Arthur J. "The Strong Fire Forces in Los Angeles County." *American City* 74 (August 1959): 100.

GOVERNMENT

GOVERNMENT—GENERAL

3907. Baerncopf, David A. "Regional Interest Rates: Municipal Bonds in California, 1900-1957." Doctoral dissertation, Stanford University, 1961. 273 pp.

3908. Baker, Benjamin. "Municipal Autonomy: Its Relationship to Metropolitan Government." *Western Political Quarterly* 13 (1960): 83-98.

3909. Bollens, John C. *Appointed Executive Local Government: The California Experience.* Los Angeles, 1952. 233 pp.

3910. Crouch, Winston W. "American State and Local Government: Extraterritoral Powers of Cities as Factors in California Metropolitan Government." *American Political Science Review* 31 (1937): 286-91.

3911. ——, and Bollens, John C. *Your California Governments in Action.* 2nd ed. Berkeley, 1960. 296 pp.

3912. ——, and Dinerman, Beatrice. *Southern California Metropolis, A Study in Development of Government for a Metropolitan Area.* Berkeley, 1964. 443 pp.

Advocates centralization of municipal functions, metropolitan government.

3913. ——, and Maccoby, Wendell. *Sanitation Administration in the Los Angeles Metropolitan Area: A Study in Development of Public Policy and Administrative Organization.* Los Angeles, 1952. 100 pp.

3914. ——; McHenry, Dean E.; Bollens, John C., and Scott, Stanley. *California Government and Politics.* Englewood Cliffs, N. J., 1956. 292 pp.

3915. ——; ——; ——, and ——. *State and Local Government in California.* Berkeley and Los Angeles, 1955. 232 pp.

3916. Gladfelder, Jane. "Our Emergent Counties: A Study of County Government in California." Master's thesis, California State College at Los Angeles, 1967. 251 pp.

3017. Hatfield, D. D., and Jones, Linnea, comps. *Los Angeles Public Service Guide to the City, County, State, and Federal Offices and Departments.* Los Angeles, 1946. 235 pp.

3918. Jones, Harold T. "Administration of Election Laws in Los Angeles City and County and the State of California." Master's thesis, University of Southern California, 1954. 346 pp.

3919. —— *Administration of Elections in Los Angeles City, County and State of California.* Los Angeles, 1955. 214 pp.

Based on author's master's thesis.

3920. Markey, Beatrice. "Minority Problems in Public Employment with Special Reference to the Negro." Master's thesis, University of Southern California, 1952. 117 pp.

3921. Scott, Stanley, and Bollens, John C. "Special Districts in California Local Government." *Western Political Quarterly* 3 (1950): 233-43.

3922. Taxpayers' Association of California. *City and County Consolidation for Los Angeles.* Los Angeles, 1917. 194 pp.

GOVERNMENT—COUNTY

3923. Adams, Walter H. "A Study of the Engineering Functions Carried on by the County of Los

Angeles, California." Master's thesis, University of Southern California, 1936. 133 pp.

3924. Allen, Wayne. "Los Angeles County Streamlined." *National Municipal Review* 31 (April 1942): 196-201.

Accomplishments under County Chief Administrative Officer plan.

3925. Barnett, Murray. "The Decentralization of the Los Angeles County Probation Department." Master's thesis, University of Southern California, 1957. 125 pp.

3926. Bemis, George W. *From Rural to Urban, the Municipalized County of Los Angeles.* Los Angeles, 1947. 33 pp.

3927. ———— *Los Angeles County as an Agency of Municipal Government.* The Haynes Foundation, *Monograph Series No. 10.* Los Angeles, 1947. 105 pp.

3928. Benell, Ruth. "Engineer-Planning & Computer Technology Used to Study Incorporation Feasibility by L.A.F.C." *Western City* 45 (July 1969): 17+.

L.A.F.C.—Local Agency Formation Commission of Los Angeles County.

3929. Bigger, Richard; Iverson, Evan A., and Jamison, Judith N. "Escape from the County: Recent Rush of Los Angeles Area Communities to Go It Alone May Weaken Functional Consolidation Trend." *National Municipal Review* 46 (March 1957): 124-30.

3930. Binkley, Robert W., Jr. *County Government Organization in California.* Berkeley, 1945. 69 pp.

3931. Boyd, C. T. "Auto Registration Hits New Mark." *Southern California Business* 3 (April 1924): 17+.

Statistics on motor vehicle registration in the State of California and Los Angeles County.

3932. Browell, R. Kenneth. "Some Social Implications of the National Defense Problem in Los Angeles County, with Special Reference to Three Typical Communities." Master's thesis, Claremont Graduate School, 1941. 227 pp.

3933. "California's 'Contract Cities.'" *American City* 75 (December 1960): 100.

Twenty-two cities that contract with Los Angeles County to provide municipal services.

3934. Campion, Alfred H. "Budget Dates Advanced: Los Angeles County Improves Procedure." *Tax Digest* 18 (January 1940): 9+.

3935. Chadsey, Howard B. "A Study of the Mechanization of the Assessment Roll Procedures for the County of Los Angeles." Master's thesis, University of Southern California, 1942. 211 pp.

3936. "City-County Contracts." *American City* 52 (February 1937): 95+.

Municipal services provided by Los Angeles County on a contract basis.

3937. Cloner, Alexander. "The Joint Salary Survey as a Study in Intergovernmental Cooperation in the Los Angeles Area." Master's thesis, University of Southern California, 1948. 148 pp.

3938. Collins, James H. "Old Man Work Does a Stretch: How Los Angeles County Spreads Work under Hoover—And Its Own Previous Plan." *Southern California Business* 11 (March 1932): 8-9.

"Previous Plan" was Employment Stabilization Bureau, under County Supervisor Frank Shaw.

3939. Conliffe, Archie J. "Community Organization Process in the Relationship Between the Council of Social Agencies and the Coordinating Council in Los Angeles." Master's thesis, University of Southern California, 1944. 118 pp.

3940. "Consolidation of Local Governments Pay." *American City* 51 (March 1936): 105.

Los Angeles County township consolidation program.

3941. Cottrell, Gary N. "A Study of the Organization and Administration of the County Sanitation Districts of Los Angeles County." Master's thesis, University of Southern California, 1960. 117 pp.

3942. "County Plans Long Range Construction Program to Cost $445,000,000." *Apartment Journal* 28 (July 1945): 14.

3943. "County Sanitation District Management." *Municipal League of Los Angeles Bulletin* 7 (January 1, 1930): [1-2].

3944. Crouch, Winston W. "California—Manager in Los Angeles County Halted." *National Municipal Review* 25 (November 1936): 671.

3945. ——— "The California Way: State, with Eight Metropolitan Areas, Has Approached Problem in Three Different Ways." *National Civic Review* 51 (March 1962): 139-44+.

3946. ——— "The Relationship Between the City and the County of Los Angeles, California." Master's thesis, Claremont Graduate School, 1930. 166 pp.

3947. Davis, Paul. "Population Pressure and Its Effect on the Land Use Pattern and Land Valuations in Los Angeles County from 1940 to 1953." Master's thesis, University of Southern California, 1954. 169 pp.

3948. Earl, Howard. "Dispersal Is Bridge to Survival in Present Civil Defense Approach." *Western City* 31 (May 1955): 33-4.

Los Angeles basin survey by executive office, Los Angeles County and Cities Civil Defense Planning Board.

3949. Eddy, Don. "A Citizen Army Goes into Action." *American Magazine* 133 (April 1942): 106-10.

Los Angeles County Civilian Defense organization.

3950. Erickson, Eugene R. "An Administrative Study of the Los Angeles County Department of Charities." Master's thesis, University of Southern California, 1950. 122 pp.

3951. F.S.B. "New County Courthouse—'No Progress' Report." *Los Angeles Bar Bulletin* 23 (January 1948): 150-1.

Author contends that "No tangible progress has been made in the past fifteen years to solve permanently the problem of adequate court room space."

3952. Fisher, Robert. "The Work of the Committee on the Revision of the Civil Service Provisions of the Los Angeles County Charter." Master's thesis, Occidental College, 1939. 158 pp.

3953. Frank, Elisabeth R. *Differentiating Communities in Los Angeles County*. Welfare Planning Council, Los Angeles Region, *Special Report Series No. 50.* Los Angeles, 1957. 2 vols.

3954. French, Helene P. "Burden of Growth: A Case Study of the Los Angeles County Commission on Human Relations." Master's thesis, California State College, Fullerton, 1968. 266 pp.

Minorities in Los Angeles.

3955. Genari, Breno. "An Analysis of the Consulting Process in the Reorganization Plan of the Los Angeles County Road Department." Master's thesis, University of Southern California, 1962. 144 pp.

3956. Golden, Morton J. "Dog Control by County Contract." *American City* 81 (September 1966): 197.

Los Angeles County animal shelters.

3957. "Government Functions Expand in Los Angeles County." *American City* 65 (August 1950): 7.

County takeover of various municipal services.

3958. Halferty, Guy. "A Unique Experiment in City-County Relationships: How the 'Lakewood Plan' Operates." *American City* 70 (May 1955): 134-5.

3959. Harris, Robert E.G. "5 Men for Five Million: Handicapped by a Horse-and-Buggy Charter, Los Angeles County Government Is a Confusing Tangle." *Frontier* 7 (March 1956): 13-7.

3960. Hartman, J. W. "Forty-Two Municipalities Served by Los Angeles County Tax Billing." *American City* 67 (June 1952): 83-5.

3961. Holtzman, Abraham. *Los Angeles County Chief Administrative Officer: Ten Years' Experience.* Bureau of Governmental Research, University of California, Los Angeles, *Studies in Local Government No. 10.* Los Angeles, 1948. 77 pp.

3962. ——— "The Office of the Chief Administrative Officer, Los Angeles County." Master's thesis, University of California, Los Angeles, 1947. 170 pp.

3963. "How Los Angeles Does It." *Western Construction* 44 (October 1969): 33-5.

Maintenance of Los Angeles County Road Department vehicles.

3964. Jamison, Judith N. "Neighboring Areas Join Hands: Los Angeles County and Its Communities Seek to Solve Area Problems by Contracts and Agreements for Local Services." *National Municipal Review* 35 (March 1946): 111-4.

3965. Jones, Helen L., and Wilcox, Robert F., under the direction of Edwin A. Cottrell. *Metropolitan Los Angeles: Its Governments.* Los Angeles, 1949. 224 pp.

3966. Kennedy, Harold W. "The Legal Aspects of Air Pollution Control with Particular Reference to the County of Los Angeles." *Southern California Law Review* 27 (1954): 373-414.

3967. Larson, Frances G. "A Study of the Procedure of Taxing Liens on Property by Los Angeles County Department of Charities." Master's thesis, University of Southern California, 1941. 71 pp.

3968. League of Women Voters of Los Angeles County. *Los Angeles County Government.* Los Angeles, 1964. 77 pp. Rev. ed., 1968. 79 pp.

3969. Legg, Herbert C. "Governing Los Angeles County." *California Journal of Development* 26 (July 1936): 15+.

3970. Low, J. C. "Community Association Control in Unincorporated Territory." *The Architect and Engineer* 100 (January 1930): 43-8.

Palos Verdes.

3971. Los Angeles City. Bureau of Budget and Efficiency. *A Study of a Proposed City and County Government of Los Angeles within the Present City Limits.* Los Angeles, 1932. 11 pp.

3972. Los Angeles County. Bureau of Efficiency. *Growth of County Functions, 1852-1934.* Los Angeles, 1936. 136 pp.

3973. ———. Chief Administrative Officer. *Capital Projects Program, 1945-1946 and Future Years.* Los Angeles, 1945. 280 pp.

3974. ———. Regional Planning Commission. *Guide to the Los Angeles County Zoning Ordinance, August, 1929.* [Los Angeles, 1929]. 28 pp.

3975. ———. Superintendent of Schools. *Los Angeles County; A Handbook of Its Government and Services.* Ed. by Harold T. Shafer and Frances Hall Adams. *Social Studies Curriculum Monograph No. 57.* Los Angeles, [1950]. 382 pp.

3976. "Los Angeles Channels Public Support with Fact-Laced Information Program." *American City* 73 (June 1958): 164+.

Public Information Division, Los Angeles Air Pollution Control District.

3977. "Los Angeles County Continues Gas Tax Grants to Cities." *Western City* 24 (March 1948): 33.

3978. "Los Angeles County Standardizes Specs." *Western Construction* 40 (April 1965): 98+.

Agreement reached between all major public works agencies and contractors.

3979. "Los Angeles Gets Ready." *Time* 38 (December 15, 1941): 76+.

Los Angeles County [Civilian] Defense Council.

3980. Marquardt, John F. D. "A Study of the Los Angeles County Coordinating Council's Plan Organization and Procedure." Master's thesis, University of Southern California, 1938. 111 pp.

3981. Martin, Norman R. "Los Angeles County Department of Charities." *Annals of the American Academy of Political and Social Science* 105 (January 1923): 156-9.

3982. McDiarmid, John. "Streamlined County Government—Los Angeles Style." *National Municipal Review* 28 (November 1939): 757-63.

3983. McWilliams, Carey. "The Registration of Heretics." *Nation* 171 (December 9, 1950): 526-8.

Los Angeles County ordinances requiring a loyalty oath from public employees.

3984. Mosk, Stanley. "Pattern for Local Unity." *New Republic* 112 (May 14, 1945): 674-5.

Institute on Community Relations, a program for employees of Los Angeles County.

3985. Mount, William J. "The Effects of the Provisions for Police, Fire, Health, and Special District Services by Los Angeles County in the Unincorporated Fringe Areas." Master's thesis, University of Southern California, 1951. 110 pp.

3986. Nance, Frank A. "The County Coroner's

Job." *Municipal League of Los Angeles Bulletin* 5 (October 31, 1927): 4-5.

3987. "New County Court House Plans." *Los Angeles Bar Association Bulletin* 11 (February 20, 1936): 136.

3988. "New Sanitation District Organized." *Western City* 21 (February 1945): 18-9.

Los Angeles County Sanitation District Number 15.

3989. Palmer, Selma N. "Decision Making by the Los Angeles County Board of Supervisors: The Short-Doyle Act." Master's thesis, University of Southern California, 1961. 129 pp.

3990. Petrie, Harry P. "Personnel Management under a Merit System: A Study of Civil Service in Los Angeles County." Master's thesis, University of Southern California, 1956. 192 pp.

3991. Pixley, John C. "An Investigation of the Operation and Findings of the Los Angeles County Joint Work Test Panel." Master's thesis, University of Southern California, 1942. 178 pp.

3992. *Proceedings of the Metropolitan Government Symposium.* Los Angeles, 1958. 114 pp.

Describes "the problems-in-being" of the communities, towns, and cities comprising Los Angeles County.

3993. Quam, Victor W. " 'Instant Money' for Small-Order Purchases." *American City* 80 (May 1965): 118-9.

Blank-check purchase-order system adopted by Los Angeles County Purchasing Department.

3994. Quinn, John R. "1.2 Seconds per Bill." *American City* 78 (May 1963): 105.

Los Angeles County tax administration and assessment.

3995. Radig, William A. "A Critical Analysis of Intergovernmental Metropolitan Planning Cooperation in the Los Angeles Area." Master's thesis, University of Southern California, 1965. 102 pp.

3996. Rawn, A. M. *Narraitve—C.S.D.* Los Angeles, 1965. 176 pp.

History of Los Angeles County Sanitation Districts, 1923-1961.

3997. Reed, Wave. "Problems in City and County Consolidation in Los Angeles." Master's thesis, Occidental College, 1930. [78] pp.

3998. Reiterman, Carl. "Birth-Control Policies and Practices in Fifty-Eight California County Welfare Departments." Master's thesis, University of California, Los Angeles, 1965. 251 pp.

3999. "Richmond Replaces Bowron." *Western Housing* 40 (April 1957): 19.

Delmas Richmond replaces Fletcher Bowron (who takes a seat on the Superior Court) on the Air Pollution Control Board of Supervisors.

4000. Rudel, Cha[rle]s A. "A Discussion of Local Taxation." *Los Angeles Realtor* 4 (September 1925): 13+.

Los Angeles County.

4001. Ruggie, Angelina A. "The Preparation of the Office Manual for the Large Public Agency with Particular Reference to the Work of the Los Angeles County Department of Charities." Master's thesis, University of Southern California, 1937. 30 pp.

4002. Sarnighausen, Olga. "A Study of County Government with Particular Reference to Los Angeles County." Master's thesis, University of Southern California, 1918. 106 pp.

4003. Scott, Mellier G. *Metropolitan Los Angeles: One Community.* Los Angeles, 1949. 192 pp.

Supplementary textbook for senior high schools in Los Angeles and Orange counties.

4004. Scoville, H. F. "Growth of Los Angeles County: 762 Functions Added Since 1850." *Tax Digest* 14 (February 1936): 46-9+.

4005. ———— "Los Angeles County Adopts Modified Manager Plan." *National Municipal Review* 27 (September 1938): 461-2.

4006. Scudder, K. J. "Coordinating to Beat the Devil." *Rotarian* 51 (September 1937): 21-3.

Los Angeles County Co-ordinating Council Plan.

4007. Shoemaker, Thaddeus E. "Local Agency Formation Commission of Los Angeles County." Master's thesis, University of Southern California, 1965. 110 pp.

4008. "Signs $6.4 Million Contract for New Voting System." *American City* 82 (November 1967): 50.

Los Angeles County, with more than three million registered voters, is the largest voting jurisdiction in the United States.

4009. Stafford, James G. "Tax Assessment by Scientific Methods." *American City* 15 (December 1916): 663-6.

Methods of realty valuation in Los Angeles city and county.

4010. "Standardization of Zoning Symbols for Use in the County of Los Angeles." *Los Angeles Realtor* 8 (May 1929): 6-7+.

4011. Steinberg, Warren L. "A Study of the Community Relations Conference of Southern California." Doctoral dissertation, University of California, Los Angeles, 1962. 343 pp.

Mainly on the Los Angeles County Community Relations Conference.

4012. Stewart, Frank M. "Committee on Governmental Simplification of Los Angeles County Reports." *Western City* 11 (August 1935): 9.

4013. Strathman, Earl [R.] "Fringe Benefits—As an Aspect of Salary: Los Angeles County Survey." *Western City* 30 (June 1954): 30-1.

4014. ———. "They Like Los Angeles Plan: Taxpayers and Official Feel That Chief Administrative Officer Idea Has Proved Effective over Ten Years of Use." *National Municipal Review* 37 (September 1948): 428-32.

4015. Sullivan, Michael E. "Congressional Administrative Relations in Los Angeles County." Master's thesis, University of Southern California, 1961. 141 pp.

4016. Swanson, John E. *Cooperative Administration of Property Taxes in Los Angeles County.* Bureau of Governmental Research, University of California, Los Angeles, *Studies in Local Government No. 12.* Los Angeles, 1949. 63 pp.

4017. "Taking a Look at the Question of Consolidated Health Service: Hazards to Public Well Being Are No Respectors of Political Boundaries; Experience of 36 Cities in Los Angeles County." *Western City* 10 (August 1934): 21-2.

4018. Thurman, Shirley M. "A Statistical Study of the Los Angeles County Civil Service Openings from October, 1933 Through September, 1935." Master's thesis, University of Southern California, 1936. 169 pp.

4019. Town Hall. *Pay Policies for Public Personnel.* Los Angeles, 1961. 96 pp.

A report of the Municipal and County Government Section of Town Hall.

4020. "Twenty-Five Departments Move in to New Los Angeles State Building." *California Highways and Public Works* 10 (March 1932): 32-3.

Serves Los Angeles County.

4021. Vinson, Thomas W. "The 1966 Changeover from a Civil Service to a Personnel Department in the County of Los Angeles; A Case Study." Master's thesis, University of Southern California, 1968. 348 pp.

4022. White, Jack L. "A Comparative Analysis of the City Administrative Officer of the City of Los Angeles and the Chief Administrative Officer of the County of Los Angeles." Master's thesis, University of Southern California, 1956. 127 pp.

4023. Williams, Adelaide A. "The Social Consequences of the Coordinating Council." Master's thesis, University of California, Los Angeles, 1937. 80 pp.

4024. Winjum, Orel R. "Classification in Los Angeles County Civil Service." Master's thesis, University of California, Los Angeles 1938. 73 pp.

4025. Works, Lewis R. "County Home Rule in California: The Los Angeles County Charter." *Annals of the American Academy of Political and Social Science* 47 (May 1913): 229-36.

4026. Young, James. "Non-Wage Benefits in Voluntary Health, Educational, and Welfare Agencies in Los Angeles County, California." Doctoral dissertation, University of Southern California, 1963. 260 pp.

GOVERNMENT—MUNICIPAL

4027. Abrahams, Marvin. "Functioning of Boards and Commissions in Los Angeles City Government." Doctoral dissertation, University of California, Los Angeles, 1967. 323 pp.

4028. Adams, A. H. "Long Beach Dedicates New Auditorium." *Western City* 8 (April 1932): 28.

4029. Ahl, Frances N. "Separate County Project for Los Angeles City Is Opposed." *National Municipal Review* 21 (December 1932): 704.

Movement to make Los Angeles City a separate opposed by the County Bureau of Efficiency.

4030. Alameda, Don B. "A Study of the Council Manager Form of Government of Alhambra." Master's thesis, University of Southern California, 1935. 155 pp.

4031. Albers, J. C. "Glendale's City Engineer Has Dual Duties." *Pacific Municipalities* 45 (June 1931): 283-4.

4032. Aleshire, F. D., and Ogden, Douglas K. "Pico Rivera Establishes Retirement System Patterned after 'Money Purchase' Plan." *Western City* 38 (April 1962): 35.

4033. "Alhambra Buys Acreage from Pasadena." *Western City* 26 (August 1950): 48.

4034. "American Municipal Association Names Mayors of Portland and Los Angeles." *Western City* 21 (December 1945): 21-2.

Fletcher Bowron named to Board of Trustees.

4035. Anderson, Robert T. "A Critical Examination of the Financial Organization of the City of Los Angeles." Master's thesis, University of Southern California, 1949. 124 pp.

4036. ———— "Portrait of Lakewood — After Two Years Incorporation." *Western City* 32 (January 1956): 39-41.

4037. Ashley, Chester C. "Spending the City's Millions." *Southern California Business* 3 (March 1924): 13+.

Allocation of Los Angeles tax monies.

4038. "Automation Helps Los Angeles Tend to Its Civic Affairs." *American City* 72 (June 1957): 161.

City's punch card installations and computors.

4039. Baughan, F. A. "Review of Organization

L.A. County League of Municipalities." *Pacific Municipalities* 46 (May 1932): 173-4.

4040. Beard, William. "The City Manager Plan in Pasadena, California." Master's thesis, University of California, Los Angeles, 1938. 119 pp.

4041. Beaver, Lee A. "Fringe Benefits — As an Aspect of Salary: Santa Monica Survey." *Western City* 30 (June 1954): 32-3.

4042. Beckett, Paul; Plotkin, Morris, and Pollak, George. *Governmental Purchasing*. Los Angeles, 1952. *Metropolitan Los Angeles. A Study in Integration,* Vol. XI, The Haynes Foundation, *Monograph Series No. 18.* 138 pp.

4043. Beckley, Berle R. "South Gate's 'Pay As You Go' Plan Pays Off." *Western City* 25 (June 1949): 32-5.

4044. Bemis, George W. *Intergovernmental Coordination of Public Works Programs in the Los Angeles Metropolitan Area.* The Haynes Foundation, *Pamphlet Series No. 10.* Los Angeles, 1945. 24 pp.

4045. Bennett, G. Vernon. "The Mess in L.A." *Frontier* 4 (March 1953): 15-6.

Los Angeles City government and the operation of five-man commissions.

4046. Bibb, James. " 'Dog's Life' Shows Improvement in Modern Long Beach Animal Shelter." *Western City* 30 (February 1954): 42.

4047. ———— "Long Beach Gets an Animal Shelter." *American City* 69 (January 1954): 105-7.

4048. Bigger, Richard; Dvorin, Eugene P., and Jamison, Judith N. "Branch Civic Centers." *National Municipal Review* 46 (November 1957): 511-7.

Los Angeles.

4049. ————, and Jamison, Judith N. "Suburban Cities and Metropolitan Integration Proposals." *Western City* 33 (September 1957): 52-3.

Metropolitan Water District cited as example.

4050. ————, and Kitchen, James D. "City Managers and Metro: What Is Effect of Integration on Activity, Status of City Administrators in a

Changing Environment?" *National Civic Review* 49 (March 1960) : 120-6.

Discusses Dade County, Florida, and Los Angeles County.

4051. ——— and ——— *How the Cities Grew: A Century of Municipal Independence and Expansionism in Metropolitan Los Angeles.* Los Angeles, 1952. *Metropolitan Los Angeles. A Study in Integration,* Vol II, The Haynes Foundation, *Monograph Series No. 19.* 259 pp.

4052. Bird, Frederick L. *Revenue Bonds.* Los Angeles, 1941. 43 pp.

4053. Birdsall, M. C. "How Los Angeles Purchases." *American City* 51 (December 1936) : 77+.

Los Angeles City Department of Supplies.

4054. Bisby, R. L. "Long Beach. Here's Showing How the Fastest Growing Town That's Going Grows." *Out West,* new series, 3 (June 1912) : 407-17.

4055. Blackman, John W. B. "Pre-Cast Concrete Piles for Canal Walls at Long Beach, Calif." *Civil Engineering* 10 (November 1940) : 719-22.

Naples district.

4056. Blake, Aldrich. *You Wear the Big Shoe: An Inquiry into the Politics and Government of the American City, with a Case Study of the Los Angeles Metropolitan Area.* Los Angeles, 1945. 111 pp.

4057. "Blake Ave. and Riverdale Improvement District, Los Angeles." *Western Construction News* 5 (July 25, 1930) : 357-8.

Improvements to a residential district adjacent to Elysian Park including a water system, sewers, storm drains, and paving of 15 streets.

4058. Boddy, Manchester. "Will Private Capital Complete Civic Center?" *Saturday Night* 45 (December 3, 1938) : 14-7.

Los Angeles.

4059. Bond, Harry C. "Municipal Lease-Back Financing; A Study of Court Cases and Selected Cities in the Los Angeles Metropolitan Area." Master's thesis, University of Southern California, 1963. 150 pp.

4060. Bone, Chapman L. "Health and Accident Insurance Plans Tested by Hermosa Beach Employees." *Western City* 34 (March 1958) : 37.

4061. Bonner, Richard L. "Los Angeles' New Animal Shelter . . . Utilizes New, Humane, Aviation-Developed Euthanasia Method." *American City* 73 (November 1958) : 183.

4062. Bopf, William L. "An Analysis of the Lakewood Plan's Influence on the Cities That Incorporated in Los Angeles County Since April, 1954." Master's thesis, University of Southern California, 1954. 122 pp.

4063. Borough, Reuben W. "Can Our Cities Buy at the 'Lowest and Best' Price?" *Forum* 104 (October 1945) : 108-13.

Municipal purchasing in Los Angeles, 1938-1945.

4064. Bowron, Fletcher. "How Uncle Sam Mooches on Your City." *American Magazine* 142 (July 1946) : 32-3+.

Los Angeles.

4065. ——— "Some Problems of Metropolitan Areas." *Tax Digest* 22 (May 1944) : 157-8+.

4066. Brown, George E., Jr. "Monterey Park's Job Attitude Survey Analyzes Management Operations." *Western City* 31 (September 1955) : 50-1.

4067. Bryant, David L. "Special Assessments in Los Angeles." Master's thesis, Stanford University, 1933. 182 pp.

4068. Buhrman, Robert. "Can You Trust Your Councilman . . . Whatsisname? Do These 15 Curious Characters Really Know What They're Doing? Do We?" *Los Angeles* 15 (April 1970) : 34-5.

Los Angeles City Council.

4069. ——— "The Peter Principle: Why Things Go Wrong in Los Angeles." *Los Angeles* 14 (September 1969) : 38-40+.

4070. "Burbank Builds Modern Animal Shelter." *American City* 68 (August 1953) : 127.

4071. Burton, James D. "Trends in Municipal Government Activity for the City of Los Angeles, 1910-1955." Master's thesis, University of Southern California, 1956. 146 pp.

4072. California Taxpayers' Association. "Higher Tax Rates for Cities of Los Angeles County." *Apartment Journal* 28 (October 1945): 11+.

4073. Campbell, Harold. "Liability Insurance Payments Reduced in Lynwood by Form of Self-Coverage." *Western City* 35 (July 1959): 42.

4074. Carrasco, Robert M. "A Survey of the Personnel Programs of the Smaller Cities of Southern California." Master's thesis, University of Southern California, 1950. 104 pp.

4075. Carvalho, Romulo C. "The Plight of Municipal Finance and the Search for New Resources of Revenue as Exemplified by the City of Los Angeles." Master's thesis, University of Southern California, 1963. 87 pp.

4076. Cashin, Harold J., Jr. "The Legislative Advocate and the Los Angeles City Council." Master's thesis, University of Southern California, 1964. 114 pp.

4077. Charleville, J. W. "Pasadena Completes New Civic Auditorium." *Western City* 8 (March 1932): 12.

4078. Cheuvront, Verne W. "Flat Tires Can Cost $50 Per Hour . . . So Long Beach, Calif., Develops a High-Speed Way to Repair Them." *American City* 71 (November 1956): 118-9.

4079. "Cities Plan Living War Memorials." *Western City* 24 (January 1948): 22-3.
Includes Los Angeles and Long Beach.

4080. "Cities with 85% of Population Ask 49% of Gas Tax from L. A. County." *Western City* 17 (April 1941): 30-1.

4081. " 'City of Burbank Is on the Air.' " *Western City* 27 (April 1951): 55.
Weekly transcription of city council meeting.

4082. "City Water Study Presents Data on Rates." *Western City* 7 (July 1931): 12.
Comparison of 32 cities, nearly all in Los Angeles County.

4083. "Civil Defense Ordinance Provides Bomb Shelters for City of Los Angeles." *The Architect and Engineer* 186 (October 1951): 9+.

4084. "Civilan Defense in Los Angeles." *Western City* 18 (September 1942): 20-43+.
A detailed article that treats the subject from every standpoint.

4085. Clary, William W. "New City Charter Analyzed." *Saturday Night* 5
  I. [no subtitle] (March 22, 1924): 26.
  II. "Mayor and Council" (March 29, 1924): 26.
  III. "Departmental Organization" (April 5, 1924): 26.
  IV. "Highway and Traffic" (April 12, 1924): 26.
  V. "Franchises" (April 19, 1924): 26.
  VI. "Boroughs" (April 25, 1924): 22.
  VII. [no subtitle] (May 3, 1924): 22.
Los Angeles.

4086. "A Combination City Hall and Fire Engine House: New Municipal Building in South Pasadena, Cal." *American City* 12 (May 1915): 428-9.

4087. "Combined Police and Fire Service Nothing New for City of Hawthorne." *Western City* 26 (Januray 1950): 31.

4088. Conser, E. P. "Los Angeles Views Its Budget: Cost of Government on Up-Trend after Five Years of Trimming Expenses." *Apartment Journal* 18 (July 1935): 8-9.

4089. "Contract Collection in Monterey Park and Montebello." *Western City* 28 (April 1952): 45-6.
Rubbish collection.

4090. Cook, Wilbur D. "The Los Angeles Administrative Center Problem." *The Architect and Engineer* 75 (October 1923): 70-2.

4091. Coop, F. Robert. "Job Analysis of the Municipal Service in the City of Pasadena, California." Master's thesis, University of Southern California, 1937. 220 pp.

4092. Cornett, W[illia]m F. "South Gate—University [USC] Cooperate To Develop New Overall Computer Utilization System." *Western City* 42 (January 1966): 20-1+.

4093. Cortelyou, Herman P. "Los Angeles Average Annual Bid Prices: Methods Employed for Determining, and Results Obtained from, an Index of Contract Prices on Public Work." *Western Construction News* 6 (December 25, 1931): 665-6.

4094. Cottrell, Edwin A., and Jones, Helen L. *Characteristics of the Metropolis*. Los Angeles, 1952. *Metropolitan Los Angeles. A Study in Integration*, Vol. I, The Haynes Foundation, *Monograph Series No. 18*. 123 pp.

4095. —— and —— *The Metropolis: Is Integration Possible?* Los Angeles, 1955. *Metropolitan Los Angeles. A Study in Integration*, Vol. XVI, The Haynes Foundation, *Monograph Series No. 33*. 120 pp.

4096. Crawford, Fred G. *Organizational and Administrative Development of the Government of the City of Los Angeles During the Thirty-year Period July 1, 1925 to September 30, 1955*. Los Angeles, 1955. 282 pp.

Although mimeographed, this publication by the USC School of Public Administration is included because of its importance.

4097. Crouch, Winston W. "Charter Revision in Los Angeles." *National Municipal Review* 27 (July 1938): 379-80.

4098. —— *Intergovernmental Relations*. Los Angeles, 1954. *Metropolitan Los Angeles. A Study in Integration*, Vol. XV, The Haynes Foundation, *Monograph Series No. 32*. 164 pp.

4099. ——, and McHenry, Dean E. "Los Angeles," in *Great Cities of the World, Their Government, Politics and Planning*. Ed. by William A. Robson. New York, 1955. Pp. 297-322. 2nd ed., [1957].

4100. ——; Swanson, John E.; Bigger, Richard, and Algie, James A. *Finance and Taxation*. Los Angeles, 1954. *Metropolitan Los Angeles. A Study in Integration*, Vol. XIV, The Haynes Foundation, *Monograph Series No. 31*. 154 pp.

4101. Crowley, John C. "Monterey Park's Accident Reporting and Prevention Program Reduces Cost." *Western City* 31 (January 1955): 42.

4102. —— "Three Cities Adopt Combination Group Annuity and Life Plans Tied to OASI: Monterey Park." *Western City* 30 (November 1954): 32-3+.

OASI—Old Age Survivor's Insurance.

4103. Cupp, Carl C. "City of Inglewood, Calif. Centralizes All Communications." *The American City* 74 (October 1959): 96-7.

4104. Darby, Ray [mond] V. "How Inglewood Built Its New Veterans Hall with CWA and SERA Aid." *Western City* 11 (February 1935): 24.

CWA—Civil Works Administration; SERA—State Emergency Relief Administration.

4105. Davies, J. H. "A Strikingly Located and Efficiently Designed Municipal Auditorium and Exhibit Hall." *American City* 48 (April 1933): 63-4.

Long Beach.

4106. Davis, Arthur C. "History and Analysis of the Applications of the City of Los Angeles to the Public Works Administration for Federal Works Projects [1933-1935]." Master's thesis, University of Southern California, 1935. 115 pp.

4107. Dellota, Melecio D. "A Critical Analysis of the Post Office Administration in Los Angeles." Master's thesis, University of Southern California, 1939. 71 pp.

4108. "Department of Efficiency Planned for Pasadena." *Pacific Municipalities* 25 (November 1911): 175-6.

4109. DeWolfe, Anne. "I Love You, Susan B. Anthony: An Encounter with the Los Angeles Feminist Movement." *Los Angeles* 14 (December 1969): 40-3+.

4110. Diederich, P. "Municipal Construction Program by Public Service Department of Glendale, California." *Pacific Municipalities* 45 (March 1931): 117-8.

4111. Donner, John W. "Administrative Control by Staff Agencies in the Department of Water and Power of the City of Los Angeles." Master's thesis, University of Southern California, 1933. 100 pp.

4112. Donovan, Richard. "A Town Los Angeles Can't Absorb: The Corporate Duchy of Vernon, Almost Surrounded by L.A., Boasts More Factories Than Homes; 250 Voters, 42,000 Workers." *Reporter* 5 (December 11, 1951): 22-4.

4113. Dunlop, George H. "The Political Officers of Los Angeles City." *Municipal League of Los*

Angeles Bulletin 4 (February 28, 1927): 6-7; (March 31, 1927): 5-6; (April 22, 1927): 8.

4114. Dvorin, Eugene P. *Tax Exemptions and Local Self Government; A Case Study of Santa Monica, California* . . . Los Angeles, 1958. 47 pp.

4115. Dykstra, Clarence A. "The Pending Los Angeles Charter." *National Municipal Review* 13 (March 1924): 148-51.

4116. Eckert, Ross D. "Regulatory Commission Behavior: Taxi Franchising in Los Angeles and Other Cities." Doctoral dissertation, University of California, Los Angeles, 1968. 244 pp.

4117. Edwards, Harlan H. "Low Cost Projects Use WPA Labor in Claremont Public Works Program." *Western City* 16 (April 1940): 21-3.

4118. Eghtedari, Ali M. "An Analysis of Performance Budgeting in the City of Los Angeles." Doctoral dissertation, University of Southern California, 1959. 258 pp.

4119. Eimon, Pan D. "Film Sparks PR Training." *American City* 80 (August 1965): 140+.

"With a film as a central training tool, Glendale, Calif., is improving the public service and the public image of its 1,500 civil service employees."

4120. ———— "Norwalk on Record." *American City* 82 (July 1967): 118+.

"Soundletter" produced by city of Norwalk to keep its 94,000 residents "alert and interested in the community."

4121. "Evolution of a Civic Center: Azusa's Long-Range Plans Are Realized with the Integration of Its Municipal Departments." *American City* 61 (December 1946): 102.

4122. Ferguson, Jenniellen W. *City Council Organization and Procedures in Los Angeles County.* Los Angeles, 1955. 77 pp.

4123. "Fifty Years of Municipal Cooperation in California: The League of California Cities Observes Its Golden Anniversary." *Western City* 24 (September 1948): 28-39.

4124. "Five Hundred Serve a Million and a Quarter: The Work of the Refuse Collection Divi-

sion of Los Angeles." *American City* 50 (March 1935): 47-8.

4125. Flynn, Anne. "Contract Cities." *Parks & Recreation* 5 (April 1970): 26-7+.

Municipal services provided by the County of Los Angeles on a cost plus overhead basis.

4126. "The Forces at Work on Our Next Five Years." *Los Angeles* 15 (January 1970): 26-7.

Governmental reform and planning in Los Angeles.

4127. "$45,000 Shelter Is Dedicated." *Western City* 29 (June 1953): 37.

Burbank Animal Shelter.

4128. "Four Cities Make Safety Instruction a Function of Their Departments." *Western City* 33 (September 1957): 48-9+.

Includes Glendale and Lakewood.

4129. "Garbage and Refuse Collection Motorized in Los Angeles." *American City* 27 (July 1922): 22.

City Engineering Department buys garbage trucks.

4130. Garrett, Leroy A. "The New Municipal Retail Sales Tax." *Los Angeles Bar Bulletin* 21 (August 1946): 356-8.

Los Angeles.

4131. "Gas Tax Views of Cities, Counties, and Auto Club Presented at Regional League Meeting." *Western City* 10 (April 1934): 20-1.

Cities include Los Angeles.

4132. Geib, George A. "A Survey of the History, Organization and Accomplishments of the Municipal Government of Pasadena, California [1769-1933]." Master's thesis, University of Southern California, 1935. 164 pp.

4133. "Glendale Builds for Public Convenience: City of Glendale's Public Comfort Station Located in the Central Part of the Business District." *Pacific Municipalities* 44 (October 1930): 246-7.

4134. "Glendale Establishes In-Service Training and Safety Program." *Western City* 25 (September 1949): 23.

4135. Goldbach, John C. "The Politics of Incorporation: Cityhood in Southern California." Master's thesis, Claremont Graduate School, 1964. 447 pp.

4136. "Good Government Fund of Los Angeles." *American City* 2 (April 1910): 161-2.

4137. Goudey, Raymond F. "Engineering Outlook for Southern California." *Civil Engineering* 5 (September 1935): 545-52.

Discusses Mono Basin Project; Boulder Dam-Los Angeles transmission line; Metropolitan Water District; Los Angeles flood control; need in Los Angeles for various municipal improvements, such as rapid transit, an A-1-A airport, and much else.

4138. Graves, Richard. "Council Manager Government in California Cities." *Western City* 23 (June 1947): 25-9.

Includes many cities in Los Angeles County.

4139. —— "Sales Taxes in 53 California Cities." *Western City* 23 (March 1947): 24-7.

4140. Greer, Scott A., and Kube, Ella. *"Urban Worlds: A Comparative Study of Four Los Angeles Areas."* Unpublished, Occidental College, Laboratory in Urban Culture, 1955. 224 pp.

4141. Grove, Samuel K. *The Lakewood Plan.* Urbana, Ill., 1960. 26 pp.

4142. Guiney, M. W. "The Government of the City of Santa Monica." *Western City* 12 (September 1936): 26-39.

4143. Guinn, J[ames] M. "How the Area of Los Angeles City Was Enlarged." *Annual Publication Historical Society of Southern California* 9 (1914): 173-80.

4144. Gulick H. E. "Public Service Department Opens Corporate Yard Facility in Glendale." *Western City* 37 (January 1961): 29.

4145. Haines, Aubrey B. "Jungle of Jurisdictions: How Can Los Angeles Be Governed?" *Frontier* 9 (February 1958): 5-7.

4146. Hall, Bryant. "Los Angeles—1981." *Western City* 34 (January 1958): 39-40.

Article is a portion of feature "City of the Future: Can Cities Meet the Challenge of Technological Success?"

4147. Hamilton, A. L. "A Municipal Printing Department." *American City* 20 (April 1919): 354-5. Pasadena.

4148. Hamilton, John J. "The Discussion of the Los Angeles Charter." *National Municipal Review* 1 (December 1912): 650-4.

4149. Hamner, Homer H. "Municipal Finance Problems of the City of Glendale, California: An Analysis of Their Nature, Trends, and Prospects." Doctoral dissertation, University of Southern California, 1949. 417 pp.

4150. Hansen, A. C. "Refuse Collection and Disposal for the City of Los Angeles." *Pacific Municipalities* 29 (November 1915): 232-6.

4151. Harrell, Frank L. "Local Government Participation in the Sister-City Program: A Case Study of Claremont, California." Master's thesis, Claremont Graduate School, 1966. 91 pp.

4152. Hawley, Claude E. "Big City Held in Hobble Chains: Little Hope Seen for a Revision of Los Angeles Charter Even Though Authorities Call It the 'Worst in the Nation.'" *National Municipal Review* 37 (November 1948): 538-40.

4153. Heinly, Burt A. "Los Angeles Annexes More Territory." *Engineering News* 73 (May 13, 1915): 956.

Nearly all of tillable land in San Fernando Valley.

4154. —— "Operating Cost Records Show Comparative Economy of 65 Motor Vehicles in Los Angeles Water Department." *Engineering Record* 73 (June 3, 1916): 728-32.

4155. Henderson, Keith M. "A Study of the Los Angeles Civil Service Examination." Master's thesis, University of Southern California, 1957. 135 pp.

4156. Hoffman, Paul G. "Making a City Charter Worth While." *Southern California Business* 3 (May 1924): 9+.

Vote on new Los Angeles city charter, May 6, 1924.

4157. ——— "The Traffic Commission of Los Angeles." *Annals of the American Academy of Political and Social Science* 116 (November 1924): 246-50.

Los Angeles had 430,000 automobiles in 1923, one for every 2.9 residents of city, largest percentage in world.

4158. Hogan, Chester E. "Maintenance Management in Los Angeles Using 'Methods-Time-Measurement.'" *Western City* 44 (September 1968): 48-9.

4159. Hogoboom, William C. "Management and Supervision of Refuse Collectors in the Bureau of Engineering, City of Los Angeles." Master's thesis, University of Southern California, 1940. 129 pp.

4160. Holm, A. G. "How the City of Los Angeles Buys Public Works Equipment." *Western City* 28 (August 1952): 36-7.

4161. Hopkins, A. Lowell. "A Small City Conducts an Effective and Inexpensive Safety Program." *Western City* 23 (December 1947): 32-3.

Redondo Beach.

4162. Hopkins, Francis E. "Redondo Beach Round Table Discussions Result in Community Program." *Western City* 44 (May 1968): 26-8.

4163. ———, and Leach, Joseph. "Lease and Option Features Used to Acquire Redondo Beach Police, Fire Buildings." *Western City* 35 (July 1959): 28.

4164. Hormley, John H. "Gardena Contracts for Computer Services." *Western City* 46 (February 1970): 30-1.

4165. Hornbuckle, William I. "How Four Cities Buy Cars." *The American City* 72 (May 1957): 191+.

Los Angeles is one of cities discussed.

4166. "How Four New Cities Faced Problem of 'Getting Ready for Business.'" *Western City* 33 (March 1957): 38-42+.

Includes La Puente.

4167. "How Long Beach Handles Its Relief Problem." *Western City* 9 (May 1933): 30.

4168. "How Los Angeles Keeps 'em Rolling." *Western Construction* 43 (September 1968): 70+.

City of Los Angeles equipment maintenance.

4169. "How Salvage Helps Pay the Civilian Defense Bill at Manhattan Beach." *Western City* 18 (April 1942): 24-6+.

4170. "How Santa Monica Recognizes Long and Faithful Employee Service." *Western City* 28 (January 1952): 38.

4171. "How Sierra Madre Meets Unemployment Situation—and Pays the Bill: Street Surfacing Program Gives Work to Citizens, Improves Property Values and City's Appearance, All at Low Cost." *Western City* 7 (December 1931): 27-8.

4172. "How 37 Western Cities Are Meeting 1932 Conditions." *Western City* 8 (May 1932): 7-10.

Includes Alhambra, Los Angeles, Monrovia, Pasadena and Santa Monica.

4173. Hubiak, Metro. "This City Yard Is Neighborly: Covina, Calif., Puts a Maintenance Yard in a Residential Area and Makes It Residentially Attractive." *American City* 82 (June 1967): 114-5.

4174. Hunter, Burton L. "The Evolution of Municipal Organization and Administrative Practice in the City of Los Angeles." Master's thesis, University of Southern California, 1933. 219 pp.

4175. ——— *The Evolution of Municipal Organization and Administrative Practice in the City of Los Angeles.* Los Angeles, 1933. 283 pp.

Based on the author's master's thesis.

4176. "Inglewood Has a Business Manager: Pretty Suburban City Near Los Angeles Takes the Lead in Trying Out the New Idea for Sixth Class Cities in California." *Pacific Municipalities* 28 (April 1914): 224.

4177. Jackson, Jesse A. "Facilities and Functions of Long Beach Park and Highway Commission." *Western City* 12 (March 1936): 17-8.

4178. Jamison, Judith N. *Local Election Administration in California.* Los Angeles, 1952. 60 pp.

Chapter 3, pp. 16-19, describes a typical Los Angeles City election. Table 6 illustrates organization and use of election board.

4179. Jessup, J[ohn] J. "The Cyclical Nature of Public Works." *American City* 49 (March 1934): 11.

Chart of annual value of Los Angeles public works projects, 1899-1933, shows wide swings. Peaks in 1914-1915, 1927-1928; lows in 1908-1909, 1919-1920.

4180. ——— "Los Angeles Bureau of Engineering Program." *Western Construction News and Highways Builder* 8 (January 10, 1933): 22.

Los Angeles City construction and maintenance program for 1933.

4181. Johnson, James C. "Having Identified Its Future Needs Compton Now Requires More Funds." *Western City* 46 (March 1970): 16-7.

4182. Jones, Helen L. *Personnel Management.* Los Angeles, 1952. *Metropolitan Los Angeles. A Study in Integration,* Vol. X, The Haynes Foundation, *Monograph Series No. 27.* 73 pp.

4183. Kassell, Lola. "A History of the Government of Los Angeles, 1781-1925." Master's thesis, Occidental College, 1929. 68 pp.

4184. Kay, Cecil R. "Program and Performance Budgeting for Municipal Health Services: A Case Study of the Los Angeles City Health Department." Master's thesis, University of Southern California, 1959. 235 pp.

4185. Keeley, K. V. "All Emergency PhonAlarm in Los Angeles." *American City* 72 (December 1957): 103-4.

Public alarm box system, harbor area.

4186. Kendall, Thomas R. "Repairing Truck Breakdowns before They Occur." *American City* 54 (August 1939): 46-8+.

Los Angeles refuse collection trucks.

4187. Kennedy, W. E. "Inglewood Maps Out a Long Range Program of Public Works." *Western City* 19 (February 1943): 26-7.

4188. Ketcham, Ronald M. *Intergovernmental Cooperation in the Los Angeles Area.* Bureau of Governmental Research, University of California, Los Angeles, *Studies in Local Government No. 4.* Los Angeles, 1940. 61 pp.

4189. King, Oren L. "Profile of a City: Downey—Year and Half of Progress." *Western City* 34 (September 1958): 46-7.

4190. Klein, Robert N. "Monterey Park Contracts Maintenance of City Cars, Motorcycles." *Western City* 27 (August 1951): 27.

4191. Knox, Roy A. "Detail of Los Angeles' City Budgeting Plan." *Pacific Municipalities* 43 (October 1929): 438-9.

4192. Koiner, C. W[ellington]. "The Benefits Resulting from Municipal Lighting in Pasadena." *Pacific Municipalities* 23 (January 31, 1911): 281-5.

4193. ——— "Government of the City of Pasadena: Being a Summary of the Functional Operation of Each Major Department, with an Introduction by City Manager C. W. Koiner." *Western City* 10 (September 1934): 17-23.

4194. ——— "Pasadena's Civic Auditorium." *American City* 53 (August 1938): 49-50.

4195. ——— "Pasadena's Disaster Preparedness Plan." *American City* 51 (August 1936): 93.

4196. ——— "Pasadena's Municipal Problems." *City Manager Magazine* 6 (April 1924): 14-5.

4197. ——— "Salary Schedule for City Employees: Pasadena Hires only Qualified Persons and Aims to Pay a Standard Wage for a Standard Service. No Employees Are on Pay Roll as Charity." *City Manager Magazine* 5 (September 1923): 11-4.

4198. ——— "Why Pasadena's City Manager Resigned: The Manager Would Not Stultify Himself by Tolerating Political Interference with His Prerogatives." *City Manager Magazine* 7 (August 1925): 9-11.

4199. Kraemer, Kenneth L., and Whisenand, Paul M. "Governmental Automatic Data Processing: A Survey of Cities in Los Angeles and Orange County." *Western City* 42 (August 1966): 36-7+.

4200. Krueger, Ralph A. "Business Principles in Municipal Accounting Practice." *Western City* 10 (October 1934): 11-2.

Santa Monica.

4201. "Landfill and Hospital Live in Harmony." *American City* 81 (May 1966): 38.

San Pedro "Disposal Gardens," adjacent to Kaiser Hospital.

4202. Lane, Robert G. "The Administration of Fletcher Bowron as Mayor of the City of Los Angeles." Master's thesis, University of Southern California, 1954. 173 pp.

4203. Lawson, Melvin J. "The Administrative Phases of City Manager Government in Glendale, California." Master's thesis, University of California, Los Angeles, 1940. 90 pp.

4204. Leaf, Edward G. "Los Angeles' Administration Center." *American Architect* 127 (April 8, 1925): 317-9.

4205. League of Women Voters of Long Beach, Calif. *Long Beach Versus Poverty; Employment, Education and Related Programs, Governmentally Funded for Low-Income Residents of Long Beach, California.* Long Beach, 1968. 74 pp.

4206. League of Women Voters of Los Angeles. *Los Angeles: Structure of a City.* Los Angeles, [1963?]. 62 pp. Rev. ed., 1968. 136 pp.

4207. Leever, Basil E. "About Oil and the City of Long Beach." *Western City* 21 (June 1945): 26-8.

Petroleum revenues finance numerous municipal improvements.

4208. Lewin, Molly. "A New Charter for Los Angeles." *Frontier* 2 (April 1951): 13-5.

4209. Long Beach Community Welfare Council. *The Central Area Study.* Long Beach, 1965. 26 pp.

Study of community services provided for residents of the central Long Beach area.

4210. "Long Beach Begins Training Plan." *Western City* 25 (December 1949): 33.

4211. "Long Beach Offers Citizen Report in 30-Minute Color Motion Picture." *Western City* 31 (July 1955): 53.

4212. Los Angeles. Board of Civil Service Commissioners. *Forward Through a Half Century, 1903-1953; Los Angeles City Civil Service.* [N.p., n.d.]. 20 pp.

4213. ———. Bureau of Budget and Efficiency. *A Study of Local Government in the Metropolitan Area within the County of Los Angeles.* Los Angeles, 1935. 298 pp.

4214. Los Angeles City Government Conference. *History, Duties, Organization of the Municipal Departments, City of Los Angeles, 1932-33.* Los Angeles, 1932. 71 pp.

4215. "Los Angeles Adds to Area and Irregular Shape." *Engineering News* 75 (June 29, 1916): 1252-3.

Westgate and Occidental annexations, 1916.

4216. "Los Angeles Adopts Sewer Service Charge to Repair Outfall." *Western City* 18 (July 1942): 34.

4217. "Los Angeles and Dayton [Ohio] Install Effective CD Communications System." *American City* 69 (June 1954): 13.

CD—Civilian Defense.

4218. "Los Angeles Attacks Metropolitan Problem." *National Municipal Review* 29 (July 1940): 459-66+.

4219. "Los Angeles Becomes the Largest City in Area in the United States." *American City* 15 (July 1916): 65-6.

Westgate and Occidental annexations, 1916.

4220. "Los Angeles Council Will Consider $12,-600,000 Revenue Program." *Western City* 22 (March 1946): 50.

4221. "Los Angeles Has $28,000,000 WPA Work." *Western Construction News* 11 (February 1936): 58.

1936 city construction.

4222. "Los Angeles Plans $33,500,000 Program." *Western Construction News* 14 (January 1939): 11.

Public improvements for 1939.

4223. "Los Angeles Recruits Applicants for Master Plan Project." *Western City* 19 (July 1943): 21.

4224. "Los Angeles Selects Sites for New Buildings." *American City* 62 (March 1947): 93.

War Memorial Auditorium and Opera House.

4225. "Los Angeles to Vote $6,000,000 Bonds for Sewers." *Western Construction News* 5 (October 25, 1930) : 514.

4226. "Los Angeles Votes $26,500,000 of Bonds for New Improvements." *American City* 29 (July 1923) : 20.

Major expenditures for harbor ($15 million) and city hall ($7.5 million).

4227. Mansfield, Donald W. "Moving Day at Torrance Organized to 'Keep Business Going' at City Hall." *Western City* 33 (March 1957) : 49+.

4228. Martin, Harold J. "Water Service and Repair Trucks in Los Angeles." *American City* 53 (June 1938) : 41-2.

4229. Marx, Wesley. "As If Los Angeles Didn't Have Enough Trouble." *Reporter* 27 (October 25, 1962) : 38-9.

Describes Los Angeles area's "industrial baronies" incorporated as tax-dodges: Vernon, Irwindale, City of Commerce, City of Industry.

4230. Maverick, Maury, and Harris, Robert E. G. "Los Angeles: Rainbow's End," in *Our Fair City*. Ed. by Robert S. Allen. New York, 1947. Pp. 370-87.

4231. Maxfield, George. "Governments of Cities of Los Angeles County Operating under Freeholder Charters: A Comparative Study." Master's thesis, Occidental College, 1929. 105 pp.

4232. "Mayor Eaton on City Charters." *California Municipalities* 2 (June 1900) : 157.

Los Angeles.

4233. McCardle, L. V. "A Modern City Treasury." *American City* 63 (May 1948) : 77.

Los Angeles City Treasurer.

4234. McDaniel, Wesley C. "Arcadia Opens Combined Corporation Yard to Have Three Field Service Areas." *Western City* 43 (October 1967) : 58-9.

4235. McDiarmid, John. "Los Angeles Attacks Metropolitan Problem: Finds in Functional Consolidation a Compromise Between Advantages of Unified Administration and Local Self-Government Which Can Be Put in Operation Gradually with No Political Upheaval." *National Municipal Review* 29 (July 1940) : 459-66+.

4236. McLean, Francis H. "Municipal Control of Charities in Los Angeles." *Survey* 33 (January 9, 1915) : 400-1.

Los Angeles Municipal Charties Commission.

4237. McMicken, Craig. "Glendora's Prezoning Ordinance Establishes Protective City Ring." *Western City* 33 (January 1957) : 33+.

4238. Metz, William R. "How the Nation's Fastest Growing City Is Kept Clean, and What It Costs." *Western City* 7 (February 1931) : 29-31.

Beverly Hills.

4239. Miller, A[ndrew] George. "City Manager Government in Long Beach," in *City Manager Government in Seven Cities*. Ed. by Frederick C. Mosher, et al. Chicago, 1940. Pp. 325-71.

An offprint of 47 pp. was published separately in 1940.

4240. ———— "City Manager Government in Long Beach, California." Master's thesis, University of Southern California, 1938. 107 pp.

4241. Miller, Willis H. "The Localization of Functions in the Pomona Area." Doctoral dissertation, University of Chicago, 1933. 251 pp.

4242. Mills, Earl O. "Los Angeles Again Pioneers in Zoning: Some Highlights of the New Comprehensive Zoning Ordinance Adopted by the City Council of Los Angeles, March 7, 1946." *American City* 61 (April 1946) : 113-4.

4243. "Model City Charter." *Independent* 73 (December 5, 1912) : 1326-8.

Proposed Los Angeles Charter.

4244. "A Modern Tale of Two Cities; Or, the Object Lesson Furnished by the Story of the Water Supply of Los Angeles and Denver." *Arena* 38 (October 1907) : 436-8.

Comparison of rates under public and private ownership.

4245. "Monrovia Merit System." *Western City* 29 (January 1953) : 39.

4246. "Monrovia Streamlines Public Works and Service Functions." *Western City* 22 (July 1946) : 37.

4247. "Montebello City Hall Is Part of New Civic Center Development." *Western City* 40 (July 1964) : 25.

4248. "Montebello Finds New Revenues to Meet Needs of Growing City." *Western City* 22 (July 1966) : 35.

4249. "Monterey Park's New City Hall Dedicated." *Western City* 24 (April 1948) : 48.

4250. "More Assistance to Mayors Urged by New York, Los Angeles Surveys." *Western City* 29 (June 1953) : 33.

4251. Morris, Theodore P. "An Inquiry into Supervisory Training in the City of Pasadena, California." Master's thesis, University of Southern California, 1954. [320] pp.

4252. "Motorizing the Cities." *Western City* 6 (August 1930) : 40.

City of Pasadena buys Moreland trucks.

4253. Moulton, Marjorie G. "The Government of the City of Glendale." Master's thesis, Stanford University, 1943. 93 pp.

4254. Mulrooney, Keith F. "Pomona Pays Its Employees to Be Safe: A Municipal Profit Sharing Plan in Miniature." *Western City* 40 (September 1964) : 65-6.

4255. ———— "Pomona's 24 Hour Communications Center Includes Complete Underground City." *Western City* 40 (May 1964) : 44-5.

4256. "Municipal Movies Produced in Burbank and Philadelphia." *American City* 67 (January 1952) : 112-3.

4257. "Municipal Reform in Los Angeles." *Outlook* 91 (March 13, 1909) : 570-1.

4258. Myers, Al S. "Sierra Madre Considers Consolidation." *Western City* 12 (February 1936) : 14-5+.

4259. Navarro, Charles. "200,000 Records at Our Fingertips." *American City* 78 (January 1963) : 79.

Los Angeles Records Control System.

4260. "Negroes Win City Jobs in Los Angeles." *American City* 82 (October 1967) : 89.

4261. Nehring, Earl A. "Local Political Leadership, a Study of Decision-Making in a Council-Manager City." Doctoral dissertation, University of California, Los Angeles, 1958. 360 pp.

Santa Monica.

4262. "New Charter for Los Angeles. *Survey* 28 (September 28, 1912) : 796.

4263. "New Charter for Los Angeles." *Pacific Municipalities* 29 (August 1915) : 339.

4264. "The New City Hall and the Hall of Justice." *Municipal League of Los Angeles Bulletin* 5 (January 31, 1928) : [5].

4265. "New City Hall Annex Is H-Bomb Proof." *American City* 76 (September 1961) : 112.

Burbank.

4266. "New City Hall Is Designed to Dominate Los Angeles Landscape." *American City* 27 (November 1927) : 666.

4267. "The New City Hall, Los Angeles, California." *American Architect* 131 (April 20, 1927) : 497-508.

4268. "New City Hall Marks Hawthorne's Growth and Emergence from Debt." *Western City* 24 (December 1948) : 39.

4269. "New South El Monte Civic Center Uses a 'Lease Back' Financing Program." *Western City* 43 (April 1967) : 30.

4270. Nishizaki, Ogden M. "How a City Tells Its Story: An Inquiry into the Public Relations Program of Inglewood, California." Master's thesis, University of Southern California, 1953. 122 pp.

4271. Nogueira, Flavio P. "Some Aspects of Personnel Record-Keeping in Three Departments of the City of Los Angeles; A Case Study." Master's thesis, University of Southern California, 1954. 116 pp.

4272. Ogden, Douglas K. "Azusa Modernizes Accounting System to Handle Growth." *Western City* 34 (August 1958) : 41.

4273. Olmsted, H. M. "Los Angeles Creates Office of Zoning Administrator." *National Municipal Review* 30 (October 1941) : 595.

4274. ——— "Stronger 'Manager' Urged for Los Angeles: Little Hoover Commission Issues Its Final Report." *National Municipal Review* 42 (July 1953) : 338-9.

4275. "One Year Sewer Service Charge in Prospect for Los Angeles." *Apartment Journal* 25 (July 1942) : 14.

4276. O'Rourke, Lawrence W. "The Office of Mayor in Los Angeles: An Administrative Analysis." Master's thesis, University of California, Los Angeles, 1954. 123 pp.

4277. Osterhout, Roy H. "1965 Municipal Accounting Award: San Gabriel Financial Reorganization Wins." *Western City* 43 (September 1967) : 54-5.

4278. Ostrom, Vincent; Tiebout, Charles M., and Warren, Robert. "The Organization of Government in Metropolitan Areas: A Theoretical Inquiry." *American Political Science Review* 55 (1961) : 831-42.

Latter part of article focuses on Los Angeles area.

4279. Owen, David W. "The Working Relationships Between City Managers and City Planners in Representative Portions of the Los Angeles Metropolitan Area." Master's thesis, University of Southern California, 1962. 156 pp.

4280. Owens, Robert P. "San Fernando's Community Service Officer Fulfills Requirements of Crime Commission." *Western City* 46 (February 1970) : 16+.

4281. Padgett, B. Lewis. "Construction Progress on the New Los Angeles City Hall." *Western Construction News* 3 (April 25, 1928) : 275-7.

4282. Paris, Ben R. "Los Angeles Maintenance Shop Keeps City Equipment Fit." *American City* 66 (December 1951) :92-3.

4283. "Pasadena and Altadena Agree—No Annexation." *Western City* 26 (June 1950) : 52.

4284. Patterson, Beeman C. "Political Action of Negroes in Los Angeles: A Case Study in the Attainment of Councilmanic Representation." *Phylon* 30 (1969) : 170-83.

4285. Peebles, Wade E. "Municipal Uniforms Provide Identity for Torrance Personnel." *Western City* 39 (October 1963) : 40.

4286. "People-to-People Programs: Strengthening the Bonds of International Friendship." *Western City* 39 (March 1963) : 21-34.

Sister City Program, includes: Bellflower—Los Mochis, Mexico; Downey—Guadalajara; Glendale—Hiraoka, Japan; Montebello—Ashiya, Japan; Norwalk—Hermosillo, Mexico; Santa Monica—Mazatlan, Mexico; South Gate—Southgate, England.

4287. Perkins, C. E. "Functional Consolidation Trend in Los Angeles Area Government." *Western City* 34 (November 1958) : 38-9.

4288. ——— "Glendale Tries 'Compact Cars' for Municipal Fleet Use." *Western City* 36 (August 1960) : 44.

4289. Peterson, W. C. "Municipal Fact Finding Agency: Bureau of Budget of Los Angeles Rendering Efficient Service." *Pacific Municipalities* 46 (January 1932) : 15.

4290. Peterson, Walter C. "Indexing Council Minutes: Five Years with an Orderly System." *American City* 61 (January 1946) : 80-1.

Los Angeles.

4291. Petrie, C. G., and Wheaton, James D. "Use of Propane as a Motor Fuel Tested by Monterey Park Public Works." *Western City* 37 (October 1961) : 61.

4292. Pfiffner, John M. "The Los Angeles Bureau of Budget and Efficiency." *National Municipal Review* 21 (February 1932) : 107-9.

4293. Phillips, John. "Department of Community Development Established to Meet New Challenges." *Western City* 46 (September 1970) : 27+.

Pasadena.

4294. Pinkerton, Frank B., Jr. "A Study of the Measurement of Quantity and Quality of Work Performed by the Claims Adjustors in the State Compensation Insurance Fund at Los Angeles." Master's thesis, University of Southern California, 1955. 76 pp.

4295. Porter, Evelyne N. "The Business Phase of the Bureau of Indigent Relief of Los Angeles

County." Master's thesis, University of Southern California, 1936. 98 pp.

4296. "Pouring the Foundation for the New Los Angeles City Hall." *American City* 35 (November 1926): 666.

4297. "Preparing Our Home Defenses." *Popular Mechanics* 75 (March 1941): 392-5.
Civilian defense, Los Angeles.

4298. "Prescription for Alienation: Divide & Conquer." *Los Angeles* 13 (July 1968): 48-52.
Plan for dividing Los Angeles into functional sub-communities.

4299. Pritchard, Lawrence D. "The History, Activities, and Organization of the All City Employees Association of Los Angeles [1918-1940]." Master's thesis, University of Southern California, 1940. 154 pp.

4300. "Progress of Los Angeles." *Pacific Municipalities* 16 (March 1907): 46.
Public works projects.

4301. "Propose Bond Issue for Six Large Combustible Refuse Incinerators." *Western City* 22 (February 1946): 18.
Los Angeles.

4302. "Propose Sewer Service Charge to Raise $17,580,000 for Los Angeles System." *Western City* 17 (April 1941): 34-7.

4303. "A Public Address System Which Has Proved Indispensable to Pasadena, Calif." *City Manager Magazine* 7 (February 1925): 26-7.

4304. Pyle, W. C. "How Whittier Worked Out an A. and I. Bond Cancellation Program." *Western City* 13 (June 1937): 37-8.
A. and I.—Acquisition and Improvement.

4305. Reeves, Cuthbert E. *The Valuation of Business Lots in Downtown Los Angeles.* Los Angeles, 1932. 38 pp.
On metropolitan tax structures.

4306. Rehfuss, John A. "Techniques and Procedures in Revenue Estimating, with Particular Reference to Five Selected Cities in Los Angeles County." Master's thesis, University of Southern California, 1958. 144 pp.

4307. "Revised Los Angeles Building Code Effective January 1, 1943." *Western Construction News* 17 (November 1942): 500.
Signed October 3, 1942, by Mayor Fletcher Bowron.

4308. Roberts, Myron. "Charting the New City Charter." *Los Angeles* 15 (January 1970): 28-9+.

4309. ———— "Zoning: The New Corruption." *Los Angeles* 13 (November 1968): 26-7+.
Los Angeles.

4310. Roberts, Samuel M. "Long Beach Adopted Coordinated Plan of State Retirement and Federal OASI." *Western City* 33 (March 1957): 35-7.
OASI—Old Age Survivors Insurance.

4311. Robison, Donald. "A Study of Civil Service Administration in the City of Los Angeles from 1938 to 1958." Master's thesis, University of Southern California, 1958. 114 pp.

4312. Rowlin, R. L. "Walking Is Too Costly: Los Angeles Finds That Small, Electric-Powered Cars Are the Most Effective and Rapid Means of Transporting Personnel Around the 75-Acre Hyperion Sewage-Treatment Plant." *American City* 70 (May 1955): 104-5.

4313. "Safety Program Pays Off for Los Angeles City Department of Public Works." *Western City* 40 (August 1964): 19.

4314. "Sales Simulation Program Inaugurated by Los Angeles Bureau of Water Works." *Western Construction News* 13 (October 1938): 366.

4315. "Santa Monica Dedicates New $370,000 City Hall." *Western City* 15 (December 1939): 19.

4316. "Santa Monica Votes to Join State Employees Retirement System." *Western City* 19 (December 1943): 28.

4317. Schone, Harold K., and Brown, David M. "Arcadia's New Pay Plan System—A Year's Experience." *Western City* 40 (January 1964): 15+.

4318. Schuchardt, William H. "The Civic Center," in *Los Angeles: Preface to a Master Plan.* Ed. by George W. Robbins and L. Deming Tilton. Los Angeles, 1941. Pp. 239-49.

4319. Schumann, Howard. "The Incorporation of East Los Angeles as a Separate City: Problems and Prospects." Master's thesis, University of Southern California, 1965. 114 pp.

4320. Schwab, Paul E. "Beverly Hills Dedicates New City Hall." *Western City* 8 (May 1932): 11.

4321. Seeger, Deane, Jr. "Pilot Project in Citizen Leadership Successfully Conducted in Redondo Beach." *Western City* 41 (May 1965): 48.

4322. ———, and Jones, Russell D. "Rubbish Collection Established in Culver City with Tax Levy." *Western City* 35 (May 1959): 44-5.

4323. "Sewer Service Charges in California Cities." *Western City* 29 (February 1953): 37-43.
Includes Los Angeles County cities.

4324. "Sewer Service Charges in 78 Western Cities." *Western City* 34 (April 1958): 26-31+.
Includes some Los Angeles County cities.

4325. Sharp, T. L. "The Inauguration of a New Public Personnel Agency in the City of Glendale, California." Master's thesis, University of Southern California, 1939. [?] pp.

4326. Shea, Charles G. "Three Approaches to a Selection Program in Public Personnel Administration; An Analysis of the Validity of the Contract Between the City of Burbank and Los Angeles County for Examination Services." Master's thesis, University of Southern California, 1968. 147 pp.

4327. Sherwood, Frank P. "Revolt in the Valley: Inequities in the Tax Load on the Local Level." *Frontier* 6 (February 1955): 13-4.
San Fernando Valley.

4328. ——— "Southern California Communities Have Advanced Techniques." *Western City* 30 (January 1954): 34-6+.
Performance Budgeting as recommended by 1949 Little Hoover Commission Report. Includes Los Angeles and Long Beach.

4329. ———, and Storm, William B. "Community Survey of Hawthorne Discloses Citizen Apathy, Interests." *Western City* 33 (February 1957): 44-5+.

4330. Siffert, Donald E. "A Comparative Study of City Governments in Santa Monica, California." Master's thesis, University of California, Los Angeles, 1956. 186 pp.

4331. Simons, Seward C., and Andrews, Harry. "The Proposed New Charter for Los Angeles." *Pacific Municipalities* 30 (April 1916): 141-3.

4332. Simpson, Frank, Jr. "Unique—Our 5-City Convention Plan: Through Years of Experience, These Los Angeles County Communities Have Learned Teamwork." *Southern California Business* 14 (April 1935): 8-9.
Long Beach, Pasadena, Hollywood, Santa Monica, and Los Angeles.

4333. "Six-Year City Programs: Los Angeles, Calif." *Western Construction News* 18 (February 1943): 71-2.

4334. "A Small California City Adopts the Merit System." *Western City* 14 (January 1938): 20.
Montebello.

4335. Smith, Luke M. "Relations Between the Territorial Structuring and the Local Government of a Metropolitan Suburb: The Sunland-Tujunga Valley, Los Angeles." Doctoral Dissertation, Harvard University, 1948. 690 pp.

4336. Smith, Wade S. "Los Angeles Adopts Sales Tax." *National Municipal Review* 35 (July 1946): 380-1.

4337. Smith, Will. "Cities Received $61,779,632 Last Year from Gas, 'In Lieu' Taxes, Liquor Fees." *Western City* 29 (August 1953): 37-41.
Tables includes Los Angeles County cities.

4338. Soper, Leonard G. "Regional Cooperation Initiates San Gabriel Valley Municipal Data System." *Western City* 45 (July 1969): 16+.

4339. "Soundletter Brings Award." *American City* 83 (November 1968): 22+.
"A five-minute 'Soundletter' earned the city of Norwalk, Calif., the honor of being the only city selected by the Freedom Foundations [sic] at Valley Forge to receive the George Washington Honor Medal for 1967."

4340. Spencer, Bert F. "A Case Study Comparison

of Personnel Administration in the Cities of Glendale and Pasadena." Master's thesis, University of Southern California, 1949. 132 pp.

4341. Spencer, Richard. "Cities within Cities: Problems of Streets and Other Services Complicated by Independent Areas Engulfed within a Larger Metropolis." *National Municipal Review* 37 (May 1948): 256-8.
Includes Los Angeles and Long Beach.

4342. Stenberg, George B. "Beverly Hills Is Winner of 1956 Award for New Financial Organization." *Western City* 32 (September 1956): 54-5.

4343. Stephenson, Allen B., and A'pert, Alexander. "Civil Service Rules Committee Prepares Alhambra's Regulations." *Western City* 35 (September 1959): 63.

4344. Story, Russell M. "Municipal Affairs: Proposals for Government Reorganization in the Los Angeles Metropolitan Area." *American Political Science Review* 30 (1936): 943-50.

4345. Strayer, A. D. "Bicycle Licensing Handled by Burbank Fire Department." *Western City* 35 (January 1959): 25.

4346. Strick, Anne. "Los Angeles' Golden Goose." *Nation* 209 (July 28, 1969): 87-9.
Ten percent tax levied against gross profits of Music Center.

4347. *A Study of the Los Angeles City Charter.* Los Angeles, 1963. 215 pp.

4348. "Suppose the Bond Issue Fails." *American City* 85 (March 1970): 88+.
Describes formation of non-profit corporation to build Pomona city hall and council chamber, then lease it back to the city with payment to come out of the general fund.

4349. Talbott, William G. "Long Beach, 1888-1925: A Study in Municipal Development." Master's thesis, University of Southern California, 1947. 146 pp.

4350. "Tax Rates in California Cities." *Pacific Municipalities* 9 (October 1903): 86-7.

4351. "Tax Rates in California Cities." *Pacific Municipalities* 13 (November 1905): 110-1.

4352. Taylor, Dick. "City Designs New Logo for 'New Image.'" *Western City* 46 (October 1970): 26.
Inglewood's new seal.

4353. Taylor, F. J. "Town with Too Much Money." *Saturday Evening Post* 224 (January 12, 1952): 32-3.
A slick article in which the author talks about what Long Beach faces with the tidelands' windfall.

4354. Thiel, Walter C. "Financial and Administrative Reorganization, Department of Public Works, City of Los Angeles." Master's thesis, University of Southern California, 1933. 59 pp.

4355. ——— "General Fund Revenues of Cities in Los Angeles County." *Western City* 21 (March 1945): 24-6.

4356. ——— "Revenues of Cities in Los Angeles County: 1945-6 Fiscal Year Budget." *Western City* 22 (May 1946): 32-3.

4357. Thomas, Larry. "Electric Voting System Comes to Pomona." *Western City* 43 (May 1967): 29-30.

4358. "Three New Municipal Buildings for Glendale, Calif." *Western City* 6 (January 1930): 41+.

4359. "Three-Stage Expansion of Convention Facilities Begins in Long Beach, Calif." *American City* 70 (February 1955): 120-1.

4360. Town Hall, Los Angeles. *Pay Policies for Public Personnel.* Los Angeles, 1961. 96 pp.
A report of the Municipal and County Government Section of Town Hall.

4361. ——— *A Study of the Los Angeles City Charter: A Report of the Municipal and County Government Section of Town Hall.* Los Angeles, 1963. 215 pp.

4362. ——— *Wage-Setting Methods in the Local Government Jurisdictions of the Los Angeles Area.* [Los Angeles], 1950. 22 pp.

4363. "A Transportation Center for All Modes." *American City* 83 (November 1968): 122.
Financed jointly by local, state, and federal

funds, this "Mixed-Mode Transportation Center" in the city of Pomona combines facilities for air, railroad, long distance and local bus travel, express, car rental and leasing, and other transportation services.

4364. Trygg, C. E. "Police and Fire Departments Re-established after Signal Hill Tries Contract Services." *Western City* 37 (January 1961): 17-8.

4365. Updegraff, Winston R. "California League Observes 50 Years of Municipal Cooperation in State." *Western City* 24 (October 1948): 30-44.
Portions written by Los Angeles Fire Chief John H. Alderson, General Manager George Hjelte of the City Recreation and Park Department, and Principal Planner Milton Breivogel.

4366. Urquhart, Alexander D. "Adjudication and Rule-Making in Los Angeles Municipal Administration." Doctoral dissertation, University of California, Los Angeles, 1957. 281 pp.

4367. "Use of TV for MPR in Los Angeles and Cincinnati." *American City* 65 (September 1950): 116-7.
MPR—Municipal Public Relations.

4368. Utter, James W., Jr. "The Territorial Expansion of Los Angeles." Master's thesis, University of Southern California, 1946. 155 pp.

4369. Vandervoort, Paul, II. "Burbank's New City Hall." *American City* 58 (September 1943): 55.

4370. Van Valen, Nelson S. "Power Politics: The Struggle for Municipal Ownership of Electric Utilities in Los Angeles, 1905-1937." Doctoral dissertation, Claremont Graduate School, 1963. 398 pp.

4371. Vega, Miguel A. "The Nature of Oral Testing in Government and Its Application in the Los Angeles City Civil Service Department." Master's thesis, University of Southern California, 1953. 115 pp.

4372. Vieg, John A., ed. *California Local Finance.* Stanford, 1960. 370 pp.

4473. Walker, J. P. "Montebello Department Trust Fund." *Western City* 9 (March 1933): 16-7.

4374. Walker, Mabel L. "Los Angeles Bureau [of Municipal Research] Propounds a Panacea for Tax Relief." *American City* 49 (May 1934): 81.
A hostile appraisal of plan to abolish property tax, with fees to be paid for all municipal services.

4375. Warren, Robert O. "Changing Patterns of Governmental Organization in the Los Angeles Metropolitan Area." Doctoral dissertation, University of California, Los Angeles, 1964. 590 pp.

4376. ——— *Government in Metropolitan Regions: A Reappraisal of Fractionated Political Organization.* Davis, [1966]. 327 pp.
Based on the author's doctoral dissertation cited above.

4377. Wasserman, Lauren M. "Business Licensing Practices in Contract Cities." Master's thesis, California State College, Long Beach, 1968. 119 pp.

4378. "Water Bumpers—New Automotive Safety Device." *American City* 82 (September 1967): 184+.
Installed by Culver City on its police cars.

4379. "Water Rates in California Cities." *Western City* 31 (October 1955): 50-8+; (November 1955): 50-2.

4380. Watson, Ben[jamin M.]. "Burbank Civil Defense Operations Center Undergoes Simulated Attack in Test Program." *Western City* 38 (January 1962): 22.

4381. ——— " 'Zero Zone' Civil Defense Headquarters Constructed under Burbank City Hall Annex." *Western City* 36 (September 1960): 23-4.

4382. ———, and Baker, Joseph N. "Burbank Prepares for Disaster Emergency Operations." *Western City* 42 (October 1966): 60-1.

4383. Wentz, John B. "An Analysis of the Advisability of Annexing All or a Part of the Lakewood Area to the City of Long Beach." Master's thesis, University of Southern California, 1951. 253 pp.

4384. ——— "Should Lakewood Annex to Long Beach?" *Western City* 28 (January 1952): 21-6.

4385. "Western Cities Plan Works." *Western Construction News* 18 (January 1943): 27-9.
Includes public works planned by Santa Monica, Glendale, Pasadena, Long Beach.

4386. "Western Figures from the Census of Construction." *Western Construction News* 12 (January 1937) : 19.

Includes "Los Angeles Programs $24,000,000 [Public] Expenditure" for 1937 construction program. Bulk of these expenditures were through the Work Progress Administration.

4387. "What Does a Municipal Art Commission Do?" *American City* 40 (March 1929) : 141.

Los Angeles.

4388. Whisenand, Paul M. "The Supervision of the Los Angeles Investigative Program: A Study." Master's thesis, University of Southern California, 1963. 128 pp.

4389. White, Fred G., Jr. "The Contract Method of Furnishing Personnel Services to Small Cities in Los Angeles County." Master's thesis, University of Southern California, 1941. 94 pp.

4390. White, Jack L. "A Comparative Analysis of the City Administrative Officer of the City of Los Angeles and the Chief Administrative Officer of the County of Los Angeles." Master's thesis, University of Southern California, 1956. 127 pp.

4391. White, Larry C. "Employees Public Relations Program Puts City's 'Best Foot Forward.'" *Western City* 30 (January 1954) : 27+.

Glendale.

4392. Whitnall, Gordon. "A Comment on the 'Lakewood Plan.'" *American City* 70 (May 1955) : 135.

4393. "Whittier Survey Shows Water Rates in 28 Cities." *Western City* 26 (December 1950) : 54.

All Los Angeles County cities.

4394. Wiener, Rosalind. "How a Woman of a City Council Sees Her Job." *American City* 69 (April 1954) : 119.

Miss Wiener was elected to the Los Angeles City Council at the age of 22.

4395. Wiggs, Anna. "The History of Los Angeles City Government under the Second Charter, 1889-1925." Master's thesis, University of Southern California, 1928. 139 pp.

4396. Will, Arthur G. "The Lakewood Story: A Case Study in the Annexation of a Large Inhabited Area by Long Beach." *Western City* 30 (March 1954) : 42-7.

4397. Williams, Robert L. "Busy Neighborhood Center in Santa Fe Springs Provides Community Services to Citizens." *Western City* 46 (September 1970) : 23-4.

4398. Wood, C. Raymond. "Remarks on Central Purchasing in Beverly Hills, Calif." *American City* 70 (December 1955) : 99.

4399. Wood, Clarence R. "An Analysis of the Problems of Finance Administration in Small Cities." Master's thesis, University of Southern California, 1956. 217 pp.

Beverly Hills.

4400. Wood, Richard J. "Would You Believe a Voluntary Assessment District? Cudahy Makes It Work!" *Western City* 43 (October 1967) : 40.

4401. Woodruff, Clinton R. "Civil Service Reform at Los Angeles." *National Municipal Review* 1 (December 1912) : 639-45.

4402. Woollett, William L. "Proposed Civic Center." *Saturday Night* 6 (February 20, 1926) : 1-2.
Los Angeles.

HARBORS

4403. Ahl, Frances N. "Los Angeles Harbor." *Overland Monthly* 89 (July 1931) : 19-20+.

4404. "The Airman's Check on a Busy Day at the Harbor." *Southern California Business* 11 (July 1932) : 26.

Los Angeles.

4405. Allen, Walter B. "Los Angeles Harbor: Gateway to the Pacific Southwest." *Los Angeles Saturday Night 150th Birthday of Los Angeles: Fiesta and Pre-Olympiad.* Special Issue (1931) : [6].

4406. Allison, Lawrence. "Our Warring Waterfronts: The Rival Ports—Los Angeles and Long Beach—Should Have Merged Years Ago. Now They're Battling for an Overlooked Market: The Tourist." *Los Angeles* 7 (March 1964) : 28-33+.

4407. Amar, E. J. "The City Enlarges the Navy's Home." *Southern California Business* 13 (November 1934) : 12-3.
Navy accommodations at Los Angeles Harbor.

4408. Aughinbaugh, W. E. "Good Times—But Poor Advertising: Port of Los Angeles Full of Freight, Crops in All Sections Abundant, Business Flourishing, But Lack of Publicity Sense." *Southern California Business* 1 (October 1922) : 21+.

4409. Barsness, Richard W. "The Maritime Development of San Pedro Bay, California, 1821-1921." Doctoral dissertation, University of Minnesota, 1963. 621 pp.

4410. Beecher, John. "The History of Los Angeles Harbor [1542 to 1915]." Master's thesis, University of Southern California, 1915. 61 pp.

4411. ———— "Los Angeles Harbor—Past and Present." *Out West,* new series, 11 (January 1916): 45-53; (February 1916) : 97-105.

4412. Berry, Alan. "Completed Los Angeles-Long Beach Breakwater Will Be World's Longest." *Western Construction News* 23 (August 1948): 98-100.

4413. Bjork, G. E. "Construction Review of Western Projects." *Western Construction News and Highways Builder* 9 (March 1934) : 91-4.
Includes extension of Los Angeles-Long Beach Harbor Breakwater.

4414. Bobrow, Robert. "The Changing Harbor." *Westways* 56 (March 1964) : 2-6.
Los Angeles and Long Beach harbors.

4415. "Building a Great Seaport." *Harper's Weekly* 46 (March 22, 1902) : 374.
Los Angeles Harbor.

4416. Case, Walter H. *Early History of City of Long Beach Harbor Development.* Long Beach, 1927. 32 pp.

4417. Caverly, L. E. "The Making of a Cosmopolitan Port." *Southern California Business* 1 (September 1922) : 38-9.

4418. Chandler, Paul. " 'They Laughed When I Said Seaport' and Now These Very Sea-Dogs Work Ships in the Man-Made Port of Los Angeles." *Southern California Business* 12 (March 1933) : 12-3.

4419. Cockshott, Maurice C. "Hancock Oil Terminal, Los Angeles Harbor." *Western Construction News* 4 (July 10, 1929) : 338.

4420. Collins, James H. "When A Ship Comes In— What Happens?" *Southern California Business* 10 (October 1931) : 10-1.
Los Angeles Harbor.

4421. Coxe, Lewis C. "Long Beach Naval Shipyard Endangered by Subsidence." *Civil Engineering* 19 (November 1949) : 44-7+.

4422. Cram, C. M. "$2,800,000 Construction Combines Auditorium, Pier and . . . And Also a $15,-000,000 Harbor Development Program." *Western City* 6 (March 1930) : 25-9.
Long Beach.

4423. Cramer, Tom M. "The Mormon Island Story." *Pioneer* 3 (September 1962) : 12-3.
San Pedro.

4424. Creakbaum, W. M. "Giving the Harbor a New Fireboat." *Southern California Business* 4 (December 1925) : 15+.
Los Angeles Harbor.

4425. Davis, Jehiel S. "Seaports—A Study, Illustrated by Los Angeles." *The Journal of Geography* 18 (1919) : 188-93.

4426. ———— "Seaports of San Francisco, Los Angeles and San Diego." *The Journal of Geography* 21 (1922) : 131-40.

4427. Dektar, Cliff. "Seagoing Smokeaters." *Westways* 46 (October 1954) : 6-7.
Fireboats of Los Angeles Harbor.

4428. DeVoss, Donald W. "A Comparative Analysis of Organizational and Functional Aspects of the Los Angeles and Long Beach Port Administrations." Master's thesis, University of Southern California, 1949. 249 pp.

4429. Diehl, Digby. "The Surprising Harbor." *Los Angeles* 11 (August 1966) : 24-9.
San Pedro's Ports O'Call Village.

4430. Ditzel, Paul. "The Monday Morning Banana Train." *Westways* 50 (December 1958): 10-1.
Wilmington docks.

4431. Donovan, Frank P., Jr. "Memory Port." *Westways* 35 (January 1943): 18-9.
Redondo Beach.

4432. Dotron, Robert E. "Southern California's Growing Export Trade." *Los Angeles Saturday Night* 10 (May 10, 1930): 7.
Rise of Los Angeles Harbor.

4433. Dow, Lorenzo I., Jr. "The General Cargo Ocean Trade of the Port of Los Angeles, California." Master's thesis, University of California, Los Angeles, 1952. 142 pp.

4434. "Enough Lumber to Build a Big City." *Southern California Business* 4 (June 1925): 20.
Los Angeles Harbor lumber imports.

4435. "Exports Increase 300 Times." *Southern California Business* 5 (January 1927): 12-3+.
Los Angeles Harbor, 1912-1926.

4436. "Extensive Work in Los Angeles Harbor Recommended: Chief Engineer Approves Plan to Construct Breakwater and Dredge Channel—Port District to Be Set Up." *Engineering News-Record* 93 (November 6, 1924): 740-1.

4437. Falick, Abraham J. "The Twin Ports: Los Angeles/Long Beach." Master's thesis, University of California, Los Angeles, 1967. 111 pp.

4438. "First Los Angeles Ship for Hawaii: Rapid Progress at Harbor—Transcontinental Lines Perfect Plans for Entering Heavy Import and Export Trade." *Southern California Business* 1 (April 1922): 22-3.

4439. Fitzgerald, Gerald C. "The Port of Los Angeles: An Account of Its Swift Rise to Third Place Among the Ports of the Nation." *Civil Engineering* 5 (September 1935): 519-23.

4440. Foster, Gerald I. "Tidewater Industrial Sites at Los Angeles-Long Beach Harbor, California." Master's thesis, University of California, Los Angeles, 1953. 103 pp.

4441. Friedman, Ben-Ami. "Functional Relationship Aspects of Branch Administrative Center Planning: A Case Study of the Los Angeles Harbor Area." Master's thesis, University of Southern California, 1965. 179 pp.

4442. Fries, Amos A. *Los Angeles Harbor.* Washington D. C., c1912. 35 pp.
Reprint from *Professional Memoirs, Corps of Engineers, U. S. Army and Engineer Department-at-Large.* (Washington, D. C., 1912).

4443. ——— "The Men Who Made the Harbor." *Southern California Business* 17 (June 1938): 8-9.
Los Angeles.

4444. ——— "San Pedro Harbor." *Out West* 27 (October 1907): 301-31.

4445. Gaffney, Marian A. "The International Commercial Position of the Port of Los Angeles." Master's thesis, Claremont Graduate School, 1939. 119 pp.

4446. "Getting into the Hawaiian Trade." *Southern California Business* 4 (October 1925): 8-9+.
Los Angeles-Hawaii trade.

4447. "Good News for the Harbor." *Los Angeles Saturday Night* 15 (May 25, 1935): 3.
Los Angeles designated as a permanent naval base.

4448. Gordon, C. M. "Fish Harbor Proves Profitable." *American City* 20 (February 1919): 144.
Los Angeles municipal project.

4449. Gorter, Wytze and Hildebrand, George H. *The Pacific Coast Maritime Shipping Industry, 1930-1948.* Berkeley, 1952-54. 2 vols.

4450. "The Greater Harbor Committee: How Organized—Methods of Work—Aims—Accomplishments." *Municipal League of Los Angeles Bulletin* 2 (May 1925): 5-8.
Includes "The Committee—An Introduction," by Burt A. Heinly, pp. 5-6; "The Harbor—It's Development," by Chas. Leeds, pp. 6-7; and "The Port Railroads," by F. B. Cole, pp. 7-8.

4451. Greenleaf, E. M. "Where Dry Land Becomes Sea; New Harbor for Los Angeles at Long Beach." *Overland Monthly,* new series, 55 (June 1910): 547-51.
An early account of the harbor development

and the important support of Long Beach in voting a harbor bond and in building the first municipal docks on the Pacific Coast.

4452. Grosswendt, Betty. "Ahoy, Police." *Westways* 51 (April 1959): 18-9.
Harbor police at Redondo Beach.

4453. Hager, Anna Marie. "A Salute to the Port of Los Angeles from Mud Flats to Modern Day Miracle." *California Historical Society Quarterly* 49 (1970): 329-35.

4454. Hammelton, Raynal L. "New Port Cities in Western America and Their Effect on Economic Development." Doctoral dissertation, University of Southern California, 1964. 350 pp.

4455. Hampton, Edgar L. "From Frog Pond to Second Port." *Southern California Business* 3 (October 1924): 46-7+.
Los Angeles Harbor.

4456. ———— "Why Is Los Angeles Harbor?" *Southern California Business* 3 (August 1924): 9+.

4457. "The Harbor Committee of One Hundred: Business Men Organize to Carry on Preliminary Survey on Which to Base Plans for Greatly Enlarged and Improved Port Facilities." *Southern California Business* 1 (October 1922): 19+.

4458. "Harbor Development at San Pedro, California." *Engineering Record* 67 (May 17, 1913): 549-50.

4459. Heaton, Reece. "Real Estate and Los Angeles Harbor." *Los Angeles Realtor* 5 (November 1925): 15-6.

4460. "Helping the City Build a Harbor." *Southern California Business* 4 (April 1925): 20-1+.
Trade Extension Department, Los Angeles Chamber of Commerce.

4461. "High Lights of the Harbor." *Saturday Night* 6 (January 16, 1926): 13.

4462. Holder, Charles F. "The San Pedro Breakwater." *Sunset* 13 (October 1904): 473-7.

4463. Howard, William S., Jr. "Long Beach-Los Angeles Harbor Breakwater." *Western Construction News and Highways Builder* 8 (May 10, 1933): 231-3.

4464. James, Cecil A. "Keeping Track of Ships in Port." *Southern California Business* 3 (March 1924): 13+.
Marine Exchange, Los Angeles Chamber of Commerce.

4465. Johnson, Colonel [sic]. "Harbor Improvements at Long Beach." *Pacific Municipalities* 40 (January 1926): 489-93.

4466. Karr, Albert. "The Port of Redondo Beach (1887-1926)." Master's thesis, University of Southern California, 1947. 76 pp.

4467. "Keeping Track of Ship Movements." *Southern California Business* 4 (October 1925): 24+.
Marine Exchange, Los Angeles Chamber of Commerce.

4468. Kerr, J. A. H. "A $99,000,000 Jump in Los Angeles Exports." *Southern California Business* 5 (July 1926): 18-9+.
1916 to 1926.

4469. Kohn, Walter. "Redondo Gets a Harbor." *Westways* 53 (October 1961): 16-7.

4470. Krauch, Robert A. "Ducks, Dredges and Developers." *Westways* 56 (January 1964): 10-3.
Playa del Rey.

4471. Krec, Ted. "The Longest Pier in the World." *Westways* 51 (March 1959): 32-3.
Long Beach Harbor.

4472. Kreider, Sam L. "International Trading Dawns on Horizon of Possibilities for Harbor at Los Angeles. *Los Angeles Saturday Night* 1 (December 25, 1920): section 2, page 5.

4473. Krenkel, John H. "The Development of the Port of Los Angeles." *Journal of Transport History* 7 (May 1965): 24-33.

4474. ———— "The History of the Port of Los Angeles." Master's thesis, Claremont Graduate School, 1935. 151 pp.

4475. ———— "The Port of Los Angeles as a Municipal Enterprise." *Pacific Historical Review* 16 (1947): 285-97.

4476. Lapham, Roger D. "What the Panama Canal Means to Southern California." *Southern California Business* 8 (May 1929): 18-9+.

4477. "League's Committee Report on Harbor Board Recommendations." *Municipal League of Los Angeles Bulletin* 4 (March 31, 1927): 6-7.

4478. Long Beach. Board of Harbor Commissioners. *The Port of Long Beach, California.* Long Beach, 1947. 16 pp.

4479. ———. Chamber of Commerce. *The Twin Harbors of Los Angeles and Long Beach.* Los Angeles, 1938. Unp.

4480. "Long Beach Breakwater, California." *Western Construction News* 2 (March 25, 1927): 40-1.

4481. "Long Beach Where Oil and Water Mix." *California Highways and Public Works* 45 (September-October 1966): 18-25.
States that "oil was the prime moving force which started the city on its way to prosperity, but its development of its waterfront . . . is the factor which is bringing it to the fore among the West Coast's great cities." Article also discusses tourism and recreation.

4482. Los Angeles. Board of Harbor Commissioners. *Los Angeles, the Great Seaport of the Southwest.* Los Angeles, c1920. 51 pp. 2nd ed., 1921. 62 pp. 3rd ed., 1923.

4483. ——— ——— *The Port of Los Angeles.* Los Angeles, 1917. 272 pp.

4484. ——— ——— *The Port of Los Angeles: Its History, Development, Tributary Territory, Present and Prospective Commerce.* [Los Angeles], 1913. 158 pp.

4485. ——— ——— Chamber of Commerce, Department of Foreign Commerce and Shipping. *The Story of Los Angeles Harbor; Its History, Development, and Growth of Its Commerce.* National Foreign Trade Week, May 19-25, 1935. Los Angeles, 1935. 22 pp.

4486. Los Angeles Chamber of Commerce. *The Port of Los Angeles: Its History, Development and Commerce.* Los Angeles, 1922. 95 pp.

4487. "L. A. Commerce This Year to Exceed That of Any Previous Year, Says Collector of Customs." *Los Angeles Saturday Night* 2 (June 25, 1921): 5.

4488. "Los Angeles Engineering Organization Designing U. S. Navy Fleet Facilities." *Western Construction News* 15 (October 1940): 356.
San Pedro navy facilities.

4489. "Los Angeles Harbor Development." *The Architect and Engineer* 206 (September 1956): 22-3.

4490. "L.A. Harbor Outstrips Nine Others." *Southern California Business* 3 (October 1924): 29.
Los Angeles Harbor shipping volume compared to that of other U.S. harbors.

4491. "Los Angeles Harbor Second in U.S.: Shipping Board Report Shows That in Inter-Coastal Tonnage This Port Runs Ahead of All Others in Country Except New York." *Southern California Business* 2 (April 1923): 9+.

4492. "Los Angeles Harbor Terminal." *Arts & Architecture* 80 (August 1963): 26-7.

4493. "Los Angeles Port Leads on Coast." *Southern California Business* 3 (April 1924): 13.
"The Port of Los Angeles during 1923 ran ahead of San Francisco and Seattle combined in the receipt of westbound intercoastal cargoes of general merchandise of the U.S."

4494. Lowe, Horace A. "An Economic Survey of the Port of Long Beach, California [1945-1949]." Master's thesis, University of Southern California, 1949. 96 pp.

4495. Ludwig, Ella A. *History of the Harbor District of Los Angeles: Containing also Personal Sketches of Many Men and Women.* [Los Angeles, 1928]. 938 pp.

4496. "Lumber for Two Blocks an Hour: Los Angeles Harbor Is the Greatest Import Point for Lumber, with Shipments Increasing at Tremendous Rate." *Southern California Business* 2 (August 1923): 22.

4497. Lynch, Samuel D. "Fabulous Salt Water Tour." *Westways* 46 (February 1954): 18-9.
Long Beach Harbor.

4498. Mapplebeck, John. "Now—4th Coffee Port:

Growing Trade with Latin America and Hawaii Has Made Us an International Market." *Southern California Business* 11 (March 1932) : 22.

4499. Matson, Clarence H. "The Answer Lies Over the Ocean." *Southern California Business* 11 (February 1932) : 8-9.
"Question: Why Build a World City in the Desert?—Answer: Because Los Angeles Grows with the Orient."

4500. ——— "The Beginnings of a Great Harbor." *Southern California Business* 8 (October 1929) : 18+.
Los Angeles Harbor from 1909.

4501. ——— *Building a World Gateway: The Story of Los Angeles Harbor.* Los Angeles, 1945. 255 pp.

4502. ——— "The Busy Harbor of a Metropolis: Through Young in Years, the Port of Los Angeles Is Known Throughout the World as One of Rapid Development." *Southern California Business* 1 (September 1922) : 29+.

4503. ——— "Harbor Business Is Up-and-Up." *Southern California Business* 13 (May 1934) : 7.
Los Angeles.

4504. ——— "Harbor Trade Shows Real Recovery." *Southern California Business* 14 (May 1935) : 10-1.
Los Angeles.

4505. ——— "Imports Certainly Make Jobs: More Work and Wages Arrive on Every Ship Entering the Harbor from Other Lands." *Southern California Business* 16 (May 1937) : 8-9.
Los Angeles.

4506. ——— "Los Angeles Harbor—A World Port of Call." *Los Angeles Realtor* 5 (November 1925) : 11-2+.

4507. ——— "Los Angeles Ships Around the World." *Southern California Business* 3 (June 1924) : 7-8.
Los Angeles Harbor.

4508. ——— "Speaking of International Trade *Southern California Business* 4 (December 1925) : 7-8+.
Los Angeles exports and imports.

4509. ——— "We Harbor Many More Cargoes of Merchandise: Our Healthy Growth in Manufactured Exports Is Making Up for Shrinkage in Heavy Materials." *Southern California Business* 12 (October 1933) : 8-9.
Los Angeles.

4510. ——— "What Rubber Means to the Harbor." *Southern California Business* 16 (September 1937) : 22-30.
Los Angeles.

4511. ——— "Which Is the Leading Pacific Port?" *Southern California Business* 7 (February 1928) : 14-5+.
Argues case for Los Angeles.

4512. McFee, Maynard. "Growth of Los Angeles Harbor." *The Argonaut* 96 (December 13, 1924) : 7.

4513. ——— "Pinning Faith to a Growing Harbor." *Southern California Business* 3 (February 1924) : 7-8+.
Los Angeles Harbor commerce.

4514. ——— "30 Years of Harbor Building." *Southern California Business* 5 (July 1926) : 40-2+.
Los Angeles.

4515. McGlone, R. G. "The Port of Long Beach." *Pacific Municipalities* 44 (June 1930) : 198-201.
4516. ———, and Cram, C. M. "Long Beach Improves Ocean Front." *Western Construction News* 5 (February 10, 1930) : 73-4.

4517. McGovern, Elsie. "The Growth of Los Angeles and the Long Beach Harbors and the Unification Project [1771-1930]." Master's thesis, University of Southern California, 1930. 64 pp.

4518. McGroarty, John S., and Schallert, Edwin. *Los Angeles—A Maritime City.* Los Angeles, 1912. 20 pp.
Maritime and railway futures.

4519. Measday, Walter. "Los Angeles a World Port." *California Journal of Development* 25 (May 1935) : 14+.

4520. Miller, H. S. "The Defense of Our Coast." *Southern California Business* 14 (February 1925) : 10-1.
Fort MacArthur defends Los Angeles-Long Beach Harbor.

4521. Miller, Willis H. "The Port of Los Angeles." Master's thesis, The University of Chicago, 1931. 237 pp.

4522. —— "Ports and Harbors," in *Los Angeles: Preface to a Master Plan*. Ed. by George W. Robbins and L. Deming Tilton. Los Angeles, 1941. Pp. 145-58.

4523. Mills, Eugene A. "New Business Through the Harbor." *Southern California Business* 12 (April 1933) : 12-3.
Los Angeles.

4524. "Mole Calms Navy Base Tides." *Western Construction News* 20 (October 1945) : 91-4.
Terminal Island breakwater.

4525. Moran, Edward J. "The Army in Southern California." *Southern California Business* 14 (February 1935) : 8-9.
Includes harbor defenses of Los Angeles.

4526. Morgan, Octavius. "California Architects and Engineers Inspect Government Works." *The Architect and Engineer of California* 8 (April 1907) : 43-5.
Inspection and proposed improvements to San Pedro and Wilmington harbors.

4527. Moss, Marvin A. "Long Beach Naval Shipyard." *California Engineer* 30 (April 1952) : 7+.

4528. "New Harbor Terminal at Los Angeles to Be Built at Cost of $6,000,000." *Western Construction News* 24 (November 15, 1949) : 89+.

4529. "A New Use for Vitrified Clay Pipe." *The Architect and Engineer of California* 30 (September 1912) : 85-6.
Construction of new wharfs at Terminal Island.

4530. Nicholson, G[eorge] F. "Los Angeles Harbor Construction for 1932." *Western Construction News* 7 (January 10, 1932) : 23-4.

4531. —— "Non-Military Harbor Projects in California: Los Angeles Harbor Department." *Western Construction News and Highways Builder* 8 (January 25, 1933) : 39-40.
Major construction projects for 1933.

4532. —— "West Basin Terminal, Los Angeles Harbor." *Western Construction News* 7 (February 10, 1932) : 85-6.

4533. Overton, Eugene. "World Trade Grows on Good Figures: How the Marine Exchange Keeps Track of Harbor Business, and How to Use Its Data." *Southern California Business* 11 (July 1932) : 16-7.

4534. Research Department, The First National Bank of Los Angeles, Los Angeles Trust & Savings Bank, First Securities Company, in Cooperation with The College of Commerce and Business Administration, University of Southern California. *Commerce Through Los Angeles Harbor: An Economic Survey of a Dominating Factor in the Economic Life of the Pacific Southwest*. Los Angeles, [1922?]. 62 pp.

4535. Riddiford, Henry. "Los Angeles, The Country's Greatest Lumber Port." *Southern California Business* 1 (September 1922) : 114+.

4536. Roberts, Sam[uel] M. "Water Injection System in Long Beach Harbor Has—Subsidence Halted." *Western City* 35 (June 1959) : 26-7.

4537. Robinson, Henry M. "What of Your Harbor?" *Southern California Business* 1 (February 1922) : 7+.
Los Angeles.

4538. San Pedro. Board of Trade. *San Pedro; The Harbor City*. [Los Angeles, 1903]. 16 pp.

4539. Sandeman, Frank S. "Harbor Fire in Ford Plant Tests Value of Long Beach Fireboat 'Fleet.'" *Western City* 32 (March 1956) : 42-5.

4540. Scott, Kyle, and Olmsted, Connie. "The Changing Coastline: Boats at the Back Door." *Los Angeles* 3 (March 1962) : 18-28.
Small boat harbors from Playa del Rey to Orange County.

4541. "Seaport of Los Angeles." *Bulletin of the Pan American Union* 37 (September 13, 1913) : 379-82.

4542. Shoemaker, R. R. "Impressive Construction Program at Port of Long Beach, Calif." *American City* 60 (April 1945) : 97.

4543. —— "Long Beach Plans Super Harbor: Land-Filled Piers Aided Development of Long Beach, Thus Enabling Community to Create a Great Commercial and Naval Harbor." *Western Construction News* 21 (January 1946) : 97-8.

4544. —— "Steel Sheetpile Cells Form Bulkhead for Long Beach Harbor Expansion." *Civil Engineering* 20 (September 1950): 26-9+.

4545. "Small-Craft Harbor Built with Public-Private Funds." *Western Construction* 37 (January 1962): 76.
 Marina del Rey.

4546. Smith, Jack. "A Day in the City: Captains Contagious." *Westways* 61 (October 1969): 11-3+. 47.
 Marina del Rey.

4547. Stanley, Gene. "The Island That Moved to Let the Ships Go By." *Westways* 28 (July 1936): 18-9.
 Deadman's Island, "a barren rocky peak that stood like a sentinel in the middle of old San Pedro Bay," and was removed in 1927.

4548. Stephens, Jess E. "San Pedro Harbor. A California Commercial Wonder and What the Experts Say About It—." *Out West*, new series, 4 (July 1912): 27-32.

4549. Stewart, L. H. "Discrimination Against Los Angeles in Harbor Rates." *Municipal League of Los Angeles Bulletin* 5 (December 28, 1927): 1-2.

4550. Stump, Frank V. "The Way Wilmington Stepped Out." *Southern California Business* 3 (March 1924): 10-2+.
 Growth of harbor and industry.

4551. Sutor, W. F. "Ahoy—The Shore!" *Southern California Business* 11 (February 1932): 20.
 Adaption of air-conveyor apparatus to unloading copra by Sutor & Co., Los Angeles.

4552. "Taking the Lead in Intercoastal Trade." *Southern California Business* 5 (February 1926): 30+.
 Los Angeles.

4553. Thompson, Jean H. "Relation of Foreign Trade to Southern California." *Southern California Business* 8 (May 1929): 24+.
 Los Angeles Harbor.

4554. Warden, William R. "The History and Development of the Artificial Harbor of Los Angeles." Master's thesis, University of Southern California, 1957. 121 pp.

4555. Weinstein, Robert A. "The Million Dollar Mud Flat." *American West* 6 (January 1969): 33-43.
 Primarily a pictorial record of San Pedro Bay and its conversion into the port of Los Angeles.

4556. Willard, C[harles] D. "The Inner Harbor at San Pedro." *Land of Sunshine* 14 (January 1901): 69-76.

4557. Wilson, Edgar F. "Opportunity May Come Aboard Ship." *Southern California Business* 12 (July 1933): 16.
 Unusual exports and imports at Los Angeles Harbor.

4558. Wilson, William G. "Stepping Up in Foreign Trade." *Southern California Business* 4 (August 1925): 9-10+.
 Los Angeles Harbor.

4559. Workman, Boyle. "Municipal Harbors." *Pacific Municipalities* 37 (October 1923): 373-4+.
 Los Angeles Harbor.

HISTORICAL LANDMARKS

4560. Abeloe, William N., ed. *Historic Spots in California*. 3rd rev. ed., Stanford, 1966. 642 pp.
 Valuable for researchers as well as general readers. Counties arranged alphabetically with bibiography for each.

4561. Berger, John A. *The Franciscan Missions of California*. New York, 1941. 392 pp.
 San Fernando and San Gabriel missions included.

4562. "Bring Back Our Yesterdays." *Southern California Business* 8 (August 1929): 16-7+.
 Christine Sterling and plan to preserve Olvera Street.

4563. Brown, Forman G. *Olvera Street and the Avila Adobe*. Los Angeles, 1930. 20 pp. 2nd ed., 1932. 20 pp.

4564. California Division of Beaches and Parks. *California Historical Landmarks*. Sacramento, 1936. 111 pp.

4565. Cleland, Robert G. *El Molino Viejo.* [Los Angeles], 1950. 57 pp.

Last ten pages are on Henry Huntington's purchase (1903) of the San Marino tract where old mill stands and subsequent developments.

4566. Collins, James H. "A One-Woman Revolution." *Southern California Business* 9 (June 1930): 14-5.

Christine Sterling and preservation of Olvera Street.

4567. Crowder, Farnsworth. "El Alisal." *Westways* 39 (December 1947): 2-4.

Charles F. Lummis Memorial Home.

4568. Donovan, Richard. "Los Angeles . . . the Old Plaza." *Reporter* 2 (December 20, 1949): 13-5.

4569. "Exploring Walk in Old Los Angeles." *Sunset* 142 (1969): 40-2.

4570. [Forbes, Harrie Rebecca Piper (Smith)]. *Battalla de la Mesa; "The Battle of the Mesa" 1847-1926.* [Los Angeles, 1926]. 22 pp.

4571. ———, comp. *Then and Now, 100 Landmarks within 50 Miles of Los Angeles Civic Center.* Los Angeles, 1939. 64 pp.

4572. Ford, John Anson. "Unity of Purpose Becomes Unity of Action in Unique Pioneer Memorial Project." *American City* 69 (February 1954): 122-3.

Fort Moore Pioneer Memorial.

4573. Fraser, Emil. "El Molino Aviejo [sic]." *Saturday Night* 7 (August 13, 1927): 2.

Plan of Mrs. James Brehm (formerly Mrs. Howard Huntington) to restore Old Mill in San Marino.

4574. Giffen, Helen S. *Casas & Courtyards; Historic Adobe Houses of California.* Oakland, 1955. 153 pp.

4575. Gordon, Dudley C. "El Alisal: The House That Lummis Built." *Historical Society of Southern California Quarterly* 35 (1953): 19-28.

4576. ——— *El Alisal: The Lummis Home; Its History and Architecture, California State Monument No. 531.* [Los Angeles, 1964]. 11 pp.

Lummis Memorial Home and Charles Fletcher Lummis, 1859-1928.

4577. Gorham, Jessie C. "Time Out for Olvera Street." *Los Angeles Saturday Night* 14 (December 23, 1933): 7.

Impressionistic description.

4578. Harris, L. Mildred. "History and a Hill; Los Angeles Loses a Landmark." *Historical Society of Southern California Quarterly* 32 (1950): 133-8.

Fort Moore Hill, cut away when North Broadway tunnel removed.

4579. Hastings, Don. "Casa de Los Cerritos — Bridge to the Past." *Westways* 48 (May 1956): 28-9.

4580. "How Can the Historic Leonis Adobe Be Best Restored as a Useful Public Facility?" *Community Review* 7 (October, 1963): 11-5.

San Fernando Valley Parks Institute.

4581. Hylen, Arnold. *The Vanishing Face of Los Angeles.* Los Angeles, 1968. Unp.

4582. James, George W. *In and Out of the Old Missions of California: An Historical and Pictorial Account of the Franciscan Missions.* Boston, 1905. 392 pp.

San Fernando and San Gabriel missions included.

4583. King, Elmer R., comp. *Handbook of Historical Landmarks of California.* [Los Angeles, c1938]. 150 pp.

4584. Los Angeles County. Superintendent of Schools. *Historic Landmarks in Los Angeles County, a Descriptive Guide for Teachers.* Prepared by Marie B. Dickinson. *Social Studies Curriculum Monograph No. 5.* Rev. ed., Los Angeles, 1956. 97 pp.

4585. McLean, Mildred. "San Gabriel Mission and the Mission Play," in *The Old Spanish Missions of California.* By Anne J. Nolan. Chicago, [n.d.]. Pp. 75-88.

4586. Morrow, Irving F. "The Restoration of the California Missions." *The Architect and Engineer* 60 (January 1920): 43-55.

Includes Mission San Fernando.

4587. Parks, Marion. *Doors to Yesterday; A Guide to Old Los Angeles . . .* Los Angeles, c1932. 16 pp.

4588. —— "In Pursuit of Vanished Days; Visits to the Extant Historic Adobe Houses of Los Angeles County." *Annual Publication Historical Society of Southern California* 14, Part 1 (1928): 7-[63]; 14, Part 2 (1929): 135-207.

4589. Piper, Natt. "El Paseo de Los Angeles." *The Architect and Engineer* 107 (December 1931): 33-6.
Olvera Street.

4590. *Registered Historical Landmarks, County of Los Angeles.* [Los Angeles, 1958]. [36] pp.

4591. Rolle, Andrew F. "New Flag Over Fort Moore." *Westways* 48 (September 1956): 4-5.
Design and construction of Fort Moore Memorial; recap of Mexican War in Los Angeles.

4592. Sherlock, Robert E. "Death of a Landmark." *Westways* 51 (August 1959): 28-9.
Destruction by fire of Alpine Tavern on Mt. Lowe.

4593. Shulman, Julius. *Los Angeles Historic-Cultural Landmarks.* Los Angeles, 1968. Unp.
Pictorial.

4594. Siple, Molly. "Landmarks: Is This the Best We Can Come Up With?" *Los Angeles* 12 (August 1967): 30-1.
Author asserts that Los Angeles' forty Landmarks (pictured) designated by the Cultural Heritage Board "seem somehow colorless," and suggests that the board pick more interesting ones.

4595. Smith, Jack. "A Day in the City: The Acropolis in Highland Park." *Westways* 60 (April 1968): 5-7.
El Alisal, the Southwest Museum, and the Casa de Adobe.

4596. Sterling, Christine. *Olvera Street, Its History and Restoration.* Los Angeles, 1933. 26 pp. 2nd ed., 1947. 23 pp.

4597. Sugranes, Eugene J. *The Old San Gabriel Mission; Historical Notes Taken from Old Manuscripts and Records.* San Gabriel, 1909. 104 pp.

4598. Taylor, Katherine A. "She Made a Back Alley Clean House." *American Magazine* 111 (February 1931): 84.
Christine Sterling's successful campaign to clean up and restore Olvera Street.

HISTORY

HISTORY—STATE

4599. Ainsworth, Ed[ward M.]. *California Jubilee; Nuggets from Many Hidden Veins.* Culver City, 1948. 272 pp.

4600. Bean, Walton. *California: An Interpretive History.* New York, 1968. 576 pp.

4601. Caughey, John W. *California; A Remarkable State's Life History.* Englewood Cliffs, N.J., 1970 674 pp.
Supersedes the two previous editions of the author's *California,* published in 1940 and 1953.

4602. Cleland, Robert G. *California in Our Time (1900-1940).* New York, 1947. 320 pp.

4603. —— *From Wilderness to Empire.* Ed. by Glenn S. Dumke. New York, 1962. 445 pp.
A one-volume revision of Cleland's *From Wilderness to Empire. A History of California, 1542-1900,* and *California in Our Time.* Dumke has added several chapters of his own updating the material. About twenty-five pages on Los Angeles in the twentieth century.

4604. Coy, Owen C. *California County Boundaries, a Study of the Division of the State into Counties and Subsequent Changes in Their Boundaries.* Sacramento, 1923. 335 pp.
Los Angeles County, pp. 140-56.

4605. Hartman, David N. *California and Man.* Dubuque, Iowa, 1964. 478 pp.
Numerous references to the Los Angeles area.

4606. Hunt, Rockwell D. "Fifteen Decisive Events of California History." *Historical Society of Southern California Quarterly* 50 (1958): 353-72.
Published in four parts; the last section cited here, deals with the twentieth century. Reprinted as a book, same title.

4607. Los Angeles City School District. Curriculum Division. *California Yesterday, Today, and Tomorrow.* School publication No. 468.

For use in the observance of the California centennial years 1948, 1949 and 1950. Los Angeles, 1949. 233 pp.

4608. McDow, Roberta M. "State Separation Schemes, 1907-1921." *California Historical Society Quarterly* 49 (1970): 39-46.

4609. McWilliams, Carey. *California: The Great Exception.* New York, 1949. 377 pp.

4610. Nadeau, Remi. *California: The New Society.* New York, 1963. 303 pp.

4611. Robinson, William W. *Land in California: The Story of Mission Lands, Ranchos, Squatters, Mining Claims, Railroad Grants, Land Scrip, [and] Homesteads.* Berkeley, 1948. 291 pp.

Covers period 1769-1948.

4612. Rolle, Andrew F. *California: A History.* New York, 1963. 649 pp. 2nd ed., 1969. 739 pp.

4613. Roshe, Ralph J. *Everyman's Eden. A History of California.* New York, 1968. 624 pp.

4614. Rush, Philip S. *A History of the Californians.* 2nd ed., San Diego, 1964. 277 pp.

HISTORY—REGIONAL

4615. Ainsworth, Ed[ward M.]. *California.* Los Angeles, 1951. 272 pp.

Historical sketches and anecdotes of Southern California by a long-time member of the Los Angeles *Times* editorial staff.

4616. Brackett, Frank P. *Brief Early History of the San Jose Rancho and Its Subsequent Cities, Pomona, San Dimas, Claremont, La Verne and Spadra.* Los Angeles, 1920. 203 pp.

4617. Brilliant, Ashleigh E. "Social Effects of the Automobile in Southern California During the Nineteen-Twenties." Doctoral dissertation. University of California, Berkeley, 1964. 325 pp.

4618. Cameron, Una. "The History of San Gabriel Valley." Master's thesis, University of Southern California, 1938. 130 pp.

4619. Carew, Harold D. *History of Pasadena and the San Gabriel Valley, California.* Chicago, 1930. 3 vols.

4620. Conner, Palmer. *The Romance of the Ranchos.* Los Angeles, 1941. 44 pp.

4621. Daniell, John B. *The Bay Area Pageant; The Story of the Santa Monica Bay Area, 1542-1957.* [Santa Monica, 1957]. 23 pp.

Reprinted from the Santa Monica *Evening Outlook.*

4622. [Daughters of the American Revolution, San Fernando Valley Chapter]. *The Valley of San Fernando.* [N.p., c1924]. 120 pp.

4623. Faulkner, Frederick. *San Fernando Valley and Its Thriving Communities in a Thumbnail Setting of History.* North Hollywood, 1951. 24 pp.

4624. Guinn, James M. *Historical and Biographical Record of Los Angeles and Vicinity, Containing a History of the City from Its Earliest Settlement as a Spanish Pueblo to the Closing Year of the 19th Century. Also Containing Biographies of Well-Known Citizens of the Past and Present.* Chicago, 1901. 940 pp.

Important for biographies at the turn-of-the century.

4625. ———— *Historical and Biographical Record of Southern California . . .* Los Angeles, 1902. 1019 pp.

4626. ———— *A History of California and an Extended History of Its Southern Coast Counties.* Los Angeles, 1907. 2 vols.

4627. ———— *A History of California and an Extended History of Los Angeles and Environs.* Los Angeles, 1915. 3 vols.

4628. ———— *Southern California, Its History and Its People.* Los Angeles, [c1907]. 2 vols.

Differs from 1902 edition entitled *Historical and Biographical Record of Southern California . . .*

4629. Harmon, Wendell E. "The Bootlegger Era in Southern California." *Historical Society of Southern California Quarterly* 37 (1955): 335-46.

4630. Hatch, Mabel, *et al. The Green Verdugo Hills: A Chronicle of Sunland-Tujunga . . . and How It Grew.* [Tujunga, 19--?]. [24] pp.

4631. Hayden, Dorothea (Hoaglin). *These Pioneers.* Los Angeles, 1938. 287 pp.
Pasadena and Altadena, 1870-1938.

4632. Ingersoll, Luther A. *Ingersoll's Century History, Santa Monica Bay Cities . . . with . . . a Condensed History of Los Angeles County, 1542-1908 . . .* Los Angeles, 1908. 512 pp.

4633. Keffer, Frank M. *History of San Fernando Valley. In Two Parts, Narrative and Biographical.* Glendale, 1934. 329 pp.

4634. Los Angeles County Employee's Association. *Historical Synopsis of Los Angeles County.* [Los Angeles], 1922. 54 pp.

4635. McGroarty, John Steven. *California of the South: A History.* Chicago, 1933. 4 vols.
Vol. I is a history of Los Angeles and vicinity; vols. II-IV consist of biographical sketches.

4636. ——— *History of Los Angeles County; With Selected Biography of Actors and Witnesses in the Period of the County's Greatest Growth and Achievement.* Chicago, 1923. 3 vols.
Vol. I is historical; vols. II-III are biographical.

4637. ——— *Los Angeles from the Mountains to the Sea.* Chicago and New York, 1921. 3 vols.
Vol. I is historical; vols. II and III are biographical.

4638. ——— *Southern California.* San Diego, 1914. 263 pp.
Includes historical sketch of Los Angeles County.

4639. ——— *The Valley of Our Lady; The Romantic History of Los Angeles and the San Gabriel Valley.* [N.p., 1909]. 14 pp. Reprinted from *West Coast Magazine* 6 (July 1909): 3-21.

4640. McWilliams, Carey. *Southern California Country: An Island on the Land.* New York, 1946. 387 pp.

4641. Northrup, William M., ed. *Alhambra (San Gabriel-Monterey Park) Community Book . . . In Two Parts, Narrative and Biographical.* Alhambra, 1944. 249 pp. 2nd ed., 1949. 179 pp.

4642. Oberbeck, Grace J. *History of La Cresenta-La Canada Valleys.* Montrose, 1938. 93 pp.

4643. O'Dell, Scott. *Country of the Sun. Southern California, An Informal History and Guide.* Cornwall, N. Y., 1957. 310 pp.

4644. Preston, Richard E. "The Changing Landscape of the San Fernando Valley Between 1930 and 1964." *California Geographer* 6 (1965): 59-72.

4645. Robinson, William W. *Culver City, California: A Calendar of Events in Which Is Included, also, the Story of Palms and Playa del Rey Together with Rancho de los Bueyes.* Los Angeles, 1939. 28 pp. 2nd ed., 1942. 28 pp.

4646. ——— "The Rancho Story of the San Fernando Valley." *Historical Society of Southern California Quarterly* 38 (1956): 225-39.
Covers period 1834-1910.

4647. ——— *Ranchos Become Cities.* Pasadena, 1939. 243 pp.
"The story of how San Pedro-Wilmington, Glendale, Long Beach, Whittier, the San Fernando Valley, Culver City, Inglewood, Santa Monica, Beverly Hills, Pasadena, Monrovia, and Pomona developed from ranchos to modern cities."

4648. ——— *The Spanish and Mexican Ranchos of San Fernando Valley.* Southwest Museum Museum *Leaflet No. 31.* Los Angeles, 1966. 14 pp.

4649. ——— *The Story of San Fernando Valley.* Los Angeles, 1961. 63 pp.

4650. ——— *The Story of Your Land.* Los Angeles, 1938. [13] pp.
History of land in Los Angeles County.

4651. ———, ed. *Zamorano Choice, Selections from the Zamorano Club's Hoja Volante 1934-1966.* Los Angeles, 1966. 128 pp.
Contains a number of biographical and historical sketches pertinent to the Los Angeles area.

4652. ———, and Powell, Lawrence C. *The Malibu: Ranch Topanga Malibu Sequit, An Historical Approach.* Los Angeles, 1958. 86 pp. Reprinted ed., 1970.

4653. San Fernando Valley Federal Savings and Loan Association. *Pioneer.* Los Angeles, 1961. 10 pp.

San Fernando Valley.

4654. Scheerer, Lorietta L. "History of the Sausal Redondo Rancho [1837-1936]." Master's thesis, University of Southern California, 1938. 69 pp.

4655. Security Trust and Savings Bank. Lankershim Branch. Publicity Department. *A Daughter of the Snows. The Story of the Great San Fernando Valley.* [Los Angeles], c1923. 56 pp.

4656. Shrode, Ida M. "The Sequent Occupance of the Rancho Azusa de Duarte, a Segment of the Upper San Gabriel Valley of California [1771-1948]." Master's thesis, University of Chicago, 1948. 165 pp.

4657. Simons, Patricia C. "A History of the Cucamonga Rancho [1839-1945]." Master's thesis, University of Southern California, 1946. 74 pp.

4658. "Southern California: The Story of Its Development, Resources, and Progress." *Harper's Weekly* 48 (April 2, 1904): 504-19.

4659. Spalding, William A., ed. *Historical Record and Souvenir.* Los Angeles, 1923. 283 pp.

Los Angeles County.

4660. ———, comp. *History and Reminiscences. Los Angeles City and County, California.* Los Angeles, [1931]. 3 vols. Vols. 2-3 have title: *History of Los Angeles City and County . . . Biographical.*

4661. Starr, Richard. "History of Antelope Valley, California from 1542-1920." Master's thesis, University of Southern California, 1938. 135 pp.

4662. *The Upper San Gabriel Valley in the War [1914-1918]: Azusa, Baldwin Park, Charter Oak, Covina, Glendora, Puente.* [Covina, 1919]. Unp.

4663. Van Nuys, J. Benton. "My Memories of San Fernando Valley." *Historical Society of Southern California Quarterly* 38 (1956): 235-8.

4664. Vernon, Charles C. "A History of the San Gabriel Mountains." *Historical Society of Southern California Quarterly* 38 (1956): 39-60, 141-66, 263-88, 373-84.

4665. Walker, Franklin. *A Literary History of Southern California.* Berkeley and Los Angeles, 1950. 282 pp.

HISTORY—LOCAL

4666. Adler, Pat[ricia]. *The Bunker Hill Story.* Glendale, 1963. 36 pp.

"Rise and decline of a neighborhood in central Los Angeles and its redevelopment."

4667. ——— *A History of the Venice Area: A Part of the Venice Community Plan Study.* Los Angeles, 1969. [24] pp.

4668. Ainsworth, Ed[ward M.]. *Enchanted Pueblo.* Los Angeles, 1959. 48 pp.

Story of the development of a modern metropolis around the Plaza de Los Angeles.

4669. Arnold, Benjamin F., and Clark, Artilissa D. *History of Whittier.* Whittier, 1933. 393 pp.

4670. Arnold, Frank R. *Getting to Know Your Claremont.* N.p., 1936. 19 pp.

4671. Azusa Foot-Hills Citrus Co. *Azusa Old and New; Being a True Recital of the Founding and Development of a California Community.* Azusa, 1921. 28 pp.

4672. Baker, E. N., comp. *Pasadena and Environs.* Pasadena, [19———?]. [129 pp.].

4673. Baldwin, Anita M. *Santa Anita Rancho, Los Angeles County, California.* [N.p., 1918?]. 23 pp.

4674. Barratt, Harry. "This Is Hollywood." *Los Angeles Realtor* 6 (November 1926): 15-6.

4675. Belford, Herbert E., and Montgomery, C.P. "Cahuenga Pass: Phenomenal Changes Since Days of Mission Padres." *California Highways and Public Works* 28 (March-April 1949): 20-4.

4676. Benedict, Pierce E., ed. *History of Beverly Hills . . . In Two Parts, Narrative and Biographical.* Beverly Hills, 1934. 235 pp.

4677. Benton, Elizabeth. "When Redondo Was Young and Gay." *Westways* 39 (May 1947): 18-9.

4678. Beverly Hills. City Council. *1952-1958: Five*

Years of Municipal Progress in Beverly Hills. Beverly Hills, [1958]. 16 pp.

4679. Blair, William L., ed. *Pasadena Community Book; In Two Parts, Narrative and Biographical.* Pasadena, [c1943]. 789 pp. 1947 ed., 476 pp.

Subsequent editions are cited under the name of Clarence F. Shoop.

4680. Blow, Ben. "San Fernando Pass, Historic and Forgotten." *California Highways and Public Works* 7 (July-August 1929): 11-2.

4681. Bowen, Edith B., comp. *Annals of Early Sierra Madre.* Sierra Madre, 1950. 206 pp.

4682. "Bowron's Boom Town." *Time* 52 (October 11, 1948): 27-8.

Los Angeles during Fletcher Bowron's first decade as mayor.

4683. Brode, Alverda J. "History of the University Section, Los Angeles." *Annual Publication* Historical Society of Southern California 12 (1922): 72-109.

Based on the author's master's thesis, University of Southern California, 1922. 67 pp. Same title.

4684. Cameron, Marguerite. *El Pueblo; A General History of One of America's Largest Cities.* Los Angeles and New York, 1936. 153 pp.

4685. Carpenter, Bruce R. "Rancho Encino: Its Historical Geography." Master's thesis, University of California, Los Angeles. 133 pp.

4686. Carter, Emily B., comp. *Hollywood, the Story of the Cahuengas . . .* Hollywood, 1926. 86 pp.

4687. Case, Walter H., ed. *History of Long Beach and Vicinity . . . In Which Is Incorporated the Early History Written by the Late Jane Elizabeth Harnett.* Chicago, 1927. 2 vols.

4688. ———, ed. *History of Long Beach . . . In Two Parts, Narrative and Biographical.* Long Beach, 1935. 336 pp. 2nd ed., 1942. 434 pp. 3rd ed., 1948. 431 pp.

4689. *Catalina's Yesterdays.* Los Angeles, c1926. 21 pp.

4690. Chamberlain, James F. "Los Angeles From Pueblo to Metropolis." *Overland Monthly* 89 (August-September 1931): 5-6+.

4691. Chapin, Lon F. *Thirty Years in Pasadena.* Los Angeles, 1929. 323 pp.

4692. Citizens National Bank of Claremont. *Claremont . . . Then and Now.* Claremont, c1954. Unp.

4693. Clifton, A. R. "History of the Communistic Colony Llano del Rio." *Annual Publication* Historical Society Southern California 11, Pt. 1 (1918): 80-90.

4694. Coffin, George H. "From Pasture to Metropolis." *Los Angeles Realtor* 4 (October 1925): 15. Hollywood.

4695. Colver, Seth I., ed. *The Historical Volume and Reference Works, Covering Arcadia, Azusa, Baldwin Park, Bradbury, Charter Oak, Claremont, Covina, Duarte, El Monte, Glendora, Irwindale, La Verne, Monrovia, Pomona, San Dimas, South El Monte, West Covina.* Arlington, 1964. 962 pp.

4696. Cowan, Robert C. *A Backward Glance: Los Angeles, 1901-1915.* Los Angeles, 1969. 50 pp.
Pictorial.

4697. Cowick, Kate L. *The Outlook's Story of Santa Monica.* [Santa Monica, 1932]. 40 pp.

4698. Crocker, Donald W. *Within the Vale of Annandale: A Picture History of South Western Pasadena and Vicinity.* Pasadena, 1968. 72 pp.
Pictorial.

4699. Crouch, Charles W. "Capri with a Coney Touch." *Westways* 27 (January 1935): 16-7+.
History and description of Catalina Island.

4700. Davis, Charles F., ed. *History of Monrovia and Duarte.* Monrovia, 1938. 229 pp.

4701. ———, ed. *The Monrovia Blue Book, a Historical and Biographical Record of Monrovia and Duarte.* Monrovia, 1943. 147 pp.

Based in part upon the author's *History of Monrovia and Duarte,* published in 1938.

4702. ———, ed. *Monrovia - Duarte Community Book.* Monrovia, 1957. 384 pp.

4703. Doran, Adelaide L. *The Ranch That Was*

Robbins'; Santa Catalina Island, Calif. Glendale, [c1963]. 211 pp.

4704. Dorland, Allan H. "A History of San Marino, California [1764-1933]." Master's thesis, University of Southern California, 1947. 159 pp.

4705. Driscoll, Roy L., ed. *Pomona Valley Community Book.* Pomona, 1950. 445 pp.

4706. Duarte Chamber of Commerce. *Andreas Duarte and the Community That Bears His Name, 1841-1941.* [Duarte, 1914?]. 12 pp.

4707. Eagle Rock Chamber of Commerce. *Eagle Rock, California.* [N.p., 1935?]. [41] pp.
   Includes a history of Eagle Rock by Mrs. C. W. Young.

4708. Eberly, Gordon S. *Arcadia: City of the Santa Anita.* Claremont, 1953. 239 pp.

4709. Eggert, Jerry, ed. *Proclamacion de la Natividad, el Pueblo de Nuestra Senora la Reina de Los Angeles de California, 1781-1956 . . . Historical Sketch [of Los Angeles].* Los Angeles, c1956. Unp.

4710. El Monte Lodge No. 424, Independent Order of Odd Fellows. *A History of El Monte, "The End of the Santa Fe Trail."* [El Monte], 1923. 88 pp.

4711. "El Segundo Has Its 30th Birthday." *Petroleum World* 38 (September 1941): 30-1.

4712. *El Segundo "The Standard Oil Pay Roll City."* [N.p., 1914]. 16 pp.

4713. Epley, Malcolm. *Highlights [and] Anecdotes; Long Beach's 75 Years.* Ed. by Bill Boyd. [Long Beach, c1963]. 96 pp.
   Pictorial history.

4714. Fogelson, Robert M. *The Fragmented Metropolis: Los Angeles, 1850-1930.* Cambridge, Mass., 1967. 362 pp.

4715. Forbes, James B. *The Story of Michillinda, A City Suburban.* Los Angeles, [1912]. 36 pp.

4716. French, Virginia F. *Rancho La Cienega o Paso de la Tijera.* Los Angeles, 1970. 132 pp.
   Crenshaw district in Los Angeles from early days to the present.

4717. *From Pueblo to City: Eighteen Hundred and*

Forty Nine [to] Nineteen Hundred and Ten. Los Angeles, [1910?]. 79 pp.
   Essays by Ben C. Truman, Harry Carr and others.

4718. Fryer, Roy. "El Rancho Los Nogales [Pomona Valley]." *Pomona Valley Historian* 5 (1969): 139-56.

4719. Gee, Denson W., ed. *Long Beach in the World War.* Long Beach, 1921. 156 pp.

4720. Giddings, Jennie (Hollingsworth). *I Can Remember Early Pasadena.* Los Angeles, [c1949]. 141 pp.

4721. Gilliland, Doris. "The History of Rancho Malibu." Master's thesis, University of Southern California, 1947. 105 pp.

4722. Gillingham, Robert C. *The Rancho San Pedro.* Los Angeles, 1961. 473 pp.

4723. Golden State Mutual Life Insurance Co. *Historical Murals Portray the Contribution of the Negro to the Growth of California from Exploration and Colonization through Settlement and Development.* [Los Angeles, 1952?]. 15 pp.

4724. Gregg, Adelaide. "A History of Santa Catalina Island from 1542 to 1919." Master's thesis, University of Southern California, 1934. 230 pp.

4725. Groeling, John C. "A Historical Study of the Early Development of Bellflower, California." Master's thesis, Whittier College, 1954. 111 pp.

4726. Guzman, Louis E. "San Fernando: Two Hundred Years in Transition." *California Geographer* 3 (1962): 55-8.

4727. Hager, Anna M., and Hager, Everett G. *San Pedro Harbor Highlights.* Glendale, 1968. 36 pp.
   Photographically-illustrated historical sketch of San Pedro Harbor from 1542 to modern times.

4728. Halliburton, Richard. "Half a Mile of History: Main Street in the City of Angels." *Reader's Digest* 31 (October 1937): 70-3.

4729. Hamilton, Lloyd P., ed. *Inglewood Community Book.* Inglewood, 1949. 443 pp.

4730. Hammer, Steven H. "William Wrigley, Jr.'s Santa Catalina Island, 1919-1932." Master's thesis, Claremont Graduate School, 1968. 80 pp.

4731. Hancock, Ralph. *Fabulous Boulevard*. New York, 1949. 322 pp.
Wilshire Boulevard.

4732. Hardcastle, William R. *Alamitos Bay; Golden Anniversary of Progress*. Long Beach, 1955. 32 pp.

4733. Harrington, M. R. "Pass into Yesterday." *Westways* 44 (November 1952) : 18-9.
Fremont Pass above San Fernando.

4734. Harris, Cynthia H. "Little Tokyo of Los Angeles; March 1, 1937-August 17, 1949." Master's thesis, Claremont Graduate School, 1970. 109 pp.

4735. Hathcock, Donald L. "The History of Baldwin Park, California (A Resource Unit for Teachers of Baldwin Park Schools) ; An Education Project." Master's thesis, Whittier College, 1954. Unp.

4736. Heric, Thomas M. "Rancho La Brea: Its History and Its Fossils." *Journal of the West* 8 (1969) : 209-30.

4737. Hertrich, William. *Early San Marino*. San Marino, 1945. 24 pp.

4738. Hill, Laurance L. *In the Valley of the Cahuengas; The Story of Hollywood*. [Hollywood], 1922. 48 pp.
Four subsequent printings, 1923-1924.

4739. —— *La Reina, Los Angeles in Three Centuries; A Volume Commemorating the Fortieth Anniversary of the Founding of the Security Trust & Savings Bank of Los Angeles, February 11, 1889*. Los Angeles, 1929. 208 pp. 4th ed., 1931.

4740. —— *Ranchos of the Sunset*. Long Beach, 1925. 48 pp.
Long Beach area.

4741. Hine, Robert V. "Llano del Rio." *California's Utopian Colonies*. New Haven, Conn., 1966. Pp. 114-31.
This desert communal colony was headed for a time by Job Harriman, unsuccessful socialist candidate for mayor of Los Angeles.

4742. Historical Society of Long Beach. *Journal, 1968-69: A Look at Long Beach in the Nineteen-Twenties*. [Long Beach, 1969?]. Unp.
Pictorial.

4743. *History of Pomona Valley, California, with Biographical Sketches*. Los Angeles, 1920. 818 pp.

4744. Hoffman, Hortense. *Long Beach from Sand to City*. [Long Beach?], 1953. 46 pp. Rev. and enlarged, [Long Beach], 1957. 73 pp.

4745. Holder, Charles F. *An Isle of Summer, Santa Catalina: Its History, Climate, Sports and Antiquities*. Los Angeles, 1901. 91 pp.

4746. Holstein, Walter. "A History of Wilmington." Master's thesis, University of Southern California, 1931. 109 pp.

4747. Holt, Raymond M. "Heritage of the Diamond Bar." *Westways* 54 (September 1962) : 30-2.
Diamond Bar Ranch (originally Rancho Los Nogales) in Brea Canyon, "the largest single piece of pastoral California remaining within thirty miles of downtown Los Angeles," finally sold for subdivision in 1956.

4748. Hoover, J. Howard. *Profile of San Dimas*. San Dimas, 1961. 173 pp.

4749. Hopkins-Smith, pub. *Pasadena and Pasadenans in Honor of Pasadena's Fiftieth Birthday*. [Pasadena, 1924]. 56 pp.

4750. Horvath, Ronald. "The Origin and Functional Structure of Santa Fe Springs, California." Master's thesis, University of California, Los Angeles, 1961. 100 pp.
An analysis that deals with "the areal artifactual expression of urban man's activities."

4751. Hubbard, Carson B., ed. *History of Huntington Park . . . In Two Parts, Narrative and Biographical*. Huntington Park, 1935. 257 pp.

4752. Hutchison, Louisa W. *Azusa, "The Blessed Miracle."* Azusa, 1937. 11 pp.

4753. Ives, Sarah N. *Altadena*. Compiled for the Altadena Historical and Beautification Society. Pasadena, c1938. 351 pp.

4754. James, George W. "The Building Up of an Ideal California Ranch." *Out West*, new series, 7 (May-June 1914) : 236-57.
Rancho Santa Anita.

4755. Janss Investment Co. *Short History of Los Angeles*. [Los Angeles, 1935?]. [16] pp.

4756. Jennings, David L. "Cahuenga Pass: A Significant Gateway Through an Intra-Regional Barrier in the Los Angeles Metropolitan Area." Master's thesis, University of California, Los Angeles, 1944. 81 pp.

4757. Johanect, F. W. "The Making of a City." *Out West* 42 (October 1915): 93-8.
El Segundo.

4758. Kahanek, Richard L. *A History of Norwalk, Los Angeles County, California.* [Norwalk?, 1968]. 71 pp.

4759. Kimball, Ruth P. *Glendora, California, 1887-1937. History and Souvenir Program of the Golden Get-Together Celebration, May 29, 1937.* [Glendora, 1937?]. 28 pp.

4760. [King, Lenora H.]. *Society's Yearbook; A Current History of Los Angeles' Epoch Year, with Glimpses of the Days That Were.* By Angeles Ayers [pseud.]. [Los Angeles], 1926. 304 pp.

4761. King, Oren L. "History of Downey Since Incorporation." *The Downey Historical Society Annual* 2 (1967-68): 30-41.

4762. King, William. "El Monte, 1851-1941." Master's thesis, Claremont Graduate School, 1966. 141 pp.

4763. Kleihauer, Aylsworth. " 'A Great Little City . . .' " *Westways* 57 (June 1965): 14-5.
Hollywood.

4764. Koehler, Nancy A. "An Historical Study of Canoga Park (Owensmouth) from 1912 to 1945." Master's thesis, Whittier College, 1960. Unp.

4765. Krauch, Robert A. "Ducks, Dredges and Developers." *Westways* 56 (January 1964): 10-3.
Playa del Rey.

4766. Krythe, Maymie R., ed. *The Historical Volume and Reference Works, Covering Long Beach.* Arlington, 1965. Bound with James L. Stamps, ed., *The Historical Volume and Reference Works, Covering Artesia, Bellflower, Bell Gardens, Compton, Dairy Valley, Downey, Lynwood, Montebello, Norwalk, Paramount, South Gate.*

4767. [Lanterman, Frank]. *La Canada, California.* [La Cañada, 1948]. 24 pp.

4768. Lee, Margaret E. "The History of Alhambra to 1915." Master's thesis, University of Southern California, 1935. 111 pp.

4769. Lehman, Anthony L. "Claremont's Historic Indian Hill." *Pomona Valley Historian* 3 (1967): 1-19.
Reprinted by Claremont Savings and Loan Association as a pamphlet.

4770. [Lewin, Molly, ed.]. *The City of Los Angeles, the First 100 Years, 1850-1950.* [Los Angeles, 1950]. 98 pp.
Pictorial history.

4771. Littleboy, Jeff. "Gold in the San Gabriel." *Westways* 51 (November 1959): 7.
Gold, first found on East Fork of San Gabriel River in 1844, still occasionally found in 1950s.

4772. Lockmann, Ronald F. "Burbank, California: An Historical Geography." Master's thesis, University of California, Los Angeles, 1967. 113 pp.

4773. Long Beach. Board of Harbor Commissioners. *History of Rancho Los Cerritos.* Long Beach, 1959. Unp.

4774. Los Angeles. City Board of Education. Emergency Education Program. *Historical Background of the Negro in Los Angeles (1935).* [Los Angeles, 1935]. 26 pp.

4775. Los Angeles County Museum, History Division. *Los Angeles, 1900-1960.* Los Angeles, 1961. 60 pp.

4776. Los Angeles County Pioneer Society. *Historical Record and Souvenir.* [Los Angeles], 1923. 283 pp.

4777. *Los Angeles Saturday Night. 150th Birthday of Los Angeles City and County: A Pre-Olympiad Feature, 1781-1931.* [Los Angeles], 1931. [c91] pp.
The articles in this pictorial issue have been distributed in the appropriate categories.

4778. Lummis, Charles F. "The Making of Los Angeles." *Out West* 30 (April 1909): 227-57.

4779. Magnolia Park Chamber of Commerce. *The Story of Burbank from Her Eventful Pioneer Days.* Burbank, 1954. 46 pp.

4780. Manhattan Beach, California. Fiftieth Anniversary Committee. *Direction; Fifty Years in the Right Direction, Manhattan Beach, California.* [Manhattan Beach, 1962]. 48 pp.

4781. Marx, M. Richard. "History at Santa Anita." *Westways* 47 (October 1955) : 30-1.
   History of tract on which County Arboretum is located.

4782. Mayo, Morrow. *Los Angeles.* New York, 1933. 337 pp.

4783. McCoy, Esther. "Face of the City: Wilshire Boulevard." *Western Architect and Engineer* 222 (September 1961) : 25-51.

4784. McDonald, Patricia. "A History of Beverly Hills, California." Master's thesis, University of Southern California, 1947. 127 pp.

4785. Millier, Arthur. "That Was the Town That Was." *Los Angeles* 8 (September 1964) : 26-31+.
   Los Angeles, 1908-29.

4786. Monroe, George L., ed. *Burbank Community Book. In Two Parts, Narrative and Biographical.* Burbank, 1944. 216 pp.

4787. Morris, Lucie. "The History of the Town of Lancaster, Center of Antelope Valley, California." Master's thesis, University of Southern California, 1934. 86 pp.

4788. "A Mountain Gem." *Trails Magazine* 5 (Winter 1938) : 11-4.
   A story of Colby's Ranch in Angeles National Forest, c1891-1938.

4789. Murray, Jim. "An Impolite Toast to Beverly Hills." *Los Angeles* 7 (April 1964) : 30-3+.
   Fifty-year history of Beverly Hills.

4790. Nadeau, Remi. *Los Angeles, from Mission to Modern City.* New York, 1960. 302 pp.

4791. Newhall, Ruth W. *The Newhall Ranch: The Story of the Newhall Land & Farming Company.* San Marino, 1958. 120 pp.

4792. Newmark, Harris. *Sixty Years in Southern California, 1853-1913.* Edited by Maurice H. and Marco R. Newmark. New York, 1916. 688 pp. 2nd ed., New York, 1926. 732 pp. 3rd ed., New York, 1929. 732 pp. 4th ed., rev. by W. W. Robinson. Los Angeles, 1970. 744 pp.

4793. Northrup, William M., ed. *Alhambra (San Gabriel-Monterey Park) Community Book . . . In Two Parts, Narrative and Biographical.* Alhambra, 1944. 249 pp. 2nd ed., 1949. 179 pp.

4794. ———, and Thompson, Newton W., eds. *History of Alhambra . . . In Two Parts, Narrative and Biographical.* Alhambra, 1936. 219 pp.

4795. Otis, Harrison Gray. "Los Angeles — A Sketch." *Sunset* 24 (January 1910) : 12-6.
   Following the article, pp. 17-48, sixty-four photographs are presented.

4796. Overholt, Alma (Staheli). *The Catalina Story.* Compiled and edited under the auspices of the Catalina Island Museum Society. Avalon, 1962. 96 pp.

4797. Palmer, Edwin O. *History of Hollywood.* Hollywood, 1937. 2 vols. Rev. and extended edition, 1938. 294 pp.

4798. Parcher, Carroll W., ed. *Glendale Community Book.* Glendale, 1957. 1039 pp.

4799. Parle, Alice. "Santa Anita Rancho: Its History and Personalities." Master's thesis, University of Southern California, 1939. 95 pp.

4800. Pasadena Savings and Loan Association. *Valley of the Hahamog-na; Pasadena Through Two Centuries.* [Pasadena?, 1952]. [44] pp.

4801. Peck, Sedley. "Colorful Old Days on the Upper San Gabriel." *Trails Magazine* 5 (Summer 1938) : 5-14.

4802. Petchner, William C. *Romance and Drama in the Valley of the Sunshine; Being a Story of Old Palmdale.* Los Angeles, 1914. [19] pp.

4803. Pflueger, Donald. *Glendora: The Annals of a Southern California Community.* Claremont, 1951. 262 pp.

4804. ——— *Sunflowers, Citrus, Subdivisions.* Covina, 1964. 372 pp.
   History of Covina.

4805. Popenoe, Lucile. "Downey — City with a Heritage." *Westways* 49 (June 1957) : 12-3.

4806. Potter, Bernard. *Los Angeles, Yesterday and Today.* Los Angeles, [1950]. 201 pp.

4807. Ramseyer, Norman. "A History of Lordsburg, California." Master's thesis, University of Southern California, 1938. 60 pp.

Now called La Verne.

4808. Raup, Hallock F. "The History and Development of Rancho Los Palos Verdes." *Historical Society of Southern California Quarterly* 19 (1937): 7-21.

4809. ———— *Rancho Los Palos Verdes.* Los Angeles, 1937. 17 pp.

Summarizes history, 1793-1937.

4810. Reimert, Phil, ed. *Direction; 50 Years in the Right Direction, Manhattan Beach, California.* Manhattan Beach, 1962. 48 pp.

4811. Richardson, James H. *Spring Street; A Story of Los Angeles.* Los Angeles, 1922. 418 pp.

4812. Robinson, William W. *Beverly Hills: A Calendar of Events in the Making of a City.* Los Angeles, 1938. [23] pp.

Another edition printed in 1942.

4813. ———— *The Changing Scene: A 100 Year Picture-History of Southern California.* [Los Angeles], 1965. [64] pp.

4814. ———— *Fabulous San Fernando Valley.* Los Angeles, [1963]. 16 pp.

4815. ———— *Los Angeles from the Days of the Pueblo: Together with a Guide to the Historic Old Plaza Area Including the Pueblo de Los Angeles, State Historical Monument.* San Francisco, 1959. 96 pp.

4816. ———— *Glendale: A Calendar of Events in the Making of a City* [1769-1906]. Los Angeles, 1936. [23] pp.

4817. ———— *History of the Miracle Mile.* Los Angeles, 1965. [12] pp.

4818. ———— *Inglewood: A Calendar of Events in the Making of a City.* Los Angeles, 1935. 20 pp. 2nd ed., Los Angeles, 1937. 23 pp. Subsequent editions printed in 1942, 1955, 1964.

4819. ———— *The Island of Santa Catalina.* Los Angeles, 1941. [48] pp.

4820. ———— *The Key to Los Angeles.* Philadelphia, [1963]. 128 pp.

For young readers.

4821. ———— *Little History of a Big City, Los Angeles.* Los Angeles, 1963. 32 pp.

Minature book.

4822. ———— *Long Beach: A Calendar of Events in the Making of a City.* Los Angeles, 1942. [16] pp. Other editions 1948, 1957, 1961.

4823. ———— *Los Angeles: A Profile.* Norman, Okla., 1968. 138 pp.

4824. ———— *Monrovia: A Calendar of Events in the Making of a City.* Los Angeles, 1936. [16] pp.

4825. ———— "Myth-Making in the Los Angeles Area." *Southern California Quarterly* 45 (1963): 83-94.

An effort to set the record straight concerning a number of erroneous beliefs and interpretations that pervade the historiography of the city.

4826. ———— *Our Spanish-Mexican Heritage.* Los Angeles, [1965?]. 12 pp. Reprint from *Masterkey* 39 (July-September 1965): 104-13.

4827. ———— *Panorama: A Picture History of Southern California.* Los Angeles, 1953. [158] pp.

4828. ———— *Pasadena: A Calendar of Events in the Making of a City.* Los Angeles, 1935. [19] pp. Other editions 1942, 1949, 1955, 1964.

4829. ———— *Pomona: A Calendar of Events in the Making of a City.* Los Angeles, 1936. [24] pp. 2nd ed., 1942.

4830. ———— "Profile of Los Angeles." *Museum Alliance Quarterly* 2 (1954): 1-15.

Reprinted in *A Bookman's View of Los Angeles.* Los Angeles, 1961. Pp. 3-14.

4831. ———— "San Fernando Tells California's Story." *Westways* 42 (October 1950): 10.

4832. ———— *San Fernando Valley: A Calendar of Events.* Los Angeles, 1938. [28] pp. Other editions 1942, 1951. 35 pp.

4833. ———— *San Pedro and Wilmington: A Calen-*

dar of Events in the Making of the Two Cities and the Los Angeles Harbor. Los Angeles, 1937. [24] pp.

4834. ——— *Santa Monica: A Calendar of Events.* Los Angeles, 1935. [15] pp. Other editions 1942, 1950, 1955, 1959, 1962.

4835. ——— *Whittier: A Calendar of Events.* Los Angeles, 1935. [15] pp. Other editions 1942, 1947, 1955, 1962.

4836. Rogers, Warren S. *Mesa to Metropolis; The Crenshaw Area, Los Angeles.* Los Angeles, 1959. 20 pp.
  Reprinted from a serialization in the *Angeles Mesa News-Advertiser*, September-October, 1959.

4837. Rolle, Andrew F. *Los Angeles: A Student's Guide to Localized History.* New York, 1964. 35 pp.

4838. ——— *Pasadena: Two Centuries of Growth.* Los Angeles, 1969. [22] pp.

4839. *The Romance of Rancho Santa Anita.* Los Angeles, 1940. 32 pp.

4840. Romer, Margaret. "The Story of Los Angeles" [Parts V-VIII]. *Journal of the West* 3 (January-October 1964): 1-39, 199-220, 375-400, 459-88.
  This, the second half of an eight-part historical survey of Los Angeles from its founding, deals with the city in the twentieth century.

4841. Rosenberg, Roy. *History of Inglewood . . . Narrative and Biographical.* Inglewood, 1938. 215 pp.

4842. Rowland, Leonore, comp. *Bits of California.* [La Puente, 1963]. 16 pp.
  La Puente area.

4843. ——— *The Romance of La Puente Rancho.* [La Puente, 1948]. 23 pp.

4844. ——— *The Romance of La Puente Rancho.* Including Excerpts from *La Puente Valley, Past and Present* by Janet and Dan N. Powell. [Covina, 1958]. 68 pp.

4845. Russell, J[oe] H. *Cattle on the Conejo.* Los Angeles, 1957. 135 pp.
  Approximately one-third of the Russell Ranch lies in Los Angeles County, the rest in Ventura County.

4846. *S P 75.* [N. p., 1963]. 48 pp.
  Souvenir publication of the South Pasadena Diamond Jubilee. Pp. 21-48 deal with the twentieth century.

4847. *San Marino, 50th Anniversary, 1915-1963; The Golden Years.* [San Marino, 1963]. 24 pp.
  Pictorial.

4848. Santa Catalina Island Co. *Catalina's Yesterdays.* Los Angeles, c1926. 21 pp.

4849. Security Trust and National Bank, Burbank Branch. *Ranchos de Los Santos, the Story of Burbank.* Los Angeles, 1927. 48 pp.

4850. Security Trust and Savings Bank, Glendale Branch. *First of the Ranchos; The Story of Glendale.* 2nd ed., Glendale, 1924. 48 pp. 3rd ed., 1927.

4851. ———, Highland Park Branch. *The Five Friendly Valleys: The Story of Greater Highland Park.* 2nd ed., [Los Angeles], 1923. 48 pp.

4852. ———, Hollywood Branch. *In the Valley of the Cahuengas; The Story of Hollywood.* 5th ed., Hollywood, 1924. 48 pp.

4853. ———, Long Beach Branch. *Ranchos of the Sunset; The Story of Long Beach.* Los Angeles, c1925. 48 pp.

4854. ———, Pasadena and Maryland Branches. *Crown of the Valley: The Story of Pasadena.* 3rd ed., Los Angeles, 1924. 48 pp. 4th ed., 1927.

4855. ———, Research and Publicity Departments. *"Since You Were Here Before"; A Story of the Changes That Have Come to Los Angeles Since It Was Host to the American Bankers Association in 1910-1921.* Los Angeles, 1926. [80] pp.

4856. ———, South Pasadena Branch. *On Old Rancho San Pascual; The Story of South Pasadena.* South Pasadena, [c1922]. 48 pp. 2nd ed., 1924.

4857. Seewerker, Joseph. *Nuestro Pueblo; Los Angeles, City of Romance.* Boston, 1940. 184 pp.

4858. Sherer, John C. *History of Glendale and Vicinity.* Glendale, 1922. 476 pp.

4859. Shoop, C[larence] F., ed. *Pasadena Community Book.* Pasadena, 1951. 584 pp.

4860. ———; Blair, William L.; and Arnold, Ralph, eds. *Pasadena Community Book: Ralph Arnold Edition.* Pasadena, 1955. 472 pp.

4861. Simpson, Alice F. "San Fernando Pass: Story of Historic Gateway to the San Joaquin Valley." *California Highways and Public Works* 33 (September-October 1954): 34-7+.

4862. Smith, Clifford. "The History of San Fernando Valley with Special Emphasis on the City of San Fernando." Master's thesis, University of Southern California, 1930. 182 pp.

4863. Smith, Cornelius. "The Old San Gabriel and Some of Those Who Made Its History." *Trails Magazine* 3 (Summer 1936): 6-16.
Latter part of article devoted to the twentieth century.

4864. Spalding, William A., comp. *History and Reminiscences. Los Angeles City and County, California.* Los Angeles, [1931]. 3 vols.
Vols. 2-3 have title: *History of Los Angeles City and County . . . Biographical.*

4865. Stade, Odo B. "Loomis Ranch — Last Homestead." *Trails Magazine* 5 (Spring 1938): 8-12.

4866. Stamps, James L., ed. *The Historical Volume and Reference Works, Covering Artesia, Bellflower, Bell Gardens, Compton, Dairy Valley, Downey, Lynwood, Montebello, Norwalk, Paramount, South Gate.* Arlington, 1965. 898 pp. Bound with Krythe, Maymie R., ed., *The Historical Volume and Reference Works, Covering Long Beach.*

4867. Starbuck, Margaret. *So This Is Glendale: Welcome to a New Neighbor; A Sketch of the City's Colorful History, Where to Find Schools.* Glendale, c1939. 30 pp.

4868. Sterrett, Roger J. "Los Angeles Celebrates Its Centennial." *Historical Society of Southern California Quarterly* 28 (1946): 129-33.

4869. Stewart, Maria H. *Los Encino's Past and Present.* [Encino, 1965]. 96 pp.

4870. Stone, Irving. *Rose Bowl Town.* [N.p., n.d.]. 47 pp.
An amusing history of Pasadena with interesting bits about the Rose Tournament.

4871. Studer, Robert P., ed. *The Historical Volume and Reference Works, Including Alhambra, Monterey Park, Rosemead, San Gabriel, South San Gabriel, Temple City.* Los Angeles, 1962. 836 pp.

4872. Swain, John G., ed. *The Historical Volume and Reference Works, Covering Bassett, City of Industry, La Habra, La Mirada, La Puente, Pico Rivera, Santa Fe Springs, Walnut, Whittier.* Whittier, 1963. 1052 pp.

4873. Swigart, William R. *Biography of Spring Street in Los Angeles.* Los Angeles, 1945. 190 pp.

4874. Tatum, Donn B., Jr. "The Rancho Sausal Redondo." Master's thesis, University of Southern California, 1968. 120 pp.
Inglewood-Centinela Valley area.

4875. Temple, Scott E. "Downey's First Year [1956-1957] as a City." *The Downey Historical Society Annual* 2 (1967-68): 17-29.

4876. Thacker, Mary E. "A History of Los Palos Verdes Rancho, 1542-1923." Master"s thesis, University of Southern California, 1923. 73 pp.

4877. Thompson, Edward G. "The History and Development of South Pasadena to 1917." Master's thesis, University of Southern California, 1938. 102 pp.

4878. *A Thumb Nail History of Pasadena.* [Los Angeles, n.d.]. 16 pp.

4879. Treanor, Tom. "Look Back, San Marino!" *Saturday Night* 45 (June 18, 1938): 20-1.

4880. Tuller, Carol. *The Story of Burbank from Her Eventful Pioneer Days.* Burbank, 1954. 46 pp.

4881. Walker, J. P. "A Word from Montebello." *Pacific Municipalities* 45 (August 1931): 375-6.

4882. Warren, Charles S., ed. *History of Santa Monica Bay Region. In Two Parts, Narrative and Biographical.* Santa Monica, 1934. [308] pp.

4883. Wiley, John L. *History of Monrovia.* Pasadena, 1927. 291 pp.

4884. Willard, Charles D. *The Herald's History of Los Angeles City . . .* Los Angeles, 1901. 365 pp.

4885. Windle, Ernest. *History of Santa Catalina Island [& Guide]*. Avalon, 1931. 159 pp. 2nd ed., 1940.

4886. Winslow, F. E. "City of the Angels," in *American Historic Towns: Historic Towns of the Western States*. Ed. by L. P. Powell. New York, 1901. Pp. 645-84.

4887. Wood, John W. *Pasadena, California: Historical and Personal* . . . [Pasadena], 1917. 565 pp.

4888. Workman, Boyle. *The City That Grew*. Los Angeles, 1935 [i.e. 1936]. 430 pp.
Los Angeles.

4889. Young, Hugh A. *Furlough Den*. Long Beach, 1949. 103 pp.
Long Beach.

4890. Zierer, Clifford M. "San Fernando — A Type of Southern California Town." *Annals of the Association of American Geographers* 24 (1934) : 1-28.

HORTICULTURE

4891. Boone, Andrew R. "Weather Factory for Plants." *Westways* 44 (January 1952) : 16-7.
Matching plants to climate in Pasadena laboratory.

4892. Bruner, Mrs. E. L. "Third Annual Exhibit of Landscape Architecture and Garden Sculpture, Los Angeles." *The Architect and Engineer* 86 (August 1926) : 61-3.

4893. Burtnett, G[erald] B. "Brief History of Mandeville Canyon." *Los Angeles Saturday Night* 8 (January 21, 1928) : 17.
Santa Monica Mountain Park Co. and its plans for a botanical garden.

4894. ——— "Brilliant Future of Botanic Garden Assured." *Los Angeles Saturday Night* 8 (February 4, 1928) : 2.
California Botanic Garden, located on a 3,200 acre tract in Mandeville Canyon.

4895. ——— "California Botanic Garden Institution." *Los Angeles Saturday Night* 8 (January 14, 1928) : 9.
Author's name erroneously given as E. B. Burtnett.

4896. ——— "Eden in Los Angeles." *Touring Topics* 21 (March 1929) : 44.
California Botanic Garden.

4897. ——— "A Profitless Subdivision." *Los Angeles Realtor* 8 (December 1928) : 14.
California Botanic Garden.

4898. "The Care of Trees in Los Angeles." *American City* 13 (December 1915) : 508-9.

4899. Clark, Robert. "The Old and the New Santa Anita." *Westways* 40 (January 1948) : 12-3.
Description of County Arboretum.

4900. Cook, Wilbur D. "Landscape Features of the C. W. Leffingwell Estate." *The Architect and Engineer of California* 11 (November 1907) : 48-50.
Pasadena estate.

4901. Corlett, Dudley S. "The California Botanic Garden and Trees." *California Graphic* 5 (February 4, 1928) : 5.
Deplores Los Angeles' not preserving trees and flowers.

4902. ——— "In the Devil's Garden." *Los Angeles Saturday Night* 9 (January 26, 1929) : 17.
California Botanic Garden.

4903. ——— "What a Botanic Garden Means to Business." *Southern California Business* 7 (February 1928) : 16-7+.
Mandeville Canyon.

4904. Cornell, Ralph D. "Landscaping of Pueblo Del Rio." *The Architect and Engineer* 150 (September 1942) : 21+.
Los Angeles housing project.

4905. Fellows, Donald K. "The Imprint of Japanese Buddhism on the Cultural Landscape of the Sawtelle Area of West Los Angeles, 1968." Master's thesis, San Fernando Valley State College, 1968. 119 pp.
Japanese professional landscape gardeners, and the influence of their religion on their work.

4906. Graham Photo Company, Los Angeles. *The Busch Gardens, Pasadena, California*. [Los Angeles, n.d.]. [16] pp.

4907. Haig, M. J. "A California City Beautiful Campaign." *American City* 16 (February 1917) : 168-9.

Whittier Chamber of Commerce Civics Bureau flower garden contest.

4908. Hall, L. Glenn "Los Angeles Starts Systematic Planting of Street Trees." *American City* 46 (April 1932) : 88-9.

Division of Forestry, Los Angeles Park Department.

4909. Hamilton, A. L. "Street Trees." *Pacific Municipalities* 29 (November 1915) : 537-8.

Pasadena.

4910. Hamilton, Andrew. "The Fight for Beauty: Los Angeles Citizens Prove Elimination of Eyesores Good Business, Contagious Example." *National Civic Review* 51 (February 1962) : 66-9.

Valley Knudsen and the Los Angeles Beautiful Movement.

4911. Hertrich, William. *The Huntington Botanical Gardens, 1905-1949; Personal Recollections of William Hertrich, Curator Emeritus.* San Marino, 1949. 167 pp.

4912. Jennings, Frederick. "The Architecture and Landscape Architecture of Los Angeles and Vicinity." *The Architect and Engineer* 62 (August 1920) : 47-94.

4913. Kendig, Francis. "Rare Plants in Inglewood Park Cemetery." *Los Angeles Saturday Night* 11 (May 30, 1931) : 7.

4914. Leadabrand, Russ. "A Beautiful Boon for Gardeners." *Westways* 50 (November 1958) : 11-3.

Los Angeles County Arboretum.

4915. ———— "The Garden in the Live Oak Forest." *Westways* 51 (February 1959) : 37-9.

Descanso Gardens in La Cañada.

4916. Lyndon, Joyce E. "Problem: Landscaping the Santa Monica Mountains." *Arts & Architecture* 83 (February/March 1966) : 38.

Sunset Mountain Park, a planned community.

4917. Mappelbeck, John. "Blossoming Out for the Olympics." *Southern California Business* 11 (March 1932) : 12.

Chamber of Commerce sponsored beautification program for Los Angeles County.

4918. McCarthy, John R. "Half a Million Camellias." *Westways* 39 (February 1947) : 18-9.

Rancho del Descauso in San Rafael Hills, owned by Manchester Boddy.

4919. McDowell, Evelyn. "Azalea Time in the Huntington Gardens." *Los Angeles Saturday Night* 15 (April 20, 1935) : 4.

4920. McIntire, Ross O. "Downtown Tree Planting: Los Angeles Businessmen Cooperate with the City in a Tree-Planting Beautification Program and Find It Is a Good Business Investment." *American City* 74 (August 1959) : 106-7.

4921. Merrill, E. D. "Botanic Gardens Play Big Part in Economic Life." *Southern California Business* 8 (February 1929) : 16+.

California Botanic Garden in Mandeville Canyon.

4922. ———— "The Economic Importance of California's Botanic Gardens." *Southern California Business* 6 (July 1927) : 10-1+.

Mandeville Canyon.

4923. ———— "Plants — From Every Part of the Globe." *Los Angeles Realtor* 7 (June 1927) : 15-6+.

First landscaping for California Botanic Garden in Mandeville Canyon.

4924. "More Trees for Los Angeles." *Los Angeles Realtor* 8 (March 1929) : 12+.

4925. Nelson, Howard J. "The Spread of an Artificial Landscape over Southern California." *Annals of the Association of American Geographers* 49 (1959) : 80-99.

4926. Olmsted, Frederick Law. "Palos Verdes Estates." *Landscape Architecture* 17 (July 1927) : 255-90.

4927. Padilla, Victoria. *Southern California Gardens; An Illustrated History.* Berkeley, 1961. 359 pp.

4928. "Rare Desert Plants in Huntington Botanical Gardens." *Los Angeles Saturday Night* 43 (August 15, 1936) : 15.

4929. "Rare Plants in the Huntington Gardens." *Los Angeles Saturday Night* 43 (April 11, 1936) : 9.

4930. Rowan, Charles D. "Ornamental Plants as a Factor in the Cultural Development of Southern California." Master's thesis, University of California, Los Angeles, 1957. 260 pp.

4931. Saunders, Charles F. "A City Wild-flower Park." *Sunset* 38 (May 1917) : 34.

Five-acre corner of Exposition Park set aside as public botanical garden for native California wild-flowers, shrubs and trees.

4932. Skutt, Gilbert L. "The Pasadena Flower Shows: Enthusiastic Lovers of Plant Life Gather at These Shows Which Exemplify the Flower Land of America." *City Manager Magazine* 7 (April 1925) : 17-9.

4933. Spalding, George H. "State and County Arboretum Developing at Los Angeles." *Parks and Recreation* 34 (August 1951) : 8-10.

4934. Thompson, Douglas G. *Descanso Gardens, Its History and Camellias.* Los Angeles, 1962. 64 pp.

4935. Thorpe, James. "The Creation of the Gardens." *Huntington Library Quarterly* 32 (1968-9) : 333-50.

Huntington Library.

4936. Troeger, E. L. "Santa Monica Surveys Its Trees: City Takes 'Tree Census' to Guide in the Care and Future Plantings." *American City* 66 (April 1951) : 141.

4937. Williamson, C.J.S. "A City Forester for Los Angeles." *Pacific Municipalities* 44 (May 1930) : 157.

HOUSING

4938. "Aliso Village, Los Angeles." *The Architect and Engineer* 152 (January 1943) : 13-21+.

Los Angeles housing.

4939. Allen, Ralph K. "Substandard Housing: Glendale and Pasadena, California." Master's thesis, San Fernando Valley State College, 1968. 142 pp.

4940. "Association's Long Fight Against Rent Con-trol Ends in Success." *Western Housing* 34 (January 1951) : 6-7.

Los Angeles County Apartment Association.

4941. "Association's Toughest Battle Ends as L.A. City Council Kills Rent Control." *Western Housing* 34 (August 1950) : 7+.

Los Angeles County Apartment Association.

4942. "Avalon Gardens." *The Architect and Engineer* 148 (January 1942) : 15-9.

Los Angeles housing project.

4943. Baruch, Dorothy W. "Sleep Comes Hard: Negro Housing in Los Angeles." *Nation* 160 (January 27, 1945) : 195-6.

4944. Bennett, Charles B. "Is Public Housing Needed for Urban Redevelopment?" *American City* 63 (November 1948) : 84.

4945. Bennett, Harry. "Wyvernwood and Its Rental Policies." *Insured Mortgage Portfolio* 4 (February 1940) : 8-10+.

4946. Berger, Jay S. *Profile of the Los Angeles Metropolis: Finance Census Chart Book.* Los Angeles, 1964. Unp.

4947. Berry, Graham. "Time Marches on Orange Grove Avenue." *Apartment Journal* 24 (November 1941) : 12-3.

Pasadena apartments.

4948. Brooke, Tyler. "Pickets + Neighbors = Homes for Vets." *New Republic* 117 (December 1, 1947) : 15.

Community comes to support of veterans seeking homes under VA financing.

4949. Buckley, George B. "Building a Home Minus 'Blue Sky': Here's a Center That Supplies Non-Selling Information about Sound Methods and Builders." *Southern California Business* 15 (March 1936) : 12-3.

Association for the Advancement of Home Building, Los Angeles.

4950. "Building Homes in Fair Weather." *Southern California Business* 4 (April 1925) : 17+.

4951. Bullough, Bonnie L. "Alienation Among Middle Class Negroes: Social-Psychological Factors Influencing Housing Desegregation." Doctoral dissertation, University of California, Los Angeles, 1968. 233 pp.

4952. "Burbank Acts Fast in Housing Crisis; 100 Families of Veterans under Roof." *Western City* 22 (January 1946) : 20.

4953. Burns, Leland S. *Profile of the Los Angeles Metropolis — Its People and Its Homes.* Part 3: *Intra-Metropolitan Contracts: The Island Communities.* Los Angeles, 1964. 49 pp.

4954. Byers, Charles A. "The Popular Bungalow-Court Idea." *The Architect and Engineer* 59 (October 1919) : 80-5.
    Los Angeles.

4955. "Cancellation of Public Housing Plan Expected as Result of Public's Vote." *Western Housing* 35 (June 1952) : 8.

4956. Carfagno, Edward C. "A Housing Development for the Bunker Hill Area with Special Reference to the Function of Apartment Hotels." Master's thesis, University of Southern California, 1933. 59 pp.

4957. Carpenter, Willard. "How FEPC Was Scuttled in LA by a Single Vote." *Frontier* 6 (July 1955) : 6.
    City Council rejects proposal of Edward Roybal's Public Health and Welfare Committee, by an 8 to 7 vote.

4958. Case, Frederick E. *The Housing Status of Minority Families, Los Angeles, 1956.* Los Angeles, 1958. 78 pp.

4959. ———— "UCLA Real Estate Department Asks Cooperation in Rental Market Study." *Western Housing* 37 (November 1953) : 8.

4960. "Case Studies 1102 — Apartment Development. Wyvernwood Village Housing Project, Los Angeles California." *Architectural Record* 86 (September 1939) : 101-7.

4961. "Channel Heights Housing Project." *Architectural Forum* 80 (March 1944) : 65-74.
    A Federal Public Housing Authority project, Los Angeles Housing Authority in charge, designed by Richard Neutra.

4962. "Child Ban: Los Angeles Apartment-House Boycott on Children Creates Problem." *Literary Digest* 122 (November 14, 1936) : 44-5.

4963. "City of Los Angeles to Be World's Biggest Landlord." *Western Housing* 35 (July 1951) : 18+.
    Los Angeles City Housing Authority.

4964. Claus, Cynthia. "The Franklin Plaza." *Apartment Journal* 18 (December 1935) : 8-9+.

4965. ———— "Glendale." *Apartment Journal* 17 (June 1935) : 10+.
    Housing survey.

4966. ———— "The Human Side of Housing." *Apartment Journal* 23 (January 1941) : 10-1+.
    Carmelitos, Long Beach.

4967. ———— "Pasadena." *Apartment Journal* 19 (May 1937) : 8-9+.

4968. ———— "St. Francis Terrace: How an Obsolete Property Has Been Transformed into an Ultra Modern Court." *Apartment Journal* 19 (March 1937) : 14-7.

4969. ———— "Santa Monica Bay." *Apartment Journal* 19 (December 1936) : 10-1+.
    Housing survey.

4970. Collier, Robert W. "An Analysis of the Large-Scale Single-Family Residential Builder in Los Angeles, Orange and Ventura Counties." Doctoral dissertation, University of Southern California, 1967. 213 pp.

4971. Conser, E. P. "Our Communities: Study Shows Southern California Cities Rank High in Advantages of Life." *Apartment Journal* 22 (January 1940) : 8+
    Report on a Carnegie-financed study headed by E. L. Thorndike. Pasadena ranked first in the nation in "livability"; Glendale, Santa Monica, and Long Beach also ranked high. Los Angeles designated "best metropolis."

4972. ———— "Our Part in Defense Housing: Employment Expansion Raises Question of Adequate Housing; Plan to Coordinate Thousands of Vacant Apartments with Rising Rental Demand Starts." *Apartment Journal* 23 (November 1940) : 10+
    Los Angeles area.

4973. ———— "Relative Rents Divulged: Government Surveys Show Los Angeles Rents Lower Than Other Major Cities." *Apartment Journal* 22 (November 1939) : 8-9.

4974. ———— "Rent Control Effective Today: Regulations on Rent, Services and Tenant Evictions Now Are in Effect in Los Angeles County; Registration of all Units and Rooms Required." *Apartment Journal* 25 (November 1942) : 8+.

4975. ———— "Rent Control in So. Calif." *Apartment Journal* 25 (July 1942) : 8-9+

4976. ———— "Replacement Work in Los Angeles Apartment Buildings Urged by Association Executive." *The Architect and Engineer* 123 (October 1935) : 53-6.

4977. Cook, Wilbur D. "Highbourne Gardens — A Southern California Bungalow Court." *The Architect and Engineer of California* 49 (June 1917) : 39-46.

Bungalow court in Los Angeles.

4978. Davis, W[illia]m A. "Masonry Used in L.A. Housing." *Western Construction News* 18 (June 1943) : 271-2.

4979. "Delay after Delay of Rent Decontrol in Los Los Angeles, an Unfunny Farce." *Western Housing* 34 (October 1950) : 7.

4980. Donovan, Richard. "The Great Los Angeles Public Housing Mystery." *Reporter* 6 (March 4, 1952) : 25-9.

Mayor Bowron and the City Housing Authority vs. the City Council over the issue of low-rent public housing.

4981. Dorn, Douglas, and Edwards, Burton E. "Rent Control Had Reduced Total Rental Market in Los Angeles." *Western Housing* 33 (May 1950) : 9+.

4982. Duncan, Beverly; Sabagh, George, and Van Arsdol, Maurice. "Patterns of City Growth." *American Journal of Sociology* 67 (January 1962) : 418-29.

"Cohort analysis of Los Angeles residential areas indicates that the rapidity of redistribution varies directly with both the rate of population growth and the ratio of new dwellings to incremental population."

4983. "Erection of Quonset Huts Continues at Park Despite Suit of Donor's Heir." *Western Construction News* 21 (April 1946) : 109.

Griffith Park housing.

4984. "FHA's Largest Rental Project under Way." *American City* 54 (March 1939) : 93.

Wyvernwood, Los Angeles, largest privately financed rental housing in the U.S.

4985. Ferguson, Jim. "West Coast's First Large Housing Project." *The Architect and Engineer* 135 (May 1938) : 41-3.

San Gabriel Village development.

4986. Fox, William J. "Los Angeles Project for Housing Indigents." *Civil Engineering* 8 (March 1938) : 168-9.

4987. Fuller, Elizabeth. "The Mexican Housing Problem in Los Angeles." *Studies in Sociology* 5 (November 1920) : 1-11.

Published separately as *Sociology Monograph No. 17.*

4988. Gervasi, Frank. "Housing: The Homeless Southwest." *Collier's* 118 (December 14, 1946) : 22-3+.

4989. "Giant Housing Project Announced for East Side." *Apartment Journal* 21 (August 1938) : 16.

Wyvernwood.

4990. Gill, Corringon [*sic*]. "Five Congested Production Areas Designated on West Coast." *Western City* 20 (February 1944) : 25-6.

Includes Los Angeles.

4991. Gillies, James, and Berger, Jay S. *Profile of the Los Angeles Metropolis—Its People and Its Homes.* Part 4: *Financing Homeownership: The Borrowers, the Lenders, and the Homes.* Los Angeles, 1965. 77 pp.

4992. Goetze, Sigfried. "The Housing Situation in Los Angeles." *National Municipal Review* 13 (April 1924) : 197-200.

4993. ———— "Los Angeles Tackles the Housing Problem." *American City* 43 (December 1930) : 150-1.

4994. Goldman, Ronald E. "Hillside Housing Proj-

ect." *Arts & Architecture* 80 (September 1963): 14-5+.
   Zoning and building in South Pasadena Hills.

4995. "Governor [Warren] Approves Rent Decontrol in Beverley [*sic*] Hills and South Pasadena." *Western Housing* 33 (December 1949): 6-7+.

4996. "Grand Jury Asked to Investigate Los Angeles Public Housing Plan." *Western Housing* 35 (December 1951): 6+.

4997. Grebler, Leo. *Profile of the Los Angeles Metropolis—Its People and Its Homes.* Part 1: *Metropolitan Contrasts.* Los Angeles, 1963. 55 pp.

4998. Guzman, Ralph. "The Hand of Esau." *Frontier* 7 (June 1956): 13+.
   How restrictive convenants are perpetuated under a new guise in Lynwood, Compton, and South Gate.

4999. Harmer, Ruth M. "Trick Play at City Hall: 'Socialism' and the New Los Angeles Housing Plan." *Frontier* 6 (February 1955): 11-2.
   Community Redevelopment Agency plan for Bunker Hill.

5000. Henehan, Anne. "Watts: Facing the Problems of Minority Ghettos in Today's Cities." *Senior Scholastic* 89 (January 1967): 9-12.

5001. Hoedinghaus, George E. "Report of the 1934 Housing Investigation, University of Southern California." Master's thesis, University of Southern California, 1934. 102 pp.
   Student housing.

5002. "House Sense: Los Angeles Committee on Job with Factual Yardsticks to Avert Residential Overbuilding as Result of Defense Clamor." *Business Week* (March 22, 1941): 34-5.

5003. "Housing Expeditor in All Out Effort to Prevent Decontrol in Los Angeles." *Western Housing* 33 (February 1950): 7.

5004. "Housing in Los Angeles." *Survey* 65 (March 15, 1931): 668.
   Joint Legislative Committee on Better Housing, sponsored by the Municipal League of Los Angeles.

5005. "A Housing Record—Building a Building a

Day." *Western Construction News* 15 (January 1940): 18-9.
   Wyvernwood, Los Angeles largest privately financed rental housing project in the U.S.

5006. "Housing Survey Strikes Pay Ore: So Many Modernization Jobs Have Been Found That Now a Two-Year Campaign Is under Way." *Southern California Business* 13 (December 1934): 14.
   Los Angeles.

5007. Ihlder, John. "Housing at the Los Angeles Conference." *National Municipal Review* 2 (1913): 68-75.
   Discussion of Los Angeles housing at conference of National Municipal League.

5008. Jones, Frederick W. "Pueblo Del Rio: Los Angeles' Most Recent Housing Project." *The Architect and Engineer* 150 (September 1942): 11-20.

5009. Jones, Helen L. "House-Tents in California." *Out West* 20 (March 1904): 237-47.

5010. Kienle, John E. "Housing Conditions Among the Mexican Population of Los Angeles." Master's thesis, University of Southern California, 1912. 50 pp.

5011. Kraus, Henry. *In the City Was a Garden; A Housing Project Chronicle.* New York, 1951. 255 pp.
   San Pedro.

5012. Leigh, Laura. "Wyvernwood." *Apartment Journal* 21 (June 1939): 12-3.

5013. "'Local Option' [Rent] Decontrol Campaign Launched in City of Los Angeles." *Western Housing* 33 (October 1949): 7+.

5014. "Long Beach Conducts Its Own Rental Vacancy Survey." *Western City* 25 (November 1949): 42.

5015. Los Angeles Freedom Club of the First Congregational Church. "Review of the Prolonged Los Angeles 10,000 Unit Public Housing Muddle." *Western Housing* 36 (October 1952): 9+.

5016. Los Angeles. Municipal Housing Commission. *A Brief History of Public Housing Activities in Los Angeles.* Los Angeles, 1936. 6 pp.

5017. "L.A. Citizens Fair Rent Committee Forges

Ahead with Decontrol." *Western Housing* 33 (November 1949): 7.

5018. "L.A. City Council Votes to Cancel $110,000-000 Public Housing Program." *Western Housing* 35 (January 1952): 6-7+.

5019. "Los Angeles County's Interesting Rehabilitation Housing Venture." *Western City* 15 (January 1939): 30-1.

5020. "L. A. Housing: Subsistence Homesteads." *The Architect and Engineer* 120 (January 1935): 37-40.

5021. "Los Angeles Is Not a Critical Defense Housing Area." *Western Housing* 35 (August 1951): 7.
No automatic re-control of rents under Defense Production Act.

5022. "L.A. Public Housing Authority May Get Congressional Investigation." *Western Housing* 36 (May 1953): 7.

5023. "Los Angeles Public Housing Battle Continues on Many Fronts." *Western Housing* 36 (July 1952): 7.

5024. "L.A. Public Housing Issue May Go to Public Vote on June 3rd Ballot." *Western Housing* 35 (February 1952): 7+.

5025. "L.A. Rent Decontrol Delayed by Series of Injunctions." *Western Housing* 34 (September 1950): 7+.

5026. "Los Angeles Rent Decontrol Results Reported by Apartment Association." *Western Housing* 34 (May 1951): 6+.

5027. "Low Cost Homes Built to Last." *Popular Mechanics* 75 (January 1941): 40-3+.
Los Angeles County Slum Clearance Program.

5028. Ma, Shwen Wei. "A Housing Project for a Low Income Group in the Northeast Corner of 38th Street and Wisconsin Street, Los Angeles, California." Master's thesis, University of Southern Calfornia, 1940. 44 pp.

5029. Maisel, Sherman J., *et al. California Housing Studies.* Berkeley, 1963. 230 pp.
Several of the tables and figures treat Los Angeles and Los Angeles County statistically.

5030. Matthews, William H. "The House Courts of Los Angeles." *Survey* 30 (July 5, 1913): 461-7.

5031. "Mayor Bowron Protests Housing Appointment." *Apartment Journal* 23 (March 1941): 27.

5032. McMahon, Charles A. "Concrete Formwork Totals 10,000,000 Contact Sq. Ft. on—Record Parklabrea Housing Project." *Western Construction* 25 (October 1950): 71-4.

5033. McQuiston, John M. *Negro Residental Invasion in Los Angeles County.* Master's thesis, University of Southern California, 1968. 401 pp.

5034. McWilliams, Carey. "Watts: The Forgotten Slum." *Nation* 201 (August 30, 1965): 89-90.

5035. Miller, Loren. "Housing and Racial Covenants." *Frontier* 1 (February 1, 1950): 11-3.
Los Angeles cases.

5036. Mittelbach, Frank G. *Profile of the Los Angeles Metropolis—Its People and Its Homes.* Part 2: *The Changing Housing Inventory: 1950-1959.* Los Angeles, 1963. 33 pp.

5037. Nelson, Herbert U. "Los Angeles a Leader in Local Government Principles." *Western Housing* 35 (March 1952): 16-8.
Los Angeles described as "The first great city to seek freedom from the public housing octopus."

5038. Neutra, Richard J. "Homes and Housing," in *Los Angeles: Preface to a Master Plan.* Ed. by George W. Robbins and L. Deming Tilton. Los Angeles, 1941. Pp. 180-202.

5039. ———— "Mild-Climate Housing." *Frontier* 5 (April 1954): 11-3.
Los Angeles high-rise housing.

5040. "Nickerson Gardens: Big Project of Small Neighborhoods Built by Los Angeles Housing Authority." *Journal of Housing* 11 (December 1954): 426-7.

5041. "Nine L.A. City Councilmen Vote for Fair Play to Apartment Owners." *Western Housing* 33 (March 1950): 8-9.
Favor rent decontrol.

5042. O'Conner, Tom, and Hughes, Carol. "Our Slum Problem." *Saturday Night* 45 (November 19, 1938): 14-7+.
Los Angeles.

5043. O'Donovan, Patrick J. "Fifteen Rent Advisory Boards Named for Los Angeles Defense Rental Area." *Western Housing* 31 (September 1947): 25+.

5044. O'Dwyer, Msgr. Thomas J. "Piercing the Housing Smog." *Frontier* 3 (September 1952): 8-10.
Federal Housing Program in Los Angeles. Also published in *Commonweal* 56 (October 3, 1952): 623-5.

5045. " 'Operation Junkyard' in Pasadena Corrects Sub-Standard Structures." *Western City* 28 (February 1952): 51.
Following issuance of comprehensive report of housing conditions by Pasadena Planning Commission, City Manager Don C. McMillan launches program to eliminate sub-standard housing.

5046. Patric, Gladys. *A Study of the Housing and Social Conditions in the Ann Street District of Los Angeles California.* Los Angeles, c1917. [32] pp.

5047. "Petitions for L.A. Rent Decontrol Being Circulated by Committee [of Los Angeles County Apartment Association]." *Western Housing* 33 (April 1950): 8.

5048. "Public Housing in the Far West—Three Projects Underway; 18 Loans Approved." *Western City* 16 (February 1940): 15-8.
Includes Ramona Village in Los Angeles, and Carmelitos in North Long Beach.

5049. "Public Housing Victory." *New Republic* 126 (May 12, 1952): 7.
State Supreme Court decision requiring the City of Los Angeles to meet the terms of its agreement with the Housing Authority.

5050. Raner, Guy H., Jr. "Public Housing and Politics: An Inquiry into the Historical and Political Background of Public Housing, and an Estimate of Its Future in the City of Los Angeles [1937-1957]." Master's thesis, University of Southern California, 1957. 296 pp.

5051. "Rental Vacancy Survey in Progress: L.A.

Decontrol Hearing in 6 Weeks." *Western Housing* 33 (March 1950): 7+.

5052. Rossmore, John R. "Los Angeles Betrayed: A Strange Conglomeration of Interests Is Lined Up Behind the City Council's Attempt to Scuttle the Public Housing Program." *Frontier* 3 (February 1952): 5+.

5053. Rothstein, Mignon. "A Study of the Growth of Negro Population in Los Angeles and Available Housing Facilities Between 1940 and 1946." Master's thesis, University of Southern California, 1950. 108 pp.

5054. Rutledge, J. Howard. "Vacancies Are on Rise in Los Angeles Two Months after Rent Decontrol." *Western Housing* 34 (March 1951): 7+.

5055. Saltzman, Joe, and Saltzman, Barbara. "Proposition 14: Appeal to Prejudice." *Frontier* 15 (October 1964): 5-8.
Open housing initiative; some emphasis on Los Angeles area.

5056. "Sanitary Surveys in Los Angeles." *Monthly Labor Review* 20 (June 1925): 1369-71.
Comparison of sanitary and living conditions in the Belvedere Gardens and Maravilla Park districts.

5057. Shirley, H. V. "No General Raise in Rents in Decontrolled Long Beach." *Western Housing* 33 (May 1950): 10+.

5058. "65 Year-Old Bunker Hill House Converted into Modern Apartments." *Western Housing* 37 (January 1954): 8+.

5059. "Slum-Clearance Starts: First of Los Angeles County's Low-Cost Housing Projects Now under Way." *Apartment Journal* 22 (September 1939): 12.
Carmelitos, North Long Beach.

5060. "Slum-Ending Ordinance Passed Unanimously by Los Angeles Council." *Western Housing* 36 (November 1952): 10.

5061. Smith, L. Elden. "A Statiscal Picture of the Housing Market." *Apartment Journal* 18 (October 1935): 8-9+.
Los Angeles.

5062. Sollins, J. "Systematic Inspection of Sub-standard Housing: The Experience of Five Cities Using the American Public Health Association Housing Appraisal Method." *American City* 63 (May 1948): 82-3.

Los Angeles section authored by Joseph Sollins.

5063. Spaulding, Charles B. "Housing Problems of Minority Groups in Los Angeles County." *Annals of the American Academy of Political and Social Science* 248 (November 1946): 220-5.

5064. Spicer, John L. "Housing Characteristics of Los Angeles Analyzed." *Apartment Journal* 28 (July 1945): 8+.

5065. ———" Population and Housing Data for Los Angeles City." *Apartment Journal* 28 (September 1945): 9.

5066. Stephens, Harrison. "Los Angeles Completes 5 Lanham Act Projects." *The Architect and Engineer* 154 (September 1943): 13-26.

Five federally-financed war-housing projects—Channel Heights, Banning Homes, Wilmington Hall, Normont Terrace, and Dana Strand Village —all in the harbor area.

5067. Strawn, Paul R. "The Mutual Housing Association of Los Angeles, a Case Study in Cooperation." Master's thesis, University of California, Los Angeles, 1951. 137 pp.

5068. Teetor, Josephine. "A Study of the Needs for Housing of Unattached Girls and Women in Los Angeles, California." Master's thesis, University of Southern California, 1939. 172 pp.

5069. Thomas, Don. "Housing Expansion: Huge Building Program Raises Question of Meeting Future Needs." *Apartment Journal* 22 (November 1939): 12+.

Los Angeles.

5070. "Thousand Gardens: Local Large-Scale Privately Financed Housing Project to Start Soon." *Apartment Journal* 22 (November 1939): 13+.

Los Angeles.

5071. Tomlinson, Russell P. "Mobile Home Parks as a Settlement Type in Los Angeles, Orange, and Riverside Counties." Master's thesis, California State College at Los Angeles, 1968. 178 pp.

5072. "Veterans Move into 1st Conversion Project: Red Cross and City Housing Authority Join Forces to Provide Homes for 300 Veterans with Families in Former Bachelor Quarters in Wilmington." *Western Housing* 28 (February 1946): 9.

5073. Walters, William. "Rent Control a Great Injustice to Los Angeles Property Owners." *Western Housing* 30 (May 1947): 10+.

5074. Ward, Mike. "A Man Buys a Home, and Monterey Park Won't Ever Be Quite the Same Again. *Frontier* 13 (June 1962): 7-9.

The experience of one Negro home-seeker.

5075. Weining, Clifford V. "The Fifield Manors— A New Type of Residence for Elderly People." *Western Housing* 39 (May 1956): 7+.

Non-profit corporations, the idea of Dr. and Mrs. James W. Fifield, Jr.

5076. ——— "Pleasant Apartment-Hotel Living Atmosphere at Fifield Manors." *Western Housing* 40 (July 1956): 7.

5077. Werner, Oscar G. "The Study of a Housing Development for Bunker Hill, Los Angeles." Master's thesis, University of Southern California, 1933. 90 pp.

5078. Wilkinson, Frank. "And Now the Bill Comes Due." *Frontier* 16 (October 1965): 10-2.

Declares that ". . . the real estate lobby . . . sabotaged badly needed additional public housing [in Watts] a decade ago. Any study of the Watts riots should not neglect this history of civic irresponsibility."

5079. Williams, Robert M. "The Relationship of Housing Prices and Building Costs in Los Angeles, 1900-1953." *The Journal of the American Statistical Association* 50 (1955): 370-6.

5080. Woehlke, Walter V. "Los Angeles—Homeland." *Sunset* 26 (January 1911): 3-16.

Reasons for increase in homebuilding in Los Angeles.

5081. Wolfinger, Raymond E., and Greenstein, Fred I. "The Repeal of Fair Housing in California: An Analysis of Referendum Voting." *American Political Science Review* 62 (1968): 753-69.

5082. "Worthy Ideas from Wartime Housing." *Architectural Record* 94 (November 1943): 55-60.

Normont Terrace housing project, Los Angeles.

5083. "Wyvernwood Housing Project." *The Architect and Engineer* 136 (March 1939): 31.

5084. Zuetell, Walter. "Pasadena Ends Sub-Standard Housing Problem with 'Operation Junkyard.'" *Western Housing* 35 (March 1952): 7+; (April 1952): 8+.

Reprinted from *Building Standards Monthly,* January 1952.

JOURNALISM

5085. Adler, Donald H. "Management Aspects of Establishing and Operating a Recently Organized Daily City Newspaper in Los Angeles." Master's thesis, University of Southern California, 1950. 157 pp.

The *Mirror.*

5086. Ainsworth, Edward M. *History of the Los Angeles Times.* [Los Angeles, 1941?]. 42 pp. 2nd ed., [Los Angeles, 1952?]. 64 pp.

5087. Anderson, Walt. "You Think 1968's Bad? . . . You Should Have Been Around for 1910." *Los Angeles* 13 (April 1968): 38-9+.

Includes *Times* bombing.

5088. Bliven, Bruce. "Two Newspapers in Search of a City." *Reporter* 26 (April 26, 1962): 22-3.

Los Angeles *Mirror* and *Examiner.*

5089. "Boddy Steps Out." *Newsweek* 40 (September 15, 1952): 64.

Manchester Boddy, newspaperman.

5090. Borough, Reuben W. "The Suicide of a Newspaper." *Frontier* 16 (February 1965): 13-4.

Los Angeles *Record.*

5091. Buhrman, Robert. "Is Los Angeles a Three-Newspaper Kind of Town?" *Los Angeles* 15 (June 1970): 36-8+.

Citizen-News challenges *Times* and *Herald-Examiner.*

5092. Brantley, Wilbur R. "A Comparative Analysis of Public Information Services of Three Major Law Enforcement Agencies in Los Angeles." Master's thesis, University of Southern California, 1958. 130 pp.

Los Angeles Police Department, Los Angeles County Sheriffs Department, Los Angeles County District Attorney's office.

5093. Carpenter, Bill. "Los Angeles: The Death of the [Daily] News." *New Republic* 132 (January 10, 1955): 6.

5094. Cifarelli, Anthony. "The Owens River Aqueduct and the Los Angeles Times; A Study in Early Twentieth Century Business Ethics and Journalism." Master's thesis, University of California, Los Angeles, 1969. 148 pp.

5095. Claypool, Leslie, "What Ails the Liberal Press?" *Frontier* 6 (March 1955): 24-5.

Author declares that the demise of the Los Angeles *Daily News* "leaves the 11 western states without a metropolitan daily newspaper that can be called democratic with either a large or a small "D".

5096. Conlon, Timothy J. "The Death of the Los Angeles *Mirror:* A Study in the Effects of Suburbanization upon the Community Role of a Metropolitan Newspaper." Master's thesis, Stanford University, 1962. 120 pp.

5097. Corry, John. "The Los Angeles Times." *Harper's* 239 (December 1969): 74-6+.

5098. Davenport, Robert W. "Weird Note for the Vox Populi: The Los Angeles *Municipal News.*" *California Historical Society Quarterly* 44 (1965): 3-15.

5099. Dunlop, George H. "A Municipal Newspaper." *National Municipal Review* 1 (July 1912): 441-3.

Los Angeles *Municipal News,* a weekly published by the City of Los Angeles.

5100. Ellerbe, Rose L. *History of Southern California Woman's Press Club, 1894-1929.* Los Angeles, [1930?]. 68 pp.

5101. "Experiment in Giveaways." *Time* 53 (January 24, 1949): 45-6.

James Parton's attempt to combine Los Angeles' most successful giveaway newspapers and "establish a profitable citywide newspaper with ready-made readership and advertising revenue."

5102. Feichert, Mary St. Joseph, Sister. "The History of *The Tidings,* Official Organ of the Archdiocese of Los Angeles." Master's thesis, Catholic University of American, 1951. 149 pp.

5103. Finney, Guy W. *Death Watch on The Gazette.* Los Angeles, 1933. 62 pp.

5104. ———— "Our Government by the Daily Press." *California Graphic* 5 (February 18, 1928): 7+.
Alleged Los Angeles *Times* monopoly.

5105. Gewecke, Clifford G., Jr. "The World as Seen Through Los Angeles Editorials, 1939-40 and 1954-55." Master's thesis, University of Southern California, 1956. 158 pp.

5106. Haas, Lucien C. "In the Belly of the Whale: The Daily News and Why It Died." *Frontier* 6 (February 1955): 7-10.

5107. Hassel, Damon. "Hollywood's Kept Press." *Frontier* 2 (October 1951): 7-9.
Hollywood reporters and gossip-columnists.

5108. Healey, John R. "The California Press and the Brown Act." Master's thesis, University of California, Los Angeles, 1964. 77 pp.

5109. "Hearst vs. L. A. Mirror." *Newsweek* 32 (November 8, 1948): 56+.

5110. Hill, Gladwin. "Why the New York *Times* for Los Angeles?" *Los Angeles* 3 (January 1962): 50-2.

5111. Illustrated Daily News. *Prospectus; Cornelius Vanderbilt, Jr., Publisher.* [Los Angeles, 1923]. [18] pp.

5112. James, George W. "Founding of the Overland Monthly and History of the Out West Magazine." *Overland Monthly* 81 (May 1923): 7-11.

5113. Johnson, Fern P. "Science News in the Los Angeles Press: A Curriculum Study." Master's thesis, University of Southern California, 1936. 113 pp.

5114. Kerby, Phil. "No News Is Bad News." *Frontier* 7 (July 1956): 12-4.
"The sensational and parochial press of Los Angeles."

5115. ———— "The Partisan Press and the Campaign: How the Papers of Los Angeles and San Francisco Colored and Weighted the News to Favor the Candidate of Their Choice" *Frontier* 4 (January 1953): 5-9.

5116. King, Margaret C. "The Los Angeles Newspaper Service Bureau, Incorporated: A Study of Publication Rates for Public Notice." Master's thesis, University of Southern California, 1941. 136 pp.

5117. "Los Angeles Discontinues Its Municipal Newspaper." *American City* 8 (May 1913): 555.

5118. "The Los Angeles Municipal News." *Technical World Magazine* 17 (July 1912): 522.

5119. "The L. A. Times Clock and the Crime Wave." *Municipal League of Los Angeles Bulletin* 2 (December 15, 1924): [3].
Allegation that the *Times* manufactured a bogus "crime wave" to boost circulation.

5120. Los Angeles Typographical Union No. 174. *Mr. Otis and the Los Angeles "Times."* Los Angeles, 1915. 24 pp.

5121. McCorkle, Julia N. "A History of Los Angeles Journalism." *Annual Publication* Historical Society of Southern California 10 (1915-1916): 24-43.

5122. McCoy, John H. "Educational News in the Los Angeles Press." Master's thesis, University of Southern California, 1933. 109 pp.

5123. McWilliams, Carey. "Nervous Los Angeles. I. The 'Wolf-Pack' Crusade." *Nation* 170 (June 10, 1950): 570-1.
"Lurid" press campaign against Mexican-American delinquency.

5124. Michaels, Rob. "After a Year of Strife . . . Where Does the Herald-Examiner Go from Here?" *Los Angeles* 13 (December 1968): 30-3.

5125. "A Municipal Newspaper." *Independent* 71 (December 14, 1911): 1342-4.
Los Angeles *Municipal News.*

5126. Murray, William. "The L. A. Free Press Is Rich: In a Revolutionary Society, a Few Crumbs

Can Become a Lot of Bread." *Esquire* 73 (June 1970): 54+.

5127. "The New World." *Time* 70 (July 15, 1957): 20-31.
Concentrates on the Los Angeles *Times,* its owners, and the extent of their power.

5128. Nunis, Doyce B., Jr. "A New Dress and under a New Plan." *Southern California Quarterly* 44 (1962): 1-16.
Summarizes past editorial policy and printers of the Historical Society of Southern California, with mention of the members of the Publication Committee of the *Annual,* and the previous editors of the *Quarterly,* initiated in 1935.

5129. "Passing of the Record." *Los Angeles Saturday Night* 16 (February 8, 1936): 9.
Los Angeles newspaper.

5130. Persons, A. Madelyn. "News and Editorials Concerning the Los Angeles Public Schools." Master's thesis, University of Southern California, 1952. 133 pp.

5131. Peters, Glen W. "The Sunday Supplement in Transition: An Analysis of the Sunday Supplement from Hearst's *American Weekly* to the *Los Angeles Times' West.*" Master's thesis, University of Southern California, 1969. 112 pp.

5132. "Plane Paper: Published for Workers in Southern California Factories, Los Angeles Aircraft Times Finds Market in 'City Within a City.'" *Business Week* (October 10, 1942): 64+.

5133. Prince, Virginia A. "A Sociological Analysis of the Negro Press in Los Angeles." Master's thesis, University of Southern California, 1946. 147 pp.

5134. "Public Relations—How 40 California Cities Supplement the Local Press." *Western City* 28 (February 1952): 41.
Includes several Los Angeles County cities.

5135. Rathbun, Morris M. "Newspapers Help to Build Community: Large Daily Publications of Los Angeles, the Equal of Any in the United States, Exert Every Effort to Advance City Interest." *Southern California Business* 1 (September 1922): 105+.

5136. Rathwell, Grace K. "Public School News in the Los Angeles Press." Master's thesis, University of Southern California, 1935. 105 pp.

5137. Riley, Frank. "The Changing Direction of the 'Times.'" *Los Angeles* 11 (June 1966): 28-31+.
Otis Chandler's Los Angeles *Times.*

5138. ——— "The City's Changing Newspaper World." *Los Angeles* 11 (July 1966): 26-30+.
Los Angeles' Hearst paper, *Herald-Examiner.*

5139. Ritter, Lloyd. "The *Chronicle,* Pasadena's First Newspaper, and Its Participation in the Growth of the Community." Master's thesis, Occidental College, 1950. 161 pp.

5140. Roberts, Myron. "The Poison Pen from Palos Verdes." *Los Angeles* 13 (October 1968): 30-3.
Pulitzer Prize winning Los Angeles *Times* cartoonist, Paul Conrad.

5141. Robinson, William W. "Southern California in Fifty Volumes." *Southern California Quarterly* 50 (1968): 1-4.
Review of the fifty volumes of historical annuals and quarterlies published by the Historical Society of Southern California.

5142. Roosevelt, Theodore. "Gompers, General Otis, and the Dynamite Charges." *Outlook* 98 (June 17, 1911): 330-2.

5143. Rosenstone. Robert A. "Manchester Boddy and the L. A. Daily News." *California Historical Society Quarterly* 49 (1970): 291-307.

5144. Ryan, Marian L. "Los Angeles Newspapers Fight the Water War, 1924-1927." *Southern California Quarterly* 50 (1968): 177-90.

5145. Stocker, Joseph. "The Los Angeles Mirror: Sex, Slaughter, & Liberalism." *American Mercury* 76 (January 1953): 34-41.

5146. Stotsenberg, Dorothy D. "A Man's World? Twenty-Five Years of Women's Pages in Los Angeles." Master's thesis, University of California, Los Angeles, 1950. 82 pp.

5147. "Too Many Papers in L. A.?" *Time* 58 (September 24, 1951): 77.
Discharge of Los Angeles newspaper employees as an austerity move.

5148. Tusher, William. "Hollywood's Keyhole Patrol." *Frontier* 1 (December 15, 1949): 7-9.

Journalistic "Jackals and Jackasses" who rob Hollywood personalities of their privacy.

5149. University Club of Los Angeles. *The Toreador, 1898-1948, Fiftieth Anniversary Number.* Los Angeles, 1948. 63 pp.

Publication of the club.

5150. "Uphill Climb." *Time* 63 (January 18, 1954): 51-2+.

Early years of Los Angeles *Mirror* (established 1948).

5151. "When Newspapers Die." *New Republic* 146 (January 22, 1962): 6.

Los Angeles *Examiner* and Los Angeles *Mirror*.

5152. "Where We've Been . . . Putting Out a Magazine about Los Angeles Was a Lot Easier in 1960—We Had Nowhere to Go But Up." *Los Angeles* 15 (July 1970): 34.

A decade of *Los Angeles* magazine.

5153. Wilkins, Barbara. "Miss Lonelyhearts Meets the Underground Press." *Los Angeles* 13 (January 1968): 28-9+.

Los Angeles *Free Press*.

5154. Williams, John H. "The Los Angeles Times and Public Opinion, a Study of Its Editorial Policy and the Effect on News Selection." Master's thesis, Claremont Graduate School, 1929. 107 pp.

5155. "Yortytoons." *Newsweek* 71 (February 12, 1968): 67.

Fued between Mayor Yorty and *Times* Publisher Otis Chandler.

5156. Young, Robert O. "The Stassen Incident of the 1956 Campaign, a Case Study in Newspaper Political Tactics." Master's thesis, University of California, Los Angeles, 1958. 123 pp.

Analysis of coverage given incident by the Los Angeles *Times*.

LABOR

5157. Adamic, Louis. *Dynamite: The Story of Violence in America.* Rev. ed., New York, 1934. 495 pp.

Anti-*Times*.

5158. Adams, Graham, Jr. *The Age of Industrial Violence, 1910-1915.* New York, 1966. 316 pp.

First chapter, "The Crime of the Century," pp. 1-24, is on the Los Angeles *Times* bombing of 1910.

5159. Allen, Arthur P., and Schneider, Betty V. H. *Industrial Relations in the California Aircraft Industry.* Berkeley, 1956. 59 pp.

Collective bargaining, with particular reference to Southern California.

5160. Amano, Matsukichi. "A Study of Employment Patterns and a Measurement of Employee Attitudes in Japanese Firms at Los Angeles." Doctoral disseration, University of California, Los Angeles, 1966. 485 pp.

5161. Ardon, Victor. "Piece Rate Structure in the Unionized Dress and Sportswear Industry in the Los Angeles Area." Master's thesis, University of Southern California, 1959. 86 pp.

5162. Arnett, Eugene V. "An Analysis of the Southern California Airframe Industry's Long Range Manpower Planning for Engineering Requirements." Master's thesis, University of Southern California, 1957. 113 pp.

Airplane industry workers.

5163. Atkinson, Barnett. "An Occupational Survey in the Highland Park District of Los Angeles." Master's thesis, University of Southern California, 1936. 96 pp.

5164. Baisden, Richard N. "Labor Unions in Los Angeles Politics." Doctoral dissertation, University of Chicago, 1958. 507 pp.

5165. Bassett, W. J. *Los Angeles County Federation of Labor, AFL-CIO: History and Growth.* [Los Angeles, n.d.]. 26 pp.

5166. Bernstein, Irving. *Hollywood at the Crossroads.* Los Angeles, 1957. 78 pp.

American Federation of Labor Film Council.

5167. "Big Labor Drive in Los Angeles." *Business Week* (April 10, 1937): 39-40+.

5168. Black, Frederick H., Jr. "Employee Relations Policies in Southern California." Master's thesis, University of Southern California, 1960. 196 pp.

5169. Bower, Anthony. "Films." *Nation* 152 (March 1, 1941): 249-50.

Stresses rise and growing influence of unions and guilds in Hollywood. Effectiveness of Screen Office Employees Guild said to be crippled by its inability to penetrate the ranks of Twentieth Century-Fox, Paramount or Warner Brothers.

5170. Brenner, Estelle D. "Factors in the Determination of Employability with Special Reference to Public Relief Administration in Los Angeles County." Master's thesis, University of Southern California, 1939. 151 pp.

5171. Brown, Joseph R., Jr. "Retail Clerks Unions in Los Angeles County [1887-1953]." Master's thesis, University of Southern California, 1953. 116 pp.

5172. Buzzell, J. W. "An Open Shop Citadel Falls." *American Federationist* 48 (April 1941): 6-7+.

5173. Bymers, Gwendolyn J. "A Study of Employment in Women's and Misses' Outerwear Manufacturing, Los Angeles Metropolitan Area, 1946-1954." Doctoral dissertation, University of California, Los Angeles, 1958. 307 pp.

5174. Cantrell, Lang L. "An Inquiry into the 1945-1947 Jurisdictional Strike in the Motion Picture Industry." Master's thesis, University of Southern California, 1947. 98 pp.

5175. Carlson, Oliver. "Los Angeles Grows Up." *Nation* 146 (January 8, 1938): 43-4.

Describes "sudden metamorphosis of Los Angeles from an open-shop paradise into a seething center of labor unrest."

5176. Carpenter, Willard. "Rebellion in Local 47." *Frontier* 7 (April 1956): 10+.

Los Angeles musicians and Petrillo law.

5177. Carr, Edward. "A Study of the Trends in Employee Training in the Los Angeles Area from 1941 to 1952." Master's thesis, University of Southern California, 1952. 102 pp.

5178. Citizens' Committee for the Shipowners. *The Pacific Maritime Labor Crisis.* San Francisco, 1936. 12 pp.

5179. Citizens' Manpower Committee. *History of the Los Angeles Citizens' Manpower Committee, 1943-1945.* [Los Angeles, 1945]. 31 pp.

5180. "City Is Accused: Los Angeles Is Informed That Its Wage Increase to Power Strikers Exceeded Limits Imposed by Little Steel Formula." *Business Week* (April 29, 1944): 108.

5181. Cohen, Wallace F. "An Investigation of the Unionization of Teachers in Southern California." Master's thesis, University of Southern California, 1959. 127 pp.

5182. Conference of Studio Unions. *The Hollywood Story.* Los Angeles, 1946. [?] pp.

5183. Connolly, Thomas E., Jr. "Employer-Attitudes Toward Section 7a in Southern California." Master's thesis, University of Southern California, 1935. 115 pp.

National Labor Relations Act.

5184. Corlett, Frank S. "An Analysis of Changes in Wage and Salary Relationships Among Certain Occupations in the Los Angeles Metropolitan Area, Period 1947-1960." Master's thesis, University of Southern California, 1960. 101 pp.

5185. Cosman, Ralph H. "A Study of the Industrial Recreation Program at Twentieth Century Fox Film Corporation." Master's thesis, University of California, Los Angeles, 1951. 55 pp.

5186. Crawshaw, Marshall R. "Testing the Reliability and Validity of the Los Angeles Office Employment Test." Master's thesis, University of Southern California, 1937. 59 pp.

5187. "Creation of Labor Relations Department in Superior Court of Los Angeles." *Monthly Labor Review* 53 (July 1941): 137-8.

5188. Crockett, Earl C. "The History of California Labor Legislation, 1910-1930." Doctoral dissertation, University of California, Berkeley, 1931. 329 pp.

5189. Cross, Ira B. *A History of the Labor Movement in California.* Berkeley, 1935. 354 pp.

5190. Darling, Kenneth. "A Study of the Activities of the War Manpower Commission in the Los Angeles Harbor Shipbuilding Industry." Master's thesis, Redlands University, 1952. 148 pp.

5191. Dawson, Anthony. "Patterns of Production and Employment in Hollywood." *Hollywood Quarterly* 4 (1950): 338-53.

5192. Dickert, Lois. "The Los Angeles Career Girl." *Los Angeles* 8 (November 1964): 26-31+.

5193. Dixon, Marion. "The History of the Los Angeles Central Labor Council." Master's thesis, University of California, Berkeley, 1929. 240 pp.

5194. Dunne, George H. *Hollywood Labor Dispute; A Study in Immorality.* Los Angeles, [1950?]. 44 pp.

5195. Durham, George H. "The Administration of Unemployment Compensation in California." Doctoral dissertation, University of California, Los Angeles, 1939. 321 pp.

5196. Elac, John C. "The Employment of Mexican Workers in U. S. Agriculture, 1900-1960; A Binational Economic Analysis." Doctoral dissertation, University of California, Los Angeles, 1967. 233 pp.

5197. Elliott, Clifford A. "Home Attractions Keep Track Laborers Satisfied." *Electric Railway Journal* 52 (July 27, 1918): 150-2.
Pacific Electric Railway.

5198. Ellis, William R. "Operation Bootstrap: A Case Study in Ideology and the Institutionalization of Protest." Doctoral dissertation, University of California, Los Angeles, 1969. 436 pp.
Operation Bootstrap: "A small self-help job training organization . . . a relatively direct outgrowth of previously existing protest organizations."

5199. "Employers Curbed: Barring Court Test, Order by NLRB Restraining M. & M. and Other Groups Marks End of an Era in Los Angeles Labor History." *Business Week* (December 13, 1941): 19-20+.

5200. Erb, Gertrude. "An Occupational Survey of a City Suburban to Los Angeles as a Basis for the Placement of Commercial Pupils." Master's thesis, University of Southern California, 1938. 87 pp.
Inglewood.

5201. Fitch, John A. "Los Angeles, a Militant Anti-Union Citadel." *Survey* 33 (October 3, 1914): 4-6.

5202. Flannery, Helen. "The Labor Movement in Los Angeles, 1880-1903." Master's thesis, University of California, 1929. 103 pp.

5203. Ford, Clyde E. "Agreement and Deviation of Practice and Provisions of the Plumbing-Heating Piping Labor Agreement in the Los Angeles Area." Master's thesis, University of Southern California, 1960. 114 pp.

5204. Fordyce, Robert C. "Area Wage Rate Differentials in Greater Los Angeles." Master's thesis, University of Southern California, 1960. 87 pp.

5205. Fremming, H. C. "Los Angeles Meets Unemployment." *American Federationist* 38 (July 1931): 855-7.

5206. George, Marie R. "Opportunities for Male Stenographers in the Los Angeles Area." Master's thesis, University of Southern California, 1939. 113 pp.

5207. Gilbert, Robert W. "The Wage Earners Committee: Home-Grown Fascism." *Frontier* 1 (August 15, 1950): 3-5.
An attack on "Wage Earners Committee of the U.S.A.," an anti-labor organization.

5208. Gleason, George. *The Fifth Migration . . . California Migratory Agricultural Worker Situation.* Prepared for the Los Angeles Committee for Church and Community Cooperation. [Los Angeles, 1940]. 29 pp.

5209. Goodell, Mame E. "A Critical Analysis of the Placement of Commercial High School Students in Los Angeles." Master's thesis, University of Southern California, 1930. 95 pp.

5210. Gordon, Margaret S. *Employment Expansion and Population Growth: The California Experience, 1900-1950.* Berkeley and Los Angeles, 1954. 192 pp.

5211. Greer, Scott A. "The Participation of Ethnic Minorities in the Labor Unions of Los Angeles County." Doctoral dissertation, University of California, Los Angeles, 1952. 413 pp.

5212. "Half Million Workers in Los Angeles." *Southern California Business* 3 (November 1924): 25.

5213. Hamren, Vandyce. "A Comparative Survey of the Characteristics of Two Groups of Unemployment Insurance Claimants with Respect to Acceptance or Nonacceptance of Insurance Benefits." Doctoral dissertation, University of Southern California, 1951. 182 pp.

5214. Hanna, Byron C. *Los Angeles Fights for Freedom.* Los Angeles, 1938. 44 pp.
Open and closed shop in Los Angeles.

5215. Hartman, William E. "The Relationship Between Job Adjustment and Marital Adjustment of a Selected Group of Workers." Doctoral dissertation, University of Southern California, 1950. 236 pp.

5216. Henderson, John C. "Public Recreation and Unemployment." *Western City* 9 (April 1933): 13-4.

5217. Hinsdale, Jennie R. "A Study of the Free Public Employment Agency with Special Reference to the Los Angeles Public Employment Bureau." Master's thesis, University of Southern California, 1918. 149 pp.

5218. Holman, Alfred. "In the Calcium Light: Harrison Gray Otis and His Fight for the Open Shop." *Overland Monthly* 51 (March 1908): 288-94.

5219. Horton, Helen M. "Occupations for Graduates of Los Angeles High Schools." Master's thesis, University of Southern California, 1928. 133 pp.

5220. Howell, Harry M. "Salary Survey and Job Analysis of Non-Certificated Personnel in Los Angeles City Schools." Master's thesis, University of Southern California, 1936. 81 pp.

5221. Iliff, Ruth M. "A Social Study of the Newsboys' Trade in Los Angeles." Master's thesis, University of Southern California, 1912. 23 pp.

5222. International Typographical Union of North America, Union No. 174, Los Angeles. *Mr. Otis and the Los Angeles "Times."* Los Angeles, 1915. 24 pp.

5223. International Union, United Automobile, Aircraft and Agricultural Implement Workers of America, Los Angeles Local 887. *Strike Home; A Report on the 54-Day Strike of 33,000 North American Workers.* [Los Angeles, 1953]. 42 pp.

5224. Johnson, Charles S. "Negro Workers in Los Angeles Industries." *Opportunity; A Journal of Negro Life* 6 (August 1928): 234-40.

5225. Johnston, Lyle F. "Analysis of Training Techniques for Industrial Relations Personnel in Southern California Industry." Master's thesis, University of Southern California, 1958. 157 pp.

5226. Kamei, Toshio. "An Inquiry into the Industrial Relations Program of the Restaurant Industry in Los Angeles." Master's thesis, University of Southern California, 1952. 142 pp.

5227. Lazard, Flora. "Child Workers in Street Trades in Los Angeles." Master's thesis, University of Southern California, 1939. 103 pp.

5228. Levenson, Lew. "The Case of Thomas Sharpe." *Nation* 139 (September 5, 1934): 272.
Appended is Sharpe's affidavit that he was mistreated by the Los Angeles police after being arrested for picketing at Terminal Island.

5229. Leventhal, Bertha. "Efforts Made by Clients in the Vermont District, Los Angeles County, State Relief Administration, Toward Rehabilitation by Acquiring New Skills or Improving Old Skills." Master's thesis, University of Southern California, 1939. 93 pp.

5230. Lieber, L. O. "Recreation and Welfare Work for Los Angeles Railway Employees." *Electric Railway Journal* 46 (September 11, 1915): 506-7.

5231. Liggett, Hazel M. *The Relation of Wages to the Cost of Living in Los Angeles 1915 to 1920.* Studies in Sociology, *Southern California Sociological Society Monograph No. 19,* Vol. V, No. 3. Los Angeles, 1921. 11 pp.

5232. Logan, Somerset. "The Battle of Hollywood." *New Republic* 59 (August 7, 1929): 308-10.
Actors' Equity vs. motion picture producers.

5233. ——— "Revolt in Hollywood." *Nation* 129 (July 17, 1929): 61-2.
Actors' Equity vs. motion picture producers.

5234. Los Angeles County Central Labor Council. *Golden Anniversary. Los Angeles Central Labor Council, 1901-1951.* [Los Angeles, 1951]. 71 pp.

5235. Los Angeles Industrial Union Council—CIO.

Unions Mean Higher Wages: The Story of the La Follette Committee Hearings in Los Angeles. Los Angeles, 1940. 32 pp.

Investigation of the La Follette Civil Liberties Committee into "violations of civil liberties and undue restraints on the right to organize."

5236. Los Angeles Times. *The Forty-Year War for a Free City, History of the Open Shop in Los Angeles.* [Los Angeles], 1929. 28 pp.

Elucidation of *Times'* concept of "true industrial freedom."

5237. "Los Angeles Airways Costly Strike Ends." *Aviation Week and Space Technology* 92 (May 11, 1970): 26.

5238. "Los Angeles Industries Increase Workers." *Southern Califonria Business* 1 (March 1922): 23+.

5239. "Los Angeles Open Shop Fight." *Business Week* (June 24, 1939): 28-9.

5240. "Los Angeles Stays Open Shop." *Business Week* (March 6, 1937): 15-6.

5241. "Los Angeles Studying Her Labor Conditions." *Survey* 28 (August 31, 1912): 680-1.

5242. "Los Angeles Union Drive Weaker." *Business Week* (September 25, 1937): 38.

5243. "L.A.'s Last Stand: Open-Shop Citadel Eyes San Francisco's Plan. M. & M. Reorganizing to Make the Best of Labors' Admitted Gains." *Business Week* (January 18, 1941): 48+.

5244. "L. A.'s Own War." *Business Week* (March 14, 1942): 87-8.

Open-shop battle persists in Los Angeles.

5245. Lovell, Hugh, and Carter, Tasile. *Collective Bargaining in the Motion Picture Industry.* Berkeley, 1955. 54 pp.

5246. Mabon, David W. "The West Coast Waterfront and Sympathy Strikes of 1934." Doctoral dissertation, University of California, Berkeley, 1966. 219 pp.

5247. Marine, Gene. "Los Angeles. 172,500 Jobless." *Nation* 186 (April 5, 1958): 292-3.

5248. ——— "Who Closed the Stores? The Issues in Los Angeles Strike-Lockout." *Frontier* 10 (February 1959): 9-10.

Retail Clerks Joint Council of Southern California vs. Food Employers' Council.

5249. Mathewson, Walter G. "L.A. Shows Greatest Employment Gains." *Southern California Business* 1 (November 1922): 16+.

5250. McCrea, Joan M. "Wage Determination in Retail Trade: Los Angeles Food Stores." Doctoral dissertation, University of California, Los Angeles, 1965. 92 pp.

5251. McElheney, Alice. "A Study of Existing Conditions in Household Employment in Los Angeles." Master's thesis, University of Southern California, 1937. 138 pp.

5252. McEntire, Davis. *The Labor Force in California.* Berkeley, 1952. 101 pp.

5253. McWilliams, Carey. *Factories in the Field* Boston, 1939. 334 pp.

5254. McWilliams, Carey. "Nervous Los Angeles. II. The Angry 'Wage Earners.'" *Nation* 170 (June 10, 1950): 571-2.

"Wage Earners Committee of the U.S.A.," and its anti-liberal campaigns.

5255. Meister, Dick. "No More Braceros." *Frontier* 14 (July 1963): 12-3.

5256. Merchants' and Manufacturers' Association of Los Angeles. *Los Angeles and the Open Shop.* Los Angeles, 1922. 4 pp.

5257. Michaels, Rob. "After a Year of Strife . . . Where Does the Herald-Examiner Go from Here?" *Los Angeles* 13 (December 1968): 30-3.

5258. "Minority Groups in California." *Monthly Labor Review* 86 (September 1966): 978-83.

Important labor statistics.

5259. Mitchell, Charles K. "An Analysis of Technical Recruiting in the Missile Industry of Southern California." Master's thesis, University of Southern California, 1959. 128 pp.

5260. Modell, John. "Class or Ethnic Solidarity: The Japanese American Company Union." *Pacific Historical Review* 38 (1969): 193-206.

Southern California Retail Produce Workers Union, Los Angeles.

5261. Mones, Samuel L. "An Inquiry into the Areas of Cooperation Between Management and the Warehouse, Processing and Distribution Workers Union—Local 26, (I.L.W.U.) Ind., in the Los Angeles Area." Master's thesis, University of Southern California, 1955. 155 pp.

5262. Monte, Joseph L. "Part-Time Female Employees—A Partial Solution to the Staffing Problem in the Banking Industry of the Los Angeles Metropolitan Area." Master's thesis, University of Southern California, 1958. 98 pp.

5263. Morgans, Robert D. "A History of Organized Labor in Long Beach, California." Master's thesis, University of California, Berkeley, 1940. 161 pp.

5264. Murray, Helen. "Welfare Needs of Migratory Agricultural Labor in Southern California." Master's thesis, University of Southern California, 1939. 115 pp.
Los Angeles County included.

5265. National Negro Congress. Los Angeles Council. *Jim Crow in National Defense.* [Los Angeles, 1940?]. 27 pp.

5266. "New Job Agency: Los Angeles Committee to Direct Men to Defense Work Is Made Up of Management, Labor, Government Representatives." *Business Week* (December 13, 1941): 78-9.

5267. Newton, Charles S. "A Critical Analysis of the Wage and Salary Administrator in Los Angeles Industry." Master's thesis, University of Southern California, 1961. 103 pp.

5268. Nordahl, Ruth M. "A Social Study of the Newsboys' Trade in Los Angeles." Master's thesis, University of Southern California, 1912. 23 pp.

5269. "Open Shop under Fire: La Follette Blasts Business Groups for Attempting to Keep Los Angeles Out of Union Grip." *Business Week* (January 27, 1940): 26-7.
Hearings of the La Follette Civil Liberties Committee in Los Angeles.

5270. Otis, Harrison Gray. "A Long, Winning Fight Against the 'Closed Shop': An Account of a Seventeen-Years' Conflict Between the Los Angeles

'Times' and the Typographical Union." *World's Work* 15 (December 1907): 9675-9.

5271. Palmer, Frederick. "Otistown of the Open Shop." *Hampton's Magazine* 26 (January 1911): 29-44.

5272. Perry, Louis B. "A Survey of the Labor Movement in Los Angeles, 1933-1939." Doctoral dissertation, University of California, Los Angeles, 1950. 801 pp.

5273. ——, and Perry, Richard S. *A History of the Los Angeles Labor Movement, 1911-1941.* Berkeley and Los Angeles, 1963. 622 pp.

5274. Porter, Paul T. "Handling Mexican Labor in California." *Electric Railway Journal* 72 (August 11, 1928): 221-2.
Pacific Electric Railway.

5275. Pridham, R. W. "Good Business and the Open Shop." *Southern California Business* 6 (June 1927): 18+.
Los Angeles labor policy.

5276. Pritchard, Lawrence. D. "The History, Activities, and Organization of the All City Employees' Association of Los Angeles [1918-1940]." Master's thesis, University of Southern California, 1940. 154 pp.

5277. Reed, Mary. "San Pedro." *Nation* 119 (July 9, 1924): 45-6.
Describes attack on I.W.W. members following an explosion on the S.S. *Mississippi* in Los Angeles harbor.

5278. Reynolds, William H. *Experience of Los Angeles Employers with Minority Group Employees.* [Los Angeles, 1967]. 54 pp.

5279. Rockwell, Robert C. "An Analytical Study of Employment Conditions within Los Angeles County." Master's thesis, University of Southern California, 1947. 76 pp.

5280. Roosevelt, Theodore. "Gompers, General Otis, and the Dynamite Charges." *Outlook* 98 (June 17, 1911): 330-2.

5281. Ross, Murray. "The C.I.O. Loses Hollywood." *Nation* 149 (October 7, 1939): 374-7.

5282. ——— "Labor Relations in Hollywood." *Annals of the American Academy of Political and Social Science* 254 (November 1947): 58-64.

5283. "Salaries in Various Occupations in Los Angeles." *Monthly Labor Review* 33 (August 1931): 383-5.

5284. Sangster, R. D. "Turning Out a Factory Record." *Southern California Business* 5 (January 1927): 9-10+.
Los Angeles factory employment.

5285. Schwartz, Ellen L. "Some Aspects of the Los Angeles City School District's Retirement System for the Certified Employee." Master's thesis, University of California, Los Angeles, 1943. 109 pp.

5286. Security First National Bank of Los Angeles. Research Division. *Survey of Community Employment Trends in Southern California.* [Los Angeles], 1965. 20 pp

5287. "Self-Help Activities of Unemployed in Los Angeles." *Monthly Labor Review* 36 (April 1933): 717-40.

5288. Shanks, Harriette B. "Occupational Trends in the Los Angeles Area." Master's thesis, University of Southern California, 1949. 58 pp.

5289. Shaw, John W. "The Social Phases of Industrial Recreation as They Affect Employee-Employer Relations in the Los Angeles Metropolitan Area." Doctoral dissertation, University of Southern California, 1948. 477 pp.

5290. Simpson, Roy E. "Vocational Survey of the City of Pomona, California." Master's thesis, Claremont Graduate School, 1931. 56 pp.

5291. Spaulding, Charles B. "The Mexican Strike at El Monte, California." *Sociology and Social Research* 18 (July-August 1934): 571-80.

5292. Sterkel, Elizabeth M. "Employing the 'Unemployables': A Study of Los Angeles County Rehabilitation Division." Master's thesis, University of Southern California, 1939. 73 pp.

5293. Stevens, George T. "Public Employee Credit Unions in the Los Angeles Area." Master's thesis, University of Southern California, 1940. 136 pp.

5294. Stevens, I. M. "Call Mutual 8381 and Cut Taxes: Why Employers Should Hire from the County's List of 75,000 Employables." *Southern California Business* 12 (December 1933): 8-9.

5295. Stimson, Grace H. *Rise of the Labor Movement in Los Angeles.* Berkeley and Los Angeles, 1955. 529 pp.

5296. Sullivan, Ethel (MacKenzie). "Case Studies of Employed Ninth Grade Graduates of a Los Angeles Junior High School; A Record of Seventy-Eight Employed Graduates and the Use They Make of Shop Information and Acquired Skill in Connection with Their Jobs." Master's thesis, University of Southern California, 1932. 60 pp.

5297. "A Tale of Two Cities and the Open Shop." *Current Opinion* 69 (August 1920): 248-50.
Los Angeles and San Francisco.

5298. Thomas, Milton G. "An Analytical Study of the Industrial Relations Program at Northrop Aircraft, Inc." Master's thesis, University of Southern California, 1948. 163 pp.

5299. Thompson, Morton. "Hollywood Is a Union Town." *Nation* 146 (April 2, 1938): 381-3.

5300. Tipton, Gene B. "The Labor Movement in the Los Angeles Area During the Nineteen-Forties." Doctoral dissertation, University of California, Los Angeles, 1953. 395 pp.

5301. Tormey, Mary M. "An Historical Study of Labor Relations in the Southern California Area of the Pacific Telephone and Telegraph Company." Master's thesis, University of Southern California, 1954. 181 pp.

5302. "Twelve Millions Added to Payroll." *Southern California Business* 6 (February 1927): 9-10.
Los Angeles industrial expansion 1923-1925.

5303. "Unemployment Still Critical." *Southern California Business* 13 (February 1934): 11.
Los Angeles County.

5304. "Union Climax in L.A.: Fight of Los Angeles Business Men to Defend Open Shop Is Close to Critical Stage." *Business Week* (January 29, 1938): 34-5.

5305. "Union Labor and Dynamiting." *Sunset* 35 (November 1915) : 854.

Los Angeles *Times* dynamiting.

5306. "Unionism in Filmland." *Nation* 129 (August 28, 1929) : 211.

5307. "Unionism in Los Angeles." *Survey* 42 (July 26, 1919) : 633.

5308. "Utility Is Seized: Los Angeles Take-Over May Lead to Setting a Nation-Wide Pattern for Federal Procedure in Walkouts of Municipal Workers." *Business Week* (March 4, 1944) : 21-2.

5309. Van Valen, Nelson S. "The Bolsheviki and the Orange Growers." *Pacific Historical Review* 22 (1953) : 39-50.

On a 1919 strike of orange pickers in the San Gabriel Valley initiated by the Industrial Workers of the World.

5310. ———— "The Industrial Workers of the World in the Los Angeles Area, 1919-1923." Master's thesis, Claremont Graduate School, 1951. 215 pp.

5311. Wade, Margaret H. "A Descriptive Study of the Jobs Held by Women in the Radio-Television Industry in Los Angeles." Master's thesis, University of Southern California, 1951. 374 pp.

5312. "Wage Earners Could Buy Four States." *Southern California Business* 4 (October 1925) : 19+.

Earnings of Los Angeles wage earners.

5313. Walther, Henry W. "A Survey of the Employment and Subsequent History Records of Behavior Problem Boys Who Have Passed Through the Welfare Centers of the Los Angeles City Schools." Master's thesis, University of Southern California, 1937. 111 pp.

5314. Waltz, Richard C. "Beverly Hills Municipal Picketing Ordinance Is Upheld." *Western City* 14 (February 1938) : 12-3.

5315. Weintraub, Hyman. "The I.W.W. in California, 1905-1931." Master's thesis, University of California, Los Angeles, 1947. 328 pp.

5316. Wentz, Walter B. "The Los Angeles Newspaper Guild." Master's thesis, Claremont Graduate School, 1958. 181 pp.

5317. Williams, Kenneth R. "A Critical Study of the Appearance and Behavior Characteristics That Effect the Selection of Female Applicants for Office Positions in Selected Los Angeles Companies." Master's thesis, University of California, Los Angeles, 1957. 151 pp.

5318. Wilson, Andrew A. "Wage Determination in the Los Angeles Retail Food Industry." Doctoral dissertation, Claremont Graduate School, 1966. 306 pp.

5319. Wilson, Harry A. "Correlation Between Wage Rates and Labor Turnover in the Los Angeles Area." Master's thesis, University of Southern California, 1954. 47 pp.

5320. Wolf, Jerome. "The Los Angeles Times, Labor, and the Open Shop, 1890-1910." Master's thesis, University of Southern California, 1961. 105 pp.

5321. "Women's Bombshell: Housewives' Accusations in Open Shop Fight Embarrass Los Angeles Executives." *Business Week* (October 7, 1939) : 36-7.

5322. Wuesthoff, Marie. "An Inquiry into the Activities of the Internation Ladies' Garment Workers' Union in Los Angeles [1911-1938]." Master's thesis, University of Southern California, 1938. 176 pp.

LAW—COURTS, LAWYERS AND JUDGES

5323. "Act to Establish County Courts Submitted to Supervisors." *Bar Bulletin* 14 (January 1939) : 151-60.

Proposed legislation concerning the organization of inferior courts in Los Angeles County.

5324. "Activities of 14 Los Angeles County Bar Associations in Furnishing Free Legal Services to Draftees." *Bar Bulletin* 17 (September 1941) : 1-2.

5325. "The Administration of Buron Fitts." *Municipal League of Los Angeles Bulletin* 9 (January 20, 1932) : [7-8].

District attorney.

5326. Ambrose, Thomas L. "The Municipal Court."

Municipal League of Los Angeles Bulletin 2 (June 1925) : 13-4.

5327. Anderson, W. H. "Bench and Bar of Los Angeles City and County." *Los Angeles Saturday Night 150th Birthday of Los Angeles: Fiesta and Pre-Olympiad.* Special Issue (1931) : [16].

5328. Bailie, Norman A. "The Bar Associations of Los Angeles County." *Los Angeles Bar Association Bulletin* 6 (September 18, 1930) : 3+.

5329. ——— "Purposes and Work of Los Angeles Bar Association." *The Bar Association Bulletin* 5 (March 20, 1930) : 197+.

5330. Baker, Robert. "Why the McNamaras Pleaded Guilty to the Bombing of the Los Angeles Times." Master's thesis, University of California, Berkeley, 1949. 113 pp.

5331. Bauchet, Ruth M. "Municipal Court Consolidation Plan: An Opponent's Point of View." *Long Beach Bar Bulletin* 9 (May 1963) : 15-7.

5332. ——— "Municipal Court of Long Beach, 35th Anniversary." *Long Beach Bar Bulletin* 6 (September 1960) : 13-6.
Brief history and evolution.

5333. Beecher, Daniel. "Office of District Attorney of Los Angeles County." *Bar Bulletin* 17 (February 1942) : 139-44.
History of office and evolution of duties.

5334. Beeson, John R. "The Background and Development of Domestic Relations Investigations in the County of Los Angeles." Master's thesis, University of Southern California, 1961. 180 pp.

5335. Began, William D. "Legal Aid in Long Beach." *Bar* 2 (September 1956) : 1-3+.

5336. Belcher, Frank B. "The Los Angeles Bar Association's Answer to Newspaper Attacks." *Bar Bulletin* 13 (June 1938) : 297-302.
Bar Association's opposition to the taking of pictures of court proceedings.

5337. Bishop, Edward T. "No Delays in Los Angeles Courts: Continuances Not Favored in Either Civil or Criminal Cases." *Los Angeles Bar Association Bulletin* 10 (Special Edition, July 1935) : 252-4.

5338. Bishop, S. A. "The Value of An Index Bureau in Dealing with Fraudulent Claims." *Electric Railway Journal* 42 (July 19, 1913) : 105-6.
Pacific Electric Railway.

5339. Blake, Samuel R. "The Superior Court, Lawyers and Litigants Also Have Housing Problems." *Los Angeles Bar Bulletin* 23 (January 1948) : 152-9.
Overcrowding.

5340. Bloom, Hannah. "Loyalty in Los Angeles." Two part article: "None But the Lonely Hearts." *Frontier* 1 (March 15, 1950) : 3-4; "The Great Game of Truth or Consequence." *Frontier* 1 (April 1, 1950) : 8-9.
City and county loyalty oaths, and challenges thereto.

5341. Bond, Harry C. "Municipal Lease-Back Financing; A Study of Court Cases and Selected Cities in the Los Angeles Metropolitan Area." Master's thesis, University of Southern California, 1963. 150 pp.

5342. "Bond Feature of the New California Lien Law Unconstitutional?" *The Architect and Engineer of California* 34 (September 1913) : 93-4.
Los Angeles court cases.

5343. Borough, R[e]ube[n]. "Law and Order in Los Angeles." *Nation* 125 (July 6, 1927) : 12.
Julian oil scandal.

5344. Bowers, Deloss H. "The Juvenile Court of Los Angeles." Master's thesis, University of Southern California, 1931. 126 pp.

5345. Brand, Edward R. "Getting Results in Municipal Traffic Court: How Los Angeles Is Reducing Accidents; Unique Punishment Sometimes Essential; And What the Ticket 'Fixer' Deserves." *Western City* 11 (May 1935) : 13-4.

5346. Brinkman, Lester. "Supreme Court Upholds Los Angeles Zoning Re Minimum Lot Area." *Western City* 26 (May 1950) : 50.

5347. Brockmann, Ray. "The Hobgoblin of Scattered Courts." *Los Angeles Bar Bulletin* 23 (January 1948) : 160-7.
Los Angeles Municipal Courts.

5348. Burnside, Howard S. "Los Angeles County

Zoning Ordinance Upheld." *Western Construction* 30 (March 1955): 70.

Livingston Rock & Gravel Co. vs. County of Los Angeles (272 P.2d 4).

5349. Cain, Elmer. "90% of Lawyers in Los Angeles County in 'Bench and Bar.'" *Los Angeles Bar Bulletin* 24 (October 1948): 37-8+.

Publication with photos and biographical sketches of more than 4,000 Los Angeles County lawyers described.

5350. Call, Joseph L. "Criminal Divisions of the Municipal Court of the City of Los Angeles." *Los Angeles Bar Bulletin* 21 (October 1945): 36-40.

5351. Campbell, Alan G. "Los Angeles Zoning Ordinance Ruling Viewed in Light of Legal Principles." *Western City* 31 (April 1955): 59+.

5352. Campbell, Kemper. "What Los Angeles Bar Association Is Doing." *The Bar Association Bulletin* 3 (October 6, 1927): 5-12+.

5353. "Canons of Ethnics of the Los Angeles Bar Association." *Los Angeles Bar Association Bulletin* 9 (November 16, 1933): 57-64.

5354. Clad, Clinton, and Hoose, Harned P. "The Organized Bar in Los Angeles: (A Survey of Amici Curiae in Utopis)." *Los Angeles Bar Bulletin* 28 (October 1952): 2-13+.

5355. Claggett, Helen L. "An Innovation in Courtrooms." *Bar Bulletin* 17 (August 1942): 274-5+.

Effort of Hon. Thurmond Clarke, Presiding Judge of Dept. 6 of Superior Court of Los Angeles County, "to provide a room that would be attractive to both the lawyer and the layman."

5356. Clary, William W. "A Brief History of the Los Angeles Bar Association." *The Los Angeles Bar Bulletin* 43 (October 1968): 507-10+.

5357. —— *History of the Law Firm of O'Melveny & Myers 1885-1965.* Los Angeles, 1966. 2 vols.

Los Angeles law firm.

5358. "Compensation of Los Angeles Municipal Court Judges." *Bar Bulletin* 14 (March 1939): 204-6.

5359. Connolly, Christopher P. "The Saving of Clarence Darrow: Factors and Motives That Led

to the Dramatic Close of the McNamara Case." *Collier's* 48 (December 23, 1911): 9-10+.

5360. —— "The Trial at Los Angeles: Some of the Questions and Personalities in the McNamara Case." *Collier's* 48 (October 14, 1911): 17+.

5361. Continini, A. "The Civil Judgment Division of the County Clerk's Office." *Long Beach Bar Bulletin* 5 (March 1959): 7+.

5362. Continuing Special Committee on Legal Aid of the Los Angeles Bar Association. "Legal Aid and the Local Bar." *Bar Bulletin* 14 (November 1938): 91-2.

5363. Coombs, Claire H. "The Women's Court." *Out West,* new series, 11 (March 1916): 115-7.

The brainchild of Judge Thomas P. White, a Los Angeles court with women officers and assisted by a "Woman's Court Committee" for hearing cases involving female defendants.

5364. "Cost of Establishing and Maintaining Branches of the Superior Court: Report of Bar Committee Urges Survey of All Courts of County and Their Personnel." *Los Angeles Bar Association Bulletin* 12 (February 18, 1937): 187+.

5365. "Court Room Pictures." *Bar Bulletin* 13 (August 1938): 380-2.

Comments on article by Bar Association President Frank B. Belcher in June 1938 issue of this periodical.

5366. "The Craig Judicial Scandal; Los Angeles Bar Association Takes Action." *Los Angeles Bar Association Bulletin* 12 (November 12, 1936): 79-81.

Appellate Justice Gavin Craig was convicted in May, 1935 of conspiring to obstruct justice, but remained in office; situation greatly concerned the Los Angeles Bar Association.

5367. "Creation of Labor Relations Department in Superior Court of Los Angeles." *Monthly Labor Review* 53 (July 1941): 137-8.

5368. Curtis, Wilbur C. "Pre-Trial Procedure in Los Angeles Municipal Court." *Bar Bulletin* 13 (May 1938): 227-8.

5369. Darby, Raymond V. "Los Angeles County's

Convenient Courts." *California Magazine of the Pacific* 41 (September 1951) : 10+.

5370. Darrow, Clarence S. *The Plea of Clarence Darrow in His Own Defense to the Jury at Los Angeles, August, 1912.* Los Angeles, 1912. 59 pp.

5371. David, Leon T. *Law and Lawyers, One Hundred Twenty-Eight Years in the History of Los Angeles, as Seen from the City Attorney's Office.* Los Angeles, [1950]. 35 pp.

5372. Detzer, Karl. "The Judge Didn't Throw the Book." *Reader's Digest* 37 (October 1940) : 94-6.

Los Angeles program for sending delinquent boys to mountain camp where they render useful services. From *The Kiwanis Magazine* 25 (October 1940) : 562-3+.

5373. "Divorce Mill: Los Angeles Frees Many More Mismated Couples Than Reno." *Life* 19 (July 23, 1945) : 55-9.

5374. Dorsey, R[alph] T. "Los Angeles' Depression Traffic School." *American City* 48 (July 1933) : 63.

Traffic offenders given option of attending traffic school, rather than paying fine.

5375. Dutton, Frederick G. "Survey to be Made of the Administration of Justice in Los Angeles." *Los Angeles Bar Bulletin* 29 (October 1953) : 7-8+.

5376. Elkins, J. Louis. "Report of Activities of Lawyer Reference Service Los Angeles Bar Association." *Los Angeles Bar Bulletin* 27 (January 1952) : 165-6+.

Service established in 1937 "to refer persons who do not know a lawyer to a member of the profession."

5377. Elliott, Shelden D. "Legal Aid and the Los Angeles Bar." *Los Angeles Bar Association Bulletin* 11 (October 17, 1935) : 35-7.

5378. Ellis, Arthur M. "The Legal Status of the Venice Canals." *The Bar Association Bulletin* 5 (November 21, 1929) : 78-9.

5379. Endore, Samuel G. *Justice for Salcido.* Introduction by Carey McWilliams. Los Angeles, 1948. 31 pp.

5380. —— *The Sleepy Lagoon Mystery.* Los Angeles, 1944. 48 pp.

A famous Los Angeles murder mystery involving some Mexican youths.

5381. "Enforcing the Standard Weight Bread Law in Los Angeles County." *American City* 26 (April 1922) : 318.

5382. Ennis, George W. "The Juvenile Traffic School of Los Angeles County." Master's thesis, University of Southern California, 1935. 140 pp.

5383. Feldmeier, John F. "The Los Angeles City Attorney's Office." *Bar Bulletin* 17 (March 1942) : 154-60.

History of office and evolution of duties.

5384. Finney, Guy W. *The Great Los Angeles Bubble: A Present Day Story of Colossal Financial Jugglery and of Penalties Paid.* Los Angeles, 1929. 203 pp.

Julian Petroleum Corp. scandal.

5385. —— "The Julian Verdict—A Travesty or Benefit?" *California Graphic* 5 (May 26, 1928) : 7+.

Julian stock swindlers' trial.

5386. —— "Justice Grinds Slowly at the Julian Trial." *California Graphic* 5 (January 21, 1928) : 7+.

5387. —— "Mr. Toplitzky (Julian Indictee) Threatens Suit." *California Graphic* 5 (October 1, 1927) : 9+.

Joe Toplitzky, real estate broker, and the Julian oil scandal.

5388. Ford, Patrick E., ed. *The Darrow Bribery Trial with Background Facts of the McNamara Case and Including Darrow's Address to the Jury.* Whittier, 1956. 61 pp.

5389. Gibson, Hugh C. "Probation, What It Involves or Cultivating Our Garden." *Out West,* new series, 9 (January 1915) : 3-8.

Written by the Chief Probation Officer of Los Angeles County.

5390. Gibson, La Dessa. "Juvenile Court Referee's Work Recognized Abroad." *California Graphic* 5 (July 7, 1928) : 8.

Miriam Van Waters' role.

5391. "Glendale Revenue Case Review to Be Asked of Supreme Court." *Western City* 28 (January 1952): 29.

5392. "A Guide for Public Relations Activities for the Los Angeles County Bar Association." *The Los Angeles Bar Bulletin* 37 (November 1961): 11-4.

5393. Hahn, Walter, Jr.; Cupp, Carl C., and Warner, Nicholas. "Inglewood's Centralized Communication System Services Police, Fire and City Hall Offices." *Western City* 35 (July 1959): 38+.

5394. Hannon, Philip J. "Legal Services in Southern California: A Study of the Legal Services Program in Action." Doctoral dissertation, Claremont Graduate School, 1969. 247 pp.

5395. Harris, Nicholas B. *In the Shadows. Thirty Detective Stories Showing "Why Crime Doesn't Pay." A Series of Famous Cases.* Los Angeles, 1923. 361 pp.

5396. Heath, A. H. "Family Services of Long Beach: Who & What." *Long Beach Bar Bulletin* 3 (December 1958): 6+.

5397. Hickson, A. L. *A Short History of the Pomona Valley Bar Association, 1917-1954.* N.p., 1954. 82 pp.

5398. Hindman, Jo. "Bulldozer at Your Door." *American Mercury* 87 (September 1958): 119-27.
Diatribe against "socialistic schemes for redevelopment."

5399. Holbrook, James G., *et al. A Survey of Metropolitan Trial Courts Los Angeles Area.* [Los Angeles, 1956]. 434 pp.

5400. Honnard, Ronald R., *et al. Views of Authority: Probationers and Probation Officers.* Ed. by A. W. McEachern. University of Southern California, Youth Studies Center, *Research Paper 1.* Los Angeles, 1961. 238 pp.

5401. Hutson, Donald R. "Boys Seen in Los Angeles County Juvenile Court as Incorrigible: Exploration of Factors Relevant to the Breakdown in the Parent-Child Relationship." Master's thesis, University of Southern California, 1965. 62 pp.

5402. Ivens, Charles P. "The Office of Public Defender with Special Reference to Alameda, Los Angeles, and San Francisco Counties." Master's thesis, University of California, Berkeley, 1950. 250 pp.

5403. Jorgensen, Alfred W. "A New Approach to Solving Water Disputes: The Long Beach Case [1781-1967]." Master's thesis, University of Southern California, 1967. 140 pp.

5404. "Judge Bowron's Report to Judicial Council of Work of Superior Court." *Los Angeles Bar Association Bulletin* (March 17, 1938): 220-31.
Digest of report to Judicial Council of California.

5405. "Juvenile Crime Prevention Committee of the Junior Barristers of Los Angeles Bar." *Los Angeles Bar Association Bulletin* 11 (May 21, 1936): 214.

5406. Keim, Thomas B. "The Recall of Superior Court Judges in Los Angeles in 1932." Master's thesis, University of California, Los Angeles, 1936. 176 pp.

5407. Kennedy, Harold W. "The History, Legal and Administrative Aspects of Air Pollution Control in the County of Los Angeles." Master's thesis, University of Southern California, 1954. 195 pp.

5408. ———— *The History, Legal and Administrative Aspects of Air Pollution Control in the County of Los Angeles.* Report submitted to the Board of Supervisors of the County of Los Angeles. [Los Angeles], 1953. 83 pp.
The author completed a similarly entitled study. See above entry.

5409. Kenny, Robert W. "Case Load on Superior Court Judges for the Entire State Greater in Los Angeles County." *Los Angeles Bar Association Bulletin* 9 (May 17, 1934): 197+.

5410. Kerby, Phil. "Case No. 33." *Frontier* 9 (February 1958): 18+.
Case brought before the Supreme Court on behalf of 23 "blacklisted" Hollywood actors, writers, and studio employees.

5411. Kraus, Phillip. "The Office of Public Defender in Los Angeles County." Master's thesis, University of California, Los Angeles, 1937. 123 pp.

5412. Lampton, L. E. "Is Trial Work of Superior Court Increasing or Decreasing?" *Los Angeles Bar Association Bulletin* 12 (March 18, 1937): 226-9.

The county clerk presents statistics as to the number of contested cases tried, the number of judges available for civil trial work, and changes occurring in types of civil litigation.

5413. Larrabee, Lawrence L. " 'The Bar Endorses.' " *Southern California Business* 11 (August 1932): 16.

Activities of the Los Angeles Bar Association.

5414. Larwill, George R. "Pre-Trial Hearing in Superior Court: First Six Weeks' Experiment Assures Success of New Procedural Plan." *Los Angeles Bar Association Bulletin* 12 (April 15, 1937): 257-9.

Plan inaugurated through the efforts of Presiding Judge Fletcher Bowron.

5415. Lawrence, Dorothy W. "Some Problems Arising in the Treatment of Adolescent Negro Girls Appearing Before the Los Angeles Juvenile Court." Master's thesis, University of Southern California, 1941. 106 pp.

5416. Leader, Maurice T. "Los Angeles Municipal Division 40." *The Los Angeles Bar Bulletin* 38 (June 1963): 275-7.

5417. Lembert, Edwin M., and Rosberg, Judy. *The Administration of Justice to Minority Groups in Los Angeles County.* University of California *Publications in Culture and Society,* Vol. 2, No. 1. Berkeley and Los Angeles, 1948. 27 pp.

Contents date from 1938.

5418. Levine, Mildred. "An Investigation of the Socialized Procedure in the Court in Los Angeles County Dealing with Guardianship of Minors." Master's thesis, University of Southern California, 1940. 148 pp.

5419. Levit, William H. "Pretrial Procedures in the Los Angeles Superior Court." *The Los Angeles Bar Bulletin* 38 (October 1963): 433-7+.

5420. Lomax, Almena. " 'A Drama of Extraordinary Complexity': The Muslim Trial in Los Angeles." *Frontier* 14 (July 1963): 5-7.

Trial of 14 Black Muslims on 42 charges.

5421. Los Angeles Bench and Bar. *Centennial Edition, 1949-50.* [Los Angeles, 1950]. 315 pp.

5422. Los Angeles Daily Journal. *The Bench and Bar of Los Angeles County.* Los Angeles, 1922. 44 pp.

5423. ———— *The Bench and Bar of Los Angeles County, 1928-1929.* Los Angeles, c1929. 255 pp.

5424. ———— *An Historical Review of Bench and Bar.* Los Angeles, 1907. 14 pp.

5425. "Los Angeles Bar Association Investigates Lawless Enforcement of the Law Constitutional Rights Committee Makes Startling Report on Alleged Illegal Enforcement in Connection with Deportation of Aliens." *Los Angeles Bar Association Bulletin* 6 (July 16, 1931): 354-8+.

5426. "L. A. Bar Ethics Rule Ban Lawyer-Actors." *American Bar News* 5 (April 15, 1960): 3.

Los Angeles Bar Association Board of Trustees rules it "professionally and ethically improper" for a lawyer to appear as an attorney or judge in a simulated radio, television, or movie trial.

5427. "L. A. Labor Court." *Business Week* (April 26, 1941): 55-60.

"The first labor relations department of a superior court in the United States."

5428. "The Los Angeles Water Case." *Engineering Record* 41 (June 9, 1900): 538-9.

Supreme Court rules Los Angeles cannot compel Los Angeles City Water Co. to lower its rates.

5429. Lubow, Sylvia. "The Espionage Act in Southern California." Master's thesis, University of California, Los Angeles, 1968. 224 pp.

Espionage Act of 1917.

5430. Maddock, Don. "A Newsman Looks at Long Beach Courts." *Bar Bulletin* 3 (July-August 1958): 7-9+.

5431. Maddox, C. Richard. *Beverly Hills Justice.* N.p., 1959. 70 pp.

5432. Marchetti, Joseph. "This Court Is Quick, Simple, Cheap: The Small Claims Court of Los Angeles Speeds Money Cases Involving Fifty Dollars or Less." *Southern California Business* 14 (May 1935): 12-3.

5433. Marr, Ned. "The City's Law Department." *Los Angeles Bar Association Bulletin* 12 (March 18, 1937) : 245-7.

Duties and functions of the City Attorney's Office.

5434. Martineau, Glenn B. "The Los Angeles Plan of Juror Selection." *Bar Bulletin* 15 (November 1939) : 55-61.

5435. McCoy, Philbrick. "Powers, Tenure and Compensation of the Presiding Judge of the Superior Court of Los Angeles County." *Los Angeles Bar Bulletin* 32 (January 1957) : 67-72.

5436. McKay, William R. "The Criminal Departments of the Los Angeles County Superior Court." *Los Angeles Bar Bulletin* 20 (July 1945) : 327-30.

5437. McKibbon, Thomas S. "The Origin and Development of the Los Angeles County Juvenile Court." Master's thesis, University of Southern California, 1932. 60 pp.

5438. "The McNamara Trial." *Current Literature* 51 (November 1911) : 466-8.

5439. Menzies, Austin F. M. "The Office of City Attorney in Los Angeles." Master's thesis, University of California, Los Angeles, 1935. 114 pp.

5440. Miller, John Alva. "The County Grand Jury and the Public Schools of Southern California [1958 to 1967]." Doctoral dissertation, University of Southern California, 1969. 160 pp.

5441. Moore, Ewell D. "No 'Delayed Justice' in Los Angeles Trial Courts: Litigants Able to Obtain Prompt Trial. Saving of Time and Money Accomplished under Present Master Calendar System." *Los Angeles Bar Association Bulletin* 9 (February 15, 1934) : 123+.

5442. ——— " 'What Does the Bar Association Do?' " *Bar Bulletin* 15 (March 1940) : 155-6.
Los Angeles.

5443. Moroney, J. F. "The Domestic Relations Record of Los Angeles County." *Los Angeles Bar Bulletin* 21 (February 1946) : 165-9.

5444. Morrow, John C. "The Los Angeles Bar Association Plan of Life Insurance." *Los Angeles Bar Bulletin* 33 (June 1958) : 245-6.

5445. Nelson, Dorothy W. "Should Los Angeles County Adopt a Single-Trial-Court Plan?" *Southern California Law Review* 33 (1960) : 117-62.

5446. Nelson, Kenneth E. "Curfew Legislation: With Special Reference to Los Angeles and San Francisco." Master's thesis, University of Southern California, 1952. 83 pp.

5447. Nelson, Ronald R. "The Legal Relationship of Church and State in California." *Southern California Quarterly* 46 (1964) : 11-53, 125-60.
Cases involving Spiritualism, Jehovah's Witnesses, the Salvation Army in Los Angeles, the Los Angeles Board of Education program, parochial schools, Sunday laws, and disputes of First Presbyterian Church of Los Angeles.

5448. Peterson, Virginia. "Adopted Children in Difficulty: Forty-Two Adopted Children Known to the Los Angeles County Juvenile Court." Master's thesis, University of California, 1944. 68 pp.

5449. Postlethwaite, H. A. "Supreme Court Decides Los Angeles Zoning Cases." *Pacific Municipalities* 39 (March 1925) : 71-2+.

5450. Prince, Neil F. "Inferior Court Reorganization in Los Angeles County." Master's thesis, University of Southern California, 1963. 107 pp.

5451. "The Proposed Constitution and By-Laws of the Los Angeles Bar Association." *Los Angeles Bar Association Bulletin* 6 (November 13, 1930) : 71+.

5452. Reid, William H. "Criminal Rehabilitation in Los Angeles County: A Study of the Work Furlough Program." Master's thesis, California State College at Los Angeles, 1967. 115 pp.

5453. Riley, Frank. "The Curious Case of Connor Everts: Obscenity?" *Los Angeles* 8 (September 1964) : 35-7+.

Connor Everts, Chouinard Art Institute teacher, arrested for exhibiting "obscene matter."

5454. ——— "The D.A.'s Answer to 'Police Brutality.' " *Los Angeles* 11 (March 1966) : 58-62.
District Attorney Evelle J. Younger.

5455. ——— "A New Kind of D.A." *Los Angeles* 8 (December 1964) : 36-9+.
District Attorney Evelle Younger.

5456. Robinson, William W. *Bombs and Bribery: The Story of the McNamara and Darrow Trials Following the Dynamiting in 1910 of the Los Angeles Times Building.* Los Angeles, 1969. 52 pp.

5457. —— *Lawyers of Los Angeles; A History of the Los Angeles Bar Association and of Bar of Los Angeles County.* Los Angeles, 1959. 370 pp.
Also discusses the title insurance companies and the court system.

5458. Rodman, Willoughby. *History of the Bench and Bar of Southern California.* Los Angeles, 1909. 267 pp.

5459. Saltzman, Esther R. "The Factors Influencing the Disposition of Cases of Minors Who Passed Through the Psychopathic Court of Los Angeles County During the Fiscal Year from July 1, 1939 to June 30, 1940." Master's thesis, University of Southern California, 1941. 150 pp.

5460. Sayer, Juanita. "The Coroner's Inquest." *Frontier* 17 (October 1966): 13-5.
Argues need for procedural reform in coroner's inquests.

5461. Scharf, Anna. "Effectiveness of Social Treatment of Children Brought to the Juvenile Court of Los Angeles County under Subdivisions B and D of the Juvenile Court Law of California." Master's thesis, University of Southern California, 1939. 142 pp.

5462. Scott, Robert H. "Our Juvenile Court Today." *Los Angeles Bar Association Bulletin* 11 (May 21, 1936): 221-4.

5463. Scudder, Kenyon J., and Beam, Kenneth S. *Why Have Delinquents? . . . The Los Angeles County Plan of Coordinating Councils Administered by the Juvenile Court and Probation Department . . .* [Los Angeles], c1933. 48 pp.

5464. Searing, Richard C. "The McNamara Case: Its Causes and Results." Master's thesis, University of California, Berkeley, 1951. 133 pp.

5465. Shaw, Hartley. "Appellate Departments of the Superior Court." *Los Angeles Bar Bulletin* 21 (January 1946): 144-5+.

5466. Shuler, Robert P. *Julian Thieves in Politics.* Los Angeles, [n.d.]. 64 pp.
Polemic of author (Pastor, Trinity Methodist

Church and owner of Radio station KGEF, Los Angeles) against S. C. Lewis and others in respect to C. C. Julian Petroleum scandal.

5467. Simons, Blaine N. "Unique Medico-Legal Service Established in Long Beach." *Long Beach Bar Bulletin* 12 (December 1966): 5+.
"Medico-Legal Coordinating and Consulting Service."

5468. Sleepy Lagoon Defense Committee. *The Sleepy Lagoon Case, Prepared by the Citizens' Committee for the Defense of Mexican-American Youth.* Los Angeles, [1943]. 24 pp.

5469. Sloate, Nathan. "A Study of Some Social Factors in the Background of One Hundred and Eighteen Jewish Defendants Appearing for Sentence in the Superior Courts of Los Angeles County from 1935-1937." Master's thesis, University of Southern California, 1939. 131 pp.

5470. Smith, Charles T. "The 'Nine-Court Plan' for Municipal Courts." *Long Beach Bar Bulletin* 7 (May 1961): 8.
Plan for Municipal Court reorganization in Los Angeles County.

5471. "The Southern California Law Review." *The Bar Association Bulletin* 3 (October 6, 1927): 16.
Founding of new law review at USC.

5472. "Special Report on the Holbrook Courts Survey." *Los Angeles Bar Bulletin* 32 (March 1957): 149+.
Report of committee appointed to study recommendations in James G. Holbrook's "A Survey of Metropolitan Trial Courts—Los Angeles Area."

5473. "The Status of the Craig Case." *Los Angeles Bar Association Bulletin* 12 (December 17, 1936): 123.
Judge Gavin Craig.

5474. Steffens, Lincoln. " 'An Experiment in Good Will.' " *Survey* 27 (December 30, 1911): 1434-6.
Observation on trial of McNamara brothers.

5475. Stern, William B., and Feldman, Edward S. "Income of Attorneys in Los Angeles." *Los Angeles Bar Bulletin* 25 (March 1950): 195-6+.

5476. Stoddart, Bessie B. "The Courts of Sonoratown." *Charities* 15 (December 2, 1905): 295-9. Los Angeles.

5477. "Suggestions on Practice in the Justices' Courts of Los Angeles County." *Bar Bulletin* 17 (September 1941): 4-8+.

5478. Taft, Clinton J. *Fifteen Years on Freedom's Front.* [Los Angeles, 1939]. 46 pp.
"The story of the struggle for civil liberties in Southern California from 1923 to 1939."

5479. Taylor, Frank J. "A Court to Prevent Divorce." *New Republic* 103 (August 19, 1940): 239-40.
Judge Ben Lindsey's "Children's Court of Conciliation."

5480. Thompson, Robert S. "Night Traffic Court in Los Angeles." *The Los Angeles Bar Bulletin* 41 (Februaray 1966): 184-8.

5481. Tompkins, Ida P. "A History of the Juvenile Court of Los Angeles County." Master's thesis, University of Southern California, 1936. 119 pp.

5482. "Trial by Jury on Trial." *Outlook* 99 (December 2, 1911): 794-5.
Times' bombing case.

5483. "The Trouble in Los Angeles." *Review of Reviews* 45 (January 1912): 8-12.
Times bombing and McNamara trial.

5484. *The True History of the Famous McNamara Case: Speeches of Anton Johannsen, Clarence Darrow, and Mother Jones.* [Kansas City, Mo., c1915]. 32 pp.
Speeches given at the Labor Temple, August 7, 1915, under the auspices of the Industrial Council. Published by Carpenters Local No. 61, Kansas City, Mo.

5485. Van Elgort, Howard M. "Extension of Legal Services to the Poor: A Report of the First Months of Operation of the Expanded Legal Aid Foundation of Long Beach." *Long Beach Bar Bulletin* 12 (November 1966): 9-16.

5486. Van Waters, Miriam. "When Children Sit in Judgement: The Juvenile Court as Its Own Wards See It." *Survey* 54 (June 1, 1925): 293-5+.
Los Angeles Juvenile Court.

5487. "Vigorous Action to Remove Judge Craig Taken by Los Angeles Bar Association." *Los Angeles Bar Association Bulletin* 10 (June 10, 1935): 332-3+.
Gavin Craig was convicted and sentenced to jail on a charge of conspiring to obstruct justice.

5488. Vogle, James R. "An Investigation of the Establishment and Organization of Courts of Limited Jurisdiction and Their Attachés in Los Angeles County." Master's thesis, University of Southern California, 1956. 95 pp.

5489. Waldron, Granville A. "Courthouses of Los Angeles County." *Historical Society of Southern California Quarterly* 41 (1959): 345-74.

5490. Waller, Jean L. "Contested Adoptions in Los Angeles County." *The Los Angeles Bar Bulletin* 36 (December 1960): 47-50.

5491. Walters, Byron J. "The 'One Court Plan' for Municipal Courts." *Long Beach Bar Bulletin* 7 (May 1961): 9.
Plan for Municipal Court reorganization in Los Angeles County.

5492. "We Are a County Wide Association." *Los Angeles Bar Bulletin* 28 (October 1952): 1-2.
Los Angeles Bar Association.

5493. "What the Judicial Council Really Said about Court Pictures." *Bar Bulletin* 13 (July 1938): 330-1.
Controversy over the taking of photographs of courtroom proceedings.

5494. Whitnall, Gordon. "The Significance of the Recent Supreme Court Zoning Ruling." *Los Angeles Realtor* 4 (April 1925): 19+.

5495. Whitten, Woodrow C. *Criminal Syndicalism and the Law in California, 1919-1927.* Philadelphia, 1969. *Transactions of the American Philosophical Society* 59 (1969): 73 pp.
Los Angeles *Times'* dynamiting and the organization of the Merchants and Manufacturers Association are included.

5496. Wholden, Rosalind G. "Art West." *Arts & Architecture* 82 (February 1965): 12-3.
Result of Connor Everts' obscenity trial, (deadlocked jury) along with a critique of his work.

5497. Woolwine, Thomas L. "A Story of Law Enforcement: How the Energetic Enforcement of the Statutes Led to a Political Upheaval in Los Angeles." *World's Work* 18 (July 1909): 11828-33.

5498. Wright, Kenneth K. "The New Municipal Licence Tax as It Affects Attorneys." *Los Angeles Bar Bulletin* 21 (July 1946): 235-6.
Los Angeles.

5499. "Zoning Case Voiding 'Home Industry' Prohibition to Be Appealed." *Western City* 14 (February 1938): 13.
Los Angeles County.

5500. Zwaska, Edward. "A Sociological Study of a Group of Convicted Adult Male Misdemeanants Applying for Probation in Los Angeles County." Master's thesis, University of Southern California, 1959. 99 pp.

LAW ENFORCEMENT

5501. Adams, Graham, Jr. *The Age of Industrial Violence, 1910-1915.* New York, 1966. 316 pp.
First chapter, "The Crime of the Century," pp. 1-24, is on the Los Angeles *Times* bombing of 1910.

5502. American Civil Liberties Union. Southern California Branch. *Day of Protest, Night of Violence, the Century City Peace March; A Report of the American Civil Liberties Union of Southern California.* [Los Angeles], 1967. 46 pp.
Report of events resulting from a Vietnam war protest.

5503. American Civil Liberties Union. Southern California Branch. *Police Malpractice and the Watts Riot: A Report.* [Los Angeles?, 1966?]. 67 pp.

5504. Anderson, Clinton H. *Beverly Hills Is My Beat.* Englewood Cliffs, N. J., 1960. 218 pp.
Author was one-time Beverly Hills police chief.

5505. Ashla, Mason. "Psychological Testing for Applicants to Beverly Hills Police Department." *Western City* 37 (January 1961): 18.

5506. Bailey, Robert O. "National Award for Culver City Police Facility." *Western City* 43 (October 1967): 60-1.

5507. Becker, Harold K. "Do Police Helicopters Justify Their Cost: Study Shows That They Reduce Major Crime by 8.8%." *American City* 84 (November 1969): 70-1.
"Project Sky Knight," an operation of the Los Angeles County Sheriff's Department, begun in Lakewood in June 1966.

5508. "Beverly Hills Officers Use Cameras for Police Reporting." *Western City* 15 (May 1939): 18.

5509. Boyd, Malcolm. "Violence in Los Angeles." *Christian Century* 82 (September 8, 1965): 1093-5.
Watts Riot, 1965.

5510. Brantley, Wilbur R. "A Comparative Analysis of Public Information Services of Three Major Law Enforcement Agencies in Los Angeles." Master's thesis, University of Southern California, 1958. 130 pp.
Los Angeles Police Department, Los Angeles County Sheriffs Department, Los Angeles County District Attorney's Office.

5511. Brereton, George H. "Survey of California Police Departments: Personnel, Salaries, Working Conditions, Who Hires and Fires, Retirement Provisions, Motor Vehicles and Jail Facilities in 267 Cities." *Western City* 26 (August 1950): 31-8.
Includes many Los Angeles County cities.

5512. Burns, William J. *The Masked War: The Story of a Peril That Threatened the United States, by the Man Who Uncovered the Dynamite Conspirators and Sent Them to Jail.* New York, 1913. 328 pp.
Times bombing.

5513. "A Charge of Wholesale Murder." *Outlook* 98 (May 6, 1911): 1-2.
Times bombing.

5514. Cohen, Jerry, and Murphy, William S. *Burn, Baby, Burn! The Los Angeles Race Riot, August, 1965.* New York, 1966. 318 pp.

5515. Cohen, Nathan, ed. *The Los Angeles Riots: A Socio-Psychological Study.* New York, 1970. 742 pp.

5516. Conot, Robert E. *Rivers of Blood, Years of Darkness.* Toronto and New York, 1967. 497 pp.
Watts Riot, 1965.

5517. Costain, Dave, ed. *Anarchy. Los Angeles.* Los Angeles, 1965. Unp.

Watts Riot, 1965.

5518. "Covina Works at Improving Police-Community Relations." *Western City* 43 (October 1967): 46-7.

5519. Cray, Ed. "The Police and Civil Rights." *Frontier* 13 (May 1962): 5-11.

Criticism of the Los Angeles Police Department.

5520. Crump, Spencer. *Black Riot in Los Angeles; The Story of the Watts Tragedy.* Los Angeles, [1966]. 160 pp.

Watts Riot, 1965.

5521. Cummings, Gordon R. "A Plan for Metropolitan County Police in Los Angeles County." Master's thesis, University of California, Berkeley, 1935. 185 pp.

5522. Davidson, Bill. "The Mafia Can't Crack Los Angeles." *Saturday Evening Post* 238 (July 31, 1965): 23-7.

5523. Davidson, Wayne R. "An Analysis of the Problems of Fifty Migrant Boys Who Were Known to the Los Angeles Police Department in 1944." Master's thesis, University of Southern California, 1947. 279 pp.

5524. Davis, James E. "L.A. Police Commended for Marksmanship." *Pacific Municipalities* 43 (January 1929): 13-4.

5525. ———— "Meeting the Bandit with Police Tactics: Los Angeles Police Experts Will Teach Business How to Cope with Him Safely and Surely." *Southern California Business* 10 (February 1931): 14-5.

5526. Denton, R. B. "Pasadena, Calif., Police Department Leads: With Less Than 100 Men Chief Charles H. Kelly Has Achieved National Recognition." *Pacific Municipalities* 44 (August 1930): 293-4.

5527. Detzer, Karl. "Dragnet in Real Life: Bill Parker, Los Angeles Chief of Police for Past Nine Years, Fights for Public Decency and Safety." *National Civic Review* 48 (September 1959): 403-7.

5528. Domer, Marilyn. "The Zoot-Suit Riot: A Culmination of Social Tensions in Los Angeles." Master's thesis, Claremont Graduate School, 1955. 193 pp.

A study in wartime inter-group relations of the Mexicans and Anglo-Americans as reflected in the riot of June 1943.

5529. Dykstra, C[larence] A. "Los Angeles Now Has Civil Service Police." *National Municipal Review* 13 (January 1924): 50.

5530. Earle, Howard H. "A Study of Contract Services Provided by the Los Angeles County Sheriff's Department to Municipalities in Los Angeles County." Master's thesis, University of Southern California, 1960. 138 pp.

5531. Eimon, Pan D. "Relating!—Police with People." *American City* 84 (April 1969): 142+.

County Sheriff Peter J. Pitchess' "Adopt a Deputy" Project.

5532. "Electronic Cooking Saves Time and Money in New Panorama City Jail Facility." *Western City* 42 (October 1966): 65.

5533. Endore, Samuel G. *The Sleepy Lagoon Mystery.* Los Angeles, 1944. 48 pp.

A famous Los Angeles murder mystery involving some Mexican youths.

5534. Fogelson, Robert M., comp. *The Los Angeles Riots.* New York, 1969. 187 pp.

Select documents relating to the 1965 Watts Riot.

5535. "Ford V-8's for Police." *Western City* 10 (September 1934): 38.

Los Angeles Police Department.

5536. Fulton, Max. "Rookie College." *Westways* 34 (November 1942): 12-3.

Los Angeles Police Academy.

5537. Gabard, Charles. "A Study of the History, Organization, and Function of the Crime Laboratory, Scientific Investigation Division, Los Angeles Police Department, with Emphasis on the Laboratory's Newest Unit, Blood-Alcohol [1949-1957]." Master's thesis, University of Southern California, 1957. 225 pp.

5538. Gardner, Richard T. "Coordination of Law Enforcement and Social Agencies: A Study of Nineteen Cases Referred to the Bureau of Public Assistance from the Crime Prevention Division of the Sheriff's Department in Los Angeles County." Master's thesis, University of Southern California, 1948. 119 pp.

5539. Gleason, Sterling. "Volunteer Flying Cops Aid the Law." *Popular Science* 135 (August 1939): 66-9.

County Sheriff's Department Aero Squadron.

5540. Glover, Katherine. "Project 1-E-4-15: How Unemployed Men and Women Met Juvenile Deliquency on Its Own Ground." *Survey* 71 (December 1935): 362-3.

5541. Goedhard, Neil. "Police Spend a Night in Jail." *American City* 82 (April 1967): 42+.

Covina officers submit to voluntary incarceration in order to see what it is like to be a prisoner.

5542. Gourley, G. Douglas. "Police Public Relations." *Annals of the American Academy of Political and Social Science* 291 (January 1954): 135-42.

Includes summary of survey of citizens' attitudes toward police in Los Angeles. This survey is also reported in the author's book, *Public Relations and the Police* (Springfield, Ill., 1953).

5543. Gourley, G. Douglas. "A Survey of the Attitudes of Local Residents Toward the Los Angeles Police Deparmtent, and the Utilization of Attitude Surveys in Police Administration." Master's thesis, University of Southern California, 1951. 254 pp.

5544. Governor's Commission on the Los Angeles Riots [McCone, John A., *et al*]. *Violence in the City — An End or a Beginning?* [Los Angeles?], 1965. 101 pp.

The *Report* of the Governor's Commission comprises Vol. 1 of the full transcript, which runs to eighteen volumes.

5545. Grosswendt, Betty. "Ahoy, Police." *Westways* 51 (April 1959): 18-9.

Harbor police at Redondo Beach.

5546. Hagen, Peter F. "Helicopter — The Latest Police Tool." *American City* 75 (April 1960): 123+.

Los Angeles Police Department.

5547. "Hawthorne, Calif., Gets a New Police Building." *American City* 70 (December 1955): 13.

5548. Herberg, Will. "Who Are the Guilty Ones?" *National Review* 17 (September 7, 1965): 769-70.

Watts Riots, 1965.

5549. Herrmann, William W., and Isaacs, Herbert H. "Advanced Computer Technology and Crime Information Retrieval Tested by Los Angeles Police." *Western City* 41 (January 1965): 19.

5550. Holladay, Everett F. "PACE—People's Anti-Crime Effort Instituted in Monterey Park." *Western City* 43 (July 1967): 17+.

5551. Holliday, Kate. "The L.A.P.D. Goes Back to School." *Westways* 62 (December 1970): 27-8+.

5552. Homrighausen, George. "Police, Fire and Health Departments of Los Angeles [1850-1939]." Master's thesis, University of Southern California, 1939. 290 pp.

5553. Hood, Iva. "Crime Prevention Methods of the Los Angeles Police Department with Reference to Girls under Eighteen During 1938." Master's thesis, University of Southern California, 1939. 78 pp.

5554. Houghton, Robert A., with the assistance of Theodore Taylor. *Special Unit Senator: The Investigation of the Assassination of Sen. Robert Kennedy*. New York, 1970. 305 pp.

5555. "How Burns Caught the Dynamiters." *McClure's Magazine* 38 (January 1912): 325-9.

Times bombing.

5556. Hynd, Alan. "Murder in Hollywood." *American Mercury* 69 (November 1949): 594-601.

William Desmond Taylor case, 1922.

5557. "Is Third Degree Ever Necessary? Police Officials Give Their Views." *Western City* 7 (September 1931): 27-8.

Includes opinions of Pasadena Police Chief and Los Angeles Deputy Police Chief.

5558. Iverson, Jean; Kido, Ruth; Leibner, Stanley,

and von Bloeker, Ruth. "Los Angeles County Juvenile Probation Officers' Opinions of the California Juvenile Court Law." Master's thesis, University of Southern California, 1964. 171 pp.

5559. Jackson, Robert A. "Value of Step Test in Police Recruit Physical Fitness Training." Master's thesis, University of California, Los Angeles, 1967. 56 pp.
Los Angeles Police Department.

5560. Jacobs, Paul. "Los Angeles Police." *Atlantic Monthly* 218 (December 1966): 95-101.

5561. "Watch Your Language in the Police Station!" *Reporter* 18 (March 6, 1958): 25-7.
Describes arrest of Mickey Cohen in downtown Los Angeles by officers of the Beverly Hills Police Department, on a charge of failing to register as an ex-convict.

5562. Jones, Solomon J. "The Government Riots of Los Angeles, June, 1943." Master's thesis, University of California, Los Angeles, 1969. 166 pp.

5563. Karabian, Walter J. "Who Makes the Decisions of Law Enforcement Policy in Five Los Angeles County Cities." Master's thesis, University of Southern California, 1965. 60 pp.

5564. Kemmerer, Jack B. "The Jail That Modern Science Built." *Popular Mechanics* 106 (July 1956): 79-83.
Los Angeles Police Building and its facilities.

5565. Kerby, Phil. "Riding Shotgun in Watts." *Nation* 207 (September 2, 1968): 166-7.

5566. Kimtex Corp. *Anarchy Los Angeles. Shocking Photos of the Most Terrifying Race Riot in History.* Los Angeles, c1965. [65] pp.
Mainly an illustrated decription of the Los Angeles Watts Riot.

5567. King, Veronica. *Problems of Modern Crime.* London, 1924. 284 pp.
A number of murder cases most of which occurred in Los Angeles County.

5568. Koiner, C. W[ellington]. "Prisoners Housed Near City Departments, Do City Work." *American City* 56 (February 1941): 85.
Pasadena.

5569. ——— "Wanted: Police Chief, Pasadena." *American City* 56 (January 1941): 66.

5570. Kortz, Ralph G. "Recorders and Duplicating Machines Speed Police Reporting." *American City* 79 (July 1964): 81.
Long Beach Police Department.

5571. Levenson, Lew. "The Case of Thomas Sharpe." *Nation* 139 (September 5, 1934): 272.
Appended is Sharpe's affidavit that he was mistreated by Los Angeles police after being arrested for picketing at Terminal Island.

5572. "Light on Crime Situation in Los Angeles City." *Municipal League of Los Angeles Bulletin* 7 (September 1, 1930): [1-2].

5573. Locke, Charles E. *White Slavery in Los Angeles.* [Los Angeles, c1913]. 68 pp.

5574. "The Los Angeles Atrocity." *Independent* 69 (October 6, 1910): 780-1.
Times bombing.

5575. "Los Angeles Builds New Misdemeanant Farm." *American City* 68 (April 1953): 93.
Located near Saugus.

5576. "The Los Angeles Crime." *Independent* 70 (May 4, 1911): 967-8.
Times bombing.

5577. "The Los Angeles Disclosures." *Electric Railway Journal* 38 (December 9, 1911): 1185.
McNamara brothers' confession to *Times* bombing.

5578. "Los Angeles Photographs All Persons Arrested." *American City* 68 (August 1953): 197.

5579. "Los Angeles Photographs All Persons Convicted." *American City* 68 (November 1953): 27.

5580. Manes, Hugh R. *A Report on Law Enforcement and the Negro Citizen in Los Angeles.* Hollywood, [1963?]. Various pagings.

5581. Martin, Robert E. "Straight-Shooting Cops Trained on Novel Pistol Range." *Popular Science* 132 (February 1938): 62-3+.
Los Angeles Police Department target range, Elysian Park.

5582. McCarthy, Thomas J. "Report from Los Angeles." *Commonweal* 38 (June 25, 1943): 243-4.
Attacks on "zoot-suiters."

5583. McCarty, Charles V. "A Survey of Police Training in Los Angeles County." Master's thesis, University of Southern California, 1959. 131 pp.

5584. Mc Grory, Mary. "A New Outburst in Watts." *American* 114 (April 2, 1966): 437.

5585. McManigal, Ortie. *The National Dynamite Plot.* Los Angeles, 1913. 91 pp.

5586. McWilliams, Carey. "The Big Fix in Los Angeles." *Nation* 169 (August 20, 1949): 170-2.
Alleged shakedown involving Mickey Cohen and the Vice Squad of the Los Angeles Police Department.

5587. ———— "Zoot-Suit Riots." *New Republic* 108 (June 21, 1943): 818-20.

5588. Mennig, Jan C. "Police Field Patrol Analysis in Los Angeles County—Cities 15,000 to 125,000 Population." Master's thesis, University of Southern California, 1964. 89 pp.

5589. Meyer, William J. " 'Rancho Experanza' Means New Hope for Prisoners at Long Beach Facility." *Western City* 30 (July 1954): 52.

5590. Moniot, A. M., and Wasmansdorff, C. W. "How Glendale's 'All Out' Fire and Police System Functions." *Western City* 17 (June 1941): 30-1.

5591. Morgan, Edward L. "Los Angeles M.D.T.A. —Patrolman Program: A Case Study in Intergovernmental Relations." Master's thesis, California State College, Los Angeles, 1968. 97 pp.
M.D.T.A.—Manpower Development and Training Act, Public Law 415, enacted in the 87th Cong., 2nd Sess. 1962, and amended by Public Law 214, 88th Cong., 1st Sess., 1963.

5592. Morris, Clarence H. "Pasadena's Police Cadet Program Recruits 18-21 Year Old Trainees." *Western City* 30 (December 1954): 21.

5593. "Motorcycles Equipped with Radio Used at Pasadena." *Western City* 8 (February 1932): 21.
Pasadena Police Department.

5594. Mount, William J. "The Effects of the Provisions for Police, Fire, Health, and Special District Services by Los Angeles County in the Unincorporated Fringe Areas." Master's thesis, University of Southern California, 1951. 110 pp.

5595. Naegele, Timothy D. *Civilian Complaints Against the Police in Los Angeles.* [Berkeley], 1965. 35 pp.

5596. "New Los Angeles Police Building." *Western City* 26 (January 1950): 26.

5597. O'Connor, George M. "The Negro and the Police in Los Angeles." Master's thesis, University of Southern California, 1955. 237 pp.

5598. O'Higgins, Harvey J. "The Dynamiters: A Great Case of Detective William J. Burns." *McClure Magazine* 37 (August 1911): 346-64.
Times bombing.

5599. "One Building Houses All Los Angeles Police Activities." *American City* 64 (November 1949): 17.

5600. "Operation Empathy." *Newsweek* 74 (December 15, 1969): 104+.
Project conceived by Covina Police Chief Robert Ferguson to have officers masquerade as indigents and hippies, in order to obtain "a ground-up view of life seldom available on their beat."

5601. "Out of a Cauldron of Hate — Arson and Death." *Life* 59 (August 27, 1965): 20-30.
Watts Riot, 1965.

5602. Owens, Robert P. "San Fernando's Community Service Officer Fulfills Requirements of Crime Commission." *Western City* 46 (February 1970): 16+.

5603. "Pachuco Troubles." *Inter-American* 2 (August 1943): 5-6.
"Zoot-Suit Riots" in Los Angeles.

5604. Packard, Rose Marie. "The Los Angeles Border Patrol." *Nation* 142 (April 4, 1936): 295.

5605. Parker, Ralph E. "Pomona Police Join the Hotrodders to Teach Safety, Reduce Accidents." *Western City* 33 (September 1957): 51+.
Dragstrip at County Fairgrounds.

5606. Parker, William H. *Parker on Police.* Ed. by O. W. Wilson. Springfield, Ill., 1957. 235 pp.

5607. "Parker . . . And What's Next." *Los Angeles* 10 (September 1965): 28+.

5608. "Pedaling Police Curb Street Crime." *American City* 82 (March 1967): 12.
Police in Long Beach utilize a new tool in the war against crime—the unmarked bicycle.

5609. Perham, Marshall. "Boy Sheriffs Help Fight Crime." *Popular Science* 137 (July 1940): 96-8.
"Junior Deputies" of County Sheriff's Department.

5610. Peterson, C. E. "19 Cities Operate Police Radio Exchange." *Western City* 13 (January 1937): 27-8.
Mostly Los Angeles County cities.

5611. ———— "Two-Way Police Radio in Long Beach—How It Works and What It Costs." *Western City* 11 (May 1935): 23-5.

5612. "Photographic Facilities Among Features of the Los Angeles Police Building." *Western City* 33 (February 1957): 38.

5613. Poe, Elizabeth. "Watts." *Frontier* 16 (September 1965): 5-7.

5614. "Portent of Storm." *Christian Century* 60 (June 23, 1943): 735-6.
"Zoot-Suit Riots," Los Angeles.

5615. Pratt, Anthony. "Pioneer Los Angeles, a Laggard in Prison Reform." *Municipal League of Los Angeles Bulletin* 7 (April 1, 1930): [3+].

5616. "Project Sky Knight." *American City* 82 (August 1967): 33:
County Sheriff's Department helicopters.

5617. Reddin, Thomas. "The Police and the Courts —Is There a Communication Gap?" *The Los Angeles Bar Bulletin* 42 (October 1967): 579-83.

5618. Renshaw, William B., Jr. "Arcadia Police Dept. Building Is Zoned for Functional Use." *Western City* 34 (March 1958): 38-9.

5619. Rice, Craig, ed. *Los Angeles Murders.* New York, 1947. 249 pp.

5620. Riley, Frank. "Crime and the L.A.P.D.: A Shifting Relationship." *Los Angeles* 11 (October 1966): 26-31+.

5621. Roberts, Samuel M. "Police Departments in 58 California Cities Over 10,000 Population." *Western City* 17 (January 1941): 14-9.
Includes Los Angeles County cities.

5622. "Policemen in Smaller Cities Have Wide Variety of Duties." *Western City* 17 (March 1941): 21-5.
Includes many Los Angeles County cities.

5623. Robinson, Ivan A. "Glendale Police Training Program Seeks to Encourage Higher Schooling." *Western City* 31 (July 1955): 42-3.

5624. Robinson, Louie. " 'This Would Never Have Happened . . . If They Hadn't Kicked That Man': Police Action Ignites Fiery L.A. Riot." *Ebony* 20 (October 1965): 114-24.
Watts Riot.

5625. Rogers, Ray. "Panthers and Tribesmen: Black Guns on Campus." *Nation* 208 (May 5, 1969): 558-60.
Black Panthers vs. Ron Karenga's US at UCLA.

5626. Roosevelt, T[heodore]. "Murder Is Murder." *Outlook* 98 (May 6, 1911): 12-3.
Times bombing.

5627. Rossa, Della. *Why Watts Exploded; How the Ghetto Fought Back.* New York, 1966. 21 pp.

5628. Samuels, Gertrude. "Justice in the Courtroom—Can the Poor Get It?" *Saturday Review* 49 (January 29, 1966): 25+.
The workings of the Los Angeles Public Defender's Office, first established in 1912.

5629. Sanders, Stanley. "Riot as a Weapon: The Language of Watts." *Nation* 201 (December 20, 1965): 490-3.
Author, born in Watts, was a Rhodes Scholar.

5630. Saunders, Margaret. "A Study of the Work of the City Mother's Bureau of the Los Angeles Police Department." Master's thesis, University of Southern California, 1939. 201 pp.

5631. Seiler, Conrad. "Los Angeles Must Be Kept Pure." *Nation* 122 (May 19, 1926): 548-9.

Arrest and prosecution of actors in Los Angeles production of O'Neill's "Desire Under the Elms."

5632. Severns, Harry, and Wilhelms, M. L. "Hawthorne's Modern Police Facility Viewed as Model Plant by Experts." *Western City* 31 (March 1955): 40-1+.

5633. "Sheriffs Use Bell 47s for Patrol Work." *Aviation Week and Space Technology* 71 (December 14, 1959): 95-6+.
County Sheriff's Department Aero Detail.

5634. Sollen, Robert H. "The Insurrection." *Frontier* 16 (September 1965): 1+.
Watts Riot, 1965.

5635. "South Pasadena Takes Step Toward Fire and Police Integration." *Western City* 28 (February 1952): 56.

5636. Sparr, George L. "A Study of the Feeding of County Jail Prisoners in Seven Southern California Counties." Master's thesis, University of Southern California, 1963. 112 pp.

5637. Stoker, Charles. *Thicker 'n Thieves.* Santa Monica, [c1951]. 415 pp.
This reputed "factual exposé" of graft and corruption in the Los Angeles Police Department must be used with caution. Its accuracy and charges are highly questionable.

5638. Swanson, Leland M. "A Cybernetic Law Enforcement Information System for Los Angeles County." Doctoral dissertation, University of Southern California, 1963. 240 pp.

5639. Taylor, Edward K. "The Training Program of the Los Angeles County Sheriff's Department." Master's thesis, University of California, Los Angeles, 1963. 111 pp.

5640. Taylor, Graham. "Justice Without Fear or Favor." *Survey* 26 (May 6, 1911): 214-5.
Arrest of suspects in *Times* bombing.

5641. Thompson, Louis W. "L.A.'s Crime Rate from the General to the Specific." *Los Angeles* 15 (October 1970): 32-3.

5642. Tichenor, Henry M. *A Wave of Horror; A Comparative Picture of the Los Angeles Tragedy.* St. Louis, Mo., 1912. 31 pp.
Times bombing.

5643. "The Tragedy of 'The Times.'" *Out West,* new series, 1 (December 1910): 18-21.
Times bombing.

5644. "Trail of the Lawless." *Newsweek* 53 (March 16, 1959): 24-5.
J. Edgar Hoover announces that Los Angeles has more crime than New York or Chicago.

5645. Trotter, Crawford. "Los Angeles Area Takes on Crime." *Christian Century* 75 (January 29, 1958): 149.

5646. Trygg, C. E. "Police and Fire Departments Re-established after Signal Hill Tries Contract Services." *Western City* 37 (January 1961): 17-8.

5647. "Uniform Crime Reporting Installed at Pasadena and Berkeley." *Western City* 7 (September 1931): 32-4.

5648. Walton, Frank E. "Radio Police Talk Win Friends." *American City* 55 (July 1940): 15.
"Traffic Tribunal," radio program put on by the Traffic Division of the Los Angeles Police Department.

5649. Wasserman, Lauren M. "Lakewood's Airborne Police Augment Ground Patrol." *Western City* 43 (February 1967): 21-2+.

5650. Webb, Jack. *The Badge.* Englewood Cliffs, N.J., 1958. 310 pp.
Deals with the Los Angeles Police Department.

5651. Wilcox, Robert F. *Law Enforcement.* Los Angeles, 1952. *Metropolitan Los Angeles. A Study in Integration,* Vol. IV, The Haynes Foundation, *Monograph Series No. 21.* 225 pp.

5652. Yoshioka, Ben T. "In-Service Training of the Police Officers in the Los Angeles Police Department and in the Los Angeles Sheriff's Department." Master's thesis, University of California, Berkeley, 1941. 105 pp.

5653. "Zoot-Suit Riots: 125 Hurt in Los Angeles Fights." *Life* 14 (June 21, 1943): 30-1.

LIBRARIES

5654. Algie, James, and Perkins, John. "Why a

City Library for Inglewood? A Case History of One City's Decision to Withdraw from the County System to Form Its Independent City Library Service." *Western City* 39 (November 1963): 33-4.

5655. Allerding, Johanna E. "The Pacific Aeronautical Library." *California Library Association Bulletin* 6 (March 1945): 103-4.

5656. Alliot, Hector. "The Lummis Library and Collections." *Out West* 32 (March 1910): 212-32.

5657. Archeological Institute of America, Southwest Society. *Two Great Gifts: The Lummis Library and Collections [and] Munk Library.* Los Angeles, 1910. 34 pp.
At the Southwest Museum.

5658. Archer, H. Richard. "Graphic Arts at the Clark Memorial Library." *Quarterly News Letter* of the Book Club of California 17 (1952): 56-60.

5659. Aroeste, Jean. "Engaging the Viewer's Mind." *Wilson Library Bulletin* 42 (June 1968): 1020-6.
Library exhibitions at UCLA.

5660. Baughan, Nancy. "Library Keeps Pace with Industry." *Southren California Business* 3 (March 1924): 14+; (April 1924): 34+.
Science and Industry Department of the Los Angeles Public Library.

5661. "Beautiful Books in Huntington Library." *Los Angeles Saturday Night* 44 (January 23, 1937): 5.
Exhibition in observance of National Printing Education Week.

5662. Bentson, Jim. "The Law Library in the New Courthouse." *Long Beach Bar Bulletin* 6 (July-August 1960): 5-6.
Long Beach Branch Law Library.

5663. Billington, Ray A. "The Genesis of the Research Institution." *Huntington Library Quarterly* 32 (1968-9): 351-72.
Huntington Library.

5664. Bishop, Edith P. "Young Adult Services in Los Angeles." *Wilson Library Bulletin* 33 (October 1958): 138-9.
Los Angeles Public Library.

5665. Bliss, Leslie E. "Friends of the Huntington Library." *California Library Association Bulletin* 1 (March 1940): 121-2.

5666. Bresler, Riva [T]. "Los Angeles Library Boom." *Library Journal* 83 (June 15, 1958): 1896-8.
Author's name is incorrectly spelled Bressler.

5667. —— "Special Libraries in Southern California." *California Librarian* 14 (June 1953): 240-1+.

5668. Brewitt, Theodora R. "Long Beach Library Stricken by Earthquake." *Library Journal* 58 (April 15, 1933): 366-7.
Damage from earthquake of March 10, 1933.

5669. Caldwell, Gladys. "The Staff Association of the Los Angeles Public Library." *Library Journal* 60 (June 1, 1935): 461-4.

5670. Carpenter, Edwin H., Jr. "Three Rare Book Libraries in Southern California." *California Librarian* 14 (June 1953): 224-6+.
Edward Laurence Doheny Memorial Library, William Andrews Clark Memorial Library, and Henry E. Huntington Library.

5671. Carter, Mary J. "A Victory Book Game." *Wilson Library Bulletin* 17 (May 1943): 738-9.
Game devised for children at Ascot Branch Library.

5672. Cavette, Elmer W. "An Investigation of Some Major Aspects of the Budgeting, Accounting and Purchasing Practices of Representative Medium-Sized Public Libraries in the Los Angeles Area." Master's thesis, University of Southern California, 1942. 114 pp.

5673. Chase, George. "Work for the Blind in Los Angeles." *Library Journal* 52 (November 15, 1927): 1064.
Braille Section, Los Angeles Public Library.

5674. Christeson, Frances. "The Far Corners of Pasadena." *California Librarian* 18 (October 1957): 265-6.
Pasadena library system.

5675. Claggett, Helen L. " 'Good Neighboring' at the Law Library." *Bar Bulletin* 17 (June 1942): 236.
Latin-American section of County Law Library.

5676. Clark, Robert. "Research Shangri-la." *Westways* 35 (January 1943) : 22-3.

Huntington Library.

5677. Cole, George W. "The Henry E. Huntington Library." *Annual Publication* Historical Society of Southern California 11, Pt. 3 (1920) : 24-9.

5678. Collins, Blanche. "Branch Building in Long Beach." *California Librarian* 19 (January 1958) : 22-3.

5679. Connor, Dorcas, and Taylor, Zada. "In the Heart of Hollywood." *Library Journal* 85 (January 15, 1960) : 202-5.

Hollywood Branch Library.

5680. Cooley, Laura C. "The Los Angeles Public Library." *Historical Society of Southern California Quarterly* 23 (1941) : 5-27.

5681. Cotton, Zola V. "Montebello, California, Dedicates Modern Library Building." *Pacific Municipalities* 44 (September 1930) : 365.

5682. "The County Law Library." *Los Angeles Bar Association Bulletin* 7 (March 17, 1932) : 216-7.

5683. Dabagh, Thomas S. "Future of Los Angeles County Law Library." *Bar Bulletin* 14 (March 1939) : 195-6.

5684. ———— "Let Us Reason Together." *Los Angeles Bar Bulletin* 20 (January 1945) : 136-8.

Pros and cons of various locations for new County Law Library.

5685. ———— "The Los Angeles County Law Library." *California Library Association Bulletin* 5 (March 1944) : 94-5.

5686. ———— "Yes, We Have No Million Dollars!" *Los Angeles Bar Bulletin* 20 (December 1944) : 103-5.

County Law Librarian outlines what is needed and what is feasible in a new County Law Library.

5687. Davies, Godfrey. "The Huntington Library as a Research Center, 1925-1927." *Huntington Library Quarterly* 11 (1948) : 293-306.

5688. Davis, Earl H. "News from the Long Beach Branch of the Los Angeles County Law Library." *Bar* 1 (June 1955) : 17.

5689. Davis, Edna C., and Rosenberg, Betty. "UCLA's Laboratory for Humanists." *Library Journal* 84 (January 1, 1959) : 46-9.

William Andrews Clark Library.

5690. "Dedication of New Public Library." *Saturday Night* 6 (July 17, 1926) : 2.

Los Angeles.

5691. Diveley, Ruth A. "A Program of College Library Co-operation for Southern California." *California Library Association Bulletin* 5 (September 1943) : 13-6.

5692. Dole, Arthur M. "Public Libraries of Southern California." *Out West* 22 (February 1905) : 83-95.

Includes Pasadena, Pomona, Los Angeles, and Santa Monica.

5693. Dotson, Margaret. "Huntington Library." *Apartment Journal* 20 (January 1938) : 13+.

5694. "The Eileen and Kenneth Norris Medical Library, University of Southern California." *California Librarian* 30 (1969) : 80-4.

5695. Ellerbe, Rose L. "Californiana in Huntington Library." *Saturday Night* 4 (June 2, 1923) : 17+.

5696. Fairchild, Donald S. "Low Cost, High Efficiency at L. A. Branches." *Library Journal* 77 (January 15, 1952) : 125-7.

Building program of County Public Library.

5697. Fickes, Eugene W., and Perry, E. Caswell. "Central Library, City of Burbank." *California Librarian* 26 (April 1965) : 69-77.

5698. Foye, Betsy M. "Children's Work in Los Angeles Sub-Branches." *Library Journal* 48 (April 15, 1923) : 363-5.

Los Angeles Public Library.

5699. Franklin, Alan. "Industry Finds Profit in Public Library." *Southern California Business* 6 (February 1927) : 16-7+.

Los Angeles.

5700. "Friends of Huntington Library." *Bar Bulletin* 14 (April 1939): 237.

Describes role played by lawyers in founding this organization.

5701. "From Jerusalem to the West." *Wilson Library Bulletin* 37 (June 1963): 822.

Describes acquisition by UCLA of a major Hebraic collection from defunct Bamberger and Warhman Bookstore in Israel.

5702. Fulmer, Margaret. "The Whittier Public Library." *California Librarian* 21 (July 1960): 137-40.

5703. "Glance at Clark Library." *Los Angeles Saturday Night* 11 (November 15, 1930): 28.

Description of library's major collections.

5704. Glaser, Hilda M. "Santa Monica Public Library." *California Librarian* 28 (July 1967): 135-43+.

5705. "Graduate Research Library Designed to Expand." *Architectrual Record* 140 (September 1966): 214-7.

UCLA.

5706. Hamill, Harold L. "New Program of the Los Angeles Public Library." *California Librarian* 14 (June 1953): 221-3+.

5707. Hancock, Helen R. "Reading Guidance for Parents." *Wilson Library Bulletin* 27 (May 1953): 720-3.

Program at North Hollywood Branch, Los Angeles Public Library.

5708. Harlow, Neal, and Moore, Everett T. "UCLA's New Wing But the Beginning." *Library Journal* 74 (June 15, 1949): 971-4.

Library.

5709. Haro, Robert P. "One Man Survey: How Mexican-Americans View Libraries." *Wilson Library Bulletin* 44 (March 1970): 736-42.

Survey made in East Los Angeles and Sacramento.

5710. Harris, Anne B. "By Bus to the Library." *Library Journal* 62 (June 1, 1937): 473.

Describes visit by third-graders from Seventeenth Street School to the Los Angeles Public Library.

5711. Henderson, J[ohn] D. "Expanding Los Angeles." *Library Journal* 79 (December 15, 1954): 2396-9.

Planned Norwalk and West Whittier branches of County Public Library.

5712. ——— "Los Angeles County Public Library." *California Librarian* 14 (June 1953): 233-4+.

5713. ——— "Los Angeles Emphasizes Regional Facilities." *Library Journal* 85 (December 1, 1960): 4291-4.

County Public Library.

5714. ——— "Planning, Programming and Evaluating: The Reorganization of the Los Angeles County Public Library." *Library Journal* 82 (December 15, 1957): 3144-7.

5715. Henselman, Frances. "The Bookmobile in Long Beach." *California Library Association Bulletin* 6 (September 1944): 17.

5716. ——— "Good Design Is a Feature of New Beach Libraries." *American City* 67 (February 1952): 96-7.

5717. ——— "One Million Customers: Southern California Libraries Go to the Fair." *California Librarian* 15 (September 1953): 46-7+.

5718. ——— "Triple-Purpose Bookmobile." *Wilson Library Bulletin* 21 (November 1946): 235-7.

Long Beach Public Library.

5719. Hickman, Margaret G. "Listen!" *Wilson Library Bulletin* 19 (February 1945): 403.

Foreign-language programs of the Los Angeles Public Library's Foreign Department.

5720. Hill, Elsie I. "The Library Borrows a Good Idea from the Army." *Wilson Library Bulletin* 17 (May 1943): 728-9.

Student liasion officers, Washington Irving Junior High School.

5721. Hollingsworth, Josephine B. "Los Angeles Introduces Municipal Reference Library Department." *Pacific Municipalities* 43 (April 1929): 163-4.

5722. Holmes, John W. "Los Angeles Lawyers Use More Foreign Law." *Bar Bulletin* 15 (September 1939): 5.

Increased use of foreign law materials reported by County Law Librarian.

5723. Holt, Raymond M. "Pomona Public Library." *California Librarian* 27 (April 1966): 69-79.

5724. Hughes, Erwin N., and Smith, John E. "Loyalty at the Los Angeles County Librarian." *California Librarian* 12 (December 1950): 106-7.

5725. Hume, Jessie H. "The Organization and Administration of the Los Angeles School Libraries." Master's thesis, University of Southern California, 1935. 241 pp.

5726. "Huntington Library Invites Bar to Special Exhibition of Rare Legal Manuscripts and Books." *Los Angeles Bar Association Bulletin* 11 (October 17, 1935): 39.

5727. "Huntington Library to be Specially Opened for Convention Delegates [of League of City Officials of California]." *Western City* 10 (July 1934): 15.

5728. "Huntington Library to Have Bible Exhibition." *Los Angeles Saturday Night* 16 (November 2, 1935): 3.
Commemorationg the 400th anniversary of the Coverdale Bible.

5729. "Huntington Library Visitors Number Million." *Los Angeles Saturday Night* 16 (January 25, 1936): 5.
Since opening to public January 27, 1928.

5730. Hyers, Faith H. "Beauty in Library Entrance." *Saturday Night* 6 (November 6, 1926): 6.
Flower Street entrance to Los Angeles Public Library.

5731. ———— "Expansion of Los Angeles Public Library." *Library Journal* 51 (February 1, 1926): 121-4.

5732. ———— "Features of New Public Library." *Saturday Night* 6 (July 16, 1926): 1-2.
Los Angeles.

5733. ————, comp. *Handbook of the Central Building Los Angeles Public Library.* Los Angeles, 1927. 49 pp.

5734. ———— "The New Los Angeles Library." *Libraries* 31 (February 1926): 74-7.

5735. ———— "The New Public Library, Los Angeles." *The Architect and Engineer* 87 (November 1926): 77-82.

5736. ———— "Our Public Library Investment." *Southern California Business* 8 (July 1929): 16-7.

5737. ———— "Resources for Defense." *Library Journal* 67 (March 1, 1942): 218.
"Defense Information Desk," Los Angeles Public Library.

5738. ———— "Seen from Library Windows." *Los Angeles Saturday Night* 13 (November 12, 1932): 7.
Borrowing habits of patrons of the Los Angeles Public Library.

5739. ———— "Significance of Los Angeles' New Library." *Library Journal* 51 (August 1926): 633-6.

5740. ———— "Utility and Beauty in the New Los Angeles Public Library." *Libraries* 31 (October 1926): 408-10.
Description of library, opened to public July 6, 1926.

5741. ———— "What Los Angeles Is Reading." *Los Angeles Saturday Night* 8 (June 23, 1928): 13. '
Books most frequently requested at Los Angeles Public Library.

5742. Jones, Helen L. *Public Libraries.* Los Angeles, 1953. *Metropolitan Los Angeles. A Study in Integration,* Vol. XIII, The Haynes Foundation, *Monograph Series No. 30.* 88 pp.

5743. Kemp, Emily W. "Work with Los Angeles Young People." *Wilson Bulletin for Librarians* 9 (December 1934): 192-6.
Los Angeles Public Libary.

5744. Kennedy, Helen J. "Visiting Branch Libraries in Los Angeles." *Library Journal* 48 (May 1, 1923): 403-6.

5745. Ketcham, Ronald M. *Integration of Public Library Services in the Los Angeles Area.* Bureau of Governmental Research, University of California, Los Angeles, *Studies in Local Government No. 6.* Los Angeles, 1942. 185 pp.

5746. Laich, Katherine. "Los Angeles Public

Library Wins Its Bond Election." *California Librarian* 18 (July 1957): 189-92+.

5747. "Law Library Building Favored." *Los Angeles Bar Bulletin* 20 (June 1945): 295-300.

Expresses preference of Los Angeles Bar Association for a separate building to house new County Law Library.

5748. "A Library of Music Scores at UCLA." *California Library Association Bulletin* 7 (June 1946): 148+.

5749. "Library Photographic Service." *Library Journal* 82 (January 15, 1957): 178-9.

UCLA.

5750. Los Angeles County Library. *50 Years of Service, 1912-1962*. Los Angeles, 1962. 32 pp.

5751. —— *History of the Los Angeles County Free Library, 1912-1927*. Los Angeles, 1927. 40 pp.

5752. —— *Twenty-Five Years of Growth, 1912-1937*. [Los Angeles, 1937]. 76 pp.

5753. "Los Angeles Book Jam Forces Depository Storage." *Library Journal* 93 (February 1, 1968): 502.

Los Angeles Public Library.

5754. "Los Angeles County Libraries." *Libraries* 35 (December 1930): 458-60.

5755. "Los Angeles Public Library 1872-1920." *Library Journal* 46 (April 1, 1921): 308-9.

5756. Lummis, Charles F. "Books in Harness." *Out West* 25 (September 1906): 195-225

Compares the Los Angeles Library to other libraries.

5757. Lynch, Samuel D. "Arts, Facts, and Fiction." *Westways* 40 (December 1948): 2-3.

Los Angeles Public Library.

5758. MacQuarrie, Catherine. "IBM Book Catalog." *Library Journal* 82 (March 1, 1957): 630-4.

Los Angeles County Library.

5759. "Major Library Building Program Gets under Way at UCLA." *Library Journal* 87 (September 1, 1962): 2860.

5760. Marquis, Neeta. "Salute to the Library." *Los Angeles Saturday Night* 8 (March 17, 1928): 4-5.

New Los Angeles Public Library.

5761. Matthews, Paul R. "Los Angeles County Law Library." *Los Angeles Bar Association Bulletin* 11 (October 17, 1935): 31.

5762. Miles, Paul. "UCLA in Three Stages." *Library Journal* 89 (December 1, 1964): 4746-9.

Campus library building program.

5763. Nelson, Elmer S. *Treasures of the Past*. Los Angeles, 1929. [33] pp.

This article, descriptive of the Huntington Library and Art Gallery, appeared in three parts in the *Pacific Mutual News* and is reprinted.

5764. "New Branch Libraries in Los Angeles." *The Architect and Engineer of California* 50 (July 1917): 78-83.

5765. "New Los Angeles Charter to Alter Library Status." *Library Journal* 94 (September 1, 1969): 2856.

One provision of Charter (which failed to be approved in 1970 election) would have reduced the Library Commission's status to that of an advisory body.

5766. Nimmo, Ray E. "Perret Library of Graphic Art." *Los Angeles Saturday Night* 14 (June 9, 1934): 4; (June 16, 1934): 4.

Los Angeles library of illustrations, covering such subjects as architecture, music, opera, cinema, interior decoration, color chemistry, natural history, and archaeology.

5767. "Norwalk's Library Emphasizes Minority Educational Opportunities." *Western City* 46 (November 1970): 21.

5768. "Palos Verdes Estates Library." *Los Angeles Saturday Night* 9 (November 17, 1928): 17.

5769. Parker, Thomas F. "The Burbank Western History Collection." *California Librarian* 26 (April 1965): 104-7.

5770. "Party at U.C.L.A." *Library Journal* 71 (1946): 1041.

Accession of 500,000th volume to the university library.

5771. Pearce, Stanley K. "The Los Angeles County Law Library." *The Los Angeles Bar Bulletin* 37 (December 1961): 50-2.

5772. Perry, Everett R. " 'Reading Maketh a Full Man' What the Library Means to the Real Estate Man." *Los Angeles Realtor* 7 (June 1927): 17+.
Los Angeles Public Library.

5773. ———— "What the Public Library Means to the Community." *Los Angeles Saturday Night 150th Birthday of Los Angeles: Fiesta and Pre-Olympiad.* Special Issue (1931): [17].
Los Angeles.

5774. Place, Estella M. "Erudition Among the Oranges." *Sunset* 51 (September 1923): 52+.
Huntington Library.

5775. "Plan Improvements at Huntington Library." *Los Angeles Saturday Night* 44 (May 1, 1937): 14.
Changes to improve service both to the public and to scholars.

5776. Pleasants, Martha G. "At Olive View Sanatorium." *California Library Association Bulletin* 7 (December 1945): 63-4.
Branch of Los Angeles County Public Library.

5777. Poff, Robert L. "City Library Built by Non-Profit Corporation Lease-Back System." *Western City* 42 (April 1966): 60-1.
Duarte.

5778. Pomfret, John E. *The Henry E. Huntington Library and Art Gallery from Its Beginnings to 1969.* San Marino, 1969. 241 pp.

5779. ———— "The Huntington Library: Fifteen Years' Growth, 1951-1966." *California Historical Society Quarterly* 45 (1966): 241-57.

5780. Powell, Lawrence C. "Resources Unlimited: Special Collections at UCLA." *California Librarian* 15 (September 1953): 40-1.

5781. ———— "Stop Thief: A Nocturnal Episode in Library History." *Wilson Library Bulletin* 28 (December 1953): 361-3.
Account of attempt to steal a copy of the *Bay Psalm Book* on exhibition at UCLA.

5782. ———— *Ten Years (Almost) of Rounce &*

Coffinism. Los Angeles, 1941. 15 pp.
Club of librarians.

5783. ———— "William Andrews Clark Memorial Library," in *A Bookman's View of Los Angeles.* Los Angeles, 1961. p. 19.

5784. Power, Ralph L. *Libraries of Los Angeles and Vicinity.* Los Angeles, 1921. 63 pp.

5785. Richardson, Frances C. "The Twentieth Century-Fox Research Library." *California Librarian* 28 (April 1967): 94-6.

5786. Rider, Ione M. "Neighborhood Forums." *Wilson Library Bulletin* 19 (March 1945): 488-9.
Community current-events forums at John Muir Branch of Los Angeles Public Library.

5787. Robertson, Marjorie G. "A Branch Library in a Branch Bank." *Library Journal* 56 (June 1, 1931): 476-9.
Los Angeles Library of the Bank of America National Trust & Savings Association.

5788. Russell, Amy R. "In Pursuit of California History: Huntington Library Collects Invaluable Early Days Relics." *Los Angeles Saturday Night* 43 (July 11, 1936): 8.

5789. Sanborn, Florence M. "An Example of Regional Cooperation in West Los Angeles." *California Librarian* 21 (January 1960): 41-4+.
Inter-library cooperation.

5790. Schad, Robert O. "Henry E. Huntington: The Founder and the Library." *Huntington Library Bulletin* 1 (May 1931): 3-32.

5791. ———— "The Henry E. Huntington Library," in *A Bookman's View of Los Angeles.* Los Angeles, 1961. Pp. 27-9.

5792. ———— *A Quarter Century at the Huntington Library.* [San Francisco], 1952. 8 pp.

5793. "Serving Knowledge by the Truck-Load." *Southern California Business* 7 (September 1928): 12+.
Los Angeles County Free Library.

5794. Shimar, Neljte T. "Securing and Recording Public Documents." *Library Journal* 56 (May 1, 1931): 394-6.
Los Angeles Public Library.

5795. Smith, Jack. "A Day in the City: At Mr. Huntington's Place." *Westways* 61 (July 1969): 26-8+.

Huntington Library.

5796. Smith, Mary R. "Los Angeles County Children's Work." *Wilson Library Bulletin* 29 (October 1954): 163-6.

5797. Snow, Bert N. "Los Angeles Is Still Building." *Library Journal* 84 (December 1959): 3672-5.

Program for building new branch libraries in Los Angeles.

5798. ———— "Los Angeles Shifts into High Gear." *Library Journal* 85 (December 1, 1960): 4273-6.

Progress of program for building new branch libraries in Los Angeles.

5799. ———— "28 New LAPL Branches—A Community Boon." *Wilson Library Bulletin* 33 (September 1958): 36-8.

Los Angeles public libraries.

5800. "Some Los Angeles Reading Plans." *Wilson Library Bulletin* 16 (May 1942): 743-4.

Eagle Rock Branch, Los Angeles Public Library.

5801. Stephenson, Allen B., and Perkins, John W. "Inglewood's New Main Library Built at Less Than $6 Per Sq. Ft." *Western City* 44 (June 1968): 27-8.

5802. Sweetser, L. H. "Outdoor Reading Rooms in Parks." *American City* 53 (October 1938): 91.

Pershing Square and Lafayette Park, Los Angeles.

5803. Taylor, Thelma V. "Los Angeles Harbor Junior College Library." *California Librarian* 12 (December 1950): 91-2.

5804. Thorpe, James. "The Founder and His Library." *Huntington Library Quarterly* 32 (1968-9): 291-308.

Henry E. Huntington and the library he founded.

5805. University of California, Los Angeles. William Andrews Clark Memorial Library. *William Andrews Clark Memorial Library; Report of the First Decade, 1934-1944.* Berkeley and Los Angeles, 1946. 79 pp. *Report of the Second Decade, 1945-1955.* Los Angeles, 1956. 25 pp. *Report of the Third Decade, 1956-1966.* Los Angeles, 1967. 75 pp.

5806. Vaughn, Nancy. "Library Service for Los Angeles Business Men." *Library Journal* 51 (February 1, 1926): 137-8.

5807. Vogleson, Helen E. "A Five-Step Pay Plan." *Library Journal* 66 (June 1, 1941): 472.

County Public Library.

5808. ———— *History of the Los Angeles County Free Library, 1912-1927.* Los Angeles, 1927. 40 pp.

5809. ———— "Libraries and the War Program: Los Angeles County." *Library Journal* 67 (May 1, 1942): 402.

5810. ———— "Los Angeles County Library Also Suffers." *Library Journal* 58 (April 15, 1933): 367.

Damage from earthquake of March 10, 1933.

5811. Wallace, Lura B., and Cozad, Lyman H. "Beverly Hills Library System Seeks 'Home Rule' Controls." *Western City* 42 (July 1966): 30-1+.

5812. Warren, Althea H. "Library Building Is in the Air!" *Library Journal* 69 (December 15, 1944): 1076-7.

Los Angeles branch library program.

5813. ———— "Los Angeles Has 5-Year Plan." *Library Journal* 70 (December 15, 1945): 1187.

5814. Weber, Francis J. *A Bibliophilic Odyssey: The Story of the Bibliotheca Montereyensis-Angelorum Dioeceseos.* Los Angeles, 1969. 31 pp.

5815. ———— "The Los Angeles Chancery Archives." *The Americas* 21 (1965): 410-20.

5816. Weisenberg, Charles M. "Los Angeles Public Library: Encino-Tarzana Branch." *California Librarian* 23 (January 1962): 9-12.

5817. ———— "Los Angeles Public Library Van Nuys Branch." *California Librarian* 25 (October 1964): 203-11.

5818. Whittington, Harriett E. "The Administration of Senior High School Libraries in Los Angeles." Master's thesis, University of Southern California, 1929. 136 pp.

MEDICINE; PUBLIC HEALTH

5819. Abu-Haydar, Leyla. "Some Psycho-Social Factors Related to the Voluntary Admissions of Patients to the Sepulveda Veterans Administration Hospital." Master's thesis, University of Southern California, 1960. 63 pp.

5820. Anderson, Chloe C. "A Study of the Health Work of the Schools of Long Beach, California." Master's thesis, University of Southern California, 1922. 263 pp.

5821. Andrae, Elsbeth. *The Dear Old Boys in Blue; Memories of the Early Days of the Veterans Administration Center, Los Angeles.* San Francisco, 1948. 25 pp.

5822. Appleby, John J.; Larsen, Jack G.; Muegge, John R., and Stevens, Curtis H. "Family Care Program: A Descriptive Study of the Family Care Program at the Neuropsychiatric Hospital Veterans Administration Center, Los Angeles." Master's thesis, University of Southern California, 1955. 67 pp.

5823. Barnhill, O. H. "How Los Angeles Helps Children with Weak Hearts." *Hygeia* 6 (August 1928): 452-4.

5824. Baur, John E. *The Health Seeks of Southern California, 1870-1900.* San Marino, 1959. 202 pp.

5825. —— "Los Angeles County in the Health Rush, 1870-1900." *California Historical Society Quarterly* 31 (1952): 13-33.

5826. Berry, Edna L. "Convalescent Care of Crippled Children Hospitalized in the Los Angeles Area." Master's thesis, University of Southern California, 1941. 154 pp.

5827. Binder, Gertrude. "Psycho-Charlatans . . . They Prey on Human Misery." *Survey* 88 (March 1952): 116-8.

Los Angeles as a mecca for bogus healers of mental disease.

5828. Bishop, Ernest G. "A Social and Economic Study of the Non-Resident Consumptive in the City of Los Angeles." Master's thesis, University of Southern California, 1916. 52 pp.

5829. Boettcher, Nina T. "A Survey and Critical Ananlysis of the Educational and Health Status of the Pupils in a Large Los Angeles Elementary School." Master's thesis, University of Southern California, 1938. 185 pp.

Home Gardens School.

5830. Bogen, Emil, *et al.*, eds. *A Decade of Medical Research: A Summary Report Prepared under the Auspices of the Medical Advisory and Research Committee, Showing the Progress and Results of the Medical Research Program of the Los Angeles County Tuberculosis and Health Association for the Period 1947 Through 1956.* Los Angeles, 1957. 114 pp.

5831. Boskin, Joseph, and Pilson, Victor. "The Los Angeles Riot of 1965: A Medical Profile of an Urban Crisis." *Pacific Historical Review* 39 (1970): 353-65.

5832. Bower, A. G., *et al.* "Clinical Features of Poiliomyelitis in Los Angeles." *American Journal of Public Health and the Nation's Health* 24 (December 1934): 1210-2.

5833. Boyer, Gordon. "A Short Historical Account of the Los Angeles Alcoholic Rehabilitation Clinic, 1957-1963." Master's thesis, University of Southern California, 1963. 40 pp.

5834. Bricker, Dorothy E. "An Analysis of the Community's Use of the Los Angeles Bureau of Social Work of the California State Department of Mental Hygiene as Demonstrated by Request for Information and Referral Service." Master's thesis, University of Southern California, 1950. 69 pp.

5835. Bridgwater, Alfred. "A Brief History of the Suicide Prevention Center of Los Angeles 1950-1964." Master's thesis, University of Southern California, 1964. 56 pp.

5836. Brophy, Helen E. "A Study of the Problems of Interrelationships as Reported by the School Nurses of the Pasadena City Schools." Master's thesis, University of California, Los Angeles, 1956. 123 pp.

5837. Bucknall, Nathalie. "Home Accident Prevention: The Home Safety Program of the Los Angeles City Health Department." *American Journal of Public Health and the Nation's Health* 41 (August 1951): 959-62.

5838. Carpenter, Ford A. "Why Southern California Is Free from Malaria." *Southern California Business* I (October 1922): 14+.

5839. Carter, Mark. *Okay, America.* Los Angeles, 1963.
   City of Hope, hospital in Duarte, pp. 75-165.

5840. Casey, G. Rae. "Reactivating Family Ties of Chronic Schizophrenic Patients: Analysis of Social Work Activity with a Selected Group at the Veterans Administration Neuropsychiatric Hospital at West Los Angeles, California." Master's thesis, University of Southern California, 1948. 88 pp.

5841. "Cavities Unlimited." *Time* 74 (December 28, 1959): 46.
   Southern California Dental Hospital.

5842. Chase, Melvin L. "A Survey of the Coordinated Health Services in the Pasadena Area." Master's thesis, Claremont Graduate School, 1941. 141 pp.

5843. Collins, Lucille. "The Nature of the Medical-Social Problems of Eight Female Patients Admitted to Los Angeles County General Hospital for Emergency Care of Pre-Existing Medical Conditions." Master's thesis, University of Southern California, 1954. 72 pp.

5844. Creighton, Robert C. "The Long Beach Health Center." *American City* 66 (September 1951): 122-3.

5845. Crouch, Winston W.; Maccoby, Wendell; Morden, Margaret G., and Bigger, Richard. *Sanitation and Health.* Los Angeles, 1952. *Metropolitan Los Angeles. A Study in Integration,* Vol. V, The Haynes Foundation *Monograph Series No. 23.* 163 pp.

5846. Daughters of Charity. *One Hundred Years of Service . . . 1856-1956, Dedicated to the People of Southern California.* [Los Angeles, 1956]. 36 pp.
   Dedicated to nursing.

5847. De Rosales, Eugenia. "Interaction Process Analysis of Two Small Groups of Mentally Ill Patients." Master's thesis, University of Southern California, 1959. 51 pp.
   Los Angeles County.

5848. Deutsch, Ronald M. "Patients Enjoy This Hospital." *Popular Science* 164 (March 1954): 126-8+.
   Kaiser Foundation, Los Angeles.

5849. Diamond, Susan J. "How Sick Is Our City?" *Los Angeles* 13 (January 1968): 38-41+.
   Los Angeles medical services.

5850. Edlen, Annie M. "A Study of the Economic Rehabilitation of Tuberculosis Patients Discharged from Sanitoria in Los Angeles County." Master's thesis, University of Southern California, 1938. 79 pp.

5851. Ehmann, Norman R., and Frizzi, Louis A. "Fly Control Methods in Los Angeles Area Involve Community Cooperation." *Western City* 30 (February 1954): 40-1.

5852. "Extracts from Recent Survey of Public Health Activities in Los Angeles County." *Municipal League of Los Angeles Bulletin* 6 (January 1, 1929): [7-8].

5853. Feldman, Frances (Lomas). *History of the Committee on Mental Health, Health Division, Welfare Planning Council, Los Angeles Region, 1936-1953.* [Los Angeles], 1955. 42 pp.

5854. Fite, Alan N. "Tuberculosis Case-Finding in Industry: An Analysis and Evaluation of the Mass Miniature Chest X-Ray Program of the Los Angeles County Tuberculosis and Health Association, 1943-1947." Master's thesis, University of Southern California, 1948. 132 pp.

5855. Fodor, John T. "Analysis of the School Health Program in Seventy-One Schools within the Los Angeles City School Districts." Master's thesis, University of California, Los Angeles, 1958. 151 pp.

5856. Gann, Dan M. *At Forty: The Queen of Angels Story.* Los Angeles, 1967. 73 pp.
   Los Angeles hospital.

5857. Gershoy, Elinor K., and Palanchian, Rosemarie. "A Study of Social Factors in the Lives of World War II Women Veterans Admitted to

Wadsworth General Hospital, Veterans Administartion Center, Los Angeles, from December 1, 1957, through January 15, 1958." Master's thesis, University of Southern California, 1958. 66 pp.

5858. Gilmore, Julia, Sister. *Saint John's and Its People*. St. Louis, 1967. 160 pp.
History of Catholic hospital in Santa Monica.

5859. Goldberg, Violet B. "A Study of the Home Treatment of Tuberculosis Cases with the Details of a Colony Plan in Los Angeles County and a Study of a Family Group of Ninety-Nine." Master's thesis, University of Southern California, 1939. 72 pp.

5860. Golter, Samuel H. *The City of Hope*. New York, 1954. 177 pp.
Hospital in Duarte.

5861. "Good Hope Hospital Association and Its Practical Philanthropy." *Saturday Night* 7 (April 9, 1927): 2.
Semi-charitable organization operating through Good Samaritan Hospital, Los Angeles.

5862. Gordon, Shirley. "A Way Back for Troubled Youngsters: Mental Health Volunteers in Los Angeles County Are Helping Former Psychiatric Patients to Live Again in the Outside World." *Parents Magazine* 42 (November 1967): 66-7+.

5863. Goudey, R. F. "Sanitation," in *Los Angeles: Preface to a Master Plan*. Ed. by George W. Robbins and L. Deming Tilton. Los Angeles, 1941. Pp. 203-12.

5864. Graves, Dorothy A. "Some Predisposing Factors for Poliomyelitis in Los Angeles County During the 1948 Epidemic." Master's thesis, University of Southern California, 1951. 78 pp.

5865. Gulick, Gay. "Patrons of the Los Angeles Mothers' Clinic in 1930: A Statistical Analysis of 288 Cases." Master's thesis, University of Southern California, 1936. 76 pp.

5866. Halverson, Wilton L. "War and the Health Department." *American Journal of Public Health and the Nation's Health* 33 (January 1943): 20-5.
Los Angeles County.

5867. Hamilton, Andrew. "City of Hope: A Pilot Medical Center." *Westways* 55 (September 1963): 26-7.
Located in Duarte.

5868. Hamilton, James A. *A Hospital Plan for Los Angeles County, California*. [Los Angeles, 1947?]. 51 pp.

5869. Harmon, Michael M. "The Consolidation of the Los Angeles City and County Health Departments: A Case Study." Doctoral dissertation, University of Southern California, 1968. 314 pp.

5870. Harper, Evelyn S. "A Survey of the Eugene Street Development Center in Los Angeles." Master's thesis, University of Southern California, 1934. 171 pp.
Center for mentally handicapped children.

5871. Harris, Henry. *California's Medical Story*. San Francisco, 1932. 421 pp.
Carries story to the 1920s. Scattered references to Los Angeles vicinity.

5872. Hart, Trusten M., and Luck, J. Vernon. "Orthopedic Aspect of the Los Angeles County 1934 Poliomyelitis Epidemic." *American Journal of Public Health and the Nation's Health* 24 (December 1934): 1224-8.

5873. Hassouna, Fouad Amin Sami. "Proposed Memorial Hospital for Culver City, California." Master's thesis, University of Southern California, 1950. 43 pp.

5874. Hatfield, Sally J. "The Dietary Practices of Students in Grades Seven Through Twelve in the Inglewood Unified School District." Master's thesis, University of California, Los Angeles, 1962. 157 pp.

5875. Hebel, Vernon E. "Educational Provision for the Physically Handicapped Child in the Los Angeles City Schools." Master's thesis, University of Southern California, 1933. 138 pp.

5876. Hillinger, Charles. "Medicine at Marineland." *Westways* 55 (January 1963): 11-3.

5877. Holsinger, Margaret W. "Hope for Moderate Incomes." *Survey* 60 (May 15, 1928): 239-40.
Good Hope Hospital Association, Los Angeles.

5878. Homrighausen, George. "Police, Fire and Health Departments of Los Angeles [1850-1939]." Master's thesis, University of Southern California, 1939. 290 pp.

5879. Hopmans, Walter. "A History of Dentistry in Southern California." Master's thesis, Occidental College, 1947. 162 pp.

5880. *Hospital — Sanitarium of St. John of God.* Los Angeles, 1943. Unp.
Operated by a religious nursing order.

5881. *The Hospitaller Order of St. John of God.* Los Angeles, 1950. Unp.
A religious nursing order.

5882. Hughes, Marie M. "Youth at Work on a Community Problem." *NEA Journal* 36 (March 1947): 230.
Student health conferences, Los Angeles.

5883. Ickes, Arnoldine L. "Differential Function of Public Health Nursing and Medical Social Work in the Los Angeles County Health Department." Master's thesis, University of Southern California, 1948. 151 pp.

5884. Jamison, Alice M., and Desler, John E. "John Tracy Clinic: A Brief Historical Account, 1942-1964." Master's thesis, University of Southern California, 1965. 94 pp.
Clinic for deaf children.

5885. Jeffress, Mary H. "A Historical Study of the Community Health Association of Los Angeles." Master's thesis, University of California, Los Angeles, 1949. 106 pp.

5886. Jessup, Roger W. "Los Angeles County Medical Education Center." *California Magazine of the Pacific* 46 (June 1956): 20+.

5887. Jordan, Velma, and McComic, Beverly. "Behaviour Problems of Adolescent Girls Accepted for Treatment at El Retiro and Child Guidance Clinic of Los Angeles; A Comparative Study." Master's thesis, University of Southern California, 1959. 89 pp.

5888. Kaplan, Anne, and Crummett, Duane O. *Tuberculosis in Homes for the Physically-Well Aged in Los Angeles County.* Los Angeles, 1963. 48 pp.

5889. Kay, Cecil R. "Program and Performance Budgeting for Municipal Health Services: A Case Study of the Los Angeles City Health Department." Master's thesis, University of Southern California, 1959. 235 pp.

5890. Kessel, John F.; Hoyt, Anson S., and Fisk, Roy T. "Use of Serum and the Routine and Experimental Laboratory Findings in the 1934 Poliomyelitis Epidemic." *American Journal of Public Health and the Nation's Health* 24 (December 1934): 1215-23.
Los Angeles.

5891. Kincaid, James W. "A Survey of 180 Unattached Tuberculosis Male Indigents in Los Angeles with the Emphasis on the Public Health Problem." Master's thesis, University of Southern California, 1939. 137 pp.

5892. Knox, William B. "Los Angeles's Campaign of Silence." *Nation* 121 (December 9, 1925): 646-7.
Alleged efforts of Chamber of Commerce to suppress fact that the city suffered a major infantile paralysis epidemic during summer of 1925.

5893. Korf, Jean P. "The Use of Standard Theatrical Skills in the Presentation of Three Short Scenes Acted by Patients of the Brentwood Neuropsychiatric Hospital." Master's thesis, University of California, Los Angeles, 1956. 221 pp.

5894. Krakower, Joseph D. "An Administration and Health Center Building for the City Health Department of Los Angeles, California." Master's thesis, University of Southern California, 1947. 39 pp.

5895. Kress, George H. *A History of the Medical Profession of Southern California.* Los Angeles, 1910. 209 pp. 2nd ed., Los Angeles, 1910. 209 pp.

5896. Laidlaw, Dorothy. "A Community's Use of a Mental Hygiene Clinic: A Statistical Study of One Hundred and Fifty-Five Cases Referred to the Long Beach Mental Hygiene Clinic." Master's thesis, University of Southern California, 1951. 65 pp.

5897. Land, John H., Jr. "Male Mentally Ill Patients Who Have Been Hospitalized for Twenty

Years or More: A Population Study Undertaken at Metropolitan State Hospital." Master's thesis, University of Southern California, 1957. 46 pp.

Norwalk.

5898. Landis, Edward E. "Problems of Consolidating the Sanitation Functions of the Los Angeles City and the Los Angeles County Helath Departments." Master's thesis, University of Southern California, 1960. 122 pp.

5899. Larson, Gordon P. "Medical Research and Control in Air Pollution." *American Journal of Public Health and the Nation's Health* 42 (May 1952): 549-56.

Los Angeles County Air Pollution Control District.

5900. Leitner, Roni J. "Teacher Observation of Pupil Health at Dana Junior High School, Los Angeles." Master's thesis, University of California, Los Angeles, 1956. 112 pp.

5901. Lewis, S. A. "Dentistry on Wheels for School Children in Rural Los Angeles." *American City* 50 (March 1935): 66.

City "Healthmobile."

5902. ———— "How Los Angeles Wages War on Its Rodent Population." *American City* 45 (October 1931): 104.

Los Angeles City Health Department Rodent Control Bureau.

5903. Lindsay, Doreen. "Social Concomitance of Long Term Patients at Metropolitan State Hospital." Master's thesis, University of Southern California, 1958. 43 pp.

Norwalk.

5904. Liverman, Louis W. "The Child Health Conference: Its Clientele, Its Values and Limitations. An Analysis of the Socio-Economic Characteristics of Families Using the Long Beach Department of Public Health Child Health Conferences." Master's thesis, University of Southern California, 1953. 103 pp.

5905. "Long Beach Has Best Equipped Naval Hospital in U. S." *The Architect and Engineer* 153 (April 1943): 23-6.

5906. Lorenzi, Louise L. "The Home Adjustments of Fifty Physically Handicapped Children Discharged from the Los Angeles County General Hospital." Master's thesis, University of Southern California, 1939. 88 pp.

5907. "Los Angeles Builds a School for the Crippled." *Architectural Record* 82 (November 1937): 30-1.

Washington Boulevard Orthopaedic School.

5908. "Los Angeles County General Hospital: Acute Unit." *Architectural Record* 77 (June 1935): 402-7.

5909. Los Angeles County Medical Association. *The Story of the Los Angeles County Medical Association.* Los Angeles County Medical Association *Bulletin* 79 (January 31, 1946): 75th Anniversary Number. [Los Angeles, 1946]. 202 pp.

Also, consult *A Struggle for Excellence: One Hundred Years of the Los Angeles County Medical Association.* Los Angeles, 1971. 112 pp.

5910. "L. A. Tenement Problem and the Bubonic-Pneumonic Plagues." *Municipal League of Los Angeles Bulletin* 2 (February 16, 1925): 2-6.

5911. "Low-Cost Medical Care Through Group Clinics." *American City* 51 (June 1936): 105+.

Ross-Loos Clinic for public employees.

5912. Lowenthal, Anita. "Contents of Correspondence Files at Metropolitan State Hospital." Master's thesis, University of Southern California, 1955. 45 pp.

Norwalk.

5913. Lowman, Charles L. "The Orthopaedic Medical Center—A Los Angeles Achievement, 1903-1962." *Southern California Quarterly* 44 (1962) 133-47.

5914. Marralle, James J. "A Case Study of the Patterns of Influence and Action Taken to Obtain a Hospital in Southeast Los Angeles." Master's thesis, University of Southern California, 1966. 184 pp.

Watts area.

5915. Marshall, William R. "The Municipal Rest Houses of Pasadena." *American City* 13 (November 1915): 382-3.

5916. McCann, Vernie. "Introduction of the Group Psychotherapy Program in the Mental Hygiene Clinic, Regional Office, Veterans Administration, Los Angeles, California." Master's thesis, University of Southern California, 1950. 78 pp.

5917. McDonald, Marguerite V. "Psychiatric Services for Children at the Los Angeles State Mental Hygiene Clinic." Master's thesis, University of Southern California, 1949. 104 pp.

5918. McGinnis, Katherine D. "Brief Psychiatric Services in a Public General Hospital: Reactions of Mexican-American Former Patients." Master's thesis, University of Southern California, 1965. 75 pp.

5919. "Medical Care for the Unemployed: Los Angeles County to Give Free Services to Its 400,000 Idle." *Literary Digest* 120 (August 10, 1935): 15.

5920. "Medical Computer Center." *Science News Letter* 82 (October 20, 1962): 259.
Computer for processing medical research data, UCLA Medical School.

5921. "The Methodist Hospital." *California Christian Advocate* 70 (July 7, 1921): 5.
Los Angeles.

5922. "The Methodist Hospital of Southern California." *California Christian Advocate* 61 (October 31, 1912): 3.
Los Angeles.

5923. Mount, William J. "The Effects of the Provisions for Police, Fire, Health, and Special District Services by Los Angeles County in the Unincorporated Fringe Areas." Master's thesis, University of Southern California, 1951. 110 pp.

5924. Mueller, John E. "The Politics of Fluoridation in Seven California Cities." Master's thesis, University of California, Los Angeles, 1963. 58 pp.
The cities studied include Manhattan Beach, Long Beach, Pomona, and Glendale.

5925. Mulrooney, Keith F. "Tri-City Mental Health Authority Portends Possible New Concern for Municipalities." *Western City* 38 (July 1962): 38.
Claremont, LaVerne, and Pomona enter joint agreement under the Short-Doyle Act to provide mental health services; state underwrites half of the costs.

5926. "Municipal Hospitals in California." *Western City* 21 (January 1945): 14-7.
Includes Whittier, Alhambra, Beverly Hills, Burbank, and Pasadena.

5927. Neher, Gerwin C. "A Survey of the Health Services of the Los Angeles City Schools." Master's thesis, University of Southern California, 1934. 200 pp.

5928. Nemethi, Carl E., and Balchum, Oscar. "City Employees and Private Health Agency Join in Fight on Baffling Disease." *Western City* 37 (September 1961): 56.
Joint research project of the City of Vernon and the Tuberculosis and Health Association of Los Angeles County.

5929. "New Clinic Serves Long Beach." *Long Beach Bar Bulletin* 5 (November 1959): 11-12.
Alcoholism Rehabilitation Institute.

5930. "New Rays of Light for the Old Gray Matter." *Business Week* (April 27, 1968): 62-4.
UCLA Brain Research Institute.

5931. "Orthopaedic Hospital's Growth: Some Interesting Data Concerning the Only Institution in Southern California Dedicated Exclusively to the Physical Correction and Care of the Physically Handicapped Child." *Los Angeles Saturday Night* 44 (March 27, 1937): 8-9.

5932. Osherenko, Marian. "The Social Implications of Delay in Sanatorium Placement for Tuberculosis: A Study of a Group of Cases in Los Angeles County." Master's thesis, University of Southern California, 1941. 68 pp.

5933. Overholt, Alma. "Summer Health Schools as Inaugurated in Los Angeles County." *Hygeia* 9 (June 1931): 547-50.

5934. Poe, Elizabeth, "Suicide: How the Behavioral Sciences Are Applied to a Major Socio-Psychological Problem. *Frontier* 14 (August 1963): 5-12.
Suicide Prevention Center of Los Angeles.

5935. Pomroy, J. L. "Los Angeles County Health Center Plan." *Pacific Municipalities* 45 (June 1931): 281-2.

5936. ——— "Meeting the Earthquake Health Emergency." *Western City* 9 (April 1933): 11.

5937. Queen of Angels Hospital. *Silver Jubliee, 1926-1951.* [Los Angeles, 1951]. Unp.
Los Angeles.

5938. Rainville, Helen N. "Psycho-Social Factors Involved in Requests for Discharge Against Medical Advice from a Veterans Administration Neuropsychiatric Hospital." Master's thesis, University of Southern California, 1959. 66 pp.
Los Angeles.

5939. Reeves, Frances M. "Housing Problems of the Los Angeles County Central Welfare District: A Study in Administrative Procedure." Master's thesis, University of Southern California, 1936. 79 pp.

5940. Riffel, Lydia E. "The Care of Fifty-Two Children with Rhematic Fever in Private Cardiac Clinics in Los Angeles County." Master's thesis, University of Southern California, 1943. 67 pp.

5941. Rosenhouse, Miriam. "A Study of the Los Angeles Medical Agencies Providing Care for Certain Cases of Low Income Groups." Master's thesis, University of Southern California, 1939. 125 pp.

5942. Roybark, Joyce. "Adjustment of Veterans on Trial Visit from a Veterans Administration Neuropsychiatric Hospital." Master's thesis, University of Southern California, 1961. 56 pp.
Los Angeles.

5943. Sacks, Doris C. "Trial Visit: Impact on Fathers." Master's thesis, University of Southern California, 1961. 86 pp.
Mentally ill, Los Angeles.

5944. "Sanitary Surveys in Los Angeles." *Monthly Labor Review* 20 (June 1925): 1369-71.
Comparison of sanitary and living conditions in the Belvedere Gardens and Maravilla Park districts.

5945. Schreiber, Flora R., and Herman, Melvin. "Psychiatrists Analyze the Los Angeles Riots." *Science Digest* 58 (November 1965): 18-22.

5946. Sharfman, Katherine H. "Adolescent Delinquents: A Caste Study of Thirteen Treatment Referrals to the State Mental Hygiene Clinic by the Probation Department, Los Angeles." Master's thesis, University of Southern California, 1950. 85 pp.

5947. Shepard, Charles C., and Huebner, Robert J. "Q Fever in Los Angeles County." *American Journal of Public Health and the Nation's Health* 38 (June 1948): 781-8.

5948. Silver, Myrtle E. "Medical Care for Families on Relief in Glendale District of Los Angeles County." Master's thesis, University of Southern California, 1937. 59 pp.

5949. Spett, Allen. "An Analysis of Services by the Los Angeles County Physically Handicapped Children's Program to Children with Impaired Hearing." Master's thesis, University of Southern California, 1951. 66 pp.

5950. Stangle, Esther K. "The Role of the University of California at Los Angeles in Gerontology." Master's thesis, University of California, Los Angeles, 1964. 155 pp.

5951. Stevens, George M. "The 1934 Epidemic of Poliomyelitis in Southern California." *American Journal of Public Health and the Nation's Health* 24 (December 1934): 1213-4.

5952. Stewart, Marilaton. "A Study of the Social and Emotional Adjustments Made by Fourteen Ex-Patients of Olive View Tuberculosis Sanitorium, Los Angeles County." Master's thesis, University of Southern California, 1944. 65 pp.

5953. Swartout, H. O. "Measles, Scarlet Fever and Whooping Cough in the Los Angeles County Health Department Area: A Ten Year Study." *American Journal of Public Health and the Nation's Health* 25 (August 1935): 907-12.

5954. "Taking a Look at the Question of Consolidated Health Service: Hazards to Public Well Being Are No Respectors of Political Boundaries; Experience of 36 Cities in Los Angeles County." *Western City* 10 (August 1934): 21-2.

5955. Tasem, Marjorie. "Orientation Meeting for Relatives of Patients Newly Admitted to a State Mental Hospital." Master's thesis, University of Southern California, 1959. 87 pp.
Los Angeles County.

5956. Terry, R. A. *History of the Harbor Branch, Los Angeles County Medical Society, 1905-1942.* Long Beach, 1942. 15 pp.

5957. Thompson, Clara C. "The Range and Type of Medical Social Problems Presented by Patients at the General Hospital, Veterans Administration, West Los Angeles, in Relation to Professional Education for Medical Social Work." Master's thesis, University of Southern California, 1946. 82 pp.

5958. Thompson, Louis W. "The Best Kept Secret in the Abortion Controversy." *Los Angeles* 15 (September 1970): 42-5+.
"Liberal open-door policy" of Los Angeles County Medical Center.

5959. Thompson, Marion G. "The School Adjustment of Thirty Crippled Children Known to the Orthopaedic Hospital in Los Angeles." Master's thesis, University of Southern California, 1943. 78 pp.

5960. "The 20-Hour Nuns." *Time* 64 (October 18, 1954): 67-8.
St. Anne's Maternity Hospital, a home for unwed mothers.

5961. "The Ultimate in Research." *Time* 88 (November 11, 1966): 66+.
Jules Stein Eye Institute at UCLA Medical Center.

5962. Underhill, Duncan. "Sawtelle—Fairest of Warrior's Retreats." *Westways* 48 (June 1956): 8-9.
Veterans' hospital.

5963. Van Sickle, Florence P. "The Function of the Mental Hygiene Clinic at Juvenile Hall in Los Angeles, California." Master's thesis, University of Southern California, 1944. 84 pp.

5964. Van Wart, Roy, *et al.* "1934 Epidemic of Poliomyelitis in Los Angeles: Preliminary Report on the Pathological Changes in the Nervous System." *American Journal of Public Health and the Nation's Health* 24 (December 1934): 1207-9.

5965. Vroman, Veta B. "The Pomona Clinic: The Clinical Concept as a Significant Factor in Effective Treatment of Mal-Adjusted Public School Children." Master's thesis, Claremont Graduate School, 1950. 107 pp.

5966. Watrous, Valerie. "Health on Wheels: Children of Los Angeles Far-Flung School District Eagerly Await the 'Healthmobile' Dental and Eye Clinic." *School Life* 16 (June 1931): 191-3.

5967. "A Way of Life." *Rotarian* 90 (March 1957): 21.
Rancho Los Amigos, Los Angeles, "The world's largest respitory and rehabilitation center for polio patients."

5968. "Weird Hospital." *Time* 35 (March 1940): 66.
Los Angeles County General Hospital.

5969. Wessells, Zelpha E. "The Significance of Authority for Tuberculous Patients: A Study of Quarantine Law Enforcement in Tuberculosis as Exemplified in the Los Angeles County Public Health Area." Master's thesis, University of Southern California, 1946. 138 pp.

5970. Widney, Joseph P. *The Greater City of Los Angeles; A Plan for the Development of Los Angeles City as a Great World Health Center.* Los Angeles, 1938. 8 pp.

5971. Will, Arthur J. "Seventy-Five Years of Los Angeles County Hospital Service." *California Magazine of the Pacific* 43 (June 1953): 14-5.

5972. Williams, Vivienne C. "The Probation System for the Insane with Special Reference to Los Angeles County." Master's thesis, University of Southern California, 1939. 171 pp.

5973. Yoder, Merlin D. "Case Studies of Boys in the Los Angeles Tuberculosis and Health Association Preventorium." Master's thesis, University of Southern California, 1936. 141 pp.

MINORITIES

5974. Adams, Flora A. "Chinese Student Life at the University of Southern California." Master's thesis, University of Southern California, 1935. 117 pp.

5975. Anderson, James. "The Los Angeles Black Community, 1781-1940." Los Angeles County Museum of Natural History. *America's Black*

Heritage: History Division Bulletin No. 5. Los Angeles, 1969. 64 pp.

5976. Antoniou, Mary. "Welfare Activities Among the Greek People in Los Angeles." Master's thesis, University of Southern California, 1939. 198 pp.

5977. Aquino, Valentin R. "The Filipino Community in Los Angeles." Master's thesis, University of Southern California, 1952. 117 pp.

5978. Ave, Mario P. "Characteristics of Filipino Social Organizations in Los Angeles." Master's thesis, University of Southern California, 1956. 126 pp.

5979. Baruch, Dorothy W. "Sleep Comes Hard: Negro Housing in Los Angeles." *Nation* 160 (January 27, 1945): 95-6.

5980. Berbano, M. P. "The Social Status of the Filipinos in Los Angeles County." Master's thesis, University of Southern California, 1931. 144 pp.

5981. Bingham, Edwin. "The Saga of the Los Angeles Chinese." Master's thesis, Occidental College, 1942. 185 pp.

5982. Bloom, Leonard. *Removal and Return*. Berkeley, 1949. 259 pp.
Internment of Japanese-American citizens during World War II.

5983. Bogardus, Emory S. *The Mexican in the United States*. University of Southern California School of Research Studies Number Five, *Social Science Series No. 8*. Los Angeles, 1934. 126 pp.

5984. Bond, J. Max. "The Negro in Los Angeles." Doctoral dissertation, University of Southern California, 1936. 365 pp.

5985. Borcherdt, Donn. "Armenian Folk Songs and Dances in the Fresno and Los Angeles Areas." *Western Folklore* 18 (1959): 1-12.

5986. Branham, Ethel. "A Study of Independent Adoptions by Negro Parents in Metropolitan Los Angeles." Master's thesis, University of Southern California, 1949. 62 pp.

5987. Briegel, Kaye L. "The History of Political Organizations Among Mexican-Americans in Los Angeles Since the Second World War." Master's thesis, University of Southern California, 1967. 93 pp.

5988. Broom, Leonard; Riemer, Ruth, and Creedon, Coral. *Marriages of Japanese-Americans in Los Angeles County*. Berkeley and Los Angeles, 1945. 23 pp.

5989. Brown, Walton J. "Historical Study of the Portuguese in California." Master's thesis, University of Southern California, 1944. 117 pp.

5990. Bulen, Mary H. "Molokan Colony in Los Angeles." *Los Angeles Saturday Night* 13 (June 24, 1933): 5.
Russian colony near Hollenbeck Park.

5991. Bullock, Paul, ed. *Watts: The Aftermath; An Inside View of the Ghetto People of Watts*. New York, [1969]. 285 pp.

5992. Burnight, Ralph F. *The Japanese in Rural Los Angeles County*. Southern California Sociological Society, University of Southern California, Studies in Sociology, *Sociology Monograph No. 16*. Los Angeles, 1920. 16 pp.

5993. ———— "The Japanese Problem in Agricultural Districts of Los Angeles County." Master's thesis, University of Southern California, 1920. 70 pp.

5994. Carlstrand, Robert W. "A Comparison of Negro Mobility Characteristics of Probationers in Los Angeles." Master's thesis, University of Southern California, 1955. 95 pp.

5995. Cartland, Earl F. "A Study of the Negroes Living in Pasadena." Master's thesis, Whittier College, 1948. Unp.

5996. Catapusan, Benicio T. "The Filipino Occupational and Recreational Activities in Los Angeles." Master's thesis, University of Southern California, 1934. 124 pp.

5997. ———— "The Social Adjustment of Filipinos in the United States." Doctoral dissertation, University of Southern California, 1940. 244 pp.

5998. Cayton, Horace R. "America's Ten Best Cities for Negroes." *Negro Digest* 5 (October 1947): 4-10.
Los Angeles is included.

5999. Chamberlain, J. F. "The Chinese New Year." *The Journal of Geography* 1 (April 1902): 183-4.
  Los Angeles Chinatown.

6000. Chen, Wen-Hui Chung. "Changing Socio-Cultural Patterns of the Chinese Community in Los Angeles." Doctoral dissertation, University of Southern California, 1952. 444 pp.

6001. ———— "A Study of Chinese Family Life in Los Angeles as Compared with the Traditional Family Life in China." Master's thesis, University of Southern California, 1940. 104 pp.

6002. Clark, Laurence E. "The Social Adjustment of Cuban Refugee Families." Master's thesis, University of Southern California, 1963. 70 pp.

6003. Corpus, S. F. "An Analysis of the Racial Adjustment Activities and Problems of the Filipino-American Fellowship in Los Angeles." Master's thesis, University of Southern California, 1938. 140 pp.

6004. Crawford, Doris. "A Brief History of the Japanese in California." Master's thesis, Occidental College, 1946. 216 pp.

6005. Crimi, James E. "The Social Status of the Negro in Pasadena, California." Master's thesis, University of Southern California, 1941. 136 pp.

6006. Culp, Alice B. "A Case Study of the Living Conditions of Thirty-Five Mexican Families of Los Angeles with Special Reference to Mexican Children." Master's thesis, University of Southern California, 1922. 66 pp.

6007. Day, George M. "Races and Cultural Oases." *Sociology and Social Research* 18 (March-April 1934): 326-39.
  Racial and ethnic minorities in Los Angeles.

6008. Day, George M. *The Russians in Hollywood: A Study in Culture Conflict.* [Los Angeles, 1934]. 101 pp.
  Based on the author's doctoral dissertation, same title, University of Southern California, 1930. 283 pp.

6009. Deal, Gerald V. "A Study of the Vocational Opportunities in Pomona Valley for Mexican-Americans: A Study in Counseling." Master's

thesis, Claremont Graduate School, 1951. 142 pp.

6010. De Graaf, Lawrence B. "The City of Black Angels: Emergence of the Los Angeles Ghetto, 1890-1930." *Pacific Historical Review* 39 (1970): 323-52.

6011. Dlin, Norman. "Some Cultural and Geographic Aspects of the Christian Lebanese in Metropolitan Los Angeles." Master's thesis, University of California, Los Angeles, 1961. 117 pp.

6012. Dunne, John G. "The Ugly Mood of Watts: Militant Leaders in Los Angeles' Negro Ghetto Are Trying to Win Power by Threatening Whites with Violence—And Behind Their Threats Lies Hatred." *Saturday Evening Post* 239 (July 16, 1966): 83-7.

6013. Eason, Charles L. "An Analysis of the Social Attitudes and Casual Factors of Negro Problem Boys of the Los Angeles City Schools." Master's thesis, University of Southern California, 1936. 96 pp.

6014. Elman, Richard M. *Ill-At-Ease in Compton.* New York, 1967. 207 pp.
  Negroes in the city of Compton.

6015. Ervin, James M. "The Participation of the Negro in the Community Life of Los Angeles." Master's thesis, University of Southern California, 1931. 113 pp.

6016. Ferguson, Charles K. "Political Problems and Activities of Oriental Residents in Los Angeles and Vicinity." Master's thesis, University of California, Los Angeles, 1942. 225 pp.

6017. Fiske, Walter M. "A Follow-Up Study of Six Cases of Mexican-American Parents to Explore Their Feelings about Child Placement." Master's thesis, University of Southern California, 1960. 55 pp.

6018. Foster, Nellie. "The *Corrido,* a Mexican Culture Trait Persisting in Southern California." Master's thesis, University of Southern California, 1939. 196 pp.

6019. Franklin, Ruth. "Study of the Services Needed and/or Available to Negro Newcomer Families; A Study of Perceptions of Eleven Health and Welfare Agencies Serving the Community of Watts." Master's thesis, University of Southern California, 1962. 104 pp.

6020. Freeman, George H. "A Comparative Investigation of the School Achievement and Socio-Economic Background of the Japanese-American Students and the White-American Students of Gardena High School." Master's thesis, University of Southern California, 1938. 92 pp.

6021. Friedman, Ralph. "The Negro in Hollywood." *Frontier* 9 (July 1958): 15-9.

6022. ——— "U.N. In Microcosm: Boyle Heights as an Example of Democratic Progress." *Frontier* 6 (March 1955): 11-4.

6023. Fukuoka, Fumiko. "Mutual Life and Aid Among the Japanese in Southern California with Special Reference to Los Angeles." Master's thesis, University of Southern California, 1937. 94 pp.

6024. Fuller, Elizabeth. "The Mexican Housing Problem in Los Angeles." *Studies in Sociology* 5 (November 1920): 1-11.
Published separately as *Sociology Monograph No. 17.*

6025. Girdner, Audrie, and Loftis, Anne. *The Great Betrayal: The Evacuation of the Japanese-Americans During World War II.* New York, [1969]. 562 pp.

6026. Givens, H. L. "The Korean Community in Los Angeles County." Master's thesis, University of Southern California, 1939. 85 pp.

6027. Glasgow, Douglas G. "The Sons of Watts': Analysis of Mobility Aptirations and Life-Styles in the Aftermath of the 'Watts Riot, 1965.' " Doctoral dissertation, University of Southern California, 1968. 294 pp.

6028. Gleason, George. *The Japanese on the Pacific Coast; A Factual Study of Events, December 7, 1951, to September 1, 1942, with Suggestions for the Future. Statement for the Los Angeles County Committee for Church and Community Cooperation.* [Los Angeles], 1942. 20 pp.

6029. Golden State Mutual Life Insurance Co. *Historical Murals Portray the Contribution of the Negro to the Growth of California from Explora-*

tion and Colonization through Settlement and Development. [Los Angeles, 1952?]. 15 pp.

6030. Gosting, Ken. "The Red Power Struggle." *Los Angeles* 14 (October 1969): 42-4.
Migration of American Indians to Los Angeles.

6031. Graham, Luelva B. "A Survey of Counseling Needs as Reported by Negro Female Students in the Twelfth Grade of the Los Angeles Area." Master's thesis, University of California, Los Angeles, 1967. 76 pp.

6032. Greer, Scott A. "The Participation of Ethnic Minorities in the Labor Unions of Los Angeles County." Doctoral dissertation, University of California, Los Angeles, 1952. 413 pp.

6033. Griffing, John B. "A Comparison of the Effects of Certain Socioeconomic Factors upon Size of Family in China, Southern California, and Brazil." Doctoral dissertation, University of Southern California, 1941. 177 pp.

6034. Griffith, Beatrice W. *American Me.* Boston, 1948. 341 pp.
Mexicans in the United States; Los Angeles area included.

6035. Guzman, Ralph. "The Hand of Esau." *Frontier* 7 (June 1956): 13+.
How restrictive covenants are perpetuated under a new guise in Lynwood, Compton, and South Gate.

6036. Hacker, Frederick J. "What the McCone Commission Didn't See." *Frontier* 17 (March 1966): 10-5.
Poses question, "What effect did the Watts Riots have upon Los Angeles Negroes and their conception of themselves?"

6037. Haines, Aubrey B. "Words—And Deeds." *Frontier* 7 (August 1956): 11-2.
Describes various forms of discrimination against Negoes in Los Angeles.

6038. Hall, Martin. "Roybal's Candidacy and What It Means." *Frontier* 5 (June 1954): 5-7.
Candidacy of Edward Roybal for the Los Angeles City Council.

6039. Haro, Robert P. "One Man Survey: How Mexican-Americans View Libraries." *Wilson Li-*

brary Bulletin 44 (March 1970): 736-42.
Survey made in East Los Angeles and Sacramento.

6040. Harper, Helena. "A Study of Colored Unmarried Mothers in Los Angeles." Master's thesis, University of Southern California, 1932. 61 pp.

6041. Hartmann, Sidney A. *History of the Long Beach Jewish Community.* Long Beach, 1957. 64 pp.

6042. Harvey, Louise F. "The Delinquent Mexican Boy in an Urban Area, 1945." Master's thesis, University of California, Los Angeles, 1947. 128 pp.
Based on case histories from Los Angeles Juvenile Hall records.

6043. Henehan, Anne. "On-the-Spot in Watts," in Irwin Isenberg, ed. *The City in Crisis.* New York, 1968. Pp. 54-63.

6044. —— "Watts: Facing the Problems of Minority Ghettos in Today's Cities." *Senior Scholastic* 89 (January 20, 1967): 9-12.
Reprinted as "On-the-Spot in Watts." *The City in Crisis.* Ed. by Irwin Isenberg. New York, 1968. Pp. 54-63.

6045. Hobbs, Thadeaus H. "The Dynamics of Negroes in Politics in the Los Angeles Metropolitain Area, 1945-1956." Master's thesis, University of Southern California, 1960. 189 pp.

6046. Hopkinson, Shirley. "An Historical Account of the Evacuation, Relocation and Resettlement of the Japanese in the United States, 1941-1946." Master's thesis, Claremont Graduate School, 1951. 264 pp.
Also see, Bill Hosokawa, *Nisei. The Quiet Americans.* New York, 1969. 522 pp. Los Angeles included.

6047. Hutson, William G. "Voting Attitudes of Mexican-American Residents of Belvedere—East Los Angeles." Master's thesis, University of Southern California, 1960. 116 pp.

6048. Hymer, Elizabeth E. "A Study of the Social Attitudes of Adult Mexican Immigrants in Los Angeles and Vicinity." Master's thesis, University of Southern California, 1924. 90 pp.

6049. Interchurch World Movement of North America. *The Mexican in Los Angeles.* [Los Angeles], 1920. 28 pp.

6050. Johnson, Charles S. "Negro Workers in Los Angeles Industries." *Opportunity; A Journal of Negro Life* 6 (August 1928): 234-40.

6051. Johnson, James C., and Foster, Bill. "How Do You Define Urban Success? James C. Johnson, City Manager, of Compton, Calif., the First Non-White City Manager in the Nation, Challenges Urban America in a Candid Interview with Bill Foster, Editor of the American City Magazine." *American City* 84 (December 1969): 69-71.

6052. Johnson, Milo P. "The Trade and Industrial Education of Negroes in the Los Angeles Area." Master's thesis, University of Southern California, Los Angeles, 1945. 86 pp.

6053. Jones, Robert. "How Hollywood Feels about Negroes." *Negro Digest* 5 (August 1947): 4-8.

6054. Kagiwada, George. "Ethnic Identification and Socio-Economic Status: The Case of the Japanese-Americans in Los Angeles." Doctoral dissertation, University of California, Los Angeles, 1969. 319 pp.

6055. Kaiser, Evelyn. "The Unattached Negro Woman on Relief: A Study of Fifty Unattached Negro Women on Relief in the Compton District Office of the State Relief Administration of California in Los Angeles." Master's thesis, University of Southern California, 1939. 166 pp.

6056. Kawamoto, Fumi. "Folk Beliefs Among Japanese in the Los Angeles Area." *Western Folklore* 21 (1962): 13-26.

6057. Kawasaki, Kanichi. "The Japanese Community of East San Pedro Terminal Island, California." Master's thesis, University of Southern California, 1931. 186 pp.

6058. Kendall, Robert. *White Teacher in a Black School.* New York, [1964]. 241 pp.
Los Angeles.

6059. Kerby, Phil. "Minorities Oppose Los Angeles School System: Persistent Segregation." *Christian Century* 85 (September 4, 1968): 1+.

6060. Kim, Young Il. "A Study of Some Changes in Los Angeles Japanese Settlement Since 1950 with an Analysis of Selected Communities." Master's thesis, California State College at Los Angeles, 1963. 129 pp.

6061. Kirschner, Olive P. "The Italian in Los Angeles." Master's thesis, University of Southern California, 1920. 62 pp.

6062. Kitani, Misue. "An Inquiry into the Parental Attitude of Selected Japanese-American Families Toward Their Delinquent Sons." Master's thesis, University of Southern California, 1959. 74 pp.

6063. Kurth, Myrtle. "A Study of Four Racial Groups in a Pasadena Junior High School." Master's thesis, University of Southern California, 1941. 143 pp.
McKinley Junior High School.

6064. Lacy, Eloise T. "Contributions of People of French Origin to the Historical Development of the City and County of Los Angeles [1785-1932]." Master's thesis, University of Southern California, 1946. 200 pp.

6065. Lanigan, M. C. "Second Generation Mexicans in Belvedere." Master's thesis, University of Southern California, 1932. 86 pp.

6066. Lawrence, Dorothy W. "Some Problems Arising in the Treatment of Adolescent Negro Girls Appearing before the Los Angeles Juvenile Court." Master's thesis, University of Southern California, 1941. 106 pp.

6067. Lee, Kyung. "Settlement Patterns of Los Angeles Koreans." Master's thesis, University of California, Los Angeles, 1969. 81 pp.

6068. Lee, Mabel Sam. "The Recreational Interests and Participation of a Selected Group of Chinese Boys and Girls in Los Angeles, California." Master's thesis, University of Southern California, 1939. 90 pp.

6069. Lehman, Anthony L. *Birthright of Barbed Wire: The Santa Anita Assembly Center for the Japanese.* Los Angeles, 1970. 101 pp.

6070. Lembert, Edwin M., and Rosberg, Judy. *The Administration of Justice to Minority Groups in Los Angeles County.* University of California *Publications in Culture and Society,* Vol. 2, No. 1. Berkeley and Los Angeles, 1948. 27 pp.
Data from 1938.

6071. Lipman, Henry E. "A Preliminary Study of the Economic and Social Adjustment of Jewish Displaced Persons Now Residing in Los Angeles." Master's thesis, University of Southern California, 1958. 59 pp.

6072. Los Angeles. City Board of Education. Emergency Education Program. *Historical Background of the Negro in Los Angeles (1935).* [Los Angeles, 1935]. 26 pp.

6073. "L. A. Greeks to Organize Chamber of Commerce." *Southern California Business* 1 (April, 1922): 25.

6074. Louis, K. K. "A Study of American-Born and American-Reared Chinese in Los Angeles." Master's thesis, University of Southern California, 1931. 162 pp.

6075. Lourie, Anton, "Social Adjustments of German Jewish Refugees in Los Angeles." Master's thesis, University of Southern California, 1953. 221 pp.

6076. Loyer, Fernand, and Beaudreau, Charles, assisted by Beaudreau, Catherine, eds. *Le Guide Francais de Los Angeles et du Sud de la Californie.* Los Angeles, c1932. 221 pp.

6077. Lui, Garding. *Inside Los Angeles Chinatown.* Los Angeles, 1948. 207 pp.

6078. Lyon, Laura L. "Investigation of the Program for the Adjustment of Mexican Girls to the High Schools of the San Fernando Valley." Master's thesis, University of Southern California, 1933. 74 pp.

6079. MacCarthy, C. B. H. "A Survey of the Mexican Hardship Cases Active in the Los Angeles County Department of Charities, Los Angeles, California." Master's thesis, University of Southern California, 1939. 95 pp.

6080. Manes, Hugh R. *A Report on Law Enforcement and the Negro Citizen in Los Angeles.* Hollywood, [1963?]. Various pagings.

6081. Markey, Beatrice. "Minority Problems in

Public Employment with Special Reference to the Negro." Master's thesis, University of Southern California, 1952. 117 pp.

6082. Marquis, Neeta. "Inter-Racial Amity in California: Personal Observations on the Life of the Japanese in Los Angeles." *Independent* 75 (July 17, 1913) : 138-42.

6083. Marx, Wesley. "The Negro Community: 'A Better Chance.' " *Los Angeles* 3 (March 1962) : 38-41.
　Los Angeles.

6084. Mason, William M. "The Chinese in Los Angeles." *Museum Alliance Quarterly* 6 (Fall 1967) : 15-20.

6085. ———, and Anderson, James. "Los Angeles Black Heritage." *Museum Alliance Quarterly* 8 (Winter 1969-70) : 4-9.

6086. ———, and McKinstry, John A. "The Japanese of Los Angeles." Los Angeles County Museum of Natural History *Contributions in History No. 1.* Los Angeles, 1969. [43 pp.].

6087. Matzigkeit, Wesley. "The Influence of Six Mexican Cultural Factors on Group Behavior." Master's thesis, University of Southern California, 1947. 120 pp.

6088. McCombs, Vernon M. "Friendship for Mexicans." *California Christian Advocate* 62 (October 30, 1913) : 4.
　Los Angeles program.

6089. McEuen, William W. "A Survey of the Mexicans in Los Angeles [1910 to 1914]." Master's thesis, University of Southern California, 1914. 104 pp.

6090. McQuiston, John M. "Patterns of Negro Residential Invasion in Los Angeles County." Master's thesis, University of Southern California, 1968. 401 pp.

6091. McWilliams, Carey. *Prejudice. Japanese-Americans: Symbol of Racial Intolerance.* Boston, 1944. 337 pp.

6092. "The Mexicans Are Coming." *California Christian Advocate* 67 (February 21, 1918) : 4.
　Refugees from Mexico.

6093. "Mexicans in Los Angeles." *Survey* 44 (September 15, 1920) : 715-6.

6094. Miller, Elaine K. "Mexican Folk Narrative from the Los Angeles Area." Doctoral dissertation, University of California, Los Angeles, 1967. 625 pp.

6095. "Minority Groups in California." *Monthly Labor Review* 89 (September 1966) : 978-83.

6096. Mittelbach, Frank G. *Intermarriage of Mexican-Americans.* Los Angeles, 1966. 84 pp.
　Los Angeles.

6097. Modell, John. "Class or Ethnic Solidarity: The Japanese American Company Union." *Pacific Historical Review* 38 (1969) : 193-206.
　Southern California Retail Produce Workers Union, Los Angeles.

6098. ——— "The Japanese of Los Angeles: A Study in Growth and Accommodation, 1900-1946." Doctoral dissertation, Columbia University, 1969. 463 pp.

6099. Morales, Armando. "A Study of Recidivism of Mexican-American Junior Forestry Camp Graduates." Master's thesis, University of Southern California, 1963. 169 pp.

6100. Moseley, Ruth J. "Study of Negro Families in Los Angeles." Master's thesis, University of Southern California, 1938. 115 pp.

6101. Neblo, Sandro. *Sacred Earth.* Hollywood, 1948. 126 pp.
　Russians in Los Angeles.

6102. "Negroes Win City Jobs in Los Angeles." *American City* 82 (October 1967) : 89.

6103. Nodera, Isamu. "Survey of the Vocational Activities of the Japanese in the City of Los Angeles." Master's thesis, University of Southern California, 1937. 133 pp.

6104. O'Connor, George M. "The Negro and the Police in Los Angeles." Master's thesis, University of Southern California, 1955. 237 pp.

6105. Ortegon, Samuel M. "The Religious Status of the Mexican Population of Los Angeles." Master's thesis, University of Southern California, 1932. 69 pp.

6106. Otis, Johnny. *Listen to the Lambs*. New York, [c1968]. 256 pp.

Life in the Negro communities of Berkeley and Los Angeles is described by a Greek-American native of California. Emphasis on music.

6107. Oxnam, G. Bromley. "The Mexican in Los Angeles from the Standpoint of the Religious Forces of the City." *Annals of the American Academy of Political and Social Science* 93 (January 1921): 130-3.

6108. *"La Patria" di Los Angeles*. Los Angeles, 1915. 63 pp.

Italian-Americans in Los Angeles.

6109. Patterson, Beeman C. "The Politics of Recognition: Negro Politics in Los Angeles 1960-1963." Doctoral dissertation, University of Califoria, Los Angeles, 1967. 263 pp.

6110. Peek, Rena B. "The Religious and Social Attitudes of the Mexican Girls of the Constituency of the All Nations Foundation in Los Angeles." Master's thesis, University of Southern California, 1929. 87 pp.

6111. Peñalousa, Fernando. "The Changing Mexican in Southern California." *Sociology and Social Research* 51 (1967): 405-17.

6112. ———— "Class Consciousness and Social Mobility in a Mexican-American Community." Doctoral dissertation, University of Southern California, 1963. 365 pp.

Pomona.

6113. Penrod, Vesta. "Civil Rights Problems of Mexican-Americans in Southern California." Master's thesis, Claremont Graduate School, 1948. 109 pp.

6114. Porter, Paul T. "Handling Mexican Labor in California." *Electric Railway Journal* 72 (August 11, 1928): 221-2.

Pacific Electric Railway.

6115. Powell, William J. *Black Wings*. Los Angeles, 1934. 218 pp.

Written by a Los Angeles aviator, contains reference to some local Negro aviators.

6116. "The Race Problem at Swimming Pools: A Group of Reports from Representative Cities." *American City* 47 (August 1932): 76-7.

Includes report on desegregation of Los Angeles pools, by Raymond E. Hoyt.

6117. Ransford, Harry E. "Negro Participation in Civil Rights Activity and Violence." Doctoral dissertation, University of California, Los Angeles, 1966. 262 pp.

The data for this study was gathered during the summer and fall of 1965. The 400 interviewees were drawn from two contrasting neighborhoods of Los Angeles.

6118. Richards, Eugene S. "The Effects of the Negro's Migration to Southern California Since 1920 upon His Socio-Cultural Patterns." Doctoral dissertation, University of Southern California, 1941. 309 pp.

6119. Richardson, Adeline (Claff). "A Follow-Up Study of Negro Girl Graduates of a Los Angeles High School." Master's thesis, University of Southern California, 1941. 105 pp.

6120. Roberts, Glenys, and Thomas, Gilbert. "City of Ethnics." *Los Angeles* 12 (January 1967): 44-50.

Los Angeles ethnic groups.

6121. Roberts, Myron. " 'Our Crowd'—West." *Los Angeles* 13 (April 1968): 34-7+.

Los Angeles Jewish community.

6122. ———— "Summertime: Will the Livin' Be Easy?" *Los Angeles* 13 (June 1968): 24-6+.

Councilman Tom Bradley, Assemblyman William Greene, and the Los Angeles Negro community.

6123. Robertson, Florence (Keeney). "Problems in Training Adult Negroes in Los Angeles." Master's thesis, University of Southern California, 1929. 94 pp.

6124. Ross, Robert H. "Social Distance as It Exists Between the First and Second Generation Japanese in the City of Los Angeles and Vicinity." Master's thesis, University of Southern California, 1939. 194 pp.

6125. Roth, Henry. "Hollywood and the Negro Musician." *Frontier* 15 (January 1964): 21-2.

6126. Rothstein, Mignon. "A Study of the Growth of Negro Population in Los Angeles and Available Housing Facilities Between 1940 and 1946." Master's thesis, University of Southern California, 1950. 108 pp.

6127. Rubin, Mildred S. "The French in Los Angeles: A Study of a Transplanted Culture [1534 to 1936]." Master's thesis, University of Southern California, 1936. 113 pp.

6128. Santos, Amparo E. "Marital Adjustment of Filipino Couples in Los Angeles." Master's thesis, University of Southern California, 1962. 63 pp.

6129. Sauter, Mary C. "Arbol Verde: A Cultural Conflict and Accommodation in a California Mexican Community." Master's thesis, Claremont Graduate School, 1933. 241 pp.

6130. Schuerman, Leo A. "Assimilation of Minority Subpopulations in Los Angeles County." Master's thesis, University of Southern California, 1969. 142 pp.

6131. Schwartz, Marianne P. "The Perception of Social Class and Social Status and Its Relationship to Stereotyped Perception as Evidence of Social Distance in a Selected Group of Negro Women." Master's thesis, University of Southern California, 1964. 88 pp.

Relates to Los Angelse.

6132. Scott, Woodrow W. "Interpersonal Relations in Ethnically Mixed Small Work Groups." Doctoral dissertation, University of Southern California, 1959. 260 pp.

6133. Sears, David O. "Black Attitudes Toward the Political System in the Aftermath of the Watts Insurrection." *Midwest Journal of Political Science* 13 (1969): 515-44.

6134. Sheets, Dorothy I. "Anti-Japanese Agitation in California Studied at Three Period of Crisis." Master's thesis, Whittier College, 1944. Unp.

6135. Simons, Robert A. "Problems of Dutch Nationals Resettled in Los Angeles County under the Pastore-Walter Act and Its Amendment as Seen by Helping Persons and Representatives of Helping Organizations." Master's thesis, University of Southern California, 1963. 80 pp.

6136. Smith, Clara G. "The Development of the Mexican People in the Community of Watts, California." Master's thesis, University of Southern California, 1933. 126 pp.

6137. Soffer, Virginia M. "Socio-Cultural Changes in the Lives of Five Mexican-American College Graduates." Master's thesis, University of Southern California, 1958. 82 pp.

Los Angeles.

6138. Sokoloff, Lillian. *The Russians in Los Angeles.* Southern California Sociological Society, *Sociology Monograph No. 11.* Los Angeles, 1918. 16 pp.

6139. Spaulding, Charles B. "The Mexican Strike at El Monte, California." *Sociology and Social Research* 18 (July-August 1934): 571-80.

6140. Speier, Matthew R. "Japanese-American Relocation Camp Colonization and Resistance to Resettlement: A Study in the Social Psychology of Ethnic Identity under Stress." Master's thesis, University of California, 1956. 168 pp.

6141. Spencer, William D. "Problems of Assimilation of the Holland-Dutch People in a Selected Area in Southern California." Master's thesis, University of Southern California, 1942. 219 pp.

6142. Stevenson, Janet. "Before the Colors Fade: The Return of the Exiles." *American Heritage* 20 (June 1969): 22-5+.

An interview with Robert W. Kenny, California's state attorney general in 1945, concerning his efforts on behalf of Japanese-Americans released from wartime internment camps.

6143. Stirling, James H. "Culture Shock Among Central Americans in Los Angeles." Doctoral dissertation, University of California, Los Angeles, 1968. 146 pp.

6144. Taam, Loretta. "The Arrangements of the Chinese Community in Los Angeles for Meeting People's Needs." Master's thesis, University of Southern California, 1961. 121 pp.

6145. Taylor, Dora J. "Broken Homes as a Factor in the Maladjustment of Delinquent Negro Boys in Los Angeles." Master's thesis, University of Southern California, 1936. 61 pp.

6146. tenBroek, Jacobus, *et al. Prejudice, War and*

the Constitution. Causes and Consequences of the Evacuation of Japanese Americans in World War II. Berkeley and Los Angeles, 1969. 408 pp.

6147. Thomas, Dorothy S., ed. *Japanese American Evacuation and Resettlement.* Berkeley and Los Angeles, 1946-69. 3 vols.

6148. Tom, K. F. "The Participation of the Chinese in the Community Life of Los Angeles." Master's thesis, University of Southern California, 1944. 132 pp.

6149. Trillin, Calvin. "U.S. Journal: Los Angeles New Group in Town." *New Yorker* 46 (April 18, 1970): 92+.
    Deals mainly with the social life of Los Angeles' Indians, said to number 60,000.

6150. Trillingham, C. C. "Lessons from Watts; It Can Happen Here." *PTA Magazine* 61 (October 1966): 12-4.

6151. Trotter, Velma M. "The Status of Music, Dancing, Art, and Dramatic Instruction in a Selected Group of Mexican Elementary Schools in Los Angeles County." Master's thesis, University of Southern California, 1940. 133 pp.

6152. Tschekaloff, Natalia L. "Social Service Problems of Immigration with Special Reference to Russian Immigrants in Los Angeles." Master's thesis, University of Southern California, 1945. 218 pp.

6153. Tuthill, Gretchen L. "A Study of the Japanese in the City of Los Angeles." Master's thesis, University of Southern California, 1924. 95 pp.

6154. Ullman, Paul S. "An Ecological Analysis of Social Variables of Mexican-Americans in Los Angeles County." Master's thesis, University of Southern California, 1953. 88 pp.

6155. Underhill, Ruth M. *The Indians of Southern California.* Ed. by Willard W. Beatty. [Washington, D. C., 1941]. 73 pp.

6156. Vaz, August M. *The Portuguese in California.* Oakland, [c1965]. 235 pp.
    Los Angeles area included.

6157. Voget, L. M. "The Germans in Los Angeles County, California, 1850-1900." Master's thesis, University of Southern California, 1933. 100 pp.

6158. Wallovits, Sonia E. "The Filipinos in California." Master's thesis, University of Southern California, 1966. 153 pp.

6159. Watson, Homer K. "A Study of the Causes of Delinquency Among Fifty Negro Boys Assigned to Special Schools in Los Angeles." Master's thesis, University of Southern California, 1923. 68 pp.

6160. Whitaker, Hazel G. "A Study of Gifted Negro Children in the Los Angeles City Schools." Master's thesis, University of Southern California, 1931. 86 pp.

6161. Williams, Dorothy, S. "Ecology of Negro Communities in Los Angeles County, 1940-1959." Doctoral dissertation, University of Southern California, 1961. 187 pp.

6162. Williams, Faith M., and Hanson, Alice C. "Mexican Families in Los Angeles." *Money Disbursements of Wage Earners and Clerical Workers in Five Cities of the Pacific Region.* United States Bureau of Labor Statistics *Bulletin* 639 (1939): 85-109.

6163. Williams, Robert L., Jr. "The Negro's Migration to Los Angeles, 1900-1946." *Negro History Bulletin* 19 (February 1956): 102+.

6164. Williams, William J. "Attacking Poverty in the Watts Area: Small Business Development under the Economic Opportunities Act of 1964." Doctoral dissertation, University of Southern California, 1966. 273 pp.

6165. Wirin, A. L. "The Japanese Evacuation and the Constitution." *Bar Bulletin* 18 (October 1942): 27-30.

6166. Work, Lena B. "A Different View of Watts." *Harper's Magazine* 234 (May 1967): 38.
    Lists a number of graduates of Jordan High School who have gone on to college "and who are now making contributions of which they have reason to be proud."

6167. Yamaji, Yoshiko G. "The Impact of Communication Difficulties in Family Relations Observed in Eight Japanese War-Bride Marriages." Master's thesis, University of Southern California, 1961. 95 pp.

6168. Yeretzian, Aram S. "A History of Armenian Immigration to America with Special Reference to Conditions in Los Angeles." Master's thesis, University of Southern California, 1923. 97 pp.

6169. Young, Pauline V. "Assimilation Problems of Russian Molokans in Los Angeles." Doctoral dissertation, University of Southern California, 1930. 276 pp.

6170. —— *Pilgrims of Russian-Town.* Chicago, 1932. 296 pp.
Based on author's doctoral dissertation cited above.

6171. —— "Russian Molokan Community in Los Angeles." *American Journal of Sociology* 35 (1929): 393-402.

MOVING PICTURE INDUSTRY

6172. Atkinson, Sam. "Freedom for Expression: The Beginning of the Fight to Emancipate the Films from the Domination of the Local Censors." *Out West* 10, new series (November-December 1915): 103-7.
Los Angeles Motion Picture Censor Board.

6173. Baird, Leslie. "The Unseen Hollywood Revolution." *Overland Monthly* 90 (January-February 1932): 22.
Describes improvement in quality of movies.

6174. Bardeche, Maurice, and Brassillach, Robert. *The History of Motion Pictures.* Trans. and ed. by Iris Barry. New York, 1938. 412 pp.
Republished as *History of the Films.* London, 1945. 412 pp.

6175. Barratt, Harry. "The Film Version of Hollywood." *Los Angeles Realtor* 7 (November 1927): 20-1+.

6176. —— "Hollywood—Motion Picture Capital of the World." *Los Angeles Realtor* 5 (June 1926): 16+.

6177. Beall, Harry H. "The Capitalization of Sunshine and Shadows: The Films as the Southland's Greatest Asset." *Los Angeles Realtor* 4 (December 1925): 21+.

6178. Bernstein, Irving. *Hollywood at the Crossroads.* Los Angeles, 1957. 78 pp.
American Federation of Labor Film Council.

6179. Berry, Charles F. "A 7 Week Construction Wonder." *Southern California Business* 5 (October 1926): 24+.
Burbank movie studio.

6180. Bessie, Alvah C. *Inquisition in Eden.* New York, [1965]. 278 pp.
House Committee on Un-American Activities investigation of the motion picture industry.

6181. Biberman, Herman. "The Question." *Frontier* 10 (May 1959): 14-5.
Blacklist of "Hollywood Ten."

6182. Bobrow, Robert. "What's Become of Hollywood?" *Westways* 57 (June 1965): 42-4.
Effects of television.

6183. Boone, Andrew R. "Hollywood Business: Facts and Figures of Today's Big Expansion in Motion Pictures." *California Magazine of Pacific Business* 27 (January 1937): 7-10+.
Business aspects of movie production and distribution.

6184. Bowen, James E. "Bright Future Ahead of Photoplays." *Southern California Business* 1 (September 1922): 46+.
Los Angeles film makers.

6185 Bower, Anthony. "Films." *Nation* 152 (March 1, 1941): 249-50.
Effectiveness of Screen Office Employees Guild said to be crippled by its inability to penetrate the ranks of Twentieth Century-Fox, Paramount, or Warner Brothers.

6186. Brown, Harry D. "Why Movies Will Stay in Hollywood." *Southern California Business* 4 (January 1926): 18-9+.

6187. Browne, Michael. "Survey of the Hollywood Entertainment Film During the War Years 1941-1943." Master's thesis, University of California, Los Angeles, 1951. 239 pp.

6188. Buhrman, Robert. "MGM: The Lion in Winter." *Los Angeles* 14 (February 1959): 28-32+.
"The rise and fall of MGM. Can Leo make a comeback?"

6189. ——, and Lasky, Jesse, Jr. *Curtain of Life.* By Jack Preston [pseud.] and Jesse Lasky, Jr. New York, [1934]. 244 pp.

6190. [Buschlen, John P.]. *Heil! Hollywood.* By Jack Preston [*pseud.*]. Chicago, 1939. 344 pp.

6191. Bush, Carl. "Hollywood Still Center of Picture Industry." *Los Angeles Realtor* 6 (November 1926): 18+.

6192. Cameron, Anne. "The Double Gold Rush: The Transition from Stakes to Scripts." *Saturday Review of Literature* 26 (October 30, 1943): 10-1.
    Quality of Hollywood movies.

6193. Cantrell, Lang L. "An Inquiry into the 1945-1947 Jurisdictional Strike in the Motion Picture Industry." Master's thesis, University of Southern California, 1947. 98 pp.

6194. Cantwell, John J. "Priests and the Motion Picture Industry." *American Ecclesiastical Review* 90 (1934): 136-46.
    Directs attention to "the magnitude of the moving picture interests and to the degrading influence of many of the films that are exhibited."

6195. "Cathedral Built for a Motion Picture." *The Architect and Engineer* 61 (June 1920): 76-7.
    Goldwyn Picture Corp., Culver City.

6196. Chaplin, John R. "Hollywood Goes Closed Shop." *Nation* 142 (February 19, 1936): 225-6.

6197. Cohen, Helene K. "Avenues to Professional Positions in Hollywood Theatrical Films." Master's thesis, University of California, Los Angeles, 1968. 196 pp.

6198. Collins, James H. "Making Movies on a 'Line.'" *Southern California Business* 16 (January 1937): 6-7.

6199. Conference of Studio Unions. *The Hollywood Story.* Los Angeles, 1946. [?] pp.

6200. Connell, Will. *In Pictures; A Hollywood Satire . . .* New York, 1937. 104 pp.
    Each right-hand page is a photo by Connell. Facing is a brief text by Nunnally Johnson, Patterson McNutt, Gene Fowler, and Grover Jones.

6201. Cosman, Ralph H. "A Study of the Industrial Recreation Program at Twentieth Century-Fox Film Corporation." Master's thesis, University of California, Los Angeles, 1951. 55 pp.

6202. Covington, Floyd C. "The Negro Invades Hollywood." *Opportunity* 7 (April 1929): 111-3.

6203. Cowing, George C. *This Side of Hollywood; Together with The Private Life of Goldilocks and Other Bedtime Stories for Grown-ups.* Pasadena, 1938. 152 pp.

6204. Crowther, Bosley. *The Lion's Share; The Story of an Entertainment Empire.* New York, 1957. 320 pp.

6205. Daniels, Bebe. "Hollywood as I Know It." *Los Angeles Realtor* 8 (November 1928): 25+.

6206. Dawson, Anthony. "Patterns of Production and Employment in Hollywood." *Hollywood Quarterly* 4 (1950): 338-53.

6207. Day, Beth. *This Was Hollywood; An Affectionate History of Filmland's Golden Years.* New York, 1960. 287 pp.

6208. Day, George M. "The Russian Colony in Hollywood: A Study in Culture Conflict." Doctoral dissertation, University of Southern California, 1930. 283 pp.

6209. —— *The Russians in Hollywood: A Study in Culture Conflict.* [Los Angeles, 1934]. 101 pp.
    Based on the author's doctoral dissertation.

6210. De Mille, Cecil B. "The Spotlight of Los Angeles." *Southern California Business* 5 (July 1926): 20-1+.
    Film industry.

6211. Dunne George H. *Hollywood Labor Dispute; A Study in Immorality.* Los Angeles, [1950?]. 44 pp.

6212. Dunne, John G. *The Studio.* New York, [1969]. 244 pp.

6213. Ehret, Richard C. "A Descriptive Analysis of the Hearings Held by the House Committee on Un-American Activities in 1947 and 1951 on the Communist Infiltration of the Motion Picture Industry and Their Relationship to the Hollywood

Labor Movement." Master's thesis, University of California, Los Angeles, 1969. 190 pp.

6214. Elliott, James W. "The Movies Prepare to Speak for Themselves." *Los Angeles Realtor* 8 (November 1928): 28+.
The coming of sound.

6215. Ellis, Robert. "Ida Lupino Brings New Hope to Hollywood." *Negro Digest* 8 (August 1950): 47-9.
"Italian actress, turned movie producer, vows her pictures shall be free of prejudice."

6216. F. N. "Hollywood: Censorship." *Frontier* 5 (February 1954): 23-4; (March 1954): 22.

6217. Fadiman, William. "Hollywood: Blockbusters or Bust!" *Frontier* 14 November 1962): 21-2.
"In a desperate determination to recapture a diminishing audience, Hollywood has undertaken a number of films to be manufactured at unprecedented high costs."

6218. Faulkner, Robert R. "Studio Musicians: Their Work and Career Contingencies in the Hollywood Film Industry." Doctoral dissertation, University of California, Los Angeles, 1968. 294 pp.

6219. Feller, Dan. "An Introductory Study of Related Factors Pertaining to the Education, Welfare, and Employment of Minors in Motion Pictures in the Los Angeles Area." Doctoral dissertation, University of California, Los Angeles, 1954. 186 pp.

6220. Fellig, Arthur. *Naked Hollywood by Weegee and Mel Harris.* New York, 1953. Unp.

6221. Ferguson, Otis. "To the Promissory Land." *New Republic* 105 (July 14, 1941): 49-52; (August 4, 1941): 150-3.
July 14—I: " 'NY to LA' "
August 4—II: "Hollywood Will Fool You If You Don't Watch Out (Didn't It?)"

6222. Field, Alice E. *Hollywood, U.S.A.: From Script to Screen.* New York, 1952. 256 pp.

6223. Florey, Robert. *Hollywood d'Hier et d'Aujourd'hui.* Paris, [1948]. 381 pp.
A history.

6224. Friedman, Ralph. "The Negro in Hollywood." *Frontier* 9 (July 1958): 15-9.

6225. Fulton, Albert R. *Motion Pictures: The Development of an Art from Silent Films to the Age of Television.* Norman, 1960. 320 pp.

6226. Garfield, John. "How Hollywood Can Better Race Relations." *Negro Digest* 6 (November 1947): 4-8.

6227. Gassaway, Gordon. "Scooting Stars." *Touring Topics* 13 (April 1921): 18-20.
Movie stars and their taste in autos.

6228. Gillespie, Gilbert A. "The Role of the Hollywood Talent Agency in Developing the Talent of College Trained Screen Actors." Master's thesis, University of California, Los Angeles, 1962. 225 pp.

6229. Goodman, Ezra. *The Fifty-Year Decline and Fall of Hollywood.* New York, c1961. 465 pp.

6230. Gordon, Jan, and Gordon, Cora. *Star-Dust in Hollywood.* London, 1931. 300 pp.

6231. Graham, Sheilah. *The Garden of Allah.* New York, 1970. 258 pp.
Famed Hollywood residential court and the history of its stellar residents.

6232. "The Grauman Legacy: Late Chinese Theatre Owner Really Left His Mark." *Life* 28 (March 20, 1950): 47-8.
Sid Grauman.

6233. Greene, Forrester M. "An Analysis of Factors Contributing to the Current Recession in the Hollywood Motion Picture Industry." Master's thesis, University of Southern California, 1952. 138 pp.

6234. Griffith, Linda (Arvidson). *When the Movies Were Young.* New York, 1925. 256 pp.

6235. Griffith, Richard. *The Movie Stars.* New York, 1970. 498 pp.

6236. ———— *The Movies; The Sixty Year Story of the World of Hollywood and Its Effect on America.* New York, 1957. 442 pp.

6237. Gunsell, Richard M. "An Inquiry into the Operations of the Independent Educational Film Producer in the Los Angeles Area." Master's thesis, University of Southern California, 1964. 189 pp.

6238. Halliday, Ruth S. *Stars on the Crosswalks; An Intimate Guide to Hollywood.* Sherman Oaks, 1958. 100 pp.

6239. Hampton, Benjamin B. *A History of the Movies.* New York, 1931. 456 pp.

6240. Harding, Alfred. "The Motion Pictures Need a Strong Actors' Union." *American Federationist* 36 (March 1929): 282-9.

6241. Hassel, Damon. "Hollywood's Kept Press." *Frontier* 2 (October 1951) 7-9.
Hollywood reporters and gossip columnists.

6242. Higham, Charles, and Greenberg, Joel. *Hollywood in the Forties.* London and New York, 1968. 192 pp.

6243. Hill, Laurance L., and Snyder, Silas E. *Can Anything Good Come Out of Hollywood?* Los Angeles, 1923. 64 pp.

6244. "Hollywood What Now?" *Negro Digest* 14 (December 1964): 72-8.

6245. "Hollywood's Magic Mountain: Movies for the Masses, the West Coast's Biggest Peacetime Industrial Export, Are Made on the Highest Eminence of Earned Income in History." *Fortune* 31 (February 1945): 152-6+.

6246. Holstius, Edward N. *Hollywood Through the Back Door.* New York, 1937. 419 pp.

6247. Hummel, Ralph E. "A Study of Motion Picture Production Management in the Major Studios." Master's thesis, University of California, Los Angeles, 1964. 135 pp.

6248. Hunt, Howard. *Hollywood in the Thirties.* London and New York, 1968. 160 pp.

6249. Hynd, Alan. "Murder in Hollywood." *American Mercury* 69 (November 1949): 594-601.
William Desmond Taylor case, 1922.

6250. Jacobs, Lewis. *The Rise of the American Film, a Critical History.* New York, 1968. 631 pp.

6251. Johnson, Wynonah B. "Center of Motion Picture Industry." *Los Angeles Saturday Night 150th Birthday of Los Angeles: Fiesta and Pre-Olympiad.* Special Issue (1931): [14].

6252. Jones, Robert. "How Hollywood Feels about Negroes." *Negro Digest* 5 (August 1947): 4-8.

6253. Kahn, Gordon. *Hollywood on Trial; The Story of the 10 Who Were Indicted.* New York, 1948. 229 pp.

6254. Kerby, Phil. "Hollywood Blacklist." *Frontier* 3 (July 1952): 5-7.
Film industry leaders insititute a loyalty check of certain employees, allegedly at the behest of the American Legion.

6255. [Knepper, Max]. *Sodom and Gomorrah; The Story of Hollywood.* Los Angeles, [c1935]. 236 pp.

6256. Knight, Arthur. *The Liviliest Art; A Panoramic History of the Movies.* New York, 1957. 383 pp.

6257. Lash, John S. "The Negro in Motion Pictures." *Negro History Bulletin* 8 (1944): 7-8+.

6258. Lempertz, Thomas Q. "When Hollywood Was Hollywood." *Westways* 58 (Septmber 1966): 23-5.
A memoir.

6259. Levin, Martin. *Hollywood and the Great Fan Magazines.* New York, 1970. 224 pp.

6260. Lewis, Howard T. *The Motion Picture Industry.* New York, 1933. 454 pp.

6261. Lickness, George C. *The Oscar People; From Wings to My Fair Lady.* Mendota, Ill., [1965]. 415 pp.
Motion Picture Academy of Arts and Sciences awards.

6262. Logan, Somerset. "The Battle of Hollywood." *New Republic* 59 (August 7, 1929): 308-10.
Actors' Equity vs. motion picture producers.

6263. ——— "Revolt in Hollywood." *Nation* 129 (July 17, 1929): 61-2.
Actors' Equity vs. motion picture producers.

6264. Look Magazine, eds. *Movie Lot to Beachhead, the Motion Picture Goes to War and Prepares for the Future.* Garden City, N.Y., 1945. 291 pp.

6265. Lovell, Hugh, and Carter, Tasile. *Collective Bargaining in the Motion Picture Industry.* Berkeley, 1955. 54 pp.

6266. Lyons, John H. "A General Introduction to Feature Film Financing in the Hollywood (Entertainment) Motion Picture Industry." Master's thesis, University of Southern California, 1970. 182 pp.

6267. Macgowan, Kenneth. "Motion Picture Industry," in *California and the Southwest.* Ed. by Clifford M. Zieger. New York, 1956. Pp. 272-7.

6268. MacPherson, Harry. "Back of the Laughs in Hollywood." *Touring Topics* 25 (June 1933): 8-11+.

6269. ——— "Hollywood on Wheels." *Touring Topics* 25 (November 1933): 24-5+.

6270. ——— "Hollywood Takes the Torch." *Touring Topics* 25 (July 1933): 10-3+.

6271. ——— "Seers and Superstitions in Hollywood." *Touring Topics* 23 (September 1933): 16-9+.

6272. Mangold, William P. "Hollywood Fights Its Writers." *New Republic* 87 (May 27, 1936): 70-1.
Movie producers vs. Screen Writers' Guild.

6273. Marberry, M. M. "The Overloved One." *American Heritage* 16 (August 1965): 84-7+.
An engaging article of the 1926 death of Rudolph Valentino, movie idol, his funeral, and its aftermath.

6274. Marlowe, Don. *The Hollywood That Was.* Fort Worth, Texas, 1969. 189 pp.

6275. Mayersberg, Paul. *Hollywood, the Haunted House.* New York, 1968. 188 pp.

6276. McCarthy, John R. "High Moments in Hollywood History: How Mack Sennett Awakened Uncle Albert and the Rest of America to the Beauty of the Feminine Knee." *Saturday Night* 45 (July 16, 1938): 10-1+.

6277. McDonough, Joan. "Independent Production in the American Motion Picture Industry." Master's thesis, Stanford University, 1947. 166 pp.

6278. McManus, John T., and Kronenberger, Louis. "Motion Pictures, the Theatre, and Race Relations." *Annals of the American Academy of Political and Social Science* 244 (March 1946): 152-8.
Describes in part the place of Negroes in Hollywood films.

6279. Miller, Loren. "Hollywood's New Negro Films." *Crisis* 45 (January 1938): 8-9.

6280. Miller, Max. *For the Sake of Shadows.* New York, 1936. 200 pp.
The movie business from the perspective of a Hollywood writer.

6281. Minney, Rubeigh J. *Hollywood by Starlight.* London, [1935]. 264 pp.

6282. Moses, Walter I. *Adventures of a Writer in Movieland.* [Los Angeles?, c1924]. 63 pp.

6283. "Motion Picture Producers Appreciate: Express Belief That Action Taken by Chamber of Commerce and Newspaper Publishers Will Result in Much Good." *Southern California Business* 1 (March 1922): 19+.

6284. Murray, Jim. "Billy Wilder: Hating People for Fun and Profit." *Los Angeles* 6 (October 1963): 28-31.
Wilder at Paramount Studios in Hollywood.

6285. Musun, Chris. "The Marketing of Motion Pictures." Doctoral dissertation, University of Southern California, 1970. 339 pp.

6286. Niblo, Fred. "Contact! Camera!" *Western Flying* 4 December 1928): 40-1+.
Role of flying in the film industry.

6287. ———, and Kellogg, Virginia. "When Hollywood Flies." *Western Flying* 6 (November 1929): 44-5+.

6288. Orr, James E. *The Inside Story of the Hollywood Christian Group.* Grand Rapids, Mich., [1955]. 134 pp.

6289. Owen, Willis. "Motion Pictures Build a Bigger Hollywood." *Los Angeles Realtor* 7 (November 1927): 40+.

6290. Parcher, Will C. "Ante-Cinema Hollywood." *Westways* 27 (May 1935): 24-5+.

6291. Partridge, Helen. *A Lady Goes to Hollywood.* New York, 1941. 259 pp.
"Being the casual adventures of an author's wife in the much misunderstood capital of filmland." Impressianistic letters to various friends and relatives.

6292. Pensel, Hans A. "Seastrom and Stiller in Hollywood; A Case Study of Two Swedish Directors in Silent American Film, 1923-1930." Master's thesis, University of California, Los Angeles, 1967. 147 pp.

6293. Phillips, Gifford. "Where Is Hollywood Headed?" *Frontier* 5 (February 1954): 3-4.

6294. Pike, Robert M. "A Critical Study of the West Coast Experimental Film Movement." Master's thesis, University of California, Los Angeles, 1960. 208 pp.

6295, Poe, Elizabeth. "The Hollywood Story." *Frontier* 5 (May 1954): 6-25.
I: "The Techniques of the Purge," pp. 7-15.
II: "Results of the Purge," pp. 15-25.
Loyalty investigations in film industry.

6296. Powdermaker, Hortense. *Hollywood, the Dream Factory; An Anthropologist Looks at the Movie Makers.* Boston, 1950. 342 pp.

6297. Raborn, George. *How Hollywood Rates.* Los Altos, 1955. 74 pp.

6298. Ramsaye, Terry. *A Million and One Nights; A History of the Motion Picture.* New York, 1926. 2 vols.

6299. Ray, Charles. *Hollywood Shorts, Compiled from Incidents in the Everyday Life of Men and Women Who Entertain in Pictures.* Los Angeles, 1935. 177 pp.

6300. "Retreat from Hollywood." *Outlook and Independent* 153 (September 4, 1929): 13-4.
Effort of Actors' Equity Association's to unionize Hollywood.

6301. Rivkin, Allen. *The Rivkin-Kerr Production of Hello, Hollywood! A Book about the Movies by the People Who Make Them.* New York, c1962. 571 pp.

6302. Robinson, David. *Hollywood in the Twenties.* London and New York, [1968]. 176 pp.

6303. [Rodd, Marcel]. *Souvenir-album. Los Angeles, Hollywood, and the Southland at a Glance.* Hollywood, [c1942]. 96 pp.

6304. Ross, Murray. "The C.I.O. Loses Hollywood." *Nation* 149 (October 7, 1939): 374-7.

6305. ——— "Labor Relations in Hollywood." *Annals of the American Academy of Political and Social Science* 254 (November 1947): 58-64.

6306. Rosten, Leo C. *Hollywood: The Movie Colony and the Movie Makers.* New York, 1941. 436 pp.

6307. Roth, Henry. "Hollywood and the Negro Musician." *Frontier* 15 (January 1964): 21-2.

6308. Sands, Pierre N. "A Historical Study of the Academy of Motion Picture Arts and Sciences [1927-1947]." Master's thesis, University of Southern California, 1967. 262 pp.

6309. Sauberli, Harry A., Jr. "Hollywood and World War II." Master's thesis, University of Southern California, 1967. 361 pp.

6310. Schatz, Gerald S. "Will H. Hays and the Motion Picture Industry, 1919-1922." *Historical Society of Southern California Quarterly* 43 (1961): 316-29.

6311. Schenck, Joseph M. "A Business View of Motion Pictures: Production in Los Angeles Studios Will Be Expanded on Large Scale, with Addition of Capital, During Next Twelve Months." *Southern California Business* 1 (June 1922): 9+.

6312. Schulberg, Budd. "Confessions of a Hollywood Boyhood." *Los Angeles* 10 (September 1965): 36-40+.
"A noted novelist recalls days when his father ran a studio, Clara Bow as every schoolboy's idol, and monkeys resided at the Beverly Hills Hotel."

6313. ——— "Hollywood." *Holiday* 5 (January 1949): 34-49+.

6314. Shaw, Irwin. "Hollywood People." *Holiday* 5 (January 1949): 53-9+.

6315. Sheehan, P. P. *Hollywood as a World Center.* Hollywood, c1924. 115 pp.

6316. Smith, William T. "Hollywood Report." *Phylon* 6 (1945): 13-6.
The Negro in the entertainment industry.

6317. Steele, Rufus "In the Sun Spot." *Sunset* 34 (April 1915): 690-9.
Los Angeles as a motion picture center.

6318. Still, William G. "How Do We Stand in Hollywood?" *Opportunity* 23 (April-June 1945): 74-7.
The Negro in Hollywood.

6319. Strosnider, R. H. " 'Forward' —Burbank." *Los Angeles Realtor* 8 (November 1928): 32.
Deals particularly with movies and airplane manufacture.

6320. Suber, Howard. "The Anti-Communist Blacklist in the Hollywood Motion Picture Industry." Doctoral dissertation, University of California, Los Angeles, 1968. [?] pp.

6321. —— "The 1947 Hearings of the House Committee on Un-American Activities into Communism in the Hollywood Motion Picture Industry." Master's thesis, University of California, Los Angeles, 1966. 309 pp.

6322. Symes, Lillian. "The Beautiful and Dumb." *Harper's Magazine* 163 (June 1931): 22-32.
Hollywood and the "Hollywood mentality."

6323. Thomas, Bob. *Thalberg: Life and Legend.* New York, 1969. 415 pp.
Major figure in building MGM into Hollywood's biggest film studio.

6324. Thompson, Morton. "Hollywood Is a Union Town." *Nation* 146 (April 2, 1938): 381-3.

6325. Trombley, William. "Don't Stick Your Neck Out: Politics in Hollywood." *Frontier* 14 (May 1963): 5-13.

6326. Trumbo, Dalton. "Blackface, Hollywood Style." *Crisis* 50 (December 1943): 365-7+.

6327. Tusher, William. "Hollywood's Keyhole Patrol." *Frontier* 1 (December 15, 1949): 7-9.
Journalistic "Jackals and Jackasses" who rob Hollywood personalities of their privacy.

6328. Tyler, Parker. *Hollywood Hallucination.* New York, 1944. 246 pp.

6329. [Ullback, Sylvia]. *Hollywood Undressed, Observations of Sylvia as Noted by Her Secretary.* New York, 1931. 250 pp.

6330. "Unionism in Filmland." *Nation* 129 (August 28, 1929): 211.

6331. University of Southern California, Bureau of Business Research. *An Economic Survey of Hollywood.* Directed by Thurston H. Ross. [Los Angeles, 1938]. I vol., various pagination.

6332. Wagenkecht, Edward C. *The Movies in the Age of Innocence.* Norman, Okla., 1962. 280 pp.

6333. Warner Bros. Pictures, Inc. *A Financial Review and Brief History, 1923-1945.* [N.p., 1946?]. 39 pp.

6334. Weber, Francis J. "John J. Cantwell and the Legion of Decency." *American Ecclesiastical Review* 151 (1964): 237-47.

6335. Wilson, Edmund. "Eisenstein in Hollywood," in author's *The American Earthquake: A Documentary of the Twenties and Thirties.* Garden City, N.Y., 1958. Pp. 397-413.

6336. Zierer, C[lifford] M. "Hollywood, World Center of Motion Picture Production." *Annals of the American Academy of Political and Social Science* 254 (November 1947): 12-7.

MUSEUMS

6337. Archaeological Institute of America, Southwest Society. *The Southwest Museum; Three Years of Success.* Los Angeles, 1907. 82 pp.

6338. —— *The Southwest Society . . . Something about Its Aims and Its First Year's Work.* [Los Angeles, 1904]. 30 pp.

6339. Bach, Richard F. "The Southwest Museum, Los Angeles, Cal." *Architectural Record* 42 (July 1917): 18-26.

6340. Battle, Don. "A Labor of Love." *Westways* 52 (August 1960): 26-8.
The Archaeological Survey Association, associated with Southwest Museum.

6341. Buhrman, Robert. "Portrait of the Artist as a Mad Scientist." *Los Angeles* 14 (November 1969): 42-4+.
County Museum's art and technology program.

6342. Carlton, Frederick. "A Champagne Wedding for Art and Architecture." *Los Angeles* 9 (April 1965): 26-31+.
County Museum of Art.

6343. Clark, Donavan L. "A History of the Southwest Museum, 1905-1955." Master's thesis, Claremont Graduate School, 1956. 221 pp.

6344. Cochran, Drew. "Ric the Lionhearted: Out of Controversy and Chaos, the Daring Director of the County Art Museum Has Masterminded an Artistic Revolution." *Los Angeles* 7 (June 1964): 45+.
County Museum of Art.

6345. Collins, James H. "Bring'em Back Petrified!" *Southern California Business* (February 1938): 8-9.
County Museum's fossils.

6346. ——— "So for Xmas They Bought the Zoo." *Southern California Business* 11 (September 1932): 8-9.
California Zoological Gardens, Los Angeles.

6347. Cox, W[illia]m L. "Toot. Toot Here's Travel Town." *Rotarian* 89 (August 1956): 20-1.
Transportation Museum in Griffith Park.

6348. Denzel, Carl S. "The Southwest Museum," in *A Bookman's View of Los Angeles.* Los Angeles, 1961. Pp. 33-5.

6349. Dotson, Margaret. "Pony Express Museum." *Apartment Journal* 20 (September 1937): 10-1+.
Formerly in Arcadia.

6350. Gleason, Sterling. "Push-Button Museum Shows Secrets of Science." *Popular Science* 128 (April 1936): 14-5+.
Planetarium and Griffith Observatory.

6351. Griffith Observatory. *Griffith Observatory and Planetarium Los Angeles.* Los Angeles, 1935. [48] pp.

6352. ——— *The Story of Griffith Observatory and Planetarium.* Los Angeles, [1952]. 49 pp.

6353. "Griffith Planetarium." *Los Angeles Saturday Night* 15 (July 6, 1935): 5.
Brief description of facilities and surroundings.

6354. Guinn, James M. "The Museum of History, Science, and Art." *Annual Publication* Historical Society of Southern California 8, Pts. 1-2 (1909): 5-8.

6355. Harrington, Marie. "The Museum That's Carved in the Rocks." *Westways* 47 (March 1955): 28-9.
Antelope Valley Museum of Indian Artifacts.

6356. Hill, Gladwin. "Travel Town U.S.A.: A Museum to Enjoy." *Recreation* 8 (October, 1955): 381.
Transportation museum in Griffith Park. Reprinted from *New York Times,* June 5, 1955.

6357. Hill, Laurance L. *Six Collegiate Decades— The Growth of Higher Education in Southern California. Los Angeles, 1929.* 11 pp.
Los Angeles County Museum, the Huntington Library and the Southwest Museum.

6358. Johnson, Norman K. "SC——ERA Narrow Gauge Electrics: An Up-to-Date Report on the Trolley Preservation Efforts of the SC——ERA." *Headlights* 18 (March 1956): 1-2.
Preservation of old trolley cars at Travel Town in Griffith Park by the Southern California Electric Railroaders' Association.

6359. Kuh, Katherine. "Los Angeles: Salute to a New Museum." *Saturday Review* 48 (April 3, 1965): 29-35.
County Museum of Art.

6360. Leider, Philip. "Art: Who's in Charge Here?" *Frontier* 17 (December 1965): 22-3.
County Museum of Art.

6361. Lummis, Charles F. "The Southwest Museum." *Out West* 26 (May 1907): 389-412.

6362. Lynch, Samuel D. "Science Protects Art." *Westways* 57 (August 1965): 8-10+.
Various devices and procedures for protection of treasures in the County Museum of Art.

6363. Millier, Arthur. "A Museum Comes Alive." *Magazine of Art* 33 (March 1940): 148-51.
Los Angeles Museum of History, Science and Art.

6364. ———— "The Museum Gets Its Second Wind." *Los Angeles* 12 (February 1967): 24-6+.
County Museum of Art.

6365. "Mount Hollywood Rivals the Boulevard . . . Star-Gazing in Griffith Planetarium Popular Entertainment." *Los Angeles Saturday Night* 16 (January 11, 1936): 6.

6366. "An Observatory for the Public." *Literary Digest* 119 (April 20, 1935): 28.
Griffith Planetarium and Observatory.

6367. Palmer, Frank M. "Nucleus of Southwestern Museum." *Out West* 22 (January 1905): 23-4.

6368. "Paradise for Casey Jones, Jr.: Travel Town in Griffith Park." *Popular Mechanics* 105 (April 1956): 42-3.

6369. "Planetarium Has New Comet Projector." *Los Angeles Saturday Night* 44 (November 7, 1936): 5.
Griffith Park.

6370. "Reorganization at the Los Angeles Museum." *Science* 94 (September 12, 1941): 255-6.

6371. Riley, Frank. "Maurice Tuchman: A Museum Curator Sounds Off." *Los Angeles* 10 (August 1965): 42-5.
Controversy over the role of the new County Museum of Art in the community.

6372. Robinson, William W. *The Story of the Southwest Museum.* Los Angeles, 1960. 50 pp.

6373. Rodriguez, Paul. "Flight Through the Heavens." *Westways* 31 (April 1939): 18-9.
Griffith Planetarium and Observatory.

6374. "Shooting at the Los Angeles Zoo." *Western Construction* 41 (November 1966): 74-5.
Building animal compounds of gunite.

6375. Smith Jack. "A Day in the City: The Acropolis in Highland Park." *Westways* 60 (April 1968): 5-7.
El Alisal, the Southwest Museum, and the Casa de Adobe.

6376. ———— "A Day in the City: Far Out in Pasadena." *Westways* 62 (October 1970): 14-6+.
New Pasadena Art Museum.

6377. ———— "A Day in the City: Masters and Mastodons." *Westways* 60 (July 1968): 25-7.
County Museum of Art.

6378. ———— "A Day in the City: The Zoo." *Westways* 62 (January 1970): 9-11+.
Griffith Park.

6379. Southwest Museum. *The Southwest Museum.* [Los Angeles, n.d.]. 36 pp.

6380. "The Southwest Museum at Los Angeles." *Art and Archaeology* 4 (December 1916): 341-3.

6381. Stephenson, Allen B., and Wess, William H. "Lomita's Railroad Museum for City Without Railroad." *Western City* 46 (April 1970): 38-40.

6382. Stern, Seymour, and Kunkin, Art. "The Battle of Alta Loma Terrace." *Frontier* 15 (April 1964): 11-2.
Hollywood Museum.

6383. Welles, Thomas. "The Pony Express Museum." *Overland Monthly* 91 (March 1933): 44-5+.
Formerly in Arcadia.

6384. "Wild Animals Pose at Museum." *Los Angeles Saturday Night* 44 (March 20, 1937): 8.
Display of big game animals at County Museum.

6385. Wilkins, Barbara. "The Unsung Little Museums." *Los Angeles* 14 (March 1969): 42-5.
Los Angeles area.

6386. Wing, Will E. "Founder of Los Angeles Museum Retires." *Los Angeles Saturday Night* 43 (February 15, 1936): 3.
William M. Bowen resigns as president of board of governors of Los Angeles Museum of History, Science and Art.

NATURAL HISTORY

NATURAL HISTORY—CLIMATE

6387. Bailey, Harry P. *The Climate of Southern California.* Berkeley, 1966.
Explains such phenomena as temperature inversion, prevailing westerly, Catalina eddy, and Santa Ana winds.

6388. Carpenter, Ford A. "Flying Weather in Two

American Cities." *Southern California Business* 8 (April 1929): 14-5+.
Los Angeles and Chicago.

6389. ——— "Four Reasons for the Climate of Southern California." *Los Angeles Saturday Night 150th Birthday of Los Angeles: Fiesta and Pre-Olympiad.* Special Issue (1931): [7].

6390. ——— *The Land of the Beckoning Climate.* Los Angeles, 1932. 15 pp. Other editions printed in 1936 and 1938.

6391. ——— "Start by Asking about the Climate." *Southern California Business* 17 (April 1938): 12-3.
Department of Meteorology and Aeronautics of the Los Angeles Chamber of Commerce.

6392. ——— "Where Climate Assists the Worker." *Southern California Business* 1 (September 1922): 140.

6393. ——— "Why Los Angeles Is 'The Windless City.'" *Southern California Business* 10 (February 1931): 16-7.
Explains why high winds are comparatively rare in the Los Angeles area.

6394. Dean, Gordon A. "The Climate of the Los Angeles Area According to the Koppen Classification." Master's thesis, University of California, Los Angeles, 1947. 39 pp.
Most of this thesis consists of a lengthy appendix containing numerous maps, charts, and tables.

6395. Harris, Michael F. "Effects of Tropical Cyclones upon Southern California." Master's thesis, San Fernando Valley State College, 1969. 89 pp.

6396. Hawkins, Robert N. "The Distribution of Solar Radiation, Infrared Radiation and Net Radiation in an Urban Area—Pasadena, California." Master's thesis, University of California, Los Angeles, 1969. 100 pp.

6397. Holt, L. M. "What Is Climate Worth Per Acre?" *Out West* 32 (April 1910): 304-16.
Discusses various California cities, including Los Angeles, Long Beach, and Pasadena.

6398. Holt, Raymond M. "That Devil Wind—The Santa Ana." *Westways* 50 (November 1958): 6-7.

6399. Koutnik, Ward M. "Newhall Winds of the San Fernando Valley." Master's thesis, San Fernando Valley State College, 1968. 80 pp.

6400. McAdie, Alexander. "The Los Angeles Rain-Making." *Sunset* 15 (October 1905): 575-7.
Skeptical comment on the accomplishments of a rain-maker said to have been hired by a group of Los Angeles merchants.

6401. "Rainfall and Stream Run-Off in Southern California Since 1769: Report Prepared by H. B. Lynch for Metropolitan Water District Shows No Material Change in Climatic Conditions in 162 Years." *Western City* 7 (September 1931): 19-20.

6402. Stephenson, Terry E. "The Santa Ana Wind." *California Folklore Quarterly* 2 (1943): 35-40.

6403. Thomas, Franklin. "Then Came the Deluge." *Western City* 28 (February 1952): 37-8.
Los Angeles rainfall data.

6404. Winther, Oscar O. "The Use of Climate as a Means of Promoting Migration to Southern California." *Mississippi Valley Historical Review* 33 (1946): 411-24.

6405. Wolff, John E. "Cloudburst on San Gabriel Peak, Los Angeles County, California." *Bulletin of the Geological Society of America* 38 (September 1927): 443-55.

6406. Young, Floyd. "Frost Warnings in the Early Days." *Pomona Valley Historian* 5 (1969): 171-4.
Pomona Valley.

NATURAL HISTORY—FLORA

6407. Abrams, LeRoy. *Flora of Los Angeles and Vicinity.* Stanford, 1904. 474 pp.

6408. Bauer, H. L. "Moisture Relations in the Chaparral of the Santa Monica Mountains, California." Doctoral dissertation, University of Southern California, 1934. [?] pp.

6409. Crebbin, Alfred K. "What of the Future." *Trails Magazine* 3 (Spring 1936): 19-21.
Angeles National Forest.

6410. Dawson, E. Yale. *Seashore Plants of South-*

ern California. Berkeley and Los Angeles, 1966. 101 pp.

6411. DeLisle, Harold F. *Common Plants of the Southern California Mountains.* Healdsburg, 1961. 64 pp.

6412. "Forestry in Southern California—Past—Present—Future." *Trails Magazine* 1 (Autumn 1934): 9.

6413. Fultz, Francis M. *The Elfin Forest.* Los Angeles, 1923. 267 pp.
   Includes low-lying chaparral forests in San Gabriel Mountains.

6414. Gauss, Norman M. "Distribution of Selected Plant Species in a Portion of the Santa Monica Mountains, California, on the Basis of Site." Master's thesis, University of California, Los Angeles, 1964. 119 pp.

6415. Hudson, Jack. "A Taxonomical and Ecological Study in the San Rafael Hills, California." Master's thesis, Occidental College, 1950. 55 pp.

6416. McClatchie, Alfred J. "The Eucalypts of the Southwest." *Out West* 20 (April 1904): 336-46; (May 1904): 422-35.
   Includes Abbott Kinney and eucalypts in Los Angeles.

6417. Mears, Joe. "Birthday for a Forest." *Westways* 34 (December 1942): 8-9.
   Angeles National Forest.

6418. Miller, E. H. "The Effect of Altitude and Slope Exposure on Environmental Conditions and the Growth of Chaparral Species in the San Gabriel Mountains of Southern California." Doctoral dissertation, University of Southern California, 1944. [?] pp.

6419. Miller, James E. "Vegetation and Its Relationship to Land Use in the Santa Monica Mountains, California." Master's thesis, University of California, Los Angeles, 1969. 156 pp.

6420. Munz, Philip A. *Supplement to a California Flora.* Berkely and Los Angeles, 1968. 224 pp.

6421. ——, and Keck, David D. *A California Flora.* Berkeley and Los Angeles, 1959. 1681 pp.

6422. Peterson, Peter V. *Native Trees of Southern California.* Berkeley and Los Angeles 1966. *California Natural History Guides No. 14.* 136 pp.

6423. Raven, Peter H. *Native Shrubs of Southern California.* Berkeley and Los Angeles, 1966. *California Natural History Guides No. 15.* 132 pp.

6424. Thurston, Carl. *Wildflowers of Southern California.* Pasadena, 1936. 393 pp.

NATURAL HISTORY—FOSSILS

6425. Heric, Thomas M. "Rancho La Brea: Its History and Its Fossils." *Journal of the West* 8 (1969): 209-30.

6426. Holder, Charles F. "A Saber-Tooth Tiger Hunt." *Outlook* 99 (September 23, 1911): 188-95.
   La Brea tar pits and fossils.

6427. Moore, Sidney H. "Find of Fossil Bones at Los Angeles." *Out West* 31 (December 1909): 969-80.

6428. Orcut, Mary L. "The Discovery in 1901 of the La Brea Fossil Beds." *Historical Society of Southern California Quarterly* 36 (1954): 338-41.

6429. Randau, John A. "Making Prehistory at the La Brea Tar Pits." *Westways* 59 (August 1967): 33-5.

6430. Walker, Edwin F. *Five Prehistoric Archaeological Sites in Los Angeles County, California.* Los Angeles, 1952. 116 pp.

6431. Woodside, Ethel. "Rancho La Brea Fossil Pits." *Apartment Journal* 23 August 1940): 12+.

NATURAL HISTORY— GEOLOGY AND GEOGRAPHY

6432. Anderson, Homer G. "Sunland-La Crescenta Area, Los Angeles County, California: A Geographical Study of Land Use Types." Master's thesis, University of California. Los Angeles, 1947. 86 pp.

6433. Bailey, Harry P. "Physical Geography of the San Gabriel Mountains, California." Doctoral dissertation, University of California, Los Angeles, 1950. 246 pp.

6434. Bass, Ralph O. "Geology of the Western Part of the Point Dume Quadrangle, Los Angeles County, California." Master's thesis, University of California, Los Angeles, 1960. 91 pp.

6435. Battle, Don. "The Scouts' Memorial Mountain." *Westways* 52 (March 1960) : 8-9.
Mt. Baden-Powell in the San Gabriels.

6436. Baudino, Frank J. "The Geology of the Glendale Quadrangle, Los Angeles County, California." Master's thesis, University of Southern California, 1934. 42 pp.

6437. Baugh, Ruth E. "The Antelope Valley: A Study in Regional Geography." Master's thesis, Clark University, 1926. 234 pp.

6438. —— "The Geography of the Los Angeles Water Supply." Doctoral dissertation, Clark University, 1929. 269 pp.

6439. Beatie, Robert L. "The Geology of the Sunland-Tujunga Area, Los Angeles County, California." Master's thesis, University of California, Los Angeles, 1958. 102 pp.

6440. Beer, Robert M. "Suspended Sediment over Redondo Submarine Canyon and Vicinity, Southern California." Master's thesis, University of Southern California, 1969. 131 pp.

6441. Bell, David I. "A Geologic Investigation of Landslides in a Portion of the Northern Santa Monica Mountains." Master's thesis, University of Southern California, 1967. 98 pp.

6442. Bishop, Ernest G. "Our Sierra Madre, Mother Mountains." *Los Angeles Saturday Night* 15 (December 8, 1934) : 5.

6443. Bishop, William C. "Geology of Southern Flank of Santa Susana Mountains County Line to Limekiln Canyon, Los Angeles County, California." Master's thesis, University of California, Los Angeles, 1950. 115 pp.

6444. Bissell, Malcolm H. "A Review of the Geographic Base," in *Los Angeles: Preface to a Master Plan*. Ed. by George W. Robbins and L. Deming Tilton. Los Angeles, 1941. Pp. 13-28.

6445. Brady, Thomas J. "Geology of Part of the Central Santa Monica Mountains East of Topanga Canyon, Los Angeles County, California." Master's thesis, University of California, Los Angeles, 1957. 72 pp.

6446. Brockhouse, Thomas E. "The Geology and Paleontology of a Portion of the Santa Monica Mountains." Master's thesis, University of Southern California, 1932. 55 pp.

6447. Byer, John W. "Geology and Engineering Properties of the Portugese Tuff, Palos Verdes Hills, California." Master's thesis, University of Southern California, 1969. 88 pp.

6448. Carter, Neville L. "Geology of the Fernwood-Topanga Park Area, Santa Monica Mountains, California." Master's thesis, University of California, Los Angeles, 1958. 99 pp.

6449. Clark, Bruce L. "Topography of Southern California." Master's thesis, University of California, Berkeley, 1909. 63 pp.

6450. Corbato, Charles E. "Gravity Investigation of the San Fernando Valley, California." Doctoral dissertation, University of California, Los Angeles, 1960. 62 pp.

6451. Cowan, J. M. "Geological Rambles on the Angeles." *Trails Magazine* 3 (Spring 1936) : 16+.

6452. Draine, Edwin H. "The Geographic Implications of Land Subsidence in the Long Beach, California, Harbor Area." Master's thesis, University of California, Los Angeles, 1958. 131 pp.

6453. Dudley, Paul H., Jr. "Geology of the Area Adjacent to the Arroyo Seco Parkway, Los Angeles County, California." Master's thesis, University of California, Los Angeles, 1954. 84 pp.

6454. Eaton, J. E. "Geology of the Southern California Earthquake." *Petroleum World* 30 (April 1933) : 13-4.
Long Beach earthquake of March 10, 1933.

6455. Elam, Jack G. "Geology of Seminole Quadrangle, Los Angeles County, California." Master's thesis, University of California, Los Angeles, 1948. 43 pp.

6456. Elliott, John L. "Geology of the Eastern Santa Monica Mountains Between Laurel Canyon and Beverly Glen Boulevards, Los Angeles County, California." Master's thesis, University of California, Los Angeles, 1951. 57 pp.

6457. Fairbanks, Harold W. *Southern California: The Land and Its People: A Reader for Beginners in Geography.* San Francisco, [c1929]. 344 pp.

6458. Gaal, Robert A. P. "Marine Geology of the Santa Catalina Basin Area, California." Doctoral dissertation, University of Southern California, 1966. 268 pp.

6459. Gorsline, Donn S. "Marine Geology of San Pedro and Santa Monica Basins and Vicinity, California." Doctoral dissertation, University of Southern California, 1958. 301 pp.

6460. Griffin, Paul F., and Young, Robert N. *California, the New Empire State: A Regional Geography.* San Francisco, 1957. 325 pp.
Contains 26 pages in the Los Angeles Basin.

6461. Hall, Francis R. "Geology of the Southwestern Portion of the Las Flores Quadrangle, Los Angeles County, California." Master's thesis, University of California, Los Angeles, 1952. 44 pp.

6462. Handin, John W. "The Source, Transportation, and Deposition of Beach Sediment in Southern California." Doctoral dissertation, University of California, Los Angeles, 1949. 178 pp.

6463. Harris, Herbert. "Geology of the Palomas Canyon—Castaic Creek Area, Los Angeles County, California." Master's thesis, University of California, Los Angeles, 1950. 72 pp.

6464. Heald, Weldon F. "There'll Always Be a Baldy." *Westways* 48 (April 1956): 26-7.
Mt. Baldy.

6465. Heap, Eugene N. "Typologies of the Intersection in the Los Anglees Area." Master's thesis, University of Southern California, 1964. 141 pp.

6466. Hill, Robert T. *Southern California Geology and Los Angeles Earthquakes with an Introduction to the Physical Geography of the Region.* Los Angeles, 1928. 232 pp.

6467. Jaeger, Edmund C., and Smith, Arthur C. *Introduction to the Natural History of Southern California.* Berkeley, 1968. 104 pp.
Shows that despite proliferating urbanization much of the land still remains natural.

6468. Jones, Alfred. "Geodetic Control Surveys Around Los Angeles." *Civil Engineering* 14 (May 1944): 199-202.

6469. Kaye, John P. "Avalanches Scour the San Gabriels." *Westways* 33 (May 1941): 21.

6470. Kingsley, John. "The Gravity and General Geology of the San Gabriel Valley, Los Angeles County, California." Master's thesis, University of California, Los Angeles, 1963. 31 pp.

6471. Konigsberg, Richard L. "Geology Along the San Francisquito Fault, Los Angeles County, California." Master's thesis, University of California, 1967. 84 pp.

6472. Lantis, David W., and Reith, John W. "Los Angeles." *Focus* 12 (May 1962): 1-6.
Entire issue concentrates on Los Angeles, emphasizing human, physical, and economic geography.

6473. ———; Steiner, Rodney, and Karinen, Arthur. *California: Land of Contrast.* Belmont, 1963. 509 pp.
Basic geography text.

6474. Livingston, Alfred, and Putnam, William C. *Geological Journeys in Southern California.* Los Angeles, 1933. 104 pp.

6475. Loop, Taylor H. "Physical Oceanography and Sediment Characteristics within Little and Shark Harbors, Santa Catalina Island, California." Master's thesis, University of Southern California, 1969. 143 pp.

6476. Macdonald, Gordon A. "Sediments of Santa Monica Bay." Master's thesis, University of California, Los Angeles, 1934. 37 pp.

6477. MacIvor, Keith A. "Geology of the Thousand Oaks Area, Los Angeles and Ventura Counties, California." Master's thesis, University of California, Los Angeles, 1955. 46 pp.

6478. McCurdy, Robert. "Water Motion and Sediments of Northeast San Pedro Bay, California." Master's thesis, University of Southern California, 1964. 79 pp.

6479. Mead, Richard G. "The Geology of a Portion of Point Dume Quadrangle, California." Master's thesis, University of Southern California, 1952. 55 pp.

6480. Merenbach, Simon E. "Some Leading Structural Features of Eastern Santa Monica Mountains, Los Angeles, California." Master's thesis, University of Southern California, 1931 24 pp.

6481. Merriam, Patricia D. "Geology of the El Segundo Sand Hills." Master's thesis, University of Southern California, 1949. 42 pp.

6482. Moore, David G. "The Marine Geology of San Pedro Shelf." Master's thesis, University of Southern California, 1951. 87 pp.

6483. Newton, Robert C. "The Malibu Bowl Fault Area, Santa Monica Mountains, California." Master's thesis, University of California, Los Angeles, 1958. 77 pp.

6484. Page, Gordon B. "Beach Erosion and Composition of Sand Dunes, Playa del Rey—El Segundo Area, California." Master's thesis, University of California, Los Angeles, 1950. 50 pp.

6485. Paige, Lennon T. "A Geomorphic Interpretation of the Thousand Oaks Corridor, Los Angeles and Ventura Counties, California." Master's thesis, University of California, Los Angeles, 1969. 63 pp.
  Analyzes landforms and their relation to underlying geologic patterns.

6486. Roberts, Samuel M. "Water Injection System in Long Beach Harbor Has—Subsidence Halted." *Western City* 35 (June 1959): 26-7.

6487. Robertson, George K. "The Geology of the Santa Monica Mountains in the Vicinity of Topanga Canyon, Los Angeles County, California." Master's thesis, University of Southern California, 1932. 56 pp.

6488. Smith, Valene L. "Canoga Park: A Study of Water Problems as Related to Land Use." Master's thesis, University of California, Los Angeles, 1950. 75 pp.

6489. Sonderegger, A. L. "Physiography of the Los Angeles Area." *Civil Engineering* 5 (September 1935): 536-40.

6490. Taweel, Michael E., Jr. "The Geology of the Eagle Rock and Highland Park Area, Los Angeles County, California." Master's thesis, University of Southern California, 1963. 108 pp.

6491. "Terminal Island Sinking Remains Major Problem." *Western City* 32 (April 1956): 80.

6492. Thomas, C. S. "How Los Angeles Plain Became a Basin." *Southern California Business* 9 (February 1930): 22-3+.
  Los Angeles region was referred to as a "plain" until geologists studies revealed that it was in fact geosynclinal in structure. "Wherefore, the more euphoneous name 'basin' has been applied."

6493. Valencia, Shirley M. "The Origin, Distribution, and Engineering Characteristics of Surficial Material in the San Gabriel Valley, California." Master's thesis, University of Southern California, 1966. 162 pp.

6494. Vernon, Charles C. "A History of the San Gabriel Mountains." Master's thesis, Occidental College, 1952. 216 pp.

6495. Woodford, A. O. "Why 'San Gabriels'?" *Westways* 28 (February 1936): 11.
  Why the name "San Gabriel Mountains," rather than "Sierra Madre," is correct.

NATURAL HISTORY—
NATURAL DISASTERS

6496. Baker, George E. "Tilting of City Area Found in Long Beach Level Survey." *Western Construction News* 17 (February 1942): 64-5.

6497. "Civic Committee Studies Needs Attending Major Disasters." *Enigineering News-Record* 99 (October 27, 1927): 680-1.
  Los Angeles.

6498. Davis, W. M. "Long Beach Earthquake." *Geography Reviews* 24 (January 1934): 1-11.

6499. Doehring, Donald O. "Fire-Flood Sequences in the San Gabriel Mountains of Southern California." Master's thesis, Claremont Graduate School, 1965. 75 pp.

6500. "Earthquake Valves in Los Angeles Indicate Area Affected by Shock." *Western Construction News* 16 (December 1941): 373.

6501. Eddstein, Irvin. "Mountains in Motion: When the Rains Come, Anything Can Happen — And Often Does." *Frontier* 12 (November 1960): 14-5.

6502. "Fright in Los Angeles: 'Creeping Cliff' Antics Worry 'Public Relations' Board." *Newsweek* 10 (December 1937): 17-9.
Elysian Park land slippage.

6503. Hadley, Homer M. "The Long Beach Earthquake—And Afterwards." *Western Construction News and Highways Builder* 8 (September 1933): 395-7.

6504. Iacopi, Robert. *Earthquake Country*. Menlo Park, 1964. 191 pp. Paperback ed., 1969. 160 pp.
Deals with such faults as San Andreas, Newport, and Inglewood.

6505. "Ill Wind." *Los Angeles* 2 (December 1961): 26-8.
Bel-Air fire.

6506. Lusk, Earl F. "An Analysis of the Effect of the Landsliding Problem on the Value of the Single Family Residential Properties in Pacific Palisades." Master's thesis, University of Southern California, 1963. 82 pp.

6507. McGlashan, H. D., and Ebert, F. C. *Southern California Floods of January 1916*. Washington, D.C., 1918. 80 pp.

6508. "National Rainfall Record Set in California Flood." *Western Construction News* 18 (March 1943): 128.
Los Angeles, January 22-23, 1943.

6509. Parsons, Robert H. "A Study of 1961-1962 Winter Rain Damage on Certain Firegrounds in the Major Watersheds of Los Angeles County." Master's thesis, University of Southern California, 1963. 79 pp.

6510. "The Press Goes to a Fire." *Saturday Night* 45 (December 17, 1938): 4-7.
Santa Monica Mountains.

6511. "Rebuilding under Way in Earthquake Area." *Western City* 9 (April 1933): 7-10.
Damage in 29 cities, particularly Long Beach and Compton areas.

6512. "Reviewing the Official Report on the Record Los Angeles Flood of March 2." *Western Construction News* 13 (September 1938): 328-30.

6513. Roth, Eldon S. "Landslides Between Santa Monica and Point Dume." Master's thesis, University of Southern California. 1959. 184 pp.

6514. Smith, Wade S. "Absorbing Disaster Costs." *National Municipal Review* 27 (April 1938): 230-2.
1938 Los Angeles floods.

6515. Wailes, C. D., Jr., and Horner, A. C. "Survey of Long Beach Earthquake Damage." *Western City* 9 (June 1933): 7-10.

6516. Wake, William H. "Chaparral and Man." *Journal of the West* 4 (1965): 449-57.
Author explains the ecological function of chaparral and discusses brush fires, citing as cases in point the 1964 Whiting Woods and Chevy Chase fires in the hills above Burbank and Glendale.

6517. Weide, David L. "The Geography of Fire in the Santa Monica Mountains." Master's thesis, California State College at Los Angeles, 1968. 183 pp.

6518. *When Destruction Walked Abroad.* [Oakland, 1933?]. [24] pp.
Photographs of damage caused by the Southern California earthquake of March 10, 1933, with descriptive text.

6519. "When Disaster Strikes." *Trails Magazine* 5 (Summer 1938): 16-8.
Flood of March 1938, and damage it caused in San Gabriel Mountains.

NATURAL HISTORY—WILDLIFE

6520. Booth, Ernest S. *Mammals of Southern California*. Berkeley and Los Angeles, 1968. *California History Guides No. 21*. 99 pp.

6521. Bullock, Frederick W. "A Study of Physiological Conditions Relating to the Distribution of Marine Phytoplankton at Los Angeles Harbor Using an Especially Designed Plankton and Water Sampling Apparatus." Master's thesis, University of Southern California, 1933. 93 pp.

6522. Cruickshank, Helen G. "Big City Sanctuary." *Audubon Magazine* 54 (May-June 1952): 158-63.
San Gabriel River Wildlife Sanctuary, administerd by National Audubon Society.

6523. Gill, Don A. "Coyote and Urban Man; A Geographic Analysis of the Relationship Between the Coyote and Man in Los Angeles." Master's thesis, University of California, Los Angeles, 1965. 114 pp.

6524. Hamilton, Andrew. "The Man Who Talks to Birds." *Westways* 43 (November 1951): 18-9.
Prof. Loye Miller, biologist at UCLA.

6525. Hinton, Sam. *Seashore Life of Southern California. An Introduction to the Animal Life of California Beaches South of Santa Barbara.* Berkeley and Los Angeles, 1969. *California Natural History Guides No. 26.* 181 pp.

6526. Howell, Robert S. "Bringing Orky Home." *Westways* 60 (February 1968) 13-5.
Marineland's killer whale.

6527. McCarthy, John R. *These Waiting Hills, the Santa Monicas.* Los Angeles, 1925. 73 pp.
Birds, plants, and animals.

6528. Munro, Caroline S. G. "Lucky Baldwin's Birds." *Westways* 56 (August 1964): 22-3.
Pair of Indian peacoks imported by Lucky Baldwin just before the turn of the century gave rise to the flock now at the Arboretum.

6529. *Queer Farms.* By Sixth Grade Boys and Girls of Ascot Public School, Los Angeles. Burbank, 1938. 140 pp.
"Farms" in the Los Angeles area which raise various animals.

6530. Willett. George. *Birds of the Urban Districts of Los Angeles County.* Los Angeles County Museum, *Science Series No. 7.* Zoology Publication No. 3. [Los Angeles], 1951. 40 pp.

6531. ——— *Common Birds of the Los Angeles County Coast.* Los Angeles County Museum, Sci-

ence Series No. 5. Zoology Publication No. 1. [Los Angeles, 1942]. 39 pp.

6532. ——— *Common Birds of the Los Angeles County Mountains.* 2nd ed. Los Angeles County Museum, *Science Series No. 6.* Zoology Publication No. 2. [Los Angeles], 1953. 41 pp.

PARKS; RECREATION

6533. Albrecht, Jacob. "The Entrance to Pasadena's Big Playground." *American City* 15 (July 1916): 61.
Tournament Park.

6534. Aldrich, Lloyd. "Plan Shore Line Improvement: Proposed Los Angeles Shore Line Development Provides for Recreation and Parking Areas on the Seaward Side of Scenic Drive Along 13-mile Ocean Front Bordering Santa Monica Bay." *Western Construction News* 20 (January 1945): 73-6.

6535. Allan, Fitz John. "Human Architecture Revised at L.A.A.C." *California Graphic* 5 (April 14, 1928): 12.
Physical education classes at the Los Angeles Athletic Club.

6536. Aloia, Alexander D. "Public Recreation in Inglewood, California." Master's thesis, University of Southern California, 1946. 109 pp.

6537. Arnold, David R. "Long Beach Coordinated Recreation Plan a Great Success." *Pacific Municipalities* 33 (May 1930): 154-7.

6538. Asakura, Junichi. "An Analysis of Park Work in the Los Angeles Region." Master's thesis, University of Southern California, 1950. 116 pp.

6539. Austin, Lloyd B. "When Switzer Came: Early Days of the Arroyo Seco." *Trails Magazine* 3 (Winter 1936): 6-8.
San Gabriel Mountains.

6540. Bahr, Ferdinand A. "How Huntington Park Has Organized a Public Recreation Program." *Western City* 23 (May 1947): 17-9.

6541. Baus, Herbert M. "Big Pines Carnival: All of Los Angeles and Its Guests Are Invited to Southern California's Biggest Winter Sports Event." *Apartment Journal* 20 (January 1938): 10+.

6542. "Beach Park Growing with Fill from New Los Angeles Sewage Plant Site: Seward Extension of a 13-Mile Stretch of Los Angeles Shore Line for New Park Area Is Being Coordinated with Excavation for the Hyperion Sewage Plant." *Western Construction News* 23 (May 1948): 97-9.

6543. "Beverly Hills Fountain." *Los Angeles Saturday Night* 11 (July 4, 1931): 14.
"Electric Fountain," Santa Monica and Wilshire Blvds., set in a mini-park.

6544. Bevington, Lawrence C. "Sales Tax Revenues Financed Sierra Madre Swimming Pool." *Western City* 34 (August 1958): 43.

6545. "Big Pines Sector Offers Gay Winter Lure." *Los Angeles Saturday Night* 15 (December 22, 1934): 1.
County-operated recreation area.

6546. "The Boats Around Us." *Los Angeles* 4 (July 1962): 20-9.
Pleasure boating in the Los Angeles area.

6547. Booker, Frederick J. "An Appraisal of the Public Recreational Facilities in the Pasadena Area." Master's thesis, University of Southern California, 1950. 129 pp.

6548. Bowen, William M. *Vicious Attack on Men Who Saved Exposition Park. The Issue: Bowen's "Activities" Which Recovered and Improved Park or Neylan's Vicious Political Thrust.* [Los Angeles?, 1915]. 19 pp.

6549. Brodie, Fawn M. "Parks and Politics in Los Angeles." *Reporter* 32 (February 11, 1965): 39-42.
Proposed Santa Monica Mountains State Park as a political football.

6550. Brown, Thomas M. "An Analysis of Methods Used by Local Governments in Securing Public Open Spaces for Recreation in the Los Angeles Metropolitan Area." Master's thesis, University of Southern California, 1957. 110 pp.

6551. "Burbank's Playgrounds Built According to Redevelopment Plan." *Western City* 32 (September 1956): 58.

6552. Carter, Arthur N. "Early Days in the Chillia Country." *Trails Magazine* 5 (Spring 1938): 14-7.
San Gabriel Mountains.

6553. ——— "Mt. Wilson and Sturtevant Trails from Sierra Madre." *Trails Magazine* 4 (Winter 1937): 6-12.

6554. Case, Fred E. and Case, Lola. "Saving Something for the People." *Frontier* 15 (April 1964): 5-7.
Plan for Santa Monica Mountains Park.

6555. [Cass & Johansing Insurance Brokers]. *The History of Yachting in Southern California.* [Los Angeles, 1957?]. [44] pp.

6556. Cathcart, James A. "Environmental Determinants of Per Capita Park and Recreation Expenditure Variations for Forty-Nine Los Angeles County Cities." Master's thesis, Claremont Graduate School, 1968. 39 pp.

6557. Chace, Burton W. "Los Angeles County Beach Development." *California Magazine of the Pacific* 43 (September 1953): 13+.

6558. Chace, Burton W. "Los Angeles County's Marina Del Rey: A Small Craft and Recreational Harbor." *California Magazine of the Pacific* 44 (September 1954): 16+.

6559. Chaplin, Claude M. "Beach Cleaning with Tractors." *American City* 37 (August 1927): 249.
Long Beach.

6560. "City's Recreation Camps Alluring." *Los Angeles Saturday Night* 2 (July 30, 1921): 3.
Los Angeles' Camp Radford and Camp Seeley.

6561. Clarke, Clinton C. "The John Muir Trail: California—Southern Division." *Trails Magazine* 1 (Spring 1934): 12.

6562. "Clean Beach Is Major Hermosa Asset." *Western City* 15 (October 1939): 48.

6563. Community Surveys, Inc. *A Plan for Recreation and Group Service for Long Beach.* Long Beach, 1948. 146 pp.

6564. "Concrete Piling for Santa Monica Pleasure Pier." *The Architect and Engineer of California* 13 (July 1908): 69-71.

6565. Copeland, John Q. "Sierra Madre Rangers: Students of Rescue." *Westways* 60 (March 1968): 23-5.
Mountain rescue squad.

6566. Cornell, Ralph D., and Hjelte, George. "Planning a Modern City Park." *Western City* 22 (September 1946): 42-3.
South Gate Park.

6567. Cortelyou, S. V. "Angeles Crest Highway Opens Vast Recreational Territory." *California Highways and Public Works* 15 (Septembeb 1937): 8+.

6568. ——— "Angeles Crest Highway Will Open Vast Recreational Mountain Area in Fall." *California Highways and Public Works* 12 (July 1934): 2+.

6569. Cram, C. M. "An Unusual Sea Wall Achievement: Long Beach California, Builds a Municipal Recreation Project." *Civil Engineering* 1 (February 1931): 409-12.

6570. Crenshaw, C. R. L. "La Fayette Square — Los Angeles." *Out West,* new series, 6 (July-August 1913): 69.

6571. Davis, Merrill D. "Big Pines Camp: Los Angeles County's All-Year Playground." *Los Angeles Realtor* 7 (February 1927): 16-7+.

6572. ——— "Los Angeles County Capitalizes the Snow and Ice of the Mountain Area." *California Journal of Development* 20 (November 1930): 14.

6573. Davis, Pete. "Recreational Training Opportunities in Los Angeles." Master's thesis, University of Southern California, 1940. 131 pp.

6574. "A Day Around Mt. Lowe." *Trails Magazine* 2 (Winter 1935): 4.
San Gabriel Mountains.

6575. "Decentralized Recreation Department Tried in Los Angeles County." *American City* 73 (February 1958): 173.
County Department of Parks and Recreation establishes six divisional offices.

6576. Edgerly, Florence G. "Burbank Makes Full Use of Its Parks." *Recreation* 38 (June 1944): 122+.

6577. "Engineers Make Ocean Build Mile of Bathing Beach Along Coast Highway." *California Highways and Public Works* 12 (May 1934): 12-3
Santa Monica.

6578. "Engineer's Report on Santa Monica Pier Failure." *The Architect and Engineer* 59 (December 1919): 97-102.

6579. Erdhaus, Fred. "Installation and Maintenance of Tennis Courts." *Western City* 38 (July 1962): 30.
Standards established by Los Angeles Department of Recreation and Parks.

6580. Erickson, Clarence E. *Southern California Coast: Boating, Fishing, Beaches.* [Menlo Park, 1953]. 32 pp.

6581. Erskine, Robert A. "A Survey of the Organization and Administration of Public Recreation by the Los Angeles County Government." Master's thesis, University of Southern California, 1941. 91 pp.

6582. "Exposition Park His Lifelong Hobby." *Los Angeles Saturday Night* 16 (January 4, 1936): 12.
William M. Bowen.

6583. "Failure of Santa Monica Municipal Pier." *The Archietect and Engineer* 59 (October 1919): 86-7.

6584. "The Finest Bath House on the Pacific Coast." *Out West* 17 (July 1902): 138.
Long Beach.

6585. Fisher, Philip H. "The Redevelopment of the Long Beach Shore-Line." Master's thesis, University of California, Los Angeles, 1958. 40 pp.

6586. Fiss, Walter. "Take Your Nerves to the Mountains." *Southern California Business* 7 (April 1928): 20-1+.
Big Pines Recreation Camp.

6587. Foxworthy, Rena E. "Recreation Goes Hollywood—in Hollywood." *Recreation* 35 (May 1941): 87-8.
Poinsettia Recreation Center.

6588. Frank, Melvin D. "Accidents in the Los Angeles City Playgrounds, 1947-48." Master's thesis, Stanford University, 1949. 104 pp.

6589. Frederickson, William, Jr. "Blueprint for Organization: Results of an Industrial Engineering Study of Operations in the Los Angeles Department of Recreation and Parks Have Wide Application for the Entire Field." *Recreation* 57 (October 1964): 410-4.

6590. Friedman, Samuel L. "Call of the Mountains." *Apartment Journal* 20 (July 1937): 19+.
This, and the ensuing four articles by the same author, discusses mountain camps operated by the Los Angeles City Playground and Recreation Department.

6591. —— "City Camps." *Los Angeles Saturday Night* 43 (May 30, 1936): 9.

6592. —— "High Altitude for Pale Pocketbooks." *Southern California Business* 9 (July 1930): 50.

6593. —— "Los Angeles Opens Her Summer Camps." *Southern California Business* 8 (June 1929): 26-7+.

6594. —— "Oh, for the Mountains When It's Winter." *Los Angeles Saturday Night* 44 (January 9, 1937): 3.

6595. —— "Playing for a Stronger America." *Recreation* 35 (April 1941): 21-3+.
Special physical training clubs for draft registrants established by the Los Angeles Playground and Recreation Department.

6596. —— "Winter Sports in Southern California." *California Journal of Development* 21 (December 1931): 11+.

6597. Gautier, George. "Shark Fishing from Lagoon Beaches." *Out West,* new series, 5 (March-April 1913): 185-7.
Alamitos Bay.

6598. "Gay Christmas at Santa Anita Races." *Los Angeles Saturday Night* 15 (December 22, 1934): 5.
Sanita Anita opening.

6599. George, Duane. "Long Beach, Calif. Develops . . . An Adventure Play Project." *American City* 73 (September 1958): 109.
Playground at El Dorado Park.

6600. Gilkerson, Jess D. "Long Beach Builds for Its Boatmen: Current Program Will Quadruple the Size of the City's Alamitos Bay Marina." *American City* 74 (May 1959): 189-90+.

6601. "Glendale Builds New Half Million Dollar Recreation Center." *Western City* 12 (May 1936): 17.

6602. "Glendale's Public Parks." *Pacific Municipalities* 44 (February 1930): 46.

6603. Grant, Glen O. "Los Angeles Trains for Enlarged Leisure." *Recreation* 27 (October 1933): 316-9+.
Los Angeles Department of Playground and Recreation.

6604. Grant, Harold. "A Proposed Community Recreational Program for the City of Redondo Beach." Master's thesis, University of Southern California, 1940. 119 pp.

6605. Greater Los Angeles Citizens Committee. *Shoreline Development Study, Playa del Rey to Palos Verdes, a Portion of a Proposed Master Recreation Plan for the Greater Los Angeles Region.* [Los Angeles], 1944. 39 pp.

6606. Griffith, Griffith J. *Parks, Boulevards and Playgrounds.* Los Angeles, [c1910]. 80 pp.
Griffith Park.

6607. Guinn, James M. "The True History of Central Park." *Annual Publication* Historical Society of Southern California 8 (1911): 211-6.

6608. Hall, Bryant. "Beverly Hills Acquires Unique Park and Solves Boulevard Frontage Problem." *Western City* 7 (September 1931): 9-12.

6609. Hall, L. Glenn. "Landscape Design for Playgrounds: An Outline for a Sound Program with Examples from Los Angeles." *American City* 42 (June 1930): 90-2.

6610. Hall, Lorin. "Ocean Fishing from a Pier." *Forest and Stream* 99 (January 1929): 37+.
Manhattan Beach.

6611. Hammack, Dan S. "A Tale of Old Pine Flat (Now Charlton Flat)." *Trails Magazine* 5 (Spring 1938): 5-7.
Area named for an early supervisor of Angeles Forest.

6612. "The 'Hard Luck' Marina Comes of Age." *Los Angeles* 8 (August 1964): 42-5.
Marina del Rey.

6613. Harnett, F. "Spit and Argue Club." *Recreation* 39 (December 1945): 460.
The author tells the story of an old Long Beach tradition going back to the first city pier and area set aside where men could argue and declaim.

6614. Hassler, Dorothy K. "Freeway for Horseless Vehicles." *Westways* 43 (June 1951): 4-5.
Cycleway connecting Los Angeles and Pasadena, opened January 1, 1900.

6615. ——— "Mountain Squad to the Rescue." *Westways* 46 (November 1954): 28-9.
Altadena Mountain Rescue Squad.

6616. Hayes, Mary Agnes, Sister. "A History of Griffith Park in Los Angeles [1796-1935]." Master's thesis, University of California, Berkeley, 1951. 97 pp.

6617. Haynes, Clarence E. "Interagency Cooperation in Los Angeles County. Relationships Between School Districts and City Recreation Departments." Master's thesis, Claremont Graduate School, 1970. 49 pp.

6618. Heinly, Burt A. "The Remodeling of a City Square in Los Angeles, Cal." *American City* 6 (May 1912): 728-30.
Central (later Pershing) Square.

6619. Henderson, John C. "Public Recreation and Unemployment." *Western City* 9 (April 1933): 13-4.

6620. Hjelte, George. "Bureau of Home Play Established." *American City* 38 (January 1928): 163.
Los Angeles.

6621. ——— "Facilities for Recreation," in *Los Angeles: Preface to a Master Plan.* Ed. by George W. Robbins and L. Deming Tilton. Los Angeles, 1941. Pp. 213-25.

6622. ——— "Magnitude of Projects Show That Recreation Is 'Big Business' Today in and out of Government." *Western City* 30 (July 1954): 33+.

6623. ——— "Public Recreation in Los Angeles." *Public Management* 9 (September 1927): 690-3.

6624. ——— "Public Work in Los Angeles, California." *Playground* 22 (April 1928): 23.
Report on comprehensive study for regional plan of parks, playgrounds, and beaches.

6625. Holden, Harry M. "Los Angeles Teens in Action: Bridging the Communications Gap Between Teenagers and Adults Through Recreation." *Parks and Recreation* 3 (August 1968): 41+.
Teen Executive Advisor Board to the Los Angeles Department of Recreation and Parks.

6626. Holden, William. " 'Commissioner Holden Reports. . .' " *Western City* 31 (February 1955): 35.
On accepting appointment to Los Angeles City Recreation and Park Commissioners.

6627. Holder, Charles F. "Rod, Reel and Gaff in Southern California." *Sunset* 6 (January 1901): 73-83.
Fishing at Santa Catalina Island.

6628. Hollowell, Buddy R. "A Study of the Organization and Administration of Senior Citizen Clubs and Centers in the Los Angeles Area." Master's thesis, University of Southern California, 1970. 91 pp.

6629. "How Local Historic Tradition Enriches the Recreation Life of One City." *American City* 41 (April 1930): 138.
Memory Garden in Brand Park, across from San Fernando Mission.

6630. Howard, Hazel E. "Switzer's Camp—Hikers' Paradise Lost." *Westways* 49 (May 1957): 18-9.
Sierra Madre (San Gabriel) Mountains.

6631. Hoyt, Raymond E. "Items in a Million-Dollar Recreation Program." *American City* 46 (March 1932): 110.
Facilities completed under terms of unemployment relief bond issue.

6632. ——— "Los Angeles' $335,000 Beach Playground." *American City* 48 (March 1933): 64.
Cabrillo Beach.

6633. ——— "$1,000,000 for Los Angeles Playgrounds." *Western City* 7 (May 1931): 38-9.

6634. Hunt, Charles H. "How the Famed Co-Ordinated Recreation Program at Long Beach Functions." *Western City* 7 (May 1931): 34-6.

6635. Irwin, John K. "Surfers: A Study of the Growth of a Deviant Subculture." Master's thesis. University of California, Berkeley, 1965. 116 pp.

6636. Janss, Harold. "Give Them More Parks to Romp In." *Southern California Business* 7 (September 1928): 14-5+.
Plea for more Los Angeles recreation sites.

6637. Johnson, A. G. "The Beaches Are Born Again." *Western City* 22 (May 1946): 24-31.

6638. —— "The Vanishing Beaches of Southern California." *Western City* 16 (May 1940): 22-5.

6639. Johnson, Worth. "Beach Maintenance in Long Beach." *Western City* 40 (July 1964): 32+.

6640. —— "We Use a Hay-Rake . . . To Keep Beach Sand Clean and Debris-Free on Five Miles of Ocean Frontage at Long Beach, California." *American City* 75 (March 1960): 188+.

6641. Jones, Robert B. "Administration of Public Recreation in the City of Los Angeles." Master's thesis, University of Southern California, 1933. 190 pp.

6642. Jones, Vincent. "On the Trails of Griffith Park." *Los Angeles Saturday Night* 8 (March 10, 1928): 4-5.
The joys of hiking.

6643. Kelly, K. E. "Operation 'Parkette': El Segundo, Calif., Transforms Drainage Sumps into Playground." *American City* 72 (October 1957): 179+.
Reprinted in *Western City* 34 (April 1958): 22.

6644. Kern, Jack C. "A Few Leaves from the Camp Ground History Book." *Trails Magazine* 4 (Spring 1936): 11-3.
San Gabriel Mountains.

6645. —— "Public Camp Development in the Los Angeles National Forest." *Trails Magazine* 2 (Summer 1937): 6-15.

6646. King, Fred. "New El Monte City Pool Facility Built by Bond and Sales Tax Funds." *Western City* 30 (October 1954): 85.

6647. Kohn, Walter. "Treasure Hunters of Moonstone Beach." *Westways* 42 (May 1950): 6-7.
Redondo Beach.

6648. Krec, Ted. "The Longest Pier in the World." *Westways* 51 (March 1959): 32-3.
Pier A started as a breakwater. Fill and Long Beach have converted it over the years into a peninsula.

6649. Kyne, Peter B. "Sunshine & Seabreezes, Inc. Purveyors of Cool Summers." *Sunset* 27 (July 1911): 3-18.
Los Angeles beaches.

6650. "Lakes and Rushing Streams in Snow-Clad High Sierras Lure Summer Vacationist: Source of [Los Angeles] City's Water and Power a Scenic Wonderland." *Los Angeles Saturday Night* 43 (May 23, 1936): 16.

6651. Larson, George P. "The Beaches Must Belong to the People: California's Statewide Program." *Shore and Beach* 14 (October 1946): 67-71.

6652. —— "Real Progress Continues in California." *Shore and Beach* 10 (October 1942): 44-59.

6653. Leadabrand, Russ. "Lane of Black and Yellow Gold." *Westways* 51 (May 1959): 5-7.
Placerita Canyon State Park.

6654. —— "Where They Took Their Pleasure." *Westways* 57 June 1965): 9-12.
A short history of recreation in Los Angeles.

6655. Lee, Mabel S. "The Recreational Interests and Participation of a Selected Group of Chinese Boys and Girls in Los Angeles, California." Master's thesis, University of Southern California, 1939. 90 pp.

6656. Los Angeles Citizens' Committee on Parks, Beach, and Recreational Facilities. *Parks, Beaches, and Recreational Facilities for Los Angeles County.* [Los Angeles], 1945. 18 pp.

6657. —— *Parks, Playgrounds, and Beaches for the Los Angeles Region.* Los Angeles, 1930. 178 pp.

6658. Los Angeles City School District. *Recreation, A Community Enterprise.* Los Angeles, 1940. 64 pp.

6659. Los Angeles County. Department of Parks and Recreation. *Plummer Park, Its History and Objectives.* [Los Angeles], 1950. 9 pp.

6660. Los Angeles Department of Recreation and Parks. *Progress Report, 1946-1950.* Los Angeles, 1950. 34 pp.

6661. "Los Angeles Fights Against Encroachment." *American City* 70 (February 1955): 17.
Opposition of Recreation and Parks Commission to the routing of freeways through Griffith Park.

6662. "Los Angeles' New Sports Center." *American City* 54 (September 1939): 105.
Rancho Cienega Playground.

6663. "Los Angeles Opens an Arts and Crafts Center." *Recreation* 36 (May 1942): 115.
Barnsdall Park.

6664. "Los Angeles Pilot Study of Playgrounds." *Recreation* 51 (April 1958): 129.
Report on a study of two local playgrounds, under sponsorship of the Youth Services Division of the Welfare Planning Council.

6665. Marienthal, Michael J. "Recommendations for a Program Based on the Recreational Needs and Resources of Leg Amputees in the City of Los Angeles." Master's thesis, University of California, Los Angeles, 1951. 147 pp.

6666. "Marina Del Rey: The Boom Is Finally On." *Los Angeles* 14 (May 1969): 67+.

6667. Mark, David. "Summer Snow at Mount Baldy." *Westways* 49 (July 1957): 16-7.
Man-made "snow," brought in by the sackful, permits summer skiing at Baldy Notch.

6668. McCary, H. D. "How Public Recreation in Beverly Hills Helps Pay Its Own Way." *Western City* 13 (March 1937): 31-2.

6669. McCune, Ellis. *Recreation and Parks.* Los Angeles, 1954. *Metropolitan Los Angeles, A Study in Integration,* Vol. IX, The Haynes Foundation, *Monograph Series No. 26.* 78 pp.

6670. McCurdy, Robert M. "Pasadena's Coordinated Plan for Administering Public Recreation." *Western City* 24 (September 1963): 48.

6671. Mendenhall, William V. "Mountain Recreation." *Trails Magazine* 5 (Spring 1938): 18-9.

6672. ———— "Recreation Policy of Angeles National Forest." *Trails Magazine* 1 (Spring 1934): 11.

6673. Meserve, Harold. "I Floats: Los Angeles County Finds an Inexpensive Solution to an An-noying Beach Maintenance Problem." *American City* 74 (October 1959): 113.
Polystyrene foam floats.

6674. Millar, J. D. "What About Our Parks?" *Los Angeles Realtor* 3 (August 1925): 17+.
Los Angeles.

6675. Miller, Geoff. "The Beach." *Los Angeles* 2 (June 1961): 13-7.

6676. "Model Parks and Recreation Area Dedicated by Subdivider." *American City* 48 (April 1933): 45.
Terrace Park, Los Angeles.

6677. "Modern Swimming Pool Adjoins Los Angeles Police Pistol Range." *Western City* 12 (March 1936): 39.

6678. Mohrbacker, Peter. "Maintaining 400 Acres of Park Lawn." *Western City* 7 (February 1931): 27-8.
Long Beach.

6679. Morris, Bob. "Rx for Sea Fever." *Westways* 57 (May 1965): 4-7.
Facilities and activities at Marina Del Rey.

6680. Mosauer, Walter. "Ski Touring Around Los Angeles." *Trails Magazine* 2 (Winter 1935): 6-7.

6681. Mott, B. D. "Young Citizens Improve Recreation Areas." *Recreation* 50 (June 1957): 221.
Volunteer program sponsored by the Los Angeles Recreation and Parks Department.

6682. Mott, L. C. "When the Navy Plays: How San Pedro Has Provided Athletic Facilities for 36,000 Young Men—And the Games They Play." *Southern California Business* 13 (November 1934): 16-7.

6683. "New Million Dollar Public Recreation Plant Nears Completion." *Western City* 14 (April 1938): 31-4.
Santa Anita Recreation Center.

6684. "New Pool for San Fernando." *Western City* 24 (April 1948): 46.

6685. Newmark, Marco R. "Early California Resorts." *Historical Society of Southern California Quarterly* 35 (1953): 129-52.
Includes descriptions of Santa Catalina, Syca-

more Grove, Big Bear, Arrowhead, Balboa, Washington Gardens, Sierra Madre Villa, Redondo, Raymond and Green Hotels, Mt. Lowe, Terminal Island, and Venice-Ocean Park.

6686. Nicholls, C. P. L. "Los Angeles Swims in Drinking Water." *American City* 44 (February 1931): 152.
Municipal pools.

6687. ——— "Safeguarding the Lives of Los Angeles Swimmers." *American City* 44 (June 1931): 94-6.
City lifeguard service.

6688. Noel, P. D. "Bathing Beaches and the Sewage." *Municipal League of Los Angeles Bulletin* 6 (October 1, 1928): [6-7].

6689. Norviel, John W. "A Survey of Recreation in Glendale, California." Master's thesis, University of Southern California, 1934. 172 pp.

6690. "Ocean Beaches of California." *California Magazine of the Pacific* 41 (June 1951): 28-32.
Includes Los Angeles County.

6691. Osterman, John. "A Model Recreation Department and Program for Cities of 10,000 to 20,000 Population in Southern California." Master's thesis, Occidental College, 1948. 122 pp.

6692. Overholt, Alma. "Catalina as a Winter Resort." *Los Angeles Saturday Night* 10 (November 16, 1929): 7.

6693. Pageot, Jean C. "A Study of Characteristics and Recreational Interests of the Aged Population in Culver City." Master's thesis, University of Southern California, 1970. 93 pp.

6694. Paige, Clayton W. "Burbank Moves a Mountain to Make a Golf Course." *Western City* 33 (September 1957): 46-7.

6695. Palmer, Leroy A. "Dragline Excavator Handles Earth on Los Angeles Stadium." *Engineering News-Record* 89 (August 3, 1922): 196-7.
Building of the Colesium.

6696. "Palos Verdes Estates' Fountain of Neptune." *Los Angeles Saturday Night* 10 (February 15, 1930): 7.

6697. "Parks of Los Angeles." *Parks and Recreation* 21 (August 1938): 606-13.

6698. Peebles, John. "The Construction and Application of a Recreation Director's Rating Scale for Day Camping as Conducted by the City of Los Angeles Department of Recreation and Parks." Master's thesis, University of Southern California, 1956. 72 pp.

6699. Perkins, C. E. "Cooperative Arrangement Provides Glendale Area with Refuse Disposal Site and Park." *Western City* 36 (December 1960): 22-3.

6700. "Pickering Pleasure Pier, Santa Monica." *Pacific Municipalities* 35 (May 1921): 190.

6701. "Playgrounds and Parks in Los Angeles." *Saturday Night* 5 (May 10, 1924): 38.

6702. Plumer, Melvin C. "A Survey of Public Recreation in Santa Monica." Master's thesis, University of Southern California, 1942. 127 pp.

6703. Politi, Leo. *Tales of the Los Angeles Parks.* Palm Desert, [1966]. Unp.
Pictoral.

6704. Pomeroy, Hugh R. "That We May Continue as the World's Playground." *Southern California Business* 7 (May 1928): 18-9+.
Los Angeles and vicinity.

6705. Porter, John C. "Los Angeles—The Host of the International Recreation Congress." *Recreation* 25 (November 1931): 440-4+
Description of recreation facilities in the Los Angeles Area.

6706. "Prepare the Way for More Parks." *Southern California Business* 6 (February 1927): 30.
Describes need for additional parks and playgrounds in Los Angeles.

6707. Probert, William J. "San Gabriel Experiments with Operation of Vending Machines in Recreation Areas." *Western City* 38 (July 1962): 36-7.

6708. "Program for the County of Los Angeles." *Recreation* 40 (August 1946): 279-80.
Formation (1944) and activities of the County Department of Parks and Recreation.

6709. "The Race Problem at Swimming Pools: A Group of Reports from Representative Cities." *American City* 47 (August 1932): 76-7.
   Includes report on desegragation of Los Angeles pools, by Raymond E. Hoyt.

6710. Raitt, C. B. "Municipal Recreation Camps." *Pacific Municipalities* 39 (April 1925): 103-6+.
   Los Angeles Playground Department.

6711. —— "Municipal Vacation Camps That Work the Year Round." *American City* 26 (June 1922): 567.
   Los Angeles Playground Department.

6712. —— "Now That the Saloon Has Gone." *American City* 24 (January 1921): 34-5.
   Experimental recreation building, equipped and run by Los Angeles Playground Commission.

6713. Rall, Pearl. "Big Pines Celebrates Annual Winter Sports Carnival." *Los Angeles Saturday Night* 15 (January 12, 1935): 14.

6714. —— "Recreation Camp and Playgrounds." *Los Angeles Saturday Night* 15 (May 25, 1935): 4.
   County recreation areas at Big Pines and Crystal Lake.

6715. Rankin, E. P. "The Mountains' Invitation 'Come Up Higher': Reverend E. P. Rankin's Own Story of His First Attempt to Climb Monrovia Peak, January 22, 1920." *Trails Magazine* 4 (Winter 1937): 17+.

6716. "Recreation Center, Swimming Pool Part of Burbank's 10-Year Improvement Plan." *Western City* 22 (December 1957): 43.

6717. "Recreation Facility Gifted to Santa Monica." *Western City* 31 (January 1955): 56.
   Recreation center in Palisades Park.

6718. Reid, James K. "Bridle Paths for Recreation and Beautification." *Trails Magazine* 4 (Summer 1937): 17+.

6719. —— "Why Do We Have Winter Sports?" *Trails Magazine* 2 (Autumn 1935): 8-9.

6720. Righter, Ruth V. "A Survey of Adult Recreational Facilities in the City of Los Angeles." Master's thesis, University of Southern California, 1934. 184 pp.

6721. Roach, Leonard J. "Recreation in Los Angeles County." *California Magazine of the Pacific* 42 (March 1952): 34.

6722. Robinson, Dwayne M. "An Appraisal of the Public Recreational Facilities and Services of Norwalk Park District." Master's thesis, University of Southern California, 1955. 132 pp.

6723. Robinson, William W. *The Forest and the People; The Story of the Angeles National Forest.* Los Angeles, 1946. 44 pp.

6724. —— *The Story of Pershing Square.* Los Angeles, 1931. 37 pp.

6725. Robles, Arnold J. "Monthly Water-User Assessments Built Lynwood's Recreational Facilities." *Western City* 30 (July 1954): 36-7.

6726. Rochford, Lloyd A. "Khaki and Blue Caravan." *Recreation* 39 (April 1945): 34+.
   Group of volunteer entertainers enrolled by the Recreation Division of the Citizens' Service Corps of Long Beach.

6727. —— "Spreading the News." *Recreation* 39 (April 1945): 24+.
   Publicizing recreation programs in Long Beach.

6728. Rogers, Rockwell L. "The Relationship Between the Physical Activities of Citizens of Pasadena, California, and Their Contributions to Community Welfare." Master's thesis, University of Southern California, 1936. 108 pp.

6729. Rotsch, V. E. "Population Survey Set the Pattern for Montebello Recreation Program." *Western City* 32 (July 1956): 36.

6730. "Santa Monica Beach." *Pacific Municipalities* 35 (June 1921): 234.

6731. Saunders, Charles F. "A City Wild-Flower Park." *Sunset* 38 (May 1917): 34.
   Five acre corner of Exposition Park set aside as public botanical garden for native California wild-flowers, shrubs, and trees.

6732. —— *The Story of Carmelita.* Pasadena, 1928. 54 pp.
   Pasadena park.

6733. Scannell, Patrick. "A Survey of Playground

Activities and Recreational Interests of School Children in Los Angeles City." Master's thesis, University of Southern California, 1935. 123 pp.

6734. Schneider, Walter S. "The Story of Henniger Flat and the Half-Way House." *Trails Magazine* 4 (Winter 1937): 13-6.
San Gabriel Mountains.

6735. Scott, Walter L. "The Long Beach Coordinated Plan of Municipal and School Recreation." *Western City* 12 (March 1936): 14-7.

6736. Sears, W. L. "History of the Angeles National Forest." *Trails Magazine* 3 (Spring 1936): 7-9; (Summer 1936): 18-9.

6737. Shaw, James. "Montebello Police Convert Dump-Site into Recreational Area for City." *Western City* 31 (March 1955): 43.

6738. Sides, Robert. "Surf Slaloms." *Saturday Night* 45 (February 12, 1938): 7-9+.
Surfboarding, particularly along Palos Verdes.

6739. "Small-Craft Harbor Built with Public-Private Funds." *Western Construction* 37 (January 1962): 76.
Marina del Rey.

6740. Smith, Bertha H. "Sandyland! They Who Go Down to the Sea in Summer. A Social Study Along Western Wave-Lines." *Sunset* 33 (August 1914): 291-305.

6741. Smith, Jack. "A Day in the City: Captains Contagious." *Westways* 61 (October 1969): 11-3+.
Marina del Rey and yatching.

6742. ——— "A Day in the City: Where There's a Will." *Westways* 61 (December 1969): 23-5+.
Will Rogers State Historic Park.

6743. "Southern California Leads in Forest Visitors." *Southern California Business* 4 (April 1925): 12.
Angeles National Forest.

6744. Stapleton, Charles R. "Recreation and Its Problems on the Santa Monica-Venice Shoreline, Southern California." Master's thesis, University of California, Los Angeles, 1952. 143 pp.

6745. Steiner, Rodney. "Recreation and Watershed Problems in the Southwestern San Gabriel Mountains, California." Master's thesis, University of California, Los Angeles, 1951. 88 pp.

6746. "Still More Playground within the Nation's Playground." *Southern California Business* 5 (December 1926): 20+.
Los Angeles.

6747. Stinson, Dorothy B. "A Survey Showing the Effects of the Depression on Adult Recreation in the City of Los Angeles." Master's thesis, University of Southern California, 1935. 106 pp.

6748. Stites, Howard I. "Burbank Makes a Parkland from Trash Dumps." *American City* 66 (July 1951): 13.

6749. Stocks, James L. "Survey of Public Recreation in San Marino." Master's thesis, University of Southern California, 1948. 73 pp.

6750. Stoddart, Bessie D. "The Public Playgrounds of Los Angeles." *Pacific Municipalities* 26 (April 30, 1912): 175-81.

6751. ——— "Recreative Centers of Los Angeles, California." *Annals of the American Academy of Political and Social Science* 35 (March 1910): 426-35.

6752. Stone, Ormond A. "Montebello Municipal Natatorium." *Western Construction News* 2 (October 10, 1927) 51-2.
$100,000 outdoor swimming pool.

6753. Stone, Wilson M. "The Recreational Needs of Grammar School Boys in the West Los Angeles Area." Master's thesis, University of California, Los Angeles, 1947. 46 pp.

6754. "Street-Cleaning a Beach: Hermosa Beach, Calif., Increases Interest of Bathers by Removing Debris Every Morning by Machine." *American City* 55 (July 1940): 45.

6755. "Surfing: Sports Happy Southern Californians Are Off and Surfing at Malibu — Our Answer to Waikiki." *Southern California Prompter* 1 (July 1960): 48-50.

6756. Taylor, D. W. "Southern California: Winter Sports Center." *Southern California Business* 8 (December 1929): 18+.
Mostly Los Angeles County.

6757. Thantschold, Reginald "Automatic Irrigation of Big City Park." *American City* 56 (February 1941): 65.
Grfifith Park.

6758. Thrall, Will H. "John Muir Trail Through Los Angeles County." *Trails Magazine* 1 (Summer 1934): 6-8; (Autumn 1934): 6-8.

6759. "Three Coast Cities May Offer Their Beaches to State." *Western City* 20 (March 1944): 40.
Redondo, Hermosa, and Manhattan Beaches.

6760. "Thrills and Charms of Mt. Lowe." *Los Angeles Saturday Night* 11 (May 9, 1931): 6.
Mt. Lowe said to be attracting 100,000 visitors yearly at this time.

6761. Tomche, C. L. "Relax on Two Gallons of Gas." *Recreation* 39 (May 1945): 66-9.
Recreation programs in Burbank.

6762. "Toy Loan Centers." *Recreation* 32 (October 1938): 388-91.
Los Angeles County Toy Loan program.

6763. Treadwell, W. A., Jr. "The Ski Hills of Big Pines." *Trail Magazine* 2 (Autumn 1935): 13+.

6764. Turner, Spencer D. "A Hazardous Year in the [Angeles] Forest." *Trails Magazine* 1 (Summer 1934): 9.

6765. "Unusual Design Features Mark New South Pasadena Pool." *Western City* 15 (October 1939): 38-9.

6766. Updegraff, Winston R. "Municipal Golf in 65 Western Cities." *Western City* 36 (December 1960): 26-32+; 37 (February 1961): 26-30; (March 1961): 26-31.

6767. Van Aken, Mrs. Lillian A. "History of Exposition Park." *Annual Publication* Historical Society of Southern California 9 (1914): 244-52.

6768. Van Bellehem, Harry B. "A Community's Effort to Improve Recreation Programs Through Citizen — City Cooperation." *Western City* 39 (June 1963): 40-1.
"Operation Bootstrap," Torrance.

6769. ——— "Recreation Activities Advertised by Use of Torrance Equipment." *Western City* 32 (July 1956): 38.

6770. Van Degrift, Ethel S. "Los Angeles at Home on Skis." *Trails Magazine* 2 (Winter 1941): 24-7.

6771. Vickers, Samuel E. "In Parks — Our Emphasis Is on Facilities: Long Beach, Calif., Has Embarked on a $4.9-Million Program to Provide City-Wide Recreation Facilities." *American City* 72 (May 1957): 215+.

6772. Weinstein, Robert A. "In the Good Old Summertime, 1900." *Museum Alliance Quarterly* 4 (Spring 1966): 4-9.

6773. Wells, A. J. "California Summer Resorts." *Out West* 19 (July 1903): 115-27.
Includes Catalina Island, Long Beach, and Santa Monica.

6774. "When Snow Comes to Southern California." *Trails Magazine* 2 (Autumn 1935): 15-6.

6775. "Where Campers Hug the Snow Line: Plans Are under Way to Provide Los Angeles Business Men with an Ideal Recreation Field Where Game and Fish Abound." *Southern California Business* 2 (March 1923): 16-7+.
Proposed Municipal Playground at Reds Meadows, in the Sierras, 340 miles from Los Angeles.

6776. Whitnall, Gordon. "L.A. Should Acquire Beach Frontage." *Municipal League of Los Angeles Bulletin* 3 (August 1925): 9.

6777. ——— "Saving Private Recreation Areas for Permanent Public Use." *American City* 57 (March 1942): 66.
Proposal designed to encourage owners of private country clubs to deed their holdings to the city or county of Los Angeles.

6778. Whitsett, W[illiam] P. "Our Eastern Sierra Playgrounds." *Southern California Business* 8 (February 1929): 12+.
Inyo-Mono region, source of Los Angeles Aqueduct water.

6779. Whitworth, D. M. "Eavesdropping in the Sand." *Westways* 55 (June 1963): 18-21.
Beaches of the Los Angeles area.

6780. Wiatt, Earl. "Yachting Popular Sport for Los Angeles Vacationists." *Los Angeles Realtor* 4 (May 1925): 25-6.

6781. Wickham, Verne. "Golf in Long Beach." *Pacific Municipalities* 39 (March 1925): 73-5+.

6782. Wilkins, Barbara. "In Search of an Urban Oasis: The City's Best Parks." *Los Angeles* 15 (April 1970): 38-42.
   Los Angeles.

6783. Williams, Hortense L. "Recreation for Crippled Children." *Recreation* 26 (June 1932): 139-40+.
   Orthopaedic Hospital School, Los Angeles.

6784. "Winter Sports Carnival in Big Pines." *Los Angeles Saturday Night* 44 (January 23, 1937): 5.

6785. "The World's Greatest Mountain Playground." *Trails Magazine* 3 (Summer 1936): 5.
   Angeles National Forest.

6786. Yukie, Thomas S. "An Analysis of the Administrative Factors Affecting the Use of School Facilities for Recreation During After-School Hours in Selected Communities in Los Angeles County." Master's thesis, University of California, Los Angeles, 1952. 203 pp.

PETROLEUM INDUSTRY AND TRADE

6787. "All the World Burns L.A. Kerosene." *Southern California Business* 2 (October 1923): 28.

6788. Allen, D. R. "A Study of Water Shut-Off Tester Failures in the Los Angeles Basin." *Summary of Operations California Oil Fields* 41 (July-December 1955): 49-54.

6789. Amar, E. J. "What Oil Did for the Harbor." *Southern California Business* 14 (November 1935): 14-5.

6790. American Petroleum Institute, Department of Information. *California's Oil.* New York, 1948. 28 pp.

6791. "Artifices of the Casinghead Chisler: State Investigation in Los Angeles Basin Oil Fields Reveals How Dishonest Oil Workers Employ Camouflaged Stills to Obtain Tax Free Gasoline; 102 Illegal Traps Uncovered." *Petroleum World* 35 (June 1938): 24-6.

6792. Atwood, Albert W. "When the Oil Flood Is On." *Saturday Evening Post* 116 (July 7, 1923): 3-7+.
   A lively contemporary account of the Signal Hill oil boom and its effect on the Long Beach economy.

6793. Bain, Joe S. *The Economics of the Pacific Coast Petroleum Industry.* Berkeley and Los Angeles, 1944-1947. 3 vols.

6794. ———— *War and Postwar Developments in the Southern California Petroleum Industry.* Los Angeles, 1945. 49 pp.

6795. Barnes, R. M., and Bowes, Glenn H. "Seal Beach Oil Field." *Summary of Operations California Oil Fields* 16 (October-December 1930): 9-29.

6796. Barton, Cecil L. "A Report on Playa Del Rey Oil Field." *Summary of Operations California Oil Fields* 17 (October-December 1931): 5-15.

6797.————, and Sampson, Norman N. "Placerita Oil Field." *Summary of Operations California Oil Fields* 35 (July-December 1949): 5-20.

6798. "Big Leasing Campaign in Newhall District: Havenstrite Discovering Near Castaic Stimulates Interest in Territory from Aliso Canyon to Piru and Brisk Prospecting Campaign Is Expected." *Petroleum World* 37 (October 1940): 20-1.

6799. Borough, R[e]ube[n] [W.] "Law and Order in Los Angeles." *Nation* 125 (1927): 12.
   Julian oil scandal.

6800. Brison, J. Oliver. "City of Long Beach Holds Unique Position as Big Oil Producer; Property Worth Millions." *Pacific Municipalities* 39 (February 1925): 35-6+.

6801. "Building a Success from One Small Natural Gasoline Plant at Signal Hill." *Petroleum World* 12 (August 1927): 123.
   Signal Oil Co.

6802. "California Oil 96% of Exports from Los Angeles Harbor." *Petroleum World* 13 (December 1928): 100.

6803. Case, J. B. "Report on Santa Fe Springs Oil Field." *Summary of Operations California Oil Fields* 8 (May 1923): 5-19.

6804. ——, and Keyes, Rob[er]t L. "Report on the Long Beach Oil Field." *Summary of Operations California Oil Fields* 9 (October 1923): 5-17.

6805. Chappuis, L. C. "Los Angeles Basin Still Holds Promise of New Discoveries: Encouraging Showings Point to a Second Uplift Parelleling Beverly Hills-Newport Line of Oil Fields." *Petroleum World and Oil Age* 27 (March 1930): 67-9.

6806. "[City Planning Committee of the Municipal League] Against Oil Drilling in Residential Districts." *Municipal League of Los Angeles Bulletin* 9 (January 20, 1932): [3-5].

6807. "Coast Gasoline Back on 'Pre-War' Basis; Up 6 Cents in Los Angeles; Crude Situation Threatening." *Petroluem World* 12 (May 1927): 57-9.

6808. Cole, H. S., Jr. "Long Beach Installation of California Gasoline Co. Is Milepost in Plant Design and Operation." *Petroleum World* 13 (July 1928): 102+.

6809. Collins, James H. "Douglas Puts His Heart in His Gasoline: West Coast Aircraft Builder Has Put the Famous Douglas Family Emblem into the Oil Company's 'Flying Heart'; Strong Marketing Organization Behind the New Brand." *Petroleum World* 38 (October 1941): 30-4+.

6810. Copp, W. W., and Bowes, Glenn H. "Seal Beach Oil Field." *Summary of Operations California Oil Fields* 13 (September 1927): 5-16.
Los Angeles and Orange counties.

6811. Cordova, Simon. "Castaic Junction Oil Field." *Summary of Operations California Oil Fields* 52, No. 2, Pt. 2 (1966): 55-65.

6812. —— "El Segundo Oil Field." *Summary of Operations California Oil Fields* 49, No. 2 (1963): 45-52.

6813. —— "Saugus Oil Field." *Summary of Operations California Oil Fields* 48 (July-December 1962): 81-4.

6814. Courtney, Jack. "Cristobal Was No Treasure Hunter." *Westways* 28 (April 1936): 22-3.
Underground pocket of oil and gasoline discovered by Cristobal Salcedo while digging a cesspool in Wilmington.

6815. Crowder, Robert E. "Del Amo Zone of Torrance Oil Field." *Summary of Operations California Oil Fields* 51, No. 1 (1965): 47-51.

6816. —— "Hyperion Oil Field." *Summary of Operations California Oil Fields* 46 (January-June 1960): 86-91.

6817. —— "Inglewood City Area of Potrero Oil Field." *Summary of Operations California Oil Fields* 44 (January-June 1958): 27-33.

6818. —— "Los Angeles City Oil Field." *Summary of Operations California Oil Fields* 47 (January-June 1961): 66-77.

6819. —— "Torrance Oil Field." *Summary of Operations California Oil Fields* 42 (July-December 1956): 4-18.

6820. ——, and Johnson, R. A. "Recent Developments in Jade-Buttram Area of Salt Lake Oil Field." *Summary of Operations California Oil Fields* 49 (January-June 1963): 53-9.

6821. Crown, Walter J. "Wilmington Oil Field." *Summary of Operations California Oil Fields* 26 (July 1940-June 1941): 5-11.

6822. ——; Peirce, G. G., and Howard, Paul J. "Recent Developments in the Long Beach Oil Field." *Summary of Operations California Oil Fields* 18 (October-December 1932): 5-25.

6823. "Deep Drilling Campaign at Long Beach Is Beginning to Have Its Effect on Production Curve." *Petroleum World* 13 (April 1928): 98+.

6824. Dodd, Harold V. "Dominguez Oil Field." *Summary of Operations California Oil Fields* 12 (October 1926): 7-22.

6825. Dosch, M.W., and Beecroft, G. W. "Tapia Oil Field." *Summary of Operations California Oil Fields* 45 (January-June 1959): 74-9.

6826. "Douglas Has Modern Cracking Plant." *Petroleum World* 38 (October 1941): 37-8+.
Douglas Oil and Refining Co., Wilmington.

6827. Downey, Sheridan. *Truth About the Tidelands.* San Francisco, 1948. 74 pp.
Question of off-shore ownership of submerged oil lands.

6828. Driggs, J. L., and Sampson, N. N. "Ramona Oil Field." *Summary of Operations California Oil Fields* 37 (January-June 1951): 5-19.

Los Angeles and Ventura counties.

6829. Driver, Herschel L. "Inglewood Oil Field, Los Angeles County, California." Master's thesis, University of Southern California, 1939. 40 pp.

6830. Dykstra, Clarence A. "The Future of Los Angeles," in *Los Angeles: Preface to a Master Plan.* Ed. by George W. Robbins and L. Deming Tilton. Los Angeles, 1941. Pp. 3-10.

6831. Eaton, J. E. "Alamitos Heights Extension of Seal Beach [Oil Field] Holds California Record for Drilling Activitiy." *Petroleum World* 12 (April 1927): 62-3.

6832.——— "San Clemente [Oil Company] Well Proves New High-Gravity Oil Field in West Part of Los Angeles Basin." *Petroleum World* 13 (August 1928): 52-3.

Located west of Lawndale.

6833. Elliott, J. E., and Merritt, F. C. "Core Drilling in Oil Fields of Southern California." *Summary of Operations California Oil Fields* 8 (July 1922): 5-12.

6834. Emery, Kenneth O. *The Sea Off Southern California; A Modern Habitat of Petroleum.* New York, [1960]. 366 pp.

6835. Farrand, William H. "Santa Fe Springs Blow-Out Presents Problem in Firefighting New to California." *Petroluem World* 13 (October 1928): 54-5.

6836. Finney, Guy W. *The Great Los Angeles Bubble: A Present Day Story of Colossal Financial Jugglery and of Penalties Paid.* Los Angeles, 1929. 203 pp.

Julian Petroleum Corp.

6837. "First Refinery Reborn: Standard Oil Restores 300-Bbl. Plant at Newhall as Memorial to California Industry's Pioneers." *Petroleum World and Oil Age* 27 (December 1930): 40-2.

6838. Foster, F. E. "From Spring-Pole to Rotary Drill: Here Are the High Lights in Southern California's Oil Equipment Story, Dating from the 1860's." *Southern California Business* 14 (November 1935): 12-3.

Los Angeles.

6839. Frame, R. G. "Earthquake Damage, Its Cause and Prevention in the Wilmington Oil Field." *Summary of Operations California Oil Fields* 38 (January-June 1952): 5-15.

6840. ——— "A Review of Water Flooding in the Wilmington Oil Field." *Summary of Operations California Oil Fields* 43 (January-June 1957): 59-74.

6841. Gaede, Verne F. "Central Area of Whittier Oil Field." *Summary of Operations California Oil Fields* 50, No. 1 (1964): 59-67.

6842. ——— "La Habra Area of Whittier Oil Field." *Summary of Operations California Oil Fields* 51, No. 1 (1965): 53-9.

6843. ——— "Leffingwell Oil Field." *Summary of Operations California Oil Fields* 43 (July-December 1957): 35-8.

6844. "Gasoline and Crude Oil Prices Reduced on Pacific Coast; Alamitos Height Is Storm Center." *Petroleum World* 12 (April 1927): 57-9.

6845. "Gusher Completions at Playa del Rey." *Petroleum World* 32 (April 1935): 27-8+.

6846. Haas, Lucien C. "Redondo Beach: What Oil Wants, Oil Gets." *Frontier* 7 (December 1955): 7-8+.

Alleged machinations involved in securing public approval for a slant-drilling program off the coast of this beach city.

6847. Henderson, A. B. "Town Lot Oil Operations." *The Los Angeles Bar Bulletin* 35 (July 1960): 284-9.

6848. Hendrickson, A. B., and Weaver, D. K. "Santa Fe Spirngs Oil Field." *Summary of Operations California Oil Fields* 14 (January 1929): 5-21.

6849. Higgins, Edwin. *California's Oil Industry.* Los Angeles, 1928. 39 pp.

6850. Hill, F. F. "Looking Backward at a Few Santa Fe Springs Blow-Outs." *Petroleum World* 12 (February 1927): 96.

6851. Hinton, Arthur R. "Other City Drilling Programs Proposed: Seaboard, Universal, McDuffie, and Ramsey Brothers Lease Los Angeles Properties in Search for Deep Productive Horizons in Shallow 'Ghost' Fields of Yesterday; Program Has Support of Petroleum Administration." *Petroleum World* 40 (March 1943): 64+.

6852. —— "Quiet Waters Favor Off-Shore Drilling: Several Sub-Sea Structures Declared to Have Oil Possibilities Along California Coast Between Newport and Point Conception." *Petroleum World* 35 (October 1938): 29-30.

6853. —— "State Shows Hand in Tideland Squabble: Will Base Claim to Wilmington Oil Field Lands on Common Law, Contending That It Did Not Cede Mineral Rights in Grant to Long Beach." *Petroleum World* 35 (February 1938): 40-1.

6854. Hodges, F. C. "Gas Storage and Recent Developments in the Playa del Rey Oil Field." *Summary of Operations California Oil Fields* 30 (July-December 1944): 3-10.

6855. ——, and Murray-Aaron, E. R. "Newhall-Potrero, Aliso Canyon, Del Valle, and Oak Canyon Oil Fields." *Summary of Operations California Oil Fields* 29 (January-June 1943): 5-29.

6856. "How El Segundo's Wild Well Was Capped." *Petroleum World* 37 (February 1940): 34-5+.

6857. "How Macmillan Converted Plant for War." *Petroleum World* 40 (July 1943): 72+.
Macmillan Petroleum Co., Long Beach.

6858. "How Montebello Wild Well Got That Way and How It Was Capped." *Petroleum World* 36 (June 1939): 24-5.

6859. "How Science and a Lot of Nerve Got the Best of a Bad Oil Fire." *Petroleum World and Oil Age* 26 (August 1929): 62-8.
Santa Fe Springs.

6860. "How the Old Salt Lake Pipe Line Served the Industry in Los Angeles for a Quarter of a Century." *Petroleum World* 13 (September 1928): 117.

6861. Huey, Wallace F. "Subsidence and Repressuring in Wilmington Oil Field." *Summary of Operation California Oil Fields* 50, No. 2 (1964): 5-25.

6862. Hunter, W. J. "North Whittier Heights Area of Los Angeles County." *Summary of Operations California Oil Fields* 45 (January-June 1959): 80-8.

6863. Ingram, W[illiam] L. "Aliso Canyon Oil Field." *Summary of Operations California Oil Fields* 45 (January-June 1959): 65-73.

6864. —— "Recreation Park Area of Long Beach Oil Field." *Summary of Operations California Oil Fields* 52, No. 2, Pt. 2 (1966): 67-71.

6865. —— "Rideout Heights Area of Whittier Oil Field." *Summary of Operations California Oil Fields* 48 (July-December 1962): 93-6.

6866. "Islands Get Gunite Sculpture Embellishment." *Western Construction* 44 (February 1969): 68+.
Oil-drilling rigs off Long Beach disguised as high-rise apartment buildings.

6867. Jensen, Joseph. "California Petroleum Development During 1926." *Southern California Business* 6 (March 1927): 9-11+.
Much on Los Angeles County.

6868. ——, et al. "Changes in Equipment Important Phase of Santa Fe Springs Development." *Petroleum World and Oil Age* 26 (November 1929): 60-6.
At the time, this was the greatest producing oil field in U.S.

6869. —— " 'Oil' . . . the Magic Word of Southern California." *Southern California Business* 5 (August 1926): 9-11.
Los Angeles County.

6870. ——, and Robertson, Glenn D. "A History of Petroleum Development in the Los Angeles Basin Area from 1923 to Date." *Petroleum World* 13 (April 1928): 57-9.

6871. Johnson, Charles R. "Service Station Growth Continues in California; One Company Offers Prizes for New Designs: Union Oil Invites Competition Among Architects in Order That Stations May Strike a More Harmonious Note with Surroundings." *Petroleum World* 13 (January 1928): 62-3.

6872. Johnson, R. A. "Boyle Heights Oil Field." *Summary of Operations California Oil Fields* 52, No. 1 (1966) : 69-72.

6873. ———— "East Area of Potrero Oil Field." *Summary of Operations California Oil Fields* 47 (July-December 1961) : 65-74.

6874. Julier, W. G. "How Gilmore [Oil Co.] Uses Records to Save on Motor Truck Operation." *Petroleum World and Oil Age* 26 (December 1929) : 72-4.

6875. Kegley, Howard. "San Fernando Foothills Oil Search Begins." *Petroleum World* 48 (June 1951) : 5.

6876. ———— "Wildcats Near the Santa Monica Mountains . . . California's Most Intensive Drilling Campaign?" *Petroleum World* 48 (December 1951) : 10-2.

6877. Kegley, Howard C. "Billions from Boneyards of the Musty Past." *Touring Topics* 20 (June 1928) : 40-2+.
The author recounts the oil boom and its effect on the economy of Southern California.

6878. Krec, Ted. "Island City of Gold." *Westways* 49 (August 1957) : 10-1.
Signal Hill.

6879. Langley, Nancy C. "The Land of Milk and Oil." *Westways* 36 (September 1944) : 10-1.
Gilmore Oil Company's wells tapped reserves beneath Gilmore's dairy ranch (originally part of Rancho La Brea) at Wilshire and La Brea.

6880. Leever, Basil E. "About Oil and the City of Long Beach." *Western City* 21 (June 1945) : 26-8.
Petroleum revenues finance numerous municipal improvements.

6881. Lloyd, E. C. "Seaboard's Test Well in L.A. City." *Petroleum World* 43 (September 1945) : 54-5.
Elysian Park area.

6882. Loken, Kent P. "Long Beach Airport Oil Field." *Summary of Operations California Oil Fields* 50, No. 1 (1964) : 53-8.

6883. "Long Beach Ignores State's Claim to Tidelands; Drilling Starts Soon." *Petroleum World* 35 (January 1938) : 30-1.

6884. "Los Angeles County Restricts the Erection of Wooden Derricks." *Petroleum World and Oil Age* 26 (August 1929) : 77-8.

6885. "Los Angeles, the Mining and Oil Center of the Southwest." *Out West,* new series, 5 (May 1913) : 271-82.

6886. Masters, E. W. "Pronounced Benefits Accruing from Gas Storage Experiments in the Dominguez Field." *Petroleum World* 13 (October 1928) : 72+.

6887. Matthews, John F. "The Honor Rancho Oil Field." *Summary of Operations California Oil Fields* 39 (January-June 1953) : 21-5.

6888. "Mayor Vetoes Ordinance Barring Large Storage at Service Stations: Attempt of Los Angeles City Council to Have Huge Underground Stocks of Los Angeles Price-Cutting Group Declared Menace to Safety Balked by Porter: Would Have Helped Retail Market." *Petroleum World* 29 (May 1932) : 13-4.

6889. McLaughlin, R[oy] P. "Montebello Oil Field." *Summary of Operations California Oil Fields* 5 (May 1920) : 5-27.

6890. ———— *The Tenderfoot Comes West; Half a Century of Progress in California, and the Petroleum Industry.* New York, [1968]. 124 pp.

6891. McMaster, Robert N. "Electric Power as Used by the Chanslor-Canfield Midway Oil Company in the Development of Its Properties in the Torrance Oilfield, Los Angeles County, California." Master's thesis, University of Southern California, 1931. 103 pp.

6892. Mead, Roy G., Jr., "Wilmington Boom Grows as Drilling Proves Another Big Field Has Been Discovered." *Petroleum World* 34 (April 1937) : 27-32.

6893. Mefferd, M. G. "Newhall-Potrero Oil Field." *Summary of Operations California Oil Fields* 51, No. 2 (1965) : 41-51.

6894. ————, and Cordova, S. "Mission Oil Field." *Summary of Operations California Oil Fields* 47 (January-June 1961) : 79-85.

6895. ———— and ———— "West Coyote Oil Field."

Summary of Operations California Oil Fields 48 (January-June 1962): 37-46.

Los Angeles and Orange counties.

6896. Metzner, Loyde H. "The Del Rey Hills Area of the Playa del Rey Oil Field." *Summary of Operations California Oil Fields* 21 (October-December 1935): 5-26.

6897. Miller, Max C. *Speak to the Earth.* New York, 1955. 310 pp.

Some references to Los Angeles area.

6898. Millett, E. R., Jr. "Factors in Del Rey's Early Collapse." *Petroleum World* 32 (August 1935): 13-4.

6899. ———— "New Playa del Rey Area May Be Another Major Field for Los Angeles Basin." *Petroleum World* 32 (April 1935): 13-5+.

6900. "Multiple Zone Production at Wilmington." *Petroleum World* 35 (July 1938): 32-3+.

6901. "Municipal Wildcat: Los Angeles to Drill for Oil on City Property Despite the Dry Hole Encountered by Shell on Gilmore Island." *Business Week* (June 19, 1943): 40+.

6902. Murray-Aaron, Eugene R., and Pfeil, Adolph W. "Recent Developments in the Wilmington Oil Field." *Summary of Operations California Oil Fields* 34 (July-December 1948): 5-13.

6903. Musser, E. H. "Report on the Torrance Oil Field." *Summary of Operations California Oil Fields* 11 (September 1925): 5-17.

6904. ———— "The Rosecrans Oil Field." *Summary of Operations California Oil Fields* 11 (November 1925): 5-21.

6905. "Nemesis Overtakes Oil Officials." *Los Angeles Saturday Night* 12 (May 21, 1932): 3.

Judge Leon Yankwich and trial of Richfield Oil Co. officials.

6906. "New Station Has 200,000 Gals. Storage: Huge Installation Goes Ahead When Los Angeles County Supervisors Table Proposed Emergency Ordinance Restricting Storage to 10,000 Gallons." *Petroleum World* 29 (November 1932): 36-7.

J. De Bell's "Go-Gas."

6907. "New 12-Pump Station Is Model of Efficiency." *Petroleum World* 30 (October 1933): 36.

Standard Oil Co. station on Roosevelt Highway, Santa Monica.

6908. "New Wells Reveal Wilmington Structure." *Petroleum World* 35 (February 1938): 29-32+.

6909. Noel, F[ritz] C. "Oil Industry Makes Giant Strides: While the Older Wells in Southern California Are the Old Stand-Bys, New Development Has Proved Most Startling." *Southern California Business* 1 (September 1922): 42-3.

6910. ———— "Oil Industry Offers Surprises." *Southern California Business* 2 (January 1924): 9+.

Discoveries of prolific new local fields. [Author's name is incorrectly given as E. C. Noel.]

6911. "A Noiseless Well in the Heart of the City." *Petroleum World* 40 (March 1943): 30-2+.

Shell test well in old Salt Lake Field, Wilshire District.

6912. Norris, Byron B. "Report on the Fields on or Adjacent to the Whittier Fault." *Summary of Operations California Oil Fields* 15 (April-June 1930): 5-20.

6913. "Oil Muddle in the City of Los Angeles." *Petroleum World* 40 (August 1943): 21.

Controversy over resumption of in-town drilling.

6914. "Oil Pump Concern Completing $250,000 Expansion Program." *Petroleum World* 13 (January 1928): 137.

Axelson Machine Co., Los Angeles.

6915. "Oil Wells Don Mask and Muffler: Drillers in the Los Angeles Residential and Hollywood Areas Are Camouflaging Their Operations within Soundproof Towers." *Business Week* (February 13, 1960): 32-3.

6916. "Old World Atmosphere at This New Super-Station." *Petroleum World* 12 (March 1927): 82.

California Petroleum Corp. (Calpet) Service Station in Wilshire District, Los Angeles.

6917. "One Crew Drills 20,000 Ft. at Venice in 109 Days." *Petroleum World* 32 (May 1935): 14-6.

6918. O'Neill, Edmond. "Petroleum in California." *Sunset* 6 (April 1901): 177-84.

6919. Orcutt, W. W. "Los Angeles' Rich Oil Basin Fields." *Los Angeles Saturday Night 150th Birthday of Los Angeless Fiesta and Pre-Olympiad.* Special Issue (1931): [9].

6920. Palmer, Russell R. "Gasoline Price War in California Short Lived; Long Beach Peak Begins to Look Like 225,000 [Barrels per Day]." *Petroleum World* 13 (June 1928): 47-9.

6921. ——— "Increase in Crude Prices Brightens California Sky; Santa Fe Springs Is Dark Cloud on Horizon." *Petroleum World* 13 (September 1928): 47-50.

6922. ——— "Long Beach Peak May Go Close to 200,000 Barrels; Associated Gets 1,000-Barrel Well at Potrero." *Petroleum World* 13 (May 1928): 47-9.

6923. ——— "New Fields Center Attention of Oil Industry in California; Race for Deep Sand at Long Beach." *Petroleum World* 12 (November 1927): 55-8+.

6924. "Peanuts under the Patio." *Time* 69 (June 17, 1957): 90+.
City Council authorizes drilling for oil beneath Rancho Golf Course and Hillcrest Country Club.

6925. Pike, Tom, Jr. "Wilmington Wells Create New Problems: Sand Is Causing Considerable Trouble But Equipment and Methods Have Been Provided Which Have Eliminated Most of the Difficulty." *Petroleum World* 34 (September 1937): 31-3.

6926. "Placerita Canyon Production Peak Passed." *Petroleum World* 46 (November 1949): 18-20.

6927. "Playa Del Rey Drilling Gets under Way in Earnest." *Petroleum World and Oil Age* 27 (May 1930): 63-5.

6928. Porter, L. E. "Development of El Segundo Oil Field." *Petroleum World* 34 (Octber 1937): 39-44+.

6929. "Potrero Is Most Likely Looking Candidate for California's Next Oil Field; Associated Finds Sand." *Petroleum World* 12 (February 1927): 56.

Field south of Inglewood, where Julian Petroleum, among others, was active.

6930. Preston, Harold M., and King, Vernon L. "West Montebello Oil Field." *Petroleum World* 36 (September 1939): 19-25.

6931. "Richfield's 4750-Barrel Well from Long Beach Deep Sand Is Feature of October Completions." *Petroleum World* 12 (November 1927): 63.

6932. "Richfield's Woeful Mismanagement." *Los Angeles Saturday Night* 11 (May 2, 1931): 3.
Bankruptcy of Richfield Oil Co.

6933. Rintoul, William T. "The Case of the Disappearing Derricks." *Westways* 54 (May 1962): 22-3.
Demolition of California oil derricks.

6934. Ritzius, D. E. "Southeast Area of Honor Rancho Oil Fields." *Summary of Operations California Oil Fields* 45 (July-December 1959): 5-12.

6935. Roberts, D. C. "Long Beach Oil Field." *Summary of Operations California Oil Fields* 13 (May 1928): 5-20.

6936. Robertson, Glenn D. "Santa Fe Springs Field Holds Spotlight as Nation's Most-Discussed Oil Area." *Petroleum World* 13 (November 1928): 88+.

6937. Robinson, R. R. "Unique Gas Lift Pump Gets Test in Long Beach Field." *Petroleum World and Oil Age* 26 (May 1929): 73-6.

6938. Rothermel, R. V. "Canoga Park Oil Field." *Summary of Operations California Oil Fields* 50, No. 2 (1964): 35-8.

6939. Schwarzman, Richard C. "The Pinal Dome Oil Company; An Adventure in Business, 1901-1917." Doctoral dissertation, University of California, Los Angeles, 1967. 328 pp.
Mostly on Santa Maria Valley, but one chapter on Los Angeles: Chapter VII, "Establishing the Los Angeles Distribution Station," pp. 186-216.

6940. Shuler, Robert P. *Julian Thieves in Politics.* Los Angeles, [n.d.]. 64 pp.
Polemic of author (Pastor, Trinity Methodist Church and owner of Radio KGEF, Los An-

geles) against S. C. Lewis and others in respect to C. C. Julian petroleum scandal.

6941. Sorensen, Royal W. "What California Institute of Technology Learned About Lightning Protection for Storage Tanks." *Petroleum World* 13 (September 1928): 52-5.

6942. Soyster, M. H., and Van Couvering, M. "Notes on Long Beach Oil Field, Los Angeles County." *Summary of Operations California Oil Fields* 7 (April 1922): 5-22.

6943. Stolz, H[arry] P. "West Montebello Oil Field and the Application of the State Gas Law." *Summary of Operations California Oil Fields* 25 (July 1939-June 1940): 5-23.

6944. ———, and Winckel, Edmond E. "Subsurface Correlation of a Portion of the Southwest Flank of the Long Beach Oil Field, with Particular Reference to Legal Proceedings Involving Trespass Deviational Drilling." Master's thesis, University of Southern California, 1939. 190 pp.

6945. "The Story of a Great Oil Company." *Petroleum World* 29 (August 1932): 19-50.
Richfield Oil Co.

6946. Summer, Harrison. "Acres of Oil." *Petroleum World and Oil Age* 26 (February 1929): 77.
General Petroleum refinery, Torrance.

6947. "Super-Service 'Way Back When.'" *Petroleum World and Oil Age* 28 (October 1931): 55-6+.
Brief history of gasoline stations, including National Supply of Los Angeles, established in 1913 by Earle C. Anthony and Don Lee.

6948. Swigart, T. E. "Notes on the Efficiency of Flowing Wells in the Dominguez Field, California." *Summary of Operations California Oil Fields* 10 (January 1925): 5-17.

6949. Taylor, Frank J., and Welty, Earl M. *Black Bonanza: How an Oil Hunt Grew Into the Union Oil Company of California.* New York, [1950]. 280 pp.

6950. "The Texas Tower Comes West." *Western Construction* 31 (November 1956): 50+.
Platform for off-shore oil exploration, Long Beach.

6951. "Third Fire in Year Is Costly to Santa Fe Springs Operators." *Petroleum World and Oil Age* 26 (July 1929): 63-4.

6952. Thomas, J. R. "Extension of Wilmington Oil Field." *Summary of Operations California Oil Fields* 43 (January-June 1957): 51-7.

6953. Thompson, D. R. "Haas's Blackberry Patch at Long Beach Has Produced 6,000,000 Barrels of Oil." *Petroleum World* 12 (December 1927): 65+.

6954. Thorne, Frank. "Black Gold and the Horseless Carriage." *Westways* 42 (December 1950): 14-6.
Historical sketch of the Southern California petroleum industry.

6955. Tilton, L. Deming. "The Master Plan," in *Los Angeles: Preface to a Master Plan.* Ed. by George W. Robbins and L. Deming Tilton. Los Angeles, 1941. Pp. 253-66.

6956. Tompkins, Walker A. *Little Giant of Signal Hill: An Adventure in American Enterprise.* Englewood Cliffs, N. J., [1964]. 258 pp.
History of Signal Oil and Gas Co., now the Signal Companies.

6957. Tudor, Richard B. "Las Llajas Oil Field." *Summary of Operations California Oil Fields* 49, No. 2 (1963): 53-7.

6958. ——— "Recent Developments in the Kraft-York Area of Placerita Oil Field." *Summary of Operations California Oil Fields* 48 (January-June 1962): 47-53.

6959. Union Oil Company of California. "Union Oil Co. Is Proud of Its Great Past, Looks Ahead to a Greater Future." *Petroleum World* 37 (May 1940): 40-67.
Issued as a separate: *Fifty Years of Progress, the Story of Union Oil Company.* [N.p., 1940]. 31 pp.

6960. Van Couvering, Martin. "Searching for Oil in the City When Los Angeles Was Young—and Now!" *Petroleum World* 40 (March 1943): 42+.

6961. Van Deinse, F. C. "Controlling Oil Production for Business Safety." *Southern California Business* 8 (June 1929): 16+
Los Angeles and Southern California.

6962. van Wingen, N. "Review of Wilmington Water Floods." *Summary of Operations California Oil Fields* 48 (January-June 1962): 33-6.

6963. Walling, R. W. "Report on Newhall Oil Field." *Summary of Operations California Oil Fields* 20 (October-December 1934): 5-58.

6964. Watson, Janet M. "The Petroleum Industry in California with Special Reference to Its Historical Development." Master's thesis, University of Southern California, 1930. 101 pp.
Includes the Los Angeles basin.

6965. Wells, N. C. "Pressure Drilling at Signal Hill." *Petroleum World* 35 (October 1938): 19-21.

6966. Welty, Earl M., and Taylor, Frank J. *The Black Bonanza.* New York, London and Toronto, 1958. 255 pp.
History of the Union Oil Company of California.

6967. ———— and ———— *The 76 Bonanza: The Fabulous Life and Times of the Union Oil Company of California.* Menlo Park, 1966. 351 pp.

6968. Western Oil and Gas Association. *Highlights of California's Petroleum History.* Los Angeles, 1965. 25 pp. 2nd ed., 1968. 29 pp.

6969. "Where Flow Rivers of Liquid Wealth: The Two Greatest Oil Producing Fields in the United States, Santa Fe Springs and Signal Hill, Are in Southern California Territory." *Southern California Business* 2 (February 1923): 7-8.

6970. White, Gerald T. *Formative Years in the Far West. A History of the Standard Oil Company of California and Predecessors Through 1919.* New York, 1962. 694 pp.

6971. White, J. Lloyd. "Lawndale Oil Field and Alondra Area." *Summary of Operations California Oil Fields* 36 (July-December 1950): 11-8.

6972. ———— "The Schist Surface of the Western Los Angeles Basin." *Summary of Operations California Oil Fields* 32 (January-June 1946): 3-11.

6973. "Wildcatting Booms in Los Angeles Basin." *Petroleum World* 33 (May 1936): 27-30.

6974. Williams, George C. "Torrance Deep Zone Booms Oil Field." *Petroleum World* 35 (August 1938): 31-4.

6975. "Wilmington Area Latest Hot Spot." *Petroleum World* 33 (June 1936): 24-6+.

6976. "Wilmington Drilling Boom Tapering Off." *Petroleum World* 35 (April 1938): 22+.

6977. "Wilmington Potential Expected Soon to Reach 100,000 Barrels Daily." *Petroleum World* 34 (May 1937): 36-7.

6978. Winterburn, Read. "East Los Angeles Field." *Summary of Operations California Oil Fields* 38 (January-June 1952): 16-20.

6979. Witucki, Gerard S. "A Study of Subsidence in the Wilmington Oil Field, California." Master's thesis, University of California, Los Angeles, 1959. 107 pp.

6980. Wosk, L. David. "Oil Possibilities of Newhall—Castaic Area." *Petroleum World* 37 (October 1940): 22-7.

6981. "World's Largest Water Flooding Project, Long Beach, California." *The Architect and Engineer* 217 (May 1959): 5.
Project to restore underground pressure undertaken at Wilmington Oil Field.

6982. Wride, Rosalie. "A History of the Long Beach Oil Fields." Master's thesis, Occidental College, 1949. 139 pp.

6983. Ybarra, R. A. "Recent Developments in the Santa Fe Springs Oil Field." *Summary of Operations California Oil Fields* 43 (July-December 1957): 39-45.

6984. ————, and Stockton, A. D. "Ford Pool of Fault Block I, Wilmington Oil Field." *Summary of Operations California Oil Fields* 50, No. 1 (1964): 69-79.

6985. ———— and ———— "Oak Canyon Oil Field." *Summary of Operations California Oil Fields* 44 (July-December 1958): 71-5.

6986. Zulberti, John L. "Towsley Canyon Area of Newhall Oil Field." *Summary of Operations California Oil Fields* 52, No. 1 (1966): 53-61.

PLANNING

6987. Adler, Pat[ricia]. *A History of the Venice Area: A Part of the Venice Community Plan Study.* Los Angeles, 1969. [24] pp.

6988. "Administrative Civic Center Plans." *Municipal League of Los Angeles Bulletin* 2 (January 20, 1925): 10-1.

6989. "Adoption of Administration Center Plan by Los Angeles County." *American City* 34 (February 1926): 199.

6990. Aiassa, George. "Planning-Oriented Data Bank Established by West Covina." *Western City* 44 (July 1968): 41+.

6991. ———— "West Covina Develops Civic Center Program Through Use of 'Public Authority' Legislation." *Western City* 43 (May 1967): 36-8.

6992. ". . . And the Ultimate Solution: It May, of Course, Be Necessary to Destroy Los Angeles in Order to Save It." *Los Angeles* 15 (January 1970): 34-5+.

6993. Anderson, Walt. "The Dropout Towns." *Los Angeles* 12 (November 1967): 28-30+.

Fully planned and self-contained communities on fringes of Los Angeles, such as Westlake, Valencia, and Porter Ranch.

6994. Arnebergh, Roger W. "Variances Are Trouble — Handle with Care: Zoning Exercises Police Power and It's Administrative — Not Legislative." *Western City* 27 (December 1951): 24-5.

6995. Avakian, John C. *The Property Republic: Being an Outgrowth of a Plan for the Development of the Metropolitan District of Los Angeles.* Los Angeles, 1925. 221 pp.

6996. Backhouse, Judith. "Functional Differentiation in Santa Monica." Master's thesis, University of California, Los Angeles, 1961. 158 pp.

6997. Bemis, George W. "Public Works Review Board Proposed for Area Development Coordination." *American City* 60 (December 1945): 88.

Plan for coordinating public works projects in Metropolitan Los Angeles.

6998. Bennett, Charles B. "Planning Progress in Los Angeles, California." *Town Planning Institute Journal* 36 (February 1950): 103-11.

6999. ————, and Breivogel, Milton. "Planning for the San Fernando Valley." *Western City* 21 (April 1945): 20-31.

7000. Berkshire, F. W. "Partial Plan for the Economic Development of the San Fernando Valley." *Los Angeles Realtor* 6 (October 1926): 14.

7001. Berry, Richard D. "Baldwin Hills Village— Design or Accident." *Arts & Architecture* 81 (October 1964): 18-20+.

Planned Los Angeles community.

7002. Bird, Remsen D. "On the Composing of a City." *Western City* 15 (February 1939): 20.

Plea for a Los Angeles master plan.

7003. Boddy, Manchester. "A Program for Los Angeles." *Saturday Night* 45 (October 8, 1938): 12-3.

Suggested plans for the city.

7004. Bollens, John C. "Relating City Areas to Functions: The California Experience." *American Institute of Planners Journal* 17 (1951): 13-22.

7005. Brandt, Gladys L. "The San Fernando Valley: A Study in Changing Adjustment Between Its Economic Life and Its Natural Environment." Master's thesis, University of Chicago, 1928. 160 pp.

7006. Britton, James. "Is Ours the Worst-Planned City?" *Los Angeles* 4 (September 1962): 19+.

7007. Bush, Carl. "What About Zoning?" *Los Angeles Realtor* 5 (October 1925): 17+.

Hollywood zoning.

7008. Case, Fred[erick E.], and Gillies, James. "Some Aspects of Land Planning: The San Fernando Valley Case." *The Appraisal Journal* 23 (January 1955): 15-41.

7009. Cheney, Charles H. "A Great City-Planning Project on the Pacific Coast." *American City* 27 (July 1922): 47.

Palos Verdes.

7010. ———— "Palos Verdes: Eight Years of Development." *The Architect and Engineer* 100 (January 1930): 35-42.

7011. "City Planning in Los Angeles." *Survey* 26 (July 22, 1911): 599-600.

7012. "City Planning on a Large Scale." *Playground* 18 (March 1925): 688+.
Argues that Los Angeles growth necessitates corresponding park development.

7013. Clark, Charles D. "Subdivision Control." *Western City* 7 (July 1931): 25-7.
Los Angeles County.

7014. Collins, James H. "No Quarrel with This Planning: Our New City Bureau That Plans for Possible Disaster Is the First and Best of Its Kind." *Southern California Business* 13 (September 1934): 8-9.

7015. Commons, John P. "Long Range Planning of Airports in Los Angeles County." *Western City* 21 (December 1945): 26-31.

7016. Cornell, Ralph D. "The Importance of Appearance," in *Los Angeles: Preface to a Master Plan.* Ed. by George W. Robbins and L. Deming Tilton. Los Angeles, 1941. Pp. 227-37.
Author argues need for "an official body which can set aesthetic objectives for the entire region and direct both private and public efforts towards such goals."

7017. ———, and Hjelte, George. "Planning a Modern City Park." *Western City* 22 (September 1946): 42-3.
South Gate Park.

7018. Daguerre, Norm. "LARTS: Bank for Community Planners." *Westways* 57 (April 1965): 28-30; (May 1965): 31-3; (July 1965): 6-8.
LARTS — Los Angeles Regional Transportation Study.

7019. Damon, George A. "A 'Home-Made' City Planning Exhibit and Its Results: The Cause and Effect of the 'My City' Exhibit at Pasadena, Cal." *American City* 15 (October 1916): 369-78.

7020. Daniels, Mark. "Combining the Practical and the Beautiful in City Planing." *Los Angeles Realtor* 7 (June 1928): 14+.
Hollywood Riviera section of Redondo Beach.

7021. Douglass, Enid H. "The Claremont Planning Commission: A Study of Social Backgrounds, Attitudes and Opinions of Planning Commissioners." Master's thesis, Claremont Graduate School, 1959. 73 pp.

7022. "Downtown: The Doom-Criers Foiled Again." *Los Angeles* 12 (August 1967): 27-8.
Downtown Los Angeles and the possibility of it becoming "the living core of the city."

7023. Dykstra, Clarence A. "Owens Valley — A Problem in Regional Planning." *The Community Builder* 1 (February 1928): 9-12.

7024. Eisner, Stanley. "Burbank's 'Golden Mall' Project Concludes Ten Year Planning." *Western City* 43 (January 1967): 26.

7025. Estrin, Lester D. "The Miracle Mile: An Example of Decentralization in Los Angeles." Master's thesis, University of California, Los Angeles, 1955. 66 pp.

7026. "The Forces at Work on Our Next Five Years." *Los Angeles* 15 (January 1970): 26-7.
Governmental reform and planning in Los Angeles.

7027. "40 Cities, 15 Counties and State Plan California Shoreline Development." *Western City* 22 (April 1946): 22-9.
Includes Los Angeles County.

7028. Frank, Elisabeth R. *Background for Planning.* [Los Angeles, 1949?]. 125 pp. 2nd ed., 1955. 105 pp.

7029. ——— *Differentiating Communities in Los Angeles County.* Welfare Planning Council, Los Angeles Region, *Special Report Series No. 50.* Los Angeles, 1957. 2 vols.

7030. Glendinning, Robert M. "Zoning: Past, Present and Future," in *Los Angeles: Preface to a Master Plan.* Ed. by George W. Robbins and L. Deming Tilton. Los Angeles, 1941. Pp. 173-88.

7031. Gold-Thompson and Co. *West Hollywood, Hollywood West; An Economic Feasibility Study of the Proposed City.* South Pasadena, [1960?]. 60 pp.

7032. Gray, Mary R. "Putting Your Civic House

in Order: How the Young Members of the Family Help." *Craftsman* 30 (June 1916): 283-91.
"Los Angeles City and County Improvement Contest."

7033. Greater Los Angeles Citizens Committee. *Shoreline Development Study, Playa del Rey to Palos Verdes, a Portion of a Proposed Master Recreation Plan for the Greater Los Angeles Region.* [Los Angeles], 1944. 39 pp.

7034. Gregg, Gardner W. "Los Angeles' Bold Plan for a Civic Center." *National Municipal Review* 14 (July 1925): 406-9.

7035. Griffenhagen-Kroeger. *Claremont's Future Civic Center.* Los Angeles, 1964. 25 pp.

7036. Griffin, Donald F. *Plans and Action for the Development of the Los Angeles Metropolitan Coastline.* Los Angeles, 1944. 40 pp.

7037. Gruen Associates. *Central City Development Program.* Los Angeles, 1967. 13 pp.
Long Beach.

7038 ——— *Downtown Long Beach; A Digest of the Planning Proposals.* Los Angeles, 1969. 18 pp.

7039. ——— *Reconnaisance and Programming Study of Central Long Beach for Downtown Long Beach Associates.* Los Angeles, 1967. 13 pp.
Supplements the *Central City Development Program* report and suggests means of financing including the first proposal of federal participation.

7040. Hall, Bryant. "Design Made for A Future City: Plan for Complete Self-Contained Community Is Outlined by Regional Planning Commission; Precised with Highway Program." *Western City* 7 (January 1931): 43-4.
East of Los Angeles Airport.

7041. ——— "Regional Plan Is Adopted by Seventeen Cities." *Western City* 6 (January 1930): 13-8+.
San Gabriel Valley.

7042. Hamilton, John J. *The Community Program of Greater Los Angeles.* Los Angeles, 1916. 20 pp.

7043. Harrell, Clyde P., Jr. "Comprehensive Zoning Plan for Los Angeles." *Los Angeles Bar Bulletin* 22 (January 1947): 131-8.

7044. Hjelte, George. "Public Work in Los Angeles, California." *Playground* 22 (April 1928): 23.
Report on comprehensive study for regional plan of parks, playgrounds, and beaches.

7045. Holden, Edward A. "An Analysis of the Extent of and Limitations Placed on Government Control of the Subdivision of Land in Los Angeles County—A Comparative Analysis of California State Law and City and County Subdivision Ordinances and Codes." Master's thesis, University of Southern California, 1953. 110 pp.

7046. Holland, Park. "The 'What-Ifs' of City Planning . . . The Ever-Changing Future City Plan." *Los Angeles* 15 (June 1970): 32-5+.

7047. Hultquist, Warren E. "The City Planning Movement in Santa Monica, California." Master's thesis, University of California, Los Angeles, 1953. 108 pp.

7048. Hunt, Rockwell D. "The Social Significance of Planning," in *Los Angeles: Preface to a Master Plan.* Ed. by George W. Robbins and L. Deming Tilton. Los Angeles, 1941. Pp. 283-96.
Author concludes that "to insure the largest measure of success in the metropolitan area, the self-interest principle and the incentive of private gain must be consciously geared to the social welfare ideal and made progressively subsidiary to the common weal."

7049. Hunt, Sumner. "For a Los Angeles Civic Center." *Saturday Night* 4 (May 12, 1923): 26.

7050. ——— "Is Public Housing Needed for Urban Redevelopment?" *American City* 63 (November 1948): 84-7.
Views of planners from several cities, including those of Charles B. Bennett on Los Angeles.

7051. Isen, Albert, and Stevens, George. "New Civic Center Construction for Torrance Envisions Growth." *Western City* 31 (December 1955): 50.

7052. Jamison, Judith N. "Administration of City Planning in Los Angeles." Master's thesis, University of California, Los Angeles, 1947. 95 pp.

7053. ——— *Coordinated Public Planning in the Los Angeles Region.* Bureau of Governmental Research, University of California, Los Angeles, *Studies in Local Government No. 9.* Los Angeles, 1948. 198 pp.

7054. —— *Regional Planning.* Los Angeles, 1952. *Metropolitan Los Angeles. A Study in Integration,* Vol. III, The Haynes Foundation, *Monograph Series No. 20.* 106 pp.

7055. Jermain, Nina. "The History of the Los Angeles Civic Center Movement, Los Angeles." Master's thesis, University of Southern California, 1934. 106 pp.

7056. Jessup, Roger W. "Los Angeles Looks Back and Ahead." *Tax Digest* 19 (January 1941): 9-10+.
Accomplishments and plans of Los Angeles county.

7057. —— "Plans of Los Angeles: A Great County Sets Its Course." *Tax Digest* 17 (January 1939): 8-9+.
Brief description of various projects undertaken or planned by the county.

7058. Klett, Gordon A. "Glendale, California: A Geographical Analysis of Use Variances (1947-1949)." Master's thesis, University of California, Los Angeles, 1951. 167 pp.

7059. Lambie, John A. "Hillside Subdivisions . . . Can Be Developed into the Most Beautiful Parts of Your City If Proper Precautions Are Observed." *American City* 74 (May 1959): 157-8.
The experience of Los Angeles County.

7060. Lamm, Ray J. "Azusa Rounds Out Twenty Year Civic Center Plan with New Fire Station." *Western City* 21 (November 1945): 34-5.

7061. Lawyer, Jay. "Well Planned Community Development Pays." *The Architect and Engineer California* 100 (January 1930): 49-52.
Palos Verdes.

7062. Los Angeles County. Regional Planning Commission. *Industrial Location Factors Survey.* [N.p., n.d.]. 74 pp.

7063. —— —— *The Southwest Area: An Area Land Use Plan.* Los Angeles, [1959]. 34 pp.

7064. "The Los Angeles Civic Center." *The Architect and Engineer* 73 (June 1923): 65-7.
Plans for new Civic Center.

7065. "L.A. Voters Approve Civic Center Plan." *Western Construction News* 22 (June 1947): 106.

7066. Mars, David. "Regional Activity in Los Angeles: Planning, Data Systems and City Charter Studied." *National Civic Review* 58 (April 1969): 169-70.

7067. Martin, Albert C. "How to Plan for the Urban Spirit." *American City* 85 (February 1970): 82+.
Includes brief description of author's new planning concepts for downtown Los Angeles and the San Fernando Valley.

7068. Marx, Wesley. "What Are They Doing to Catalina." *Los Angeles* 4 (July 1962): 34.
Residential and commercial planning.

7069. "A Master Planner Speaks His Mind." *Los Angeles* 4 (September 1962): 23+.
William Pereira on Los Angeles City planning.

7070. McGaffey, Ernest. "Los Angeles—Dreamer and Doer: The City That Visualizes Broadly and Then Has the Courage to Carry Out Plans for Tremendous Development." *Southern California Business* 1 (October 1922): 9-10.

7071. Meeker, Marchia. *San Fernando Valley Profile.* Van Nuys, 1964. 39 pp.

7072. *"Memo to City Planners . . . 'Let's Get on with It.'"* *Los Angeles* 13 (April 1968): 27-9.
Argues that Los Angeles should fulfill its promise as a super-city.

7073. Miller, Gifford W. "A Realistic Development Plan . . . Helps Monrovia, Calif., to Get Ready for the Inevitable Increase in Population and Higher Densities of Land Use." *American City* 80 (May 1965): 100-1.

7074. Millier, Arthur. " 'Always Plan Largely: Architect Lloyd Wright Recalls Ideas His Famous Father Had for Los Angeles, and Blasts Current Civic Planning." *Los Angeles* 3 (February 1962): 21-2.

7075. Mohler, Charles K. "Excess Condemnation and City Planning." *Engineering News* 76 (July 6, 1916): 20-2.
Examples from Los Angeles.

7076. Mullens, Robert H., Jr., "Analysis of Urban Residential Environments Using Color Infrared Aerial Photography; An Examination of Socio-

Economic Variables and Physical Characteristics of Selected Areas in the Los Angeles Basin." Master's thesis, University of California, Los Angeles, 1969. 132 pp.

7077. "A Notable City Planning Project." *The Architect and Engineer* 69 (June 1922): 88-9.
Palos Verdes.

7078. Owen, David W. "The Working Relationships Between City Managers and City Planners in Representative Portions of the Los Angeles Metropolitan Area." Master's thesis, University of Southern California, 1962. 156 pp.

7079. "Palos Verdes Carries Its Town Plan into Execution." *American City* 33 (December 1925): 666-7+.

7080. Pastier, John. "Mastering the Master Plan." *Los Angeles* 15 (January 1970): 30-1+.

7081. Phillips, John. "Department of Community Development Established to Meet New Challenges." *Western City* 46 (September 1970): 27+.
Pasadena.

7082. "Plan for Pedestrians." *Architectural Forum* 76 (March 1942): 10.
Plans for C. B. Troedsson's "Safety Town" exhibited at Los Angeles County Museum.

7083. "The Plan for the San Fernando Valley Developed by the Los Angeles Planning Commission." *Pencil Points* 26 (June 1945): 93-8.
New zoning system worked out by Charles B. Bennett, director of planning, Milton Breivogel, principal planner, and others.

7084. "Planning a City's Civic Center: Voters Will Decide Whether Grouping of Public Buildings Shall Be More in North Part of Downtown District." *Southern California Business* 2 (April 1923): 19+.

7085. "Post-War Building Program for City of South Gate." *The Architect and Engineer* 161 (May 1944): 33-6.

7086. "Postwar Public Works and Planning." *Western City* 20 (March 1944): 22-7; (April 1944): 26-8; (May 1944): 28-9+; (June 1944): 26-7; (July 1944): 40-1; (August 1944): 26-7.
Includes many cities in Los Angeles County.

7087. "Projects from a Masterplan for a Shoreline Development." *Arts & Architecture* 72 (June 1955): 12-5.
Long Beach.

7088. Radig, William A. "A Critical Analysis of Intergovernmental Metropolitan Planning Cooperation in the Los Angeles Area." Master's thesis, University of Southern California, 1965. 102 pp.

7089. Richards, C. Arnold. "How the Geologist Can Help Your City." *American City* 85 (June 1970): 84-6.
Author formerly worked as a geologist for several Los Angeles city departments, advising them on such matters as oil-drilling permits, hillside building permits, and design of reservoirs and pipeline systems.

7090. Richardson, John L. "A Critical Analysis of Zoning Ordinances in Los Angeles County." Master's thesis, University of Southern California, 1950. 122 pp.

7091. Ridings, Willard A. "A Model for City Planning." *Engineering News-Record* 127 (July 17, 1941): 107-8.
Scale model of Los Angeles for use in solving planning problems. A reprint of this article appears in *The Builder* 161 (October 3, 1941): 300-1.

7092. Riley, Frank. "The Cry to 'Save Los Angeles': Is Anyone Listening?" *Los Angeles* 10 (December 1965): 42-5.
Difficulty of arousing local interest in beautification, planning, and historical preservation.

7093. —— "The Man Who Will Remake Our City." *Los Angeles* 9 (February 1965): 28-32+.
Los Angeles City Planning Director, Calvin S. Hamilton.

7094. Rineer, James S. "A Study of the Administration of Zoning in the Unincorporated Areas of Los Angeles County." Master's thesis, University of Southern California, 1938. 150 pp.

7095. Robbins, George W., and Tilton, L. Deming, eds. *Los Angeles: Preface to a Master Plan*. Los Angeles, 1941. 303 pp.
Because of the importance of the individual chapters, contributed by notable experts, separate entries have been prepared and distributed in the appropriate subject categories.

7096. Roberts, Myron. "The Ambivalent City: Which Way Is It Going?" *Los Angeles* 14 (September 1969): 28-31+.

"What do the men who are actually designing, building, and planning tomorrow's Los Angeles see ahead? More congestion, smog, crime, ugliness? Or a new and better city, rebuilt on a human scale?"

7097. ———— " 'Damn It, We'd Rather Do It Ourselves. . .' " *Los Angeles* 14 (April 1969): 32-5+.

"While the city pushes forward an ambitious renewal plan, the citizens of Venice are fighting to determine their own environment . . . the outcome will be a test of many things, including the entire philosophy guiding the Planning Department."

7098. ———— "The End of the Suburbs and the Beginning of Metropolis: Can We Bring It All Together." *Los Angeles* 15 (October 1970): 28-31+.

7099. ———— "Getting Off Dead Center in Central City." *Los Angeles* 15 (January 1970): 32-3.

7100. Rockey, Ordean. "The Los Angeles Institute of Public Affairs." *American Political Science Review* 20 (1926): 866-9.

Report on a week-long series of conferences and lectures at the Southern Branch of the University of California dealing with such subjects at traffic, planning, minorities, and criminal justice.

7101. "San Gabriel Civic Center Plan Unifies New and Old." *Western City* 24 (August 1948): 20-1.

7102. Scott, Mellier G. *Metropolitan Los Angeles: One Community.* Los Angeles, 1949. 192 pp.

7103. "Seven Points of Agreement." *American City* 58 (February 1943): 5.

Summary of post-war plan for Los Angeles, prepared at behest of Mayor Fletcher Bowron by Remsen D. Bird and William H. Schuchardt.

7104. Smith, Morris D. "A Preliminary Statement of Significant Data and Issues Relating to the Development of a Master Plan for the Antelope Valley Area of Los Angeles County." Master's thesis, University of Southern California, 1958. 120 pp.

7105. "Student Research on City Planning Useful to Manhattan Beach." *Western City* 27 (July 1951): 41.

7106. "Subdivision Redesign Pays Off in Los Angeles: City's Design Experts Provide Savings to Taxpayers and Developers." *American City* 69 (September 1954): 102.

7107. "10 Ideas to Make the City Great." *Los Angeles* 13 (January 1968): 24-7.

Los Angeles.

7108. "Twelve Civic Centers for Los Angeles." *American City* 65 (June 1950): 108.

Plans for twelve branch administrative centers developed by the City Planning Commission.

7109. Wall, Henry V. "Unique Commuinty Planning Follows Expansion of Defense Industries." *American City* 57 (January 1942): 55-6.

East of Los Angeles Airport.

7110. Walter, Allan M. "Tarzana; A Community Problem; Its Analysis and Solution." Master's thesis, University of Southern California, 1947. 2 vols: thesis, 67 pp.; plans unp.

7111. Watson, Richard A. "Open Space and Planning in the San Fernando Valley." Master's thesis, University of California, Los Angeles, 1969. 157 pp.

7112. Wharton, Mel. "Burbank Has Always Known Planning: For This City 'In the Valley' Was Planned by David Burbank Nigh 50 Years Ago." *Southern California Business* 12 (July 1933): 12-3.

7113. Whitnall, Gordon. "Importance of Broad City Planning." *Southern California Business* 1 (February 1922): 9+.

Los Angeles.

7114. ———— "Regional Planning in Los Angeles." *National Municipal Review* 12 (June 1923): 333.

7115. ———— "Regional Planning Progress in the Los Angeles District." *American City* 29 (December 1923): 578-9.

7116. Willard, Walter. "Moving the Factory Back to the Land." *Sunset* 30 (March 1913): 299-304.

Mainly about the industrial town of Torrance, planned by Frederick Law Olmsted, Jr.

7117. Withey, Henry F. "Reasons Why a Municipality Needs a City Planning Department." *The Architect and Engineer of California* 46 (July 1916): 89-93.

Los Angeles city planning.

7118. Zierer, Clifford M. "The Land Use Patterns," in *Los Angeles: Preface to a Master Plan*. Ed. by George W. Robbins and L. Deming Tilton. Los Angeles, 1941. Pp. 43-59.

POLITICS

POLITICS — STATE

7119. Anderson, Totten J. "The 1956 Election in California." *Western Political Quarterly* 10 (1957): 102-16.

7120. ———, and Lee, Eugene C. "The 1964 Election in California." *Western Political Quarterly* 18 (1965): 451-74.

7121. ——— and ——— "The 1966 Election in California." *Western Political Quarterly* 20 (1967): 535-54.

7122. Barclay, Thomas S. "Reapportionment in California." *Pacific Historical Review* 5 (1936): 93-129.

Much of this article concerns the position of Los Angeles regarding various plans for altering the distribution of legislative apportionment.

7123. ——— "The Reapportionment Struggle in California in 1948." *Western Political Quarterly* 4 (1951): 313-24.

7124. Barrett, Edward L., Jr. *The Tenney Committee*. Ithaca, N.Y., 1951. 400 pp.

History of controversial state senate investigating committee.

7125. Batman Richard D. "The Road to the Presidency: Hoover, Johnson, and the California Republican Party, 1920-1924." Doctoral dissertation, University of Southern California, 1965. 314 pp.

7126. Bemis, George W. "Sectionalism and Representation in the California State Legislature, 1911-1931." Doctoral dissertation, University of California, Berkeley, 1934. 265 pp.

7127. Bennett, David H. *Demagogues in the Depression*. New Brunswick, N.J., 1969. 341 pp.

The best over-view of Francis Townsend and the background which brought about his pension plan.

7128. ——— "The Year of the Old Folk's Revolt." *American Heritage* 16 (December 1964): 48-51+.

Dr. Francis E. Townsend and his plan to aid the elderly during the depression of the 1930s. Some details of Townsend's residence in Long Beach are included.

7129. Berkowitz, Madelon H. "Progressivism and the Anti-Japanese Agitation in California." Master's thesis, University of California, Berkeley, 1966. 112 pp.

7130. Bird, Frederick L., and Ryan, Frances M. *The Recall of Public Officers: A Study of the Operation of the Recall in California*. New York, 1930. 403 pp.

7131. Burke, Robert E. "Cross-Filing in California Elections, 1914-1946." Master's thesis, University of California, Berkeley, 1947. 110 pp.

7132. Callan, Patrick M. "William Gibbs McAdoo and the California Democrats, 1932-38." Master's thesis, University of Santa Clara, 1966. 135 pp.

7133. Canterbury, John B. " 'Ham and Eggs' in California." *Nation* 147 (October 22, 1938): 408-10.

7134. Crawford, James M. "The Democratic Party of California and Political Reform, 1902-1910." Master's thesis, University of California, Berkeley, 1959. 143 pp.

7135. Davenport, F. M. "Did Hughes Snub Johnson?" *American Political Science Review* 43 (1949): 321-32.

Famous political incident in Long Beach, 1916.

7136. "Differences Between the 1938 and 1939 'Ham and Eggs' Constitutional Amendments." *Bar Bulletin* 15 (September 1939): 2-4.

7137. Erickson, George. "From Townsend to McLain: Twenty Years of Pension Planning in California, 1933-1953." Master's thesis, University of Redlands, 1953. 106 pp.

7138. Findley, James C. "Cross-Filing and the Progressive Movement in California Politics." *Western Political Quarterly* 12 (1959): 699-711.

7139. Fitzgerald, Bill. "Pension Politics in California." Master's thesis, University of California, 1951. 112 pp.

Movement especially strong in the Los Angeles area from the 1930s through the 1950s.

7140. Friedman, Lawrence J. "Reapportionment of the California Senate." Master's thesis, University of California, Los Angeles, 1965. 118 pp.

7141. Gaydowski, J. D., ed. "Eight Letters to the Editor: The Genesis of the Townsend National Recovery Plan." *Southern California Quarterly* 52 (December 1970): 365-82.

Letters published in the Long Beach press.

7142. George, Marcel. "The Townsend Plan in California, 1933-1936." Master's thesis, University of Southern California, 1953. 124 pp.

7143. Gridley, Nina. "Southern California's Attitude on Political Issues, 1910-1926." Master's thesis, University of Southern California, 1931. 93 pp.

7144. "Ham 'n Eggs: $30 Every Thursday Pension Plan Endangers Apartment House Operation." *Apartment Journal* 21 (October 1938): 22+.

7145. Hardy, Leroy C. "The California Reapportionment of 1951." Doctoral dissertation, University of California, Los Angeles, 1955. 495 pp.

7146. Harmon, Wendell E. "A History of the Prohibition Movement in California." Doctoral dissertation, University of California, Los Angeles, 1955. 371 pp.

7147. Harris, Joseph P., ed. "The 1950 Elections in the West." *Western Political Quarterly* 4 (1951): 67-96.

Included in this collection is an analysis of "The 1950 Elections in California," by Burton R. Brazil, pp. 67-75.

7148. Harris, Robert E. G. "California's Democratic Party: A Health Report." *Frontier* 7 (February 1956): 5-12.

Author concludes that the "patient is up and around but a little wobbly."

7149. Hill, Gladwin. *Dancing Bear. An Inside Look at California Politics.* Cleveland and New York, 1968. 303 pp.

7150. Hutchinson, W. H. "Prologue to Reform, the California Anti-Railroad Republicans, 1899-1905." *Southern California Quarterly* 44 (1962): 175-218.

Author describes role of Los Angeles Republicans in the fight against Southern Pacific domination.

7151. "Is the Townsend Plan a Racket?" *Los Angeles Saturday Night* 43 (March 7, 1936): 4.

7152. Larsen, Charles. "The 'EPIC' Movement in California Politics, 1933-1934." Master's thesis, University of California, Berkeley, 1945. 64 pp.

7153. Layne, Joseph G. "The Lincoln-Roosevelt League: Its Origin and Accomplishments." *Historical Society of Southern California Quarterly* 25 (1943): 97-101.

The major organ of progressives in California and Los Angeles.

7154. Lee, Eugue C., and Buchanan, William. "The 1960 Election in California." *Western Political Quarterly* (1961): 309-26.

7155. McDow, Roberta B. "A Study of the Proposals to Divide the State of California from 1860 to 1952." Master's thesis, College of the Pacific, 1952. 118 pp.

7156. McHenry, Dean E. "Urban vs. Rural in California." *National Municipal Review* 35 (July 1946): 350-4.

Struggle over legislative reapportionment.

7157. McIntosh, Clarence F. "Upton Sinclair and the Epic Movement, 1933-1936." Doctoral dissertation, Stanford University, 1955. 385 pp.

7158. McWilliams, Carey. "Lobbyist for the Aged." *Frontier* 2 (April 1951): 5-12.

George McLain's activies in behalf of old-age pensions.

7159. Merrill, M. R., ed. "The 1954 Elections in the Eleven Western States." *Western Political Quarterly* 7 (1954): 589-635.

7160. Mowry, George. *The California Progressives.* Berkeley and Los Angeles, 1951. 349 pp.

Though the emphasis on Los Angeles is limited, this is the major work on this topic.

7161. Petersen, Eric F. "Prelude to Progressivism: California Election Reform, 1870-1909." Doctoral dissertation, University of California, Los Angeles, 1969. 262 pp.

7162. Pitchell, Robert J. "The Electoral System and Voting Behavior: The Case of California's Cross-Filing." *Western Political Quarterly* 12 (1959): 459-84.

7163. —— "The Influence of Professional Campaign Management Firms in Partisan Elections in California." *Western Political Quarterly* 11 (1958): 278-300.

7164. —— "Reapportionment as a Control of Voting in California." *Western Political Quarterly* 14 (1961): 214-35.

7165. Ranstead, Donald D. "District 13: A History of the Activities of the California Communist Party, 1929-1940." Master's thesis, University of California, Davis, 1963. 222 pp.

Although this treatise deals with the party's activities on a statewide basis, it contains a good deal of information pertaining to Los Angeles County.

7166. Riley, Richard. "Upton Sinclair and the 1934 Califorina Gubernatorial Elections." Master's thesis, Chico State College, 1952. 111 pp.

7167. Rose, Alice. "Rise of California Insurgency; Origins of the League of Lincoln-Roosevelt Republican Clubs, 1900-1907." Doctoral dissertation, Stanford University, 1942. 408 pp.

7168. Saltzman, Joe, and Saltzman, Barbara. "Proposition 14: Appeal to Prejudice." *Frontier* 15 (October 1964): 5-8.

Open housing initiative; some emphasis on Los Angeles area.

7169. Shaffer, Ralph E. "Radicalism in California, 1869-1929." Doctoral dissertation, University of California, Berkeley, 1962. 400 pp.

7170. Shields, Currin V. "A Note on Party Organi-zation: The Democrats in California." *Western Political Quarterly* 7 (1954): 673-83.

7171. Sinclair, Upton. *The Epic Plan for California.* New York, 1934. [194] pp. Contents: *I, Governor of California. EPIC Answers. The Lie Factory Starts. Immediate Epic.*

7172. Singer, Donald L. "Upton Sinclair and the California Gubernatorial Campaign of 1934." Master's thesis, University of Southern California, 1966. 153 pp.

7173. Slome, Stanley M. "The Press Against Upton Sinclair: The 1934 California Gubernatorial Campaign." Master's thesis, University of California, Los Angeles, 1968. 103 pp.

7174. Townsend, Helen M. "The History of the Epic Movement, 1933-1934." Master's thesis, University of Southern California, 1940. [?] pp.

Movement was launched and centered in the Los Angeles area.

7175. Waters, Laughlin E., and Waters, Hinderaker. "A Case Study in Reapportionment—California, 1951." *Law and Contemporary Problems* 17 (1952): 440-69.

7176. Weber, Francis J. "The California Bishops and Proposition 14." *Front Line* 3 (1965): 176-84.

7177. Whiteman, Luther, and Lewis, Samuel L. *Glory Roads: The Psychological State of California.* New York, 1936. 267 pp.

Discusses a variety of political movements, many launched in Los Angeles County.

7178. Wolfinger, Raymond E., and Greenstein, Fred I. "The Repeal of Fair Housing in California: An Analysis of Referendum Voting." *American Political Science Review* 62 (1968): 753-69.

7179. Wolfson, Daniel F. "A History of the Socialist Party of Los Angeles from 1900 to 1912." Master's thesis, University of Southern California, 1964. 115 pp.

7180. Zanger, Martin. "Politics of Confrontation. Upton Sinclair and the Launching of the ACLU in Southern California." *Pacific Historical Review* 38 (1969): 383-406.

POLITICS — COUNTY

7181. Almy, Timothy A. "Campaign Spending, Los Angeles County Congressmen." Master's thesis, California State College, Long Beach, 1968. 136 pp.

7182. Bayes, Jane H. "Political Participation and Geographic Mobility in Los Angeles County, 1965." Doctoral dissertation, University of California, Los Angeles, 1967. 283 pp.

7183. Beli, Ida May P. "Voting Behavior in Los Angeles County." Master's thesis, California State College, Long Beach, 1969. 94 pp.

7184. Bell, Charles G. "Suburban Political Behavior in Los Angeles County, California." Doctoral dissertation, University of Southern California, 1966. 346 pp.

7185. Bliven, Bruce. "How Did Southern California Get That Way?" *Reporter* 26 (January 18, 1962): 39-40.
   Speculation on roots of right-wing extremism in Los Angeles area.

7186. Doss, Jesse P. "A Study of Voting Procedures and Results of Trustee Elections in Los Angeles County in 1946, 1947, and 1948." Master's thesis, University of Southern California, 1949. 109 pp.

7187. Duke, John H. "The County Committeeman and His Role in California Politics." Doctoral dissertation, University of Southern California, 1956. 320 pp.

7188. Ford, John Anson. *Thirty Explosive Years in Los Angeles County.* San Marino, 1961. 232 pp.

7189. Halberg, June E. "The Fitts-Palmer Campaign for District Attorney in Los Angeles County, 1936." Master's thesis, University of California, Los Angeles, 1940. 160 pp.

7190. Hobbs, Thadeaus H. "The Dynamics of Negroes in Politics in the Los Angeles Metropolitan Area: 1945-1956." Master's thesis, University of Southern California, 1960. 189 pp.

7191. Kinkead, Robert B. "The Attitudes Held by Employees in the Classified Service of Los Angeles County Toward Provisions Limiting Political Activity; A Preliminary Survey." Master's thesis, University of Southern California, 1965. 181 pp.

7192. Noetzli, Fred A. "Retaining Reagan to Cost $10,000,000?" *Municipal League of Los Angeles Bulletin* 2 (January 20, 1926): 2-6.
   The League's opposition to J. W. Reagan, Chief Engineer of the County Flood Control District, and the controversy over the site of the San Gabriel Dam.

POLITICS — MUNICIPAL

7193. "Abusing a Privilege." *Los Angeles Saturday Night* 12 (November 21, 1931): 3.
   Robert P. Shuler and his "presumptuous intolerance."

7194. Ahl, Frances N. "Los Angeles Mayor Survives Recall." *National Municipal Review* 21 (June 1932): 400.
   John C. Porter.

7195. Allen, Sarah. "Long Beach Recalls Its Council." *National Municipal Review* 23 (September 1934): 478.

7196. Ashkenazy, Elinor. "Peace March in Los Angeles." *Frontier* 11 (September 1960): 9-10.

7197. Baker, Lorin L. *That Imperiled Freedom.* Los Angeles, 1932. 448 pp.
   Deals with Julian Oil scandal and corruption in Los Angeles politics.

7198. Begelman, Kenneth J. "Political Activity of Appointed City Officials." Master's thesis, University of Southern California, 1964. 65 pp.
   Los Angeles.

7199. "Bitter Victory." *Time* 93 (June 6, 1969): 28-9.
   Samuel Yorty reelected mayor of Los Angeles.

7200. Blackburn, Mark. "The Carpetbaggers Take Los Angeles." *New Republic* 128 (June 15, 1953): 13-4.
   Bowron-Poulson mayoralty campaign.

7201. Blight, Reynold E. "The Recall of the Mayor of Los Angeles." *Independent* 66 (April 22, 1909): 861-3.
Recall of Arthur C. Harper.

7202. Bonelli, William G. *Billion Dollar Blackjack.* Beverly Hills, [1954]. 230 pp.
A political tirade against the Los Angeles Times and its publisher.

7203. Bowen, William M. *Vicious Attack on Men Who Saved Exposition Park. The Issue: Bowen's "Activities" Which Recovered and Improved Park or Neylan's Vicious Political Thrust.* [Los Angeles?, 1915]. 19 pp.

7204. "Bowron Beaten." *Newsweek* 41 (June 8, 1953): 32-3.
Norris Poulson wins mayoralty by 35,000 votes.

7205. "Bowron's Biggest Battle." *Newsweek* 41 (February 23, 1953): 30.
Personality sketch of Los Angeles Mayor Fletcher Bowron, his fight for federal public housing, and his then-upcoming campaign against Rep. Norris Poulson.

7206. Briegel, Kaye L. "The History of Political Organizations Among Mexican-Americans in Los Angeles Since the Second World War." Master's thesis, University of Southern California, 1967. 93 pp.

7207. Brownell, Robert C. "The Who, What, Where, When and Why of Manchester Boddy." *Frontier* 1 (May 15, 1950): 7-8.
Broddy's political views and speculation on his motives for entering the 1950 U.S. senatorial race.

7208. Caplan, Jerry S. "The CIVIC Committee in the Recall of Mayor Frank Shaw." Master's thesis, University of California, Los Angeles, 1947. 142 pp.

7209. Carew, Harold D. "Technocracy as Graham Laing Views It." *Touring Topics* 25 (March 1933): 12-3+.
Laing, a Cal Tech economics professor, was author of *Towards Technocracy.*

7210. Carney, Francis M. "The Decentralized Politics of Los Angeles." *Annals of the American Academy of Political and Social Science* 353 (May 1964): 107-21.

7211. Carpenter, Willard. "Liberal v. Conservative: The Issues Are Clear in California's 16th District." *Frontier* 11 (October 1960): 8-10.
Alphonzo Bell vs. Jerry Pacht.

7212. Charles, Jack. "Why They Call the City Council Chambers the Cave of the Winds." *Los Angeles* 2 (November 1961): 16-9.
Los Angeles councilmanic system.

7213. *Chronological Record of City Officials — Supplement —July 1, 1937 —June 30, 1965.* Comp. by the Municipal Reference Department, Los Angeles Public Library. Los Angeles, 1966. Unp. (approx. 450 pp.)

7214. *Chronological Record of Los Angeles City Officials. 1850-1939.* Comp. under the direction of the Municipal Reference Library. Los Angeles, 1938. 2 vols.
Vol. II covers period 1889-1939. An index is available, entitled *Los Angeles City Officials. 1850-1936. Alphabetical Index.* Comp. under the direction of the Municipal Reference Library. Los Angeles, 1938. 164 pp.

7215. Clinton, Clifford E. *The Clock Strikes Twelve: A Little Journey into Los Angeles As It Was, As It Is and As It Can Be.* Los Angeles, 1945. 14 pp.

7216. ——— "Has Los Angeles a New Boss?" *American Mercury* 52 (May 1941): 633-5.

7217. Clodius, Albert H. "The Quest for Good Government in Los Angeles, 1890-1910." Doctoral dissertation, Claremont Graduate School, 1953. 567 pp.

7218. Clover, Sam T. "Miles S. Gregory: Alert Compromise Candidate for Mayor." *Saturday Night* 5 (May 2, 1925): 1.
Includes an outline of Gregory's political program.

7219. Collins, James A. "An Analysis of Some Characteristics of Voters in the Covina School Bond Election of 1956." Master's thesis, Claremont Graduate School, 1956. 64 pp.

7220. Collins, James H. "Mayor Porter and His Job." *Southern California Business* 9 (July 1930): 10-1.

7221. Cook, Beverly B. "Political Organization and Ideology in a Nonpartisan City: A Case Study of Claremont, California." Doctoral dissertation, Claremont Graduate School, 1962. 202 pp.

7222. Cray, Ed. "Rock, Sand and Politics." *Frontier* 12 (September 1961): 7-9.
The influence of Consolidated Rock Products, Inc., on politics in the town of Irwindale.

7223. ——— "Should the Police Engage in Politics: The Issues in the Hannon Case." *Frontier* 16 (August 1965): 5-7.
Author accuse police officials of condoning right-wing activities of officers, while attempting to purge Michael Hannon, a leftist activist.

7224. Creel, George. "Unholy City: Los Angeles Is Up to Its Civic Ears in a Fight on Political Corruption and All-Around Sin. It Has Gone after Its Woes at the Source and, Between Bombings, Results Are Beginning to Show. *Collier's* 104 (September 2, 1939): 12-3+.

7225. Criswell, R. L. "Election Plan for Los Angeles City." *Pacific Municipalities* 34 (November 1920): 435-8.

7226. Crouch, Winston W. "John Randolph Haynes and His Work for Direct Government." *National Municipal Review* 28 (September 1938): 434-40+.

7227. Dahan, Arthur W. "Electoral and Population Geography of South Central Los Angeles, 1932-1966." Master's thesis, University of California, Los Angeles, 1970. Unp.

7228. DeWolfe, Anne. "I Love You, Susan B. Anthony: An Encounter with the Los Angeles Feminist Movement." *Los Angeles* 14 (December 1969): 40-3+.

7229. Dimock, Marshall E. "Recall Movement Against Mayor Porter of Los Angeles." *National Municipal Review* 20 (December 1931): 742-3.

7230. Donovan, Richard A. "Roybal Rouses the Ninth: A Los Angeles Mexican-American District Learns How to Make Its Political Voice Heard." *Reporter* 2 (January 17, 1950): 7-9.
Congressman Edward Roybal.

7231. Douglas, Helen Gahagan. "They Come of Age." *Frontier* 1 (November 15, 1949): 5-6.

Election of Edward Roybal to Los Angeles City Council, and speculation on the significance of this event.

7232. Duncan, Ray. "What Makes Jimmy Run?" *Los Angeles* 9 (March 1965): 26-30+.
James Roosevelt's challenge to Samuel Yorty for Los Angeles mayoralty.

7233. Dunlop, George H. "Proportional Representation at Los Angeles." *National Muniicipal Review* 3 (1914): 92-5.

7234. Dykstra, C[larence] A. "Los Angeles Returns to the Ward System." *National Municipal Review* 14 (April 1925): 210-2.

7235. "Elephant with a Headache: Mayor Poulson, in Office Two Years, Finds Problems of Los Angeles Multiplying at a Frightening Tempo." *Frontier* 6 (September 1955): 13-8.

7236. Emmett, William. "Mania in Los Angeles." *Nation* 106 (January 17, 1918): 58-9.
Prosecution of the leaders of the Conference of Christian Pacifists.

7237. "Fallen Angels." *New Republic* 160 (June 9, 1969): 7.
Yorty-Bradley mayoralty contest.

7238. "Feels the Halter Draw." *Los Angeles Saturday Night* 13 (January 21, 1933): 3.
Robert P. Shuler's plan to run for governor.

7239. Finney, Guy W. *Angel City in Turmoil: A Story of the Minute Men of Los Angeles in Their War on Civic Corruption, Graft and Privilege.* Los Angeles, 1945. 211 pp.

7240. Gaddis, Tom. "Recall in Lawndale." *Frontier* 3 (September 1952): 24.
Recall of president of school board, who had opposed additional school expenditures.

7241. Germond, Jack W. "L.A.'s About to Say 'So Long Sam!' " *New Republic* 160 (May 24, 1969): 10.
Mayoraalty election, 1969: "All signs indicate that Bradley soon will be mayor."

7242. Gouldner, Helen B. "The Organization Woman: Patterns of Friendship and Organizational Commitment." Doctoral dissertation, University

of California, Los Angeles, 1959. 221 pp.
League of Women Voters of Los Angeles.

7243. Haas, Lucien C. "Los Angeles: The Issues at Stake in the City Election." *Frontier* 6 (April 1955): 7-9.
Discussion of various contests, with focus on how liberal candidates are "up against the usual propaganda."

7244. ———— "Redondo Beach: What Oil Wants, Oil Gets." *Frontier* 7 (December 1955): 7-8+.
Alleged machinations involved in securing public approval for a slant-drilling program off the coast of this beach city.

7245. Hall, Martin. "Roybal's Candidacy and What It Means." *Frontier* 5 (June 1954): 5-7.
Candidacy of Edward Roybal for the Los Angeles City Council.

7246. Henley, David C. "The Clerical Conservative; A Study of Conservative and Ultra-Rightist Protestant Ministers and Organizations of the Los Angeles Area." Master's thesis, University of Southern California, 1964. 128 pp.

7247. Hindman, Jo. "Los Angeles: City in Turmoil." *American Mercury* 84 (April 1957): 141-7.

7248. Hobbs, Thadeaus H. "The Dynamics of Negroes in Politics in the Los Angeles Metropolitan Area, 1945-1956." Master's thesis, University of Southern California, 1960. 189 pp.

7249. Hooker, Phyllis A. "Voting Behavior in Sixteen Cities in Los Angeles County, 1920-1940." Master's thesis, University of California, Los Angeles, 1946. 82 pp.

7250. "House-Cleaning in Los Angeles." *Outlook* 91 (April 3, 1909): 757-8.
Recall of Mayor Arthur C. Harper.

7251. "How Los Angeles Is Misserved." *Los Angeles Saturday Night* 12 (August 6, 1932): 3.
Allegation that, due to the influence of Senators Johnson and Shortridge, nearly all naval supplies for San Pedro are purchase in San Francisco.

7252. Huckshorn, Robert J., and Young, Charles E. "Study of Voting Splits on City Councils in Los Angeles County." *Western Political Quarterly* 13 (1960): 479-97.

7253. Hutson, William G. "Voting Attitudes of Mexican-American Residents of Belvedere—East Los Angeles." Master's thesis, University of Southern California, 1960. 116 pp.

7254. "The Intellectual Discovers City Hall." *Los Angeles* 14 (January 1969): 27+.
Author contends that Los Angeles intellectuals should involve themselves in local politics.

7255. Jaques, Janice. "The Political Reform Movement in Los Angeles, 1900-1909." Master's thesis, Claremont Graduate School, 1948. 125 pp.

7256. Kalionzes, George W. "Some Aspects of Intergovernmental Lobbying in California with Special Emphasis on the Los Angeles Area." Doctoral dissertation, University of Southern California, 1951. 214 pp.

7257. Kerby, Phil. "Race, Television and Yorty." *Nation* 208 (March 31, 1969): 403-5.
Assessment of some of the candidates in the 1969 mayoralty primary.

7258. ———— "Victory for a Specter." *Nation* 208 (June 16, 1969): 749-50.
Yorty's defeat of Bradley in 1969 mayoralty election.

7259. Lissner, Meyer. *Reform in Los Angeles; Retrospective—Prospective; an Address . . . Before the City Club of Los Angeles, Saturday, April 10, 1909.* [Los Angeles, 1909]. 15 pp.

7260. "The Los Angeles Primary." *Sunset* 34 (June 1915): 1078-9.
Mayoralty primary of 1915.

7261. "Los Angeles, Where the People Rule." *Hampton's Magazine* 26 (May 1911): 657-8.
Laudatory assessment of various forms of direct democracy.

7262. Macfarlane, Peter C. "What Is the Matter with Los Angeles?" *Collier's* 48 (December 2, 1911): 28+.
Question refers to the fact that, since Job Harriman won a plurality in the December 5 primary. Los Angeles might well elect as its mayor this exponent of "pronounced radicalism."

7263. "Magnet in the West." *Time* 88 (September 2, 1966): 14-9.
Los Angeles political scene.

7264. Mayo, Charles G. "The 1961 Mayoralty Election in Los Angeles; The Political Party in a Nonpartisan Election." Doctoral dissertation, University of Southern California, 1963. 231 pp.

7265. ———— "The 1961 Mayoralty Election in Los Angeles: The Political Party in a Nonpartisan Election." *Western Political Quarterly* 16 (1964): 325-37.

7266. McCurtain, Marilyn E. "Political Ecology of Three Metropolitan Areas of California: San Francisco, Los Angeles, San Diego, 1850-1950." Master's thesis, University of California, Berkeley, 1955. 133 pp.

7267. Metcalf, Allen C. "A Negro Congressman from Los Angeles." *Frontier* 9 (April 1958): 7-11.
Argues that an equitable redrawing of congressional district boundaries in Los Angeles would result in the election of a Negro congressman.

7268. Mobilization for Democracy. *Los Angeles Against Gerald L. K. Smith: How a City Organized to Combat Native Fascism.* [Los Angeles, 1945]. [36] pp.

7269. "A Negro Mayor for Los Angeles?" *U.S. News & World Report* 66 (April 14, 1969): 12.
Tom Bradley's showing in April primary.

7270. Nelson, Howard J. "The Vernon Area, California—A Study of the Political Factor in Urban Geography." *Annals of the Association of American Geographers* 42 (June 1952): 177-91.

7271. Norton, Edmund. "Politics in Los Angeles." *The Public* 14 (November 24, 1911): 1190-2.
Mayoralty campaign of 1911, Owens Valley project, and single-taxers.

7272. Norton, Richard H. *Reminiscences of an Agitator; With a Diagnosis and a Remedy for Present Economic Conditions.* Los Angeles, 1912. 91 pp.
On the use of direct legislation and recall in Los Angeles City.

7273. "The Old Corruption: The Year Los Angeles Created Las Vegas.' *Los Angeles* 13 (November 1968): 29.

7274. Patterson, Beeman C. "The Politics of Recognition: Negro Politics in Los Angeles 1960-1963."

Doctoral dissertation, University of California, Los Angeles, 1967. 263 pp.

7275. Pfiffner, J. M. "Entire City Council Recalled in Long Beach." *Public Management* 16 (September 1934): 283-4.

7276. Poe, Elizabeth. "Spring Street Massacre." *Frontier* 4 (July 1953): 23-4.
Discrepancy in amount and fairness of coverage given by the *Times* to Fletcher Bowron and Norris Poulson in the 1953 mayoralty campaign.

7277. Pomeroy, Eltweed. "The First Discharge of a Public Servant." *Independent* 58 (January 12, 1905): 69-71.
Recall of Councilman J. P. Davenport.

7278. Quint, Howard H. "Gaylord Wilshire and Socialism's First Congressional Campaign." *Pacific Historical Review* 26 (1957): 327-40.

7279. "The 'Recall' of the Mayor of Los Angeles." *Independent* 66 (February 25, 1909): 432-3.
Proposed recall of Mayor Arthur C. Harper.

7280. "Reform over Los Angeles." *Time* 32 (December 5, 1938): 14.
First weeks of the Bowron administration.

7281. "Renegade's Triumph." *Time* 77 (June 9, 1961): 15.
Yorty defeats Poulson, 1961 mayoralty election.

7282. Riegler, Gordon. "The Attitudes of the People of Los Angeles Toward Prohibition from the Recommendation of the Eighteenth Amendment by Congress to the Time of Its Adoption." Master's thesis, University of Southern California, 1924. 118 pp.

7283. Riha, Jeanne. "The Bitter Bread: What Happens to Victims of a Witchhunt?" *Frontier* 9 (February 1958): 9-11.
What happend to victims of House Committee in Los Angeles. Brief interviews with 15 Southern Californias (nearly all Angelenos) who had been investigated by HUAC and/or the State Senate Fact-Finding Committee on Un-American Activities: what they thought of their experience and what had happened to them since.

7284. Riley, Frank. "The Power Structure." *Los Angeles* 11 (December 1966): 28-31.
Los Angeles.

7285. "Rise of New Political Figure Seen in Mayor Bowron's Election." *Apartment Journal* 27 (May 1945): 13.

7286. Roberts, Myron. "If It's Bradley . . ." *Los Angeles* 14 (May 1969): 26-9+.
If he is elected mayor, "what kind of administration and leadership can we expect from [Thomas] Bradley . . . ?"

7287. ———— "The Plot to Seize Los Angeles." *Los Angeles* 14 (January 1969): 24-6+.
Mayoralty contest of 1969.

7288. ———— "Summertime: Will the Livin' Be Easy?" *Los Angeles* 13 (June 1968): 24-6+.
Councilman Tom Bradley, Assemblyman William Greene, and the Los Angeles Negro community.

7289. Roberts, Smith. "Culver City Circus." *Frontier* 7 (November 1955): 12-3.
Culver City politics.

7290. Rogers, Stanley. "The Attempted Recall of the Mayor of Los Angeles." *National Municipal Review* 21 (July 1932): 416-9.
John C. Porter.

7291. "Roosevelt vs. Yorty." *Frontier* 16 (March 1965): 5-10.
Mayoralty election, 1965.

7292. "Sad Sam." *Time* 93 (April 11, 1969): 28-9.
Thomas Bradley outpolls 13 other candidates, including Samuel Yorty, in 1969 mayoralty primary election.

7293. Sanders, Leonard R. "Los Angeles and Its Mayors, 1850-1925." Master's thesis. University of Southern California, 1968. 189 pp.

7294. Scigliano, Robert G. "Democratic Political Organization in Los Angeles." Master's thesis, University of California, Los Angeles, 1952. 131 pp.

7295. Sherwood, Frank P. "That Curious Prop. 13 and Vernon, Los Angeles' Tax-Proof Island." *Frontier* 5 (October 1954): 10-1.
Proposition 13—a measure to permit Vernon to write its own charter.

7296. Shuler, Robert P. *The Strange Death of Charlie Crawford.* Los Angeles, [c1931]. 64 pp.

Crawford's death in 1931 was linked to political corruption in the city.
The Rev. Shuler wrote a series of pamplets, published in Los Angeles, on a variety of politically oriented subjects: *Contempt and the Judge* [c1930], 64 pp.; *The Criminal Lawyer* [c1930], 64 pp.; *Jailed* [c1930], 96 pp.; *Millionaries and "Hired Girls"* [c1930], 64 pp., and *Silenced* [c1932]. 64 pp.

7297. "Shuler's Excessive Ego." *Los Angeles Saturday Night* 12 (December 19, 1931): 3.
Robert P. Shuler's plan to run for the Senate.

7298. Sloan. Dolores. "Public Relations in the 1964 Campaign of Robert A. Chrisman, 49th Assembly District." Master's thesis, Claremont Graduate School, 1965. 113 pp.

7299. Smith, Roy L. "Reform Election in Los Angeles." *Christian Century* 53 (September 1936): 1293.
Harlan Palmer vs. Buron Fitts for the office of district attorney.

7300. "Sun and Shade." *Time* 32 (September 26, 1938): 12.
Fletcher Bowron elected mayor of Los Angeles.

7301. Taft, Clinton J. "City of Fallen Angeles." *Forum* 99 (May 1938): 259-65.
Comment on Los Angeles politics during administration of Mayor Frank L. Shaw.

7302. "Tighe Woods May Be Held in Contempt of Congress Because of L.A. Action. *Western Housing* 34 (November 1950): 6-7.
Los Angeles Housing Expeditor accused, among other things, of collusion with Los Angeles Tenants' Council.

7303. Vale, Rena M. "A New Boss Takes Los Angeles." *American Mercury* 52 (March 1941): 299-307.
Clifford E. Clinton, allegedly "the person to 'see' in Los Angeles."

7304. Weisenberg, Charles M. "Delegates Bumper to Bumper." *Reporter* 23 (July 7, 1960): 19-20.
Speculation on effect that Los Angeles' spatial dispersion and traffic problems might have on 1960 Democratic Convention.

7305. "Why Regan [sic] Should Go." *Municipal*

League of Los Angeles Bulletin 2 (November 15, 1924): [2-5].

League's reasons for advocating dismissal of J. W. Reagan, Chief Engineer of the County Flood Control District.

7306. Willard, Charles D. "A Political Experiment." *Outlook* 78 (October 22, 1904): 472-5.

First use of the recall, against Los Angeles Councilman J. W. Davenport.

7307. ——— "The Recall in Los Angeles." *La Follette's* 1 (August 7, 1909): 7-9+.

7308. Wilson, James Q. "Los Angeles: The Search for Power," in *The Amateur Democrats Club Politics in Three Cities.* Chicago, 1962. Pp. 96-127.

7309. Works, John D. "A City's Struggle for Political and Moral Freedom." *Arena* 41 (March 1909): 353-7.

Recall of Los Angeles Mayor Arthur C. Harper.

7310. "Yortytoons." *Newsweek* 71 (February 12, 1968): 67.

Feud between the mayor of Los Angeles and Los Angeles *Times* publisher Otis Chandler.

POPULATION

7311. Beach, Frank L. "The Transformation of California, 1900-1920: The Effects of the Westward Movement on California's Growth and Development in the Progressive Period." Doctoral dissertation, University of California, Berkeley, 1963. 349 pp.

7312. Bechdolt, Burley V. "Some External Diseconomies of Urban Growth and Crowding: Los Angeles." Doctoral dissertation, University of Southern California, 1970. 402 pp.

7313. Bell, Wendell. "A Comparative Study in Methodology of Urban Analysis." Doctoral dissertation, University of California, Los Angeles, 1952. 207 pp.

7314. California. Commission on Immigration and Housing. *Community Survey Made in Los Angeles.* San Francisco, 1919. 74 pp.

7315. Champlin, C. D. "Our Disappearing Land:

The Population Upsurge Continues; Will Los Angeles Run Out of Land?" *Southern California Prompter* 1 (November 1960): 16-8.

7316. Clarke, E. P. "Growth of California Cities." *Overland Monthly* 88 (October 1930): 303+.

Comparative study of rates of population growth.

7317. Clyne, Anthony. "Los Angeles." *Contemporary Review* 132 (October 1927): 491-6.

Principally about reasons for tremendous growth.

7318. Collins, James H. "Census Surprises of 1930 —and 1940." *Southern California Business* 9 (June 1930): 20.

Growth of Southern California communities.

7319. Copeland, Clem A. *Population of the City of Los Angeles from 1890 to 1932.* [Los Angeles], c1926. [19] pp.

7320. Cunnigham, Ray M. "A Pupil Population Study in the City of Long Beach, California." Master's thesis, University of Southern California, 1931. 36 pp.

7321. Dahan, Arthur W. "Electoral and Population Geography of South Central Los Angeles, 1932-1966." Master's thesis, University of California, Los Angeles, 1970. Unp.

7322. Davis, Jehiel S. "Los Angeles, the New Fifth City [in Population Rank]." *The Journal of Geography* 30 (May 1931): 190-200.

Disusses, among other things, location, industries, harbor, and "checkerboard City Limits."

7323. Davis, Paul. "Population and Its Effect on the Land Use Pattern and Land Valuations in Los Angeles County from 1940 to 1953." Master's thesis, University of Southern California, 1954. 169 pp.

7324. ——— "Population Pressure and Its Effect on the Land Use Pattern and Land Valuations in Los Angeles County from 1940 to 1953." Master's thesis, University of Southern California, 1954. 169 pp.

7325. De Graaf, Lawrence B. "Negro Migration to Los Angeles, 1930 to 1950." Doctoral dissertation, University of California, Los Angeles, 1962. 358 pp.

7326. Duncan, Beverly; Sabagh, George, and Van Arsdol, Maurice D., Jr. "Patterns of City Growth." *American Journal of Sociology* 67 (1962): 418-29.
"Cohort analysis of Los Angeles residential areas indicates that the rapidity of redistribution varies directly with both the rate of population growth and the ratio of new dwellings to incremental population."

7327. Fisher, J. Donald. "A Historical Study of the Migrant in California [to 1940]." Master's thesis, University of Southern California, 1945. 100 pp.

7328. Gaertner, Miriam L. "A Study of Transient Girls in Los Angeles Including Fifty-Eight Case Digests." Master's thesis, University of Southern California, 1939. 251 pp.

7329. Gordon, Margaret S. *Employment Expansion and Population Growths. The California Experience, 1900-1950.* Berkeley and Los Angeles, 1954. 192 pp.

7330. "The Growth of Los Angeles." *Out West* 19 (November 1903): 534-5.

7331. Hall, Nason E. "Similarity of Social Characteristics and Neighboring Behavior: A Study of Four Metropolitan Neighborhoods." Doctoral dissertation, University of California, Los Angeles, 1962. 181 pp.

7332. Hamilton, Helen. "A Study of the Transient Boy in Los Angeles County in 1939." Master's thesis, University of Southern California, 1939. 119 pp.

7333. Hanson, Earl. *Los Angeles County Population and Housing Data; Statistical Data from the 1940 Census.* Los Angeles, 1944. 30 pp.

7334. ———, and Beckett, Paul. *Los Angeles: Its People and Its Homes.* Los Angeles, 1944. 206 pp.

7335. Hightower, Sharon W. "The Changing Structure of the Los Angeles Metropolitan Area: An Investigation of Demographic and Functional Patterns." Master's thesis, Claremont Graduate School, 1966. 127 pp.

7336. "How Fast Is Los Angeles Growing?" *Southern California Business* 1 (December 1922): 14.

7337. "Inglewood Gains 710% in 5 Years." *Southern California Business* 5 (September 1926): 20+.

7338. James, T. F. "New World in the West." *Cosmopolitan* 146 (May 1959): 25-33.
Migration to California since 1940.

7339. Jones, Elizabeth J. "Familism, Suburbanization, and Residential Mobility in a Metropolis." Doctoral dissertation, University of Southern California, 1967. 173 pp.
Los Angeles.

7340. Koehler, Freed W. "The Unattached Transient: A Study of 2000 Unattached Adult Male Transients Registered by the Los Angeles, California Area of the Federal Transient Service." Master's thesis, University of Southern California, 1937. 72 pp.

7341. Lofstedt, Anna C. "A Study of the Mexican Population in Pasadena, California." Master's thesis, University of Southern California, 1923. 42 pp.

7342. Los Angeles. Chamber of Commerce. Research Department. *Impact of Future Population Growth on Employment, Retail Sales, Personal Income, Bank Deposits, Motor Vehicles. Projections from 1960 by 5-Year Intervals.* Los Angeles, [1961]. 24 pp.

7343. ——— ——— Research Department. *Population Projections to 1980 By Five Year Intervals, 14 Southern California Counties.* Los Angeles, [1958?]. 36 pp.

7344. "Los Angeles—A City of Cities." *Southern California Business* 14 (August 1935): 26.
Los Angeles' eleven statistical areas.

7345. "Los Angeles Climbs to Fifth Place: New Figures Show That Only Four Cities, All of Them East of the Rockies, Have More Residents Than Pacific Coast Metropolis." *Southern California Business* 2 (February 1923): 9-10.

7346. "L.A. Crowding for Fourth Place." *Southern California Business* 2 (January 1924): 11.
Population statistics.

7347. "Los Angeles, Fifth City in the United States, Facts and Figures to Support the Claim:

An Interview with Sydney I. Wailes." *Los Angeles Realtor* 7 (August 1927): 20-1.
Results of a survey prepared by Wailes-Smith Company of Los Angeles.

7348. "Los Angeles Has Third of Population." *Southern California Busines* 2 (November 1923): 38.
"Los Angeles County has more than one-third of all the school pupils in the state of California."

7349. "Los Angeles Reaches 900,000 Mark: Computations, Based on Building Operations and Utilities Installations, Show Large Gain in Past Five Months." *Southern California Business* 2 (June 1923): 19.

7350. Lummis, Charles F. "A Lesson in the Census." *Land of Sunshine* 14 (January 1901): 61.
Population of Los Angeles compared with other California cities.

7351. Marion, Guy E. "What of the Future? Population Growth, Its Development, and What It Means to the Apartment Industry." *Apartment Journal* 19 (October 1936): 14-5+.
Los Angeles and suburbs.

7352. Martin, Helen B. "A Youth Survey of Downey, California." Master's thesis, University of Southern California, 1941. 128 pp.

7353. Mattison, Dick. "The Many Faces of L.A." *Westways* 57 (June 1965): 40-1.
Ethnic polyglot of Los Angeles.

7354. Maxwell, Laurence E. "Residential Distribution of Occupations in Los Angeles." Master's thesis, University of California, Los Angeles, 1966 108 pp.

7355. "The Metropolitan T." *Los Angeles* 11 (January 1966): 28-30.
"Outlined by freeways, the high density, high rise 'center' for Los Angeles now assumes a definite shape and structure, beginning downtown and stretching to the ocean."

7356. Miller, Curtis R. "A Typology of Spanish Surname Census Tracts in Los Angeles County." Master's thesis, University of Southern California, 1960. 132 pp.

7357. Mitchell, John W. "Los Angeles: In the Making." *American City* 2 (1910): 149-57.
Growth of population and public facilities.

7358. Mittelbach, Frank G., and Burns, Leland S. *Profile of the Los Angeles Metropolis; Census Chart Book.* Los Angeles, 1963. Unp.

7359. Panunzio, Constantine. "Growth and Character of the Population," in *Los Angeles: Preface to a Master Plan.* Ed. by George W. Robbins and L. Deming Tilton. Los Angeles, 1941. Pp. 29-42.

7360. Pegrum, Dudley F. *Residential Population and Urban Transport Facilities in the Los Angeles Metropolitan Area.* Los Angeles, 1964. 42 pp.

7361. Phelps, G. Allison. "The Bubble That Never Broke." *Southern California Business* 5 (March 1926): 14+.
Los Angeles growth.

7362. "Population of Los Angeles County—1930." *California Journal of Development* 20 (September 1930): 23.
California State Chamber of Commerce Research Department Economic Survey Report No. 11, Series 1930-1931.

7363. Shevky, Eshref, and Lewin, Molly. *Your Neighborhood: A Social Profile of Los Angeles.* The Haynes Foundation, *Phamplet Series No. 14.* Los Angeles, 1950. 35 pp.

7364. ———, and Williams, Marilyn. *Social Areas of Los Angeles: Analysis and Typology.* Berkeley and Los Angeles, 1949. 172 pp.

7365. "A Short Story About a City's Seven League Boots." *Southern California Business* 7 (February 1928): 30-1.
Los Angeles growth.

7366. Smith, Elizabeth C. "The Transient Family in Southern California." Master's thesis, University of Southern California, 1935. 71 pp.

7367. Smith, R. L. P. "The Index of a Great City." *Southern California Business* 5 (December 1926): 14-5+.
Compilation of Los Angeles City Directory.

7368. Spaulding, Charles B. "The Development of Organization and Disorganization in the Social

Life of a Rapidly Growing Working-Class Suburb Within a Metropolitan District." Doctoral dissertation, University of Southern California, 1939. 380 pp.

7369. Stein, Walter J. "California and the 'Dust Bowl' Migration." Doctoral dissertation, University of California, Berkeley, 1969. 513 pp.

7370. Thomas, William L., Jr. *Man, Time, and Space in Southern California: A Symposium.* Washington, D. C., 1959. 120 pp.
A supplement to the *Annals of American Geographers,* 1959.

7371. Tilden, Freeman. "Los Angeles: The Tenth Tourist Never Goes Home." *World's Work* 60 (September 1931): 51-7.

7372. Uono, Koyoshi. "The Factors Affecting the Geographical Aggregation and Dispersion of the Japanese Residences in the City of Los Angeles [1885-1926]." Master's thesis, University of California, 1927. 149 pp.

7373. Van Loan, Wallace. "An Analytical Study of the Physical Distribution of Population in Los Angeles County [1946-1956]." Master's thesis, University of Southern California, 1957. 138.

7374. Williams, Dean L. "Some Political and Economic Aspects of Mexican Immigration into the United States Since 1941; With Particular Reference to This Immigration in the State of California." Master's thesis, University of California, Los Angeles, 1950. 93 pp.

7375. Woehlke, Walter V. "The Corn Belt in California: How Climate Is Moving the Middle West to the Shores of the Pacific." *Sunset* 47 (August 1921): 29-32.
Los Angeles growth.

7376. ———— "How Long, Los Angeles? An Examination of the Root System That Feeds the Angel City's Astonishing Growth." *Sunset* 52 (April 1924): 8-11+.

7377. Woodhead, William. "Los Angeles: The Most Rapidly Growing City in America." *Sunset* 26 (January 1911): 124.

7378. "The World's Greatest City—in Prospect. *Worlds Work* 47 (December 1923): 140-2.

Current population growth indicates that Los Angeles is destined to become the world's largest city.

7379. Yeatman, Walter C. *A Study of Population Trends in Los Angeles and the Nation.* Los Angeles, 1933. 45 pp.

7380. Zeronian, Joseph P. "A Narrative History of Migrating Oklahomans in California, 1935-1940." Master's thesis, University of Southern California, 1965. 103 pp.

PUBLIC TRANSPORTATION

PUBLIC TRANSPORTATION — LOCAL AND SUBURBAN MASS TRANSIT

7381. "The Abandonment of the Watts Line." *Headlights* 21 (December 1959): 5.
Los Angeles Metropolitan Transit Authority (ex-Pacific Electric) trolley car line from Downtown Los Angeles to Watts.

7382. Ames, Neil. "The Street Car." *Los Angeles Saturday Night* 43 (March 7, 1936): 9.
Humorous impressions of Los Angeles streetcars.

7383. Andrus, Alec V. "Mass Transportation in the Los Angeles Metropolis, a Case Study." Master's thesis, Claremont Graduate School, 1968. 94 pp.

7384. "Another Huntington Project in California." *Street Railway Journal* 21 (June 27, 1903): 951.
Los Angeles Interurban Railway.

7385. Arnold, Bion J. *Report on the Transportation Problem of Los Angeles.* [N.p.], 1911. 20 pp.
From *The California Outlook* 11 (November 4, 1911): Supplement.

7386. "Auto Snipers and Trolley Cars." *Sunset* 34 (January 1915): 47.
About Jitneys, which were private automobiles whose operators solicited riders waiting for streetcars. Their first appearance in the United States was in Los Angeles in July 1914.

7387. "Bad Mass Transit a Factor in Watts Riots." *American City* 81 (November 1966): 32+.

7388. Batman, D. "Wartime Transportation in Los Angeles." *Civil Engineering* 13 (November 1943): 537-40.

7389. Bauer, John. "Public Utilities: Los Angeles Five-Cent Fare Franchises Invalid." *National Municipal Review* 19 (February 1930): 110-2.
Los Angeles Railway.

7390. "Board Reports on Grade Crossings: Interurban Line in Los Angeles Shold Elevate or Depress Tracks—City Line Should Use Viaducts or Subways in Business Districts." *Electric Railway Journal* 46 (July 24, 1915): 160-1.

7391. Borbridge, J. J., and Veysey, Laurence. "The Mount Lowe Railway." *Headlights* 13 (June 1951): 3-5.
Line operated to mountain resort by Pacific Electric.

7392. Bradbury, Ray. "Los Angeles: Orange Without a Navel." *Frontier* 15 (February 1964): 7-8+.
Proposes a 14-point program for solving the mass transit problem in Los Angeles.

7393. "Bus Radio 'Silent Alarms' Bring Help Fast." *American City* 84 (June 1969): 170.
Emergency equipment installed in 200 busses operated by the Southern California Rapid Transit District.

7394. "Buses Replacing Street Cars." *Los Angeles Saturday Night* 15 (February 23, 1935): 3.
Contention is that, although New York is replacing streetcars, this is not necessarily the way to improve Los Angeles' public transportation.

7395. Central Business District Association, Los Angeles. *Transit Study, Los Angeles Metropolitan Area.* Los Angeles. 1944. 39 pp.

7396. "Constructive Ideas Advanced by Business Men." *Electric Railway Journal* 73 (February 2, 1929): 189-90.
Los Angeles City Club report on local transportation.

7397. Crump, Spencer. *Henry Huntington and the Pacific Electric: A Pictorial Album.* Los Angeles, 1970. 112 pp.

7398. ——— *Ride the Big Red Cars: How Trolleys Helped Build Southern California.* Los Angeles, 1962. 240 pp. New ed., [Costa Mesa, 1970]. 256 pp.

7399. "Danger in Bus Proposition." *Los Angeles Saturday Night* 15 (May 4, 1935): 3.
Expresses opposition to Proposition 2, a measure to establish a municipally owned local bus system.

7400. Dektar, Cliff. "End of the Line." *Westways* 55 (March 1963): 26-8.
Los Angeles' last streetcars replaced with buses.

7401. "Discussion of Proposed Franchise Ordinance in Los Angeles." *Electric Railway Journal* 38 (September 9, 1911): 437.

7402. Donovan, Frank P., Jr. "Huntington's Palace on Wheels." *Westways* 45 (December 1953): 8-9.
Henry E. Huntington's private trolley car, the *Alabama.*

7403. Duke, Donald. "Mount Lowe Railway." *Pacific Railway Journal* 1 (February 8, 1955): 1-12.

7404. ———, comp. "Pacific Electric Railway; A Pictorial Album of Electric Railroading." *Pacific Railway Journal* 2 (September 1958): 1-63.

7405. ——— "Two Angels on a String; The Story of Angels Flight, Los Angeles' Funicular Railway." *Pacific Railway Journal* 2 (February 1958): 1-12.

7406. Dumke, Glenn S. "Early Interurban Transportation in the Los Angeles Area [to 1911]." *Historical Society of Southern California Quarterly* 22 (1940) 131-49.
A condensation of author's thesis at Occidental (next entry).

7407. ——— "The Growth of the Pacific Electric and Its Influence Upon the Development of Southern California to 1911." Master's thesis, Occidental College, 1939. 131 pp.

7408. Dunn, W[illiam]. E. "The Application of Established Legal Principles to the Jitney." *Electric Railway Journal* 46 (September 11, 1915): 503-5.

7409. *Electric Line Trips: Balloon Route.* Los Angeles, n.d. Unp.
Pacific Electric trolley excursion.

7410. "Electric Railways at Los Angeles." *Electric Railway Journal* 34 (October 2, 1909): 568-70.
Discusses the Pacific Electric Los Angeles Railway, and Los Angeles and Mt. Washington Cable Railway.

7411. Elliott, Clifford A. "Construction and Maintenance of Grade Crossings on Pacific Electric." *Electric Railway Journal* 55 (May 15. 1920): 995-8.

7412. —— "Dual Control Signals on the Pacific Electric." *Electric Railway Journal* 56 (August 14, 1920): 321-2.

7413. —— "Home Attractions Keep Track Laborers Satisfied." *Electric Railway Journal* 52 (July 27, 1918): 150-2.
Pacific Electric.

7414. —— "Pacific Electric Adopts Flood-Control Measures." *Electric Railway Journal* 52 (August 17, 1918): 297.

7415. —— "Pacific Electric Has Complete Parking Program." *Electric Railway Journal* 54 (September 13, 1919): 517.

7416. —— "Shelters and Stations on Pacific Electric's Interurban Lines." *Electric Railway* 53 (April 12, 1919): 733-4.

7417. —— "Shockless Crossing on Pacific Electric." *Electric Railway Journal* 56 (August 21, 1920): 361.

7418. —— "Terminal at San Pedro Completed." *Electric Railway Journal* 56 (December 4, 1920): 1147-8.
Pacific Electric.

7419. "Expansion by Los Angeles Railway." *Electric Railway Journal* 71 (February 4, 1928): 215.

7420. "The Facts of the Huntington Deal in California." *Street Railway Journal* 25 (January 21, 1905): 136.
Acquisition by Henry E. Huntington of minority interests giving him half-ownership of the Pacific Electric and Los Angeles Interurban Railway.

7421. "Fifty-Million-Dollar Holding Company for Southern California Lines Abandoned." *Street Railway Journal* 22 (August 22, 1903): 274.
Hellman-Huntington interurbans.

7422. "Financing in Los Angeles." *Electric Railway Journal* 42 (December 13, 1913): 1258.
Los Angeles Railway.

7423. "Fire Destroys Mt. Lowe Property." *Street Railway Journal* 26 (December 23, 1905): 118.
Mountain resort served by Pacific Electric.

7424. "First Subway West of New York Opened." *Electric Railway Journal* 66 (December 19, 1925): 1087.
Pacific Electric Subway Terminal on Hill Street between Fourth and Fifth.

7425. "The Fitzgeralds Go West." *Time* 44 (December 18, 1944): 82+.
Report of the sale of the Los Angeles Railway to American City Lines, Inc., along with a brief description of the city's public transportation facilities.

7426. Fizell, Russell W. "A Study of Certain Economic Aspects of the Transportation System of Los Angeles." Master's thesis, University of Southern California, 1924. 116 pp.

7427. "414 Buses Now Used by Pacific Electric Railway: Growth of Operation at Los Angeles Recited by Official at Interstate Commerce Commission Hearing." *Electric Railway Journal* 75 (August 1931): 431+.

7428. "4,000,000 Expenditure Before Public: Pershing Square Subway Franchise for Pacific Electric to Be Determined by Los Angeles Voters." *Electric Railway Journal* 61 (May 26, 1923): 899.
Subway Terminal built on Hill Street between Fourth and Fifth.

7429. "A Four-Track Line on the Pacific Coast." *Street Railway Journal* 27 (June 9, 1906): 926.
Pacific Electric line to Watts.

7430. "Funeral Car of the Los Angeles Railway Company." *Electric Railway Journal* 34 (July 17, 1909): 110.

7431. Garfain, Daniel. "An Aggregate Time-Series Analysis of Public Transportation Usage in the Los Angeles Metropolitan Area." Master's thesis, University of Southern California, 1968. 104 pp.

7432. "George A. Damon on Needs at Los Angeles." *Electric Railway Journal* 39 (March 2, 1912): 363.

Discussion by the Dean of the School of Engineering, Throop Polytechnic Institute Institute, of street railway problems in the Los Angeles vicinity.

7433. Gilliss, C. M. "New District Formed in Los Angeles." *Western City* 41 (May 1965): 24-6.
Southern California Rapid Transit District.

7434. "Good Night, Sweet Streetcar." *Los Angeles* 5 (March 1963): 40-1.
Los Angeles' last streetcars replaced with buses.

7435. Harper, Howard K. "A Survey of Public Transportation in the Los Angeles City School Districts." Master's thesis, University of Southern California, 1934. 130 pp.

7436. Haverlin, Carl. *Romance of Transportation and the Story of the Packard Building.* Los Angeles, 1929. 32 pp.

7437. Heald, Weldon F. "The Pasadena Mountain Railway." *Westways* 42 (January 1950): 10-1.
Pacific Electric line to Mt. Lowe.

7438. Hilton, George W., and Due, John F. *The Electric Interurban Railways in America.* Stanford, 1960. 463 pp.

Deals mainly with the Midwest interurban lines, but has a brief sketch (pp. 406-13) of the Pacific Electric and its antecedent companies.

7439. Hoodenpyl, Geo[rge] L. "Long Beach Sells a Jitney Bus Franchise." *Pacific Municipalities* 31 (January 1917): 565.
Jitney "buses" were simply large automobiles.

7440. "How Santa Monica Successfully and Profitably Operates Bus System." *Western City* 14 (December 1938): 15-7.

7441. Hungerford, Edward. "California and Her Tractions — Part II." *Electric Railway Journal* 56 (September 11, 1920): 490-3.

Deals mainly with the Pacific Electric and Los Angeles Railway. (Part I deals with San Francisco.)

7442. Hutchinson, W. M. "Control Equipment for Pacific Electric Railway." *Electric Railway Journal* 59 (June 24, 1922): 991-5.

7443. "Interlocking Installation on Pacific Electric." *Electric Railway Journal* 45 (May 15, 1915): 946-7.

7444. Interurbans. *Official Car Records, Pacific Electric Railway Co.* [Los Angeles, 1964]. 64 pp. *Interurbans Special* 38.

7445. Israel, Lazear. "Los Angeles: Abandonment Due in March." *Headlights* 24 (November 1962): 3.
Los Angeles' last streetcars to be replaced with buses.

7446. —— "Los Angeles: Narrow-Gauge Streetcar Service Ends." *Headlights: The Magazine of Electric Railways* 25 (April 1963): 8-12.
Abandonment of last Metropolitan Transit Authority (ex-Los Angeles Railway) trolley lines, March 31, 1963.

7447. James, George W. *Scenic Mount Lowe and Its Wonderful Railway.* 5th ed., Los Angeles, 1905. 126 pp.

7448. Jeffrey, J. G. "Merit System Works Well in Los Angeles." *Electric Railway Journal* 61 (April 28. 1923): 721-2.
Los Angeles Railway.

7449. —— "The Street Railway as a City Builder." *Los Angeles Realtor* 5 (January 1926): 17+.
Mainly history of Los Angeles Railway.

7450. —— "Training Platform Men: New Plan at Los Angeles Involves Practical Instruction on Several Lines of a Division in Turn." *Electric Railway Journal* 56 (August 14, 1920): 322.

7451. "The Jitney Bus Situation." *Sunset* 34 (May 1915): 863-4.
Los Angeles.

7452. Johnson, Norman K. "The First LAMTA Streetcar Extension." *Headlights* 20 (July 1958): 6.
LAMTA — Los Angeles Metropolitan Transit Authority.

7453. —— "A Look at 'LAMTA.'" *Headlights* 20 (November 1958): 5-6.

7454. Joseph, James. "Business Machines Keep L.A. Transit's Stock Room Coordinated." *Bus*

Transportation 30 (January 1951): 31-3.
Los Angeles Transit Lines, successor to Los Angeles Railway.

7455. ———— "Pasadena Knows Where It's Going." *Bus Transportation* 29 (July 1950): 36-8.
Pasadena City Lines bus system.

7456. Kaplan, Walter. "The Rise of Interurban Motor Bus Transportation in California." Master's thesis, Stanford University, 1950. [?] pp.

7457. La Barbera, Joseph. "Joe Fawkes and the Aerial Swallow." *Westways* 56 (February 1964): 26-7.
Ill-fated transportation innovation at Burbank.

7458. Lanham, Stanley M. "Re-Zoning Ups Revenue for L.A. Transit." *Bus Transportation* 30 (March 1951): 30-3+.

7459. "Leading in Street-Car Installation." *Southern California Business* 5 (June 1926): 30.
Los Angeles.

7460. League of Women Voters of Los Angeles County. *Too Many Wheels: The Transit Dilemma in Los Angeles County.* [Los Angeles], 1967. 14 pp.

7461. Lewis, E[dwin] L. "The Rise and Decline of the Jitney in Its Birthplace." *Electric Railway Journal* 46 (September 11, 1915): 500-2.

7462. Locke, William J. "Jitney Bus Ordinances." *Pacific Municipalities* 29 (March 1915): 121-3.
Ordinances in six western cities, including Los Angeles, Long Beach and Pasadena.

7463. Los Angeles. Metropolitan Traffic Association. *Express Busses on Freeways: Transit Study, 1953, Los Angeles Metropolitan Area.* [Los Angeles, 1953]. 41 pp.

7464. ————. Transportation Engineering Board. *A Transit Program for the Los Angeles Metropolitan Area.* Los Angeles, [1939]. 67 pp.

7465. Los Angeles Railway Corp. *Fare and Service of the Los Angeles Railway.* [Los Angeles], 1921. Unp.

7466. "Los Angeles: Future of Streetcars Dim." *Headlights* 24 (July 1962): 3-4.

Impending replacement of Los Angeles' last trolleys with buses.

7467. "Los Angeles Interurban Railways." *Street Railway Journal* 19 (June 14, 1902): 754.

7468. "Los Angeles: SCRTD to Replace LAMTA." *Headlights: The Magazine of Electric Railways* 26 (July 1964): 9-10.
Los Angeles Metropolitan Transit Authority superseded by Southern California Rapid Transit District.

7469. "Los Angeles Works to Solve Traffic Problem." *American City* 62 (April 1947): 137.
Los Angeles Transit Lines orders 120 new trackless trolleys.

7470. MacMurray, G. J. "Parking Places at Electric Railway Stations Help to Relieve Downtown Congestion." *American City* 43 (December 1930): 142-3.
Some discussion of Pacific Electric.

7471. "Mayor Cryer and the Street Railway Problem." *Municipal League of Los Angeles Bulletin* 4 (February 28, 1927): 3-4.
Concerns petition of Los Angeles Railway for a raise in fares.

7472. McClees, E. D. *Suburban Trips: Eight Delightful Trips out of Los Angeles via Pacific Electric and L.A. Inter-Urban Railways.* Los Angeles, 1904. 64 pp.

7473. McClintock, Miller. "Reducing Delays to Street Car Traffic." *Electric Railway Journal* 70 (October 8, 1927): 656-8.
Los Angeles.

7474. McGroarty, John S. "A Pageant of Transportation." *Sunset* 33 (October 1914): 749-52.
Pacific Electric.

7475. "More About Municipal Busses or Not." *Pacific Electric Magazine* 17 (April 10, 1937): 3.
The management of the Pacific Electric and the Los Angeles Railway adamantly opposed the municipal bus system periodically proposed for Los Angeles.

7476. Moreau, Jeffrey. *The Los Angeles Railway Pictorial.* [Los Angeles, 1964]. Unp.
This entry and the three which follow are issues

of the *Western Traction Quarterly* devoted to the subjects indicated.

7477. —— *The Mount Lowe Pictorial.* [Los Angeles, 1964]. 51 pp.

7478. —— *The Pacific Electric Pictorial.* [Los Angeles 1964]. 69 pp.

7479. ——, and Walker, James, Jr. *Glendale and Montrose.* [Los Angeles, 1966]. 64 pp.
Electric Railway.

7480. Munger, D. A. *The Trolley Trail Through the Heart of Southern California.* Los Angeles, 1910. Unp.
Description of Pacific Electric's special tours.

7481. " 'Muni' Operation Again Confronts Us." *Pacific Electric Magazine* 20 (October 10, 1939): 5.
Municipal bus system proposal.

7482. "The Municipal Bus Operation—A Dying Institution?" *Western City* 37 (December 1961): 18-25.
Includes: "Culver City Among First to Set Up System," by W. W. Chandler; " 'Rags to Riches' Story for Montebello Line," by Leslie L. Doolittle; "Santa Monica Bus Lines Show $200,000 Profit," by George Bundy; "Torrance Bus System Operates Since 1941," by M.A. Chamberlain.

7483. Nadeau, Remi. "Remember the Big Red Cars?" *Westways* 52 (March 1960): 20-1.
Pacific Electric.

7484. "New California Line Opened." *Street Railway Journal* 22 (November 21, 1903): 922-3.
Pacific Electric to Whittier.

7485. "New Pacific Electric Repair Shops." *Electric Railway Journal* 50 (July 21, 1917): 95-9.
Torrance.

7486. Olin, Blaine. "Municipal Buses: Santa Monica Solves Its Transportation Problem." *Public Ownership of Public Utilities* 17 (January 1935): 3-4.

7487. O'Rourke, Lawrence W. "[City of] Commerce Provides Free Public Transit System." *Western City* 42 (July 1966): 50.

7488. Oswald, Harry C. "Pacific Electric." *Headlights* 23 (May 1961): 1-5.

7489. Pacific Electric Railway Company. *Rules and Regulations of the Transportation Department.* Los Angeles, 1913. 98 pp.

7490. "Pacific Electric Completes Repair Layout at Long Beach." *Electric Railway Journal* 74 (July 1930): 496.

7491. "The Pacific Electric Railway Company's System." *Street Railway Journal* 23 (February 27, 1904): 308-18.

7492. "The Pacific Electric Railway Equipment." *Street Railway Journal* 20 (August 23, 1902): 246-8.

7493. "Pacific Electric Railway Experiments with Motor Bus Feeders." *Electric Railway Journal* 48 (August 19, 1916): 314.

7494. "Pacific Electric Railway Terminal at Los Angeles." *Electric Railway Journal* 50 (August 25, 1917): 307-9.

7495. "Pacific Electric Subway Terminal, Los Angeles." *The Architect and Engineer* 82 (July 1925): 68-70.

7496. Pegrum, Dudley F. *Residential Population and Urban Transport Facilities in the Los Angeles Metropolitan Area.* Los Angeles, 1964. 42 pp.

7497. "Photoplay Projected Publicity Plan of Pacific Electric Railway." *Electric Railway Journal* 60 (July 29, 1922): 165.

7498. Pontius, D. W. "California Interurbans and the Bus." *Electric Railway Journal* 60 (October 7, 1922): 556-7.

7499. —— "Municipal Busses or Not?" *Pacific Electric Magazine* 17 (April 10, 1937): 2-3.

7500. —— "Railroad Looks into the Future." *Southern California Business* 3 (October 1924): 24+.
Pacific Electric.

7501. Post, Robert C. "The Fair Fare Fight: An Episode in Los Angeles History." *Southern California Quarterly* 52 (1970): 275-98.

Legal battle over attempt of Los Angeles Railway to increase its fares.

7502. ——— "Street Railways in Los Angeles: Robert Widney to Henry Huntington [1874-1910]." Master's thesis, University of California, Los Angeles, 1967. 311 pp.

7503. "Power Station, Rolling Stock and Dispatching System of the Pacific Electric Railway." *Street Railway Journal* 23 (March 12, 1904): 397-405.

7504. Price, C. E. "A Unique Railway." *Scientific American* 87 (August 9, 1902): 86.
Angels Flight.

7505. Prior, Tom. "Santa Monica's Big Blue Buses Don't 'Smell.'" *Western City* 41 (August 1965): 50-1.
Malabite odor-control program.

7506. "Putting the Brakes on the Motor Bus." *Sunset* 34 (April 1915): 645-6.
Los Angeles Jitneys.

7507. Ramsay, Robert A., and Veysey, Laurence. "Pacific Electric: Battle to Save Subway On." *Headlights: America's Popular Electric Railway Magazine* 16 (March 1954): 6.
Reaction to announced plan of Metropolitan Coach Lines to abandon the ex-Pacific Electric Subway Terminal.

7508. "Rapid Transit Between Los Angeles and Glendale." *Electric Railway Journal* 73 (February 23, 1929): 336.
Pacific Electric.

7509. "Recent Jitney Data from Los Angeles." *Electric Railway Journal* 48 (July 22, 1916): 139.

7510. "Recent Work of the Los Angeles Railway." *Street Railway Journal* 17 (June 1, 1901): 642-6.

7511. "Recommendation for Municipal Ownership Provision in New Los Angeles Charter." *Electric Railway Journal* 40 (August 10, 1912): 225.

7512. "Reinforced Concrete Paint Shop." *Electric Railway Journal* 40 (July 27, 1912): 126.
Los Angeles Railway.

7513. "Repair Shop Practice of the Pacific Electric Railway Company." *Street Railway Journal* 23 (March 19, 1904): 30-9.

7514. "Report on Los Angeles." *Electric Railway Journal* 73 (February 2, 1929): 218.
Los Angeles City Club recommendations expected to promote interest in street railway problem.

7515. "Roping the Wild Jitney." *Sunset* 34 (March 1915): 432-3.
Legal attempts of Los Angeles Railway to curb Jitneys.

7516. "Report on Los Angeles Transit Conditions: B[ion] J. Arnold Finds Great Traffic Congestion in Los Angeles and Recommends the Construction of Additional Tracks by the Municipality." *Electric Railway Journal* 38 (October 21, 1911): 907-9.

7517. Reynolds, Del [M.]. "Around the Trolley Trail." *Out West,* new series, 1 (December 1910): 41-8.
Trolley lines of the Pacific Electric and the Los Angeles Pacific.

7518. Ronnie, Art. "Cable Car Days on Mt. Washington." *Westways* 48 (December 1956): 14-5.
Funicular railway that ran up Mt. Washington in Highland Park from terminus at Marmion Way and Ave. 43 between 1909 and 1919.

7519. Sachse, Richard. "Transit: The Movement of People," in *Los Angeles: Preface to a Master Plan.* Ed. by George W. Robblns and L. Deming Tilton. Los Angeles, 1941. pp. 101-13.

7520. Sanders, Eric. "Last Western Interurban." *Dispatcher* (Railway Historical Society of San Diego) Issue 35 (March 19, 1961): 1-8.
LAMTA (ex-Pacific Electric) line to Long Beach, last interurban electric railway line west of Chicago.

7521. Schofield, Miles. "Angels Ride for a Nickel." *Westways* 53 (December 1961): 28-9.
Angels Flight.

7522. Shonerd, Roscoe E. "Investigation of Los Angeles Electric Railway Traffic Conditions." Bachelor's thesis, University of Southern California, 1912. 15 pp.

7523. Shoup, Paul. "An Electric Railway Paradise." *Electric Railway Journal* 46 (September 11, 1915): 475-80.
Pacific Electric.

7524. "Shuttle Bus Parking System Used by Inglewood at Christmas Peak." *Western City* 31 (January 1955): 49.

7525. "Significance of Pacific Electric Deal." *Out West,* new series, 1 (December 1910): 69-70.
Speculation on consequences of Henry E. Huntington's sale of his half-interest in the Pacific Electric to E. H. Harriman.

7526. "Significance of Subway Opening." *Saturday Night* 6 (December 5, 1925): 3.
Pacific Electric terminal on Hill Street.

7527. Sims, Donald. "Los Angeles Transit." *Railroad Magazine* 62 (January 1954): 36-59.
Los Angeles Transit Lines (successor to the Los Angeles Railway), at the time the largest streetcar operation in the western United States.

7528. "Skip-Stops as Seen by L. A. Railway." *Municipal League of Los Angeles Bulletin* 2 (December 15, 1924): [7].
Explains why the Los Angeles Railway continued to pursue a policy that was supposed to be a temporary wartime power-conservation measure.

7529. Smith, Howard G. "The Role of Interurban Railways in the Los Angeles Area." Master's thesis, San Fernando Valley State College, 1964. 123 pp.

7530. "Southern California on the Move: Electric Transportation Lines Handle a Larger Number of People in a Year Than Reside in America and Europe." *Southern California Business* 1 (May 1922): 22+.
Los Angeles Railway and Pacific Electric.

7531. Steele, Rufus. "The Red Car of Empire." *Sunset* 31 (October 1913): 710-7.
Pacific Electric.

7532. "Street Car Fares Here and Abroad." *Los Angeles Saturday Night* 8 (April 14, 1928): 4.
Comparisons cast doubt on the fairness of the California Railroad Commission's denial of a fare boost to the Los Angeles Railway.

7533. Swett, Ira L. *Cars of Pacific Electric.* Volume I, *City & Suburban Cars.* Los Angeles, 1962. Volume II, *Interurban & Deluxe Cars.* Los Angeles, 1965. 445 pp.
This and the ensuing thirteen entires were published as "Interurbans Specials" of *Interurbans Magazine,* which is edited by Swett. In nearly all cases the title indicates the subject matter of the entire publication, although in some instances there are a few pages of non-related material included at the end.

7534. ——— *Die Day in Los Angeles.* Los Angeles, 1964. 144 pp.
The last day of streetcar operation in Los Angeles.

7535. ——— *Lines of Pacific Electric.* Los Angeles, 1953, *et seq.* Various pagination.
This publication was issued in four main parts with six supplements over a period of more than a decade. The total number of pages is a approximately 260.

7536. ——— *Los Angeles and Redondo Electric Railway.* Los Angeles, 1956. 72 pp.
A company eventually consolidated into the Pacific Electric.

7537. ——— *Los Angeles Pacific.* Los Angeles, 1956. 112 pp.
A company eventually consolidated into the Pacific Electric.

7538. ——— *Los Angeles Pacific Album.* Los Angeles, 1967. 148 pp.

7539. ——— *Los Angeles Railway.* Los Angeles, 1952. 84 pp.

7540. ——— *Los Angeles Railway Roster of Cars.* Los Angeles, 1953. 72 pp.

7541. ——— *Los Angeles Railway's Pre-Huntington Cars, 1890-1902.* Los Angeles, 1962. 72 pp.

7542. ——— *Pacific Electric Album of Cars.* Los Angeles, 1967. 210 pp.

7543. ——— *Pacific Electric All Time Roster.* Los Angeles, 1953. 48 pp.

7544. ——— *Pacific Electric Box Motors and Locomotives.* Los Angeles, 1966. 302 pp.
Freight-hauling equipment.

7545. ——— *Pacific Electric in Pomona.* Los Angeles, 1969. 117 pp.

7546. —— *Pacific Electric Roster of Cars.* Los Angeles, 1945. 32 pp.

7547. Tax Relief Association of California. *Tax Facts* 5 (November 1926): 25+.
On the Los Angeles Railway's fare-increase application.

7548. Titcomb, H. B. "The Bus and the Trolley." *Electric Railway Journal* 57 (January 8, 1921): 81-3.
Pacific Electric.

7549. "Traffic and Transportation: Mr. [Henry] Huntington's Reasons for Opposing Rate-Making Ordinance." *Electric Railway Journal* 39 (June 8, 1912): 993.

7550. "Traffic Features of Some of the Pacific Coast Roads." *Electric Railway Journal* 36 (October 8, 1910): 630-42.
Includes Los Angeles interurbans.

7551. "Transportation Facilities of Southern California." *Los Angeles Saturday Night 150th Birthday of Los Angeles: Fiesta and Pre-Olympiad.* Special Issue (1931): [13].

7552. "Transportation Problem of Los Angeles." *Electric Railway Journal* 38 (November 18, 1911): 1063-7.
Recommendations for street railway improvement.

7553. "A Trip to Mount Lowe: A World-Famed Mountain and Railway Lies at Los Angeles' Doorstep." *Apartment Journal* 19 (July 1936): 17+.

7554. "Union Depot at Los Angeles Built for Long-Haul Buses." *Engineering News-Record* 83 (December 25, 1919): 1080.
Located at Fifth and Los Angeles Streets, utilized initially by seven interstate and local bus companies.

7555. [Van Norden, Rudolph W.]. *Pacific Electric Railway Company.* [Los Angeles, 1912]. [109] pp.

7556. —— "Pacific Electric Railway Consolidation." *Journal of Electricity, Power and Gas* 28 (March 23, 1912): 261-7.

7557. Veysey, Laurence R. "Changes and Talk of Future Changes on LAMTA." *Headlights* 20 (May 1958): 6.
Los Angeles Metropolitan Transit Authority.

7558. —— *A History of the Rail Passenger Service Operated by the Pacific Electric Railway Since 1911 and by Its Successors Since 1953.* Los Angeles, 1958. 144 pp.
"Interurbans Special," No. 21, published by *Interurbans.* Based on author's "The Pacific Electric Railway Company, 1910-1953: A Study in the Effects of Economic, Social, and Political Forces Upon American Local Transportation." (B.A. thesis, Yale University, 1953). 549 pp.

7559. —— "Los Angeles MTA in Business, States Policies." *Headlights* 20 (April 1958): 4-5.
MTA takes over operation of city's two major public transportation companies, Los Angeles Transit Lines (ex-Los Angeles Railway), and Metropolitan Coach Lines (ex-Pacific Electric).

7560. —— "Los Angeles Transit Lines Announces New Bus Substitution Program." *Headlights: America's Popular Electric Railway Magazine* 16 (October 1954): 7.
Conversion of six of the eleven remaining streetcar lines.

7561. —— "PE Santa Ana, Newport Lines Quit." *Headlights* 12 (July 1950): 5.
Discontinuance of last Pacific Electric rail passenger service to penetrate outside Los Angeles County.

7562. —— "Pacific Electric Today." *Headlights: America's Popular Electric Railway Magazine* 15 (May 1953): 1.

7563. —— "West Basin Line Enjoys Freak Passenger Runs." *Headlights: America's Popular Electric Railway Magazine* 17 (November 1955): 4.
Because harbor drawbridge demaged after being rammed by a ship, Los Angeles-San Pedro Red Cars rerouted around West Basin of harbor.

7564. —— "Yes, Los Angeles Has a Subway: P. E's. Hill St. Subway Terminal is the Heart of Busy Suburban Traffic." *Headlights* 13 (September 1951): 1-4.

7565. Walker, J. P. "Montebello's New [Municipal] Bus Lines." *Pacific Municipalities* 45 (September 1931): 448.

7566. Walker, James W., Jr. "Los Angeles: Remaining PCCs Sold to Cairo." *Headlights: The Magazine of Electric Railways* 27 (August 1965) : 2.
Last streetcars owned by Southern California Rapid Transit District sold to Cairo Transport Authority.

7567. Waterhouse, Alfred J. "The Trolley-Man and the Angel Hosts." *Sunset* 30 (April 1913) : 390-3.
Henry E. Huntington.

7568. Wheelock, Walt[er]. *Angels Flight.* Glendale, 1961. 36 pp.
Los Angeles funicular railway.

7569. "Whittier Sets Up Municipal Bus System to Get Workers to Their Jobs." *Western City* 18 (June 1942) : 18-9.

7570. Wiggins, Wallace S. "Remember the Miniature Railway?" *Westways* 41 (May 1949) : 6-7.
Three-mile loop railway built at Venice by Abbott Kinney.

7571. Wilcox, Delos F. "Memoranda on Purchase of Los Angeles Railway." *Municipal League of Los Angeles Bulletin* 4 (June 25, 1927) : 4-5.

7572. —— *Preliminary Report on Local Transportation Policy.* Los Angeles, 1927. [18] pp.
Recommendation that City of Los Angeles purchase Los Angeles Railway.

7573. "Wilcox's Conclusions on Street Railway Problem." *Municipal League of Los Angeles Bulletin* 4 (June 25, 1927): 1.
Delos F. Wilcox was an independent consultant hired by the City of Los Angeles to advise it in a fare dispute with the Los Angeles Railway.

7574. Willard, Walter. "Moving the Factory Back to the Land." *Sunset* 30 (March 1913) : 299-304.
Includes discussion of the Pacific Electric.

7575. Willis, Richard B. "The First LAMTA Abandonment." *Headlights* 20 (July 1958) : 6.
Buses substituted for trolleys on the Los Angeles-Bellflower line (ex-Pacific Electric).

7576. Wootton, William. "Last of the Yellow Cars." *Dispatcher* (Railway Historical Society of San Diego) Issue 42 (March 3, 1963) : 1-14; Issue 45 (December 31, 1963) : 1-8.
Los Angeles' last streetcars replaced with buses.

7577. "Would Retain Dr. Wilcox, Franchise Expert, to Advise City." *Municipal League of Los Angeles Bulletin* 4 (December 31, 1926): 1+.

7578. Wright, Mabel L. "The History of the Pacific Electric Railway." Master's thesis, University of Southern California, 1930. 73 pp.

PUBLIC TRANSPORTATION — RAILROADS

7579. Anderson, Willard V. "$7.50 to L. A." *Trains* 10 (August 1950) : 36-42.
Southern Pacific passenger service between Los Angeles and San Francisco.

7580. Arnebergh, Roger W. "U.S. Supreme Court Rulings Hold Grade Separation Costs Must Be Shared." *Western City* 29 (December 1953) : 28-9.
Cases involve Los Angeles grade crossings.

7581. Brashear, H. R. "Los Angeles Takes Hand in Rates." *Southern California Business* 4 (November 1925) : 22+.
Freight rates.

7582. Charlton, Robert. "The Story of a Great Tunnel." *Sunset* 13 (July 1904) : 219-24.
The Southern Pacific's Santa Susana tunnel.

7583. Creakbaum, W. M. "Experts Tackle an Important Job." *Southern California Business* 3 (June 1924) : 15+.
Problem of establishing competitive freight rates.

7584. Deming, Bill. "The Malibu Line." *Los Angeles* 2 (April 1961) : 22-3.
Malibu and Port Los Angeles Railroad, 1905-30.

7585. Ditzel, Paul. "Forty Trains a Day." *Westways* 57 (March 1965) : 39-41.
Southern Pacific's Taylor Yard, along the east bank of the Los Angeles River.

7586. —— "The Monday Morning Banana Train." *Westways* 50 (December 1958) : 10-1.
Connecting with Wilmington docks.

7587. "Elevated Tracks a Necessity." *Saturday Night* 3 (November 18, 1922) : 3.
Argues that elimination of railroad grade-crossings is essential to the continued progress of Los Angeles.

7588. Gilman, H. L. "Southland Ticket Office: Santa Fe Railway System, Hollywood, California." *The Architect and Engineer* 180 (February 1950): 14-5.

7589. "Greatest Diesel Locomotive to Hasten California Travel." *Los Angeles Saturday Night* 16 (October 19, 1935): 5.
Diesel locomotives begin powering certain Santa Fe trains to and from Los Angeles.

7590. Gregson, Fred P. "Southwest Shippers Want Equal Rates: All Los Angeles Asks Is Fairness and a Guarantee That the Best of Service Will Be Rendered." *Southern California Business* 1 (March 1922): 11+.

7591. Heinly, Burt A. "The Case of the Santa Fe Railroad." *Municipal League of Los Angeles Bulletin* 3 (August 1925): 3+.
Controversy over building Santa Fe branch line to the harbor district.

7592. ———. "Santa Fe Enters Harbor." *Municipal League of Los Angeles Bulletin* 3 (May 31, 1926): 6-7.

7593. "Here Is the S. P.'s Challenge to Travel Competition." *Los Angeles Saturday Night* 44 (April 17, 1937): 5.
New 90-mph San Francisco-Los Angeles "Daylight" streamliners.

7594. "How About a Railroad Right Down Your Main Street?" *Western City* 7 (July 1931): 11.
One-time Union Pacific line on Ocean Avenue in Long Beach.

7595. "League for Acquiring Rights of Way to Complete Harbor Belt Line." *Municipal League of Los Angeles Bulletin* 5 (January 31, 1928): [3].

7596. Lightner, D. Roy. "Los Angeles as a Railway Center." Master's thesis, University of Southern California, 1916. 99 pp.

7597. Moody, Charles A. "Railroad Building Between Los Angeles and Salt Lake City." *Land of Sunshine* 14 (June 1901): 513-21.

7598. Murphy, Janice K. "A History of Local Steam Railroads of Los Angeles, 1870-1900." Master's thesis, University of Southern California, 1930. 70 pp.

7599. "PE's Bustling Freight." *Trains* 8 (June 1948): 18-21.
Freight-hauling and switching activities of Pacific Electric Railway (a Southern Pacific subdivision).

7600. Peck, Tom C. "In the Old Days of Terminal Fame." *Southern California Business* 1 (August 1922): 11-2.
Los Angeles Terminal Railway, now part of Union Pacific.

7601. "Plan of Joint Railroads to Give Traffic Relief." *Saturday Night* 6 (January 2, 1926): 11.
Plan for re-routing railroads in central Los Angeles.

7602. "Railroad Freight Yard Goes Modern: Remotely-Controlled Car Retarders and Power Switches Being Installed at What Is to Be the West Coast's Most Modern Freight Yard." *Western Construction News* 24 (September 15, 1949): 89+.
Southern Pacific's Taylor Yard, Los Angeles.

7603. Rose, Howard B. "Union Pacific Builds Long Beach Cutoff." *Western Construction News and Highways Builder* 7 (August 25, 1932): 475-7.

7604. Seidman, Laah. "The History of the Santa Fe Railroad in California." Master's thesis, University of Southern California, 1930. 57 pp.

7605. Sharpe, Edward H. "Growth of Interurban Freight Service." *Southern California Business* 1 (March 1922): 27+.

7606. Sims, Donald. "The L. A. Story: Diesels Where the Dodgers Went." *Trains* 19 (July 1959): 16-23.
Comprehensive description of railroad operations in and around Los Angeles.

7607. ———. "The L. A. Story: Over the Mountains to the City of Angels." *Trains* 19 (August 1959): 42-50.

7608. "Southern Pacific's New 'Daylight' Streamliners." *Western Machinery and Steel World* 28 (April 1937): 145.

7609. Stump, Frank V. "All Trains Unload in Los Angeles." *Southern California Business* 1 (September 1922): 33.

7610. ——— "The Great Southwest Moves Closer: Los Angeles Has Become the Center of a Rapid Freight Shipping System That Proves of Value to a Large Trade Territory." *Southern California Business* 1 (December 1922): 15-6.

7611. "Union Pacific's New Broadway Office." *Saturday Night* 7 (February 26, 1927): 17.
　　Los Angeles ticket office.

7612. "When Santa Fe's Super Chief Flashes Over the Rails." *Los Angeles Saturday Night* 44 (May 8, 1937): 9.
　　New Chicago-Los Angeles streamliner.

7613. Willard, C[harles] D. "Salt Lake and Los Angeles Railway." *Land of Sunshine* 13 (October 1900): 301-5.

PUBLIC TRANSPORTATION — RAILROAD TERMINALS

7614. Butler, Merrill. "Los Angeles Union Railroad Terminal . . . Solution of a Major Municipal Problem: Construction under Way by City and Southern Pacific, Santa Fe and Union Pacific Companies on Project Discussed Since 1911." *Western Construction News* 11 (August 1936): 256-9.

7615. Dunlop, George H. "League's Position on Union Terminal." *Municipal League of Los Angeles Bulletin* 2 (August 15, 1924): [15-6].

7616. Goudge, Herbert J. "History of the Union Terminal Controversy." *Municipal League of Los Angeles Bulletin* 6 (October 1, 1928): [3+].

7617. "Handsome New Freight Depot of Los Angeles-Pacific Railroad Company." *Street Railway Journal* 25 (May 6, 1905): 825.

7618. "Hearing on Los Angeles [Union] Terminal Adjourned." *Electric Railway Journal* 67 (February 6, 1926): 261.

7619. Hill, George S. "The Los Angeles Union Passenger Terminal." *The Architect and Engineer* 75 (December 1923): 95-7.

7620. "Los Angeles Terminal Plan Is Ordered: State Commission Adopts Plaza Union Station Project." *Engineering News-Record* 86 (May 12, 1921): 829-30.

7621. "Los Angeles Terminal Station Rehearing Resumed." *Electric Railway Journal* 58 (July 2, 1921): 26.

7622. "Los Angeles Union Terminal Order Upset by Supreme Court." *Engineering News-Record* 90 (January 25, 1923): 180.

7623. "Los Angeles Voters Approve Union Depot at Plaza Site." *Engineering News-Record* 96 (May 13, 1926): 786.

7624. "New Los Angeles Station Provides Unusual Conveniences for Passengers." *Engineering Record* 72 (December 25, 1915): 783-4.
　　Southern Pacific Depot.

7625. "Next Step in Los Angeles Terminal Plan." *Electric Railway Journal* 72 (August 25, 1928): 315.
　　Union Station.

7626. Stimson, Marshall. "The Battle for a Union Station at Los Angeles." *Historical Society of Southern California Quarterly* 21 (1939): 37-44.

7627. "A Symposium on the L. A. Grade Crossing and Union Terminal Problems." *Municipal League of Los Angeles Bulletin* 3 (January 30, 1926): 1+.
　　Includes:
　　"The North End or So Called Plaza Site," by Samuel Storrow, pp. 3-5;
　　"Site Urged for Consideration by the League," by Geo[rge] H. Dunlop, pp. 5-7.
　　"High Lights of the 'Daum Plan,'" by W. H. Daum, pp. 7+;
　　"The Common Carriers' Plan," by D. W. Pontius, pp. 10-3;
　　"Argument Against Any Union Terminal," by Herbert J. Goudge, pp. 13-4;
　　"The Noerenberg Plan," by C. E. Noerenberg, pp. 14-5.

7628. "Union Station Humbug." *Los Angeles Saturday Night* 13 (December 17, 1932): 3.
　　Opposition to Union Station plan.

7629. "Union Station Project Determined." *Los Angeles Saturday Night* 11 (May 23, 1931): 3.
　　Supreme Court decision upholding California Railroad Commission order for railroads to build jointly a Union Station.

7630. "Union Station Tommyrot." *Los Angeles Saturday Night* 13 (February 25, 1933): 4.
Opposition to Union Station plan.

7631. "Union Station Toy Achieved." *Los Angeles Saturday Night* 13 (September 16, 1933): 3.
Station depicted as "another evidence of the economic waste that the country has so long confronted."

7632. "Union Terminal for Los Angeles: Pacific Electric Railway, Southern Pacific Company and Salt Lake Railroad to Combine Entrances to the City." *Electric Railway Journal* 49 (May 5, 1917): 838.

7633. Yankwich, Leon R. "The Present Status of the [Union] Terminal Fight." *Municipal League of Los Angeles Bulletin* 3 (June 30, 1926): 1+.

PUBLIC TRANSPORTATION — RAPID TRANSIT

7634. "The Big Decision: Part and Parcel of Los Angeles' Fabulous Future Is a Satisfactory Rapid Transit System." *Southern California Prompter* 1 (October 1960): 16-9.

7635. Black, Glenn L. "Monorail for Los Angeles." *Railroad Magazine* 62 (December 1953): 88-91.
An idea for rapid transit much discussed during the 1950s.

7636. Britton, James. "The Wilshire Corridor . . . Key to Rapid Transit?" *Los Angeles* 4 (October 1962): 22-3+.

7637. Buhrman, Robert. "What Time's the Next Air Cushion to the Airport?" *Los Angeles* 15 (August 1970): 38-9.
Projected rapid transit line to International Airport.

7638. Burpee, George W. "A Monorail System for Los Angeles: Study Shows That Rapid Transit Line 45.7 Miles Long Could Cut Commuting Time in Half." *Civil Engineering* 25 (April 1955): 205-8.

7639. "California's Two Big Cities Ponder Subways in the Sky." *Popular Science Monthly* 163 (October 1953): 168-70.
Proposed monorail systems.

7640. Daniel, Mann, Johnson Mendenhall. *Los Angeles Metropolitan Transit Authority Rapid Transit Program*. [Los Angeles], 1960. 22 pp.

7641. ———— *Planning and Economic Considerations Affecting Transportation in the Los Angeles Region*. [Los Angeles], 1965. Various pagings.

7642. De Kanter, Hendrik. "An Elevated Monorail Rapid-Transit System for Los Angeles Viewed as a Challenging Industrial-Design Problem." Master's thesis, University of Southern California, 1960. 177 pp.

7643. Dykstra, C[larence] A. "Congestion De Luxe —Do We Want It?" *National Municipal Review* 15 (July 1926): 394-8.
Argues against rapid transit for Los Angeles.

7644. Ehrenreich, Joseph W. "Some Implications of the Projected Transit Plan Upon the Movement of Retail Trade in the Los Angeles Metropolitan Area." Master's thesis, University of Southern California, 1948. 100 pp.

7645. "Elevated Tracks Bugaboo Laid." *Saturday Night* 6 (April 24, 1926): 3.
D. W. Pontius, General Manager of the Pacific Electric, assures Traffic Commission that his company "would never make an attempt to build elevated railways west of Main Street."

7646. "Elevated Tracks for Los Angeles." *Street Railway Journal* 27 (February 10, 1906): 259.
The first of many such proposals that came to naught.

7647. Fagerberg, Elliott P. "The Transit Problem of Metropolitan Los Angeles: A Study in Pressure Politics." Master's thesis, University of Southern California, 1955. 445 pp.

7648. Gilstrap, Jack R. "The Los Angeles Metropolitan Transit Authority and the State Legislative Process; A Case Study." Master's thesis, University of Southern California, 1962. 127 pp.

7649. Hilton, George W. "Transportation: What's Ahead for Southern California?" *Westways* 60 (April, 1960): 27-8+.
Views of the most articulate opponent of rapid transit for Los Angeles.

7650. Himmel, Nieson S. "Aerospace Firms Design

Cars for Los Angeles Transit Link." *Aviation Week & Space Technology* 92 (June 15, 1970): 18.

7651. Ingersoll, Alfred C. "Transportation: What's Ahead for Southern California?" *Westways* 60 (March 1968): 12-5+.
Views of an ardent proponent of rapid transit.

7652. Kelker, De Leuw & Co., Chicago. *Report and Recommendation on a Comprehensive Transit Plan for the City and County of Los Angeles*. [Los Angeles], 1925. 202 pp.

7653. Linscott, Philip M. "$529,700,000 Rapid Transit System Recommended for Los Angeles." *Traffic Quarterly* 15 (1961): 295-305.

7654. "Los Angeles: LAMTA Pushes Rapid Transit." *Headlights* 25 (February 1963): 5.
Los Angeles Metropolitan Transit Authority asks California Legislature for special taxation to finance 58-mile rapid transit system.

7655. "Los Angeles Plans 100 MPH Monorail Train." *Science Digest* 34 (December 1953): 28.

7656. "Los Angeles Rejects Monorail Proposal." *American City* 77 (June 1962): 143.

7657. McMillan Don C. "Rapid Transit Programing for LA County Is a By-Product of Municipal Participation." *Western City* 44 (October 1968): 64-5

7658. Michaels, Rob. "Would You Accept a Ride from This Stranger?" *Los Angeles* 13 (October 1968): 27-9+.
Proposed rapid transit system of SCRTD.

7659. "Modern Transit Proposed for Los Angeles." *American City* 76 (January 1961): 88.
Monorail.

7660. "Monorail Is Latest Relief Proposed for Los Angeles Traffic." *American City* 68 (March 1953): 155.

7661. "Monorail Trains Planned to Speed Los Angeles Traffic." *Popular Science* 158 (June 1951): 120.

7662. Moreau, Jeffrey. "Los Angeles: Rapid Transit Defeated." *Headlights: The Magazine of Electric Railways* 31 (January 1969): 7-8.

$2.5 billion plan receives a 45% "yes" vote; 60% necessary for passage.

7663. ——— "Los Angeles: Routes Chosen." *Headlights: The Magazine of Electric Railways* 27 (May 1965): 14.
Southern California Rapid Transit District unveils 160-mile Rapid Transit Master Plan.

7664. ——— "Los Angeles: Transit Bill Killed." *Headlights: The Magazine of Electric Railways* 27 (July 1965): 5-6.
Special taxation measure defeated in committee of California Legislature.

7665. Newcomer, Milton V. "A Subway for Los Angeles as a Solution of the Traffic Problem: Its Cost and Who Must Pay." Master's thesis, University of Southern California, 1927. 110 pp.

7666. "Points in Need of Clarification as to Rapid Transit." *Municipal League of Los Angeles Bulletin* 7 (June 1, 1930): [7].

7667. Ramsay, Robert A. "Monorail by 1959 Seen for Los Angeles." *Headlights: America's Popular Electric Railway Magazine* 16 (May 1954): 4.
Coverdale & Colpitts monorail plan released; "many experts predicted" that it would materialize by 1959.

7668. "Rapid Transit Issues in Los Angeles." *Electric Railway Journal* 68 (August 21, 1926): 317-8.

7669. Scott, George W. "More Light on the Kelker De-Leuw Traffic Survey." *Municipal League of Los Angeles Bulletin* 3 (November 25, 1925): 1+.
Rapid transit plan.

7670. Southern California Research Council. *An Approach to an Orderly and Efficient Transportation System for the Southern California Metropolis*. Los Angeles, 1960. 48 pp.

7671. Southwick, A. F. "The Kelker L. A. Traffic Plan." *Municipal League of Los Angeles Bulletin* in Southern California." *California Librarian* 14 3 (September 25, 1925): 7-8.
Kelker, De Leuw & Co. rapid transit plan for Los Angeles.

7672. "Subway Permits in Los Angeles to [E.H.] Harriman." *Street Railway Journal* 29 (January 12, 1907): 85.
Subways never built.

7673. "Subways in Los Angeles." *Street Railway Journal* 29 (February 16, 1907): 307.

7674. Thomas, Evan W. "An Analysis of Proposals to Provide Rapid and Adequate Mass Transportation for the Los Angeles Area." Master's thesis, University of California, Los Angeles, 1939. 192 pp.

PUBLISHERS, BOOKSELLERS

7675. Archer, H. Richard. "Notes on Fine Printing." (June 1953): 242-5+.

7676. ——— *The Private Press of Thomas Perry Stricker.* [Los Angeles, 1947]. 12 pp.

7677. Bobrow, Robert. "Jake the Bookie." *Los Angeles* 7 (May 1964): 33-5.
In a red barn on La Cienega, Jake Zeitlin, a former cowboy, runs one of the world's great rare book emporiums.

7678. "Branch Office of Supervisor of Documents to Be Established in Los Angeles." *Bar Bulletin* 15 (August 1940): 291-2.
Government Printing Office agency.

7679. Bulen, Mary H. "Jake Zeitlin's Alluring Book Shop." *Los Angeles Saturday Night* 15 (March 2, 1935): 13.

7680. Cheney, William M. *A Natural History of the Typestickers of Los Angeles.* Comp. from the Letters of Wm. M. Cheney, by Edwin H. Carpenter. Los Angeles, 1960. 62 pp.

7681. Edelstein, J.M., ed. *A Garland for Jake Zeitlin.* Los Angeles, 1967. 131 pp.
Several contributions relate to Mr. Zeitlin's activities as a renowned bookseller.

7682. "The First Book Publisher Comes." *Southern California Business* 9 (October 1930): 32.
Arthur H. Clark Co. relocates from Cleveland, Ohio, to Glendale.

7683. Frampton, Jane. "Fine Printing in Southern California." Master's thesis, Occidental College, 1940. 124 pp.

7684. Grivas, Theodore. "The Arthur H. Clark Company, Publisher of the West." *Arizona and the West* 5 (1963): 63-78.

A brief history of the Glendale-based publishing firm drawn primarily from company records.

7685. Haines, Helen E. "Los Angeles as a Book Market." *Publishers Weekly* 117 (April 19, 1930): 2089-95.

7686. Harmsen, Tyrus G. *The Plantin Press of Saul and Lillian Marks.* Los Angeles, 1960. 21 pp.

7687. "The Huntington Goes to Press." *Saturday Night* 45 (April 23, 1938): 26-7.
Huntington Library's publication program.

7688. International Association of Printing House Craftsmen, Los Angeles Club. *Craftsmanship in Los Angeles, 1922-1947: Printing History in Los Angeles.* Los Angeles, 1947. 22 pp.

7689. ——— *The Story of Printing in Los Angeles.* Los Angeles, 1949. 54 pp.

7690. "Parnassus on Wilshire." *Saturday Night* 44 (June 26, 1937): 15.
Rare book shop on Wilshire Blvd.

7691. Powell, Lawrence Clark. *Vroman's of Pasadena.* Pasadena, 1953. 14 pp. A second printing: Garden City, N. Y., 1953.
Story of one of Southern California's pioneer bookstores.

7692. Ritchie, Ward. *Bookmen and Brothels: Recollections of Los Angeles in the 1930s.* Los Angeles, 1970. 38 pp.

7693. ——— "Fine Printing in Southern California," in *A Bookman's View of Los Angeles.* Los Angeles, 1961. Pp. 39-87.

7694. ——— "The Primavera Press," in *Influences on California Printing.* Los Angeles, 1970. Pp. 37-64.

7695. ——— "Tradition and the Printers of Southern California," in *Modern Fine Printing.* Los Angeles, 1968. Pp. 19-40.

7696. ——— *The Ward Ritchie Press and Anderson, Ritchie & Simon.* Los Angeles, 1961. 156 pp.
This renowned press and publishing firm's history is discussed, pp. 3-65.

7697. Roberts Russell A. "The Arthur H. Clark Company and Its Contributions." *California Librarian* 22 (January 1961): 35-8.

7698. ———— "Books of the West . . . from the West': The Westernlore Press." *California Librarian* 26 (October 1965): 236-41.

7699. ———— "Dawson's Book Shop: Publisher of Western Americana and Patron of the Book Arts." *California Librarian* 25 (April 1964): 97-101.

7000. Shochat, Fern Dawson. *The Fiftieth Anniversary of Dawson's Book Shop, 1905-1955.* Los Angeles, 1955. 23 pp.

7701. Suggs, Wayne L. "The Story of Saunders Press." *Pomona Valley Historian* 5 (1969): 1-21.

7702. Zeitlin, Jake [Jacob]. "The Bookseller and the Librarian." *California Librarian* 23 (April 1962): 91-4.

7703. ———— "Small Renaissance: Southern California Style." *The Papers of the Bibliographical Society of America* 50 (1956): 17-27.

7704. ZuTavern, A. B. "Now We Publish School Books." *Southern California Business* 12 (March 1933): 20.
Commercial Textbook Co., Ltd., South Pasadena.

RADIO, TELEVISION

7705. Ames, Neil "Radio Mystery Unsolved When Television Enters." *Los Angeles Saturday Night* 44 (December 5, 1936): 9.
Description of equipment and operation of radio station KHJ and pioneer TV station W6XAO.

7706. Armstrong, F .W. "Where Words Have Wings: What a Visitor to Santa Catalina Island Saw and Heard of the Practical Workings of Wireless Telegraphy." *Sunset* 10 (January 1903): 225-7.

7707. Beck, John F. "Is Radio the Antidote to the Partisan Press?" *Frontier* 4 (March 1953): 5-7.
Author claims that since the local newspapers "have lost the confidence of the public," it has turned to radio "as the prime source of its unbiased information."

7708. Blythe, Stuart O. "Hollywood Broadcast: Radio Companies Erect Big New Studies as Many Programs Move to the West Coast." *California Magazine of the Pacific* 28 (January 1938): 5-8+.

7709. Buhrman, Robert. "Fighting Flames, Bullets and Ratings with Los Angeles' TV Newsmen." *Los Angeles* 15 (November 1970): 36-9+.

7710. Burton, Russ. "Blurred Screen at KCET." *Frontier* 17 (March 1966): 7-8.
Los Angeles educational television station.

7711. Chiljan, Diane G. "An Investigation of the Utilization of the Education Radio Series, 'People, Places, and Things,' in Schools of Los Angeles County." Master's thesis, University of California, Los Angeles, 1958. 116 pp.

7712. Dager, Eleanor T. "A Descriptive Study of the Development of Educational Television Production and Policy at the University of California at Los Angeles, 1950-1954." Master's thesis, University of California, Los Angeles, 1956. 126 pp.

7713. Denton, Charles, and Cassyd, Sid. "The TV Traffic Jam." *Los Angeles* 6 (November 1963): 40-2.
Los Angeles television.

7714. Drake, Robert O. "A Survey of the Effectiveness of Retail Advertising via Television in the Los Angeles Marketing Area January 1947 to December 1, 1949." Master's thesis, University of Southern California, 1949. 87 pp.

7715. Duncan, Ray. "The Curious, Costly, Cutthroat Battle Over Pay-TV." *Los Angeles* 7 (May 1964): 44-6+.
Los Angeles pay television.

7716. ———— "Will Success Spoil ETV?" *Los Angeles* 8 (September 1964): 48-50.
Los Angeles Channel 28, educational television.

7717. ———— "The Zany Comeback of Los Angeles Radio." *Los Angeles* 8 (July 1964): 44-7+.

7718. Fagan, Walter M. "Making a New Conquest of the Air." *Southern California Business* 8 (March 1929): 20-1+.
Los Angeles broadcasting stations.

7719. Friedman, Samuel L. "Television as a New Aid to Recreation." *Recreation* 34 (August 1940): 305+.
Describes programs presented by the Los Angeles Playground and Recreation Department over station W6XAO.

7720. Furukawa, Fred M. "An Analysis and Appraisal of Transfer Credit Courses via a Commercial Television Channel from Selected Community Colleges in Los Angeles County." Doctoral dissertation, University of Southern California, 1969. 143 pp.

7721. Ganimian, Sammy E. "A Descriptive Study of the Development of KCET-TV, Channel 28, Los Angeles." Master's thesis, University of California, Los Angeles, 1966. 174 pp.

7722. Goggin, Richard J. "Radio and Television in Los Angeles," in *California and the Southwest.* Ed. by Clifford M. Zierer. New York, 1956. Pp. 278-86.

7723. Harper, James. "Radio in Hollywood." *Pacific Saturday Night* 45 (October 23, 1937): 12-3.

7724. Huse, Douglas R. "A Study of Employment Practices and Standards of the Seven VHF Commercial Television Stations in Los Angeles." Master's thesis, University of California, Los Angeles, 1966. 197 pp.

7725. [Huyck, Charles L.]. *"Die Walkure," a Classic Feat of Broadcasting, October 18, 1926.* [Los Angeles?, 1926]. 13 pp.
  Transmission from Los Angeles to San Francisco of the first opera broadcast by telephone.

7726. "Is Educational Television Going Down the Tube?" *Los Angeles* 13 (September 1968): 46-9.
  Channel 28, KCET.

7727. Johnson, Clifton W. "Survey of Documentary Programs on Film Produced and Broadcast by Selected Los Angeles Television Stations." Master's thesis, University of California, Los Angeles, 1969. 295 pp.

7728. Kieffer, Dorothy L. "A Descriptive Study of the Role of the Producer of Dramatic Television in Hollywood in 1966." Master's thesis, University of California, Los Angeles, 1967. 135 pp.

7729. Lane, James A. "A Descriptive Study of Spanish-Language Television Station KMEX and the Spanish-Speaking Audience of Los Angeles." Master's thesis, University of California, Los Angeles, 1966. 183 pp.

7730. Leach, J. Merritt. "KCET: Medium with a Message." *Westways* 59 (October 1967): 24-7.
  Educational television.

7731. McWilliams, Carey. "Put This on Our Air." *Frontier* 1 (May 1, 1950): 3-4.
  Allegation that C.A. Richards, owner of radio station KMPC, was consistently guilty of news "distortion."

7732. Michaels, Rob. "Escalating the Television News War." *Los Angeles* 11 (October 1966): 42-4+.
  Competition between Los Angeles television outlets.

7733. Moss, Marvin A. "Television in Southern California." *California Engineer* 27 (February 1949): 12+.

7734. Orme, Frank. "Prejudice in the Air: An Analysis of Los Angeles Radio-TV News." *Frontier* 5 (July 1954): 10-2.

7735. ———— "Prejudice in the Air: Radio Propagandists and News Analysts." *Frontier* 5 (September 1954): 13-4.

7736. Perrow, Maxwell V. "A Descriptive Analysis of the Religious Programing Policies of the Radio and the Television Stations in Los Angeles Area, 1957." Master's thesis, University of Southern California, 1960. 158 pp.

7737. Pickering, Robert L. "Eight Years of Television in California." *California Magazine of the Pacific* 29 (June 1939): 9-10+.

7738. Polon, Martin I. "Automation at KNXT and Its Impact on the Structures and Polices of the Television Industry." Master's thesis, University of California, Los Angeles, 1968. 173 pp.

7739. Power, Ralph L. "Hollywood Has a New Baby: It's Network Radio Programs, Born a Year Ago, and Getting to Be a Great Big Kid." *Southern California Business* 15 (December 1936): 10-1.

7740. ———— "Reckoning Up Our Radio Resources." *Southern California Business* 14 (July 1935): 10-1.
  Los Angeles, "the radio capital of the west."

7741. ———— "'This Is a Transcribed Program': Made by Our Transcription Industry, Which Has Now Reached the Million-Dollar Class." *Southern California Business* 16 (July 1937): 12-3.
  Los Angeles.

7742. Ross, Marc D. "A Descriptive Study of the Multi-Channel Television Station KZH-31 Established and Operated by the Long Beach Unified School District." Master's thesis, University of California, Los Angeles, 1968. 113 pp.

7743. Rue, James J. "Analysis of Television News Techniques in the Los Angeles Area." Master's thesis, University of Southern California, 1951. 112 pp.

7744. Russnow, Michael A. "A Descriptive Analysis of Alan Cranston's Use of Broadcasting Media in His Winning Senatorial Campaign of 1967." Master's thesis, University of California, Los Angeles, 1967. 140 pp.

7745. Saettler, L. Paul. "A Comparative Study of Frequency Modulation Programs in Los Angeles." Master's thesis, University of Southern California, 1949. 236 pp.

7746. Sauer, Jane A. "The Application of Selected Critera to Pre-School Children's Television Programs in the Los Angeles Area During January, February, and March, 1961." Master's thesis, University of California, Los Angeles, 1961. 154 pp.

7747. Schmidt, A. E. "Rock Anchors Hold TV Tower on Mt. Wilson." *Civil Engineering* 26 (January 1956): 56-8.
  532-foot NBC transmitter.

7748. Sheperd, Howard. "Disaster: Ham Disaster Communications in Los Angeles County." *Electronics World* 62 (August 1959): 68-9.

7749. "Shuler Practices Scored." *Los Angeles Saturday Night* 13 (December 3, 1932): 3.
  Court of Appeals upholds cancellation of Rev. Robert P. Shuler's broadcasting license.

7750. "Sierra Madre Wrestles Master Antenna Installation Problem." *Western City* 29 (June 1953): 60.

7751. Smith, Bernard. "Station KECA—Los Angeles." *California Magazine of the Pacific* 28 (May 1938): 19+.

7752. Stacher, Leslee N. "The History of Radio Stations KGIL-AM, KKHI-AM and FM, and KOL-AM and Their Development by the Buckley Broadcasting Corporation of California." Master's thesis, University of California, Los Angeles, 1969. 120 pp.

7753. "TV Antennas Go Underground." *American City* 80 (December 1965): 100.
  Manhattan Beach.

7754. "Use of TV for MPR in Los Angeles and Cincinnati." *American City* 65 (September 1950): 116-7.
  MPR—Municipal Public Relations.

7755. Wade, Margaret H. "A Descriptive Study of the Jobs Held by Women in the Radio-Television Industry in Los Angeles." Master's thesis, University of Southern California, 1951. 374 pp.

7756. Wood, Barbara L. "A Comparative Analysis of Children's Radio and Television Programs in the Los Angeles Area." Master's thesis, University of Southern California, 1950. 111 pp.

7757. Yates, Peter. "KPFK: A Listeners' Subscription Station." *Arts & Architecture* 76 (October 1959): 4+.
  Los Angeles FM radio station.

REAL ESTATE

7758. "Advantages of Rancho Malibu La [sic] Costa." *Los Angeles Saturday Night* 9 (August 10, 1929): 7.
  Real estate subdivision.

7759. Allen-Pinchon, Mary. *Beverly Hills, Southern California.* [Los Angeles, 1911?]. 23 pp.

7760. Anderson, Arnold T. "Subdivision Activity in and around Los Angeles." *Los Angeles Realtor* 8 (April 1929): 7.

7761. "Annandale—Taking Shape as an Exclusive Residential Colony." *Saturday Night* 6 (September 4, 1926): 1.
  Western Pasadena subdivision.

7762. Arnold, Mrs. M. "What's New in Hollywood." *Los Angeles Realtor* 7 (November 1927): 28-30+.
  Enumerates such matters as number and value of new buildings devoted to a variety of functions, rise in property values, increase in public works projects, and growth in bank clearings.

7763. ——— "What's New in Hollywood." *Los Angeles Realtor* 8 (November 1928): 26.

New businesses, banks, churches, factories, apartments, homes, and studios.

7764. "Artistic Plan for Residence Park." *Pacific Municipalities* 14 (March 1906): 39.

Brentwood Park.

7765. Ashmun, R. M. "The East Side and the Home Buyer." *Los Angeles Realtor* 7 (March 1927): 17+.

Describes East Side of Los Angeles as a desirable residential section.

7766. Ayers, Harold M. *Redondo Beach on the Rim of the Western Sea.* Redondo Beach, [c1915]. [32] pp.

7767. Baker, George W. "The East Side of Los Angeles." *Los Angeles Realtor* 7 (April 1928): 12-3+.

7768. Barnett, Thomas D. "Hollywood—A City within a City." *Los Angeles Realtor* 9 (November 1928): 23+.

7769. Bayne, E. G. "North Hollywood." *Los Angeles Realtor* 8 (November 1928): 29+.

7770. "Beach Homesites at Desirable Rancho Malibu la Costa." *Los Angeles Saturday Night* 10 (May 17, 1930): 7.

Rancho Malibu subdivision.

7771. "Beach Property Withdrawn from Sale by Pacific Electric." *Electric Railway Journal* 71 (April 28, 1928): 716.

Three-fourths of a mile of Redondo Beach frontage.

7772. "Beauties and Future of Wilshire Boulevard." *Los Angeles Saturday Night* 10 (January 11, 1930): 7.

Includes figures on increase in property values along Wilshire.

7773. Becker, Louis L. "History of Apartment Association [of Los Angeles County] Reviewed on 40th Anniversary." *Western Housing* 39 (June 1956): 8-9.

7774. ——— "Story of the Apartment Association of Los Angeles County, Inc." *Apartment Journal* 44 (November 1961): 14-5.

7775. "Bel-Air Canyon's Ready Accessibility." *Los Angeles Saturday Night* 12 (June 18, 1932): 11.

Subdivision of Stone Canyon.

7776. "Bel-Air: Picturesque Domain of Attractive Homes." *Los Angeles Saturday Night* 8 (February 18, 1928): 2.

Suburb promoted by Alphonzo Bell, Sr.

7777. Benmar Hills Corp. *Benmar Hills, Burbank; The Ideal City Beautiful.* Burbank, c1926. 11 pp.

A developer's brochure.

7778. "Benmar Hills 'City Beautifal!'" [sic] *Saturday Night* 4 (May 26, 1923): 21+.

Burbank subdivision.

7779. Bergh, H. R. "The Los Angeles Realty Advisors—Who, Why and What They Are." *Los Angeles Realtor* 8 (September 1929): 16+.

7780. Bobrow, Robert. "Land Speculation: A Science All Its Own." *Los Angeles* 7 (February 1964): 42-3.

Los Angeles.

7781. Bogardus, Emory S. "The House-Court Problem." *American Journal of Sociology* 22 (November 1916): 391-9.

Study of 1,202 Los Angeles house-courts, which are characterized as parcels of land with three or more habitations that share in common the vacant portions thereof.

7782. Britton, James. "Santa Monica's Real Estate Revolution." *Los Angeles* 6 (July 1963): 26-31+.

7783. "Built-in Salesmanship and Canny Construction Gear This 2,000 Unit Development for a Bearish Market. Thoughtful Design Lowers the Height of the House and the Price Tag." *Architectural Forum* 90 (April 1949): 118-22.

Article descriptive of Panorama City, where project is located.

7784. Burrud, L. J. "The Golden Harvest of the Hill-Tops." *Los Angeles Realtor* 4 (April 1925): 9-10.

Hilltop subdivisions in Los Angeles and vicinity.

7785. Burtnett, Gerald B. "Growing Community of

Garden Homes." *Los Angeles Saturday Night* 15 (June 22, 1935): 4.
Lakewood Village.

7786. ——— "Los Angeles' Woodlands Surprise Long-Time Residents." *Los Angeles Saturday Night* 15 (May 11, 1935): 4.
Subdivision in Bel-Air area.

7787. "California Beach Sale under Way." *Electric Railway Journal* 68 (October 23, 1926): 785.
Sale of Redondo Beach property by Pacific Electric Railway.

7788. "California's Outstanding Residential Community." *Los Angeles Saturday Night* 9 (June 15, 1929): 7.
Palos Verdes Estates.

7789. "Carlton Terrace Choice Hillside Property." *Los Angeles Saturday Night* 10 (April 12, 1930): 7.
Hollywood subdivision.

7790. Case, Frederick E. *Cash Outlays and Economic Costs of Homeownership.* Los Angeles, c1957. 58 pp.

7791. Champlin, C. D. "Our Disappearing Land: The Population Upsurge Continues; Will Los Angeles Run Out of Land?" *Southern California Prompter* 1 (November 1960): 16-8.

7792. Clark, Arthur E. "Beverly Crest's Attractive Vista." *Los Angeles Saturday Night* 8 (July 14, 1928): 2.
Subdivision adjoining Doheny Ranch.

7793. ——— "Desirable Canoga Estates." *Los Angeles Saturday Night* 9 (November 3, 1928): 7.
San Fernando Valley subdivision.

7794. ——— "Glance at Rancho Malibu." *Los Angeles Saturday Night* 8 (April 21, 1928): 2.
Opening of Malibu beaches for development.

7795. ——— "Historic Rancho Malibu Seashore Project under Way." *Los Angeles Saturday Night* 9 (February 16, 1929): 10.

7796. ——— "Rancho Malibu's New Seashore Colony." *Los Angeles Saturday Night* 8 (June 2, 1928): 2.

7797. Clark, Charles D. "Land Subdivision," in Los Angeles: Preface to a Master Plan. Ed. by George W. Robbins and L. Deming Tilton. Los Angeles, 1941. Pp. 159-71.

7798. Claus, Cynthia. "Wilshire's Parks: An Apartment-Hotel District That Hasn't Lost Its Quality in Twenty-Five Years of Los Angeles Growth." *Apartment Journal* 20 (June 1938): 10-1+.

7799. Coffin, George H. "Tremendous Gains in Realty Values Mark Past Twenty Years in Hollywood." *Los Angeles Realtor* 6 (November 1926): 17.

7800. "Contractors Tackle Century City: Construction Is in Full Swing at Century City, the Nation's Largest Privately-Financed Urban Development." *Western Construction* 38 (March 1963): 51-4.

7801. "Country-City Contentment at Canoga Estates." *Los Angeles Saturday Night* 10 (May 3, 1930): 7.
San Fernando Valley subdivision.

7802. Darling, Arthur. "East of Western in Hollywood." *Los Angeles Realtor* 8 (November 1928): 18+.

7803. "Delightful Homes of Flintridge." *Los Angeles Saturday Night* 8 (March 24, 1928): 2+.
Los Angeles boom of twenties and the development of Hollywood tract homes.

7804. De Mille, Cecil B. "The Birth of a Giant." *Southern California Business* 2 (December 1923): 19+.

7805. du Bois, Ayers J. "Hollywood—Where Nature Smiles and Opportunity Beckons." *Los Angeles Realtor* 8 (November 1928): 13-4.

7806. ——— "Los Angeles Real Estate—A Good Investment." *Los Angeles Realtor* 8 (April 1929): 8-9+.

7807. Elliott, Gaylord W. "Office Buildings of Hollywood." *Los Angeles Realtor* 6 (November 1926): 23+.

7808. Fader, Edmund F. "Hollywood, a City of Prosperous Home Owners." *Los Angeles Realtor* 6 (November 1926): 39+.

7809. Finney, Guy W. "Real Estate Promotion via Religious Induction." *California Graphic* 5 (March 31, 1928): 7+.

7810. Foster, Parker. "Why Hollywood Grows." *Los Angeles Realtor* 8 (November 1928): 21+.

7811. Garland, William M. "A Glimpse into the Past and Forecast for the Future." *Los Angeles Realtor* 8 (December 1928): 11+.
From a radio talk by Garland.

7812. Garner, William C. "The Importance of Tourist Travel to Los Angeles Real Estate Men." *Los Angeles Realtor* 4 (April 1925): 14-5+.

7813. Gianni, Stephen A. "A Study of the Real Estate Prices and Apartment House Construction Trends in the San Fernando Valley, 1940-1957." Master's thesis, University of Southern California, 1958. 258 pp.

7814. Gillies, James. "Land . . . A Bigger Squeeze Is Coming." *Los Angeles* 7 (February 1964): 40+.
How the price of land in Los Angeles is forcing a change in the shape and form of the city.

7815. Green, Gael. "For the Single Girl: A New Way of Life in California; South Bay Club, in a Los Angeles Suburb." *Ladies Home Journal* 83 (July 1966): 58-9+.
Singles apartment complex.

7816. Gregor, Howard F. "Urban Pressures on California Land." *Land Economics* 33 (1957): 311-25.
Explains reasons for shrinkage in amount of land devoted to agriculture.

7817. Guinn, James M. "The Romance of Rancho Realty." *Annual Publication* Historical Society of Southern California 8 (1911): 234-42.

7818. Hallam, Clark. "The Effect of Sales Promotion on Land Values in the Los Angeles Area from 1922 to 1932." Master's thesis, University of Southern California, 1933. 90 pp.

7819. Harries, Keith D. "An Analysis of Inter-Ethnic Variations in Commercial Land-Use in Los Angeles." Doctoral dissertation, University of California, Los Angeles, 1969. 187 pp.

7820. Harrison, George B. "Twenty Years in and over Los Angeles." *Los Angeles Realtor* 7 (May 1928): 15+.

7821. Hashem, Erfan. "Development of the University Neighborhood, the University of Southern California [1930 to 1954]." Master's thesis, University of Southern California, 1954. 177 pp.

7822. Heaton, Reece. "Real Estate and Los Angeles Harbor." *Los Angeles Realtor* 5 (November 1925): 15-6.

7823. Height, Lewis H., Jr. "Settlement Patterns of the San Fernando Valley, Southern California." Master's thesis, University of California, Los Angeles, 1953. 197 pp.

7824. "Here the Sun Rises and Sets." *Out West,* new series, 5 (May 1913): 283-8.
Real estate development in Los Angeles.

7825. "Hippies Hurt More Than Riots in Los Angeles." *American City* 83 (July 1968): 47.
Presence of hippies allegedly detrimental to value of commercial and residential land.

7826. "Hollywood—Los Angeles Other Half." *Los Angeles Realtor* 7 (November 1927): 35-9+.

7827. "Homes Beautiful at California Riviera." *Los Angeles Saturday Night* 9 (March 16, 1929): 11.
Beverly Blvd. subdivision.

7828. "Huge Deal: Century City Resold." *Western Housing* 43 (June 1960): 6-7.
Land sold by 20th Century-Fox to Krattner Corp. for $42 million.

7829. "Ideal Homes and Gardens of Picturesque Bel-Air." *Los Angeles Saturday Night* 8 (April 28, 1928): 2.

7830. "Ideal Westwood Center Abutting University Campus." *Los Angeles Saturday Night* 9 (July 6, 1929): 10.
Westwood Village under construction.

7831. Ingold, Ernest. "Home-Building and the Southland." *Out West,* new series, 1 (March 1911): 233-9.
Los Angeles tract homes.

7832. "Janss Investment Corporation Success."

Los Angeles Saturday Night 9 (February 2, 1929):
7.
> Said to be "the foremost community development organization in the country."

7833. Jennings, Frederick W. "Los Angeles the Home of Many High Class Apartment Houses." *The Architect and Engineer of California* 34 (September 1913): 65-75.

7834. Keim,W[illia]m C. "The Office Rental Situation in Los Angeles." *Los Angeles Realtor* 4 (March 1925): 22-3.

7835. Kenyon, C. E. "Homes in the Hollywood Hills." *Los Angeles Realtor* 6 (November 1926): 37+.

7836. Klissner, Harry. "How Agencies of Comunications Can Convert a Gigantic Real Estate Operation (Lakewood) into a Socially Cohesive Community." Master's thesis, University of California, Los Angeles, 1954. 145 pp.

7837. Lane, D. D. "Featuring Hollywood—A First Magnitude Star.' *Los Angeles Realtor* 8 (November 1928): 15+.

7838. "Laying Out a Complete New City."*Southern California Business* 2 (May 1923): 21.
> Declare that "enough land has been sub-divided in Los Angeles County in the last year to make two cities the size of St. Louis city proper."

7839. Lesperance, Leo B. "Out in the San Fernando Valley." *Southern California Business* 4 (January 1926): 15-6.
> Growth and planning for further growth.

7840. "Los Angeles Realty Board Passes Milestone in Laying Cornerstone for New Home." *Los Angeles Realtor* 7 (June 1928): 15.

7841. Lusk, Earl F. "An Analysis of the Effect of the Landsliding Problem on the Value of the Single Family Residential Properties in Pacific Palisades." Master's thesis, University of Southern California, 1963. 82 pp.

7842. Marion, Guy E. "Planning Sales on Actual Buying Power: The Whole 450 Square Miles of Los Angeles Plotted by Family Income, in 115 Tracts." *Southern California Business* 12 (April 1933): 14.

7843. ———— "What of the Future? Population Growth, Its Development, and What It Means to the Apartment Industry." *Apartment Journal* 19 (October 1936): 14-5+.
> Los Angeles and suburbs.

7844. Marx, Wesley. "A Kingdom Is Laid to Rest." *Los Angeles* 2 (July 1961): 38-40.
> 20th Century Fox backlot gives way to high rise apartments and office buildings.

7845. McClenahan, Bessie A. "The Changing Nature of an Urban Residential Area." Doctoral dissertation, University of Southern California, 1928. 374 pp.
> Los Angeles.

7846. McClure, Paul T. "Some Projected Effects of Jet Noise on Residential Property Near Los Angeles International Airport by 1970." Master's thesis, University of Southern California, 1969. 155 pp.

7847. Mines, W. W. " 'The Home City' of America." *Out West,* new series, 11 (April 1916): 158-9.
> Los Angeles.

7848. "Miramar Estates—High Above the Sea." *Los Angeles Saturday Night* 9 (April 27, 1929): 7.
> Santa Monica subdivision.

7849. Montgomery, O. L. "West Hollywood." *Los Angeles Realtor* 8 (November 1928): 24+.

7850. "A 'Motor-Safe' Residential District: Cerritos Park, California." *American City* 53 (April 1938): 87+.
> A Long Beach subdivision.

7851. Myers, William H. "The Apartment Association of Los Angeles County, Inc.: What It Is Doing for the Apartment Owner and What It Is Dedicated to Do." *Western Housing* 40 (November 1956): 7+.

7852. Nelson, Howard J. "The Spread of an Artificial Landscape over Southern California." *Annals of the Association of American Geographers* 49 (1959): 80-92.
> Dispersal of urban centers in the evolution of settlement.

7853. *The Ocean Park Improvement Company.* Los Angeles, [c1904]. 16 pp.

7854. O'Melveny, Staurt, "How Is Los Angeles Real Estate?" *Southern California Business* 7 (December 1928): 12-3+.

7855. "Outpost Estates, Originally Won by the Pathfinder." *Los Angeles Saturday Night* 8 (June 16, 1928): 2.
Hollywood Hills subdivision developed by C. E. Toberman.

7856. Owen, Willis. "Motion Pictures Build a Bigger Hollywood." *Los Angeles Realtor* 7 (November 1927): 40+.

7857. Pappas, George R. "Some Socio-Geographic Factors Pertaining to the Spread of Urbanism in the San Fernando Valley, Los Angeles, California." Doctoral dissertation, University of Maryland, 1952. 290 pp.

7858. "Pomona Requires Disposal Units in New and Remodeled Homes." *Western City* 29 (March 1953): 47.

7859. "Providing Space for the Newcomer." *Southern California Business* 7 (July 1928): 22+.
Los Angeles residential concentration.

7860. Rachal, Charles E. " 'Road of Good Fortune': Ventura Boulevard." *Los Angeles Realtor* 7 (February 1928): 11-2+.

7861. "Rancho Malibu la Costa Improvements." *Los Angeles Saturday Night* 9 (June 1, 1929): 7.
Malibu subdivision.

7862. Raskoff, Richard M. "A Study of the Land Use Structure of the Central Business District of Los Angeles, California." Master's thesis, San Fernando Valley State College, 1965. 126 pp.

7863. "Record in Property Values." *Southern California Business* 8 (May 1929): 30-1.
Comparative valuation in Los Angeles County and other counties.

7847. McNeil, Lawrence G. "Should Los Angeles Maintain Its Limit Height on Office Buildings?" *Los Angeles Realtor* 7 (January 1927): 15+.

7864. Roberts, Glenys. "How to Sell a $150,000 White Elephant: Wheeling and Dealing in the Mansions of Hancock Park." *Los Angeles* 11 (December 1966): 58-9.

7865. Roberts, Myron. "The Coming Post-War Boom." *Los Angeles* 13 (August 1968): 32-5.
Los Angeles real estate.

7866. Robinson, William W. *Land Titles in Long Beach.* Los Angeles, 1935. [8] pp.

7867. ———— "The Southern California Real Estate Boom of the Twenties." *Historical Society of Southern California Quarterly* 24 (1942): 25-30.

7868. Selzer, Fred, Jr. *The San Fernando Valleys Past, Present, and Future.* Los Angeles, 1953. 20 pp.
Market analyst's optimistic appraisal of valley realty.

7869. Sengel, Jerome "Jerry". "Hollywood's Building Outlook." *Los Angeles Realtor* 6 (November 1926): 29+.

7870. Siebert, Paul E. "An Empirical Study Comparing Lot Improvement Costs in Developed and Undeveloped Areas of Los Angeles and Riverside Counties." Master's thesis, University of Southern California, 1970. 98 pp.

7871. Smith, Jack. "A Day in the City: A Place of This Century." *Westways* 61 (April 1969): 21-3+.
Century City.

7872. Smith, Robert L. "Is Hollywood on Its Great White Way?" *Los Angeles Realtor* 7 (November 1927): 16-9.
Hopeful speculation that Hollywood is to become the western counterpart of Times Square.

7873. Staats, William R. "About Oneonta." *Sunset* 13 (September 1904): 453-5.
Oneonta Park, between Pasadena and Los Angeles on the Pacific Electric, "an incomparable spot" that Staats was promoting for homesites.

7874. Stewart, Marion. "To Demonstrate Right to Become Resident in This Charmed Area Prospective Client Must Pass a Searching Examination . . . Rolling Hills (Rancho Palos Verdes) County Estates a Select Neighborhood." *Los Angeles Saturday Night* 43 (May 2, 1936): 8-9.

7875. Stiles, George L. "Miramar Estates—Nestled High above the Sea." *Los Angeles Saturday Night* 8 (August 11, 1928): 2+.
Subdivision in Santa Monica Hills.

7876. Stiller, George. "Cooperative Advertising: Building Address-Prestige Foreseen as Logical Development in Los Angeles Multiple Housing." *Apartment Journal* 18 (December 1935): 6-7+.

7877. Stump, Frank V. "The Great Southwest Trade Field: Farm Land Values of Los Angeles County and Neighboring States Far Outstrip Figures of Large Eastern Territory." *Southern California Business* 1 (June 1922): 12-3.

7878. ———— "Pomona Makes Most of Rare Gifts." *Southern California Business* 4 (September 1925): 12-3+.
Favorable location and fertile soil.

7879. "Survey of Glendale Houses." *Apartment Journal* 17 (January 1935): 20.

7880. "Survey Shows Los Angeles County Leads in Real Estate Activity." *Los Angeles Realtor* 7 (August 1928): 19.

7881. Takizawa, Bill H. "West Covina, California: Differentiation of a Suburb from Central Cities with Emphasis on Land-Use." Master's thesis, University of California, Los Angeles, 1961. 132 pp.

7882. Tennant, Frank A. "History of Los Angeles Apartments Revealed by Title Company's Records." *Western Housing* 37 (December 1953): 18+.

7883. "3,000 New Apartments Being Built at Parklabrea Site." *Western Housing* 33 (January 1950): 29.

7884. Tomlin, Edwin A. "Rancho Vega Offers Country Life in the City." *Western Housing* 28 (December 1945): 8+.
Apartment house complex in Burbank.

7885. "20th Century City." *Time* 71 (January 13, 1958): 81.
20th-Century Fox real estate development.

7886. Vreeland, Francis W. "City Should Acquire All of Olive Hill." *California Graphic* 5 (March 31, 1928): 5+.

7887. Wall, Bernard J. "Appraising Property in Hollywood—and Elsewhere." *Los Angeles Realtor* 8 (November 1928): 30+.

7888. Ware, Alan. "Luxurious Apartments in Westwood Feature Outdoor Swimming Pool." *Western Housing* 31 (October 1947): 12+.

7889. Waters, Heber W. "Broadway from First to Twelfth Worth Nearly Two Hundred Million." *Los Angeles Realtor* 4 (June 1925): 19+.

7890. ———— "Los Angeles Skyscraper Projects for 1925 Total $87,000,000." *Los Angeles Realtor* 4 (January 1925): 26-8+.

7891. "What Does It Cost to Build in Los Angeles?" *Los Angeles Realtor* 7 (June 1928): 22-3.

7892. "Where Property Values Run Highest." *Southern California Business* 4 (September 1925): 28.
Los Angeles County.

7893. "Where They Own Their Own Homes." *Southern California Business* 4 (May 1925): 21.
Los Angeles home ownership compared with other cities.

7894. Wilkins, Barbara. "Surviving the Great Apartment Squeeze." *Los Angeles* 13 (December 1968): 34-7+.
Los Angeles apartments.

7895. Williams, Dorothy S. "Ecology of Negro Communities in Los Angeles County, 1940-1959." Doctoral dissertation, University of Southern California, 1961. 187 pp.

7896. Williams, W. J. "Los Angeles Grows Up." *Apartment Journal* 44 (June 1961): 6+.
High-rise buildings necessary if Los Angeles is to maintain its present growth, says vice-president of Tishman Realty & Construction Company.

7897. Wilson, George "Washington." "Sump Hole to Home in a Year." *Los Angeles Realtor* 4 September 1925): 16-7+.
From oil wells to residences on property of G. Allan Hancock.

7898. Winnick, Sam. "The San Fernando Valley Apartment Industry." *Western Housing* 43 (February 1961): 9.

7899. Wray, Albert. "Complete New Suburban Community Being Built in Long Beach." *Western Housing* 31 (March 1948): 9+.
Bixby Knolls.

7900. ——— "New Luxury Apartments in West-wood Designed for Town and Country Life." *Western Housing* 31 (June 1948): 14+.
Sherry Wilshire Apartments.

7901. Wright, H. S. "Open Air Swimming Pool on Roof of Langham Apartments, Los Angeles." *Western Construction News* 3 (June 10, 1928): 362-3.

7902. Zent, George W. "Hello World! Hollywood Realtors Broadcasting." *Los Angeles Realtor* 8 (November 1928): 17.

RELIGION

7903. Alker, Henry. *Golden Jubilee—St. Agnes Church, Los Angeles, 1903-1953.* Los Angeles, 1953. Unp.

7904. Allen, Kring. "Integration by the Cross." *Christian Century* 75 (August 20, 1958): 943-5.
Integration of McCarthy Memorial Christian Church, Los Angeles.

7905. Andrews, Ailleen. *St. Hilary Parish History.* Pico Rivera, 1958. 60 pp.
An earlier study, no author given, was published in 1952, 29 pp.

7906. Antczak, Al. "The See of Los Angeles." *Catholic Market* 3 (January 1964): 20-7.

7907. Appelgate, Joseph M. "An Inductive Study of Selected Groups of Young People's Religious Activities in the Southwest Section of Los Angeles." Master's thesis, University of Southern California, 1932. 75 pp.

7908. Arant, Francis M. "A Study of the History and Development of the Disciples of Christ in Southern California." Master's thesis, University of Southern California, 1936. 83 pp.

7909. Arrow Research Institute. *Cults, Sects, Philosophical Groups, and Small Denominations in Los Angeles and Southern California.* Los Angeles, 1958. 16 pp.

7910. Baggot, M[ary] Reginald, Sister. "A History of the Sisters of the Immaculate Heart of Mary in California." Master's thesis, University of Southern California, 1937. 204 pp.

7911. Bardaouil, Michael. *Saint Anne's Melchite Church.* Los Angeles, 1965. Unp.

7912. Baughman, Pearl K., and West, Donald F. *History of the First Christian Church of Pomona, California, 1883-1943.* [Pomona, c1943]. 94 pp.

7913. "Beautiful Churches House Hollywood's Congregations." *Los Angeles Realtor* 6 (November 1926): 25+.

7914. Bell, Lorne W. "A Study of the Christian Citizenship Program in Certain Churches of Southwest Los Angeles." Master's thesis, University of Southern California, 1930. 111 pp.

7915. Beverly Hills. Community Presbyterian Church. *The Story of the Beverly Hills Community Presbyterian Church; The First Twenty-Five Years, 1921-1946.* [Beverly Hills, n.d.]. 32 pp.

7916. Bigbee, Morris R. "The Aims, Methods, and Results of the Church Loyalty Crusade in the City of Los Angeles." Master's thesis, University of Southern California, 1929. 87 pp.

7917. Bissell, Shelton. "Vaudeville at Angelus Temple." *Outlook* 149 (May 23, 1928): 126-7+.

7918. *Bodas de Plata, 1923-1948.* Los Angeles, 1948. 36 pp.
Commemorates silver anniversary of Church of Our Lady of Guadalupe.

7919. Bomberger, David R. "A Program of Religious Education for Young Men (Ages 18-25) with Special Reference to the Los Angeles Young Men's Chirstian Association." Master's thesis, University of Southern California, 1922. 60 pp.

7920. Bramble, Keith. *St. Christopher Parish.* Covina, 1962. 112 pp.

7921. Brennan, John L. *The Church of St. Peter and St. Paul.* Wilmington, 1965. Unp.

7922. Brennan, Robert E. *St. Elizabeth Parish. A History of Early Rancho Days and of Fifty Parish Years, 1918-1968.* Altadena, 1968. 152 pp.

7923. ——— *A Visit to St. Paul's Church.* Los Angeles, 1947. 63 pp.

7924. "A Brief History of California Methodism." *California Christian Advocate* 75 (September 16, 1926): 16.

7925. Brouwers, Anthony J. "See How the World Suffers." *Linacre Quarterly* 29 (1962): 118-21.
Description of Mission Doctors Association of the Archdiocese of Los Angeles.

7926. Burdette, Clara (Bradley). *The Rainbow and the Pot of Gold.* Pasadena, 1908. 147 pp.
Story of Temple Baptist Church.

7927. Burns, Charles, O.M.I. *La Sagrada Familia, 1929-1969.* Wilmington, 1969. Unp.

7928. "A Cathedral from Charlie: A Generous Skouras Shows His Devotion." *Life* 33 (November 3, 1952): 54-7.
Charles P. Skouras, theatre magnate, and his two brothers, Spyros and George, build a $2 million cathedral for Los Angeles' 12,000 Orthodox Greeks.

7929. "A Change in the Los Angeles District Superintendency." *California Christian Advocate* 66 (December 20, 1917): 4.

7930. Chapman, Ernest E. "Contemporary Theological Approaches and the Political Role of the Anglo-American Protestant Denominations in an Urban Complex." Doctoral dissertation, University of Southern California, 1967. 288 pp.

7931. Chi Rho Researchers, San Pedro, California. *A Report on Manhattan Beach Community Church.* [San Pedro, 1961]. 32 pp.

7932. "Children Crowd This Sunday School . . ." *Ladies Home Journal* 74 (September 1957): 43.
Congregational Church of the Chimes, Van Nuys.

7933. Chromoga, Eugene A. *St. Mary's Byzantine Catholic Church.* Van Nuys, 1966. Unp.
Tenth anniversary of the parish.

7934. "Church Life of Los Angeles." *Los Angeles Saturday Night 150th Birthday of Los Angeles: Fiesta and Pre-Olympiad.* Special Issue (1931): [18].

7935. *Church of the Blessed Sacrament.* Hollywood, 1954. 52 pp.
There is also a 1953 pictorial edition relating to the church, published by Mellenger Studio, Hollywood. Unp.

7936. *Church of the Epiphany.* El Monte, 1959. 60 pp.

7937. Clark, Stephen C. *The Diocese of Los Angeles, a Brief History.* [Pasadena], 1945. 92 pp.
Account of the early Episcopal Church in Southern California.

7938. Clarke, John K. *St. Anselm's Parish—Silver Jubilee, 1925-1950.* Los Angeles, 1950. 32 pp.

7939. Clifford, John J. *Church of the Nativity.* Los Angeles, 1924. 36 pp.

7940. Coffin, T. Eugene. "History of California Yearly Meeting of Friends Churches, 1895-1955." Master's thesis, University of Southern California, 1956. 93 pp.

7941. Cohen, Thomas. "First Jewish Community Site—Los Angeles." *Western States Jewish Historical Quarterly* 1 (1969): 89-108.

7942. Cole, Clifford A. *The Christian Churches (Disciples of Christ) of Southern California; A History.* [St. Louis], 1959. 324 pp.

7943. Collins, Leonard W. *Seventy-Five Years of Service, 1885-1960.* [Pasadena?, 1960]. 23 pp.
Pasadena First Congregational Church.

7944. Conmy, Charles C. *The Centennial, 1840-1940.* Los Angeles, 1940. 200 pp.
Catholicism in Southern California.

7945. Cook, Francis E. "The Problem of Authority in Contemporary Protestant Preaching with Special Reference to the Pulpits of Los Angeles." Master's thesis, University of Southern California, 1928. 87 pp.

7946. Cordill, Tunis S. "Church Life Activities and Attitudes of San Dimas High School Students; A Socio-Religious Survey Made in San Dimas, California, 1932-1933." Master's thesis, Claremont Graduate School, 1933. 134 pp.

7947. Cossentine, Erwin E. "A Brief Survey of the Seventh-Day Adventist Work in Southern California." Master's thesis, Claremont Graduate School, 1933. 103 pp.

7948. Cottman, Gail. "The Nuns' Rebellion." *Los Angeles* 13 (March 1968): 34-7+.
Liberal vs. conservative Catholics in Los Angeles.

7949. "Crowning of a Cult." *Newsweek* 55 (January 11, 1960): 59.

Opening of Founder's Church of Religious Science, Los Angeles.

7950. Cunningham, Harold R. "The Modern Tendencies of Adult Religious Education as Found in the Local Churches of Los Angeles and Vicinity." Master's thesis, University of Southern California, 1929. 116 pp.

7951. Daley, Richard, Brother. "The Beginnings of the Brothers of the Holy Cross in California, 1941-55." Master's thesis, University of Santa Clara, 1965. 122 pp.

7952. Daughters of Charity. *One Hundred Years of Service . . . 1856-1956, Dedicated to the People of Southern California.* [Los Angeles, 1956]. 36 pp.

7953. Davis, James R. "A History of the Evangelical United Brethren Church in California, 1849-1962." Doctoral dissertation, University of Southern California, 1963. 389 pp.

7954. Davis, Royal G. *Light on a Gothic Tower: First Congregational Church of Los Angeles.* Los Angeles, 1967. 188 pp.

7955. Dee, Maurice P. *Immaculate Conception Church.* Monrovia, 1955. 58 pp.

7956. De Martini, Edward, S.D.B. *The Story of St. Patrick's.* Los Angeles, 1954. 64 pp.

7957. *Diamond Jubilee. St. Mary's of the Assumption.* Whittier, 1968. Unp.

7958. Dignam, John. *Fifteenth Anniversary and Dedication Souvenir of St. Rose of Lima Church.* Maywood, 1937. Unp.

7959. Dignan, Patrick J. *St. Cecilia's Church Golden Jubilee.* Los Angeles, 1959. 10 pp.

7960. Diomartich, Felix. *55th Anniversary. St. Anthony's Croatian Church.* Los Angeles, 1965. 44 pp.

7961. Dohrman, H. T. *California Cult. The Story of "Mankind Unlimited."* Boston, 1958. 163 pp.
    History of the Christ Church of the Golden Rule, founded in Los Angeles in 1934.

7962. Done, G. Byron. "The Participation of the Latter-Day Saints in the Community Life of Los Angeles." Doctoral dissertation, University of Southern California, 1939. 299 pp.

7963. Duke, Keith E. "Geographical Factors in the Location of Church Sites in Urban Los Angeles." Doctoral dissertation, University of California, Los Angeles, 1965. 357 pp.

7964. Edmondson, William. "Fundamentalist Sects of Los Angeles, 1900-1930." Doctoral dissertation, Claremont Graduate School, 1969. 462 pp.

7965. Ellis, Ivan C. "The Origin and Development of Baptist Churches and Institutions in Southern California." Master's thesis, University of Southern California, 1938. 194 pp.

7966. Enriquez, Angel. *12a Solemne Procesion del Corpus.* Los Angeles, 1938. 24 pp.
    A commemorative booklet issued at the annual procession honoring Our Lady of Guadalupe, containing historical background of the parish of Our Lady of Guadalupe.

7967. Esch, I. Lynd. "A Historical Study of the Church of the United Brethren in Christ in California." Master's thesis, University of Southern California, 1941. 166 pp.

7968. Fan, Chan Hon. "History of Chinese Methodism on the Pacific Coast." *California Christian Advocate* 75 (October 28, 1926): 2-3.

7969. Fellers, Donald R. "The Problem of a Language Church in Transition: A Survey of Trinity Methodist Church, Pasadena, California." Master's thesis, University of Southern California, 1947. 78 pp.
    Swedish people.

7970. "Fighting Nuns." *Newsweek* 71 (April 1, 1968): 100.
    Dispute Between Sisters of the Immaculate Heart of Mary and Cardinal McIntyre.

7971. First A[frican] M[ethodist] E[piscopal] Church. *Milestones of Progress, 1872, 1903, 1953; 81st Anniversary of Founding and 50th Year at 8th and Town . . .* Los Angeles, [1953]. [50] pp.

7972. First Christian Reformed Church, Los Angeles. *Silver Anniversary . . . 1914-1939, Los Angeles.* [Los Angeles, 1939?]. 23 pp.

7973. First English Lutheran Church, Los Angeles. *Golden Jubilee and Dedication Service.* [Los Angeles, 1937?]. 11 pp.

7974. First Methodist Episcopal Church. *The Horizon*. Written by The Pages' Club and compiled by Harold G. Black. Los Angeles, 1938. 95 pp.
History of the First Methodist Episcopal Church.

7975. First Presbyterian Japanese Church, Los Angeles. *A Glimpse of Institutional Japanese First Presbyterian Church*. Los Angeles, 1905. [10] pp.

7976. Fish, Merle E., Jr. "Adjustment of Large Downtown and Boulevard Churches in Los Angeles to Socio-Cultural Factors in the Community." Doctoral dissertation, University of Southern California, 1959. 137 pp.

7977. Foley, Thomas J. *Saint Barnabas*. Long Beach, 1951. 27 pp.

7978. ——— *Twenty-Fifth Anniversary — Saint Barnabas Parish*. Long Beach, 1964. 35 pp.

7979. *Fortieth Anniversary—St. Anthony's Parish, 1903-1943*. Long Beach, 1943. 130 pp.

7980. Fujiyoshi, Donald H. "A Study of the Educational Program of the Church School of the Japanese Christian Church and Institute of Los Angeles." Master's thesis, University of Southern California, 1942. 161 pp.

7981. Galvin, Michael J. *Holy Family Church*. Glendale, 1968. Unp.

7982. Gelbach, Alice M. "The Catholic Church in Pomona." *Pomona Valley Historian* 3 (1967): 112-23.

7983. Gibson, La Dessa. "An Interview with Clergyman Frank Dyer." *California Graphic* 5 (June 9, 1928): 8+.
Pastor of the Wilshire Blvd. Congregational Church.

7984. Ginty, Denis. *Nativity Church*. El Monte, 1955. 100 pp.

7985. Glennon, James J. *Saint Anthony's Parish*. San Gabriel, 1957. 52 pp.

7986. Gliauda, Jurgis. *Sv. Kazimiero Parapija*. New York, 1966. 231 pp.
Commemorates the silver anniversary of Saint Casmir's Parish, Los Angeles.

7987. *Golden Jubilee of Saint Anthony's Croatian Roman Catholic Church*. Los Angeles, 1960. Unp.

7988. *Golden Jubilee of St. Joseph Church, Los Angeles, California, 1903-1953*. Los Angeles, 1953. 118 pp.

7989. "Great Churches of America: VIII. First Presbyterian, Hollywood, California." *Christian Century* 67 (September 20, 1950): 1098-1105.

7990. Green, J. B. "Genesis of the Southern California Annual Conference." *California Christian Advocate* 75 (September 16, 1926): 12.

7991. Greene, Austin J. *St. Joseph the Worker Church*. Canoga Park, 1961. Unp.

7992. Guzman, Frank A. "Bi-Weekly Reports of Social Group Workers, Content and Use in the Church Welfare Bureau of the Church Federation of Los Angeles." Master's thesis, University of Southern California, 1950. 84 pp.

7993. Hackel, Stuart M. "The Implications of the Exemption from Property Taxation of Religious Property in Los Angeles County." Doctoral dissertation, University of California, Los Angeles, 1967. 273 pp.

7994. Hall, Martin. "What God Hath Wrought; Experiment in Church Integration in Los Angeles." *Frontier* 8 (September 1957): 17-8.

7995. Hanrahan, Peter T. *Golden Anniversary— All Souls Parish*. Alhambra, 1962. 96 pp.

7996. Haran, Michael J. *Diamond Jubilee, 1909-1969. St. John Evangelist Church*. Los Angeles, 1969. 167 pp.

7997. ——— *Golden Jubilee, 1917-1967, Saint Paul's Parish*. Los Angeles, 1967. 98 pp.

7998. Harkness, Elizabeth. "A History of the Presbytery of Los Angeles, 1850-1928." Master's thesis, University of Southern California, 1929. 122 pp.

7999. Harlan, Morgan M. "Religion in the Homes of Six Hundred Eighty College Students." Master's thesis, University of Southern California, 1947. 104 pp.

8000. Harrington, C. Henry, ed. *Marching Along;*

A History of the Highland Park Presbyterian Church, 1898-1948. [N.p.], 1948. 34 pp.

8001. Haskell, George W. "Formative Factors in the Life and Thought of Southern California Congregationalism, 1850-1908." Doctoral dissertation, University of Southern California, 1947. 223 pp.

8002. Haussler, John C. "The History of the Seventh-Day Adventist Church in California." Doctoral dissertation, University of Southern California, 1945. 468 pp.

8003. Hayes, Thomas G. *Saint Marcellius.* Los Angeles, 1959. Unp.

8004. Henley, David C. "The Clerical Conservative; A Study of Conservative and Ultra-Rightist Protestant Ministers and Organizations of the Los Angeles Area." Master's thesis, University of Southern California, 1964. 128 pp.

8005. Henry, Helen E. "A Study of Attitudes and Social Values of the Youth of Four Selected Negro Churches of Los Angeles." Master's thesis, University of Southern California, 1945. 108 pp.

8006. Henry, Helga B. *Mission on Main Street.* Boston, 1955. 200 pp.
Union Rescue Mission.

8007. Hessel, Josephine. "The History of the Catholic Church in Los Angeles [1850-1930]." Master's thesis, University of Southern California, 1938. 110 pp.

8008. Hine, Leland D. *Baptists in Southern California.* Valley Forge, Pa., 1966.
Chapters 7-10 (pp. 77-181) detail period from 1892 to 1966, with emphasis on the greater Los Angeles area.

8009. *Historia de la Parroquia de la Asuncion.* Los Angeles 1961. Unp.

8010. *History of the Church of Saint Vincent de Paul.* Los Angeles, 1925. Unp.

8011. Hoick, John E. *The Fruitage of Fifty Years in California; A History of the Evangelical Lutheran Synod of California, in Connection with the United Lutheran Church in America, 1891-1941 ... Together with a Brief Sketch of Each of the Congregations of the Synod, and a Biography of the*

Sons and Daughters of the Synod. [N.p., 1941]. 179 pp.

8012. Hollywood. Blessed Sacrament Church. *History of Blessed Sacrament Parish, 1904-1954. Golden Jubilee Souvenir, October 15-16-17, 1954.* Hollywood, [1954]. 51 pp.

8013. *Hospital—Sanitarium of St. John of God.* Los Angeles, 1943. Unp.
Operated by a religious nursing order.

8014. *The Hospitaller Order of St. John of God.* Los Angeles, 1950. Unp.
A religious nursing order, Los Angeles.

8015. Houghton, Frank B. *History of the Plaza Church.* Hollywood, [c1945?]. [16] pp.

8016. Hourihan, James. *St. Luke the Evangelist Church.* Temple City, 1946. 48 pp.

8017. —— *St. Luke's Church.* Temple City, 1951. 55 pp.

8018. Householder, Donald H. "The Place of Evangelism in the Church School (Sunday School) of a Certain Protestant Denomination (Methodist Episcopal Church South) in the Los Angeles District." Master's thesis, University of Southern California, 1929. 107 pp.

8019. Huebner, Paul F. "A Study of the Programs of the Rural Supply Charges of the Methodist Episcopal Church on the Long Beach District." Master's thesis, University of Southern California, 1922. 109 pp.

8020. Hunter, Allan A. "Attack on Crime Gains Ground: Los Angeles Churchmen Make Headway in Fight on Gangster Rule." *Christian Century* 54 (December 8, 1937): 1534.

8021. —— "Auspicious Start for Weekday Plan: Los Angeles Registers 5,000 Children in Religious Classes." *Christian Century* 61 (November 1, 1944): 1264.

8022. Hutchins, Jennings. "A History of Quaker Social Thought and Action in Southern California." Master's thesis, University of Southern California, 1947. 293 pp.

8023. *Iglesia del Santo Nino.* Los Angeles, 1942. Unp.

8024. Ines, Doroteo B. "Influence of Motion Pictures Upon Sunday School Children (Ages 11-17) of Christian Churches of Los Angeles, California." Master's thesis, University of Southern California, 1938. 93 pp.

8025. Jackson, George F. "The History of Seventh-Day Adventist Education in California." Doctoral dissertation, University of Southern California, Los Angeles, 1959. 354 pp.

8026. Jervey, Edward D. *The History of Methodism in Southern California and Arizona.* Nashville, Tenn., [1960]. 247 pp.
Numerous references to the Los Angeles area.

8027. —— "The Methodist Church and the University of Southern California." *Historical Society of Southern California Quarterly* 40 (1958): 59-69.

8028. Jones, Dilys. "Pilgrim's Progress." *Westways* 42 (August 1950): 14-5.
Pilgrim Place, a home for retired ministers and missionaries in Claremont.

8029. *Jubileo de Plata de la Iglesia de Ntra. Sra. de la Soledad.* Los Angeles, 1950. 30 pp.

8030. Kaiser, Robert B. "The McIntyre Controversy." *Los Angeles* 8 (August 1964): 28-31+.
Archbishop James Cardinal McIntyre, Los Angeles.

8031. Kelley, Douglas O. *History of the Diocese of California from 1849 to 1914 . . . Together with Sketches of the Dioceses of Sacramento and Los Angeles, and of the District of San Joaquin from Their Organization.* San Francisco, [1915]. 471 pp.

8032. Kelley, Robert K. "The Church's Ministry to College Students in the United Presbyterian Churches of Southern California." Doctoral dissertation, University of Southern California, 1960. 288 pp.
Episcopal Church.

8033. Kempin, Albert J. "Leadership Education in the Churches of God in Southern California." Master's thesis, University of Southern California, 1940. 87 pp.

8034. Kloepfer, W. Wesley. *St. Frances of Rome Church.* West Los Angeles, 1967. 44 pp.
Pictorial history of parish church in Azusa.

8035. Krebs, A. V., Jr. "Catholicism in Los Angeles—I: A Church of Silence." *Commonweal* 80 (July 10, 1964): 467-76.

8036. Kucinskas, John A. *The Tenth Anniversary of St. Casmir's Lithuanian Parish.* Los Angeles, 1951. 58 pp.

8037. Lamott, Kenneth. "A Quiet Revolt." *Horizon* 12 (Winter 1970): 68-72.
Archdiocese of Los Angeles.

8038. Lani, Mathias. *St. Stephen's Roman Catholic Church.* Los Angeles, 1953. Unp.

8039. Leo, John. "Catholicism in Los Angeles — II: The DuBay Case." *Commonweal* 80 (July 10, 1964): 477-82.

8040. LeShana, David C. *Quakers in California.* Newberg, Ore., [1969]. 186 pp.
Scattered references to the Los Angeles area.

8041. Lewis, James. "An Historical Survey of Radical Sectarianism in Los Angeles." Master's thesis, Occidental College, 1950. 283 pp.

8042. Lindsay, Harry A. "Political Aspects of Church Social Action Committees at the Local Level in Los Angeles County." Master's thesis, University of Southern California, 1964. 192 pp.

8043. Looney, Floyd. *History of California Southern Baptists.* Fresno, 1954. 494 pp.

8044. Los Angeles Baptist City Mission Society. *Twenty-Fifth Anniversary, 1906-31.* [Los Angeles, 1931?]. 46 pp.

8045. —— *Twenty-Five Years of Building into a City.* Los Angeles, 1930. 45 pp.

8046. Mannix, Dolorosa, Sister. *The Congregation of the Sisters of Saint Joseph of Carondolet.* Los Angeles, 1950. Unp.

8047. Marquis, Neeta. *Immanuel and the Fifty Years, 1888-1938.* Los Angeles, 1938. 76 pp.
Immanuel Presbyterian Church, Los Angeles.

8048. Marshall, Thomas C. *Into the Streets and Lanes: The Beginnings and Growth of the Social Work of the Episcopal Church in the Diocese of Los Angeles, 1887-1947.* Claremont, 1948. 178 pp.

8049. McDonald, Tom. "The Priest and the Cardinal." *Frontier* 15 (August 1964): 10-3.

Father DuBay, Cardinal McIntyre, and the controversy over racial policy in the Archdiocese of Los Angeles.

8050. McGarvey, Vincent J., O.S.A. *Our Mother of Good Counsel Church.* Hollywood, 1962. Unp.

8051. McGoldrick, Patrick. *St. Bridget of Sweden.* Van Nuys, 1958. Unp.

8052. McGroarty, John S. *Silver Jubilee—All Souls Parish.* Alhambra, 1938. 98 pp.

8053. McHenry, Henry J. *Our Lady of the Rosary Church.* Paramount, 1950. Unp.

8054. McHugh, Pat, and Schultz, Karen. *25th Anniversary. St. Finbar Parish.* Burbank, 1963. 42 pp.

8055. McNicholas, Thomas. *Souvenir Booklet of Saint Jerome Parish.* Los Angeles, 1953. 28 pp.

8056. McPherson, Aimee Semple. "Foursquare." *Sunset* 58 (February 1927): 14-6+.

Mrs. McPherson outlines the tenets of her faith, analyzes the drawing power of Angelus Temple, and describes her methods of preaching.

8057. McWilliams, Carey. "Battle for the Clergy." *Nation* 166 (February 7, 1948): 150-2.

Dr. James W. Fifield's "Spiritual Mobilization."

8058. ——— "Dianetics: The Trouble-Born Quick-Cure, Without the Religious Trappings, Brings Back Memories of Aimee and the Utopians." *Frontier* 2 (January 1951): 8-11.

A "Home Psychoanalysis" cult founded by L. Ron Hubbard, a writer of science-fiction.

8059. Miller, Elaine H. "The Use of Pastoral Case-Work by Twenty-Five Protestant or Evangelical Churches in the City of Los Angeles." Master's thesis, University of Southern California, 1941. 143 pp.

8060. Miller, Geoff. "Our Churches . . . and Their Leaders." *Los Angeles* 2 (December 1961): 21-5.

8061. Mission Covenant Church, Los Angeles. *A Half Century . . . 1889-1939.* Los Angeles, 1939. 56 pp.

8062. Mitchell, James W. "A Program for Single Young Adults at the First Methodist Church of Los Angeles." Master's thesis, University of Southern California, 1956. 213 pp.

8063. Mixon, Mrs. John L. "The Presbyterian Church, U.S.A., in the Inner City of Los Angeles, California [1930-1956]." Los Angeles, 1956-57. 165 pp. Mimeographed.

8064. Monrovia, California, First Presbyterian Church. *Golden Jubilee. 1888-1938.* [Monrovia, 1938?]. [24] pp.

8065. Moran, Thomas. *St. John Chrysostom Church.* Inglewood, 1961. 28 pp.

8066. Morning Star Missionary Baptist Church. *Thirty-Eighth Anniversary, 1928-1966.* Los Angeles, 1966. 56 pp.

Los Angeles.

8067. Moss, Edwin. *Sixty Years, the Church of the Angels, the Bishop's Chapel.* [Pasadena, 1951]. 51 pp.

Episcopal Church, Highland Park District, Los Angeles.

8068. Muir, Leo J. *A Century of Mormon Activities in California.* Salt Lake City, 1952. 2 vols.

Vol. I is historical; Vol. II, biographical.

8069. Neal, Thomas A. *Saint Vibiana's Los Angeles Cathedral, 1876-1950.* Los Angeles, 1950. 11 pp.

8070. Newmark, Marco R. "Wilshire Boulevard Boulevard Temple: Congregation B'nai B'rith 1862-1947." *Historical Society of Southern California Quarterly* 38 (1956): 167-84.

8071. O'Callaghan, James A. *Our Lady of Malibu.* Malibu, [n.d.]. 24 pp.

8072. O'Donnell, Edmond. *The Church of the American Martyrs.* Manhattan Beach, 1958. Unp.

8073. O'Donnell, Terence M., C.M. *St. Vincent de Paul Church.* Los Angeles, c1968. Unp.

8074. O'Dowd, Patrick J. *A Brief History of St. Alphonsus Parish.* Montebello, n.d. Unp.

8075. O'Gara, Joseph G., S.J. *Blessed Sacrament Parish. Church and Family Pictorial.* Hollywood, 1968. Unp.

    Mostly pictorial.

8076. Ogura, Kosei. "A Sociological Study of the Buddhist Churches in North America; With a Case Study of Gardena, California, Congregation." Master's thesis, University of Southern California, 1933. 90 pp.

8077. O'Halloran, Michael. *The Tenth Anniversary of the Church of the Most Precious Blood of Jesus, 1926-1936.* Los Angeles, 1936. 48 pp.

8078. O'Keefe, Gerald M. *Church of the Holy Angels.* Arcadia, 1966. Unp.

8079. O'Keefe, Timothy. *Sacred Heart Church.* Altadena, 1954. 20 pp.

8080. Omark, Edwin J. "A History of the Swedish Baptist Churches of California." Master's thesis, University of Southern California, 1944. 147 pp.

8081. Orr, James E. *The Inside Story of the Hollywood Christian Group.* Grand Rapids, Mich., [1955]. 134 pp.

8082. Ortega, Alicia. *La Santisima Virgen de Talpa, Titular de la Parroquia Rodeada de los Emblemas de las Asociaciones y Grupos que han existido en la Parroquia duarte estos Veinticinco Anos de 1938 a 1963.* Los Angeles, 1964. 78 pp.

8083. Osaki, Norio. "A Survey of Interdenominational Cooperation Within Each of Three Japanese Religions in Los Angeles, Shinto, Buddhism, and Christianity." Master's thesis, University of Southern California, 1941. 131 pp.

8084. O'Toole, Thomas N. *St. Ambrose Church.* Hollywood, 1951. 68 pp.

8085. Pasadena. Presbyterian Church. *Fifty Years, 1875-1925.* [Pasadena, 1925]. 19 pp.

8086. ———— *The Story of the Pasadena Presbyterian Church.* Pasadena, 1945. 24 pp.

8087. *Pearl of Great Price.* Los Angeles, 1953. Unp.

    History of the Little Sisters of the Poor.

8088. [Perry, John D. K.]. *A History of the First Unitarian Church of Los Angeles, California, 1877-1937.* Los Angeles, [1937?]. 31 pp.

8089. Phillips, Grace D., and Cole, Myron C. *Seventy-Five Romantic Years. Hollywood-Beverly Christian Church, 1888-1963.* Hollywood, 1963. 160 pp.

    History of the first Protestant church in Hollywood.

8090. Power, T. Franklin. *The Blessed Sacrament Church, a Sketch.* [Hollywood, c1927?]. [29] pp.

8091. "Presbyterian Church: A Vigorous Agency for a Sober Faith Grows Big in Hollywood." *Life* 26 (January 10, 1949): 75-84.

    Rev. Louis Hadley Evans and the First Presbyterian Church of Hollywood.

8092. "Presbyterian in Hollywood." *Time* 50 (August 25, 1947): 58-9.

    Rev. Louis Hadley Evans of the First Presbyterian Church of Hollywood, largest U.S. Presbyterian congregation.

8093. Redford, M. E. *The Rise of the Church of the Nazarene.* Kansas City, Mo., 1948. 110 pp.

    Chapter II (pp. 29-48) details the founding of this church in Los Angeles by Phineas F. Bresee.

8094. Rider, Arthur W. *Historical Address on the Occasion of the 50th Anniversary of the Organization of the Southern California Baptist Convention.* Los Angeles, [1941]. 27 pp.

8095. Ritter, Elizabeth. "The History of the Protestant Episcopal Church in Southern California." Master's thesis, University of Southern California, 1936. 176 pp.

8096. Roloff, H. Wesley. "A Study of Contemporary Doctrines of Universal Restoration with Particular Reference to the Los Angeles Area." Master's thesis, University of Southern California, 1944. 223 pp.

    A study of reconciliation of religions from a theological view point.

8097. Rose, Mary L. "The Chief Objectives and Program Elements in a Selected Group of Philosophic and Religious Organizations in Los Angeles." Master's thesis, University of Southern California, 1933. 100 pp.

8098. "Round the Clock Vigil." *American Magazine* 157 (October 1954): 56.
   All-night church services in the Little Brown Church in the Valley (North Hollywood).

8099. Ruether, Rosemary. "Crisis in Los Angeles." *Continuum* 2 (1965): 652-62.
   Revolt of Father DuBay and Father Coffield against Cardinal McIntyre.

8100. Ryan, Maurice J. *Saint Rose of Lima.* Maywood, 1954. 80 pp.

8101. Sacon, Y. H. "A Study of the Religious Organizations in Japanese Communities in America." Report to the Department of Religious Education, University of Southern California, 1932. 231 pp.

8102. *Sacred Heart Church.* Lancaster, 1956. Unp.

8103. *Saint Ambrose Church.* Los Angeles, 1954. 38 pp.

8104. *St. Benedict.* Montebello, 1959. Unp.

8105. *St. Bernadette's Parish—21 Years.* Los Angeles, 1968. Unp.

8106. *St. Cornelius Parish.* Long Beach, 1960. 56 pp.

8107. *Saint Ferdinand's Church.* San Fernando, 1949. Unp.

8108. *Saint James.* Torrance, 1961. Unp.

8109. "Saint John's Church, Los Angeles, Calif." *Liturgical Arts* 16 (August 1948): 128-9.

8110. *Saint Luke's Roman Catholic Church.* Temple City, 1956. 56 pp.

8111. *St. Therese Church.* Alhambra, 1951. 64 pp.

8112. San Fernando, Presbyterian Church. *Presbyterian Church, San Fernando, California, 1889-1939.* San Fernando, 1939. 16 pp.

8113. *Santa Teresita. Silver Jubilee Celebration.* Duarte, 1955. Unp.
   Catholic convent, Carmelite Sisters of the Third Order.

8114. Scaff, Marilee K., ed. *Perspectives on a College Church; A Report of the College Church Study in Claremont, California.* [By] Theodore M. Greene [and others]. New York, [1961]. 239 pp.

8115. Schneiders, Joseph G. *Our Lady of Peace.* Sepulveda, n.d. 39 pp.

8116. Scranton, Cathryn C. *History of the Highland Park Methodist Episcopal Church.* Los Angeles, 1935. 28 pp.

8117. *75th Anniversary of the First Methodist Church, Long Beach, California, 1884-1959.* Long Beach, 1959. Unp.

8118. Shaughnessy, John and Cupp, Norbert. *The Church of St. Peter and St. Paul.* Wilmington, 1965. Unp.

8119. Shear, Patrick. *Golden Jubilee—St. Matthias Parish, 1913-1963.* Huntington Park, 1963. 103 pp.

8120. Shuler, Robert P. *"McPhersonism," A Study of Healing Cults and Modern Day "Tongues" Movements, Containing Summary of Facts as to Disappearance and Reappearance of Aimee Semple McPherson.* Los Angeles, [1926?]. 128 pp.

8121. *Silver Jubilee and Dedication of Incarnation Church.* Glendale, 1952. 76 pp.

8122. *Silver Jubilee of Our Lady of the Rosary of Talpa Parish.* Los Angeles, 1953. 79 pp.

8123. *Silver Jubilee of St. Turibius Church.* Los Angeles, 1952. 44 pp.

8124. *Silver Jubilee—Sacred Heart Church.* Covina, 1936. Unp.

8125. *Sixty Years in Our Parish, 1889-1949.* San Pedro, 1949. 55 pp.
   Commemorates the diamond anniversary of Mary Star of the Sea Church.

8126. Smith, Harry I. "A Study of the Oxford Group Movement and Its Influence in Southern California." Master's thesis, University of Southern California, 1934. 163 pp.

8127. Smith, S. Raynor, Jr. "The Attitudes and Practices of the Methodist Church in California with Reference to Certain Significant Social Crises, 1847 Through 1949." Doctoral dissertation,

University of Southern California, 1955. 487 pp.

8128. Southern California Baptist Convention. *We the Baptists of Southern California.* Los Angeles, [n.d]. 89 pp.

8129. *Souvenir of the Silver Jubilee of St. Joseph's Church, Twelfth and Los Angeles Streets, Los Angeles.* Los Angeles, 1928. 75 pp.

8130. *Souvenir Program Commemorating the One Hundredth Anniversary of the Sisters of the Immaculate Heart of Mary, 1848-1948.* Los Angeles, 1948. Unp.

8131. Stack, Daniel J., S.J. *Church of the Blessed Sacrament.* Hollywood, 1923. Unp.

8132. Stilson, Mary E. "Dana Bartlett, the Modern Mission Father." *Out West,* new series, 3 (April 1912): 222-6.
Bethlehem Mission on Vignes Street, Los Angeles.

8133. Stocker, Joseph. "The Real Cool Preacher of East L. A." *American Mercury* 81 (September 1955): 22-6.
"Reverend Andy" Griffin and his "unorthodox one-man crusade against delinquency and juvenile gang life."

8134. Stroup, Paul E. *Our Lady of Lourdes.* Northridge, 1960. Unp.

8135. Takahashi, Kyojiro. "A Study of the Japanese Shinto and Buddhism in Los Angeles." Master's thesis, University of Southern California, 1937. 134 pp.

8136. Tarver, David F. "A Critical Evaluation of the Church Through the Story and Study of the Imperial Heights Methodist Church, Los Angeles, California." Master's thesis, University of Southern California, 1953. 128 pp.

8137. *Tenth Anniversary. St. Dominic's Parish.* Eagle Rock, 1931. 23 pp.

8138. Thacker, Ernest W. "The Methodist Church in Southern California in Relation to the 'Social Gospel,' 1928 Through 1941." Doctoral dissertation, University of Southern California, 1952. 435 pp.

8139. "Trinity—An All-Around Church: A Great Hotel - Clubhouse - Gymnasium - Theatre - Hospital -Auditorium in Los Angeles." *Independent* 84 (October 25, 1915): 154.

8140. Trinity Evangelical Church, Los Angeles. *Golden Anniversary.* [Los Angeles?, 1932?]. [31] pp.

8141. "Triumphant Campaign." *Time* 40 (August 3, 1942): 38.
Success of Dr. James W. Fifield's campaign to liquidate debt of First Congregational Church.

8142. Truxaw, Joseph J. *Church of the Immaculate Conception.* Los Angeles, 1954. Unp.
Pictorial edition.

8143. "Unique Endowment Fund to Perpetuate St. John's [Episcopal] Church." *Los Angeles Saturday Night* 11 (April 4, 1931): 7.

8144. Valakis, A. P. D. *The Cathedral of Saint Sophia in Los Angeles, and the Greek Orthodox Church; Its History and Its Faith.* [N.p.], 1955. 52 pp.

8145. Vandenberg, Hugh. *Our Lady of Refuge.* Long Beach, 1962. Unp.

8146. Walker, Brooks R. "The Ultra-Protestant Patrioteers." *Frontier* 13 (September 1962): 11-3.
"Fulminations of right-wing Christians" in Los Angeles area.

8147. [Washburn, Josephine M.]. *History and Reminiscences of the Holiness Church Work in Southern California and Arizona.* South Pasadena, [1911?]. 463 pp.

8148. Weber, Francis J. *Christ on Wilshire Boulevard. Saint Basil's Catholic Church.* Los Angeles, 1969. 32 pp.

8149. ——— "An Historical Sketch of Saint Vibiana's Cathedral." *Southern California Quarterly* 44 (1962): 43-56.

8150. ——— *A Pictorial History of Saint Victor's Parish.* Los Angeles, 1961. 64 pp.
The story of pioneer Catholicism in West Hollywood.

8151. Wells, Carl D. "A Changing Social Institution in an Urban Environment: A Study of the Changing Behavior Patterns of the Disciples of

Christ in Los Angeles." Doctoral dissertation, University of Southern California, 1931. 276 pp.

8152. Wells, Mariann K. "Chinese Temples in California." Master's thesis, University of California, 1962. 190 pp.

8153. West, W. B., Jr. "Origin and Growth of the Churches of Christ in California." Master's thesis, University of Southern California, 1936. 82 pp.

8154. Wheaton, Nathaniel. "Glance at Churches of Los Angeles." *Los Angeles Saturday Night* 11 (January 3, 1931): 4.
Description of a variety of Los Angeles churches.

8155. White, Lawrence B. "The Claremont Study: Monograph No. 1—. . . A Study of the Claremont Community Church." Master's thesis, Claremont Graduate School, 1931. 153 pp.

8156. Wicher, Edward A. *The Presbyterian Church in California, 1849-1927.* New York, 1927. 360 pp.

8157. Wilcox, William W. *Throop Memorial Universalist Church [Pasadena] . . . 1886-1936.* Pasadena, 1936. 48 pp.

8158. Wilson, Edmund. "The City of Our Lady the Queen of the Angels," in *The American Earthquake: A Documentary of the Twenties and Thirties.* Garden City, N. Y., 1958. Pp. 379-96.
Discusses Rev. Robert Shuler and his rival, Dr. Gustav A. Briegleb.

8159. Winters, Esther M. "A Study of Young People's Society Programs in Selected Churches California." Master's thesis, University of Southern California, 1942. 197 pp.

8160. Wirt, Williston. "Missionaries' Haven: Claremont's Pilgrim Place." *Pomona Valley Historian* 6 (1970): 87-92.

8161. Younger, Paul P. "A Study of Education for Christian Avocations in Selected Protestant Churches of Los Angeles and Vicinity." Master's thesis, University of Southern California, 1943. 106 pp.

SOCIAL AND FRATERNAL ORGANIZATIONS

8162. Arlt. Gustave O. "Thoughts on the Eve of Our Diamond Jubilee." *Historical Society of Southern California Quarterly* 40 (1958): 203-10.
Traces the efforts of the Historical Society of Southern California to find attractive and suitable quarters. Sketches of early society members.

8163. "Attractive Belmont, with Club Appendages." *Los Angeles Saturday Night* 9 (September 28, 1929): 7.
Belmont Country Club, La Tuna Canyon.

8164. Boskin, Joseph. "Associations and Picnics as Stabilizing Forces in Southern California." *California Historical Society Quarterly* 44 (1965): 17-26.

8165. California Federation of Women's Clubs. *California Federation of Women's Clubs Organized at Los Angeles, January 18th, 1900 . . .* Los Angeles, 1901. 31 pp.

8166. Cohoon, Burton W. "Historical Society of Pomona Valley." *Pomona Valley Historian* 2 (1966): 47-64.

8167. Crahan, Marcus E., comp. *The Wine and Food Society of Southern California; A History with a Bibliography of Andre L. Simon.* [Los Angeles], 1957. 60 pp.

8168. Crowther, Mrs. Henry C. *High Lights, the Friday Morning Club, Los Angeles, California, April 1891-1938.* [Los Angeles, 1939]. 62 pp.

8169. Ellerbe, Rose L. *History of Southern California Woman's Press Club, 1894-1929.* Los Angeles, [1930?]. 68 pp.

8170. Ellis, Arthur M., comp. *Historical Review, Seventy-Fifth Anniversary, May 5, 1929, Los Angeles Lodge No. 42, F. & A. M.* [Los Angeles], 1929. 129 pp.

8171. Freemasons. Los Angeles. Holland Lodge No. 20. *Tenth Anniversary Number . . . Jurisdiction of M. W. Sovereign Grand Lodge of California . . . September, A.D. 1921.* [Los Angeles?, 1921]. [6] pp.
Includes a short history of the lodge.

8172. Garrett, Sara G. "The Woman's City Club of Los Angeles." *Out West* New Series, 11 (March 1916): 132.

8173. Gouldner, Helen B. "The Organization Woman: Patterns of Friendship and Organizational Commitment." Doctoral dissertation, University of California, Los Angeles, 1959. 221 pp.
League of Women Voters of Los Angeles.

8174. Grivas, Theodore. "A History of the Los Angeles Young Men's Christian Association: The First Twenty Years." *California Historical Society Quarterly* 44 (1965): 205-27.

8175. "Handsome New Home of California Club." *Los Angeles Saturday Night* 10 (September 6, 1930): 7.
Includes history of club.

8176. Harmsen, Tyrus G. "The Zamorano Club: 1927 to 1961," in *A Bookman's View of Los Angeles*. Los Angeles, 1961. Pp. 91-107.

8177. Hubbell, Thelma L. and Lothrop, Gloria R. "The Friday Morning Club: A Los Angeles Legacy." *Southern California Quarterly* 50 (1968): 59-90.

8178. Jack, Emma L. "Ebell, of Los Angeles." *Woman's Journal* 13 (September 1928): 26-7.
New clubhouse for Ebell Club.

8179. Jonathan Club. *Jonathan Club of Los Angeles, 1909-1910*. [Los Angeles, 1910?]. 62 pp.

8180. Kaitt, C. B. "Success of Los Angeles Men's Club." *National Municipal Review* 9 (August 1920): 520.

8181. Knights of Pythias. California Brigade, Third Regiment. *Souvenir of Its Organization and of Southern California*. [Los Angeles, 1902]. 127 pp.

8182. Long Beach Elks Lodge. *Sixty Years*. Long Beach, 1964. 150 pp.

8183. Los Angeles County Club. *History of the Los Angeles Country Club*. Beverly Hills, 1936. 40 pp.

8184. *The Los Angeles Girls' Council, Los Angeles, Califonia, 1927-1935*. [Los Angeles, 1935]. 59 pp.

8185. Macrate, Arthur N., Jr. *The History of the Tuna Club, Avalon, Santa Catalina Island*. N.p., 1948. 197 pp.

8186. McCord, Clara, ed. *Sixty Years. Long Beach Elks Loge No. 888, 1904-1964*. [Long Beach, 1964]. 160 pp.

8187. Newmark, Marco R. "Pioneer Clubs of Los Angeles Founded During the Nineteenth Century." *Historical Society of Southern California Quarterly* 31 (1949): 299-317.

8188. Pacific Coast Club, Long Beach. *Inaugural Volume*. Long Beach, 1926. 283 pp.

8189. Packman, Ana Begue de. "A Brief Society History." *Historical Society of Southern California Quarterly* 40 (1958): 223-64.
Describes the thirty pilgrimages of the Historical Society of Southern California.

8190. Parks, Marion. "Women's Athletic Club of Los Angeles." *Los Angeles Saturday Night* 14 (July 14, 1934): 6.

8191. Powell, Lawrence Clark. "The Sense of the Past." *Historical Society of Southern California Quarterly* 40 (1958): 325-36.
An address given at the seventy-fifth anniversary meeting of the Historical Society of Southern California in November 1958.

8192. ———— *Ten Years (Almost) of Rounce & Coffinism*. Los Angeles, 1941. 15 pp.
Club of libarians and bookmen.

8193. Robbins, Margaret E. "Functions of the Personnel Committee of the Los Angeles YWCA as Revealed in the Minutes for 1947-1951." Master's thesis, University of Southern California, 1952. 63 pp.

8194. Rotary Club of Los Angeles. *History of the Rotary Club of Los Angeles. Organized June 25, 1909, Club No. 5, Rotary International*. Los Angeles, 1955. 311 pp.

8195. Salley, Robert L. "Activities of the Knights of the Ku Klux Klan in Southern California: 1921-1925." Master's thesis, University of Southern California, 1963. 199 pp.

8196. Schwend, Ted C. "A Short Account of the Junípero Serra Boys' Club of Los Angeles." Master's thesis, University of Southern California, 1965. 72 pp.

8197. Scott, Joseph, III. "The Deb Deluge." *Los Angeles* 12 (December 1967): 28-31+.
The ritual of "coming out" in Los Angeles.

8198. Shochat, Fern D. "The Voluntary Cooperative Association of Los Angeles, 1913-1922." *Southern California Quarterly* 45 (1963): 169-80.
George Millar and Ernest Dawson and their work with the VCA.

8199. Sneed, Virgil. "A Study of the Organization, Operation, and Program of the YMCA of Metropolitan Los Angeles." Master's thesis, University of Southern California, 1970. 55 pp.

8200. Sojourner Truth Industrial Club, Inc. *Golden Anniversary 1905-1954. Ootober17-21, 1954.* [Los Angeles, 1954]. [16] pp.

8201. Steckhan, H. O. "Comic Artists Have Social Dinner Club." *California Graphic* 5 (April 14, 1928): 8+.
The Cartoonists Club.

8202. Stewart, Wendall O. "Mineralogical Society of Southern California." *Trails Magazine* 3 (Winter 1936): 18-9.

8203. Sunset Club of Los Angeles. *Final Meeting of Our First Forty Years, June 28, 1895-May 31, 1935.* [Los Angeles], 1935. 32 pp.

8204. ——— *Sunset Club 1895-1905.* Los Angeles, [1905]. 134 pp.

8205. Trabue, Anne. *History of the Los Angeles Country Club.* Beverly Hills, 1936. 40 pp.

8206. Turlo, Bernice P. "The Use of Professional Time by Eight Staff Workers of a Metropolitan Girl Scout Council." Master's thesis, University of Southern California, 1950. 105 pp.

8207. Union League Club. *Twenty-Fifth Anniversary, Union League Club of Los Angeles, 1914.* Los Angeles, 1914. 154 pp.

8208. University Club of Los Angeles. *The Toreador, 1898-1948, Fiftieth Anniversary Number.* Los Angeles, 1948. 63 pp.

8209. ——— *Twenty-Fifth Anniversary Year Book.* Los Angeles, 1924. 95 pp.

8210. Waddell, Al. "1950 Shrine Convention to Bring 150,000 Shriners to Los Angeles." *Western Housing* 33 (November 1949): 8+.

8211. Wilkins, Barbara. "The Club Glut." *Los Angeles* 13 (May 1968): 30-3.
Private clubs in Los Angeles.

8212. [Wilshire Country Club]. *25th Anniversary Issue, 1919-1944.* Los Angeles, 1944. 19 pp.
Separate reprint of *Wilshire Club News* 11 (September 1944).

8213. Wirt, Florence M. "An Evaluation of the Personal Services of the Young Women's Christian Association of Los Angeles, California." Master's thesis, University of Southern California, 1938. 191 pp.

SOCIAL PROBLEMS

8214. Allen, Gary. "The Plan to Burn Los Angeles." *American Opinion* 10 (May 1967): 31-40.
Describes the "Watts rebellion" as a Communist conspiracy.

8215. "Another Civil-Rights Headache—Plight of Mexican-Americans." *U. S. News and World Report* 60 (June 6, 1966): 46-8.
"Los Angeles, already plagued with Negro violence, sees a new kind of racial danger developing."

8216. Aptheker, Herbert. "The Watts Ghetto Uprising." *Political Affairs* 44 (October 1965): 16-29; (November 1965): 28-44.

8217. Bartlett, Dana W. *The Better City; A Sociological Study of a Modern City.* Los Angeles, 1907. 248 pp.

8218. Baruch, Dorothy (Walter). *Glass House of Prejudice.* New York, 1946. 205 pp.
Race problems in Los Angeles.

8219. Bates, Dorothy. "A Study of Delinquent Girls in a Pasadena High School." Master's thesis, University of Southern California, 1940. 137 pp.
McKinley Junior High School.

8220. Bernstein, Saul. *Alternatives to Violence:*

Alienated Youth and Riots, Race, and Poverty.
New York, [1968, c1967]. 192 pp.
A study of disturbances in various U. S. cities including Los Angeles.

8221. Bianchi, Eugene C. "Los Angeles: Tragedy and Opportunity." *America* 113 (September 11, 1965): 260-1.
Watts Riot, 1965.

8222. Bice, Margaret L. "A Study of the Effects of Replacements in Foster Homes and Institutions on Dependent Children in Los Angeles County." Master's thesis, University of Southern California, 1937. 292 pp.

8223. Bogardus, Emory S. *The City Boy and His Problem; A Survey of Boy Life in Los Angeles...* Los Angeles, 1926. 148 pp.

8224. Bogo, Tulio R. "Social Backgrounds in Los Angeles City and the Communities They Represent." Master's thesis, University of Southern California, 1963. 117 pp.

8225. Boyd, Malcolm. "Violence in Los Angeles." *Christian Century* 82 (September 8, 1965): 1093-5.
Watts Riot, 1965.

8226. Buggs, John A. "Report from Los Angeles." *Journal of Intergroup Relations* 5 (1966): 27-40.
A report on the Watts Riot.

8227. Bullock, Paul. "Poverty in Los Angeles." *Frontier* 17 (September 1966): 5-7.

8228. Bullough, Bonnie. "Alienation in the Ghetto." *American Journal of Sociology* 72 (March 1967): 469-78.
Los Angeles and the San Fernando Valley.

8229. Burma, John H. "Interethnic Marriage in Los Angeles, 1948-1959." *Social Forces* 42 (1963): 156-65.

8230. Casriel, Daniel. *So Fair a House; The Story of Synanon.* Englewood Cliffs, N.J., [1963]. 224 pp.
Synanon Foundation for rehabilitation of drug addicts, begun in Santa Monica.

8231. Cohen, Jerry, and Murphy, William S. *Burn, Baby, Bun! The Los Angeles Race Riot, August, 1965.* New York, 1966. 318 pp.

8232. Cohen, Nathan, ed. *The Los Angeles Riots; A Socio-Psychological Study.* New York, 1970. 742 pp.

8233. Conot, Robert E. *Rivers of Blood, Years of Darkness.* Toronto and New York, 1967. 497 pp.
Watts Riot, 1965.

8234. Costain, Dave, ed. *Anarchy. Los Angeles.* Los Angeles, 1965. Unp.
Watts Riot, 1965.

8235. Crump, Spencer. *Black Riot in Los Angeles; The Story of the Watts Tragedy.* Los Angeles, [1966]. 160 pp.
Watts Riot, 1965.

8236. Dahl, Virgil D. "Geographical Concentration of Juvenile Delinquency in Los Angeles County." Master's thesis, University of Southern California, 1932. [?] pp.

8237. Davidson, Wayne R. "An Analysis of the Problems of Fifty Migrant Boys Who Were Known to the Los Angeles Police Department in 1944." Master's thesis, University of Southern California, 1947. 279 pp.

8238. "Does Anyone Really Care?" *Christian Century* 82 (September 22, 1965): 1148.
Inquires into causes of Watts Riot, 1965.

8239. Domer, Marilyn. "The Zoot-Suit Riot: A Culmination of Social Tensions in Los Angeles." Master's thesis, Claremont Graduate School, 1955. 193 pp.
A study in wartime inter-group relations of the Mexicans and Anglo-Americans as reflected in the riot of June 1943.

8240. Duncan, Ray, and Rau, William. "The Party Liners: Equipped with Electronics and a Strange New Status, the Los Angeles Call Girl Leads an Easy But Empty Life in Some of the Best Parts of Town." *Los Angeles* 9 (April 1965): 48-51+.

8241. Dunne, John G. "The Ugly Mood of Watts: Militant Leaders in Los Angeles' Negro Ghetto Are Trying to Win Power by Threatening Whites with Violence—And Behind Their Threats Lies Hatred." *Saturday Evening Post* 239 (July 16, 1966): 83-7.

8242. Du Vall, Everett W. "A Sociological Study

of Five Hundred Underprivileged Children in a Selected Area of Los Angeles." Doctoral dissertation, University of Southern California, 1936. 432 pp.

8243. Ellis, William R. "Operation Bootstrap: A Case Study in Ideology and the Institutionalization of Protest." Doctoral dissertation, University of California, Los Angeles, 1969. 436 pp.
    Operation Bootstrap: "a small self-help job training organization . . . a relatively direct outgrowth of previously existing protest organizations."

8244. Endore, Samuel G. *Synanon*. Garden City, N. Y., 1968. 360 pp.
    Private drug rehabitation institution founded in Santa Monica.

8245. Evans, Joseph P. "Professional Leadership in the Initiation of Social Community Organization Work in an Area in Transition: An Analysis of a Process Record, Willowbrook, Los Angeles County." Master's thesis, University of Southern California, 1950. 84 pp.

8246. Ferderber, Murray. " 'The 'Games' at Synanon." *Los Angeles* 13 (October 1968) : 41-3+.

8247. "The Fire That Time." *New South* 20 (November 1965) : 2-10.
    The Los Angeles Watts Riot, 1965, pp. 3-5.

8248. Fisher, Lloyd H. *The Problem of Violence; Obsevations on Race Conflict in Los Angeles.* [San Francisco, 1946]. 20 pp.

8249. Fogelson, Robert M., comp. *The Los Angeles Riots.* New York, 1969. 187 pp.
    Select documents relating to the 1965 Watts Riot.

8250. Freudenberg, Edward, and Street, Lloyd. *Social Profiles: Los Angeles County.* For the Welfare Planning Council, Los Angeles Region. Research Department. Los Angeles, 1965. Various paging.

8251. Garfield, John. "How Hollywood Can Better Race Relations." *Negro Digest* 6 (November 1947) : 4-8.

8252. Glover, Katherine "Project 1-E4-15: How Unemployed Men and Women Met Juvenile Delinquency on Its Own Ground." *Survey* 71 (December 1935) : 362-3.

8253. ———— "Stopping Crime at Its Source: Neighborhood Councils of Los Angeles." *Woman's Home Companion* 63 (September 1936) : 28+.

8254. Good, John H. "A History of the Delinquency Control Institute: Its Program to Combat Juvenile Delinquency." Master's thesis, University of Southern California, 1967. 152 pp.

8255. Gordon, Edmond D. "Problem Boys in the Special Schools of Los Angeles." Master's thesis, University of Southern California, 1936. 123 pp.

8256. Governor's Commission on the Los Angeles Riots [McCone, John A., *et al*]. *Violence in the City—An End of a Beginning?* [Los Angeles?], 1965. 101 pp.
    The *Report* of the Governor's Commission comprises Vol. 1 of the full transcript, which runs to eighteen volumes.

8257. Griffing, John B. "A Comparison of the Effects of Certain Socioeconomic Factors upon Size of Family in China, Southern California, and Brazil." Doctoral dissertation, University of Southern California, 1941. 177 pp.

8258. Habecker, Viola A. "A Study of One Hundred Unmarried Mothers in Los Angeles." Master's thesis, University of Southern California, 1935. 89 pp.

8259. Haines, Aubrey. "Skid Row, Los Angeles." *Frontier* 7 (September 1956) : 15+.

8260. Hanley, Anne. "D.C.I.—The Self-Fulfilling Prophecy." *Westways* 61 (November 1969) : 17-20.
    Delinquency Control Institute of University of Southern California's School of Public Administration—background and prospects.

8261. Harper, Helena H. "A Study of Colored Unmarried Mothers in Los Angeles." Master's thesis, University of Southern California, 1932. 61 pp.

8262. Harrod, Merrill L. "A Study of Deviate Personalities as Found in Main Street of Los Angeles." Master's thesis, University of Southern California, 1939. 102 pp.

8263. Harvey, Louise F. "The Delinquent Mexican Boy in an Urban Area, 1945." Master's thesis, University of California, Los Angeles, 1947. 128 pp.
    Based on case histories from Los Angeles Juvenile Hall Records.

8264. Haworth, Shirley I. "Socio-Economic Characteristics of the Potential Unmarried Minor Mother: A Study of Twenty-Two Cases in Jewish Family Service of Los Angeles." Master's thesis, University of Southern California, 1963. 48 pp.

8265. Herberg, Will. "Who Are the Guilty Ones?" *National Review* 17 (September 7, 1965): 769-70.
Watts Riot, 1965.

8266. Honnard, Ronold R., *et al. Views of Authority: Probationers and Probation Officers.* Ed. by A. W. McEachern. University of Southern California, Youth Studies Center, *Research Paper No. 1.* Los Angeles, 1961. 238 pp.

8267. Hopkins, Francis E. "Concern for Problems of Youth Is Prime Project of Redondo Beach." *Western City* 46 (March 1970): 17-8.

8268. "How Culver City Is Successfully Meeting Its Juvenile Problem." *Western City* 11 (December 1935): 14.

8269. Isenberg, Irwin, ed. *The City in Crisis.* New York, 1968. 246 pp.
Contains two essays on Los Angeles: "Watts— 'Remarkably the Same,' " by John C. Waugh, pp. 50-4; and "On-the-Spot in Watts," by Anne Henehan, pp. 54-63.

8270. Jackson, Maurice. "Conformity and Reference Groups in Metropolitan Los Angeles." Doctoral dissertation, University of California, Los Angeles, 1966. 456 pp.

8271. Johns, Dorothy. *Victims of the System; How Crime Grows in Jail and City Hall.* [Los Angeles, 1908]. 20 pp.

8272. Johnson, Virginia. "Boys Who Play with Fire—For Keeps." *Westways* 37 (June 1945): 8-9.
Juvenile offenders sent to County forestry camps instead of to reform school.

8273. Jones, Solomon J. "The Government Riots of Los Angeles, June, 1943." Master's thesis, University of California, Los Angeles, 1969. 166 pp.

8274. Kitani, Misue. "An Inquiry into the Parental Attitude of Selected Japanese-American Families Toward Their Delinquent Sons." Master's thesis, University of Southern California, 1959. 74 pp.

8275. Knoll, Robert E. "Delinquency and Rationalization: A Study of the Delinquent Act." Doctoral dissertation, University of Southern California, 1965. 257 pp.
Data for this study was obtained at the Los Angeles County Probation Department, California Youth Authority, in Norwalk and Chino, and at a Southern California high school.

8276. Kopkind, Andrew. "Watts—Waiting for D-Day." *New Republic* 154 (June 11, 1966): 15-7.

8277. "The Lash, Club, and Mailed Fist." *Nation* 178 (January 9, 1954): 21-2.
Alleged over-reaction of the Los Angeles Press and public to a crime incident involving some local Mexican-Americans.

8278. Lessin, Sylvia. "Adoptive Parents Tell Their Children." Master's thesis, University of Southern California, 1959. 42 pp.

8279. Locke, Charles E. *White Slavery in Los Angeles.* [Los Angeles, c1913]. 68 pp.

8280. Longmoor, Elsa S., and Young, Erle F. "Ecological Interrelationships of Juvenile Delinquency, Dependency, and Population Mobility: A Cartographic Analysis of Data from Long Beach, California." *American Journal of Sociology* 41 (March 1936): 598-610.
Population data taken from 1930 census.

8281. Loren, Eugene L. *Economic Background— the Los Angeles Riot Study.* Los Angeles, c1967. 48 pp.

8282. Los Angeles. Chamber of Commerce. Research Committee. *The Dynamics of the Youth Explosion—A Look Ahead.* [N.p., n.d.]. 64 pp.

8283. Los Angeles Coordinating Councils. Juvenile Research Committee. *Youth's New Day, the Juvenile Problem in Los Angeles and Tools for Its Solution.* Los Angeles, 1935. 95 pp.

8284. Marshall, Thomas C. *Into the Streets and Lanes: The Beginnings and Growth of the Social Work of the Episcopal Church in the Diocese of Los Angeles, 1887-1947.* Claremont, 1948. 178 pp.

8285. Marx, Wesley. "Divorce—Los Angeles Style." *Los Angeles* 6 (October 1963): 24-7+; (November 1963): 41-7+.

8286. Masotti, Louis H., and Bowen, Don R., eds. *Riots and Rebellion; Civil Violence in the Urban Community.* Beverly Hills, [c1968]. 459 pp.
Includes William McCord and John Howard, "Negro Opinions in Three Riot Cities [Houston, Los Angeles, Oakland]," and T. M. Tomlinson, "Riot Ideology Among Urban Negroes," based on data from a study of the Los Angeles Watts Riot of 1965.

8287. Mathison, Richard. "Troubled Generation." *Newsweek* 57 (May 22, 1961): 26+.
Juvenile delinquency in Los Angeles County, and the attempts of an organization called Group Guidance to combat it.

8288. Maxwell, William C. "An Investigation of Boy Delinquency in Long Beach, California, and Its Implications for the Public Schools." Master's thesis, University of Southern California, 1936. 356 pp.

8289. McAllister, Joy T. "A Study of Delinquent Jewish Youth in Los Angeles County." Doctoral dissertation, University of California, Los Angeles, 1968. 185 pp.

8290. McCarthy, Thomas J. "Report from Los Angeles." *Commonweal* 38 (June 25, 1943): 243-4.
Attacks on "zoot-suiters."

8291. McClenahan, Bessie A. *The Changing Urban Neighborhood: From Neighbor to Nigh-Dweller, A Sociological Study.* Los Angeles, 1929. 140 pp.

8292. Mc Grory, Mary. "A New Outburst in Watts." *America* 114 (April 2, 1966): 437.

8293. McWilliams, Carey. "Los Angeles' Pachuco Gangs." *New Republic* 108 (January 18, 1943): 76-7.

8294. ——— "Nervous Los Angeles. I. The 'Wolf-Pack' Crusade." *Nation* 170 (June 10, 1950): 570-1.
"Lurid" press campaign against Mexican-American delinquency.

8295. ——— "Suicide Bridge." *Frontier* 5 (November 1953): 9-11.
Colorado Street Bridge in Pasadena, originally called Arroyo Seco Bridge.

8296. ——— "Watts: The Forgotten Slum." *Nation* 201 (August 30, 1965): 89-90.

8297. ——— "Zoot-Suit Riots." *New Republic* 108 (June 21, 1943): 818-20.

8298. Meriwether, Louise. "What the People of Watts Say." *Frontier* 16 (October 1965): 7-9.
Quotes from various residents.

8299. Mesnick, Charles. "Social Problems Presented by 200 Unattached Men with Jail Records Receiving Unemployment Relief in Los Angeles County, October, 1939, to April, 1940." Master's thesis, University of Southern California, 1944. 101 pp.

8300. Meyer, Larry L. "D.C.I. and the Problem of Juvenile Crime." *Westways* 56 (July 1964): 12-5; (August 1964): 12-4.
Delinquency Control Institute at University of Southern California—past, present, future.

8301. Milich, Cynthia S. "Watts, 1965: A Content Analysis of Student Responses." Master's thesis, Whittier College, 1967. 293 pp.

8302. Mittelbach, Frank G. *Intermarriage of Mexican-Americans.* Los Angeles, 1966. 84 pp.
Los Angeles.

8303. Morgan, Leo. "Marriage Consents for Minors: Attitudes of Deputy Probation Officers Toward Responsibility and Decision Making." Master's thesis, University of Southern California, 1965. 52 pp.

8304. Moseley, Ruth J. "Study of Negro Families in Los Angeles." Master's thesis, University of Southern California, 1938. 115 pp.

8305. Moser, Don. "There's No Easy Place to Pin the Blame." *Life* 59 (August 27, 1965): 31-3.
Watts Riot, 1965.

8306. Mosk, Stanley. "Pattern for Local Unity; Institute on Community Relations, Los Angeles County." *New Republic* 112 (May 1945): 674-5.

8307. Nimkoff, Meyer F. "Social Distance Between Child and Parent with Special Reference to Processes of Parent-Child Interaction and Certain of Their Origins." Doctoral dissertation, University of Southern California, 1928. 402 pp.

8308. Oberschall, Anthony R. "Los Angeles Riot of August, 1965." *Social Problems* 15 (1968): 322-41.

8309. "Out of a Cauldron of Hate—Arson and Death." *Life* 59 (August 27, 1965): 20-30.
Watts Riot, 1965.

8310. "Pachuco Troubles." *Inter-American* 2 (August 1943): 5-6.
"Zoot-suit riots" in Los Angeles.

8311. Panunzio, Constantine. "Intermarriage in Los Angeles, 1924-33." *American Journal of Sociology* 47 (March 1942): 690-701.

8312. Perry, Glenn E. "Juvenile Delinquency in the Junior and Senior High Schools of Los Angeles: Its Prevalence, Manifestations, and Causes." Master's thesis, University of Southern California, 1937. 75 pp.

8313. Pheifer, Phyllis. "Village for Youth: A Successful Experiment in Democratic Living." *Frontier* 5 (July 1954): 17-8.
Ormsby Village for youth in Topanga Canyon, where "young people of high-school are live and work together for two weeks each summer, learning through the intimate association of camp life that brotherhood can be a reality now, not a dream of the future." Idea initiated by Los Angeles County Unitarian Council.

8314. Poe, Elizabeth. "Watts." *Frontier* 16 (September 1965): 5-7.

8315. "Portent of Storm." *Christian Century* 60 (June 23, 1943): 735-6.
"Zuit-soot riots," Los Angeles.

8316. Ranker, Jess E., Jr. "A Study of Juvenile Gangs in the Hollenbeck Area of East Los Angeles." Master's thesis, University of Southern California, 1957. 127 pp.

8317. Ransford, Harry E. "Isolation, Powerless, and Violence: A Study of Attitudes and Participation in the Watts Riot." *American Journal of Sociology* 73 (1968): 581-91.

8318. Reese, John. "Scoundrels Among the Angels." *Westways* 57 (June 1965): 37-9.
Various "confidence men," pickpockets, and petty crooks of Los Angeles.

8319. "Report from Los Angeles, the Watts Riot of 1965." *Journal of Intergroup Relations* 5 (1966): 27-40.

8320. Riley, Frank. "The Student Drug Kick." *Los Angeles* 10 (October 1965): 58-61.
Drug use by Los Angeles students.

8321. "Riot and Premise Protection." *Security World* 2 (September 1965): 10-4.
Concerns the Los Angeles Watts Riot.

8322. Roberts, Myron. "The New Los Angeles Woman: Some Forces That Shaped Her [A Man's View]." *Los Angeles* 12 (April 1967): 28-9+.

8323. ———— "The New Violence: An Age of 'Freaky' Crime." *Los Angeles* 14 (October 1969): 30-2+.
Reaction of Los Angeles to Sharon Tate case.

8324. Robinson, Duane M. *Chance to Belong: Story of the Los Angeles Youth Project, 1943-1949.* New York, 1949. 173 pp.

8325. Robinson, Elizabeth H. "An Inquiry into the Immediate Social Situations of Twelve Adolescent Unmarried Mothers Receiving Public Assistance." Master's thesis, University of Southern California, 1949. 59 pp.
Los Angeles.

8326. Robinson, Willian W. *Tarnished Angels: Paradisiacal Turpitude in Los Angeles.* [Los Angeles, 1964]. [16] pp.
Brief history of Los Angeles organized prostitution, 1890s to 1900s.

8327. Rossa, Della. *Why Watts Exploded: How the Ghetto Fought Back.* [Los Angeles, 1966]. 21 pp.

8328. Rustin, Bayard. "Some Lessons from Watts." *Journal of Intregroup Relations* 5 (1966): 41-8.

8329. Sanders, Stanley. "Riot as a Weapon: The Language of Watts." *Nation* 201 (December 20, 1965): 490-3.
Author, born in Watts, was a Rhodes Scholar.

8330. Saperstein, M. J., and Blank-Shapira, Irene "The New Los Angeles Woman. The Mature Woman: Mosaic of Mommy." *Los Angeles* 12 (April 1967): 33+.

8331. Schreiber, Flora R., and Herman, Melvin. "Psychiatrists Analyze the Los Angeles Riots." *Science Digest* 58 (November 1965): 18-22.

8332. Schulberg, Budd. "The Angry Voices of Watts." *Los Angeles* 11 (June 1966): 32-4+.

8333. Scoble, Harry M. "McCone Commission and Social Science." *Phylon* 29 (1968): 167-81.
Concerns Los Angeles Watts Riot, 1965.

8334. Scudder, Kenyon J., and Beam, Kenneth S. *Who Is Delinquent?* Los Angeles, 1936. 56 pp.

8335. Selby, Earl, and Selby, Anne. "Watts: Where Welfare Bred Violence." *Reader's Digest* 88 (May 1966): 67-71.

8336. Sherman, Jimmie. "From the Ashes: A Personal Reaction to the Revolt of Watts." *Antioch Review* 27 (1967): 285-93.

8337. Sherwood, Frank P., and Markey, Beatrice. *The Mayor and the Fire Chief: The Fight over Integrating the Los Angeles Fire Department.* The Inter-University Case Program, Case Series No. 43. University, Alab., 1959. 24 pp.

8338. Shevky, Eshref, and Lewin, Molly. *Your Neighborhood: A Social Profile of Los Angeles.* The Haynes Foundation, *Pamphlet Series No. 14.* Los Angeles, 1950. 35 pp.

8339. ———, and Williams, Marilyn. *Social Areas of Los Angeles: Analysis and Typology.* Berkeley and Los Angeles, 1949. 172 pp.

8340. Silberman, Charles E. "The Deepening Crisis in Metropolis." *Journal of Intergroup Relations* 4 (1965): 119-31.
Anticipates the Los Angeles Watts Riot.

8341. Smallenburg, Harry W. "Selection, Segregation and Training of Behavior Problem Boys in Los Angeles." Master's thesis, University of Southern California, 1935. 211 pp.

8342. Sniderman, Dan A. "Sources of Referral of 74 Families Who Applied to Jewish Family Service in the San Fernando Valley for Help with Their Adolescent Children." Master's thesis, University of Southern California, 1964. 73 pp.

8343. Sollen, Robert H. "The Insurrection." *Frontier* 16 (September 1965): 1+.
Watts Riot, 1965.

8344. Steinberg, Warren L. "Race Relations: Opportunity for Los Angeles." *Frontier* 16 (January 1965): 14-6.

8345. Stephens, Ruth M. B. "Practices in the Los Angeles City Schools in Dealing with Socially Maladjusted Girls." Master's thesis, University of Southern California, 1940. 131 pp.

8346. Stevens, Edwin A. "Opportunities for Re-education of the Juvenile Delinquent in Los Angeles County." Master's thesis, University of Southern California, 1951. 93 pp.

8347. "Synanon vs. Santa Monica." *Los Angeles* 2 (May 1961): 14-6.
Drug addiction center.

8348. Taylor, Dora J. "Broken Homes as a Factor in the Maladjustment of Delinquent Negro Boys in Los Angeles." Master's thesis, University of Southern California, 1936. 61 pp.

8349. Taylor, William C. "Storm over Los Angeles." *Political Affairs* 44 (1965): 8-15.
Concerns the Los Angeles Watts Riot.

8350. Tuck, Ruth D. "Behind the Zoot Suit Riots." *Survey Graphic* 32 (August 1943): 313-6+.
Los Angeles and its Mexicans.

8351. Van Arsday, Maurice D., Jr., and Lourie, Anton. *Social Characteristics of Santa Monica, with Special Reference to Youth.* University of Southern California, Youth Studies Center. Los Angeles, 1961. 68 pp.

8352. "Vandal Squad." *Time* 64 (November 8, 1954): 90.
Effort to curtail school vandalism in Los Angeles.

8353. Vernon, Robert. and Novack, George. *Watts and Harlem; The Rising Revolt in the Black Ghettos.* [New York, 1965]. 15 pp.

8354. Walsma, John P. "The Problem of Runaways at El Retiro School for Girls." Master's thesis, University of Southern California, 1960. 92 pp.

8355. Walther, Henry W. "A Survey of the Employment and Subsequent History Records of Behavior Problem Boys Who Have Passed Through the Welfare Centers of the Los Angeles City Schools." Master's thesis, University of Southern California, 1937. 111 pp.

8356. Watson, Homer K. "A Study of the Causes of Delinquency Among Fifty Negro Boys Assigned to Special Schools in Los Angeles." Master's thesis, University of Southern California, 1923. 68 pp.

8357. "Watts and the 'War on Poverty'—Editorial Comment." *Political Affairs* 44 (October 1965): 1-7.

8358. Waugh, John C. "Watts—Remarkably the Same." *Christian Science Monitor,* July 13, 1967. Reprinted in Irwin Isenberg, ed. *The City in Crisis.* New York, 1968. Pp. 50-4.

8359. Webster, Argow. "Formula for Explosion." *Frontier* 16 (October 1965): 12-5.
   Watts Riots, 1965.

8360. Wells, Vernon. "A Study of Delinquency Concentration in the Newton Street Division of Los Angeles." Master's thesis, University of Southern California, 1948. 55 pp.

8361. "West Coast, Too, Has Its Race Problems." *United States News & World Report* 40 (June 29, 1956): 36-40+.
   "America's race problem, reaching across the nation, now turns up in a Far Western City—Los Angeles."

8362. Wheelock, Charles C. "Coordinating Council Guidelines for the Prevention of Juvenile Delinquency." Doctoral dissertation, University of California, Los Angeles, 1968. 331 pp.

8363. Woods, Betty. "An Historical Survey of the Women's Christian Temperance Union of Southern California." Master's thesis, Occidental College, 1950. 217 pp.

8364. Yamaji, Yoshiko G. "The Impact of Communication Difficulties in Family Relations Observed in Eight Japanese War-Bride Marriages." Master's thesis, University of Southern California, 1961. 95 pp.

8365. "The Year of the Rebels . . . And the Riots." *Los Angeles* 10 (September 1965): 30-1.
   Watts Riot and Hell's Angels (a motorcycle club).

8366. Youth Opportunities Board of Greater Los Angeles. *Expanding Opportunities for Youth: South Central Study Area.* [Los Angeles, 1964]. 2 vol.

8367. ———— *A Program for Youth; South Central Study Area. A Proposal.* [Los Angeles?, 1963]. 6 vol.

8368. "Zoot-Suit Riots: 125 Hurt in Los Angeles Fights." *Life* 14 (June 21, 1943): 30-1.

SPORTS

8369. Adams, Richard L. "Current Practices and Recommendations in Relation to Interscholastic Athletics in Selected Junior High Schools in the Los Angeles Area." Master's thesis, University of California, Los Angeles, 1958. 68 pp.

8370. Baus, Herbert M. "12 Years' Development of Sports." *Southern California Business* 16 (December 1937): 10-1.
   Los Angeles.

8371. Bobrow, Robert. "The Colisum . . . Candidate for Immortality." *Westways* 62 (October 1970): 28-30.

8372. Brodie, S. Dan. *66 Years on the California Gridiron 1882-1948.* Oakland, 1949. 477 pp.

8373. Buchtel, Jack. "Winter Sports Fiesta: Eight Champion Athletic Events Are Scheduled with Santa Anita Season Getting the Adjectives." *Saturday Night* 45 (December 31, 1938): 14-7.

8374. Buhrman, Robert. "O'Malley the Younger." *Los Angeles* 14 (May 1969): 46-8+.
   Peter O'Malley, son of Walter O'Malley owner of Los Angeles Dodgers in the same business.

8375. "Building an International City for Headliners in Sport." *Literary Digest* 109 (June 13, 1931): 40.
   "Olympic Village" for 1932 Olympic Games.

8376. Burtnett, Gerald B. "First in 1934—The 'L.A. Open.'" *Southern California Business* 12 (December 1933): 16.
   Golf.

8377. Cassidy, Patrick. "A Check List of Los Angeles Sports." *Southern California Business* 12 (August 1933): 20.

8378. ———— "Name Your Sport! No Let-Down

after the Olympics in This Region of Sports All the Year and Every Year." *Southern California Business* 11 (July 1932): 18.

8379. ———— " 'Varsity' Depends on Spectators." *Southern California Business* 12 (July 1933): 14.
   National Intercollegiate Crew Race, Long Beach Marine Stadium.

8380. Chamberlain, Arthur H. "Los Angeles Olympic Games of 1932." *Overland Monthly* 90 (August 1932): 164-5.

8381. "Christmas Races at Santa Anita Park." *Los Angeles Saturday Night* 15 (December 15, 1934): 9.
   Background of track's opening.

8382. Cochran, Kent. "Santa Anita's 'Big 'Uns.' " *Thoroughbred of California* 16 (February 1953): 138-40+.
   Race track's $100,000 horse races.

8383. "Coliseum Contract Violates State Constitution." *Municipal League of Los Angeles Bulletin* 6 (September 1, 1929): [8].

8384. "Coliseum Lighting for Color TV." *American City* 83 (February 1968): 126.

8385. "Collegiate Crew Races at Long Beach a National Event." *Los Angeles Saturday Night* 15 (June 22, 1935): 5.

8386. Collins, James H. "After All, a Race Track Is a 'Plant.' " *Southern California Business* 16 (February 1937): 8-9.
   Santa Anita.

8387. Cook, Frank A. "Megaphone: When Motor Racing in Los Angeles Was Young." *Touring Topics* 17 (August 1925): 27+.

8388. "Death of a Conference." *Newsweek* 50 (December 23, 1957): 54.
   UCLA, USC and UC Berkeley withdraw from Pacific Coast Conference.

8389. Dyer, Braven. "The Unforgettable Olympics of '32." *Los Angeles* 8 (October 1964): 29-31+.

8390. Estes, Richard G. "The Development of Thoroughbred Horse Racing in Southern California." Master's thesis, University of Southern California, 1949. 76 pp.

8391. "Floodlighting the [Los Angeles] Olympic Stadium." *American City* 45 (November 1931): 139.

8392. Fox, Fred W. "Pegasus Comes to Parnassus: Society Mingles with Cinema Gods and Goddesses to Hail Debut of Olympian Equines at Santa Anita." *Los Angeles Saturday Night* 15 (December 29, 1934): 7.

8393. Frank, Wallace. "History of Thoroughbred Racing in California." Doctoral dissertation, University of Southern California, 1964. 483 pp.

8394. Garland, William M. "Just What We May Expect in 1932." *Southern California Business* 9 (November 1930): 10-1.
   Los Angeles Olympics.

8395. ———— "Tenth Olympic Games, Los Angeles 1932." *Los Angeles Saturday Night 150th Birthday of Los Angeles: Fiesta and Pre-Olympiad.* Special Issue (1931): [5].

8396. Gates, Charles F. "The Birth of the Racing Game in Southern California." *Touring Topics* 12 (February 1920): 16-8.
   Automobile racing.

8397. Grey, Zane. *Great Game Fishing at Catalina.* [Santa Catalina], 1919. 32 pp.

8398. Hahn, Kenneth. "Los Angeles Sports Auditorium." *California Magazine of the Pacific* 46 (March 1956): 26+.

8399. Hamilton, Andrew. "Games Scotsmen Play." *Westways* 61 (June 1969): 39-41.
   Thirty-Sixth Annual Gathering and Games, presented by the United Scottish Societies of Southern California at Corsair Field, Santa Monica.

8400. Hanna, Paul A. "Blood, Sweat and Tears." *Frontier* 7 (January 1956): 16-7.
   Suit filed against Cal Eaton, operator of the Olympic Auditorium, for conspiring to monopolize wrestling exhibitions in the Los Angeles area.

8401. Hassler, Dorothy K. "The Great Pasadena-Altadena Hill Climb." *Westways* 54 (January 1962): 30-1.
   Auto race up Santa Rosa Avenue, held annually between 1906 and 1909.

8402. "Hollywood [American] Legion Building 8000 Seat Tournament Stadium." *Los Angeles Saturday Night* 2 (August 6, 1921): 7.

8403. Knight, Emerson. "Outdoor Theatres and Stadiums in the West." *The Architect and Engineer* 78 (August 1924): 53-92.
Includes many in Los Angeles area.

8404. Lange, Fred W. *History of Baseball in California and Pacific Coast Leagues, 1847-1938.* Oakland, 1938. 231 pp.
Interesting history illustrated with many photos of old-time players. Los Angeles and Hollywood had P.C.L. teams.

8405. Lardner, John. "The War for Chavez." *Newsweek* 50 (December 16, 1957): 78.
Walter O'Malley's efforts to obtain Chavez Ravine as site for Dodger Stadium.

8406. Libby, Bill. "The Season at Chavez: A Fifty Mile Hike to Hysteria." *Los Angeles* 5 (April 1963): 30-2.
Dodgers and Angels baseball teams.

8407. "Lighting the Olympic Swimming Pool." *Western City* 8 (July 1932): 15-6.
Los Angeles.

8408. Long Beach Yacht Club. *Pictorial Log.* [Long Beach, 1963]. 256 pp.

8409. Los Angeles Athletic Club. *Pictorial Tour of the Los Angeles Athletic Club and Allied Institutions: Los Angeles Athletic Club; Pacific Coast Club, Long Beach; Hollywood Athletic Club; Santa Monica Athletic Club; Surf and Sand Club, Hermosa.* [Los Angeles, 1930?]. 40 pp.

8410. "Los Angeles Swimming Stadium, Los Angeles, California." *American Architect* 144 (March 1934): 63-4.

8411. Lynch, Samuel D. "Coliseum City." *Westways* 41 (January 1949): 2-4.
Los Angeles Memorial Coliseum.

8412. Marcy, John. "Behind the Scenes at Santa Anita." *Westways* 27 (March 1935): 30+.
Horse racing.

8413. Mathison, Richard R. "Santa Anita: City Within a City." *Westways* 52 (January 1960): 4-6.
The Santa Anita Race Track.

8414. McCoy, G. T. "All Roads Will Lead to California for Olympiad; 250,000 Cars Expected." *California Highways and Public Works* 9 (September 1931): 15-7+.

8415. McEachron, Gordon T. "A Survey of the Availability of Commercial Golfing Facilities for Use by Private Educational Institutions of Los Angeles." Master's thesis, University of Southern California, 1953. 51 pp.

8416. McKinstry, F. D. "An Illuminating Article." *Western City* 6 (April 1930): 18.
Lighting Rose Bowl and the Los Angeles Municipal Airport.

8417. Momyer, George R. "The Olympic Games, Ancient and Modern." *Touring Topics* 24 (July 1932): 10-2.

8418. "New Santa Anita Being Made Ready for Opening Races on Christmas Day." *Los Angeles Saturday Night* 16 (December 14, 1935): 16.
Track said to have been "completely remodeled, beautified and enlarged."

8419. Nichols, C. P. "Los Angeles Olympic Swimming Stadium." *Western City* 7 (May 1931): 17-8.

8420. ——— "Olympic Athletes Will Swim in Pure Water." *American City* 45 (July 1931): 131-2.
Los Angeles Swimming Stadium.

8421. Oates, Robert M. *The Los Angeles Rams.* [Culver City, 1955]. 96 pp.

8422. "Das Olympische Stadion in Los Angeles." *Wasmuths Monatshefte Fur Baukunst* 16 (1932): 153-8.

8423. Parks, Marion. "When Olympic Park Was a Jack-Rabbit Course." *Overland Monthly* 90 (July 1932): 151+.
Site of Tenth Olympiad.

8424. "Pasadena's Dignified Stadium." *Saturday Night* 3 (November 4, 1922): 4.
Rose Bowl.

8425. "Pleasant Echo of 1932 Olympiad Cheers Courageous Californians." *Los Angeles Saturday Night* 43 (June 27, 1936): 9.
After prolonged litigation, Los Angeles receives first profit on Olympics, checks totaling $1.260 million.

8426. "Pomona and the Hot-Rodders." *Western City* 28 (February 1952): 51.
Fairgrounds drag-strip, for timing quarter-mile acceleration contests.

8427. Poulson, Norris. "The Untold Story of Chavez Ravine." *Los Angeles* 3 (April 1962): 14-7+.
Walter O'Malley and Dodger Stadium.

8428. Probert, William J. "New Golf Course Complex in Pasadena Doubles Income from Related Uses." *Western City* 44 (August 1968): 24-6.
Brookside Golf Course.

8429. "Proposed Home of the New Santa Monica Tennis Club." *Saturday Night* 7 (May 21, 1927): 1.
What club's facilities and policies will be.

8430. "Ralph DePalma Sets New Record at Beverly Hills." *Touring Topics* 13 (March 1921): 24-5+.
Automobile races, Los Angeles Speedway.

8431. Rogers, Si. "USC vs. UCLA." *Los Angeles* 2 (October 1961): 16-9.
History of traditional football game, 1936-1961.

8432. Ronnie, Art. "Life and Death of a Village." *Westways* 52 (August 1960): 10-1.
1932 Olympic Village.

8433. Samuelsen, Rube. *The Rose Bowl Game.* Garden City, N. Y., 1951. 299 pp.

8434. Sanders, Everett L. "The Olympic Games." *Overland Monthly* 89 (November 1931): 10+.

8435. "Santa Anita: It Started as a Monument to Lucky Baldwin . . . It Became America's Greatest Racetrack . . . It Was Dr. Strub's Stubborn Idea.'" *Southern California Prompter* 2 (Holiday Issue [December 1960-January 1961]): 45-7.

8436. Schulberg, Budd. "Before We Went Big League." *Los Angeles* 10 (November 1965): 28-32+.
Los Angeles sports history, mainly 1930s and 1940s.

8437. Seim, Charles. "Southern California Timing Association." *California Engineer* 29 (December 1950): 12-3+.
Los Angeles-based organization initiated in 1937 to sponsor race-car time-trials on dry lake beds in the Mojave Desert and at the Bonneville Salt Flats in Utah.

8438. Sergiuff, Alex G. "A Study of Municipal Sports in Los Angeles." Master's thesis, University of Southern California, 1957. 141 pp.

8439. Smith, Jack. "A Day in the City: The Greens of Arcady." *Westways* 60 (March 1968): 2-4.
Santa Anita Race Track.

8440. Somerby, Grace A. "When Los Angeles Was Host to the Olympic Games of 1932." *Historical Society of Southern California Quarterly* 34 (1952): 125-32.

8441. Sorver, Edwin R. *Tournament of Roses, the Rose Bowl Game; Our First 70 Years.* Pasadena, 1959. 58 pp.

8442. "Spring Training at Catalina." *Los Angeles Saturday Night* 11 (February 28, 1931): 7.
Chicago Cubs baseball team.

8443. Stebbins, Barton A. "Attracting Golfers to Fast Field." *Southern California Business* 4 (November 1925): 24+.
Los Angeles Country Club.

8444. Stiles, Maxwell. *The Rose Bowl; A Complete Action and Pictorial Exposition of Rose Bowl Football.* Ed. by Ward B. Nash. Los Angeles, [1946?]. 128 pp.

8445. "Summer Horse Racing Begins." *Southern California Business* 17 (June 1938): 12.
Hollywood Park's initial season.

8446. "Summer Polo at Uplifters Club Field." *Los Angeles Saturday Night* 8 (May 12, 1928): 2.
Located on Beverly (now Sunset) Blvd. in Santa Monica.

8447. Sutton, Horace. "Turn West, Turn Blue." *Saturday Review* 37 (January 9, 1954): 42-4.
UCLA football and the Rose Bowl game.

8448. Tobin, John G. "The Pacific Coast Conference Football Scandal and the Los Angeles Press." Master's thesis, University of California, Los Angeles, 1959. 223 pp.

8449. "Under-Water Lighting for Olympic Pool." *American City* 47 (August 1932): 105.
Los Angeles.

8450. "Where Speed Will Be Enthroned." *Touring Topics* 12 (February 1920): 19-20+.
Los Angeles Speedway, Beverly Hills.

8451. Williams, Roger. "The Apathy in Smogsville." *Sports Illustrated* 15 (November 13, 1961): 22-3.

Speculation on why attendance at Los Angeles spectator sports is suffering.

8452. Witt, Ralph W. "A Comparative Analysis of Athletic Injuries Incurred in Selected Varsity Sports at the University of California, Los Angeles." Master's thesis, University of California, Los Angeles, 1953. 84 pp.

8453. "World's Championship Cowboy Contest: Western Fiction Characters Come to Life." *Los Angeles Saturday Night* 15 (July 13, 1935): 4.

Championship rodeo, Gilmore Stadium.

8454. Zimmerman, Paul. *The Los Angeles Dodgers.* New York, 1960. 221 pp.

TRAFFIC
TRAFFIC—BRIDGES AND TUNNELS

8455. Albers, J. C. " 'Bottle Neck' Removed by Widening and Road Alignment." *Western City* 8 (December 1932): 11.

Canada Boulevard Bridge across Verdugo Wash, Glendale.

8456. —— "Rigid Frame Bridge on Main Traffic Route in Los Angeles Metropolitan Area." *American City* 48 (February 1933): 57-8.

Canada Boulevard Bridge across Verdugo Wash.

8457. Annin, R. Howard. "Ford Avenue Bascule Bridge Jacked Up 7½ Ft. in Four Days: Subsidence Caused Tops of Piers and Bridge Rockers to Be Awash at High Tide." *Civil Engineering* 20 (June 1950): 20-2.

8458. "Arroyo Seco Freeway Project Required 26 Bridge Structures." *California Highways and Public Works* 18 (November 1940): 14-5+.

8459. "Atlantic Avenue Bridge, Los Angeles County." *Western Construction News* 6 (October 10, 1931): 536.

8460. Bacon, Robert H. "Fifty Pedestrian Subways Planned for Los Angeles." *Engineering News-Record* 96 (June 10, 1926): 949-50.

8461. —— "Improvements Made in Design for Pedestrian Subways in Los Angeles." *Western Construction News* 10 (July 1935): 196-7.

8462. —— "Los Angeles Will Soon Have 44 Pedestrian Subways." *Engineering News-Record* 100 (May 17, 1928): 785.

8463. —— "Tunnel Making and Second Street Bore." *Saturday Night* 3 (January 6, 1923): 5+; (January 13, 1923): 5+.

Los Angeles.

8464. Barton, Robert M. "Prestressed Bridge: First of Its Kind in State Is Built in Los Angeles." *California Highways and Public Works* 30 (March-April 1951): 1-5+.

Pedestrian bridge over Arroyo Seco.

8465. "Bridge Bonds Sold for Terminal Island Span." *California Highways and Public Works* 40 (May-June 1961): 79.

8466. Butler, Merrill. "The City of Los Angeles Building 'Million-Dollar' Bridges." *Pacific Municipalities* 43 (June 1929): 256-7.

First and Fourth Street bridges across railroad yards and Los Angeles River.

8467. —— "Sixth Street Viaduct, Los Angeles." *Western Construction News and Highways Builder* 7 (July 10, 1932): 385-91.

8468. Calhoun, Chad F. "Fourth Street Viaduct, Los Angeles." *Western Construction News* 5 (August 10, 1930): 377-8.

8469. Cortelyou, H[erman]. P. "Strength of Concrete in Bridge Construction at Los Angeles." *Western Construction News* 3 (April 25, 1928): 270-1.

8470. Cortelyou, S[pencer] V. "Santa Monica Grade Separation Project Solves Coast Route Problem." *California Highways and Public Works* 17 (August 1939): 6-7+.

8471. Curran, J. M. "Rio Hondo Bridge: Santa Ana Freeway Structure Calls for Unusual Construction." *California Highways and Public Works* 32 (January-February 1953): 21-3.

8472. Darby, C. H. "Colorado Freeway: Bridge Over Arroyo Seco Has Unusual Design Problems."

California Highways and Public Works 30 (January-February 1951): 22-7.

8473. Denning, Ernest. "Long Beach Rebuilds Crossing." *Western Construction News* 22 (August 1947): 79-82.
Long Beach Boulevard Bridge over Los Angeles River flood control channel.

8474. Dickinson, Thomas A. "Two-Inch Pier Separation Means Knotty Problems on—'Two-for-One' Bridge at Long Beach." *Western Construction News* 24 (July 1949): 78-9.
Bridge built in mirror-image halves.

8475. "Erecting the West's First Prestressed Concrete Bridge." *Western Construction* 26 (April 1951): 76-7.
Pedestrian bridge over Arroyo Seco.

8476. "Floating Bridge—Pontoons Retract under Approaches." *Western Construction News* 20 (July 1945): 83-5.
Bridge between Long Beach and Terminal Island Naval Base.

8477. "For the Biggest Concrete Bridge in California—Three Arches to Span 780 Feet." *Western Construction* 27 (March 1952): 65-7.
Colorado Freeway Bridge, Pasadena.

8478. Fox, William J. "Grade-Crossing Control and Grade-Separation Programs." *American City* 46 (May 1932): 95-6.
Los Angeles County.

8479. "Grade Separation of Sunset and Glendale Avenues Completed." *California Highways and Public Works* 12 (October 1934): 24-5.

8480. Gutleben, Phil. "The Malibu Bridge, Coast Highway, California." *Western Construction News* 2 (May 10, 1927): 31-3.

8481. Hatch, James N. "Widening San Gabriel River Bridge, California." *Western Construction News* 5 (February 25, 1930): 99-101.

8482. Hokin, Frederic. "Bridge Problem: Los Angeles County Making Good Use of F.A.S. Funds." *California Highways and Public Works* 28 (May-June 1949): 34+.
Florence Avenue Bridge across Los Angeles River. F.A.S.—Federal Aid Secondary.

8483. Hollister, Leonard C. "California Division of Highways Building the West's—First Bridge of Prestressed Concrete." *Western Construction* 25 (December 1950): 67-9.
Pedestrian bridge over Arroyo Seco.

8484. James, Warren B. "Prestressed Girders: San Bernardino-Santa Ana Freeway Bridge Interchange." *California Highways and Public Works* 34 (March-April 1955): 30-3+.

8485. Jones, C[harles] W. "Building a Viaduct under Difficulties Where Teeming Traffic Lanes Cross." *California Highways and Public Works* 12 (June 1934): 14+.
Intersection of Sunset and Glendale boulevards.

8486. ———. "Eighteen Bridge Structures Will Span Arroyo Seco Parkway." *California Highways and Public Works* 15 (December 1937): 10-1+.

8487. Kennedy, R. C. "Ground Broken: Construction of Colorado Street Bridge in Pasadena Is Started." *California Highways and Public Works* 30 (May-June 1951): 5-6+.

8488. ———. "New Pasadena Bridge Opened to Traffic." *California Highways and Public Works* 32 (November-December 1953): 48.

8489. "Los Angeles' Highway By-Pass Tunnels." *American City* 46 (April 1932): 95.
North Figueroa Street tunnels through Elysian Park, now used by outbound Pasadena Freeway.

8490. "Los Angeles' Prestressed Pedestrian Bridge." *American City* 66 (September 1951): 118-9.
Bridge over Arroyo Seco.

8491. "Los Angeles Traffic Uses Rebuilt Highway Tunnel." *Engineering Record* 73 (April 1, 1916): 451-2.
North Broadway Tunnel.

8492. Mayberry, Edward L. "Unique Reinforced Concrete Bridge." *The Architect and Engineer of California* 19 (November 1909): 73-9.
Linda Vista Bridge, Pasadena.

8493. McClintock, Miller. "Pedestrian Tunnels for School Children." *American City* 34 (January 1926): 81-2.
Los Angeles.

8494. McCoy, George T. "39 Grade Crossings on California Highways Being Eliminated with $7,-500,000 Federal Funds." *California Highways and Public Works* 13 (October 1935): 1-7.
Includes eight in Los Angeles County.

8495. McWilliams, Carey. "Suicide Bridge." *Frontier* 5 (November 1953): 9-11.
Colorado Street Bridge, Pasadena, originally called Arroyo Seco Bridge.

8496. Mitchell, Stewart. "Twenty Grade Separation Projects Being Built in Southern California." *California Highways and Public Works* 14 (May 1936): 2+.
Nine in Los Angeles Metropolitan area.

8497. Myers, R[alph] C. "Figueroa-Temple Street Grade Separation in City of Los Angeles." *California Highways and Public Works* 17 (November 1939): 14-5.

8498. ———— "Santa Monica Grade Separation." *California Highways and Public Works* 18 (September 1940): 18-20.

8499. "New Bridge Completed on Historic Whittier Boulevard." *California Highways and Public Works* 3 (March 1926): 5.

8500. "New $5,000,000 Aliso Street Viaduct Heralds Era of Freeway Construction." *California Highways and Public Works* 22 (September-October 1944): 18-9.

8501. Obermuller, J. H. "Pomona Grade Separations Involve Channelized Ramp Approach System." *California Highways and Public Works* 17 (October 1939): 16-7.

8502. "On California's Biggest Job . . . Belts Are Key to Bridge Deck Pour." *Western Construction* 45 (November 1970): 54.
Interchange between U.S. Highways 14 and 5 at southern end of Ridge Route.

8503. Panhorst, F.W. "Sixty-Eight Grade Separation Projects Aggregate 11,000,000." *California Highways and Public Works* 17 (May 1939): 11-4+.

8504. Peterson, J. M., and Clinton, H. Ross. "Progress Report: Hollywood Freeway Structure Rapidly Nearing Completion." *California Highways and Public Works* 29 (January-February 1950): 22-3+.
Western Avenue overcrossing.

8505. "Pomona Grade Separations Will Provide New Highway Connection." *California Highways and Public Works* 18 (May 1940): 6-7.

8506. Poppe, John B. "Cable Spinning: Terminal Island Bridge Suspension Cables Completed." *California Highways and Public Works* 42 (January-February 1963): 9-13.

8507. Saph, A. V. "A Discussion of a Reinforced Concrete Arch." *The Architect and Engineer of California* 6 (August 1906): 51-5.
Concrete arch bridge in South Pasadena.

8508. Scott, H. J. "L.A. River Bridge Will Form East End of Freeway Viaduct." *California Highways and Public Works* 38 (July-August 1959): 39-41.
Santa Monica Freeway.

8509. Shaw, John C. "Los Angeles' Bridge and Tunnel Program." *Pacific Municipalities* 43 (January 1929): 20-1.

8510. ———— "Sepulveda Tunnnel under Mulholland Highway, Los Angeles." *Western Construction News* 4 (December 25, 1929): 667-9.

8511. Smith, G. C. "Span Lift: Novel Method Used to Raise San Gabriel River Bridge." *California Highways and Public Works* 41 (May-June 1962): 59-60.
Pacific Coast Highway near Long Beach.

8512. Stover, H. D. "New San Gabriel River Bridge an Example of Construction Economy." *California Highways and Public Works* 11 (December 1933): 26-7.

8513. Stump, Frank V. "The Transformation of a Grade Crossing." *American City* 15 (September 1916): 317.
Viaduct and park in South Pasadena.

8514. Tilton, G. A., Jr. "Boring 2 Tunnels on Angeles Crest Highway." *California Highways and Public Works* 19 (December 1941): 8+.

8515. Walsh, E. L. "Railroad Grade Separations Completed on Rosemean Arterial." *California*

Highways and Public Works 16 (December 1938): 22-4.

8516. Warren, Don. "Four Grade Crossing Projects Completed in Los Angeles." *California Highways and Public Works* 15 (February 1937): 2-3+.

8517. Watson, Paul R. "Figueroa Street Viaduct, Los Angeles." *The Architect and Engineer* 129 (May 1937): 49-51.

8518. ———— "Figueroa Street Viaduct Project in Los Angeles Crosses 2 Railroads, River and Highway." *California Highways and Public Works* 15 (April 1937): 14-5+.

8519. ———— "Santa Monica Tunnel Being Built in Open Cut on Footing of Concrete Piles." *California Highways and Public Works* 13 (November 1935): 2+.

8520. ———— "Spectacular Steel Erection Job on Arroyo Seco Extension Bridge." *California Highways and Public Works* 21 (November-December 1943): 4-5+.

8521. Whitney, M. E. "San Gabriel River Bridge Near Azusa: Another Bottleneck Eliminated by California Division of Highways." *Western Construction News* 5 (September 10, 1930): 433-4.

TRAFFIC—CONTROL

8522. Albers, J. C. "Traffic Checks in Glendale." *Western City* 8 (June 1932): 7+.

8523. "Alhambra to Install Street Name Signs with County Gas Tax Funds." *Western City* 22 (August 1946): 36.

8524. Baker, Donald M. "Traffic Problems in Los Angeles Today and Tomorrow." *Western City* 9 (December 1933): 19-20.

8525. Bergstrom, Edwin. "Relief of Traffic Congestion Seen in Acceptance of Civic Center Plan: Comprehensive Arrangement of Streets Will Afford Many Outlets for Downtown Section." *Los Angeles Realtor* 4 (February 1925): 12-3.

8526. Boddy, Manchester. "Los Angeles and Her Traffic Problem." *Saturday Night* 45 (November 45 (November 5, 1938): 14-5+.

8527. Braff, Lloyd M. "Electronic Traffic Control System Installed at Freeway Bottleneck." *Western City* 32 (June 1956): 42-3.
Temporary terminus of Hollywood Freeway at Ventura Boulevard.

8528. ———— "Los Angeles Uses Thermo Compound for Street-Marking at 20 Sites." *Western City* 33 (July 1957): 52.

8529. ———— "The Vehicles Regulate L.A.'s Ventura Boulevard Traffic Lights." *American City* 71 (April 1956): 149+.

8530. Brown, Richard V. "San Fernando's Mall Allows Limited Vehicular Traffic to Revitalize Its Downtown Business District." *Western City* 43 (January 1967): 22-3+.

8531. Butler, John L. "Traffic Congestion Materially Relieved." *American City* 17 (July 1917): 32-4.
Los Angeles.

8532. Caldwell, B. R. "Los Angeles Adds 24 New Patrol Cars and 108 Motorcycles in Campaign to Cut Deaths." *Western City* 17 (October 1941): 25+.

8533. ———— "Police Motors of Los Angeles." *American City* 57 (January 1942): 13.

8534. Clark, Robert. "Policeman in the Sky." *Westways* 38 (December 1946): 24.
Traffic control by blimp.

8535. Cortelyou, S[pencer] V. "Congestion of Traffic Big Problem: Increase in Vehicular Transportation and Population in District VII Creates Complex Highway Situation." *California Highways and Public Works* 16 (December 1938): 1-5.
District VII complises Ventura, Los Angeles, and Orange counties.

8536. Dorsey, Ralph T. "Cost Reduced and Safety Increased by New 'Balanced Light' Traffic Signals." *American City* 67 (March 1952): 139.

8537. ———— "Extra Center Signal Halves Violations." *American City* 53 (April 1938): 125.
Intersection of Wilshire and La Brea.

8538. ———— "Maintaining Traffic Speed in Los Angeles." *American City* 65 (August 1950): 141.

8539. ———— "Narrow Steel Divider Makes Street Safer." *American City* 55 (April 1940): 117.
Ramona Boulevard, Los Angeles.

8540. ———— "Three Lanes West and One Lane East." *American City* 53 (September 1938): 107.
Plan for expediting rush-hour traffic.

8541. ———— "Traffic Control Progress in the West." *Western City* 23 (September 1947): 42-3.

8542. ———— "The Use of Off-Center Land Movement in Los Angeles." *Traffic Quarterly* 2 (1948): 291-302.

8543. East, E. E. "Los Angeles' Street Traffic Problem." *Civil Engineering* 12 (August 1942): 435-8.

8544. Ervin, Frank. "Regulating Pedestrian Traffic." *Western City* 7 (August 1931): 32-3.
Includes Los Angeles.

8545. "Fighting Death in the Street." *Popular Mechanics* 75 (February 1941): 194-6+.
Stringent measures adopted by Los Angeles to reduce high traffic accident rate.

8546. "Four Hundred More Traffic Officers in Los Angeles." *American City* 62 (August 1947): 111.

8547. Frampton, Virgil. "Analysis of Reported Automobile Accidents in the City of Los Angeles." Master's thesis, University of Southern California, 1937. 126 pp.

8548. "Glendale Installs New Traffic Signal System and 4,000 Street Name Signs." *Western City* 18 (June 1942): 27-9.

8549. "Governor [Knight] Wants Stricter Traffic Laws." *California Highways and Public Works* 36 (May-June 1957): 43+.
Refers mostly to Los Angeles.

8550. Heath, Cleveland. "Down-Town Traffic Regulations: Some Rules and Improvements Which Have Helped to Reduce Congestion in the Down-Town Streets of Los Angeles." *American City* 31 (September 1924): 200.

8551. Helliwell, George F. "Loading Zones, Painted Yellow, Eliminate Double-Line Parking in Los Angeles." *American City* 37 (November 1927): 634-5.
Measure for expediting traffic flow.

8552. Himelhoch, A. L. "Case History: High Capacity Through Medians and Signals." *California Highways and Public Works* 36 (July-August 1957): 8-13+.
Expediting traffic flow in vicinity of the Los Angeles Airport.

8553. Hoffman, Paul G. "The Traffic Commission of Los Angeles." *Annals of the American Academy of Political and Social Science* 116 (November 1924): 246-50.
Los Angeles had 430,000 automobiles in 1923, one for every 2.9 residents of city, the largest percentage in world.

8554. ———— "Wider Streets and Better Streets." *Southern California Business* 3 (November 1924): 13+.
Author, head of the Los Angeles Traffic Comcission, favored passage of the Major Traffic Street Plan.

8555. Holmes, Donald L. "Los Angeles Lays Built-in Traffic Marker." *Western Construction News and Highways Builder* 7 (July 10, 1932): 401-2.

8556. Hooper, P. A. "Pasadena Conducts Safety Campaign: A Splendid Method for Obtaining Reliable Data for the Regulation of Street Traffic." *City Manager Magazine* 6 (August 1924): 12-3.

8557. Horrall, C. B. "Four Hundred More Traffic Officers in Los Angeles." *American City* 62 (August 1947): 111.

8558. "How Southern California Cities Are Saving Money on Traffic Signs: Municipalities Afforded Opportunity to Purchase Traffic Equipment at Cost by Arrangement with Motoring Organization [Automobile Club of Southern California]." *Western City* 6 (September 1930): 34.

8559. "Installing Lights and Signals in Los Angeles." *American City* 75 (July 1960): 118+.

8560. "Interconnected Signals Speed Traffic Flow." *American City* 84 (June 1969): 134.
One step in Los Angeles' master traffic control supervision system that will tie together all principal signalized intersections by 1974.

8561. Joseph, James. "$350,000 Traffic-Paint Bill Leads to Tests by Los Angeles." *American City* 66 (July 1951): 135+.

8562. "Lawdale Traffic Median Developed of Monsanto's AstroGrass Rolls." *Western City* 46 (March 1970): 34-5.

8563. Lefferts, E. B. "Effective Regulation of Pedestrians." *American City* 37 (October 1927): 434-6.
  Los Angeles.

8564. "Los Angeles and Its Motor-Jam." *Literary Digest* 81 (April 26, 1924): 68-71.

8565. "Los Angeles Doubles Motorcycle Force." *American City* 56 (September 1941): 15.

8566. Lynch, Samuel D. "The Signal That Alerts." *Westways* 49 (September 1957): 6-7.
  "Sigalert" system for warning of freeway congestion.

8567. MacKenzie, Douglas C. "Traffic Markings: Pasadena Experiment on Colorado Street a Success." *California Highways and Public Works* 35 (July-August 1956): 33-4+.

8568. McClintock, Miller. "Interesting Features of Los Angeles' New Traffic Ordinance." *American City* 32 (March 1925): 333+.

8569. ———— "Relieve Traffic Congestion— How?" *Southern California Business* 3 (September 1924): 9+.
  Los Angeles.

8570. "Miniature Metropolitan Facilities Traffic and Transportation Study." *Western City* 15 (February 1939): 44.
  WPA-built scale model of downtown Los Angeles.

8571. Morris, Clarence H. "Directing Traffic from a Blimp." *Western City* 22 (March 1946): 30-3.
  New Year's Day traffic in Pasadena.

8572. "Nation's Worst Traffic City: Los Angeles Fights Accident Rise." *Life* 19 (December 17, 1945): 43-4+.

8573. "New Machine Speeds Traffic Striping." *Western City* 7 (February 1931): 23-4.
  Designed by R. T. Dorsey of the Los Angeles Street Traffic Engineering Bureau.

8574. "New Street Ordinance in Los Angeles." *Electric Railway Journal* 41 (April 26, 1913): 765.

Length of no-parking zones at intersections increased as a means of expediting traffic flow.

8575. "New Type Road Divider Developed to Make Driving Safer." *Western City* 15 (January 1939): 35-6.
  Ramona Boulevard.

8576. Olmsted, Frederick Law. *A Major Traffic Street Plan for Los Angeles: Prepared for the Committee on Los Angeles Plan of Major Highways of the Traffic Commission of the City and County of Los Angeles.* Los Angeles, 1924. 69 pp.

8577. "Operation Airwatch." *Newsweek* 51 (June 2, 1958): 56.
  Radio station KABC's helicopter freeway patrol.

8578. "Operation of New Traffic Signal System on Wilshire Boulevard, Los Angeles." *Western City* 7 (December 1931): 25-6.

8579. Osborne, Henry Z., Jr. "Traffic Congestion and Business." *Southern California Business* 1 (June 1922): 21+.

8580. "Pedestrians Move with Traffic at Los Angeles Intersections." *Engineering News-Record* 94 (May 7, 1925): 761.
  Pedestrians required to obey semaphores.

8581. "Pertinent Facts as to the Major Traffic Commission and Plan." *Municipal League of Los Angeles Bulletin* 4 (August 31, 1927): 1+.

8582. "Public Demands Elimination of Grade Crossings." *Municipal League of Los Angeles Bulletin* 6 (September 1, 1928): [1].

8583. Richards, C. H. "Los Angeles Mapped from Air to Aid Traffic Studies." *Engineering News-Record* 88 (June 8, 1922): 961-3.

8584. Richards, William. "Arcadia Leads New Trend in Street Signs." *Western City* 29 (April 1953): 49.

8585. "The Sharing of the Green in Los Angeles." *American City* 73 (October 1958): 145.
  Method of cycling pedestrian and vehicle traffic at intersections.

8586. Sharples, Philip P. "Traffic Counts by Boy Scouts in Los Angeles." *American City* 31 (September 1924): 197-200.

8587. Snethen, Clarence R. "Los Angeles Making Scientific Study to Relieve Traffic Congestion." *American City* 31 (September 1924): 116-7.

8588. —— "Tackling a Metropolitan Traffic Jam." *Southern California Business* 2 (October 1923): 17+.
Organization and duties of Los Angeles Traffic Commission.

8589. "Suggested Solution of Los Angeles Traffic Problems." *The Architect and Engineer* 78 (August 1924): 125-6.

8590. Sullivan, H. W. "L.A.'s Police Helicopter Detects Fires and Traffic Jams." *American City* 75 (August 1960): 169.

8591. Taylor, S. S. "Moving the Most Cars the Fastest." *American City* 75 (December 1960): 109.
Radio-coordinated traffic signal control in Los Angeles.

8592. "Traffic Congestion in Los Angeles." *Journal of Electricity, Power and Gas* 27 (October 14, 1911): 343-5.

8593. "Traffic Control Crosses over Heavy Continuous Traffic." *American City* 72 (February 1957): 153+.
Underpass linking two sections of Long Beach City College campus.

8594. "A Traffic Controller for Any Intersection." *American City* 84 (May 1969): 152.
Santa Monica obtains new four-phase solid-state digital-timed traffic controller.

8595. "Traffic Safety Measures on World's Busiest Boulevard." *Pacific Municipalities* 44 (September 1930): 362-4.
Wilshire Boulevard.

8596. Tufte, Edward E. "Putting Traffic-Control Practices to Work." *American City* 80 (August 1965): 125-6.
Beverly Hills.

8597. Welch, W. L. "Long Beach Traffic Circle Improvement Eliminates Bad Intersection Bottleneck." *California Highways and Public Works* 20 (June 1942): 8-9.

8598. Whitnall, Gordon. "More in Relation to the Major Traffic Problem." *Municipal League of Los Angeles Bulletin* 5 (October 31, 1927): 8; (December 28, 1927): [8]; (January 31, 1928): [8].

8599. —— " 'No Parking of Autos!' " *American City* 22 (May 1920): 484.
Plan to expedite downtown Los Angeles traffic flow by prohibiting parking during certain hours.

TRAFFIC—FREEWAYS

8600. Adams, Arthur H. "Los Angeles County Is Ready with Limited Access Highway Plans." *American City* 60 (September 1945): 96-7.

8601. Adams, Kenneth C., ed. *From Trails to Freeways.* Sacramento, 1950. 167 pp.
Highway and freeway development in California.

8602. Aldrich, Lloyd. "Increasing Traffic in Los Angeles Metropolitan Area Demands Adequate Freeway and Parkway System." *Civil Engineering* 17 (May 1947): 28-31+.

8603. "Another Mile of Ramona Freeway Opened to Traffic." *California Highways and Public Works* 33 (March-April 1954): 47.
Now San Bernardino Freeway.

8604. *The Arroyo Seco Parkway, "The West's First Freeway."* [N.p., 1940]. [16] pp.
Now Pasadena Freeway.

8605. Automobile Club of Southern California, Engineering Department. *An Appraisal of Freeways vs. Surface Streets in the Los Angeles Metropolitan Area.* [Los Angeles?], 1954. 28 pp.

8606. Baker, Harrison R. "The Colorado Freeway." *California Highways and Public Works* 29 (November-December 1950): 1-2+.

8607. —— "Hollywood Freeway: Third Unit of Construction Between Grand Avenue and Silver Lake Boulevard Dedicated and Opened to Public Traffic." *California Highways and Public Works* 30 (January-February 1951): 12-6.

8608. Balfour, Frank C. "Freeway Agreement Signed with City of Pomona." *California Highways and Public Works* 29 (July-August 1950): 28.

8609. Beer, C. G. "Traffic Studies: Need for Network of Freeways in Los Angeles Area Clearly Evident." *California Highways and Public Works* 32 (September-October 1953): 31-6.

8610. Bezzone, Albert P., and Morse, Gordon. "Elysian Viaduct: Key Structure in Complex L. A. Interchange Nears Completion." *California Highways and Public Works* 40 (September-October 1961): 11-4.

8611. "Billions for Freeways—But Traffic Gets Worse." *U. S. News and World Report* 50 (March 20, 1961): 90-3.
Los Angeles.

8612. Bozzani, Amerigo. "Governor Olson Dedicates and Opens Arroyo Seco Freeway." *California Highways and Public Works* 19 (January 1941): 3-8+.

8613. Brady, W. V. "Firm Foundation: Ingenuity Displayed on Santa Ana Freeway." *California Highways and Public Works* 28 (March-April 1949): 7-9.

8614. Bush, Carl. "Freeway System to Link L. A. Areas by Rapid Transit." *Western Housing* 28 (December 1945): 6-7+.

8615. Butler, Robert H. "Golden State Freeway: Progress at Junction with Four Major Highway Routes." *California Highways and Public Works* 33 (January-February 1954): 38-41.

8616. Camp, Maurice E., and Collins, Ray. "Harbor Freeway: Construction Progress on Important Project." *California Highways and Public Works* 35 (September-October 1956): 19-23+.

8617. Central Business District Association, Los Angeles. *Los Angeles Parkway System.* Los Angeles, 1946. 40 pp.

8618. Cessna, M. E. "Moving Forward: Los Angeles River Freeway Plans for Future Are Comprehensive." *California Highways and Public Works* 30 (May-June 1951): 13-6+.
Los Angeles River (now Long Beach) Freeway, 16.2 miles in length between Pacific Coast Highway and Santa Ana Freeway.

8619. —— "Norwalk Diagonal: Strategic Link of Santa Ana Freeway Now Being Constructed."
California Highways and Public Works 31 (November-December 1952): 16-23+.

8620. Cohon, Barry. "Banks of the San Gabriel: Interstate 605 Will Serve Historic, Fast-Developing Area as Easterly Leg of Los Angeles Metropolitan Freeway Loop." *California Highways and Public Works* 43 (July-August 1964): 34-41.

8621. "Colorado Parkway: Studies Being Made for Los Angeles Unit." *California Highways and Public Works* 27 (May-June 1948): 21-3.

8622. Compagnon, Henry. "Unique Project: Four-Level Grade Separation in Los Angeles First of Kind." *California Highways and Public Works* 27 (November-December 1948): 20-3.

8623. "Construction under Way on New Arroyo Seco Parkway." *Western City* 14 (May 1938): 36.

8624. Cooley, Roy, and Lendecke, H. R. "Ramona Freeway: Another Unit of This Project Now under Construction." *California Highways and Public Works* 29 (May-June 1950): 30-1.
1.8 mile section just east of Los Angeles city limits.

8625. Cortelyou, S[pencer] V. "Arroyo Seco Parkway Unit Open." *California Highways and Public Works* 18 (August 1940): 14-7.

8626. —— "Arroyo Seco Parkway Will Include a Six Mile Double Lane Depressed Arterial." *California Highways and Public Works* 14 (August 1936): 4-5+.
Reprinted as: Cort[e]lyou, S. V. "Building the Arroyo Seco Parkway." *Los Angeles Saturday Night* 43 (September 12, 1936): 5.

8627. —— "Arroyo Seco 6-Lane Freeway." *California Highways and Public Works* 17 (June 1939): 10-3.

8628. —— "Cahuenga Freeway Unit Opened." *California Highways and Public Works* 18 (July 1940): 2-4+.

8629. —— "Fort Moore Hill: Part of Historic Site Will Be Raised for Hollywood Freeway." *California Highways and Public Works* 28 (May-June 1949): 17-21.

8630. —— "Four Level Grade Separation for

Los Angeles Parkways Intersection." *California Highways and Public Works* 22 (May-June 1944): 8-9+.

8631. ——— "New Freeway: East Los Angeles Motorists Are Saved Driving Time." *California Highways and Public Works* 27 (July-August 1948): 1+.
Santa Ana Freeway.

8632. ——— "Ramona and Santa Ana Parkways Proposed for Los Angeles Area." *California Highways and Public Works* 22 (July-August 1944): 2+.

8633. Crawford, W. H. "Full Freeway: San Bernardino Freeway Now Continuous for 60 Miles." *California Highways and Public Works* 39 (May-June 1960): 43-6.

8634. Cressy, Frank B. "Last Link: San Bernardino Freeway in District VII Completed." *California Highways and Public Works* 36 (May-June 1957): 24-6+.

8635. ———; Belford. H. E., and Ayanian, Haig. "Hollywood Freeway." *California Highways and Public Works* 29 (July-August 1950): 17+.

8636. Crumm, Fred J. "California's Plan for Freeways in Metropolitan Areas." *Civil Engineering* 11 (October 1941): 569-72.
Includes Los Angeles.

8637. Curran, J. M. "Terminal Island Freeway Structure." *California Highways and Public Works* 26 (November-December 1947): 27-9+.

8638. Decker, Ralph E., and Muller, H. W. "Cable Moving: New 'Skidding' Technique Saves State $146,000." *California Highways and Public Works* 41 (January-February 1962): 44+.
San Diego Freeway.

8639. Dickinson, Thomas A. "Removing a Million Cubic Yard Hilltop for—Hollywood Parkway Grading Project: Landscape Feature of Downtown Los Angeles Removed by Shovel-and-Truck Operation—Old Broadway Tunnel Concrete Demolished by Hydraulic Pressure Equipment." *Western Construction News* 24 (October 1949): 62-5.

8640. Eckhardt, J. E., and Van Voorhis, L. S. "San Fernando Valley Freeways." *California Highways and Public Works* 35 (September-October 1956): 1-8.

8641. Fahey, W. L. "Long Beach Freeway." *California Highways and Public Works* 31 (November-December 1952): 9-15+.

8642. ——— "Rapid Progress on Harbor Freeway: Multimillion-Dollar Project Reviewed." *California Highways and Public Works* 33 (May-June 1954): 1-15+.

8643. ——— "Santa Ana Freeway Has Induced Industrial and Recreational Development." *California Highways and Public Works* 34 (September-October 1955): 1-13.

8644. ——— "Santa Ana Freeway: Rapid Progress Is Being Made on Important Project." *California Highways and Public Works* 31 (January-February 1952): 20-4+.

8645. ——— "17 Contracts: Hollywood Freeway Construction under Way Is Extensive and Varied." *California Highways and Public Works* 30 (May-June 1951): 17-22.

8646. "Finishing the West's Biggest Cut." *Western Construction* 37 (July 1962): 50-2.
Sepulveda-Mulholland section of San Diego Freeway.

8647. "First Parkway for Los Angeles: New Grade-Separated, Divided-Lane Route Will Extend 6 Miles Up Arroyo Seco from Monumental Figueroa St. Viaduct in Los Angeles to Pasadena." *Engineering News-Record* 121 (July 21, 1938): 79-82.

8648. "First Section of Long Beach Freeway Opened to Traffic." *California Highways and Public Works* 32 (January-February 1953): 37.

8649. "Four-Level Grade Separation in Los Angeles." *American City* 64 (April 1949): 159.
Downtown interchange.

8650. "Four Level Grade Separation Structure on Los Angeles Metropolitan Freeway System." *California Highways and Public Works* 31 (September-October 1952): 22+.
Downtown interchange.

8651. "Freeway Interchange: Intricate Three-Level Structure Progresses." *California Highways and Public Works* 36 (March-April 1956): 30-1.
Long Beach and Santa Ana freeways.

8652. "Freeway Leaflets: Boy Scouts Help Distribute Them." *California Highways and Public Works* 43 (September-October 1964) : 42-3.
District VII freeways.

8653. "Freeways in the Los Angeles Metropolitan Area." *Traffic Quarterly* 1 (January 1947) : entire issue.

8654. "Freeways Relieve Traffic Congestion and Conserve Property Values." *Western City* 20 (December 1944) : 34-6+.
Mainly Arroyo Seco.

8655. Frischer, Donald. "New Lanes: Minor Improvements Aid Freeway Traffic Flow." *California Highways and Public Works* 38 (September-October 1959) : 21-3+.
Vicinity of Los Angeles Civic Center.

8656. Frischer, Don[ald]. "Tough Job: Santa Ana Freeway Widening Carried Out under Heavy Traffic Conditions." *California Highways and Public Works* 35 (May-June 1956) : 58-9.
2.3-mile section of Santa Ana Freeway between Camulos Street and Olympic Boulevard in East Los Angeles.

8657. Frykland, B. N. "Ramona Freeway Engineering Personnel Is Organized Efficiently." *California Highways and Public Works* 31 (January-February 1952) : 17-9.

8658. George, A. N. "Arroyo Seco Parkway Extension Adds Four Southbound Traffic Lanes." *California Highways and Public Works* 22 (January-February 1944) : 2-4.

8659. ———. "Easterly Gateway to Los Angeles Involves Structure for Freeways." *California Highways and Public Works* 19 (February 1941) : 13-6.
Aliso Street.

8660. ———. "Work on New Santa Ana Freeway in Los Angeles Is Well under Way." *California Highways and Public Works* 24 (March-April 1946) : 25-6.

8661. Gillis, Lyman R. "Freeway Loop: New Eight-Lane Roadway Will Encircle L. A. Downtown Area." *California Highways and Public Works* 38 (September-October 1959) : 11-20+.

8662. ———. "San Bernardino Freeway." *California Highways and Public Works* 35 (July-August 1956) : 37-48.

8663. Goodwin, H. Marshall, Jr. "The Arroyo Seco: From Dry Gulch to Freeway." *Southern California Quarterly* 47 (1965) : 73-102.

8664. ———. "California's Growing Freeway System." Doctoral dissertation, University of California, Los Angeles, 1969. 714 pp.

8665. Green, J. W. "Key Problem in the Los Angeles Area Is—Freeway Structure Practice." *Western Construction* 28 (February 1953) : 57-60.

8666. ———. "Santa Ana Freeway: Another Major Unit Is Opened to Public Travel." *California Highways and Public Works* 29 (May-June 1950) : 32-3.
La Verne to Eastland avenues.

8667. Griffin, A. D. "Arroyo Seco: Pasadena Freeway, First in West, Has 20th Birthday." *California Highways and Public Works* 40 (January-February 1961) : 57-63+.

8668. ———. "Hollywood Freeway Project Is Truly Cooperative Effort." *California Highways and Public Works* 33 (September-October 1954) : 7-19.

8669. ———. "Proposed Arroyo Seco Parkway Extension to Los Angeles Business Center Through Elysian Park." *California Highways and Public Works* 18 (October 1940) : 6-9+.

8670. Griswold, Wesley S. "Los Angeles Prepares for More Traffic." *Popular Science Monthly* 161 (December 1952) : 139-41.
Freeway construction program.

8671. "Ground Breaking: Governor Launches Two Major Freeway Projects." *California Highways and Public Works* 33 (September-October 1954) : 20-1.
Sections of Sepulveda (San Diego) and Ramona (San Bernardino) freeways.

8672. Gustafson, Charles F. "First Night Paving Job." *California Highways and Public Works* 45 (September-October 1966) : 26-9.
Widening of Long Beach Freeway.

8673. Hanson, E. G. "Plan and Design: Eight Years History of Long Beach Freeway Told." *California Highways and Public Works* 36 (November-December 1957) : 5-10+.

8674. "Harbor Freeway: Governor Knight Opens New Four-Mile Section." *California Highways and Public Works* 36 (May-June 1957): 41-3.

8675. "Harbor Freeway: Important New Section Is Opened to Traffic." *California Highways and Public Works* 31 (September-October 1952): 23.

8676. "Harbor Freeway Project Wins Bonneroo Award in Los Angeles." *California Highways and Public Works* 40 (May-June 1961): 78.
Prize for high-quality workmanship.

8677. "Harbor Parkway Is under Construction." *California Highways and Public Works* 26 (November-December 1947): 17.

8678. Harding, P[aul] O. "Big Job: Role of Division of Highways in Development of the Freeway System for the Los Angeles Metropolitan Area." *California Highways and Public Works* 31 (March-April 1952): 1-16.

8679. ———— "District VII Freeways Developments in the Los Angeles Area." *California Highways and Public Works* 34 (January-February 1955): 14-30.

8680. ———— "District VII Freeways Report: Appraisal of Work During Past Five Years." *California Highways and Public Works* 35 (January-February 1956): 54-66.

8681. ———— "Harbor Freeway: Progress Report on Multi-Million Dollar Project in Los Angeles." *California Highways and Public Works* 30 (March-April 1951): 11-3+.

8682. ———— "Harbor Freeway Temporary Field for Helicopters." *California Highways and Public Works* 31 (July-August 1952): 58-9+.

8683. ———— "Highway Department Makes Progress Report on Los Angeles Freeways." *Western Housing* 37 (March 1954): 6-7+.

8684. ———— "Problems and Progress on Los Angeles Freeway System." *California Highways and Public Works* 32 (March-April 1953): 1-17.

8685. ———— "Ramona Freeway: Report of Accomplishments in Los Angeles County." *California Highways and Public Works* 30 (September-October 1951): 12-6.

8686. ———— "Santa Ana Freeway: Another Unit Is Opened to Traffic." *California Highways and Public Works* 28 (May-June 1949): 44-7+.

8687. ———— "Southern Freeways: Progress Report on Los Angeles Highways." *California Highways and Public Works* 33 (January-February 1954): 1-16.

8688. Hatfield, Robert J. "Arroyo Seco Freeway Extension Becomes a $4,000,000 Defense Highway Project." *California Highways and Public Works* 19 (September 1941): 6-8+.

8689. Heckeroth, Heinz. "Traffic Relief: Loop Freeways Ease Congestion in Metropolitan Los Angeles." *California Highways and Public Works* 41 (September-October 1962): 16-8.

8690. Hill, Stuart L. "Glendale Report: Preconstruction Study Shows Freeway Benefits." *California Highways and Public Works* 43 (March-April 1964): 42-7.

8691. Himelhock, A. L. "Long Beach: 16½-Mile Freeway Connects Los Angeles with Area to the South." *California Highways and Public Works* 37 (September-October 1958): 49-57.

8692. ———— "Loop Progress: L. A. Freeway Completions Will Bring Traffic Relief." *California Highways and Public Works* 40 (January-February 1961): 13-23.

8693. Hollister, L[eonard] C. "Careful Design Cuts Construction Costs on Los Angeles Freeway Structures." *Civil Engineering* 20 (May 1950): 72-6.

8694. ———— "New Freeway Structures Show Twisting and Turning Designs." *California Highways and Public Works* 21 (March-April 1943): 18-9.
Ramona (San Bernardino) Freeway.

8695. "How to Build a Freeway on Legs." *Western Construction* 36 (June 1961): 100-1+.
Santa Monica Freeway viaduct through Los Angeles.

8696. "Hub of the Los Angeles Freeways." *Western Construction* 29 (June 1954): 79.
Downtown four-level interchange.

8697. Innis, R. M. "Slipform Paving—L. A.: New

Technique Used on Harbor Freeway." *California Highways and Public Works* 39 (May-June 1960): 47-50.

8698. James, Warren B., and Munger, A. H. "Cable Relocation: New Technique Used, Savings Total $240,000." *California Highways and Public Works* 39 (September-October 1960): 36-9.
Golden State Freeway from Mission Road to Pasadena Avenue, Los Angeles.

8699. Kapono, J. O. "Central Mix: Revised Method Speeds Road Paving Operations." *California Highways and Public Works* 41 (July-August 1962): 29-32.
San Diego Freeway in Carson-Dominguez area.

8700. Kelly, John F., and Reilly, Edward P. "Industry and Frontage Roads: Property Owners Acclaim Santa Ana Freeway an Advantage to Industrial Business." *California Highways and Public Works* 33 (July-August 1954): 19-22+.
Los Angeles.

8701. Kennedy, R. C. "Busy Day: Highway Commissioners Break Ground for Two Major Freeway Projects in South." *California Highways and Public Works* 30 (July-August 1951): 15-6+.
Los Angeles River (Long Beach) Freeway and Harbor Freeway between Temple and Fourth streets.

8702. ———— "Christmas Gift: Hollywood Freeway Through Los Angeles Civic Center Open to Traffic." *California Highways and Public Works* 31 (January-February 1952): 13-6.

8703. ———— "New Link: Two Additional Miles of Hollywood Freeway Opened." *California Highways and Public Works* 30 (September-October 1951): 17-8+.

8704. Kimoto, James K. "El Monte: City's Post-Freeway Progress Refutes 'Chinese Wall' Fears." *California Highways and Public Works* 38 (January-February 1959): 15-9.

8705. Knittel, Deway W., and McCauley, Marvin L. "Seismic Tests—Followup Report Compares 1960 Prediction with Results." *California Highways and Public Works* 42 (May-June 1963): 54-8.
Antelope Valley Freeway between Saugus and Palmdale.

8706. Kretzer, Carole. "Antelope Valley Freeway." *California Highways and Public Works* 43 (January-February 1964): 2-8.

8707. Laird, G[eorge] L. "New Pacific Coast Highway Will Be Portion of Terminal Island Freeway." *California Highways and Public Works* 26 (November-December 1947): 25-6.

8708. ————, and Frykland, B. N. "Santa Ana Freeway: Another Major Unit under Construction." *California Highways and Public Works* 28 (May-June 1949): 48+.

8709. ————; McCullough, C. J., and Bannister, E. A. "New Freeway: Ramona-99 Project Through Pomona, Claremont, Ontario and Upland Now Completed." *California Highways and Public Works* 33 (November-December 1954): 7-12+.

8710. "Landscaping Arroyo Freeway." *California Highways and Public Works* 18 (December 1940): 14-5.

8711. Langsner, George. "Terminal Island Access Road Is Completed as Freeway at Cost of $10,-242,000." *California Highways and Public Works* 27 (September-October 1948): 11-5+.

8712. Lefferts, E. B. "Correcting Los Angeles Traffic Snarls." *American City* 54 (May 1939): 99+.
Proposal for system of grade-separated "motorways."

8713. Lendecke, H. R. "Foothill Freeway Will Relieve Traffic Congestion at Devil's Gate Dam." *California Highways and Public Works* 33 (July-August 1954): 49-51.

8714. ————, and Beer, C. G. "Four Level: Construction Advancing on Unique Highway Project." *California Highways and Public Works* 28 (January-February 1949): 61-4.
Downtown interchange.

8715. Leonard, Harold W. "Right-of-Way Clearance: District VII Program Moves Ahead Steadily." *California Highways and Public Works* 37 (January-February 1958): 21-4+.

8716. "Long Beach Freeway Link Opened by Governor [Knight]." *California Highways and Public Works* 33 (November-December 1954): 34.

8717. "A Look at Los Angeles Planning Reports Shows . . . Freeway Building Has Just Begun." *Western Construction* 43 (June 1968): 71-2+.

8718. Los Angeles County. Regional Plannnig Commission. *Freeways for the Region*. Los Angeles, 1943. 53 pp.

8719. "Los Angeles Freeway Call Box System Saves Lives." *Western City* 43 (July 1967): 19.

8720. "Los Angeles Makes Recommendations." *California Highways and Public Works* 34 (September-October 1955): 54-5.
  Chamber of Commerce and Downtown Business Men's Association recommendations for new freeway projects.

8721. "Los Angeles Parkway—First Four-Level Grade Separation." *Western Construction News* 23 (September 1948): 75-8.
  Downtown interchange.

8722. "Los Angeles Plans Freeways: Traffic Congestion in Business Areas of Los Angeles County Forces Planning Commission to Devise a System of Freeways and Parkways to Speed Inter-Community Travel, Reduce Accident Rate and Protect Investment of the Motoring Public." *Western Construction News* 18 (October 1943): 457-8.

8723. "Los Angeles Plans Parkways: To Expedite the Safe and Rapid Movement of Vehicular Traffic, the City of Los Angeles Has Planned an Extensive Parkway System, without Cross Streets, Traffic Signals, or Left Turns, Which Will Be Coordinated with and Form an Integral Part of the State-Wide System of Limited Access Freeways." *Western Construction News* 20 (January 1945): 83-6.

8724. "Los Angeles Plans Unusual Four-Level Grade Separation." *American City* 59 (November 1944): 17.
  Downtown freeway interchange.

8725. "Los Angeles Traffic Board Urges Super-Highway Start: Recommendations in Report Include Extensive Plan for Express Highway Routes of Parkway Type in Metropolitan Area—Initial Los Angeles-Hollywood Unit Would Cost $20,000,-000." *Western Construction News* 15 (February 1940): 54-5.

8726. Ludlow, Warren S. "Freeway Model: Construction of Complex Interchange Model Described." *California Highways and Public Works* 37 (November-December 1958): 19-23+.
  Golden State and Santa Ana freeways.

8727. Maghetti, C. A. "El Monte: Governor Knight Opens New Section of Freeway in South." *California Highways and Public Works* 35 (July-August 1956): 52-3.

8728. Martin, James E. "San Diego Freeway: Half of 90-mile Route Completed or under Way." *California Highways and Public Works* 41 (January-February 1962): 45-59.

8729. McCullough. C. J.; Britton, R. F., and Holl, C. R., Jr. "Final Link: Last Unit on Santa Ana Provides 42 Miles Continuous Freeway." *California Highways and Public Works* 37 (September-October 1958): 13-6.

8730. McElhiney, Paul T. "The Freeways of Metropolitan Los Angeles; An Evaluation in Terms of Their Objectives." Doctoral dissertation, University of California, Los Angeles, 1959. 238 pp.

8731. McIntyre. W. A. "Harbor Freeway: Retaining Walls and Bridge Structures Are Important." *California Highways and Public Works* 33 (July-August 1954): 46-8+.

8732. McKnight, Wallace M.; Lynn, A. J. A., and Kennelly, Patrick J. "Progress Report: On Santa Ana Freeway from Norwalk to Miraflores." *California Highways and Public Works* 29 (November-December 1950): 20-1+.

8733. McMahon, J. E. "New Colorado Freeway Is Opened to Traffic." *California Highways and Public Works* 33 (July-August 1954): 18.

8734. "The Metropolitan T." *Los Angeles* 11 (January 1966): 28-30.
  "Outlined by freeways, the high density, high rise 'center' for Los Angeles now assumes a definite shape and structure, beginning downtown and stretching to the ocean."

8735. Meyer. John G. "Extending Arroyo Seco Parkway into Los Angeles Business Center." *California Highways and Public Works* 19 (April 1941): 8+.

8736. Meyer, Larry L. "Design in Concrete." *Westways* 56 (May 1964): 22-3.
San Diego-Santa Monica Freeway interchange.

8737. ——— "Sinews of a Super City." *Westways* 57 (June 1965): 26-8+.
Los Angeles freeways.

8738. " 'Mixmaster' for Los Angeles Traffic: Four Freeways Are Joined in a $10,000,000 Interchange, the Largest Contract Let by the California Division of Highways." *Western Construction* 34 (October 1959): 78+.
East Los Angeles interchange.

8739. Moss, Marvin A. "Los Angeles Freeways." *California Engineer* 26 (June 1948): 8-9.

8740. "Nine Mile 'Freeway' Being Built by State and Three Cities." *Western City* 15 (July 1939): 14-5.
Arroyo Seco.

8741. "Old Fort Moore Hill in Los Angeles Gives Way to Freeway." *California Highways and Public Works* 30 (January-February 1951) 17+.
Hollywood Freeway.

8742. Pierce, R. E. "Study Shows Accidents on Arroyo Seco Parkway Are Less Than on Some Los Angeles City Streets." *California Highways and Public Works* 23 (July-August 1945): 1-3+.

8743. "Progress Report—Los Angeles Freeway System." *Western Construction* 27 (March 1952): 84-5.

8744. "Prohibition of Billboards Along Freeways in Los Angeles." *American City* 67 (January 1952): 159.

8745. "Ramona Freeway Construction Completed from Los Angeles City to Alhambra Front Door." *California Highways and Public Works* 32 (July-August 1953): 15-6+.

8746. "Route Actions: Freeway Locations for Malibu, Other L.A. County Areas Chosen." *California Highways and Public Works* 43 (September-October 1964): 68-9.

8747. Schmidt, Robert H. "The Impact of Freeways on California's Rural Landscape." Doctoral dissertation, University of California, Los Angeles, 1968. 231 pp.

8748. "Slip-Form Paving on L.A. Freeway." *Western Construction* 35 (March 1960): 56-8.
Harbor Freeway.

8749. Smith, J. F., and Woodbridge, C. J. "Golden State Freeway." *California Highways and Public Works* 36 (September-October 1957): 20-5.

8750. Spooner, Robert A. "Huge Job: Right of Way Clearance in the Los Angeles Metropolitan. Area." *California Highways and Public Works* 28 (May-June 1949): 35-41+.

8751. Stark, Milton. "L. A. Renaissance: Freeway Service Key Factor in Downtown Growth, Renewal." *California Highways and Public Works* 40 (September-October 1961): 29-45.

8752. "State Wins Los Angeles Beautiful Awards." *California Highways and Public Works* 33 (January-February 1954): 37.
Awards for landscaping on Hollywood Freeway and Arroyo Seco Parkway.

8753. Sturgeon, F. E. "Harbor Freeway Construction in the Wilmington-San Pedro Area." *California Highways and Public Works* 34 (July-August 1955): 57-9+.

8754. ———, and Mock, K. P. "Ventura Freeway: Last Two Sections in the San Fenando Valley Opened." *California Highways and Public Works* 39 (May-June 1960): 2-10.

8755. "System of Super Highways Proposed for Los Angeles: Solution of Vehicular Traffic Problem Attacked by Comprehensive Study Which Recommends Plan for Multi-Lane Express 'Motorways.' " *Western Construction News* 13 (March 1938): 115-6.

8756. Taylor, Frank J. "The World's Worst Traffic Tangle." *Saturday Evening Post* 226 (March 13, 1954): 42-3+.
Freeways seen as the solution to Los Angeles' traffic problem.

8757. Telford, E[dward] T. "District VIII Freeway Completions, Current Construction Add Up to Encouraging Progress Picture." *California Highways and Public Works* 40 (March-April 1961): 3-22+.

8758. ——— "District VII Freeways." *California*

Highways and Public Works 42 (March-April 1963): 20-41.

8759. ——— "District VII Freeways Report: Accomplishments During 1956 and Outlook for Future." *California Highways and Public Works* 36 (January-February 1957): 1-18+.

8760. ——— "District VII Progress." *California Highways and Public Works* 43 (March-April 1964): 14-35.

8761. ———"District 7 Progress." *California Highways and Public Works* 44 (March-April 1965): 30-51.

8762. ——— "District VII Progress: 430 Miles of Freeway Now Open in Los Angeles Region." *California Highways and Public Works* 43 (January-February 1964): 14-35.

8763. ——— "Freeways in District VII." *California Highways and Public Works* 39 (January-February 1960): 3-19+.

8764. ——— "Long Beach Freeway Phenomenal Traffic Increase Gives Impetus to Project." *California Highways and Public Works* 32 (July-August 1953): 17-23+.

8765. ——— "L. A. Freeways." *California Highways and Public Works* 41 (March-April 1962): 42-57+.

8766. ——— "Report from District VII: Freeway System Taking Shape in Greater Los Angeles Area." *California Highways and Public Works* 37 (January-February 1958): 1-16.

8767. ———, *et al.* "Long Beach Freeway: What Is Happening on This Huge Project." *California Highways and Public Works* 33 (July-August 1954): 23-31+.

8768. ———, *et al.* "Report from District VII." *California Highways and Public Works* 38 (January-February 1959): 23-44+.

8769. "Terminal Island: Highway Commission Votes Needed Funds." *California Highways and Public Works* 38 (May-June 1959): 39.

8770. "Toll Parkway Proposed for Los Angeles."

Engineering News-Record 124 (February 29, 1940): 332-3.
Six-lane Los Angeles-Hollywood tollway proposed as initial project of $250,000,000 traffic-relief plan.

8771. "Traffic Safeguards: Improvements on Arroyo Seco Parkway Are Recommended." *California Highways and Public Works* 27 (May-June 1948): 8+.

8772. Verner, C. J. "Foothill Freeway: Narrow Devil's Gate Roadway Is Eliminated." *California Highways and Public Works* 34 (September-October 1955): 40-1.

8773. "Widening the San Diego Freeway." *Western Construction* 43 (September 1968): 80+.
Los Angeles.

8774. Winter, Hugo H. "Development of a Freeway System in Los Angeles Metropolitan Area." *Traffic Quarterly* 3 (1949): 105-18.

8775. Woodbridge, C. J. "Progress: Next to Last Section of Hollywood Freeway Is Opened to Traffic." *California Highways and Public Works* 32 (September-October 1953): 27-8.

TRAFFIC—LIGHTING

8776. Aiassa. George. "A Booklet That Sells Street Lights." *American City* 83 (March 1968): 36+.
Pamphlet titled "A Bright City Is a Safe City" said to have persuaded West Covina property owners to finance adequate street lighting.

8777. Albers, J. C. "Street Lighting and Tree Planting in Beverly Hills, California." *City Manager Magazine* 8 (August 1926): 19-21.

8778. "Alhambra, San Marino, Monterey Park and San Gabriel Use Vapor Lights." *Western City* 12 (March 1936): 31.

8779. Baumgardner, George. "How South Gate Is Re-Lighting City Streets on Assessment Basis." *Western City* 15 (July 1939): 36.

8780. Bettannier, E. L. "Sodium Vapor Highway Lighting Results Record and Economy at Pasadena." *Western City* 11 (May 1935): 17.

8781. "A Brighter Image Through Lighting." *American City* 84 (June 1969): 124.
Installation of some 20,000 ornamental street lights by Los Angeles during 1969.

8782. "Burbank Banks on Good Lighting." *American City* 84 (August 1969): 122+.

8783. Cartmell, A. W. "Pasadena's Street Lights Fit Each Area." *American City* 75 (October 1960): 116-8.

8784. Crowther, Fred D. "Safety with Sodium." *American City* 55 (March 1940): 103.
Sodium-vapor lighting and the reduction of accidents.

8785. "Darkness Dangers Stressed by City Traffic Report." *American City* 57 (February 1942): 97.
Report on study prepared by traffic engineer R. T. Dorsey.

8786. Dorsey, Ralph T. "Do You Want to Reduce Accidents? Los Angeles Is Doing It." *American City* 53 (September 1938): 139.
Sodium-vapor street lighting.

8787. ——— "Safety Lighting Proves Itself." *American City* 53 (May 1938): 97.
Los Angeles.

8788. ——— "Yellow Light Saves Money." *American City* 57 (January 1942): 95.
Sodium-vapor lighting, Los Angeles.

8789. "Four New Street Lighting Jobs Part of PWA Projects in Los Angeles." *Western City* 13 (February 1937): 29-30.

8790. Gentry, Francis H. "Long Beach Lights American Avenue." *American City* 55 (January 1940): 103.

8791. Hansen, Frank A. "Single System Lights Street and Park: Beverly Hills Develops System of Unique Design and Usefulness for Santa Monica Boulevard and Paralleling Park." *Western City* 8 (June 1932): 16-7.

8792. Hill, C. G. "The Lighting of a Residential Section in a California City of 600." *American City* 19 (April 1918): 120-1.
Beverly Hills.

8793. Huot, Louis L. "Lighting the New Sixth Street Viaduct." *Western City* 9 (July 1933): 19-20.
Los Angeles.

8794. "Improved Illumination in Pasadena." *American City* 33 (November 1925): 488.
East Green Street.

8795. "Installing Lights and Signals in Los Angeles." *American City* 75 (July 1960): 118+.

8796. Jarrett, W. M. "Accident Toll Reduced at Alhambra Intersections." *American City* 62 (January 1947): 115.
Experimental lighting installation.

8797. Julian, Marshall. "Shatterproof Plastic Light Bowls Used in San Fernando to Avoid Replacement." *Western City* 35 (September 1959): 58.

8798. Keebaugh, Harry B. "Street Light Improvement Program Increases City's Downtown Business." *Western City* 30 (October 1954): 56+.
San Gabriel.

8799. Kennedy, Bartlett L. "A Master Plan That Means Modern Lighting." *American City* 77 (July 1962): 129.
Santa Monica.

8800. Koiner, C. Wellington. "South Pasadena's First Installation of Ornamental Street Lighting." *American City* 13 (September 1915): 249-51.

8801. ——— "Street Lighting in Pasadena." *American City* 8 (January 1912): 51.

8802. Lauer, W[illiam]. E. "City-Owned Lighting in Los Angeles." *American City* 62 (September 1947): 145.
Author of this and the ensuing five articles was principal street lighting engineer for the City of Los Angeles.

8803. ——— "How Bright Are Los Angeles Streets?" *American City* 59 (July 1944): 109+.

8804. ——— "Los Angeles, Calif. Tailored Lighting at Intersections Wipes Out Pedestrian Fatalities." *American City* 64 (January 1949): 133+.

8805. ——— "Los Angeles Parkway Lighting." *American City* 61 (July 1946): 115-6.

8806. ——— "Modern Street Lighting Reduces Accidents and Fatalaties." *Western City* 21 (January 1945): 18-20.

8807. ——— " 'Operation Safety' How Los Angeles Saves Lives with Street Lighting." *Western City* 24 (April 1948): 24-7.

8808. "Lighting in Los Angeles." *American City* 55 (December 1940): 105.
Statistics on street lights.

8809. "The Long Beach, Calif., Street-Lighting Installation." *American City* 38 (May 1928): 191.
Redondo Avenue.

8810. Mimmack, Arthur A. "Improvements Above and Below Ground Increase Efficiency: Beverly Hills Lamp Life Shows Gains Made in Two Year Period; Fifty Miles of Wiring Replaced; Conduit Experience Record." *Western City* 12 (February 1936): 16-8.

8811. Nevin, George J. "Huntington Park Flood Lights City Hall, Intersections and Recreation Areas." *Western City* 7 (September 1931): 38.

8812. "New Santa Monica Highway Tunnel Example of Modern Lighting." *Western City* 12 (June 1936): 40.

8813. "New Street Lights Increase Trade 25 Per Cent: The Story of the Better-Lighting Movement Sponsored by the Western Avenue Business Association, Los Angeles." *American City* 30 (February 1924): 173.

8814. "New System of Tunnel Lighting." *Western City* 8 (December 1932): 19.
North Figueroa Street tunnels, Los Angeles.

8815. Nightingale, F. B. "Sodium and Mercury Vapor Installations in United States; Experience in Europe." *Western City* 10 (October 1934): 15-6.
Includes two portions of Highway 66 east and west of Pasadena.

8816. ——— "Utility and Decorative Lighting as Used in the Crown City—Pasadena." *Western City* 10 (September 1934): 25-6.

8817. Rathbun, Morris M. "The New Lighting System in Los Angeles, Calif." *American City* 18 (May 1918): 639.

8818. Shepherd, Theodore H. "The World's Best-Lighted City." *Southern California Business* 11 (December 1932): 14.
Los Angeles streets.

8819. Simonds, C. L., and Van Alstine, R. D. "Long Beach Turns Darkest Street into Brilliant Boulevard." *American City* 36 (January 1927): 42-3.
Atlantic Avenue.

8820. Singer, D. R. "Lakewood Uses 100 Watt Mercury Vapor Luminaires for Area Park Lighting." *Western City* 37 (November 1961): 55.

8821. "Street Lighting Conversion Job in Alhambra Proves Worth." *Western City* 22 (March 1946): 48.

8822. Tufte, Edward E. "Beverly Hills Citizens Decide to Pay Extra for Residential Street Lightnig Modernization." *Western City* 39 (September 1963): 64+.

8823. Victoria, Vesta. "Bright Future for a Big City." *Public Works* 88 (August 1957): 127.
Los Angeles' ten-year $27,000,000 street lighting improvement program.

8824. Watson, Glenn B. "Arcadia Installs New Street Lighting to Help Handle Acute Traffic Needs." *Western City* 23 (February 1947): 42-3.

8825. Wentz, John B. Initiative Is the Key to Beverly Hills' Alley Improvement, Lighting Projects." *Western City* 30 (August 1954): 40-1+.

8826. ——— "Relighting Wilshire Boulevard." *American City* 70 (April 1955): 171-2.

8827. "Wilshire Street Light Conversion Job Far Exceeds I.E.S. Standards." *Western City* 33 (August 1957): 58.
I.E.S.—Illuminating Engineering Society.

8828. "The World's Brightest Street." *American City* 83 (February 1968): 128.
Award for "World's Brightest Lighted Street" goes to three-way intersection in Westwood.

TRAFFIC—MAINTENANCE

8829. Allin, J. H. "Pavement Maintenance

Methods in City of Pasadena." *Western City* 12 (March 1936): 20-2.

8830. Carroza, M. J. "Arcadia Develops Plastic Fiber Broom for Street Sweeping." *Western City* 32 (August 1956): 46.

8831. Davis, Don C. "Hawthorne Adopts Systematic Plan for Street Rehabilitation." *Western City* 25 (December 1949): 34.

8832. "Downtown Merchants Beat Dirty Sidewalk Problems." *American City* 85 (May 1970): 50.
Plan for systematic sidewalk cleaning devised by Downtown Long Beach Associates.

8833. "Findings of Street Sweeping Survey Show Operations of 60 Western Cities." *Western City* 32 (February 1956): 38-41.
Includes many cities in Los Angeles County.

8834. Garber, Lewis W., Jr. "Asphalt Remix Overlay Assures Strength of Vernon's Streets." *Western City* 42 (December 1966): 40-1+.

8835. ——— "To Rejuvenate Old Streets: Heat, Plane, Remix and Overlay." *American City* 83 (January 1968): 88-90.
Vernon.

8836. Greeley, Douglas H. "Prevention of Slides as a Safety Factor." *California Highways and Public Works* 18 (May 1940): 13-4.
Santa Monica.

8837. Hamlin, Homer. "Vacuum Street Cleaning." *American City* 16 (January 1917): 61-2.
Los Angeles.

8838. "How Sierra Madre Meets Unemployment Situation—and Pays the Bill: Street Surfacing Program Gives Work to Citizens, Improves Property Values and City's Appearance, All at Low Cost." *Western City* 7 (December 1931): 27-8.

8839. "How 64 Western Cities Clean Their Streets; A Survey and an Analysis." *Western City* 15 (August 1939): 16-23.
Includes many cities in Los Angeles County.

8840. Joyner, F. H. "The Los Angeles County Road Department Warehouse System." *American City* 39 (October 1928): 88-91.

8841. Kennedy, W. E., and Peebles, W. E. "Inglewood Stretches Its Maintenance Dollars by Use of Low Cost Pavements." *Western City* 30 (August 1954): 50-1.

8842. Lackey, J. M. "Sunset Boulevard Surfacing Removed by Burners Covering 900 Yards a Day." *California Highways and Public Works* 14 (January 1936): 26+.

8843. Lockman, W. J. "Monterery Park Saves $35,000 Street Costs by Utilizing Old Pavement Materials." *Western City* 36 (August 1960): 40.

8844. "L. A. Municipal Asphalt Plant." *Western Construction News* 22 (August 1947): 96-7.

8845. "Los Angeles' New Asphalt Plant." *American City* 62 (August 1947): 96-7.
The third such plant put in operation by the city.

8846. "Los Angeles Report on Riverside Streets." *Pacific Municipalities* 14 (April-May 1906): 74.
Reports on road-oiling techniques.

8847. "Maintaining the Toll Road on Mount Wilson, Pasadena, Calif." *American City* 35 (October 1926): 609.

8848. Meyer, M[osier] M. "Laying 2000 Tons of Asphalt a Day for Los Angeles Street Resurfacing." *Western Construction News* 12 (December 1937): 473-5.

8849. ——— "Street-Cleaning Problems, Los Angeles." *American City* 52 (October 1937): 73-5.

8850. "More Motorized [Street] Sweeping in Los Angeles." *American City* 51 (September 1936): 74.

8851. "The Municipal Asphalt and Oil Heating Plant of Los Angeles." *American City* 40 (January 1929): 11.

8852. Nash, Charles E. "Los Angeles Saves $60,000 Annually by Motorizing Its [Street] Flushers." *American City* 32 (January 1925): 19-20.

8853. "New Economic Street Resurfacing Method Developed by Los Angeles." *Western City* 26 (September 1950): 32.

8854. "New Los Angeles Asphalt Plant." *Western City* 23 (September 1947): 44.

8855. "Object Lesson in Street Oiling Over at Monrovia." *Pacific Municipalities* 12 (March 1905): 44.

8856. O'Malley, John. "Angeles Crest: 55 Miles Now under General Maintenance." *California Highways and Public Works* 36 (March-April 1957): 69-72.

8857. ——— "Snow in the South: Maintenance Crews Meet Unusual Challenge." *California Highways and Public Works* 41 (March-April 1962): 37-9.

District VII maintenance procedures in Los Angeles and vicinity.

8858. Paris, Ben R. "Just One Pass with Two Engines." *American City* 77 (May 1962): 102-4.

Twin-engine sweepers reduce cost of street cleaning in Los Angeles.

8859. Peebles, W[ade] E. "Inglewood Saves Maintenance Costs by Use of a Slurry on the Top." *Western City* 32 (February 1956): 45+.

8860. ——— "Save the Street with Slurry: Inglewood, Calif., Uses a Plaster Mixer and 'Squeegee' to Spruce Up Cracking Asphalt Streets." *American City* 71 (March 1956): 132-3.

8861. "Repairing Freeway Median Barriers." *Western Construction* 42 (June 1967): 74+.

District VII.

8862. "Repairing Lynwood's Major Streets System." *Western City* 40 (May 1964): 34+.

8863. "Road Maintenance Plans and Practice On the Los Angeles County System: A Review of the Organization and Field Procedure Required for the Upkeep of 4,000 Mi. of Highway Serving a County of 3,952-Sq. Mi. Area and 2,300,000 Population." *Western Construction News* 14 (July 1939): 227-9.

8864. Shelby, W. W. "Road Oil-Heating Plant for Los Angeles County." *Engineering News-Record* 103 (July 18, 1929): 100-3.

8865. "Speed in Resurfacing Prevents Traffic Congestion in Down Town Los Angeles." *Western City* 6 (November 1930): 27-8.

8866. "Suction Sweeping of City Streets." *American City* 18 (April 1918): 524-6.

Los Angeles.

8867. Thompson, M. I. "Dump Truck Versatility Increased: Los Angeles County Road Department Has Developed a Commercial Dump Truck Unit That Will Travel and Can Be Safely Handled in Reverse Speeds as High as Forward Speeds by the Addition of Auxiliary Throttle and Brake Controls and Special Gearing." *Western Construction News* 17 (June 1942): 258-9.

8868. "Two Cities Adopt New Street-Sweeping Method: Culver City and Claremont, Calif., Use Central Dumping to Lower Costs and Increase the Efficiency of the Work." *American City* 65 (June 1950): 104-5.

8869. "Well-Designed Maintenance Equipment and Methods at Pasadena, Calif.: [Street] Patches of Asphalt and Concrete." *American City* 54 (November 1939): 41.

8870. Wentz, John B. "Beverly Hills Inaugurates Program of Alley Sweeping." *Western City* 32 (February 1956): 41.

8871. Wilhelms, Meno. " 'Closed On Saturday, Opened by Thursday' Is the Claim of Hawthorne Alley Program." *Western City* 33 (December 1957): 45.

8872. Wright, A. W. "Los Angeles Broom Rebuilding Shop Operates Two 8-Hr. Shifts per Day." *Western Construction News* 14 (October 1939): 348.

Street-sweeper brooms.

8873. ——— "Problems and Practices of Street Cleaning in Los Angeles." *Western City* 20 (February 1944): 20-2.

TRAFFIC—PARKING

8874. Adsit, Ted B., and Jones, Frank A. "Pasadena's New Auto Parking Plan." *Western City* 23 (December 1947): 23.

8875. "Airport Builds Parking Structure with Tomorrow in Mind." *Public Works* 100 (July 1969): 71.

Relocatable, three-deck, 800-car parking structure at Los Angeles International Airport.

8876. "Authorize 1650-Car Underground Parking Station in Los Angeles." *Western City* 26 (September 1950): 33.
Pershing Square.

8877. "Beverly Hills Considers Rear Lot Parking in 30 Block Area." *Western City* 18 (March 1942): 37.

8878. "Construction Begins on 2000 Car Underground Garage in Los Angeles." *Western City* 27 (February 1951): 36.
Pershing Square.

8879. "Continuous Ramp Parking Garage Being Built in Los Angeles." *Western City* 24 (July 1948): 29.
General Petroleum Building, Eight and Flower streets.

8880. "Continuous Ramp Parking Garage Is Planned for Downtown Los Angeles." *Western Construction News* 23 (March 1948): 100.
Pershing Square.

8881. Dorton, Randall M. "Parking Meters Win Quick Approval in City of Long Beach." *Western City* 13 (February 1937): 16-8.

8882. Douglass, Ken. "Multi-Deck Parking Garage Added to Whittier's Downtown System." *Western City* 36 (January 1969): 28-9.

8883. Elliott. Clifford A. "Pacific Electric Has Complete Parking Program." *Electric Railway Journal* 54 (September 13, 1919): 517.

8884. "Five More Metered Lots Placed in Operation." *Western City* 29 (September 1953): 50+.
Pomona.

8885. Gallas, Edward. "Parking Meters in California Cities." *Western City* 23 (May 1947): 20-7.
Includes many cities in Los Angeles County.

8886. Hahn, Walter, Jr., and Julian, Marshall. "Inglewood Parking Check Is Left to the Girls." *Western City* 33 (June 1957): 44+.

8887. "Huntington Park Opens Municipal Metered Parking Lot." *Western City* 25 (January 1949): 21.

8888. "Inglewood Study Leads to Purchase of Two Off-Street Parking Lots." *Western City* 27 (July 1951): 52.

8889. Kincaid, James. "16 Years of Experience with Parking Meters in Long Beach." *Western City* 28 (September 1952): 22-3.

8890. Lillard, Richard G. "Life in the Parking Lot." *Nation* 201 (December 6, 1965): 435-7.
Los Angeles.

8891. Lindersmith, Walter R. "Less Parking— More Purchasing, in Los Angeles." *American City* 43 (December 1930): 120-1.
Author states that parking restrictions do no reduce number of autos entering central business district.

8892. McMahon, Charles A. "Acres of Concrete Floors for the Underground Garage in Los Angeles." *Western Construction* 27 (February 1952): 80-3.
Pershing Square.

8893. ———. "Los Angeles Constructs 2,000-Car Underground Garage." *Civil Engineering* 21 (December 1951): 25-30.
Pershing Square.

8894. "Municipal Off-Street Parking in 79 California Cities." *Western City* 27 (March 1951): 25-30.
Includes many cities in Los Angeles County.

8895. "Off-Street Parking in California." *Western City* 24 (May 1948): 19-23; (June 1948): 20-1+.
Includes many cities in Los Angeles County.

8896. "Parking Meter Rental Plan Worked Out for Alhambra Municipal Lots." *Western City* 25 (March 1949): 29.

8897. "Parking Meter Survey of 281 Cities Shows Increased Use for Regulation." *Western City* 33 (September 1957): 40-3.
Includes several cities in Los Angeles County.

8898. "The Portable Garage . . . A Recent Technological Breakthrough in Garage Construction Provides a Low Cost Flexible Solution to Today's Off-Street Parking Problems." *American City* 85 (January 1970): 108+.
Describes, among other examples, the Los An-

geles County Garage at First and Grand, and a new facility at Los Angeles International Airport.

8899. "Precast Units Support Excavation, Then Form Permanent Walls at West's Largest Underground Garage." *Western Construction* 26 (July 1951): 61-5.
Pershing Square.

8900. "Programmed Parking: How 7 Cities Resolve Off-Street Parking under California's Statutes." *Western City* 32 (March 1956): 36-41.
Includes description of facilities in Los Angeles by Lloyd M. Braff, pp. 3617; Pomona by Frederick W. Sharp, pp. 37-9; Alhambra by Charles Lortz, p. 39; Inglewood by F. Robert Coop, pp. 39-40; and Beverly Hills by John B. Wentz, p. 41.

8901. "The Results of Off-Street Parking and Meter Rates Questionnaire from 269 Western Cities Point to Increased Income." *Western City* 33 (July 1957): 38-43.
Includes several cities in Los Angeles County.

8902. Richerson, John L. "Burbank Sells $825,000 Parking District Bonds to Help Revive Central Business District." *Western City* 37 (March 1961): 22-3.

8903. Scott, Perry. "Santa Wouldn't Provide 2,000 Free Parking Spaces . . . So Local Merchants and Property Owners Built Six Downtown Parking Garages for Santa Monica." *American City* 84 (May 1969): 145-6.

8904. Sharp, Fred [W.]. "New Parking, Lighting and Paving for Pomona Shopping Center." *Western City* 28 (September 1952): 27-8.

8905. ———— "Pomona Tackles Its Off-Street Parking Problem by Assessment District Plan." *Western City* 27 (March 1951): 30-2.

8906. Sherrod, Clinton E. "Planning for Downtown Parking with Empasis Upon the Los Angeles Metropolitan Area." Master's thesis, University of Southern California, 1963. 141 pp.

8907. "Shuttle Bus Parking System Used by Inglewood at Christmas Peak." *Western City* 31 (January 1955): 49.

8908. "Solving the Parking Problem in Los An-

geles." *Los Angeles Saturday Night* 8 (March 3, 1928): 2.
Building large-capacity downtown garages, such as Hill's Garage on South Spring Street.

8909. "Triple Decker Garage Beneath Public Square Proposed as Traffic Aid." *Western City* 7 (April 1931): 25+.
Pershing Square.

8910. "Twin-Stall Curb Parking at Monterey Park." *Western City* 27 (February 1951): 36.

8911. Wood, C. Raymond. " 'Parkettes' + Punch Cards = 300% Revenue Gain: Beverly Hills, Calif. Redesigns Its Parking-Meter Enforcement and Collection System—and the Resulting Benefits Surpass All Predictions." *American City* 75 (March 1960): 122-3.

8912. "Work Starts on Underground Pershing Square Garage, Los Angeles, California." *The Architect and Engineer* 184 (February 1951): 12-5+.

TRAFFIC—HIGHWAYS

8913. "Aggregates for Paving Ridge Route Alternate." *Western Construction News and Highways Builder* 8 (July 1933): 317.
Between Castaic and Gorman.

8914. Albers, J. C. "Widening and Repaving of Wilshire Boulevard through Beverly Hills, Los Angeles County, California." *Western Construction News* 2 (May 25, 1927): 45.

8915. Aldrich, Lloyd. "Highway Subway Constructed under Runways of Los Angeles International Airport." *Civil Engineering* 23 (April 1953): 48-52.

8916. "Angeles Crest Highway Construction Stopped as Unessential to War Effort." *California Highways and Public Works* 20 (December 1942): 18-9.

8917. Ayanian, Haig. "Artesia Street: Progress in Converting Route 175 into Four-Lane Divided Highway." *California Highways and Public Works* 33 (September-October 1954): 50-2+.

8918. Barney, W. E. "Boulevard Construction in Pasadena." *American City* 39 (November 1928): 140.
Linda Vista Avenue.

8919. Barnhill, O. H. "Venice Canals Converted into Paved Streets." *Western Construction News* 5 (December 10, 1930): 609-11.

8920. Bauders, M. L. "Unusual Drainage Features on the Angeles Crest Highway." *California Highways and Public Works* 17 (April 1939): 20+.

8921. Bezzant. R. G. "Alhambra Improves an Abandoned Right-of-Way to Aid Traffic Flow." *Western City* 35 (June 1959): 66.
Ex-Pacific Electric right-of-way.

8922. Blow, Ben. *California Highways; A Descriptive Record of Road Development by the State and Such Counties as Have Paved Highways.* San Francisco, 1920. 308 pp.
Includes Los Angeles County.

8923. Brent, W. L. "Good Streets for Less Money." *Southern California Business* 7 (August 1928): 19+.
Los Angeles.

8924. "Brick Pavements on the Pacific Coast." *The Architect and Engineer of California* 14 (August 1908): 52-4.
Los Angeles.

8925. Burrud, L. J. "Mulholland Highway a Civic Achievement." *Saturday Night* 3 (November 3, 1923): 22.

8926. Burt, E. A. "Building the Angeles Forest Highway." *Civil Engineering* 12 (March 1942): 147-9.

8927. ———— "Long Beach Blvd. Improvement, Los Angeles County, California." *Western Construction News* 3 (May 10, 1928): 306.

8928. Busch, Carl. "To and Through Hollywood." *Los Angeles Realtor* 7 (November 1927): 25-6.
Improvement of street system.

8929. "Canals Are Filled to Become Modern Traffic Arteries." *Western City* 6 (January 1930): 23-6.
Venice.

8930. Childs, J. H. "Comparison and Analysis of Unit Bids on Street Paving Contracts in Los Angeles and Vicinity." *Western Construction News* 2 (December 25, 1927): 45-6.

8931. "Clear the Way for Traffic: Los Angeles Removes Jogs in Major Highway to Ocean." *American City* 54 (September 1939): 75.
Olympic at Figueroa.

8932. Collins, Ray A. "Malibu Project: Improvement on Coast Highway Traffic Benefit." *California Highways and Public Works* 28 (March-April 1949): 32-3+.

8933. "Contractor Is Required to Complete $760,-000 Highway Job in 4½ Months." *Western Construction News* 15 (May 1940): 164-7.
Cahuenga Boulevard.

8934. "Cooperative Project Completes New Whittier Boulevard." *California Highways and Public Works* 3 (June 1926): 5+.

8935. Cortelyou, Herman P. "Los Angeles Makes Concrete Pavement Tests." *Western Construction News and Highways Builder* 7 (September 25, 1932): 529-31.

8936. ———— "Secondary Residential Street Becomes Metropolitan Business Artery: Widening, Re-Alignment, Paving. Sewers, Drains, Lighting and New Underground Structures Are Involved in Los Angeles Project [Eight Street]." *Western City* 7 (January 1931): 27-9.

8937. Cortelyou, S[pencer] V. "Angeles Crest Highway Opens Vast Recreational Territory." *California Highways and Public Works* 15 (September 1937): 8+.

8938. ———— "Angeles Crest Highway Will Open Vast Recreational Mountain Area in Fall." *California Highways and Public Works* 12 (July 1934): 2+.

8939. ———— "Breaking the Newhall Bottleneck." *California Highways and Public Works* 5 (May-June 1928): 7-8.
Relocating a portion of the Ridge Route.

8940. ———— "Firestone Boulevard Bottleneck in Graham Widened and Open to Traffic." *California Highways and Public Works* 12 (October 1934): 6+.

8941. ——— "Foothill Boulevard Cutoff Relieves Traffic Congestion in San Fernando." *California Highways and Public Works* 12 (November-December 1934): 20-1+.

8942. ——— "New $2,119,000 L. A.-Pomona Arterial Will Save Traffic $876,000 Annually." *California Highways and Public Works* 12 (February 1934): 2+.
Ramona Boulevard, later part of Ramona (San Bernardino) Freeway.

8943. ——— "Olympic Boulevard Developing as Major Los Angeles Arterial." *California Highways and Public Works* 15 (February 1937): 6-8+.

8944. Denning, Ernest. "Malibu Shore Road Rebuilt." *Western Construction News* 22 (December 1947): 82-5.
Pacific Coast Highway.

8945. Donovan, J. L. "Sepulveda Boulevard Tunnel, Los Angeles." *Western Construction News* 5 (August 10, 1930): 381-5.

8946. East, E. E. "Streets: The Circulatory System," in *Los Angeles: Preface to a Master Plan.* Ed. by George W. Robbins and L. Deming Tilton. Los Angeles, 1941. Pp. 91-100.

8947. Edwards, Harlan H. "Designing Flood-Proof Streets to Carry Water Flows." *Public Works* 71 (April 1940): 16-8.
Claremont.

8948. Edwards, R. W. "La Canada-Mt. Wilson State Highway, California." *Western Construction News* 5 (August 25, 1930): 393-6.

8949. "F. A. S. Highway Program in Los Angeles County." *California Highways and Public Works* 31 (July-August 1952): 1-8.
F. A. S.—Federal Aid Secondary.

8950. "Fast Slipform Paving for City Street." *Western Construction* 43 (February 1968): 68.
90th St., Crenshaw to Prairie, access to the Forum sports center.

8951. "Fourth Vehicular Tunnel to Improve Major Traffic Route in Los Angeles." *Western Construction News* 10 (November 1935): 308-9.
North Figueroa Street tunnels through Elysian Park.

8952. Friedman, Samuel L. "A Scenic Drive Along a 200-Foot Beach." *American City* 50 (October 1935): 69.
Proposed link of Roosevelt (now Pacific Coast) Highway between Santa Monica and Playa Del Rey.

8953. Gallagher, John D. "Newhall Tunnel Replaced by Cut." *California Highways and Public Works* 18 (January 1940): 16-8+.
Santa Susana Mountains.

8954. George, A. N. "Day-Labor Camp for Angeles Crest Highway." *Western Construction News* 6 (December 25, 1931): 680-1.

8955. Glass, E. Earl. "Replacing an Oiled Earth Road with a Special Type of Light Macadam." *American City* 19 (July 1918): 23-4.
Duarte Avenue, Los Angeles County Road Dept.

8956. "Grading and Paving Ridge Route Alternate: California Division of Highways Finishing 28 Mi. of Grading, Paving, and Bridges Between Castaic School and Gorman, Los Angeles County." *Western Construction News and Highways Builder* 8 (May 10, 1933): 223-5.

8957. "Grading San Gabriel High-Line Road." *Western Construction News and Highways Builder* 7 (November 25, 1932): 649-51.

8958. Hagerman, Perry S. "Street Design Principles in Los Angeles." *American City* 66 (August 1951): 120-1.

8959. Harding, P[aul] O. "No Small Job: Four Million Dollars Spent on Lakewood-Rosemead Project." *California Highways and Public Works* 29 (January-February 1950): 16-8+.

8960. Hatfield, R. J. "Building Divided Highway Link on L. A.-Pomona Airline Lateral." *California Highways and Public Works* 15 (April 1937): 4-5+.

8961. Heckeroth, Heinz, and Cohon, Barry. "The Ridge Route: Construction History, Future Plans Summarized." *California Highways and Public Works* 44 (September-October 1965): 20-31.

8962. Helliwell, George F. "Traffic Capacity of 6- and 8-Lane Thoroughfares at a Busy Intersection."

American City 38 (June 1928): 98.
Wilshire and Western, Los Angeles.
geles.

8963. Hill, Harlan H. "History of the Ridge Route." Master's thesis, Occidental College, 1954. 90 pp.

8964. Hoffman, Abraham. "Angeles Crest: The Creation of a Forest Highwest System in the San Gabriel Mountains." *Southern California Quarterly* 50 (1968): 309-39.

8965. Hoffman, Alice M. "The Evolution of the Highway from Salt Lake City to Los Angeles." Master's thesis, University of Southern California, 1936. 128 pp.

8966. "Hollywood's Appian Way — Mulholland Drive." *Los Angeles Realtor* 6 (November 1926): 33.

8967. "Hollywood's Paving Program." *Los Angeles Realtor* 6 (November 1926): 36+.

8968. Holmes, Donald L. "Five-Finger Plan Improvement, Hollywood." *Western Construction News* 6 (July 25, 1931): 386-8.
Street widening and paving program.

8969. "Improvements on U.S. 101 & 101A from Santa Barbara to Laguna." *California Highways and Public Works* 27 (November-December 1948): 36-8.

8970. Jellick, J. E. "Los Angeles Buys Most Pavements Cheapest." *Pacific Municipalities* 43 (May 1929): 218-20.

8971. ———— "New Developments in Concrete Pavement Construction: A Feature in Construction of Whittier Boulevard, Los Angeles County, on Coast Route, California State Highway." *Western Construction News* 2 (August 25, 1927): 42-3.

8972. ———— "Roosevelt Highway, Southern California." *Western Construction News* 4 (February 10, 1929): 75-7.
Now Pacific Coast Highway.

8973. Jessup, John J. "Financing Arterial Highways in Cities." *Western City* 8 (December 1932): 21-2.
Los Angeles.

8974. Jones, Charles W. "End Barrier to Los Angeles Traffic." *The Architect and Engineer* 124 (March 1936): 42-4.
Completion of North Figueroa Street tunnels through Elysian Park and viaducts over Los Angeles River and Southern Pacific Railroad yards.

8975. ———— "Tunnel of Unusual Design to Carry Coast Highway Through Santa Monica." *California Highways and Public Works* 13 (July 1935): 6+.

8976. Kincaid, James. "Low-Cost Streets in Long Beach, Calif." *American City* 65 (September 1950): 130.

8977. Lackey, J. M. "Two Mountain Tunnels Necessary on the Angeles Crest Highway." *California Highways and Public Works* 19 (March 1941): 28-31.

8978. Langsner, George. "Angeles Crest Highway Opened: Half Century Dream of Engineers Realized." *California Highways and Public Works* 35 (November-December 1956): 1-17.

8979. "Largest Municipal Concrete Paving Project Completed." *Pacific Municipalities* 41 (March 1927): 105.
7¾ miles of Pico Boulevard, Los Angeles.

8980. "Last Unit of $1,235,000 Coast Highway Project under Way at Santa Monica." *California Highways and Public Works* 13 (June 1935): 4+.

8981. Leadabrand, Russ. "Highway into History." *Westways* 50 (March 1958): 8-9.
East fork of San Gabriel River.

8982. LeTourneau, R. G. "Heavy Highway Grading Equipment on the Newhall Alternate, California." *Western Construction News* 4 (September 10, 1929): 467-8.

8983. Lewis, K. D., and Akin, Robert W. "Topanga Canyon: Major Reconstruction Project on Sign Route 27 Is Completed." *California Highways and Public Works* 35 (July-August 1956): 23-5.
From Pacific Coast Highway in Malibu to Ventura Boulevard in Woodland Hills.

8984. Lindersmith, Walter R. "Ironing Out the Traffic Wrinkles on Wilshire Boulevard in Los

Angeles." *Western City* 7 (November 1931): 7-8.

8985. Los Angeles County. Regional Planning Commission. *Report of a Highway Traffic Survey in the County of Los Angeles.* Los Angeles, 1934. 32 pp.

8986. ———— *Report of a Highway Traffic Survey in the County of Los Angeles.* Los Angeles, 1937. 62 pp.

8987. Los Angeles. Park Commission. *The Arroyo Seco Parkway . . . Its Relation to a Boulevard from the Mountains to the Sea.* Los Angeles, [1913?]. 19 pp.

8988. "Los Angeles Improves Riverside Drive." *Western Construction News* 5 (June 25, 1930): 303.

8989. "Los Angeles Is Site of Experiment, Laying the—West's First Natural Rubber Road." *Western Construction* 27 (October 1962): 68-9.
Figueroa Street and Venice Boulevard, Los Angeles.

8990. "Los Angeles' R-3 Ordinance . . . Provides Proper Street Widths and Improvements Ahead of Time While the Cost Is Low." *American City* 78 (December 1963): 95.

8991. "Los Angeles Raises Vermont Avenue 18 Feet: Fill Made 'Free of Cost.'" *Western Construction News* 3 (December 10, 1928): 755.

8992. "Los Angeles Safeguards Underpass Air Purity." *American City* 68 (June 1953): 96-7.
Carbon monoxide detectors in Sepulveda Boulevard underpass, Los Angeles Airport.

8993. "Los Angeles Will Get New Building to House State Highway Offices." *California Highways and Public Works* 19 (August 1941): 6-7.

8994. Marshall, Frank F., and MacBride, Dexter. "Outer Highways: A Study in Successful Planning for Major Retail Business Development." *California Highways and Public Works* 27 (May-June 1948): 1-7.
Crenshaw Shopping Center.

8995. Mattoon, E. W. "The Improvement Ordinance of Los Angeles." *Pacific Municipalities* 34 (March 1920): 107-9.

8996. McCoy, G. T. "Three California Cities Complete Street Projects." *American City* 60 (February 1945): 61.
Los Angeles, Burbank, and San Diego.

8997. McCune, Bernard E. "Residential Streets in Long Beach—Their Design and Performance." *Western City* 29 (May 1953): 31-3+.

8998. McDonald, P. A. "Elimination of Newhall Tunnel Bottleneck Soon to Be Realized." *California Highways and Public Works* 16 (January 1938): 10+.
Transformation of tunnel through Santa Susana Mountains into open cut.

8999. ———— "Governor Dedicates Link in Roosevelt Highway in South." *California Highways and Public Works* 15 (June 1937): 8+.
Final section of Santa Monica-Seal Beach Highway, at Wilmington.

9000. ———— "Manchester-Firestone Boulevard Is Opened by Governor Merriam." *California Highways and Public Works* 15 (July 1937): 14.

9001. ———— "Sepulveda Boulevard Key Link Opened and Dedicated by Governor Merriam." *California Highways and Public Works* 13 (November 1935): 4+.
Between Ventura and Sunset boulevards.

9002. McGinnis, William D. "Artesia Street: State Highway Route 175 in Los Angeles Is Standardized." *California Highways and Public Works* 32 (July-August 1953): 11-4+.

9003. Mock, Kenneth. "On the Malibu: New Highway Construction on US 101 Alternate Completed." *California Highways and Public Works* 34 (May-June 1955): 33-5.

9004. Mohr, William H. "Sepulveda Boulevard in San Fernando Valley Rebuilt as Divided Highway." *California Highways and Public Works* 18 (October 1940): 24-6.

9005. Montgomery, C. P. "Highway Construction Through Famous Rancho Malibu." *California Highways and Public Works* 4 (January 1927): 6-7+.

9006. Mount, William. "Burbank Builds Mountain Road, Parking Area with Rubbish Reclamation Fill." *Western City* 26 (February 1960): 30-5.

9007. Mueller, A. J. "Road Development on the Angeles National Forest." *Trails Magazine* 3 (Spring 1936): 18+.

9008. Myers, Ralph C. "Angeles Crest Link Completed by U. S. Bureau [of Public Roads]." *California Highways and Public Works* 14 (August 1936): 2+.

9009. ———— "Building Mint Canyon Cut-Off." *California Highways and Public Works* 18 (March 1940): 8+.

9010. ———— "City, County, U. S. and State Building San Gabriel Canyon Scenic Highway." *California Highways and Public Works* 11 (May-June 1933): 8-9+.

9011. ———— "Coast Highway Along Malibu Reconstructed with Divided Lanes." *California Highways and Public Works* 16 (August 1938): 22-3.
Author's name misspelled Meyers.

9012. ———— "Eliminating a Tunnel Bottleneck." *California Highways and Public Works* 16 (November 1938): 4-6+.
Newhall Tunnel through Santa Susana Mountains transformed into open cut.

9013. ———— "Monterey Park Celebrates Completion of Los Angeles-Pomona Highway Link." *California Highways and Public Works* 13 (June 1935): 12+.

9014. ———— "Ramona Boulevard a 6-Mile 'Airline' Urban Route Without Grade Crossings." *California Highways and Public Works* 13 (February 1935): 6-7+.

9015. ———— "Two Olympic Boulevard Units Completed in Los Angeles City." *California Highways and Public Works* 19 (January 1941): 12-5+.

9016. "New 'Airline' Urban Highway Serves Many Cities; Grade Crossings Eliminated: Ramona Boulevard into Los Angeles. . . ." *Western City* 11 (May 1935): 19-21.

9017. "Olive and 23rd Street Improvement District, Los Angeles." *Western Construction News* 5 (July 10, 1930): 329-30.

9018. Osborne, H[enry] Z., Jr. "Good Roads and the Vrooman Act." *The Architect and Engineer of California* 12 (February 1908): 59.
Los Angeles street work.

9019. Pardee, Lyall A. "Fourth Street Project: Traffic Barrier in Los Angeles Removed." *California Highways and Public Works* 35 (May-June 1956): 14-20.

9020. Parker, E. A. "Final Link: Extension of Olympic Boulevard Completed." *California Highways and Public Works* 28 (January-February 1949): 58-9.

9021. Paul, Alfred L., and Clements, V. H. "Three Large District Improvements in Los Angeles." *Western Construction News* 3 (November 10, 1928): 687-9.
Subheads are: "Meyler Street and Twenty-First Street Improvement District, Los Angeles Harbor District—A 400,000 Residential Improvement." "South Sherman Way and Tyrone Avenue Improvement District, Hollywood District." "Westgate Avenue and Iowa Avenue Improvement District, Sawtelle District." First two are by Paul; latter is by Clements.

9022. "Proposed Scenic Drive and Its Enginee[r]." *Saturday Night* 4 (March 3, 1923): 26.
Dewitt Raeburn and Mulholland scenic drive.

9023. "Protecting the Highway from Ocean Waves." *California Highways and Public Works* 1 (August 1924): 4.
Santa Monica.

9024. "Reconstruction of San Gabriel Boulevard, Los Angeles." *Western Construction News* 2 (August 10, 1927): 33.

9025. "Relocation of Roosevelt Highway Is Proceeding at Rapid Rate." *California Highways and Public Works* 25 (March-April 1947): 18-9+.
Malibu Creek to Latigo Canyon.

9026. Richardson, A. T. "Two New Highway Links Opened and Armory Dedicated at Pomona." *California Highways and Public Works* 11 (July-August 1933): 18+.

9027. Ritter, John. "On Angeles Crest: Work on Recreational Highway Is Resumed." *California Highways and Public Works* 27 (September-October 1948): 6-7+.

9028. "The Road Yesterday and Today." *Southern California Business* 5 (March 1926): 26+.
Route between Los Angeles and Wilmington.

9029. Rook, R. H. "Los Angeles Builds 10-Inch Concrete Pavement on Cahuenga Pass Road." *American City* 35 (August 1926): 200-2.

9030. Rose, Howard B. "New Washington Blvd.—El Segundo Highway." *Western Construction News and Highways Builder* 7 (May 10, 1932): 245-6.

9031. "Rosemead Boulevard Job Completed." *California Highways and Public Works* 24 (September-October 1946): 26-8.

9032. Roussel, Julien D. "Completion of Manchester Blvd. Fruition of 13 Years of Effort." *California Highways and Public Works* 15 (May 1937): 18-9+.

9033. Rugen, Otto N. "How Low-Priced and Durable Residential Streets Are Developed in Alhambra." *Western City* 8 (April 1932): 11-3+.

9034. "San Gabriel 'High-Line' Road." *Western Construction News* 7 (March 25, 1932): 163-4.

9035. "San Gabriel High-Line Road Nears Completion." *Western Construction News and Highways Builder* 8 (May 10, 1933): 217.

9036. "Santa Monica Coast Highway Widened to 80 Feet Eliminating Bad Bottleneck." *California Highways and Public Works* 12 (August 1934): 12+.

9037. Schulte, John T. "Street Improvement Project in Manhattan Beach Is Associated with Beautification Planning." *Western City* 40 (July 1964): 28-9.

9038. Shaw, John C. "City of Los Angeles Orders $29,000,000 [Street] Improvements Program." *Pacific Municipalities* 43 (August 1929): 226-7.

9039. ——— "Curing Cement-Concrete Pavement in Los Angeles." *American City* 38 (April 1928): 119-20.

9040. ——— "Los Feliz Boulevard, Los Angeles: Reconstruction Provides Major Highway for Western Section of City." *Western Construction News* 3 (March 10, 1928): 156-7.

9041. "Special Concrete Highway Built for Motor Trucks." *Engineering News-Record* 87 (July 14, 1921): 55-6.
Downtown Los Angeles to San Pedro.

9042. "Special Concrete Pavement for Motor Trucks; Los Angeles." *Engineering News* 76 (October 5, 1916): 639.
Downtown Los Angeles to San Pedro.

9043. "Steep Slopes at Angeles Crest: California Pushes Mountain Highway Through Inaccessible Section of Los Angeles County by Full Cooperation of Corrections and Public Works Departments—Year-Around Prison Camp Is Maintained for 100 of the Workers as Construction of Tunnels and 5-Mi. Section Goes into High Gear During Summer Months." *Western Construction News* 24 (June 1949): 84-6.

9044. Stone, Ormand A. "Improvement of Beverly Boulevard, Montebello, California." *Western Construction News* 3 (March 10, 1928): 154-5.

9045. Sturgeon, F. E. "San Fernando: New Highway Construction in Southern City Is under Way." *California Highways and Public Works* 29 (May-June 1950): 28-9.

9046. Sullivan, E. Q. "New Foothill Boulevard Will Be Four Lanes." *California Highways and Public Works* 15 (September 1937): 6.

9047. Templin, Newton H. "Two-County Link: Divided Highway Connects Katella Avenue, Willow Street." *California Highways and Public Works* 41 (September-October 1962): 28-30.
Willow Street is in Los Angeles County.

9048. Thrall, Will H. "Mount Wilson—the Observatory and the Toll Road Company." *Trails Magazine* 4 (Summer 1937): 6-10.

9049. "Topanga Canyon Road, Los Angeles County, California." *Western Construction News* 5 (May 10, 1930): 233-4.

9050. "Ventura Boulevard, Los Angeles." *Western Construction News* 5 (March 10, 1930): 140.

9051. Whitnall, Gordon. "Saving Money in Street Widening." *American City* 40 (February 1929): 122-3.
Los Angeles.

9052. Wilcox, Robert F. *Highways.* Los Angeles, 1953. *Metropolitan Los Angeles. A Study in Integration,* Vol. VII, The Haynes Foundation, Monograph Series No. 24. 64 pp.

9053. Workman, Boyle. "Abusing the Street Work Petition." *Southern California Business* 5 (April 1926): 9-11+.
 Alleged abuses in present method of initiating public improvements in Los Angeles.

URBAN RENEWAL

9054. Adler, Patricia. *The Bunker Hill Story.* Glendale, Calif., 1963. 36 pp.
 "Rise and decline of a neighborhood in central Los Angeles and its redevelopment."

9055. —— *A History of the Venice Area.* Los Angeles, 1969. [24] pp.

9056. Alberg, Lyle. "City Hall Attracts Development in New Area." *Western City* 44 (June 1968): 34+.
 Montebello.

9057. Alexander, Robert E. *Rebuilding a City; A Study of Redevelopment Problems in Los Angeles.* The Haynes Foundation, *Monograph Series No. 16.* Los Angeles, 1951. 69 pp.

9058. "Apartment Association Opposes Bunker Hill Redevelopment." *Western Housing* 40 (July 1956): 10+.

9059. "Association Opposes Bunker Hill Redevelopment, Asks Rehabilitation." *Western Housing* 38 (May 1955): 7+.

9060. Babcock, Henry A. *Report on the Feasibility of Redeveloping the Bunker Hill Area, Los Angeles, for the Community Redevelopment Agency of the City of Los Angeles.* Los Angeles, 1951. 55 pp.

9061. Babcock, Wm. H., & Sons. *Report on the Economic and Engineering Feasibility of Regrading the Bunker Hill Area, Los Angeles, to the City Council of the City of Los Angeles and the Board of Supervisors of Los Angeles County.* [Chicago], 1931. 96 pp.

9062. Bill, Joseph T. "Federal Approval of Los Angeles' Bunker Hill Project Received." *Western City* 34 (June 1958): 24.

9063. Bloom, Murray T. "One Way to Stop Slums: Los Angeles Gets Legal Big Stick But Speaks Softly to Win Voluntary Action by Blight Area Home Owners." *National Municipal Review* 45 (February 1956): 54-9.
 A condensation appeared as: "Los Angeles Shows How Slums Can Be Stopped." *Readers Digest* 68 (March 1956): 101-5.

9064. "Bunker Hill Leveling Project." *Los Angeles Saturday Night* 9 (October 6, 1928): 5.
 "Bigelow Plan."

9065. Carfagno, Edward C. "A Housing Development for the Bunker Hill Area with Special Reference to the Function of Apartment Hotels." Master's thesis, University of Southern California, 1933. 59 pp.

9066. "City and Homeowners Unite for Neighborhood Betterment." *American City* 69 (December 1954): 124.
 Los Angeles Department of Building and Safety spurs rehabilitation on a neighborhood basis.

9067. Duncan, Ray. "The Painful Rejuvenation of Downtown." *Los Angeles* 6 (November 1963): 28-33+.
 Los Angeles Civic Center.

9068. Eliot, Charles W. *Citizen Support for Los Angeles Development.* Los Angeles, 1945. 12 pp.

9069. Faull, Harry A. "Pomona's Downtown Redevelopment Program Shifts into High Gear." *Western City* 39 (May 1963): 28-9.

9070. Harris, Robert J. "Venice, California; Urban Rehabilitation in a Small American Community." Master's thesis, University of California, Los Angeles, 1966. 112 pp.

9071. Hazelleaf, Robert. "High Hopes for the Historic Hill." *Westways* 58 (July 1966): 7-9.
 Signal Hill renaissance.

9072. Hindman, Jo. "Homes into Kindling: Urban Renewal, Our Latest Demolition Team 'Home Wrecking a Specialty.'" *American Murcury* 89 (December 1959): 20-4.

Chavez Ravine affair used as the basis for a general attack on the "Urban Renewal Behemoth."

9073. Joyce, Cynthia. "Bunker's Comeback." *Los Angeles* 13 (May 1968): 38-40.
New Bunker Hill residence structures.

9074. Koski, Karl L. "New Pedestrian Malls in Temple City Constitute Part of Business District Revitalization." *Western City* 43 (January 1967): 34+.

9075. "Lights Add Esthetics to a Mall." *American City* 84 (June 1969): 128.
Burbank shopping mall.

9076. Los Angeles City Community Redvelopment Agency. *Report on the Feasibility of Redeveloping the Bunker Hill Area, Los Angeles.* Los Angeles, 1951. 55 pp.

9077. "Los Angeles City Council OK's Spectacular Renewal Project." *American City* 74 (August 1959): 96.
Bunker Hill.

9078. "Los Angeles Plans Redevelopment Bond Issue for Bunker Hill." *Western City* 27 (January 1951): 31.
Mayor Fletcher Bowron recommends $5 million bond issue.

9079. "Mall Gives Pomona 'New Look': Pomona Replaces Congested City 'Core' with the Tree Lined Pedestrian Mall." *Western Construction* 38 (February 1963): 78.

9080. Marine, Gene. "Bunker Hill: Pep Pill for Downtown Los Angeles." *Frontier* 10 (August 1959): 5-8+.
Poses question of who stands to benefit from redevelopment plan for Bunker Hill.

9081. Martin, Albert C., *et al. City of San Fernando Business Redevelopment Study.* San Fernando, 1961. 39 pp.

9082. Morris, Gilbert E. "What Los Angeles Does to Prevent Growth of Slums." *Western City* 32 (March 1956): 46-7.

9083. Owen, C. A. "The Bunker Hill Project. . . . Would You Say It's Good Business?" *Western Housing* 40 (October 1956): 8+.

9084. Pooler, Richard C. "Urban Redevelopment Comes to Santa Fe Springs." Master's thesis, University of Southern California, 1966. 207 pp.

9085. "Razing of Bunker Hill, Los Angeles." *Western Construction News* 4 (July 10, 1929): 339-40.
"Bigelow Plan" to level Bunker Hill.

9086. "A Semi-Pedestrian Mall . . . Is Better Than No Mall at All, a Lot Better, Finds El Monte, Calif." *American City* 82 (August 1967): 102.

9087. Sigurdson, Herbert, *et al.* "Crenshaw Project: An Experiment in Urban Community Development." *Sociology and Social Research* 51 (1967): 432-4.

9088. Smith, Miles C. "A Unique Method of Financing the Regrading and Rebuilding of a Large Downtown Area." *American City* 41 (August 1929): 148.
"Bigelow Plan" for Bunker Hill.

9089. Solnit, Albert. "A Study and Redevelopment Plan for the Ocean Park District of the City of Santa Monica." Master's thesis, University of Southern California, 1957. 105 pp.

9090. "The Status of Urban Renewal Programs in Western Cities." *Western City* 34 (February 1958): 43-52.
Includes several Los Angeles County cities.

9091. Thomas, Gil[bert]. "Civic Center's Rebirth: Uptown at the Downtown." *Los Angeles* 11 (March 1966): 40-3.

9092. ———— "Los Angeles: Doomed to Ugliness?" *Los Angeles* 10 (July 1965): 24-31.
"Needed: A Unified Effort to Change the City's Face."

9093. Tucker, C. H. "Moving a Mountain to Build a City." *Professional Engineer* 14 (July 1929): 5. Reprinted as "Get Out of My Way, Mountain!" *Literary Digest* 102 (September 7, 1929): 19-20.
"Bigelow Plan" to level Bunker Hill.

9094. Walker, Earl M. "The Impact of Urban Renewal on the Los Angeles Subcommunity of Sawtelle." Master's thesis, University of California, Los Angeles, 1968. 107 pp.

9095. " 'We'd Rather Do It Ourselves' Say Pico

Rivera Residents on Area Improvements." *Western City* 44 (February 1968): 32-3.

9096. Werner, Oscar G. "The Study of a Housing Development for Bunker Hill, Los Angeles." Master's thesis, University of Southern California, 1933. 90 pp.

UTILITIES

9097. Allen, Clayton M. "San Francisquito Power Plant No. 2: Reconstructed in Record Time by Use of Slip Forms, by Bureau of Power & Light, Los Angeles, Following St. Francis Dam Failure." *Western Construction News* 4 (March 25, 1929): 163-4.

9098. "The Automatic Telephone in Los Angeles." *Out West,* new series, 9 (April 1915): 172.

9099. Banks, F. M. "Southern California Gas Supplies." *California Magazine of the Pacific* 42 (March 1952): 26.

9100. Bauer, John. "Public Utilities: Consider the Case of Los Angeles." *National Municipal Review* 20 (December 1931): 729-32.
    Los Angeles Bureau of Power and Light.

9101. Bendinger, Leonard L. "Municipal Gas—Good for Long Beach . . . But Not Necessarily for All Cities." *American City* 70 (June 1955): 138-9.

9102. Bennett, G. Vernon. "The Lion and the Lamb: Can Private and Public Power Peacefully Coexist." *Frontier* 5 (October 1954): 12-3.
    Cooperative arrangement between Southern California Edison and the Los Angeles Department of Water and Power.

9103. Bird, Frederick L., and Ryan, Frances M. *Public Ownership on Trial. A Study of Municipal Light and Power in California.* New York, 1930. 186 pp.
    Los Angeles included.

9104. "Breakfast Deal." *Time* 29 (February 15, 1937): 73-4.
    Los Angeles Bureau of Power and Light buys Los Angeles Gas and Electric Corp. for $46 million.

9105. Burkhart, H. W. "Municipal Gas in Long Beach Proving a Success." *Pacific Municipalities* 39 (April 1925): 107-8.

9106. Catren, Robert J. "A History of the Generation, Transmission, and Distribution of Electrical Energy in Southern California." Doctoral dissertation, University of Southern California, 1951. 481 pp.

9107. ———— "Hydroelectric Developments in Southern California." Master's thesis, University of Southern California, 1942. 113 pp.

9108. Chadwick, W. L. "Steam Power Plant Protected Against Subsidence Below High Tides." *Civil Engineering* 20 (June 1950): 17-20.
    Southern California Edison Co., Long Beach.

9109. "City Buys Electric System in Record Transaction." *Western City* 13 (March 1937): 44-5.
    Los Angeles Bureau of Power and Light buys Los Angeles Gas and Electric Corp.

9110. Cockfield, R. H., and Eardley, M. V. "Utility Service to Large Refineries: Electric System of City of Los Angeles Has Provided Generation, Transmission and Distribution Facilities That Insure Adequate and Reliable Supply of Power." *Petroleum World* 29 (May 1932): 26+.

9111. "Complex Transmission Tower Lift Handled by Four Truck Cranes." *Western Construction* 29 (April 1954): 57.
    Raising transmission lines to give clearance for Colorado Freeway at Eagle Rock.

9112. "Contract Helicopter Service . . . Speeds Transmission-Line Patroling for the Los Angeles Department of Water and Power." *American City* 77 (June 1962): 211-2+.

9113. "Copper Helps to Bind Two States: Development of Public Utilities in Southern California Calls for Rapidly Increasing Supplies of Copper Materials." *Southern California Business* 2 (February 1923): 26.

9114. "The Cradle of Electric Energy: Los Angeles Lays Claim to Being the Pioneer City in Many of the Utilities That Use Hydro-electric Power." *Southern California Business* 2 (February 1923): 13-4+.

9115. Cromwell, Leslie. "A Study of the Development of Hydroelectric Power in Southern California [1892-1949]." Master's thesis, University of California, Los Angeles, 1951. 148 pp.

9116. Day, Addison B. "Growth of the Natural Gas Industry in Los Angeles." *California Journal of Development* 21 (September 1931): 10+.

9117. DeLanty, B. F. "Pasadena's Experiment in Municipal Ownership." *Pacific Municipalities* 43 (April 1929): 152-4.
Pasadena Municipal Light and Power Department.

9118. Diederich, Peter. "A Modern Steam Generating Station for the Glendale City System." *Western City* 16 (April 1940): 24-5.

9119. Dietz, Lawrence. "My Telephone Company, Right or Wrong." *Los Angeles* 11 (May 1966): 40-2.
Pacific Telephone and Telegraph Company.

9120. "Discussion Following the Address of E. F. Scattergood on Some of the Engineering and Economic Features of the Municipal Electric System of Los Angeles." *Pacific Municipalities* 35 (January 1921): 5-7.

9121. Drescher, Thomas B. "The Electric Power Supply for the Los Angeles-San Bernardino Lowland." Master's thesis, University of California, Los Angeles, 1951. 99 pp.

9122. Dykstra, C[larence] A. "Los Angeles Municipal Power Making Money on Low Rates." *National Municipal Review* 13 (September 1924): 483-5.

9123. *From Pueblo to Metropolis: Water and Power in the Story of Los Angeles.* [Los Angeles, 1965?]. [12] pp.

9124. "Gas for Los Angeles." *Newsweek* 28 (November 11, 1946): 30-1.
Difficulties in securing pipe for building a line to tap Texas reserves.

9125. Hampton, Edgar L. "Cheap Power as a City Developer: Men of Broad Vision Saw to It That the Waters of Distant Mountains Were Brought Down for the Use of Industrial Plants." *Southern California Business* 2 (May 1923): 12-3+.

9126. Hatch, James N. "Pasadena Gets Low-Cost Power: Doubling of Generating Capacity Is Accompanied by Greatly Increased Efficiency, with Unusually Low Rates to Consumers." *American City* 42 (April 1930): 116-8.

9127. Heinze, Carl A. "How Los Angeles Is Spending Her Power Bonds." *National Municipal Review* 14 (May 1925): 281-3.

9128. Hichborn, Franklin. "Political Activities of the Power Trust in California." *Public Ownership* 14 (January, 1932): 3-16.

9129. "Highest Pressure Gas Line." *Western Construction News* 20 (January 1945): 79-82.
Line between La Goleta and Hollywood.

9130. Hinrichsen, Kenneth. "Pioneers in Southern California Hydroelectric Waterpower: Chaffey and Baldwin." Master's thesis, University of California, Berkeley, 1949. 117 pp.
San Antonio Light [&] Power Co., and its background.

9131. Jones, William C. "Corporate Evolution of the Southern California Edison Company and Its Financial History from 1909 to 1928." Master's thesis, University of Southern California, 1929. 134 pp.

9132. Karpain, Felix. "Upgrading an Island Paradise: By Re-Shaping the Basic Structure of Its Public Services and Utilities." *Western City* 38 (October 1962): 29+.
Avalon.

9133. Koiner, C. Wellington. *History of Pasadena's Municipal Light and Power Plant.* Pasadena, 1925. 36 pp.

9134. ——— "Municipal Lighting Plant." *California Outlook* 10 (February 1911): 2-25.
Pasadena.

9135. Labarre, Robert V. "Foundation Tests for Los Angeles Steam Plant." *Civil Engineering* 11 (December 1941): 711-4.
Harbor steam plant, Wilmington.

9136. Lacy, William. "Where Los Angeles Gets Some of Its Power." *Southern California Business* 6 (October 1927): 14-5+.
Southern California Edison's Big Creek-San Joaquin Project.

9137. Lewis, Harold H. "Pasadena Builds an Ornamental Cooling Tower." *Western City* 15 (April 1939): 45-6.
Fountain designed to cool water for the generator air coolers at the powerhouse of the Municipal Light and Power Department.

9138. Los Angeles Department of Water and Power. *A Brief Summary of Important Historical Data and Current Facts Concerning the Municipally Owned Department of Water and Power, City of Los Angeles.* Published annually beginning 1945.

9139. ——— *Water and Power, 1902-1952; Five Decades That Transformed Los Angeles.* Los Angeles, [1953?]. 8 pp.

9140. "Los Angeles Aqueduct Power Utilization." *Electrical World* 57 (May 4, 1911): 1080.

9141. "Los Angeles Bureau of Power and Light Building Highest Voltage Transmission Line in World." *Western Construction News and Highways Builder* 9 (February 1934): 65.
From Boulder Dam to Los Angeles, 270 miles.

9142. "Los Angeles Gas and Electric Corporation's New Pasadena Structure." *Los Angeles Saturday Night* 9 (April 6, 1929): 7.

9143. "Los Angeles Gets More Electrical Power." *American City* 63 (February 1948): 112-3.
Inauguration of Harbor Steam Plant, Wilmington.

9144. "Los Angeles Goes Underground." *American City* 84 (March 1969): 161-2.
Department of Water and Power program for placing utility wires underground.

9145. "The Los Angeles Lighting Company." *Journal of Electricity, Power and Gas* 12 (February 1902): 28-9.

9146. "Los Angeles Nears Realization of 'City Power' Plan." *Engineering Record* 72 (August 7, 1915): 167.
First Los Angeles Aqueduct power plant, San Francisquito Canyon No. 1.

9147. "Los Angeles Observes Fifty Years of City Ownership of Utilities." *Western City* 28 (January 1952): 34.

9148. "Los Angeles Starts to Construct Owens Gorge Power." *Engineering News-Record* 83 (November 13-20, 1919): 904.

9149. "Los Angeles to Build Three Hydroelectric Plants." *American City* 63 (October 1948): 117.
Owens Gorge.

9150. "Los Angeles Will Buy Unused Boulder Power." *Western Construction News* 19 (August 1944): 78.

9151. Low, George P. "The Generating, Transmission and Distribution Systems of the Edison Electric Company of Los Angeles, California." *Journal of Electricity, Power and Gas* 12 (January 1903): 9-46.

9152. Marriott, Crittenden. "Power and the City: Some Facts and Figures on How Los Angeles Has Harnessed the Distant Mountain Streams." *Scientific American* 123 (December 18, 1920): 608+.

9153. Marvin, Cloyd H. "The Telephone Situation in Los Angeles." Master's thesis, University of Southern California, 1916. 93 pp.

9154. Mason, H. A. "Municipal Electrical Plants in California." *Pacific Municipalities* 33 (August 1919): 287-90.

9155. ——— "Should Los Angeles Be Punished for Promoting Public Ownership." *Pacific Muncipalities* 35 (July 1921): 246-8.

9156. Mason, W. C. "Los Angeles Builds Three Hydro Plants in Owens River Gorge." *Civil Engineering* 19 (December 1949): 24-7+.
Hydroelectric power plants.

9157. ——— "Tunnel Records Broken at Owens River Gorge." *Civil Engineering* 20 (April 1950): 22-4.
Owens River Gorge Power Project, Los Angeles Department of Water and Power.

9158. ——— "Tunneling at World Record Speed Completed at Owens Gorge." *Western Construction* 27 (February 1952): 76+.

9159. Masser, H. L. "Natural Gas Production and Utilization in Southern California." *Summary of Operations California Oil Fields* 8 (March 1923): 5-37.

9160. McCambridge, J[ames] H. "Burbank's Power Story." *American City* 62 (September 1947): 108-10.

9161. McCurdy, Howard. "A Model Diesel-Engine Central Station." *Civil Engineering* 5 (September 1935): 585-7.
Vernon municipal power plant.

9162. McGarry, D. F. "Viewing the Source of Municipal Power Supply." *Southern California Business* 6 (January 1928): 16-7+.

9163. Mersereau, John D.; Fogg, W. K., and Hotaling, H. C. "Municipal Lighting in Pasadena." *Out West*, new series, 1 (March 1911): 227-31.

9164. Mohler, Charles K. "Public Utility Regulation by Los Angeles." *The Annals of the American Academy of Politcal and Social Sciences* 53 (May, 1914): 108-18.

9165. Moody, Burdett. "Abundant Low-Priced Electric Power." *Southern California Business* 1 (September 1922): 37+.
Los Angeles Bureau of Power and Light.

9166. Morris, Samuel B. "As Big as Hoover Dam: Los Angeles' New Valley Steam Plant Will Produce as Much Electric Power as Is Allotted by Hoover Dam." *American City* 69 (October 1954): 94-6.
Generating plant in San Fernando Valley.

9167. —— "How Los Angeles Washes Insulators . . . on Energized High-Voltage Lines." *American City* 66 (October 1951): 101.

9168. "Morris to Succeed Van Norman as Head of Los Angeles Utilities." *Western City* 20 (September 1944): 26.
Samuel Morris succeeds H. A. Van Norman.

9169. Morrow, Burdett. "Industries Make Huge Power Demand." *Southern California Business* 3 (January 1925): 9+.
Los Angeles.

9170. Moss, Marvin A. "The Owens Gorge Project." *California Engineer* 28 (March 1950): 14+.

9171. Mullendore, William C. "The Relation of Boulder Dam to Southern California Power Supply." *Southern California Business* 8 (September 1929): 48+.

9172. "Municipal Ownership in Pasadena. A Study of the Failure of an Ambitious Scheme." *Out West*, new series, 1 (December 1910): 26-36.
Depicts Pasadena's municipally-owned electric plant as a financial failure and a political football.

9173. Myers, Charles. "Capital Expenditures of the Los Angeles Public Utilities as an Aspect of Public Utility Economics." Master's thesis, Occidental College, 1947. 228 pp.

9174. Nally, Timothy F. "Long Distance, Please." *Pomona Valley Historian* 6 (1970): 110-7.
Pomona's telephone system, 1885-1968.

9175. "New Home of Los Angeles Gas and Electric Corporation." *The Argonaut* 96 (January 31, 1925): 21.
810 S. Flower Street.

9176. "New Operating Bases of the Southern California Gas Co." *The Architect and Engineer* 192 (February 1953): 22-6.
Van Nuys and Redondo Beach.

9177. "New Vernon Power Plant." *Western City* 9 (June 1933): 15.

9178. Northmore, E. R. "The Lighting Companies of Los Angeles." *Journal of Electricity, Power and Gas* 24 (March 26, 1910): 284.

9179. Partridge, William H., and Bryant, Edwin S. "Long Beach Municipal Gas System." *Pacific Municipalities* 44 (July 1930): 341-5.

9180. "Pasadena's Municipal Lighting Works." *Pacific Municipalities* 19 (November 1908): 66.

9181. "Power and Light Bureau Efficiency." *Los Angeles Saturday Night* 8 (March 10, 1928): 3.
This periodical strongly defended Los Angeles' municipal power operation.

9182. "Power and Light Bureau's Efficiency." *Los Angeles Saturday Night* 13 (April 29, 1933): 16.
Price, Waterhouse and Co. audit indicates Bureau of Power and Light is efficiently managed.

9183. "Pressure Switches Monitor Electrical Distribution System: Los Angeles Uses Pressure-Actuated Switches to Protect Its High-Voltage Circuits." *American City* 80 (June 1965): 117.

9184. "Rebuilding Power Plant No. 2 After the St. Francis Dam Break." *Engineering News-Record* 102 (March 28, 1929): 494-5.
Los Angeles Bureau of Power and Light.

9185. Redinger, David H. *The Story of Big Creek.* Los Angeles, 1949. 182 pp.
Author was resident engineer at Big Creek hydroelectric plant, begun by Pacific Light and Power in 1911 and completed by Southern California Edison in 1929. As of 1949, it provided more than a quarter of Edison's generating capacity.

9186. Reynolds, Del M. "The West and Its Power Problem." *Out West,* new series, 1 (January 1911): 93-102.
Discusses Southern California Edison and Pacific Light and Power.

9187. Scattergood, E[zra] F. "Another Splendid Power Bureau Accomplishment: City's Power Plant No. 2, Wiped Out by Flood March 13, 1928, Rebuilt and Running Again November 1, 1928." Rebuilt and Running Again November 1, 1928." *Municipal League of Los Angeles Bulletin* 6 (February 1, 1929): [1-3].

9188. ———— "Edison Company Propaganda Answered." *Municipal League of Los Angeles Bulletin* 8 (December 1, 1930): [1-2].

9189. ———— "Los Angeles Buys Local Gas Company's Electric System." *American City* 52 (April 1937): 71-2.

9190. ———— "The Power Phase of It." *Southern California Business* 8 (September 1929): 20-1.
Boulder Canyon project.

9191. ———— "Rebuilding San Francisquito Power House." *Pacific Municipalities* 43 (March 1929): 100-2.
Power Plant No. 2.

9192. ———— "Some Engineering and Economic Features of the Municipal Electric System of Los Angeles." *Pacific Municipalities* 34 (November 1920): 429-32.

9193. ———— "Why L. A. Needs a 'Stand-By' Steam Plant." *Municipal League of Los Angeles Bulletin* 4 (December 31, 1926): 3.

9194. Scott, W. S. "Municipal Lighting in Pasadena." *Out West,* new series, 1 (April 1911): 293-6.

9195. Sewell, William. "Studies in the Development of Irrigation and Hydro-Electric Power in California." Master's thesis, Occidental College, 1928. 159 pp.

9196. Shettel, W. R. "Substation Construction of Los Angeles Gas & Electric Corporation." *Western Construction News* 2 (December 25, 1927): 54-5.

9197. Southern California Edison Company. *The Antelope Valley; An Area Inventory.* [Los Angeles], 1963. Various pagings.
Utility needs.

9198. "Steam Plant Units in Service: New Station Is One of the Most Modern and Efficient of Its Type in the World." *Western Construction News* 23 (June 1948): 112-4.
Southern California Edison at Redondo Beach.

9199. Stuart, John. "San Francisco and Los Angeles Linked by a $10,000,000 Cable: Longest Telephone Line West of Mississippi Is Completed." *Pacific Municipalities* 45 (May 1931): 231.

9200. "Success of the Los Angeles Power Plant No. 2." *Pacific Municipalities* 36 (July 1922): 236-7.
San Francisquito Canyon.

9201. "The System of the Los Angeles Electric Company." *Journal of Electricity, Power and Gas* 12 (February 1902): 23-7.

9202. "'Tax Free'—A New Interpretation." *American City* 50 (November 1935): 71.
Los Angeles Bureau of Power and Light meets all obligations without aid of tax funds.

9203. "Transmission Line to Carry Power from Boulder Dam: Los Angeles Builds 2,700 Steel Towers to Support 270-Mi. Line for Delivering First 240,000 kw. Block of Power." *Western Construction News* 11 (February 1936): 38-9.

9204. "Utilization of Proposed Power Development of Los Angeles Aqueduct." *Electrical World* 56 (October 27, 1910): 978-9.

9205. Vance, C. S. "The Emergency Service of the Los Angeles Gas and Electric Corporation." *Journal of Electricity, Power and Gas* 23 (October 9, 1909): 327-8.

9206. Van Norman, H. A. "When Should a Municipality Operate Its Own Utilities?" *American City* 59 (June 1944): 69-71.

Sketches development of municipal utilities in Los Angeles.

9207. van Valen, Nelson S. "Power Politics. The Struggle for Municipal Ownership of Electric Utilities in Los Angeles, 1905-1937." Doctoral dissertation, Claremont Graduate School, 1963. 398 pp.

9208. Vickers, Samuel E. "Long Beach Expands Gas System." *American City* 73 (November 1958): 121.

9209. "Water and Power Attract Industries." *Southern California Business* 4 (March 1925): 12-3+.

Los Angeles.

9210. "Water Power on the Los Angeles Aqueduct." *Engineering Record* 65 (February 3, 1912): 126-7.

9211. West, Joy. "Paraplegics Man Consolidated Communications Center: Hawthorne, El Segundo and Telephone Company Combine to Provide Area-Wide Service Unit." *Western City* 42 (February 1966): 26+.

9212. Wilcox, Raymond. "Long Beach Steam Plant No. 3 of the Southern California Edison Company." *Western Construction News* 2 (June 10, 1927): 28-31.

9213. Willard, C[harles] D. "The Los Angeles Rate-Making Episode." *Pacific Municipalities* 25 (October 31, 1911): 97-101.

Los Angeles Board of Public Utilities, headed by Meyer Lissner, resigns as a body after "the Mayor and [City] Council finally got themselves into an attitude toward the Utilities Commission that amounted to a 'lack of confidence' vote."

9214. Woehlke, Walter V. "Live Wires: The Electric Motor Can Do the World's Work More Efficiently Than Any Other Form of Power. The Time Is Coming When the Degree of Civilization Will Be Measured by the Consumption of Kilowatt-Hours. This Is the Story of the Men Who Are Making Life in the West Brighter, Broader, Easier by Carrying the Energy of the Snowflake Melting in the High Sierra to the Cities and Farms of the Wide Valleys." *Sunset* 31 (August 1913): 267-80.

9215. "The Work of the Board of Public Utilities of Los Angeles." *Electric Railway Journal* 36 (December 3, 1910): 1116-7.

9216. "Work Peak Reached at Scattergood." *Western Construction* 33 (May 1958): 40+.

Steam plant of Los Angeles Department of Water and Power, El Segundo.

9217. "The World's Largest Municipal Distributor of Electricity: A Statement Furnished to the American City by the Department of Public Service, Los Angeles." *American City* 27 (October 1922): 333-4.

9218. "World's Largest Municipal Utility Sets Up Four-Way Guard System." *Western City* 19 (February 1942): 24-5.

Los Angeles Department of Water and Power.

WATER

WATER SUPPLY—GENERAL

9219. Baugh, Ruth E. "The Geography of the Los Angeles Water Supply." Doctoral dissertation, Clark University, 1929. 269 pp.

9220. Bogart, Ernest L. *The Water Problem of Southern California.* Urbana, Ill., 1934. 132 pp.

9221. Bookman, Max. "Planning to Meet the Growing Need for Water in Southern California." *Western City* 29 (October 1953): 41-4+.

9222. Brooks, Thomas. *Notes on Los Angeles Water Supply.* Los Angeles, 1938. [9] pp.

9223. Bunnell, Victoria D. "The Water Structure of the San Pedro Basin, California Borderland." Master's thesis, University of Southern California, 1969. 142 pp.

9224. Cantor, Leonard M. "The California Water Plan." *The Journal of Geography* 68 (September 1969): 366-71.

9225. "Chamber Opposes Water Power Bill: Organization of Sound Business Men Objects to Placing Huge Development Project in Hands of

Five Unknown Men." *Southern California Business* 1 (November 1922): 12-3+.

Water and Power Act providing for control of state water resources by a five-man appointive commission.

9226. Conkling, Harold. "The Depletion of Underground Water Supplies in California." *Western City* 11 (January 1935): 31-3.

Includes Los Angeles area.

9227. Diemer, Robert B. "Southern California's Domestic Water Supply Problem." *Western City* 30 (October 1954): 35+.

9228. Elder, C. C. "Why Southern California Coastal Plain Requires Supplementary Water Supply." *Western City* 14 (June 1938): 14.

9229. Eliot, Charles. *Waterlines, Key to Development of Metropolitan Los Angeles.* The Haynes Foundation, *Monograph Series No. 9.* Los Angeles, 1946. 39 pp.

9230. Fredricks, Agatha. "Development of Irrigation in California [1781-1926]." Master's thesis, University of Southern California, 1928. 132 pp.

Includes San Fernando Valley.

9231. *From Pueblo to Metropolis: Water and Power in the Story of Los Angeles.* [Los Angeles, 1965?]. [12] pp.

9232. Garnsey, Morris E. "The Struggle for Water: California vs. the Mountain West." *Frontier* 1 (July 1, 1950): 3-5; (July 15, 1950): 8-9.

The author writes as a confessed "partisan of the Mountain West," who suspects that Los Angeles "will stop short of nothing to take all the water she can possibly get to feed her insatiable appetite for expansion."

9233. Heald, Weldon F. "Water! Water!" *Westways* 40 (August 1948): 2-4.

Describes how California has "squandered its water resources with amazing profligacy."

9234. Hurlbut, W[illiam] W. "The Domestic Water Supply of Los Angeles." *Western Construction News* 2 (July 25, 1927): 55-6.

9235. —— "Los Angeles Bureau of Water Works and Supply." *Western Construction News* 7 (January 10, 1932): 16-7.

9236. —— "Water Requirements and Sources of Supply for California." *Western City* 27 (October 1951): 29-42.

9237. "Investigating the Water Resources of Southern California." *California Highways and Public Works* 8 (February 1930): 1-2.

9238. Jorgensen, Alfred W. "A New Approach to Solving Water Disputes: The Long Beach Case." Master's thesis, University of Southern California, 1967. 140 pp.

9239. Kennedy, Harold W. "New State Water Resources Act Will Have Far Reaching Effect." *Western City* 21 (September 1945): 54.

9240. Kilpatrick, Vernon. "Southern California's Struggle for Water." *Frontier* 7 (March 1956): 7-9.

Discusses legal problems involved in tapping Northern California sources for delivery to Southern California.

9241. Kinsey, Don J. *Romance of Water and Power.* Los Angeles, 1926. 39 pp.

History of the Los Angeles water supply from Spanish days to 1926.

9242. Leonard, Robert L. "Integrated Management of Ground and Surface Water in Relation to Water Importation: The Experience of Los Angeles County." Doctoral dissertation, University of California, Berkeley, 1964. 157 pp.

9243. Lippincott, J. B. "Mountain Stream Characteristics of Southern California." *Out West* 23 (July 1905): 75-82.

Discusses local sources of water supply for Los Angeles and Southern California.

9244. Los Angeles. Department of Water and Power. *Water and Power, 1902-1952; Five Decades That Transformed Los Angeles.* Los Angeles, [1953?]. 8 pp.

9245. Lynch, Henry B. *Rainfall and Stream Run-Off in Southern California Since 1769.* Los Angeles, 1931. 31 pp.

9246. Matthew, Raymond. "A Threat Against Southern California's Future Water Supply." *California Magazine of the Pacific* 36 (June 1946): 13+.

9247. McBride, Conrad L. "Federal-State Relations in the Development of the Water Resources of the Colorado River Basin." Master's thesis, University of California, Los Angeles, 1962. 493 pp.

9248. McGlashan, H. D. *Surface Water Supply of the Pacific Slope of Southern California.* Washington, D.C., 1921. 557 pp.

U. S. Geological Survey, Water Supply Paper No. 447.

9249. Morris, Samuel B. "The Water Problem of Los Angeles." *Western City* 25 (May 1949): 23-32.

Reprinted as a separate pamphlet.

9250. —— "Water Problems of the Metropolitan Area," in *Los Angeles: Preface to a Master Plan.* Ed. by George W. Robbins and L. Deming Tilton. Los Angeles, 1941. Pp. 77-89.

9251. Mulholland, William. "History of Water Supply Development for the Metropolitan Area of Los Angeles." *Hydraulic Engineering* 4 (July 1928): 432-3.

9252. —— "The Municipal Water Supply of Los Angeles." *Pacific Municipalities* 29 (November 1915): 539-44.

9253. Nadeau, Remi. "Water + Land = People." *Westways* 57 (June 1965): 22-5.

History of Los Angeles water supply.

9254. —— *The Water Seekers.* New York, 1950. 309 pp.

9255. Nelson, Samuel B. "Increase Water Supply —Don't Allocate Shortages: Los Angeles Suggests a Bold Plan to Bolster an Over-Burdened Colorado River the Better to Serve a Three-State Area." *American City* 80 (March 1965): 96-7+.

9256. —— "A Program of Regional Planning Can Solve Water Problems of the West." *Western City* 42 (October 1966): 23-6.

9257. Ostrom, Vincent A. "Government and Water: A Study of the Influence of Water Upon Governmental Institutions and Practices in the Development of Los Angeles." Doctoral dissertation, University of California, Los Angeles, 1950. 588 pp.

9258. —— *Water and Politics: A Study of Water Policies and Administration in the Development of Los Angeles.* Los Angeles, 1953. 297 pp.

9259. —— *Water Supply.* Los Angeles, 1953. *Metropolitan Los Angeles. A Study in Integration,* Vol. VIII, The Haynes Foundation, *Monograph Series No. 25.* 181 pp.

9260. Randau, John A. "Bringing Rivers to the People." *Westways* 60 (May 1968): 3-8+.

California Water Project.

9261. Rozell, Arthur, and Wigglesworth, David. "Springs of Water." Master's thesis, Occidental College, 1953. 246 pp.

Historical survey, 1850-1950, detailing significant water developments.

9262. "Sales Simulation Program Inaugurated by Los Angeles Bureau of Water Works." *Western Construction News* 13 (October 1938): 366.

9263. Sewell, William. "Studies in the Development of Irrigation and Hydro-Electric Power in California." Master's thesis, Occidental College, 1928. 159 pp.

9264. Smith, Bert. "Ground Water and the California Water Plan." *California Magazine of the Pacific* 45 (September 1955): 13+.

9265. Snyder, James. "Floods Upon Dry Ground: A History of Water Law and Water Resource Development in California, 1900-1928." Master's thesis, University of California, Davis, 1967. 179 pp.

Los Angeles County treated briefly.

9266. Sonderegger, A. L. "Rainfall Phenomena as a Factor in Water Supply for Coastal Plain." *Hydraulic Engineering* 5 (August 1929): 28-33+.

9267. "Sources of Water Supply for the City of Los Angeles." *American City* 51 (June 1936): 71.

9268. "Southern California's Growing Thirst." *Western Construction* 43 (November 1968): 70.

Growing gap between water supply and demand in Los Angeles-San Diego area.

9269. Thomas, Franklin. "Value of Water in Southern California: A Historical Résumé of the Cost of Its Development for Irrigation and Domestic Use." *Civil Engineering* 3 (October 1933): 555-9.

> Mostly on water projects in Los Angeles and vicinity.

9270. Valentine, Edward R. "Southland's Water Supply in Jeopardy." *California Magazine of the Pacific* 37 (September 1947): 16+.

9271. "Water Rates in California Cities." *Western City* 31 (October 1955): 50-8+; (November 1955): 50-2.

9272. "Water: State's Most Acute Problem." *California Highways and Public Works* 9 (October 1931): 19-21.

> Part 3 of a series. Other parts not relevant to Los Angeles.

9273. White, Magner. "Thirsty Cities." *Saturday Evening Post* 201 (May 18, 1929): 18-9+.

> Water supply of Los Angeles and Southern California.

WATER SUPPLY—FLOOD CONTROL

9274. Aldrich, Lloyd. "Storm-Water Station Saves Space with Submersible Pumps." *American City* 67 (May 1952): 105.

> Sepulveda Boulevard subway under runways of Los Angeles International Airport.

9275. Armstrong, L. W. "Cities Have a Stake in Flood Control, Too." *Western City* 15 (February 1939): 38-42.

9276. ———— "Los Angeles Storm Drain Design." *Western Construction News* 5 (January 25, 1930): 42-7.

9277. Baumann, Paul. "Devil's Gate Dam—Sluiceway Driven Through Structure: Silt Deposition in Los Angeles County Flood Control Dam, with Consequent Interruption of Percolation and Loss of Water Storage Space, Necessitates Construction of New 60-In. Sluiceway." *Western Construction News* 19 (November 1944): 67-9.

> Devil's Gate on the Arroyo Seco was the first major dam built by the County Flood Control District (1920).

9278. "Beat Scheduled Time Five Months in Building Huge De la Brea Sewer." *Engineering Record* 72 (July 31, 1915): 130-2.

> Los Angeles storm drain, said to be the largest in the West.

9279. Beebe, James L. "Control and Disposal of Storm Waters." *Western Construction News and Highways Builder* 7 (April 25, 1932): 228-9.

9280. Bennett, Ralph. "Engineer Suggests a 100% Saving on the Big Dalton Dam Project." *Municipal League of Los Angeles Bulletin* 5 (July 1, 1928): [5].

> County Flood Control District.

9281. "Bids Called for Dam at Los Angeles to Contain 13,000,000 Cu. Yd. of Earthfill." *Western Construction News* 13 (July 1938): 255.

> Hansen Dam on Tujunga Wash.

9282. "The Big Dalton Multiple-Arch Dam." *Western Construction News* 2 (October 25, 1927): 44-5.

> County Flood Control District.

9283. "Big Tujunga Dam No. 1, California: Los Angeles County Flood Control District Completes First Dam in Its Second Largest Watershed." *Western Construction News* 6 (July 10, 1931): 343-9.

9284. Bigger, William R. "Flood Control in Metropolitan Los Angeles." Doctoral dissertation, University of California, Los Angeles, 1954. 406 pp.

9285. "Board Reports on Los Angeles Flood Control Projects: Approve Forks Dam Site on San Gabriel River for 180,000 Acre-Ft. for Flood Control and Conservation — District's Policy 'Not Based on Sound Engineering Principles.'" *Engineering News-Record* 98 (April 7, 1927): 570-2.

> Report of special board of consulting engineers disputes conclusions of County Flood Control District's engineers.

9286. Boone, Andrew R. "River Rebuilt to Curb Floods: Engineers Are Protecting Los Angeles and Surrounding Area . . . Flood Control and Water Conservation Dual Aim." *Scientific American* 161 (November 1939): 264-5.

> Lining the bed of the Los Angeles River with concrete.

9287. Borgen, C. G., and Smith, Charles A. "By-

Pass Used for Nuisance Flows at Gardena Intersections." *Western City* 34 (September 1958): 44-5.

9288. Bower, Chalmers. "New Pumping Station Handles City's Storm Water." *Western City* 6 (April 1930): 15-7.

Long Beach.

9289. ——— "Second Storm Water Pumping Plant Built: City of Long Beach Drains Area for Business and Residential Development; Operation of Station Is Entirely Automatic." *Western City* 7 (February 1931): 15-6.

9290. "Building a High Concrete Arch Dam in a Narrow Canyon." *Engineering News-Record* 99 (August 4, 1927): 168-70.

Pacoima Dam.

9291. "California Contractor's Dream Job." *Western Construction* 44 (March 1969): 74-5+.

Removing 22,000,000 tons of debris behind San Gabriel Dam No. 1.

9292. Christison, W. E. "Asphaltic Paving Used on Flood Control Revetments: Experimental Work in Los Angeles County Undertaken to Develop Surfacing with Characteristics of Low First Cost, Flexibility, Long Life and Small Maintenance." *Western Construction News* 12 (June 1937): 224-5.

9293. ——— "Trapping Flood Debris in Excavated Detention Basins." *Western Construction News* 11 (July 1936): 220-1.

Describes County Flood Control District reservoirs at mouths of foothill canyons.

9294. Collins, Albert B. "The Sierra Madre Dam; Its Inception and Design [1889-1932]." Master's thesis, University of Southern California, 1932. 32 pp.

9295. Collins, James H. "Among Our Souvenirs—Storm Drains." *Southern California Business* 15 (November 1936): 8-9.

Los Angeles County.

9296. ——— "Fact-Finding Over 17,000 Acres: San Dimas Forest Has the First Big-Scale 'Lab' for Flood and Water Research." *Southern California Business* 16 (June 1937): 8-9.

9297. "Concrete Flood Control Channel for L.A. River." *Western Construction News* 23 (January 1948): 77-80.

9298. Conkling, Harold. "San Gabriel Water Problems." *California Highways and Public Works* 4 (December 1927): 6+.

Legal and physical aspects of flood control.

9299. "Contractor's Maintenance Program for Equipment Used on San Gabriel Dam." *Western Construction News* 12 (August 1937): 298-301.

9300. "Controlling the Floods of Los Angeles County: How Motor Trucks Helped in the Construction of the Big Dam, Which Impounds 6,600 Acre-Feet of Water." *American City* 23 (September 1920): 301-3.

Devil's Gate Dam.

9301. "County Flood Control Plan of Los Angeles Aided by U.S. Engineers with Federal Funds." *Western Construction News* 10 (December 1935): 348-9.

9302. Cowper, William R. "The Story of San Antonio Dam." *Pomona Valley Historian* 3 (1967): 158-64.

Completed by Army Corps of Engineers in 1956.

9303. Cummings, Naomi J. "The Civil Functions of the Corps of Engineers of the United States Army as Related to the Los Angeles County Flood Control District." Master's thesis, University of Southern California, 1953. 117 pp.

9304. "Dam Politics." *Municipal League of Los Angeles Bulletin* 7 (November 1, 1929): [1-2+].

Controversy over safety of locating dam at the Forks of the San Gabriel River.

9305. Darwin, A. Gilbert. "Preliminary Work on the World's Largest Rockfill Dam." *Western Construction News* 9 (May 1934): 159-61.

San Gabriel Dam No. 1, built two miles below the Forks, the site originally selected for this project.

9306. ——— "San Gabriel Rock-Fill Dams No. 1 and 2." *Western Construction News and Highways Builder* 8 (May 10, 1933): 241-6.

Dams designed to provide flood control and conservation on the largest single watershed in the county.

9307. "Digging Out of San Gabriel Canyon." *Western Construction* 44 (July 1969): 43-5+.

Floods swamp silt-removal project at San Gabriel Dam No. 1.

9308. "Drainage District Improvement No. 29, Los Angeles County." *Western Construction News* 5 (April 25, 1930): 215-6.

9309. "Earth Handling Equipment Operations at Hansen Dam." *Western Construction News* 15 (June 1940): 202-4.

9310. Eaton, E. C. "Big Santa Anita Dam for the Los Angeles County Flood Control District." *Western Construction News* 2 (November 25, 1927): 44-8.

9311. ———— "Eaton Wash Debris Dam Near Pasadena." *Western Construction News and Highways Builder* 8 (June 10, 1933): 262.

County Flood Control District.

9312. ———— "Flood Control Measures Undertaken by County of Los Angeles Have Proven Very Successful." *Hydraulic Engineering* 5 (January 1929): 11-5.

9313. ———— "Los Angeles County Flood Control District: Progress of Construction on Various Projects." *Western Construction News* 2 (December 25, 1927): 29-35.

9314. ———— "Los Angeles Flood Control District to Build San Gabriel Dams No. 1 and 2." *Western Construction News* 7 (January 10, 1932): 14.

9315. ———— "Plans Approved for San Gabriel Dam No. 1." *Western Construction News and Highways Builder* 7 (June 10, 1932): 332-6.

Site two miles below the Forks.

9316. ———— "San Gabriel Dam for Los Angeles County Flood Control District." *Western Construction News* 4 (July 25, 1929): 373.

This and the subsequent three entries deal with the Forks site, subsequently abandoned as unsafe.

9317. ———— "San Gabriel Dam for Los Angeles County Flood Control District, California." *Western Construction News* 4 (June 10, 1929): 295-6.

9318. ———— "San Gabriel Dam, Los Angeles Flood Control District: Bids on World's Biggest Dam to Be Opened July 11." *Western Construction News* 2 (May 25, 1927): 53-4.

9319. Elliott Clifford A. "Pacific Electric Adopts Flood-Control Measures." *Electric Railway Journal* 52 (August 17, 1918): 297.

9320. "Engineers Find Mulholland and Other Los Angeles Water Department Dams Safe Structures." *Western Construction News* 3 (August 10, 1928): 515.

Investigation following St. Francis collapse.

9321. "Experts' Verdict on Flood Control Plans: Quotations from the Marx-Fowler-Paul Report." *Municipal League of Los Angeles Bulletin* 4 (March 31, 1927): 1+.

9322. "First Flood Control Engineer in Los Angeles Is Honored." *Western Construction News* 19 (July 1944): 80.

Pacoima Dam named for James W. Reagan.

9323. "First Step Toward Taming San Gabriel River." *Western Construction* 25 (August 1950): 75-6.

Whittier Narrows Dam.

9324. Fisher, S. M. "San Gabriel Dam." *Western Construction News* 2 (July 10, 1927): 47-50.

Forks site.

9325. Fix, Don. "Wellpoints Save the Day on Los Angeles River Job." *Western Construction* 29 (March 1954): 65-6.

Deepening and improving river channel near Long Beach to protect city from danger of flooding.

9326. "Flood-Control Channel Lines: Long Project in Pasadena, Calif., Built to Prevent Further Flood Damage." *American City* 54 (September 1939): 65+.

Arroyo Seco.

9327. "Flood Control Controversy in Los Angeles County." *Engineering News-Record* 96 (June 3, 1926): 890-2.

Board of consulting engineers questions conclusions of County Flood Control District regarding safety of Folks site for San Gabriel Dam.

9328. "Flood Control Levee on Los Angeles River." *Western Construction News* 7 (February 25, 1932): 100.

9329. "Flood Control Program for Los Angeles." *Western Construction News* 14 (April 1939): 148.
$200,000,000 plan, 85 projects.

9330. "Foundation Movements at San Gabriel Damsite." *Western Construction News* 4 (November 10, 1929): 598-9.
Forks site proves unsafe.

9331. "4,250,000 Flood-Prevention Plan Presented." *Engineering Record* 75 (January 6, 1917): 37.
Los Angeles County.

9332. Fraim, H. W. "Flood Control and Parkway Project Along Arroyo Seco at Los Angeles." *Western Construction News* 13 (June 1938): 233-6.

9333. Gilkerson, Jess D. "The State Helped Build the Storm-Water Pump Station: Financing Was Only One of the Significant Features in Long Beach's City-State Storm Water Project." *American City* 71 (October 1956) 132-3.

9334. Hahn, Walter, Jr., and Farnam, William. "Inglewood Attacks Flood Water Problem as Part of $4.5 Million Total Job." *Western City* 36 (March 1960): 29.

9335. "Hansen Dam Preliminaries Started by Guy F. Atkinson Grading Operations Started on Large Rolled Earthfill Structure Being Built by U. S. Engineers for Flood Control Near Los Angeles." *Western Construction News* 13 (November 1938): 414-5.

9336. Hart, Alan S. "The San Gabriel Dam." *The Architect and Engineer* 102 (July 1930): 94-5.
Description of plans for the Forks site dam, and the reasons why State Engineer Edward Hyatt denied the County Flood Control District permission to proceed with its construction.

9337. —— "The San Gabriel Dam: An Account of the Investigation of What Was to Have Been the World's Highest Dam." *California Engineer* 8 (February 1930): 10+.

9338. Henning, Lee R. "Concrete Lining for River Channel." *Western Construction* 33 (February 1958): 31-4.
Los Angeles River.

9339. "High Dam for Flood Control on San Gabriel River." *Engineering News-Record* 99 (October 6, 1927): 563.
Forks site.

9340. Hincks, Harvey W. "Comparison of San Gabriel Dam Sites." *Municipal League of Los Angeles Bulletin* 3 (October 28, 1925): 7-9.

9341. Hoult, Thomas. "The Whittier Narrows Dam: A Study in Community Competition and Conflict." Master's thesis, Whittier College, 1948. 183 pp.

9342. Hovater, Louis R. "Flood Channel Paved with Asphaltic Concrete." *Civil Engineering* 26 (December 1956): 33-4.
Bull Creek, San Fernando Valley.

9343. Hyatt, Edward. "Largest Earth and Rock Fill Dam Dedicated by Governor Merriam." *California Highways and Public Works* 15 (August 1937): 8-9+.
San Gabriel Dam No. 1.

9344. —— "$31,904,000 Dam Building Program under Way in Southern California." *California Highways and Public Works* 10 (August 1932): 1+.
Several major dams in San Gabriel Mountains included.

9345. Jarmuth, J. A. "Damming San Gabriel's Flood Waters." *Southern California Business* 3 (May 1924): 20+.

9346. Jessup, Roger. "Southern California Flood Control: Why It Adds Up to $501,000,000." *California Magazine of the Pacific* 29 (November 1939): 12-3+.

9347. Lee, Elsworth. "The Creek That Never Touches Land." *Westways* 58 (September 1966): 28-9.
Ballona Creek.

9348. Legg, Herbert C. "Los Angeles County Flood Control District." *California Magazine of the Pacific* 42 (September 1952): 11+.

9349. "Los Angeles County Flood District: Special Board of Consulting Engineers Submits Report Containing Drastic Recommendations." *Western Construction News* 2 (April 10, 1927): 55-7.
Controversy over site of San Gabriel Dam.

9350. "Los Angeles Flood Control Plans Reviewed." *Engineering News-Record* 98 (March 24, 1927): 501.
Controversy over site of San Gabriel Dam.

9351. "Los Angeles Flood Projects Completed by U.S. Engineers." *Western Construction News* 12 (February 1937): 75-6.

9352. "Los Angeles Pushes Work to Improve Conditions in Olympic Boulevard District by Open Cut and Tunnel for New Storm Drain." *American City* 54 (November 1939): 44-5.

9353. "L.A. River Channel To Be Completed." *Western Construction News* 16 (October 1941): 308-9.

9354. "Los Angeles Tests Flood Control Defense with Simulated Storm Record Runoff." *Western Construction News* 24 (November 15, 1949): 70.

9355. "A Master Flood Control Plan Demanded." *Municipal League of Los Angeles Bulletin* 9 (January 20, 1932): [1-2].

9356. Mears, Joe. "Moving Day in the Canyon." *Westways* 36 (January 1944): 12-3.
Flood control measures in Arroyo Seco Canyon necessitate abandonment or removal of private cabins by end of 1943.

9357. "More Dam Politics." *Municipal League of Los Angeles Bulletin* 9 (October 25, 1932): [8].
Controvery over San Gabriel Dam.

9358. "More Los Angeles Flood Control Dams." *Western Construction News* 14 (November 1939): 392.

9359. Morgan, J. G. "Earthfill Flood Control Dam." *Western Construction News* 18 (October 1943): 441-5.
Santa Fe Dam on San Gabriel River near Azusa.

9360. Noetzli, Fred A. "Gravity Dams Subject to Internal Stresses Which Often Result in Undesirable Fractures: Compensation Made in San Gabriel Dam Design by Providing Internal Contraction Joints Parallel to Stress Planes." *Hydraulic Engineering* 4 (December 1928): 726-9.
Forks dam site, later abandoned.

9361. "Novel Combined Dragline-Conveyor Speeds Hansen Dam Earth Handling." *Western Construction News* 14 (April 1939): 121-3.

9362. O'Melveny, Stuart. *It's Best to Divide with Our Friends.* Los Angeles, 1955. 33 pp.
History and reminiscences of San Gabriel Canyon, including dam construction.

9363. Oppenheimer, Phillip F. "Rubio Flood Works Complete." *Western Construction News* 19 (January 1944): 81-2.
Canyon above Altadena.

9364. Outland, G. W. "Record Needle Valves Installed in San Gabriel Dam Outlet Works." *Western Construction News* 14 (May 1939): 162-5.

9365. Perkins, Ralph. "Torrance Solves Flood Problem by Joint Citizen-Community Effort." *Western City* 34 (August 1958): 36.

9366. "Preliminary Report on San Gabriel Dam No. 1 Unfavorable." *Western Construction News* 10 (January 1935): 22.

9367. "Pre-Placed Aggregate for Spillway Grouted to Form 'Prepakt' Concrete." *Western Construction* 26 (July 1951): 69-72.
Whittier Narrows Dam.

9368. "Rate of Fill at San Gabriel Dam Exceeds 525,000 Cu. Yd. per Month." *Western Construction News* 11 (October 1936): 336-9.

9369. "Redesign of San Gabriel Dam No. 1 Submitted to State Engineer." *Western Construction News* 10 (May 1935): 141.

9370. "Resume Work on San Gabriel Dam." *Western Construction News* 10 (September 1935): 259.

9371. "Revised Plan for San Gabriel Dam Rejected by State Engineer." *Western Construction News* 10 (June 1935): 166.

9372. Salazar, Dean. "Those Dog-Gone Measurements." *American City* 77 (January 1962): 38.
Dachshund used to carry tape-measure through storm-drains by County Flood Control District.

9373. "San Gabriel Dam." *Western Construction News* 3 (October 10, 1928): 639-40.

9374. "San Gabriel Dam." *Western Construction News* 4 (December 10, 1929): 657.

Abandonment of Forks site.

9375. "San Gabriel Dam." *Western Construction News* 5 (December 25, 1930): 628.

Search for substitute location after abandonment of Forks site.

9376. "The San Gabriel Dam Issue." *Municipal League of Los Angeles Bulletin* 5 (January 31, 1928): [6].

9377. "San Gabriel Dam No. 1 Work Is Resumed Following Approval of New Design." *Western Construction News* 10 (November 1935): 324-6.

9378. "The San Gabriel Dam Report." *California Highways and Public Works* 7 (December 1929): 14-5+.

Text of report from State Engineer Edward Hyatt disapproving Los Angeles County's request to continue construction of dam at Forks site.

9379. "San Gabriel Project to Get Another Hearing." *Engineering News-Record* 97 (July 1, 1926): 29-30.

Controversy over location of dam.

9380. "San Gabriel River Project of Los Angeles County Flood Control District District." *Western Construction News* 6 (August 25, 1931): 457.

9381. "Santa Fe Dam Construction Started with Ground-Breaking Ceremonies." *Western Construction News* 16 (December 1941): 371.

San Gabriel River near Azusa.

9382. "Second Record Rainfall Tests L.A. Flood Control." *Western Construction News* 18 (April 1943): 175.

9383. Shaw, John C. "Storm Drain Construction Program for the City of Los Angeles." *Pacific Municipalities* 43 (June 1929): 262.

9384. ———— 'The Verdugo Road and Glassell Avenue Storm Drain." *Western Construction News* 3 (April 25, 1928): 264-5.

9385. "Simple Plant Makes Good Record in Dam Construction." *Engineering News-Record* 85 (July 29, 1920): 202-3.

Devil's Gate Dam, Arroyo Seco.

9386. "$16,000,000 Required for Los Angeles County Flood Protection." *Engineering Record* 72 (August 14, 1915): 204-6; (August 21, 1915): 232-3.

9387. "Slip-Form Paver on Slope Helps Beat Winter Rains on Rio Hondo." *Western Construction* 30 (March 1955): 49-50.

Flood control channel, part of Whittier Narrows Project.

9388. Stewart, R. W. "Controlling an Erratic Stream with Concrete." *American City* 19 (December 1918): 482-4.

Concrete lining for a portion of Arroyo Seco.

9389. Stewart, Ralph W. "The 'World's Record' Catch Basin, Los Angeles." *Western Construction News* 3 (March 25, 1928): 213.

Beverly Boulevard and Kenmore Avenue, Los Angeles.

9390. "Symposium on Flood Control of Los Angeles County." *Municipal League of Los Angeles Bulletin* 7 (February 1, 1930): [1-2+].

Includes:

"In Case of Flood," by Walter E. Jessup, pp. [1-2+];

"Check Dams with Special Reference to Water Conservation," by F. E. Trask, pp [4-5];

"Reforestation and Flood Control," by George H. Barnes, pp. [5-6]; and

"Theory and Practice in Flood Control," by Frank Olmstead, pp. [6-7].

9391. Thomas, Charles W. "Grid of Channels to Control Floods: Expected to Serve as a Model for Future Flood Control Work in the Nation, a Grid of Channels from Mountains to Sea Will Protect Thousands of Acres in Los Angeles River Watershed." *Western Construction News* 24 (May 1949): 83-5.

9392. Tscharner, P. J. "Building One of the World's Largest Dams." *Southern California Business* 8 (June 1929): 24+.

Forks site, San Gabriel River, abandoned shortly thereafter.

9393. Tulloch, Thomas P. "Los Angeles County Flood Control." *California Engineer* 10 (November 1931): 5-6+.

9394. "A Twisted Flood Control Program." *Mu-

nicipal League of Los Angeles Bulletin 7 (December 1, 1929): [3-6].

9395. "Uncle Sam Studies Flood Control: His Responsibility Starts in a National Forest and Runs to a Vital Pacific Harbor." *Southern California Business* 15 (May 1936): 12-3.
Los Angeles County.

9396. White, D. O. "Storm Drain Installed under Busy Street Without Traffic Interruption." *Western City* 9 (May 1933): 19-20.
Hawthorne.

9397. "Whittier Flood Control Project Is on Schedule." *Western Construction* 30 (April 1955): 32.

9398. "Who Delays the San Gabriel Dam?" *Municipal League of Los Angeles Bulletin* 3 (July 31, 1926): 1+.

9399. Wood, Walter J. "Los Angeles County Flood Control and the Early 1969 Storms." *Civil Engineering* 40 (January 1970): 58-61.

9400. "World's Highest Dam Completed: Pacoima Dam, 365 Feet High, Built at Cost of $1,564,421, Is the Latest Achievement of the Los Angeles County Flood Control District." *Hydraulic Engineering* 5 (March 1929): 33+.

9401. Wyman, Theodore. *Flood Control in the Los Angeles County Drainage Area.* Washington, D.C., 1938. 131 pp.

WATER SUPPLY—LOCAL SOURCES, STORAGE, AND DISTRIBUTION FACILITIES

9402. Ackerman, Theodore V. "Pasadena's Cross-Connection Control Program." *Public Works* 97 (August 1966): 109-11+.
Pasadena Water Department.

9403. Anderson, M. W. "All-Welded Tank for Maywood: First All-Welded Steel Water Tank on the Pacific Coast Has Been Erected by the City of Maywood to Increase the Storage Capacity of the Municipal Utility System and to Regulate Pressure Head in the Distribution System—the Structure Has Been Especially Designed to Resist Earthquakes." *Western Construction News* 21 (October 1946): 87-8.

9404. Bateman, Ivan L. "Recording All Talks with City Water and Power Trucks." *American City* 69 (October, 1954): 116-7.
Mobile radio dispatching, Los Angeles Department of Water and Power.

9405. Boggs, E. M. *A Study of Water Rights on the Los Angeles River, California.* Washington, D.C., 1901. 83 pp.

9406. Brown, Walter M. "50 Years of Growing Pains: In Long Beach, Calif. New Storage Capacity and Transmission Mains Overcome Water Problems Aggravated by Booming Population Curve." *American City* 64 (August 1949): 110-1.

9407. "Cast-Iron Service Pipe in Los Angeles." *Western Construction News* 4 (October 25, 1929): 543-4.
Los Angeles Bureau of Water Works and Supply pioneers in the use of small-diameter cast-iron service pipe.

9408. Clark, Alfred. "The San Gabriel River: A Century of Dividing the Waters." *Southern California Quarterly* 52 (1970): 155-69.

9409. Clough, Frank H. "New Type Elevated Steel Tank for South Pasadena Water Department." *Western City* 12 (February 1936): 32-3.

9410. "Dam Fails in Los Angeles." *Western Construction* 39 (January 1964): 55-8.
Baldwin Hills.

9411. Derby, R[ay] L. "New Water Softening Plant for Beverly Hills, California." *Western Construction News* 2 (October 25, 1927): 31-4.

9412. "Desalted Water from the Sea . . . Washes Away the Fear of Drought on Catalina Island." *American City* 81 (June 1966): 12.

9413. Dollison, Don H. "The City of South Pasadena . . . Reconditions 7000 Feet of Water Pipe . . . Awards Contract for Second Similar Job." *Western City* 27 (June 1951): 46-7.

9414. ———— "South Pasadena Relines Pipe in 'No-Man's Zone.'" *American City* 67 (February 1952): 83-4.
Water mains.

9415. Dunn, S. M. "Los Angeles Method of Well

Testing." *Western Construction News and Highways Builder* 7 (July 10, 1932): 383.
Describes novel method of developing water wells.

9416. ——— "New North Hollywood Pumping Plant Taps Natural Storage Water." *Western City* 7 (June 1931): 32-3+.

9417. "El Segundo Pumping Plant Station Disguised as Residential Unit." *Western City* 42 (May 1966): 56.

9418. "First Report on Causes of Dam Failure." *Western Construction* 39 (June 1964): 134-5+.
Baldwin Hills.

9419. "Getting Around Charity Rates for Water Service: The Problem and How It Has Been Solved in Los Angeles, Where Cut Rates Are Illegal." *American City* 56 (March 1941): 75+.

9420. Gilman, H[erbert] S. "Water Development in San Dimas." *Pomona Valley Historian* 3 (1967): 124-35.
Reprint of 1929 article written by an official of both the San Dimas Co. and the San Dimas Orange Growers Association.

9421. ——— "Water Problems in San Dimas Valley." *Pomona Valley Historian* 4 (1968): 139-48.
Reprint of a 1929 article.

9422. "Glorietta Avenue Reservoir, Glendale." *Western Construction News* 6 (October 10, 1931): 521-4.

9423. Goerlick, Henry L. "New City Department Established as Lakewood Purchases Water System." *Western City* 35 (August 1959): 40+.

9424. Harnish, C. P. "Small Filtration Plants for Southern California Water." *Western Construction News* 11 (June 1936): 191-3.
Los Angeles area.

9425. Hovater, Louis R. "Reservoir Lining at Lower Stone Canyon Features Asphalt Lining on 2:1 Slope." *Western Construction* 31 (April 1956): 60-1.
Los Angeles Department of Water and Power.

9426. "How Big a 'Sugar Daddy' Should a Water Works Be?" *American City* 60 (August 1945): 97.

Fees paid by the Long Beach Water Department to the city treasury.

9427. "How Wartime Conditions Affect Water Department Shown in Pasadena Report." *Western City* 22 (January 1946): 23-4.

9428. Hurlbut, William W. "Use of Cast Iron Service Lines from Main to Curb by Los Angeles Water Department." *Hydraulic Engineering* 4 (July 1928): 430-1+.

9429. "Interesting Installations of Cast-Iron Pipe in Los Angeles." *Western Construction News* 4 (May 25, 1929): 262.
Various projects of Los Angeles Bureau of Water Works and Supply.

9430. Johnson, J. B. "Burbank Builds Reservoir." *Western Construction News* 22 (July 1947): 97-8.

9431. Jones, Morris. "Water is Popular in Pasadena . . . and the Pasadena Water Department Provides Service That Makes This Popularity Permanent." *American City* 62 (July 1947): 137-9.

9432. Jones, Willis S. "Our Important Natural Resource—Water." *Pomona Valley Historian* 5 (1969): 175-84.
Pomona Valley.

9433. Jorgensen, Alfred. "A New Approach to Solving Water Disputes: The Long Beach Case [1781-1967]." Master's thesis, University of Southern California, 1967. 140 pp.

9434. King, Maurice M. "Two Water Reservoirs Being Built under Streets in Santa Monica." *Western City* 25 (May 1949): 34-7.

9435. Leadabrand, Russ. "The Day the Dam Broke." *American Forests* (February 1964): 30-3+.
Baldwin Hills.

9436. Lippincott, J[oseph] B. "Water Supply Development on Santa Catalina Island." *Western City* 6 (February 1930): 27-9+.

9437. Los Angeles. Department of Water and Power. *A Brief Summary of Important Historical Data and Current Facts Concerning the Municipally Owned Department of Water and Power, City of Los Angeles.*
Published annually beginning 1945.

9438. "Los Angeles Develops Water Wells in San Fernando Valley." *Western City* 25 (May 1949): 39.

9439. "Los Angeles Installs Its 300,000th Meter." *American City* 56 (April 1941): 125.
Includes statistics on number of water meters in city, 1902-1940.

9440. "Los Angeles Reservoir Storage Capacity Increased." *Pacific Municipalities* 44 (April 1930): 122.
Lower San Fernando and Chatsworth reservoirs.

9441. "Los Angeles Water-Works Grow." *Engineering News-Record* 80 (May 23, 1918): 992.
Los Angeles becomes the fourth-ranking city in the nation in pipeline mileage.

9442. "Los Angeles Will Build New Reservoir in Baldwin Hills." *Western Construction News* 22 (January 1947): 94.

9443. Marshall, Henry L. "Covina Concerning Modern Wizardry." *Out West,* new series, 3 (March 1912): [211-5].
Conserving water and tapping new sources help Covina and San Gabriel Valley to prosper.

9444. Martin, Harold J. "Water Service and Repair Trucks in Los Angeles." *American City* 53 (June 1938): 41-2.
Los Angeles Bureau of Water Works and Supply.

9445. Maynard, Glyde. "The Development of San Antonio Canyon." *Pomona Valley Historian* 1 (1965): 33-9; 73-87; 125-33.
From the author's 1935 master's thesis at USC entitled "A History of the Development of San Antonio Canyon California." Part of the second and most of the third installments deal with the twentieth century, water and forests being the principal topics.

9446. McCambridge, James C. "Burbank's Water Developments." *American City* 62 (July 1947): 114-6.

9447. Mini, T. R., and Liming, H. R. "Burbank's 7,000,000-Gallon Concrete Lined Reservoir." *Western Construction News* 3 (October 25, 1928): 653-4.

9448. "A Modern Tale of Two Cities; Or, the Object Lesson Furnished by the Story of the Water Supply of Los Angeles and Denver." *Arena* 38 (October 1907): 436-8.
Comparison of rates under public and private ownership.

9449. Morris, Samuel B. "All-Welded Steel Pipe Line Brings Water to Pasadena from Morris Reservoir." *Western Construction News* (October 1934): 310-15.

9450. "The Mulholland Dam of the Los Angeles Water-Supply." *American City* 33 (September 1925): 258.

9451. "New Elevated Tank and Automatic Pump Station for South Pasadena." *Western City* 17 (March 1941): 35.

9452. Olmos, Robert. "The River: The Mighty 'River of Angels' As It Looked to a Boy in the '30s." *Los Angeles* 2 (August 1961): 18.

9453. Padick, Clement. "Control and Conservation of Natural Runoff Water in the San Fernando Valley, California." Master's thesis, University of California, Los Angeles, 1956. 178 pp.

9454. "Pasadena (California) Water Works." *Western Construction News* 4 (February 10, 1929): 87-8.

9455. "Pasadena Water Department Report Is Informative Document." *Western City* 26 (January 1950): 26-7.
35th Annual Report said to be "one of the most comprehensive, informative and interesting documents issued by any utility."

9456. Patten, R. S. "How Santa Monica Cut Water Losses with Meter and Reservoir Programs." *Western City* 31 (September 1955): 58-60+.

9457. Porter, Fred S. "Long Beach Water System Improvements." *Western Construction News and Highways Builder* 7 (April 25, 1932): 205-10.

9458. ———— "Steel Reservoirs for Long Beach." *Western Construction News* 9 (October 1934): 327.

9459. "Private Water Systems Bought by Municipality." *Western Construction News* 22 (January 1947): 98.
Los Angeles.

9460. "Profits of Los Angeles Water System." *Pacific Municipalities* 13 (September 1905): 38.

9461. Read, George. "Maintenance and Testing of Meters as Practiced in the City of Los Angeles." *Western City* 6 (October 1930): 12-5+.
Water meters, Bureau of Water Works and Supply.

9462. Renner, Geo[rge] O. "Monrovia's Water Regulations." *California Municipalities* 2 (July 1900): 181-3.

9463. "Reports of Engineers on Stability of Los Angeles Water Department Dams and Reservoirs." *Western Construction News* 3 (September 10, 1928): 553-4.
Investigation following St. Francis collapse.

9464. Riggs, Eugene H. "West Covina Plans a Municipal Water System." *Western City* 24 (October 1948): 52-3.

9465. "Safety Is Main Item on—First Membrane-Lined Earth Reservoir: Uncontrolled Drainage Will Be Zero on the Los Angeles Dept. of Water and Power Membrane-Lined Baldwin Hills Reservoir." *Western Construction News* 24 (May 1949): 81-2+.

9466. "Small Reservoir Is Enlarged." *Western Construction News* 18 (July 1943): 300-1.
Elysian Park Reservoir, Los Angeles.

9467. Snyder, John H. "Factors Affecting the Ground-Water Economy of the Antelope Valley, Los Angeles County, California." Doctoral dissertation, University of California, Berkeley, 1954. 415 pp.

9468. Socha, Max K. "The Desperate Fight to Save the Baldwin Hills Dam." *Western Construction* 39 (March 1964): 84+.

9469. "Solving Our Water Problem: Saturday Night Has Just Completed a Survey of Southern California's Major Three-Way Problem — Water Supply, Fire Protection and Flood Control. Facts Favoring the Erection of a Dam in Santa Ynez Canyon Are Offered Herewith." *Saturday Night* 45 (December 31, 1938): 18-21.

9470. Spriggs, Elisabeth. "The History of the Domestic Water Supply of Los Angeles [1871-1902]." Master's thesis, University of Southern California, 1931. 80 pp.

9471. "State Report on Dam Failure: Land Subsidence Both Local and General Led to the Failure of Baldwin Hills Dam." *Western Construction* 39 (August 1964): 71-2+.

9472. "Submarine Pipe Line Laid under Los Angeles Harbor." *Western Construction News* 12 (October 1937): 393.
Augmenting Terminal Island water supply.

9473. Taylor, Arthur. "Economic Results of Water Softening and Purification in Beverly Hills." *Western City* 9 (January 1933): 11-3.

9474. Taylor, Nelson. "Two City Reservoirs Involve Distinctive Types of Concrete Roof Design." *Hydraulic Engineering* 5 (November 1929): 36-8.
Beverly Hills and Ventura.

9475. "Testing Enamel Lining of 36-Inch Pipe: Los Angeles Department of Water and Power Has Novel Perambulator." *American City* 52 (June 1937): 81.

9476. Thomas, Brennan S. "Long Beach, Calif., Builds a Multi-Tank Water Reservoir." *American City* 66 (July 1951): 96-7.

9477. ———, and Schafer, Frederick. "Expansion, Progressive Design Keys Long Beach Water Department System." *Western City* 30 (October 1954): 48-51+.

9478. "The Use of Water Meters at Los Angeles." *Pacific Municipalities* 13 (August 1905): 12-3.

9479. Van Wagner, James H. "Pomona's Filtration Plant Marks Historic Shift of Water Use for City." *Western City* 36 (October 1960): 36-7.

9480. Vollmer, Robert, and Moffitt, William. "Topography Complicates Beverly Hills Water System." *Western City* 40 (October 1964): 44-5.

9481. W. S. B. "The Record of the Owens River Project." *Out West* 30 (April 1909): 259-77.

9482. Warne, William E. "The Baldwin Hills Dam Failure." *Western Construction* 39 (February 1964): 78+.

9483. "Water Revenue Bonds Assure Growth of Los Angeles System." *Western City* 27 (June 1951): 44.
$18 million improvements to local storage and distribution system.

9484. "The Water Supply System of Los Angeles, Cal." *Engineering Record* 57 (February 20, 1908): 228-32.

9485. "Water Works Construction at Long Beach." *American City* 60 (November 1945): 117.

9486. Wells, C. Kenyon. "40,000,000-Gal. Stored in 12 Steel Tanks at Long Beach: Addition to Reservoir System of City Required by Population Growth and Increasing Load on Municipal System." *Western Construction* 25 (October 1950): 80-1.

9487. Wheatfill, Edward L. "The Possibilities of Locating and Developing Deeper Aquifers to Augment the Water Well Production for Long Beach, California." Master's thesis, University of California, Los Angeles, 1957. 58 pp.

9488. Wilson, Carl. "Control of Algal Growths in the Water Storage Reservoirs of Los Angeles." *Western Construction News* 3 (June 10, 1928): 355-6.

WATER SUPPLY—LOS ANGELES AQUEDUCT, MONO BASIN, AND OWENS VALLEY

9489. "Additions to Los Angeles Water System." *Western Construction News* 11 (September 1936): 290.

9490. "All St. Francis Dam Reports Agree as to Reason for Failure: Defective Foundations Generally Accepted as the Cause of Failure of Structure." *Engineering News-Record* 100 (May 10, 1928): 639.
Dam was designed and built by the Los Angeles Bureau of Water Supply as part of the Los Angeles Aqueduct System.

9491. "Aqueduct Barge Fleet—Canal Relined by Crews on Floating Platforms: After 30 Yrs. of Service Sections of the Los Angeles Aqueduct in Owens Valley Are Being Reconditioned with 5 In. of Concrete—Two-Stage Operations with Final Step Carried Out from Barges." *Western Construction News* 15 (October 1940): 331-3.

9492. Bannister, E. W. "Construction Work on the Los Angeles Aqueduct." *Engineering Record* 59 (April 3, 1909): 393-7.

9493. Bennett, Ralph. "St. Francis Dam Failure—An Engineer's Study of the Site." *Engineering News-Record* 100 (March 22, 1928): 517-8.

9494. "Better Prospects for Settlement of Owens Valley Dispute: Clearing House Association Acts as Mediator in Fight Between Ranchers and Los Angeles Over City Water Rights." *Engineering News-Record* 94 (May 7, 1925): 767-8.

9495. "Bids Received for Dam on Mono Basin Project." *Western Construction News* 14 (May 1939): 165.
Tapping sources north of Owens Valley to augment flow of aqueduct.

9496. "Big Water Scheme for Los Angeles." *Pacific Municipalities* 13 (August 1905): 15.
Aqueduct from Owens Valley.

9497. Bliss, H. P. "Mono Craters Tunnel Taps New Water Supply for Los Angeles: Construction Started on $7,000,000 Project to Bring Water from Mono Basin in Central California to Los Angeles, a Distance of 350 Miles." *Western Construction News* 10 (February 1935): 33-5.

9498. "Bouquet Canyon Dam and Conduit." *Western Construction News and Highway Builder* 8 (November 1933): 461.
This dam and storage reservoir was built to replace St. Francis.

9499. "Bouquet Canyon Dam Started." *Western Construction News and Highways Builder* 7 (May 10, 1932): 246.

9500. "Bo[u]quet Canyon Earth-Fill Dame for Los Angeles Water Supply." *Western Construction News and Highways Builder* 7 (October 25, 1932): 599-600.

9501. "Bouquet Canyon Reservoir and Outlet Works." *Western Construction News and Highways Builder* 8 (May 10, 1933): 226-30.

9502. Bowen, E. R. 'Designing Steel Pipe for Minimum Weight of Metal Consistent with Safety: Studies for the Jawbone Inverted Siphon of the Los Angeles Aqueduct, Which Operates under a Maximum Head of 850 Feet." *Engineering Record* 68 (December 20, 1913): 682-5.

9503. Bowers, Nathan A. "St. Francis Dam Catastrophe — A Great Foundation Failure." *Engineering News-Record* 100 (March 22, 1928): 466-72.

9504. ———— "St. Francis Dam Catastrophe—A Review Six Weeks After." *Engineering News-Record* 100 (May 10, 1928): 727-36.

9505. Breed, L. C. "The Los Angeles Aqueduct." *Pacific Municipalities* 18 (July 1908): 103-5.

9506. Brennecke, Olga. "How Los Angeles Built the Greatest Aqueduct in the World: A Story of Interesting Municipal Activity." *Craftsman* 23 (November 1912): 188-96.

9507. "Builders Blamed for Failure of St. Francis Dam: Governor's Commission Finds Dam Built on Rock Which Softened in Water." *Engineering News-Record* 100 (March 29, 1928): 527-8.

9508. "Cable Tramways Used on Construction Work." *Engineering News* 75 (June 29, 1916): 1236-7.
Los Angeles Aqueduct.

9509. "California's Little Civil War." *Literary Digest* 83 (December 6, 1924): 15.
Owens Valley residents retaliate against alleged "unscrupulous machinations" of the Los Angeles Department of Water and Power.

9510. "The Cement Mill of the Los Angeles Aqueduct." *Engineering Record* 62 (September 17, 1910): 331-2.

9511. Cifarelli, Anthony. "The Owens River Aqueduct and the Los Angeles Times; A Study in Early Twentieth Century Business Ethics and Journalism." Master's thesis, University of California, Los Angeles, 1969. 148 pp.

9512. "City's Dealings with Owens Valley." *Municipal League of Los Angeles Bulletin* 3 (April 30, 1926): 5-7.
Report from the Owens Valley Land Purchasing Committee, composed of W. B. Mathews, H. A. Van Norman, and E. F. Leahey.

9513. "Commission Finds Failure of St. Francis Dam Due to Defective Foundations." *Engineering News-Record* 100 (April 5, 1928): 553-5.

9514. "Concrete Flume Culverts, Los Angeles Aqueduct." *Engineering Record* 65 (June 22, 1912): 698-9.

9515. "Congressional Act Settles Los Angeles Water Dispute." *American City* 63 (July 1948): 9.
Poulson Bill on Inyo and Mono County water resources.

9516. "Construction on the Los Angeles Aqueduct: A Review of the Methods of Excavating and Concreting in Desert Land." *Engineering Record* 65 (January 6, 1912): 6-8.

9517. Cowan, James G. "Mortar Lining 11-Ft. Steel Siphons: First Use in the West of In-Place Lining Process for Thin-Walled Large Diameter Pipe." *Western Construction* 26 (May 1951): 72-3.
Los Angeles Aqueduct, Placerita and Quigley canyons.

9518. Cross, Frederick C. "My Days on the Jawbone." *Westways* 60 (May 1968): 3-8.
Personal memoir of construction of the aqueduct.

9519. "Dam Building at 7 Cents a Yard." *Engineering Record* 70 (July 11, 1914): 46-7.
San Fernando Dam, Los Angeles Aqueduct.

9520. Davison, Frank B. *Commemorative of the Official Opening, the Los Angeles Aqueduct and Exposition Park, November Fifth and Sixth, Nineteen Hundred Thirteen.* Los Angeles, 1913. Unp.

9521. "Destroy Standing Section of St. Francis Dam." *Engineering News-Record* 102 (May 23, 1929): 845.

9522. "Dynamite Blast Damages Los Angeles Aqueduct." *Engineering News-Record* 92 (June 5, 1924): 991.
Three miles north of Lone Pine.

9523. "Engineering World Seeks to Learn Lesson from Collapse of St. Francis Dam, California." *Hydraulic Engineering* 4 (March 1928): 145.

9524. Flandreau, John. "The Los Angeles Aqueduct: A Study of Its Significance in the History of the City of Los Angeles." Master's thesis, Occidental College, 1947. 116 pp.

9525. Forbes, Hyde. "Geological Formation at the St. Francis Dam Site." *Engineering News-Record* 100 (April 12, 1928): 596-7.

9526. ———— "Geology of the St. Francis Damsite." *Western Construction News* 3 (April 10, 1928): 234-5.

9527. —— "Most Damsites Are Geologically Safe: Failure of St. Francis Dam Should Occasion No Uncertainty as to the Stability of Foundations at Most Existing Dams." *Western Construction News* 3 (May 10, 1928): 301-2.

9528. Ford, Thomas F. "Los Angeles Votes Extension of Water Supply System." *National Municipal Review* 19 (July 1930): 457-8.
Owens Valley and Mono Basin.

9529. "Forty-Three Miles of Tunnels in One Aqueduct." *Independent* 75 (August 28, 1913): 518-9.
General description of the aqueduct.

9530. "Foundations of St. Francis Dam Again Indicated." *Engineering News-Record* 100 (April 12, 1928): 605.
Cause of collapse.

9531. Gerry, M. H., Jr. "St. Francis Dam Failure." *Western Construction News* 3 (July 10, 1928): 442-3.

9532. Goldman, Don. "Owens Valley and Its Water." Master's thesis, University of California, Los Angeles, 1960. 149 pp.

9533. "The Great Water Project of Los Angeles." *Engineering Record* 54 (November 3, 1906): 488.

9534. Grunsky, C. E., and Grunsky, E. L. "St. Francis Dam Failure at Midnight, March 12-13, 1928." *Western Construction News* 3 (May 25, 1928): 314-24.

9535. Heinly, Burt A. "Aqueduct Outlet Cascades." *Engineering News* 74 (September 2, 1915): 455-6.
Outlet of last aqueduct tunnel, northern San Fernando Valley. Author of this and the ensuing dozen articles was secretary to William Mulholland.

9536. —— "An Aqueduct Two Hundred and Forty Miles Long: How Steel and Concrete Siphons Will Supply Los Angeles with Water." *Scientific American* 106 (May 23, 1912): 476.

9537. —— "Carrying Water Through a Desert: The Story of the Los Angeles Aqueduct." *National Geographic* 21 (July 1910): 568-96.

9538. —— "Combined Water-Supply, Irrigation, and Power Project." *Engineering Magazine* 38 (December 1909): 161-74.

9539. —— "The Completion of the Los Angeles Aqueduct." *Engineering News* 69 (June 19, 1913): 1257-68.

9540. —— "Completion, Testing and Dedication of the Los Angeles Aqueduct." *Engineering News* 70 (November 6, 1913): 920-3.

9541. —— "Construction and Completion of the Los Angeles Aqueduct." *Engineering Magazine* 45 (April 1913): 1-17.

9542. —— "The Longest Aqueduct in the World." *Outlook* 93 (September 25, 1909): 215-20.

9543. —— "The Los Angeles Aqueduct." *Pacific Municipalities* 20 (May 1909): 101-12.

9544. —— "The Los Angeles Aqueduct: Causes of Low Cost and Rapidity of Construction." *The Architect and Engineer of California* 19 (January 1910): 70-9.

9545. —— "Los Angeles—A City in Business." *National Municipal Review* 3 (1914): 97-102.
Los Angeles Aqueduct and its ramifications.

9546. —— "Municipal Progressiveness and the Los Angeles Aqueduct." *American City* 6 (April 1912): 662-4.

9547. —— "Water for Millions: Building the Great Aqueduct That Is to Supply Los Angeles—What the Task Means." *Sunset* 23 (December 1909): 631-8.

9548. Henry, D. C. "Important Lessons of Construction Taught by Failure of St. Francis Dam." *Hydraulic Engineering* 4 (December 1928): 731-5+.

9549. "History and General Features of the Owens Gorge Project." *Western Construction* 27 (February 1952): 77.

9550. "How Los Angeles Meters Aqueduct Water for Irrigation." *Engineering News-Record* 85 (September 2, 1920): 451.
San Fernando Valley.

9551. "How to Meet St. Francis Flood Damages." *Municipal League of Los Angeles Bulletin* 5 (April 1, 1928): [8].

9552. Hurlbut, William W. "Antelope Valley Siphon, Los Angeles Aqueduct." *Engineering Record* 68 (July 19, 1913) : 60-2.

9553. ——— "Completion of Los Angeles Aqueduct." *Engineering Record* 68 (November 1, 1913) : 482-6.

Includes a bibliography of articles on that project published by this periodical.

9554. ——— "Completion of San Fernando Siphon, Los Angeles: Steel Pipe That Forms the Connecting Link Between the Aqueduct and the City's Present Distribution System." *Engineering Record* 70 (July 11, 1914) : 4819.

9555. "Inverted Siphons on the Los Angeles Aqueduct." *Engineering Record* 65 (June 29, 1912) : 722.

9556. "Investigations under Way on St. Francis Dam Failure." *Engineering News-Record* 100 (March 22, 1928) : 491.

9557. "Inyo County's Gesture." *Saturday Night* 7 (July 16, 1927) : 3.

Grand jury investigation of various assaults on aqueducts.

9558. "Irrigation by Los Angeles Aqueduct Water." *Engineering News* 74 (November 25, 1915) : 1053-4.

9559. Jorgensen, Lars R. "St. Francis Dam Failure Analyzed." *Western Construction News* 3 (July 10, 1928) : 443-5.

9560. Kelly, Allen. *Historical Sketch of the Los Angeles Aqueduct*. [Los Angeles], 1913. Unp.

9561. Kinsey, Don J. *The Water Trail; The Story of Owens Valley and the Controversy Surrounding the Efforts of a Great City to Secure the Water Required to Meet the Needs of an Ever-Growing Population*. Los Angeles, 1928. 39 pp.

9562. Lancaster, Hugh. "The San Francisquito Dam Failure." *California Engineer* 6 (April 1928) : 217+.

9563. Lee, Charles H. *An Intensive Study of the Water Resources of a Part of Owens Valley, California*. Washington, D.C. 1912. 135 pp.

9564. ——— "Theories of the Cause and Sequence

of Failure of the St. Francis Dam." *Western Construction News* 3 (June 25, 1928) : 405-8.

9565. Lippincott, J[oseph] B. "The South Haiwee Earth Dam and Reservoir of the Los Angeles Aqueduct." *Engineering Record* 65 (February 3, 1912) : 116-8.

Storage facility in Owens Valley.

9566. "The Location and Design of Conduits on the Los Angeles Aqueduct." *Engineering Record* 64 (December 16, 1911) : 716-7.

9567. "Long Valley Dam Started on Mono Basin Project." *Western Construction News* 10 (June 1935) : 166.

Dam impounds reservoir named Crowley Lake.

9568. Los Angeles. Board of Public Service Commissioners. *Complete Report on Construction of the Los Angeles Aqueduct: With Introductory Historical Sketch*. Los Angeles, 1916. 319 pp.

9569. ——— Department of Water and Power. *Facts Concerning the Owens Valley Reparations*. Los Angeles, [n.d.]. 20 pp.

9570. "Los Angeles Aqueduct Dynamited." *Engineering News-Record* 96 (May 20, 1926) : 827.

Incident occurred near Lone Pine, not far from where the aqueduct was blown up in May 1924, and was seized and the flow diverted in November 1924.

9571. "Los Angeles Aqueduct Seized and Waste Gates Opened." *Engineering News Record* 93 (November 30, 1924) : 845.

9572. "Los Angeles Aqueduct Water Used for Irrigation." *Engineering Record* 74 (July 29, 1916) : 154.

San Fernando Valley.

9573. "Los Angeles Completes $200,000,000 Addition to Aqueduct System." *Western City* 17 (November 1941) : 16-7.

Tunnel tapping Mono Basin.

9574. "Los Angeles Provides Water Supply for 2,250,000 with Mono Basin Project." *Western City* 12 (June 1936) : 46-7.

9575. "Los Angeles Repairs Its Aqueducts: Precast Slab Construction Makes Repair Work Fast and Efficient." *American City* 64 (June 1949) : 118.

9576. "Los Angeles Taps Mono Basin Water by Means of 11.5-Mile Tunnel." *Western Construction News* 11 (June 1936): 170-2.

9577. "Los Angeles to Spend $39,000,000 for Water Works." *Western Construction News* 5 (May 25, 1930): 259-60.

9578. "Los Angeles Votes for the Aquisition of the Owens River Water Supply." *Pacific Municipalities* 13 (September 1905): 48.

9579. "Los Angles' 'Water Crop' Below Normal." *American City* 63 (August 1948): 9.
    1948 Owens Valley-Mono Basin runoff 64% of normal.

9580. "Los Angeles's Giant Water Scheme." *Scientific American* 93 (December 9, 1905): 462.

9581. Mamrelli, E. S. "Replacing 11-Ft. Steel Siphons." *Western Construction News* 15 (December 1940): 409-11.
    Sections of aqueduct between Haiwee and San Fernando reservoirs.

9582. McGaffey, Ernest. "The Harvest of the Snows." *Touring Topics* 14 (October 1922): 24-6+.
    Los Angeles Aqueduct.

9583. "Mono Craters Tunnel Progress in 1936." *Western Construction News* 12 (February 1937): 74.

9584. Moody, Charles A. "Los Angeles and the Owens River." *Out West* 23 (October 1905): [416]-42.

9585. "A Moral Responsibility Accepted." *American City* 38 (April 1928): 11
    St. Francis Dam disaster.

9586. Mulholland, William. "Floods Damage Antelope Siphon, Los Angeles Aqueduct." *Engineering Record* 69 (April 18, 1914): 447.

9587. "Municipal Water Works." *Sunset* 34 (June 1915): 1081-3.
    Criticizes administration of aqueduct facilites.

9588. Nadeau, Remi. "The Water War." *American Heritage* 13 (December 1961): 30-5+.
    The "Little Civil War" between Los Angeles and Owens Valley.

9589. Newell, F. H. "The Reclamation Service and the Owens Valley." *Out West* 23 (October 1905): 454-61.

9590. Osborne, Henry Z. 'The Completion of the Los Angeles Aqueduct: Bringing 265,000,000 Gallons of Water Per Day 234 Miles from the Sierras to Los Angeles." *Scientific American* 109 (November 8, 1913): 364-5+.

9591. Outland, Charles F. *Man-Made Disaster. The Story of St. Francis Dam, Its Place in Southern California's Water System, Its Failure and the Tragedy of March 12 and 13, 1928, in the Santa Clara River Valley.* Glendale, 1963. 211 pp.

9592. "The Owens Valley 'Background.' " *Municipal League of Los Angeles Bulletin* 2 (August 15, 1924): [9-10].
    Report of an address by R. E. Chadwick, a member of the League's executive committee, in which he discussed the dynamiting of the aqueduct in May 1924, and the background for the Owens Valley proposal that the city buy 28,000 acres of land in the Bishop district.

9593. "The Owens Valley Situation." *Municipal League of Los Angeles Bulletin* 5 (March 1, 1928): [8].

9594. Phillips, Robert V. "Building Second Los Angeles Aqueduct as New Water Lifeline to Los Angeles." *Western City* 43 (October 1967): 24-6+.

9595. ——— "Los Angeles Undertakes $825 Million Water Expansion Program." *Western City* 45 (May 1969): 34+.
    Mainly on the Second Los Angeles Owens River [sic] Aqueduct.

9596. "Power Development on the Los Angeles Aqueduct." *Engineering Magazine* 39 (May 1910): 261-3.

9597. "Preliminary Work on the Los Angeles Aqueduct." *Engineering Record* 57 (February 8, 1908): 144-7.

9598. Reames, Paul E. "Safety of Dams: Lesson from the Failure of the St. Francis Dam." *Western Construction News* 4 (January 25, 1929): 58-9.

9599. "Rehabilitating the Owens River Aqueduct." *Western Construction* 43 (January 1968): 110.

9600. "Report on Future Water Supply for Los Angeles." *Engineering News-Record* 93 (September 11, 1924): 442.

Owens Valley and Mono Basin.

9601. "Resume of Reports Covering Causes for Failure of St. Francis Dam." *Hydraulic Engineering* 4 (July 1928): 444-6.

Reports of Los Angeles Section of the American Society Civil Engineers.

9602. Richards, John R. "Owens Valley." *Municipal League of Los Angeles Bulletin* 5 (September 30, 1927): 1-2.

Pro-Los Angeles side of "Little Civil War" by a Department of Water and Power Commissioner.

9603. ———— "Why Not Settle the Owens Valley Trouble?" *Municipal League of Los Angeles Bulletin* 4 (July 30, 1927): 1.

9604. Ryan, Marian L. "Los Angeles Newspapers Fight the Water War, 1924-1927." *Southern California Quarterly* 50 (1968): 177-90.

Author emphasizes that the newspapers, especially the *Record* and the *Times,* were more interested in defending their editorial positions than presenting the real issues, a factor keeping California's "Little Civil War" alive.

9605. "The St. Francis Dam." *Public Works* 59 (April 1928): 160-2.

9606. "St. Francis Dam Disaster Chapter Closed." *Engineering News-Record* 105 (August 28, 1930): 346.

9607. "St. Francis Dam Disaster Due to Poor Foundation." *American City* 38 (May 1928): 11.

9608. "St. Francis Dam Disaster to Cost Los Angeles $7,000,000." *Engineering News-Record* 104 (June 19, 1930): 1029.

9609. "St. Francis Dam Fails." *Western Construction News* 3 (March 25, 1928): 210-2.

9610. "St. Francis Dam Failure." *Western Construction News* 3 (April 10, 1928): 224-33.

9611. "St. Francis Dam of Los Angeles Water-Supply System Fails under Full Head." *Engineering News-Record* 100 (March 15, 1928): 456.

9612. "St. Francis Damage Claims Being Settled Speedily Out of Court." *Engineering New-Record* 101 (August 23, 1928): 293.

9613. Scattergood, E[zra] F. "Electric Power in the Construction of the Los Angeles Aqueduct." *Journal of Electricity, Power* and Gas 25 (August 27, 1910): 185-9.

9614. "The Second Los Angeles Aqueduct." *Western Construction* 44 (May 1969): 43-6.

9615. "Seeking a Scapegoat for the Santa Clara Flood." *Literary Digest* 97 (April 14, 1928): 34+.
St. Francis Dam disaster.

9616. "Shaft Completed on Mono Craters Tunnel Adds Two Headings on 11-Mi. Bore." *Western Construction News* 10 (December 1935): 351.

9617. Shelley, W. Frank. "Recent Progress on the Aqueduct." *Out West,* new series, 1 (May 1911): 361-7.

9618. Shrader, E. Roscoe. "A Ditch in the Desert." *Scribner's Magazine* 51 (May 1912): 538-50.
Describes aqueduct under construction.

9619. Shuey, George R. "Sinking, Cleaning and Testing Wells on the Los Angeles Aqueduct." *Engineering News-Record* 94 (May 14, 1925): 820-2.
Owens Valley.

9620. ———— "Well Sinking and Tests for the City of Los Angeles." *Engineering News-Record* 97 (July 1, 1926): 8-9.
Owens Valley.

9621. "Sixth Report on St. Francis Dam Offers New Theories: Abutments Lifted by Landslide at Left Bank and Swelling under Right — Cracks Permitted Underscour." *Engineering News-Record* 100 (June 7, 1928): 895.

9622. Smythe, William E. 'The Social Significance of the Owens River Project." *Out West* 23 (October 1905): 443-53.

9623. Socha, Max K. "Second Owens River Aqueduct Planned for Los Angeles." *Western City* 41 (June 1965): 35-8.

9624. Spilman, W. T. *The Conspiracy: An Exposure*

of the Owens River Water and San Fernando Land Frauds. Los Angeles, 1912. 71 pp.

9625. "Standing Section of St. Francis Dam Razed with Dynamite." *Engineering News-Record* 103 (July 11, 1929): 51.

9626. Stewart, William R. "A Desert City's Far Reach for Water: A $23,000,000 Aqueduct for Los Angeles to Bring Water 240 Miles from Mountain Peaks to the Sea-Shore, for City Use and for Irrigation." *World's Work* 15 (November 1907): 9538-40.

9627. "Subterranean Water Storage in Owens Valley." *Engineering Record* 66 (December 21, 1912): 687-8.

9628. "Text of the Report to Governor Young on Causes of St. Francis Dam Failure." *California Highways and Public Works* 5 (April 1928): 6-7+.

9629. "Tunnel Plans for San Fernando Valley." *Touring Topics* 2 (April 1910): 20.
Delivery of Owens Valley water.

9630. "Valuable Watershed Lands Acquired." *Los Angeles Saturday Night* 14 (October 28, 1933): 11.
Mono Basin.

9631. Van Norman, H. A. "Bouquet Canyon Reservoir and Dams: Large Earth-Fill Structure Provides Needed Storage for Domestic Supply of Los Angeles." *Civil Engineering* 4 (August 1934): 393-7.

9632. ———— "The Mono Basin Project: Aqueduct to Supply Los Angeles with Additional Water Now under Construction." *Civil Engineering* 6 (May 1936): 306-8.

9633. ———— 'The New Los Angeles Reservoir." *American City* 48 (May 1933): 7.
Bouquet Canyon.

9634. ———— "$38,000,000 Will Provide Needed Water for Los Angeles." *Pacific Municipalities* 44 (June 1930): 202-3.
Purchase of Owens Valley and Mono Basin lands.

9635. ———— "Water Works Ski-Troopers: Los Angeles Board of Water and Power Uses Snow

Survey to to Forecast Water Supply." *American City* 59 (October 1944): 67-9.
Eastern Sierra Nevadas, watershed supplying the aqueduct.

9636. ———— "Why Los Angeles Voted $38,800,000 for Water and How It Will Be Spent." *Western City* 6 (June 1930): 17-9.
Main items included: purchase of Owens Valley and Mono Basin lands and water rights, purchase of Owens Valley towns, and enlargement of aqueduct storage capacity.

9637. "West's Largest Pipe Line." *Southern California Business* 13 (March 1934): 20.
Connection between aqueduct and Bouquet Canyon Reservoir, 4½ miles in length.

9638. "Where Los Angeles Goes for Drink: Working in Snows of High Sierra to Bring More Water." *Los Angeles Saturday Night* 15 (September 21, 1935): 3+.
Beginning of Mono and Owens Gorge projects.

9639. "Where the Los Angeles Aqueduct Was Dynamited." *Saturday Night* 7 (June 4, 1927): 1.
Description of dynamiting at No-Name Canyon.

9640. Widney, Erwin W. "We Build a Railroad: Scenes and Incidents, Humorous and Otherwise, in the Camp Life of a Roustabout During the Construction of the Los Angeles Aqueduct." *Touring Topics* 23 (March 1931): 36-41+.

9641. Wilkes, Kenneth G. "Tunnel Concrete Car Design: Necessity for Lining Short Sections of Mono Craters Tunnel on Los Angeles Aqueduct Required the Development of a Special Car Design to Transport Concrete Quickly in Limited Space." *Western Construction News* 16 (March 1941): 87-8.

9642. Willey, Dan A. "Los Angeles 200-Mile Conduit Water Supply." *Scientific American* 100 (June 19, 1909): 460+.

9643. Willis, Bailey. "Report on the Geology of St. Francis Damsite, Los Angeles County, California." *Western Construction News* (June 25, 1928): 409-13.

9644. Wilson, Carl. "San Fernando Chlorination Plant, Los Angeles: Unusual Automatic Features of New Installation to Chlorinate Owens River

Aqueduct Water." *Western Consturction News* 2 (October, 1927): 73-5.

9645. Winther, Oscar O. "Los Angeles: Its Aquatic Life Lines." *The Journal of Geography* 49 (February 1950): 45-56.

9646. Wood, Richard C. "The History of the Owens Valley and the Los Angeles Water Controversy." Master's thesis, University of the Pacific, 1934. 91 pp.

9647. Wyckoff, W. W. "Mono Craters Tunneling Has Involved Struggle with Water and Gas Flows: Major Feature of the Project to Develop a Supplemental Water Supply for the City of Los Angeles Has Been the Driving of the 11-1/3-Mi. Bore Through the Crest of the Sierra Nevada." *Western Construction News* 13 (December 1938): 438-42.

9648. "A Year's Work in Arbitrating St. Francis Damage Claims." *Engineering News-Record* 102 (May 30, 1929): 880.

WATER SUPPLY—COLORADO RIVER AQUEDUCT AND METROPOLITAN WATER DISTRICT

9649. "Aqueduct Builders Span the State: How the Metropolitan Water District Speeds Gigantic Work Is Revealed." *Los Angeles Saturday Night* 43 (September 5, 1936): 9.

9650. "Aqueduct Water Softening Plant Contract Award." *Western City* 15 (December 1939): 31.

9651. "Aqueduct Work Progresses." *Western City* 9 (February 1933): 29.

9652. Aultman, William W. "Colorado River Aqueduct Water Softening and Filtration Plant." *Western City* 16 (February 1940): 21-4.

9653. ———. "First Colorado River Water Delivered to Southern California Cities." *Western City* 17 (July 1941): 18-25.

9654. ———. "Water Works Men to Inspect Aqueduct Softening and Filtration Plant." *Western City* 16 (October 1940): 16-22.
La Verne.

9655. Bailey, Phillip L., and Hovater, Louis R. "First Use of Mechanical Spreader for Paving on 3:1 Reservoir Slope." *Western Construction* 29 (November 1954): 68-9.
Garvey Reservoir of Metropolitan Water District Monterey Park.

9656. Barrows, H[enry] D. "Water for Domestic Purposes Versus Water for Irrigation." *Annual Publication* 8 (1911): 208-18.
Warns that city should sell surplus Owens Valley water for irrigation on an interim basis only.

9657. Bigger, Richard, and Jamison, Judith N. "Suburban Cities and Metropolitan Integration Proposals." *Western City* 33 (September 1957): 52-3.
Metropolitan Water District cited as example.

9658. Bradshaw, Frank. "Pasadena Votes $10,-000,000 for Dam and Additional Water Supply." *Hydraulic Engineering* 5 (July 1929): 11-4.
Dam, built in Pine Canyon of San Gabriel River, was completed in 1934 and subsequently sold to the Metropolitan Water District for use as a storage facility.

9659. Cecil, George H. "Our Changing Water Picture: Industry's Larger Demands Have Been Fully Met in the New Aqueduct Plans." *Southern California Business* 16 (July 1937): 10-1.
Los Angeles area.

9660. "City Water Study Presents Data on Rates." *Western City* 7 (July 1931): 12.
Comparison of 32 cities, nearly all in Los Angeles County.

9661. Clark, Walter G. "All-Tunnel, All-Gravity Aqueduct Proposed from Black Canyon to Los Angeles." *Hydraulic Engineering* 5 (September 1929): 23-7+.

9662. "Colorado River Aqueduct: Metropolitan Water District of Southern California by Vote of 5 to 1 Approves $220,000,000 Bond Issue." *Western Construction News* 6 (October 25, 1931): 542-4.

9663. "Colorado River Aqueduct Route Selected for Metropolitan Water District of Southern California." *Western Construction News* 6 (January 10, 1931): 21-2+.

9664. "Colorado River Aqueduct Work under Way." *Western City* 9 (January 1933): 14.

9665. "The Colorado River Aqueduct—World's Greatest Hydraulic Engineering Job." *Western City* 15 (February 1939): 24-5.

9666. "The Colorado River Aqueduct—World's Largest Construction Program." *Western City* 11 (January 1935): 34-6.

9667. "Colorado River Water for More Cities." *Western City* 24 (June 1948): 51.

West Basin Municipal Water District: El Segundo, Manhattan Beach, Hermosa Beach, Redondo Beach, and Palos Verdes Estates.

9668. "Colorado River Water for Our Cities: Why the Metropolitan Water District Is Prepared to Finance and Build the Colorado River Aqueduct Works." *Los Angeles Saturday Night 150th Birthday of Los Angeless Fiesta and Pre-Olympiad.* Special Issue (1931): [20].

9669. "Colorado River Water Suitable for All Uses." *Western Construction News* 5 (October 25, 1930): 515.

9670. Conkling, Harold. "San Gabriel Water Problems Occupy Attention of Hydraulic Engineer." *Hydraulic Engineering* 4 (February 1928): 92.

Legal and physical issues involved in diversion of water from the San Gabriel River.

9671. "Consulting Board Is Named to Advise on Pasadena Dam." *California Highways and Public Works* 8 (October 1930): 19.

Dam, located in Pine Canyon, is now owned by the Metropolitan Water District, which uses its reservoir for storage.

9672. Cooper, Erwin. *Aqueduct Empire.* Glendale, 1968. 2 vols.

9673. Daugherty, Robert L. "Aqueduct Pump Testing at California Institnte of Technology." *Western City* 12 (June 1936): 15-8.

9674. ——— "Aqueduct Pumping Problems Investigated at California Institute of Technology." *Western City* 11 (January 1935): 29+.

9675. Diemer, Robert B. "Colorado River Aqueduct Capacity Being Double to Fill Needs Until 1980." *Civil Engineering* 26 (December 1956): 58-61.

9676. "Director John G. Bullock, of Metropolitan Water District, Explains Its Chief Functions." *Los Angeles Saturday Night* 11 (March 14, 1931): 7.

9677. Dyksra, Clarence A., ed. "Colorado River Development and Related Problems." *Annals of the American Academy of Political and Social Science* 148 (March 1930): 1-48.

9678. "Filtering and Softening of Colorado Aqueduct Water Being Considered." *Western City* 15 (January 1939): 36.

9679. "5 Aqueduct Pumping Plants Will Lift Billion Gallons Daily 1634 Feet." *Western City* 13 (October 1937): 21-4+.

9680. "Frank E. Weymouth—General Manager and Chief Engineer, Metropolitan Water District of Southern California—His Engineering Skill and Ability as an Organizer Have Carried the Colorado River Aqueduct Through Its Design and Financing Stages into Actual Construction." *Western Construction News and Highways Builder* 8 (August 1933): 330.

9681. Fuss, Oscar R. "Big Water Is Big Business." *Frontier* 2 (July 1951): 5-8.

Author questions motives of the Colorado River Association, a private organization "functioning ostensibly to safeguard the Southern California water supply."

9682. Grayson, King H. "Parker Dam to Furnish Water for Thirteen California Cities." *American City* 50 (March 1935): 59-60.

9683. Haynes, John R. "A Canyon and a City." *Survey* 52 (June 1, 1924): 279-83.

A plea for passage of the Swing-Johnson Bill.

9684. Hinds, Julian. "The Distribution System for the Colorada River Aqueduct." *Western Construction News* 11 (June 1936): 175-6.

Describes facilities for delivering water to member cities of the Metropolitan Water District.

9685. "Features of the Colorado River Aqueduct." *Western City* 7 (June 1931): 13-6.

9686. "Increased Colorado River Water Supply for Seventy-Seven Cities." *Western City* 33 (August 1957): 59.

9687. Kleinsorge, Paul L. *The Boulder Canyon Projects Historical and Economic Aspect.* Stanford, 1941. 330 pp.

9688. La Rue, E. C. "$296,000,000 Aqueduct Plan to Secure Water for Southern California." *Hydraulic Engineering* 5 (May 1929) : 21-8+.

9689. "Los Angeles Installs Super-Size Cone Valves." *American City* 68 (July 1953) : 17.
Eagle Rock-Hollywood pipeline, the City of Los Angeles, first major connection with the Colorado River Aqueduct.

9690. "Manhattan Beach Doubles *Since* War; New Water Supply from Colorado River." *Western City* 25 (October 1949) : 32-5.

9691. McKenney, J. Wilson. "Heat and Hardrock Not Terrifying to These Desert Invaders." *The Desert Magazine* 1 (January 1934) : 16-8+.
Building the aqueduct.

9692. Metropolitan Water District of Southern California. *Colorado River Aqueduct.* Los Angeles, 1950. 77 pp.

9693. *The Great Aqueduct. The Story of the Planning and Building of the Colorado River Aqueduct.* Los Angeles, [1941]. 69 pp.

9694. —— *History and First Annual Report.* Los Angeles, 1939. 353 pp.

9695. —— *Water from Colorado River.* Los Angeles, 1931. 31 pp.

9696. "Metropolitan Aqueduct Has World's Biggest Pipe Line: 392-Mile Aqueduct Now Reaching into District Cities." *Los Angeles Saturday Night* 43 (April 18, 1936) : 16.

9697. "Metropolitan Water District Gives Instructions on Aqueduct Survey." *Hydraulic Engineering* 5 (October 1929) : 25+.

9698. Milliman, Jerome W. "The History, Organization, and Economic Problems of the Metropolitan Water District of Southern California." Doctoral dissertation, University of Southern California, Los Angeles, 1956. 536 pp.

9699. Mills, Henry J. "M. W. D. Programs Its Plans for Completion of State Water Plan." *Western City* 43 (October 1967) : 29-30.

9700. Moller, Beverley B. "Phil Swing in Washington: The Boulder Canyon Project Legislation." Doctoral dissertation, University of Southern California, Los Angeles, 1968. 310 pp.

9701. Morris, Samuel B. "Pasadena Builds Canyon Dam." *Civil Engineering* 3 (June 1933) : 309-13.
Dam now part of Metropolitan Water District.

9702. "Notable Engineering Figures in Councils of Metropolitan Water District." *Western City* 8 (February 1932) : 22.
Royal W. Sorensen, Arthur Davis, and Harvey S. Mudd.

9703. "Parker Route Costing $200,644,000 Recommened for Colorado River Aqueduct." *Western City* 6 (December 1930) : 37-41.

9704. "Pasadena Pipe Line Nears Completion: Pine Canyon Dam and Water Carrier Project Built under $7,500,000 City Bond Issue; To Be Unit of Metropolitan Water District System." *Western City* 10 (February 1934) : 12-5.

9705. Peuch, Verne L. "Construction of Morris Dam." *Civil Engineering* 5 (September 1935) : 549-52.
Dam located in Pine Canyon of the San Gabriel River, christened Samuel Morris Dam upon completion, and subsequently sold to the Metropolitan Water District as a storage facility. The ensuing four entries are descriptive of the financing and construction of this project.

9706. "Pine Canyon Dam for Domestic Water Supply of Pasadena—Bond Election Voted June 18, for $10,000,000." *Western Construction News* 4 (July 10, 1929) : 336-7.

9707. "Pine Canyon Dam for Pasadena Water Supply." *Western Construction News* 7 (February 10, 1932) : 81-3.

9708. "Pine Canyon Water Supply Dam for Pasadena." *Western Construction News and Highways Builder* 7 (October 25, 1932) : 609-12.

9709. "Pine Canyon Water Supply Dam for Pasadena." *Western Construction News and Highways Builder* 8 (May 10, 1933) : 237-40.

9710. "Preliminary Work Started on World's

Greatest Water Supply Project." *Western City* 7 (October 1931): 28-9+.
  Colorado River Aqueduct.

9711. "Progress on Aqueduct." *Los Angeles Saturday Night* 16 (November 30, 1935): 9.

9712. "Record-Size Mortar-Lined Steel Pipe for Distribution System." *Western Construction News* 13 (October 1938): 354-7.
  Palos Verdes Feeder of Metropolitan Water District.

9713. Reed, Harold J. "Colorado River Water for the Los Angeles Metropolitan Area, 1922 to 1928: With Special Reference to the Legislative Enactments." Master's thesis, Claremont Graduate School, 1939. 224 pp.

9714. Roher, Miriam. "Cities Built on Water." *Western City* 23 (March 1947): 21-3.
  Notes effects of Boulder Dam and the Metropolitan Water District on Los Angeles.

9715. "Santa Monica Uses Colorado River Water for Entire Supply." *Western City* 19 (October 1943): 38-9.

9716. Scattergood, E[zra] F. "Community Development in the Southwest as Influenced by the Boulder Canyon Project." *Annals of the American Academy of Political and Social Science* 148 (March 1930): 1-5.

9717. "What Development of Boulder Dam Means to Southern California." *Western City* 9 (September 1933): 31-2.

9718. "Second Water Softening Plant under Construction in Southern California." *Western Con-News* 23 (December 1948): 89-91.
  Metropolitan Water District plant at LaVerne.

9719. Smith, Lynn D. "392 Miles for a Drink to Make Southland Blossom Like the Rose Thousands of Workmen Push Construction Across the Desert and Through Mountains of World's Greatest Aqueduct." *Los Angeles Saturday Night* 44 (February 13, 1937): 8.

9720. "Southern California's Growth Stunted If Colorado River Water Is Diverted." *Western Housing* 32 (July 1948): 8-9+.
  Claims that "a grasping neighbor," Arizona,

threatens to thwart progress of Metropolitan Water District cities.

9721. Speers, Robert D. "Carrying on Ages-Old Fight with Desert: Army of 8000 Men Building Colorado River Aqueduct." *Los Angeles Saturday Night* 16 (October 19, 1935): 3.

9722. "The Story of the Colorado River Aqueduct Project." *Western City* 8 (October 1932): 17-25.

9723. Streicher, Lee. "Filter Backwash Gets Special Treatment . . . in an Unusual Plant That Reduces Wash-Water Losses to a Record Low and Produces Other Benefits." *American City* 82 (November 1967): 94-5.
  F. E. Weymouth Memorial Softening and Filtration Plant, Los Angeles.

9724. Taylor, Arthur. "Significance of Colorado River Aqueduct Water Supply to Southern California." *Western City* 12 (June 1966): 23-30.

9725. ———— "Water Quality Problem of Metropolitan District of Southern California." *Western City* 12 (January 1936): 9-10+.
  Discusses "hardness" of Colorado River water compare to other sources utilized by M.W.D. cities.

9726. Thomas, Franklin. "California Cities Fast Developing Plans for Immense Aqueduct." *Hydraulic Engineering* 5 (July 1929): 30-4+.

9727. "Metropolitan Water Distribution in the Los Angeles Area." *Annals of the American Academy of Political and Social Science* 148 (March 1930): 6-11.

9728. Tune, Newell W. "The Proposed Los Angeles Aqueduct." *California Engineer* 8 (November 1929): 9+.
  Actually, Colorado River Aqueduct.

9729. Twilegar, Bert I. "Mulholland's 'Pipe' Dream." *Westways* 41 (January 1949): 16-7.
  Colorado River Aqueduct.

9730. "$220,000,000 Colorado Aqueduct Bond Issue Approved Five To One." *Western City* 7 (October 1931): 37.

9731. "Unprecedented Progress of Colorado River

Construction." *Los Angeles Saturday Night* 14 (January 13, 1934): 9.

The aqueduct.

9732. Updegraff, Winston R. "The Colorado River Aqueduct Guarantees Water for Fifty Cities: $52 Million Expansion Underway." *Western City* 30 (May 1954): 46-55.

9733. Van Norman, H. A. "Then, There Is the Great Aqueduct to Build." *Southern California Business* 8 (September 1929): 16-7+.

9734. Water for People. *An Outline of the Metropolitan Water District Aqueduct from the Colorado River.* [Los Angeles, 1962]. 19 pp.

9735. "Water from the Colorado River." *Municipal League of Los Angeles Bulletin* 2 (October 20, 1924): [11-12].

A report of remarks made by A. L. Sonderegger, William Mulholland, and H. A. Van Norman.

9736. Watkins, T. H. "Conquest of the Colorado." *American West* 6 (July 1969): 5-9+.

9737. Weymouth, F[rank] E. "Colorado River Aqueduct for the Metropolitan Water District of Southern California." *Western Construction News* 5 (October 25, 1930): 511-6.

9738. "Colorado River Aqueduct: Route Selected for Metropolitan Water District Requires Pumping." *Civil Engineering* 1 (February 1931): 371-6.

9739. Wheeler, Fred C. "Why Los Angeles Favors the Boulder Dam." *Pacific Municipalities* 38 (May 1924): 167-8+.

9740. Whitsett, W[illiam] P. "Bringing Water from the Colorado River." *Municipal League of Los Angeles Bulletin* 6 (March 1, 1929): [1-2].

9741. —— "The Metropolitan Water District of Southern California." *Western City* 6 (September 1930): 21-3.

9742. —— "What Is the Metropolitan Water District?" *Southern California Business* 8 (September 1929): 22-3+.

9743. "Why Colorado River Water Is a Vital Necessity for Southern California." *Western City* 7 (August 1931): 7-8.

9744. Wilson, Carl. "Los Angeles Water Supply Problem Solved by Construction of Aqueduct." *Western Construction News* 10 (April 1935): 112.

9745. "Work Underway on Distribution System of Colorado River Aqueduct." *Western City* 14 (October 1938): 22-3.

9746. "World's Greatest Municipal Water Project Nears Construction: Eleven Cities Expected to Be Called upon Next April to Vote $200,000,000 in Bonds for Colorado Aqueduct." *Western City* 7 (January 1931): 31-3.

WELFARE

9747. Agan, Ruth M. "The Use of Relief by the Three Non-Sectarian Private Family Welfare Agencies in the Los Angeles Community Chest Area, Family Welfare Department of the Volunteers of American." Master's thesis, University of Southern California, 1941. 101 pp.

9748. Aikman, Duncan. "California Sunshine." *Nation* 132 (April 22, 1931): 448-50.

Relief efforts in Los Angeles and Southern California.

9749. Alexander, Arthur M. "Data Communications Fight Rising Welfare Costs." *American City* 83 (July 1968): 108-9.

"The Department of Public Social Services coorinates and administers all federal, state and county aid in sprawling Los Angeles County."

9750. Allen, Dorothy F. "The Changing Emphasis in Protective Services to Children with an Account of the Children's Protective Association of Los Angeles." Master's thesis, University of Southern California, 1943. 167 pp.

9751. Anderman, Loretta E. "The Use of Relief by a Nonsectarian Family Agency in Los Angeles." Master's thesis, University of Southern California, 1941. 107 pp.

9752. Antoniou, Mary. "Welfare Activities Among the Greek People in Los Angeles." Master's thesis, University of Southern California, 1939. 198 pp.

9753. "Arroyo Seco Emergency Relief Camp

Operating Full Quota of Workers." *California Highways and Public Works* 10 (December 1932): 2+.

9754. Bice, Martha A. "A Study of the Effects of Replacements in Foster Homes and Institutions on Dependent Children in Los Angeles County." Master's thesis, University of Southern California, 1937. 287 pp.

9755. Birge, Margaret L. "Some Social Work Techniques Indicated in an Analysis of Twenty-Five Case Histories Known to the Bureau of County Welfare, Deparment of Charities, Los Angeles County, for a Period of Ten Years or More." Master's thesis, University of Southern California, 1936. 234 pp.

9756. Blake, Lewis L. "A Study of the Resources for Vocational and Avocational Training Now Available to Blind Persons in Los Angeles County." Master's thesis, University of Southern California, 1939. 88 pp.

9757. Blue, Phyllis E. "The Use of Relief by Three Non-Sectarian Private Family Welfare Agencies in the Los Angeles Community Chest Area. The Family Welfare Department of the Assistance League of Southern California." Master' thesis, University of Southern California, 1941. 118 pp.

9758. Blumberg, Murray T. "Community Relations as Recognized and Practiced by the Jewish Centers Association of Los Angeles and Its Four Institutional Members." Master's thesis, University of Southern California, 1952. 129 pp.

9759. Bohem, Paul. "Post Release Success of Boys in Junior Camp Programs of Los Angeles Probation Department: A Survey of 345 Graduates with a Follow-Up Study of Sixty." Master's thesis. Claremont Graduate School, 1951. 135 pp.

9760. Boothe, Barbara, and Pollard, Shirley. "The Role of the Child Welfare and Attendance Worker in the Los Angeles City Schools." Master's thesis, University of Southern California, 1960. 61 pp.

9761. Bornet, Vaughn D. *California Social Welfare.* Englewood Cliffs, N. J., 1956. 520 pp.

9762. Bradley, Esther R. "A Study of the Coorinating Council Movement in Los Angeles County, with Particular Emphasis upon Its Sociological

and Educational Implications." Master's thesis, Claremont Graduate School, 1941. 133 pp.

9763. Branham, Ethel. "A Study of Independent Adoptions by Negro Parents in Metropolitan Los Angeles." Master's thesis, University of Southern California, 1949. 62 pp.

9764. Bulen, Mary H. "Romance Background of Goodwill Industries." *Los Angeles Saturday Night* 15 (June 1, 1935): 7.

History of Los Angeles plant of Goodwill Industries, philanthropic enterprise.

9765. Burgess, J. Stewart. "Living on a Surplus." *Survey* 69 (January 1933): 6-8.

Unemployed Cooperative Relief Association, with 31 branches in Los Angeles County.

9766. Cahn, Frances, and Bary, Veleska. *Welfare Activities of Federal, State, and Local Governments in California, 1850-1934.* Berkeley, 1936. 422 pp.

9767. Campbell, Cheryl B. "A Study of the Federal Transient Program with Special Reference to Fifty Transient Families in Los Angeles." Master's thesis, University of Southern California, 1936. 143 pp.

9768. Carlstrand, Robert W. "A Comparison of Negro Mobility Characteristics of Probationers in Los Angeles." Master's thesis, University of Southern California, 1955. 95 pp.

9769. Carodine, Charlene D. "A Study of the Socioeconomic Characteristics of Clients Who Use Central District Family Service of Los Angeles Area, September 1962." Master's thesis, University of Southern California, 1963. 105 pp.

9770. Carter, Leland C. "The Los Angeles County Bureau of Public Assistance and the Aid to Needy Children Program." *Long Beach Bar Bulletin* 6 (December 1960): 5-10.

9771. Carter, Shirley B. "A Comparison of Socio-Economic Characteritics of Fee-Paying and Non-Fee-Paying Clientele of San Fernando District of Family Service of Los Angeles Area, October 1961." Master's thesis, University of Southern California, 1962. 104 pp.

9772. Carver, Ransom F. "The Financial Problems

of a Community Chest in a Suburban Residential City, as Illustrated by the Twelve Independent Chests Near Los Angeles." Master's thesis, University of Southern California, 1940. 152 pp.

9773. Chang, Tse Hua. "Comparative Study of Child Day Care Centers in Los Angeles, California, and Canton, China." Master's thesis, Claremont Graduate School, 1949. 255 pp.

9774. Cherwynak, Helen A. "Boarding Home Care as Used by the Los Angeles County Probation Department." Master's thesis, University of Southern California, 1942. 102 pp.

9775. Citizens Adoption Committee, Los Angeles County. *Children Without Homes of Their Own; A Study of Children Needing Adoption and Other Foster Care in Los Angeles County.* Los Angeles, 1953. 60 pp.

9776. ——— *Gleanings from Twenty-Two Months of Activity by Mary Stanton.* Los Angeles, 1952. 21 pp.

9777. Clover, Madge. "Fifty Years of Los Angeles Orphans' Home Society." *Los Angeles Saturday Night* 10 (July 26, 1930): 7.

9778. Cocks, Robert W. "An Analysis of Methods of Determining Case Loads for the Professional Staff of Four Public Welfare Agencies in Los Angeles County Government." Master's thesis, University of Southern California, 1953. 105 pp.

9779. Cohen, Benjamin L. "Evaluation of the Jewish Youth Council of Los Angeles by Its Constituent Groups." Master's thesis, University of Southern California, 1947. 112 pp.

9780. Cohen, Bernard L. "Sociological Aspects in the Welfare Activities Among American Jews with Special Reference to Welfare Activities in Los Angeles." Master's thesis, University of Southern California, 1949. 146 pp.

9781. Conrad, Gertrude J. "The Need for and Availability of Social Work Programs for the Aged, with Special Reference to the City of Los Angeles." Master's thesis, University of Southern California, 1950. 108 pp.

9782. Cooper, Marie T. "A Follow-Up Study of Fifty-Two Cases Involving Financial Assistance

Which Were Not Accepted by the Jewish Social Service Bureau of Los Angeles." Master's thesis, University of Southern California, 1938. 80 pp.

9783. Copleston, Marion D. "The Procedures Used by the Los Angeles Probation Department in the Disposition of One Hundred Nonresident Cases." Master's thesis, University of Southern California, 1945. 126 pp.

9784. Corr, William E. *The Santa Rita Settlement.* Los Angeles, c1920. 38 pp.
    History and operational procedures of a Catholic Welfare agency.

9785. Cottrell, Edwin A. Assisted by Prudence Kwiecien, Walter H. Brown, and Edward C. Jenkins. *Pasadena Social Agencies Survey.* Pasadena, 1940. 378 pp.
    Pasadena charities.

9786. Council of Social Agencies of Los Angeles, Division of Social Studies. *The Bill for Social Welfare in Los Angeles, 1938. How Much Is It? Who Pays It? How Is It Spent?* [Los Angeles, 1939]. 23 pp.

9787. Dalmas, Herbert. "Woman Guardian of L. A. Charities." *Coronet* 37 (April 1955): 73-6.
    Evelyn Spaulding, General Manager of the Los Angeles Social Service Department, and her fight against charity rackets.

9788. Deupree, Robert P. "An Analysis of the Opinions Regarding Social Welfare Planning of Eight Laymen Active in the Welfare Council of Metropolitan Los Angeles." Master's thesis, University of Southern California, 1952. 82 pp.

9789. Douglas, L. N. "A Study of the Goodwill Industries Movement, with Analysis of the Goodwill Industries of Southern California." Master's thesis, University of Southern California, 1926. 143 pp.

9790. Dwyer, Mercedes M. "A Descriptive Study of Case Histories of Families Who Are Receiving Relief and Have Received Relief from Los Angeles County over a Period of Twenty Years or More." Master's thesis, University of Southern California, 1939. 95 pp.

9791. Eaton, Constance H. "A Study of the Prevailing Policies and Practices of Twelve Los Angeles Agencies in Respect to the Unmarried

Mother and Her Child." Master's thesis, University of Southern California, 1940. 121 pp.

9792. Erickson, George. "From Townsend to Mc-Lain: Twenty Years of Pension Planning in California, 1933-1953." Master's thesis, University of Redlands, 1953. 106 pp.

9793. Feldman, Albert G. "Statisical Trends in Programs of Certain Private Child Care Agencies in Los Angeles County, 1936-1940." Master's thesis, University of Southern California, 1943. 193 pp.

9794. Feldman, Frances. *History of the Committee on Mental Health, Health Division, Welfare Planning Council, Los Angeles Region, 1936-1953.* [Los Angeles], 1955. 42 pp.

9795. Fenley, Robert F. "An Anaysis of the Legislative Activity of the Welfare Council of Metropolitan Los Angeles, 1942-1947." Master's thesis, University of Southern California, 1948. 62 pp.

9796. Fiske, Walter M. "A Follow-Up Study of Six Cases of Mexican-American Parents to Explore Their Feelings About Child Placement." Master's thesis, University of Southern California, 1960. 55 pp.

9797. Franklin, Ruth. "Study of the Services Needed and/or Available to Negro Newcomer Families; A Study of Perceptions of Eleven Health and Welfare Agencies Serving the Community of Watts." Master's thesis, University of Southern California, 1962. 104 pp.

9798. Friedman, Frances H. "Some Factors Involved in Re-Applications for Service at the Jewish Social Service Bureau of Los Angeles." Master's thesis, University of Southern California, 1941. 85 pp.

9799. Fukuoka, Fumiko. "Mutual Life and Aid Among the Japanese in Southern California with Special Reference to Los Angeles." Master's thesis, University of Southern California, 1937. 94 pp.

9800. Gardner, Richard T. "Coordination of Law Enforcement and Social Agencies: A Study of Nineteen Cases Referred to the Bureau of Public Assistance from the Crime Prevention Division of the Sheriff's Department in Los Angeles County." Master's thesis, University of Southern California, 1948. 119 pp.

9801. Gelber, Sophie. "A Comparison of Twenty-Five Extra-Mural Cases with Twenty-Five Intramural Cases with Special Reference to the Rehabilitative Factors of Rancho Los Amigos." Master's thesis, University of Southern California, 1939. 174 pp.
One of five divisions of Los Angeles County Department of Charities.

9802. Gerstel, Edna C. "An Analysis of Factors Seen in Replacecents of Children in Foster Care Programs." Master's thesis, University of Southern California, 1950. 51 pp.

9803. Gibbs, Jeanie W. *Memoirs of the Pasadena Children's Training Society.* Pasadena, 1930. 44 pp.

9804. Glane, Sam. "The Administration of Public Aid to Indigent Aged in California with Special Reference to Los Angeles County." Master's thesis, University of Southern California, 1937. 172 pp.

9805. Glass, John. "Organizational Dilemmas in the War on Poverty: Contrasts in the Neighborhood Youth Corps." Doctoral dissertation, University of California, Los Angeles, 1968. 327 pp.

9806. Glazer, Mike. *The L.A. CSO Story; American Democracy Is Not a Fake.* Los Angeles, 1965. 14 pp.
Los Angeles Community Service Organization.

9807. Goldberg, Charles. "A Study of Intake Procedure in Social Group Work and Its Practice in Los Angeles." Master's thesis, University of Southern California, 1950. 76 pp.

9808. "Good Work of the Rescue Home." *Los Angeles Saturday Night* 8 (March 31, 1928): 15.
Salvation Army appeal for funds to rebuild Truelove Rescue Home for Girls on North Griffin Avenue.

9809. Goodwin, Jeanie. "The Relation of Juvenile Delinquency and Family Dependency. A Case Study of Fifty Children from Families Assisted by the Los Angeles County Department of Charities." Master's thesis, University of Southern California, 1939. 177 pp.

9810. Griswold, Tom. "A Bum's Guide to Los Angeles." *American Mercury* 51 (December 1940): 408-13.
Charities.

9811. Groggs, Blanche P. "An Analysis of Social Group Work with Senior-Age Girls in Five Los Angeles Agencies." Master's thesis, University of Southern California, 1944. 92 pp.

9812. Hanson, Elsie M. "How Los Angeles Family Welfare Agencies Met the Requests of Discharged Servicemen: An Analysis of 595 Requests Made to the Veterans' Referral Desk in the United States Employment Service During the Period of July 24, 1944 to December 28, 1944." Master's thesis, University of Southern California, 1947. 100 pp.

9813. Harmer, Ruth M. "Price Tag on Youth." *Frontier* 9 (July 1958): 5-7.
Group Guidance Section of the Los Angeles County Juvenile Probation Department.

9814. Harper, Helena H. "A Study of Colored Unmarried Mothers in Los Angeles." Master's thesis, University of Southern California, 1932. 61 pp.

9815. Harriman, William R. "Easing the Sunset Years: A Picture of the 'Rancho of the Friends,' County Home for the Sick and Aged Who Have No Financial Resources." *Apartment Journal* 23 (December 1940): 8-9+.
Rancho Los Amigos.

9816. Hawes, Bess L. "La Llorona in Juvenile Hall." *Western Folklore* 27 (1968): 153-70.
"Ghost lore . . . told by inmates of Las Palmas School for Girls, a residential facility of the Department of Corrections of the County of Los Angeles."

9817. Hicks, Frederick J. "An Analysis of the Directorates of Sixty Los Angeles Welfare Agencies." Master's thesis, University of Southern California, 1936. 77 pp.

9818. Hirschhorn, Pearl A. "The Development of the Home Service Department of the Los Angeles Chapter of the American National Red Cross, 1916 to 1944." Master's thesis, University of Southern California, 1944. 144 pp.

9819. Hobbs, Irene. "An Analysis of the Problems of and Direct Services Offered to Unattached Clients 65 Years of Age or Older by Family Service of Los Angeles Area." Master's thesis, University of Southern California, 1951. 86 pp.

9820. Holbrook, W. Sumner, Jr.; Maxwell, Roland, and Rourke, James G. "Fifield Manor Tax Refund Cases: True Meaning of 'Charity' under California Welfare Tax Exemption Restated." *Southern California Law Review* 35 (1962): 276-99.

9821. Hollenbeck Home. *Hollenbeck Home for the Aged.* Los Angeles, [1930?]. 42 pp.

9822. Iverson, Jean; Kido, Ruth; Leibner, Stanley, and von Bloeker, Ruth. "Los Angeles County Juvenile Probation Officers' Opinions of the California Juvenile Court Law." Master's thesis, University of Southern California, 1964. 171 pp.

9823. Jackson, Wesley. "How Pleasant Was Our Valley." *Frontier* 7 (April 1956): 7-9.
Dispute over plan to rezone the western San Fernando Valley for industry.

9824. Kaiser, Evelyn. "The Unattached Negro Woman on Relief: A Study of Fifty Unattached Negro Women on Relief in the Compton District Office of the State Relief Administration of California in Los Angeles." Master's thesis, University of Southern California, 1939. 166 pp.

9825. Kaplan, Lillian P. "The Use of the Child Guidance Clinic of Los Angeles by Vista Del Mar Child-Care Service, 1935-1940." Master's thesis, University of Southern California, 1941. 134 pp.

9826. Kincaid, Ronald D. "Public Work Relief Activities in Los Angeles County, March, 1933 to June 30, 1938." Master's thesis, University of Southern California, 1967. 169 pp.

9827. King, Louis J. "Relationship Between Group Workers and Parents of Group Members: A Study of Five Selected Settlements and Centers within Metropolitan Los Angeles." Master's thesis, University of Southern California, 1951. 67 pp.

9828. King, Ruby L. "Program Content in Three Groups of Teenage Girls: An Analysis of Records from Special Service Unit of the Los Angeles Youth Project." Master's thesis, University of Southern California, 1951. 87 pp.

9829. La Rosa, Nina. "Foster Homes Closed After Being in Use for Two Years or Less." Master's thesis, University of Southern California, 1957. 42 pp.

9830. Leddel, Helen G. "Adolescent Girls' Perceptions of Casework Services: A Follow-Up Study." Master's thesis, University of Southern California, 1964. 48 pp.

9831. Levan, Goldie L. "The Services of the Los Angeles Social Service Exchange as an Aid in Case Work." Master's thesis, University of Southern California, 1939. 203 pp.

9832. Levin, Ray. "Factors Determining Institutional (Cottage Plan) and Foster Home Placement." Master's thesis, University of Southern California, 1949. 66 pp.

9833. Li, Kuan. "A Study of Selected Child Caring Agencies in Los Angeles and Vicinity." Master's thesis, University of Southern California, 1940. 108 pp.

9834. Lieber, L. O. "Recreation and Welfare Work for Los Angeles Railway Employees." *Electric Railway Journal* 46 (September 11, 1915): 506-7.

9835. Long, William S. "The Child Guidance Clinic of Los Angeles: Its Historical Development, 1923-1947." Master's thesis, University of Southern California, 1948. 115 pp.

9836. Los Angeles, Bureau of Engineering, Federal Coordination Division. *Survey of Unemployment Relief Activities in the City of Los Angeles, California, 1932-1938.* Los Angeles, 1938. 48 pp.

9837. Los Angeles Community Welfare Federation. *Social Service as Administered by Public and Private Agencies in Membership in the Council of Social Agencies of Los Angeles.* Los Angeles, 1934. 124 pp.

9838. Los Angeles Coordinating Councils, Juvenile Research Committee. *Youth's New Day, the Juvenile Problem in Los Angeles and Tools for Its Solution.* Los Angeles, 1935. 95 pp.

9839. MacCarthy, C. B. H. "A Survey of the Mexican Hardship Cases Active in the Los Angeles County Department of Charities, Los Angeles, California." Master's thesis, University of Southern California, 1939. 95 pp.

9840. Mackenzie, Dorthea M. "A Survey and Analysis of Fifty Selected American Families Receiving Aid in 1939 from the State Relief Adminis-

tration." Master's thesis, University of Southern California, 1939. 158 pp.

9841. Mangold, George B. *Life — in Long Beach; a Survey of Community Welfare Services and Needs* . . . Long Beach, 1939. 108 pp.

9842. Marshall, Dale R. "The Politics of Participation in Poverty: A Case Study of the Board of Economic and Youth Opportunities Agency of Greater Los Angeles." Doctoral dissertation, University of California, Los Angeles, 1969. 406 pp.

9843. Marshall, Thomas C. *Into the Streets and Lanes: The Beginnings and Growth of the Social Work of the Episcopal Church in the Diocese of Los Angeles, 1887-1947.* Claremont, 1948. 178 pp.

9844. Martin, Norman R. "Experiences with Unemployed on Road Rock Breaking." *Engineering News* 76 (October 19, 1916): 755.
By the Los Angeles County Superintendent of Charities.

9845. Mathison, Richard. "Troubled Generation." *Newsweek* 57 (May 22, 1961): 26+.
Juvenile delinquency in Los Angeles County, and the attempts of an organization called Group Guidance to combat it.

9846. Matson, Allen D. "Foster Home Placement of Adolescent Age Children." Master's thesis, University of Southern California, 1959. 124 pp.

9847. McAfee, Ethel M. "Veterans' Problems at Intake in a Private Family Agency." Master's thesis, University of Southern California, 1949. 80 pp.

9848. McCool, John W. "An Evaluation of the Forestry Camp Program of the Los Angeles County Probation Department." Master's thesis, Claremont Graduate School, 1945. 75 pp.

9849. McCoy, Georgia F. "A Study of Removal and Placement of Dependent Children in Foster Homes and Institutions in Los Angeles County, California, with Special Reference to Boarding Home Removals." Master's thesis, University of Southern California, 1937. 183 pp.

9850. McMullen, Dora. "The Place of the Study Home in a Child Care Program, with Special Reference to Bluegate Cottage of the Children's Bureau of Los Angeles." Master's thesis, University of Southern California, 1943. 112 pp.

9851. Melinkoff, Sidney I. "Economic Rehabilitation of the Unemployed through Cooperative Production: A Study of the Los Angeles County Rehabilitation Department." Master's thesis, University of Southern California, 1936. 69 pp.

9852. Milliken, W. W. "How Santa Monica Helped Its Unemployed Citizens and Obtained a Permanent Street Improvement." *Western City* 9 (March 1933): 18-9.

9853. Montelius, Marjorie. "Dislocated Children: A Study of Twenty Evacuated and Refugee Children in Los Angeles under the Auspices of National Organizations and with Supervision by Local Agencies." Master's thesis, University of Southern California, 1944. 132 pp.

9854. Morales, Armando. "A Study of Recidivism of Mexican-American Junior Forestry Camp Graduates." Master's thesis, University of Southern California, 1963. 169 pp.

9855. Mueller, Edward. "What the Civilian Conservation Corps Means to 115 Los Angeles Boys Who Were Honorably Discharged on March, 1940." Master's thesis, University of Southern California, 1941. 235 pp.

9856. "Municipal Control of Charity in Los Angeles." *Survey* 31 (October 4, 1913): 1-2.

9857. Munoz, Rosalio F. "An Adoption Agency's Services to the Unadoptable Child." Master's thesis, University of Southern California, 1949. 63 pp.

9858. Murphy, Ellis P. "An Analysis of Certain Factors in Unadaptability: A Study of Thirty-One Cases Referred to the Children's Home Society of California." Master's thesis, University of Southern California, 1949. 118 pp.

9859. Nesbitt, Florence. *Study of a Minimum Standard of Living for Dependent Families in Los Angeles, Made . . . for the Los Angeles Community Welfare Federation.* Los Angeles, 1927. 36 pp.

9860. "Nursery Building for the Children's Home Society of California, Los Angeles." *Pencil Points* 26 (August 1945): 70-3.

Article also describes activities of this society, which deals mainly in adoptions.

9861. Ohse, Francis. "A Study of Children Who Have Received Long Term Public Foster Care: An Inquiry into the Social Situations of Recently Terminated Cases." Master's thesis, University of Southern California, 1960. 71 pp.

9862. O'Reilly, Patrick J. "Adolescent Attitudes Toward Institutional Sleeping Arrangements." Master's thesis, University of Southern California, 1955. 82 pp.

Junipero Serra Boys' Club, Los Angeles.

9863. O'Rourke, Kathleen C. "Factors in the Discontinuance of Parents at a Child Guidance Clinic after Two Visits." Master's thesis, University of Southern California, 1963. 85 pp.

9864. Ostomel, Anne M. "Use of Evaluations of Case Work Personnel in Los Angeles Agencies." Master's thesis, University of Southern California, 1947. 153 pp.

9865. Patti, Rino J. "Child Protection in California, 1850-1966: An Analysis of Public Policy." Doctoral dissertation, University of Southern California, 1967. 404 pp.

9866. Peairs, Myra A. "Personal and Social Adjustments of Girls Who Were Placed in Work Homes by the Girls' Placement and Supervision Division, Church Federation of Los Angeles During the Period of January 1936 to January 1938." Master's thesis, University of Southern California, 1939. 125 pp.

9867. Phadke, Sindhu V. "Licensing of Child Care in California: 1911-1961." Doctoral dissertation, University of Southern California, 1963. 355 pp.

9868. Porter, Evelyne N. "The Business Phase of the Bureau of Indigent Relief of Los Angeles County." Master's thesis, University of Southern California, 1936. 98 pp.

9869. Porter, Florence C., ed. *The Story of the McKinley Home for Boys.* Los Angeles, 1921. 76 pp.

9870. "Problems of the Aged Recognized in City Senior Citizen Programs." *Western City* 35 (August 1959): 19+.

Includes reports on many Los Angeles County cities.

9871. Putnam, Glenn D. "Fee Charging as Perceived and Practiced by Methodist and Presbyterian Community Centers in Metropolitan Los Angeles." Master's thesis, University of Southern California, 1962. 49 pp.

9872. Reid, Daniel. "The Early History of the Fred C. Nelles School for Boys [1927-1957]." Master's thesis, University of Southern California, 1964. 92 pp.

Reform School in Whittier.

9873. Reifman, Eli. "Socio-Economic Aspects of 125 'Continued Service' Cases in the San Fernando Valley Office of the Jewish Family Service Agency." Master's thesis, University of Southern California, 1963. 107 pp.

9874. Richards, Eylfa R. "Group Development as a Basis for Transferral of Three Groups of the Special Service Unit of the Los Angeles Youth Project to Community Agencies." Master's thesis, University of Southern California, 1950. 115 pp.

9875. Richards, Lenora A. "A Study of the Social Welfare Activities of the Los Angeles Urban League." Master's thesis, University of Southern California, 1941. 79 pp.

9876. Rock, John E. *Twenty Years on Skid Row.* Los Angeles, n.d. 12 pp.

9877. Roffinello, Lena C. "Married Parents Who Considered Adoption for Their Child." Master's thesis, University of Southern California, 1949. 61 pp.

Los Angeles.

9878. Rosenfield, Leon A., Jr. "Governing Board Organization in Voluntary Social Agencies: A Study of the By-Laws of Forty-Four Agencies in the Los Angeles Area." Master's thesis, University of Southern California, 1951. 71 pp.

9879. Saunders, Margaret. "A Study of the Work of the City Mother's Bureau of the Los Angeles Police Department." Master's thesis, University of Southern California, 1939. 201 pp.

9880. Selby, Earl and Selby, Anne. "Watts: Where Welfare Bred Violence." *Reader's Digest* 88 (May 1966): 67-71.

9881. Smith, Marguerite J. "A Study of Requests for Petitions on Behalf of Neglected Children Receiving Public Assistance in Los Angeles County." Master's thesis, University of Southern California, 1965. 90 pp.

9882. Steel-Brooke, Gertrude. "The Single Woman on Relief: A Study of the Status of Two Hundred Sixty Single, Unattached, American-Born, White Women on Relief in the Heart of Downtown Los Angeles." Master's thesis, University of Southern California, 1936. 109 pp.

9883. Stonecypher, William R. "Large Families on Relief: A Comparative Study of the Dependency, Occupational, Social and Economic Factors Relating to 173 Large Families Receiving Assistance in June, 1940, from the Harbor District of the California State Relief Administration in Los Angeles County." Master's thesis, University of Southern California, 1942. 133 pp.

9884. Strimling, Hilda. "Incidental Services, Jewish Social Service Bureau of Los Angeles, California." Master's thesis, University of Southern California, 1937. 72 pp.

9885. Stumpf, Jack E. A. "The Role of a Community Organization Worker as Revealed by a Process Record of a Welfare Council Committee." Master's thesis, University of Southern California, 1949. 171 pp.

Los Angeles.

9886. Taylor, Frank J. "Jobs for Women with Money." *Reader's Digest* 40 (January 1942): 49-51.

Assistance League of Southern California, which provides "Leisure Class Women" with charitable pursuits. Condensed from *Mademoiselle.*

9887. Trecker, Harley B. "Pioneering in Coordi-

nation." *Survey Midmonthly* (January 1947): 15-7.
Los Angeles Youth Project, under sponsorship of Welfare Council of Metropolitan Los Angeles.

9888. Tschekaloff, Natalia L. "Social Service Problems of Immigration with Special Reference to Russian Immigrants in Los Angeles." Master's thesis, University of Southern California, 1945. 218 pp.

9889. U.S. Citizens Service Corps. *Report of Civilian War Services by the Citizens Service Corps for the Period of 1941 to December 31, 1944. . . .* [Los Angeles, 1945]. 16 pp.

9890. Unker, Lillian. "Conflict Between Parent and Foster Parent as a Factor Contributing Towards Replacements in Foster Homes at the Children's Bureau of Los Angeles." Master's thesis, University of Southern California, 1944. 123 pp.

9891. Wallis, Marie P. "A Study of Dependency in One Hundred Cases Taken from Files of Bureau of County Welfare, Catholic Welfare Bureau, Los Angeles County Relief Administration [Torrance and Watts Districts]." Master's thesis, University of Southern California, 1935. 81 pp.

9892. Webber, Jane. "An Evaluation of One Hundred Juvenile Probation Cases Studied by a Child Guidance Clinic: A Study of Los Angeles and Pasadena Child Guidance Clinic Case Histories and Yearly Follow-Ups Over a Five Year Period." Master's thesis, University of Southern California, 1941. 106 pp.

9893. Wells, Grace H. "A Study of the Problems Existing in the Families of Three Hundred Current 'Aid to Dependent Children' Cases in the Compton District of the Bureau of Indigent Relief." Master's thesis, University of Southern California, 1939. 100 pp.

9894. White, Vivian E. "The Social Contributions of a Welfare Center for Negro Girls in the City of Los Angeles, California." Master's thesis, University of Southern California, 1947. 127 pp.

9895. Young, William S. *A History of Hollenbeck Home.* Los Angeles, 1934. 270 pp.
Home for the Aged, Los Angeles.

Author Index

Subject Index